Frommer's

W9-BVR-657

California

2005

**by Harry Basch, Erika Lenkert,
Matthew Richard Poole
& David Swanson**

Here's what the critics say about Frommer's:

"Amazingly easy to use. Very portable, very complete."
—*Booklist*

"Detailed, accurate, and easy-to-read information for all price ranges."
—*Glamour Magazine*

"Hotel information is close to encyclopedic."
—*Des Moines Sunday Register*

"Frommer's Guides have a way of giving you a real feel for a place."
—*Knight Ridder Newspapers*

WILEY

Wiley Publishing, Inc.

Published by:

Wiley Publishing, Inc.
111 River St.
Hoboken, NJ 07030-5774

Copyright © 2005 Wiley Publishing, Inc., Hoboken, New Jersey. All rights
reserved. No part of this publication may be reproduced, stored in a retrieval system or transmitted in any form or by any means, electronic, mechanical, photo-
copying, recording, scanning or otherwise, except as permitted under Sections 107
or 108 of the 1976 United States Copyright Act, without either the prior written
permission of the Publisher, or authorization through payment of the appropriate
per-copy fee to the Copyright Clearance Center, 222 Rosewood Drive, Danvers,
MA 01923, 978/750-8400, fax 978/646-8600. Requests to the Publisher for permission should be addressed to the Legal Department, Wiley Publishing, Inc.,
10475 Crosspoint Blvd., Indianapolis, IN 46256, 317/572-3447, fax 317/572-
4355, E-Mail: brandreview@wiley.com.

Wiley and the Wiley Publishing logo are trademarks or registered trademarks of
John Wiley & Sons, Inc. and/or its affiliates. Frommer's is a trademark or registered
trademark of Arthur Frommer. Used under license. All other trademarks are the
property of their respective owners. Wiley Publishing, Inc. is not associated with
any product or vendor mentioned in this book.

ISBN 0-7645-7152-4

Editor: Richard Goodman
Production Editor: Bethany André
Cartographer: Elizabeth Puhl
Photo Editor: Richard Fox
Production by Wiley Indianapolis Composition Services

Front cover photo: Man leaping for Frisbee®
Back cover photo: The Giant Dipper roller coaster in Mission Bay, San Diego

For information on our other products and services or to obtain technical support,
please contact our Customer Care Department within the U.S. at 800/762-2974,
outside the U.S. at 317/572-3993 or fax 317/572-4002.

Wiley also publishes its books in a variety of electronic formats. Some content that
appears in print may not be available in electronic formats.

Manufactured in the United States of America

5   4   3   2   1

Contents

1 The Best of California   10

by Harry Basch, Erika Lenkert, Matthew Richard Poole & David Swanson

2 Planning Your Trip to California   23

by Matthew Richard Poole

3 For International Visitors   52

8 The Far North: Lake Tahoe, the Shasta Cascades & Lassen Volcanic National Park   243

by Matthew Richard Poole

9 The High Sierra: Yosemite, Mammoth Lakes & Sequoia/Kings Canyon   286

by Matthew Richard Poole

10 Sacramento, the Gold Country & the Central Valley   321

by Matthew Richard Poole

11 The Monterey Peninsula & the Big Sur Coast   355

by Matthew Richard Poole

15 The Southern California Desert   627

by Harry Basch

16 San Diego & Environs   671

by David Swanson

Index   741

List of Maps

About the Authors

Harry Basch, and his wife Shirley Slater, have been a husband-and-wife travel-writing team whose books, articles, and photographs have been published internationally over the past 25 years. He and Shirley are the authors of *Frommer's Exploring America by RV, RV Vacations For Dummies,* and have contributed to *Frommer's USA.*

A native San Franciscan, **Erika Lenkert** spends her time traipsing through San Francisco and across the globe in search of adventure and great food. She has written for *Travel + Leisure, Food & Wine, Bride's, Wine Country Living, San Francisco Magazine, Los Angeles Magazine,* and *Time Out.* Her latest work is an entertaining and cooking guide called *The Last-Minute Party Girl: Fashionable, Fearless, and Foolishly Simple Entertaining* (www.lastminutepartygirl.com), which mixes fun, humor, and recipes into a tasty, useful guide to living large, Bay Area–style.

Matthew Richard Poole, a native Californian, has authored more than two dozen travel guides to California, Hawaii, and abroad, and is a regular contributor to radio and television travel programs, including numerous guest appearances on the award-winning *Bay Area Backroads* television show. Before becoming a full-time travel writer and photographer, he worked as an English tutor in Prague, ski instructor in the Swiss Alps, and scuba instructor in Maui. Highly allergic to office buildings and mortgage payments, he spends most of his time traveling the globe searching for new adventures. His other Frommer's titles include *California from $70 a Day, San Francisco from $70 a Day, Los Angeles, Portable Los Angeles,* the *Irreverent Guide to San Francisco,* and *Portable Disneyland®.*

San Diego native **David Swanson's** first travels were in the back of a Volkswagen bus with his parents through Yosemite and the Sierras, San Francisco, and Santa Barbara. His stories and photography have appeared in *the Los Angeles Times, Chicago Tribune, Boston Globe, Miami Herald, Dallas Morning News,* and *The Globe and Mail* among many others. His work also appears in *National Geographic Traveler, Bride's, TravelAge West,* and he is a contributing editor at *Caribbean Travel & Life.*

An Invitation to the Reader

In researching this book, we discovered many wonderful places-hotels, restaurants, shops, and more. We're sure you'll find others. Please tell us about them, so we can share the information with your fellow travelers in upcoming editions. If you were disappointed with a recommendation, we'd love to know that, too. Please write to:

Frommer's California 2005
Wiley Publishing, Inc. • 111 River St. • Hoboken, NJ 07030-5774

An Additional Note

Please be advised that travel information is subject to change at any time-and this is especially true of prices. We therefore suggest that you write or call ahead for confirmation when making your travel plans. The authors, editors, and publisher cannot be held responsible for the experiences of readers while traveling. Your safety is important to us, however, so we encourage you to stay alert and be aware of your surroundings. Keep a close eye on cameras, purses, and wallets, all favorite targets of thieves and pickpockets.

Frommer's Star Ratings, Icons & Abbreviations

Every hotel, restaurant, and attraction listing in this guide has been ranked for quality, value, service, amenities, and special features using a **star-rating system.** In country, state, and regional guides, we also rate towns and regions to help you narrow down your choices and budget your time accordingly. Hotels and restaurants are rated on a scale of zero (recommended) to three stars (exceptional). Attractions, shopping, nightlife, towns, and regions are rated according to the following scale: zero stars (recommended), one star (highly recommended), two stars (very highly recommended), and three stars (must-see).

In addition to the star-rating system, we also use **seven feature icons** that point you to the great deals, in-the-know advice, and unique experiences that separate travelers from tourists. Throughout the book, look for:

Finds	Special finds—those places only insiders know about
Fun Fact	Fun facts—details that make travelers more informed and their trips more fun
Kids	Best bets for kids, and advice for the whole family
Moments	Special moments—those experiences that memories are made of
Overrated	Places or experiences not worth your time or money
Tips	Insider tips—great ways to save time and money
Value	Great values—where to get the best deals

The following **abbreviations** are used for credit cards:

AE	American Express	DISC	Discover	V	Visa
DC	Diners Club	MC	MasterCard		

Frommers.com

Now that you have the guidebook to a great trip, visit our website at **www.frommers.com** for travel information on more than 3,000 destinations. With features updated regularly, we give you instant access to the most current trip-planning information available. At Frommers.com, you'll also find the best prices on airfares, accommodations, and car rentals-and you can even book travel online through our travel booking partners. At Frommers.com, you'll also find the following:

- Online updates to our most popular guidebooks
- Vacation sweepstakes and contest giveaways
- Newsletter highlighting the hottest travel trends
- Online travel message boards with featured travel discussions

What's New in California

From small hotels in San Francisco to a new ballpark in San Diego, change is afoot in the regions of California. Here's a quick overview:

SAN FRANCISCO Where to Stay Hotel rates in San Francisco are still substantially discounted. Shop the Internet and call hotels directly for the best bargains.

There's a new luxury boutique hotel, the **Argonaut Hotel,** 495 Jefferson St. (© **866/415-0704** or 415/563-0800; www.argonauthotel.com), at the Maritime National Historic Park, half a block from the bay. The four-story timber-and-brick landmark building built in 1909 is now a slick place to sleep. Suites come fully loaded with telescopes and spa tubs. Rates range from $159 to $339 double and suites go from $249 to $499.

Where to Dine The past year left hundreds of restaurant closures in its wake. But there is a bright side. **Campton Place Hotel,** 340 Stockton St. (© **800/235-4300** or 415/781-5555), is serving European-inspired cuisine that's rooted in Provence with an emphasis on pureness, simplicity, and the Bay Area's local bounty now that young Swiss-born Daniel Humm is in the kitchen.

Last year downtown's Shannon Court got a new name—**Hotel Adagio,** 550 Geary St. (© **800/228-8830** or 415/775-5000)—and new interiors under the creative eye of the Joie de Vivre hotel group. Its restaurant and bar **Cortez** (© **415/292-6360**) is the creation of one of the city's favorite restaurateurs, Pascal Rigo of Pacific

Heights's **Chez Nous.** His Mediterranean-inspired menu features what he's best at: small plates of tasty tapas, great breads, and reasonable prices starting around $6 and topping out at $16. The dinner-only joint is luring theatergoers and downtown diners.

Attractions The **Ferry Plaza Farmers' Market,** Embarcadero, at Market Street (© **415/353-5650**), now at the renovated **Ferry Building Marketplace,** keeps getting better and is a must-visit. Not only do they have an enormous organic market hawking the bounties of local farmers, florists, and specialty food purveyors, they also host myriad cooking demonstrations. The outdoor market is open 4 days a week (see www.ferrybuildingmarket place.com for hours), but the interior gourmet shopping emporium is open daily. This is a great place just to come, hang out, and graze.

The **Conservatory of Flowers,** Golden Gate Park, reopened in September 2003 after a major renovation to its delicate and dazzling glass design. Drop by for a stunning peruse of the 1878 glass building and its treasure trove of the planet's most gorgeous plants.

The **Cliff House,** at Ocean Beach, is still undergoing renovation, but remains open to visitors.

THE WINE COUNTRY Fab food is still a big draw in Napa Valley, and two new additions up the culinary ante. Famed French Laundry chef Thomas Keller has opened **Bouchon Bakery,** 6528 Washington St., Yountville (© **707/944-2253**), next to his happening bistro Bouchon. Drop in anytime for bread baked twice daily, killer treats (think éclairs, cookies, tarts, and more), coffee drinks, and all-around pricy but near-perfect pastry. Also new and hot in Yountville, is **Père Jeanty,** 6725 Washington St. (© **707/945-1000**), the sister restaurant to popular Bistro Jeanty. Here, Philippe Jeanty directs his skills to Provençal-inspired fare, served in beautiful French-country surroundings.

On the Sonoma side, **La Poste,** 599 Broadway, just south of the plaza (© **707/939-3663**), may be the town's tiniest dining room, but it's already got a big reputation going for it. The shoebox-size French bistro with 26 chairs and maple banquettes is a Francophile's dream with a chalkboard announcing chef Rob Larman's daily changing menu, which might include seared scallops seasoned with tomato-herb vinaigrette over truffled mashed potatoes; or braised veal cheeks with cream, Calvados, English peas, and chanterelles. Make reservations for the dinner-only spot, which is open Wednesday through Saturday.

Nearby, the **Harmony Club,** 480 First St. E. (© **707/996-9779**), is not only a looker with its elegant Italianate dining room, it also offers great food and live entertainment. Drop in anytime after their gourmet breakfast for "small plates" such as tender Moroccan spiced lamb loin with saffron couscous, grapes, and mint; French fries with tarragon aioli; and Scharffen Berger chocolate and orange Muscat torte. A musician entertains nightly. Open daily for breakfast, lunch, and dinner. Upstairs are six superluxury rooms, under the name of the Ledson Hotel.

THE NORTHERN COAST You'll find loads of new stuff in the Northern Coast chapter, starting with **Johnson's Oyster Farm** (© **415/669-1149**), in Point Reyes National Seashore. Buy a sack of right-out-of-the-water oysters and a bottle of Special Oyster Sauce, head to the beach, crack a beer, and shuck away. Also newly added is the romantic **Olema Inn & Restaurant,** 10000 Sir Francis Drake Blvd. (© **415/663-9559**). Built in 1876, it's a modern luxury that still retains much of its period charm, and the inn's restaurant is superb.

Point Reyes is full of expensive B&Bs, but the homey, well-maintained **Motel Inverness,** 12718 Sir Francis Drake Blvd. (© **888/669-6909**), is an exception and perfect for the budget-minded outdoor adventurer. I've also included a trio of side-trip sidebars: hanging out in **Point Reyes Station,** a former rail town just across the bay from the national seashore; tips on mountain biking in **Point Reyes;** and sunning yourself at nearby **Stinson Beach.**

Further up the coast I've added info about **Sea Ranch Home Rentals** (© **888/732-7262**), where you can rent a furnished home at one of the most beautiful seaside communities in the nation for as little as $150 per night. Also newly listed is the **St. Orres Restaurant,** 36601 Hwy. 1 (© **707/884-3335**), where chef Rosemary Campiformio has been wowing fans and food writers for years with her version of North Coast cuisine.

The newest addition to Mendocino lodging is the **Brewery Gulch Inn,** 9401 Coast Hwy. 1 N. (© **800/578-4454**), a three-story inn set high on a bluff overlooking Mendocino's Smuggler's Cove, built almost entirely from eco-salvaged old-growth redwood. I also included a sidebar on **Mendocino Nightlife,** from drinkin' Buds with the locals at **Dick's Place,** 45080 Main St. (© **707/937-5643**), to rock-n-reggae at the **Caspar Inn,** 14957 Caspar Rd. (© **707/964-5565;** www.casparinn.com).

Up near Eureka in the small town of Ferndale is the newly renovated **Shaw House Inn Bed and Breakfast,** 703 Main St. (© **800/557-SHAW**). This gorgeous B&B is the oldest B&B in California and one of the prettiest Victorian homes I've ever seen.

THE FAR NORTH South Lake Tahoe's $1-billion redevelopment plan reached new heights with the completion of the 464-room **Marriott's Timber Lodge & Grand Residence Club,** 4100 Lake Tahoe Blvd. (© **800/ 845-5279**), a sprawling "alpine village" next to the casinos. I prefer the far humbler **Zephyr Cove Resort,** Highway 50 at Zephyr Cove (© **775/ 589-4907**), a lakeside bargain with everything you need for a relaxing vacation on the lake (such as a beach bar, for example).

I've also included a couple of my favorite new South Lake restaurants: **The Naked Fish,** 3940 Lake Tahoe Blvd. (© **530/541-3474**), by far the best sushi bar in Tahoe, complete with Japanese chefs who love to party; and **Ivano's,** 605 Hwy. 50 (© **775/586-1070**), an intimate 10-table room serving Tahoe's best Italian cuisine.

The new **Wild Goose,** 7320 N. Lake Blvd. (© **530/546-3640**), is not only the finest restaurant in Lake Tahoe, it's made my top-10-in-the-state list. Trust me, you *have* to dine here if you come to Tahoe.

I've also added a couple of great cabin-style lodgings on the lake: the **North Lake Lodge,** 8716 N. Lake Blvd. (© **888/923-5253**), offering lakeside cabins for as little as $60 a night; and the **Tamarack Lodge,** 2311 N. Lake Blvd. (© **888/824-6323**), which has been around so long that Clark Gable and Gary Cooper played poker in these gleaming knotty-pine cabins secreted among pines.

Over in Redding I've discovered an amazing roadside seafood stand (yes, in landlocked Redding). For more than 30 years, the signature seafood baskets at **Buz's Crab Stand,** 2159 East St. (© **530/243-2120**), have everyone who's in on the secret stopping in Redding for lunch and dinner.

THE HIGH SIERRA Lots of new restaurants and lodgings in this chapter, starting with Groveland. On your way to Yosemite, stop by the 150-year-old **Iron Door Saloon,** 18763 Main St. (© **209/962-6244**), for a charbroiled buffalo burger and a try at tacking a $1 bill to the ceiling. Or stay the night at the historic **Hotel Charlotte,** 18736 Main St. (© **800/961-7799**), an inexpensive little charmer built in 1921 and listed on the National Register of Historic Places.

Another good deal is **The Yosemite Bug Lodge,** 6979 Calif. 140 (© **209/ 966-6666**), a cross between a mountain lodge and summer camp that's perfect for young families that are into the outdoors. Romantics will prefer the new **Big Creek Inn,** 1221 Hwy. 41 (© **559/641-2828**), an idyllic riverside B&B just 2 miles from the south entrance to Yosemite National Park.

On the east side of Yosemite is one of my favorite sights in the state, eerie Mono Lake, so I've added a bit on the **Mono Basin Scenic Area Visitors Center** (© 760/647-3044; www. monolake.org) and lodging in pretty June Lake: the **Fern Creek Lodge,** 4628 Hwy. 158 (© **800/621-9146**), a spread of simple yet fully furnished cabins on the sunrise side of the Eastern High Sierra.

In the mountain town of Mammoth, I've added a couple of dining spots: **Berger's Restaurant,** 6118 Minaret Rd. (© **760/934-6622**), a cabinlike cafe serving a huge array of burgers, steak, ribs, chicken, and such; and **Grumpy's Saloon and Eatery,** 361 Mammoth Rd. (© **760/934-8587**), a massive log "sports restaurant" with 35 TVs, a great selection of beers on tap, barbecued ribs, and table games.

Dan Braun has added a slew of new cabins at his **Evergreen Lodge** in Groveland (33160 Evergreen Rd.; © 800/935-6343), on the border of Yosemite National Park. His lodge is so fun and affordable that it fills up quickly, so make a reservation ASAP.

SACRAMENTO & THE GOLD COUNTRY I used to live in Sactown so I know the scoop. Ergo, I added an entire page of Sacramento bests—best burgers, best coffee joint, best Mexican, best breakfast, and—of course—the best brewpub. I also added the **Best Western Sutter House,** 1100 H St. (© 800/830-1314), a modern hotel with a pool, central location, and far better rates than the Hyatt or Hilton.

In the Gold Country I've added the **Nevada City Inn,** 760 Zion St. (© 800/977-8884), a charmer with cabinlike rooms and a park setting with barbecues, picnic tables, and a horseshoe pit. If you can't afford the pricey Nevada City B&B experience, the simple, clean **Holiday Lodge,** 1221 E. Main St. (© 800/742-7125), has a pool, sauna, and even a 9-hole golf course across the street. In Grass Valley is the new **212 Bistro at the Holbrooke,** 212 W. Main St. (© 530/273-1353), the most authentic and nostalgic restaurant in town serving mesquite-smoked prime rib and Cajun-rubbed steaks.

Further south on Highway 49 in Sonora is the newly renovated **Gunn House Hotel,** 286 S. Washington St. (© 209/532-3421), one of the best deals in the Gold Country. It's loaded with charm, history, quality antiques, and a pretty pool and patio.

THE MONTEREY PENINSULA I would have never found the **Fern River Resort,** 5250 Hwy. 9 (© 831/335-4412), on my own. It's a mountain retreat on the San Lorenzo River, only 4 miles from Santa Cruz town, but surrounded by redwood groves.

Also new to the Santa Cruz section is **Rosa's Rosticeria,** 439 Lake Ave. (© 831/479-3536), where Latin music goes well with the sunny seating, harbor view, Cuban cuisine, and wickedly good Black Margaritas; and **The Crepe Place,** 1134 Soquel Ave. (© 831/429-6994), a local favorite serving 15 styles of delicious crepes.

New additions to Monterey and Pacific Grove sections include the **Casa Munras Garden Hotel,** 700 Munras Ave. (© 800/222-2558), the original hacienda to the last Spanish diplomat to California; the **Butterfly Grove Inn,** 1073 Lighthouse Ave. (© 800/337-9244), a seaside place so peaceful butterflies migrate here and deer wander the streets; **Rosine's,** 434 Alvarado St. (© 831/375-1400), local favorite for its charbroiled pork chops and down-to-earth prices; **Thai Bistro,** 159 Central Ave. (© 831/372-8700), the most popular Thai restaurant in the region; and **Toastie's Cafe,** 702 Lighthouse Dr. (© 831/373-7543), which makes a mean eggs Benedict and addictive waffles

In Carmel I discovered two quality lodgings charging moderate rates: the **Pine Inn Hotel,** Ocean Avenue (© 800/228-3851), with its turn-of-the-20th-century-bordello-meets-the-Far-East decor, and the **Vagabond House,** Fourth Street (© 800/262-1262), a warm, homey English Tudor inn. As for new restaurants in Carmel, I discovered two gems: **Club Jalapeño,** San Carlos Avenue (© 831/626-1997), the best, hippest, and most authentic Mexican restaurant in town; and **Tommy's Wok,** Mission Street (© 831/624-8518), a little Chinese restaurant with a make-it-all-from-scratch philosophy and a Mongolian lamb dish that'll blow your taste buds. I've also included a trio of longtime favorites: **The Hog's Breath Inn,** San Carlos Street (© 831/625-1044), Clint's Eastwood old hangout; **Little**

Swiss Cafe, Sixth Street (© 831/624-5007), where the village's best breakfast is served all day; and **Neilsen Brothers Market,** San Carlos Street (© 831/624-6263), the top deli in town.

As for things to do in Carmel, we're now hip to **Carmel Walks** (© 831/642-2700), a tour guide company offering 2-hour guided walks through Carmel's gardens, hidden pathways, and fairy-tale-like cottages of bohemian writers, artists, and movie stars.

Since most visitors prefer to camp in Bur Sur, I've included **The Big Sur Center Deli,** on Highway 1 (© 831/667-2225), the best place to stock up on chicken, enchiladas, fresh-baked goods, strong coffee, and cold beer.

THE CENTRAL COAST If you're headed to the coastal minitown of Cambria, the rustic, secluded cabins and an awesome Olympic-size pool are two good reasons to stay at the **Cambria Pines Lodge,** 2905 Burton Dr. (© 800/445-6868), and the lobster bisque alone is worth a trip to Cambria's **Bistro Solé,** 1980 Main St. (© 805/927-0887).

Down in Paso Robles I discovered **Busi's on the Park,** 1122 Pine St. (© 805/238-1390), a cozy tavern with a pretty outdoor patio and tasty saffron mussels.

Lots of new stuff in Santa Barbara: The **Four Seasons Biltmore,** 1260 Channel Dr. (© 800/332-3442), just built a multimillion-dollar, 10,000-square-foot Spanish-style spa. **Nu,** 1129 State St. (© 805/965-1500), is my new favorite restaurant for lobster risotto and cocktails; and **Don Pepe,** 701 Chapala St. (© 805/730-1612), is another delicious reason why I'm always on the prowl for authentic Mexican taco stands. I've added several of Santa Barbara's best nightlife venues as well (old stomping grounds from my college days). Also new to this chapter is the **San Ysidro Ranch,**

900 San Ysidro Lane (© 800/368-6788), near Santa Barbara. Considered one of the most romantic destinations in the world, it's been a hideaway for the rich and famous for decades.

I've also added a fantastic moderately priced lodge in pricey Ojai, the **Blue Iguana Inn,** 11794 N. Ventura Ave. (© 805/646-5277). Its colorful Southwestern decor, pool, and large lawn are a winning combo.

A couple of new additions to Ventura: **Deco,** 394 E. Main St. (© 805/667-2120), serves a mean San Francisco–style cioppino and wasabe-spiced crab cakes; and **Taquería Vallarta,** 278 E. Main St. (© 805/643-3037), is another authentic order-at-the-counter locals-only hot spot serving excellent enchiladas.

LOS ANGELES Where to Stay It seems like wherever you turn, L.A.'s hotels are upping the ante with multi-million-dollar face-lifts and mood-enhancing feng shui elements. The new **Ambrose,** 1255 20th St., Santa Monica (© 877/262-7673), blends Arts & Crafts movement with Asian influences such as a Japanese garden, a koi pond, and fountains. Rates start at a very reasonable $165 for an upscale boutique, so book a room while it's still a bargain.

Also new to this edition is **Le Merigot,** 1740 Ocean Ave., Santa Monica (© 800/228-9290), a low-key luxury hotel and spa right on the ocean. Package deals include convertible Porsche Boxster or BMW Z4 Roadster rentals, surfing lessons, and full-session Swedish massages—*if* you can drag yourself out of your "Cloud Nine" bed.

I also discovered a great budget motel: the **Farmer's Daughter,** 115 S. Fairfax Ave., midtown (© 800/334-1658). It's a cheery lodge with lots of bright colors, a country-kitsch theme, and plenty of free perks. Across the street is the Farmers Market—easy access to an entire block of inexpensive foodstuffs, great shopping, and weekend entertainment

Where to Dine It's been an insane year for the L.A. restaurant scene, with so many excellent restaurants opening in the past 12 months that they're calling it the "Golden Age" of dining in L.A. I've included 10 of the best, such as **Le Dôme**, 8720 Sunset Blvd., West Hollywood (© **310/659-6919**), an old Sunset Strip hangout that recently reopened after $2-million makeover by designer *du moment* Dodd Mitchell. Feast on Japanese black pig baby back ribs and Kumamoto oysters with L.A.'s pretty people at the outdoor terrace while the tourists walk by.

Maple Drive, 345 N. Maple Dr., Beverly Hills (© **310/274-9800**), has a new look and new menu by chef Eric Klein, the former executive sous chef at Spago. Celebrities and entertainment bigwigs arrive nightly to dine on Klein's signature thin-crusted tarte flambées while listing to live jazz.

I finally made it to **La Cachette,** 10506 Santa Monica Blvd., Century City (© **310/470-4992**), a very elegant, romantic French restaurant presided over by Jean Francois Meteigner, one of America's most influential French chefs. His *cuisine naturelle* is light on cream and butter but heavy on flavor (the braised Kurobuta black pork shank with braised baby back ribs and Banyul vinegar sauce is le bomb).

Being a fan of a good steak, I've included two great steakhouses this year: **Mastro's Steakhouse,** 246 N. Canon Dr., Beverly Hills (© **310/888-8782**), where even big eaters have trouble finishing the Fred Flintstone–size slabs of beef. And some of the finest and most authentic Mexican food I've ever had is being served at **Frida,** 236 S. Beverly Dr., Beverly Hills (© **310/278-7666**), a newcomer to the Beverly Hills dining scene (the mole dishes alone are worth the drive over here).

Joachim Splichal's **Patina,** 141 S. Grand Ave., downtown (© **213/972-3331**), has been relocated to the new Walt Disney Concert Hall and is more popular than ever. The après-show crowd creates quite a din as they dine on sautéed black truffled Brussels sprouts with a sweet-potato purée and crispy-skinned yellowtail snapper served on a bed of fava-bean purée.

If you love sushi as much as I do, you're in luck: I've included two new Asian restaurants. **Koi,** 730 N. La Cienega Blvd., West Hollywood (© **310/659-9449**), is one of L.A.'s hottest new eateries with regulars ranging from George Clooney to Jennifer Garner, and Demi and Ashton. Start with the baked crab roll with edible rice paper and a glass of Koi sake.

Dodd Mitchell strikes again at the opium-den-like **Zen Grill & Sake Lounge,** 1051 Broxton Ave., Westwood Village (© **310/209-1994**). Bathed in a soothing amber glow, this sexy new restaurant serves wonderful pan-Asian cuisine and more than 50 brands of premium sake.

Attractions Universal Studios Hollywood (© **818/662-3801**) has a new thrill ride called **Revenge of the Mummy,** a super-high-tech indoor rollercoaster with creepy animatronic Warrior Mummies that drop down and scare the heck out of you. **Six Flags Magic Mountain** (© **661/255-4500**) beefed up their ride selection with Scream!, a 'coaster where riders are strapped into a "flying chair" and raced upside down at 65 mph.

The beautiful **Walt Disney Concert Hall,** First Street and Grand Avenue (© **323/850-2000**), designed by world-renowned architect Frank O. Gehry, now offers 45-minute audio walking tours narrated by actor John Lithgow.

The Autry Museum of Western Heritage has been renamed the **Museum of the American West,** 4700 Western Heritage Way (© 323/667-2000), but it's still one of the country's finest museums of the American West.

Red Line Tours (© 323/402-1074) is now offering two 90-minute great walking tours of downtown L.A.: the Inside Historic Downtown L.A. Tour, and Contemporary Downtown L.A., which includes the new Walt Disney Concert Hall

Paramount Pictures, 5555 Melrose Ave. (© 323/956-1777), the only major studio still located in Hollywood, is again offering a 2-hour walking tour around its Hollywood headquarters on a first-come, first-served basis, giving visitors a real-life behind-the-scenes look at working movie and television facilities.

I've also added a few fun day trips, including **Topanga Canyon,** where the itinerary includes horseback riding, shopping for vintage clothes, accessories, and plenty of cold margaritas; and spending the day under a big oak while watching polo matches at **Will Rogers Polo Club,** 1501 Will Rogers State Park Rd., Pacific Palisades (© 310/573-5000).

On a final note, the **Griffith Observatory** is still closed for a major renovation and expansion and probably won't reopen until 2006. However, a **"Griffith Observatory Satellite,"** south of the Los Angeles Zoo at 4800 Western Heritage Way (© 323/664-1181), hosts planetarium shows and provides a telescope to view the stars at night

Shopping This year I enlisted my resident L.A. shopping expert, Tracy Larrua, to fill me in on all the hot new stores. Some highlights include: **Cloud's,** 2719 Main St. (© 310/399-2059), where you'll find heavenly scented candles; **Arts & Letters,** 2665

Main St. (© 310/314-7345), a stationery haven, including invitations by the owner herself, Marilyn Golin; **Sun Precautions,** 1600 Montana Ave. (© 310/451-5858), specializing in 100% UV protection apparel; **GR2,** 2062 Sawtelle Blvd. (© 310/445-9276) and **Giant Robot,** 2015 Sawtelle Blvd. (© 310/478-1819), two Japantown stores specializing in Asian-American pop culture items.

I've also added new stores along my favorite shopping street, **Abbot Kinney Boulevard:** For one-of-a-kind jewelry aka "metals with an edge," check out **Nagual,** 1326 Abbott Kinney Blvd. (© 310/396-8500); **Strange Invisible Perfumes,** 1209 Abbot Kinney Blvd. (© 310/314-1505), can make you a custom scent; and **Firefly,** 1413 Abbot Kinney Blvd. (© 310/450-6288), is that one store you can go into and find that great baby gift, stationery, books, quirky handbags, and clothing.

After Dark There's no shortage of weird and wonderful in this city. Nightclubs I've included are **The Avalon Hollywood,** 1735 N. Vine St., Hollywood (© 323/462-8900), a good place to imbibe, dance, and cavort until the wee hours; **Babe's & Ricky's Inn,** 4339 Leimert Blvd., Leimert Park (© 323/295-9112), where great blues guitarists are the rule; and **Nacional,** 1645 Wilcox Ave., Hollywood (© 323/962-7712), Hollywood's hottest dance floor and a magnet for the hip crowd

As for cool bars, newcomers this edition include **Hank's Bar,** 840 S. Grand Ave. (© 213/396-7718), a classic downtown watering hole on the ground floor of the Stillwell Hotel; and **The Standard Downtown,** 550 S. Flower St. (© 213/892-8080), an ultrahip rooftop hotel bar where lovely ladies sip exotic cocktails amid waterbeds and bent-plastic loungers.

And be sure to catch a movie at the "The World's Most Private Public Theater," the new **ArcLight Cinemas,** 6360 W. Sunset Blvd. (© **323/464-4226**), where each seat is reserved, ushers keep it quiet, late arrivals are forbidden, and there's a full bar and lounge serving appetizers.

SIDE TRIPS FROM LOS ANGELES Everything new in the Side Trips chapter is about romance and adventure, starting with **The Sky Room** restaurant in Long Beach, 40 S. Locust Ave. (© **562/983-2703**). You'll get a sense of what fine dining must have been like during Hollywood's golden age at this romantic retro supper club.

Further south in Laguna Beach is a spectacular new 30-acre resort called **Montage Resort & Spa,** 30801 S. Coast Hwy. (© **888/715-6700**). This neo-Craftsman-style hotel and spa is on the beach, and everything about it is spacious, immaculate, tasteful, and expensive—but worth the splurge.

As for the adventure part, I risked my life to review **Barnstorming Adventures** (© **800/759-5667**), an aviation company in Carlsbad that gives nonpilots the chance to fly in a 1920s-era biplane ride, and to actually fly—as in control the stick—a World War II fighter plane.

THE SOUTHERN CALIFORNIA DESERT Palm Springs' historic 74-room **Viceroy Palm Springs,** 415 S. Belardo Rd. (© **800/237-3687;** www.viceroypalmsprings.com), the former Estrella, built in the 1930s, has a glam face-lift. The inn has been lavished with modern design elements, a cutting-edge spa, and a new restaurant and bar, **Citron,** which features a fusion of California and French sensibilities.

The nine-unit **Calla Lily Inn** (© **888/888-5787;** www.callalily palmsprings.com) opened recently after an extensive renovation. Each of the units that surround the pool varies from a king-size double to a two-bedroom suite. The Calla Lily serves an evening cordial or brandy to top off your evening.

SAN DIEGO & ENVIRONS San Diego has two big new attractions. First is a new home for the Padres baseball team, **PETCO Park** (www.padres.com). Across the street from the convention center downtown, the ballpark's construction was steeped in political squabbles and legal delays but has drawn sellout crowds since it opened.

Also new is the **San Diego Aircraft Carrier Museum** (© **619/544-9600;** www.midway.org), the city's first museum devoted to naval history, located at the Embarcadero. You can't miss this attraction—just drive south on Harbor Drive and look for the 1,001-foot-long aircraft carrier parked at Navy Pier. Climb aboard the USS *Midway* and explore this piece of military history.

With the downtown ballpark open, a roster of hotel projects is hot on the heels. At the head of the list is the new **Omni San Diego Hotel,** 675 L St. (© **800/THE-OMNI** or 619/231-6664; www.omnihotels.com), the only hotel connected (via skybridge) to a Major League ballpark. The Omni's rooftop terrace—with its swimming pool, Jacuzzi, and fireplace—is a snazzy perch for sunning and socializing, and 12 rooms even offer ballpark views. Then there's **500 West,** at 500 W. Broadway (© **619/234-5252;** www.500west hotel.com), which opened following a $9-million makeover of downtown's old YMCA building and offers 260 rooms geared to the budget traveler, with an eye-catching price-range of $69 to $89 for doubles.

Summer nights in the Gaslamp have only gotten busier with the opening of the ballpark, and **Mister Tiki Mai Tai Lounge,** 801 Fifth Ave., at F Street (© **619/233-1183**), is one of the latest arrivals. The eatery has more than a dozen affectionately kitschy Tiki gods and masks custom-carved by San Diego Poly-pop lover Bosko Hrnjak. No one visits San Diego without experiencing one of the city's fantastic animal parks, and there's news at all three this year. Continuing its move toward ride-type enhancements, **SeaWorld,** 500 SeaWorld Dr. (© **619/226-3901**), debuted **Journey to Atlantis,** a water-coaster taking guests on a splash-filled ride. At the **San Diego Zoo,** 2920 Zoo Dr. (© **619/234-3153;** www.sandiego zoo.org), the $28-million Heart of the Zoo project will be completed in 2005, offering bioclimatically correct (and multispecies) exhibits. And at the zoo's sibling, the **Wild Animal Park,** San Pasqual Valley Rd. in Escondido (© **760/747-8702**), a crew of seven young African elephants were imported from Swaziland, rescuing them from probable culling.

1

The Best of California

by Harry Basch, Erika Lenkert, Matthew Richard Poole & David Swanson

California's allure is understandable. It really is warm and sunny most of the year, movie stars do abound in Los Angeles, and you can't swing a cat by its tail without hitting a rollerblading babe in Venice Beach. This part of the California mystique—however exaggerated it may be—does exist, and it's not hard to find.

But there's more—a lot more—to California that isn't scripted, sanitized, and broadcast to the world's mesmerized masses. Beyond the glitter and glamour is an incredibly diverse state that, if it ever seceded from the Union, would be a productive and powerful nation. We've got it all: redwood forests, an incredibly verdant Central Valley, the Sierra Nevada, deserts, a host of world-renowned cities, and hundreds of miles of stunning coastline.

And despite the crime, pollution, traffic, and earthquakes for which California is famous, we're still the golden child of the United States: America's spoiled rich kid everyone else either loves or loathes. (Neighboring Oregon, for example, sells lots of license-plate rims that proudly state, "I hate California.") But, truth be told, we really don't care. Californians *know* they live in one of the most diverse and interesting places in the world, and we're proud of the state we call home.

Granted, there's no guarantee that you'll bump into Arnold Schwarzenegger or learn how to surf, but if you have a little time, a little money, and—most importantly—an adventurous spirit, then Erika, David, Harry and I will help guide you through one of the most fulfilling vacations of your life. The four of us travel the world for a living, but we *choose* to live in California, because there's no other place on earth that has so much to offer.

—*Matthew Richard Poole*

1 The Best of Natural California

- **Redwood National & State Parks:** Come see the largest of all living things, the *Sequoia sempervirens*. Within the old-growth forests that line the northern California coast are acres and acres of unbelievably massive and majestic redwood trees, all of which shade a thick, lush canopy of huge ferns, mosses, and wild orchids. See "Redwood National & State Parks" in chapter 7.

- **Lake Tahoe:** One of the world's most magnificent bodies of fresh water, sparkling Lake Tahoe is famous for its pure, azure water and incredible volume. See "Lake Tahoe" in chapter 8.

- **Yosemite National Park:** You're in for the ultimate treat at Yosemite. Nothing in the state—maybe even the world—compares to this vast wilderness and its miles of rivers, lakes, peaks, and valleys. With 3 out of 10 of the world's tallest waterfalls, the largest granite monolith in the world, and some of the world's largest trees, Yosemite is one of the most fantastic natural places on the planet. See "Yosemite National Park" in chapter 9.

- **Big Sur:** Rock-strewn beaches, towering cliffs, and redwood forests combine to form what may be the world's most dramatic coastal panorama. Our favorite vantage point for taking it all in is Garrapata State Park, a 2,879-acre preserve. See "The Big Sur Coast" in chapter 11.
- **The Elkhorn Slough Safari:** When you're sick of schlepping your way through Monterey, take a 20-minute drive north and embark on a safe, friendly voyage best described as stepping into the pages of *National Geographic*. The up-close views of "rafts" of otters, harbor seals, and hundreds of bird species are priceless. See "Monterey" in chapter 11.
- **Cachuma Lake:** On mountainous and scenic Calif. 154, halfway between Solvang and Santa Barbara, is this winter home to dozens of American bald eagles. Loons, white pelicans, and Canada geese are some of the other migratory birds that call this glassy lake home part of the year. See "The Central Coast Wine Country: Paso Robles & the Santa Ynez Valley" in chapter 12.
- **Joshua Tree National Park:** You'll find awesome rock formations, groves of flowering cacti and stately Joshua trees, ancient Native American petroglyphs, and shifting sand dunes in this desert wonderland. See "Joshua Tree National Park" in chapter 15.
- **Torrey Pines State Reserve:** Poised on a majestic cliff overlooking the Pacific Ocean, this state park is set aside for the rarest pine tree in North America. The reserve has short trails that immerse hikers into a delicate and beautiful coastal environment. See chapter 16.

2 The Best Beaches

- **Drake's Beach:** This is a massive stretch of white sand at Point Reyes National Seashore. Winds and choppy seas make it rough for swimmers, but sun worshippers can have their Marin County tan for the day. See "Point Reyes National Seashore" in chapter 7.
- **Santa Cruz's Beaches:** Santa Cruz has 29 miles of beaches that are varied enough to please all comers: surfers, swimmers, fishers, sailboarders, the sand-pail-and-shovel set, and the bikini and biceps crowd. For starters, walk down the steps from the famous Santa Cruz Beach Boardwalk to the mile-long Main Beach, complete with summer lifeguards and golden-oldie tunes drifting over the sand. See "Santa Cruz" in chapter 11.
- **Santa Barbara's East Beach:** This wide swath of white sand hosts beach umbrellas, sand-castle builders, and volleyball games. On Sundays local artists display their wares beneath the elegant palm trees. See "Santa Barbara" in chapter 12.
- **Malibu's Legendary Beaches:** Zuma and Surfrider beaches served as inspiration for the 1960s surf music that embodies the Southern California beach experience. Surfrider, just up from Malibu Pier, is home to L.A.'s best waves. Zuma is loaded with amenities, including snack bars, restrooms, and jungle gyms. In addition to some of the state's best sunbathing, you can walk in front of the Malibu Colony, a star-studded enclave of multimillion-dollar

homes. See "L.A.'s Beaches & Coastal Attractions" in chapter 13.

- **La Jolla's Beaches:** Roughly translated, *La Jolla* means "the jewel," and the beaches of La Jolla's bluff-lined coast truly are gems. Each has a distinct personality: Surfers love Windansea's

waves, harbor seals have adopted the Children's Pool, La Jolla Shores is popular for swimming and sunbathing, while the Cove is a top snorkeling spot and your best chance to spot the rare California state fish, the garibaldi. See "Beaches" in chapter 16.

3 The Best Golf Courses

- **Pebble Beach Golf Links:** The famous 17-Mile Drive is the site of 10 national championships and the celebrity-laden AT&T Pebble Beach National Pro-Am. The nearby Pacific and a backdrop of the Del Monte Forest justify astronomical greens fees. See "Pebble Beach & the 17-Mile Drive" in chapter 11.
- **PGA West TPC Stadium Course** (La Quinta): The par-3 17th hole has a picturesque island green where Lee Trevino made Skins Game history with a hole-in-one. The rest of Pete Dye's 7,261-yard

design is flat with huge bunkers, lots of water, and severe mounding throughout. See "The Palm Springs Desert Resorts" in chapter 15.

- **Torrey Pines Golf Course** (La Jolla): Two 18-hole championship courses overlook the ocean and provide players with plenty of challenge. In February the Buick Invitational Tournament is held here. The rest of the year, these popular municipal courses are open to everybody. See "Outdoor Pursuits" in chapter 16.

4 The Best Californian Travel Experiences

- **Hot-Air Ballooning over Napa Valley:** Sure, you have to rise at dawn, but there's no better way to view Napa Valley than drifting over the vineyards in a balloon. Flights are offered in the morning on clear days, when the air is calm and cool. You can book a trip through your hotel or with **Bonaventura Balloon Company** (© 800/FLY-NAPA) or **Adventures Aloft** (© 800/944-4408). See "Hot-Air Ballooning over the Valley" in chapter 6.
- **Rafting Scenic Northern California Rivers:** You can whitewater raft through thrilling cascades of raging Class IV water or float through tranquil vistas of blue skies, deep forests, and wildlife. Depending on the river and the time of year, some trips

are okay for children over age 6. See chapters 7 and 8.

- **Exploring a Real Gold Mine:** Don your hardhat, "tag in," board the mine shuttle, and experience what it's like to be a gold miner. The **Sutter Gold Mine** tour company (© 866/762-2837) takes you deep into a mine that's loaded with gold deposits. You'll get an opportunity to sluice for some real gold. See "A Modern Gold Mine Tour" in chapter 10.
- **Taking a Studio Tour:** Studio tours are an opportunity to see the actual stage sets for shows such as *ER* and *The West Wing,* and you never know who you're going to see emerging from his or her Star Wagon. See "Exploring the City" in chapter 13.

- **Visiting Venice Beach's Ocean-front Walk:** You haven't visited L.A. properly until you've rented some skates in Venice and embarrassed yourself in front of thousands while taking in the human carnival around you. Nosh on a Jody Maroni's haute dog; buy some cheap sunglasses, silver jewelry, or ethnic garb, all while enjoying the wide beach, blue sea, and performers along the boardwalk. See "Exploring the City" in chapter 13.
- **Flying a World War II Fighter Aircraft:** Don your parachute, strap yourself into the 600-horsepower fighter aircraft, and prepare to have your mind blown as you (yes, you) perform aerobatic maneuvers—loops, rolls, lazy-8s—high above the Carlsbad coastline. It's an experience you'll never forget. See p. 620.
- **Getting Up Close to the Desert's Gigantic Windmills:** Anyone who's driven through the desert near Palm Springs has marveled at these structures. Now visitors have a chance to see, touch, and learn about the efficient power generators, and why they're clustered here. See "En Route to the Palm Springs Resorts" in chapter 15.
- **Explore Wreck Alley** (San Diego): Five drowned vessels sit on the sea floor, 2 miles off Mission Beach, providing a chance for certified divers to investigate an exciting nautical graveyard that includes a 366-foot Canadian destroyer, the *Yukon* (intentionally sunk in 2000). See "Outdoor Pursuits" in chapter 16.

5 The Best of Small-Town California

- **St. Helena:** In the heart of the Napa Valley, St. Helena is known for its Main Street, lined with Victorian storefronts featuring intriguing wares. In a horse and buggy, Robert Louis Stevenson and his bride once made their way down this street. Come for the old-timey, tranquil mood and the food. See "Napa Valley" in chapter 6.
- **Arcata:** Arcata has it all: its own redwood forest and bird marsh, a charming town square, great family-owned restaurants, and even its own minor-league baseball team, which draws the whole town together for an afternoon of pure camaraderie. See "Eureka & Environs" in chapter 7.
- **Nevada City:** The whole town is a National Historic Landmark and the best place to understand gold fever. Settled in 1849, it offers fine dining and shopping and a stock of Victorian frame houses. Relics of the cannibalistic Donner Party are on display at the 1861 Firehouse No. 1. See "The Gold Country" in chapter 10.
- **Pacific Grove:** You can escape the Monterey crowds by heading 2 miles west to Pacific Grove, known for its tranquil waterfront and unspoiled air. Thousands of monarch butterflies flock here between October and March. See "Pacific Grove" in chapter 11.
- **Cambria:** Near Hearst Castle, Cambria benefits from a stream of visitors, who bring the right amount of sophistication to this coastal town. Moonstone Beach holds a string of seaside lodges; farther north are dozens of sunbathing elephant seals, while the village is filled with B&Bs, artists' studios and galleries, and shops. See "San Simeon: Hearst Castle" in chapter 12.
- **Santa Catalina Island:** Taking a day trip to the small town of Catalina makes for a most adventurous day: a scenic boat ride, shopping, snorkeling and diving,

golfing, hiking, ice cream, sun-
burns, and DUI-free barhopping.
Tip: The helicopter taxi is cheaper
than you'd expect. See "Santa
Catalina" in chapter 14.

- **Julian:** This old mining town
in the Cuyamaca Mountains
near San Diego has long been
known for its wildflower fields,
the apple harvest, and charming
bed-and-breakfasts. Julian and the

surrounding communities were
shaken by forest fires in October
2003, but—from a touring stand-
point—most of the community is
back to normal. There's plenty of
pioneer history here, including a
local-history museum, an 1888
schoolhouse, and mining demonstrations. See "Julian: Gold, Apple
Pies & a Slice of Small-Town California" in chapter 16.

6 The Best Family Vacation Experiences

- **San Francisco:** The City by the
Bay is filled with pleasures for
every family member. Ride the
cable cars that "climb halfway to
the stars," visit the Exploratorium,
the Metreon, the zoo, the ships at
the National Maritime Museum,
Golden Gate Park, and much
more. See chapter 4.
- **Lake Tahoe:** Lake Tahoe has loads
of family-fun things to do. Skiing,
snowboarding, hiking, toboggan-
ing, swimming, fishing, boating,
water-skiing, mountain biking—
the list is nearly endless. See "Lake
Tahoe" in chapter 8.
- **Yosemite National Park:** Camping or staying in a cabin in
Yosemite is a premier family
attraction in California. Sites are
scattered over 17 campgrounds,
and the rugged beauty of the
Sierra Nevada surrounds you.
During the day, the family calendar is packed with hiking, bicycling, white-water rafting, and
even mountaineering to rugged,
snowy peaks. See "Yosemite
National Park" in chapter 9.
- **Santa Cruz:** Surfing, sea kayaking, hiking, fishing, and shopping,
not to mention those fantastic
beaches and the legendary amusement park on the boardwalk—
this funky bayside town has everything you need for the perfect

family vacation. See "Santa Cruz"
in chapter 11.
- **Big Bear Lake:** Families flock
year-round to this lake in the San
Bernardino Mountains, and not
just for the skiing. Horseback riding, watersports, and the Alpine
Slide (kind of a snowless bobsled)
are fun alternatives, and you can
see and learn about wildlife at the
Moonridge Animal Park. The village has a movie theater, arcade,
and dozens of cutesy bear-themed
businesses. The area's cabins are
perfect for families. See "Big Bear
Lake & Lake Arrowhead" in chapter 14.
- **Disneyland:** The "Happiest Place
on Earth" is enhanced by its sister
theme park, **California Adventure.** Whether you're wowed by
Disney animation, thrilled by the
roller-coaster rides, or interested
in the history and secrets of this
pop-culture icon, you won't walk
away disappointed. Get a FAST-
PASS to skip those long lines! See
"The Disneyland Resort" in chapter 14.
- **San Diego Zoo, Wild Animal
Park & SeaWorld:** San Diego
boasts three of the world's best
animal attractions. At the zoo,
animals live in naturalistic habitats such as Tiger River and Polar
Bear Plunge, and it's one of only

three zoos in the U.S. where you can see giant pandas. At the Wild Animal Park, most of the 3,500 animals roam freely over a 1,800-acre spread. And SeaWorld, with its water-themed rides, flashy animal shows, and detailed exhibits, is an aquatic wonderland of pirouetting dolphins and 4-ton killer whales with a fetish for drenching visitors. See "The Three Major Animal Parks" in chapter 16.

7 The Best Architectural Landmarks

- **The Golden Gate Bridge** (San Francisco): More tomato red than golden, the famous bridge remains a stunning visual for the San Francisco skyline. It's also an excellent expanse to walk. See "Exploring the City" in chapter 4.

- **The Carson Mansion** (Eureka): This house is a flamboyant Victorian—and one of the state's most photographed Queen Anne–style structures. It was built in 1885. See "Eureka & Environs" in chapter 7.

- **California State Capitol** (Sacramento): Built in 1869 and renovated in 1976, the dazzling white capitol has the original statuary restored along its eaves, historical rooms furnished with antiques from the original offices, a strangely interesting collection of portraits of California governors (don't miss Jerry Brown's), and a dome that from the inside looks like a Faberge egg. See "Sacramento" in chapter 10.

- **Mission San Carlos Borromeo del Río Carmelo** (Carmel): The second mission founded in California in 1770 by Father Junípero Serra is perhaps the most beautiful. Its stone church and tower dome have been restored, and a garden of poppies adjoins the church. See "Carmel-by-the-Sea" in chapter 11.

- **Hearst Castle** (San Simeon): This 165-room estate of publishing magnate William Randolph Hearst is one of the last great estates of America's Gilded Age. It's an astounding, over-the-top monument to wealth and power. See "San Simeon: Hearst Castle" in chapter 12.

- **Walt Disney Concert Hall:** Simply amazing. You would have to fly to Spain to see Frank O. Gehry's other architectural masterpiece. The dramatically curvaceous stainless-steel exterior houses one of the most acoustically perfect concert halls in the world. See p. 524.

- **The Theme Building** (Los Angeles): The *Jetsons*-style "Theme Building," which once loomed over LAX, still holds court in the center of the airport and signals your arrival. Enjoy the view of arriving and departing jets from the building's observation deck or its groovy *Star Trek*–ish **Encounter LAX** restaurant and bar, whose purple neon lights flood the area after dark. See "Exploring the City" in chapter 13.

- **Balboa Park** (San Diego): These Spanish-revival style buildings along El Prado were originally built as temporary structures for the Panama-California Exposition (1915–16). Set amidst the beautifully landscaped terrain of mesas and canyons that comprise one of the country's finest city parks, the ornately decorated and imposing facades have a special magic, creating a romantic fantasia abounding with Mediterranean flourishes. The buildings also house many of San Diego's best museums. See "Exploring the Area" in chapter 16.

8 The Best Museums

- **California State Railroad Museum** (Sacramento): Old Sacramento's biggest attraction, the 100,000-square-foot museum was once the terminus of the Transcontinental and Sacramento Valley railways. It displays 21 locomotives and railroad cars, among other attractions. See p. 324.

- **J. Paul Getty Museum at the Getty Center** (Los Angeles): Since its opening in 1997, the Getty has been deluged by visitors eager to see whether this complex fulfills its promise as the cultural cornerstone of L.A. Besides boasting a permanent art collection and notable visiting exhibits, the center is a striking—and starkly futuristic—architectural landmark. From its picturesque vantage point, the Getty offers panoramic city and ocean views. See p. 517.

- **Museum of the American West** (Los Angeles): Relive California's historic cowboy past and see how the period has been depicted by Hollywood, from Disney cartoon re-creations to founder Gene Autry's "singing cowboy" films to popular 1960s TV series. Highlights include a glimmering vault of ornate frontier firearms. See p. 526

- **Petersen Automotive Museum** (Los Angeles): This museum is a natural for Los Angeles, a city whose personality is so entwined with the popularity of the car. Impeccably restored vintage autos are displayed in life-size dioramas accurate to the last period detail (including an authentic 1930s–era service station). Upstairs galleries house movie star and motion-picture vehicles, car-related artwork, and exhibits. See p. 526.

- **The Museums of Balboa Park** (San Diego): In a relaxed, verdant setting, these venues offer a variety of cultural experiences. My favorites include the Aerospace Museum, the Museum of Photographic Arts, the Model Railroad Museum, the Botanical Building, the Timken Museum of Art, and the Mingei International Museum of Folk Art. Check in at the House of Hospitality for a map and "Passport to Balboa Park," a low-cost combination pass to the museums. See "Exploring the Area" in chapter 16.

9 The Best Luxury Hotels & Resorts

- **Ritz-Carlton San Francisco** (✆ 800/241-3333): Two blocks from the top of Nob Hill, San Francisco's Ritz is world-renowned for its accommodating staff, luxurious amenities, and top-rated restaurant. Another bonus is the most lavish brunch in town, served on Sundays in the Terrace Room or on the patio amidst blooming rose bushes. See p. 86.

- **Auberge du Soleil** (Rutherford; ✆ 800/348-5406): The "Inn of the Sun," a Relais & Châteaux member in a 33-acre olive grove, stands above the vineyards of Napa Valley. This French country–style inn is the Wine Country's best resort. Each of the villas is named after a region of France and exudes an ambience of romantic exclusivity. And the spa is to die for. See p. 177.

- **Meadowood Napa Valley** (St. Helena; ✆ 800/458-8080): An utterly luxurious retreat, this 256-acre Wine Country estate was inspired by New England's grand cottages. With its plethora of sports facilities and stress-relieving treatments, it attracts such clients as megabuck novelist Danielle Steele. See p. 178.

- **The Estate by the Elderberries** (Oakhurst; ✆ 559/683-6860): Close to Yosemite, the Château du Sureau and Erna's Elderberry House evoke the best of Europe. Exquisite furnishings, individually decorated rooms, and a cuisine worthy of the stars make for a memorable lodging and dining experience. See p. 291.

- **Casa Palmero Resort** (Pebble Beach; ✆ 800/654-9300): A small, ultraluxury resort on the first tee of the Pebble Beach Golf Course, Casa Palmero has 24 cottages and suites, all very intimate and private. In addition, you have the splendors of Pebble Beach to amuse you. See p. 380.

- **Post Ranch Inn** (Big Sur; ✆ 800/527-2200): Perched 1,200 feet above the Pacific, the elevated wood-and-glass guest cottages at this romantic cliff-side retreat give guests the illusion that they're living at cloud level. See p. 394.

- **Shutters on the Beach** (Santa Monica; ✆ 800/334-9000) and **Casa del Mar** (Santa Monica; ✆ 800/898-6999): If an ocean-front room at either of these hotels doesn't put a spring in your relationship, it's hard to imagine what will. Which one is best for you depends on your taste: Shutters is dressed up like a rich friend's contemporary-chic beach house, while glamorous Casa del Mar is an impeccably restored Deco-era delight. See p. 474 and p. 473.

- **Beverly Hills Hotel and Bungalows** (Beverly Hills; ✆ 800/283-8885): It's well worth the heavy hit to your credit card for the opportunity to take afternoon tea in the famous Polo Lounge next to Ozzy Osbourne, swim laps in the same pool Katharine Hepburn once dove into fully clothed, and eat pancakes in the fabled Fountain Coffee Shop. See p. 479.

- **La Quinta Resort & Club** (La Quinta; ✆ 800/598-3828): This luxury resort, set in a grove of palms at the base of the Santa Rosa Mountains, is in the midst of some of the desert's best golf courses. Spanish-style cottages are surrounded by a gardenlike setting and 24 "private" swimming pools. The lounge and library in the original hacienda hearkens back to the early days of the resort, when Clark Gable, Greta Garbo, and other luminaries escaped to the seclusion of La Quinta. See p. 648.

- **The Lodge at Torrey Pines** (La Jolla; ✆ 858/777-6690): You don't need to know much about Craftsman-style architecture to appreciate the taste and artistry that went into creating this luxury resort. The lodge sits next to the Torrey Pines Golf Course, and you can enjoy a fireplace in your room, sunset ocean views from your balcony, and superb meals at the hotel's A.R. Valentine restaurant. See p. 692.

10 The Best Affordable Small Hotels & Inns

- **St. Orres** (Gualala; ✆ 707/884-3303): Designed in a Russian style—complete with two Kremlinesque onion-domed towers—St. Orres offers secluded accommodations constructed from century-old timbers salvaged from a nearby mill. One of the most eye-catching inns on California's North Coast. See p. 212.

- **Albion River Inn** (Albion; ☎ **800/ 479-7944**): One of the best rooms-with-a-view on the coast, the Albion River Inn is perched on a cliff overlooking the rugged shoreline. Most of the luxuriously appointed rooms have Jacuzzi tubs for two, elevated to window level. Add champagne and you're guaranteed to have a night you won't soon forget. See p. 220.
- **River Ranch Lodge** (Lake Tahoe; ☎ **800/535-9900**): Alongside the Truckee River, the River Ranch has long been one of our favorite affordable inns at Lake Tahoe. It has everything you'd want in a mountain lodge: rustic decor, a great bar and outdoor deck overlooking the river, and a restaurant serving wood-oven-roasted Montana elk loin and other hearty dishes. See p. 262.
- **Evergreen Lodge** (Yosemite; ☎ **800/935-6343**): Scattered throughout a wooded grove of towering pines near the entrance to Yosemite are 18 rustic cabins, a beautiful old bar and restaurant, and easy access to dozens of outdoor adventures. Enjoy a pitcher of beer and a game of Ping-Pong on the patio, or sit around the campfire telling stories and roasting marshmallows—it's all part of the Evergreen experience. See p. 287.
- **The Mosaic** (Beverly Hills; ☎ **800/463-4466**): This Beverly Hills boutique is a perfect blend of art, luxury, service, location, and value. Huge rainforest showerheads, Frette linens, Bvlgari bath products, Wolfgang Puck refreshments, and piles of pillows add up to hotel heaven. See p. 482.
- **Casa Malibu** (Malibu; ☎ **800/ 831-0858**): This beachfront motel will fool you from the front.

Its cheesy 1970s entrance on Pacific Coast Highway belies the quiet, restful charm within. Around the courtyard garden are 21 rooms, many with private decks above the sands. Rooftops and balconies are festooned with bougainvillea vines. There's easy beach access, and a suite that was Lana Turner's favorite. See p. 478.
- **Olallieberry Inn** (Cambria; ☎ **888/927-3222**): Nestled in the charming town of Cambria, this 1873 Greek Revival house, furnished in a floral-and-lace Victorian style, is a perfect base for exploring Hearst Castle. The gracious innkeepers provide everything from directions to Moonstone Beach to restaurant recommendations—and a scrumptious breakfast in the morning. See p. 406.
- **Casa Cody** (Palm Springs; ☎ **760/ 320-9346**): You'll feel more like a house guest at this 1920s Spanish-style *casa* that's blessed with peaceful, blossoming grounds and two swimming pools. The Southwestern-style rooms are large and equipped for extended stays, and the hotel is a couple of blocks from the heart of the action. See p. 646.
- **La Pensione Hotel** (San Diego; ☎ **800/232-4683**): In the Little Italy neighborhood, on the fringe of downtown, this find feels like a small, modern European hotel and offers tidy lodgings at bargain prices. There's an abundance of great dining in the surrounding blocks, and you'll be perfectly situated to explore the rest of town by car. The neighborhood is filled with art galleries and some of the city's most dashing new architecture. See p. 684.

11 The Best Places to Stay with the Kids

- **The Lost Whale Bed and Breakfast Inn** (Trinidad; ✆ 800/677-7859): Parents will love the beautiful inn and the outdoor spa, and kids will love the play area and the menagerie of horses, goats, and other animals down the road. It has a private beach, and it's near interesting redwood parks. Best of all, a fabulous breakfast is included. See p. 235.

- **KOA Kamping Kabins** (Point Arena; ✆ 800/562-4188): Once you see the adorable log cabins at this KOA campground, you can't help but admit that this is one cool way to spend the weekend on the coast. Rustic is the key word: mattresses, a heater, and a light bulb are the standard amenities. All you need is some bedding (or sleeping bags), cooking and eating utensils, and charcoal for the barbecue out front. See p. 215.

- **City Hotel** and **Fallon Hotel** (Columbia; ✆ 800/532-1479): Some parents may roll their eyes at this preserved Gold Rush town, but it's rather remarkable, with rides on a 100-year-old stage-coach, a blacksmith shop, and lots of relics from mining. And these reasonably priced Victorian hotels dish up a great buffet breakfast. Cars are barred from the dusty main street. See p. 347.

- **Grey Squirrel Resort** (Big Bear Lake; ✆ 800/381-5569): Like a camp for kids and adults alike, this cluster of kitchen-equipped cottages near the lake and Big Bear's village offers economical lodgings for a night or the entire season (winter or summer). Enjoy a heated, enclosed pool, barbecues, volleyball and basketball courts—plus skiing, boat rental, and plenty of other family recreation. See p. 591.

- **Disneyland Resort Hotels** (Anaheim; ✆ 714/956-MICKEY): The Holy Grail of Disney-goers has always been the "Official Hotel of the Magic Kingdom," the original **Disneyland Hotel** (p. 602) and newcomers **Paradise Pier Hotel** (p. 602) and the **Grand Californian** (p. 601). An easy monorail or tram ride to the parks' gates (the Grand Californian opens directly into California Adventure) means you'll be able to return to your room anytime, whether to take a much-needed nap or to change your soaked shorts after a water ride.

- **Marriott's Desert Springs Spa & Resort** (Palm Desert; ✆ 800/331-3112): In the spirit of Disneyesque resorts, this oasis welcomes with a whimsical lobby "rainforest" that features tropical birds and gondolas ferrying guests to their rooms. Once settled, kids will find hours worth of fun at the lagoonlike pools and play areas (supervised children's programs are available), while grown-ups luxuriate on the golf course, tennis court, or in the 30,000-square-foot day spa. See p. 638.

- **Crystal Pier Hotel** (San Diego; ✆ 800/748-5894): Occupying a historic pier that extends into the Pacific Ocean, this property affords guests the experience of sleeping *over* the ocean in a cottage. Ideal for beach-loving families, who can enjoy the sound of waves or head out for boardwalk action; beach gear is available for rental. See p. 689.

12 The Best Restaurants

- **San Francisco's Finest:** We can't choose! It's practically sacrilege to even attempt to name the "top" restaurant. But for a perfect combo of food and atmosphere, we count on **Boulevard** (© 415/543-6084; p. 96), **Restaurant Gary Danko** (© 415/749-2060; p. 102), and **Zuni Café** (© 415/552-2522; p. 106).

- **Chez Panisse** (Berkeley; © 510/548-5525): This is the domain of Alice Waters, "the queen of California cuisine." Her food captivates the senses and the imagination. Originally inspired by the Mediterranean, her kitchen has found its own style. Chez Panisse delights include dishes like grilled fish wrapped in fig leaves with red-wine sauce, and Seckel pears poached in red wine with burnt caramel. See p. 142.

- **Bistro Don Giovanni** (Napa; © 707/224-3300): *Shhh . . .* Don't tell anyone, but in this Napa Valley dining room you can get an incredible meal without a reservation. Just drop in to the cheery, large restaurant, wait for a seat at the bar, and order off the fantastic Italian menu. See p. 183.

- **Restaurant 301** (Eureka; © 800/404-1390): Mark and Christi Carter are passionate about food and wine, which is why their hotel restaurant is considered the best on the Northern Coast. Most of the herbs and many vegetables served are picked fresh from the hotel's organic gardens. Indulge in their prix-fixe five-course dinner menu, where each course is paired with a recommended wine by the glass (Mark is a Grand Award recipient from *Wine Spectator* magazine). See p. 232.

- **Erna's Elderberry House** (Oakhurst; © 559/683-6800): It's like a beacon shining across the culinary wasteland of the region around Yosemite. The six-course menu—which changes nightly—is an almost perfect blend of Continental and Californian. The food is bountiful and as fully satisfying as the elegant European ambience. See p. 291.

- **bouchon santa barbara** (Santa Barbara; © 805/730-1160): With an always-intriguing seasonal menu derived from Santa Barbara County's wine country, this intimate restaurant (whose name means "wine cork") lies hidden behind a shrubbery portal in the heart of downtown. The food and service are impeccable, and an experienced staff stands ready to help coordinate by-the-glass (or even half-glass) wines for each course. See p. 437.

- **The Hump** (Santa Monica; © 310/313-0977): The chefs here are deadly serious about their sushi. Flown in daily from Tokyo's Tsukijii and Fukuoka fish markets in oxygen-filled containers, it's so fresh that there's a sign at the entrance warning the faint-of-heart that the meat's still moving. See p. 494.

- **Koi Restaurant** (West Hollywood; © 310/659-9449): The hottest new restaurant in L.A. has the A-list celebrities arriving here nightly to nosh on addictive dishes such as baked crab rolls with edible rice paper. A killer combination of soothing feng shui ambience and superb Asian fusion cuisine. See p. 519.

- **Laurel** (San Diego; © 619/239-2222): The polished service and elegant setting at this restaurant near Balboa Park are urbane and discriminating. The food is prepared with inventive flair and the

Rhône-heavy wine list soars, making Laurel a rewarding splurge for a special occasion. See p. 701.

- **George's at the Cove/George's Ocean Terrace** (La Jolla; © 858/454-4244): Tasty smoked chicken–broccoli–black-bean soup is an enduring dish; it's on the menu at the fancy downstairs dining room *and* the breezy upstairs cafe. The two share an *aah*-inspiring ocean view. The downstairs kitchen turns up the finesse factor for inventive and formal California cuisine, while the cafe offers crowd-pleasing versions. See p. 707.

13 The Best Culinary Experiences

- **Grazing at San Francisco's Farmers Market:** In 2003 San Francisco's favorite outdoor culinary fair moved to the Ferry Building Marketplace where some of the best artisan food producers and restaurants have opened new storefronts. Stop by anytime to peruse the shops or visit during open-air market days—Tuesday and Thursday—to join the locals as they feast on the freshest vegetables, fruits, and prepared foods from some of the city's beloved restaurants. See "Exploring the City" in chapter 4.

- **A Decadent Meal in the Wine Country:** The Wine Country atmosphere sets a better stage for indulgent dining than anywhere else in the state. Add the best wines and some of the most talented chefs in the nation and you've got what we consider the ultimate dining experience. Deep-pocketed diners must reserve an evening at **The French Laundry** in St. Helena (© 707/944-2380); see p. 182. More moderately priced memories can be made at **Bistro Jeanty** (© 707/944-0103; p. 183) and **Terra** (© 707/963-8931; p. 183).

- **Tomales Bay Oysters: Johnson's Oyster Farm** (© 415/669-1149) sells its farm-fresh oysters—by the dozen or the hundreds—for a fraction of the price you'd pay at a restaurant. Our modus operandi is to 1) buy a couple dozen, 2) head for an empty campsite along the bay, 3) fire up the barbecue pit (don't forget the charcoal), 4) split and 'cue the little guys, 5) slather them in Johnson's special sauce, and then 6) slurp 'em down—yum. See "Point Reyes National Seashore" in chapter 7.

- **Grand Central Market** (Los Angeles; © 213/624-2378): Fresh-produce stands, exotic spice and condiment vendors, butchers and fishmongers, and prepared-food counters create a noisy, fragrant, vaguely comforting atmosphere in this L.A. mainstay. The gem of the cavernous complex is the fresh juice bar at the southwest corner. A market fixture for many years, it dispenses dozens of varieties from an elaborate system of wall spigots, deftly blending unlikely but heavenly combinations. See "Shopping" in chapter 13.

- **Sunday Champagne Brunch Aboard the *Queen Mary*** (Long Beach; © 562/435-3511 or 562/432-6964): This elegant ocean liner was the largest, finest vessel when she was built in 1934, and the grandeur of those Atlantic-crossing days remains. A buffet-style feast, accompanied by a harp soloist and ice sculpture, is presented in the wood-furnished, first-class dining room. Walk off your indulgence on the teak decks and through the Art Deco interiors. See p. 573.

- **A Date with the Coachella Valley:** Some 95% of the world's dates are farmed here. While the groves of date palms make evocative scenery, it's their fruit that draws visitors to the National Date Festival in Indio each year. You can feast on an array of plump Medjool, amber Deglet Noor, caramel-like Halawy, and buttery Empress dates. The rest of the year, date farms and markets sell dates from the season's harvest, as well as date milkshakes, date coconut rolls, and more. See "Sweet Treat of the Desert: The Coachella Valley Date Gardens" in chapter 15.

14 The Best of the Performing Arts & Special Events

- **The San Francisco Opera:** This world-class company performs at the War Memorial Opera House, modeled after the Opéra Garnier in Paris. The season opens with a gala in September and runs through December. This was the first municipal opera in the United States, and its productions and members have been acclaimed throughout the world. See p. 132.
- **The American Conservatory Theater** (San Francisco): The A.C.T. is one of the nation's leading regional theaters. It's been called the American equivalent of the British National Theatre, the Berliner Ensemble, and the Comédie Française in Paris. See p. 132.
- **World Championship Great Arcata to Ferndale Cross-Country Kinetic Sculpture Race** (Arcata; © **800/346-3482**): One of California's most bizarre outdoor events, the Kinetic Sculpture Race is a 3-day event every Memorial Day weekend where people-powered vehicles trudge over land, sand, mud, and water. The competition draws more than 10,000 spectators. See "The Avenue of the Giants" in chapter 7.
- **The Monterey Jazz Festival** (© **800/307-3378**): When the third weekend of September rolls around, the Monterey Fairgrounds hosts this classic, drawing jazz fans from around the world. The 3-day festival (which is usually sold out about a month in advance) is known for presenting the sweetest jazz west of the Mississippi. See "California Calendar of Events" in chapter 2.
- **The Hollywood Bowl** (Los Angeles): This iconic outdoor amphitheater is the summer home of the Los Angeles Philharmonic, a stage for visiting virtuosos—including the occasional pop star—and the setting for splendid fireworks shows throughout the summer. See p. 565.
- **Festival of Arts & Pageant of the Masters** (Laguna Beach): These events draw crowds to the Orange County coast every July and August. Begun in 1932 by a handful of painters, the festival has grown to showcase hundreds of artists. In the evening, crowds marvel at the Pageant of the Masters' *tableaux vivants,* in which costumed townsfolk pose inside a giant frame and depict famous works of art, accompanied by music and narration. See "The Orange Coast" in chapter 14.
- **The Old Globe** (San Diego): This Tony Award–winning theater, fashioned after Shakespeare's original stage, produced recent stage hits *The Full Monty* and the revival of *Damn Yankees* before they hit Broadway, and has billed such notable performers as John Goodman, Hal Holbrook, and Ellen Burstyn. The outdoor Shakespeare each summer is often a winner. See p. 732.

2

Planning Your Trip to California

by Matthew Richard Poole

In the pages that follow, we've compiled everything you need to know to handle the practical details of planning your trip—from making campsite reservations to finding great deals on the Internet, plus a calendar of events and much more.

1 Visitor Information

VISITOR INFORMATION

For information on the state as a whole, contact **California Tourism,** 1102 Q St., Suite 6000, Sacramento, CA 95814 (© **800/GO-CALIF;** www.visitcalifornia.com), and ask for a free information packet. In addition, almost every city and town in the state has a tourist bureau or chamber of commerce that will send you information on its particular area. These are listed under the appropriate headings in the geographically organized chapters that follow.

International travelers should also see chapter 3 for entry requirements and other pertinent information.

INFORMATION ON CALIFORNIA'S PARKS To find out more about California's national parks, contact the **Pacific West Region Information Center,** National Park Service, 1111 Jackson St., Suite 700, Oakland, CA 94607 (© **510/817-1300;** www.

nps.gov). Reservations can be made at national park campsites by calling © **800/365-CAMP** (800/436-PARK for Yosemite) or logging on to http://reservations.nps.gov from 7am to 7pm (Pacific time).

For information on state parks, contact the **Department of Parks and Recreation,** P.O. Box 942896, Sacramento, CA 94296-0001 (© **800/777-0369;** http://cal-parks.ca.gov). Thousands of campsites are on the department's reservation system and can be booked up to 8 weeks in advance by calling **Park-Net** at © **800/444-PARK.** You can also get reservations information online at www.reserveamerica.com.

For information on fishing and hunting licenses, contact the **California Department of Fish and Game,** License and Revenue Branch, 3211 S St., Sacramento, CA 95816 (© **916/227-2245;** www.dfg.ca.gov).

2 Money

ATMs

The easiest and best way to get cash away from home is from an ATM (automated teller machine). The

Cirrus (© **800/424-7787;** www.mastercard.com) and **PLUS** (© **800/843-7587;** www.visa.com) networks span the country; look at the back of your bank card to see which network you're on, then call or check online for ATM locations at your destination. Be sure you know your personal identification number (PIN) before you leave home and be sure to find out your daily withdrawal limit before you depart. Also keep in mind that many banks impose a fee every time a card is used at a different bank's ATM, which can be around $1.50 per transaction. On top of this, the bank from which you withdraw cash may charge its own fee.

TRAVELER'S CHECKS

Traveler's checks are something of an anachronism from the days before the ATM made cash accessible at any time. Traveler's checks used to be the only sound alternative to traveling with dangerously large amounts of cash. They were as reliable as currency, but, unlike cash, could be replaced if lost or stolen.

These days, traveler's checks are less necessary because most cities have 24-hour ATMs that allow you to withdraw small amounts of cash as needed. However, keep in mind that you will likely be charged an ATM withdrawal fee if the bank is not your own, so if you're withdrawing money every day, you might be better off with traveler's checks—provided that you don't mind showing identification every time you want to cash one.

You can get traveler's checks at almost any bank. **American Express** offers denominations of $20, $50, $100, $500, and (for cardholders only) $1,000. You'll pay a service charge ranging from 1% to 4%. You can also get American Express traveler's checks over the phone by calling ℂ **800/221-7282;** Amex gold and platinum cardholders who use this number are exempt from the 1% fee.

Visa offers traveler's checks at Citibank locations nationwide, as well

as at several other banks. The service charge ranges between 1.5% and 2%; checks come in denominations of $20, $50, $100, $500, and $1,000. Call ℂ **800/732-1322** for information. AAA members can obtain checks without a fee at most AAA offices. **MasterCard** also offers traveler's checks. Call ℂ **800/223-9920** for a location near you.

If you choose to carry traveler's checks, be sure to keep a record of their serial numbers separate from your checks in the event that they are stolen or lost. You'll get a refund faster if you know the numbers.

CREDIT CARDS

Credit cards are a safe way to carry money, they provide a convenient record of all your expenses, and they generally offer good exchange rates. You can also withdraw cash advances from your credit cards at banks or ATMs, provided you know your PIN. If you've forgotten yours, or didn't even know you had one, call the number on the back of your credit card and ask the bank to send it to you. It usually takes 5 to 7 business days, though some banks will allow you to reset it over the phone if you tell them your mother's maiden name or some other personal information.

Almost every credit card company has an emergency toll-free number to call if your card is stolen. Be sure to block charges against your account immediately and file a police report. Your credit card company may be able to wire you a cash advance off your credit card, and in many places, they can deliver an emergency credit card in a day or two. To report a lost or stolen card, contact **Visa** at ℂ 800/336-8472; **American Express,** ℂ 800/221-7282; **MasterCard,** ℂ 800/307-7309; **Discover,** ℂ 800/347-2683; or **Diners Club,** ℂ 800/234-6377.

3 When to Go

CLIMATE

California's climate is so varied that it's impossible to generalize about the state as a whole.

San Francisco's temperate marine climate means relatively mild weather year-round. In summer, temperatures rarely top 70°F (21°C; pack sweaters, even in Aug), and the city's famous fog rolls in most mornings and evenings. In winter the mercury seldom falls below freezing, and snow is almost unheard of. Because of the fog, summer rarely sees more than a few hot days in a row. Head a few miles inland, though, and it's likely to be clear and hot.

The Central Coast shares San Francisco's climate, although it gets warmer as you get farther south. Seasonal changes are less pronounced south of San Luis Obispo, where temperatures remain relatively stable year-round. The northern coast is rainier and foggier; winters tend to be mild but wet.

Summers are refreshingly cool around Lake Tahoe and in the Shasta Cascades—perfect for hiking, camping, and other outdoor activities and a popular escape for residents of the sweltering deserts and valleys who are looking to beat the heat. Skiers flock to this area for terrific snowfall from late November to early April.

Southern California—including Los Angeles and San Diego—is usually much warmer than the Bay Area, and it gets significantly more sun. This is the place to hit the beach. Even in winter, daytime thermometer readings regularly reach into the 60s (15°C–20°C) and warmer. Summers can be stifling inland, but Southern California's coastal communities are always comfortable. The area's limited rainfall is generally seen between December and mid-April, and is rarely intense enough to be more than a slight inconvenience. It's possible to sunbathe throughout the year, but only die-hard enthusiasts and wet-suited surfers venture into the ocean in winter. The water is warmest in summer and fall, but even then, the Pacific is too chilly for many.

The deserts, including Palm Springs and the desert national parks, are sizzling hot in summer; temperatures regularly top 100°F (38°C). Winter is the time to visit the desert resorts (and remember, it gets surprisingly cold at night in the desert).

San Francisco's Average Temperatures

	Jan	Feb	Mar	Apr	May	June	July	Aug	Sept	Oct	Nov	Dec
Avg. High (°F)	56	59	60	61	63	64	64	65	69	68	63	57
Avg. High (°C)	13	15	16	16	17	18	18	18	21	20	17	14
Avg. Low (°F)	46	48	49	49	51	53	53	54	56	55	52	47
Avg. Low (°C)	8	9	9	9	11	12	12	12	13	13	11	8

Los Angeles's Average Temperatures

	Jan	Feb	Mar	Apr	May	June	July	Aug	Sept	Oct	Nov	Dec
Avg. High (°F)	65	66	67	69	72	75	81	81	81	77	73	69
Avg. High (°C)	18	19	19	21	22	24	27	27	27	25	23	21
Avg. Low (°F)	46	48	49	52	54	57	60	60	59	55	51	49
Avg. Low (°C)	8	9	9	11	12	14	16	16	15	13	11	9

AVOIDING THE CROWDS

If you're planning a summertime visit, you're not alone. The period between Memorial Day and Labor Day is the height of the tourism season virtually everywhere—except for desert areas like Palm Springs and Death Valley, where sizzling temperatures keep all but the hardiest bargain hunters away. California's pleasant summer weather (with relatively low humidity) has a lot to do with these numbers, but the season is also popular simply because that's when most people, especially families with kids, get to take that precious vacation time. So, naturally, prices are highest between Memorial Day (late May) and Labor Day (early Sept) in much of the state, and can fall dramatically outside of that period—exceptions to this rule include the aforementioned deserts and winter ski resorts. *Insider tip:* Californians know the best time to travel the state is autumn. That's roughly from late September to early December, when crowds drop off, "shoulder season" rates kick in, and before winter rains loom on the horizon.

CALIFORNIA CALENDAR OF EVENTS

January

Tournament of Roses, Pasadena. A spectacular parade down Colorado Boulevard, with lavish floats, music, and equestrian entries, followed by the Rose Bowl Game. Call ✆ **626/449-4100** or visit www.tournamentofroses.com for details, or watch it on TV (you'll have a better view). January 1.

Bob Hope Chrysler Classic, Palm Springs Desert Resorts. The 46th year of this weeklong PGA golf tournament takes place in 2005. The event raises money for charity and includes a celebrity-studded Pro-Am. For spectator information

and tickets, call ✆ **888/MR-BHOPE** or 760/346-8184. Mid- to late January.

AT&T Pebble Beach National Pro-Am, Pebble Beach. A PGA-sponsored tour where pros are teamed with celebrities to compete on three famous golf courses. Call ✆ **800/541-9091** or 831/649-1533, or visit www.attpbgolf.com. Late January.

February

Chinese New Year Festival & Parade. The largest Chinese New Year festival in the U.S. is in San Francisco. The celebration includes a Golden Dragon parade with lion dancing, bands, a street fair, flower sales, and food. Call ✆ **415/982-3000** or visit www.chineseparade.com for the 2005 schedule.

L.A.'s celebration is colorful as well, with dragon dancers parading through the streets of Chinatown. For this year's schedule, contact the Chinese Chamber of Commerce at ✆ **213/617-0396** or www.lachinese chamber.org.

National Date Festival, Indio. Crowds gather to celebrate the Coachella Valley desert's most beloved cash crop with events like camel and ostrich races, the Blessing of the Date Garden, and Arabian Nights pageants. Plenty of date-sampling booths are set up, along with rides, food vendors, and other county-fair trappings. Call ✆ **800/811-3247** or 760/863-8247, or visit www.datefest.org. Two weeks mid-February.

Mardi Gras, West Hollywood. The festivities—including live jazz and lots of food—take place along Santa Monica Boulevard, from Doheny Drive to La Brea Avenue, and in the alley behind Santa Monica Boulevard. Contact the West Hollywood Convention & Visitors Bureau at

Watching the Whales

Each winter, pods of California gray whales making their annual migration to breeding lagoons at the southern tip of Baja pass close by California shores. If you've ever been lucky enough to spot one of these graceful behemoths, you'll understand why whale-watching is such an eagerly anticipated activity. From December to March you can view this great parade from land or sea. Recommended spots include **Point Reyes National Seashore** (© 415/669-1534), where a historic lighthouse offers whale- and elephant-seal viewing; **Monterey Peninsula,** where January's WhaleFest (© 831/644-7588) celebrates these mammals from the Monterey Aquarium down through Big Sur; and San Diego's **Cabrillo National Monument** (© 619/557-5450; www.nps. gov/cabr), which offers a glassed-in observatory and educational whale exhibits.

Excursions depart from many locations, including **Morro Bay** (Virq's Landing, © 805/772-1222), **Santa Barbara** (The Condor, © 888/77-WHALE or 805/963-3564), **Ventura Harbor** (Island Packers, © 805/642-1393; www.islandpackers.com), and **San Diego** (San Diego Harbor Excursions, © 800/442-7847 or 619/234-4111, or Hornblower Cruises, © 800/ON-THE-BAY or 619/686-8715; www.hornblower.com). Also in San Diego, the **Natural History Museum** (© 619/255-0203; www. sdnhm.org) offers multi-day whale-watching trips to Baja California.

© 800/368-6020. Late February or early March.

Mustard Festival, Napa Valley. Celebrating the blossom of yellow-petaled mustard flowers, which coat the valley during February and March, the event was conceived to drum up visitors during this once-slow season. The festival has evolved into 6 weeks of events from a kickoff gourmet gala to a wine auction, recipe and photography competitions, and plenty of food and wine. For information and a schedule, call © 707/259-9020 or 707/938-1133, or visit www. mustardfestival.com. February and March.

March

Return of the Swallows, San Juan Capistrano. Each St. Joseph's Day, visitors flock to this charming village for the arrival of the mission's loyal flock of swallows that nest and remain until October. The celebration includes a parade, dances, and special programs. Call © 949/234-1300 for details. March 19.

Santa Barbara International Film Festival. For 10 days each March, Santa Barbara does its best impression of Cannes. There's a flurry of foreign and independent film premieres, appearances by noted actors and directors, and symposia on hot cinematic topics. Call © 805/963-0023 or visit www.sbfilmfestival. org. Mid-March.

Kraft Nabisco Championship, Rancho Mirage. This 33-year-old LPGA golf tournament takes place near Palm Springs. After the celebrity Pro-Am early in the week, the best female pros get down to business. For further information, call © 760/324-4546 or visit www.nabiscochampionship.com. Other special-interest events for women usually take place around the tournament, including the country's largest annual lesbian gathering. Last week of March.

Redwood Coast Dixieland Jazz Festival, Eureka. Three days of jazz featuring 12 of the best Dixieland groups. Call ℂ **707/445-3378.** Late March.

April

San Francisco International Film Festival. One of the oldest film festivals in the country, featuring more than 100 films and videos from over 30 countries. Tickets are inexpensive, and screenings accessible to the general public. Call ℂ **415/931-FILM** or visit www.sffs.org. Mid-April to early May.

Toyota Grand Prix, Long Beach. A weekend of Indy-class auto racing and entertainment in and around downtown Long Beach, drawing world-class drivers from the United States and Europe. Contact the **Grand Prix Association** at ℂ **888/82-SPEED** or 562/981-2600, or www.longbeachgp.com. Mid-April.

Renaissance Pleasure Faire, San Bernardino. One of America's largest Renaissance festivals, this annual happening is in Glen Helen Regional Park in L.A.'s relatively remote countryside. Performers (and many attendees) dress in 16th-century costume in this re-creation of a medieval English village. For information, call ℂ **800/52-FAIRE** or log on to http://renaissance-faire.com. Weekends from late April to Memorial Day.

Ramona Pageant, Hemet. A unique outdoor play that portrays the lives of the Southern California Mission Indians. Performed each spring since 1923, the play was adapted from Helen Hunt Jackson's 1884 novel *Ramona*. Call ℂ **800/645-4465** or 909/658-3111, or

visit www.ramonapageant.com for details. Mid April to early May.

May

Cinco de Mayo. A weeklong celebration of one of Mexico's most jubilant holidays takes place throughout Los Angeles near May 5. The carnival-like atmosphere is created by large crowds, live music, dances, and food. The main festivities are held in El Pueblo de Los Angeles State Historic Park, with other events around the city. Call ℂ **213/485-6855** for information.

There's also a Cinco de Mayo celebration in Old Town, San Diego, featuring folkloric music, dance, food, and historical reenactments. Call ℂ **619/296-3161** for more information.

Calaveras County Fair and Jumping Frog Jubilee, Angels Camp. The event is inspired by Mark Twain's story "The Celebrated Jumping Frog of Calaveras County." Entrants from all over arrive with their frog participants. There's also a parade, livestock competition, rodeo, carnival, and fireworks. Call ℂ **209/736-2561** or visit www.frogtown.org. Third weekend in May.

Paso Robles Wine Festival. What began as a small, neighborly gathering has grown into the largest outdoor wine tasting in California. The 3-day event features winery open houses and tastings, a golf tournament, 5K run and 10K bike ride, and concerts, plus a festival in downtown's City Park. For a schedule, call ℂ **800/549-WINE** or visit www.pasowine.com. Third weekend in May.

Bay to Breakers Foot Race, San Francisco. One of the city's most popular annual events, it's more fun than run. Thousands of entrants show up dressed—or undressed—in their best costumes for the 7.5-mile run. Call ℂ **415/777-7770** or log on to www.baytobreakers.com. Third Sunday of May.

Carnival, San Francisco. The Mission District's largest annual event is a 2-day series of festivities that culminates with a parade on Mission Street over Memorial Day weekend. More than half a million spectators line the route, and the samba musicians and dancers continue to play on 14th Street, near Harrison, at the end of the march. Call the hot line at ☎ **415/920-0125** or visit www.carnavalsf.com. Memorial Day weekend.

June

Playboy Jazz Festival, Los Angeles. Bill Cosby is the traditional master of ceremonies, presiding over top artists at the Hollywood Bowl. Call ☎ **310/449-4070.** Mid-June.

San Francisco Lesbian, Gay, Bisexual, Transgender Pride Parade. It's celebrated over various weekends throughout the state in June and July, but San Francisco's party draws up to half a million participants. The parade heads west from Market Street and Beale to Market and Eighth Street where hundreds of food, art, and information booths are set up around several stages. Call ☎ **415/864-3733** or visit www.sfpride.org for info. Usually the third or last weekend of June.

Ojai Music Festival. This weekend event has been drawing world-class classical and jazz personalities to the open-air Libbey Bowl since 1947. Past events have featured Igor Stravinsky, Aaron Copland, and the Juilliard String Quartet. Seats (and local lodgings) fill up quickly; call ☎ **805/646-2094** for more information, or log on to www.ojai festival.org. Early June.

Mariachi USA Festival, Los Angeles. A 2-day family-oriented celebration of Mexican culture and tradition at the Hollywood Bowl, where festival goers pack their picnic baskets and enjoy music, ballet *folklórico* (Mexican folk dancing), and related performances by special guests. Call ☎ **323/848-7717.** Late June.

San Diego County Fair. Referred to as the Del Mar Fair by locals, this is the other big happening (besides horse racing) at the Del Mar Fairgrounds. The whole county turns out for the 3-week event, with livestock competitions, rides, flower and garden shows, food and craft booths, carnival games, and home-arts exhibits; concerts by name performers are included with admission. Call ☎ **858/793-5555,** or check www.sdfair.com. Mid-June through early July.

July

Mammoth Lakes Jazz Jubilee. A 4-day festival featuring 20 bands on 10 different stages, plus food, drink, and dancing—all under the pine trees and stars. Call ☎ **800/367-6572** or 760/934-2478. Second weekend in July.

World Championship Over-the-Line Tournament, San Diego. The beach softball event dates from 1953 and is renowned for boisterous, beer-soaked, anything-goes behavior—over 1,000 three-person teams compete, and upwards of 50,000 attend. It's a heap of fun for the open-minded but a bit much for small kids. It takes place on Fiesta Island in Mission Bay; admission is free. For more details, call ☎ **619/688-0817** or visit www.ombac.org. Mid-July.

Festival of Arts & Pageant of the Masters, Laguna Beach. A fantastic performance-art production in which actors recreate famous old-masters paintings. Other festivities include live music, crafts sales, art demonstrations and workshops, and the grassroots Sawdust Festival across the street. Grounds admission is $3 to $5; pageant tickets range from $15 to $80. Call ✆ **800/487-FEST** or 949/494-1145, or visit www.foapom.com. July through August.

Gilroy Garlic Festival. A gourmet food fair with more than 85 booths serving garlicky food from almost every ethnic background, plus close to 100 arts, crafts, and entertainment booths. Call ✆ **408/842-1625** or visit www.gilroygarlic festival.com. Last full weekend in July.

Thoroughbred Racing Season, Del Mar. The "turf meets the surf" during the Thoroughbred racing season at the Del Mar Race Track. Post time is 2pm most days; the track is dark on Tuesdays. Keep your eyes out for the occasional celeb. For this year's schedule, call ✆ **858/792-4242** or 858/755-1141. Mid-July to mid-September.

Beach Festival, Huntington Beach. Two straight weeks of fun in the sun, featuring surfing competitions—the U.S. Open of Surfing *and* the world-class Pro of Surfing—plus several extreme-sport events. Includes entertainment, food, tons of product booths and giveaways—and plenty of tanned, swimsuit-clad bodies of both sexes. For more info, call ✆ **714/969-3492** or log on to www.hbvisit. com. End of July.

U.S. Open Sandcastle Competition, San Diego. The quintessential beach event: a parade and children's castle-building contest on Saturday, followed by the main event on Sunday. Creations of astounding complexity are the rule, but castles are usually plundered after the awards ceremony. For details, call ✆ **619/424-6663** or visit www.usopen sandcastle.com. Late July.

August

Old Spanish Days Fiesta, Santa Barbara. The city's biggest annual event, this 5-day festival features a parade with horse-drawn carriages, music and dance performances, *mercados* (marketplaces), and a rodeo. Call ✆ **805/962-8101** or visit www.oldspanishdays-fiesta.org. Early August.

Nisei Week Japanese Festival, Los Angeles. This weeklong celebration of Japanese culture and heritage is held in Little Tokyo at the Japanese American Cultural and Community Center Plaza. Festivities include parades, food, music, arts, and crafts. Call ✆ **213/687-7193.** Mid-August.

California State Fair, Sacramento. At the California Exposition Grounds, a gala celebration with livestock, food, exhibits, and entertainment on 10 stages, plus thoroughbred racing and a 1-mile monorail for panoramic views over it all. Call ✆ **916/263-FAIR** or visit www.bigfun.org. Late August to early September.

September

Los Angeles County Fair. Horse racing, arts, agricultural displays, celebrity entertainment, and rides are among the attractions of the largest county fair in the world, held at the Los Angeles County Fair and Exposition Center, in Pomona. Call ✆ **909/623-3111** or visit www.fairplex.com for information. Throughout September.

Sausalito Art Festival. A juried exhibit of more than 180 artists. It's accompanied by music provided by Bay Area jazz, rock, and blues performers and international cuisine enhanced by wines from some 50 Napa and Sonoma producers. Call ✆ **415/331-3757** or log on to www.sausalitoartfestival.org for information. Labor Day weekend.

San Diego Street Scene. The historic Gaslamp Quarter is transformed by this 3-day extravaganza featuring food, dance, international character, and live music on 12 stages. Sunday is set aside as an all-ages day; attendees must be 21 or over for Friday and Saturday performances. Call © **800/260-9985** for more information, or see www.street-scene.com. First weekend after Labor Day.

Monterey Jazz Festival. Features top names in traditional and modern jazz. One of the oldest annual jazz festivals in the world. Log on to the festival's website for more information: www.montereyjazzfest.com. Mid-September.

Danish Days, Solvang. Since 1936 this 3-day event has been celebrating old-world customs and pageantry with a parade, gymnastics exhibitions by local schoolchildren, demonstrations of Danish arts and crafts, and plenty of *aebleskivers* (Danish fritters) and *medisterpolse* (Danish sausage). Call © **800/ GOSOLVANG** for further information. Mid-September.

Watts Towers Day of the Drum Festival, Los Angeles. Celebrating the historic role of drums and drummers, this event features a variety of unique performances, from Afro-Cuban *folklóricos* to East Indian tabla players. Call © **213/ 847-4646.** Late September.

October

Catalina Island Jazz Trax Festival. Contemporary jazz artists travel to the island to play in the legendary Avalon Casino Ballroom. The festival is held over two consecutive 3-day weekends. Call © **760/323-1171** or visit www.jazztrax.com for advance ticket sales and a schedule of performers. Early October.

Sonoma County Harvest Fair, Sonoma County Fairgrounds. A 3-day celebration of the harvest with exhibitions, art shows, and annual judging of the local wines. Call © **707/545-4203.** Dates vary.

The Half Moon Bay Art & Pumpkin Festival, Half Moon Bay. The festival features a Great Pumpkin Parade, pie-eating contests, a pumpkin-carving competition, arts and crafts, and all manner of squash cuisine. The highlight of the event is the Giant Pumpkin weigh-in. For exact date and details, call the Pumpkin Hot Line at © **650/726-9652.**

Western Regional Final Championship Rodeo, Lakeside. Top cowboys compete in rodeo events including calf roping, barrel racing, bull riding, team roping, and steer wrestling. At the Lakeside Rodeo Grounds, at Calif. 67 and Mapleview Avenue in Lakeside. Call © **619/561-4331.** Mid-October.

Halloween, San Francisco. The City by the Bay celebrates with a fantastic parade starting at Market and Castro, and a mixed gay-straight crowd revels in costumes of extraordinary imagination. October 31.

West Hollywood Halloween Costume Carnaval. One of the world's largest Halloween parties. Over 400,000 people, many dressed in outlandish drag couture, party all night along Santa Monica Boulevard. Call © **310/289-2525** (www.visitwesthollywood.com) for info. October 31.

November

Doo Dah Parade, Pasadena. An outrageous spoof of the Rose Parade, featuring participants such as the Precision Briefcase Drill Team and a kazoo band. Call © **626/440-7379.** Near Thanksgiving.

Hollywood Christmas Parade. This star-studded parade marches through the heart of Hollywood.

For more info, call © 323/469-2337. Sunday after Thanksgiving.

December

Balboa Park December Nights, San Diego. The city's urban park is decked out in holiday splendor for a weekend of evening events, including a candlelight procession, caroling and baroque music, craft displays, ethnic food, and hot cider. The event and the park's 13 museums are free these evenings. For more information, call © 619/239-0512 or visit www.balboapark. org. First weekend in December.

Christmas Boat Parade of Lights. Following long-standing tradition, sailors decorate their crafts with colorful lights. Several Southern California harbors hold nighttime parades to showcase the creations, which range from tiny dinghies draped with a single strand of lights to showy yachts with entire Nativity scenes twinkling on deck. Contact the following for schedules and information: **Ventura Harbor** (© 805/382-3001), **Long Beach** (© 562/435-4093), **Huntington Harbour** (© 714/840-7542), and **San Diego Bay** (www.sdparadeof lights.org).

New Year's Eve Torchlight Parade, Big Bear Lake. Watch dozens of nighttime skiers follow a serpentine path down Snow Summit's ski slopes bearing glowing torches—it's one of the state's loveliest traditions. Afterward, the party continues indoors with live bands and plenty to eat and drink. For more information on this 21-and-over event, call © 909/866-5766 or visit www.big bearmountainresorts.com.

4 Travel Insurance

Check your existing insurance policies and credit card coverage before you buy travel insurance. You may already be covered for lost luggage, canceled tickets, or medical expenses. The cost of travel insurance varies widely, depending on the cost and length of your trip, your age, health, and the type of trip you're taking.

TRIP-CANCELLATION INSURANCE Trip-cancellation insurance helps you get your money back if you have to back out of a trip, if you have to go home early, or if your travel supplier goes bankrupt. Allowed reasons for cancellation can range from sickness to natural disasters to the State Department declaring your destination unsafe for travel. In this unstable world, trip-cancellation insurance is a good buy if you're getting tickets well in advance—who knows what the state of the world, or of your airline, will be in 9 months? Insurance policy details vary, so read the fine print—and especially make sure that your airline or cruise line is on the list of carriers covered in case of bankruptcy. For information, contact one of the following insurers: **Access America** (© 866/807-3982; www.access america.com); **Travel Guard International** (© 800/826-4919; www.travel guard.com); **Travel Insured International** (© 800/243-3174; www.travel insured.com); and **Travelex Insurance Services** (© 888/457-4602; www. travelex-insurance.com).

MEDICAL INSURANCE Most health insurance policies cover you if you get sick away from home—but check, particularly if you're insured by an HMO.

LOST-LUGGAGE INSURANCE On domestic flights, checked baggage is covered up to $2,500 per ticketed passenger. If you plan to check items more valuable than the standard liability, see if your valuables are covered by your homeowner's policy. You might want to get baggage insurance as part of your comprehensive travel-insurance package or buy Travel Guard's "BagTrak" product (for contact info, see above). Don't buy insurance at the airport, as it's usually overpriced. Put any valuables or irreplaceable items in your carry-on luggage, as many items (including books, money, and electronics) aren't covered by airline policies.

If your luggage is lost, immediately file a lost-luggage claim at the airport, detailing the luggage contents. For most airlines, you must report delayed, damaged, or lost baggage within 4 hours of arrival. The airlines are required to deliver luggage, once found, to your house or destination free of charge.

5 Health & Safety

WHAT TO DO IF YOU GET SICK AWAY FROM HOME

In most cases, your existing health plan will provide the coverage you need. But double-check: You may want to buy **travel medical insurance** instead. (See the section on insurance, above.) Bring your insurance ID card with you when you travel.

If you suffer from a chronic illness, consult your doctor before your departure. For conditions like epilepsy, diabetes, or heart problems, wear a **MedicAlert Identification Tag** (© 800/825-3785; www.medicalert. org), which will immediately alert doctors to your condition and give them access to your records through MedicAlert's 24-hour hot line.

Pack **prescription medications** in your carry-on luggage, and carry prescription medications in their original containers, with pharmacy labels—otherwise they won't make it through airport security. Also bring along copies of your prescriptions in case you lose your pills or run out. Don't forget an extra pair of contact lenses or prescription glasses.

STAYING SAFE

An unscientific survey indicates that the issue most on the minds of would-be visitors to California is earthquakes, but in fact, the incidence of earthquakes is far surpassed by the paranoia. Refer to "Earthquakes" in Fast Facts, later in this chapter, for general tips on what to do in the event of an earthquake, but avoid letting these fears dominate your thoughts before or during a California vacation. Major quakes are rare, and they're localized enough that it is highly unlikely you will ever feel one.

Driving issues specific to California include winter driving on mountain roads. Chains may be required in the Sierras during icy weather at elevations above 3,000 feet. The **California Department of Transportation** provides 24-hour info at © **916/445-1534.**

Conversely, driving in desert areas carries its own hazards: Always be aware of the distance to the next gas station. In some areas, they may be 50 miles apart and summer temperatures well above 100°F (38°C) can turn a scenic drive into a disaster.

Penalties in California for drunk driving are among the toughest in the country. The legal limit is .08% blood alcohol level. In some areas, freeway speed limits are aggressively enforced after dark, partly as a pretext for nabbing drivers who might have imbibed.

California Traveler Assistance is a good resource in emergency situations, and multi-language service is available at © **888/871-4636.**

6 Specialized Travel Resources

TRAVELERS WITH DISABILITIES

California's spirit of tolerance and diversity has made it a welcoming place for travelers with disabilities. Building codes make most public facilities and attractions accessible (though some historic sites and older buildings can't accommodate drastic remodeling), and the state provides many services for those with disabilities.

The U.S. National Park Service offers a **Golden Access Passport** that gives free lifetime entrance to all properties administered by the National Park Service (of which there are many in California) for persons who are blind or permanently disabled, regardless of age. This includes national parks, monuments, historic sites, recreation areas, and national wildlife refuges. You may pick up a Golden Access Passport at any NPS entrance-fee area by showing proof of medically determined disability and eligibility for receiving benefits under federal law. Besides free entry, the Golden Access Passport also offers a 50% discount on federal-use fees charged for such facilities as camping, swimming, parking, boat launching, and tours. For more information, go to www.nps.gov/fees_passes.htm or call ℂ 888/467-2757.

Many travel agencies offer customized tours and itineraries for travelers with disabilities. **Flying Wheels Travel** (ℂ 507/451-5005; www.flyingwheelstravel.com) offers escorted tours and cruises that emphasize sports and private tours in mini-vans with lifts. **Accessible Journeys** (ℂ 800/846-4537 or 610/521-0339; www.disabilitytravel.com) caters specifically to slow walkers and wheelchair travelers and their families and friends.

Organizations that offer assistance to travelers with disabilities include the **Moss Rehab Hospital** (www.mossresourcenet.org), which provides a library of accessible-travel resources online; the **Society for Accessible Travel and Hospitality** (ℂ 212/447-7284; www.sath.org; annual membership fees: $45 adults, $30 seniors and students), which offers a wealth of travel resources for all types of disabilities and informed recommendations on destinations, access guides, travel agents, tour operators, vehicle rentals, and companion services; and the **American Foundation for the Blind** (ℂ 800/232-5463; www.afb.org), which provides information on traveling with Seeing Eye dogs.

For more information specifically targeted to travelers with disabilities, the community website **iCan** (www.icanonline.net/channels/travel/index.cfm) has destination guides and several regular columns on accessible travel. Also check out the quarterly magazine *Emerging Horizons* ($15 per year, $20 outside the U.S.; www.emerginghorizons.com); and *Open World Magazine,* published by the Society for Accessible Travel and Hospitality (see above; subscription $18 per year, $35 outside the U.S.).

Many of the major car-rental companies now offer hand-controlled cars for drivers with disabilities. **Avis** (ℂ 800/230-4898; www.avis.com) can provide such a vehicle at any of its locations in the United States with 48-hour advance notice; **Hertz** (ℂ 800/654-3131; www.hertz.com) requires between 24 and 72 hours of advance reservation at most of its locations. **Wheelchair Getaways** (ℂ 800/642-2042; www.wheelchair-getaways.com) rents specialized vans with wheelchair lifts and other features for those with disabilities in more than 100 cities across the United States.

GAY & LESBIAN TRAVELERS

California is one of the country's most progressive states when it comes to anti-discrimination legislation and workplace benefits for domestic partners. The gay and lesbian community spreads well beyond the famed enclaves of San Francisco, West Hollywood, and San Diego's Hillcrest. Gay travelers (especially men) will find a number of gay-owned inns in Palm Springs and the Russian River, north of the Bay Area.

The **International Gay & Lesbian Travel Association (IGLTA)** (© 800/448-8550 or 954/776-2626; www.iglta.org) is the trade association for the gay and lesbian travel industry, and offers an online directory of gay-and lesbian-friendly travel companies.

Many agencies offer tours and travel itineraries specifically for gay and lesbian travelers. **Above and Beyond Tours** (© 800/397-2681; www.abovebeyondtours.com) is the exclusive gay and lesbian tour operator for United Airlines. **Now, Voyager** (© 800/255-6951; www.nowvoyager.com) is a well-known San Francisco–based gay-owned and -operated travel service.

Out and About (© 800/929-2268 or 415-644-8044; www.outandabout.com) offers guidebooks and a newsletter 10 times a year packed with solid information on the gay and lesbian travel scene.

The *Damron* guides, with separate, annual books for gay men and lesbians, offer state-by-state listings and resources.

SENIOR TRAVEL

Mention the fact that you're a senior when you make your travel reservations. Although all of the major U.S. airlines except America West have canceled their senior discount and coupon book programs, many hotels still offer discounts for seniors. In most cities, people over the age of 60 qualify for reduced admission to theaters, museums, and other attractions, as well as discounted fares on public transportation.

Members of **AARP** (formerly known as the American Association of Retired Persons), 601 E St. NW, Washington, DC 20049 (© 800/424-3410 or 202/434-2277; www.aarp.org), get discounts on hotels, airfares, and car rentals. AARP offers members a range of benefits, including *AARP The Magazine* and a monthly newsletter. Anyone over 50 can join; annual dues are $13.

The **U.S. National Park Service** offers a **Golden Age Passport** that gives seniors 62 or older lifetime entrance to all properties administered by the National Park Service— national parks, monuments, historic sites, recreation areas, and national wildlife refuges—for a one-time processing fee of $10. This must be purchased in person at any NPS facility that charges an entrance fee. Besides free entry, a Golden Age Passport also offers a 50% discount on federal-use fees charged for such facilities as camping, swimming, parking, boat launching, and tours. For more information, go to www.nps.gov/fees_passes.htm or call © 888/467-2757.

Many reliable agencies and organizations target the 50-plus market. **Elderhostel** (© 877/426-8056; www.elderhostel.org) arranges study programs for those ages 55 and over (and a spouse or companion of any age) in the U.S. and in more than 80 countries around the world. Most courses last 5 to 7 days in the U.S. (2–4 weeks abroad), and many include airfare, accommodations in university dormitories or modest inns, meals, and tuition. **ElderTreks** (© 800/741-7956; www.eldertreks.com) offers small-group tours to off-the-beaten-path or adventure-travel locations, restricted to travelers 50 and older.

Recommended publications offering travel resources and discounts for seniors include: the quarterly magazine *Travel 50 & Beyond* (www.travel50andbeyond.com); *Travel Unlimited: Uncommon Adventures for the Mature Traveler* (Avalon); *101 Tips for Mature Travelers,* available from Grand Circle Travel (© 800/221-2610 or 617/350-7500; www.gct.com); *The 50+ Traveler's Guidebook* (St. Martin's Press); and *Unbelievably Good Deals and Great Adventures That You Absolutely Can't Get Unless You're Over 50* (McGraw-Hill).

FAMILY TRAVEL

If you have enough trouble getting your kids out of the house in the morning, dragging them thousands of miles away may seem like an insurmountable challenge. But family travel can be immensely rewarding, giving you new ways of seeing the world through smaller pairs of eyes.

Familyhostel (© 800/733-9753; www.learn.unh.edu/familyhostel) takes the whole family, including kids ages 8 to 15, on moderately priced domestic and international learning vacations. Lectures, field trips, and sightseeing are guided by a team of academics.

You can find good family-oriented vacation advice on the Internet from sites like the **Family Travel Network** (www.familytravelnetwork.com); **Traveling Internationally with Your Kids** (www.travelwithyourkids.com), a comprehensive site offering sound advice for long-distance and international travel with children; and **Family Travel Files** (www.thefamilytravel files.com), which offers an online magazine and a directory of off-the-beaten-path tours and tour operators for families.

Several books offer tips on traveling with kids. *Family Travel* (Lanier Publishing International) and *How to Take Great Trips with Your Kids* (The Harvard Common Press) are full of good general advice. *The Unofficial Guide to California with Kids* (Wiley Publishing, Inc.) is an excellent resource that covers the entire state. It rates and ranks attractions for each age group, lists dozens of family-friendly accommodations and restaurants, and suggests lots of beaches and activities that are fun for the whole clan.

Helpful websites include Family Travel Network (www.familytravel network.com), which offers travel tips and reviews of family-friendly destinations, vacation deals, and thoughtful features; and Family Travel Files (www.thefamilytravelfiles.com), which offers an online magazine and a directory of off-the-beaten-path tours and tour operators for families.

7 Planning Your Trip Online

SURFING FOR AIRFARES

The "big three" online travel agencies, **Expedia.com, Travelocity,** and **Orbitz** sell most of the air tickets bought on the Internet. (Canadian travelers should try Expedia.ca and Travelocity.ca; U.K. residents can go for Expedia.co.uk and opodo.co.uk.)

Each has different business deals with the airlines and may offer different fares on the same flights, so it's wise to shop around. Expedia and Travelocity will also send you **e-mail** notification when a cheap fare becomes available to your favorite destination. Of the smaller travel agency websites, **SideStep** (www.sidestep.com) has gotten the best reviews from Frommer's authors. It's a browser add-on that purports to "search 140 sites at once," but in reality only beats competitors' fares as often as other sites do.

Also remember to check **airline websites,** especially those for low-fare carriers such as Southwest, JetBlue, AirTran, WestJet, or Ryanair, whose fares are often misreported or simply missing from travel agency websites. Even with major airlines, you can often shave a few bucks from a fare by booking directly through the airline and avoiding a travel agency's transaction fee. But you'll get these discounts only by **booking online:** Most airlines now offer online-only fares that even their phone agents know nothing about. For the websites of airlines that fly to and from your destination, go to "Getting There," later in this chapter.

Great **last-minute deals** are available through free weekly e-mail services provided directly by the airlines. Most of these are announced on Tuesday or Wednesday and must be purchased online. Most are only valid for travel that weekend, but some (such as Southwest's) can be booked weeks or months in advance. Sign up for weekly e-mail alerts at airline websites or check megasites that compile comprehensive lists of last-minute specials, such as **Smarter Living** (www.smarterliving.com). For last-minute trips, site59.com often has better deals than the major-label sites.

If you're willing to give up some control over your flight details, use an **opaque fare service** like **Priceline** (www.priceline.com; www.priceline.co.uk for Europeans) or **Hotwire** (www.hotwire.com). Both offer rockbottom prices in exchange for travel on a "mystery airline" at a mysterious time of day, often with a mysterious change of planes en route. The mystery airlines are all major, well-known carriers—and the possibility of being sent from Philadelphia to San Francisco via Tampa is remote; the airlines' routing computers have gotten a lot better than they used to be. But your chances of getting a 6am or 11pm flight are pretty high. Hotwire tells you flight prices before you buy; Priceline usually has better deals than Hotwire, but you have to play their

"name our price" game (though the site has recently added a feature that lets you purchase fares knowing the airline and flight for a slightly higher set price). If you're new at this, the helpful folks at **BiddingForTravel** (www.biddingfortravel.com) do a good job of demystifying Priceline's prices. Priceline and Hotwire are great for flights within North America and between the U.S. and Europe.

For much more about airfares and savvy air-travel tips and advice, pick up a copy of *Frommer's Fly Safe, Fly Smart* (Wiley Publishing, Inc.).

SURFING FOR HOTELS
Shopping online for hotels is much easier in the U.S., Canada, and certain parts of Europe than it is in the rest of the world. Of the "big three" sites, **Expedia** may be the best choice, thanks to its long list of special deals. **Travelocity** runs a close second. Hotel specialist sites **hotels.com** and **hotel discounts.com** are also reliable. An excellent free program, **TravelAxe** (www.travelaxe.net), can help you search multiple sites at once, even ones you may never have heard of.

Priceline and Hotwire are even better for hotels than for airfares; with both, you're allowed to pick the neighborhood and quality level of your hotel before offering up your money. *Note:* Hotwire overrates its hotels by one star—what Hotwire calls a fourstar is a three-star anywhere else.

SURFING FOR RENTAL CARS
For booking rental cars online, the best deals are usually found at rentalcar company websites, although the major online travel agencies also offer rental-car reservations services. Priceline and Hotwire work well for rental cars, too; the only "mystery" is which major rental company you get, and for most travelers the difference between Hertz, Avis, and Budget is negligible.

Frommers.com: The Complete Travel Resource

For an excellent travel-planning resource, we highly recommend Frommers.com (www.frommers.com). We're a little biased, of course, but we guarantee that you'll find the travel tips, reviews, monthly vacation giveaways, and online-booking capabilities indispensable. Among the special features are our popular **Message Boards,** where Frommer's readers post queries and share advice (sometimes we authors even show up to answer questions); **Frommers.com Newsletter,** for the latest travel bargains and insider travel secrets; and **Frommer's Destinations Section,** where you'll get expert travel tips, hotel and dining recommendations, and advice on the sights to see for more than 3,000 destinations around the globe. When your research is done, the **Online Reservations System** (www.frommers.com/book_a_trip) takes you to Frommer's preferred online partners for booking your vacation at affordable prices.

8 The 21st-Century Traveler

INTERNET ACCESS AWAY FROM HOME

Travelers have any number of ways to check their e-mail and access the Internet on the road. Of course, using your own laptop—or even a PDA (personal digital assistant) or electronic organizer with a modem—gives you the most flexibility. But even if you don't have a computer, you can still access your e-mail and even your office computer from cybercafes.

WITHOUT YOUR OWN COMPUTER

It's hard nowadays to find a city that *doesn't* have a few cybercafes. Although there's no definitive directory for them, three places to start looking are at **www.cybercaptive.com**, **www.netcafeguide.com**, and **www.cybercafe.com**.

Aside from formal cybercafes, most **public libraries** offer Internet access free or for a small charge. **Hotels** that cater to business travelers often have **in-room dataports** and **business centers,** but the charges can be exorbitant. Also, most **youth hostels** nowadays

have at least one computer where you can access the Internet.

Most major airports now have **Internet kiosks** scattered throughout their gates. These kiosks, which you'll also see in shopping malls, hotel lobbies, and tourist information offices around the world, give you basic Web access for a per-minute fee that's usually higher than cybercafe prices. The kiosks' clunkiness and high price means they should be avoided whenever possible.

To retrieve your e-mail, ask your **Internet Service Provider (ISP)** if it has a Web-based interface tied to your existing e-mail account. If your ISP doesn't have such an interface, you can use the free **mail2web** service (www.mail2web.com) to view (but not reply to) your home e-mail. For more flexibility, you may want to open a free, Web-based e-mail account with **Yahoo! Mail** (http://mail.yahoo.com). (Microsoft's Hotmail is another popular option, but Hotmail has severe spam problems.) Your home ISP may be able to forward your e-mail to the Web-based account automatically.

If you need to access files on your office computer, look into a service called **GoToMyPC** (www.gotomypc. com). The service provides a Web-based interface for you to access and manipulate a distant PC from anywhere—even a cybercafe—provided your "target" PC is on and has an always-on connection to the Internet (such as with Road Runner cable). The service offers top-quality security, but if you're worried about hackers, use your own laptop rather than a cybercafe to access the GoToMyPC system.

WITH YOUR OWN COMPUTER

Major Internet Service Providers (ISPs) have **local access numbers** around the world, allowing you to go online by simply placing a local call. Check your ISP's website or call its toll-free number and ask how you can use your current account away from home, and how much it will cost.

If you're traveling outside the reach of your ISP, the **iPass** network has dial-up numbers in most of the world's countries. You'll have to sign up with an iPass provider, who will then tell you how to set up your computer for your destination(s). For a list of iPass providers, go to www.ipass. com and click on "Individuals." One solid provider is **i2roam** (www.i2 roam.com; ℂ **866/811-6209** or 920/235-0475), where you'll get a list of iPass providers that take U.S. customers.

Wherever you go, bring a **connection kit** of the right power and phone adapters, a spare phone cord, and a spare Ethernet network cable.

Most business-class hotels offer dataports for laptop modems, and a few thousand hotels in the U.S. now offer high-speed Internet access using an Ethernet network cable. You'll have to bring your own cables either way, so **call your hotel in advance** to find out what the options are.

Many business-class hotels also offer a form of Web browsing through the room TV set. We've successfully checked Yahoo! and Hotmail on these systems.

If you have an 802.11b/**Wi-fi** card for your computer, several commercial companies have made wireless service available in airports, hotel lobbies, and coffee shops, primarily in the U.S. **T-Mobile Hotspot** (www.t-mobile. com/hotspot) serves up wireless connections at more than 1,000 Starbucks coffee shops nationwide. **Boingo** (www.boingo.com) and **Wayport** (www.wayport.com) have set up networks in airports and high-class hotel

---

Useful Sites for Travelers

Veteran travelers usually carry some essential items to make their trips easier. Following is a selection of online tools to bookmark and use:

- **Visa ATM Locator** (www.visa.com), for locations of Plus ATMs worldwide, or **MasterCard ATM Locator** (www.mastercard.com), for locations of Cirrus ATMs worldwide.
- **Intellicast** (www.intellicast.com) and **Weather.com** (www.weather. com). Gives weather forecasts for all 50 states and for cities around the world.
- **Mapquest** (www.mapquest.com). This best of the mapping sites lets you choose a specific address or destination, and in seconds it will return a map and detailed directions.

lobbies. IPass providers (see above) also give you access to a few hundred wireless hotel lobby setups. Best of all, you don't need to be staying at the Four Seasons to use the hotel's network; just set yourself up on a nice couch in the lobby. Unfortunately, the companies' pricing policies are Byzantine, with a variety of monthly, per-connection, and per-minute plans.

Community-minded individuals have also set up **free wireless networks** in major cities around the U.S., Europe, and Australia. These networks are spotty, but you get what you (don't) pay for. Each network has a home page explaining how to set up your computer for their particular system; start your explorations at www.personal telco.net/index.cgi/Wireless Communities.

USING A CELLPHONE ACROSS THE U.S.

Just because your cellphone works at home doesn't mean it'll work elsewhere in the country (thanks to our nation's fragmented cellphone system). It's a good bet that your phone will work in major cities. But take a look at your wireless company's coverage map on its website before heading out—T-Mobile, Sprint, and Nextel are particularly weak in rural areas. If you need to stay in touch at a destination where you know your phone won't work, **rent** a phone that does from **InTouch USA** (© 800/872-7626; www.intouchglobal.com) or a rental-car location, but beware that you'll pay $1 a minute or more for airtime.

If you're venturing deep into national parks, you may want to consider renting a **satellite phone ("satphone")**, which is different from a cellphone in that it connects to satellites rather than to ground-based towers. A satphone is more costly than a cellphone but works where there's no cellular signal. Unfortunately, you'll pay at least $2 per minute to use the phone, and it only works where you can see the horizon (that is, usually not indoors). In North America you can rent Iridium satellite phones from **RoadPost** (www.roadpost.com; © **888/290-1606** or 905/272-5665). InTouch USA (see above) offers a wider range of satphones but at higher rates.

If you're not from the U.S., you'll be appalled at the poor reach of our **GSM (Global System for Mobiles) wireless network,** which is used by much of the rest of the world. Your phone will probably work in most major U.S. cities; it won't work in many rural areas. (To see where GSM phones work in the U.S., check out www.t-mobile.com/coverage/national_popup.asp.) And you may or may not be able to send SMS (text messaging) home—something Americans tend not to do anyway, for various cultural and technological reasons. (International budget travelers like to send text messages home because it's much cheaper than making international calls.) Assume nothing—call your wireless provider and get the full scoop. In a worst-case scenario, you can always rent a phone; InTouch USA delivers to hotels.

9 Getting There

BY PLANE

All major U.S. carriers serve the San Francisco, Sacramento, San Jose, Los Angeles, John Wayne (Orange County), and San Diego airports. They include **American** (© 800/433-7300; www.

aa.com), **America West** (© 800/235-9292; www.americawest.com), **Continental** (© 800/525-0280; www.continental.com), **Delta** (© 800/221-1212; www.delta.com), **JetBlue** (© 800/538-2583; www.jetblue.com),

Northwest (© 800/225-2525; www.nwa.com), **Southwest** (© 800/435-9792; www.southwest.com), **United** (© 800/241-6522; www.united.com), and **US Airways** (© 800/428-4322; www.usairways.com). The lowest round-trip fares to the West Coast from New York fluctuate between about $350 and $500; from Chicago, they range from $300 to $400. International travelers should also see "Getting to the U.S." in chapter 3 for information on overseas flights into California. For details on air travel within California, see "Getting Around," below.

GETTING THROUGH THE AIRPORT

With the federalization of airport security, security procedures at U.S. airports are more stable and consistent than ever. Generally, you'll be fine if you arrive **1 hour** before a domestic flight; if you show up late, tell an airline employee and he or she'll probably whisk you to the front of the line.

Bring a **current, government-issued photo ID** such as a driver's license or passport, and if you've got an e-ticket, print out the **official confirmation page;** you'll need to show your confirmation at the security checkpoint, and your ID at the ticket counter or the gate. (Children under 18 do not need photo IDs for domestic flights, but the adults checking in with them do.)

Security lines are getting shorter than they were during 2003, but some doozies remain. If you have trouble standing for long periods of time, tell an airline employee; the airline will provide a wheelchair. Speed up security by **not wearing metal objects** such as big belt buckles or clanky earrings. If you've got metallic body parts, a note from your doctor can prevent a long chat with the security screeners. Keep in mind that only **ticketed passengers** are allowed past security, except for folks escorting passengers with disabilities, or children.

Federalization has stabilized **what you can carry on** and **what you can't.** The general rule is that sharp things are out, nail clippers are okay, and food and beverages must be passed through the X-ray machine. Bring food in your carry-on rather than checking it, as explosive-detection machines used on checked luggage have been known to mistake food (especially chocolate, for some reason) for bombs. Travelers in the U.S. are allowed one carry-on bag, plus a "personal item" such as a purse, briefcase, or laptop bag. Carry-on hoarders can stuff all sorts of things into a laptop bag; as long as it has a laptop in it, it's still considered a personal item. The Transportation Security Administration (TSA) has issued a list of restricted items; check its website (www.tsa.gov/public/index.jsp) for details.

In 2003 the TSA phased out **gate check-in** at all U.S. airports. Passengers with e-tickets and without checked bags can still beat the ticket-counter lines by using **electronic kiosks** or even **online check-in.** Ask your airline which alternatives are available, and if you're using a kiosk, bring the credit card you used to book the ticket. If you're checking bags, you will still be able to use most airlines' kiosks; call your airline for up-to-date information. **Curbside check-in** is a good way to avoid lines, although a few airlines still ban curbside check-in entirely; call before you go.

At press time, the TSA also recommends that you **not lock your checked luggage** so screeners can search it by hand if necessary. The agency says to use plastic "zip ties," which can be bought at hardware stores and can be easily cut off.

FLYING FOR LESS: TIPS FOR GETTING THE BEST AIRFARE

Passengers sharing the same airplane cabin rarely pay the same fare. Travelers who need to purchase tickets at the

---

Tips Travel in the Age of Bankruptcy

At press time, two major U.S. airlines were struggling in bankruptcy court and most of the rest weren't doing very well either. To protect yourself, **buy your tickets with a credit card**, as the Fair Credit Billing Act guarantees you can get your money back from the credit card company if a travel supplier goes under (and if you request the refund within 60 days of the bankruptcy). **Travel insurance** can also help, but make sure it covers against "carrier default" for your travel provider. And be aware that if a U.S. airline goes bust midtrip, a 2001 federal law requires other carriers to take you to your destination (on a space-available basis) for a fee of no more than $25, if you rebook within 60 days of the cancellation.

---

last minute, change their itinerary at a moment's notice, or fly one-way often get stuck paying the premium rate. Here are some ways to keep your airfare costs down.

- Passengers who can book their tickets **long in advance,** who can **stay over Saturday night,** or who **fly midweek** or **at less-trafficked hours** will pay substantially less than "full" fare. If your schedule is flexible, say so, and ask if you can secure a cheaper fare by changing your flight plans.
- You can also save on airfares by keeping an eye out in local newspapers for **promotional specials** or **fare wars,** when airlines lower prices on their most popular routes. You rarely see fare wars offered for peak travel times, but if you can travel in the off-months, you may snag a bargain.
- Search **the Internet** for cheap fares (see "Planning Your Trip Online," earlier in this chapter).
- **Consolidators,** also known as bucket shops, are great sources for international tickets, although they usually can't beat the Internet on fares within North America. Start by looking in the travel sections of major newspapers at home. *Beware:* Bucket shop tickets are usually nonrefundable or have stiff cancellation penalties,

often as high as 50% to 75% of the price, and some put you on charter airlines with questionable safety records. Several reliable consolidators are worldwide and available on the Net. **STA Travel** (**www.statravel.com**) is now the world's leader in student travel, thanks to its purchase of Council Travel. It also offers good fares for travelers of all ages. **Flights. com** (www.flights.com) started in Europe and now has excellent fares worldwide. **FlyCheap** (© **800/ FLY-CHEAP**; www.1800flycheap. com) is owned by package-holiday megalith **MyTravel** and so has especially good access to fares for sunny destinations. **Air Tickets Direct** (© **800/778-3447**; www. airticketsdirect.com) is based in Montreal and leverages the currently weak Canadian dollar for low fares.

- For more tips about air travel, including a rundown of the major frequent-flier credit cards, pick up a copy of *Frommer's Fly Safe, Fly Smart* (Wiley Publishing, Inc.).

BY CAR

If you're planning a road trip, it's a good idea to be a member of the **Automobile Association of America (AAA).** Members (who carry their cards with them) receive free roadside assistance, and have access to a wealth of free travel

A Tale of Two States

It doesn't take a psychiatrist to figure out that California suffers from an acute case of bipolar schizophrenia. We Californians may, on the surface, appear to be one big *Happy Days* family, but in reality we've divided our state into separate factions worthy of Montague and Capulet. That is, you're either a Northern Californian or a Southern Californian, two opposing tribes that have little in common. In fact, which side you even choose to visit may reveal something about yourself.

All the California glamour, wealth, fame, fast cars, surf scenes, and buxom blondes you see on television are of southern invention. If this is the California you're looking for, head due south—assuming you're not terribly interested in intellectual stimulation, you won't be disappointed. In fact, it's nearly impossible not to be swept up by the energy and excitement that places like West Hollywood and Venice Beach exude. It's a narcotic effect, the allure of flashy wealth, gorgeous bodies, and celebrity status. Even watching it all as a bystander imparts a heady mixture of thrill and envy.

Northern California may be frightfully demure in comparison, but in the long run, its subdued charms and natural beauty prevail. Wealth is certainly in abundance, but rarely displayed. The few hard bodies that exist are usually swathed in loose jeans and shirts. The few celebrities who live here keep very low profiles, and are more likely to be on their ranches than on Rodeo Drive. Ostentation in any form is looked down upon (of course, it's okay to own a BMW, as long as it's slightly dirty), and unlike Los Angeles, you can actually explore smog-free San Francisco on foot.

Ironically, it's the Northern Californians who think of themselves as superior for having prudently eschewed the trappings of wealth and status (L.A.-bashing is a popular pastime). Southern Californians, on the other hand, couldn't care less what the northerners think of them; it's all sour grapes as they bask poolside 300 sunny days of the year. In fact, most Southern Californians would be perfectly content as their own state were it not for one key factor: water. Northern California holds two-thirds of the state's watershed, and without the incredibly complex system of aqueducts, reservoirs, and dams that keep huge flows going southward, Southern California's 14 million citizens would be in a world of hurt.

Will Californians ever agree to a legally mutual breakup? The idea has been bandied about the state capital for years, but it meets its Waterloo when it comes to water rights, always a hotly contested issue. But regardless of our polarized views and lifestyles, most Californians do agree on one thing: We're still the best damn dysfunctional state in America.

—*Matthew Richard Poole*

information, including detailed maps. Also, many hotels and attractions throughout California offer discounts to AAA members—always ask. Call © **800/922-8228** or visit www.aaa.com for membership information.

Here are some handy driving times if you're on one of those see-the-USA car trips. From Phoenix, it's about 6 hours to Los Angeles on I-10. Las Vegas is 265 miles northeast of Los Angeles (about a 4-hr. drive).

San Francisco is 227 miles southwest of Reno, Nevada, and 577 miles northwest of Las Vegas. It's a long day's drive 640 miles south from Portland, Oregon, on I-5. The drive between San Francisco and L.A. takes about 6 hours on I-5, closer to 8 hours on the more scenic U.S. 101.

BY TRAIN

Amtrak (© **800/USA-RAIL;** www.amtrak.com) connects California with about 500 American cities. The Sunset Limited is Amtrak's regularly scheduled transcontinental service, originating in Florida and making 52 stops along the way as it passes through Alabama, Mississippi, Louisiana, Texas, New Mexico, and Arizona before arriving in Los Angeles 2 days later. The train, which runs three times weekly, features reclining seats, a sightseeing car with large windows, and a full-service dining car. Round-trip coach fares begin at around $300; several varieties of sleeping compartments are also available for an extra charge.

10 Packages for the Independent Traveler

Before you start your search for the lowest airfare, you may want to consider booking your flight as part of a travel package. Package tours are not the same thing as escorted tours. Package tours are simply a way to buy the airfare, accommodations, and other elements of your trip (such as car rentals, airport transfers, and sometimes even activities) at the same time and often at discounted prices—kind of like one-stop shopping. Packages are sold in bulk to tour operators—who resell them to the public at a cost that usually undercuts standard rates.

One good source of package deals is the airlines themselves. Most major airlines offer air/land packages, including **American Airlines Vacations** (© 800/321-2121; www.aavacations.com), **Continental Airlines Vacations** (© 800/301-3800; www.coolvacations.com), **Delta Vacations** (© 800/221-6666; www.deltavacations.com), **Southwest Airlines Vacations** (© 800/423-5683; www.southwest.com and www.swavacations.com), and **United Vacations** (© 888/854-3899; www.unitedvacations.com). And don't forget to look at the local websites: For instance, the **San Diego Convention and Visitors Bureau** (© 800/350-6205; www.sandiego.org) has its own booking engine for packages incorporating air, hotel, and activities. Also note that the **Walt Disney Travel Company** (© 714/520-5047; www.disney.com) is one of the state's largest tour operators, featuring packages that go well beyond the Magic Kingdom.

Several big **online travel agencies**—Expedia, Travelocity, Orbitz, Site59, and Lastminute.com—also sell a lot of packages. If you're unsure about the pedigree of a smaller packager, check with the Better Business Bureau, or go online at www.bbb.org. If a packager won't tell you where it's based, don't fly with them.

Travel packages are also listed in the travel section of your Sunday newspaper. Or check ads in travel magazines such as *Arthur Frommer's Budget Travel, Travel + Leisure, National Geographic Traveler,* and *Condé Nast Traveler.*

Package tours can vary by leaps and bounds. Some offer a better class of hotels than others. Some offer the same hotels for lower prices. Some offer flights on scheduled airlines, while others book charters. Some limit your choice of accommodations and travel days. You are often required to make a large payment up front. On the plus side, packages can save you money, offering group prices but allowing for independent travel. Some even let you add on a few guided excursions or escorted day trips (also at prices lower than if you booked them yourself) without booking an entirely escorted tour.

Before you invest in a package tour, get some answers. Ask about the **accommodations choices** and prices for each. Then look up the hotels' reviews in a Frommer's guide and check their rates for your specific dates of travel online. You'll also want to find out what **type of room** you get. If you need a certain type of room, ask for it; don't take whatever is thrown your way. Request a nonsmoking room, a quiet room, a room with a view, or whatever you fancy.

Finally, look for **hidden expenses.** Ask whether airport departure fees and taxes, for example, are included in the total cost.

11 Getting Around

BY CAR

California's freeway signs frequently indicate direction by naming a town rather than a point on the compass. If you've never heard of Canoga Park, you might be in trouble—unless you have a map. The best state road guide is the comprehensive *Thomas Guide California Road Atlas,* a 300-plus-page book of maps with schematics of towns and cities statewide. It costs about $25, a good investment if you plan to do a lot of exploring. Smaller, accordion-style maps are handy for the state as a whole or for individual cities and regions; you'll find a very useful one inserted in the back of this book.

If you're heading into the Sierra or Shasta-Cascades for a winter ski trip, top up on antifreeze and carry snow chains for your tires. (Chains are mandatory in certain areas.)

See the full-color driving distance chart inside the front cover of the book for an idea of the distance between the state's popular destinations.

DRIVING RULES California law requires both drivers and passengers to wear seat belts. A law that took effect January 1, 2004, requires an approved safety seat for children under 6 or weighing less than 60 pounds. Motorcyclists must wear helmets. Auto insurance is mandatory; the car's registration and proof of insurance must be carried in the car.

You can turn right at a red light, unless otherwise indicated—but be sure to come to a complete stop.

Many California freeways have designated carpool lanes, also known as high-occupancy vehicle (HOV) lanes or "diamond" lanes. Some require two passengers, others three. Most on-ramps are metered during even light congestion to regulate the flow of traffic onto the freeway; cars in HOV lanes can pass the signal without stopping. All other drivers are required to observe the stoplights—fines begin at around $271.

CAR-RENTAL AGENCIES California is one of the cheapest places in the United States to rent a car. The best-known firms, with locations throughout the state and at most major airports, include **Alamo** (© 800/462-5866; www.alamo.com), **Avis** (© 800/230-4898; www.avis.com), **Budget** (© 800/527-0700; www.budget.com), **Dollar** (© 800/800-3665; www.dollar.com), **Hertz** (© 800/654-3131; www.hertz.com), **National** (© 800/227-7368; www.nationalcar.com), and **Thrifty** (© 800/847-4389; www.thrifty.com).

Many rental agencies have begun offering a variety of essential or just helpful extras, such as cellphones, child seats, and specially equipped vehicles for travelers with disabilities.

DEMYSTIFYING RENTER'S INSURANCE Before you drive off in a rental car, be sure you're insured. Hasty assumptions about your personal auto insurance or a rental agency's additional coverage could end up costing you tens of thousands of dollars—even if you're involved in an accident that was clearly the fault of another driver.

If you already hold a **private auto insurance** policy, you are most likely covered in the United States for loss of or damage to a rental car, and liability in case of injury to any other party involved in an accident. Be sure to find out whether you're covered in the area you're visiting, whether your policy extends to all persons who will be driving the rental car, how much liability is covered in case an outside party is injured in an accident, and whether the type of vehicle you are renting is included under your contract. (Rental trucks, sport-utility vehicles, and luxury vehicles or sports cars may not be covered.)

Most **major credit cards** provide some degree of coverage as well—provided they were used to pay for the rental. Terms vary widely, however, so be sure to call your credit card company directly before you rent.

The *Coast Starlight:* All Aboard for Nostalgia

If you're considering travel by rail along the California coast, or even as far north as Seattle, treat yourself to a ride aboard Amtrak's luxurious *Coast Starlight.* In an effort to recapture the glory days of 1940s Streamline luxury liners, Amtrak has pulled out all the stops on these doubledecker Superliners, complete with a gourmet dining car, first-class and coach lounge cars, standard and deluxe sleeping compartments, and enough diversions (including feature-length films, live entertainment, games for kids and adults, and a full bar) to make the 35-hour trip a pleasure. All sleeping-car fares include three meals daily, prepared onboard with an emphasis on regional flavor, and wines from Washington, Oregon, and California, as well as seasonal specials from along the *Coast Starlight*'s route.

While coach tickets are comparable to airplane fares, the surcharge for sleeping compartments adds considerably to the cost of the trip. Coach fare buys assigned seating in comfortable upper-level reclining chairs. Blankets and pillows are offered in the evening, and fold-up leg rests help make sleeping more comfortable than you might imagine. Between Seattle and Los Angeles, one-way adult coach fare ranges from $91 to $188. Children ages 2 to 15 travel for half-price, and seniors 62 and older receive a 15% discount. A standard sleeping compartment for two adds $169 to $377, a deluxe with private bathroom is $385 to $900.

It's advisable to book several months ahead for peak periods (summer, weekends, and holidays) and to get the best rates. Since the splendid views depend on daylight, also consider it carefully before traveling during the shorter days of winter. For information and tickets, call **Amtrak** (© **800/USA-RAIL;** www.amtrak.com).

Finds Bicycling Tours

Combine an interest in biking with views of California's spectacular scenery by signing up for a tour with **Backroads,** 801 Cedar St., Berkeley, CA 94710 (© **800/GO-ACTIVE** or 510/527-1555; www.backroads.com). Focusing on coastal routes, wine country rides, and even a microbrew program, the tours vary in difficulty and comfort; some are camping trips, while others accommodate you in B&Bs. Professional leaders accompany each group, while a van trails with gear, baggage, and provisions. Tours include meals and overnight accommodations, and range from $150 to $275 per day, per person.

If you're **uninsured,** your credit card may provide primary coverage as long as you decline the rental agency's insurance. This means that the credit card may cover damage or theft of a rental car for the full cost of the vehicle. (In a few states, however, theft is not covered; ask specifically about state law where you will be renting and driving.) If you already have insurance, your credit card may provide secondary coverage—which basically covers your deductible.

Credit cards **will not cover liability,** or the cost of injury to an outside party and/or damage to an outside party's vehicle. If you do not hold an insurance policy, you may want to consider purchasing additional liability insurance from your rental company. Be sure to check the terms, however: Some rental agencies only cover liability if the renter is not at fault.

The basic insurance coverage offered by most car-rental companies, known as the **Loss/Damage Waiver (LDW)** or **Collision Damage Waiver (CDW),** can cost as much as $20 per day. It usually covers the full value of the vehicle with no deductible if an outside party causes an accident or other damage to the rental car. Liability coverage varies according to the company policy and state law, but the minimum is usually at least $15,000. If you are at fault in an accident, however, you will be covered

for the full replacement value of the car but not for liability. In California, you can buy additional liability coverage for such cases. Most rental companies will require a police report in order to process any claims you file, but your private insurer will not be notified of the accident.

BY PLANE

In addition to the major carriers listed earlier in this section, several airlines provide service within the state, including **American Eagle** (© 800/433-7300), **Southwest** (© 800/435-9792), **United Express** (© 800/241-6522), and **US Airways Express** (© 800/428-4322). The round-trip fare between Los Angeles and San Francisco ranges from $79 to $200. See "Orientation" or "Getting There" in each city's chapter for further information.

BY TRAIN

Amtrak (© **800/USA-RAIL;** www.amtrak.com) runs trains up and down the California coast, connecting San Diego, Los Angeles, and San Francisco, and all points in between. There are multiple trains each day, and rates fluctuate according to season and special promotions. One-way fares for the most popular segments can range from $17 (L.A.–Santa Barbara), to $24 (L.A.–San Diego), to $46 to $78 (San Francisco–L.A.).

12 Tips on Accommodations

SAVING ON YOUR HOTEL ROOM

The **rack rate** is the maximum rate that a hotel charges for a room. Hardly anybody pays this price, however. To lower the cost of your room:

- **Ask about special rates or other discounts.** Always ask whether a room less expensive than the first one quoted is available, or whether any special rates apply to you. You may qualify for corporate, student, military, senior, or other discounts. Mention membership in AAA, AARP, frequent-flier programs, or trade unions, which may entitle you to special deals as well. Find out the hotel policy on children— do kids stay free in the room or is there a special rate?

- **Dial direct.** When booking a room in a chain hotel, you'll often get a better deal by calling the individual hotel's reservation desk than at the chain's main number.

- **Book online.** Many hotels offer Internet-only discounts, or supply rooms to Priceline, Hotwire, or Expedia at rates much lower than the ones you can get through the hotel itself.

- **Remember the law of supply and demand.** Resort hotels are most crowded and most expensive on weekends, so discounts are usually available for midweek stays. Business hotels are busiest during the week, so you can expect discounts on the weekends. Many hotels have high- and low-season prices, and booking the day after "high season" ends can mean big discounts.

- **Look into group or long-stay discounts.** If you come as part of a large group, you should be able to negotiate a bargain rate, since the hotel can then guarantee occupancy in a number of rooms. Likewise, if you're planning a long stay (at least 5 days), you might qualify for a discount. As a general rule, expect 1 night free after a 7-night stay.

- **Avoid excess charges and hidden costs.** When you book a room, ask whether the hotel charges for parking. Use your own cellphone, pay phones, or prepaid phone cards instead of dialing direct from hotel phones. And don't be tempted by the room's minibar offerings: Most hotels charge through the nose for water, soda, and snacks. Finally, ask about local taxes and service charges, which can increase the cost of a room by 15% or more. If a hotel insists upon tacking on a surprise "energy surcharge" that wasn't mentioned at check-in or a "resort fee" for amenities you didn't use, you can often make a case for getting it removed.

- **Book an efficiency.** A room with a kitchenette allows you to cook your own meals. This is a big money saver, especially for families on long stays.

LANDING THE BEST ROOM

Somebody has to get the best room in the house. It might as well be you. You can start by joining the hotel's frequent-guest program, which may make you eligible for upgrades. A hotel-branded credit card usually gives its owner "silver" or "gold" status in frequent-guest programs for free. Always ask about a corner room. They're often larger and quieter, with more windows and light, and they often cost the same as standard rooms. When you make your reservation, ask if the hotel is renovating; if it is, request a room away from the construction. If you're a light sleeper, request a quiet room away from vending machines, elevators, restaurants, bars, and discos. Ask for one of the rooms that have been most recently renovated or redecorated.

If you aren't happy with your room when you arrive, say so. If another room is available, most lodgings will be willing to accommodate you.

13 Recommended Reading

There's no shortage of reading material about the history and culture of California, one of the most romanticized places on earth. Almost from the beginning, novelists and poets were part of California's cultural mosaic, and the works they've created offer a fascinating window into the lives and legends of the huge, diverse state and its state of mind.

HISTORICAL PERSPECTIVES

Readers are spoiled for choices when it comes to fictionalized accounts of California's pioneers. Salinas native John Steinbeck, one of the state's best-known authors, paints a vivid portrayal of proletarian life in the early to mid-1900s. His *Grapes of Wrath* remains the classic account of itinerant farm laborers coming to California in the midst of the Great Depression. *Cannery Row* has forever made the Monterey waterfront famous, and *East of Eden* offers insight into the way of life in the Salinas Valley.

Famed humorist and storyteller Mark Twain penned vivid tales during California's Gold Rush era, including one of his most popular works, "The Celebrated Jumping Frog of Calaveras County" (an annual Gold Country competition that still has legs). Other good gold-rush reads include Bret Harte's *The Luck of Roaring Camp*, a sentimental tale of hard-luck miners and their false toughness, and J. S. Holliday's *The World Rushed In*, one of the finest nonfiction accounts of the Gold Rush still in print.

San Francisco was also a popular setting for many early works, including Twain's *San Francisco*, a collection of articles that glorified "the liveliest, heartiest community on our continent." It was also the birthplace of Jack London, who wrote several short stories of his younger days as an oyster pirate on the San Francisco Bay, as well as *Martin Eden*, his semi-autobiographical account of life along the Oakland shores.

An excellent anthology containing selections from writers representing all the varied cultures in California's diverse history, *The Literature of California: Writings from the Golden State*, is published by the University of California Press.

Finally, for what some critics consider the best novel ever written about Hollywood, turn to Nathanael West's *The Day of the Locust*, a savage and satirical look at 1930s life on the fringes of the film industry.

MYSTERY & MAYHEM

For you mystery buffs headed to California, two must-reads include Frank Norris's *McTeague: A Story of San Francisco*, a tale of love and greed set at the turn of the 20th century, and Dashiell Hammett's *The Maltese Falcon*, a detective novel that captures the seedier side of San Francisco in the 1920s. Another favorite is Raymond Chandler's *The Big Sleep*, in which Philip Marlowe explores the darker side of Los Angeles in the 1930s.

California has always been a hotbed for alternative—and, more often than not, controversial—literary styles. Joan Didion, in her novel *Slouching Toward Bethlehem*, and Hunter S. Thompson, in his columns for the *San Francisco Examiner* (brought together in the collection *Generation of Swine*), both used a "new journalistic" approach in their studies of San Francisco in the 1960s. Tom Wolfe's early work *The Electric Kool-Aid Acid Test* follows the Hell's Angels, the Grateful Dead, and Ken Kesey's Merry Pranksters as they ride through the hallucinogenic 1960s. Meanwhile, Beat writers Allen Ginsberg and Jack Kerouac were penning protests against political conservatism—and promoting their bohemian lifestyle—in the former's controversial poem "Howl" (daringly published by Lawrence Ferlinghetti, poet and owner of City Lights in San Francisco's North Beach district) and the latter's famous tale of American adventure, *On the Road.*

CONTEMPORARY FICTION

If you're interested in a contemporary look back at four generations in the life of an American family, you can do no better than Wallace Stegner's *Angle of Repose.* The winner of the Pulitzer Prize in 1971, this work chronicles the lives of pioneers on the western frontier. Among Stegner's many other works of fiction and nonfiction about the West is his novel *All the Little Live Things,* which is set in the San Francisco Bay Area of the 1960s.

SPECIAL-INTEREST READS

Geology buffs will want to pack a copy of *Assembling California,* John McPhee's observation of California's geological history. Mike Davis's *City of Quartz* and *Ecology of Fear* offer a critical perspective on the social and natural history of Los Angeles.

Outdoor enthusiasts have dozens of sporting books to choose from, but most comprehensive is Foghorn Press's outdoor series—*California Camping, California Fishing, California Golf, California Beaches,* and *California Hiking*—available at every major bookstore in the state.

FAST FACTS: California

Earthquakes In the rare event of an earthquake, if you're in a tall building, don't run outside; instead, move away from windows and toward the building's center. Crouch under a desk or table, or stand against a wall or under a doorway. If you're in bed, get under the bed or stand in a doorway, or crouch under a sturdy piece of furniture. When exiting the building, use stairwells, *not* elevators.

If you're in your car, pull over to the side of the road and stop, but wait until you're away from bridges or overpasses, as well as telephone or power poles and lines. Stay in your car.

If you're out walking, stay outside and away from trees, power lines, and the sides of buildings.

Emergencies To reach the police, ambulance service, or fire department, dial ℃ 911. No coins are needed at pay phones for 911 calls.

Liquor Laws Liquor and grocery stores, as well as some drugstores, can sell packaged alcoholic beverages between 6am and 2am. Most restaurants, nightclubs, and bars are licensed to serve alcoholic beverages during the same hours. The legal age for the purchase and consumption of alcoholic beverages is 21; proof of age is strictly enforced.

Lost & Found Be sure to tell all of your credit card companies the minute you discover your wallet has been lost or stolen and file a report at the nearest police precinct. Your credit card company or insurer may require a police report number or record of the loss. Most credit card companies have an emergency toll-free number to call if your card is lost or stolen; they may be able to wire you a cash advance immediately or deliver an

emergency credit card in a day or two. Visa's U.S. emergency number is
© **800/847-2911** or 410/581-9994. American Express cardholders and traveler's check holders should call © **800/221-7282.** MasterCard holders
should call © **800/307-7309** or 636/722-7111. For other credit cards, call
the toll-free number directory at © **800/555-1212.**

If you need emergency cash over the weekend when all banks and
American Express offices are closed, you can have money wired to you via
Western Union (© **800/325-6000;** www.westernunion.com).

Taxes California's state sales tax is 7.25%. Some cities include an additional percentage or fraction, so the tax varies throughout the state; for
example, it's 7.75% in San Diego, 8.25% in Los Angeles, and 8.5% in San
Francisco. Hotel taxes are almost always higher than tariffs levied on
goods and services.

Time Zone California and the entire West Coast are in the Pacific time
zone, 3 hours earlier than the East Coast.

3

For International Visitors

Whether it's your 1st visit or your 10th, a trip to the United States may require an additional degree of planning. This chapter will provide you with essential information, helpful tips, and advice for the more common problems that some visitors encounter.

1 Preparing for Your Trip

ENTRY REQUIREMENTS

Check at any U.S. embassy or consulate for current information and requirements. You can also obtain a visa application and other information online at the **U.S. State Department**'s website, at **www.travel.state.gov**.

VISAS The U.S. State Department has a **Visa Waiver Program** allowing citizens of certain countries to enter the United States without a visa for stays of up to 90 days. At press time these included Andorra, Australia, Austria, Belgium, Brunei, Denmark, Finland, France, Germany, Iceland, Ireland, Italy, Japan, Liechtenstein, Luxembourg, Monaco, the Netherlands, New Zealand, Norway, Portugal, San Marino, Singapore, Slovenia, Spain, Sweden, Switzerland, and the United Kingdom. Citizens of these countries need only a valid passport and a round-trip air or cruise ticket in their possession upon arrival. If they first enter the United States, they may also visit Mexico, Canada, Bermuda, and/or the Caribbean islands and return to the United States without a visa. Further information is available from any U.S. embassy or consulate. Canadian citizens may enter the United States without visas; they need only proof of residence.

Citizens of all other countries must have (1) a valid passport that expires at least 6 months later than the end of their visit to the United States, and (2) a tourist visa, which may be obtained from any U.S. consulate.

To obtain a visa, the traveler must submit a completed application form (either in person or by mail) with a 1½-inch-square photo, and must demonstrate binding ties to a residence abroad. Usually you can obtain a visa at once or within 24 hours, but it may take longer during the summer rush from June through August. If you cannot go in person, contact the nearest U.S. embassy or consulate for directions on applying by mail. Your travel agent or airline office may also be able to provide you with visa applications and instructions.

British subjects can obtain up-to-date visa information by calling the **U.S. Embassy Visa Information Line** (© **0891/200-290**) or by visiting the "Visas to the U.S." section of the American Embassy London's website at www.usembassy.org.uk.

Irish citizens can obtain up-to-date visa information through the **Embassy of the USA Dublin,** 42 Elgin Rd., Dublin 4, Ireland (© **353/1-668-8777**), or by checking the "Visas to the U.S." section of the website at http://dublin.usembassy.gov/.

Australian citizens can obtain up-to-date visa information by contacting the **U.S. Embassy Canberra,** Moonah Place, Yarralumla, ACT 2600 (© **02/6214-5600**), or by checking the U.S. Diplomatic Mission's website at http://usembassy-australia.state.gov/consular.

Citizens of **New Zealand** can obtain up-to-date visa information by contacting the **U.S. Embassy New Zealand,** 29 Fitzherbert Terr., Thorndon, Wellington (© **644/472-2068**), or get the information directly from the "For New Zealanders" section of the website at http://usembassy.org.nz.

MEDICAL REQUIREMENTS

Unless you're arriving from an area known to be suffering from an epidemic (particularly cholera or yellow fever), inoculations or vaccinations are not required for entry into the United States. If you have a medical condition that requires **syringe-administered medications,** carry a valid signed prescription from your physician—the Federal Aviation Administration (FAA) no longer allows airline passengers to pack syringes in their carry-on baggage without documented proof of medical need. If you have a disease that requires treatment with **narcotics,** you should also carry documented proof with you—smuggling narcotics aboard a plane is a serious offense that carries severe penalties in the U.S.

For **HIV-positive visitors,** requirements for entering the United States are somewhat vague and change frequently. According to the latest publication of *HIV and Immigrants: A Manual for AIDS Service Providers,* the Immigration and Naturalization Service (INS) doesn't require a medical exam for entry into the U.S., but INS officials may stop individuals because

they look sick or because they are carrying AIDS/HIV medicine.

If an HIV-positive noncitizen applies for a nonimmigrant visa, the question on the application regarding communicable diseases is tricky no matter which way it's answered. If the applicant checks "no," INS may deny the visa on the grounds that the applicant committed fraud. If the applicant checks "yes" or if INS suspects the person is HIV-positive, it will deny the visa unless the applicant asks for a special waiver for visitors. This waiver is for people visiting the United States for a short time, to attend a conference, for instance, to visit close relatives, or to receive medical treatment. For up-to-the-minute information, contact **AIDSinfo** (© **800/448-0440** or, outside the U.S., 301/519-0459; www.aidsinfo.nih.gov) or the **Gay Men's Health Crisis** (© **212/ 367-1000;** www.gmhc.org).

DRIVER'S LICENSES Most foreign driver's licenses are recognized in the U.S., although you may want to get an international driver's license if yours is not written in English.

PASSPORT INFORMATION

Safeguard your passport in an inconspicuous, inaccessible place like a money belt. Make a copy of the critical pages, including the passport number, and store it in a safe place, separate from the passport itself. If you lose your passport, visit the nearest consulate of your native country as soon as possible for a replacement.

Note: The International Civil Aviation Organization has recommended a policy requiring that *every* individual who travels by air have a passport. In response, many countries are now requiring that children must be issued their own passport to travel internationally, where before those under 16 or so may have been allowed to travel on a parent or guardian's passport.

FOR RESIDENTS OF CANADA

You can pick up a passport application at one of 28 regional passport offices or most travel agencies. Canadian children who travel must have their own passport. However, if you hold a valid Canadian passport issued before December 11, 2001, that bears the name of your child, the passport remains valid for you and your child until it expires. Passports cost C$85 for those 16 years and older (valid 5 years), C$35 for children 3 to 15 (valid 5 years), and C$20 for children under 3 (valid 3 years). Applications, which must be accompanied by two identical passport-size photographs and proof of Canadian citizenship, are available at travel agencies throughout Canada or from the central **Passport Office,** Department of Foreign Affairs and International Trade, Ottawa, ON K1A 0G3 (𝒞 **800/567-6868;** www. dfait-maeci.gc.ca/passport). Processing takes 5 to 10 days if you apply in person, or about 3 weeks by mail.

FOR RESIDENTS OF THE UNITED KINGDOM

As a member of the European Union, you need only an identity card, not a passport, to travel to other EU countries. However, if you already possess a passport, it's always useful to carry it. To pick up an application for a standard 10-year passport (5-year passport for children under 16), visit the nearest passport office, major post office, or travel agency. You can also contact the **United Kingdom Passport Service** at 𝒞 **0870/571-0410** or visit its website at www.passport.gov.uk. Passports are £33 for adults and £19 for children under 16, with another £30 fee if you apply in person at a passport office. Processing takes about 2 weeks (1 week if you apply at the passport office).

FOR RESIDENTS OF IRELAND

You can apply for a 10-year passport, costing €57, at the **Passport Office,** Setanta Centre, Molesworth Street, Dublin 2 (𝒞 **01/671-1633;** www.ir gov.ie/iveagh). Those under age 18 and over 65 must apply for a €12 3-year passport. You can also apply at 1A South Mall, Cork (𝒞 **021/272-525**), or over the counter at most main post offices.

FOR RESIDENTS OF AUSTRALIA

You can get an application from your local post office or any branch of Passports Australia, but you must schedule an interview at the passport office to present your application materials. Call the **Australian Passport Information Service** at 𝒞 **131-232,** or visit the government website at www.passports.gov.au. Passports for adults are A$144 and for those under 18 A$72.

FOR RESIDENTS OF NEW ZEALAND

You can pick up a passport application at any New Zealand passports office or download it from their website. Contact the **Passports Office** at 𝒞 **0800/225-050** in New Zealand or 04/474-8100, or log on to www. passports.govt.nz. Passports for adults are NZ$80 and for children under 16 NZ$40.

CUSTOMS
WHAT YOU CAN BRING IN

Every visitor more than 21 years of age may bring in, free of duty, the following: (1) 1 liter of wine or hard liquor; (2) 200 cigarettes, 100 cigars (but not from Cuba), or 3 pounds of smoking tobacco; and (3) $100 worth of gifts. These exemptions are offered to travelers who spend at least 72 hours in the United States and who have not claimed them within the preceding 6 months. It is forbidden to bring in foodstuffs (particularly fruit, cooked meats, and canned goods) and plants (vegetables, seeds, tropical plants, and the like). Foreign tourists may bring in or take out up to $10,000 in U.S. or foreign currency with no formalities; larger sums must be declared to U.S. Customs, which includes filing form CM 4790. For more specific information regarding U.S. Customs and Border Protection, contact your nearest U.S. embassy or consulate, or the **U.S. Customs** office (℘ **202/927-1770** or www.customs.ustreas.gov).

WHAT YOU CAN TAKE HOME

U.K. citizens returning from a non-EU country have a customs allowance of: 200 cigarettes; 50 cigars; 250 grams of smoking tobacco; 2 liters of still table wine; 1 liter of spirits or strong liqueurs (over 22% volume); 2 liters of fortified wine, sparkling wine, or other liqueurs; 60 cubic centimeters (ml) perfume; 250 cubic centimeters (ml) of toilet water; and £145 worth of all other goods, including gifts and souvenirs. People under 17 cannot have the tobacco or alcohol allowance. For more information, contact HM Customs & Excise at ℘ **0845/ 010-9000** (from outside the U.K., 020/8929-0152), or consult their website at www.hmce.gov.uk.

For a clear summary of **Canadian** rules, request the booklet *I Declare,* issued by the **Canada Customs and Revenue Agency** (℘ **800/461-9999** in Canada, or 204/983-3500; www. ccra-adrc.gc.ca). Canada allows its citizens a C$750 exemption, and you're allowed to bring back duty-free 1 carton of cigarettes, 1 can of tobacco, 40 imperial ounces of liquor, and 50 cigars. In addition, you're allowed to mail gifts to Canada valued at less than C$60 a day, provided they're unsolicited and don't contain alcohol or tobacco (write on the package "Unsolicited gift, under $60 value"). All valuables should be declared on the Y-38 form before departure from Canada, including serial numbers of valuables you already own, such as foreign cameras. *Note:* The $750 exemption can only be used once a year and only after an absence of 7 days.

The duty-free allowance in **Australia** is A$400 or, for those under 18, A$200. Citizens age 18 and over can bring in 250 cigarettes or 250 grams of loose tobacco, and 1,125 milliliters of alcohol. If you're returning with valuables you already own, such as foreign-made cameras, you should file form B263. A helpful brochure available from Australian consulates or Customs offices is *Know Before You Go.* For more information, call the **Australian Customs Service** at ℘ **1300/363-263,** or log on to www. customs.gov.au.

The duty-free allowance for **New Zealand** is NZ$700. Citizens over 17 can bring in 200 cigarettes, 50 cigars, or 250 grams of tobacco (or a mixture of all three if their combined weight doesn't exceed 250g); plus 4.5 liters of wine and beer, or 1.125 liters of liquor. New Zealand currency does not carry import or export restrictions. Fill out a certificate of export, listing the valuables you are taking out of the country; that way, you can bring them back without paying duty. Most questions are answered in a free pamphlet available at New Zealand consulates and Customs offices: *New Zealand Customs Guide for Travellers, Notice no. 4.* For more information, contact **New Zealand Customs,** The Customhouse, 17–21 Whitmore St., Box 2218, Wellington (℘ **0800/ 428-786** or 04/473-6099; www. customs.govt.nz).

HEALTH INSURANCE

Although it's not required of travelers, health insurance is highly recommended. Unlike many European countries, the United States does not usually offer free or low-cost medical care to its citizens or visitors. Doctors and hospitals are expensive, and in most cases will require advance payment or proof of coverage before they render their services. Policies can cover everything from the loss or theft of your baggage and trip cancellation to the guarantee of bail in case you're arrested. Good policies will also cover the costs of an accident, repatriation, or death. See "Travel Insurance" in chapter 2 for more information. Packages such as **Europ Assistance's "Worldwide Healthcare Plan"** are sold by European automobile clubs and travel agencies at attractive rates. **Worldwide Assistance Services, Inc.** (© **800/821-2828;** www.worldwide-assistance.com) is the agent for Europ Assistance in the United States.

Though lack of health insurance may prevent you from being admitted to a hospital in nonemergencies, don't worry about being left on a street corner to die: The American way is to fix you now and bill the living daylights out of you later.

INSURANCE FOR BRITISH TRAVELERS Most big travel agents offer their own insurance and will probably try to sell you their package when you book a holiday. Think before you sign. **Britain's Consumers' Association** recommends that you insist on seeing the policy and reading the fine print before buying travel insurance. **The Association of British Insurers** (© **020/7600-3333;** www.abi.org.uk) gives advice by phone and publishes *Holiday Insurance,* a free guide to policy provisions and prices. You might also shop around for better deals: Try **Columbus Direct** (© **020/7375-0011;** www.columbusdirect.net).

INSURANCE FOR CANADIAN TRAVELERS Canadians should check with their provincial health plan offices or call **Health Canada** (© **613/957-2991;** www.hc-sc.gc.ca) to find out the extent of their coverage and what documentation and receipts they must take home in case they are treated in the United States.

MONEY

CURRENCY The U.S. monetary system is very simple: The most common **bills** are the $1 (colloquially, a "buck"), $5, $10, and $20 denominations. There are also $2 bills (seldom encountered), $50 bills, and $100 bills (the last two are usually not welcome as payment for small purchases). All the paper money was recently redesigned, making the famous faces adorning them disproportionately large. The old-style bills are still legal tender.

There are seven denominations of coins: 1¢ (1 cent, or a penny); 5¢ (5 cents, or a nickel); 10¢ (10 cents, or a dime); 25¢ (25 cents, or a quarter); 50¢ (50 cents, or a half dollar); and the gold-colored "Sacagawea" coin worth $1.

Note: The "foreign-exchange bureaus" so common in Europe are rare even at airports in the United States, and nonexistent outside major cities. It's best not to change foreign money (or traveler's checks in a currency other than U.S. dollars) at a bank; in fact, leave any currency other than U.S. dollars at home—it may prove a greater nuisance to you than it's worth.

TRAVELER'S CHECKS Though traveler's checks are widely accepted, make sure that they're denominated in U.S. dollars, as foreign-currency checks are often difficult to exchange. The three traveler's checks that are most widely recognized—and least likely to be denied—are **Visa, American Express,** and **Thomas Cook.** Be sure to record the numbers of the checks, and keep that information in a separate place in case they get lost or stolen. Most businesses are good about taking traveler's checks, but you're better off cashing them in at a bank (in small amounts) and paying in cash. *Remember:* You'll need identification, such as a driver's license or passport, to change a traveler's check.

CREDIT CARDS & ATMs Credit cards are the most widely used form of payment in the United States: **Visa** (Barclaycard in Britain), **MasterCard** (EuroCard in Europe, Access in Britain, Chargex in Canada), **American Express, Diners Club, Discover,** and **Carte Blanche.** There are, however, a handful of stores and restaurants that do not take credit cards, so ask in advance. Most businesses display a sticker near their entrance to let you know which cards they accept. (*Note:* Businesses may require a minimum purchase, usually around $10, to use a credit card.)

It is strongly recommended that you bring at least one major credit card. You must have a credit or charge card to rent a car. Hotels and airlines usually require a credit card imprint as a deposit, and in an emergency a credit card can be priceless.

You'll find **automated teller machines (ATMs)** in just about every town in California, and on every block in the business districts of the big cities. Some ATMs will allow you to draw U.S. currency against your bank and credit cards. Check with your bank before leaving home, and remember that you will need your personal identification number (PIN) to do so. Most accept Visa, MasterCard, and American Express, as well as ATM cards from other U.S. banks. Expect to be charged up to $3 per transaction, however, if you're not using your own bank's ATM.

One way around these fees is to ask for cash back at grocery stores that accept ATM cards and don't charge usage fees. Of course, you'll have to purchase something first. The same is true at most U.S. Post Offices.

ATM cards with major credit card backing, known as "debit cards," are now a commonly acceptable form of payment in most stores and restaurants. Debit cards draw money directly from your checking account. *Tip:* Many stores and post offices enable you to receive "cash back" on your debit card purchases as well.

SAFETY
GENERAL   SUGGESTIONS
Although California's tourist areas are generally safe, you should always stay alert, particularly for petty thefts such as pickpocketing and scams. This is particularly true of large American cities. If you're in doubt about which neighborhoods are safe, don't hesitate to make inquiries with the hotel's front-desk staff or the local tourist office.

Avoid deserted areas, especially at night, and don't go into parks after dark unless there's a concert or similar occasion that will attract a crowd.

Avoid carrying valuables with you on the street, and keep expensive cameras or electronic equipment bagged up or covered when not in use. If you're using a map, try to consult it inconspicuously—or better yet, study it before you leave your room. Hold on to your pocketbook, and place your billfold in an inside pocket. In theaters, restaurants, and other public places, keep your possessions in sight.

Always lock your room door—don't assume that once you're inside the hotel you are safe and no longer need to be aware of your surroundings. Hotels are open to the public, and in a large hotel, security may not be able to screen everyone who enters.

DRIVING SAFETY Driving safety is important, too, and carjacking is not unprecedented. Question your rental agency about personal safety and ask for a traveler-safety brochure when you pick up your car. Obtain written directions—or a map with the route clearly marked—from the agency showing how to get to your destination. (Many agencies now offer the option of renting a cellphone for the duration of your car rental; check with the rental agent when you pick up the car. Otherwise, contact **InTouch USA** at ✆ **800/872-7626** or www.intouch usa.com for short-term cellphone rental.) If possible, arrive and depart during daylight hours.

If you drive off a highway and end up in a dodgy-looking neighborhood, leave the area as quickly as possible. If you have an accident, even on the highway, stay in your car with the doors locked until you assess the situation or until the police arrive. If you're bumped from behind on the street or are involved in a minor accident with no injuries, and the situation appears to be suspicious, motion to the other driver to follow you. Never get out of your car in such situations. Go directly to the nearest police precinct, well-lit service station, or 24-hour store.

Park in well-lit and well-traveled areas whenever possible. Always keep your car doors locked, whether the vehicle is attended or unattended. Never leave any packages or valuables in sight. If someone attempts to rob you or steal your car, don't try to resist the thief/carjacker. Report the incident to the police department immediately by calling ✆ **911.**

2 Getting to the U.S.

AIRLINES In addition to the domestic U.S. airlines listed in chapter 2, many international carriers serve LAX and other U.S. gateways. These include, among others: **Aer Lingus** (✆ **01/886-8888** in Dublin; www. aerlingus.ie), **Air Canada** (✆ **800/776-3000;** www.aircanada.ca), **British Airways** (✆ **0845/77 33-377** in the U.K.; www.british-airways.com), **Canadian Airlines** (✆ **800/426-7000**), **Japan Airlines** (✆ **0354/89-1111** in Tokyo; www.jal.co.jp), **Qantas** (✆ **13-13-13** in Australia; www.qantas.com.au), and **Virgin Atlantic** (✆ **01293/747-747** in the U.K.; www.fly.virgin.com). British Airways and Virgin Atlantic offer direct flights to San Francisco and Los Angeles from London. **Air New**

⎧Tips Prepare to Be Fingerprinted

Starting in January 2004, many international visitors traveling on visas to the United States will be photographed and fingerprinted at Customs in a new program created by the Department of Homeland Security called **US-VISIT.** Non–U.S. citizens arriving at airports and on cruise ships must undergo an instant background check as part of the government's ongoing efforts to deter terrorism by verifying the identity of incoming and outgoing visitors. Exempt from the extra scrutiny are visitors entering by land or those from 28 countries (mostly in Europe) that don't require a visa for short-term visits. For more information, go to the Homeland Security website at **www.dhs.gov/dhspublic.**

Zealand (© 73-7000 in New Zealand; www.airnewzealand.co.nz) also flies direct to California.

Overseas visitors can take advantage of the APEX (Advance Purchase Excursion) reductions offered by major U.S. and European carriers. For more money-saving tips, see "Getting There," in chapter 2.

IMMIGRATION & CUSTOMS CLEARANCE Visitors arriving by air, no matter what the port of entry, should cultivate patience and resignation before setting foot on U.S. soil. Getting through immigration control can take as long as 2 hours on some days, especially on summer weekends, so be sure to carry this guidebook or something else to read. This is especially true in the aftermath of the September 11, 2001, terrorist attacks, when security clearances have been considerably beefed up at U.S. airports.

People traveling by air from Canada, Bermuda, and certain countries in the Caribbean can sometimes clear Customs and Immigration at the point of departure, which is much quicker.

3 Getting Around the U.S.

BY PLANE Some large airlines (for example, Northwest and Delta) offer travelers on their transatlantic or transpacific flights special discount tickets under the name **Visit USA,** allowing mostly one-way travel from one U.S. destination to another at very low prices. These discount tickets are not on sale in the United States and must be purchased abroad in conjunction with your international ticket. This system is the best, easiest, and fastest way to see the United States at low cost. You should obtain information well in advance from your travel agent or the office of the airline concerned, since the conditions attached to these discount tickets can be changed without advance notice.

BY TRAIN International visitors (excluding Canada) can also buy a **USA Rail Pass,** good for 15 or 30 days of unlimited travel on Amtrak (© 800/USA-RAIL; www.amtrak. com). The pass is available through many overseas travel agents. Prices in 2004 for a 15-day pass were $295 off peak, $440 peak; a 30-day pass costs $385 off peak, $550 peak. With a foreign passport, you can also buy passes at some Amtrak offices in the United States, including locations in San Francisco, Los Angeles, Chicago, New York, Miami, Boston, and Washington, D.C. Reservations are generally required and should be made for each part of your trip as early as possible. Regional rail passes are also available.

BY BUS Although bus travel is often the most economical form of public transit for short hops between U.S. cities, it can also be slow, uncomfortable, and chock-full of nutcases—certainly not an option for everyone (particularly when Amtrak, which is far more luxurious, offers similar rates). **Greyhound/Trailways** (© 800/231-2222; www.greyhound. com), the sole nationwide bus line, offers an **International Ameripass** that must be purchased before coming to the United States, or by phone through the Greyhound International Office at the Port Authority Bus Terminal in New York City (© 212/971-0492). The pass can be obtained from foreign travel agents or through Greyhound's website (order at least 21 days before your departure to the U.S.) and costs less than the domestic version. Passes were priced as follows in 2004: 4 days ($160), 7 days ($219), 10 days ($269), 15 days ($329), 21 days ($379), 30 days ($439), 45 days ($489), or 60 days ($599). You can get more info on the pass at the website or by calling © **402/330-8552.** In addition, special rates are available for seniors and students.

BY CAR Unless you plan to spend the bulk of your vacation time in a city where walking is the best and easiest way to get around (read: New York City or New Orleans), the most cost-effective, convenient, and comfortable way to travel around the United States is by car. The interstate highway system connects cities and towns all over the country; in addition to these high-speed, limited-access roadways, there's an extensive network of federal, state, and local highways and roads. Some of the national car-rental companies include **Alamo** (© 800/462-5266; www.alamo.com), **Avis** (© 800/230-4898; www.avis.com), **Budget** (© 800/527-0700; www.budget.com), **Dollar** (© 800/800-3665; www.dollar.com), **Hertz** (© 800/654-3131; www.hertz.com), **National** (© 800/227-7368; www.nationalcar.com), and **Thrifty** (© 800/847-4389; www.thrifty.com).

If you plan to rent a car in the United States, you probably won't need the services of an additional automobile organization. If you're planning to buy or borrow a car, automobile-association membership is recommended. **AAA, the American Automobile Association** (© 800/222-4357), is the country's largest auto club and supplies its members with maps, insurance, and, most important, emergency road service. The cost of joining runs from $63 for singles to $87 for two members, but if you're a member of a foreign auto club with reciprocal arrangements, you can enjoy free AAA service in America. See "Getting There," in chapter 2 for more information.

FAST FACTS: For the International Traveler

Automobile Organizations Auto clubs will supply maps, suggested routes, guidebooks, accident and bail-bond insurance, and emergency road service. The **American Automobile Association (AAA)** is the major auto club in the United States. If you belong to an auto club in your home country, inquire about AAA reciprocity before you leave. You may be able to join AAA even if you're not a member of a reciprocal club; to inquire, call AAA (© **800/222-4357**). AAA is actually an organization of regional auto clubs; so look under "AAA Automobile Club" in the White Pages of the telephone directory. AAA has a nationwide emergency road service telephone number (© **800/AAA-HELP**).

Business Hours Offices are usually open weekdays from 9am to 5pm. Banks are open weekdays from 9am to 3pm or later and sometimes Saturday mornings. Stores typically open between 9 and 10am and close between 5 and 6pm from Monday through Saturday. Stores in shopping complexes or malls tend to stay open late: until about 9pm on weekdays and weekends, and many malls and larger department stores are open on Sundays.

Currency & Currency Exchange See "Entry Requirements" and "Money" under "Preparing for Your Trip," earlier in this chapter.

Drinking Laws The legal age for purchase and consumption of alcoholic beverages is 21; proof of age is required and often requested at bars, nightclubs, and restaurants, so it's always a good idea to bring ID when you go out. Beer and wine often can be purchased in supermarkets, but liquor laws vary from state to state.

Do not carry open containers of alcohol in your car or any public area that isn't zoned for alcohol consumption. The police can fine you on the spot. And nothing will ruin your trip faster than getting a citation for DUI ("driving under the influence"), so don't even think about driving while intoxicated.

Electricity   Like Canada, the United States uses 110–120 volts AC (60 cycles), compared to 220–240 volts AC (50 cycles) in most of Europe, Australia, and New Zealand. If your small appliances use 220–240 volts, you'll need a 110-volt transformer and a plug adapter with two flat parallel pins to operate them here. Downward converters that change 220–240 volts to 110–120 volts are difficult to find in the United States, so bring one with you.

Embassies & Consulates   All embassies are located in the nation's capital, Washington, D.C. Some consulates are located in major U.S. cities, and most nations have a mission to the United Nations in New York City. If your country isn't listed below, call for directory information in Washington, D.C. (② **202/555-1212**) or log on to **www.embassy.org/embassies**.

The embassy of **Australia** is at 1601 Massachusetts Ave. NW, Washington, DC 20036 (② **202/797-3000**; www.austemb.org). There are consulates in New York, Honolulu, Houston, Los Angeles, and San Francisco.

The embassy of **Canada** is at 501 Pennsylvania Ave. NW, Washington, DC 20001 (② **202/682-1740**; www.canadianembassy.org). Other Canadian consulates are in Buffalo (N.Y.), Detroit, Los Angeles, New York, and Seattle.

The embassy of **Ireland** is at 2234 Massachusetts Ave. NW, Washington, DC 20008 (② **202/462-3939**; www.irelandemb.org). Irish consulates are in Boston, Chicago, New York, and San Francisco.

The embassy of **Japan** is at 2520 Massachusetts Ave. NW, Washington, DC 20008 (② **202/238-6700**; www.embjapan.org). Japanese consulates are located in many cities including Atlanta, Boston, Detroit, New York, San Francisco, and Seattle.

The embassy of **New Zealand** is at 37 Observatory Circle NW, Washington, DC 20008 (② **202/328-4800**; www.nzemb.org). New Zealand consulates are in Los Angeles, Salt Lake City, San Francisco, and Seattle.

The embassy of the **United Kingdom** is at 3100 Massachusetts Ave. NW, Washington, DC 20008 (② **202/462-1340**; www.britainusa.com). Other British consulates are in Atlanta, Boston, Chicago, Cleveland, Houston, Los Angeles, New York, San Francisco, and Seattle.

Emergencies   Call ② **911** to report a fire, call the police, or get an ambulance anywhere in California. This is a toll-free call (no coins are required at public telephones).

If you encounter serious problems, contact the **Traveler's Aid International** (② **202/546-1127**; www.travelersaid.org) to help direct you to a local branch. This nationwide, nonprofit, social-service organization geared to helping travelers in difficult straits offers services that might include reuniting families separated while traveling, providing food and/or shelter to people stranded without cash, or even emotional counseling. If you're in trouble, seek them out.

Gasoline (Petrol) Petrol is known as gasoline (or simply "gas") in the United States, and petrol stations are known as both gas stations and service stations. Gasoline costs about half as much here as it does in Europe (about $2.10–$2.50 per gallon in California at press time), and taxes are already included in the printed price. One U.S. gallon equals 3.8 liters or .85 imperial gallons.

Holidays Banks, government offices, post offices, and many stores, restaurants, and museums are closed on the following legal national holidays: January 1 (New Year's Day), the third Monday in January (Martin Luther King, Jr., Day), the third Monday in February (Presidents' Day, Washington's Birthday), the last Monday in May (Memorial Day), July 4 (Independence Day), the first Monday in September (Labor Day), the second Monday in October (Columbus Day), November 11 (Veterans' Day/Armistice Day), the fourth Thursday in November (Thanksgiving Day), and December 25 (Christmas). Also, the Tuesday following the first Monday in November is Election Day and is a federal government holiday in presidential-election years (held every 4 years, and next in 2008).

Legal Aid If you are "pulled over" for a minor infraction (such as speeding), never attempt to pay the fine directly to a police officer; this could be construed as attempted bribery, a much more serious crime. Pay fines by mail, or directly into the hands of the clerk of the court. If accused of a more serious offense, say and do nothing before consulting a lawyer. Here the burden is on the state to prove a person's guilt beyond a reasonable doubt, and everyone has the right to remain silent, whether he or she is suspected of a crime or actually arrested. Once arrested, a person can make one telephone call to a party of his or her choice. Call your embassy or consulate.

Mail If you aren't sure what your address will be in the United States, mail can be sent to you, in your name, c/o General Delivery at the main post office of the city or region where you expect to be. (Call ✆ **800/ 275-8777** for information on the nearest post office.) The addressee must pick up mail in person and must produce proof of identity (a driver's license or passport, for example). Most post offices will hold your mail for up to 1 month and are open Monday to Friday from 8am to 6pm, and Saturday from 9am to 3pm.

Generally found at intersections, mailboxes are blue with a red-and-white stripe and carry the inscription U.S. MAIL. If your mail is addressed to a U.S. destination, don't forget to add the five-digit postal code (or zip code), after the two-letter abbreviation of the state to which the mail is addressed. This is essential to prompt delivery.

At press time, domestic postage rates were 23¢ for a postcard and 37¢ for a letter. For international mail, a first-class letter of up to one-half ounce costs 80¢ (60¢ to Canada and Mexico); a first-class postcard costs 70¢ (50¢ to Canada and Mexico); and a preprinted postal aerogramme costs 70¢.

Measurements There are a number of easy-to-use websites for converting metric measurements to U.S. equivalents. See, for example, *www.onlineconversion.com*.

Taxes The United States has no value-added tax (VAT) or other indirect tax at the national level. Every state, county, and city has the right to levy its own local tax on all purchases, including hotel and restaurant checks, airline tickets, and so on.

Telephone, Telegraph, Telex & Fax The telephone system in the United States is run by private corporations, so rates, especially for long-distance service and operator-assisted calls, can vary widely. Generally, hotel surcharges on long-distance and local calls are astronomical, so you're usually better off using a **public pay telephone,** which you'll find clearly marked in most public buildings and private establishments as well as on the street. Convenience grocery stores and gas stations always have them. Many convenience groceries and packaging services sell **prepaid calling cards** in denominations up to $50; these can be the least expensive way to call home. Many public phones at airports now accept American Express, MasterCard, and Visa credit cards. **Local calls** made from public pay phones in most locales cost either 25¢ or 35¢. Pay phones do not accept pennies, and few will take anything larger than a quarter.

You may want to look into leasing a cellphone for the duration of your trip.

Most long-distance and international calls can be dialed directly from any phone. **For calls within the United States and to Canada,** dial 1 followed by the area code and the seven-digit number. **For other international calls,** dial 011 followed by the country code, city code, and the telephone number of the person you are calling.

Calls to area codes **800, 888, 877,** and **866** are toll-free. However, calls to numbers in area codes **700** and **900** (chat lines, bulletin boards, "dating" services, and so on) can be very expensive—usually a charge of 95¢ to $3 or more per minute, and they sometimes have minimum charges that can run as high as $15 or more.

For **reversed-charge or collect calls,** and for person-to-person calls, dial 0 (zero, not the letter O) followed by the area code and number you want; an operator will then come on the line, and you should specify that you are calling collect, or person-to-person, or both. If your operator-assisted call is international, ask for the overseas operator.

For **local directory assistance** ("information"), dial ℭ 411; for long-distance information, dial 1, then the appropriate area code and 555-1212.

Telegraph and telex services are provided primarily by Western Union. You can bring your telegram into the nearest Western Union office (there are hundreds across the country) or dictate it over the phone (ℭ **800/325-6000**). You can also telegraph money, or have it telegraphed to you, very quickly over the Western Union system, but this service can cost as much as 15% to 20% of the amount sent.

Most hotels have **fax machines** available for guest use (be sure to ask about the charge to use it). Many hotel rooms are even wired for guests' fax machines. A less expensive way to send and receive faxes may be at stores such as **The UPS Store** (formerly Mail Boxes Etc.), a national chain of retail packing service shops. (Look in the Yellow Pages directory under "Packing Services.")

There are two kinds of telephone directories in the United States. The so-called **White Pages** list private households and business subscribers in alphabetical order. The inside front cover lists emergency numbers for police, fire, ambulance, the Coast Guard, poison-control center, crime-victims hot line, and so on. The first few pages will tell you how to make long-distance and international calls, complete with country codes and area codes. Government numbers are usually printed on blue paper within the White Pages. Printed on yellow paper, the so-called **Yellow Pages** list all local services, businesses, industries, and houses of worship according to activity with an index at the front or back. (Drugstores/pharmacies and restaurants are also listed by geographic location.) The Yellow Pages also include city plans or detailed area maps, postal zip codes, and public transportation routes.

Time California is in the Pacific time zone. When it is 9am in Los Angeles or San Francisco (PST), it is noon in New York (EST), 5pm in London (GMT), and 2am the next day in Sydney.

Daylight saving time is in effect from 1am on the first Sunday in April to 1am on the last Sunday in October. Daylight saving time moves the clock 1 hour ahead of standard time.

For the correct time, call "POP CORN" (© **767-2676**) in any California area code.

Tipping Tips are a very important part of certain workers' income, and gratuities are the standard way of showing appreciation for services provided. (Tipping is certainly not compulsory if the service is poor!) In hotels, tip **bellhops** at least $1 per bag ($2–$3 if you have a lot of luggage) and tip the **chamber staff** $1 to $2 per day (more if you've left a disaster area for him or her to clean up). Tip the **doorman** or **concierge** only if he or she has provided you with some specific service (for example, calling a cab for you or obtaining difficult-to-get theater tickets). Tip the **valet-parking attendant** $1 every time you get your car.

In restaurants, bars, and nightclubs, tip **service staff** 15% to 20% of the check, tip **bartenders** 10% to 15%, tip **checkroom attendants** $1 per garment, and tip **valet-parking attendants** $1 per vehicle.

As for other service personnel, tip **cab drivers** 15% of the fare; tip **skycaps** at airports at least $1 per bag ($2–$3 if you have a lot of luggage); and tip **hairdressers** and **barbers** 15% to 20%.

Toilets You won't find public toilets or "restrooms" on the streets in most California cities (except San Francisco), but they can be found in hotel lobbies, bars, restaurants, museums, department stores, railway and bus stations, and service stations. Large hotels and fast-food restaurants are probably the best bet for good, clean facilities. If possible, avoid the toilets at parks and beaches, which tend to be dirty; some may be unsafe. Restaurants and bars in resorts or heavily visited areas may reserve their restrooms for patrons. Some establishments display a notice indicating this. You can ignore this sign or, better yet, avoid arguments by paying for a cup of coffee or a soft drink, which will qualify you as a patron.

4

San Francisco

by Erika Lenkert

Consistently rated one of the top tourist destinations in the world, San Francisco abounds in multiple dimensions. Its famous, thrilling streets go up, and they go down; its citizens—and their adopted cultures, architectures, and cuisines—hail from San Antonio to Singapore. Even something as mundane as fog takes on a new dimension as it creeps from the ocean and envelops the city in a resplendent blanket of mist.

From an outsider's perspective, San Francisco is still very much the city it's reputed to be. The restaurant scene is booming, boutiques abound, the Castro is the Castro, political correctness is hip, and all the goings-on in the unique neighborhoods take place against backdrops of bridges, bay vistas, cable cars, and colorful city life.

But from an insider's view, the City by the Bay is still recovering from an evolution spawned by the rise and fall of high-tech and dot-commercialization and the aftermath of the terrorist attacks of September 11, 2001, and a slumped economy that affects our ever-important tourist industry. The result? San Francisco is much cheaper to visit these days.

Now hotel deals abound, dining reservations are easier to come by, and traffic, though still prevalent, is less horrific. On top of that, you'll still encounter classic San Francisco: Feel the cool blast of salt air as you stroll across the Golden Gate, stuff yourself on dim sum, and walk along the beach, pierce your nose, see a play, rent a Harley. It's all happening in San Francisco, and everyone's invited.

1 Orientation

ARRIVING

BY PLANE

Two major airports serve the Bay Area: San Francisco International and Oakland International. All the major car-rental companies have desks at the airports; see "Getting Around," later in this chapter, for details on car rentals.

SAN FRANCISCO INTERNATIONAL AIRPORT San Francisco International Airport (© 650/821-8211; www.flysfo.com), 14 miles south of downtown on U.S. 101, is served by almost four dozen major scheduled carriers. Travel time to downtown during rush hours is about 50 minutes; at other times it's about 20 to 25 minutes.

The airport offers a hot line Monday through Friday from 7:30am to 5pm (PST) for information on ground transport (© 415/817-1717). Also, each of the three main terminals has a transportation information desk.

A cab from the airport to downtown will cost $30 to $35, plus tip. **SFO Airporter** buses (© 650/246-8942; www.sfoairporter.com) depart from outside the lower-level baggage claim area to downtown every 30 minutes from 5:35am to 9:05pm. Shuttles on the 30-minute circuit stop at several Union Square–area hotels, including the San Francisco Hilton, San Francisco Marriott, Westin St. Francis, Renaissance Parc Fifty-Five, Hyatt Regency, Hotel Nikko, and Sheraton Palace. A shuttle running every 60 minutes stops at the Palace Hotel, Crowne Plaza, Hyatt Regency, and Grand Hyatt. No reservations are needed. The cost is $14 each way, $22 round-trip; children under age 3 ride free.

Other private shuttle companies offer door-to-door airport service, in which you share a van with a few other passengers. **SuperShuttle** (© 415/558-8500; www.supershuttle.com) will take you anywhere in the city, charging $14 to a residence or business, plus $8 for each additional person, and $65 plus $1 per passenger to charter a van for up to seven people. Keep in mind that this shuttle demands they pick you up 2 hours before your flight, 3 hours during holidays.

For the budget traveler, **BART** (Bay Area Rapid Transit; © 415/989-2278; www.bart.gov) now runs from SFO to downtown San Francisco. Rates from the airport to downtown San Francisco are around $6 per person depending on where you're headed, and the trip takes just under half an hour.

The San Mateo County Transit system, **SamTrans** (© 800/660-4287 in Northern California, or 650/508-6200; www.samtrans.com), runs two buses between the airport and the Transbay Terminal at First and Mission streets. The no. 292 bus costs $1.25 and makes the trip in about 55 minutes. The KX bus costs $3.50 and takes only 35 minutes but permits only one carry-on bag. Both buses run daily. The no. 292 starts at 5:27am, and the KX starts at 6:03am. Both run frequently until 8pm, then hourly until about midnight.

OAKLAND INTERNATIONAL AIRPORT   About 5 miles south of downtown Oakland, at the Hagenberger Road exit off Calif. 17 (I-880), Oakland International Airport (© 510/563-3300; www.oaklandairport.com) is used primarily by passengers with East Bay destinations. Many San Franciscans, however, prefer this less-crowded, accessible airport. Without traffic, a car or taxi ride to the airport is a quick 20 to 30 minutes; with traffic, give yourself at least an hour. It's also accessible by BART (see below for details), which is not influenced by traffic because it travels on its own tracks.

Taxis from the airport to downtown San Francisco are expensive, costing approximately $50, plus tip.

Bayporter Express (© 877/467-1800 or 415/467-1800) is a shuttle service that charges $26 for the first person, $12 for each additional person, to downtown San Francisco (it costs more to outer areas of town). Shuttles, usually located to the right of the airport exit, will take you to the city for around $20 per person. Children under 13 ride for $5. These are independently owned and prices vary, so ask and make any negotiations (sometimes possible) before you ride.

The cheapest way to downtown San Francisco (and easiest during traffic snarls) involves taking the shuttle bus from the airport to **BART** (Bay Area Rapid Transit; © 510/464-6000; www.bart.gov). The **AirBART** shuttle bus runs about every 15 minutes Monday through Saturday from 6am to 11:30pm and Sunday from 8:30am to 11:30pm, stopping in front of Terminals 1 and 2 near the ground-transportation signs. The cost is $2 for the 10-minute ride to BART's Coliseum terminal, and tickets must be purchased at the airport's vending machines. BART fares vary, depending on your destination; the trip to downtown San Francisco costs $2.75 and takes 20 minutes once onboard. The entire excursion should take around 45 minutes.

BY CAR

San Francisco is accessible via several major highways: **U.S. 101** and **Calif. 1** from the north and south; and **I-80** and **I-580** from the northeast and east, respectively. If you drive from Los Angeles, you can either take the longer coastal route along Calif. 1/U.S. 101 (437 miles, 11 hr.), or the inland route along I-5 to I-580 (389 miles, 6½ hr.). From Mendocino, it's a little over 3 hours along Calif. 1, and about 3¼ hours along U.S. 101; and from Sacramento, it's 88 miles, or 1½ hours, along I-80.

BY TRAIN

San Francisco–bound **Amtrak** (© **800/USA-RAIL;** www.amtrak.com) trains leave from New York and cross the country via Chicago. The journey takes about 3½ days, and seats sell quickly. At this writing, the lowest round-trip fare costs anywhere from $266 from New York and from $244 from Chicago. Round-trip tickets from Los Angeles can be purchased for as little as $100. Trains actually arrive in Emeryville, just north of Oakland, and connect with regularly scheduled buses to San Francisco's Ferry Building and Caltrain station in downtown San Francisco.

Caltrain (© **800/660-4287** or 415/546-4461; www.caltrain.com) operates train services between San Francisco and the towns of the peninsula. The city depot is at 700 Fourth St., at Townsend Street.

VISITOR INFORMATION

The **San Francisco Visitor Information Center,** Hallidie Plaza, 900 Market St. (at Powell St.), Lower Level, San Francisco, CA 94102 (© **415/283-0177;** www.sfvisitor.org), is the best source for any kind of specialized information about the city. Even if you don't have a specific question, you may want to request the free *Visitors Planning Guide* and *San Francisco Visitors.*

CITY LAYOUT

San Francisco occupies the tip of a 32-mile-long peninsula between San Francisco Bay and the Pacific Ocean. Its land area measures about 46 square miles. Twin Peaks, in the geographic center of the city, is over 900 feet high.

San Francisco may seem confusing at first, but it quickly becomes easy to negotiate. The city's downtown streets are laid out in a simple grid pattern, with the exception of Market Street and Columbus Avenue, which cut across the grid at right angles to each other. Hills appear to distort this pattern, however, and can be disorienting. But as you learn your way around, these same hills will become your landmarks and reference points.

MAIN ARTERIES & STREETS   Market Street is San Francisco's main thoroughfare. Most of the city's buses travel this route on their way to the Financial District from the outer neighborhoods to the west and south. The tall office buildings clustered downtown are at the northeast end of Market; 1 block beyond lie the Embarcadero and the San Francisco Bay.

The **Embarcadero** curves along San Francisco Bay from south of the Bay Bridge to the northeast perimeter of the city and terminates at Fisherman's Wharf, the famous tourist-oriented pier. Aquatic Park, Fort Mason, and the Golden Gate National Recreation Area are located farther on around the bay, occupying the northernmost point of the peninsula.

From the eastern perimeter of Fort Mason, **Van Ness Avenue** runs due south, back to Market Street.

San Francisco at a Glance

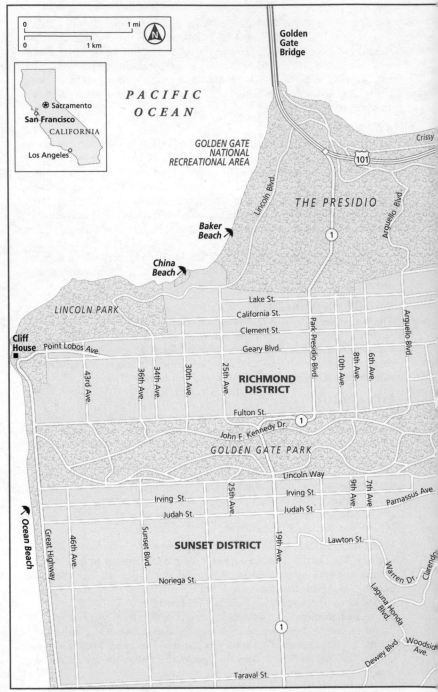

0   1 mi
0   1 km
N

PACIFIC
OCEAN

Sacramento
San Francisco
CALIFORNIA
Los Angeles

Golden
Gate
Bridge

Crissy

GOLDEN GATE
NATIONAL
RECREATIONAL AREA

101

Lincoln Blvd.

THE PRESIDIO

Arguello Blvd.

Baker
Beach

1

China
Beach

LINCOLN PARK

Lake St.
California St.
Clement St.
Geary Blvd.

Cliff
House

Point Lobos Ave.

43rd Ave.
36th Ave.
34th Ave.
30th Ave.
25th Ave.

Park Presidio Blvd.
10th Ave.
8th Ave.
6th Ave.

Arguello Blvd.

RICHMOND
DISTRICT

Fulton St.

1

John F. Kennedy Dr.

GOLDEN GATE PARK

Lincoln Way

9th Ave.
7th Ave.

Parnassus Ave.

Irving St.
Judah St.

25th Ave.

Irving St.
Judah St.

Ocean Beach

Great Highway
46th Ave.
Sunset Blvd.

SUNSET DISTRICT

19th Ave.

Lawton St.

Warren Dr.
Clarendo

Noriega St.

Laguna Honda Blvd.

1

Woodside Ave.
Dewey Blvd.

Taraval St.

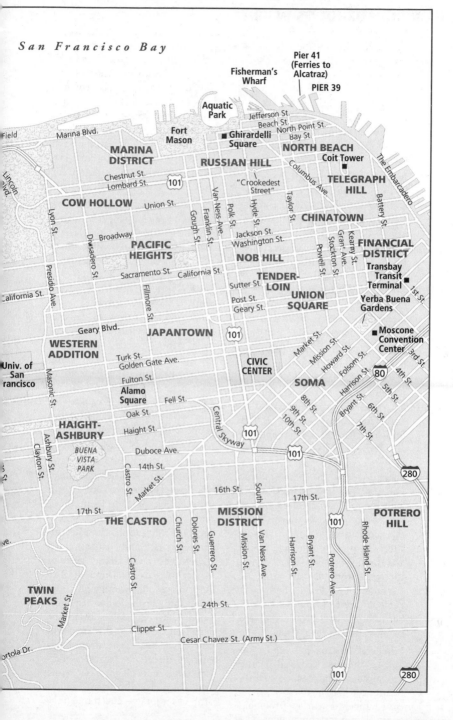

San Francisco Bay

Fisherman's Wharf

Pier 41 (Ferries to Alcatraz)

PIER 39

Aquatic Park

Jefferson St.
Beach St.
North Point St.
Bay St.

Field

Marina Blvd.

Fort Mason

■ Ghirardelli Square

NORTH BEACH

Coit Tower ■

The Embarcadero

MARINA DISTRICT

RUSSIAN HILL

Chestnut St.
Lombard St.

101

"Crookedest Street"

TELEGRAPH HILL

Lincoln Blvd.

COW HOLLOW

Union St.

Van Ness Ave.

Franklin St.

Polk St.

Hyde St.

Taylor St.

Columbus Ave.

Battery St.

CHINATOWN

Lyon St.

Broadway

PACIFIC HEIGHTS

Gough St.

Jackson St.
Washington St.

Kearny St.

Grant Ave.

Stockton St.

Powell St.

FINANCIAL DISTRICT

Divisadero St.

Presidio Ave.

California St.

Sacramento St.

California St.

NOB HILL

TENDER-LOIN

Transbay Transit Terminal ■

1st St.

Sutter St.

UNION SQUARE

Yerba Buena Gardens

Fillmore St.

Post St.
Geary St.

Geary Blvd.

JAPANTOWN

101

■ Moscone Convention Center

3rd St.

WESTERN ADDITION

Turk St.
Golden Gate Ave.

CIVIC CENTER

Market St.

Mission St.

Howard St.

Folsom St.

Harrison St.

80

4th St.

Univ. of San Francisco

Masonic St.

Fulton St.

SOMA

Bryant St.

5th St.

Alamo Square

Fell St.

8th St.

9th St.

6th St.

Oak St.

10th St.

7th St.

HAIGHT-ASHBURY

Ashbury St.

Clayton St.

Haight St.

Duboce Ave.

Central Skyway

101

BUENA VISTA PARK

14th St.

Castro St.

Market St.

101

280

16th St.

South

17th St.

17th St.

THE CASTRO

Church St.

Dolores St.

Guerrero St.

MISSION DISTRICT

Mission St.

Van Ness Ave.

Harrison St.

Bryant St.

Potrero Ave.

Rhode Island St.

POTRERO HILL

101

TWIN PEAKS

Market St.

Castro St.

24th St.

Clipper St.

Cesar Chavez St. (Army St.)

ortola Dr.

101

280

NEIGHBORHOODS IN BRIEF

Union Square Union Square is the commercial hub of the city. Most major hotels and department stores are crammed into the area surrounding the square (named for a series of violent pro-Union demonstrations held here on the eve of the Civil War), with a plethora of boutiques, restaurants, and galleries tucked between the larger buildings.

Nob Hill/Russian Hill Bounded by Bush, Larkin, Pacific, and Stockton streets, Nob Hill is the genteel, well-heeled district of the city, occupied by the power brokers and the neighborhood businesses they frequent. Russian Hill extends from Pacific to Bay and from Polk to Mason. It's marked by steep streets, lush gardens, and high-rises occupied by both the moneyed and the more bohemian.

SoMa No part of San Francisco has been more affected by recent development than South of Market (called "SoMa"). The once desolate area grew to be the hub of dot-commercialization and $750,000 lofts, as well as urban entertainment a la Yerba Buena Gardens and the Museum of Modern Art. It is demarcated by the Embarcadero, Highway 101, and Market Street, with the greatest concentrations of interest around Yerba Buena Center, along Folsom and Harrison streets between Steuart and Sixth, and Brannan and Market. Along the waterfront are an array of restaurants and Pacific Bell Park. Farther west, around Folsom between 7th and 11th streets, are many of the city's nightclubs.

Financial District East of Union Square, this area bordered by the Embarcadero and Market, Third, Kearny, and Washington streets is the city's business district and stomping grounds for major corporations. The TransAmerica Pyramid, at Montgomery and Clay streets, is one of the area's most conspicuous features. To its east stands the sprawling Embarcadero Center, an 8½-acre complex housing offices, shops, and restaurants. Farther east still is the World Trade Center, standing adjacent to the old Ferry Building, the city's pre-bridge transportation hub. Ferries to Sausalito and Larkspur still leave from this point.

Chinatown The official entrance to Chinatown is marked by a large red-and-green gate on Grant Avenue at Bush Street. Beyond lies a 24-block labyrinth, bordered by Broadway, Bush, Kearny, and Stockton streets, filled with restaurants, markets, temples, and shops—and a substantial percentage of San Francisco's Chinese residents. Chinatown is a great place for urban exploration all along Stockton, Grant, and Portsmouth Square, and the alleys that lead off them like Ross and Waverly. This area is jam-packed, so don't even think about driving around here.

North Beach The Italian quarter, which stretches from Montgomery and Jackson to Bay Street, is one of the best places in the city to grab some coffee, pull up a cafe chair, and do some serious people-watching. Nightlife also abounds: Restaurants, bars, and clubs along Columbus and Grant avenues attract folks from all over the Bay Area to fight for a parking place and romp through the festive neighborhood. Down Columbus toward the Financial District are the remains of the city's Beat generation landmarks, including Lawrence Ferlinghetti's City Lights Bookstore and Vesuvio bar. Broadway—a short strip of sex joints—cuts through the heart of the district. Telegraph Hill looms over the east side of North Beach, topped by Coit Tower, one of San Francisco's best vantage points.

Fisherman's Wharf North Beach runs into Fisherman's Wharf, which was once the busy heart of the city's great harbor and waterfront industries. Today it is a tacky-but-attractive tourist area with little if any authentic waterfront life, except for recreational boating and some friendly sea lions.

Marina District Created on landfill for the Panama-Pacific Exposition of 1915, the Marina boasts some of the best views of the Golden Gate, as well as grassy fields along San Francisco Bay (check out newly restored Crissy Fields). Streets are lined with Mediterranean-style homes and apartments, where the city's well-to-do singles and families live. Here, too, are the Palace of Fine Arts, the Exploratorium, and Fort Mason Center. The main street is Chestnut between Franklin and Lyon, which is lined with shops and cafes.

Cow Hollow West of Van Ness Avenue, between Russian Hill and the Presidio, this flat area supported 30 dairy farms in 1861. Today, Cow Hollow is largely residential and occupied by the city's young and yuppie. Its two primary commercial thoroughfares are Lombard Street, known for its many relatively inexpensive motels; and Union Street, a flourishing shopping sector filled with restaurants, pubs, cafes, and shops.

Pacific Heights The ultra-elite, such as the Gettys and Danielle Steel—and those lucky enough to buy before the real-estate boom— reside in the mansions and homes of Pacific Heights. When the rich

meander out of their fortresses, they wander down to Union Street, a long stretch of boutiques, restaurants, cafes, and bars.

Japantown Bounded by Octavia, Fillmore, California, and Geary streets, Japantown shelters only a small percentage of the city's Japanese population, but it's still a cultural experience to explore these few square blocks and the shops and restaurants within them.

Civic Center Although millions have been expended on brick sidewalks, lampposts, and street plantings, the southwestern section of Market Street remains dilapidated. The Civic Center, at the "bottom" of Market Street, is an exception. This complex includes the domed City Hall, the Opera House, Davies Symphony Hall, the Asian Art Museum, and the city's main library. The landscaped plaza connecting the buildings is the staging area for San Francisco's demonstrations for or against just about everything.

Haight-Ashbury Part trendy, part nostalgic, part funky, the Haight, as it's known, was the soul of the psychedelic '60s and the center of the counterculture movement. Today the neighborhood straddling upper Haight Street on the eastern border of Golden Gate Park is more gentrified, but the commercial area still harbors all walks of life. Leftover hippies mingle outside Ben & Jerry's with grungy, begging street kids, marijuana dealers, and people with Day-Glo hair. But you don't need to be a freak or wear tie-dye to enjoy the Haight: The food, shops, and bars cover all tastes. From Haight Street, walk south on Cole Street for a more peaceful neighborhood experience.

Richmond & Sunset Districts San Francisco's suburbs of sorts, these are the city's largest and most populous districts, consisting mainly of homes, shops, and neighborhood restaurants. Though both districts border Golden Gate Park and Ocean Beach, not many tourists venture into "The Avenues," as locals call these areas.

The Castro One of the liveliest streets in town, Castro is synonymous with San Francisco's gay community. Located at the end of Market Street between 17th and 18th streets, the Castro supports dozens of shops, restaurants, and bars catering to the gay community. Open-minded straight people are welcome, too.

Mission District This is another area greatly affected by the city's new wealth. The Mexican and Latin American populations, along with their cuisine, traditions, and art, still make the Mission District a vibrant area to visit. Some parts of the neighborhood are still poor and sprinkled with the homeless, gangs, and drug addicts, but young urbanites are infiltrating, and forging the oh-so-hot restaurants and bars that stretch from 16th Street and Valencia to 25th and Mission streets. Less adventurous tourists still duck into Mission Dolores, cruise by a few of the 200-plus amazing murals, and head back downtown. Don't be afraid to visit this area, but do use caution at night.

2 Getting Around

BY PUBLIC TRANSPORTATION

The San Francisco Municipal Railway, better known as **Muni** (© 415/ 673-6864; www.sfmuni.com), operates the city's cable cars, buses, and Metro streetcars. These public transportation services crisscross the city, making San Francisco accessible to everyone. Buses and Metro streetcars cost $1.25 for adults, 35¢ for children ages 5 to 17, and 35¢ for seniors over 65. Cable cars cost $3 for people over 5 years old ($1 for seniors 6–7am and 9pm–midnight). They're packed primarily with tourists. Exact change is required on all vehicles except cable cars.

For detailed route information, phone Muni or consult the bus map at the front of the Yellow Pages. If you plan on making extensive use of public transportation, you may want to invest in a comprehensive route map ($2), sold at the San Francisco Visitor Information Center (see "Visitor Information" in "Orientation," earlier in this chapter) and in many downtown retail outlets.

Muni **discount passes,** called "Passports," entitle holders to unlimited rides on buses, Metro streetcars, and cable cars. A Passport costs $9 for 1 day, and $15 or $20 for 3 or 7 consecutive days. Muni's "City Pass," which costs $40 for adults, $31 for seniors 65 and older, and $24 for kids 5 to 17, entitles you to unlimited rides for 7 days and admission at the California Academy of Sciences, Museum of Modern Art, Exploratorium, Palace of the Legion of Honor, and Blue & Gold Fleet Bay Cruise. You can buy a Passport or City Pass at the San Francisco Visitor Information Center, the Holiday Inn Civic Center, and the TIX Bay Area booth at Union Square. For the Blue & Gold Fleet tour to be included, you must purchase tickets from the Blue & Gold Fleet at © 415/ 705-5555 and pay an extra $2.25 fee.

BY CABLE CAR San Francisco's cable cars may not be the most practical means of transport, but these rolling historic landmarks sure are fun to ride.

There are only three lines in the city, and they're concentrated in the downtown area. The most scenic, and exciting, is the **Powell-Hyde line,** which follows a zigzag route from the corner of Powell and Market streets, over both Nob Hill and Russian Hill, to a turntable at gaslit Victorian Square in front of Aquatic Park. The **Powell-Mason line** starts at the same intersection and climbs over Nob Hill before descending to Bay Street, just 3 blocks from Fisherman's Wharf. The least scenic is the **California Street line,** which begins at the foot of Market Street and runs a straight course through Chinatown and over Nob Hill to Van Ness Avenue. All riders must exit at the last stop and wait in line for the return trip. The cable-car system operates daily from approximately 6:30am to 1:30am.

BY BUS   Buses reach almost every corner of San Francisco and travel over the bridges to Marin County and Oakland. All are numbered and display their destinations on the front. Stops are designated by signs, curb markings, and yellow bands on utility poles. Most bus shelters exhibit Muni's transportation map and schedule. Many buses travel along Market Street or near Union Square and run daily from about 6am to midnight, after which there is infrequent all-night "Owl" service. For safety and convenience, avoid taking buses late at night.

Popular tourist routes are nos. 5, 7, and 71, all of which run to Golden Gate Park; 41 and 45, which travel along Union Street; and 30, which runs between Union Square and Ghirardelli Square.

BY METRO STREETCAR   Five of Muni's Metro streetcar lines, designated F, J, K, L, M, N, and S, run underground downtown and on the street in the outer neighborhoods. The sleek railcars make the same stops as BART (see below) along Market Street, including Embarcadero Station (in the Financial District), Montgomery and Powell streets (both near Union Sq.), and the Civic Center (near City Hall). Past the Civic Center, the routes branch off in different directions: The J line will take you to Mission Dolores; the K, L, and M lines to Castro Street; and the N line parallels Golden Gate Park and now extends all the way to the Embarcadero. Streetcars run about every 15 minutes, more frequently during rush hours. Service is offered Monday through Friday from 5am to 12:30am, on Saturday from 6am to 12:20am, and on Sunday from 8am to 12:20am. The L and N lines operate all day and all night.

The most recent streetcar additions are not newcomers at all, but San Francisco's beloved 1930s streetcars. The beautiful, rejuvenated multicolored cars on the F Market line now run along the Embarcadero from Fisherman's Wharf to Market Street, and then to the Castro and back. It's a quick and charming way to get up- and downtown without any hassle.

BY BART   BART, an acronym for **Bay Area Rapid Transit (℃ 415/989-2278;** www.bart.gov), is a high-speed rail network that connects San Francisco with the East Bay—Oakland, Richmond, Concord, and Fremont. Four stations are located along Market Street (see "By Metro Streetcar," above). Fares range from $1.25 to $7.10, depending on how far you go. Tickets are dispensed from machines in the stations and are encoded with a dollar amount. Computerized exits deduct the correct fare. Children 4 and under ride free. Trains run every 15 to 20 minutes, Monday through Friday from 4am to midnight, Saturday from 6am to midnight, and Sunday from 8am to midnight.

Note: The $2.5-billion, 33-mile BART extension, which debuted in mid-2003, includes a southern line that extends to San Francisco International Airport.

BY TAXI

If you're downtown during rush hour or leaving from a major hotel, it won't be hard to hail a cab—just look for the lighted sign on the roof that indicates if one is available. Otherwise, it's a good idea to call one of the following companies to arrange a ride: **Veteran's Cab** (© 415/552-1300), **Luxor Cabs** (© 415/282-4141), or **Yellow Cab** (© 415/626-2345). Rates are approximately $2.85 for the first mile and $2.25 for each mile thereafter.

BY CAR

In this crowded and compact city, a car can be your worst nightmare. You're likely to end up stuck in traffic with lots of aggressive and frustrated drivers (especially downtown), pay upward of $30 a day in parking, and spend a good portion of your vacation looking for a parking space. But if you want to range outside of the city, driving is the best way to go.

RENTALS   The major car-rental companies in the city include **Alamo** (© 800/327-9633; www.goalamo.com), **Avis** (© 800/331-1212; www.avis.com), **Budget** (© 800/527-0700; www.budget.com), **Dollar** (© 800/800-4000; www.dollar.com), **Enterprise** (© 800/325-8007; www.enterprise.com), **Hertz** (© 800/654-3131; www.hertz.com), **National** (© 800/227-7368; www.nationalcar.com), and **Thrifty** (© 800/367-2277; www.thrifty.com).

PARKING   If you want to have a relaxing vacation, don't even attempt to find street parking downtown or in Nob Hill, North Beach, Chinatown, by Fisherman's Wharf, or on Telegraph Hill. Park in a garage or take a cab or a bus. If you do find street parking, pay attention to street signs that explain when you can park and for how long. Be especially careful not to park in zones that are tow areas during rush hours.

When parking on a hill, apply the hand brake, put the car in gear, and *curb your wheels*—toward the curb when facing downhill, away from it when facing uphill. Curbing your wheels will not only prevent a possible "runaway," but also keep you from getting a ticket—an expensive fine that is aggressively enforced.

FAST FACTS: San Francisco

American Express For travel arrangements, traveler's checks, currency exchange, and other member services, American Express has an office at 455 Market St., at First Street (tel] 415/536-2600). It's open Monday through Friday from 9am to 5:30pm and Saturday from 10am to 2pm. To report lost or stolen traveler's checks, call © 800/221-7282. For American Express Global Assist, call © 800/554-2639.

Dentist In the event of an emergency, see your hotel concierge or contact the San Francisco Dental Office, 131 Steuart St. (© 415/777-5115), between Mission and Howard streets, which offers emergency service and comprehensive dental care Monday and Tuesday from 8am to 4:30pm, Wednesday and Thursday from 10:30am to 6:30pm, and Friday from 8am to 2pm.

Doctor Saint Francis Memorial Hospital, 900 Hyde St., between Bush and Pine streets on Nob Hill (© 415/353-6000), provides 24-hour emergency-care service. The hospital also operates a physician-referral service (© 800/333-1355).

Emergencies Dial ℂ **911** for the police, an ambulance, or the fire department.

Pharmacies There are **Walgreens** drugstores all over town, including one at 135 Powell St. (ℂ **415/391-4433**). The store is open Monday through Friday from 7am to midnight and Saturday and Sunday from 8am to midnight, but the pharmacy has more-limited hours: Monday through Friday from 8am to 9pm, Saturday from 9am to 5pm, and it's closed Sunday. The branch on Divisadero Street at Lombard (ℂ **415/931-6415**) has a 24-hour pharmacy.

Police For emergencies, dial ℂ **911** from any phone; no coins are needed. For other matters, call ℂ **415/553-0123**.

Post Office There are dozens of post offices all around the city. The closest to Union Square is in Macy's department store, 170 O'Farrell St. (ℂ **800/275-8777**).

Safety Few locals would recommend walking alone late at night in certain areas, particularly the Tenderloin, between Union Square and the Civic Center. Compared to other cities, however, even this section of San Francisco is relatively tranquil. Other areas where you should be alert are the Mission District, around 16th and Mission streets; the lower Fillmore area, around lower Haight Street; and SoMa (south of Market St.).

Taxes An 8.5% sales tax is added at the register for all goods and services purchased in San Francisco. The city hotel tax is a whopping 14%.

Transit Information Call **Muni** at ℂ **415/673-6864** Monday through Friday between 7am and 5pm and Saturday and Sunday between 9am and 5pm. At other times, recorded information is available.

Useful Telephone Numbers **Tourist information** (ℂ 415/283-0176); **highway conditions** (ℂ 800/427-7623); **Moviefone** (ℂ 415/777-FILM).

Weather Call ℂ **831/656-1725** or visit www.nws.noaa.gov to find out when the next fog bank is rolling in.

3 Where to Stay

San Francisco is an extensive—and expensive—hotel town, especially considering its relatively small size. I can't cover all the options in this guide, so if you'd like a larger selection, check out *Frommer's San Francisco 2005* and *Frommer's San Francisco from $70 a Day,* which have dozens of other choices.

Most of the hotels listed below are within walking distance of Union Square and accessible via cable car. Union Square is near the city's major shops, the Financial District, and all transportation. Prices listed below do not include state and city taxes, which total 14%.

The price categories below reflect the prices of double rooms during the high season, which runs approximately April through September. (In reality, rates vary greatly these days.) So remember: These are rack (or published) rates; you can almost always get a much better deal if you inquire about promotions, packages, weekend discounts, corporate rates, and family plans, and call the hotel directly, rather than a number for the entire chain.

San Francisco Accommodations

Alisa Hotel **34**
The Andrews Hotel **21**
Argonaut Hotel **9**
Beck's Motor Lodge **1**
Best Western Tuscan Inn **12**
Campton Place Hotel **33**
Cartwright Hotel **20**
The Commodore Hotel **23**
Edward II Inn & Suites **5**
The Fairmont Hotel & Tower **17**
Fitzgerald **23**
The Four Seasons San Francisco **35**
The Golden Gate Hotel **20**
Handlery Union Square Hotel **29**
The Harbor Court **37**
Hotel Adagio **23**
Hotel Bijou **27**
The Hotel Bohème **14**
Hotel Del Sol **7**
The Hotel Majestic **3**
Hotel Vintage Court **18**
The Huntington Hotel **19**
King George Hotel **28**
The Laurel Inn **4**
The Mandarin Oriental **15**
The Marina Inn **8**
The Mark Hopkins Intercontinental **17**
The Mosser **39**
The Palace Hotel **36**
The Parker Guest House **2**
The Phoenix Hotel **40**
Prescott Hotel **30**
The Queen Anne Hotel **3**
The Ritz-Carlton **16**
The San Remo Hotel **13**
The Savoy Hotel **25**
Sheraton Fisherman's Wharf Hotel **11**
Sir Francis Drake **32**
Union Street Inn **6**
W San Francisco Hotel **38**
The Warwick Regis **26**
Westin St. Francis **31**
The Wharf Inn **10**
York Hotel **22**

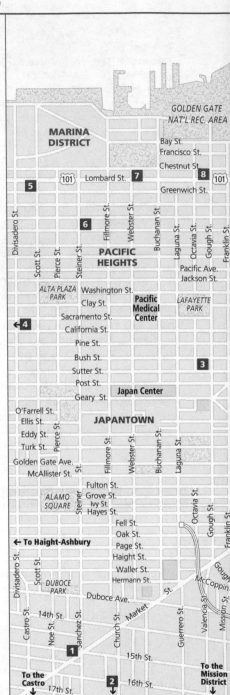

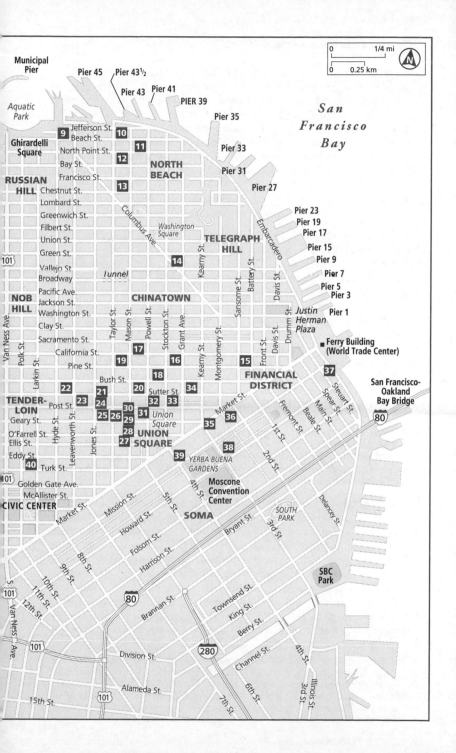

Municipal Pier

Aquatic Park

Ghirardelli Square

RUSSIAN HILL

NOB HILL

101

Polk St.

Van Ness Ave.

Larkin St.

TENDER-LOIN

CIVIC CENTER

101

S. Van Ness Ave.

101

101

280

Pier 45   Pier 43½   Pier 43   Pier 41
PIER 39
Pier 35
Pier 33
Pier 31
Pier 27
Pier 23
Pier 19
Pier 17
Pier 15
Pier 9
Pier 7
Pier 5
Pier 3
Pier 1

San Francisco Bay

0   1/4 mi
0   0.25 km

Jefferson St.
Beach St.
North Point St.
Bay St.
Francisco St.
Chestnut St.
Lombard St.
Greenwich St.
Filbert St.
Union St.
Green St.
Vallejo St.
Broadway
Pacific Ave.
Jackson St.
Washington St.
Clay St.
Sacramento St.
California St.
Pine St.
Bush St.
Sutter St.
Post St.
Geary St.
O'Farrell St.
Ellis St.
Eddy St.
Turk St.
Golden Gate Ave.
McAllister St.

NORTH BEACH

Columbus Ave.

Washington Square

TELEGRAPH HILL

Tunnel

CHINATOWN

Taylor St.
Mason St.
Powell St.
Stockton St.
Grant Ave.
Kearny St.
Montgomery St.
Sansome St.
Battery St.
Davis St.
Front St.
Davis St.
Drumm St.

Kearny St.

Justin Herman Plaza

Ferry Building (World Trade Center)

FINANCIAL DISTRICT

San Francisco-Oakland Bay Bridge

80

Steuart St.
Spear St.
Beale St.
Main St.

Hyde St.
Leavenworth St.
Jones St.

Market St.

Union Square

UNION SQUARE

YERBA BUENA GARDENS

Moscone Convention Center

SOMA

Mission St.
Howard St.
Folsom St.
Harrison St.

5th St.
4th St.
Bryant St.
3rd St.
2nd St.
1st St.
Fremont St.

SOUTH PARK

Delancey St.

8th St.
9th St.
10th St.
11th St.
12th St.

Market St.

Brannan St.

Division St.

Alameda St.

15th St.

Townsend St.
King St.
Berry St.
Channel St.

7th St.
6th St.
4th St.
3rd St.
Illinois St.

SBC Park

9 10 11 12 13 14 15 16 17 18 19 20 21 22 23 24 25 26 27 28 29 30 31 32 33 34 35 36 37 38 39 40

77

San Francisco Reservations, 360 22nd St., Suite 300, Oakland, CA 94612 (© 800/677-1500 or 510/628-4450; www.hotelres.com), arranges reservations at more than 300 of San Francisco's hotels and often offers discounted rates.

In addition to the hotels below, I also recommend those represented by the reasonably priced and fashionable Joie de Vivre chain (© 800/SF-TRIPS; www.sftrips.com) and Personality Hotels (© 800/553-1900; www.personality hotels.com), which spiffs up older buildings in central locales. Pricier options include the Kimpton Group, which owns the Juliana Hotel (© 800/ 328-3880) and the Hotel Serrano (© 415/885-2500), and the Donatello (© 800/227-3184). The Hilton San Francisco (© 800/HILTONS) and San Francisco Marriott (© 800/228-9290) both have convention-hotel ambience but are conveniently located and have enough rooms to sleep thousands. Ditto the Pan Pacific (© 800/533-6465), which despite its size exudes elegance.

UNION SQUARE
VERY EXPENSIVE

Campton Place Hotel 🏵🏵🏵   With a $15-million room renovation completed in 2001, this already fabulous luxury boutique hotel offers some of the best accommodations in town—not to mention the most expensive. Rooms were completely gutted, and old furnishings were replaced with limestone, pear wood, and more Italian-modern decor. The two executive suites and one luxury suite push the haute envelope to even more luxurious heights. Discriminating returning guests will still find superlative service, extra-large beds, exquisite bathrooms, bathrobes, top-notch toiletries, slippers, and every other necessity and extra that's made Campton Place a favored temporary address.

Chef Daniel Humm delights diners with delicately prepared and very sculpted cuisine at the excellent Campton Place Restaurant.

340 Stockton St. (between Post and Sutter sts.), San Francisco, CA 94108. © 800/235-4300 or 415/781-5555. Fax 415/955-5536. www.camptonplace.com. 110 units. $345–$475 double; $550–$2,000 suite. American breakfast $17. AE, DC, MC, V. Valet parking $35. Cable car: Powell-Hyde and Powell-Mason lines (1 block west). Bus: 2, 3, 4, 30, or 45. Amenities: Restaurant; health club; concierge; courtesy car; secretarial services; 24-hr. room service; laundry service; same-day dry cleaning. In room: A/C, TV w/pay movies, dataport, minibar, hair dryer, iron, safe, T1 line.

Prescott Hotel 🏵🏵   It may be small and lack common areas, but the boutique Prescott Hotel has some big things going for it. The staff treats you like royalty, rooms are attractively unfrilly and masculine, the location (just a block from Union Sq.) is perfect, and limited room service is provided by one of the most popular downtown restaurants, Postrio. Ralph Lauren fabrics in dark tones of green, plum, and burgundy blend well with the cherrywood furnishings in each of the soundproof rooms; the view, alas, isn't so pleasant. The very small bathrooms contain terry robes and Aveda products, and the suites have Jacuzzi bathtubs. Concierge-level—i.e., higher-paying—guests are pampered with a free continental breakfast, evening cocktails and hors d'oeuvres, and, 3 days per week, even head-and-shoulders massages.

545 Post St. (between Mason and Taylor sts.), San Francisco, CA 94102. © 800/283-7322 or 415/563-0303. Fax 415/563-6831. www.prescotthotel.com. 164 units. $275–$340 double; $300 concierge-level double (including breakfast and evening cocktail reception); from $365 suite. AE, DC, DISC, MC, V. Valet parking $35. Cable car: Powell-Hyde and Powell-Mason lines (1 block east). Bus: 2, 3, 4, 30, 38, or 45. Amenities: Restaurant/bar; small exercise room; concierge; limited courtesy car; limited room service. In room: TV w/pay movies, fax/printer, dataport, minibar, hair dryer, iron, safe, video games, high-speed Internet access.

Westin St. Francis 🏵🏵 (Kids)   Although the St. Francis is too massive to offer the personal service you get at the smaller deluxe hotels, few other hotels in San

Francisco can match its majestic aura. It sounds corny, but the St. Francis is so much a part of the city's past that it truly *is* San Francisco: Stroll through the vast, ornate lobby and you can feel 100 years of history oozing from its hand-carved redwood paneling. The hotel has spent millions on major renovations in the last 7 years, replacing the carpeting, furniture, and bedding in every main-building guest room, gussying up the lobby, and restoring the facade. Today the rooms in the Tower, which was built in the 1970s and renovated in 2001, evoke a contemporary design. The main building accentuates its history with tradi-tional, more elegant ambience, high ceilings, and crown molding. Alas, the tea-room is no longer, but in its place is new fancy restaurant **Michael Mina** (by the famed chef of Aqua), which debuted in 2004. The Westin Kids Club program means that when families check in, the kids receive age-specific gifts.

335 Powell St. (between Geary and Post sts.), San Francisco, CA 94102. © 800/WESTIN-1 or 415/397-7000. Fax 415/774-0124. www.westin.com. 1,195 units. Main building: $199–$499 double; Tower (Grand View): $219–$549 double; from $550 suite. Extra person $30. Continental breakfast $15–$18. AE, DC, DISC, MC, V. Valet parking $42. Cable car: Powell-Hyde and Powell-Mason lines (direct stop). Bus: 2, 3, 4, 30, 38, 45, or 76. Pets under 35 lb. accepted for $75 fee. **Amenities:** 2 restaurants; bar; large health club and spa; concierge; car-rental desk; business center; 24-hr. room service. *In room:* A/C, TV, dataport, minibar, fridge, hair dryer, iron.

EXPENSIVE

Handlery Union Square Hotel ⭑ A half block from Union Square, the Handlery was already a good deal before the 1906 building and its more mod-ern annex underwent a complete overhaul in 2002. Now you'll find every amenity, plus lots of extras, in the tasteful and modern (although sedate and a little dark) rooms. Everything's relatively new: mattresses, alarm radios, voice mail, refrigerators, light fixtures, paint, carpets, and furnishings. Perks include adjoining decent restaurant **The Daily Grill,** an outdoor heated pool, and club-level options (in the newer building) that include larger rooms, a complimen-tary morning newspaper, turndown service, bathroom scale, robes, two phones, and adjoining doors that make them great choices for families. Downsides? Not a lot of direct light, no grand feeling in the lobby, and lots of trekking if you want to go to and from the adjoining buildings that make up the hotel.

351 Geary St. (between Mason and Powell sts.), San Francisco, CA 94102. © 800/843-4343 or 415/781-7800. Fax 415/781-0269. www.handlery.com. 377 units. Club section from $289 dou-ble, from $280 suite. Extra person $10. AE, DC, DISC, MC, V. Parking $28. Cable car: Powell-Hyde and Powell-Mason lines (direct stop). Bus: 2, 3, 4, 30, 38, or 45. **Amenities:** Restaurant; heated outdoor swimming pool; access to nearby health club ($10 per day); sauna; barber shop; room service (7am–10pm); babysitting; same-day laundry. *In room:* A/C, TV w/Nintendo and pay movies, dataport, fridge, complimentary coffee/tea-mak-ing facilities, hair dryer, iron, safe, wireless Internet access, voice mail.

Hotel Adagio ⭑⭑ Now under new management and after an $11-million renovation, this 1929 Spanish Revival hotel has a new name and a gorgeous modern style to match its youthful and fashionable clientele. Local hip hoteliers Joie de Vivre revamped its 171 large, bright guest rooms, swathing them in a chocolate brown and mocha color palette and adorning them with chic dark-wood furnishings, firm mattresses, double-paned windows that open, voice mail, and lots and lots of elbowroom. Bathrooms are old but clean and most have tubs, and corporate floors (12 and 16) include irons, robes, and free conti-nental breakfast. Feel like splurging? Go for one of the five penthouse-level suites, which have lovely terraces with a New York vibe. Or simply step into the restaurant/bar **Cortez** at night—it serves up good "small plates" and a full bar amidst *très* chic surroundings. *Tip:* Rooms above the ninth floor have good, but not great, southern views of the city.

550 Geary St., San Francisco, CA 94102. © **800/228-8830** or 415/775-5000. www.thehoteladagio.com. 173 units. $209 double. AE, DISC, MC, V. Valet parking $29. **Amenities:** Restaurant; bar; fitness center; concierge; business center w/free wireless Internet; room service; laundry service; dry cleaning; luggage storage room. *In room:* TV w/pay movies and Nintendo, dataport, minibar, fridge, hair dryer, iron, safe, CD player, complimentary high-speed Internet access.

Hotel Vintage Court 🅡🅡 *Value*   Consistent personal service and great value attract a loyal clientele at this European-style hotel 2 blocks north of Union Square. The lobby, accented with comfy couches, is welcoming enough to actually spend time in, especially when California wines are being poured each evening from 5 to 6pm, free of charge. But the varietals don't stop at ground level. Each tidy room is named after a winery and has a modern country look where greens and earth tones reign supreme, with cream duvets and lovely mahogany-slat blinds. Niebaum-Coppola (named after the winery owned by the movie maverick), the deluxe two-room penthouse suite, has an original 1912 stained-glass skylight, wood-burning fireplace, whirlpool tub, complete entertainment center, and panoramic views of the city. *Note:* Smoking is prohibited in all rooms. **Masa's** (p. 92), one of the city's top restaurants, serves fantastic—and very expensive—contemporary French dinners here.

650 Bush St. (between Powell and Stockton sts.), San Francisco, CA 94108. © **800/654-1100** or 415/392-4666. Fax 415/433-4065. www.vintagecourt.com. 107 units. $150–$199 single or double; $325–$350 penthouse suite. Rates include continental breakfast and evening wine service. AE, DC, DISC, MC, V. Valet parking $34; self-parking $24. Cable car: Powell-Hyde and Powell-Mason lines (direct stop). Bus: 2, 3, 4, 30, 45, or 76. **Amenities:** Restaurant; access to off-premises health club ($12 per day); concierge; in-room massage; same-day laundry service/dry cleaning. *In room:* A/C, TV, dataport, minibar, coffeemaker, hair dryer, iron, video games.

Sir Francis Drake 🅡🅡   The Sir Francis Drake, whose owners have spent millions for renovations over the past 10 years, is a glorious hotel for people who are willing to trade a chipped bathroom tile or mixed furniture for the opportunity to vacation in pseudo-grand fashion. Allow Tom Sweeny, the ebullient (and legendary) Beefeater doorman, to handle your bags as you enter the elegant lobby. Sip cocktails or swing-dance to a live orchestra at the chic retro Starlight Room overlooking the city. Dine at **Scala's Bistro** (p. 92), one of the most festive restaurants downtown, and get comfortable in a room amidst the historic hotel's 21 floors. Live like the king or queen of Union Square without all the pomp, circumstance, and credit card bills.

450 Powell St. (at Sutter St.), San Francisco, CA 94102. © **800/227-5480** or 415/392-7755. Fax 415/391-8719. www.sirfrancisdrake.com. 417 units. $219–$259 double; $500–$700 suite. AE, DC, DISC, MC, V. Valet parking $35. Cable car: Powell-Hyde and Powell-Mason lines (direct stop). Bus: 2, 3, 4, 45, or 76. **Amenities:** 2 restaurants; bar; exercise room; concierge; limited room service; same-day laundry service/dry cleaning. *In room:* A/C, TV w/pay movies and Nintendo, dataport, minibar, hair dryer, iron.

MODERATE

A few worthy hotel companies operate properties throughout the city. **Holiday Inn** (© **800/465-4329;** www.holiday-inn.com) has several locations.

The Andrews Hotel 🅡   For location and price, the Andrews is a safe bet for an enjoyable stay. Two blocks west of Union Square, the Andrews was a Turkish bath before its conversion in 1981. As is typical in Euro-style hotels, the rooms are small but well maintained and comfortable, with nice touches like lace curtains and fresh flowers. Recent upgrades included new mattresses, carpets (in most rooms), and fresh paint in the bathrooms.

624 Post St. (between Jones and Taylor sts.), San Francisco, CA 94109. © **800/926-3739** or 415/563-6877. Fax 415/928-6919. www.andrewshotel.com. 48 units (some with shower only). $109–$129 double;

$149–$159 superior rooms. Rates include continental breakfast and evening wine. AE, DC, MC, V. Valet parking $28. Cable car: Powell-Hyde and Powell-Mason lines (3 blocks east). Bus: 2, 3, 4, 30, 38, or 45. **Amenities:** Restaurant; access to nearby health club; concierge; room service (5:30–10pm); babysitting; laundry service; dry cleaning; coffee in lobby; nearby self-service laundromat. *In room:* TV/VCR w/video library, dataport, fridge in suites only, hair dryer on request, iron, high-speed Internet access $10 per day.

The Cartwright Hotel 🏨🏨

Remarkably quiet, despite its convenient location near one of the busiest downtown corners, the eight-story hotel looks not unlike it did when it opened some 80 years ago. High-quality antiques collected during its decades of faithful service furnish the lobby and the individually decorated rooms, all of which were completely renovated in 2004 (think new paint and new furniture finishes). *Tip:* Request a room with a view of the backyard; they're the quietest. Complimentary wine is served in the small library each night, and afternoon tea and cookies are a daily treat, as are the apples and hot beverages in the lobby. A breakfast room added in 2004 serves complimentary expanded continental breakfast.

524 Sutter St. (at Powell St.), San Francisco, CA 94102. ℂ 800/227-3844 or 415/421-2865. Fax 415/398-6345. www.cartwrighthotel.com. 114 units. $89–$159 double; $139–$189 family/business suite (sleeps 4). Rates include 24-hr. tea, coffee, and apples in the lobby, continental breakfast, nightly wine hour, weekday newspapers, and afternoon cookies. AE, DC, DISC, MC, V. Valet parking $30; self-parking $22. Cable car: Powell-Hyde and Powell-Mason lines (direct stop). Bus: 2, 3, 4, 30, or 45. **Amenities:** Access to nearby health club; concierge; pay-for-use Internet access. *In room:* TV, dataport, minibar, fridge, hair dryer, iron.

The Commodore Hotel 🏨🏨

If you're looking for a little fun and fantasy in your vacation, check out this six-story low-budget trendy spot. The "Neo-Deco" rooms feature bright colors, whimsical furnishings, and tasteful artwork. Stealing the show is the Red Room, a swank and dim bar and lounge that's redder than Dorothy's ruby slippers. Adjoining is the **Titanic Café,** a cute diner serving buckwheat griddlecakes, Vietnamese tofu sandwiches, and salads.

825 Sutter St. (at Jones St.), San Francisco, CA 94109. ℂ 800/338-6848 or 415/923-6800. Fax 415/923-6804. www.thecommodorehotel.com. 110 units. $125–$169 double. AE, DC, DISC, MC, V. Parking $25. Bus: 2, 3, 4, 19, 27, 47, or 49. **Amenities:** Diner; bar; access to nearby health club ($15 per day); concierge; Internet access in lobby. *In room:* TV w/pay movies, dataport, fridge, coffeemaker, hair dryer, iron.

The Fitzgerald 🏨 *Value*

The Fitzgerald's guest accommodations may be outfitted with newish furniture and sweet striped wallpaper, and accented with bright bedspreads and patterned carpet, but some of the rooms are really small. (One I saw had a dresser less than a foot from the bed.) Of course, at $80 a night there's no room for complaining. But do ask for a larger room. If you can live without a sizable closet, you'll find that the price, breakfast (home-baked breads, muffins, juice, tea, and coffee), and cleanliness make it a good value. *Note:* The view of the Golden Gate on their brochure is not actually visible from the hotel.

620 Post St. (between Jones and Taylor sts.), San Francisco, CA 94109. ℂ 800/334-6835 or 415/775-8100. Fax 415/775-1278. www.fitzgeraldhotel.com. 47 units. $65–$125 double. Extra person $10. Rates include continental breakfast. Lower rates in winter. AE, DC, DISC, MC, V. Self-parking $22. Cable car: Powell-Hyde and Powell-Mason lines. Bus: 2, 3, 4, or 27. **Amenities:** Access to a nearby indoor pool and exercise room; dry cleaning. *In room:* TV, dataport, hair dryer.

King George Hotel 🏨🏨 *Value*

Built in 1914 for the Panama-Pacific Exhibition, this delightful hotel has fared well over the years, continuing to draw a mostly European clientele. The location—surrounded by cable-car lines, the Theater District, Union Square, and dozens of restaurants—is superb, and the rooms are surprisingly quiet for such a busy area. Though the very clean rooms can be small, a renovation in 1999 made the most of the space with new mattresses, desks, and a handsome studylike ambience. In 2002, new textiles were added. A big hit since it started a few years back is the hotel's English afternoon tea, served in the **Windsor Tea Room** Saturday, Sunday, and holidays from 2 to 5pm. Other perks include a pub and 24-hour business center.

334 Mason St. (between Geary and O'Farrell sts.), San Francisco, CA 94102. ✆ **800/288-6005** or 415/781-5050. Fax 415/835-5991. www.kinggeorge.com. 153 units. $140 double; $240 suite. Breakfast $6.50–$8. Special-value packages available seasonally. AE, DC, DISC, MC, V. Valet parking $25; self-parking $22. Cable car: Powell-Hyde and Powell-Mason lines (1 block west). Bus: 1, 2, 3, 4, 5, 7, 30, 38, 45, 70, or 71. **Amenities:** Tearoom; evening lounge/bar; access to health club ½ block away; concierge; 24-hr. business center; secretarial services; 24-hr. room service; same-day laundry/dry cleaning; wireless Internet access in lobby. *In room:* TV w/pay movies and Nintendo, dataport, hair dryer, iron, safe, complimentary high-speed Internet access.

The Savoy Hotel 🎯🎯 *Value*   The European-style Savoy is one of my favorite moderately priced downtown hotels (the Warwick Regis is my other top pick). With a cozy apartment-like feel to each room, old well-cleaned bathrooms with original tile, 18th-century period furnishings, featherbeds, and goose-down pillows, it's easy to relax here. Not all rooms are alike—they can be small, but each has white wood shutters, triple sheets, full-length mirrors, and two-line telephones. Guests also enjoy concierge service and access to the newly relocated **Millennium** restaurant, San Francisco's only gourmet vegan dining room.

580 Geary St. (between Taylor and Jones sts.), San Francisco, CA 94102. ✆ **800/227-4223** or 415/441-2700. Fax 415/441-0124. www.thesavoyhotel.com. 83 units. $119–$139 double; $149–$169 junior suite. Complimentary wine and cheese 4:30–6pm daily. Ask about package (like an extra $30 for parking and continental breakfast), government, senior, and corporate rates. AE, DC, DISC, MC, V. Parking $26. Bus: 2, 3, 4, 27, or 38. **Amenities:** Restaurant; bar; concierge; laundry service; dry cleaning. *In room:* TV, dataport, hair dryer, iron, safe.

The Warwick Regis 🎯🎯 *Value*   Louis XVI might have been a rotten monarch, but he certainly had taste. Fashioned in the style of pre-Revolutionary France, the Warwick is awash with French and English antiques, Italian marble, chandeliers, four-poster beds, hand-carved headboards, and the like. The result is an expensive-looking hotel that, for all its perks, is surprisingly affordable compared to its Union Square contemporaries. Rooms can be on the small side, but they're some of the city's most charming. Bathrooms are charming but small. Honeymooners should splurge on the fireplace rooms with canopy beds. Adjoining the lobby is **La Scene Café,** a beautiful place to start your day with a latte and end it with a nightcap.

490 Geary St. (between Mason and Taylor sts.), San Francisco, CA 94102. ✆ **800/827-3447** or 415/928-7900. Fax 415/441-8788. www.warwicksf.com. 80 units. $119–$159 double; $159–$269 suite. AE, DC, DISC, MC, V. Parking $28. Cable car: Powell-Hyde and Powell-Mason lines. Bus: 2, 3, 4, 27, or 38. **Amenities:** Restaurant; access to nearby health club ($15 per day); concierge; business center; secretarial services; 24-hr. room service; babysitting; laundry service; dry cleaning. *In room:* TV, dataport, minibar, hair dryer, iron, safe, wireless Internet access.

INEXPENSIVE

Alisa Hotel 🎯🎯 *Value*   The five-story Alisa Hotel is definitely a budget gem. While it has a small lobby, narrow hallways, and cramped rooms, the owners here have distanced themselves from the discount competition by including a pleasing dose of artistry. The lobby hosts art exhibits and has groovy furnishings. Guest rooms are adorned with quality Pan-Asian furnishings and tasteful accouterments. And you'll love the location as well: across the street from the entrance to Chinatown, 2 blocks from Union Square. Considering the price (rooms with a very clean shared bathroom start at $49), quality, and location, it's possibly the best budget hotel in the city. Don't sweat it if they're booked. Their sister property, **The Olympic Hotel** (call the 800 number or see www.olympichotelsf.com), is nearby and equally priced and hospitable.

447 Bush St. (at Grant St.), San Francisco, CA 94108. ℂ 800/956-4322 or 415/956-3232. Fax 415/956-0399. www.alisahotel.com. 51 units, 26 with private bathroom. $69–$119 double with bathroom; $49–$69 double without bathroom. Rates include continental breakfast. AE, DC, MC, V. Nearby parking $20. Cable car: Powell-Hyde and Powell-Mason lines. Bus: All Market St. buses. **Amenities:** 24-hr. concierge; fax and copy services. *In room:* TV, 2-line direct-dial telephone with dataport and voice mail, small fridge and microwave in some rooms, hair dryer, iron and board, wireless Internet.

The Golden Gate Hotel ✿✿
Among San Francisco's small hotels occupying historic buildings are some real gems, and the Golden Gate Hotel is one of them. It's 2 blocks north of Union Square and 2 blocks down (literally) from the crest of Nob Hill, with cable-car stops at the corner for easy access to Fisherman's Wharf and Chinatown. (The city's theaters and best restaurants are within walking distance.) But the best thing about the Golden Gate is that it's a family-run establishment: John and Renate Kenaston and daughter Gabriele are hospitable innkeepers who take pleasure in making their guests comfortable. Each individually decorated room has antique furnishings (plenty of wicker), quilted bedspreads, and fresh flowers. (Request a room with a claw-foot tub if you enjoy a good, hot soak.) Complimentary afternoon tea is served daily from 4 to 7pm, and guests are welcome to use the house fax and computer with wireless DSL free of charge.

775 Bush St. (between Powell and Mason sts.), San Francisco, CA 94108. ℂ 800/835-1118 or 415/392-3702. Fax 415/392-6202. www.goldengatehotel.com. 25 units, 14 with bathroom. $85 double without bathroom; $130 double with bathroom. Rates include continental breakfast and afternoon tea. AE, DC, MC, V. Self-parking $15. Cable car: Powell-Hyde and Powell-Mason lines (1 block east). Bus: 2, 4, 30, 38, or 45. BART: Powell and Market. **Amenities:** Access to health club 1 block away; activities desk; office equipment available; laundry service/dry cleaning next door. *In room:* TV, dataport, hair dryer and iron upon request, wireless Internet access.

Hotel Bijou ✿ ⓥalue
Three words sum up this hotel: clean, colorful, and cheap. Although it's on the periphery of the gritty Tenderloin (3 blocks off Union Sq.), this 1911 hotel is cheery, bright, and perfect for the budget traveler who wants a little style, too. The hotel's age is disguised with lively decor, a Deco theater theme, and a lot of vibrant paint. Off the small lobby is a "theater" where guests can watch San Francisco–based movies nightly (on old-fashioned theater seating in front of a TV showing videos). Upstairs, rooms named after local films are small but clean and colorful (think buttercup, burgundy, and purple), and have all the basics from clock radios, dressers, and small desks to tiny bathrooms. Some mattresses could be firmer and there's one small, slow elevator.

111 Mason St., San Francisco, CA 94102. ℂ 800/771-1022 or 415/771-1200. www.hotelbijou.com. 65 units. $95–$139 double. Rates include continental breakfast. AE, DC, DISC, MC, V. Valet parking $21. Metro: Powell St. station. Bus: All Market St. buses. **Amenities:** Concierge; limited room service; same-day laundry service/dry cleaning. *In room:* TV, dataport, hair dryer, iron.

The York Hotel ✿✿
Even as a local, I drop in the York frequently because it's home to **The Empire Plush Room,** the city's best jazz and cabaret club, and also features *Va Va Voom,* a disappointing burlesque show. But for the visitor, the 1922 hotel, featured in Hitchcock's *Vertigo,* is a boon because it's a great deal. Awarded Three Diamonds by AAA, the hotel has a helpful staff, a workout room, and promotional rates, which include continental breakfast served in the lobby. Rooms swathed in terra cotta and green are cheery and come loaded with nice touches like coffeemakers, dark-wood writing desks, newly upholstered and comfy chairs, Internet access, alarm clocks, tub/showers, and walk-in closets.

940 Sutter St. (between Leavenworth and Hyde sts.), San Francisco, CA 94109. ℂ 800/808-9675 or 415/885-6800. Fax 415/885-2115. www.yorkhotel.com. 96 units. $119–$149. Rates include continental

breakfast. AE, DC, DISC, MC, V. Valet parking $35, $25 self-parking. Bus: 4. **Amenities:** Jazz club; bar; work-out room; valet or self-serve laundry. *In room:* TV w/pay movies, coffeemaker, hair dryer, iron on request, safe, Internet access.

SOMA
VERY EXPENSIVE
The Four Seasons Hotel San Francisco 🌟🌟🌟   A perfect combination of elegance and luxury, Four Seasons does everything right. Take the elevators up to the lobby and you're surrounded by calm, cool, and collected hotel perfection and a sexy cocktail lounge that's sure to be your second home. Not too trendy, not too traditional, rooms are just right, with custom-made mattresses and pillows that guarantee a great night's sleep, works of art, and huge luxury marble bathrooms with deep tubs. Many of the oversize rooms (starting at 460 sq. ft. and including 46 suites) overlook Yerba Buena Gardens. Adding to the perks are free access to the building's huge **Sports Club L.A.,** round-the-clock business services, a 2-block walk to Union Square and the Moscone Convention Center, and a vibe that combines sophistication and hipness.

757 Market St. (between 3rd and 4th sts.), San Francisco, CA 94103. ✆ **800/332-3442** or 415/633-3000. Fax 415/633-3001. www.fourseasons.com. 277 units. $469–$600 double; $800 executive suite. AE, DC, DISC, MC, V. Parking $39. Streetcar: F and all underground streetcars. Bus: All Market St. buses. BART: All trains. **Amenities:** Restaurant; bar; huge fitness center; spa; 24-hr. multilingual concierge; high-tech business center; secretarial services; salon; 24-hr. room service; in-room massage; overnight dry-cleaning and laundry service. *In room:* A/C, TV w/pay movies, fax, minibar, hair dryer, safe.

The Harbor Court 🌟🌟   When the Embarcadero Freeway was torn down after the Big One in 1989, one of the major benefactors was this hotel, whose backyard view went from a wall of cement to a view of the Bay Bridge (a bay-view room costs extra). Just off the Embarcadero at the edge of the Financial District, this former YMCA books a lot of corporate travelers, but anyone who prefers stylish, high-quality accommodations—half-canopy beds, large armoires, writing desks, soundproof windows—and a lively scene will be content here.

165 Steuart St. (between Mission and Howard sts.), San Francisco, CA 94105. ✆ **800/346-0555** or 415/882-1300. Fax 415/882-1313. www.harborcourthotel.com. 131 units. $165–$399 double. Continental breakfast $15. AE, DC, MC, V. Parking $32. Muni Metro: Embarcadero. Bus: 14, 32, or 80X. Pets accepted. **Amenities:** Access to adjoining health club and large, heated indoor pool; courtesy car; room service (breakfast only); same-day laundry service/dry cleaning. *In room:* A/C, TV, fax, dataport, minibar, hair dryer, iron, safe.

W San Francisco Hotel 🌟🌟🌟   This 31-story, 423-room property adjacent to the San Francisco Museum of Modern Art is one of the most hip hotels in town. Sophisticated, sleek, and stylish, its octagonal, three-story glass entrance and lobby give way to a great lounge and two bars. The interior has a residential feel in the guest rooms, and a hip, urban style throughout. All guest rooms offer a "luxury" featherbed with goose-down comforters and pillows, an oversize dark-wood desk, and upholstered chaise lounge, plus louvered blinds opening to usually great city views. Rooms also feature a compact media wall complete with CD and videocassette players with an extensive CD library, 27-inch color TV, plus Internet service via an infrared keyboard and portable two-line phones. Bathrooms are supersleek and stocked with Aveda products.

181 Third St. (between Mission and Howard sts.), San Francisco, CA 94103. ✆ **800/877-WHOTEL** or 415/777-5300. Fax 415/817-7823. www.whotels.com/sanfrancisco. 423 units. From $469 double; from $1,000 suite. AE, DC, DISC, MC, V. Valet parking $40. Streetcar: J, K, L, or M to Montgomery. Bus: 15, 30, or 45. **Amenities:** Restaurant; 2 bars; heated atrium pool and Jacuzzi; fitness center; spa; concierge; business center; secretarial services; 24-hr. room service; same-day laundry service/dry cleaning; WiFi in public spaces. *In room:* A/C, TV/VCR w/pay movies and Internet access, fax, dataport, minibar, coffeemaker, hair dryer, iron, safe, CD player, wireless phone.

MODERATE

The Mosser *Value* "Hip on the Cheap" might best sum up the Mosser, a highly atypical budget hotel that incorporates Victorian architecture with modern interior design. It originally opened in 1913 as a luxury hotel, but a major multimillion-dollar renovation in the fall of 2001 transformed this aging charmer into a sophisticated, stylish, and surprisingly affordable option. Guest rooms are replete with original Victorian flourishes—bay windows, high ceilings, hand-carved moldings—and contemporary custom-designed furnishings, granite showers, stainless-steel fixtures, ceiling fans, Frette linens, and modern electronics. The least expensive rooms share a bathroom but are great deals with rates starting at $60. The location is excellent as well—3 blocks from Union Square, 2 blocks from MOMA and Moscone Convention Center, and half a block from the cable-car turnaround.

54 Fourth St. (at Market St.), San Francisco, CA 94103. © 800/227-3804 or 415/986-4400. Fax 415/495-4091. www.themosser.com. 166 units, 112 with bathroom. $109–$179 with bathroom; $59–$89 without bathroom. Rates include safe-deposit boxes, fax, and mail services. AE, DC, MC, V. Parking $27. Metro: F, and all underground Muni and BART **Amenities:** Restaurant/bar; 24-hr. concierge; same-day laundry service/dry cleaning. *In room:* TV, direct-dial telephone with dataport and voice mail, hair dryer, iron and board, AM/FM stereo with CD player, ceiling fan.

FINANCIAL DISTRICT
VERY EXPENSIVE

The Mandarin Oriental *Finds* The common areas here are limited, but the rooms are superfluously appointed and the views divine, making this a top choice for luxury travelers. The larger rooms are between the 38th and 48th floors of a high-rise, which affords them extraordinary views. Not all units have tub-side views (get one that does and you'll never forget it!), but all have well-stocked marble bathrooms that include such luxuries as terry- and cotton-cloth robes, makeup mirrors, and silk slippers. The less opulent rooms are done in a kind of reserved contemporary decor with Asian accents. Don't miss out on the Asian teatime, complete with a bento box of uncommonly delicious goodies.

222 Sansome St. (between Pine and California sts.), San Francisco, CA 94104. © 800/622-0404 or 415/276-9888. Fax 415/433-0289. www.mandarinoriental.com. 158 units. $470–$655 double; $675–$725 signature rooms; from $1,400 suite. Continental breakfast $21; American breakfast $32. AE, DC, DISC, MC, V. Valet parking $36. Muni Metro: J, K, L, or M to Montgomery. Bus: All Market St. buses. **Amenities:** Restaurant; bar; fitness center; concierge; car rental; business center; 24-hr. room service; in-room massage; laundry service; same-day dry cleaning. *In room:* A/C, TV w/pay movies, fax, dataport, minibar, hair dryer, iron, safe, CD player, high-speed Internet access.

The Palace Hotel When you walk through these doors, you'll be reminded how majestic old luxury really is. The original 1875 Palace was rebuilt after the 1906 quake; the most spectacular attribute is the old regal lobby and the Garden Court, a San Francisco landmark that has been restored to its original grandeur. Thankfully, the rooms were recently renovated with mahogany four-poster beds, warm gold paint and upholstery, and tasteful artwork.

2 New Montgomery St. (at Market St.), San Francisco, CA 94105. © 800/325-3589 or 415/512-1111. Fax 415/543-0671. www.sfpalace.com. 552 units. $550–$650 double; from $775 suite. Extra person $40. Children under 18 sharing existing bedding stay free in parent's room. Weekend rates and packages available. AE, DC, DISC, MC, V. Parking $40. Streetcar: All Market St. streetcars. Bus: All Market St. buses. **Amenities:** 4 restaurants; bar; health club with skylight-covered heated lap pool; spa; Jacuzzi; sauna; concierge; business center; conference rooms with wireless Internet access; 24-hr. room service; laundry; dry cleaning. *In room:* A/C, TV w/pay movies, dataport, minibar, hair dryer, iron, safe.

NOB HILL
VERY EXPENSIVE

The Fairmont Hotel & Tower 🏵🏵 The granddaddy of Nob Hill's ritzy hotels, the Fairmont wins top honors for the most awe-inspiring lobby in San Francisco. Even if you're not staying here, it's worth a trip to gape at its massive marble columns, vaulted ceilings, velvet chairs, gilded mirrors, and spectacular wraparound staircase. Thanks to an $85-million renovation in 2001, the glamour carries to guest rooms where everything is new, opulent, and in good taste. In addition to the expected luxuries, you'll find goose-down pillows, electric shoe buffers, walk-in closets, and multiline phones with voice mail. Whatever you do, try to visit the **Tonga Room,** a fantastically kitschy tropical bar and restaurant where happy hour hops and rain falls every 20 minutes.

950 Mason St. (at California St.), San Francisco, CA 94108. © 800/441-1414 or 415/772-5000. Fax 415/391-4833. www.fairmont.com. 591 units. Main building $289–$409 double; from $500 suite. Tower $269–$359 double; from $800 suite. Extra person $30. AE, DC, DISC, MC, V. Parking $39. Cable car: California St. line (direct stop). **Amenities:** 3 restaurants; bar; health club ($15 daily); concierge; tour desk; car-rental desk; business center; shopping arcade; salon; 24-hr. room service; massage; babysitting; same-day laundry service/dry cleaning; wireless Internet in lobby. *In room:* A/C, TV w/pay movies and PlayStation, fax, dataport, kitchenette in some units, minibar, coffeemaker, hair dryer, iron, safe.

The Huntington Hotel 🏵🏵🏵 The Huntington has long been a favorite retreat for Hollywood stars and VIPs who desire privacy and security. Family-owned since 1924—a rarity among large hotels—this place eschews pomp and circumstance; absolute privacy and unobtrusive service are its mainstays. Though the 19th-century-style lobby is rather petite, the apartment-like guest rooms are large and feature Brunschwig and Fils fabrics, antiques, and city views.

1075 California St. (between Mason and Taylor sts.), San Francisco, CA 94108. © 800/227-4683 or 415/474-5400. Fax 415/474-6227. www.huntingtonhotel.com. 135 units. $315–$460 double; $490–$1,120 suite. Continental breakfast $14. Special packages available. AE, DC, DISC, MC, V. Valet parking $29. Cable car: California St. line (direct stop). Bus: 1. **Amenities:** Restaurant; lounge; indoor heated pool (for ages 16 and up); health club; spa; steam room; sauna; concierge; massage; babysitting; same-day laundry service/dry cleaning. *In room:* A/C, TV w/pay movies, fax, dataport, kitchenette in some units, minibar, fridges in some units, hair dryer, iron, safe.

The Mark Hopkins Intercontinental 🏵🏵 Built in 1926 on the spot where railroad millionaire Mark Hopkins's turreted mansion once stood, the 19-story landmark is one of the city's most classy historic hotels. A renovation in 2000 resulted in exceedingly comfortable neoclassical rooms with all the amenities you'd expect from a world-class hotel, including custom furniture, plush fabrics, sumptuous bathrooms, and extraordinary city views. Luxury suites, added in 2001, are twice the size of most San Francisco apartments and cost close to a month's rent per night. The **Top of the Mark,** a fantastic bar and lounge, where Pacific-bound servicemen went to toast good-bye to the States during World War II, underwent a major renovation. Now, dancing to live jazz or swing is done in spruced up, old-fashioned style. (Romantics, this place is for you.)

1 Nob Hill (at California and Mason sts.), San Francisco, CA 94108. © 800/327-0200 or 415/392-3434. Fax 415/421-3302. www.markhopkins.net. 380 units. $395–$525 double; from $650 suite; from $3,000 luxury suite. Continental breakfast $20; breakfast buffet $35. AE, DC, DISC, MC, V. Valet parking $35, some oversize vehicles prohibited. Cable car: California St. and Powell lines (direct stop). Bus: 1. **Amenities:** 2 restaurants; bar; exercise room; concierge; car-rental desk; business center; secretarial services; 24-hr. room service; massage; babysitting; laundry service/dry cleaning; concierge-level floors. *In room:* A/C, TV w/pay movies, VCR in suites only, dataport, minibar, coffeemaker, hair dryer, iron, safe, 3 phones.

The Ritz-Carlton 🏵🏵🏵 Ranked among the top hotels in the world (as well as the top hotel in the city) by readers of *Condé Nast Traveler,* the Ritz-Carlton has been the benchmark of San Francisco luxury hotels since it opened in 1991. A Nob Hill landmark, it's outfitted with the finest furnishings, fabrics, and artwork, and the rooms offer every amenity and service, from Italian-marble bathrooms with double sinks to plush terry robes. The more expensive rooms offer good views of the city. Club rooms have a dedicated concierge, separate elevator-key access, and complimentary buffet meals throughout the day.

600 Stockton St. (between Pine and California sts.), San Francisco, CA 94108. © 800/241-3333 or 415/296-7465. Fax 415/986-1268. www.ritzcarlton.com. 336 units. $395–$695 double; $475–$695 club-level double; from $695 suite. Buffet breakfast $27; Sun Champagne brunch $65. Weekend discounts and packages available. AE, DC, DISC, MC, V. Parking $45. Cable car: Powell-Hyde and Powell-Mason lines (direct stop). **Amenities:** 2 restaurants; bar; indoor heated pool; outstanding health club; Jacuzzi; sauna; concierge; courtesy car; business center; secretarial services; 24-hr. room service; in-room massage and manicure; babysitting; same-day laundry service/dry cleaning. *In room:* A/C, TV w/pay movies, dataport, minibar, hair dryer, iron, safe, high-speed Internet access.

NORTH BEACH
MODERATE

The Hotel Bohème ★★ *(Finds* North Beach romance awaits you at the Bohème. Although located in the center of North Beach, this hotel's style and demeanor are more reminiscent of a prestigious home in upscale Nob Hill. The decor evokes the Beat generation, which flourished here in the 1950s; rooms are small but hopelessly romantic, with gauze-draped canopies and walls artistically accented with lavender, sage green, black, and pumpkin. The staff is ultra-hospitable, and bonuses include free sherry in the lobby each afternoon. *Take note:* While the bathrooms are sweet, they're also absolutely tiny (no tubs). *Tip:* Request a room off the street side; they're quieter.

444 Columbus Ave. (between Vallejo and Green sts.), San Francisco, CA 94133. © 415/433-9111. Fax 415/362-6292. www.hotelboheme.com. 15 units. $149–$169 double. Rates include afternoon sherry. AE, DC, DISC, MC, V. Parking $31 at nearby public garage. Cable car: Powell-Mason line. Bus: 12, 15, 30, 41, 45, or 83. **Amenities:** Concierge. *In room:* TV, dataport, hair dryer.

INEXPENSIVE

The San Remo Hotel ★★ *(Value* In a quiet North Beach neighborhood and within walking distance of Fisherman's Wharf, this small European-style *pensione* is one of the best budget hotels in San Francisco. The rooms are small and bathrooms are shared, but all is forgiven when it comes time to pay the bill. Rooms are decorated in a cozy country style with brass and iron beds, armoires, and wicker furnishings; most have ceiling fans. The shared bathrooms, each immaculately clean, feature tubs and brass pull-chain toilets with oak tanks and brass fixtures. If the penthouse is available, book it: You won't find a more romantic place to stay in San Francisco for so little money. (It's got its own bathroom, TV, fridge, and patio.)

2237 Mason St. (at Chestnut St.), San Francisco, CA 94133. © 800/352-REMO or 415/776-8688. Fax 415/776-2811. www.sanremohotel.com. 62 units, 61 with shared bathroom. $55–$95 double; $155–$175 penthouse suite. AE, DC, MC, V. Self-parking $10–$14. Cable car: Powell-Mason line. Streetcar: F. Bus: 10, 15, 30, or 47. **Amenities:** Access to nearby health club; self-service laundry; TV room. *In room:* Ceiling fan.

FISHERMAN'S WHARF
EXPENSIVE

Argonaut Hotel ★★ King of luxury boutiques, the Kimpton Hotel Group gives visitors a new reason to stay at Fisherman's Wharf with this gem at the very cool Maritime National Historic Park. A half block from the bay, the four-story timber-and-brick landmark building originally built in 1909 for the California Fruit Canners Association has 239 rooms and 13 suites whimsically decorated and stocked with minibars, flat-screen TVs, and all the standard amenities. Suites come fully loaded with telescopes and spa tubs, and the restaurant, Blue Mermaid Chowder House & Bar, features seafood with a smidgeon of seaside fun.

495 Jefferson St., San Francisco, CA 94109. (℃ 866/415-0704 or 415/563-0800. www.argonauthotel.com. 252 units. $159–$339 double; $249–$599 suites. Rates include evening wine in the lobby, daily newspaper, and kid-friendly perks like cribs and strollers. AE, DC, DISC, MC, V. Parking $32. Cable car: Powell-Hyde line. **Amenities:** Restaurant/bar; concierge; exercise room; laundry; dry cleaning; yoga video and mats. *In room:* TV w/pay movies, DVD player, minibar, coffeemaker, hair dryer, iron, safe.

Best Western Tuscan Inn 🐱🐱   The Tuscan is one of the best options at Fisherman's Wharf. Like an island of respectability in a sea of touristy schlock, it offers a level of style and comfort far beyond its neighbors. Splurge on parking—cheaper than the wharf's outrageously priced garages—and then make your way toward the plush lobby warmed by a grand fireplace. Even the rooms, each equipped with writing desks and armchairs, are a cut above competing neighborhood hotels. The only caveat is the lack of views—a small price to pay for a good hotel in a great location. The adjoining **Cafe Pescatore,** which is open for breakfast, lunch, and dinner, serves lovely Italian fare in an airy setting.

425 N. Point St. (at Mason St.), San Francisco, CA 94133. (℃ 800/648-4626 or 415/561-1100. Fax 415/561-1199. www.tuscaninn.com. 221 units. $189–$269 double; $229–$369 suite. Rates include coffee, tea, and evening fireside wine reception. AE, DC, DISC, MC, V. Parking $26. Cable car: Powell-Mason line. Bus: 10, 15, or 47. Pets welcome for $50 fee. **Amenities:** Access to nearby gym; concierge; courtesy car; secretarial services; limited room service; same-day laundry service/dry cleaning. *In room:* A/C, TV w/pay movies and Nintendo, dataport, minibar, coffeemaker, hair dryer, iron.

Sheraton Fisherman's Wharf Hotel 🐱   Built in the mid-1970s, this contemporary, four-story hotel offers the reliable comforts of a Sheraton in San Francisco's most popular tourist area. In other words, the clean, modern rooms are comfortable and well equipped but nothing unique to the city. The Corporate Floor caters exclusively to business travelers.

2500 Mason St. (between Beach and N. Point sts.), San Francisco, CA 94133. (℃ 800/325-3535 or 415/362-5500. Fax 415/956-5275. www.sheratonatthewharf.com. 529 units. $239–$274 double; $550–$1,000 suite. Extra person $20. Continental breakfast $11. AE, DC, DISC, MC, V. Valet parking $30. Cable car: Powell-Mason line (1 block east, 2 blocks south). Streetcar: F. Bus: 10 or 49. **Amenities:** Restaurant; bar; outdoor heated pool; exercise room; concierge; car-rental desk; business center; limited room service; laundry; dry cleaning. *In room:* A/C, TV, fax (in suites only), dataport, coffeemaker, hair dryer, high-speed Internet access.

MODERATE

The Wharf Inn 🐱🐱 *Kids*   My top choice for good-value lodging at Fisherman's Wharf, The Wharf Inn boasts newly refurbished rooms, done in tones of forest green, burgundy, and pale yellow, that come with all the standard amenities, including complimentary coffee and tea. Its main attribute, however, is its location—smack dab in the middle of the wharf, 2 blocks away from PIER 39 and the cable-car turnaround, and within walking distance of the Embarcadero and North Beach. The inn is ideal for those with cars, as parking is free (that saves $25 a day right off the bat) and there's no charge for an extra person.

2601 Mason St. (at Beach St.), San Francisco, CA 94133. (℃ 800/548-9918 or 415/673-7411. Fax 415/776-2181. www.wharfinn.com. 51 units. $95–$199 double; $299–$425 penthouse. AE, DC, DISC, MC, V. Free parking. Cable car: Powell-Mason line. Streetcar: F. Bus: 10, 15, 39, or 47. **Amenities:** Access to nearby health club ($10 per day); concierge; tour desk; car-rental desk; complimentary coffee/tea and newspapers. *In room:* TV, dataport, coffeemaker, hair dryer, iron (on request).

COW HOLLOW/PACIFIC HEIGHTS
EXPENSIVE

Union Street Inn 🍵🍵   Who would have guessed that one of the most delightful B&Bs in California would be in San Francisco? This two-story 1903 Edwardian fronts perpetually busy (and trendy shopping and barhopping stop) Union Street, but it's quiet as a church on the inside. The individually decorated rooms are furnished with down comforters, fresh flowers, and bay windows (ask for one with a garden view). A few have Jacuzzi tubs. An extended full breakfast is served in the parlor, in your room, or on an outdoor terrace overlooking the English garden. The ultimate honeymoon retreat is the private carriage house behind the inn, but any room at this warm, friendly inn is guaranteed to please.

2229 Union St. (between Fillmore and Steiner sts.), San Francisco, CA 94123. ℭ 415/346-0424. Fax 415/922-8046. www.unionstreetinn.com. 5 units, 1 cottage. $169–$279 standard double; $269 cottage. Rates include breakfast, hors d'oeuvres, and evening beverages. AE, MC, V. Nearby parking $15. Bus: 22, 28, 41, or 45. *In room:* TV.

MODERATE

Hotel Del Sol 🍵🍵 *Value*   Two-level Hotel Del Sol's sunshine theme attracts a youngish clientele to its hip motel, 2 blocks off busy (and bland) Lombard Street. With a centerpiece courtyard and pool and the Miami Beach–style use of vibrant color—as in the yellow, red, orange, and blue exterior—the atmosphere at the del Sol is unexpectedly festive. Fair-weather fun doesn't stop at the front door of the 57 spacious rooms, which boast colorful (read: loud) interior decor and unexpected extras like a CD player and tips to the town's happenings and shopping meccas. Sorry smokers, you'll have to step outside to puff.

3100 Webster St. (at Greenwich St.), San Francisco, CA 94123. ℭ 877/433-5765 or 415/921-5520. Fax 415/931-4137. www.thehoteldelsol.com. 57 units, including 10 1-bedroom suites. $119–$165 double; $160–$235 suite. Rates include continental breakfast. AE, DC, DISC, MC, V. Free parking. Bus: 22, 28, 41, 43, 45, or 76. **Amenities:** Heated outdoor pool; dry cleaning. *In room:* TV/VCR, dataport, kitchenette in some units, iron, CD player, wireless high-speed Internet access ($10 per day).

The Laurel Inn 🍵🍵   If you don't mind being out of the downtown area, this motel is one of the most tranquil, lovely, and affordable places to rest your head. Tucked beyond the southernmost tip of the Presidio and its winding roads shaded by eucalyptus, the outside isn't impressive. But inside it's *très* chic and modern, with Zen-like influences. Some rooms have excellent views and all have CD players, VCRs, and spiffy bathrooms. But wait! There's more: concierge services, 24-hour coffee and tea service, pet-friendly rooms, and topping it off, free parking and a hip bar/lounge called **G.**

444 Presidio Ave. (at California Ave.), San Francisco, CA 94115. ℭ 800/552-8735 or 415/567-8467. Fax 415/928-1866. www.thelaurelinn.com. 49 units. $155–$180 double. Rates include continental breakfast and afternoon lemonade and cookies. AE, DC, DISC, MC, V. Free parking. Muni Metro: 1, 3, 4, or 43. Pets accepted; no deposit required. **Amenities:** Adjoining bar; concierge; valet service. *In room:* TV/VCR, dataport, kitchenette in some rooms, hair dryer, iron, CD player.

INEXPENSIVE

Edward II Inn & Suites 🍵🍵   This three-story, self-styled "English Country" inn has a room for almost anyone's budget, ranging from *pensione* rooms with shared bathrooms to luxuriously appointed suites and cottages with living rooms, kitchens, and whirlpool tubs. Originally built for houseguests who attended the 1915 Pan-Pacific Exposition, it's now a good place to shack up in clean and comfortably appointed rooms with antique furnishings. The only caveat is that its Lombard Street location is usually congested with traffic, but nearby Chestnut and Union streets offer some of the best shopping and dining in the city. The adjoining pub serves evening drinks.

3155 Scott St. (at Lombard St.), San Francisco, CA 94123. ℂ **800/473-2846** or 415/922-3000. Fax 415/931-5784. www.edwardii.com. 32 units, 21 with bathroom. $83–$88 double with shared bathroom; $115 double with private bathroom; $185–$235 suite. Extra person $25. Rates include continental breakfast and evening sherry. AE, MC, V. Self-parking $12 a block away. Bus: 28, 30, 43, or 76. **Amenities:** Pub (open Fri–Sat). *In room:* TV, hair dryer and iron available on request.

The Marina Inn ★★ *Value*   How this 1924 four-story Victorian offers so much for so little is mystifying. Each room looks as though it's been culled from a country-furnishings catalog, complete with pinewood furniture, a four-poster bed with a silk-soft comforter, and pretty wallpaper. There are even high-class touches that many expensive hotels don't include: remote-control TVs discreetly hidden in pine cabinetry, and full bathtubs with showers. Add to that complimentary continental breakfast, afternoon sherry, friendly service, and an armada of nearby shops and restaurants, and there you have it: my number-one choice for Best Overall Value. *Note:* Be sure to request one of the quieter rooms away from Lombard Street.

3110 Octavia St. (at Lombard St.), San Francisco, CA 94123. ℂ **800/274-1420** or 415/928-1000. Fax 415/928-5909. www.marinainn.com. 40 units. Nov–Feb $65–$105 double; Mar–May $75–$125 double; June–Oct $85–$135 double. Rates include continental breakfast. AE, DC, MC, V. Bus: 28, 30, 43, or 76. *In room:* TV, hair dryer and iron on request.

JAPANTOWN & ENVIRONS
EXPENSIVE
The Hotel Majestic ★★ *Value*   The Majestic, built in 1902, meets every professional need while retaining the opulent ambience of a luxurious old-world boutique hotel. The lobby will sweep you into another era with its tapestries, brocades, Corinthian columns, and intricate details. Rooms are furnished with French and English antiques, the centerpiece of each a four-poster canopy bed; you'll also find mirrored armoires and antique reproductions. Extras include a well-lit desk and bathrobes; fireplaces (in some rooms); and easy access to a fantastic and intimate bar.

1500 Sutter St. (between Octavia and Gough sts.), San Francisco, CA 94109. ℂ **800/869-8966** or 415/441-1100. Fax 415/673-7331. www.thehotelmajestic.com. 58 units. $150 double; from $250 suite. Rates include complimentary continental breakfast in lobby 7–10am, and wine and appetizers 4–6pm. Group, government, corporate, and relocation rates available. AE, DC, DISC, MC, V. Valet parking $19. Bus: 2, 4, 47, or 49. **Amenities:** Bar; access to nearby health club ($10 per day); concierge; 24-hr. room service; in-room massage; babysitting; same-day laundry/dry-cleaning service. *In room:* TV, dataport, fridge in some rooms, hair dryer, iron, wireless Internet access.

MODERATE
The Queen Anne Hotel ★★ *Value*   This majestic 1890 Victorian is a charming boutique hotel that remains true to its heritage and emulates San Francisco's golden days. The lavish "grand salon" greets you with oak paneling and antiques; rooms follow suit with armoires, marble-top dressers, and other period pieces. Some have corner turret bay windows that look out onto tree-lined streets, plus separate parlor areas and wet bars; others have cozy reading nooks and fireplaces. All rooms have phones in the bathroom, computer hookups, and fridges. You can relax in the parlor, with its floor-to-ceiling fireplace, or in the hotel library. Amenities include complimentary afternoon tea and sherry.

1590 Sutter St. (between Gough and Octavia sts.), San Francisco, CA 94109. ℂ **800/227-3970** or 415/441-2828. Fax 415/775-5212. www.queenanne.com. 48 units. $99–$199 double; $185–$205 suite. Extra person $10. Rates include continental breakfast, afternoon tea and sherry, and morning newspaper. AE, DC, DISC, MC, V. Parking $14. Bus: 2, 3, or 4. **Amenities:** Access to nearby health club; 24-hr. concierge; business center; same-day dry cleaning; front desk safe. *In room:* TV, dataport, hair dryer, iron.

CIVIC CENTER
MODERATE

The Phoenix Hotel 𝒓   On the fringes of the less-than-pleasant Tenderloin District, this retro 1950s-style choice is a gathering place for visiting rockers, writers, and filmmakers who crave a Southern California vibe during their San Francisco visits. The focal point of the pastel-painted Palm Springs–style hotel is a heated, paisley-muraled pool in a modern-sculpture garden. The rooms, while far from plush, are currently being updated but are comfortably outfitted with bamboo furnishings and original local art. In addition to the usual amenities, the inn's own closed-circuit channel shows films exclusively made in or about San Francisco. Services include on-site massage and—*woo hoo!*—free parking. A hot restaurant and lounge, **Bambuddha,** revitalized the hotel's reputation as a hot nightspot with Southeast Asian cuisine and cocktail lounge flair.

601 Eddy St. (at Larkin St.), San Francisco, CA 94109. ℂ **800/248-9466** or 415/776-1380. Fax 415/885-3109. www.thephoenixhotel.com. 44 units. $149–$169 double; $185–$205 suite. Rates include continental breakfast. AE, DC, MC, V. Free parking. Bus: 19, 31, 38, or 47. **Amenities:** Bar; heated outdoor pool; concierge; tour desk; in-room massage; same-day laundry service/dry cleaning. *In room:* TV, VCR on request, dataport, fridge and microwave in some rooms, hair dryer, iron on request.

THE CASTRO
MODERATE

The Parker Guest House 𝒓𝒓   This is the best B&B option in the Castro, and one of the best in the entire city. The gay-friendly, 5,000-square-foot, beautifully restored Edwardian home is a few blocks from the heart of Castro's action. The bright, cheery urban compound boasts period antiques, and spacious guest rooms are wonderfully appointed with smart, patterned furnishings, voice mail, robes, and a spotless private bathroom (plus amenities) en suite or across the hall. A fire burns nightly in the cozy living room, and guests are welcome to make themselves at home in the wood-paneled common library (with fireplace and piano), sunny breakfast room overlooking the garden, and spacious garden with fountains and a steam room.

520 Church St. (between 17th and 18th sts.), San Francisco, CA 94114. ℂ **888/520-7275** or 415/621-3222. Fax 415/621-4139. www.parkerguesthouse.com. 21 units. $119–$200 double; $200 junior suite. Rates include extended continental breakfast and evening wine and cheese. AE, DISC, MC, V. Self-parking $15. Streetcar: J Church. Bus: 22 or 33. **Amenities:** Access to nearby health club; steam room; concierge, wireless computer access. *In room:* TV, dataport, hair dryer, iron.

INEXPENSIVE

Beck's Motor Lodge 𝒓   A run-of-the-mill motel swathed in vibrant color, here the ultra-tidy rooms are standard but contemporary with motel furnishings, a sun deck overlooking upper Market Street's action, and free parking. Unless you're into B&Bs, this is really your only choice in the area—fortunately, it's very well maintained.

2222 Market St. (at 15th St.), San Francisco, CA 94114. ℂ **800/227-4360** in the U.S. (except California), or 415/621-8212 (within California, call collect to make reservations). Fax 415/241-0435. 58 units. $119–$145 double. AE, DC, DISC, MC, V. Free parking. Metro: F. Bus: 8 or 37. **Amenities:** Coin-operated washing machines. *In room:* TV, dataport, fridge, coffeemaker, free Internet access in some rooms.

4 Where to Dine

San Francisco's dining scene is one of the best in the world. Below is a cross section of San Francisco's best restaurants in every price range. For a greater selection of reviews, see *Frommer's San Francisco 2005* or *Frommer's San Francisco from $70 a Day.*

UNION SQUARE
VERY EXPENSIVE

Masa's ✦✦✦ FRENCH   One of the city's veteran contenders for best French restaurant stays in the spotlight with executive Chef Ron Siegel's three-, six-, and nine-course tasting menus and an almost startlingly trendy (think hip hotelier Ian Schrager) room. Beyond the tiny bar and backlit white curtains is the dark, sleek, and minimalist dining room with delightedly well spaced tables and cozy refinement. Menus vary, but are always creative. Think delicate seared scallops elevated both literally and figuratively by microgreens and a dab of decadent *uni* (sea urchin) or savory skate balanced atop a short-rib ravioli bathed in a mushroom jus. In addition to the dessert menu, the candy cart adds a sweet finale as it's wheeled by so you can select lollipops, chocolates, and minicookies.

In the Hotel Vintage Court, 648 Bush St. (at Stockton St.). ✆ 415/989-7154. Reservations required and accepted up to 3 months in advance. Fixed-price dinner $65–$115; 6-course vegetarian dinner $85. AE, DC, DISC, MC, V. Tues–Sat 5:30–9:30pm. Closed 1st 2 weeks in Jan and 1st week in July. Valet parking $15. Cable car: Powell-Mason and Powell-Hyde lines. Bus: 2, 3, 4, 30, or 45.

EXPENSIVE

Grand Café ✦✦ FRENCH BISTRO   If you want a huge dose of atmosphere with your seared salmon, Grand Café is your best bet. It's an enormous turn-of-the-20th-century grand ballroom–like dining oasis that's a magnificent combination of old Europe and Art Nouveau, a festive bar and bistro area, and the talents of Chef Paul Arenstam. If it's on the menu, don't miss his wild-mushroom tart with black truffle *sabayon* (egg custard). Likewise his indulgent sautéed skate wing with braised cabbage and bacon in a browned butter capers sauce. Want all the fun at half the price? Dine in the bar—aka the **Petit Café,** which offers dishes from $3 to $12 (including stuffed *piquillo* peppers with feta cheese, steak tartare, pizzas, and a duck confit tart with grilled bread, mashed potatoes, and shredded duck confit). Libation lovers stop here for the great selection of small-batch American whiskeys and single-malt scotches.

501 Geary St. (at Taylor St., adjacent to the Hotel Monaco). ✆ 415/292-0101. Reservations recommended. Main courses $15–$25. AE, DC, DISC, MC, V. Mon–Fri 7–10:30am; Sat 8–11am; Sun 8am–2:30pm; Mon–Sat 11:30am–2:30pm; Sun–Thurs 5:30–10pm; Fri–Sat 5:30–11pm. Valet parking $10 for 3 hr., $3 each additional ½ hr. Bus: 2, 3, 4, 27, or 38.

MODERATE

Scala's Bistro ✦ FRENCH/ITALIAN   This polished Italian dining room with high ceilings and big booths is a downtown favorite. The Parisian-bistro/old-world atmosphere has just the right balance of elegance and informality, which means it's

---

⟮Tips⟯ Make Reservations in Advance

If you want a table at a top restaurant, make your reservation weeks in advance—perhaps through **www.opentable.com**, which provides real-time reservations to many Bay Area establishments.

okay to have some fun here (and apparently most people do). Expect a fantastic array of Italian and French dishes that are reasonably priced. Start with the Earth and Surf calamari appetizer or grilled portobello mushrooms. Generous portions of the moist, rich duck-leg confit will satisfy hungry appetites, but if you can only order one thing, make it Scala's signature dish: the seared salmon.

In the Sir Francis Drake hotel, 432 Powell St. (at Sutter St.). ℂ 415/395-8555. Reservations recommended. Breakfast $7–$10; main courses $12–$24 lunch and dinner. AE, DC, DISC, MC, V. Mon–Fri 7–10:30am; Sat–Sun 8–10:30am; daily 11:30am–4pm and 5:15pm–midnight. Cable car: Powell-Hyde line. Bus: 2, 3, 4, 30, 45, or 76.

INEXPENSIVE

Café Claude 𝓡𝓡 FRENCH Euro transplants love Café Claude, a crowded and lively restaurant tucked into a narrow (and very European feeling) side street near Union Square. Seemingly everything—every table, spoon, saltshaker, and waiter—is imported from France. With prices topping out at about $18 on the menu, featuring classics like steak tartare, steamed mussels, duck confit salad, escargot, and New York steak with spinach gratin and crisp potatoes, it's a great deal. There is live jazz on Saturday from 7:30 to 10:30pm. Atmospheric sidewalk seating is available when the weather permits.

7 Claude Lane (off Sutter St.). ℂ 415/392-3515. www.cafeclaude.com. Reservations recommended. Main courses $12–$18. AE, DC, DISC, MC, V. Mon 11:30am–5:30pm; Tues–Thurs 11:30am–10pm; Fri–Sat 11:30am–10:30pm. Cable car: Powell-Mason and Powell-Hyde lines.

Mocca 𝓡 ITALIAN If you're like me and can't be bothered with a long lunch when there's serious shopping to be done, head to this classic Italian deli on pedestrian-only Maiden Lane. Here it's counter service and cash only for sandwiches, *caprese* (Italian tomato and mozzarella salad), and big leafy salads. You can enjoy them at the few indoor tables or the pedestrian-only-street-front tables shaded by umbrellas, which look onto Union Square.

175 Maiden Lane (at Stockton St.). ℂ 415/956-1188. Reservations not accepted. Main courses $7–$13. No credit cards. Pastry and coffee daily 9:30am–4:30pm; lunch daily 11am–4:30pm. Bus: All Union Sq. buses.

Phở Hóa 𝓡 *Value* VIETNAMESE Although it's only a few blocks off Union Square, the walk to this simple cafeteria-like Vietnamese restaurant in the downtrodden Tenderloin District is quite an adventure, often characterized by crack-smoking loiterers (literally) and plenty of people down on their luck. Thing is, the arrival promises huge, killer bowls of Vietnamese soup with all the classic fixings (basil, bean sprouts, and the like) at absurdly low prices. Any of the dozens of selections is a meal in itself, be it my favorite—the seafood soup with rice noodles—or those with beef balls (not literally), chicken, shrimp, or flank steak. There are also rice dishes—with beef, vegetables, deep-fried egg rolls, or barbecued pork—and intensely strong iced coffee.

431 Jones St. (between O'Farrell and Ellis sts.). ℂ 415/673-3163. Reservations not accepted. Soups and main courses $5.50–$9. No credit cards. Daily 8am–7pm. Bus: 27 or 38.

Sanraku Japanese Restaurant 𝓡 *Value* JAPANESE/SUSHI A perfect combination of great Japanese dishes and sushi at bargain prices makes this bright, busy restaurant one of my favorites. A box lunch might include a California roll, soup, seaweed salad, deep-fried salmon roll, and beef with noodles and steamed rice, all for just $8.50. The main menu features irresistible sesame chicken with teriyaki sauce and rice, tempura, a vast selection of rolls, and delicious combination plates that mix sushi, sashimi, and teriyaki. Dinner does brisk business, too, but there always seems to be an available table.

San Francisco Dining

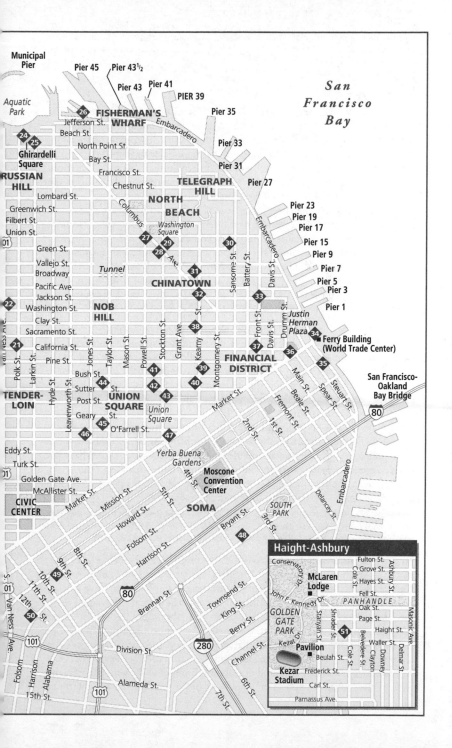

Municipal Pier

Aquatic Park

RUSSIAN HILL

Ghirardelli Square

FISHERMAN'S WHARF

Pier 45 Pier 43¹/₂
Pier 43 Pier 41
PIER 39
Pier 35
Pier 33
Pier 31
Pier 27

San Francisco Bay

Jefferson St.
Beach St.
North Point St
Bay St.
Francisco St.
Chestnut St.
Lombard St.
Greenwich St.
Filbert St.
Union St.

Embarcadero

TELEGRAPH HILL

NORTH BEACH

Washington Square

Columbus

Green St.
Vallejo St.
Broadway
Pacific Ave.
Jackson St.
Washington St.
Clay St.
Sacramento St.
California St.
Pine St.

Tunnel

CHINATOWN

NOB HILL

Polk St.
Larkin St.
Hyde St.
Leavenworth St.
Jones St.
Taylor St.
Mason St.
Powell St.
Stockton St.
Grant Ave.
Kearny St.
Montgomery St.

Pier 23
Pier 19
Pier 17
Pier 15
Pier 9
Pier 7
Pier 5
Pier 3
Pier 1

Embarcadero

Sansome St.
Battery St.
Front St.
Davis St.
Drumm St.

Justin Herman Plaza

Ferry Building (World Trade Center)

FINANCIAL DISTRICT

Main St.
Beale St.
Spear St.
Steuart St.

San Francisco-Oakland Bay Bridge

80

TENDER-LOIN

Bush St.
Sutter St.
Post St.
Geary St.
O'Farrell St.

UNION SQUARE

Union Square

Market St.
2nd St.
1st St.
Fremont St.

Eddy St.
Turk St.
Golden Gate Ave.
McAllister St.

CIVIC CENTER

Market St.
Mission St.
Howard St.
Folsom St.
Harrison St.

Yerba Buena Gardens

Moscone Convention Center

SOMA

4th St.
5th St.
3rd St.
Bryant St.

SOUTH PARK

Delancey St.
Embarcadero

Van Ness Ave.

8th St.
9th St.
10th St.
11th St.
12th St.

80

Brannan St.
Townsend St.
King St.
Berry St.

Folsom
Harrison
Alabama

101

Division St.

280

Channel St.
6th St.
7th St.

Alameda St.

101

15th St.

Haight-Ashbury

Conservatory Dr.
John F. Kennedy Dr.

McLaren Lodge

GOLDEN GATE PARK

Kezar Dr.

Pavilion

Kezar Stadium

Fulton St.
Grove St.
Hayes St.
Fell St.
PANHANDLE
Oak St.
Page St.
Haight St.
Waller St.
Beulah St.
Frederick St.
Carl St.
Parnassus Ave.

Stanyan St.
Shrader St.
Cole St.
Clayton
Belvedere St.
Downey
Masonic Ave.
Ashbury St.
Delmar St.

95

704 Sutter St. (at Taylor St.). ℂ 415/771-0803. www.sanraku.com. Main courses $6.25–$11 lunch, $10–$21 dinner. AE, DISC, MC, V. Mon–Sat lunch 11am–4pm, dinner 4–10pm; Sun 4–10pm. Cable car: Powell-Mason line. Bus: 2, 3, 4, 27, or 38.

SOMA
EXPENSIVE

bacar ⭐⭐ AMERICAN BRASSERIE   No other dining room makes wine as integral to the meal as popular bacar. Up to 250 eclectic, fashionable diners pack into the warehouse-restaurant's three areas—the casual (loud) downstairs salon, the bustling bar and loud mezzanine, or the more quiet upstairs, which looks down on the mezzanine's action—for chef Arnold Eric Wong's "American Brasserie" (that is, French Bistro with a California twist) cuisine. I'm a fan of the creamy salt-cod and crab *brandade* (purée) and zesty roasted mussels with a chile-and-garlic sauce that begs to be soaked up by the accompanying grilled bread. Ditto the braised beef short ribs. Just as much fun is the wine selection, which gives you 1,300 choices. Around 100 come by the glass, 2-ounce pour, or 250- or 500-milliliter decanter. If you want a festive night out, this is the place to come—especially when jazz is playing Monday through Saturday eves.

448 Brannan St. (at Third St.). ℂ 415/904-4100. www.bacarsf.com. Reservations recommended. Main courses lunch $14–$17, dinner $22–$38. AE, DC, DISC, MC, V. Sun 5:30–11pm; Mon–Sat 5:30pm–midnight; Fri 11:30am–2:30pm. Valet parking (Mon–Sat beginning at 6pm) $10. Bus: 15, 30, 45, 76, or 81.

Boulevard ⭐⭐⭐ *Finds* AMERICAN   Master restaurant designer Pat Kuleto and chef Nancy Oaks are behind one of my—and the city's—all-time favorites. What's the winning combination? The dramatic Belle Epoque interior combined with Oaks's mouthwatering dishes. Starters alone could make a perfect meal, especially the sweetbreads wrapped in prosciutto on watercress and Lola Rose lettuce with garlic croutons and a whole-grain mustard vinaigrette; and Sonoma foie gras with elderberry syrup, toast, and Bosc-pear salad. The main courses are equally creative and might include pan-roasted miso-glazed sea bass with asparagus salad, Japanese rice, and shiitake-mushroom broth, or spit-roasted cider-cured pork loin with sweet-potato–swirled mashed potatoes and sautéed baby red chard. Vegetarian items, such as wild-mushroom risotto with fresh chanterelles and Parmesan, are also offered. Three levels of formality—bar, open kitchen, and main dining room—keep things from getting too snobby.

1 Mission St. (between Embarcadero and Steuart sts.). ℂ 415/543-6084. Reservations recommended. Main courses $9–$17 lunch, $24–$32 dinner. AE, DC, DISC, MC, V. Mon–Fri 11:30am–2:15pm; Sun–Thurs 5:30–10pm; Fri–Sat 5:30–10:30pm. Valet parking $12 lunch, $10 dinner. Bus: 15, 30, 32, or 45.

Fifth Floor Restaurant ⭐⭐⭐ MODERN FRENCH   Executive chef Laurent Gras made his way through Michelin-star restaurants in France, spent 5 years as *chef de cuisine* at Restaurant Alain Ducasse, and forged his own ground at the Waldorf Astoria's Peacock Alley before wowing diners at this swank French spot. Like the club-style decor—rich colors and fabrics, red leather and velvet banquettes, and zebra-striped carpeting—Gras's menu is luxurious. But it's his creativity and attention to detail that makes this place one of the city's top restaurants. Here nearly everything is original and incredibly well executed, from an avocado dome hiding a mound of crabmeat brought to life with jalapeño and basil to the "lobster cappuccino" of lobster broth emulsified with chestnuts, prawns, and sautéed lobster. Main courses, like veal tournedos caramelized with sweetbread, black pepper *jus,* and braised potato; or slow-baked lamb with truffle, pistachio, and olives with steamed cabbage are also precisely prepared. The wine list is one of the most prestigious and expensive lists around.

In the Hotel Palomar, 12 Fourth St. (at Market St.). ⓒ 415/348-1555. www.fifthfloor.citysearch.com. Reservations required. Main courses $31–$65; tasting menu $95. AE, DC, DISC, MC, V. Mon–Wed 5:30–9:30pm; Thurs–Sat 5:30–10pm. Valet parking $12. Bus: All Market St. buses.

MODERATE
The Slanted Door 🍴🍴 *(Finds)* VIETNAMESE   This restaurant is so popular that Mick Jagger and former President Clinton made stopovers when they hit town. Why? The restaurant serves incredibly fresh and flavorful Vietnamese food. No doubt it's even more of a hot spot since its April 2004 relocation to its spacious bay-inspired custom-designed space in the Ferry Building Marketplace. Make a reservation to pull up a chair and order anything from clay-pot catfish or amazing green papaya salad to one of the lunch rice dishes, which come in a large ceramic bowl and are topped with such options as grilled shrimp and stir-fried eggplant. Dinner items, which change seasonally, might include beef with garlic and organic onions, grapefruit, and jícama salad. Whatever you order, it's bound to be wholesome, flavorful, and outstanding. There's also an eclectic collection of teas, which come by the pot for $3 to $5.

1 Ferry Plaza (at Embarcadero and Market). ⓒ 415/861-8032. Reservations recommended. Lunch main courses $8.50–$16; most dinner dishes $9–$27. AE, MC, V. Mon–Sun 11:30am–2:30pm; Sun–Thurs 5:30–10pm; Fri–Sat 5:30–10:30pm. Streetcar: F or N. Bus: All Market St. buses.

Yank Sing 🍴🍴 CHINESE/DIM SUM   Loosely translated as "a delight of the heart," cavernous Yank Sing is the best dim sum restaurant in the downtown area. Confident, experienced servers take the nervousness out of novices—they're good at guessing your gastric threshold as they wheel carts carrying small plates of exotic dishes past each table. Most dim sum dishes are dumplings, filled with tasty concoctions of pork, beef, fish, or vegetables. *Congees* (porridges), spareribs, stuffed crab claws, scallion pancakes, shrimp balls, pork buns, and other palate-pleasers complete the menu. While the food is delicious, the location makes this the most popular tourist spot and weekday lunch spot; at other times residents generally head to **Ton Kiang** (p. 108), the undisputed top choice for these Chinese delicacies. A second location, open during weekdays for lunch only, is at 49 Stevenson St., off First Street (ⓒ **415/541-4949**).

101 Spear St. (at Mission St. at Rincon Center). ⓒ 415/957-9300. Dim sum $2.80–$4.50 for 2–4 pieces. AE, DC, MC, V. Mon–Fri 11am–3pm; Sat–Sun 10am–4pm. Free validated parking in Rincon Center Garage on weekends. Cable car: California St. line. Streetcar: F. Bus: 1, 12, 14, or 41. BART: Embarcadero.

INEXPENSIVE
AsiaSF 🍴 CALIFORNIA/ASIAN   At AsiaSF you'll be entertained by Asian men—dressed as women—who lip-sync show tunes as they serve excellent grilled-shrimp-and-herb salad, Asian-influenced hamburgers, potstickers, duck quesadillas, and chicken sate. Fortunately, the food and the atmosphere are as colorful as the staff, which means a night here is more than a meal—it's an event.

201 Ninth St. (at Howard St.). ⓒ 415/255-2742. www.asiasf.com. Reservations recommended. Main courses $9–$19. AE, DISC, MC, V ($25 minimum). Sun–Thurs 6–10pm; Fri–Sat 5–10pm. Streetcar: Civic Center on underground streetcar. Bus: 9, 12, or 47. BART: Civic Center.

Manora's ✿ THAI   Ever-bustling Manora's cranks out dependable Thai to an eclectic mix of local diners. It's perpetually packed (unless you come early), so you'll be seated sardinelike at one of the cramped but well-appointed tables. During the dinner rush, the noise level can make conversation among larger parties almost impossible, but the food is so good, you'll probably prefer to turn toward your plate and stuff your face. Start with tangy soup or chicken satay. Follow with any of the wonderful dinner dishes—which should be shared—and a side of rice. There are endless options, including a vast array of vegetarian plates. *Tip:* Come before 7pm or after 9pm if you don't want a loud, rushed meal.

1600 Folsom St. (at 12th St.). © 415/861-6224. Reservations recommended for 4 or more. Main courses $7–$12. MC, V. Mon–Fri 11:30am–2:30pm; Mon–Sat 5:30–10:30pm; Sun 5–10pm. Bus: 9, 12, or 47.

FINANCIAL DISTRICT
EXPENSIVE

Aqua ✿✿ SEAFOOD   Without question, Aqua remains San Francisco's finest seafood restaurant. In 2003, heralded chef Laurent Manrique arrived from Campton Place to preside over the tasty traditions of previous chefs Michael Mina and George Marrone, and he continues to dazzle with a bewildering juxtaposition of earth and sea. The *ahi* (tuna) tartare—my favorite all-time rendition, period—is mixed tableside with pears, pine nuts, quail egg, and spices. Sculptural grilled medallions of ahi tuna with foie gras in pinot sauce are beyond decadent. Desserts are equally impressive. The large dining room with high ceilings, one big floral arrangement, and otherwise stark decor can be seriously loud, but that doesn't stop power-lunchers from powwowing by day and well-dressed gourmands from feasting in style at night. Steep prices prevent most people from making a regular appearance, but for special occasions or billable lunches, Aqua is on my top-10 list. Keep in mind that there's no valet or street parking at lunch, so you'll have to pull into one of the Embarcadero lots 2 blocks away.

252 California St. (near Battery). © 415/956-9662. Reservations recommended. Main courses $29–$39; 5-course tasting menu $90 or $100; vegetarian tasting menu $55. AE, DC, MC, V. Mon–Fri 11:30am–2pm; Mon–Sat 5:30–10:30pm; Sun 5:30–9:30pm. Bus: All Market St. buses.

MODERATE

Kokkari ✿✿✿ *Value* GREEK   It figures that it would take a French chef to make Greek food fabulous, and executive chef Jean Alberti, the mastermind behind the moussaka who departed in early 2004, did exactly that. Thankfully, he left his secret recipes behind, and at least for the meantime Kokkari (Ko-*car*-ee) is still wonderful in fashion and flavor. The love affair starts with the setting: a rustic living room–like dining area with a commanding fireplace and oversize furnishings, and ends with Alberti's traditional Aegean dishes. Hearty eaters should opt for the to-die-for moussaka (eggplant, lamb, potato, and béchamel). Another boon: quail stuffed with winter greens served on oven-roasted leeks, orzo, and wild-rice *pilafi*. Don't leave without sinking your fork into an order of *Kalithopita,* the most velvety chocolate cake you'll ever eat.

200 Jackson St. (at Front St.). © 415/981-0983. www.kokkari.com. Reservations recommended. Main courses $14–$23 lunch, $19–$35 dinner. AE, DC, DISC, MC, V. Lunch Mon–Fri 11:30am–2:30pm; bar menu 2:30–5:30pm; dinner Mon–Thurs 5:30–10pm, Fri 5:30–11pm, Sat 5–11pm. Valet parking (dinner only) $8. Bus: 12, 15, 41, or 83.

Finds **Dining with the Sun on Your Face at Belden Place**

San Francisco has always been lacking in the alfresco dining department. One exception, however, is Belden Place, an adorable brick alley in the heart of the Financial District closed to everything but foot traffic. When the weather is agreeable, the restaurants that line the alley break out the umbrellas, tables, and chairs a la Boulevard St-Michel and *voilà*—a bit of Paris just off Pine Street.

A handful of adorable cafes line Belden Place and offer a wide variety of cuisine. There's **Cafe Bastille**, 22 Belden Place (© **415/986-5673**), your classic French bistro and fun speakeasy basement serving excellent crepes, mussels, and French onion soup along with live jazz on Fridays; **Cafe Tiramisu**, 28 Belden Place (© **415/421-7044**), a stylish Italian hot spot serving addictive risottos and gnocchi; and **Plouf**, 40 Belden Place (© **415/986-6491**), which specializes in big bowls of mussels slathered in a choice of seven sauces as well as fresh seafood. **B44**, 44 Belden Place (**415/986-6287**), serves up a side order of Spain alongside its revered paella and other seriously zesty Spanish dishes.

Come at night for a Euro-speakeasy vibe with your dinner.

CHINATOWN
INEXPENSIVE
House of Nanking ✿ CHINESE   To its legion of fans, the wait at this dive—sometimes up to an hour—is worth what's on the plate. When the line is reasonable, I drop by for a plate of potstickers and chef-owner Peter Fang's signature shrimp-and-green-onion pancake, served with peanut sauce. You can select from a good number of pork, rice, beef, seafood, chicken, or vegetable dishes, but I suggest you trust the waiter when he recommends a special, or simply point to what looks good on someone else's table. Even with an expansion that doubled the space, seating is tight, so prepare to be bumped around a bit and don't expect good service—it's all part of the Nanking experience.

919 Kearny St. (at Columbus Ave.). © 415/421-1429. Reservations accepted for groups of 8 or more. Main courses $6–$12. MC, V. Mon–Fri 11am–10pm; Sat–Sun noon–10pm. Bus: 9, 12, 15, or 30.

R&G Lounge ✿✿ CHINESE   If you want a sure thing in Chinatown, go to R&G Lounge. During lunch, both newly redecorated floors are packed with neighborhood workers who go straight to the $5 rice-plate specials. But you can also order from the dinner menu, which features legendary (and very greasy and rich) deep-fried salt-and-pepper crab. My favorites include R&G's melt-in-your-mouth Special Beef, which explodes with the tangy flavor of the accompanying sauce; savory seafood in a clay pot; and delicious classic roast duck.

631 Kearny St. (at Clay St.). © 415/982-7877. Reservations recommended. Main courses $9–$30. AE, DC, DISC, MC, V. Mon–Thurs 11am–9:30pm; Fri 11am–10pm; Sat 11:30am–10pm; Sun 11:30am–9:30pm. Parking validated across the street at Portsmouth Sq. garage or Holiday Inn after 5pm. Bus: 1, 9AX, 9BX, 12, or 15.

NOB HILL/RUSSIAN HILL
EXPENSIVE
House of Prime Rib ★★ PRIME RIB   Anyone who loves a slab of meat and old-school–style dining will feel right at home at this shrine to prime (rib). It's a fun and ever-packed affair within the men's club–like dining rooms (fireplaces included), where drinks are stiff, waiters are loose, and all the beef is roasted in rock salt and sliced tableside. It's served with salad dramatically tossed tableside, followed by creamed spinach and either mashed potatoes or a baked potato and Yorkshire pudding, all of which accompany the entree. To placate the occasional nonmeat eater, they offer a fish-of-the-day special. Another bonus: Kids' prime-rib dinners are a paltry $8.95.

1906 Van Ness Ave. (near Washington St.). © 415/885-4605. Reservations recommended. Complete dinners $24–$30. AE, DC, MC, V. Mon–Thurs 5:30–10pm; Fri–Sat 5–10pm; Sun 4–10pm. Valet parking: $6. Bus: 47 or 49.

INEXPENSIVE
Swan Oyster Depot ★★ *Finds* SEAFOOD   Swan Oyster Depot is a San Francisco experience you shouldn't miss. Opened in 1912, this hole-in-the-wall boasts 20 or so seats, jammed cheek-by-jowl along a marble bar. Most patrons come for a cup of chowder or a plate of oysters that arrive chilling on crushed ice. The menu is limited to fresh crab, shrimp, oyster, clam cocktails, Maine lobster, and Boston-style clam chowder, all of which are exceedingly fresh. *Note:* Don't let the lunchtime line dissuade you—it moves fast.

1517 Polk St. (between California and Sacramento sts.). © 415/673-1101. Reservations not accepted. Seafood cocktails $7–$15; clams and oysters on the half shell $7–$7.50 per half dozen. No credit cards. Mon–Sat 8am–5:30pm. Bus: 19.

NORTH BEACH
MODERATE
Enrico's ★ MEDITERRANEAN   Enrico's is the most fun sidewalk restaurant and supper club destination on this North Beach strip. Families might want to skip this one, but anyone with an appreciation for live jazz (played nightly), late-night noshing, and people-watching from the patio would be quite content spending an alfresco evening under the heat lamps. (However, the best view of the band is from inside.) Chewy brick-oven pizza, a handful of pastas, zesty tapas, and thick steaks are hot items on the menu, which changes monthly.

504 Broadway (at Kearny St.). © 415/982-6223. www.enricossidewalkcafe.com. Reservations recommended. Main courses $7–$12 lunch, $11–$23 dinner. AE, MC, V. Sun–Thurs 11:30am–11pm; Fri–Sat 11:30am–midnight; bar daily 11:30am–1:30am or earlier depending on patronage. Valet parking (dinner only) $10. Bus: 9X, 12, or 15.

Piperade ★★ WEST COAST BASQUE   This casual spot on the outskirts of North Beach is an exciting recent addition. Chef Gerald Hirigoyen, once chef/partner at longtime favorite Fringale, goes it alone in the comfy room with a wood beam–lined ceiling, oak floors, and soft sconce lighting. The large plates are best shared. My personal favorites are crabmeat coddled in a paper-thin crepe accompanied by a sweet and sassy mango-and-red-pepper salsa; a bright and simple salad of giant white beans, egg, chives and marinated anchovies; and braised seafood and shellfish stew with a sweet and savory red-pepper sauce. Do yourself a favor: Save room for orange blossom beignets. Light and airy with a delicate and moist web of dough within and a kiss of orange essence, it's dessert at its finest. *Note:* The wine list has a lovely and appropriately paired by-the-glass and bottle selection, and there's a community table for drop-in diners.

1015 Battery St. (at Green St.). (€ 415/391-2555. www.piperade.com. Reservations recommended. Main courses $15–$18. AE, DC, DISC, MC, V. Mon–Fri 11:30am–3pm; Mon–Sat 5:30–10:30pm. Bus: 10, 12, 30, or 82x.

INEXPENSIVE

L'Osteria del Forno ★★ ITALIAN L'Osteria del Forno might be only slightly larger than a walk-in closet, but it's one of the top authentic Italian restaurants in North Beach. Peer in the window facing Columbus Avenue and you'll see two Italian women with their hair up, sweating from the heat of the brick-lined oven, which cranks out the best focaccia (and focaccia sandwiches) in the city. There's no pomp or circumstance: Locals come here strictly to eat. The menu features a variety of pizzas, salads, soups, and fresh pastas, plus a selection of daily specials (pray for the roast pork braised in milk), which includes a roast of the day, pasta, and ravioli. Small baskets of focaccia keep you going until the arrival of the entrees, which should always be accompanied by a glass of Italian red. Good news for folks on the go: You can get pizza by the slice.

519 Columbus Ave. (between Green and Union sts.). (€ 415/982-1124. Reservations not accepted. Sandwiches $5.50–$6.50; pizzas $10–$14; main courses $6–$11. No credit cards. Sun, Mon, and Wed–Thurs 11:30am–10pm; Fri–Sat 11:30am–10:30pm. Bus: 15 or 41.

Mario's Bohemian Cigar Store ★ *Finds* ITALIAN Across the street from Washington Square is one of North Beach's most popular neighborhood hangouts. The century-old bar—small, well worn, and always busy—is best known for its focaccia sandwiches, including meatball and eggplant. Wash it all down with an excellent cappuccino or a house Campari as you watch the tourists stroll by. And no, they do not sell cigars.

566 Columbus Ave. (at Union St.). (€ 415/362-0536. Sandwiches $6.75–$7.25. MC, V. Daily 10am–11pm. Closed Dec 24–Jan 1. Bus: 15, 30, 41, or 45.

Pasta Pomodoro ★★ *Kids* *Value* ITALIAN If you're looking for a good, cheap meal in North Beach—or anywhere else in town, for that matter—this San Francisco chain can't be beat. There's usually a 20-minute wait for a table, but after you're seated, you'll be surprised at how promptly you're served. Every dish is fresh and sizable, and best of all, they cost a third of what you'll pay elsewhere. Winners include the spaghetti *frutti di mare* made with calamari, mussels, scallops, tomato, garlic, and wine, or *cavatappi pollo* with roast chicken, sun-dried tomatoes, cream, mushrooms, and Parmesan—both are under $7.

655 Union St. (at Columbus Ave.). (€ 415/399-0300. www.pastapomodoro.com. Reservations not accepted. Main courses $6–$11. AE, MC, V. Sun–Thurs 11am–10:30pm; Fri–Sat 11am–11pm. Cable car: Powell-Mason line. Bus: 15, 30, 41, or 45. There are 7 other locations, including 2304 Market St., at 16th St. ((€ 415/558-8123); 3611 California St. ((€ 415/831-0900); and 816 Irving St., between 9th and 10th sts. ((€ 415/566-0900).

Tommaso's 👧👧 *Kids* ITALIAN   From the street, Tommaso's looks unappealing—a drab brown facade sandwiched between sex shops. Then why are people always waiting to get in? Because everyone knows Tommaso's has been packing them in since 1935. The center of attention in the dining room is the chef, who continuously tosses huge hunks of garlic and mozzarella onto pizzas before sliding them into the brick oven. Nineteen toppings make pizza the dish of choice, even though Italian classics such as veal Marsala, chicken cacciatore, lasagna, and calzones are available. Tommaso's also offers half-bottles of house wines, homemade manicotti, and Italian coffee. If you can overlook the seedy surroundings, this fun, boisterous restaurant is a great place to take the family.

1042 Kearny St. (at Broadway). © 415/398-9696. www.tommasosnorthbeach.com. Reservations not accepted. Pasta and pizza $14–$24; main courses $11–$18. AE, DC, DISC, MC, V. Tues–Sat 5–10:30pm; Sun 4–9:30pm. Closed Dec 15–Jan 15. Bus: 15 or 41.

FISHERMAN'S WHARF
EXPENSIVE

Restaurant Gary Danko 👧👧👧 *Finds* MODERN CLASSIC   Gary Danko, who received the James Beard Foundation award for best chef in California and made San Francisco's Ritz-Carlton Dining Room the top dining destination from 1991 to 1996, still ranks as my favorite fancy dining experience. Within the romantic yet unfussy wood, split-dining room, thoughtfulness is woven into the experience. The three- to five-course fixed-price menu is freestyle, so whether you want a sampling of appetizers or a flight of meat courses, you need only ask. Top picks? Glazed oysters, which were as creamy as the light accompanying sauce graced with leeks and intricately carved "zucchini pearls"; seared foie gras with peaches, caramelized onions, and *verjus* sauce; and adventurous Moroccan spiced squab with *chermoula* (a thick, spicy sauce) and orange-cumin carrots. Diners at the bar have the option of ordering a la carte, and everyone has access to the stellar, but expensive, wine list. If after dinner you have the will to pass on the cheese cart or caramel-almond peaches with buttermilk ice cream prepared tableside, a plate of petit fours reminds you that Gary Danko is one sweet and memorable meal.

800 N. Point St. (at Hyde St.). © 415/749-2060. www.garydanko.com. Reservations required. 3- to 5-course fixed-price menu $55–$78. AE, DC, MC, V. Sun–Wed 5:30–9:30pm; Thurs–Sat 5:30–10pm. Valet parking $10. Cable car: Hyde. Bus: 10. Metro: F.

Scoma's 👧 SEAFOOD   A throwback to the dining of yesteryear, Scoma's eschews trendier trout preparations and fancy digs for old-fashioned seafood served in huge portions amidst a casual waterfront setting. Gourmands should skip this one. But if your idea of heaven is straightforward seafaring classics like fried calamari, raw oysters, pesto pasta with rock shrimp, and lobster thermidor served with old-time hospitality, this is as good as tourist restaurants get. Unfortunately, a taste of tradition will cost you. Prices are as steep as some of the finest restaurants in town. I'd rather splurge at Gary Danko or Masa's. But many of my guests from out of town insist we meet at Scoma's, which is fine by me since it's a change of pace from today's chic spots and the parking is free.

Pier 47. (between Jefferson and Jones sts.). © 415/771-4383. www.scomas.com. Reservations recommended. Most main courses $18–$38. AE, MC, V. Sun–Thurs noon–10pm; Fri–Sat 11:30am–10:30pm; hours change seasonally so call to confirm. Valet parking free. Streetcar: F. Bus: 10 or 47.

MODERATE
Ana Mandara 👧👧 VIETNAMESE   Don Johnson is part owner, but the real star is the Vietnamese food in a beautiful setting. Amid a shuttered room with

mood lighting, palm trees, and Vietnamese-inspired decor, diners (mostly tourists) splurge on spring rolls; Dungeness crab with lemon sauce; Chilean sea bass, lovingly wrapped and steamed in banana leaf with shiitake mushrooms and miso sauce; lobster with sweet-and-sour sauce and black sticky rice; and wok-charred tournedos of beef tenderloin with sweet onions and peppercress.

891 Beach St. (at Polk St.). ℂ 415/771-6800. www.anamandara.com. Reservations recommended. Main courses $17–$29. AE, DISC, MC, V. Mon–Fri 11:30am–2pm; Sun–Thurs 5:30–9:30pm; Fri–Sat 5:30–10:30pm. Valet parking Tues–Sun $9. Bus: 19 or 32. Metro: F.

INEXPENSIVE

Frjtz Fries 𝕲 BELGIAN-CALIFORNIA   Deep-fried offerings are as abundant as sea lions in the Fisherman's Wharf area, but thankfully this funky-artsy "Belgian fries, crepes, and DJ/Art teahouse" features killer, fat french fries with a barrage of exotic dipping sauces that are head and flippers above the rest. Grab a bag of the addictively crisp and thick fried potatoes—perhaps with chipotle rémoulade or balsamic mayo—or swerve toward less lardy options such as a sweet or savory crepe, which range from Nutella, banana, and whipped cream to grilled rosemary chicken and Swiss cheese. Or choose a leafy salad or a focaccia sandwich packed with roasted peppers, red onions, pesto mayo, grilled eggplant, and melted Gorgonzola. Wash it down with Belgian ale. A second, equally groovy location is in Hayes Valley at 579 Hayes St., at Laguna Street (ℂ **415/ 864-7654**).

Ghirardelli Sq., 900 N. Point St. (between Larkin and Polk sts). ℂ **415/928-3886**. www.frjtzfries.com. No reservations. Fries $3–$4.50; crepes $4.25–$7.50; sandwiches $5.95–$7.25. AE, MC, V. Sun–Thurs 10am–6pm; Fri–Sat 10am–7pm; open later during summer so call for hours.

MARINA DISTRICT, COW HOLLOW & PACIFIC HEIGHTS
EXPENSIVE

Quince 𝕲𝕲 CALIFORNIA-ITALIAN   Its discreet location in a quiet residential neighborhood hasn't stopped this tiny and predominantly white restaurant from becoming one of the city's hottest reservations since it opened in late 2003. Since there are only 15 tables, diners are clamoring for seats in order to savor the pristine nightly-changing Italian-inspired menu by Michael Tusk, who mastered the art of pasta while working at the East Bay's famed Chez Panisse and Oliveto restaurants. Regardless, it's worth the effort—especially if you love simple food that honors a few high-quality ingredients. Dining divinity might start with a pillowy spring garlic soufflé or white asparagus with a lightly fried egg and brown butter, but it really hits heavenly notes with the pasta course, be it *garganelli* with English peas and prosciutto, tagliatelle with veal ragu and fava beans, or artichoke ravioli. Meat selections don't fall short either, with delicately prepared mixed grill plates, tender Alaskan halibut with fava beans, and juicy lamb with fennel and olives. Desserts, though tasty, aren't as celestial, which is just fine since it may leave room for an extra pasta course.

1701 Octavia St. (at Bush St.). ℂ **415/775-8500**. www.quincerestaurant.com. Reservations necessary. Main courses $16–$27. AE, MC, V. Thurs–Sun 5:30–10pm; Fri–Sat 5:30–10:30pm. Valet parking $8. Bus: 1, 31, or 38.

MODERATE

A16 𝕲𝕲 ITALIAN   This sleek spot featuring Neapolitan-style pizza and cuisine from the Campania region has been so hot since its 2004 opening that on my first visit tables were filled with chefs and critics. Even without the fanfare, it feels exciting to be at A16, which is named after the motorway that traverses the region. The divided space boasts a full bar up front, a larger dining area and open kitchen in the back, and a wall of wines in between. But its secret weapon is chef Christophe Hille, who whips up outstanding appetizers, pizza, and entrees. Even if you must have the insanely good braised pork breast with olives, herbs, and caramelized chestnuts to yourself, start by sharing dried fava beans with fennel salad and tuna *conserva* with braised dandelion greens and crunchy bread crumbs. Shortly after opening, a few items were ho-hum (ricotta and chard *involtini*, desserts). But even with its shortcomings, the restaurant still fell under the "great" category—especially factoring in Shelley Lindgren, who guides diners through the exciting wine list featuring 40 wines by the half-glass, glass, and carafe.

2355 Chestnut St. (between Divisadero and Scott sts.). © 415/771-2216. www.a16sf.com. Reservations recommended. Main courses lunch $8–$10, dinner $14–$19. Wed–Fri 11:30am–2:30pm; Sun–Thurs 5–10pm; Fri–Sat 5–11pm. Bus: 30 or 30X.

Ella's 🌟🌟 *Kids* AMERICAN/BREAKFAST   Although this homey restaurant serves (quiet) dinners on weeknights, it's known throughout town as the king of breakfasts. Unfortunately, its acclaim means you're likely to wait up to an hour on weekends. But midweek and in the wee hours, it's possible to slide into a counter or table seat in the colorful dining room and lose yourself in outstanding, generous servings of chicken hash, crisped to perfection and served with eggs any way you like them, with fluffy buttermilk biscuits. Pancakes, omelets, and the short list of other essentials are equally revered. Service can be slow, but at least the busboys are quick to fill coffee cups. Come lunchtime and the far more mellow dinner, solid entrees like salads or grilled salmon with mashed potatoes remind you what's great about good old American cooking.

500 Presidio Ave. (at California St.). © 415/441-5669. www.ellassanfrancisco.com. Reservations accepted for lunch. Main courses $5.50–$11 breakfast, $6–$12 lunch. AE, MC, V. Mon–Fri 7am–4pm; Sat–Sun 8:30am–2pm. Bus: 1, 5, or 43.

Florio 🌟🌟 FRENCH/ITALIAN BISTRO   When I'm in the mood for a good meal without hoopla, I head to bistrolike Florio. It's not only because the staff is friendly, or because if it's booked, I can always eat at the bar, or because the place is small enough that I don't feel like I'm being rushed in and out. The real reason is because I'm addicted to the shrimp-and-white-bean salad, steak *frites*, and virtually every other little comfort dish that makes its way to the table. The wines by the glass (and by the bottle) always disappoint, but I don't care. I pull up a chair, make myself at home, and enjoy casual and cozy surroundings and consistently satisfying food. I suggest you do the same.

1915 Fillmore St. (between Pine and Bush sts.). © 415/775-4300. www.floriosf.com. Reservations accepted. Most main courses $13–$28. AE, MC, V. Sun–Wed 5:30–10pm; Thurs–Sat 5:30–11pm. Bus: 3, 22, 41, or 45.

Greens Restaurant 🌟🌟 *Finds* VEGETARIAN   Knowledgeable locals swear by Greens, where executive chef Annie Somerville (author of *Fields of Greens*) cooks with the seasons, using produce from Green Gulch Farm and other local organic farms. In an old warehouse, with enormous windows overlooking the bridge and the bay, the restaurant is both a pioneer and a legend. A weeknight dinner might start with such appetizers as mushroom faro soup with asiago cheese and tarragon or grilled-portobello-and-endive salad. Entrees run the gamut from pizza with wilted escarole, red onions, lemon, asiago, and Parmesan to Vietnamese yellow curry or risotto with black trumpet mushrooms, leeks, savory spinach, white truffle oil, Parmesan Reggiano, and thyme. A four-course dinner is served on Saturday. Adjacent to the restaurant, **Greens to Go** bakery sells homemade breads, sandwiches, soups, salads, and pastries, and is a great place to stop and grab a bite if you're wandering the Marina waterfront.

Building A, Fort Mason Center (enter Fort Mason opposite the Safeway at Buchanan and Marina sts.). 📞 415/771-6222. Reservations recommended. Main courses $9.50–$14 lunch, $15–$20 dinner; fixed-price dinner $46; Sun brunch $8–$14. DISC, MC, V. Tues–Sat noon–4pm; Sun 10:30am–2pm; Mon–Fri 5:30–9:30pm; Sat 5:30–9pm. Greens to Go Mon–Thurs 8am–8pm; Fri–Sat 8am–5pm; Sun 9am–4pm. Free parking. Bus: 28 or 30.

Isa ★★ FRENCH TAPAS   Luke Sung has captured many locals' hearts by creating the kind of menu that foodies dream of: a smattering of small dishes that allow you to try numerous items in one sitting. It's a good thing the menu, considered "French tapas," offers snack sizes at reasonable prices. It's a lot to ask a diner to choose between sweetbreads and mushroom ragout, seared foie gras with caramelized apples, potato-wrapped sea bass in brown butter, and rack of lamb. But here a table for two could choose all of them and one or two more and not need to be rolled out the door afterward. Adding to the allure is the warm boutique dining environment—60 seats scattered amidst a very small dining room in the front and a tented, heated patio out back that sets the mood with a warm yellow glow. Cocktailers, drink elsewhere: Isa serves beer and wine only.

3324 Steiner St. (between Lombard and Chestnut). 📞 415/567-9588. Reservations recommended. Main courses $9–$16, MC, V. Mon–Thurs 5:30–10pm; Fri–Sat 5:30–10:30pm. Bus: 22, 28, 30, 30X, 43, or 76.

INEXPENSIVE

Andale Taquería ★★ (Kids) (Value) MEXICAN   Andale (Spanish for "hurry up") offers incredible high-end fast food for the health-conscious and the plain hungry in an attractive and casual setting. Lard, preservatives, or canned items are eschewed for salad dressings made with virgin olive oil; vegetarian beans (not refried); skinless chicken; salsas and *aguas frescas* (fruit drinks) made from fresh fruits and veggies; and mesquite-grilled meats. Add the location (on a sunny shopping stretch), sophisticated decor, full bar, and check-me-out patio seating (with corner fireplace), and it's no wonder the fitness-fanatic Marina District considers this place home. Cafeteria-style service keeps prices low.

2150 Chestnut St. (between Steiner and Pierce sts.). 📞 415/749-0506. Reservations not accepted. Most dishes $5.25–$9.50. MC, V. Mon 11am–9pm; Tues–Thurs and Sun 11am–10pm; Fri–Sat 11am–10:30pm. Bus: 22, 28, 30, 30X, 43, 76, or 82X.

Chez Nous ★★ FRENCH   Diners are crammed into the 45-seat dining area of this cheery small dining room, but the French tapas are so delicious and affordable, no one seems to care. Indeed, this friendly, fast-paced neighborhood haunt has become a blueprint for other restaurants that understand the allure of small plates. But Chez Nous stands out as more than a petite-portion trendsetter. Most of its Mediterranean dishes taste so clean and fresh you can't wait to come back again. Start with the soup, whatever it is; don't skip tasty french fries with harissa aioli; savor the lamb chops with lavender sea salt; and save room for their famed dessert, the mini custard cake–like *canneles de Bordeaux*.

1911 Fillmore St. (between Pine and Bush sts.). 📞 415/441-8044. Reservations recommended. Main courses $3.50–$12. MC, V. Daily 11:30am–3pm and 5:30–10pm (Fri–Sat until 11pm). Bus: 22, 41, or 45.

Eliza's ★★ (Value) CHINESE   Despite the incongruous design of modern architecture, glass art, and color, this packed neighborhood haunt serves some of the freshest, best-tasting California-influenced Chinese in town. Unlike most comparable options, here the atmosphere (albeit unintentionally funky) and presentation parallel the food. The fantastically fresh soups, salads, seafood, pork, chicken, duck, and such specials as spicy eggplant are outstanding and served on beautiful Italian plates. (Get the sea bass with black-bean sauce and go straight to heaven!) I often come at midday and order the Kung Pao chicken lunch special: a mixture of tender chicken, peanuts, chile peppers, subtly hot sauce, and perfectly crunchy vegetables. It's 1 of 32 main-course choices that come with rice and soup for around $5. The place is also jumping at night, so prepare to stand in line.

2877 California St. (at Broderick St.). ℂ **415/621-4819.** Reservations not accepted. Main courses $4.95–$5.75 lunch, $6.50–$13 dinner. MC, V ($10 minimum). Mon–Fri 11am–3pm and 5–9:45pm; Sat–Sun 4:30–9:45pm. Bus: 6, 7, 21, 66, or 71.

Mel's Diner 🎇 (Kids) AMERICAN   Sure, it's contrived, touristy, and nowhere near healthy, but when you get that urge for a chocolate shake and banana cream pie at midnight—or when you want to entertain the kids—no other place comes through like Mel's Diner. Modeled after a 1950s diner, down to the jukebox at each table, Mel's harks back to the days when cholesterol and fried foods didn't jab your conscience with every greasy, wonderful bite. Too bad the prices don't reflect the '50s: A burger with fries and a Coke runs about $9.50.

There's another Mel's at 3355 Geary St., at Stanyan Street (ℂ **415/387-2244**); it's open Thursday through Saturday from 6am to 3am.

2165 Lombard St. (at Fillmore St.). ℂ **415/921-3039.** Main courses $4–$6 breakfast, $6–$8 lunch, $8–$12 dinner. MC, V. Sun–Wed 6am–2am; Thurs 6am–3am; Fri–Sat 24 hr. Bus: 22, 30, or 43.

CIVIC CENTER
MODERATE
Hayes Street Grill 🎇🎇 SEAFOOD   For well over a decade, this small, no-nonsense seafood restaurant (owned and operated by revered food writer and chef Patricia Unterman) has maintained a solid reputation among San Francisco's epicureans for its fresh and straightforwardly prepared fish. Choices ranging from Hawaiian swordfish to Puget Sound salmon—cooked to perfection—are matched with your sauce of choice (Szechuan peanut, tomatillo salsa, or shallot butter) and a side of their signature french fries. Fancier seafood specials are available, too, such as paella with clams, mussels, scallops, calamari, chorizo, and saffron rice, as well as an impressive selection of garden-fresh salads and local grilled meats. Finish with the outstanding crème brûlée.

320 Hayes St. (near Franklin St.). ℂ **415/863-5545.** Reservations recommended. Main courses $14–$20 lunch, $16–$23 dinner. AE, DC, DISC, MC, V. Mon–Fri 11:30am–2pm; Mon–Thurs 5–9:30pm; Fri 5–10:30pm; Sat 5:30–10:30pm; Sun 5–8:30pm. Bus: 19, 21, 31, or 38.

Zuni Café 🎇🎇🎇 (Finds) MEDITERRANEAN   Delicious, trendsetting Zuni Café is and probably always will be a local favorite. Its expanse of windows and lower Castro location guarantee good people-watching, but even better is the action within: 30- and 40-somethings crowding in for the flavors of chef Judy Rodgers's satisfying Mediterranean-influenced menu. For the full effect, stand at the copper-topped bar and order a glass of wine and a few oysters from the oyster menu. (A dozen or so varieties are on hand.) Then take a seat amidst the exposed-brick, two-level maze of little dining rooms. Although the changing menu always includes meat (such as New York steak with Belgian endive gratin) and fish (grilled or braised in the kitchen's brick oven), the proven winners are Rodgers's brick oven–roasted chicken for two with Tuscan-style bread salad, the polenta with mascarpone, and the hamburger on grilled rosemary focaccia bread.

1658 Market St. (at Franklin St.). ℂ **415/552-2522.** Reservations recommended. Main courses $10–$19 lunch, $15–$29 dinner. AE, MC, V. Tues–Sat 11:30am–midnight; Sun 11am–11pm. Valet parking $8. Streetcar: All Market St. streetcars. Bus: 6, 7, 71, or 75.

HAIGHT-ASHBURY
MODERATE
RNM ✿✿ AMERICAN   Lower Haight is not known for glamour, and that's just what makes this swank restaurant such a nice surprise. Beyond the full-length silver mesh curtain is a glitzy diversion that looks like it belongs in New York City rather than this funky 'hood. Warmly lit with dark-wood floors and tables, a full bar, and a lounge mezzanine, it's the perfect setting for the equally appealing Italian- and French-inspired American tapas-style menu by chef Justine Miner, who sharpened her culinary skills and knives at San Francisco's Postrio, Café Kati, and Globe. Anticipate appetizers such as ahi tuna tartare with waffle chips, quail egg, and microgreens; and caramelized-onion-and-wild-mushroom pizza with Fontina cheese and truffle oil. Entrees include porcini-crusted day-boat scallops on a purée of artichokes with shiitake-mushroom ragout and a salad of mache greens and watermelon radishes with Meyer lemon vinaigrette; and pan roasted rib-eye steak with pancetta-wrapped red Irish potatoes, wild nettles, Oakville ranch cabernet butter, and shaved black Himalayan truffles.

598 Haight St. (at Steiner St.). ✆ 415/551-7900. www.rnmrestaurant.com. Reservations recommended. Small plates and pizza $7–$14; Main courses $12–$22. MC, V. Tues–Wed 5–10pm; Thurs–Sat 5–11pm. Closed Sun–Mon. Bus: 7 or 22.

INEXPENSIVE
Cha Cha Cha ✿✿ Value CARIBBEAN   Put your name on the mile-long list, crowd into the tiny bar, and drink sangria while you wait. When you finally get seated (generally about an hour later), you'll dine in a loud—and I mean *loud*—dining room with Santería altars, banana trees, and plastic tablecloths. Do as I do and order from the tapas menu, sharing such dishes like some of the city's best fried calamari, fried new potatoes, Cajun shrimp, and mussels in saffron broth, all of which are accompanied by luscious sauces. This is the kind of place where you can take friends in a partying mood, let your hair down, and make an evening of it. If you want the flavor without the festivities, come during lunch.

A second, larger location is open in the Mission at 2327 Mission St., between 19th and 20th streets (✆ 415/648-0504).

1801 Haight St. (at Shrader St.). ✆ 415/386-7670. Reservations not accepted. Tapas $5–$9; main courses $13–$15. MC, V. Daily 11am–4pm; Sun–Thurs 5–11pm; Fri–Sat 5–11:30pm. Streetcar: N. Bus: 6, 7, 66, 71, or 73.

Thep Phanom ✿✿ THAI   By successfully incorporating flavors from India, China, Burma, Malaysia, and the West, Thep Phanom has risen through the ranks to become one of the best Thai restaurants in San Francisco. (The line out the front door proves it's no secret.) Start with the signature dish, *ped swan*—boneless duck in a honey sauce served on a bed of spinach. *Larb ped* (minced duck salad), velvety basil-spiked seafood curry served on banana leaves, and spicy *yum plamuk* (calamari salad) are also recommended. The Haight location attracts an eclectic crowd; the atmosphere is informal, and the decor quite tasteful.

400 Waller St. (at Fillmore St.). ✆ 415/431-2526. Reservations recommended. Main courses $7–$12. AE, DC, DISC, MC, V. Daily 5:30–10:30pm. Bus: 6, 7, 22, 66, or 71.

RICHMOND & SUNSET DISTRICTS
MODERATE
Aziza ✿✿ MOROCCAN   If you're looking for something really different—or a festive spot for a large party—head deep into the Avenues for an exotic taste

of Morocco. Chef-owner Mourad Lahlou creates an excellent dining experience through colorful, distinctly Moroccan surroundings and his modern, but still authentic, take on the food of his homeland. In any of the three opulently adorned dining rooms, you might glimpse belly dancers gyrating (Thurs–Sun) as you indulge in the affordable five-course tasting menu ($39) or individual treats such as saffron Cornish hen with preserved lemon and olives, or lavender honey-braised squab. Finish off with the rhubarb galette with rose- and geranium-scented crème frâiche, vanilla aspic, and rhubarb consommé.

5800 Geary Blvd. (at 22nd Ave.). © 415/752-2222. www.aziza-sf.com. Reservations accepted. Main courses $11–$20; 5-course menu $39. AE, MC, V. Wed–Mon 5:30–10:30pm. Valet parking: $8 weekdays, $10 weekends. Bus: 29 or 38.

Kabuto A&S 🦀🦀 JAPANESE/SUSHI   In a town overflowing with seafood and pretentious taste buds, you'd think it would be easier to find great sushi. But the truth is, finding an outstanding sushi restaurant in San Francisco is more challenging than spotting a parking space in Nob Hill. Still, chop-sticking these fish-and-rice delicacies is one of the most joyous and adventurous ways to dine, and Kabuto, which moved across the street from its original location in 2003, is one of the best (and most expensive) places to do it. Chef Sachio Kojima, who presides over the small, crowded sushi bar, constructs each dish with smooth, lightning-fast movements known only to master chefs. If you're big on wasabi, ask for the stronger stuff Kojima serves on request.

5121 Geary Blvd. (at 16th Ave.). © 415/752-5652. Reservations not accepted. Sushi $3–$10; main courses $11–$18. MC, V. Thurs–Sat and Mon–Tues 11:30am–2:30pm and 5:30–11pm; Sun 11:30am–2:30pm and 5:30–10pm. Bus: 2, 28, or 38.

Straits Café 🦀 SINGAPOREAN   Straits Café is what I like to call "adventure dining" because you never know quite what you're going to get. Burlap palm trees, pastel-painted *trompe l'oeil* houses, faux balconies, and clotheslines strung across the walls evoke a surreal image of a Singaporean village. The cuisine, however, is the real thing. Among chef Chris Yeo's spicy Malaysian-Indian-Chinese offerings are *murtabak* (stuffed Indian bread), chile crab, basil chicken, *nonya daging rendang* (beef simmered in lime leaves), *ikan pangang* (fish stuffed with chile paste), and, hottest of all, *sambal udang* (prawns sautéed in chile-shallot sambal sauce). For dessert, try the sago pudding.

3300 Geary Blvd. (at Parker St.). © 415/668-1783. Reservations recommended. Main courses $14–$22. AE, DC, MC, V. Mon–Thurs noon–2:30pm and 5:30–10pm; Fri–Sat noon–11pm; Sun noon–10pm. Bus: 2, 3, 4, or 38.

INEXPENSIVE

Ton Kiang 🦀🦀 *Kids* *Finds* CHINESE/DIM SUM   Ton Kiang is the number-one place in the city to do dim sum. Wait in line (which is out the door anytime between 11am and 1:30pm), get a table on the first or second floor, and say yes to dozens of delicacies, which are brought to the table for your approval. From stuffed crab claws, roast Peking duck, and a gazillion dumplings (including scallop and vegetable, shrimp, and beef) to the delicious and hard-to-find *doa miu* (snow pea sprouts flash-sautéed with garlic and peanut oil), shark-fin soup, and mango pudding, every tray of morsels coming from the kitchen is a delight. Though it's hard to get past the dim sum, which is served all day every day, the full menu of Hakka cuisine is worth investigation as well. This is definitely one of my favorite places to do lunch, and it happens to have an unusually friendly staff.

5821 Geary Blvd. (between 22nd and 23rd aves.). © 415/387-8273. www.tonkiang.net. Reservations accepted for parties of 8 or more. Dim sum $2–$5.50; main courses $9–$13. AE, MC, V. Daily 10am–10pm. Bus: 38.

THE CASTRO
MODERATE

Mecca 👁👁 *Finds* AMERICAN   Mecca is the kind of industrial-chic supper club that makes you want to order a martini just so you'll match the ambience. A decadent swirl of chocolate-brown velvet, stainless steel, cement, and brown Naugahyde, it's a chic spot where the DJ spins hot grooves, and a fine American meal is served at tables tucked into several dining nooks. Menu options include such classic starters as Osetra caviar, oysters on the half shell, and Caesar salad. Main courses range from seared ahi tuna to wood oven–roasted pork tenderloin. The food is good, but it's that only-in–San Francisco vibe that makes this place smokin' hot in the Castro.

2029 Market St. (by 14th and Church sts.). ✆ **415/621-7000.** www.sfmecca.com. Reservations recommended. Main courses $15–$29. AE, DC, MC, V. Tues–Thurs 5:30–10pm; Fri–Sat 6–11:30pm, bar remains open later; Sun 5–9:30pm. Valet parking $10. Streetcar: F, K, L, or M. Bus: 8, 22, 24, or 37.

INEXPENSIVE

Chow 👁👁 *Value* AMERICAN   Chow claims to serve American cuisine, but the management must be thinking of today's America, because the menu is not exactly meatloaf and apple pie. And that's just fine for eclectic and cost-conscious diners. After all, what's not to like about starting with a Cobb salad before moving on to Thai-style noodles with steak, chicken, peanuts, and spicy lime-chile garlic broth, or linguine with clams? Better yet, everything except the fish of the day costs under $15. More traditional are the daily sandwich specials, which come with salad, soup, or fries. While the food and prices alone would be a good argument for coming here, beer on tap, a great inexpensive wine selection, and the fun, tavernlike environment clinch the deal. A second location, **Park Chow,** is at 1240 Ninth Ave. (✆ **415/665-9912**). You can't make reservations unless you've got a party of eight or more, but if you're headed their way, you can call ahead to place your name on the wait list (recommended).

215 Church St. (near Market St.). ✆ **415/552-2469.** Reservations not accepted. Main courses $7–$15. MC, V. Sun–Thurs 11am–11pm; Fri–Sat 11am–midnight. Streetcar: F, J, K, L, or M. Bus: 8 or 37.

MISSION DISTRICT
MODERATE

Delfina 👁👁 *Finds* SEASONAL ITALIAN   Delfina eschews bells, whistles, big-time design, and fancy preparations for something that used to be utterly San Francisco: chic but straightforward simplicity and a small-business feel. Unpretentious atmosphere, reasonable prices, and chef and co-owner Craig Stoll's ultrafresh seasonal Italian cuisine mean you're in for a price-painless and delicious experience from the minute you're seated by Craig's wife, Ann Spencer, to the time you receive your surprisingly low (by local standards) bill. Winter might welcome slow-roasted pork shoulder or gnocchi with squash and chestnuts, while spring could bring sand dabs with frisée, fingerling potatoes and lemon-caper butter, or lamb with polenta and sweet peas. Trust me: Order the buttermilk *panna cotta*. The only downside: It's impossible to find parking—literally—and there's no valet, so cab it or face the consequences.

3621 18th St. (between Dolores and Guererro sts.). ✆ **415/552-4055.** Reservations recommended. Main courses $13–$22. MC, V. Sun–Thurs 5:30–10pm; Fri–Sat 5:30–11pm. Streetcar: J. Bus: 26 or 33.

INEXPENSIVE

Taquería La Cumbre 👁👁 MEXICAN   While most restaurants gussy up their goods with high-priced decor and gimmicks, La Cumbre's celebrity is the burrito. Craftily constructed with fresh pork, steak, chicken, or vegetables, plus cheese, beans, rice, salsa, and maybe a dash of guacamole or sour cream, there is hardly a better cheap meal. That it's served in a cafeteria-like brick-lined room with shellacked tables and chairs is all the better: There's no mistaking the attraction here.

515 Valencia St. (between 16th and 17th sts.). © 415/863-8205. Reservations not accepted. Tacos and burritos $3.50–$6.50; dinner plates $5–$7. No credit cards. Mon–Sat 11am–9pm; Sun noon–9pm. Bus: 14, 22, 33, 49, or 53. BART: Mission.

5 The Top Attractions
TOP SAN FRANCISCO SIGHTS

Alcatraz Island ✪✪✪   Visible from Fisherman's Wharf, Alcatraz (aka "The Rock") has seen a checkered history. Juan Manuel Ayala, who named it after the pelicans that nested on the island, discovered it in 1775. From the 1850s to 1933, when the army vacated the island, it served as a military post protecting the bay shoreline. In 1934 the buildings were converted into a maximum-security prison. Given the sheer cliffs, treacherous currents, and frigid temperatures of the waters, it was believed to be an escape-proof prison. Among the gangsters who were penned in cell blocks A through D were Al Capone; Robert Stroud, the so-called Birdman of Alcatraz (because he was an expert in ornithological diseases); Machine Gun Kelly; and Alvin Karpis. It cost a fortune to keep them imprisoned here because all supplies, including water, had to be shipped in. In 1963, after an apparent escape in which no bodies were recovered, the government closed the prison. In 1969 a group of American Indians chartered a boat to the island to symbolically reclaim it for the Indian people. They occupied the island until 1971, and in 1972 the Rock became part of the Golden Gate National Recreation Area. The wildlife driven away during the military and prison years has begun to return—the black-crested night heron and other seabirds nest here again—and a trail has been built that passes through the island's nature areas. Tours, including an audio tour of the prison block and a slide show, are given by the park's rangers, who entertain their guests with interesting anecdotes.

It's a ridiculously popular excursion and space is limited, so purchase tickets as far in advance as possible. The tour is operated by **Blue & Gold Fleet** (© **415/705-5555;** www.blueandgoldfleet.com) and can be charged to American Express, MasterCard, or Visa ($2.25 per ticket service charge on phone orders). You can also buy tickets in advance from the Blue & Gold ticket office on Pier 41 or online at www.telesales.com. Wear comfortable shoes and take a heavy sweater or windbreaker—even when the sun's out, it's cold. The National Park Service also notes that there are a lot of steps to climb on the tour.

Pier 41, near Fisherman's Wharf. © 415/773-1188 (info only). Admission (includes ferry trip and audio tour) $16 adults with headset, $12 without; $15 seniors 62 and older with headset, $9.75 without; $11 children 5–11 with headset, $8.25 without. Winter daily 9:30am–2:15pm; summer daily 9:30am–4:15pm. Ferries depart 15 and 45 min. after the hour. Arrive at least 20 min. before sailing time.

Cable Cars ✪✪✪   Designated historic landmarks by the National Park Service in 1964, the beloved cable cars clank across the hills like mobile museum pieces. Each weighs about 6 tons and is hauled by a cable under the street in a center rail. They move at a constant 9½ mph—never more, never less. This may strike you as slow, but it doesn't feel that way when you're cresting an almost perpendicular hill and looking down at what seems like a bobsled dive into the ocean. But in spite of the thrills, they're perfectly safe.

Powell-Hyde and Powell-Mason lines begin at the base of Powell and Market sts.; California St. line begins at the foot of Market St. $3 per ride.

Coit Tower ★★   In a city known for its panoramic views and vantage points, Coit Tower is "The Peak." If it's a clear day, it's wonderful to get here by walking up the Filbert Steps (avoiding a traffic nightmare), and then taking in the panoramic views of the city and bay at the base of the tower. (In fact, I'd recommend not paying the admission to go to the top; the view is just as good from the parking area and you can see the murals for free.) Completed in 1933, the tower is the legacy of Lillie Hitchcock Coit, a wealthy eccentric who left San Francisco a $125,000 bequest. Inside the base of the tower are the WPA murals titled *Life in California, 1934,* completed during the New Deal by more than 25 artists, many of whom had studied under master muralist Diego Rivera.

Telegraph Hill. ✆ 415/362-0808. www.coittower.org. Admission to the top $3.75 adults, $2.50 seniors, $1.50 children 6–12. Daily 10am–6pm. Bus: 39 ("Coit").

Ferry Building Marketplace and Farmers' Market ★★ *Finds*   There's no better way to enjoy a San Francisco morning than strolling this gourmet marketplace in the Ferry Building and snacking your way through breakfast or lunch. Tasty tenants, open daily, include many of the best of Northern California's gourmet bounty: Cowgirl Creamery's Artisan Cheese Shop, Recchiuti Confections (amazing!), Scharffen Berger Chocolate, Acme breads, the Wine Country's gourmet diner Taylor's Refresher, famed Vietnamese restaurant The Slanted Door, and myriad other restaurants, eateries, and wine bars.

An added bonus and San Francisco favorite is the Farmers' Market, which is open alfresco on Saturday from 8am to 2pm and Tuesday and Thursday from 10am to 2pm. Drop by to peruse stands hawking the finest Northern California fruit, vegetable, bread, dairy, and flower vendors, and ready-made snacks by a few local restaurants. Visit on Sunday from 8am to 2pm for the gardeners market, which focuses on plants but also has a bit of produce. Even when the market's closed, the glistening Ferry Building is now a worthy stop.

Embarcadero, at Market St. ✆ 415/291-3276. Sat 8am–2pm; Tues, Thurs, and Sun 10am–2pm.

Golden Gate Bridge ★★★   With its gracefully swung single span, spidery bracing cables, and sky-high twin towers, the bridge looks more like a work of abstract art than one of the great engineering feats of the 20th century. Construction began in May 1937 and was completed at the then-colossal cost of $35 million. Contrary to pessimistic predictions, the bridge neither collapsed in a gale or earthquake nor proved to be a white elephant. A symbol of hope when the country was afflicted with widespread unemployment, the Golden Gate changed the Bay Area's economic life, encouraging the development of areas north of San Francisco. The mile-long steel link (longer if you factor in the approach), which reaches a height of 746 feet above the water, is an awesome bridge to cross. You can park in the lot at the foot of the bridge on the city side, and then make the crossing by foot. Back in your car, continue to Marin's Vista Point, at the bridge's northern end. Look back and you'll be rewarded with one of the most famous cityscape views in the world. Millions of pedestrians walk across each year. You can walk out onto the span from either end. *Note:* It's usually windy and cold, and the bridge vibrates. Still, walking even a short way is one of the best ways to experience the immense scale of the structure.

Hwy. 101 N. www.goldengatebridge.org. $5 cash toll collected when driving south. Bridge-bound Golden Gate Transit buses (✆ 415/923-2000) depart every 30–60 min. during the day for Marin County, starting from the Transbay Terminal (Mission and First sts.) and stopping at Market and Seventh sts., at the Civic Center, and along Van Ness Ave. and Lombard St.

Top San Francisco Sights

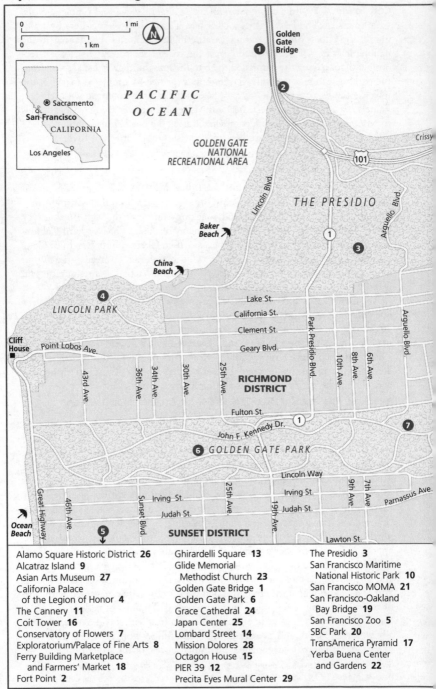

0 — 1 mi
0 — 1 km

PACIFIC OCEAN

San Francisco
CALIFORNIA
⊛ Sacramento
Los Angeles

GOLDEN GATE
NATIONAL
RECREATIONAL AREA

Golden Gate Bridge ❶
❷

Crissy

101

THE PRESIDIO

Baker Beach ↗

China Beach ↗

Lincoln Blvd.

Arguello Blvd.

❶ ❸

Lake St.
California St.
Clement St.
Geary Blvd.

LINCOLN PARK ❹

Cliff House ■

Point Lobos Ave.

43rd Ave.
36th Ave.
34th Ave.
30th Ave.
25th Ave.

RICHMOND DISTRICT

Park Presidio Blvd.

10th Ave.
8th Ave.
6th Ave.

Arguello Blvd.

Fulton St.
John F. Kennedy Dr. ❶

❻ GOLDEN GATE PARK

❼

Lincoln Way

Irving St.
Judah St.
25th Ave.

19th Ave.

Irving St.
Judah St.

9th Ave.
7th Ave.

Parnassus Ave.

Ocean Beach ↗↓

Great Highway

46th Ave.
Sunset Blvd.

SUNSET DISTRICT

Lawton St.

❺

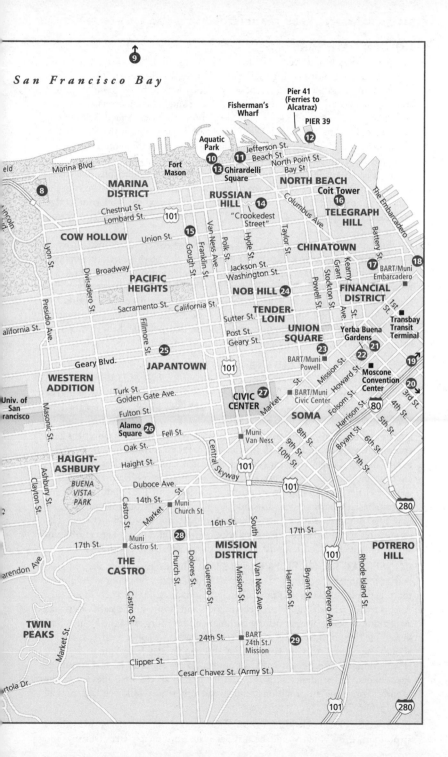

San Francisco Bay

Fisherman's Wharf

Pier 41 (Ferries to Alcatraz)

PIER 39

Aquatic Park

Jefferson St.
Beach St.
North Point St.
Bay St.

Fort Mason

Ghirardelli Square

NORTH BEACH

Coit Tower

Marina Blvd.

MARINA DISTRICT

RUSSIAN HILL

TELEGRAPH HILL

Chestnut St.
Lombard St.

"Crookedest Street"

Columbus Ave.

COW HOLLOW

Union St.

CHINATOWN

BART/Muni Embarcadero

Broadway

Divisadero St.

PACIFIC HEIGHTS

Van Ness Ave.
Franklin St.
Gough St.
Polk St.
Hyde St.

Jackson St.
Washington St.

Taylor St.

Kearny St.
Grant Ave.
Stockton St.
Powell St.

FINANCIAL DISTRICT

Lyon St.

NOB HILL

Battery St.

The Embarcadero

Presidio Ave.

Sacramento St.
California St.

NOB HILL

TENDER-LOIN

Transbay Transit Terminal

alifornia St.

Fillmore St.

Sutter St.
Post St.
Geary St.

UNION SQUARE

Yerba Buena Gardens

1st St.

Geary Blvd.

JAPANTOWN

BART/Muni Powell

Mission St.
Howard St.
Folsom St.
Harrison St.

Moscone Convention Center

3rd St.

WESTERN ADDITION

Turk St.
Golden Gate Ave.

CIVIC CENTER

BART/Muni Civic Center

4th St.
5th St.

Univ. of San Francisco

Masonic Ave.

Fulton St.

Market St.

SOMA

Alamo Square

Fell St.

Bryant St.

6th St.
7th St.

HAIGHT-ASHBURY

Oak St.

Haight St.

Muni Van Ness

Central Skyway

8th St.
9th St.
10th St.

Ashbury St.
Clayton St.

BUENA VISTA PARK

Duboce Ave.

14th St.

Market St.

Muni Church St.

16th St.

South Van Ness Ave.

17th St.

POTRERO HILL

arendon Ave.

17th St.

Muni Castro St.

THE CASTRO

Castro St.

Church St.
Dolores St.
Guerrero St.
Mission St.
Van Ness Ave.
Harrison St.
Bryant St.
Potrero Ave.
Rhode Island St.

MISSION DISTRICT

TWIN PEAKS

Market St.

Castro St.

24th St.

BART 24th St./ Mission

Clipper St.

Cesar Chavez St. (Army St.)

rtola Dr.

GOLDEN GATE PARK

Everybody loves Golden Gate Park: people, dogs, birds, frogs, turtles, bison, trees, bushes, and flowers. Literally everything feels unified here in San Francisco's enormous arboreal front yard, conveniently located between Fulton Street and Lincoln Way with the main entrance at Fell and Stanyan streets.

Totaling 1,017 acres, Golden Gate Park is a magical place. Spend a sunny day stretched out on the grass along JFK Drive, have a good read in the Shakespeare Garden, or stroll around Stow Lake and you will understand the allure. It's an interactive botanical symphony—and everyone is invited to play in the orchestra.

The park is made up of hundreds of gardens and attractions linked by wooded paths and roads. While many sites worth seeing are clearly visible, the park has infinite hidden treasures, so make your first stop the **McLaren Lodge and Park Headquarters** (© 415/831-2700) if you want detailed information on the park.

Of the dozens of gardens in the park, most recognized are the Conservatory of Flowers, Rhododendron Dell, the Rose Garden, the Strybing Arboretum (see below), and, at the western edge, a springtime array of thousands of tulips and daffodils around the Dutch windmill. An incredible, lower-key attraction is AIDS Memorial Grove, a place for reflection near the northeastern side of the park.

In addition to the highlights discussed below, the park contains several recreational facilities: tennis courts; baseball, soccer, and polo fields; a golf course; riding stables; and fly-casting pools. Bus: 16AX, BX, 5, 6, 7, 66, or 71.

OTHER PARK HIGHLIGHTS

BEACH CHALET   First listed on the National Register of Historic places in 1981, the Spanish-Colonial Beach Chalet, 1000 Great Hwy., at the west end of Golden Gate Park near Fulton Street (© 415/386-8439), was designed by Willis Polk in 1925. Built with a 200-seat restaurant upstairs and a public lounge and changing rooms on the first floor, it was a popular stopover for generations of beachgoers. In the 1930s the Works Progress Administration (WPA) commissioned Lucien Labaudt (who also painted Coit Tower's frescoes) to create frescoes, mosaics, and wood carvings of San Francisco life. After decades of use, the chalet grew old and worn, forcing its closure in 1981; but in 1996 the historic Beach Chalet reopened its doors, and through the original mosaics and new literature and displays, it continues to celebrate the city's heritage. The upstairs restaurant is far too modern to wax historical, but it's a great place to stop for a house-made brew and a glimpse of the expansive Pacific.

CONSERVATORY OF FLOWERS (1878)   This striking assemblage of glass and iron, modeled on the glass house at Kew Gardens in London, exhibits a rotating display of plants and shrubs, including an astounding variety of orchids. After years of remodeling, it opened in 2003 and is one of the park's must-see attractions. If you're around during summer and fall, don't miss the Dahlia Garden to the right of the entrance in the center of what was once a carriage roundabout. The conservatory is open Tuesday through Sunday from 9am to 4:30pm, closed Mondays. Admission is $5 for adults; $3 for children 12 to 17 years of age, seniors, and students with ID; and it's free to all the first Tuesday of the month. For more information, visit www.conservatoryofflowers.org or call © 415/666-7001.

JAPANESE TEA GARDEN (1894)   Developed for the 1894 Midwinter Exposition, this garden would be a quiet place with cherry trees, shrubs, and

Golden Gate Park

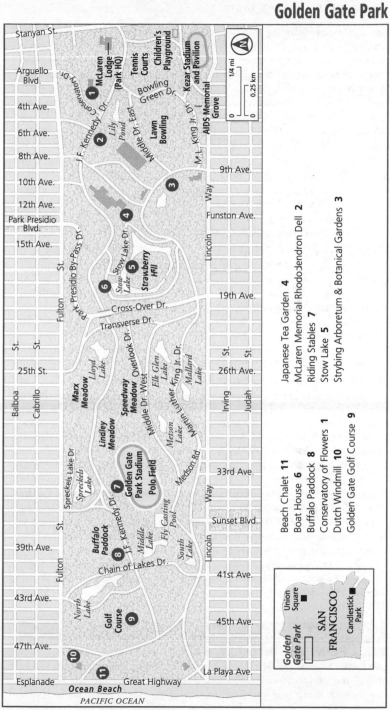

Japanese Tea Garden **4**
McLaren Memorial Rhododendron Dell **2**
Riding Stables **7**
Stow Lake **5**
Strybing Arboretum & Botanical Gardens **3**

Beach Chalet **11**
Boat House **6**
Buffalo Paddock **8**
Conservatory of Flowers **1**
Dutch Windmill **10**
Golden Gate Golf Course **9**

bonsai crossed by winding paths and high-arched bridges—were it not for the hordes of tourists and screaming children who can all but destroy any semblance of peace. Come early to enjoy the places for contemplation, including the bronze Buddha that was cast in Japan in 1790 and donated by the Gump family, the Buddhist pagoda, and the Wishing Bridge, which reflected in the water looks as though it completes a circle. The garden is open daily November through February from 8:30am to 5pm (teahouse 10am–4:30pm), March through October from 8:30am to 6pm (teahouse 10am–5:30pm). For information on admissions, call © **415/752-4227.** For the teahouse, call © **415/ 752-1171.**

STRYBING ARBORETUM & BOTANICAL GARDENS Some 6,000 plant species grow here, among them rare species, very ancient plants in a special "primitive garden," and a grove of California redwoods. Open Monday through Friday from 8am to 4:30pm, and Saturday and Sunday from 10am to 5pm. For more information, call © **415/753-7090** or visit www.strybing.org.

STOW LAKE & STRAWBERRY HILL 🎯 *(Kids)* Rent a paddleboat, rowboat, or motorboat here and cruise around the circular lake as painters create still lifes and joggers pass along the shoreline. Ducks waddle around waiting to be fed, and turtles bathe on rocks and logs. Strawberry Hill, the 430-foot-high artificial island at the center of Stow Lake, is a perfect picnic spot and boasts a bird's-eye view of San Francisco and the bay. It also has a waterfall and peace pagoda. To reach the boathouse, call © **415/752-0347.** Boat rentals are available daily from 10am to 4pm, weather permitting, with four-passenger rowboats for $13 and four-person paddleboats running $17 per hour (cash only).

Yerba Buena Center for the Arts & Yerba Buena Gardens 🎯🎯 *(Kids)* An interactive wonderland across from the Museum of Modern Art, Yerba Buena could keep you busy all day with its 5-acre garden, cafes, and art-related attractions. This includes the **Center for the Arts,** which presents music, theater, dance, and visual arts; **Galleries and Arts Forum,** which features three galleries and a dance space; **Zeum** (© **415/777-2800;** www.zeum.org), a part of the children's addition that includes a cafe, interactive cultural center, ice-skating rink, fabulous 1906 historic carousel, and interactive play and learning garden. You'll also find Sony's futuristic retail-and-entertainment mecca **Metreon Entertainment Center** (© **415/537-3400;** www.metreon.com), a 350,000-square-foot complex housing movie theaters, an **IMAX** theater, small restaurants, interactive attractions (including a restaurant and attraction that features Maurice Sendak's *Where the Wild Things Are*), shops, a virtual bowling alley, and a child-care center.

701 Mission St. © 415/978-ARTS (box office). www.yerbabuenaarts.org. Admission $6 adults, $3 seniors and students. Free to all 1st Tues of each month. Free for seniors and students with ID every Thurs. Tues–Sun 11am–5pm; 1st Thurs of each month 11am–8pm. Streetcar: Powell or Montgomery lines. Bus: 5, 9, 14, 15, 30, or 45.

6 Exploring the City

MORE POINTS OF INTEREST

Lombard Street Known (erroneously) as the "crookedest street in the world," the whimsically winding block of Lombard Street between Hyde and Leavenworth streets puts smiles on the faces of thousands of visitors each year. The elevation is so steep that the road has to snake back and forth to make a descent possible. This short stretch is one-way, downhill, and fun to drive. Take the curves slowly and in low gear, and expect a wait during the weekend. Save your film for the bottom, where, if you're lucky, you can find a parking space and take a few snapshots of the spectacle. You can also take staircases (without curves) up or down on either side of the street.

Between Hyde and Leavenworth sts.

Mission Dolores ⓖ This is the oldest structure in the city, built on order of Franciscan Father Junípero Serra by Father Francisco Palou. It was constructed of 36,000 sunbaked bricks and dedicated in June 1776 at the northern terminus of El Camino Real, the Spanish road from Mexico to California. It's a moving place to visit, with its cool, serene buildings with thick adobe walls and especially the cemetery and gardens where the early settlers are buried.

16th St. (at Dolores St.). ⓒ 415/621-8203. Donations appreciated. May–Oct daily 9am–4:30pm; Nov–Apr daily 9am–4pm; Good Friday 9am–noon. Closed Thanksgiving and Dec 25. Muni Metro: J. Bus: 14, 26, or 33 to the corner of Church and 16th sts.

ARCHITECTURAL HIGHLIGHTS

The **Alamo Square Historic District** contains many of the city's 14,000 Victorian **"Painted Ladies,"** homes that have been restored and ornately painted by residents. The small area—bordered by Divisadero Street on the west, Golden Gate Avenue on the north, Webster Street on the east, and Fell Street on the south, about 10 blocks west of the Civic Center—has one of the city's largest concentrations of these. One of the most famous views of San Francisco, which you'll see on postcards and posters all around the city, depicts sharp-edged Financial District skyscrapers behind a row of Victorians. This view can be seen from Alamo Square at Fulton and Steiner streets.

Built in 1881 to a design by Brown and Bakewell, **City Hall** and the **Civic Center** are part of a "City Beautiful" complex done in the Beaux Arts style. The newly renovated City Hall dome rises to a height of 308 feet on the exterior and is ornamented with oculi (round windows) and topped by a lantern. The rotunda soars 112 feet and is finished in oak, marble, and limestone with a marble staircase leading to the second floor.

The **Flood Mansion,** 1000 California St., at Mason Street, was built between 1885 and 1886 for James Clair Flood, who, thanks to the Comstock Lode, rose from being a bartender to one of the city's wealthiest men. The house cost $1.5 million (the fence alone carried a price tag of $30,000!). It was designed by Augustus Laver and modified by Willis Polk to accommodate the Pacific Union Club.

The **Octagon House,** 2645 Gough St., at Union Street (ⓒ 415/441-7512), is an eight-sided, cupola-topped house dating from 1861. Its features are extraordinary, especially the circular staircase and ceiling medallion. Inside, you'll find furniture, silverware, and American pewter from the colonial and Federal periods. There are also some historic documents, including signatures of 54 of the 56 signers of the Declaration of Independence. Even if you're not able to visit during open hours, this strange structure is worth a look. It's open February through December on the second Sunday and second and fourth Thursdays of each month from noon to 3pm, closed January and holidays.

The **Palace of Fine Arts,** on Baker between Jefferson and Bay streets, is the only building to survive from the Pan-Pacific Exhibition of 1915. Constructed by Bernard Maybeck, it was rebuilt in concrete using molds taken from the original in the 1950s. It now houses the **Exploratorium** (p. 118).

The **TransAmerica Pyramid,** 600 Montgomery St., between Clay and Washington streets, is the tallest structure in San Francisco's skyline—it's 48 stories tall and capped by a 212-foot spire.

Although the **San Francisco–Oakland Bay Bridge** is visually less appealing than the Golden Gate Bridge, it is in many ways more spectacular. Opened in 1936, before the Golden Gate, at 8¼ miles long it's one of the world's longest steel bridges. It's not a single bridge at all, but actually a dovetailed series of spans joined in midbay—at Yerba Buena Island—by one of the world's largest (in diameter) tunnels. To the west of Yerba Buena, the bridge is really two separate suspension bridges, joined at a central anchorage. East of the island is a 1,400-foot cantilever span, followed by a succession of truss bridges.

A CHURCH

Glide Memorial United Methodist Church ★ *Moments*   There would be nothing special about this Tenderloin-area church if it weren't for its pastor, Cecil Williams. Williams's enthusiastic and uplifting preaching and singing with the homeless and poor of the neighborhood crosses all socioeconomic boundaries and has attracted national fame. Go for an exhilarating experience.

330 Ellis St. (west of Union Sq.). ℂ **415/771-6300.** Services Sun at 9 and 11am. Muni Metro: Powell. Bus: 37.

MUSEUMS

Asian Art Museum ★   Reopened in its new Civic Center home in March of 2003, the Asian Art Museum is one of the Western world's largest museums devoted to Asian art. Its collection boasts more than 13,000 art objects such as world-class sculptures, paintings, bronzes, ceramics, jades, and decorative objects spanning 6,000 years of history and regions of South Asia, West Asia, Southeast Asia, the Himalayas, China, Korea, and Japan. Previously in Golden Gate Park, the museum's new home in the city's Beaux Arts–style central library has been renovated under Italian architect Gae Aulenti and includes 29,000 square feet of permanent gallery space showcasing 2,500 objects at any given time. Add temporary exhibitions, live demonstrations, learning activities, and a new cafe and store and you've got one very good reason to head to the Civic Center.

200 Larkin St. (between Grove and McAllister sts.). ℂ **415/581-3500.** www.asianart.org. Admission $10 adults, $7 seniors 65 and over, $6 youths 12–17, free for children under 12, $5 flat rate after 5pm on Thurs evenings. Free 1st Tues of the month. Tues, Wed, and Fri–Sun 10am–5pm; Thurs 10am–9pm. Metro: Civic Center stop. Bus: All Market St. buses.

California Palace of the Legion of Honor ★★   Even without going inside the building, this spot is one of San Francisco's most beautiful. Designed as a memorial to California's World War I casualties, the neoclassical structure is an exact replica of the Legion of Honor Palace in Paris, down to the inscription HONNEUR ET PATRIE above the portal. Reopened after a 2-year, $29-million renovation and upgrading project that was stalled by the discovery of almost 300 coffins, the museum's collection contains paintings, sculpture, and decorative arts from Europe, as well as tapestries, prints, and drawings. The chronological display of more than 800 years of European art includes a collection of Rodin sculpture. The clincher: Grassy expanses and astounding views of the Golden Gate.

In Lincoln Park (34th Ave. and Clement St.). ℂ **415/750-3600,** or 415/863-3330 (recorded information). www.thinker.org. Admission $8 adults, $6 seniors 65 and over, $5 youths 12–17, free for children under 12. Fees may be higher for special exhibitions. Free to all on Tues. Tues–Sun 9:30am–5pm. Bus: 18 or 38.

The Exploratorium ★ *Kids*   This fun, hands-on science fair contains more than 650 exhibits that explore everything from color theory to Einstein's theory of relativity. Optics are demonstrated in booths where you can see a bust of a statue in three dimensions—but when you try to touch it, you discover it isn't there! The same experience occurs with an image of yourself: When you stretch

Travel Tip: He who finds the best hotel deal has more to spend on facials involving knobbly vegetables.

Hello, the Roaming Gnome here. I've been nabbed from the garden and taken round the world. The people who took me are so terribly clever. They find the best offerings on Travelocity. For very little cha-ching. And that means I get to be pampered and exfoliated till I'm pink as a bunny's doodah.

travelocity®

1-888-TRAVELOCITY / travelocity.com / America Online Keyword: Travel

04 Travelocity.com LP. All rights reserved. TRAVELOCITY, the Stars Design and The Roaming Gnome are trademarks of Travelocity.com LP. CST# 2056372-50

@ www.Thrifty.com

Now that you

know where to go...

how ya gonna

get there?|

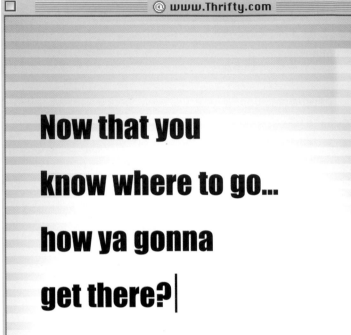

Our lowest rates.

Visit us online or call **800.THRIFTY** or your professional travel agent.

© 2004 Thrifty Rent-A-Car System, Inc. Thrifty.com is a trademark of Thrifty, Inc. All rights reserved.
Thrifty features quality products of DaimlerChrysler and other fine cars.

your hand forward, a hand comes out to touch you, and the hands pass in midair. Every exhibit is designed to be used. You can whisper into a concave reflector and have a friend hear you 60 feet away, or you can design your own animated abstract art—using sound. The museum is at the **Palace of Fine Arts** ⚸, the only building left standing from the Panama-Pacific Exposition of 1915. The adjoining park and lagoon—the perfect place for an afternoon picnic—are home to ducks, swans, seagulls, and grouchy geese, so bring bread.

3601 Lyon St., in the Palace of Fine Arts (at Marina Blvd.). (℃ **415/563-7337** or 415/561-0360 (recorded information). www.exploratorium.edu. Admission $10 adults; $7.50 seniors, youths 13–17, and college students with ID; $6 children 4–12; free for children under 4. Free to all 1st Wed of each month. AE, MC, V. Tues–Sun 10am–5pm. Closed Mon except Martin Luther King, Jr., Presidents', Memorial, and Labor days. Free parking. Bus: 30 from Stockton St. to the Marina stop.

San Francisco Maritime National Historical Park *(Kids* Shaped like an Art Deco ship and located near Fisherman's Wharf, the National Maritime Museum is filled with sailing, whaling, and fishing lore. Exhibits include model craft, scrimshaw, and a collection of shipwreck photographs and historic marine scenes, including an 1851 snapshot of hundreds of abandoned ships, deserted en masse by crews dashing off to participate in the Gold Rush. The museum's walls are lined with finely carved, painted wooden figureheads from old windjammers.

Two blocks east, at Aquatic Park's Hyde Street Pier, are several historic ships that are open to the public. The *Balclutha,* one of the last surviving square-riggers, was built in Glasgow in 1886 and carried grain from California around Cape Horn at a near-record speed of 300 miles a day; it rounded the treacherous cape 17 times in its career. Visitors are invited to spin the wheel, squint at the compass, and imagine they're weathering a mighty storm. Kids can climb into the bunking quarters, visit the "slop chest" (galley to you, matey), and read the sea chanteys (clean ones only) that decorate the walls.

The 1890 *Eureka* still carries a cargo of nostalgia for San Franciscans. It was the last of 50 paddle-wheeled ferries that regularly plied the bay; it made its final trip in 1957. Restored to its original splendor, the side-wheeler is loaded with deck cargo, including antique cars and trucks.

At the pier's small-boat shop, visitors can follow the restoration progress of historic boats from the museum's collection. It's behind the maritime bookstore on your right as you approach the ships.

At the foot of Polk St. (near Fisherman's Wharf). (℃ **415/561-7100**. www.nps.gov. Museum free. Tickets to board ships $5, free for children under 16. Museum daily 10am–5pm. Ships on Hyde St. Pier open Memorial Day to Oct 1 daily 9:30am–5:30pm; Oct 2 to day before Memorial Day daily 9:30am–5pm. Cable car: Powell-Hyde St. line to the last stop. Bus: 19, 30, or 47.

San Francisco Museum of Modern Art (SFMOMA) ⚸ SFMOMA is a fine museum, but it doesn't come close to those in New York City. That said, its collection consists of more than 23,000 works, including close to 5,000 paintings and sculptures by artists such as Henri Matisse, Jackson Pollock, and Willem de Kooning. (Alas, they only show a small amount of their collection at any given time.) Other artists represented include Diego Rivera, Georgia O'Keeffe, Paul Klee, the Fauvists, and holdings of Richard Diebenkorn. SFMOMA was also one of the first to recognize photography as a major art form; its collection includes more than 12,000 photographs by such notables as Ansel Adams, Alfred Stieglitz, Edward Weston, and Henri Cartier-Bresson. Phone for details of special exhibits, and whatever you do, check out the fabulous MuseumStore and cafe.

151 Third St. (2 blocks south of Market St., across from Yerba Buena Gardens). © 415/357-4000. www.sfmoma.org. Admission $10 adults, $7 seniors, $6 students over 12 with ID, free for children 12 and under. Half price for all Thurs 6–8:45pm; free to all 1st Tues of each month. Thurs 11am–8:45pm; Fri–Tues 11am–5:45pm. Closed Wed and major holidays. Streetcar: J, K, L, or M to Montgomery. Bus: 15, 30, or 45.

NEIGHBORHOODS WORTH SEEKING OUT

For self-guided walking tours of San Francisco's neighborhoods, pick up a copy of *Frommer's Memorable Walks in San Francisco.*

THE CASTRO   Castro Street around Market and 18th streets is the center of the city's gay community, which is catered to by the many stores, restaurants, bars, and other institutions here. Among the landmarks are Harvey Milk Plaza, the Quilt Project, and the Castro Theatre, a 1920s movie palace.

CHINATOWN   California Street to Broadway and Kearny to Stockton Street are the boundaries of today's Chinatown. San Francisco is home to the second-largest community of Chinese in the U.S., but the majority do not live and work in these 24 blocks, although they return to shop and dine here on weekends.

The gateway at Grant and Bush marks the entry to Chinatown. Walk up Grant, the tourist face of Chinatown, to California Street and Old St. Mary's.

The heart of Chinatown is at **Portsmouth Square,** where you'll find Chinese-American locals playing board games (often gambling) or just sitting quietly. This square was the center of early San Francisco and the spot where the American flag was first raised on July 9, 1846. From the square, Washington Street leads up to Waverly Place, where you can see three temples.

Explore the area at your leisure, or see "Organized Tours," below if you'd like to join a special-interest walking tour.

FISHERMAN'S WHARF & THE NORTHERN WATERFRONT   Few cities in America are as adept at wholesaling their historical sites as San Francisco, which has converted Fisherman's Wharf into one of the most popular tourist destinations in the world. Unless you come really early, you won't find any traces of the traditional waterfront life that once existed here; the only serious fishing going on is for tourist dollars. A fleet of fewer than 30 boats still operates from here, but basically Fisherman's Wharf has been converted into one long shopping mall stretching from Ghirardelli Square at the west end to PIER 39 at the east. Some love it, others can't get far enough away from it, but most agree that Fisherman's Wharf, for better or for worse, has to be seen at least once.

Ghirardelli Square, at 900 N. Point St., between Polk and Larkin streets (© 415/775-5500), is best known as the former chocolate-and-spice factory of Domingo Ghirardelli. The factory has been converted into a 10-level mall containing more than 50 stores and 11 dining establishments. Scheduled street performers play regularly in the West Plaza. The stores generally stay open until 8 or 9pm in the summer and 6 or 7pm in the winter.

PIER 39, on the waterfront at Embarcadero and Beach Street (© 415/ 981-8030), is a 4½-acre waterfront complex, a few blocks east of Fisherman's Wharf. Ostensibly a re-creation of an early-20th-century street scene, it features walkways of aged and weathered wood salvaged from demolished piers. But don't expect a slice of old-time maritime life. This is the busiest mall of the group, with more than 100 touristy stores. In addition, there are 20 or so restaurants and snack outlets, some with good views of the bay.

In recent years, some 600 California **sea lions** have taken up residence on the adjacent floating docks. They sun themselves and honk and bellow. The latest addition to Fisherman's Wharf is **Aquarium of the Bay,** a $38-million, 1-million gallon marine attraction filled with sharks, stingrays, and more, all witnessed via a moving footpath that transports visitors through clear acrylic tunnels.

The shops are open daily from 10:30am to 8:30pm. Cable car: Powell-Mason line to Bay Street.

THE MISSION DISTRICT   Once inhabited almost entirely by Irish immigrants, the Mission is now the center of the city's Latino community and the city's dot-commercialization, an oblong area stretching roughly from 14th to 30th streets between Potrero Avenue in the east and Dolores on the west. Some of the city's finest Victorians still stand in the outer areas, though many seem out of place in the mostly lower-income neighborhoods. The heart of the community lies along 24th Street between Van Ness and Potrero, where dozens of ethnic restaurants, bakeries, bars, and specialty stores attract a hip crowd from all over the city. Strolling through the Mission District at night should be done cautiously on the outskirts, but it's quite safe during the day and highly recommended.

For even better insight into the community, go to the **Precita Eyes Mural Arts Center,** 2981 24th St., between Harrison and Alabama streets (© **415/285-2287**), and take one of the 1½-hour tours conducted on Saturday and Sunday at 11am and 1:30pm, which costs $10 for adults, $8 for students with ID, $5 for seniors, and $2 for under-18s. You'll see 85 murals in an 8-block walk. Every year it also holds a Mural Awareness Month (usually in May) when tours are given daily. Most tours leave from 2981 24th St.; call ahead to confirm.

At 16th and Dolores is the **Mission San Francisco de Assisi** (better known as **Mission Dolores;** p. 117), which is the city's oldest surviving building and the district's namesake.

NOB HILL   When the cable car was invented in 1873, this hill became the most exclusive residential area in the city. The Big Four and the Comstock Bonanza kings built their mansions here, but the structures were all destroyed by the 1906 earthquake and fire. Only the Flood Mansion, which serves today as the Pacific Union Club, and the Fairmont (which was under construction when the earthquake struck) were spared. The area is now home to some of the city's most upscale hotels, as well as Grace Cathedral, which stands on the Crocker Mansion site. Stroll around and enjoy the views, and pay a visit to Huntington Park.

NORTH BEACH   In the late 1800s, an influx of Italian immigrants into North Beach established this aromatic area as San Francisco's "Little Italy." Today, dozens of Italian restaurants and coffeehouses continue to flourish in what is still the center of the city's Italian community. Walk down Columbus Avenue any given morning and you're bound to be bombarded with the wonderful aromas of roasting coffee and savory pasta sauces. Though there are some interesting shops and bookstores in the area, it's the eclectic little cafes, delis, bakeries, and coffee shops that give North Beach its Italian-bohemian character.

For a proper perspective of North Beach, sign up for **Javawalk** with coffee-nut Elaine Sosa (p. 123).

PARKS, GARDENS & ZOOS

In addition to **Golden Gate Park** and **Golden Gate National Recreation Area** and the **Presidio** (see "Golden Gate National Recreation Area & the Presidio," below), San Francisco boasts more than 2,000 additional acres of parkland, most of which are perfect for picnicking.

Lincoln Park, at Clement Street and 34th Avenue, occupies 270 acres on the northwestern side of the city and contains the California Palace of the Legion of

Honor (see "Museums," above) and an 18-hole municipal golf course. But the most dramatic features of the park are the 200-foot cliffs that overlook the Golden Gate Bridge and San Francisco Bay. Take bus no. 38 from Union Square to 33rd and Geary streets, and then transfer to bus no. 18 into the park.

San Francisco Zoo & Children's Zoo   Located between the Pacific Ocean and Lake Merced, in the southwest corner of the city, the San Francisco Zoo houses more than 1,000 inhabitants in landscaped enclosures guarded by concealed moats. The Primate Discovery Center is noteworthy for its many rare and endangered species. Expansive outdoor atriums, sprawling meadows, and a midnight world for exotic nocturnal primates house such species as the ruffed-tailed lemur, black-and-white colobus monkeys, patas monkeys, and emperor tamarins, pint-size primates distinguished by their long, majestic mustaches.

Other highlights include Koala Crossing, housing kangaroos, emus, and walleroos; Gorilla World, one of the world's largest exhibits of these gentle giants; and Penguin Island, home to a large breeding colony of Magellanic penguins. The Feline Conservation Center is a wooded sanctuary and breeding facility for the zoo's endangered snow leopards, Persian leopards, and other jungle cats. The Lion House is home to rare Sumatran and Siberian tigers, a rare white Bengal tiger, and the African lions (you can watch them being fed at 2pm Tues–Sun). The latest exhibit, which opened in mid-2004, is African Savanna, a 3-acre mixed-species habitat with giraffes, zebras, antelope, and birds.

At the Children's Zoo, adjacent to the main park, the barnyard is alive with domestic animals such as sheep, goats, ponies, and a llama. Also of interest is the Insect Zoo, which showcases a multitude of insect species, including the hissing cockroach and walking sticks.

Sloat Blvd. at 47th Ave. and Great Hwy. Ⓒ 415/753-7080. www.sfzoo.org. Admission to main zoo and Children's Zoo $10 adults, $7 seniors and youths 12–17, $4 children 3–11, free for children under 3 accompanied by an adult; $1 discount with valid Muni transfer. Free to all 1st Wed of each month, except $2 fee for Children's Zoo. Carousel $2. Main zoo daily 10am–5pm. Children's Zoo Mon–Fri 11am–4pm; weekends and summer 10:30am–4:30pm. Metro: L from downtown Market St. to the end of the line.

7 Organized Tours

ORIENTATION TOURS
THE 49-MILE SCENIC DRIVE
The self-guided, 49-mile drive is one easy way to orient yourself and to grasp the beauty of San Francisco and its location. Beginning in the city, it follows a rough circle around the bay and passes the best-known sights, from Chinatown and the Golden Gate Bridge to Ocean Beach, Seal Rocks, Golden Gate Park, and Twin Peaks. Originally designed for the benefit of visitors to San Francisco's 1939 and 1940 Golden Gate International Exposition, the route is marked with blue-and-white seagull signs. Although it makes an excellent half-day tour, this miniexcursion can easily take longer if you decide, for example, to walk across the Golden Gate Bridge or to have tea in Golden Gate Park's Japanese Tea Garden.

The San Francisco Visitor Information Center, at Powell and Market streets, distributes free route maps. Since a few of the Scenic Drive marker signs are missing, the map will come in handy. Try to avoid the downtown area during the weekday rush hours from 7 to 9am and 4 to 6pm.

BOAT TOURS
One of the best ways to look at San Francisco is from a boat on the bay. The **Blue & Gold Fleet** tours the bay year-round in a sleek, 350-passenger sightseeing

boat, with food and beverage facilities. The fully narrated, 1¼-hour cruise passes beneath the Golden Gate Bridge, and comes within yards of Alcatraz Island. Frequent daily departures from PIER 39 (not to be confused with their service to Alcatraz, which departs from Pier 41) begin at 10am in summer and 11am in winter. Tickets cost $20 for adults, $16 for kids 12 to 17 and seniors over 62, and $12 for kids 5 to 11; children under 5 cruise for free. For recorded information, call © **415/773-1188;** for tickets, which cost an additional $2.25 each when ordered via phone, call © **415/705-5555** or visit www.blueandgoldfleet.com.

The **Red & White Fleet** also offers daily bay cruises (narrated in various languages), which depart from Pier 43½ and travel under the Golden Gate Bridge and past the Marin Headlands, Sausalito, Tiburon, Angel Island, and Alcatraz. Prices are $20 for adults, $16 for seniors over 60 and kids 12 to 18, $12 for children 5 to 11, and free for children under 5. Call © **415/447-0597** for information, or check out their website at www.redandwhite.com for discounts and additional information.

SPECIAL-INTEREST WALKING TOURS

AN INSIDER'S TOUR OF CHINATOWN   Founded by author, TV personality, cooking instructor, and restaurant critic Shirley Fong-Torres, **Wok Wiz Chinatown Walking Tours** (© **650/355-9657;** www.wokwiz.com) takes you into nooks and crannies not usually seen by tourists. Each guide is intimately acquainted with all of Chinatown's back ways, alleys, and small businesses, as well as the area's history, folklore, culture, and food. The 2½-hour tours are conducted daily from 10am to 1:30pm and include a dim sum lunch. Groups are generally kept to a maximum of 12, and reservations are essential. Prices (including lunch) are $40 for adults, $35 for seniors 60 and older, and $35 for children under 11. Additional tours are offered, and prices are lower without lunch.

NORTH BEACH CAFE SOIREE   Self-described "coffeehouse lizard" Elaine Sosa leads **Javawalk,** a 2-hour walking tour. Aside from visiting cafes, Javawalk also serves up a good share of historical and architectural trivia. Sosa keeps the tour interactive and fun, and it's obvious that she knows a wealth of tales and trivia about the history of coffee and its North Beach roots. Tours are given Tuesday through Saturday at 10am and Tuesday through Friday for private parties of six or more. The price is $20 for adults and $10 for kids 12 and under. For information and reservations, call © **415/673-9255.**

THE VICTORIAN LEGACY   Jay Gifford, founder of **Victorian Homes Historical Walking Tour** (© **415/252-9485**) and San Francisco resident for 2 decades, portrays his enthusiasm and love of San Francisco throughout this entertaining 2½-hour tour. Set at a leisurely place, it incorporates a wealth of interesting facts about San Francisco's Victorian architecture, as well as the city's storied history—particularly the periods before and after the great earthquake and fire of 1906. You'll stroll through Japantown, the Western Addition (where you can take a break to cruise the trendy shops on Fillmore St.), and onward to Pacific Heights and Cow Hollow. In the process you'll see more than 200 meticulously restored Victorians, including the one where *Mrs. Doubtfire* was filmed. Jay's guests often find they are the only ones on the quiet neighborhood streets, where tour buses are forbidden. The tour ends with a trolley ride back to Union Square, passing though North Beach and Chinatown. Tours, which start at Union Square at 11am, are offered daily April through December and Thursday through Monday from January through March, and cost $20 per person. Reservations are required. You can preview the tour at **www.victorianwalk.com.**

8 Golden Gate National Recreation Area & the Presidio

GOLDEN GATE NATIONAL RECREATION AREA

No urban shoreline is as stunning as San Francisco's. The Golden Gate National Recreation Area, which wraps around the northern and western edges of the city and is run by the National Park Service, lets visitors fully enjoy it. Along this shoreline are several landmarks, and from its edge visitors have views of the bay and the ocean. The San Francisco Municipal Railway (Muni) provides transportation to most sites, including Aquatic Park, the Cliff House, and Ocean Beach. For more information, see "Outdoor Pursuits," below or contact the **National Park Service** (© 415/556-0560).

Here's a brief rundown of the major features of the recreation area, starting at the northern section and moving westward around the coastline:

Aquatic Park, adjacent to the Hyde Street Pier, is a small swimming beach, although it's not that appealing and the water's ridiculously cold.

Fort Mason Center occupies an area from Bay Street to the shoreline and consists of several buildings and piers, which were used during World War II. Today they're occupied by a variety of museums, theaters, and organizations, as well as by **Greens Restaurant** (p. 104), which affords views of the Golden Gate Bridge. For information on Fort Mason Center events, call © **415/441-5706.**

Farther west along the bay at the northern end of Fillmore, **Marina Green** is a favorite spot for flying kites or watching the sailboats on the bay. Next stop along the bay is the St. Francis Yacht Club. From here begins the 3½-mile paved **Golden Gate Promenade,** a favorite biking-and-hiking path that defines the outer limits of the Presidio (see below) and leads to the fantastic and recently reestablished marshland preserve **Crissy Field,** which is the city's latest favorite playground and a seriously spectacular destination (make a point of it!), complete with sandy beach, lots of native birds, and jogging paths.

Fort Point (© **415/556-1693**), a National Historic Site sitting under the Golden Gate Bridge, was built in 1853 to protect the entrance to the harbor. You might recognize it from Alfred Hitchcock's *Vertigo.* During the Civil War the brick Fort Point was manned by 140 men and 90 pieces of artillery to prevent a Confederate takeover of California. Rangers in Civil War regalia lead regular tours and sometimes fire the old cannons.

Lincoln Boulevard sweeps around the western edge of the bay to two of the most popular beaches in San Francisco. **Baker Beach,** a small, beautiful strand where the waves roll ashore, is a fine spot for sunbathing, walking, or fishing—it's packed on sunny days. Because of the cold water and the roaring currents that pour out of the bay twice a day, swimming is not advised here for any but the most confident. (You'll also see some nude sunbathers here.) Here you can pick up the **Coastal Trail,** which leads through the Presidio (see below). A short distance from Baker, **China Beach** is a small cove where swimming is permitted. Changing rooms, showers, a sun deck, and restrooms are available.

A little farther around the coast appears **Land's End,** looking out to Pyramid Rock. Both a lower and an upper trail provide hiking opportunities amid windswept cypress and pines on the cliffs above the Pacific.

Still farther along the coast lie **Point Lobos,** the **Sutro Baths,** and the **Cliff House.** The latter has been serving refreshments to visitors since 1863 and is slated to undergo renovation in the coming year. Here you can view the **Seal Rocks,** home to a colony of sea lions and marine birds. Only traces of the Sutro

Baths remain today northeast of the Cliff House. This swimming facility was a major attraction that could accommodate 24,000 people, but it burned down in 1966. A little farther inland at the western end of California Street is **Lincoln Park,** which contains a golf course and the Palace of the Legion of Honor.

From the Cliff House, the Esplanade continues south along the 4-mile-long **Ocean Beach,** which is not suitable for swimming. At the southern end of Ocean Beach is another area of the park around **Fort Funston** where there's an easy loop trail across the cliffs (for information, call the ranger station at © 415/239-2366). Here, too, you can watch the hang gliders taking advantage of the high cliffs and strong winds.

Farther south along I-280, **Sweeney Ridge,** which can only be reached by car, affords sweeping views of the coastline from the many trails that crisscross these 1,000 acres of land. It was from here that the expedition led by Don Gaspar de Portolá first saw San Francisco Bay in 1769. It's located in Pacifica and can be reached via Sneath Lane off Calif. 35 (Skyline Blvd.) in San Bruno.

THE PRESIDIO

In 1994 the Presidio was transferred from the U.S. Army to the National Park Service and became one of a handful of urban national parks that combines historical, architectural, and natural elements into one giant arboreal expanse—not to mention a previously private golf course and a home for George Lucas's production company.

The 1,480-acre area incorporates a variety of terrain—coastal scrub, dunes, and prairie grasslands that shelter many rare plants and more than 150 species of birds, some of which nest here. There are also more than 350 historic buildings, a national cemetery, and a variety of terrain and natural habitats. The National Park Service offers a number of walking and biking tours around the Presidio; reservations are required.

Walkers and joggers will enjoy the forests of the Presidio. It was once a bleak field of wind-blasted rock, sand, and grass, but in a strangely humanitarian gesture, 60,000 trees were planted in the 1880s to make the place more livable for the troops. Today, on the 2-mile **Ecology Loop Trail,** walkers can see more than 30 different species of those trees, including redwood, spruce, cypress, and acacias. Hikers can follow the 2.5-mile **Coastal Trail** from Fort Point along this part of the coastline all the way to Land's End. It follows the bluff top from Baker Beach to the southern base of the Golden Gate Bridge.

Crissy Field is a former airfield that in recent years has become known as one of the see-and-be-seen proving grounds of California's windsurfing culture. Between March and October, hundreds come to try their hand. The beach here provides easy water access and plenty of room to rig up, but is not recommended for the inexperienced. This is also a popular place for joggers en route from the Marina District to Fort Point and back, with great picnic spots and a sweet cafe along the path to Fort Funston. At the west end of Crissy Field is a pier that can be used for fishing and crabbing.

The Presidio is currently undergoing major changes so that it may pay for its upkeep. For schedules, maps, and general information about ongoing developments at the Presidio, the best source is the **Golden Gate National Recreation Area Headquarters** at Fort Mason, Building 102, San Francisco, CA 94123 (© 415/561-4700). For additional information, call the **Presidio Visitor Center** at © 415/561-4323. Take the no. 28, 45, 76, or 82X bus.

Golden Gate National Recreation Area & the Presidio

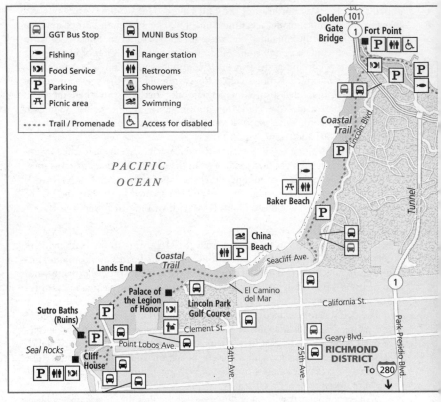

9 Outdoor Pursuits

The prime places to enjoy all kinds of recreational activities in San Francisco have already been described earlier in this chapter. See "The Top Attractions," earlier in this chapter for a complete description of Golden Gate Park, and "Golden Gate National Recreation Area & the Presidio" above for complete details on these sights.

BEACHES   There are only two beaches in San Francisco that are safe for swimming: **Aquatic Park,** which is a patch of sand adjacent to the Hyde Park Pier, and **China Beach,** a small cove on the western edge of the South Bay. But dip in at your own risk—there are no lifeguards, and the water is painfully cold.

Baker Beach, a small, beautiful strand outside the Golden Gate, isn't the best place for swimming due to strong currents, but it's great for sunning, walking, or fishing. It's wonderful to sit here on a sunny day and take in the view of the bridge. You'll climb down a long flight of stairs from the street to the beach.

Ocean Beach, at the end of Golden Gate Park, on the westernmost side of the city, is San Francisco's largest beach (4 miles long). Just offshore, at the northern end of the beach in front of the Cliff House, are the jagged Seal Rocks, inhabited by shorebirds and a large colony of barking sea lions. Bring binoculars for a close-up view. Ocean Beach is for strolling or sunning, but don't swim here—tides are tricky, and each year bathers and surfers drown in the rough waters.

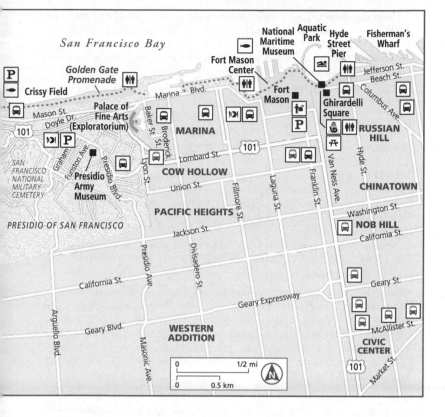

BICYCLING   Two city-designated bike routes are maintained by the Recreation and Parks Department. One winds for 7½ miles through Golden Gate Park to Lake Merced; the other traverses the city, starting in the south, and follows a route over the Golden Gate Bridge. A map is available from the San Francisco Visitor Information Center and from bike shops all around town.

A massive new seawall, constructed to buffer Ocean Beach from storm-driven waves, doubles as a public walk and bikeway along 5 waterfront blocks of the Great Highway between Noriega and Santiago streets. It's an easy ride from the Cliff House or Golden Gate Park.

There's also great biking in the Presidio. From here, you can venture across the Golden Gate Bridge and into the Marin hills.

Avenue Cyclery at 756 Stanyan St., at Waller Street (© **415/387-3155**), rents bikes for $5 per hour or $25 per day and is open daily April through September from 10am to 7pm and October through March from 10am to 6pm.

CITY STAIR-CLIMBING   You don't need a StairMaster in San Francisco. The **Filbert Street Steps,** 377 of them between Sansome Street and Telegraph Hill, scale the eastern face of Telegraph Hill, from Sansome and Filbert past 19th-century cottages and lush gardens. Napier Lane, a wooden plank walkway, leads to Montgomery Street. Turn right and follow the path to the end of the cul-de-sac, where another stairway continues to Telegraph's panoramic summit.

The **Lyon Street Steps,** between Green Street and Broadway, comprise another historic stairway street, containing four steep sets of stairs totaling 288 steps. Begin at Green Street and climb all the way up, past manicured hedges and flower gardens, to an iron gate that opens into the Presidio. A block east, on Baker Street, another set of 369 steps descends to Green Street.

GOLF **Golden Gate Park Course,** 47th Avenue and Fulton Street (© 415/ 751-8987 or www.goldengateparkgolf.com), is a 9-hole, par-27 course over 1,357 yards. All holes are par 3, tightly set, and well trapped with small greens. Greens fees are very reasonable: $13 per person Monday through Friday and $17 Saturday and Sunday. The course is open daily from 6:30am to dusk.

Lincoln Park Golf Course, 34th Avenue and Clement Street (© 415/ 221-9911), San Francisco's prettiest municipal course, has terrific views and fairways lined with Monterey cypress trees. Its 18 holes encompass 5,081 yards, for a par 68. Greens fees are $31 per person Monday through Friday and $35 Saturday and Sunday with rates decreasing after 2pm. The course is open daily from daybreak to dusk.

Presidio Golf Course (© 415/561-4664 or www.presidiogolf.com), one of the city's finest, charges $42 Monday through Thursday, $52 on Friday, and $72 Saturday and Sunday; carts are included and rates decrease later in the day.

SKATING Although people skate in Golden Gate Park all week, Sunday is best, when John F. Kennedy Drive, between Kezar Drive and Transverse Road, is closed to cars. A smooth "skate pad" is on your right, just past the Conservatory. **Skates on Haight,** 1818 Haight St. (© 415/752-8376), is the best place to rent in-line or conventional skates and is only a block from the park. Wrist guards and kneepads are included free. The cost is $6 per hour for in-line or "conventionals," $24 for all-day use. A credit card and ID deposit are required.

10 Shopping

Store hours vary, but are generally Monday through Saturday from 10am to 6pm and Sunday from noon to 5pm. Most department stores stay open later, as do shops around Fisherman's Wharf.

Sales tax in San Francisco is 8.5%. If you live out of state and buy an expensive item, consider having the store ship it home for you. You'll have to pay for its transport, but will escape paying the sales tax.

UNION SQUARE & ENVIRONS San Francisco's most congested and popular shopping mecca is centered around Union Square. Most of the big department stores and many high-end specialty shops are in this area. Be sure to venture to Grant Avenue, Post and Sutter streets, and Maiden Lane.

If you're into art, pick up *The San Francisco Gallery Guide,* a comprehensive, bimonthly publication listing the city's current shows (most of which are downtown). It's available free by mail; send a self-addressed stamped envelope to San Francisco Bay Area Gallery Guide, 1369 Fulton St., San Francisco, CA 94117 (© 415/921-1600). You can also pick one up at the San Francisco Visitor Information Center at 900 Market St. (at Powell St.).

One of my favorite galleries is the **Catharine Clark Gallery,** on the second floor at 49 Geary St., between Kearny and Grant streets (© 415/399-1439). It exhibits up-and-coming contemporary artists, mainly from California, and nurtures beginning collectors by offering an unusual interest-free purchasing plan.

Of the area's specialty stores, century-old **Gump's,** 135 Post St., between Kearny Street and Grant Avenue (© 415/982-1616), is a must-visit. A virtual treasure trove of household items and gifts, it offers a collection of Asian antiquities, contemporary art glass, exquisite jade and pearl jewelry, and more.

Music aficionados will choose to get lost in **Virgin Megastore,** Market Street at Stockton (© 415/397-4525), with thousands of CDs (including an impressive collection of imports), videos, laser discs, and a multimedia department. Its literary equivalent is nearby **Borders Books & Music,** 400 Post St., at Powell (© 415/399-1633), which has thousands of titles and a cafe.

While the department stores have plenty of clothes, real fashion fiends will want to check out the boutiques. For men, **Cable Car Clothiers,** 246 Sutter St., between Grant Avenue and Kearny Street (© 415/397-4740), is a popular stop for traditional attire, such as three-button suits with natural shoulders, Aquascutum coats, McGeorge sweaters, and Atkinson ties. The most fashionable-modern-rather-than-corporate man heads to **MAC,** 5 Claude Lane, off Sutter Street between Grant Avenue and Kearny Street (© 415/837-0615), where imported tailored suits come in designs by London's Paul Smith, Belgium's SO, and New York's John Bartlett. (An additional location is at 387 Grove St., at Gough St., © 415/863-3011, and their women's store is located at 1543 Grant Ave., between Filbert and Union sts., © 415/837-1604.)

Wilkes Bashford, 375 Sutter St., at Stockton Street (© 415/986-4380), is one of the most expensive and well-known clothing stores in the city, offering fashions for both sexes. It stocks only the finest clothes (which were often worn by former mayor Willie Brown), including men's Kiton and Brioni suits (at $2,500 and up, they're considered some of the most expensive suits in the world).

For what I consider the best in women's fashions, check out **Métier,** 355 Sutter St., between Grant and Stockton streets (© 415/989-5395). Its inventory of European ready-to-wear lines is expensive, but in the best taste; featured designers include Italian designer Anna Molinari and Alberto Biani, as well as a distinguished collection of antique-style, high-end jewelry from L.A.'s Kathie Waterman and ultrapopular custom-designed poetry jewelry by Jeanine Payer.

CHINATOWN When you pass under the gate to Chinatown on Grant Avenue, say hello to a swarm of cheap shops selling everything from linen and jade to plastic toys and $2 slippers. The real gems are tucked on side streets or in small, one-person shops selling Chinese herbs, original art, and jewelry. Grant Avenue is the area's main thoroughfare, and side streets between Bush Street and Columbus Avenue are full of restaurants, markets, and eclectic shops. Walking is best, since traffic through this area is slow at best and parking is next to impossible. Most of the stores in Chinatown are open daily from 10am to 10pm. The area is serviced by bus lines 9X, 15, 30, 41, and 45.

Of the endless array of trinket shops scattered through the neighborhood, two worth noting are **Eastwind Books & Arts,** 1435 Stockton St., at Columbus Avenue (© 415/772-5877 Chinese department, or 415/772-5899), which carries an incredible selection of Chinese books, stationery, and stamps, as well as Asian-American and English books covering everything from health and cooking to martial arts and medicine. At **Ten Ren Tea Company,** 949 Grant Ave., between Washington and Jackson streets (© 415/362-0656), you can enjoy a steaming cup of roselle tea, made of black tea and hibiscus, while you browse the selection of almost 50 traditional and herbal teas and related paraphernalia.

SOMA Though this area isn't suitable for strolling, you'll find almost all the discount shopping in warehouse spaces south of Market. You can pick up a discount-shopping guide at most major hotels. Many buses pass through this area, including nos. 9, 12, 14, 15, 19, 26, 27, 30, 42, 45, and 76.

An all-time favorite is the **SFMOMA MuseumStore,** 151 Third St., 2 blocks south of Market Street, across from Yerba Buena Gardens (© **415/357-4035**). Its array of artistic cards, books, jewelry, housewares, knickknacks, and creative tokens of San Francisco makes this one of the locals' favorite shops. It also offers far more tasteful mementos than most Fisherman's Wharf options.

Fashionable bargain hunters head to **Jeremys,** 2 S. Park, at Second Street between Bryant and Brannan streets (© **415/882-4929**), where top designer fashions from shoes to suits come at rock-bottom prices. Another worthy stop is the **Wine Club San Francisco,** 953 Harrison St., between 5th and 6th streets (© **415/512-9086**), which offers bargain prices on more than 1,200 domestic and foreign wines. Bottles cost from $4 to $1,100.

HAYES VALLEY It may not be the prettiest area in town, but while most neighborhoods cater to more conservative or trendy shoppers, lower Hayes Street, between Octavia and Gough, celebrates anything vintage, artistic, or downright funky. Though still in its developmental stage, it's definitely the most interesting new shopping area in town, with furniture and glass stores, thrift shops, trendy shoe stores, and men's and women's clothiers. There are also lots of great antiques shops south on Octavia and on nearby Market Street. Bus lines include nos. 16AX, 16BX, and 21.

If you have a fetish for foot fashions, check out **Bulo,** 437A Hayes St., at Gough Street (© **415/864-3244**), which carries Italian men's and women's shoes that run the gamut from casual to dressy, reserved to wildly funky, and ultrahip and also expensive **Gimme Shoes,** 416 Hayes St. (© **415/864-0691**). Shop for the sale items unless you're ready to drop around $200 per pair.

THE CASTRO You could easily spend all day wandering through the house-wares and men's-clothing shops of the Castro. Buses serving this area include nos. 8, 24, 33, 35, and 37.

Citizen Clothing, 536 Castro St., between 18th and 19th streets (© **415/558-9429**), is a popular shop for stylish casual clothing.

Our favorite chocolate shop, **Joseph Schmidt Confections,** 3489 16th St., at Sanchez Street (© **415/861-8682**), adds a whole new dimension to designer chocolate. Here the sinful sweets take the shape of exquisite sculptural master-pieces that are so beautiful you'll be hesitant to bite the head off your adorable chocolate panda bear. Prices are also remarkably reasonable.

UNION STREET Union Street, from Fillmore to Van Ness, caters to the upper-middle-class crowd. It's a great place to stroll; to window-shop the plethora of boutiques, cafes, and restaurants; and to watch the beautiful people parade by. Bus lines include nos. 22, 41, 42, and 45.

Among the dozens of fashion and home boutiques is **Three Bags Full,** 2181 Union St., at Fillmore (© **415/567-5753**), where expensive, handmade, and one-of-a-kind knitwear is both playful and extravagant.

CHESTNUT STREET Parallel to and a few blocks north of Union Street, Chestnut is similar to Union Street with endless shopping and dining choices, and the superfit population of postgraduate singles who hang around cafes and eye each other. The area is serviced by bus lines 22, 28, 30, 41, 42, 43, and 76.

FISHERMAN'S WHARF & ENVIRONS The tourist-oriented malls—Ghirardelli Square, PIER 39, the Cannery, and the Anchorage—run along Jefferson Street and include hundreds of shops, restaurants, and attractions.

Locals tend to avoid this part of town, but do venture to **Cost Plus Imports,** 2552 Taylor St., between North Point and Bay streets (© **415/928-6200**), a vast warehouse crammed to the rafters with Chinese baskets, Indian camel bells, Malaysian batik scarves, and innumerable other items from Algeria to Zanzibar. There's also a decent wine section. Adjoining is a **Barnes & Noble** "superstore," at 2550 Taylor, between Bay and North Point (© **415/292-6762**).

FILLMORE STREET   Some of the best shopping in town is packed into 5 blocks of Fillmore Street in Pacific Heights. From Jackson to Sutter streets, Fillmore is the perfect place to grab a bite and peruse the boutiques, crafts shops, and housewares stores. It's serviced by bus lines 1, 2, 3, 4, 12, 22, and 24.

One of my favorite housewares shops is **Zinc Details,** 1905 Fillmore St., between Bush and Pine streets (© **415/776-2100**), which has an amazing collection of handcrafted glass vases, pendant lights, ceramics, and furniture. Each piece is created specifically for the store (except vintage items).

HAIGHT STREET   Green hair, spiked hair, no hair, or mohair—even the hippies look conservative next to Haight Street's dramatic fashion freaks. The shopping in the 6 blocks of upper Haight Street, between Central Avenue and Stanyan Street, reflects its clientele and offers everything from incense and European and American street styles to furniture and vintage and übertrendy clothing. Bus lines 7, 66, 71, and 73 run down Haight Street. The Muni Metro N line stops at Waller Street and at Cole Street.

Less wearable but equally collectable are the oldies-but-goodies at **Recycled Records,** 1377 Haight St., between Central and Masonic streets (© **415/626-4075**). Easily one of the best used-record stores in the city, this loud shop has a good selection of promotional CDs and cases of used classic rock LPs. Sheet music, tour programs, and old *TV Guides* are also sold.

NORTH BEACH   Along with a great cup of coffee, Grant and Columbus avenues cater to their hip clientele with a small but worthy selection of boutiques and specialty shops.

You can pick up a great gift for yourself or anyone else at **Biordi Art Imports,** 412 Columbus Ave., at Vallejo Street (© **415/392-8096**). Its Italian Majolica pottery is both exquisite and unique.

For a dose of local color, join the literary types who browse **City Lights Booksellers & Publishers,** 261 Columbus Ave., at Broadway (© **415/362-8193**), the famous bookstore owned by renowned Beat-generation poet Lawrence Ferlinghetti. The shelves here are stocked with a comprehensive collection of art, poetry, and political paperbacks, as well as more mainstream books.

11 San Francisco After Dark

For up-to-date nightlife information, turn to the *San Francisco Weekly* and the *San Francisco Bay Guardian,* both of which contain comprehensive current listings. They're available free at bars and restaurants, and from street-corner boxes around the city. *Where,* a free tourist monthly, also has information on programs and performance times; it's available in most of the city's finer hotels. The Sunday editions of the *San Francisco Examiner* and the *Chronicle* also feature a "Datebook" section, on pink paper, with information and listings.

GETTING TICKETS   Half-price tickets to theater, dance, and music performances are available from **Tix Bay Area** (© **415/433-7827** or www.tixbayarea.org) on the day of the show only; tickets for Sunday and Monday events, if available, are sold on Saturday. Tix also sells advance, full-price tickets for most performance halls, sporting events, concerts, and clubs. A service charge, ranging from $2 to $5, is levied on each ticket. Only cash or traveler's checks are accepted for half-price tickets; Visa and MasterCard are accepted for full-price tickets. Tix, located on Powell between Geary and Post, is open Tuesday through Thursday from 11am to 6pm, Friday and Saturday from 11am to 7pm, and Sunday from 11am to 3pm. Tickets to most theater and dance events can also be obtained through **City Box Office,** 180 Redwood St., Suite 100, between Golden Gate and McAllister streets off Van Ness Avenue (© **415/392-4400;** www.cityboxoffice.com). MasterCard and Visa are accepted.

Tickets.com (© **415/478-2277** or 510/762-2277; www.tickets.com) sells computer-generated tickets to concerts, sporting events, plays, and special events, and it imposes a hefty service charge of $3 to $15 per ticket. Call for the local office nearest you.

For information on local theater, check out **www.bayareatheatre.org**.

THE PERFORMING ARTS

American Conservatory Theater (A.C.T.) A.C.T. made its debut in 1967 and quickly established itself as the city's premier resident theater group. The troupe is so venerated that A.C.T. has been compared to the superb British National Theatre, the Berliner Ensemble, and the Comédie Française. The A.C.T. season runs September through July and features both classical and experimental works. At the Geary Theater, 415 Geary St. (at Mason St.). © **415/749-2ACT.** www.act-sfbay.org. Tickets $19–$68.

The Magic Theatre The acclaimed Magic Theatre continues to be a major West Coast company dedicated to presenting the works of new playwrights; over the years it has nurtured the talents of such luminaries as Sam Shepard and Jon Robin Baitz. Shepard's Pulitzer Prize–winning play *Buried Child* premiered here. The season usually runs September through July; performances are offered Tuesday through Sunday. At Building D, Fort Mason Center, Marina Blvd. (at Buchanan St.). © **415/441-8822.** www.magictheatre.org. Tickets $20–$53. Discounts for students and seniors.

Philharmonia Baroque Orchestra Acclaimed by the *New York Times* as "the country's leading early music orchestra," Philharmonia Baroque performs in San Francisco and around the Bay Area. The season runs from September to April. At Herbst Theater, 401 Van Ness Ave. © **415/392-4400** (box office) or 415/252-1288 (administrative offices). www.philharmonia.org. Tickets $28–$62.

San Francisco Ballet Founded in 1933, the San Francisco Ballet is the oldest professional ballet company in the United States and one of the country's finest, performing an eclectic repertoire of full-length, neoclassical, and contemporary ballets. Even the *New York Times* proclaimed, "The San Francisco Ballet under Helgi Tomasson's leadership is one of the spectacular success stories of the arts in America." The 2005 season runs February through May. All performances are accompanied by the San Francisco Ballet Orchestra. War Memorial Opera House, 301 Van Ness Ave. (at Grove St.). © **415/865-2000** for tickets and information. Tickets $10–$165.

San Francisco Opera The San Francisco Opera was the second municipal opera in the United States, and is one of the city's cultural icons. All productions have English supertitles. The season starts in September and lasts just 14 weeks. Performances are held most evenings, except Monday, with matinees on Sunday. Tickets go on sale as early as June for subscribers and August for the general public, and the best seats quickly sell out. Unless Pavarotti or Domingo is in town,

---

Tips **Teatro ZinZanni**

Hungry for dinner and a damned good time? It ain't cheap, but Teatro ZinZanni is a rollicking ride of food, whimsy, drama, and song within an elegant 1926 tent on the Embarcadero. Part musical theater and part comedy, the 3½-hour show includes a four-course meal served by dozens of performers who weave the audience and astounding physical acts (think Cirque du Soleil) into their wacky, playful world. Shows are Wednesday through Sunday and tickets are $99 to $125 including dinner. The tent is located at Pier 29 on the Embarcadero at Battery Street. Call ℂ **415/438-2668** or visit www.teatrozinzanni.org for more details.

---

some less-coveted seats are usually available until curtain time. War Memorial Opera House, 301 Van Ness Ave. (at Grove St.). ℂ **415/864-3330** (box office). www.sfopera.com. Tickets $25–$195. Standing room $15–$30.

San Francisco Symphony   Founded in 1911, the internationally respected San Francisco Symphony has long been an important part of this city's cultural life under such legendary conductors as Pierre Monteux and Seiji Ozawa. In 1995 Michael Tilson Thomas took over from Herbert Blomstedt and has led the orchestra to new heights, crafting an exciting repertoire of classical and modern music. The season runs September through June; tickets are hard to come by, but there's usually someone outside the hall trying to sell their tickets the night of the show. Summer symphony activities include a Composer Festival and a Summer in the City series. At Davies Symphony Hall, 201 Van Ness Ave. (at Grove St.). ℂ **415/864-6000** (box office). www.sfsymphony.org. Tickets $12–$97.

COMEDY & CABARET

Beach Blanket Babylon *Moments*   Now a San Francisco tradition, *Beach Blanket Babylon* is best known for its outrageous costumes and oversize headdresses. It's been playing almost 31 years, and almost every performance still sells out. It's wise to write for tickets at least 3 weeks in advance, or buy them through Tix (ℂ **415/433-7827**). At Club Fugazi, Beach Blanket Babylon Blvd., 678 Green St. (between Powell St. and Columbus Ave.). ℂ **415/421-4222**. Tickets $20–$55.

THE CLUB & MUSIC SCENE
ROCK & BLUES CLUBS

Biscuits & Blues   With a crisp, blow-your-eardrums-out sound system, a New Orleans–speakeasy (albeit commercial) appeal, and a nightly lineup of live entertainment, there's no better place to muse the blues than at this basement-cum-nightclub. 401 Mason (at Geary St.). ℂ **415/292-2583**. Cover $5–$15.

Lou's Pier 47 Club   There are few locals in the place, but Lou's happens to be a good old-fashioned casual spot where you can let your hair down with Cajun seafood (downstairs), other tourists, and live jazz, blues, rock, and country bands (upstairs). A vacation attitude makes the place one of the more sloppy happy spots near the wharf. There's a $5 cover on weekdays and a $10 cover on weekends for the first band, which plays nightly from 4 to 7pm. Arrive in time for the second, which comes on at 9pm, and it will cost you $10. 300 Jefferson St. (at Jones St.). ℂ **415/771-5687**. www.louspier47.com. Cover $5–$10.

Pier 23 If there's one good-time destination that's an anchor for the party people, it's Embarcadero's Pier 23. Part ramshackle patio spot and part dance floor with a heavy dash of dive bar, here it's all about fun for a startlingly diverse clientele. The well-worn box of a restaurant and tented patio is a prime sunny-day social spot for white collars, but on weekends, it's a straight-up people zoo where every age and persuasion coexist more peacefully than the cast in a McDonald's commercial. Expect to boogie down shoulder-to-shoulder to live bands playing blues or funk. Pier 23, at the Embarcadero and Greenwich St. *C* **415/362-5125.** www.pier23cafe.com. Cover $5 to $8 during performances.

JAZZ & LATIN CLUBS

Cafe du Nord *(Finds* Although it's been around since 1907, this basement-cum-supper-club has finally been recognized as a respectable jazz venue. With a younger generation now appreciating the music, the place is often packed, from the 40-foot mahogany bar to the back room with a pool table. 2170 Market St. (at Sanchez St.). *C* **415/861-5016.**

Jazz at Pearl's This is one of the best venues for jazz in the city. Ribs and chicken are served with the sounds, too, with prices ranging from $6 to $14. The live jams last until 1:30am nightly. 256 Columbus Ave. (at Broadway). *C* **415/291-8255.** www.jazzatpearls.com. No cover. 2-drink minimum.

DANCE CLUBS

Nickie's Bar-be-cue Don't come here for dinner—the only hot thing you'll find is the small, crowded dance floor. But don't let that stop you from checking it out. Every time I come here, the old-school hits are in full force, casually dressed dancers lose all inhibitions, and the crowd is mixed with all types of friendly San Franciscans. This place is perpetually hot, so dress accordingly, and don't expect a full bar—it's beer and wine only. 460 Haight St. (between Fillmore and Webster sts.). *C* **415/621-6508.** www.nickies.com. Cover $3–$5.

Paradise Lounge Labyrinthine Paradise features three dance floors simultaneously vibrating to different beats. Smaller, auxiliary spaces include a pool room with half a dozen tables. Poetry readings are also given. Open Friday and Saturday nights only. 1501 Folsom St. (at 11th St.). *C* **415/861-6906.** Cover $3–$15.

Ruby Skye Downtown's most glamorous and gigantic nightspot is all aglitter thanks to a dramatic renovation and the addition of killer light and sound systems within the 1890s Victorian playhouse previously known as The Stage Door. Inside, hundreds of partiers boogie on the ballroom floor, mingle on the mezzanine, and puff freely in the smoking room while DJs or live music bring the dancing house down Thursday through Saturday. Big spenders should book the VIP lounge, which offers a glitzy place to kick it and bird's-eye views of the whole club scene. 420 Mason St. (between Geary and Post sts.). *C* **415/693-0777.** www.rubyskye.com. Cover $10–$25.

Ten 15 Get decked out and plan for a late night if you're headed to this party warehouse. Three levels, a full-color laser system, and a gigantic dance floor make for an extensive variety of dancing venues, complete with a 20- and 30-something gyrating mass who live for the DJs' pounding house, disco, and acid-jazz music. Each night is a different club that attracts its own crowd, ranging from yuppie to hip-hop. A recent $1.5-million renovation added 6,000 square feet of dance floor and a VIP area. Call ahead for a complete schedule of events. 1015 Folsom St. (at Sixth St.). *C* **415/431-1200.** www.1015.com. Cover $5–$15.

SUPPER CLUBS

If you can eat dinner, listen to live music, and dance (or at least wiggle in your chair) in the same room, it's a supper club—that's my criteria.

Harry Denton's Starlight Room   Come dressed to the nines or in casual attire to this old-fashioned cocktail-lounge-turned-nightclub, where tourists and locals sip drinks at sunset and boogie down to live swing and big-band tunes after dark. The room is classic 1930s San Francisco, with red-velvet banquettes, chandeliers, and fabulous views. But what really attracts flocks of all ages is a night of Harry Denton–style fun, which usually includes plenty of drinking and unrestrained dancing. Atop the Sir Francis Drake hotel, 450 Powell St., 21st floor. ℂ 415/395-8595. www.harrydenton.com. Cover $10 Wed after 7pm; $5 Thurs after 8pm; $10 Fri after 8pm; $15 Sat after 8pm.

Julie's Supper Club   Julie's is a longtime standby for cocktails and late dining. Divided into two rooms, the vibe is very 1950s cartoon, with a space-aged *Jetsons* appeal. Good-looking singles prowl, cocktails in hand, as live music plays by the front door. The food is hit-or-miss, but the atmosphere is definitely a casual and playful winner with a little interesting history. This building is one location where the Symbionese Liberation Army held Patty Hearst hostage back in the 1970s. Menu items range from $6 to $20. 1123 Folsom St. (at Seventh St.). ℂ 415/861-0707. www.juliessupperclub.com. $5 cover on weekends.

RETRO CLUB

Club Deluxe   Before the recent 1940s trend hit the city, Deluxe and its fedora-wearing clientele had been celebrating the bygone era for years. And fortunately, even with all the retro-hype, the vibe here hasn't changed. Expect an eclectic mix of throwbacks and generic San Franciscans in the intimate, smoky bar and adjoining lounge, and live jazz or blues most nights. Although many regulars dress the part, there's no attitude here—so come as you like. 1511 Haight St. (at Ashbury St.). ℂ 415/552-6949. Cover $2–$10.

THE BAR SCENE

Finding your idea of a comfortable bar has a lot to do with picking a neighborhood filled with your kind of people and investigating that area. There are hundreds of bars throughout San Francisco, and although many are obscurely located and can't be classified by their neighborhood, the following is a general description of what you'll find and where:

- **Chestnut and Union Street** bars attract a post-collegiate crowd.
- Young alternatives frequent **Mission District** haunts.
- **Upper Haight** caters to eclectic neighborhood cocktailers.
- **Lower Haight** is skate- and snowboarder grungy.
- Tourists mix with theatergoers and thirsty businesspeople in **downtown** pubs.
- **North Beach** serves all types.
- **Castro** caters to gay locals and tourists.
- **South of Market (SoMa)** offers an eclectic mix.

BARS WITH DJ GROOVES

Bambuddha Lounge *(Finds*   The hottest place for the young and the trendy to feast, flirt, or just be fabulous is this restaurant/bar adjoining the funky-cool Phoenix Hotel. With a 20-foot reclining Buddha on the roof, ultramodern San-Francisco-meets-Southeast-Asian decor (including waterfalls in the dining room and outdoor poolside cocktail lounge), very affordable and above-average Pan-Asian cuisine served late into the eve and topping out at $15, and a state-of-the-art sound system streaming ambient, down-tempo, hip-hop, funk, and house music, this is the "it" joint of the moment. 601 Eddy St. (at Polk St.). ℂ 415/885-5088. www.bambuddhalounge.com.

The Bliss Bar Surprisingly trendy for sleepy family-oriented Noe Valley, this small, stylish, and friendly bar is a great place to stop for a varied mix of locals, colorful cocktail concoctions, and a DJ spinning at the front window from 4 to 11pm 4 nights per week (call for days). If it's open, take your cocktail into the too-cool back Blue Room. And if you're on a budget or a roll, stop by from 4:30 to 7pm when martinis, lemon drops, cosmos, watermelon cosmos, and apple martinis are $3. 4026 24th St. (between Noe and Castro sts.). ℂ 415/826-6200. www.blissbarsf.com.

The Monkey Club Casual and tucked away in a quiet section of the Mission, this hip locals bar (think 20s through 30s) is an ever fun and rather red spot to kick it on plush and comfy couches backed by giant picture windows, nibble on decent and inexpensive appetizers, and down stiff drinks while a DJ spins grooving house, jazz, and world music Wednesday through Sunday. 2730 21st St. (at Bryant St.). ℂ 415/647-6546.

Wish Bar Flirtation, fun, and an attractive staff await at this mellow, narrow bar in the popular area around 11th and Folsom streets. Swathed in burgundy and black with exposed cinderblock walls and cement floors, all's aglow a la candlelight and red-shaded sconces. With a bar in the front, a DJ spinning housey lounge music in the back, and seating—including cushy leather couches—in between, it's often packed with a diverse (albeit youthful) crowd and ever filled with eye candy. 1539 Folsom St. (between 11th and 12th sts.). ℂ 415/278-9474.

OTHER BARS

The Bubble Lounge Toasting the town is a nightly event at this champagne bar. With 300 champagnes (and around 30 by the glass), brick walls, couches, and velvet curtains within its two levels, there's plenty of pop in this fizzy lounge. 714 Montgomery St. (at Columbus Ave.). ℂ 415/434-4204. www.bubblelounge.com.

Spec's Its incognito locale on Saroyan Place, a tiny alley at 250 Columbus Ave., makes Spec's less of a walk-in bar and more of a lively locals' hangout. Its funky decor—maritime flags that hang from the ceiling, exposed-brick walls lined with posters, photos, and various oddities—gives it character that intrigues every visitor. A "museum," displayed under glass, contains memorabilia and items brought back by seamen who drop in between sails, and the clientele is funky enough to keep you preoccupied while you drink a beer. 12 Saroyan Place (off Columbus Ave.). ℂ 415/421-4112.

The Tonga Room & Hurricane Bar *(Finds* It's kitschy as all get out, but there's no denying the goofy Polynesian pleasures of the Fairmont Hotel's tropical oasis. Drop in and join the crowds for an umbrella drink, a simulated thunderstorm and downpour, and a heavy dose of whimsy that escapes most San Francisco establishments. If you're on a budget, you'll definitely want to stop by for the weekday happy hour from 5 to 7pm, when you can stuff your face at the all-you-can-eat bar-grub buffet (chicken wings, chow mein, potstickers) for $6 and the cost of one drink. Settle in and you'll catch live top-40s music after 8pm, when there's a $3 cover. In the Fairmont Hotel, 950 Mason St. (at California St.). ℂ 415/772-5278. www.tongaroom.com.

Tosca *Finds*   Open daily from 5pm to 2am, Tosca is a low-key and large popular watering hole for local politicos, writers, media types, incognito visiting celebrities such as Johnny Depp or Nicolas Cage, and similar cognoscenti of unassuming classics. Equipped with dim lights, red leather booths, and high ceilings, it's everything you'd expect an old North Beach legend to be. 242 Columbus Ave. (between Broadway and Pacific Ave.). ℭ 415/986-9651.

Vesuvio   Along Jack Kerouac Alley across from the City Lights Bookstore, this beatnik hangout isn't just riding its historic reputation. Popular with writers, artists, songsters, and wannabes, Vesuvio is crowded with self-proclaimed philosophers, along with everyone else from longshoremen and cab drivers to businesspeople. 255 Columbus Ave. (at Broadway). ℭ 415/362-3370.

BREWPUBS

Gordon Biersch Brewery Restaurant   Popular with the young Republican crowd (loose ties and tight skirts predominate), this modern, two-tiered brewery and restaurant attracts a more upscale clientele than your typical beer garden. The food—beer-braised lamb shank, baby back ribs, lemon roasted half chicken—is pretty good, but it's the gourmet lagers and ales that account for the line out the door. *One caveat:* When the lower-level bar fills up, you practically have to shout to be heard. 2 Harrison St. (on the Embarcadero). ℭ 415/243-8246. www.gordonbiersch.com.

San Francisco Brewing Company   The bar is one of the city's few remaining old saloons, aglow with stained-glass windows, tile floors, skylights, a mahogany bar, and a massive overhead fan running the full length of the bar—a bizarre contraption crafted from brass and palm fronds. Menu items range from $3.70 (curiously, for *edamame,* or soybeans) to $20 for a full rack of baby back ribs with all the fixings. The happy-hour special, a dollar per 8.5-ounce microbrew beer (or $2.50 a pint), runs daily from 4 to 6pm and midnight to 1am. 155 Columbus Ave. (at Pacific St.). ℭ 415/434-3344. www.sfbrewing.com.

Thirsty Bear Brewing Company   Seven superb, handcrafted varieties of brew are always on tap at this stylish high-ceilinged brick edifice. Excellent Spanish food, too. Pool tables and dartboards are upstairs, and flamenco music can be heard on Sunday nights. 661 Howard St. (1 block east of the Moscone Center). ℭ 415/974-0905. www.thirstybear.com.

COCKTAILS WITH A VIEW

In addition to these options, see p. 135 for a full review of **Harry Denton's Starlight Room.**

The Carnelian Room   On the 52nd floor of the Bank of America building, the Carnelian Room offers uninterrupted views of the city. From a window-front table, you feel as if you can reach out, pluck up the TransAmerica Pyramid, and stir your martini with it. *Note:* The restaurant has the most extensive wine list in the city—1,600 selections. 555 California St., in the Bank of America Building (between Kearny and Montgomery sts.). ℭ 415/433-7500. www.carnelianroom.com. Jacket and tie required for men.

Cityscape   When you sit under the glass roof and sip a drink here, it feels as though you're out under the stars and enjoying views of the bay. There's nightly dancing to a DJ's picks from 10pm. The mirrored columns and floor-to-ceiling draperies help create an elegant and romantic ambience. Atop Hilton Tower I, 333 O'Farrell St. (at Mason St.), 46th floor. ℭ 415/923-5002.

Equinox   The sales "hook" of the Hyatt's rooftop Equinox is a revolving floor that gives each table a 360-degree panoramic view of the city every 45 minutes. In addition to cocktails, dinner is served daily. In the Hyatt Regency Hotel, 5 Embarcadero Center. © 415/788-1234.

Top of the Mark *(Finds)*   This is one of the most famous cocktail lounges in the world. During World War II it was considered de rigueur for Pacific-bound servicemen to toast their good-byes to the States here. The spectacular glass-walled room features an unparalleled view. Live entertainment is offered Friday and Saturday from 8:30pm, when there's a $7 to $10 cover. Drink prices range from $5 to $10. In the Mark Hopkins Intercontinental, 1 Nob Hill (between California and Mason sts.). © 415/616-6916.

GAY & LESBIAN BARS & CLUBS

The Café   When this place first got jumping, it was the only predominantly lesbian dance club on Saturday nights in the city. But once the guys found out how much fun the girls were having, they joined the party. Today it's still a very happening mixed gay and lesbian scene with three bars; a steamy, free-spirited dance floor; and a small heated patio. 2367 Market St. (at Castro St.). © 415/861-3846. www.cafesf.com.

The EndUp   It's a different nightclub every night of the week, but regardless of who's throwing the party, the place is always jumping with the DJs blasting tunes. There are two pool tables, a flaming fireplace, an outdoor patio, and a mob of gyrating souls on the dance floor. Some nights are straight, so call for gay nights. 401 Sixth St. (at Harrison St.). © 415/357-0827.

The Stud   The Stud has been around for over 30 years, is one of the most successful gay establishments in town, and is mellow enough for straights as well as gays. The interior has an antiques-shop look and a miniature train circling over the bar and dance floor. Music here is a balanced mix of old and new, and nights vary from cabaret and oldies to disco. Call in advance for the evening's venue. Drink prices range from $3 to $15. 399 Ninth St. (at Harrison St.). © 415/863-6623. www.studsf.com. Cover $2–$6 Fri–Sat.

Twin Peaks Tavern   Right at the intersection of Castro, 17th, and Market streets is one of the Castro's most famous gay hangouts. At 40 years of age, it caters to an older crowd and is considered the first gay bar in America. Because of its relatively small size and desirable location, the place becomes fairly crowded and convivial by 8pm, earlier than many neighboring bars. 401 Castro St. (at 17th and Market sts.). © 415/864-9470. No cover.

5

The San Francisco Bay Area

by Erika Lenkert

The Bay City is captivating, but don't ignore its environs, which contain a multitude of natural spectacles like Mount Tamalpais and Muir Woods; scenic communities like Tiburon, Sausalito, and Half Moon Bay; and cities like Oakland and its youth-oriented next-door neighbor, Berkeley. Farther north stretch the valleys of Napa and Sonoma, the finest wine region in the nation (see chapter 6, "The Wine Country"). To the south lie high-tech Silicon Valley and San Jose, Northern California's largest city.

1 Berkeley

10 miles NE of San Francisco

Until the 1990s, the University of California at Berkeley with its first-rate academic standards, its 18 Nobel Prize winners, and its protests that led to the most well-known student riots in U.S. history was the primary reason that Berkeley became more than a sleepy town east of the big city. But the race to find affordable Bay Area housing has made the East Bay even more of a hub. Today there's still hippie idealism in the air, but the radicals have aged; the 1960s are largely present in tie-dye and paraphernalia shops (which are joined by national chains along Telegraph Ave.). Meanwhile, communities and upscale restaurants and shops continue to flourish. All in all, it's an entertaining town with all types of people, a beautiful campus, vast parks, and some incredible restaurants.

ESSENTIALS

GETTING THERE   The Berkeley **BART** (Bay Area Rapid Transit) station is 2 blocks from the university. The fare from San Francisco is less than $3. For information, call BART at © **510/793-2278** or log on to www.bart.gov.

If you're coming **by car** from San Francisco, take I-80 east to the University Avenue exit. Count on walking some distance, as you won't find a parking spot near the university.

VISITOR INFORMATION   The **Berkeley Convention & Visitors Bureau,** 2015 Center St., Berkeley, CA 94703 (© **800/847-4823** or 510/549-7040; www.berkeleycvb.com), can answer your questions and even find accommodations for you.

EXPLORING THE UNIVERSITY & ENVIRONS

Hanging out is the Berkeley pastime, and the best place to do it is on **Telegraph Avenue,** the street that leads to the campus's southern entrance. Most of the action is between Bancroft Way and Ashby Avenue, where coffeehouses, restaurants, shops, book and record stores, and crafts booths swarm with life.

Pretend you're a local: Plant yourself at a cafe, sip a latte, and ponder something intellectual while you survey the populace bustling by. Bibliophiles must stop at **Cody's Books,** 2454 Telegraph Ave. (© **510/845-7852;** www.cody books.com), to peruse its huge selection of titles, independent-press books, and magazines. For used and antique books, stop by **Moe's Books,** 2476 Telegraph Ave. (© **510/849-2087;** www.moesbooks.com). With four floors of new, used, and out-of-print books, you're not likely to leave empty-handed.

UC Berkeley itself is worth a stroll. It's a beautiful old campus with plenty of woodsy paths, architecturally noteworthy buildings, and 33,000 students scurrying to and from classes. Among the architectural highlights of the campus are buildings by Bernard Maybeck, Bakewell and Brown, and John Galen Howard. Contact the **Visitor Information Center,** 101 University Hall, 2200 University Ave., at Oxford Street (© **510/642-5215;** www.berkeley.edu/visitors), to join a free campus tour. Tours are Monday through Saturday at 10am and Sunday at 1pm; $40 electric-cart tours are available with reservations (no tours mid-Dec to mid-Jan), or pick up a self-guided walking-tour brochure. If you're interested in notable off-campus buildings, contact the **Berkeley Convention & Visitors Bureau** (© **510/549-7040;** www.berkeleycvb.com) for an architectural-walking-tour brochure.

You'll find the university's southern entrance at the north end of Telegraph Avenue, at Bancroft Way. Walk through the main entrance into **Sproul Plaza.** When school is in session, you'll encounter the gamut of Berkeley's inhabitants as well as the **Student Union,** with a bookstore, cafes, and an information desk on the second floor, where you can pick up a free map of Berkeley along with the local student newspaper (also found in dispensers throughout campus). You might be lucky enough to stumble upon some impromptu musicians or a heated—and sometimes absurd—debate. There's always something going on, so stretch out on the grass for a few minutes and take in the Berkeley vibe.

For viewing more traditional art forms, there are some noteworthy museums. The **Lawrence Hall of Science,** Centennial Drive near Grizzly Peak (© **510/ 642-5132;** www.lawrencehallofscience.org), offering hands-on science exploration, is open from 10am to 5pm daily and is a great place to watch the sunset. Admission is $8.50 for adults; $6.50 for seniors, students, and children 7 to 18; $4 for children 3 to 6; and free for kids under 3. The **UC Berkeley Art Museum,** 2626 Bancroft Way (© **510/642-0808;** www.bampfa.berkeley.edu), is open Wednesday through Sunday from 11am to 5pm. Admission is $8 for adults; $5 for seniors, students, and children ages 12 to 17; and free for kids under 12 and UC students. This museum includes a collection of Hans Hofmann paintings, a sculpture garden, and the **Pacific Film Archive,** main entrance at 2625 Durant Ave. (© **510/642-1124**).

OFF-CAMPUS ATTRACTIONS

PARKS   Berkeley has some of the most extensive and beautiful parks around. If you enjoy hiking, getting a breath of California air, and sniffing a few roses, jump in your car and make your way to **Tilden Park** (© **510/562-PARK**). You'll find plenty of flora and fauna, hiking trails, an old steam train and merry-go-round, a farm and nature area for kids, and a chilly tree-encircled lake. On the way, stop at the colorful terraced **Rose Garden** in north Berkeley on Euclid Avenue between Bay View and Eunice Street.

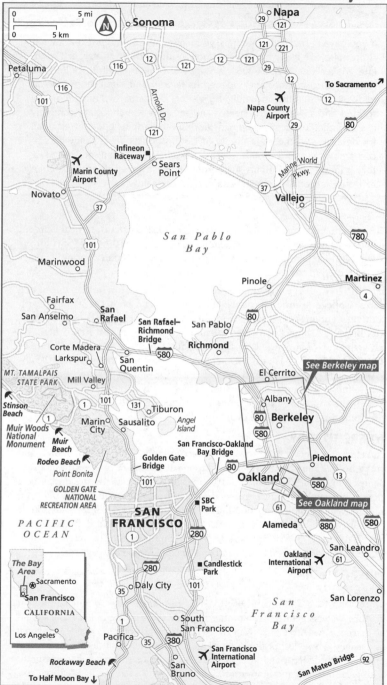

The San Francisco Bay Area

(Finds Sweet Sensations at Berkeley's Chocolate Factory

If you haven't had chocolate nibs, you haven't lived—at least that's what chocoholics are likely to discover upon visiting **Scharffen Berger Chocolate Maker** (© 510/981-4050; www.scharffenberger.com). California's runaway success chocolatier opened its factory and retail shop doors in mid-2001. Within the brick building, visitors can taste the "nibs" (crunchy roasted and shelled cocoa beans) and see how the chocolate company uses vintage European equipment during regularly scheduled tours (call for details). And there are plenty of tasty products, from candy bars to cocoa powder and chocolate sauce, available in the retail shop. The factory is located at 914 Heinz Ave.; from I-80 East, take the Ashby Avenue exit, turn left on Seventh Street and right on Heinz.

Another nature excursion is the **University of California Botanical Garden,** in Strawberry Canyon on Centennial Drive (© **510/643-2755;** http://botanicalgarden.berkeley.edu), which features a vast collection of plant life ranging from cacti to redwoods.

SHOPPING   If you're itching to exercise your credit cards, head to one of two places. **College Avenue** from Dwight to the Oakland border is crammed with boutiques, antiques shops, and restaurants. The other option is **Fourth Street** in west Berkeley, 2 blocks north of the University Avenue exit off I-80, where you can grab a cup of java, read the paper at a patio table, and then hit the **Crate & Barrel Outlet,** 1785 Fourth St., between Hearst and Virginia (© **510/528-5500**), where prices are 30% to 70% off retail. Or wander into any of the small, wonderful stores crammed with imported and locally made housewares. Nearby is **REI,** the Bay Area's favorite outdoor outfitter, at 1338 San Pablo Ave., near Gilman Street (© **510/527-4140**).

WHERE TO STAY

Berkeley's not a good hotel town. Most accommodations are basic motels and funky B&Bs. The exception is **The Claremont Resort & Spa,** 41 Tunnel Rd., Berkeley (© **800/551-7266** or 510/843-3000; www.claremontresort.com), a grand Victorian hotel with upgrades that include modern rooms, a spa and gym, a hip bar, and grandiose surroundings. Prices range from $270 to $400 double occupancy. Another option is to contact **Berkeley & Oakland Bed and Breakfast Network** (© **510/547-6380;** www.bbonline.com/ca/berkeley-oakland), which books visitors into homes and apartments in the East Bay area.

WHERE TO DINE
EXPENSIVE
Chez Panisse ★★★ CALIFORNIA   California cuisine is so much a product of Alice Waters's genius that all other restaurants following in her wake should be dated A.A.W. (After Alice Waters). Read the menus posted outside and you'll understand why. Most of the produce and meat comes from local farms and is organically produced, and after all these years, Alice still tends her restaurant with great integrity and innovation. Chez Panisse is a redwood-and-stucco cottage with a brick terrace filled with potted plants. The two dining areas, the cafe and the restaurant, both serve Mediterranean-inspired cuisine.

Berkeley

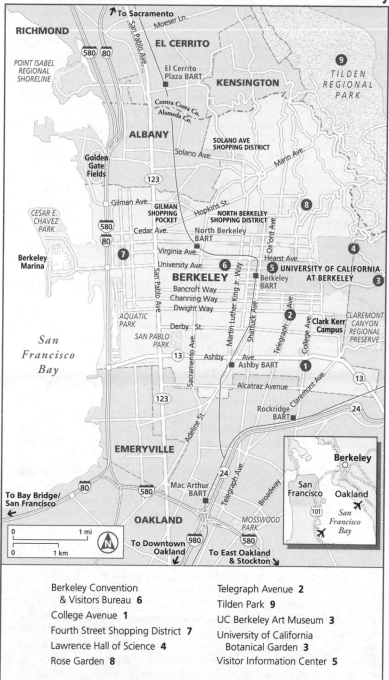

Berkeley Convention
 & Visitors Bureau **6**

College Avenue **1**

Fourth Street Shopping District **7**

Lawrence Hall of Science **4**

Rose Garden **8**

Telegraph Avenue **2**

Tilden Park **9**

UC Berkeley Art Museum **3**

University of California
 Botanical Garden **3**

Visitor Information Center **5**

In the upstairs cafe are displays of pastries and fruit and an oak bar adorned with large bouquets of fresh flowers. At lunch or dinner, the menu might feature delicately smoked gravlax or roasted eggplant soup with pesto, followed by lamb ragout garnished with apricots, onions, and spices and served with couscous.

The cozy downstairs restaurant, strewn with floral bouquets, is a warm environment in which to indulge in the $65 fixed-price four-course gourmet dinner, which is served Tuesday through Thursday. Friday and Saturday it's $75 for four courses, and Monday is bargain night, with a three-course dinner for $50.

The restaurant posts the following week's menu every Saturday. There's also an excellent wine list, with bottles ranging from $18 to $300.

1517 Shattuck Ave. (between Cedar and Vine). © **510/548-5525**; cafe reservations 510/548-5049. Fax 510/548-0140. www.chezpanisse.com. Reservations required. Restaurant fixed-price menu $50–$75; cafe main courses $15–$25. AE, DC, DISC, MC, V. Restaurant seatings Mon–Sat 6–6:30pm and 8:30–9:30pm. Cafe Mon–Thurs 11:30am–3pm and 5–10:30pm; Fri–Sat 11:30am–3:30pm and 5–11:30pm. BART: Berkeley. From I-80 north, take the University Ave. exit and turn left onto Shattuck Ave.

MODERATE

Cafe Rouge ★★ MEDITERRANEAN   After cooking at San Francisco's Zuni Cafe for 10 years, chef-owner Marsha McBride launched her own restaurant, a sort of Zuni East. She brought former staff members and some of the restaurant's flavor with her, and now her loftlike dining room serves salads, rotisserie chicken with oil and thyme, grilled lamb chops, steaks, and homemade sausages. East Bay carnivores are happy with the top-notch burger.

1782 Fourth St. (between Delaware and Hearst). © **510/525-1440.** www.caferouge.net. Reservations recommended. Main courses $9.50–$24. MC, V. Daily 11:30am–3pm; Tues–Sat 3–5pm (interim menu); Tues–Thurs 5:30–9:30pm; Fri–Sat 5:30–10:30pm; Sun 5–9:30pm.

O Chamé ★★ JAPANESE   Spare and plain in its decor, with ochre-colored walls etched with patterns, this spot has a meditative air to complement the traditional, experimental, and very fresh and clean Japanese-inspired cuisine. The menu, which changes daily, offers meal-in-a-bowl dishes ($9–$13) that allow a choice of soba or udon noodles in a clear soup with a variety of toppings—from shrimp and wakame seaweed to beef with burdock root and carrot. Appetizers include a flavorful melding of grilled shiitake mushrooms, as well as portobello mushrooms, watercress, and green-onion pancakes. There are also specials ($10–$18), which always include delicious roasted salmon.

1830 Fourth St. (near Hearst). © **510/841-8783.** Reservations recommended Fri–Sat dinner. Main courses lunch $9–$19, dinner $18–$24. AE, DC, MC, V. Mon–Sat 11:30am–3pm; Mon–Thurs 5:30–9pm; Fri–Sat 5:30–9:30pm.

Rivoli ★★★ *(Finds* CALIFORNIA   One of the favored dinner destinations in the East Bay, Rivoli offers top-notch food at reasonable prices. In an otherwise uninteresting space, the owners have created a warm, intimate dining room, which overlooks a little garden with visiting raccoons and possums and a wine bar near the entrance. Aside from a few house favorites, the menu changes entirely every 3 weeks to feature whatever's freshest and in season; the wine list follows suit with around a dozen by-the-glass options handpicked to match the food. While many love it, I'm not a fan of the portobello-mushroom fritter, a gourmet variation of the fried zucchini stick. However, plenty of dishes shine, including roast chicken roulade stuffed with pistachios, *mirepoix* (diced vegetables and seasonings) and herbs with Bing cherry jus; artichoke lasagna with ricotta, mint salsa, and tomato sauce; and braised lamb shank with green garlic risotto, sautéed spinach, and oven-dried tomatoes. Finish the evening with an assortment of cheeses or a warm chocolate truffle torte with hazelnut ice cream, orange crème anglaise, and chocolate sauce.

1539 Solano Ave. (© 510/526-2542. www.rivolirestaurant.com. Reservations recommended. Main courses $16–$20. AE, DC, DISC, MC, V. Mon–Thurs 5:30–9:30pm; Fri 5:30–10pm; Sat 5–10pm; Sun 5–9pm.

2 Oakland

10 miles E of San Francisco

Although it's less than a dozen miles from San Francisco, the city of Oakland is worlds apart from its sister city. Originally a cluster of ranches and farms, its size and stature exploded practically overnight as the last mile of transcontinental railroad track was laid down in 1869. Major shipping traffic soon followed, and to this day Oakland is one of the busiest industrial ports on the West Coast.

The price for all this success, however, has been Oakland's lowbrow reputation as a working-class city famous for its crime and forever in the shadow of San Francisco's chic spotlight. However, with housing prices and weather far more inviting than they are in San Francisco, "Oaktown" is in a renaissance and offers plenty of pleasant surprises for those who venture this way. Rent a sailboat on Lake Merritt, stroll along the waterfront, explore the fantastic Oakland Museum—they're all great reasons to hop the bay and spend a fog-free day exploring one of California's largest and most ethnically diverse cities.

ESSENTIALS

GETTING THERE   Bay Area Rapid Transit (BART) makes the trip from San Francisco to Oakland through one of the longest underwater transit tunnels in the world. Fares range from $1 to $4, depending on your station of origin; children 4 and under ride free. BART trains operate Monday through Friday from 4am to midnight, Saturday from 6am to midnight, and Sunday from 8am to midnight. Exit at the 12th Street station for downtown Oakland.

By car from San Francisco, take I-80 across the San Francisco–Oakland Bay Bridge and follow the signs to downtown Oakland. Exit at Grand Avenue South for the Lake Merritt area.

VISITOR INFORMATION   A calendar of events and a free copy of the 60-page *Destination Oakland* guide are available online or by mail from the Oakland Convention and Visitors Bureau, 463 11th St., Oakland, CA 94607 (© 510/839-9000; www.oaklandcvb.com). The city also sponsors free guided tours, including African-American Heritage and neighborhood tours; call © 510/238-3234 for details.

CITY LAYOUT   Downtown Oakland is bordered by Grand Avenue on the north, I-980 on the west, Inner Harbor on the south, and Lake Merritt on the east. Between these landmarks are three BART stations (12th St., 19th St., and Lake Merritt), City Hall, the Oakland Museum, Jack London Square, and other sights.

WHAT TO SEE & DO

Lake Merritt is Oakland's primary tourist attraction, along with Jack London Square (see below). Three and a half miles in circumference, the tidal lagoon was bridged and dammed in the 1860s and is now a refuge that's home to flocks of migrating ducks, herons, and geese. The 122-acre Lakeside Park, a popular place to picnic, to feed the ducks, and to escape the fog, surrounds it on three sides.

At the **Municipal Boathouse** (© **510/238-2196**) along the north shore, you can rent sailboats, rowboats, pedal boats, and canoes for $6 to $12 per hour. Another option is to take an hour-long gondola ride with **Gondola Servizio** (© **510/663-6603;** www.gondolaservizio.com). Experienced gondoliers will serenade you as you glide across the lake; the hourly rate for two varies from $45 for your basic Venetian fling, to $225 for a customized photo-op package for weddings and other celebrations.

Another site worth visiting is Oakland's **Paramount Theatre,** 2025 Broadway (© **510/893-2300;** www.paramounttheatre.com), an outstanding example of Art Deco architecture and decor. Built in 1931 and restored in 1973, it functions as the city's main performing-arts center, featuring talent like Alicia Keys as well as gospel music, symphony orchestras, and classic movies. Guided tours of the 3,000-seat theater are given the first and third Saturdays of each month, excluding holidays. Reservations are not necessary; just show up at 10am at the box-office entrance on 21st Street at Broadway. Cameras are allowed, and admission is $1.

If you take pleasure from strolling sailboat-filled wharves or are a die-hard fan of Jack London, you might enjoy a visit to **Jack London Square** (© **866/ 295-9853;** www.jacklondonsquare.com). Oakland's only blatant tourist area, this low-key version of San Francisco's Fisherman's Wharf shamelessly plays up the fact that Jack London spent most of his youth along this waterfront. The square fronts the harbor, housing a tacky complex of boutiques and eateries that are about as far away from the "call of the wild" as you can get. Most are open Monday through Saturday from 10am to 7pm (some restaurants stay open later). One of the best options is live jazz at **Yoshi's World Class Jazz House & Japanese Restaurant** 🏨, 510 Embarcadero W. (© **510/238-9200;** www.yoshis. com), which also serves decent sushi in its adjoining restaurant. In the center of the square is a small reconstructed version of the Yukon cabin in which Jack London lived while prospecting in the Klondike during the Gold Rush of 1897.

In the middle of Jack London Square, you'll find a more authentic memorial, **Heinold's First and Last Chance Saloon** (© **510/839-6761**)—a funky, friendly bar and landmark worth a visit. This is where London did some of his writing and most of his drinking; the corner table he used has remained as it was nearly a century ago. Also in the square are the mast and nameplate from the USS *Oakland,* a ship that saw extensive action in the Pacific during World War II.

The square is at Broadway and Embarcadero. Take I-880 to Broadway, turn south, and go to the end. Via BART, get off at the 12th Street station, walk south along Broadway (about ½ mile) or take bus no. 51a to the foot of Broadway.

Oakland Museum of California 🏨   Two blocks south of Lake Merritt, the Oakland Museum of California incorporates just about everything you'd want to know about the state and its people, history, culture, geology, art, environment, and ecology. Inside a low, modern building set among sweeping gardens and terraces, it's actually three museums in one: exhibitions of works by California artists from Bierstadt to Diebenkorn; collections of historic artifacts, from Pomo Indian basketry to Country Joe McDonald's guitar; and re-creations of California habitats from the coast to the mountains. The museum holds major shows of California artists and exhibitions dedicated to major California movements and also frequently shows photography from its huge collection.

Oakland

To 580
Bay Bridge/San Francisco

Grand Ave.

Children's
Fairyland

LAKESIDE PARK

23rd St.

W. Grand Ave.

21st St.

22nd St.

21st St.

20th St.

Harrison St.

Municipal
Boathouse
(Rentals)

Greyhound
Bus Depot

20th St.

Williams St.

19th St.
BART

SNOW
PARK

Lakeside Dr.

19th St.

Lake
Merritt

19th St.

18th St.

18th St.

17th St.

Brush St.

Castro St.

17th St.

16th St.

15th St.

Broadway

Franklin St.

Webster St.

Harrison St.

Alice St.

Jackson St.

Madison St.

Oak St.

Camron–
Stanford
House

The
Rotunda

City
Hall

14th St.

15th St.

14th St.

Preservation
Park

City
Center

13th St.

12th St.

12th St./
City Center
BART

Post
Office

12th St.

Oakland
Museum
of California

Martin Luther King Jr. Way

11th St.

Oakland
Convention
Center

11th St.

LINCOLN
SQUARE

10th St.

10th St.

CHINATOWN

9th St.

OLD
OAKLAND

Asian Cultural Center

MADISON
PARK

9th St.

Lake Merritt
BART

8th St.

8th St.

Brush St.

Castro St.

7th St.

7th St.

Fallon St.

Laney
College

JEFFERSON
SQUARE

6th St.

CHINESE
GARDEN

6th St.

To Bay Bridge/
San Francisco

880

5th St.

5th St.

880

To Oakland
International
Airport

4th St.

4th St.

Jefferson St.

Clay St.

Washington St.

Broadway

Franklin St.

Webster St.

Harrison St.

Alice St.

Jackson St.

Madison St.

Oak St.

3rd St.

3rd St.

Victory Ct.

2nd St.

2nd St.

Embarcadero

Amtrak
Terminal

Embarcadero

Jack London Square

Alameda/
Oakland
Ferry
Terminal

Water
Taxi

Webster St. Tube

Posey Tube

ESTUARY
PARK

Ferry to Alameda
& San Francisco

■ BART Station
ⓘ Information

0 ——————— 1/4 mi
0 ——————— 0.25 km

Area of
detail

Berkeley

San
Francisco

Oakland

101

San
Francisco
Bay

DINING ◆
À Côté **1**
Citron **1**
Oliveto Cafe
& Restaurant **2**
Yoshi's World Class Jazz
House and Japanese
Restaurant **7**

ATTRACTIONS ●
Jack London Square **8**
Lake Merritt **5**
Lakeside Park **4**
Oakland Museum of
California **6**
Paramount Theatre **3**

Forty-five-minute guided tours leave from the information desks on request or by appointment. There's a cafe, a **gallery** (© **510/834-2296**) that sells works by California artists, and a book and gift shop. The cafe is open Wednesday through Friday from 10:30am to 4:30pm, Saturday from 1:30 to 4:30pm.

1000 Oak St. (at 10th St.). © **888/625-6873** or 510/238-2200 for recorded information. www.muse-umca.org. Admission $8 adults; $5 students and seniors; free for children under 6. 2nd Sun of the month is free for everyone. Wed–Sat 10am–5pm; Sun noon–5pm; open until 9pm 1st Fri of the month. Closed Jan 1, July 4, Thanksgiving, and Dec 25. BART: Lake Merritt station; walk 1 block north. From I-880 north, take the Oak St. exit; the museum is 5 blocks east. Or take I-580 to I-980 and exit at the Jackson St. ramp.

WHERE TO STAY

Two fine midrange hotel options in Oaktown are the **Waterfront Plaza Hotel,** 10 Washington St., Jack London Square, Oakland (© **800/729-3638** or 510/836-3800; www.waterfrontplaza.com), and the **Oakland Marriott City Center,** 1001 Broadway, Oakland (© **510/451-4000;** www.marriott.com). Most major motel chains also have locations (and budget prices) around town and near the airport.

WHERE TO DINE

Citron ✿ FRENCH/CALIFORNIA   This adorable French bistro was a smash when it opened in 1992 and continues to earn raves for its small yet enticingly eclectic menu. The menu, which draws the flavors of France, Italy, and Spain with fresh California produce for results you aren't likely to have tasted elsewhere, changes every few weeks. Dishes might range from aioli-breadcrumb-crusted Sonoma rack of lamb atop grilled ratatouille, to spicy bayou seafood stew brimming with fried oysters, shrimp, snapper, and bell-pepper-and-tomato sauce, to rich saffron artichoke risotto. *A word of advice:* If you're into classic foods you can identify by name, head elsewhere. It's all about creative cooking here.

5484 College Ave. (north of Broadway between Taft and Lawton sts.). © 510/653-5484. www.citron-acote.com. Reservations recommended. Main courses $20–$26; 3- to 5-course fixed-price menu (Sun–Fri only) $35–$46. AE, DC, DISC, MC, V. Mon–Tues 5:30–9pm; Wed–Thurs 5:30–9:30pm; Fri 5:30–10pm; Sat 5–10pm; Sun 5–9pm.

Oliveto Cafe & Restaurant ✿✿✿ ITALIAN   Paul Bertolli, former chef at Chez Panisse, jumped ship to open one of the top Italian restaurants in the Bay Area (certainly the best in Oakland). During the week it's a madhouse at lunchtime, when local workers pile in for the wood-fired pizzas and tapas in the lower-level cafe. The upstairs restaurant—with neo-Florentine decor—is slightly more civil, packed nightly with fans of Bertolli's house-made pastas, sausages, and prosciutto. Oliveto has a wood-burning oven, flame-broiled rotisserie, and a good wine list. You might begin your meal with a special cocktail (evenings only), such as Vodka Nero, made with pinot noir grape juice and lime. An assortment of pricey grills, braises, and roasts anchor the daily changing menu, but it's the heavenly pastas that will truly send you. Still, the Arista (classic Italian pork with garlic and rosemary and pork jus) is insanely good; and no one does fried calamari, onion rings, and lemon slices better than Oliveto. *Tip:* There's free parking in the lot at the rear of the Market Hall building.

Rockridge Market Hall, 5655 College Ave. (off the northeast end of Broadway at Shafter/Keith St., across from the Rockridge BART station). © 510/547-5356. www.oliveto.com. Reservations recommended for restaurant. Main courses $9–$15 lunch, $16–$30 dinner. AE, DC, MC, V. Tues–Fri 11:30am–2pm; Tues–Wed 5:30–9:30pm; Thurs–Sat 5:30–10pm; Sun 5–9pm.

MODERATE

À Côté ⭒⭒ FRENCH TAPAS   Christopher Rossi, who also owns neighboring Citron (see above), looks to chef Matthew Colgan to serve up killer rustic Mediterranean-inspired small plates at this loud, festive, and warmly lit joint. A "no reservations" policy means there's usually a long wait during prime dining hours, but once seated you can join locals in a nosh fest featuring the likes of croque-monsieur; *pommes frites* with aioli; wood-oven cooked mussels in Pernod; grilled pork tenderloin with creamy polenta; traviso cheese; and pancetta. Remember the cheese plates, too. Wash it down with excellent by-the-glass or bottle selections from the great wine list or perky cocktails.

5478 College Ave. (at Taft Ave.). (℃ **510/655-6469.** www.citron-acote.com. Reservations not accepted. Small plates $5–$14. AE, DC, DISC, MC, V. Sun and Tues–Wed 5:30–10pm; Thurs 5:30–11pm; Fri–Sat 5:30pm–midnight. Closed Mon.

3 Sausalito

5 miles N of San Francisco

Just off the northern end of the Golden Gate Bridge is the eclectic little town of Sausalito, a slightly bohemian, nonchalant, and quaint adjunct to San Francisco. With approximately 8,000 residents, Sausalito feels rather like St. Tropez on the French Riviera—minus the starlets and the European aristocracy. It has its quota of paper millionaires, but they rub permanently suntanned shoulders with a good number of hard-up artists, struggling authors, shipyard workers, and fishers. Next to the swank restaurants, plush bars, and antiques shops and galleries, you'll see hamburger joints, beer parlors, and secondhand bookstores.

Above all, Sausalito has scenery and sunshine, for once you cross the Golden Gate Bridge, you're out of the San Francisco fog patch and under blue California sky (I hope). Almost all the tourist action, which is basically limited to window-shopping and eating, takes place at sea level on Bridgeway.

ESSENTIALS

GETTING THERE   The **Golden Gate Ferry Service** fleet, Ferry Building (℃ **415/923-2000;** www.goldengateferry.org), operates between the San Francisco Ferry Building, at the foot of Market Street, and Sausalito. Service is frequent, departing at reasonable intervals every day except New Year's Day, Thanksgiving, and Christmas Day. Phone for an exact schedule. The ride takes a half-hour, and one-way fares to Sausalito are $5.60 for adults; $2.45 on weekdays and $4.20 on weekends for kids 6 to 12; $2.80 for seniors and passengers with disabilities; and free for children under 6. Family rates are available on weekends.

Ferries of the **Blue & Gold Fleet** (℃ **415/705-5555;** www.blueandgold-fleet.com) leave from Pier 41 (Fisherman's Wharf) and cost $6.50 one-way, $4 for kids 5 to 11, and free for children under 5. Boats run on a seasonal schedule; phone or check out the website for departure information.

By car from San Francisco, take U.S. 101 north, then the first right after the Golden Gate Bridge (Alexander exit). Alexander becomes Bridgeway in Sausalito.

EXPLORING THE TOWN

Sausalito is a mecca for shoppers seeking handmade, original, and offbeat clothes and footwear, as well as arts and crafts. The town's best shops are found in the alleys, malls, and second-floor boutiques reached by steep, narrow staircases on and off **Bridgeway,** Sausalito's main touring strip, which runs along the water. Those in the know make a quick detour to **Caledonia Street,** which runs parallel to and 1 block inland from Bridgeway. Not only is it less congested, but there's also a far better selection of cafes and shops.

Bay Model Visitors Center *(Kids)*   The U.S. Army Corps of Engineers once used this high-tech, 1½-acre model of San Francisco's bay and delta to analyze problems and observe the impact of changes in water flow. The model reproduces (in scale) the rise and fall of tides, the flows and currents of water, and the mixing of fresh and salt water, and indicates trends in sediment movement. There's a 10-minute film and a tour, but the most interesting time to visit is when it's in use, so call ahead.

2100 Bridgeway. ℂ 415/332-3871. www.spn.usace.army.mil/bmvc. Free admission, but $3 donation requested. Labor Day to Memorial Day Tues–Sat 9am–4pm; Memorial Day to Labor Day Tues–Fri 9am–4pm, Sat–Sun and holidays 10am–5pm.

WHERE TO STAY

Casa Madrona *(★★)*   Sooner or later most visitors to Sausalito look up and wonder at the ornate mansion on the hill. It's part of Casa Madrona, a hideaway by the bay built in 1885 by a lumber baron. Successive renovations and extensions have added a rambling, New England–style building to the hillside below the main house. Now a landmark, the hotel offers rooms, suites, and cottages, accessed by steep, landscaped pathways. The 16 freestanding units were recently gussied up with contemporary flavor, four-poster beds, and marble bathrooms. Other rooms in the mansion are decorated in a variety of styles; some have Jacuzzis and others have fireplaces. The newest rooms overlook the water with views of the San Francisco skyline and bay. The classy **Poggio** restaurant (see below) has been Sausalito's hottest new thing since its late-2003 opening.

801 Bridgeway, Sausalito, CA 94965. ℂ **800/567-9524** or 415/332-0502. Fax 415/332-2537. www. casamadrona.com. 63 units. $255–$340 double; $430 suite. AE, DC, DISC, MC, V. Valet parking $20. Ferry: Walk across the street from the landing. From U.S. 101 north, take the 1st right after the Golden Gate Bridge (Alexander exit); Alexander becomes Bridgeway. **Amenities:** Restaurant; Jacuzzi; concierge; room service (breakfast and dinner); babysitting; laundry service; dry cleaning. *In room:* TV, VCR upon availability, minibar, coffeemaker, hair dryer, robes.

The Inn Above Tide *(★★)*   Perched over the bay atop well-grounded pilings, this former luxury apartment complex underwent a $4-million transformation into one of Sausalito's finest accommodations. It's the view that clinches it: Every room comes with a panorama of the San Francisco Bay, including a vista of the city glimmering in the distance. Should you manage to tear yourself away from your private deck, you'll find that 23 of the sumptuously appointed rooms sport a romantic little fireplace; some have a vast sunken tub with Jacuzzi jets, remote-control air-conditioning, and wondrously comfortable queen- or king-size beds. Soothing shades of pale green and blue highlight the decor, which blends in well with the bayscape outside. Be sure to request that your breakfast and newspaper be delivered to your deck, and then cancel your early appointments: On sunny mornings, nobody checks out early.

30 El Portal (next to the Sausalito Ferry Landing), Sausalito, CA 94965. ℂ **800/893-8433** or 415/332-9535. Fax 415/332-6714. www.innabovetide.com. 29 units. $255–$795 double. Rates include continental breakfast and evening wine and cheese. AE, DC, MC, V. Valet parking $12. **Amenities:** Concierge; in-room massage; same-day laundry service/dry cleaning. *In room:* A/C, TV, dataport, minibar, fridge, hair dryer, free high-speed wireless Internet access.

WHERE TO DINE
EXPENSIVE

Poggio ★★ ITALIAN   Sausalito has long been low on upscale dining options, but all that changed with the late-2003 opening of elegant Poggio, which is a loose Italian translation for "special hillside place." Adjoining the Casa Madrona hotel and across the street from the marina, everything *is* special here. Floor-to-ceiling doors open to an interior with arches and earthen colors, mahogany accents, and well-directed light. The centerpiece wood oven is manned by a cadre of chefs, and dining is enhanced by the fine wine cellar, terra-cotta-tiled floors, comfy mohair banquettes, and white linen-draped tables. Executive chef and partner Christopher Fernandez ensures the food is equally elegant with his superb salad of endive, Gorgonzola, walnuts, figs, and honey; pizzas; addictively excellent pastas (try the garganelli with squab Bolognese or spinach ricotta gnocchi with beef ragout); and yummy entrees. Think roasted halibut with faro, snap peas, mushrooms, and spring onion *brodo* (broth) and grilled lamb chops with roasted fennel and gremolata. With a full bar, great, well-priced wine list, and tasty desserts, this is Sausalito's premier dining destination—excluding more casual and decidedly Asian restaurant Sushi Ran (see below).

777 Bridgeway (at Bay St.). ℂ 415/332-7771. www.casamadrona.com. Continental breakfast pastries $2.50; main courses lunch $7.50–$16, dinner $7.50–$20. AE, MC, V. Continental breakfast daily 6:30–11:30am; lunch 11:30am–5:30pm; dinner Sun–Thurs 5:30–10pm, Fri–Sat 5:30–11pm. Free valet parking.

MODERATE

Guernica ★ FRENCH/BASQUE   Established in 1974, Guernica is one of those funky old restaurants that you'd probably pass up for something more chic and modern down the street if you didn't know better. What? You don't know about Guernica's legendary paella Valenciana? Well, now you do, so call ahead and order it in advance, and bring a partner because it's served for two but will feed three. Begin with an appetizer of mussels or escargots. Other main courses include grilled lamb shank and roasted duckling with orange sauce. Rich desserts include such specialties as crème brûlée, bread pudding, and crème caramel.

2009 Bridgeway. ℂ 415/332-1512. Reservations recommended. Main courses $12–$18. AE, DC, MC, V. Daily 5–10pm. From U.S. 101 north, take the 1st right after the Golden Gate Bridge (Alexander exit); Alexander becomes Bridgeway in Sausalito.

Sushi Ran ★★ SUSHI/JAPANESE   San Franciscans often cross the bridge just to cram into the bar, window seats, and more roomy back dining area of this top-quality favorite. They journey here for the standard rolls (yellowtail, unagi, maguro, and the like) or the specialty rolls (crab, avocado, and beyond). You'll also find a slew of creative dishes, such as generously sized, unbelievably moist and buttery miso-glazed black cod, oysters on the half shell with ponzu sauce and tobiko, and a Hawaiian-style *ahi* (tuna) poke salad with seaweed dressing. Pay the extra $2.50 or so for fresh wasabi, select from the fine sake and wine list, and don't miss dessert, because here they are more creative and delicious than those served at most Japanese restaurants.

107 Caledonia St. ℂ 415/332-3620. www.sushiran.com. Reservations recommended. Sushi $5–$14; main courses $8.50–$16. AE, DC, MC, V. Mon–Fri 11:45am–2:30pm and 5:30–11pm; Sat 5:30–11:30pm; Sun 5–10:30pm. From U.S. 101 north, take the 1st right after the Golden Gate Bridge (Alexander exit); Alexander becomes Bridgeway in Sausalito. At Johnson St. turn left, then right onto Caledonia.

Finds The Raw Deal

If you're in Marin and want a taste of the latest rage in modern cooking—or rather uncooking—head for Larkspur, home of the nation's top raw, organic, vegan restaurant, **Roxanne's** (320 Magnolia Ave., Larkspur; © 415/924-5004; www.roxraw.com). This over-the-top natural, elegant, and very PC dining experience has L.A. models and actresses flying up for dinner. Why? Because every dish—from the lasagna terrine layered with Roma tomato sauce, mushrooms, baby spinach, corn, and cashew cheese to the spicy stuffed chiles with *ensalada de Buena noche* and mole poblano—is guiltlessly decadent. Every item is made from organic unprocessed ingredients that are never heated above 115° (to preserve the enzymes). The healthy and environmentally sensitive menu is meatless, flourless, and sugarless, but it bursts with outstanding flavor and an equally impressive wine list. Don't miss the pad Thai made with raw baby coconut noodles. Skip the desserts, which tend to disappoint, and book well in advance: This is one of Northern California's hottest tickets. Open Tuesday through Sunday from 5:30 to 10pm, two courses here cost $36, three courses are $44, and four courses cost $52. American Express, MasterCard, and Visa are accepted.

4 Angel Island & Tiburon

8 miles N of San Francisco

A federal and state wildlife refuge, **Angel Island** is the largest of the San Francisco Bay's three islets (the others being Alcatraz and Yerba Buena). The island has been a prison, a quarantine station for immigrants, a missile base, and even a site for duels. Nowadays, though, most of the people who visit here are content with picnicking on the large green lawn that fronts the docking area. Loaded with the necessary recreational supplies, they claim a barbecue, plop their fannies down on the lush green grass, and while away an afternoon free of televisions and traffic. Hiking, mountain biking, and guided tram tours are also popular activities.

Tiburon, on the peninsula of the same name, looks like a cross between a fishing village and a Hollywood western set—imagine San Francisco reduced to toy dimensions. This seacoast town rambles over a series of green hills and ends up at a spindly, multicolored pier on the waterfront, like a Fisherman's Wharf in miniature. But in reality, it's a plush patch of yacht-club suburbia, as you'll see by both the marine craft and the homes of their owners. **Main Street** is lined with color-splashed old frame houses that shelter chic boutiques, souvenir stores, antiques shops, and art galleries. Other roads are narrow, winding, and hilly, leading up to dramatically situated homes. The view of San Francisco's skyline and the islands in the bay is a good enough reason to pay the price to live here.

ESSENTIALS

GETTING THERE   Ferries of the **Blue & Gold Fleet** (© 415/705-5555; www.blueandgoldfleet.com) leave from Pier 41 (Fisherman's Wharf) and travel to both Angel Island and Tiburon. Boats run on a seasonal schedule; phone for departure information. The round-trip fare is $12 to Angel Island or Tiburon, $7.50 for kids ages 6 to 11, and free for kids under 6.

By car from San Francisco, take U.S. 101 to the Tiburon/Highway 131 exit, then follow Tiburon Boulevard downtown, a 40-minute drive from San Francisco.

ANGEL ISLAND

Passengers disembark from the ferry at **Ayala Cove,** a small marina abutting a huge lawn area equipped with tables, benches, barbecue pits, and restrooms. Also at Ayala Cove are a small store, gift shop, cafe (with surprisingly good grub), and an overpriced mountain-bike rental shop (helmets included).

Among the 12 miles of Angel Island's hiking and mountain-bike trails is the **Perimeter Road,** a partly paved path that circles the island and winds its way past old troop barracks, former gun emplacements, and other military buildings; several turnoffs lead up to the top of Mount Livermore, 776 feet above the bay.

Sometimes referred to as the "Ellis Island of the West," from 1910 to 1940 Angel Island was used as a holding area for Chinese immigrants awaiting their citizenship papers. You can still see some faded Chinese characters on the walls of the barracks where the immigrants were held. During the warmer months, you can camp at a limited number of sites; reservations are required and can be obtained by calling © **800/444-7275.**

Also offered are guided **sea-kayak tours.** The all-day trips, which include a catered lunch, combine the thrill of paddling stable one-, two-, or three-person kayaks with a naturalist-led tour that encircles the island (conditions permitting). All equipment is provided, kids are welcome, and no experience is necessary. Rates run about $110 per person; a shorter trip takes 2½ hours and costs $75 per person. For more information, call **Sea Trek** (© **415/332-8494;** www.seatrekkayak.com).

The most recent tour addition is the 1-hour **Angel Island Tram Tour** (© **415/897-0715;** www.angelisland.com), which costs $13 for adults, $11 for seniors, and $7.50 for children ages 6 to 12; children under 6 ride free. For recorded information on **Angel Island State Park,** call © **415/435-1915.** It's the lazy man's (or woman's) way to check out the island's flora and fauna.

TIBURON

The main thing to do in Tiburon is stroll along the waterfront, pop in to the stores, and spend an easy $50 on drinks and appetizers before heading back to the city. For a taste of the Wine Country, stop in at **Windsor Vineyards,** 72 Main St. (© **800/214-9463** or 415/435-3113; www.windsorvineyards.com), which has a Victorian tasting room dating back to 1888. Thirty-five choices are available for a free tasting. Wine accessories and gifts—glasses, cork pullers, gourmet sauces, posters, and maps—are also for sale. Carry-packs (which hold six bottles) are available; ask about personalized labels for your own selections. The shop is open Sunday through Thursday from 10am to 6pm, Friday and Saturday until 7pm.

WHERE TO DINE

Guaymas MEXICAN   Guaymas offers authentic Mexican regional cuisine and a spectacular panoramic view of San Francisco and the bay. In good weather the two outdoor patios are almost always packed with diners soaking in the sun. Inside, colorful Mexican artwork aids the festive scene. Should you feel chilled, to the rear of the dining room is a beehive-shaped adobe fireplace.

Guaymas is named after a fishing village on Mexico's Sea of Cortez, and both the town and the restaurant are famous for their *camarones* (giant shrimp). The restaurant also features ceviche, handmade tamales, and charcoal-grilled beef, seafood, and fowl. In addition to a good selection of California wines, the restaurant offers an exceptional variety of tequilas, Mexican beers, and mineral waters flavored with flowers, grains, and fruits.

5 Main St. ⓒ 415/435-6300. www.guaymas.com. Reservations recommended. Main courses $13–$23. AE, DC, DISC, MC, V. Mon–Thurs 11:30am–10pm; Fri–Sat 11:30am–11pm; Sun 10:30am–10pm. Ferry: Walk about 10 paces from the landing. From U.S. 101, exit at Tiburon/Hwy. 131; follow Tiburon Blvd. 5 miles and turn right onto Main St. Restaurant is behind the bakery.

Sam's Anchor Café 🐀 *Finds* SEAFOOD   Summer Sundays are liveliest in Tiburon, when weekend boaters tie up at the docks of waterside restaurants like this one. Sam's is the kind of place where you and your cronies can take off your shoes and have a fun, relaxed time eating burgers and drinking margaritas outside on the pier—once you survive the wait for a highly coveted patio table. The fare is typical—sandwiches, salads, and such—but the quality and selection are inconsequential: Beers, burgers, and a designated driver are all you really need.

27 Main St. ⓒ 415/435-4527. www.samscafe.com. Main courses $9–$13 brunch, $9–$21 lunch, $15–$24 dinner. AE, DC, DISC, MC, V. Mon–Fri 11am–10pm; Sat–Sun 9:30am–10pm. Ferry: Walk from the landing. From U.S. 101, exit at Tiburon/Hwy. 131; follow Tiburon Blvd. 4 miles and turn right onto Main St.

5 Muir Woods & Mount Tamalpais

12 miles N of the Golden Gate Bridge

While the rest of Marin County's redwood forests were being devoured to feed the building spree in San Francisco around the turn of the 20th century, the trees of Muir Woods, in a remote ravine on the flanks of Mount Tamalpais, escaped destruction in favor of easier pickings.

MUIR WOODS

Although the magnificent California redwoods have been transplanted to five continents, their homeland is a 500-mile strip along the mountainous coast of southwestern Oregon and Northern California. The coast redwood, or *Sequoia sempervirens,* is the tallest tree in the region, and the largest-known specimen (located in the Redwood National Forest) towers 368 feet high. Soaring toward the sky like a wooden cathedral, seeing it is an experience you won't soon forget.

Muir Woods is tiny compared to the Redwood National Forest farther north, but you can still get a good idea of what it must have been like when these giants dominated the coastal region. What is truly amazing is that they exist a mere 6 miles (as the crow flies) from San Francisco; close enough, unfortunately, that tour buses arrive in droves on the weekends. You can avoid the masses by hiking up the **Ocean View Trail** and returning via the **Fern Creek Trail**—a moderate hike that shows off the woods' best sides and leaves the tour-bus crowd behind.

To reach Muir Woods from San Francisco, cross the Golden Gate Bridge heading north on U.S. 101, take the Stinson Beach/Calif. 1 exit heading west, and follow the signs. The park is open daily from 8am to sunset; the entrance fee is $3 per person 17 years or older. There's a gift shop, educational displays, and docent-led tours that you're welcome to follow. For more information, call the **Muir Woods information line** (ⓒ 415/388-2595; www.visitmuir woods.com).

If you don't have a car, you can book a bus trip with the **Red & White Fleet,** which takes you to Muir Woods via the Golden Gate Bridge, and on the way back makes a short stop in Sausalito. The 3½-hour tours run several times daily and cost $56 for adults, $31 for children ages 5 through 11, and are free for kids under 5. Call for more information and specific departure times (© 877/855-5506 or 415/447-0597; www.redandwhite.com).

MOUNT TAMALPAIS

The birthplace of mountain biking, Mount Tam—as the locals call it—is the Bay Area's favorite outdoor playground and the most dominant mountain in the region. Most every local has his or her secret trail and scenic overlook, as well as an opinion on the dilemma between mountain bikers and hikers (a touchy subject around here). The main trails—mostly fire roads—see a lot of foot and bicycle traffic on the weekends, particularly on clear, sunny days when you can see a hundred miles in all directions, from the foothills of the Sierra to the western horizon. It's a great place to escape from the city for a leisurely hike and to soak in the breathtaking views of the bay.

To get to Mount Tamalpais **by car,** cross the Golden Gate Bridge heading north on U.S. 101 and take the Stinson Beach/Calif. 1 exit. Follow the shoreline highway about 2½ miles and turn onto the Panoramic Highway heading west. After about 5½ miles, turn onto Pantoll Road and continue for about a mile to Ridgecrest Boulevard. Ridgecrest winds to a parking lot below East Peak. From here, it's a 15-minute hike up to the top.

6 Half Moon Bay

28 miles SW of San Francisco

A 45-minute drive from the teeming streets of San Francisco is a heavenly little hamlet called Half Moon Bay, one of the finest—and friendliest—small towns on the California coast. While other communities like Bolinas make tourists feel unwelcome, Half Moon Bay residents are disarmingly amicable, bestowing greetings on anyone and everyone who stops for a visit.

Half Moon Bay has only recently begun to capitalize on its beaches, mild climate, and proximity to San Francisco, so it's still not tourist-tacky. Visitors will find it a peaceful slice of classic California: pristine beaches, redwood forests, nature preserves, fishing harbors, horse ranches, organic farms, and a host of superb inns and restaurants—everything for the perfect weekend getaway.

Note: Temperatures rarely venture past the 70s (20s Celsius) in Half Moon Bay, so be sure to pack for cool (and often wet) weather.

ESSENTIALS

GETTING THERE   There's no public transportation from San Francisco to Half Moon Bay. There are two ways to get here by car: the fast way and the scenic way. To save time, take Calif. 92 west from I-280 or U.S. 101 out of San Francisco, which will take you over a small mountain range and drop you into Half Moon Bay. A better—and prettier—route is via Calif. 1, which starts at the south end of the Golden Gate Bridge and veers southwest to the shoreline a few miles south of Daly City. Both routes to Half Moon Bay are clearly marked, so don't worry about getting lost.

Downtown Half Moon Bay, however, is easy to miss since it's not on Calif. 1, but a few hundred yards inland. Head 2 blocks up Calif. 92 from the Calif. 1 intersection, then turn south at the Shell gas station onto Main Street until you cross a small bridge. For more information, call the **Half Moon Bay Coastside Chamber of Commerce** (© 650/726-8380; www.halfmoonbaychamber.org).

EXPLORING HALF MOON BAY & ENVIRONS

The best things to do in Half Moon Bay are the same things the locals do. There's a wonderful **paved beach trail** that winds 3 miles from Half Moon Bay to Pillar Point Harbor, where you can watch the trawlers unload their catch. Walking, biking, jogging, and skating are all de rigueur, and be sure to keep a lookout for dolphins and whales.

Half Moon Bay is also known for its organically grown produce, and the best place to stock up on fruits and vegetables is the **Andreotti Family Farm,** 329 Kelly Ave., off Calif. 1 (© 650/726-9151), an old-fashioned outfit in business since 1926. Every Friday, Saturday, and Sunday, a member of the Andreotti family slides open the door to their old barn at 10am sharp to reveal a cornucopia of strawberries, artichokes, cucumbers, and more. Head toward the beach and you'll see the barn on your right-hand side. It's open until 6pm year-round.

BEACHES & PRESERVES   The 4-mile arc of golden-colored sand that rings Half Moon Bay is broken up into three state-run beaches—Dunes, Venice, and Francis—all part of **Half Moon Bay State Beach.** There's a $5-per-vehicle entrance fee for all three beaches. Though surfing is allowed, swimming isn't a good idea unless you happen to be cold-blooded.

About 7 miles farther north on Calif. 1 is the **Fitzgerald Marine Reserve,** one of the most diverse tidal basins on the West Coast, as well as one of the safest, thanks to a wave-buffering rock terrace 50 yards from the beach. Call © 650/728-3584 before coming to find out when it's low tide (all the sea creatures are hidden at high tide) and to get information on the docent-led tour schedules (usually offered on Sat). Rubber-soled shoes are recommended. It's at the west end of California Avenue off Calif. 1 in Moss Beach. Reservations are required for all groups of 10 or more. Call © 650/363-4021. *Also note:* Dogs, open fires, or barbecue pits are prohibited, as is collecting of any kind.

Sixteen miles south of Half Moon Bay on Calif. 1 (at the turnoff to Pescadero) is the **Pescadero Marsh Natural Preserve,** one of the few remaining natural marshes on the central California coast. Part of the Pacific flyway, it's a resting stop for nearly 200 bird species, including great blue herons that nest in the northern row of eucalyptus trees. Passing through the marsh is the mile-long **Sequoia Audubon Trail,** accessible from the parking lot at Pescadero State Beach on Calif. 1 (the trail starts below the Pescadero Creek Bridge). Docent-led tours are held every Saturday at 10:30am and every Sunday at 1pm, weather permitting.

Starting in December and continuing through March, the **Año Nuevo State Reserve** is home to one of California's most amazing animal attractions: the breeding grounds of the northern elephant seal. Every winter, people reserve tickets for a chance to witness a fearsome clash between the 2½-ton bulls over mating privileges among the females. Reservations are required for the 2½-hour naturalist-led tours (held rain or shine Dec 15–Mar 31). For tickets, which cost $4 per person (free for children under 3), and information, call © 800/444-4445 or visit www.anonuevo.org. Even if it's not mating season, you can still see the elephant seals lolling around the shore almost year-round, particularly between April and August when they come ashore to molt.

OUTDOOR PURSUITS   One of the most popular activities in town is horseback riding along the beach. **Sea Horse Ranch** (aka Friendly Acres Horse Ranch), on Calif. 1 a mile north of Half Moon Bay (© 650/726-2362), offers kids' pony rides and guided and unguided rides along the beach or on well-worn trails starting at $40. A $30 "early-bird special" includes a 2-hour ride from 8 to 10am. Hours are daily from 8am to 6pm.

For golfers, there's **Half Moon Bay Golf Links,** 2000 Fairway Dr., at the south end of Half Moon Bay next to the Half Moon Bay Lodge (© **650/726-4438;** www.halfmoonbaygolf.com). Designed by Arnold Palmer, the ocean-side 18-hole course has been rated among the top 100 courses in the country, as well as the best in the Bay Area. Greens fees range from $145 to $170. Reserve your tee time as far in advance as possible.

SHOPPING   Main Street is a shopper's paradise. Dozens of small stores and boutiques line the quarter-mile strip, selling everything from feed and tack to custom furniture and camping gear. From north to south, must-see stops include the **Buffalo Shirt Company,** 604 Main St. (© **650/726-3194**), which carries a fine selection of casual wear, Indian rugs, and outdoor gear; **Cartwheels,** 330 Main St. (© **650/726-6060**), a nifty store specializing in rustic wood furniture; and **Half Moon Bay Feed & Fuel,** 331 Main St. (© **650/726-4814**), a great place to pick up a treat for your pet.

Cunha's Country Store, 448 Main St. (© **650/726-4071**), the town's beloved grocery and general store, is a mandatory stop for visitors from the Bay Area. Half Moon Bay also has a good bookstore, **Coastside Books,** 432B Main St. (© **650/726-5889**), which carries a fair selection of children's books and postcards. End your shopping spree with a stop at **Cottage Industries,** 621 Main St. (© **650/712-8078**), to marvel at the high-quality handcrafted furniture.

WHERE TO STAY

Beach House Inn ⭐   While the facade has a rather unimaginative Cape Cod look, the rooms at this three-story hotel are surprisingly well designed and decorated with modern prints, stylish furnishings, soothing yellow tones, and spectacular views of the bay and harbor. Every room comes fully loaded with a wood-burning fireplace, king-size bed and sleeper sofa, large bathroom, and stereo with CD player. Wait, there's more: Private patio or deck access, two color TVs, *four* telephones with dataports and voice mail, and a kitchenette with microwave and fridge. Opt for one of the corner rooms, which offer a more expansive view for the same price.

4100 N. Cabrillo Hwy. (Hwy. 1), Half Moon Bay, CA 94019. © **800/315-9366** or 650/712-0220. Fax 650/712-0693. www.beach-house.com. 54 units. $185–$365 double. Rates include continental breakfast and Fri–Sat evening wine hour. AE, DC, DISC, MC, V. From Half Moon Bay, go 3 miles N on Hwy. 1. **Amenities:** Heated outdoor pool; exercise room; oceanview whirlpool; concierge; in-room massage; same-day laundry and dry cleaning. *In room:* TV, minibar, kitchenette, fridge, coffeemaker, hair dryer, iron, CD player, free high-speed Internet access.

Cypress Inn on Miramar Beach ⭐⭐   A favorite place to stay in Half Moon Bay, this three-building compound is free of Victorian charm (nary a lace curtain in *this* joint). Instead you have one modern, artistically designed and decorated building infused with colorful folk art and rustic furniture made of pine and heavy wicker. Each room has a feather bed, private balcony, gas fireplace, private bathroom, and unobstructed ocean view. Adjacent is the Beach House building, which has rooms equipped with built-in stereo systems and hidden TVs, though they lack the Santa-Fe-meets-California effect that I adore in the main house. In 2002 six new Lighthouse rooms were added, complete with whirlpool spas. This is the one of the only B&Bs perched right on the beach.

407 Mirada Rd., Half Moon Bay, CA 94019. © **800/83-BEACH** or 650/726-6002. Fax 650/712-0380. www.cypressinn.com. 18 units. $215–$365 double. Rates include breakfast; tea, wine, and hors d'oeuvres; and after-dinner treats. AE, DISC, MC, V. From the junction of Highways 92 and 1, go 3 miles north, then turn

west and follow Medio to the end; hotel is at Medio and Mirada. **Amenities:** Room service (breakfast only). *In room:* TV, VCR, coffeemakers in some rooms, hair dryer, iron/ironing board, CD player, robes.

Seal Cove Inn ★★   Before Karen Herbert and her husband, Rick, opened this top-notch B&B, she was the writer and publisher of *Karen Brown's Guides,* so she knows what it takes to create and run a superior bed-and-breakfast. The result is a stately, sophisticated B&B that blends California, New England, and European influences in a spectacular setting. All rooms have fireplaces, antiques, watercolors, grandfather clocks, hidden televisions with VCRs, and refrigerators stocked with free beverages. They overlook distant cypress trees and a colorful half-acre wildflower garden dotted with birdhouses. You'll find coffee and a newspaper outside your door in the morning, wine, appetizers, brandy, and sherry by the living-room fireplace in the evening, and chocolates beside your turned-down bed at night. The ocean is just a short walk away.

221 Cypress Ave., Half Moon Bay, CA 94038. ℂ 650/728-4114. Fax 650/728-4116. www.sealcoveinn.com. 10 units. $200–$300 double. Rates include breakfast, wine and snacks, and sherry. AE, DISC, MC, V. The inn is 6 miles north of Half Moon Bay off Hwy. 1; follow signs to Moss Beach Distillery. **Amenities:** Concierge. *In room:* TV/VCR, minibar, fridge, hair dryer.

WHERE TO DINE

Downtown's Main Street is a walkable and charming street with a handful of good restaurants, many of which don't require reservations. If you're not in the mood for Italian, cruise the street and pick a spot you like.

Cetrella Bistro & Café ★★ MEDITERRANEAN   Cetrella is about as close to big-city dining as Half Moon Bay gets. Within the stunningly designed dining rooms—with a centerpiece fireplace—locals and visitors mingle over executive chef Erik Anton Cosselmon's excellent dishes. These range from hearts of romaine salad with white anchovy dressing to wood-oven focaccia bread with Bellwether Farms Crescenza cheese and a drizzle of white truffle oil to vegetarian paella to milk-braised lamb shank over soft polenta and Daylight Farms Swiss chard. Added bonuses include a killer cheese program and live weekend jazz. Attached is the more casual and cheaper cafe, which offers the likes of small plates (pizza, soups, salads) and entrees like burgers, steamed mussels, and cassoulet. Brunch is decadent and gourmet—think brioche French toast with huckleberries and chantilly cream, Tuscan-style baked eggs, or a nice juicy burger with grilled onions and arugula and crisp fries. If you're in the 'hood, definitely check it out, but do reserve first (online at their site if you like)—everyone from *Gourmet* to *San Francisco Chronicle* have trumpeted the tastiness of this small town gem, so it's no secret.

845 Main St. (at Monte Vista Lane). ℂ 650/726-4090. www.cetrella.com. Reservations recommended. Main courses dinner $19–$24, brunch $8–$17. Bistro: Sun 10:30am–2pm; Sun–Thurs 5:30–9:30pm; Fri–Sat 5:30–10pm. Cafe: Sun–Tues 5:30–10pm; Wed–Sat 5pm–midnight.

Pasta Moon ★ ITALIAN   Nouveau Italian Pasta Moon makes everything from scratch and uses only fresh ingredients. Pasta dishes, which are always freshly made and perfectly cooked, earn the highest recommendations. They include house-made linguine with sea scallops, anchovies, garlic, chile flakes, and olive oil; and penne with spicy lamb sausage in Swiss chard tomato sauce and fresh ricotta cheese. For dessert, try the wonderful tiramisu, with its layers of Marsala-and-espresso-soaked ladyfingers and creamy mascarpone.

315 Main St., Half Moon Bay. ℂ 650/726-5125. Reservations recommended. Main courses lunch $10–$23, dinner $15–$25. AE, DC, DISC, MC, V. Mon–Fri 11:30am–2:30pm; Sat noon–3pm; Sun–Thurs 5:30–9:30pm; Fri–Sat 5:30–10pm.

7 San Jose

45 miles SE of San Francisco

Some may mourn the San Jose of yesterday, a sleepy town of orchards, crops, and cattle, but those days are long gone. Founded in 1717 and once hidden in the shadows of San Francisco, San Jose is now Northern California's largest city. With surveys that declare it one of the safest and sunniest cities in the country and rank it the fifth-most-popular place to live in America, San Jose is a force to be reckoned with. Today the prosperity of Silicon Valley has transformed what was once an agricultural backwater into a thriving city of restaurants, shops, a state-of-the-art light-rail system, a sports arena (go Sharks!), and a reputable art scene.

ESSENTIALS

GETTING THERE   BART (© 510/465-2278; www.bart.gov) travels from San Francisco to Fremont in 1¼ hours; you can take a bus from there. **Caltrain** (© 800/660-4287; www.caltrain.com) operates frequently from San Francisco and takes about 1 hour and 25 minutes.

VISITOR INFORMATION   Contact the **San Jose Convention & Visitors Bureau,** located in the San Jose McEnery Convention Center, 150 W. San Carlos St., San Jose, CA 95113 (© 800/SAN-JOSE or 408/977-0900; www.sanjose.org).

GETTING AROUND   Light Rail (© 408/321-2300) is your best option for getting around. A ticket is good for 2 hours and stops include Paramount's Great America, the convention center, and downtown museums. Fares are $1.50 for adults, $1.25 for children ages 5 to 17, 75¢ for seniors and travelers with disabilities, and children age 4 and under ride for free. Day passes run $4.50 for adults, $3.75 for children, $1.75 for seniors. Or you can use the historic trolleys, which operate in a loop around downtown (in summer only). Tickets can be purchased at Light Rail stations and must be acquired before boarding.

MUSEUMS WORTH SEEKING OUT

Children's Discovery Museum _Kids_   The kids will find more than 150 interactive exhibits here, as well as shows and workshops, which explore science, humanities, arts, and technology. **ZOOMZone** consists of science and art activities designed by kids for kids; **Bubbalogna,** an exhibit that explores the whimsical and scientifically intriguing world of bubbles, draws rave reviews. Smaller kids enjoy dressing up in costumes and playing on the fire truck.

180 Woz Way. © 408/298-5437. www.cdm.org. Admission $7 children and adults, $6 seniors 60 and up, free for children under 2. Tues–Sat 10am–5pm; Sun noon–5pm.

Rosicrucian Egyptian Museum & Planetarium   The Rosicrucian is associated with an educational organization that traces its origins back to the ancient Egyptians, who strongly believed in the afterlife and reincarnation. On display are human and animal mummies, funerary boats, and canopic jars, as well as jewelry, pottery, and bronze tools. There's also a replica of a noble Egyptian's tomb. *Note:* In March 2004 the planetarium reopened after 8 years of renovation and has shows daily at 2pm Tuesday through Sunday. There's a second show on Saturday and Sunday at 3:30pm.

1342 Naglee Ave. © 408/947-3636. www.egyptianmuseum.org. Museum admission $9 adults, $7 seniors and students, $5 children 5–10, free for children under 5. Planetarium free admission. Tues–Fri 10am–5pm; Sat–Sun 11am–6pm. Closed Mon and major holidays.

San Jose Historical Museum   Twenty-six original and replica buildings on 25 acres in Kelley Park have been restored to represent life in 1880s San Jose. The usual cast of characters is here—the doctor, the printer, the postmaster— with an occasional local surprise, such as the 1888 Chinese temple and the original Stevens fruit barn.

1650 Senter Rd. (℃ **408/287-2290.** Admission $6 adults, $5 seniors, $4 children 6–17, free Tues–Fri and for children under 6. Tues–Sun noon–5pm.

San Jose Museum of Art 𝕘   This contemporary-art museum features revolving exhibitions, post-1980 works as well as older contemporary art from its permanent collection. The Historic Wing includes a cafe, bookstore, and education center. Tours of exhibitions are offered every day at 12:30 and 2:30pm. On the second Saturday of each month at 12:30pm, the public gallery tour is signed for deaf and hearing-impaired visitors. Groups are asked to call and make reservations at least 1 week in advance.

110 S. Market St. (℃ **408/294-2787** or 408/271-6840. www.sjmusart.org. Free admission. Tues–Sun 11am–5pm; Fri 11am–10pm except in Dec when it closes at 5pm. Closed major holidays.

Tech Museum of Innovation 𝕘 *Kids*   Housed in a 132,000-square-foot facility, the Tech Museum allows visitors to create their own virtual roller-coaster ride, survive an earthquake on a giant shake table, operate an underwater ROV (remotely operated vehicle), and play with tons of other cool high-tech stuff. There's also an IMAX Dome Theater, Jet Pack simulator, and Virtual Bobsled ride, the same used to train Olympic competitors. A genetics gallery, which delves into DNA details, science, and politics, opened in March 2004.

201 S. Market St., downtown at the corner of Park and Market sts. (℃ **408/294-TECH.** www.thetech.org. Admission $9 adults, $8 seniors 65 and over, $7 children 3–12, free for children under 3; additional fee for IMAX shows; a combo ticket (IMAX and museum) is $16 adults, $13 children, and $15 seniors. Daily 10am–5pm. IMAX has extended hours on weekends.

THEME PARK THRILLS

Paramount's Great America, Great America Parkway (off U.S. 101), Santa Clara (℃ **408/988-1776;** www.pgathrills.com), provides 100 acres of family entertainment. A pretty cool place to lose your lunch, the park includes such favorites as the *Top Gun* suspended jet coaster, a 3-acre Nickelodeon Center for children, "Drop Zone" (the world's tallest free-fall ride), the Xtreme Skyflyer, which combines skydiving with hang gliding, and the new Pyscho Mouse roller coaster and go-carts. Be sure to check for concerts and special events. New as of 2004 is an 11-slide three-acre water park, called Crocodile Dundee's Boomerang Bay, which is included in admission. Admission is $48 for adults and children ages 7 to 59, $40 for seniors age 60 and over, $34 for children 3 to 6, and free for children under 2. Check their website for discounted tickets. Parking is $10 per vehicle. Seasonal hours and open days vary according to season and the weather, but it's open daily June through August. From San Francisco, take U.S. 101 south for about 45 miles to the Great America Parkway exit.

WHERE TO STAY

The Fairmont San Jose   Situated near the San Jose McEnery Convention Center and the Center of Performing Arts, this hotel is in a landmark building. A popular spot to have afternoon tea or cocktails, the lobby attracts many who are just passing through. The hotel places an emphasis on comfort: The guest rooms, located in two 13-story towers—one of which was constructed and opened in 2002, offer many modern features such as fax and high-speed modem

The Winchester Mystery House: A Monument to One Woman's Paranoia

Begun in 1884, the **Winchester Mystery House,** 525 S. Winchester Blvd., at the intersection of I-280 and Highway 17, San Jose (© **408/ 247-2101;** www.winchestermysteryhouse.com), is the legacy of Sarah L. Winchester, widow of the son of the famous rifle magnate. After the deaths of her husband and baby daughter, Mrs. Winchester consulted with a seer, who proclaimed that the family had been targeted by the evil spirits of those killed with Winchester repeaters, who would only be appeased by perpetual construction on the Winchester mansion. Convinced that she'd live as long as the building continued, the widow used much of her $20-million inheritance to finance the construction, which went on 24 hours a day, 7 days a week, 365 days a year, for 38 years.

As you can probably guess, this is no ordinary home. With 160 rooms, it sprawls across half a dozen acres. And it's full of disturbing features: a staircase leading nowhere, a Tiffany window with a spider's web design, and doors that open onto blank walls. There are 13 bathrooms, 13 windows and doors in the old sewing room, 13 palms lining the main driveway, 13 hooks in the séance room, and chandeliers with 13 lights. Such schemes were designed to confound the spirits that seemed to plague the heiress.

Sixty-five-minute tours of the mansion and grounds are $20 for adults, $17 for seniors age 65 and over, $14 for children 6 to 12, and free for kids under 6; a 55-minute behind-the-scenes tour (a separate fee of $17 for adults, $16 kids and seniors) is also offered for guests over 10. An Estate Tour (a mansion plus behind-the-scenes 2½-hr. tour) costs $25 for adults, $22 for kids 10 to 12 and seniors. Tours leave about every 20 to 30 minutes. The house is open daily from 9am to 7pm in the summer; winter hours vary, so call ahead.

lines, while other amenities include 24-hour room service and a fourth-floor rooftop pool surrounded by tropical foliage. The most high-end of the hotel's three restaurants is **The Grill** steakhouse. There's also a Chinese restaurant, an upscale seafood restaurant, and a coffee shop that's nicely accented with a massive marble soda fountain.

170 S. Market St., San Jose, CA 95113. © **800/527-4727** or 408/998-1900. Fax 408/287-1648. www.fairmont. com. 805 units. $189–$400 double; $359–$1,800 suite. AE, DC, DISC, MC, V. **Amenities:** 5 restaurants; bar; heated outdoor pool; health club; spa; sauna; concierge; car-rental desk; business center; secretarial services; 24-hr. room service; in-room massage; same-day laundry service and dry cleaning. *In room:* A/C, TV w/pay movies, VCR and fax in suites, minibar, hair dryer, iron, safe in tower rooms, high-speed Internet access.

WHERE TO DINE

Santana Row, located at Winchester and Stevens Creek boulevards, is an upscale mall and hotbed for dining, shopping, and strolling. Check it out at www.santanarow.com/dining_restaurants.shtml or call © **408/551-4600.** Two good bets include all-American **Yankee Pier** and Asian-inspired **Strait's Café.**

Emile's 🌟🌟 CONTEMPORARY EUROPEAN   More than 30 years after opening in 1973, this fancy place still ranks among the Bay Area's best because the kitchen creates exceptional contemporary cuisine. Mirrors, recessed lighting, and large, bold floral arrangements create an elegant atmosphere. To start, try seared Sonoma foie gras on caramelized brioche with huckleberry-port reduction, baby arugula, and blood-orange vinaigrette. Follow with veal tenderloin medallions and white gulf prawns, sautéed with shallots and green peppercorns, wild-mushroom risotto, and a light cream sauce. For dessert, go with the warm chocolate truffle cake with raspberry sorbet. As of mid-2004 they're offering "small plate" versions of entrees; a "taste" costs about two-thirds of the entree price and allows diners to snack through the menu.

545 S. Second St. ℂ 408/289-1960. www.emiles.com. Reservations recommended. Main courses $17–$32. AE, DC, DISC, MC, V. Tues–Sat 5:30–10pm.

Paolo's 🌟 NORTHERN ITALIAN   Paolo's attracts a business crowd at lunchtime and a cultured crowd in the evening. The cuisine is refined northern Italian, with innovative flourishes. Among the appetizers, for instance, is the tuna carpaccio with capers, olives, anchovy, sage, basil, and basil oil. The main dishes might include sea scallops baked in foil with romaine lettuce, black truffle, herbs, and pancetta or veal saltimbocca (veal stuffed with sage, fontina, and Vald'osta cheese and covered with Marsala wine sauce and forest mushrooms). Desserts also stretch beyond the typical Italian favorites to include a chocolate torte with orange-caramel sauce, or *semifreddo* of cookies and cream with vanilla bean gelato and shaved Italian chocolate. An extensive wine list features more than 600 selections.

333 W. San Carlos St. ℂ 408/294-2558. Reservations recommended. Main courses lunch $15–$22, dinner $18–$34. AE, DC, DISC, MC, V. Mon–Fri 11am–2:30pm; Mon–Sat 5:30–10pm.

6

The Wine Country

by Erika Lenkert

California's Napa and Sonoma valleys are two of the most famous winegrowing regions in the world, and two of my favorite places to visit in the state. In fact, I liked Napa so much I moved there. The workaday valleys that are a way of life for thousands of vintners are also the ultimate retreat for wine and food lovers and romantics. Hundreds of wineries are nestled among the vines, and most are open to visitors. But even if you don't want to wine-taste, the country air, rolling countryside, and world-class restaurants and spas are reasons enough to come. If you can, plan on spending a couple of days just to get to know one of the valleys. No matter how long you stay, you'll probably never get enough of the romantic, indulgent lifestyle.

While Napa and Sonoma are close to each other (about a 30-min. drive apart), each is attraction-packed enough that your best bet is to focus on just one of the valleys, especially if your time is limited. I recommend that you read about each below, then decide which one is right for you—unless, of course, you're lucky enough to have time to explore both.

1 Napa Valley

The most obvious distinction between the two valleys is size—Napa Valley dwarfs Sonoma Valley in population, number of wineries, and sheer volume of tourism (and in summertime, serious traffic). Napa is definitely the more commercial of the two, with dozens more wineries, spas, and a far superior selection of fine restaurants, hotels, and quintessential Wine Country activities like hot-air ballooning. All of these are set amidst rolling, mustard flower–covered hills and vast stretches of vineyards. And if your goal is to really learn about the wonderful world of winemaking, world-class wineries such as Sterling and Robert Mondavi offer the most interesting and edifying wine tours in North America, if not in the world. The combined attractions make Napa the place to come for the ultimate Wine Country experience.

Napa Valley is relatively condensed. It's just 35 miles long, which means you can venture from one end to the other in around half an hour (traffic permitting). Conveniently, most of the large wineries—as well as most of the hotels, shops, and restaurants—are located along a single road, Calif. 29, which starts at the mouth of the Napa River, near the north end of San Francisco Bay, and continues north to Calistoga and the top of the growing region. Every Napa Valley town and winery can be reached from this main thoroughfare.

ESSENTIALS

GETTING THERE From San Francisco, cross the Golden Gate Bridge and head north on U.S. 101. Turn east on Calif. 37 (toward Vallejo), then north on Calif. 29, the main road through Napa Valley. Or take the scenic route: Calif. 37 to Highway 121/12, following the signs toward Napa, turn left onto Highway 29.

⟮Tips⟯ The Ins & Outs of Shipping Wine Home

Perhaps the only thing more complex than that $800 case of cabernet you just purchased are the rules and regulations regarding shipping it home. Due to absurd and forever fluctuating "reciprocity laws"— which were supposedly created to protect the business of the country's wine distributors—wine shipping is limited by state regulations that vary in each of the 50 states. Shipping rules also vary from winery to winery. Hence, depending on which state you live in, sending even a single bottle of wine can be a truly Kafkaesque experience.

To avoid major hassles, do your homework before you buy. Talk to wineries, shipping companies, and the companies below about whether they can ship. Be skeptical of any winery that tells you it can ship to nonreciprocal states—if they run into problems, you'll never get your wine. Find out if you can order the wine on the Internet. If you have to find a shipping company yourself, keep in mind that it's technically illegal to box your own wine and send it to a nonreciprocal state; the shippers could lose their license, and you could lose your wine. However, if you do get stuck shipping illegally (not that I'm recommending you do that), you might want to disguise your box and head to a post office, UPS, or other shipping company outside of the Wine Country area; it's far less obvious that you're shipping wine from, say, Vallejo or San Francisco than from Napa Valley.

The UPS Store, at 3212 Jefferson St. in the Grape Yard Shopping Center (✆ 707/259-1398), claims to pack and ship anything anywhere. Rates for a case of wine were quoted at approximately $28 for ground shipping to Los Angeles and $69 to New York.

St. Helena Mailing Center, 1241 Adams St., at Highway 29, St. Helena (✆ 707/963-2686), says they will pack and ship anywhere in the United States. Rates are around $30 per case for ground delivery to Los Angeles, $85 to New York. While those who live in reciprocal states get their package insured for up to $100, the Mailing Center does not insure packages shipped to nonreciprocal states. However, it's no big deal: Each bottle is packed in Styrofoam and should make it home without a problem.

In Sonoma, **Mail Boxes, Etc.,** 19229 Sonoma Hwy., at Verano Street (✆ 707/935-3438), claims it will ship your wine to any state, via UPS (which currently ships to only a dozen states) or Federal Express. Prices vary from $22 to Los Angeles to as much as $73 to the East Coast.

The **Wine Exchange of Sonoma,** 452 First St. E., between East Napa and East Spain streets, Sonoma (✆ 707/938-1794), will ship your wine, but there's a catch: You must buy an equal amount of any wine at the store. Shipping rates range from $20 to Los Angeles to $50 to the East Coast.

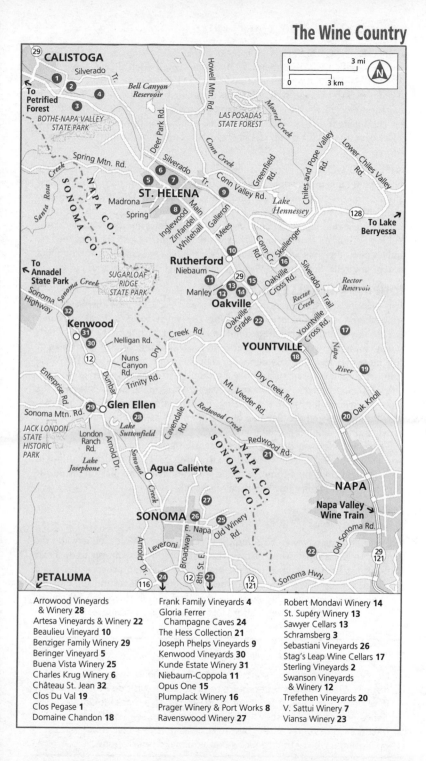

The Wine Country

CALISTOGA ①
Silverado ②
To Petrified Forest ④
③
BOTHE-NAPA VALLEY STATE PARK
Bell Canyon Reservoir
LAS POSADAS STATE FOREST
0   3 mi
0   3 km
N

Spring Mtn. Rd.
⑤ ⑥ ⑦
ST. HELENA
Madrona
Spring ⑧
⑨
Silverado Tr.
Conn Valley Rd.
Lake Hennessey
128
To Lake Berryessa

To Annadel State Park
SUGARLOAF RIDGE STATE PARK
Rutherford
Niebaum ⑩
⑪
⑯
29 ⑮
⑫ ⑬ ⑭
Manley
Oakville
⑳
Oakville Grade ⑳
Oakville Cross Rd.
Rector Reservoir

NAPA CO.
SONOMA CO.

Kenwood
③①
③⓪
12
Nelligan Rd.
Nuns Canyon Rd.
Trinity Rd.
Creek Rd.
YOUNTVILLE
⑱
⑰
Napa River
⑲

Enterprise Rd.
Sonoma Mtn. Rd.
㉙ Glen Ellen
㉘
Lake Suttonfield
JACK LONDON STATE HISTORIC PARK
London Ranch Rd.
Lake Josephone
Mt. Veeder Rd.
Dry Creek Rd.
Redwood Creek
Redwood Rd.
㉑
Oak Knoll
⑳

Agua Caliente
SONOMA CO.
NAPA CO.

㉗
SONOMA ㉖
㉕
E. Napa
Old Winery Rd.
NAPA
Napa Valley Wine Train

PETALUMA
116
㉔
12
㉓
12 121
Old Sonoma Rd.
29 121
㉒
Sonoma Hwy.

Arrowood Vineyards & Winery 28
Artesa Vineyards & Winery 22
Beaulieu Vineyard 10
Benziger Family Winery 29
Beringer Vineyard 5
Buena Vista Winery 25
Charles Krug Winery 6
Château St. Jean 32
Clos Du Val 19
Clos Pegase 1
Domaine Chandon 18

Frank Family Vineyards 4
Gloria Ferrer Champagne Caves 24
The Hess Collection 21
Joseph Phelps Vineyards 9
Kenwood Vineyards 30
Kunde Estate Winery 31
Niebaum-Coppola 11
Opus One 15
PlumpJack Winery 16
Prager Winery & Port Works 8
Ravenswood Winery 27

Robert Mondavi Winery 14
St. Supéry Winery 13
Sawyer Cellars 13
Schramsberg 3
Sebastiani Vineyards 26
Stag's Leap Wine Cellars 17
Sterling Vineyards 2
Swanson Vineyards & Winery 12
Trefethen Vineyards 20
V. Sattui Winery 7
Viansa Winery 23

VISITOR INFORMATION Once in Napa Valley, stop first at the **Napa Conference & Visitors Bureau,** 1310 Town Center Mall, Napa, CA 94559 (© **707/226-7459**), and pick up the slick *Napa Valley Guide,* or call in advance to order its $10 package, which includes the guide plus a bunch of brochures, a map, and *Four Perfect Days in the Wine Country* itinerary. If you don't want to pay the bucks for the official publications, point your browser to **www.napa valley.com,** the NVCVB's official site, which has much of the same information for free.

WHEN TO GO The beauty of the valley is striking any time of year, but it's most memorable in September and October when the grapes are being pressed and the wineries are in full production. Another great time to come is the spring, when the mustard flowers are in full bloom and the tourist season hasn't yet begun; you'll find less traffic and fewer crowds at the wineries and restaurants, and better deals on hotel rooms. While winter is beautiful and promises the best budget rates, the vines are dormant and rain is likely, so bring appropriate shoes and an umbrella. Summer? Say hello to hot weather and lots of traffic.

TOURING THE VALLEY & WINERIES

The Napa Valley has more than 280 wineries, each offering distinct wines, atmosphere, and experience—so touring the valley takes a little planning. Decide what you're most interested in and chart your path from there. Ask locals which vintners have the type of experience you're looking for. And don't plan to visit more than four or five wineries in a day. Above all, take it slowly. The Wine Country should never be rushed; like a great glass of wine, it should be savored.

Most wineries offer tours daily from 10am to 4:30pm. Tours usually chart the process of winemaking from the grafting and harvesting of the vines to the pressing of the grapes and the blending and aging in oak casks. They vary in length, detail, and formality, depending on the winery. Most tours are free.

The towns and wineries below are organized geographically, from south to north along Calif. 29, from Napa village to Calistoga. I've included a handful of my favorites below; for a complete list of wineries, be sure to pick up one of the free guides to the valley (see "Essentials," above).

NAPA

55 miles N of San Francisco

The city of Napa serves as the commercial center of the Wine Country and the gateway to Napa Valley. Most visitors whiz right past it on their way to the heart of the valley, but if you do veer off the highway, you'll be surprised to discover a small but burgeoning community of nearly 73,000 residents and some of the most affordable accommodations in the area. It is also in the process of gentrification, thanks to (relatively) affordable housing, a charming old-fashioned

---

Tips Reservations at Wineries

Plenty of wineries' doors are open to everyone between 10am and 4:30pm. Most wineries that require reservations to visit do so because of local permitting laws. A few limit guests to create a more intimate experience. In many cases, they'll be just as happy to see you if you arrive unannounced, but it's always best to call ahead if you have your heart set on visiting a winery that requests that you make reservations.

downtown, and recently added restaurants and attractions like Copia: The American Center for Wine, Food & the Arts. Heading north on either Highway 29 or the Silverado Trail leads you to Napa's wineries and the more quintessential Wine Country atmosphere of vineyards and wide-open country views.

The biggest new attraction in Napa Valley, **Copia: The American Center for Wine, Food & the Arts** ⚘, 500 First St. (℃ **707/259-1600**), operates with a mission to explore how wine and food influence our culture. This $50-million multifaceted facility tackles the topic in myriad ways, including visual arts a la rotating exhibits, vegetable and herb gardens, culinary demonstrations, wine classes, concerts, and opportunities to dine and drink on the premises. Day passes include entrance into the building and gardens, exhibitions, tours, and free 30-minute introductory classes. More advanced food, wine, garden, and art classes cost extra. A cafe offers gourmet picnic items, and a killer wine bar offers tastes of hard-to-find gems, while the adjoining restaurant, **Julia's Kitchen,** named after chef Child, is a more formal French-California affair.

If you're around in summer or fall, definitely check out the Monday night outdoor concert series. I often grab a lawn chair and head to the amphitheater for spectacular vocal and dance performances under Napa's soothing night sky. It's casual Wine Country at its best.

Admission is $13 for adults, $10 for students and seniors 62 and over, and $7.50 for children ages 6 to 12. The center is open Wednesday through Monday from 10am to 5pm. The restaurant stays open until 9:30pm Thursday through Sunday. Wednesday admissions are half-price.

Anyone with an appreciation for art absolutely must visit the **di Rosa Preserve,** which through a private tour explores the collection and 53-acre grounds of Rene and Veronica di Rosa, who have been collecting contemporary American art for more than 40 years. Their world-renowned collection features over 2,000 works in all media by more than 800 Greater Bay Area artists. Their treasures are displayed practically everywhere, from along the shores of their 30-acre lake to each nook and cranny of their century-old winery-turned-residence, adjoining building, two additional galleries, and gardens. It's located at 5200 Sonoma Hwy. (Calif. 121/12). Visits are by appointment only, when a maximum of 25 guests are guided through the preserve. Each tour lasts 2 to 2½ hours and costs $12 per person. (Free the first and third Wed of each month.) Call ℃ **707/226-5991** for reservations.

Discount shoppers should pull off Highway 29 at Napa's First Street exit to find the **Napa Premium Outlets** (℃ **707/226-9876;** www.premiumoutlets. com). Along with Barneys New York, you'll find multiple places to part with your money including Tse (killer cashmere at basement prices!), Nine West, Jones New York, BCBG, a few kitchenware shops, a food court, and a decent (but expensive) sushi restaurant. The shops are open Monday through Saturday from 10am to 8pm and Sunday from 10am to 6pm.

Antiques hounds should plan to spend at least an hour at **Red Hen**'s co-op collection of antiques, which is further north on Highway 29. You'll find everything from baseball cards to living-room sets, and prices are remarkably affordable. You can't miss this enormous red barn–style building at 5091 St. Helena Hwy., on Calif. 29 at Oak Knoll Avenue West (℃ **707/257-0822**). It's open daily from 10am to 5:30pm.

South of downtown Napa, 1½ miles east of Calif. 29 on Calif. 12, is the **Chardonnay Golf Club** (℃ **707/257-8950**), a 36-hole land-links golf complex with first-class service. There are three nines of similar challenge, all starting at the clubhouse so that you can play the 18 of your choice. You pay just one fee, which makes you a member for the day. Privileges include the use of a golf cart, the practice range (including a bucket of balls), and services usually found only at a private club. Starting times can be reserved up to 2 weeks in advance. Greens fees (including mandatory cart and practice balls) are $80 Monday through Friday, $95 weekends and holidays; at 2pm, fees go down to around $50. Limited space is available to play the private course, which goes for $130 per person.

Artesa Vineyards & Winery *(Finds)* Views, modern architecture, seclusion, and region-specific pinot noir discoveries are the reasons this is one of my favorite stops. Arrive on a day when the wind is blowing less than 10 mph, and the fountains are captivating; they automatically shut off with higher winds. Inside the cescue-grass covered winery is a very tasteful gift shop, a room outlining history and details on the Carneros region, and a long bar where $5 to $8 tastes include everything from chardonnays and pinot noirs to sauvignon blanc, cabernet sauvignon, zinfandel, and sparkling wine. Sorry, but their permits don't allow for picnicking. To find the winery, turn north on Dealy Lane from Old Sonoma Road off Highway 12/121 and turn right on Henry Road.

1345 Henry Rd., Napa. ✆ **707/224-1668.** www.artesawinery.com. Daily 10am–5pm; tours daily at 11am and 2pm.

The Hess Collection ★★ *(Finds)* No place in the valley brings together art and wine better than this combination winery and art gallery on the side of Mount Veeder. Swiss art collector Donald Hess acquired the old Christian Brothers Winery in 1978; along with producing wine, he also funded a huge restoration and expansion project to honor wine and the fine arts. The result is a working winery interspersed with gloriously lit rooms that exhibit his truly stunning art collection; the free self-guided tour takes you through these galleries as it introduces you to the winemaking process.

For a $5 tasting fee, you can sample the winery's current cabernet and chardonnay as well as one other featured wine. If you want to take some with you, by-the-bottle prices start at $10 for the second-label Hess select brand, while most other selections range from $15 to $35.

4411 Redwood Rd., Napa. ✆ **707/255-1144.** www.hesscollection.com. Daily 10am–4pm., except some holidays. From Hwy. 29 north, exit at Redwood Rd. west, and follow Redwood Rd. for 6½ miles.

Trefethen Vineyards Listed on the National Register of Historic Places, the vineyard's main building was built in 1886 and is Napa's only wooden, gravity-flow winery. Although Trefethen is one of the valley's oldest wineries, it didn't produce its first chardonnay until 1973—but thank goodness it did. The award-winning whites and reds are a pleasure to the palate. Tastings are $10 for four estate wines, but if you want to sample a reserve wine, it'll cost you $20.

1160 Oak Knoll Ave. (east of Hwy. 29), Napa. ✆ **707/255-7700.** www.trefethen.com. Daily 10am–4:30pm. From Hwy. 29 north, take a right onto Oak Knoll Ave.

Clos Du Val The ivy-covered building and well-manicured rose garden set the scene for a romantic wine-tasting experience. Inside, the friendly atmosphere completes the all-around welcoming ambience. Bordeaux-born founder and winemaker Bernard Portet and his newer, younger counterpart John Clews are responsible for what ends up in the glass; Portet has garnered a reputation for his cabernet (which makes up 70% of the winery's production). Other varietals include chardonnay, pinot noir, and merlot. You can try them all in the rather matter-of-fact tasting room. There's a $5 tasting charge (refunded with purchase) for about four wines. Lovely picnic facilities and the game *pétanque,* which is played in parks all over France and is practically a religion there, are available in grassy nooks along the grounds. A bonus is the friendly, helpful staff, which happily offers directions to other wineries, along with a small map.

5330 Silverado Trail (north of Oak Knoll Ave.), Napa. ✆ 707/259-2200. Daily 10am–5pm. Tours by appointment only.

Stag's Leap Wine Cellars   Founded in 1972, Stag's Leap shocked the oenological world in 1976 when its 1973 cabernet won first place over French wines in a Parisian blind tasting. Visit the charmingly landscaped, unfussy winery and its cramped "tasting room" where, for $10 per person, you can judge the four to six current releases; or you can fork over up to $30 for estate samples. A 1-hour tour and tasting runs through everything from the vineyard and production facilities to the ultraswank $5-million wine caves (used to store and age wine), which premiered in mid-2001.

5766 Silverado Trail, Napa. ✆ 707/944-2020. www.cask23.com. Daily 10am–4:30pm. Tours by appointment only. From Hwy. 29, go east on Trancas St. or Oak Knoll Ave., then north to the cellars.

YOUNTVILLE
70 miles N of San Francisco

The town of Yountville was founded by the first white American to settle in the valley, George Calvert Yount. While it lacks the small-town charm of neighboring St. Helena and Calistoga—primarily because its main street is rather sprawling and sprinkled with attractions rather than packed with sites—it does serve as a good base for exploring the valley, and it's home to a handful of excellent wineries, inns, boutiques, and a small stretch of fab restaurants, including the world-renowned French Laundry.

Domaine Chandon ★★ *Finds*   Founded in 1973 by French champagne house Moët et Chandon, the valley's most renowned sparkling winery rises to the occasion with elegant grounds and atmosphere. Here, manicured gardens showcase locally made sculpture, while guests linger—their glasses fizzing with bubbly—under the patio's umbrella shade, and in the restaurant diners indulge in a formal French-inspired meal. If you can pull yourself away from the Salon's bubbly (sold in tastings for $9–$14 and served with complimentary bread and spread), the comprehensive tour of the facilities is interesting, very informative, and friendly. There's a shop, a small gallery housing artifacts from Moët et Chandon that depict the history of champagnes, and revolving art exhibits (available for purchase). Check the website for events; Chandon often hosts live music and has extended salon hours during summer. *Note:* You should call or e-mail for reservations if you want to eat at the restaurant.

1 California Dr. (at Hwy. 29), Yountville. ✆ 707/944-2280. www.chandon.com. Daily 10am–6pm; hours vary by season, so call to confirm. Call for free tour schedules.

OAKVILLE
68 miles N of San Francisco

Driving farther north on the St. Helena Highway (Calif. 29) brings you to the Oakville Cross Road and the famous picnic-fare favorite **Oakville Grocery Co.** (see "Gourmet Picnics, Napa-Style" on p. 186).

PlumpJack Winery   If most wineries are like a Brooks Brothers suit, PlumpJack stands out as the Todd Oldham of wine tasting: chic, colorful, a little wild, and popular with a young, hip crowd as well as with a growing number of

Moments   Hot-Air Ballooning over the Valley

Admit it—floating across lush green pastures in a hot-air balloon is something you've always dreamed of doing. Well, here's your chance, because, believe it or not, Napa Valley is the busiest hot-air balloon "flight corridor" in the *world*. Northern California's temperate weather allows for ballooning year-round, and on summer weekends in the valley, it's a rare day when you don't see at least one of the colorful airships floating above the vineyards.

Trips usually depart early in the morning, when the air is cooler and the balloons have better lift. (*Note:* When weather conditions aren't optimal, balloon companies often launch flights from locations up to an hour's drive outside of the valley. You won't know until the morning of the flight, but you should be able to cancel on the spot if you desire.) Flight paths vary with the direction and speed of the changing breezes, so "chase" crews on the ground must follow the balloons to their undetermined destinations. Most flights last about an hour and end with a traditional champagne celebration and breakfast. Reservations are required and should be made far in advance. Prices run close to $200 per person for the basic package, which includes shuttle service from your hotel. Wedding, wine tasting, picnic, and lodging packages are also available. For more information or reservations, call Napa's **Bonaventura Balloon Company** (© 800/FLY-NAPA) or **Adventures Aloft** (© 800/944-4408 or 707/944-4408; www.nvaloft.com).

aficionados. Like the franchise's PlumpJack restaurant and wine shop in San Francisco, and its resort at Lake Tahoe, this playfully medieval winery is a welcome diversion. With Getty bucks behind what was once Villa Mt. Eden winery, the budget covers far more than just atmosphere: There's some serious winemaking going on here, too. For $5 you can sample the cabernet, merlot, and chardonnay—each an impressive product from a winery that's only been open to the public since mid-1997. There are no tours or picnic spots, but this refreshingly stylized, friendly facility will make you want to hang out for a while nonetheless.

620 Oakville Cross Rd. (just west of the Silverado Trail), Oakville. © 707/945-1220. www.plumpjack.com. Daily 10am–4pm.

Robert Mondavi Winery ⚲ *Finds*   Mission-style Mondavi gives the most comprehensive tours in the valley. Basic jaunts, which last about an hour, take you through the vineyards—complete with examples of varietals—and through their newest winemaking facilities. Ask the guides anything; they know a heck of a lot. After the tour, you can taste the results of all this attention to detail in selected current wines ($10). If you're really into learning more about wine, ask about in-depth tours. The "essence tasting" includes the opportunity to compare wine with the scents of fruits, spices, nuts, and more. An "appellation tour" includes a picnic lunch in the vineyards. You can also taste without taking a tour in the **Appellation Room** (an outdoor tasting area open in summer) and **ToKalon Room,** where a 3-ounce taste will cost you $5, a rare wine taste, $30.

The "Art of Wine and Food" program on Friday includes a slide presentation on the history of wine, a tour of the winery, and a three-course luncheon with wine pairing; the cost is around $95, and you must reserve in advance. In summer the winery also schedules some great outdoor concerts, which often sell out far in advance. Call about upcoming events.

7801 St. Helena Hwy. (Hwy. 29), Oakville. © **800/MONDAVI** or 707/226-1395. www.robertmondaviwinery.com. Daily 10am–4pm. Reservations recommended for guided tour; book 1 week ahead, especially for weekend tours.

Opus One   A visit to Opus One is a serious and stately affair. The winery was developed from a partnership between Robert Mondavi and Baron Phillipe de Rothschild, who, after years of discussion, embarked on this state-of-the-art collaboration. Architecture buffs in particular will appreciate the tour, which takes in both the impressive Greco-Roman-meets-20th-century building and the no-holds-barred ultra-high-tech production and aging facilities.

This entire facility caters to one ultrapremium wine, which is offered here for a whopping $25 per 4-ounce taste (and a painful $150 per bottle). But wine lovers should happily fork over the cash: It's a memorable red. Grab your glass and head to the redwood rooftop deck to enjoy the view.

7900 St. Helena Hwy. (Hwy. 29), Oakville. © **707/944-9442.** www.opusonewinery.com. Daily 10am–4pm. Tours by appointment only; in high season, book a month in advance.

RUTHERFORD
3 miles N of Oakville

If you blink after Oakville, you're likely to overlook Rutherford, the next small town that borders on St. Helena. Rutherford has its share of spectacular wineries, but you won't see most of them while driving along Calif. 29.

Swanson Vineyards & Winery ✦ *(Finds)*   The valley's most posh and unique wine tasting is yours with a reservation and a $25 to $45 fee at Swanson. Here the shtick is more like a private party, which they call a "SA-lon." You and up to seven other guests sit at a centerpiece round table in a coral parlor adorned with huge paintings, seashells, and a fireplace, and take in the uncommonly refined yet whimsical atmosphere. The table's set more for a dinner party than for a tasting, with Reidel stemware, slivers of a fine cheese or two, crackers, and one superb chocolate Alexis ganache-filled bonbon, which you will be glad to know can be purchased on the premises. Over the course of the hour-or-more snack-and-sip event, a winery host will pour four to seven wines and discuss the history and fine points of each. You're likely to be in store for a bright pinot grigio, merlot, and hearty Alexis, their signature cab-syrah blend. Just as important to the experience are the conversation and the making of new friends (which almost invariably occurs, because the experience puts everyone in such a festive mood). Definitely a must-do for those who don't mind spending the money.

1271 Manley Lane, Rutherford. © **707/967-3500.** www.swansonvineyards.com. Appointments available Wed–Sun 11am, 1:30pm, and 4pm.

Sawyer Cellars *(Finds)*   The most attractive thing about Sawyer, aside from its clean and tasty wines, is its dedication to extremely high quality while it maintains a humble, accommodating attitude. Step into the simple restored 1920s barn to see what I mean. Whatever you ask, the tasting-room host will answer. Whatever your request, they do their best to accommodate it. Want to picnic on the back patio overlooking the vineyards? Be their guest. Like to participate in a grape crushing? Come on over and get your hands dirty. Reserve their charming wine library for a private luncheon? Pay a minimal fee and make yourself at home. Here you can tour the property on a little tram or learn more about winemaker Brad Warner, who spent 30 years at Mondavi before embarking on this exclusive endeavor. Plunk down $5 to taste delicious estate-made wines: sauvignon blanc, merlot, cabernet sauvignon, and Meritage ($15–$46 for current releases), which some argue are worth twice the price. With a total production of only 4,200 cases and a friendly attitude, this winery is a rare treat.

8350 St. Helena Hwy. (Hwy. 29), Rutherford. ✆ 707/963-1980. www.sawyercellars.com. Tastings by appointment. Tours by appointment.

St. Supéry Winery (Kids)

The outside looks like a modern corporate office building, but inside you'll find a functional, welcoming winery that encourages first-time tasters to learn more about oenology. On the self-guided tour, you can wander through the demonstration vineyard, where you'll learn about growing techniques. Inside, kids gravitate toward coloring books and "SmellaVision," an interactive display that teaches you how to identify different wine ingredients. Adjoining it is the Atkinson House, which chronicles more than 100 years of winemaking history. For $5 you'll get lifetime tasting privileges and a tour, which includes samples of delicious sauvignon blanc, chardonnay, cab, and more. Even the prices make visitors feel at home: Many bottles go for around $22, although the tag on the 1997 Dollarhide Ranch cabernet says $70.

8440 St. Helena Hwy. (Hwy. 29), Rutherford. ✆ 800/942-0809 or 707/963-4507. www.stsupery.com. Daily 10am–5pm (until 5:30pm during summer). $5 tour at 1 and 3pm daily.

Niebaum-Coppola

Hollywood meets Napa Valley at Francis Ford Coppola's Inglenook Vineyards, now known as Niebaum-Coppola (*Nee*-bom *Coh*-pa-la). From the outside, the 1880s ivy-draped stone winery and grounds are historic grandeur. From the inside, it's one big retail center promoting Coppola's products and, more subtly, films. On display are Academy Awards and memorabilia from *The Godfather* and *Bram Stoker's Dracula;* the Centennial Museum chronicles the history of the estate and its winemaking as well as Coppola's filmmaking. Wine, food, and gift items dominate the cavernous tasting area, where wines such as an estate-grown blend, cabernet Franc, merlot, chardonnay, zinfandel, and others made from organically grown grapes are sampled for a steep $12 to $30 (price includes a souvenir glass). Bottles range from around $10 to more than $100. The château and garden tour is one of the most expensive in the valley at $25 a pop, though the 1½-hour journey includes a private tasting and a glass. *Tip:* Drop by, snoop around on your own, and spend the cash you save on one more bottle for your vacation collection.

1991 St. Helena Hwy. (Hwy. 29), Rutherford. ✆ 707/968-1100. www.niebaum-coppola.com. Daily Sept–May 10am–5pm; June–Aug 10am–6pm. Tours daily at 10:30am, 12:30pm, and 2:30pm.

Beaulieu Vineyard

Bordeaux native Georges de Latour founded the third-oldest continuously operating winery in Napa Valley in 1900. With the help of legendary oenologist André Tchelistcheff, he has produced world-class, award-winning wines that have been served by every president of the United States since Franklin D. Roosevelt. The brick-and-redwood tasting room isn't much to look at, but with Beaulieu's (*Bowl*-you) stellar reputation, it has no need to visually impress. Tastings cost $5, and a variety of bottles sell for under $20. The Private Reserve Tasting Room offers a "flight" of five reserve wines to taste for $25, but if you want to take a bottle to go, it may cost as much as $130.

1960 St. Helena Hwy. (Hwy. 29), Rutherford. ✆ 707/967-5230. www.bvwines.com. Daily 10am–5pm.

ST. HELENA
73 miles N of San Francisco

This quiet, attractive little town, located 17 miles north of Napa on Calif. 29, is home to a slew of beautiful old homes as well as first-rate restaurants and accommodations. The former Seventh-Day Adventist village manages to maintain a pseudo Old West feel while simultaneously catering to upscale shoppers with deep pockets—hence **Vanderbilt and Company,** 1429 Main St., between Adams and Pine streets (℃ **707/963-1010**), purveyor of gorgeous cookware and fine housewares; it's open daily from 9:30am to 5:30pm.

Shopaholics won't be able to avoid at least one sharp turn off Calif. 29 for a stop at the **St. Helena Premium Outlets,** located 2 miles north of downtown St. Helena (℃ **707/963-7282**), whose stores include Donna Karan, Coach, Movado, Escada, and more, open daily from 10am to 6pm.

One last favorite stop: **Napa Valley Olive Oil Manufacturing Company,** 835 Charter Oak Rd. (℃ **707/963-4173**), at the end of the road behind Tra Vigne restaurant. This market presses and bottles its own oils and sells them at a fraction of the price you'll pay elsewhere. They also have an extensive selection of Italian cooking ingredients, imported snacks, and excellent deals on exotic mushrooms.

If you'd like to go **bicycling,** the quieter northern end of the valley is an ideal place to rent a bike and ride the Silverado Trail. **St. Helena Cyclery,** 1156 Main St. (℃ **707/963-7736**), rents bikes for $7 per hour or $30 a day, including rear rack, helmet, and picnic bag.

V. Sattui Winery *(Kids)*   At this combination winery and enormous gourmet deli (pronounced "Vee Sa-*too*-ee"), you can fill up on wine, pâté, and cheese samples without ever reaching for your pocketbook. The gourmet store stocks more than 200 cheeses, sandwich meats, breads, exotic salads, and delicious desserts, such as a white chocolate cheesecake.

Meanwhile, the long wine bar in the back offers everything from chardonnay, sauvignon blanc, Riesling, cabernet, and zinfandel to a Madeira and a muscat dessert wine. Their wines aren't distributed, so if you taste something you simply must have, buy it. (If you buy a case, ask to talk with a manager, who'll give you access to the less crowded, more exclusive private tasting room.) Wine prices start around $9, with many in the $15 range; reserves top out at around $75. V. Sattui's expansive, lively, and grassy picnic facilities make this a favorite for families. *Note:* To use the facilities, food and wine must be purchased here.

1111 White Lane (at Hwy. 29), St. Helena. ℃ **707/963-7774**. www.vsattui.com. Winter daily 9am–5pm; summer daily 9am–6pm.

Joseph Phelps Vineyards ⚐   Visitors interested in intimate, comprehensive tours and a knockout tasting should schedule a tour at this stellar winery. The winery was founded in 1973 and has since become a major player in both the region and the worldwide wine market. Phelps himself is attributed with a long list of valley firsts, including launching the syrah varietal in the valley and extending the 1970s Berkeley food revolution (led by Alice Waters) up to the Wine Country by founding the **Oakville Grocery Co.** (see "Gourmet Picnics, Napa-Style" on p. 186). The tour and tasting are only available via reservation, and the location—a quick and unmarked turn off the Silverado Trail in Spring Valley—is impossible to find unless you're looking for it.

Those in the know come to this modern, state-of-the-art winery and find an air of seriousness that hangs heavier than harvest grapes. Fortunately, the mood lightens as the well-educated tour guide explains the details of what you're tasting while pouring samples of five to six wines, which may include sauvignon blanc, viogner, syrah, chardonnay, merlot, and cab. Unfortunately, some wines are so popular that they sell out quickly; come late in the season and you may not be able to taste or buy them. The three excellently located picnic tables, on the terrace overlooking the valley, are available to those who join their wine club.

Taplin Rd. (off the Silverado Trail), P.O. Box 1031, St. Helena. ℂ **800/707-5789.** www.jpvwines.com. Mon–Sat 9am–5pm; Sun 9am–4pm. $20 seminars and tastings by appointment only; tastings $10 per person for 5 wines, $10 per person for 2-oz. pour of Insignia.

Prager Winery & Port Works If you want a real down-home, off-the-beaten-track experience, Prager can't be beat. Turn the corner from Sutter Home and roll into the small gravel parking lot. Pull open the creaky old wooden door, pass the oak barrels, and you'll quickly come upon the clapboard tasting room. Most days, your host will be one of the Prager kids who'll ask for $10 (includes a complimentary glass) for samples of late-harvest Johannesburg Riesling and tawny port (which costs $45 per bottle). Also available is "Prager Chocolate Drizzle," a chocolate liqueur that tops ice creams and other desserts.

1281 Lewelling Lane (just west of Hwy. 29, behind Sutter Home), St. Helena. ℂ **800/969-PORT** or 707/963-7678. www.pragerport.com. Daily 10:30am–4:30pm.

Beringer Vineyards ⚑ *(Finds)* Follow the line of cars just north of St. Helena's business district to Beringer Vineyards, where everyone heads to taste wine and view the hand-dug tunnels in the mountainside. Founded in 1876 by brothers Jacob and Frederick, this is the oldest continuously operating winery in Napa Valley—it was open even during Prohibition, when Beringer stayed afloat by making "sacramental" wines. White zinfandel is the winery's most popular nationwide seller, but plenty of other varietals are available to enjoy. Tastings of current vintages ($5) are conducted in new facilities, where there's also a large selection of bottles for less than $20. Reserve wines are available for tasting for $3 to $12 in the remarkable Rhine House. Tours range from the $5 standard or $18 historical to the $30 1½-hour vintage legacy tour.

2000 Main St. (Hwy. 29), St. Helena. ℂ **707/963-7115.** www.beringervineyards.com. Off season daily 10am–5pm (last tour 4pm, last tasting 4:30pm); summer 10am–6pm (last tour 5pm, last tasting 5:30pm). $5 for 30-min. tours every 30 min. (free for anyone under 21 and accompanied by an adult).

Charles Krug Winery Founded in 1861, Krug was the first winery built in the valley. The family of Peter Mondavi (yes, Robert is his brother) owns it today. It's worth paying your respects here by dropping $5 to sip current releases, $8 to sample reserves. On the grounds are picnic facilities with umbrella-shaded tables overlooking vineyards or the wine cellar.

2800 Main St. (St. Helena Hwy.; just north of the tunnel of trees at the northern end of St. Helena), St. Helena. ℂ **707/963-5057.** www.charleskrug.com. Daily 10:30am–5pm.

CALISTOGA
81 miles N of San Francisco

The last tourist town in Napa Valley was named by Sam Brannan, entrepreneur extraordinaire and California's first millionaire. After making a bundle supplying miners during the Gold Rush, he went on to take advantage of the natural geothermal springs at the north end of the Napa Valley by building a hotel and spa in 1859. Flubbing up a speech in which he compared this natural California wonder to New York State's Saratoga Springs resort, he serendipitously coined the name "Calistoga," and it stuck. Today, this small, simple resort town with 5,190-plus residents and an old-time main street (no building along the 6-block stretch is more than two stories high) is popular with city folk who come here to unwind. Calistoga is a great place to relax and indulge in mineral waters, mud baths, Jacuzzis, massages, and, of course, wine. The vibe is more casual—and a little groovier—than you'll find in neighboring towns to the south.

NATURAL WONDERS   **Old Faithful Geyser of California,** 1299 Tubbs Lane (© **707/942-6463;** www.oldfaithfulgeyser.com), is one of only three "old faithful" geysers in the world. It's been blowing off steam at regular intervals for as long as anyone can remember. The 350°F (176°C) water spews at a height of about 60 feet every 40 minutes, day and night. The performance lasts about 3 minutes, and you can bring a picnic lunch to munch on between spews. An exhibit hall, gift shop, and snack bar are open every day. Admission is $8 for adults, $7 for seniors, $3 for children 6 to 12, and free for children under 6. The geyser is open daily from 9am to 6pm (to 5pm in winter). To get there, follow the signs from downtown Calistoga; it's between Highway 29 and Calif. 128.

You won't see thousands of trees turned into stone, but you'll still find many petrified specimens at the **Petrified Forest,** 4100 Petrified Forest Rd. (© **707/ 942-6667;** www.petrifiedforest.org). Volcanic ash blanketed this area after an eruption near Mount St. Helena 3 million years ago. You'll find redwoods that have turned to rock through the slow infiltration of silicas and other minerals, as well as petrified seashells, clams, and marine life indicating that water covered this area before the redwood forest appeared. Admission is $5 for adults, $4 for seniors and youths 12 to 17, $3 for children 5 to 11, and free for children under 4. The forest is open daily from 9am to 6pm (to 5pm in winter). Heading north from Calistoga on Calif. 128, turn left onto Petrified Forest Road, just past Lincoln Street.

Cycling enthusiasts can rent bikes from **Getaway Adventures BHK** (Biking, Hiking, and Kayaking), 1117 Lincoln Ave. (© **800/499-BIKE** or 707/763-3040; www.getawayadventures.com). Full-day tours cost $115 and include lunch and a visit to four or five wineries; downhill cruises (about half the price) are available for people who hate to pedal. Bike rental without a tour costs $9 an hour, $20 per half day, or $28 per day.

If you like horses and venturing through cool, misty forests, then $50 will seem like a bargain for a 1½-hour ride with a friendly tour guide from **Sonoma Cattle Company** (© **707/255-2900;** www.napasonomatrailrides.com). After you've been saddled and schooled in the basics of horse handling at the stable, you'll be led on a leisurely stroll through beautiful Skyline Park in Napa.

Frank Family Vineyards ★ *Finds*   "Wine dudes" Dennis, Tim, Jeff, Grant, and Pat will do practically anything to maintain their rightfully self-proclaimed reputation as the "friendliest winery in the valley." In recent years the name may have changed from Kornell Champagne Cellars to Frank-Rombauer to Frank Family, but the vibe's remained constant; it's all about down-home fun. No muss, no fuss, no intimidation. At Frank Family, you're part of their family—no joke. They'll greet you like a long-lost relative and serve you all the bubbly you want (three to four varieties: blanc de blanc, blanc de noir, and reserve rouge, at $20–$70 a bottle). Still-wine lovers can slip into the casual back room to sample chardonnay and a cabernet sauvignon. Behind the tasting room is a choice picnic area, situated under the oaks and overlooking the vineyards.

1091 Larkmead Lane (just off the Silverado Trail), Calistoga. © 707/942-0859. Daily 10am–5pm. Tours by appointment.

Schramsberg ★★ *Finds*   This 217-acre champagne estate, a landmark once frequented by Robert Louis Stevenson, has a wonderful old-world feel and is one of the valley's all-time best places to explore. Schramsberg is the label that presidents serve when toasting dignitaries from around the globe, and there's plenty of historic memorabilia in the front room to prove it. But the real mystique begins when you enter the champagne caves, which wind 2 miles (reputedly the longest in North America) and were partly hand-carved by Chinese laborers in the 1800s. The caves have an authentic Tom Sawyer ambience, complete with dangling cobwebs and seemingly endless passageways; you can't help but feel you're on an adventure. The comprehensive, unintimidating tour ends in a charming tasting room, where you'll sit around a big table and sample four surprisingly varied selections of bubbly. Tastings are a bit dear ($20 per person), but it's money well spent. Note that tastings are offered only to those who take the free tour, and you must reserve in advance.

1400 Schramsberg Rd. (off Hwy. 29), Calistoga. © 707/942-2414. www.schramsberg.com. Daily 10am–4pm. Tours and tastings by appointment only.

Sterling Vineyards ★ *Kids* *Finds*   No, you don't need climbing shoes to reach this dazzling white Mediterranean-style winery, perched 300 feet up on a rocky knoll. Just fork over $10 and take the aerial tram, which offers stunning bucolic views along the way. If you've been here before, even before embarking you'll notice major changes due to a complete renovation in 2001. Once you're back on land, follow the self-guided tour (one of the most comprehensive in the Wine Country) of the winemaking process. If you're not into taking the tram or you have kids in tow, visit anyway: There's an elevator that can take you to the tasting room, and kids get a goodie bag and a hearty welcome (a rarity at wineries). Wine tastings of four varietals in the panoramic tasting room are included in the tram fare, but more sophisticated sips—a la limited releases or reserve flights—will set you back $10 and $25, respectively. Expect to pay anywhere from $14 to $75 for a souvenir bottle ($20 is the average).

1111 Dunaweal Lane (off Hwy. 29, just south of downtown Calistoga), Calistoga. © 707/942-3344. www.sterlingvineyards.com. Daily 10:30am–4:30pm.

Clos Pegase ★ *Finds*   Renowned architect Michael Graves designed this incredible oasis, which integrates art, 20,000 square feet of aging caves, and a luxurious hilltop private home. Viewing the art is as much the point as tasting the wines—which, by the way, don't come cheap: Prices range from $13 for the 2000 Vin Gris merlot to as much as $80 for the 1998 Hommage Artist Series Reserve, an extremely limited blend of the winery's finest lots of cabernet sauvignon and merlot. Tasting current releases costs $7.50 for samples of three premium wines. The grounds at Clos Pegase (Clo Pey-*goss*) feature an impressive sculpture garden as well as scenic picnic spots.

1060 Dunaweal Lane (off Hwy. 29 or the Silverado Trail), Calistoga. © 707/942-4981. www.clospegase.com. Daily 10:30am–5pm. Tours daily at 11am and 2pm.

WHERE TO STAY

Accommodations here run the gamut—from motels and B&Bs to world-class luxury retreats—and all are accessible from the main highway. While I recommend the more romantically pastoral areas like St. Helena, you're definitely going to find better deals in the towns of Napa or laid-back Calistoga.

Keep in mind that during the high season—between June and November—most hotels charge peak rates and sell out completely on weekends; many have

Moments **Find the New You—in a Calistoga Mud Bath**

The one thing you should do while you're in Calistoga is what people have been doing here for the last 150 years: Take a mud bath. The natural baths are composed of local volcanic ash, imported peat, and naturally boiling mineral hot-springs water, all mulled together to produce a thick mud that simmers at a temperature of about 104°F (40°C). Follow your soak in the mud with a warm mineral-water shower, a whirlpool bath, a visit to the steam room, and a relaxing blanket-wrap. The outcome: a rejuvenated, revitalized, squeaky-clean new you.

Indulge yourself at any of these Calistoga spas: **Dr. Wilkinson's Hot Springs,** 1507 Lincoln Ave. (© 707/942-4102); **Golden Haven Hot Springs Spa,** 1713 Lake St. (© 707/942-6793); **Calistoga Spa Hot Springs,** 1006 Washington St. (© 707/942-6269); **Calistoga Village Inn & Spa,** 1880 Lincoln Ave. (© 707/942-0991); **Indian Springs Resort,** 1712 Lincoln Ave. (© 707/942-4913); **Nance's Hot Springs,** 1614 Lincoln Ave. (© 707/942-6211); or **Roman Spa Motel,** 1300 Washington St. (© 707/942-4441).

a 2-night minimum. If you need help organizing your Wine Country vacation, contact one of the following companies: **Accommodation Referral Bed & Breakfast Exchange** (© 800/240-8466 or 707/965-3400; www.accommodations referral.com), which also represents hotels and inns; **Bed & Breakfast Inns of Napa Valley** (© 707/944-4444), an association of B&Bs that provides inn descriptions and makes reservations; or **Napa Valley Reservations Unlimited** (© 800/251-NAPA or 707/252-1985), which is a source for everything from balloon rides to wine-tasting tours by limousine.

VERY EXPENSIVE

Auberge du Soleil ✦✦✦   This spectacular Relais & Châteaux property, set high above the Napa Valley in a 33-acre olive grove, is quiet, indulgent, and luxuriously romantic. The Mediterranean-style rooms are large enough to get lost in—and you might want to once you discover all the amenities. The bathtub alone—an enormous hot tub with a skylight overhead—will entice you to grab a glass of complimentary California red and settle in for a while. A wood-burning fireplace is surrounded by oversize, cushy furniture—the ideal place to relax and listen to CDs (the stereo comes with a few selections, and there's also a VCR). Fresh flowers, art, terra-cotta floors, and natural-wood and leather furnishings whisk you out of the Wine Country and into the Southwest. Each private deck has views of the valley that are nothing less than spectacular. Those with money to burn should opt for the cottage suite; the 1,800-square-foot hideaway's got two fireplaces, two full bathrooms, a den, and a patio Jacuzzi. Now *that's* living. All guests have access to a celestial swimming pool, new exercise room, and the most fabulous spa in the Wine Country, which opened in 2001. Only guests can use the spa, but if you want to get all the romantic grandeur of Auberge, have lunch on the patio at the wonderful restaurant overlooking the valley.

180 Rutherford Hill Rd., Rutherford, CA 94573. © 800/348-5406 or 707/963-1211. Fax 707/963-8764. www.aubergedusoleil.com. 50 units. $400–$750 double; $675–$1,275 suite. AE, DC, DISC, MC, V. From Hwy. 29 in Rutherford, turn right on Calif. 128 and go 3 miles to the Silverado Trail; turn left and head north about 600 ft. to Rutherford Hill Rd.; turn right. **Amenities:** Restaurant; 3 outdoor pools ranging from hot to cold; 3 tennis courts; health club and full-service spa; sauna; steam room; bikes; concierge; secretarial services; salon; 24-hr. room service; massage; same-day laundry service/dry cleaning, free Internet access. *In room:* A/C, TV/DVD w/pay movies, dataport, kitchenette, minibar, fridge, coffeemaker, hair dryer, iron.

Cottage Grove Inn ★★   Standing in two parallel rows at the end of the main strip in Calistoga is the perfect retreat. These adorable cottages—though on a residential street with a paved road running between two rows of accommodations—seem removed from the action once you've stepped across the threshold. Each compact guesthouse has a wood-burning fireplace, homey furnishings, cozy quilts, and an enormous bathroom with a skylight and a deep, two-person Jacuzzi tub. Guests enjoy such niceties as gourmet coffee, a stereo with CD player, a VCR (the inn has a video library), and a wet bar. Several major spas are within walking distance. This is a top pick if you want to do the Calistoga spa scene in comfort and style. Smoking is allowed only in the gazebos.

1711 Lincoln Ave., Calistoga, CA 94515. © 800/799-2284 or 707/942-8400. Fax 707/942-2653. www.cottagegrove.com. 16 cottages. $250–$325 double. Rates include continental breakfast and evening wine and cheese. AE, DC, DISC, MC, V. *In room:* A/C, TV/VCR, dataport, fridge, coffeemaker, hair dryer, free Internet access.

Meadowood Napa Valley ★★★ *(Finds)*   Less reclusive than Auberge du Soleil, Meadowood is summer camp for wealthy grown-ups. The resort, on 250 acres of pristine mountainside amidst a forest of madrone and oak trees, is quiet and exclusive enough to make you forget that busy wineries are just 10 minutes away. Rooms, furnished with American country classics, have beamed ceilings, private patios, stone fireplaces, and wilderness views; many are individual suite-lodges so far removed from the common areas that you must drive to get to them (lazier folks can opt for more centrally located accommodations). You can spend your days playing golf, tennis, or croquet; lounging around the pools or spa; or hiking the area. Those who actually want to leave the property to do some wine tasting can check in with the hotel's wine tutor.

900 Meadowood Lane, St. Helena, CA 94574. © 800/458-8080 or 707/963-3646. Fax 707/963-3532. www.meadowood.com. 85 units. Double $375–$790; 1-bedroom suite from $865; 2-bedroom from $1,500; 3-bedroom from $2,000; 4-bedroom from $3,585. Ask about promotional offers and off-season rates. 2-night minimum stay on weekends. AE, DC, DISC, MC, V. **Amenities:** 2 restaurants; 2 large heated outdoor pools; golf course; 7 tennis courts; health club and full-service spa; Jacuzzi; sauna; concierge; secretarial services; complimentary Internet access in business center; room service; same-day laundry service/dry cleaning; 2 croquet lawns. *In room:* A/C, TV, dataport, kitchenette in some rooms, minibar, coffeemaker, hair dryer, iron.

Napa Valley Lodge ★★ *(Finds)*   Many frequent visitors compare this contemporary hotel to the nearby upscale Vintage Inn, noting that it's even more personable and accommodating. The lodge is off Highway 29, beyond a wall that does a good job of disguising the road. Guest rooms are large, ultraclean, and better appointed than many in the area. Many have vaulted ceilings, and 39 have fireplaces. Each comes with a king- or queen-size bed, wicker furnishings, robes, and a private balcony or a patio. The least expensive units, at ground level, are smaller and get less sunlight than those on the second floor. Extras are a concierge, afternoon tea and cookies in the lobby, Friday-evening wine tasting in the library, and a full champagne breakfast—with all this, it's no wonder AAA gave the Napa Valley Lodge the Four Diamond award for excellence. Ask about winter discounts, which can be as high as 30%.

2230 Madison St., Yountville, CA 94599. ☎ **800/368-2468** or 707/944-2468. Fax 707/944-9362. www.napavalleylodge.com. 55 units. $252–$445 double. Rates include champagne breakfast buffet, afternoon tea and cookies, and Fri-evening wine tasting. AE, DC, DISC, MC, V. **Amenities:** Heated outdoor pool; small exercise room; Jacuzzi; redwood sauna; concierge; free high-speed Internet access. *In room:* A/C, TV w/pay movies, dataport, minibar, coffeemaker, hair dryer, iron.

MODERATE

Cedar Gables Inn *Finds* This grand, romantic B&B in Old Town Napa is in a stunning Victorian built in 1892. Rooms reflect that era, with rich tapestries and stunning gilded antiques. Four rooms have fireplaces, five have whirlpool tubs, and all feature queen-size brass, wood, or iron beds. Guests meet each evening in front of the roaring fireplace in the lower parlor for wine and cheese. At other times, the family room is a perfect place to cuddle up and watch the large-screen TV. Bonuses include a full breakfast each morning, port in every room, and VIP treatment at many local wineries.

486 Coombs St., Napa, CA 94559. ☎ **800/309-7969** or 707/224-7969. Fax 707/224-4838. www.cedar gablesinn.com. 9 units. $189–$309 double; winter specials available. Rates include full breakfast, evening wine and cheese, and port. AE, DISC, MC, V. From Hwy. 29 north, exit onto First St. and follow signs to downtown; turn right onto Coombs St.; the house is at the corner of Oak St. **Amenities:** Dataport in living room. *In room:* A/C, hair dryer, iron.

Christopher's Inn *Kids* A cluster of five buildings makes up one of Calistoga's more attractive accommodations options. Ten years of renovations and expansions by architect-owner Christopher Layton have turned sweet old homes into hotel rooms with a little pizzazz. Options range from simple but tasteful rooms with colorful and impressive antiques and small bathrooms to lavish abodes with four-poster beds, rich fabrics and brocades, and sunken Jacuzzi tubs facing a gas fireplace. Room no. 3 impresses you with its commanding 9-foot-tall black-wood carved Asian panels. Most rooms have gas fireplaces, and some have quirks like small, older TVs (with cable). Outstanding bouquets attest that the management goes the distance on the details. Those who prefer homey accommodations will feel comfortable, since the property doesn't have corporate polish or big-business blandness. The two plain but very functional two-bedroom units are ideal for families, provided you're not expecting the Ritz. An extended continental breakfast is delivered to your room daily.

1010 Foothill Blvd., Calistoga, CA 94515. ☎ **866/876-5755** or 707/942-5755. Fax 707/942-6895. www.christophersinn.com. 22 units. $175–$425 double; $330–$350 house sleeping 5. Rates include continental breakfast. AE, V. *In room:* TV, dataport.

Maison Fleurie Maison Fleurie, one of the prettiest hotels in the Wine Country, is a trio of beautiful 1873 brick-and-fieldstone buildings overlaid with ivy. The main house—a charming Provençal replica with thick brick walls, terracotta tile, and paned windows—holds seven rooms; the rest are in the old bakery building and the carriage house. Some feature private balconies, patios, sitting areas, Jacuzzi tubs, and fireplaces. Breakfast is served in the quaint little dining room; afterward, you're welcome to wander the landscaped grounds or hit the wine-tasting trail, returning in time for afternoon hors d'oeuvres and wine. It's impossible not to enjoy your stay at Maison Fleurie.

6529 Yount St. (between Washington St. and Yountville Cross Rd.), Yountville, CA 94599. ☎ **800/788-0369** or 707/944-2056. Fax 707/944-9342. www.foursisters.com. 13 units. $120–$275 double. Rates include full breakfast and afternoon hors d'oeuvres. AE, DC, MC, V. **Amenities:** Heated outdoor pool; Jacuzzi; free use of bikes. *In room:* A/C, TV, dataport, hair dryer, iron.

Rancho Caymus Inn ⚐ This Spanish-style hacienda, with two floors open-ing onto wisteria-covered balconies, was the creation of sculptor Mary Tilden Morton (of Morton Salt). Morton wanted each room in the hacienda to be a work of art, so she hired the most skilled craftspeople of her day. She designed the adobe fireplaces herself, and wandered through Mexico and South America purchasing artifacts for the property.

Guest rooms are situated around a whimsical garden courtyard with an enor-mous outdoor fireplace. The mix-and-match interior decor is on the funky side, with overly varnished dark-wood furnishings and braided rugs. The inn is cozy, however, and rooms are decent-size, split-level suites with queen beds. Other amenities include wet bars, sofa beds in the sitting areas, and small private patios. Most of the suites have fireplaces, and five have kitchenettes and whirlpool tubs. A complimentary continental breakfast, which includes fresh fruit, granola, orange juice, and breads, is served in the inn's dining room.

Since chef Ken Frank's formal French **La Toque** restaurant opened here, this funky inn has also become a dining destination.

1140 Rutherford Rd. (P.O. Box 78), Rutherford, CA 94573. © **800/845-1777** or 707/963-1777. Fax 707/963-5387. www.ranchocaymus.com. 26 suites. $195–$390 double; $255–$430 master suite; $385 2-bed-room suite. Rates include continental breakfast. AE, MC, V. From Hwy. 29 north, turn right onto Rutherford Rd./Calif. 128 east; the hotel is on your left. **Amenities:** Restaurant. *In room:* A/C, TV, dataport, kitchenette in some rooms, minibar, fridge, hair dryer, iron in some rooms.

Wine Country Inn ⚐⚐ Just off the highway behind Freemark Abbey vine-yard, this wood-and-stone inn, complete with a French-style mansard roof and turret, overlooks a landscape of vineyards. The individually decorated rooms contain iron or brass beds, antiques, and handmade quilts; most have fireplaces and private terraces overlooking the valley, and others have private hot tubs. One of the inn's best features (besides the absence of TVs) is the heated outdoor pool, which is attractively landscaped into the hillside. Another favorite feature is the selection of suites, which come with stereos, plenty of space, and lots of privacy. The family that runs this place puts personal touches everywhere and makes every guest feel welcome. They serve wine and plenty of appetizers nightly, along with a big dash of hotel-staff hospitality in the inviting living room. A full buf-fet breakfast is served there, too. Five luxury cottages opened in mid-2003.

1152 Lodi Lane, St. Helena, CA 94574. © **888/465-4608** or 707/963-7077. Fax 707/963-9018. www.wine-country-inn.com. 24 units (12 with shower only). $185–$595 double. Rates include breakfast and appetizers. MC, V. **Amenities:** Heated outdoor pool; Jacuzzi; concierge; free Internet access. *In room:* A/C, hair dryer.

INEXPENSIVE

Along with the listings below, I also recommend **Napa Valley Railway Inn,** 6503 Washington St., Yountville, adjacent to the Vintage 1870 shopping com-plex (© **707/944-2000**), which rents private railway cars converted into adorable hotel rooms; and **Dr. Wilkinson's Hot Springs,** 1507 Lincoln Ave., Calistoga (© **707/942-4102**), which underwent a major renovation 3 years ago.

Calistoga Spa Hot Springs ⚐ *Kids Value* Very few hotels in the Wine Coun-try cater specifically to families with children, which is why I recommend Cal-istoga Spa Hot Springs if you're bringing the little ones. They classify themselves as a family resort and are very accommodating to visitors of all ages. In any case, it's a great bargain, offering unpretentious yet comfortable rooms, as well as a plethora of spa facilities. All of Calistoga's best shops and restaurants are within easy walking distance, and you can even whip up your own grub at the barbe-cue grills near the large pool and patio area.

1006 Washington St. (at Gerrard St.), Calistoga, CA 94515. © **866/822-5772** or 707/942-6269. www.
calistogaspa.com. 57 units, 1 suite. Winter $99 double, $154 family unit; summer $121 double, $176 suite.
MC, V. **Amenities:** 3 heated outdoor pools; kids' wading pool; exercise room; spa. In room: A/C, TV, kitchenette, fridge, coffeemaker, hair dryer on request, iron.

Chablis Inn ☆

There's no way around it: If you want to sleep cheaply in a
town where the *average* room rate tops $200 per night in high season, you're des-
tined for a motel. Look on the bright side: Because your room is likely to be little more than a crash pad after a day of eating and drinking, a clean bed and a
remote control are all you'll really need. And Chablis offers much more than that.
All of the motel-style rooms are superclean, and some even boast kitchenettes or
whirlpool tubs. Guests have access to an outdoor heated pool and hot tub.

3360 Solano Ave., Napa, CA 94558. © **707/257-1944.** Fax 707/226-6862. www.chablisinn.com. 34 units.
May to mid-Nov $125–$235 double; mid-Nov to Apr $70–$120 double. AE, DC, DISC, MC, V. **Amenities:**
Heated outdoor pool; Jacuzzi. In room: A/C, TV, dataports in some rooms, kitchenettes in some rooms, fridge,
coffeemaker, hair dryer.

El Bonita Motel ☆ (Kids) (Value)

This 1930s Art Deco motel is a bit too close to
Highway 29 for comfort, but the 2½ acres of beautifully landscaped gardens
behind the building help even the score. The rooms, while small and nothing
fancy, are spotlessly clean (and sometimes smell strongly of air freshener). They
are decorated with newer furnishings and kitchenettes, and some have a
whirlpool bathtub. Many families consider El Bonita one of the best values in
Napa Valley—especially considering the pool, Jacuzzi, and sauna.

195 Main St. (at El Bonita Ave.), St. Helena, CA 94574. © **800/541-3284** or 707/963-3216. Fax
707/963-8838. www.elbonita.com. 41 units. $89–$259 double. Rates include continental breakfast. AE, DC,
DISC, MC, V. **Amenities:** Heated outdoor pool; spa; Jacuzzi; free Internet access. In room: A/C, TV, fridge, coffeemaker, hair dryer, iron, microwave.

White Sulphur Springs Retreat & Spa ☆

If your idea of the ultimate vaca-
tion is a cozy cabin on 45 acres, paradise is a short, winding drive away from
downtown St. Helena. Established in 1852, Sulphur Springs claims to be the
oldest resort in California. The property holds creeks, waterfalls, a naturally
heated sulfur hot spring, and redwood, madrone, and fir trees. Guests stay in
different-size creek-side cabins, the inn, or the Carriage House. The cabins are
decorated with simple but homey furnishings; cabin no. 9 has two queen beds
and a kitchenette. From here you can take a dip in the natural hot sulfur spring;
lounge by the large outdoor unheated pool; sit under a tree and watch for deer,
fox, raccoon, spotted owl, or woodpecker; or schedule a day of massage (fantastic massage!), aromatherapy, and other spa treatments in their spa. *Note:* No RVs
are allowed without advance notice. All rooms are nonsmoking. Call well in
advance; the resort is often rented by large groups.

3100 White Sulphur Springs Rd., St. Helena, CA 94574. © **800/593-8873** in California, or 707/963-8588.
Fax 707/963-2890. www.whitesulphursprings.com. 37 units (14 with shared bathroom); 9 cottages. Carriage
House (shared bathroom) $100–$200 double; inn $115–$140 double; creek-side cottages $175–$200. Rates
include continental breakfast. Off-season and midweek discounts available. 2-night minimum stay on weekends Apr–Oct and all holidays. AE, DC, DISC, MC, V. **Amenities:** Heated outdoor pool; soaking pool; full-service spa; Jacuzzi; free Internet hook-up in hospitality room. In room: A/C in some rooms, hair dryer on request.

Wine Valley Lodge ☆ (Value)

Dollar for dollar, the Wine Valley Lodge offers
a great deal. At the south end of town in a quiet residential neighborhood, the
Mission-style motel is extremely well kept and accessible, just a short drive from
Highway 29 and the wineries to the north. The reasonably priced deluxe units,
which are two bedrooms connected by a bathroom, are great for families.

200 S. Coombs St. (between First and Imola sts.), Napa, CA 94559. © **800/696-7911** or 707/224-7911. www.winevalleylodge.com. 54 units. $79–$135 double; $150–$165 deluxe. AE, DC, DISC, MC, V. **Amenities:** Heated outdoor pool. *In room:* A/C, TV.

WHERE TO DINE

To best enjoy Napa's restaurant scene, keep one thing in mind: *reserve*—especially for seats in a more renowned room.

EXPENSIVE

Auberge du Soleil ★★ *(Finds)* WINE COUNTRY CUISINE   There is no better restaurant view than the one at Auberge du Soleil, perched on a hillside overlooking the valley. Alfresco dining rises to an entirely new level here, particularly on warm summer afternoons at sunset. In fact, I recommend coming during the day (request terrace seating) to join the wealthy patrons, many of whom have emerged from their überluxury guest rooms and are slinking to a table to dine above the vines. The kitchen, previously overseen by the very talented chef Richard Reddington, is now in the hands of Joseph Humphrey, a veteran of various well-regarded San Francisco establishments. Devoted fans will look to him to continue to turn out superb seasonal dishes such as well-prepared sautéed sweetbreads, venison loin with butternut squash, stuffed squab, and roasted saddle of lamb. The interior is warm, bustling, and formal enough that some folks wear ties. The only drawback: Service is unsteady.

180 Rutherford Hill Rd., Rutherford. © **707/963-1211**. Reservations recommended. Main courses $19–$23 lunch, $28–$34 dinner; 4-course fixed-price dinner $79. AE, DISC, MC, V. Daily breakfast 7–11am; lunch 11:30am–2:30pm; dinner Sun–Thurs 6–9:30pm, Fri–Sat 5:30–9:30pm.

The French Laundry ★★★ CLASSIC AMERICAN/FRENCH   Several years after renowned chef-owner Thomas Keller bought the place and caught the attention of epicureans worldwide (including the judges of the James Beard Awards, who named him Chef of the Nation in 1997), this discreet restaurant is the hottest dinner ticket *in the world.*

Plainly put, the French Laundry is unlike any other dining experience, period. Part of it has to do with the intricate preparations, often finished tableside and always presented with uncommon artistry and detail, from the food itself to the surface it's delivered on. Other factors are the service (superfluous, formal, and attentive) and the sheer length of time it takes to ride chef Keller's culinary magic carpet. The atmosphere is as serious as the diners who quietly swoon over the ongoing parade of bite-size delights. Seating ranges from downstairs to upstairs to seasonal garden tables. The prix-fixe menu offers a choice of five or nine courses (including a vegetarian menu), and signature dishes include Keller's "tongue in cheek" (a marinated and braised round of sliced lamb tongue and tender beef cheeks) and "macaroni and cheese" (sweet butter-poached Maine lobster with creamy lobster broth and orzo with mascarpone cheese).

The staff is well acquainted with the wide selection of regional wines; there's a $50 corkage fee if you bring your own bottle. On warm summer nights, request a table in the flower-filled garden. *Hint:* If you can't get a reservation, try walking in—on occasion folks don't keep their reservation and tables open up, especially during lunch on rainy days. Also, Auberge du Soleil (p. 177) reserves two tables nightly which are doled out on a first-come, first-served basis. Reservations are accepted 2 months in advance of the date, starting at 10am. Anticipate hitting redial many times for the best chance. Also, insiders tell me that fewer people call on weekends, so you have a better chance at getting through the busy signal.

6640 Washington St. (at Creek St.), Yountville. ℂ **707/944-2380.** Reservations required. Vegetarian menu $80; 5-course menu $105; chef's 9-course tasting menu $120. AE, MC, V. Fri–Sun 11am–1pm; daily 5:30–9:30pm.

Terra ★★★ CONTEMPORARY AMERICAN Terra is one of my favorite restaurants because it manages to be humble even though it serves some of the most extraordinary food in Northern California. The creation of Lissa Doumani and her husband, Hiro Sone, a master chef who hails from Japan, is a culmination of talents brought together more than 15 years ago, after the duo worked at L.A.'s Spago. Today the menu reflects Sone's full use of the region's bounty and his formal training in classic European and Japanese cuisine. Dishes—all of which are incredible and are served in the rustic-romantic dining room with fieldstone walls—range from understated and refined (broiled sake-marinated cod with shrimp dumplings and shiso broth) to rock-your-world flavorful (petit ragout of sweetbreads, prosciutto, mushroom, and white truffle oil; or grilled squab with leek-and-bacon bread pudding and roasted garlic foie gras sauce). I cannot express the importance of saving room for dessert (or forcing it even if you didn't). Doumani's recipes, which include tiramisu and an out-of-this-world heavenly orange risotto in a brandy snap cookie with passion-fruit sauce, are some of the best I've ever tasted.

1345 Railroad Ave. (between Adams and Hunt sts.), St. Helena. ℂ **707/963-8931.** www.terrarestaurant. com. Reservations recommended. Main courses $19–$29. AE, DC, MC, V. Sun–Mon and Wed–Thurs 6–9:30pm; Fri–Sat 6–10pm. Closed for 2 weeks in early Jan.

MODERATE

All Seasons Café ★★ CALIFORNIA Wine Country devotees wend their way to the All Seasons Café in downtown Calistoga because of its extensive wine list and knowledgeable staff. The trick is to buy a bottle of wine from the cafe's wine shop, then bring it to your table; the cafe adds a corkage fee of around $15 instead of tripling the price of the bottle (as most restaurants do). The diverse menu dances with decadences such as seared Maine scallops with truffle-scented risotto, or red-wine-braised short ribs. Culinary director Sonja Murphy saves guests from any major faux pas by matching wines to dishes on the menu, so you know just what's right for smoked salmon and Crescenza cheese pizza.

1400 Lincoln Ave. (at Washington St.), Calistoga. ℂ **707/942-9111.** Reservations recommended on weekends. Main courses $10–$14 lunch, $16–$26 dinner. DISC, MC, V. Lunch Wed–Sun 11am–3pm; dinner nightly 6–9pm.

Bistro Don Giovanni ★★★ (Value REGIONAL ITALIAN Donna and Giovanni Scala own this bright, bustling, cheery Italian restaurant, which happens to be one of my favorite restaurants in Napa Valley. The menu features pastas, risottos, pizzas (baked in a wood-burning oven), and a half-dozen other main courses. Every time I grab a menu, I can't get past the beet and haricots verts salad and pasta with duck Bolognese. On the rare occasion that I do, I am equally smitten with thin-crust pizzas fresh from the wood-burning oven, seared salmon filet perched atop buttermilk mashed potatoes, and steak *frites*. Alfresco dining on the patio is available—and highly recommended on a warm, sunny day.

4110 Howard Lane (at St. Helena Hwy.), Napa. ℂ **707/224-3300.** Reservations recommended. Main courses $12–$24. AE, DC, DISC, MC, V. Sun–Thurs 11:30am–10pm; Fri–Sat 11:30am–11pm.

Bistro Jeanty ★★ FRENCH BISTRO This casual, warm bistro with muted buttercup walls and two dining rooms divided by the bar is the brainchild of chef Phillipe Jeanty, who a few years back left his highly reputed 18-year post at

Domaine Chandon to open one of the hottest (and most moderately priced) new restaurants in town. Jeanty was previously known for formal French cooking, but his charming and cheery bistro offers far more laid-back but equally worship-worthy fare. Outstanding classic (albeit heavy) French bistro fare comes in the form of an all-day menu, which includes his legendary tomato soup in a puff pastry, foie gras pâté, steak tartare, and house-smoked trout with potato slices basking in a light olive oil and vinegar bath; daube de boeuf simmered in red wine and served with mashed potatoes, fresh peas, and baby carrots; and cassoulet with white beans, fennel sausage, pork, and duck leg. I'll return frequently for the decadent fall-off-the-bone coq au vin with an earthy, smoky red-wine sauce and delicate deep-fried smelt special, which comes in a wax-paper cone accompanied by a seasoned mayo dipping sauce.

6510 Washington St., Yountville. ⓒ 707/944-0103. www.bistrojeanty.com. Reservations recommended. Appetizers $6.50–$11; most main courses $14–$23. AE, MC, V. Daily 11:30am–10:30pm.

Bouchon ★★ FRENCH BISTRO   French Laundry owner Thomas Keller is behind this more casual, but still delicious, and polished-looking French brasserie. Along with a raw bar, expect superb renditions of steak *frites,* mussels *marinière,* croque-monsieur (grilled cheese sandwich), and other French classics (try the expensive and rich foie gras pâté, which is made at French Laundry). My all-time favorite must-orders: the Bibb lettuce salad (seriously, trust me on this), french fries (perhaps the best in the valley), and roasted chicken bathed in wild-mushroom ragout. Prices and atmosphere are far more down-to-earth than those at French Laundry. A bonus, especially for restless residents and off-duty restaurant staff, is the late hours, although they offer a more limited menu when the crowds dwindle. Another plus: Sunday brunch featuring Granny Smith apple beignets, cold-poached salmon, and fresh-squeezed juices.

6534 Washington St. (at Humbolt), Yountville. ⓒ 707/944-8037. Reservations recommended. Main courses $14–$23. AE, MC, V. Mon–Sat 11:30am–1am; Sun 11am–1am.

Tra Vigne Restaurant ★★ ITALIAN   Tra Vigne's combination of good ultra-fresh food, high-energy atmosphere, gorgeous patio seating, and "reasonable" prices makes this restaurant a favorite among visitors and locals. Add to that plenty of seating and service running from lunch through dinner, and it's no wonder the dining room packs 'em in. Whether guests are in the Tuscany-evoking courtyard, terrace (heated on cold nights), or in the center of the bustling scene, they're usually thrilled just to have a seat. Even though the wonderful bread (served with house-made flavored olive oils) is tempting, save room for the robust California dishes, cooked Italian-style. The menu features about one daily oven-roasted pizza special, standbys like short ribs, *fritto misto,* and irresistible whole roasted fish. Equally tempting are the fresh pastas—such as spaghettini with cuttlefish Bolognese and spring onions—and delicious desserts.

1050 Charter Oak Ave., St. Helena. ⓒ 707/963-4444. Reservations recommended. Main courses $13–$22. DC, DISC, MC, V. Daily 11:30am–10pm.

Wappo Bar & Bistro GLOBAL   One of the best alfresco dining venues in the Wine Country is under Wappo's jasmine-and-grapevine-covered arbor. Unfortunately, food and service are a very distant second. But much can be forgiven when the wine's flowing and you're surrounded by pastoral splendor. The menu offers a global selection, from tandoori chicken to roast rabbit with oven tomato tagliarini. Desserts of choice are black-bottom coconut cream pie and strawberry rhubarb pie.

1226B Washington St. (off Lincoln Ave.), Calistoga. ℂ 707/942-4712. www.wappobar.com. Main courses $14–$22. AE, MC, V. Wed–Mon 11:30am–2:30pm and 6–9:30pm.

Wine Spectator Greystone Restaurant 🐾 CALIFORNIA This place offers a combination visual and culinary feast that's unparalleled in the area, if not the state. The room itself is an enormous stone-walled former winery, but the festive decor and heavenly aromas warm the space up. Cooking islands—complete with scurrying chefs, steaming pots, and rotating chicken—provide edible entertainment. The "tastings" (appetizer) menu features fresh ingredient-inspired dishes, including a perfect calamari sautéed with smoked paprika, garlic, and rosemary; a fine seafood-and-white-bean salad; and an unimpressive mushroom piroshki with caramelized onions. Portions are small but affordable; pastas and salads are a bit heftier. Main courses, such as a crispy fried lamb shank with cranberry beans, cherry tomatoes, and spinach, are well portioned. But I recommend you opt for a barrage of appetizers for your table to share. While the food is serious, the atmosphere is playful—casual enough that you'll feel comfortable in jeans or shorts. If you want to ensure a meal here, reserve far in advance. I prefer to stop by, have a snack at the bar, and eat big meals elsewhere.

At the Culinary Institute of America at Greystone, 2555 Main St., St. Helena. ℂ 707/967-1010. Reservations recommended. Tastings $8.50; main courses $7–$27. AE, DC, MC, V. Daily 11:30am–10pm.

INEXPENSIVE

Market 🐾🐾 AMERICAN San Francisco veterans Nick Peyton (of Restaurant Gary Danko, p. 102) and Douglas Keane (chef at Jardinière) aim to fill a much-needed niche of affordable dining with this upscale but cheap ode to American comfort food. Mimicking its wealthy farming environs, it's a marriage of contradictions, where stone-wall and Brunswick bar surroundings are paired with clunky steak knives and simple white-plate presentations. Try Dungeness crab cakes with avocado coulis; barbecue sauce–glazed meatloaf over gravy, mashed potatoes, and carrots; or toast-it-yourself s'mores with homemade graham crackers. Trust me: This is the ultimate find for anyone who wants great atmosphere and a nice meal at an absurdly low price—especially if you drop by for their very cheap ($13) three-course lunch.

1347 Main St., St. Helena. ℂ 707/963-3799. Most main courses $7–$15. AE, MC, V. Wed–Mon lunch 11:30am–2pm, bar menu 2–4:30pm; dinner 5:30–9pm, bar menu 9–11pm. Closed Tues.

Taylor's Refresher 🐾 DINER It isn't every day that a burger shack gets a huge spread in *Food & Wine* magazine, but then again, Taylor's Refresher isn't your average fast-food stop. At this completely outdoor diner built in 1949, you order at the counter, settle at a picnic table in the front facing Highway 29 or the relatively more pastoral back, and wait for your name to be called. When it is, you'll receive an excellent burger on a surprisingly soft but sturdy bun, fries, and creamy shakes. Those who are less carnivorous can opt for an *ahi* tuna burger.

933 Main St., St. Helena. ℂ 707/963-3486. www.taylorsrefresher.com. Main courses $4–$13. AE, MC, V. Daily 11am–8pm (9pm in summer).

ZuZu 🐾🐾 TAPAS This downtown spot is a local favorite for its delicious small plates of Spanish fare ($2–$11!). Here no reservations are taken and residents crowd into the cramped wine bar until they can be seated downstairs or up. The environment is comfortable and warm, and the food is seriously good. Chef

Charles Weber presides over the tiny kitchen cranking out sizzling symphonies. They include fantastic paella; fresh, clean corn soup; sizzling prawns with requisite bread-dipping sauce; light and delicate sea-scallop-ceviche salad; and Moroccan barbecued lamb chops with a sweet and spicy sauce guaranteed to make you swoon. Desserts aren't as fab, but who cares? I'm such a regular here that if you sit at the bar, you might end up dining next to me—and even if you don't, most folks who perch there are just as friendly and chatty.

Tips   Gourmet Picnics, Napa-Style

You could easily plan your whole trip around restaurant dining. But put together a gourmet picnic, and the valley's your oyster.

One of the finest gourmet food stores in the Wine Country, if not all California, is the **Oakville Grocery Co.**, 7856 St. Helena Hwy., at Oakville Cross Road (© **707/944-8802**). Here you can put together the provisions for a memorable picnic—or, if you give them at least 24 hours' notice, the staff can prepare a basket for you. The store, with its small-town vibe and claustrophobia-inducing crowds, is crammed with the best breads and choicest selection of cheeses in the northern Bay Area, as well as pâtés, cold cuts, crackers, top-quality olive oils, fresh foie gras, smoked Norwegian salmon, fresh caviar (Beluga, Sevruga, Osetra), and an exceptional selection of California wines. The Grocery Co. is open daily from 9am to 6pm; it also has an espresso bar (open daily 7am–6pm), offering breakfast and lunch items, house-baked pastries, and 15 wines by the glass.

Another of my favorite places to fill a picnic basket is New York City's version of a swank European marketplace, **Dean & Deluca**, 607 S. Main St. (Calif. 29), north of Zinfandel Lane and south of Sulphur Springs Road in St. Helena (© **707/967-9980**). The ultimate gourmet grocery store is more like a World's Fair of foods, where everything is beautifully displayed and often painfully pricey. But even if you choose not to buy, this place is worth a browse. Check out the 200 domestic and imported cheeses; shelves of tapenades, pastas, oils, hand-packed dried herbs and spices, chocolates, sauces, and cookware; an espresso bar; one hell of a bakery section; and more. The wine shop boasts a 1,200-label collection. Open daily from 9am to 7pm (the espresso bar opens Mon–Sat at 7:30am and Sun at 9am).

My favorite stop, **Palisades Market**, 1506 Lincoln Ave., Calistoga (© **707/942-9549**), is a much more intimate affair and serves the best sandwiches I've ever had (outside of Italy). You can also drop in for wine, juice, soda, cheese, tamales, green salads, lasagna, soup, picnic items, and every kind of treat you can think of, but under no circumstances skip the sandwiches. Hours are Sunday through Wednesday from 7:30am to 6pm and Thursday through Saturday from 7:30am to 7pm.

829 Main St., Napa. (*©* 707/224-8555. Reservations not accepted. Tapas $2–$11. AE, MC, V. Mon–Thurs
11:30am–10pm; Fri 11:30am–midnight; Sat 4pm–midnight; Sun 4–9pm.

2 Sonoma Valley

Sonoma is often thought of as the "other" Wine Country, forever in the shadow
of Napa Valley. Truth is, it's a very different experience. Sonoma still manages to
maintain a backcountry ambience thanks to its lower density of wineries, restaurants, and hotels; because it's far less traveled than its neighbor, it offers a more
genuine escape. Small, family-owned wineries are its mainstay, just like in the
old days of winemaking, when everyone started with the intention of going
broke and loved every minute of it. Unlike the rigidly structured tours at many
of Napa Valley's corporate-owned wineries, tastings and tours on the Sonoma
side of the Mayacamas Mountains are usually free and low-key, and come with
plenty of friendly banter between the winemakers and their guests.

ESSENTIALS

GETTING THERE   From San Francisco, cross the Golden Gate Bridge and
stay on U.S. 101 north. Exit at Calif. 37; after 10 miles, turn north onto Calif.
121. After another 10 miles, turn north onto Calif. 12 (Broadway), which will
take you directly into the town of Sonoma.

VISITOR INFORMATION   While you're in Sonoma, stop by the **Sonoma
Valley Visitors Bureau,** 453 First St. E. (*©* **707/996-1090;** www.sonomaval-
ley.com). It's open daily from 9am to 7pm in summer; from 9am to 5pm in winter. An additional **visitors bureau** is located a few miles south of the square at
25200 Arnold Dr. (Calif. 121), at the entrance to Viansa Winery (*©* **707/
935-4747**); it's open daily from 9am to 4pm, from 9am to 5pm in summer.

If you prefer some advance information, you can contact the Sonoma Valley
Visitors Bureau to order the free *Sonoma Valley Visitors Guide,* which lists most
every lodging, winery, and restaurant in the valley.

WHEN TO GO   See "When to Go" in the Napa section, earlier in this chapter.

TOURING THE VALLEY & WINERIES

Sonoma Valley is currently home to about 35 wineries (including California's
first winery, Buena Vista, founded in 1857) and 13,000 acres of vineyards,
which produce roughly 25 types of wines totaling more than five million cases
a year.

The towns and wineries covered below are organized geographically from
south to north, starting at the intersection of Calif. 37 and Calif. 121 in the
Carneros District and ending in Kenwood. The wineries here tend to be a little
more spread out than they are in Napa, but they're easy to find. Still, it's best to
decide which wineries you're most interested in and devise a touring strategy
before you set out so you don't find yourself doing a lot of backtracking.

I've reviewed some my favorite Sonoma Valley wineries here—more than
enough to keep you busy tasting wine for a long weekend. For a complete list of
local wineries, pick up one of the free guides to the valley available at the
Sonoma Valley Visitors Bureau (see "Visitor Information" above).

THE CARNEROS DISTRICT

As you approach the Wine Country from the south, you must pass through the
Carneros District, a cool, wind-swept region that borders the San Pablo Bay and
marks the entrance to both Napa and Sonoma valleys. Until the latter part of

the 20th century, this mixture of marsh, sloughs, and hills was mainly used as sheep pasture (*carneros* means "sheep" in Spanish). After experimental plantings yielded slow-growing yet high-quality grapes—particularly chardonnay and pinot noir—several Napa and Sonoma wineries expanded here, eventually establishing the Carneros District as an American Viticultural Appellation.

Viansa Winery and Italian Marketplace ♠ *Finds*   The first major winery you'll encounter as you enter Sonoma Valley from the south, this sprawling Tuscan-style villa perches atop a knoll overlooking the entire lower valley. Viansa is the brainchild of Sam and Vicki Sebastiani, who left the family dynasty to create their own temple to food and wine. (*Viansa* is a contraction of "Vicki and Sam.") While Sam, a third-generation winemaker, runs the winery, Vicki manages the marketplace, a large room crammed with a cornucopia of high-quality preserves, mustards, olive oils, pastas, salads, breads, desserts, Italian tableware, cookbooks, and wine-related gifts.

The winery, which does an extensive mail-order business through The Tuscan Club, features cabernet, sauvignon blanc, and chardonnay as well as Italian grape varieties such as vernaccia, sangiovese, and nebbiolo, most of which are sold exclusively at the winery. Free tastings are poured at the east end of the marketplace, and the self-guided tour includes a trip through the underground barrel-aging cellar adorned with colorful hand-painted murals. Guided tours, held at 11am and 2pm, will set you back $5.

Viansa is also one of the few wineries in Sonoma Valley that sells deli items—the focaccia sandwiches are delicious. You can dine alfresco under the grape trellis while you admire the bucolic view.

25200 Arnold Dr. (Calif. 121), Sonoma. ℂ **800/995-4740** or 707/935-4700. www.viansa.com. Daily 10am–5pm. Daily self-guided tours.

Gloria Ferrer Champagne Caves ♠ *Finds*   When you have had it up to here with chardonnays and pinots, it's time to pay a visit to Gloria Ferrer, the grande dame of the Wine Country's sparkling-wine producers. Who's Gloria? She's the wife of José Ferrer, whose family has made sparkling wine for 5 centuries. The family business, Freixenet, is the largest producer of sparkling wine in the world; Cordon Negro is its most popular brand. That equals big bucks, and certainly a good chunk went into building this palatial estate. Glimmering like Oz high atop a gently sloping hill, it overlooks the verdant Carneros District. On a sunny day, enjoying a glass of dry brut while soaking in the magnificent views is a must.

If you're unfamiliar with the term *méthode champenoise,* be sure to take the free 30-minute tour of the fermenting tanks, bottling line, and caves brimming with racks of yeast-laden bottles. Afterward, retire to the tasting room for a flute of brut or cuvée ($5–$9 a glass, $20 and up per bottle), find an empty chair on the veranda, and say, "Ahhh. *This* is the life." There are picnic tables, but it's usually too windy for comfort, and you must buy a bottle of wine to reserve a table.

23555 Carneros Hwy. (Calif. 121), Sonoma. ℂ 707/996-7256. www.gloriaferrer.com. Daily 10am–5:30pm. Tours daily 11am–4pm.

SONOMA

At the northern boundary of the Carneros District along Calif. 12 is the centerpiece of Sonoma Valley, the midsize town of Sonoma, which owes much of its appeal to Mexican general Mariano Guadalupe Vallejo. It was Vallejo who fashioned this pleasant, slow-paced community after a typical Mexican village—right down to its central plaza, Sonoma's geographical and commercial center. The plaza sits at the top of a T formed by Broadway (Calif. 12) and Napa Street. Most of the surrounding streets form a grid pattern around this axis, making Sonoma easy to negotiate. The plaza's Bear Flag Monument marks the spot where the crude Bear Flag was raised in 1846, signaling the end of Mexican rule; the symbol was later adopted by the state of California and placed on its flag. The 8-acre park at the center of the plaza, complete with two ponds populated with ducks and geese, is perfect for an afternoon siesta in the cool shade.

The best way to see the town of Sonoma is to follow the **Sonoma Walking Tour** map, provided by the Sonoma League for Historic Preservation. Tour highlights include General Vallejo's 1852 Victorian-style home; the Sonoma Barracks, erected in 1836 to house Mexican army troops; and the Blue Wing Inn, an 1840 hostelry built to accommodate travelers—including John Fremont, Kit Carson, and Ulysses S. Grant—and new settlers while they erected homes in Sonoma. You can purchase the $2.75 map at the Mission (see below).

The **Mission San Francisco Solano de Sonoma,** on Sonoma Plaza at the corner of First Street East and Spain Street (© **707/938-9560**), was founded in 1823. It was the northernmost mission built in California. It was also the only one established on the northern coast by the Mexican rulers, who wished to protect their territory from Russian fur traders. It's now part of Sonoma State Historic Park. Admission is $2 for adults, free for children ages 16 and under. It's open daily from 10am to 5pm except Thanksgiving, Christmas, and New Year's Day.

Sebastiani Vineyards & Winery   What started in 1904, when Samuele Sebastiani began producing his first wines, has in three generations grown into a small empire, producing some 300,000 cases a year. After a few years of major retrofitting, the original 1904 winery now offers more extensive educational tours, an 80-foot S-shaped tasting bar, and lots of shopping in the gift shop. The contemporary tasting room's minimuseum area shows the winery's original turn-of-the-20th-century crusher and press, as well as the world's largest collection of oak-barrel carvings, crafted by local artist Earle Brown. If it's merely wine that interests you, you can sample an extensive selection of wines for $6 to $15, the latter of which includes a keepsake glass. Bottle prices are reasonable, ranging from $8 to $90. A picnic area adjoins the cellars; a far more scenic spot is across the parking lot in Sebastiani's Cherryblock Vineyards.

389 Fourth St. E., Sonoma. © 800/888-5532 or 707/938-5532. www.sebastiani.com. Daily 10am–5pm. Tours Mon–Fri 11am and 3pm; Sat–Sun 11am, 1pm, and 3pm.

Buena Vista Winery   Count Agoston Haraszthy, the Hungarian émigré who is universally regarded as the father of California's wine industry, founded this historic winery in 1857. A close friend of General Vallejo, Haraszthy returned from Europe in 1861 with 100,000 of the finest vine cuttings, which he made available to all growers. Although Buena Vista's winemaking now takes place at an ultramodern facility in the Carneros District, the winery maintains a tasting room inside the restored 1862 Press House. The beautiful stone-crafted room brims with wines, wine-related gifts, and accessories.

Tastings are $5 for four wines with complimentary glass, $10 for a flight of three of the really good stuff. You can take the self-guided tour any time during operating hours; a "Historical Tour and Tasting," offered daily at 11am and 2pm, details the life and times of Count Haraszthy. After tasting, grab your favorite bottle, a selection of cheeses from the Sonoma Cheese Factory, salami, bread, and pâté (all available in the tasting room), and plant yourself at one of the many picnic tables in the lush, verdant setting.

18000 Old Winery Rd. (off E. Napa St., slightly northeast of downtown), Sonoma. ℭ **800/926-1266** or 707/938-1266. www.buenavistawinery.com. Daily 10am–5pm. Self-guided tours only.

Ravenswood Winery   Ravenswood established itself as the *sine qua non* of zinfandel, the versatile grape that's quickly gaining ground on the rapacious cabernet sauvignon. In fact, Ravenswood was the first winery in the United States to focus primarily on zins, which make up about three-quarters of its 500,000-case production; it also produces merlot, cabernet sauvignon, and a small amount of chardonnay.

The winery is smartly designed—recessed into the hillside to protect its treasures from the simmering summers. Tours follow the winemaking process from grape to glass and include a visit to the aromatic oak-barrel aging rooms. You're welcome to bring your own picnic basket to any of the tables. Tastings are $5 for four wines, which is refundable with purchase.

18701 Gehricke Rd. (off Lovall Valley Rd.), Sonoma. ℭ **888/NO-WIMPY** or 707/938-1960. www. ravenswood-wine.com. Daily 10am–4:30pm. Tours by reservation only at 10:30am.

GLEN ELLEN

About 7 miles north of Sonoma on Calif. 12 is the town of Glen Ellen, which, though just a fraction of the size of Sonoma, is home to several of the valley's finest wineries, restaurants, and inns. Aside from the addition of a few new restaurants, this charming Wine Country town hasn't changed much since the days when Jack London settled on his Beauty Ranch, about a mile west. If you haven't yet decided where you want to set up camp during your visit to the Wine Country, I highly recommend this lovable little town.

Hikers, horseback riders, and picnickers will enjoy **Jack London State Historic Park,** 2400 London Ranch Rd., off Arnold Drive (ℭ **707/938-5216**). Within its 800 acres, which were once home to the renowned writer, you'll find 9 miles of trails, the remains of London's burned-down dream house, preserved structures, a museum, and plenty of ideal picnic spots. The park is open daily from 9:30am to 5pm. Admission is $5 per car or $4 per seniors' car.

Arrowood Vineyards & Winery   This picturesque winery stands on a gently rising hillside lined with manicured vineyards. Tastings take place in the Hospitality House, the newer of Arrowood's two gray-and-white buildings. They're fashioned after New England farmhouses, complete with wraparound porches. The focus here is on making world-class wine with minimal intervention, and results have scored very well with critics like those in *Wine Spectator* magazine. Mind you, excellence doesn't come cheap: a taste is $5 or $10 for limited-production wines, but if you're curious about what near-perfection tastes like, it's worth it. *Note:* No picnic facilities are available here.

14347 Sonoma Hwy. (Calif. 12), Glen Ellen. ℭ 707/935-2600. www.arrowoodvineyards.com. Daily 10am–4:30pm. Tours by appointment only, daily at 10:30am and 2:30pm.

Benziger Family Winery ℛ *Finds*   At any given time, two generations of Benzigers (*Ben*-zigger) may be running around tending to chores, and they instantly make you feel as if you're part of the clan. The pastoral, user-friendly property features an exceptional self-guided tour ("The most comprehensive tour in the wine industry," according to *Wine Spectator*), gardens, a spacious tasting room staffed by amiable folks, and an art gallery. The fun and informative 40-minute tram tour, pulled by a beefy tractor, winds through the estate vineyards and into caves, and ends with a tasting of one estate wine. *Tip:* Tram tickets—a hot item in the summer—are available on a first-come, first-served basis, so either arrive early or stop by in the morning to pick up afternoon tickets.

Tastings of the standard-release wines are $5. Tastes of limited-production wines or reserve or estate wines cost $10. The winery offers several picnic spots.

1883 London Ranch Rd. (off Arnold Dr., on the way to Jack London State Historic Park), Glen Ellen. ℭ 800/989-8890 or 707/935-3000. www.benziger.com. Tasting room daily 10am–5pm. Tram tours daily (weather permitting) $10 adults and $5 children at 11:30am and at 12:30, 1:30, 2:30, and 3:30pm.

KENWOOD

A few miles north of Glen Ellen along Calif. 12 is the tiny town of Kenwood, the northernmost outpost of the Sonoma Valley. The town itself consists of little more than a few restaurants, wineries, and modest homes recessed into the wooded hillsides.

Kunde Estate Winery Expect a friendly, unintimidating welcome at this scenic winery, run by Kundes since 1904—now the fourth generation. One of the largest grape suppliers in the area, the Kunde family (pronounced "*kun*-dee") converted 800 acres of their 2,000-acre ranch to growing ultra-premium grapes, which they provide to about 30 Sonoma and Napa wineries. Hence, all their wines are "estate" (made from grapes grown on their property). The $5 new-release tastings and $10 reserve (with glass) are offered in a 17,000-square-foot winemaking facility. Private tours are available by appointment, but the picnic tables and pond can be spontaneously enjoyed. Tasting fees are refunded with purchase.

10155 Sonoma Hwy., Kenwood. ℭ 707/833-5501. www.kunde.com. Tastings daily 10:30am–4pm. Cave tours Mon–Thurs 11am and Fri–Sun approximately every half-hour from 11am–3pm.

Kenwood Vineyards Kenwood's history dates to 1906, when the Pagani brothers made their living selling wine straight from the barrel and into the jug. In 1970 the Lee family bought the property and dumped a ton of money into converting the aging winery into a modern, high-production facility (most of it cleverly concealed in the original barnlike buildings). Since then, Kenwood has earned a solid reputation for consistent quality with each of its varietals: cabernet sauvignon, chardonnay, zinfandel, pinot noir, merlot, and, most popular, sauvignon blanc—a crisp, light wine with hints of melon.

Although the winery looks rather modest in size, its output is staggering: nearly 500,000 cases of ultrapremium wines fermented in steel tanks and French and American oak barrels. Popular with collectors is winemaker Michael Lee's Artist Series cabernet sauvignon, a limited production from the winery's best vineyards, featuring labels with original artwork by renowned artists. The tasting room, housed in one of the old barns, offers $2 to $5 tastings of most varieties and sells gift items. FYI: The Lees no longer own the winery.

9592 Sonoma Hwy. (Calif. 12), Kenwood. ℭ 707/833-5891. www.kenwoodvineyards.com. Daily 10am–4:30pm.

Château St. Jean ⚡ *Finds* Château St. Jean is notable for its beautiful buildings, expansive landscaped grounds, and gourmet marketlike tasting room. Among California wineries, it's a pioneer in vineyard designation—the procedure of making wine from, and naming it for, a single vineyard. A private drive takes you to what was once a 250-acre country retreat built in 1920; a well-manicured lawn overlooking the meticulously maintained vineyards is now a picnic area, complete with a fountain and umbrella-shaded picnic tables.

In the huge tasting room—where there's also a charcuterie shop and plenty of housewares for sale—you can sample Château St. Jean's wide array of wines from chardonnays and cabernet sauvignon to fumé blanc, merlot, Johannesburg Riesling, and gewürztraminer. Tastings are $5 per person, $10 per person for reserve wines.

8555 Sonoma Hwy. (Calif. 12), Kenwood. © 800/543-7572 or 707/833-4134. www.chateaustjean.com. Tastings daily 10am–5pm. Tours 11am and 3pm. At the foot of Sugarloaf Ridge, just north of Kenwood and east of Hwy. 12.

WHERE TO STAY

If you're having trouble finding a vacancy, try calling the **Sonoma Valley Visitors Bureau** at © **707/996-1090.** They'll try to refer you to a lodging that has a room to spare, but they won't make reservations for you. Another option is calling the **Bed and Breakfast Association of Sonoma Valley** (© **800/969-4667**), which will refer you to a member B&B and make reservations for you.

VERY EXPENSIVE

Fairmont Sonoma Mission Inn, Spa & Country Club ★★★   The Wine Country's most extensive super-resort and spa, the Sonoma Mission Inn consists of a massive three-story replica of a Spanish mission (well, aside from the pink paint job) built in 1927, an array of satellite wings housing numerous superluxury suites, and, of course, the world-class spa facilities, which include pools filled with naturally heated artesian mineral water. It's a popular retreat for the wealthy and the well known—last time I visited I bumped into *Melrose Place*'s Tiffany Amber Thiessen. Big changes have occurred since the resort changed ownership a few years ago, including 70 new guest rooms and suites, a $20-million spa facility (you won't even recognize the old one), and the acquisition of the Sonoma Golf Club.

The modern rooms are furnished with plantation-style shutters, ceiling fans, down comforters, and such amenities as oversize bathroom towels. The Wine Country rooms feature king-size beds, desks, refrigerators, and huge limestone and marble bathrooms; some offer wood-burning fireplaces, and many have balconies. The older, slightly smaller Historic Inn rooms are sweetly appointed with homey furnishings, and most have queen-size beds. For the ultimate in luxury, however, the opulently appointed Mission Suites are the way to go.

Corner of Boyes Blvd. and Calif. 12 (P.O. Box 1447), Sonoma, CA 95476. © 800/441-1414 or 707/938-9000. Fax 707/938-4250. www.fairmont.com/sonoma. 228 units. $199–$1,000 double. AE, DC, MC, V. Valet parking is free for day use (spagoers) and $12 for overnight guests. From central Sonoma, drive 3 miles north on Hwy. 12 and turn left on Boyes Blvd. **Amenities:** 2 restaurants; 2 large heated outdoor pools; golf course; health club and spa; Jacuzzi; sauna; bike rental; concierge; business center; salon; room service (6am–11pm); babysitting; same-day laundry service and dry cleaning. *In room:* A/C, TV, dataport, minibar, hair dryer, iron, safe, high-speed Internet access ($13 per day) in most rooms, complimentary bottle of wine upon arrival.

Gaige House Inn ★★★ *Finds*   The Gaige House is the best B&B I've ever stayed in. The inn's owners, Ken Burnet, Jr., and Greg Nemrow, turned what was already a fine bed-and-breakfast into the finest in the Wine Country, and they've done it by offering a level of service, amenities, and decor normally associated with outrageously expensive resorts (and without the snobbery). Breakfast and afternoon appetizers are made with herbs from the inn's garden and prepared by a chef who was featured at the James Beard House in 2001. Firm mattresses are graced with wondrously silk-soft linens and premium down comforters, and even the furniture and artwork are of museum quality. Behind the inn is a 1½-acre oasis with perfectly manicured lawns, a 40-foot-long swimming pool, and a creek-side hammock shaded by a majestic Heritage oak. All rooms, each artistically designed in a plantation theme with Asian and Indonesian influences, have private bathrooms and king- or queen-size beds; two rooms have Jacuzzi tubs, and several have fireplaces. On sunny days, breakfast is served at individual tables on the large terrace. Evenings are best spent in the reading parlor sipping premium wines.

Greg and Ken also manage four long-term rentals (private guesthouses on private estates) for those who want more privacy and fewer services and are adding eight new deluxe spa garden suites in late 2004.

13540 Arnold Dr., Glen Ellen, CA 95442. © **800/935-0237** or 707/935-0237. Fax 707/935-6411. www.gaige.com. 15 units. Summer $275–$525 double, $475–$575 suite; winter $175–$325 double, $325–$525 suite. Rates include full breakfast and evening wines. AE, DC, DISC, MC, V. **Amenities:** Large heated pool; in-room massage; free Internet access. *In room:* A/C, TV, fax, dataport, hair dryer, iron, safe.

Kenwood Inn & Spa 🏵🏵   Inspired by the villas of Tuscany, the honey-colored Italian-style buildings, flower-filled courtyard, and pastoral views of vineyard-covered hills are enough to make any northern Italian homesick. Every room here is lavishly and exquisitely decorated with tapestries, velvets, and antiques; each has a fireplace, balcony (unless you're on the ground floor), feather bed, and down comforter—but no phone or TV. A minor caveat is road noise, which you're unlikely to hear from your room but can be slightly heard over the piped-in music around the courtyard and pool. Longtime guests will be surprised to find more bodies in the lounge chairs—18 new guest rooms and an adjoining building joined this slice of pastoral heaven in June 2003. But anyone with a hefty credit card limit can buy seclusion by renting the inn's nearby two-bedroom villa. An impressive two-course gourmet breakfast is served poolside or in the Mediterranean-style dining room; my meal consisted of a poached egg accompanied by light, flavorful potatoes, red bell peppers, and other roasted vegetables, followed by a homemade scone with fresh berries and a lemon tart.

10400 Sonoma Hwy., Kenwood, CA 95452. © **800/353-6966** or 707/833-1293. Fax 707/833-1247. www.kenwoodinn.com. 30 units. Apr–Oct $400–$725 double; Nov–Mar $375–$675 double; $800–$1,000 villa. Rates include gourmet breakfast and bottle of wine. 2-night minimum on weekends. AE, MC, V. **Amenities:** Heated outdoor pool; full-service spa; concierge; free Internet access. *In room:* Hair dryer, iron, CD player.

MODERATE

Beltane Ranch 🏵🏵 *Finds*   The word "Ranch" conjures up an image of a big ol' two-story house in the middle of hundreds of rolling acres; the kind of place where you laze away the day in a hammock or pitching horseshoes in the garden. Well, friend, you can have all that and more at the Beltane Ranch, a century-old, buttercup-yellow manor that's been everything from a bunkhouse to a brothel to a turkey farm. You can't help but feel your tensions ease away as you loll on the wraparound porch overlooking the vineyards, sipping a cool, fruity chardonnay. Each room is uniquely decorated with American and European antiques; all have private bathrooms, sitting areas, and separate entrances. A big country breakfast is served on the porch overlooking the vineyards. You can play tennis on the private court or hike the trails meandering through the 400-acre estate. *Tip:* Request one of the upstairs rooms, which have the best views.

11775 Sonoma Hwy. (Hwy. 12), Glen Ellen, CA 95442. © **707/996-6501**. www.beltaneranch.com. 5 units, 1 cottage. $130–$180 double; $220 cottage. Rates include full breakfast. No credit cards. Personal checks accepted. **Amenities:** Tennis court. *In room:* No phone.

El Dorado Hotel 🏵🏵   This 1843 Mission Revival building may look like a 19th-century Wild West relic from the outside, but inside it's all 21st-century deluxe. Each modern, handsomely appointed guest room—designed by the same folks who put together the exclusive Auberge du Soleil (p. 177) in Rutherford—has French windows and tiny balconies. Some rooms offer views of the plaza; others overlook the private courtyard and heated lap pool. All rooms (except those for guests with disabilities) are on the second floor and were upgraded in 2004. The four rooms on the ground floor are off the private courtyard, and each has a partially enclosed patio. Though prices reflect its prime location on Sonoma Square, this is still one of the more charming options within its price range.

405 First St. W., Sonoma, CA 95476. © 800/289-3031 or 707/996-3030. Fax 707/996-3148. www.hotel eldorado.com. 27 units. Summer $170–$190 double; winter $135–$155 double. AE, MC, V. **Amenities:** Restaurant; heated outdoor pool; free access to nearby health club; concierge; room service (11:30am–10pm); laundry service; dry cleaning. In room: A/C, TV/DVD, dataport, fridge, hair dryer, iron, CD player.

Glenelly Inn 🐾🐾 The rates are reasonable, particularly when you factor in the included breakfast and afternoon snacks, but more importantly, this former railroad inn, built in 1916, is positively drenched in serenity. Located well off the main highway on an oak-studded hillside, the peach-and-cream inn comes with everything you would expect from a country retreat. Long verandas with wicker chairs offer views of the Sonoma hillsides; a country breakfast is served beside a cobblestone fireplace; and bright, immaculate units contain old-fashioned claw-foot tubs, Scandinavian down comforters, and ceiling fans. The staff understands that it's the little things that make the difference; hence, the good reading lights and a simmering hot tub in a grapevine-and-rose-covered arbor. All rooms, decorated with antiques and country furnishings, have queen beds, terry robes, and private entrances. Top picks are the Vallejo and Jack London family suites, both with large private patios, although I also like the rooms on the upper veranda—particularly in the spring, when the terraced gardens below are in full bloom. The new freestanding garden cottages are for those who want to splurge.

5131 Warm Springs Rd. (off Arnold Dr.), Glen Ellen, CA 95442. © 707/996-6720. Fax 707/996-5227. www.glenelly.com. 10 units. $150–$250 double; $250 cottage. Rates include full breakfast and free Internet access. AE, DISC, MC, V.

INEXPENSIVE

Sonoma Hotel 🐾🐾 This charming historic hotel on Sonoma's tree-lined town plaza emphasizes 19th-century elegance and comfort. Built in 1880 by German immigrant Henry Weyl, it has attractive guest rooms decorated in early California style, with French country furnishings, antique beds, and period decorations. In a bow to modern luxuries, recent additions include private bathrooms, cable TV, phones with dataports, and air-conditioning. Perks include fresh coffee and pastries in the morning and wine in the evening. The lovely restaurant, **the girl & the fig** (p. 195), serves California-French cuisine.

110 W. Spain St., Sonoma, CA 95476. © 800/468-6016 or 707/996-2996. Fax 707/996-7014. www.sonoma hotel.com. 16 units. Summer $110–$245 double; winter Sun–Thurs $95–$170 double, Fri–Sat $115–$195 double. Rates include continental breakfast and evening wine. AE, DC, MC, V. In room: A/C, TV, dataport.

Victorian Garden Inn 🐾🐾 Here, proprietor Donna Lewis runs the cutest B&B in Sonoma Valley. A picket fence, a wall of trees, and an acre of gardens enclose a Victorian garden brimming with violets, roses, camellias, and peonies, all shaded under flowering fruit trees. It's truly a marvelous sight in the springtime. The guest units—three in the century-old water tower and one in the main building (an 1870s Greek Revival farmhouse), as well as a cottage—continue the Victorian theme, with wicker furniture, floral prints, padded armchairs, and claw-foot tubs. The most popular units are the Top o' the Tower and the Woodcutter's Cottage. Each has its own entrance and a garden view; the cottage boasts a sofa and armchairs in front of the fireplace. After a hard day of wine tasting, spend the afternoon in the pool or on the shaded wraparound porch, enjoying a mellow merlot while soaking in the sweet garden smells. *New parents, take note:* The property recommends you leave young tots behind.

316 E. Napa St., Sonoma, CA 95476. (℃) **800/543-5339** or 707/996-5339. Fax 707/996-1689. www.victorian gardeninn.com. 3 units, 1 cottage. $139–$259 double. Rates include continental breakfast. AE, DC, MC, V. **Amenities:** Outdoor pool; hot tub; concierge; business center; room service (8am–5pm); laundry service; dry cleaning. *In room:* A/C, fireplaces in some rooms.

WHERE TO DINE

Though Sonoma Valley has far fewer visitors than Napa Valley, its restaurants are often equally as crowded, so be sure to make reservations in advance.

EXPENSIVE

the girl & the fig COUNTRY FRENCH   Well established in its downtown Sonoma digs (it used to be in Glen Ellen), this modern, attractive, and cozy eatery, with lovely patio seating, is the home for Sondra Bernstein's ("the girl") beloved restaurant. Here the cuisine, orchestrated by *chef de cuisine* Matt Murray, is nouveau country with French nuances, and yes, figs are sure to be on the menu in one form or another. The wonderful winter fig salad contains arugula, pecans, dried figs, Laura Chenel goat cheese, and fig-and-port vinaigrette. Murray uses garden-fresh produce and local meats, poultry, and fish whenever possible, in dishes such as pork tenderloin with a potato-leek pancake and roasted beets, and sea scallops with lobster-scented risotto. For dessert, try the warm pear galette topped with gingered crème fraîche, a glass of Jaboulet

---

Tips Gourmet Picnics, Sonoma-Style

When the weather's warm, there's no better way to have lunch in the Wine Country than by toting a picnic basket to your favorite winery and basking under the sweet Sonoma sunshine. Sonoma's central plaza, with its many picnic tables, is a good spot to set up a gourmet spread.

But first you need grub, so head to the **Sonoma Saveurs,** on the plaza at 487 First St. ((℃) **707/996-7007;** www.sonomasaveurs.com), to stock up for an alfresco fete. The restaurant offers an extraordinary selection of charcuterie, mousse, and other take-out treats. And if you can't wait, you can pull up a chair in the casual dining room or in the airy back garden. It's open Tuesday through Sunday from 11:30am to 7:30pm. If you're looking for something a little more sandwich-casual, head to the venerable **Sonoma Cheese Factory,** on the plaza at 2 Spain St. ((℃) **707/996-1000**), which offers award-winning house-made cheeses and imported meats and cheeses; a few are set out for tasting every day. Also available are caviar, gourmet salads, pâté, and home-made Sonoma Jack cheese. Pick up some good, inexpensive sandwiches, such as fire-roasted pork loin or New York steak. The Factory is open daily from 8:30am to 5:30pm.

muscat, and a sliver of raclette from the cheese list. Sondra knows her wines and will be happy to choose the best accompaniment for your meal.

110 W. Spain St., Sonoma. (𝐂) **707/938-3634.** www.thegirlandthefig.com. Reservations recommended. Main courses $18–$23. AE, MC, V. Daily 11:30am–11pm.

Harmony Club ★★ (Finds) CONTINENTAL   The most welcome addition to Sonoma's dining scene in 2003, the Harmony Club is not only a looker with its elegant Italianate dining room with dark woods, high ceilings, marble flooring, and a wall of giant doors opening to sidewalk seating and Sonoma's plaza. It also delivers in great food and live entertainment. Drop in anytime after their gourmet breakfast for fantastic "small plates" such as tender Moroccan spiced lamb loin with saffron couscous, grapes, and mint; french fries with tarragon aioli; seared scallops with vegetable ragout and truffle beurre blanc; and Scharffen Berger chocolate and orange Muscat tort. Go for sidewalk seating during warmer weather (they also have heat lamps), sit inside, or hang at the carved wood bar. Either way you'll want to face the piano when the nightly performer is tinkling the keys and singing jazz standards. Alas, the only bummer is the wine list, which leaves little in the way of options since this spot, owned by Steve Ledson of Ledson Winery, naturally features only Ledson wines.

480 First St. E. (at the plaza), Sonoma. (𝐂) **707/996-9779.** Reservations not accepted. Small plates $6–$14. AE, MC, V. Sun–Thurs 11:30am–10pm; Fri–Sat 11:30am–11:30pm.

La Poste ★ FRENCH BISTRO   It's a gastronome's game of sardines at this shoebox-size French bistro. The original Williams-Sonoma storefront is now downtown Sonoma's tiniest dining room with 26 chairs and maple banquettes squeezed amidst brass sconces, mahogany wainscoting, a whitewashed press-tin ceiling, and just enough space on the concrete-tiled floor for staff to refill wine glasses. The ever-changing chalkboard menu announces chef Rob Larman's generously portioned offerings, which change faster than you can say "Pass the profiteroles," but recent winners included seared scallops seasoned with tomato-herb vinaigrette over truffled mashed potatoes; and braised veal cheeks with cream, Calvados, English peas, and chanterelles. Desserts, such as chocolate mousse, aren't as fab, but will placate any chocoholic. Oh, and when weather permits, you'll find 14 more seats on the sidewalk.

599 Broadway (just south of the plaza), Sonoma. (𝐂) **707/939-3663.** Reservations recommended. Main courses $16–$25. AE, MC, V. Sun and Wed–Thurs 5:30–9pm; Fri–Sat 5:30–10pm.

MODERATE

Cafe La Haye ★★ ECLECTIC   Well-prepared and wholesome food, an experienced waitstaff, friendly owners, a soothing atmosphere, and reasonable prices—including a modestly priced wine list—make La Haye a favorite. In truth, everything about this cafelike restaurant is charming. The atmosphere within the small split-level dining room, pleasantly decorated with hardwood floors, an exposed-beam ceiling, and revolving contemporary artwork, is smart and intimate. The vibe is small business—a welcome departure from Napa Valley's big-business restaurants. The straightforward, seasonally inspired cuisine, which chefs bring forth from the tiny open kitchen, is delicious and wonderfully well priced. Expect a risotto special; pasta such as fresh tagliarini with butternut squash, prosciutto, sage, and garlic cream; and pan-roasted chicken breast, perhaps with goat cheese–herb stuffing, caramelized shallot *jus,* and fennel mashed potatoes. Meat eaters are sure to be pleased with filet of beef seared with black pepper–lavender sauce and served with Gorgonzola-potato gratin.

140 E. Napa St., Sonoma. ⓒ 707/935-5994. Reservations recommended. Main courses $14–$24. MC, V. Tues–Sat 5:30–9pm.

Della Santina's ⭐⭐ TUSCAN   Follow the locals to this friendly, traditional Italian restaurant. How traditional? Ask father-and-son team Dan and Robert: When I last dined here, they pointed out Signora Santina's hand-embroidered linen doilies as they proudly told me about her Tuscan recipes. (Heck, even the dining room looks like an old-fashioned, elegant Italian living room.) And their pride is merited: Every dish my party tried was authentic and well flavored, without overbearing sauces or one *hint* of California pretentiousness. Be sure to start with traditional antipasti, especially sliced mozzarella and tomatoes, or delicious white beans. The nine pasta dishes are, again, wonderfully authentic (gnocchi lovers, rejoice!). The spit-roasted meat dishes are a local favorite (although I found them a bit overcooked); for those who can't choose between chicken, pork, turkey, rabbit, or duck, there's a selection that offers a choice of three. Don't worry about breaking your bank on a bottle of wine, because many choices here go for under $40. Portions are huge, but be sure to save room for a wonderful dessert.

133 E. Napa St. (just east of the square), Sonoma. ⓒ 707/935-0576. Reservations recommended. Main courses $9–$18. AE, DISC, MC, V. Daily 11:30am–3pm and 5–9:30pm.

Swiss Hotel ⭐ CONTINENTAL/NORTHERN ITALIAN   With its slanting floors and beamed ceilings, the historic Swiss Hotel, right in the town center, is a Sonoma landmark and very much the local favorite for fine food served at reasonable prices. The turn-of-the-20th-century oak bar is adorned with black-and-white photos of pioneering Sonomans. The white dining room and sidewalk patio seats are pleasant spots to enjoy lunch specials such as penne with chicken, mushrooms, and tomato cream; hot sandwiches; and California-style pizzas fired in a wood-burning oven. But the secret spot is the very atmospheric back garden patio, a secluded oasis shaded by a wisteria-covered trellis and adorned with plants, a fountain, gingham tablecloths, and a fireplace. Dinner might start with a warm winter salad of radicchio and frisée with pears, walnuts, and bleu cheese. Main courses run the gamut; I like the linguine and prawns with garlic, hot pepper, and tomatoes; the filet mignon wrapped in bleu-cheese crust; and roasted rosemary chicken. The food is all very simply satisfying.

18 W. Spain St. (at First St. W.), Sonoma. ⓒ 707/938-2884. Reservations recommended. Main courses lunch $8.50–$16, dinner $10–$24. AE, MC, V. Daily 11:30am–2:30pm and 5–9:30pm. (Bar, daily 11:30am–2am.)

Wolf House ⭐ ECLECTIC   The most polished-looking dining room in Glen Ellen is elegant yet relaxed whether you're seated in the handsome dining room—smartly adorned with maple floors, gold walls, dark-wood wainscoting, and a corner fireplace—or outside on the multilevel terrace under the canopy of trees with serene views of the adjacent Sonoma Creek. The lunch menu adds fancy finishes to old favorites such as the excellent chicken Caesar salad, fresh grilled ahi tuna nicoise sandwich, or a juicy half-pound burger with Point Reyes Original blue cheese. During dinner, head straight for seared Sonoma lamb sirloin with roasted eggplant, chickpea ragout, and tomato confit; or pan-seared day-boat scallops with heirloom tomatoes and avocado-cucumber emulsion. The reasonably priced wine list offers many by-the-glass options as well as a fine selection of Sonoma wines. Locals love the brunch, complete with huevos rancheros, steak and eggs, omelets, and brioche French toast. During my visits, service was rather languid, but well meaning.

13740 Arnold Dr., at the base of London Branch Road, Glen Ellen. © **707/996-4401.** Reservations recommended. Main courses brunch and lunch $8–$12, dinner $18–$20. AE, DISC, MC, V. Brunch Sat–Sun 10:30am–3pm; lunch Mon–Fri 11am–3pm; dinner nightly 5:30–9:30pm.

INEXPENSIVE

Black Bear Diner *Kids* DINER   When you're craving a classic Americana breakfast with all the cholesterol and the fixin's, bee-line to this old-fashioned diner. First, it's fun with its over-the-top bear paraphernalia, gazette-style menu listing local news from 1961 and every possible diner favorite, and absurdly friendly waitstaff. Second, it's darned cheap. Third, helpings are huge. Kids get a kick out of coloring books, old-timers reminisce over Sinatra on the jukebox, and everyone leaves stuffed on omelets, scrambles, and pancakes. Lunch and dinner feature steak sandwiches, salads, and comfort food faves like barbecued pork ribs, roast beef, fish and chips, and spaghetti with meat sauce. That said, you can load up here on the cheap, especially since dinners come with salad or soup, bread, and two sides, and seniors can order from a specially priced menu.

201 West Napa St. (at Second St.), Sonoma. © **707/935-6800.** Main courses breakfast $5–$8.50, lunch and dinner $5.50–$17. AE, DISC, MC, V. Sun–Thurs 6am–10pm; Fri–Sat 6am–midnight.

The Northern Coast

by Matthew Richard Poole

Heading north from San Francisco, you'll reach a California that hardly resembles the southern part of the state. It's a different landscape, in climate as well as flora and fauna. You can forget about the surfing-and-bikini scene; instead, you'll find miles of rugged coastline with broad beaches and tiny bays harboring fantastic rock formations—from chimney stacks to bridges and blowholes—carved by the ocean waves.

You may think you've arrived in Alaska when you hit the beaches of Northern California. Take a dip and you'll soon agree with the locals: When it comes to swimming, the Arctic waters along the northern coast are best left to the sea lions. But that doesn't mean you can't enjoy the beaches, whether by strolling along the water or taking in the views of towering cliffs and seascapes. And unlike their southern counterparts,

the beaches here are not likely to be crowded, even in summer.

The best time to visit is in the spring or fall. In spring the headlands are carpeted with wildflowers—golden poppy, iris, and sea foam—and in fall the sun shines clear and bright. Summers are typically cool and windy, with the ubiquitous fog burning off by the afternoon.

The most scenic way to reach Stinson Beach, Gualala, Mendocino, and points north is to drive along the coast via Calif. 1. U.S. 101 runs inland through Healdsburg and Cloverdale and is much faster but doesn't provide the spectacular coastal views. A good compromise if you're headed to, say, Mendocino, is to take U.S. 101 to Cloverdale, then cut over to the coast on Calif. 128

Oh, and one last thing: Dress warmly.

1 Point Reyes National Seashore ★★★

35 miles NW of San Francisco

The national seashore system was created to protect rural and undeveloped stretches of the coast from the pressures brought on by soaring real-estate values and increasing population. Nowhere is the success of the system more evident than at Point Reyes. Residents of the surrounding towns—**Inverness, Point Reyes Station,** and **Olema**—have steadfastly resisted runaway development. You won't find any strip malls or fast-food joints here—just laid-back coastal towns with cafes and country inns where gentle living prevails.

The park, a 71,000-acre hammer-shaped peninsula jutting 10 miles into the Pacific and backed by Tomales Bay, is loaded with wildlife, ranging from tule elk, birds, and bobcats to gray whales, sea lions, and great white sharks. Aside from its scenery, it also boasts historical treasures that offer a window into California's coastal past, including lighthouses, dairies and ranches, the site of Sir Francis Drake's 1579 landing, plus a replica of a coastal Miwok Indian village.

Though the peninsula's people and wildlife live in harmony above the ground, the situation beneath the soil is more volatile. The San Andreas Fault separates Point Reyes—the northernmost landmass on the Pacific Plate—from the rest of California, which rests on the North American Plate. Point Reyes is making its way toward Alaska at a rate of about 2 inches per year, but there have been times when it has moved faster. In 1906 Point Reyes jumped north almost 20 feet in an instant, leveling San Francisco and jolting the rest of the state. The half-mile **Earthquake Trail,** near the Bear Valley Visitor Center, illustrates this geological drama with a loop through an area torn by the fault. Shattered fences, rifts in the ground, and a barn knocked off its foundation illustrate how alive the earth is here. If that doesn't convince you, a seismograph in the visitor center will.

ESSENTIALS

GETTING THERE Point Reyes is 35 miles northwest of San Francisco, but it takes at least 90 minutes to reach by car (it's the small towns that slow you down). The easiest route is via Sir Francis Drake Boulevard from U.S. 101 south of San Rafael; it takes its time getting to Point Reyes, but does so without any detours. For a longer but more scenic route, take the Stinson Beach/Calif. 1 exit off U.S. 101 just south of Sausalito and follow Calif. 1 north.

VISITOR INFORMATION As soon as you arrive at Point Reyes, stop at the **Bear Valley Visitor Center** (© 415/464-5100; www.nps.gov/pore, www.point reyes.net, or www.pointreyes.org) on Bear Valley Road (look for the small sign just north of Olema on Calif. 1) and pick up a free Point Reyes trail map. The rangers here are helpful and can answer any questions you have about the national seashore. Be sure to check out the great natural-history and cultural displays as well. It's open Monday through Friday from 9am to 5pm, Saturday and Sunday from 8am to 5pm.

FEES & PERMITS Entrance to the park is free. Camping is $12 per site per night year-round, and permits are required; reservations can be made up to 3 months in advance by calling © 415/663-8054 Monday through Friday from 9am to 2pm.

WHAT TO SEE & DO

When heading out to any part of the Point Reyes coast, expect to spend the day surrounded by nature. The park encompasses several surf-pounded beaches, bird estuaries, open swaths of land with roaming elk, and the Point Reyes lighthouse—a favorite among visitors who are awestruck by the spectacular views of the coast. But bear in mind that, as beautiful as the wilderness can be, it's also untamable. Waters in these areas are not only bone chilling and home to a vast array of sea life, including sharks, but are also unpredictable and dangerous. There are no lifeguards on duty, and waves and riptides strongly discourage swimming. Pets are not permitted on any of the area's trails.

By far the most popular—and crowded—attraction at Point Reyes National Seashore is the venerable **Point Reyes Lighthouse** ⚓ at the westernmost tip of Point Reyes. Even if you plan to forego the 308 steps down to the lighthouse, it's still worth the visit to marvel at the dramatic scenery, which includes thousands of common murres and prides of sea lions that bask on the rocks far below (binoculars come in handy). The lighthouse visitor center (© **415/669-1534**) is open Thursday through Monday from 10am to 4:30pm, weather permitting.

The Northern Coast

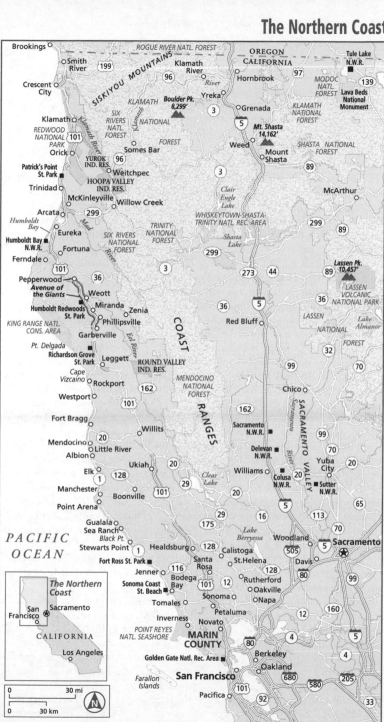

Tips **Whale Sightings**

Rangers suggest that during the southern migration (Jan), you should go to the lighthouse for the best view, and during the northern migration (Mar), you can see the whales from any of the area's beaches.

The lighthouse is also the top spot on the California coast to observe **gray whales** as they make their southward and northward migrations along the coast from January to April. The annual round-trip is 10,000 miles—one of the longest mammal migrations known. The whales head south in December and January, and return north in March. *Tip:* If you plan to drive out to the lighthouse to whale-watch, arrive early as parking is limited. If possible, come on a weekday. On a weekend or holiday from December to April (weather permitting), it's wise to park at the Drake's Beach Visitor Center and take the shuttle bus to the lighthouse, which costs $3.50 for adults and is free for kids age 12 and under. Dress warmly—it's often quite cold and windy—and bring binoculars.

Whale-watching is far from the only activity offered. Rangers conduct many different tours on weekends: You can walk along the **Bear Valley Trail,** spotting the wildlife at the ocean's edge; see the waterfowl at **Fivebrooks Pond;** explore tide pools; view some of North America's most beautiful ducks in the wetlands of **Limantour;** hike to the promontory overlooking **Chimney Rock** to see the sea lions, elephant seals, harbor seals, and seabirds; or take a self-guided walk along the **San Andreas Fault** to observe the site of the epicenter of the 1906 earthquake and learn about the regional geology. Since tours vary seasonally, you can either call the **Bear Valley Visitor Center** (© **415/464-5100**) or request a copy of *Park Paper,* which includes a schedule of activities and other useful information. Many of the tours are suitable for travelers with disabilities.

North and South **Point Reyes Beaches** face the Pacific and withstand the full brunt of ocean tides and winds—so much so that the water is far too rough for even wading. Until a few years ago, entering the water was illegal, but persistent surfers went to court for their right to shred the mighty waves. Today the park service strongly advises against taking on the tides, so play it safe and stroll the coastline. Along the southern coast, the waters of **Drake's Beach** ⚝ can be as tranquil and serene as Point Reyes's are turbulent. Locals come here to sun and picnic; occasionally a hearty soul ventures into the cold waters of Drake's Bay. But keep in mind that storms generally come inland from the south and almost always hit Drake's before moving north or south. A powerful weather front can turn wispy waves into torrential tides.

Some of the park's best—and least crowded—highlights can only be approached on foot, such as **Alamere Falls** ⚝, a freshwater stream that cascades down a 40-foot bluff onto Wildcat Beach, or **Tomales Point Trail** ⚝, which passes through the Tule Elk Reserve, a protected haven for roaming herds of tule elk that once numbered in the thousands. Hiking most of the trails usually ends up being an all-day outing, however, so it's best to split a 2-day trip within Point Reyes National Seashore into a "by car" day and a "by foot" day.

If you're a bird-watcher, definitely visit the **Point Reyes Bird Observatory** ⚝ (© **415/868-1221;** www.prbo.org), one of the few full-time ornithological research stations in the United States, at the southeast end of the park on Mesa Road. This is where ornithologists keep an eye on more than 400 species. Admission to the visitor center and nature trail is free, and visitors are welcome

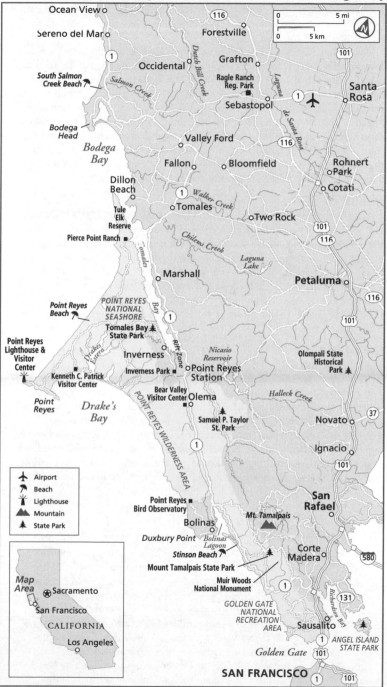

Point Reyes National Seashore & Bodega Bay

Ocean View
Sereno del Mar
Forestville
116
0   5 mi
0   5 km

South Salmon Creek Beach
Occidental
Dutch Bill Creek
Grafton
Ragle Ranch Reg. Park
Salmon Creek
Santa Rosa
101
1
Sebastopol

Bodega Head
Bodega Bay
Valley Ford
de Santa Rosa
116
Fallon
Bloomfield
Rohnert Park
Cotati

Dillon Beach
Walker Creek
Tule Elk Reserve
Tomales
Two Rock
101
116

Pierce Point Ranch
Chileno Creek
Laguna Lake
1
Tomales Bay
Marshall
Petaluma
116
101

Point Reyes Beach
POINT REYES NATIONAL SEASHORE
Tomales Bay State Park
Bay
Rift Zone
Nicasio Reservoir
Olompali State Historical Park

Point Reyes Lighthouse & Visitor Center
Drakes Estero
Inverness
Inverness Park
Point Reyes Station
Halleck Creek

Kenneth C. Patrick Visitor Center
Bear Valley Visitor Center
Olema
Novato
37

Point Reyes
Drake's Bay
Samuel P. Taylor St. Park
Ignacio
101

POINT REYES WILDERNESS AREA
1

Airport
Beach
Lighthouse
Mountain
State Park

Point Reyes Bird Observatory
San Rafael

Bolinas
Mt. Tamalpais
580

Duxbury Point
Bolinas Lagoon
Stinson Beach
Corte Madera

Mount Tamalpais State Park

Muir Woods National Monument
131
Richardson Bay

Map Area
Sacramento
San Francisco
CALIFORNIA
Los Angeles

GOLDEN GATE NATIONAL RECREATION AREA
Sausalito
ANGEL ISLAND STATE PARK

Golden Gate
101
1

SAN FRANCISCO
1
101

203

to observe the tricky process of catching and banding the birds. It's open daily from 15 minutes after sunrise until sunset. Banding hours vary seasonally; call ℂ **415/868-0655** for exact times.

One of my favorite things to do in Point Reyes is paddle through placid Tomales Bay, a haven for migrating birds and marine mammals. **Tamal Saka Tomales Bay Kayaking** ✵ (ℂ **415/663-1743;** www.tamalsaka.com) organizes kayak trips, including 3-hour sunset outings, 3½-hour full-moon paddles, yoga tours, day trips, and longer excursions. Instruction, clinics, and boat delivery are available, and all ages and levels are welcome. Prices for tours start at $65. Rentals begin at $35 for one person, $50 for two. Don't worry—the kayaks are very stable, and there are no waves to contend with. The launching point is on Highway 1 at the Marshall Boatworks in Marshall, 8 miles north of Point Reyes Station. Open daily from 9am to 6pm and by appointment.

WHERE TO STAY

If you're having trouble finding a vacancy, **Inns of Marin** (ℂ **800/887-2880** or 415/663-2000; www.innsofmarin.com) and **West Marin Network** (ℂ **415/ 663-9543**) are two reputable services that will help you find accommodations, ranging from one-room cottages to inns and complete vacation homes. The **West Marin Chamber of Commerce** (ℂ **415/663-9232;** www.pointreyes.org) is also a good source for lodging and visitor information. Keep in mind that many places here have a 2-night minimum, although in slow season they may make an exception. They'll also refer you to restaurants, hiking, and attractions in the area.

EXPENSIVE

Blackthorne Inn ✵✵   This redwood home with its octagonal widow's walk, spiral staircase, turrets, and multiple decks looks more like a deluxe treehouse than a B&B. My favorite—and the most expensive—unit is the Eagle's Nest, an octagonal room enclosed by glass and topped with a sun deck with a catwalk leading to the bathroom. The largest room is the Forest View, a two-room suite complete with deck, which has a private entrance and a sitting area facing the woods; it's furnished with wicker and natural rattan, and decorated with floral fabrics and modern lithographs. All have private bathrooms. The main sitting room in the house features a stone fireplace, skylight, wet bar, and stained-glass

---

Finds   **Johnson's Oyster Farm**

One of my favorite things to do in Point Reyes is swing by Johnson's Oyster Farm, buy a sack of right-out-of-the-water oysters and a bottle of "Johnson's Special Sauce," head to one of the beaches, whip out the folding chair, crack an ice cold beer, prop my feet up, and chow down. The oyster farm resides within Drakes Estero, a large saltwater lagoon on the Point Reyes peninsula that produces nearly 20 percent of California's commercial oyster yield. Located off Sir Francis Drake Boulevard about 6 miles west of Inverness, you'll know you've found it when you see a cluster of rather odiferous oyster tanks surrounded by huge piles of oyster shells. It's open 8am to 4pm Tuesday through Sunday, ℂ **415/669-1149.**

Moments   **Living the Low-Tech Life at Point Reyes Station**

Progress is taking its sweet time at Point Reyes Station, a tiny West Marin community across the bay from the national seashore. When you stroll along the 3-block-long Main Street at this former rail town, it's not hard to imagine what life was like back when the town was founded in the 1890s. Toby's Feed Barn emits that comforting aroma of hay, feed, and horse tack. The hardworking gals at the Cowgirl Creamery make organic handcrafted cheeses the old-school way from local dairy milk. The cook gets up early at the Pine Cone Diner to whip up biscuits and gravy every morning. Brawls still spill into the street once in a while at the Western Saloon, a rough-and-ready bar where townies and ranch hands shoot pool in the back. Yep, you sure ain't in the city anymore, so turn off that damn cellphone, mosey on up to the old oak bar at the saloon, and order a Bud (no glass).

windows and is surrounded by a huge deck. A country buffet breakfast, included in the room rate, is served on the upper deck when the sun's out.

266 Vallejo Ave. (off Sir Francis Drake Blvd., south of Inverness), Inverness Park (P.O. Box 712), Inverness, CA 94937. © **415/663-8621.** Fax 415/663-8635. www.blackthorneinn.com. 4 units. $225–$325 double. Rates include buffet breakfast. MC, V. **Amenities:** Nearby golf course; Jacuzzi. *In room:* Coffeemaker.

Manka's Inverness Lodge *&&&*   If there were ever a reason to pack your bags and leave San Francisco for a day or two, this is it. A former hunting-and-fishing lodge, Manka's Inverness Lodge looks like something out of a Hans Christian Andersen fairy tale, down to the tree-limb bedsteads and cooks roasting venison sausage in front of the hearth. It's all romantic in a Jack London sort of way, and tastefully done. The lodge consists of an excellent restaurant on the first floor (see "Where to Dine" below), four rooms upstairs (nos. 1 and 2 come with large private decks), four rooms in the Redwood Annex, and two spacious one-bedroom cabins located behind the lodge. For the ultimate romantic splurge, inquire about these secluded cabins: Fishing and Manka's, or at the water's edge, the Boathouse and Chicken Ranch.

30 Callendar Way (on Argyle St. off Sir Francis Drake Blvd., 1½ blocks north of downtown Inverness), P.O. Box 1110, Inverness, CA 94937. © **800/58-LODGE** or 415/669-1034. Fax 415/669-1598. www.mankas.com. 12 units. $185–$465. MC, V. **Amenities:** Restaurant; bike rental; limited room service; in-room massage. *In room:* TV in some units, kitchenette, fridge, coffeemaker, hair dryer, no phone.

MODERATE

An English Oak Bed and Breakfast *&*   This two-story turn-of-the-20th-century farmhouse has survived everything from a major earthquake to a recent forest fire, which is lucky for you because you'll be hard-pressed to find a better B&B for the price in Point Reyes. Loaded with charm, down to the profusion of flowers and vines outside and comfy chairs fronting a toasty-warm woodstove inside, it's in a great location, too, with two good restaurants within walking distance and the entire national seashore at your doorstep. One of the units is a private cottage with two futon couches in the living area, suitable for children.

88 Bear Valley Rd., Olema, CA 94950. (C) 415/663-1777. www.anenglishoak.com. 4 units. $95–$120 double; $120–$160 cottage. Rates include breakfast. AE, DISC, MC, V. *In room:* A/C, TV, kitchen in cottage, some units with coffeemaker, hair dryer, iron.

Olema Inn & Restaurant 🐟🐟

Built in 1876, the pretty Olema Inn has an interesting history. It opened on July 4, 1876, as a gathering place for farmers and ranchers, was lost in gambling debt, and survived the 1906 earthquake (Olema was the epicenter). Today it still retains much of its period charm, combining modern luxuries such as European Sleepworks mattresses, down comforters, and Ralph Lauren linens with antique furniture and light fixtures, Victorian-style white porcelain and chrome bathrooms, and those great high ceilings you find in old Bay Area buildings. The decor is simple and elegant—pastels, beige wool carpeting, and floral patterns. Views are of the beautiful back garden—site of many weddings—and Olema Valley. After checking in, take a stroll on the stone pathways behind the inn to the orchard and flower gardens. The inn's romantic candle-lit restaurant features local produce and meats such as Bellweather Farms ricotta gnocchi with pine nuts and sage brown butter, pan-roasted Sonoma duck breast with a crispy potato galette, and a grilled center-cut Niman Ranch pork chop with a cider glaze and a side of crispy corn cake. Much of the restaurant's produce is grown at the inn's organic garden and orchard. *Tip:* Try to reserve room no. 3, which overlooks the garden and is the quietest of the six.

10000 Sir Francis Drake Blvd., Olema, CA 94950. (C) 415/663-9559. Fax 415/663-8783. www.theolemainn. com. 6 units. $145–$185 double. Rates include continental breakfast. AE, MC, V. Checks okay. Dogs are welcome at no extra charge. **Amenities:** Restaurant; gardens. *In room:* Antique furniture and tile, natural lighting, large tub and/or shower.

Point Reyes Country Inn & Stables 🐟

Are you and your horse dreaming of a country getaway? Then book a room at Point Reyes Country Inn & Stables, a ranch-style home on 4 acres that offers pastoral accommodations for two- and four-legged guests (horses only), plus access to plenty of hiking and riding trails. Each of the six B&B rooms has a private bathroom and either a balcony or a garden. The innkeepers have also added two studios (with kitchens) above the stables, plus they rent out two cottages on Tomales Bay equipped with decks, stocked kitchens, fireplaces, and a shared dock.

12050 Calif. 1 (P.O. Box 501), Point Reyes Station, CA 94956. (C) 415/663-9696. Fax 415/663-8888. www. ptreyescountryinn.com. 10 units. $95–$115 studio; $110–$170 double; $190–$200 cottage. $10–$15 per horse. Rates include breakfast in the B&B rooms, breakfast provisions in the cottages. MC, V. **Amenities:** Nearby golf course. *In room:* No phone.

INEXPENSIVE

Motel Inverness 🐟*Kids*

Finding an inexpensive place to stay in Point Reyes is next to impossible, because hoity-toity B&Bs reign supreme. There is, however, one exception—Motel Inverness, a homey, well-maintained lodging fronting Tomales Bay. For the outdoor adventurer who plans on spending as little time indoors as possible, it's the perfect place to hole up. (Those seeking a little romance should dig a little deeper into their pockets and opt for An English Oak Bed and Breakfast; see above.) Attached to the hotel is a giant great room, complete with fireplace and pool table to distract the kids; parents can relax on the back lawn overlooking the bay, bird sanctuary, and rolling green hills beyond. The two-bedroom suite with a kitchenette is ideal for families as is the Dacha cottage, which is on the water and boasts three bedrooms.

12718 Sir Francis Drake Blvd., Inverness, CA 94937. (C) 888/669-6909 or 415/669-1081. 8 units. $99–$175 double; $300–$350 suite. MC, V. *In room:* TV, coffee.

Point Reyes Hostel *(Kids)* Located deep within Point Reyes National Seashore, this beautiful old ranch-style complex has 44 dormitory-style accommodations, including one room that's reserved for families (though at least one child must be 5 years old or younger). There are also two common rooms, each warmed by wood-burning stoves on chilly nights, as well as a fully equipped kitchen, barbecue (BYO charcoal), and patio. If you don't mind sharing your sleeping quarters with strangers, this is a deal that can't be beat. Reservations (and earplugs) are strongly recommended.

Off Limantour Rd. (P.O. Box 247), Point Reyes Station, CA 94956. © **415/663-8811.** www.norcalhostels.org. 44 bunks, 1 private unit. $16 per adult, $9 per child under 17 with parents. 5 nights out of 30 maximum stay. MC, V. Reception hours 7:30–10am and 4:30–9:30pm daily.

WHERE TO DINE

Manka's Inverness Lodge *(🟊🟊)* CALIFORNIA/WILD GAME   Manka's reputation is built in large part on its restaurant, which dominates the bottom floor of the lodge. The dinners are prix fixe, and the specialty of the house is fire-grilled wild game, although if you call ahead, you may be able to arrange something tamer. The seasonal menu features such things as pheasant with a Madeira *jus*, mashed potatoes, and a wild-huckleberry jam; black buck antelope chops with sweet-corn salsa; or everybody's favorite, pan-seared elk tenderloin. The restaurant's boast is that the majority of the fish, fruits, and vegetables it serves are grown and raised or caught within 15 minutes of its kitchen. The wine cellar features more than 150 selections.

On Argyle St. (off Sir Francis Drake Blvd., 1½ blocks north of downtown Inverness), Inverness. © **800/58-LODGE** or 415/669-1034. www.mankas.com. Reservations recommended. Prix-fixe menu Thurs, Fri, and Sun $48 per person; Sat $68 per person; Mon $32 per person. MC, V. Thurs–Mon 6–9pm (spring hours may vary—call ahead).

Station House Café *(🟊🟊)* AMERICAN   For more than 2 decades, the Station House Café has been a favorite pit stop for Bay Areans headed to and from Point Reyes. It's a friendly, low-key place with an open kitchen, an outdoor garden dining area (key on sunny days), and live music on weekend nights. Breakfast dishes include a Hangtown omelet with local oysters and bacon, and eggs with creamed spinach and mashed-potato pancakes. Lunch and dinner specials might include fettuccine with fresh local mussels steamed in white-wine-and-butter sauce, two-cheese polenta served with fresh spinach sauté and grilled garlic-buttered tomato, or a daily fresh salmon special—all made from local produce,

---

Point Reyes Mountain Biking

Marin was the birthplace of mountain biking, so it's no surprise that Point Reyes National Seashore is crisscrossed with miles of meandering mountain-bike trails. The challenge-level varies from easy to oh-my-god, with mostly fire roads and a few single-track trails winding through densely forested knolls and sunny meadows with pretty ocean views. Since many of the hiking trails are off-limits to bikes, you'll need a bike map to figure out which ones are bike-legal. They're available for free at the Bear Valley Visitor Center (see above). To rent a bike, call David Barnett at **Cycle Analysis** (© **415/663-9164** or 415/663-1645; www.cyclepointreyes.com).

(*Finds*)   **Stinson Beach: The Bay Area's Best**

One of the most popular beaches in Northern California, this 3-mile-wide stretch of sand at the western foot of Mount Tamalpais is packed with Bay Area residents (and their dogs) on those rare fog-free summer weekends. Granted, it lacks the hard bodies and soft golden sand of Southern California, but it still makes for an enjoyable day trip via the scenic drive on Calif. 1. Although swimming is allowed and lifeguards are on duty from May to mid-September, notices about riptides (and the cold water) usually discourage beachgoers from venturing too far into the water. Adjoining the beach is the small town of Stinson Beach, where you can have an enjoyable alfresco lunch at the numerous cafes along Calif. 1.

To reach Stinson Beach from San Francisco, cross the Golden Gate Bridge heading north on U.S. 101, take the Stinson Beach/Calif. 1 exit heading west, and follow the signs (it's a 20-mile trip that's full of curves). The beach is open daily from 9am to 10pm, and there's no charge for admission. For more information, contact the Stinson Beach ranger and lifeguard station at © **415/868-0942.**

---

seafood, and organically raised Niman Ranch beef. The cafe has an extensive list of fine California wines and local as well as imported beers.

Main St., Point Reyes Station. © **415/663-1515.** Reservations recommended. Breakfast $4.50–$8.50; main courses $7–$11 lunch, $9–$25 dinner. DISC, MC, V. Sun–Tues and Thurs 8am–9pm; Fri–Sat 8am–10pm.

Taqueria La Quinta (*Value*) MEXICAN   Fresh, fast, good, and cheap: What more could you ask for in a restaurant? Taqueria La Quinta has been one of my favorite lunch stops in downtown Point Reyes for years. A huge selection of Mexican-American dishes are posted above the counter. My favorite is chile verde in a spicy tomatillo sauce with a side of handmade corn tortillas. Those in the know inquire about the seafood specials. Since it's all self-serve, you can skip the tip, but watch out for the salsa—that sucker's *hot.*

11285 Calif. 1 (at Third and Main sts.), Point Reyes Station. © **415/663-8868.** Main courses $5–$9. No credit cards. Wed–Mon 11:30am–7:30pm.

2 Along the Sonoma Coast

BODEGA BAY

Beyond the tip of the Point Reyes peninsula, the road curves around toward the coastal village of Bodega Bay, which supports a fishing fleet of around 300 boats. It's a good place to stop for lunch or a stroll. Despite the droves of tourists on summer weekends, Bodega Bay is still a mostly working-class fishing town—the sort of place where most people start their day before dawn mending nets, rigging fishing poles, and talking shop. There are several interesting shops and galleries, though the best show in town—especially for kids—is at **Tides Wharf,** where the fishing boats come in to unload their catch, which is gutted and packed in ice.

Bodega Head State Park (✦) is a great vantage point for whale-watching during the migration from January to April. At **Doran Beach,** there's a large bird sanctuary (willets, curlews, godwits, and more), and the **U.C. Davis Bodega**

Bay Marine Laboratory (© 707/875-2211; www.bml.ucdavis.edu) next door conducts guided tours of its lab projects on Friday afternoons between 2 and 4pm. (Suggested donation is $2.)

The **Bodega Harbour Golf Links,** at 21301 Heron Dr. (© 707/875-3538; www.bodegaharbourgolf.com), offers a panoramic ocean-side setting. It's an 18-hole Scottish-style course designed by Robert Trent Jones, Jr. A warm-up center and practice facility is free for registered golfers. Rates range from $60 with cart Monday through Thursday, $70 on Friday, and $90 on weekends. If golfing isn't your thing, you can go horseback riding through some spectacular scenery by contacting **Chanslor Horse Stables** (© 707/875-3333; www.chanslor.com), which also has pony rides for kids. It's open daily from 9am to 5pm.

One of the bay's major events is the **Fisherman's Festival** in April. Local fishing boats, decorated with ribbons and banners, sail out for a Blessing of the Fleet, while up to 25,000 landlubbers enjoy music, a lamb-and-oyster barbecue, and an arts-and-crafts fair. For more information about this festival and other goings-on, call or stop in at the **Sonoma Coast Visitors Center,** 860 Calif. 1, Bodega Bay, CA 94923 (© 707/875-3866; www.bodegabay.com or www.visit sonomacoast.com). Open daily, it has lots of brochures about the town and the surrounding area, including maps of the Sonoma Coast State Beaches and the best local fishing spots.

A few miles inland on Calif. 1 (toward Petaluma) is the tiny town of **Bodega** (pop. 100), famous as the setting of Alfred Hitchcock's *The Birds,* filmed here in 1961. Fans will want to visit the Potter School House and St. Teresa's Church.

WHERE TO STAY

Bodega Bay Lodge and Spa 🐦🐦   Near Doran Beach State Park, this is the best hotel in Bodega Bay. Each room has plush furnishings, a fireplace, and a private balcony with sweeping views of the bay and bird-filled marshes. If you can afford it, opt for one of the large luxury suites. Guests have complimentary access to a fitness center and sauna, as well as to a fieldstone spa and heated pool above the bay, surrounded by gardens. The lodge's **Duck Club Restaurant** enjoys a reputation as Bodega Bay's finest. Picture windows take advantage of the bay view, a romantic setting for Sonoma County cuisine such as roasted Petaluma duck and fresh fish caught by the Bodega fleet.

103 Calif. 1, Bodega Bay, CA 94923. © 800/368-2468 or 707/875-3525. Fax 707/875-2428. www.bodega baylodge.com. 84 units. Sun–Thurs $210–$240 double, $400 suite; Fri–Sat $235–$285 double, $450 suite. 2-night minimum on weekends. AE, DC, DISC, MC, V. **Amenities:** Restaurant; heated outdoor pool with ocean view; nearby golf course; full-service spa and fitness center; concierge; room service; in-room massage; babysitting; coin-op laundry. *In room:* A/C, TV w/pay movies, fax, dataport, minibar, fridge, coffeemaker, hair dryer, iron, safe.

Inn at the Tides 🐦   The larger of Bodega Bay's two upscale lodgings (the other being Bodega Bay Lodge), the Inn at the Tides consists of a cluster of condolike wood complexes on the side of a gently sloping hill. The selling point is the view; each unit is staggered just enough to guarantee a view of the bay across the highway. The rooms are modern and the inn's amenities are first-rate, like the attractive indoor-outdoor pool, but I would only stay here if I couldn't get a room at the Bodega Bay Lodge. The **Bay View Restaurant** is open Wednesday through Sunday for dinner only, offering ocean views, a well-prepared albeit traditional choice of entrees, and a romantic, somewhat formal ambience. Be sure to check their website for special package deals.

800 Coast Hwy. 1 (P.O. Box 640), Bodega Bay, CA 94923. © 800/541-7788 or 707/875-2751. Fax 707/875-3285. www.innatthetides.com. 86 units. Summer Sun–Thurs $169–$249, Fri–Sat $199–$284. Winter rates

---

Fun Fact Hitchcock Haunt

Alfred Hitchcock fans will want to make the pilgrimage to Bodega, located off Highway 1 a few miles southeast of Bodega Bay. Drive past the roadside shops, turn the corner, look right, and *voilà!* A bird's-eye view of the hauntingly familiar Potter School House and St. Teresa's Church, both immortalized in Hitchcock's *The Birds,* filmed here in 1961.

---

drop about 20%. Rates include continental breakfast. Golf packages available. AE, DC, DISC, MC, V. **Amenities:** Restaurant; indoor-outdoor heated pool; nearby golf course; exercise room; Jacuzzi; Finnish sauna; room service; in-room massage; babysitting (with advance notice); self-service laundry. *In room:* TV w/pay movies, minibar, coffeemaker, hair dryer, iron.

WHERE TO DINE

In addition to the following, see "Where to Stay," above, for hotel restaurants.

Lucas Wharf Deli 🎇 *(Value* DELI   I always stop here when I pass through Bodega Bay. Most visitors don't even give it a glance as they head into the adjacent restaurant, but that's because they don't know about the big bowls of fresh, tangy crab cioppino doled out, in season, for about $5.50 a pint—a third of the restaurant price. It's a messy affair, best devoured at the nearby picnic tables. Great fish and chips are available year-round. The deli is also open for breakfast.

595 Calif. 1, Bodega Bay. ✆ 707/875-3562. Deli items $4–$10. MC, V. Sun–Thurs 9am–6pm; Fri–Sat 9am–7pm.

Tides Wharf Restaurant SEAFOOD/PASTA   In summer, as many as 1,000 diners a day pass through the Tides Wharf. Back in the early '60s, it served as a set for Hitchcock's *The Birds,* but don't expect the weather-beaten, board-and-batten luncheonette you saw in the movie—a $6-million renovation gentrified, enlarged, and redecorated the place beyond recognition. The best tables offer views overlooking the ocean, and the fare is what you might expect at a seaside eatery: oysters on the half shell, clam chowder, and all the fish that the owners (who send their own fishing boat out into the Pacific every day) can dredge up from the cold blue waters. Prime rib, pasta, and poultry are available as well. Next to the restaurant are a fish-processing plant, snack bar, and gift shop.

835 Calif. 1. ✆ 707/875-3652. www.innatthetides.com/tideswharf.html. Main courses $14–$37. AE, DISC, MC, V. Mon–Fri 7:30am–9pm; Sat–Sun 7am–9:30pm.

THE SONOMA COAST STATE BEACHES, JENNER & FORT ROSS STATE HISTORIC PARK 🎇🎇

Along 13 winding and picturesque miles of Calif. 1—from Bodega Bay to Goat Rock Beach in Jenner—stretch the Sonoma Coast State Beaches. These beaches are ideal for walking, tide-pooling, abalone picking, fishing, and bird-watching for such species as great blue heron, cormorant, osprey, and pelican. Each beach is clearly marked from the road, and numerous pullouts are provided for parking. Even if you don't stop at any of the beaches, the drive alone is spectacular.

At **Jenner,** the Russian River empties into the ocean. **Penny Island,** in the river's estuary, is home to otters and many species of birds; a colony of harbor seals lives out on the ocean rocks. **Goat Rock Beach** is a popular breeding ground for the seals; pupping season begins in March and lasts until June.

From Jenner, an 11-mile drive along some dramatic coastline will bring you to **Fort Ross State Historic Park** (✆ 707/847-3286; www.parks.sonoma.net), a reconstruction of the fort established in 1812 by the Russians as a base for seal and otter hunting (it was abandoned in 1842). At the visitor center, you can view the Russians' samovars and table services. The compound contains several buildings, including the first Russian Orthodox church on the North American continent outside Alaska. A short history lesson about the fort is offered at 11:30am, 1:30pm, and 3:30pm between Memorial Day and Labor Day, and at noon and 2pm the rest of the year. Call ahead to be sure. The park also offers beach trails and picnic grounds on more than 1,000 acres. Admission to the park is $2 per car per day.

North from Fort Ross, the road continues to **Salt Point State Park** (© 707/ 847-3221). This 3,500-acre expanse contains 30 campsites, 14 miles of trails, dozens of tide pools, and old Pomo village sites. Your best bet is to pull off the highway any place that catches your eye and start exploring. At the north end of the park, head inland on Kruse Ranch Road to the **Kruse Rhododendron Reserve** (© 707/847-3286), a forested grove of wild pink and purple flowers where the *Rhododendron californicum* grow up to a height of 18 feet under the redwood-and-fir canopy. Admission to the park is $2 per car per day.

WHERE TO STAY

Jenner Inn & Cottages ⽊   The worst-kept secret on the Northern Coast is Jenner Inn, a hodgepodge of individually designed and decorated houses and cottages along the coast and inland along the Russian River. Couples from the Bay Area who want to stay along the coast for a night, but dread the long drive to Mendocino, wend their way here. Most of the houses are subdivided into suites, while second honeymooners vie for the ultraprivate oceanfront cottages. Wicker furniture, wood paneling, and private bathrooms and entrances are standard, though each lodging has its own personality: Some have kitchens, while others have fireplaces, porches, or private decks. The private cottages overlooking the Pacific are the priciest, but for about $130, most people are content with one of the small suites. The inn offers yoga classes several times weekly and has a small meditation cabin. A complimentary full breakfast is served in the main lodge. In addition to the B&B accommodations, the inn rents out vacation homes along the river, within Jenner Canyon, or overlooking the ocean.

10400 Calif. 1 (P.O. Box 69), Jenner, CA 95450. © 800/732-2377 or 707/865-2377. Fax 707/865-0829. www. jennerinn.com. 20 units (plus several vacation homes). $95–$375 double. Rates include full breakfast. AE, MC, V. *In room:* Kitchen in some units, fridge, coffeemaker, hair dryer, iron, phones in cottages only.

WHERE TO DINE

River's End INTERNATIONAL   Outwardly unpretentious yet deceptively urbane, this seaside restaurant offers an artfully rustic setting, with big windows overlooking the coast (seals and sea lions might happen to be cavorting offshore). The menu, which changes monthly, is wonderfully eclectic, offering everything from coconut shrimp, pheasant breast, racklets of elk, seafood, and steaks. Local Sonoma products—game, lamb, poultry, vegetables—are used whenever possible, including Sonoma microbrews and wines. After dinner, take the remainder of your wine to the deck and enjoy the sunset. *Note:* The hours tend to vary as much as the menu, so be sure to call ahead if you're planning to dine here.

Calif. 1, Jenner. © 707/865-2484. Reservations recommended. Main courses $13–$28. MC, V. Summer Thurs–Mon 11:30am–9pm; winter (Nov–Apr) Fri–Sun noon–9pm.

Sizzling Tandoor *(Value* INDIAN   Along a rather desolate stretch of Calif. 1 between Bodega Bay and Jenner, the Sizzling Tandoor serves huge, inexpensive plates of Indian cuisine. The lonely location, though peculiar, is superb: Perched high atop a wind-swept hill, the restaurant boasts an exquisite view of the Russian River far below. The large array of curries and kabobs are accompanied by soup, vegetables, pulao rice, and the best naan (Indian bread) I've ever had. Even if you're not hungry, order some naan to go—it makes the perfect road snack.

9960 Calif. 1 (at the south end of the Russian River Bridge), Jenner. ℂ 707/865-0625. Main courses $9–$14. AE, DISC, MC, V. Mon–Thurs 11:30am–9pm; Fri–Sun 11:30am–9:30pm.

GUALALA & POINT ARENA

Back on Calif. 1 heading north, you'll pass through Sea Ranch, a series of condominium beach developments, before you reach the small coastal community of Gualala (pronounced "Wah-*la*-la"). In the old days, Gualala was a vivacious logging town. A few real-life suspender-wearing lumberjacks still end their day at the Gualala Hotel's saloon, but for the most part the town's role is providing gas, groceries, and hardware for area residents. Just outside of town are several parks, hiking trails, and about 10 or so beaches ideal for sunbathing.

The **Gualala River,** adjacent to the town of the same name, is suitable for canoeing, rafting, and kayaking, because all powerboats and jet skis are forbidden. Along its banks you're likely to see osprey, herons, egrets, and ducks; steelhead, salmon, and river otters make their homes in the waters. Canoes and kayaks can be rented in Gualala for 2 hours, a half-day, or a full day from **Adventure Rents** (ℂ **888/881-4386** or 707/884-4386; www.adventurerents. com), in downtown Gualala on Calif. 1, north of the Chevron. Prices range from $25 for a few hours on a river canoe to $70 for a full day on a tandem ocean kayak.

Point Arena lies a few miles north of Gualala. Most folks stop here for the view at the **Point Arena Lighthouse** ★ (ℂ **707/882-2777;** www.mcn.org/1/palight), which was built in 1870 after 10 ships ran aground here on a single night during a storm. A $5-per-person fee ($1 for children under 12) covers parking, entrance to the lighthouse museum, and a surprisingly interesting tour of the six-story, 145-step lighthouse (the view through the dazzling 6-ft.-wide, lead-crystal lens is worth the hike alone). The lighthouse is open daily 10am to 4:30pm April–September and 10am to 3:30pm October–March; the half-hour tours are given every 20 minutes.

WHERE TO STAY

St. Orres ★★ *Finds*   An extraordinary Russian-style building—complete with two onion-domed towers—St. Orres lies 1½ miles north of Gualala. The complex was built in 1972 with century-old timbers salvaged from a nearby mill. It offers cottage-style accommodations on 42 acres, as well as eight rooms in the main building (these rooms are handcrafted and share three bathrooms decorated in brilliant colors). Other units are very private. Some have wet bars, sitting areas with Franklin stoves, and French doors leading to decks with a distant ocean view. Seven cottages border St. Orres Creek and have exclusive use of a spa facility that includes a hot tub, sauna, and sun deck. The most luxurious is Pine Haven, with two bedrooms, two redwood decks, two bathrooms, a tiled breakfast area, a beach-stone fireplace, and a wet bar. The Black Chanterelle is as exotic as it sounds, with domes, a sauna and Jacuzzi, a fireplace, and an ocean view. Full breakfast is delivered to the cottages. The hotel's restaurant (see review below), open for dinner only, is in a dramatic setting below one of the main building's domes. Light filters through stained-glass windows onto strands of ivy that cascade down from the balcony. The menu is inspired by Pacific Northwest cuisine and includes wild boar, pheasant, venison, quail, and rack of lamb.

> ## (Tips) Renting a Home at the Beach
>
> If you're taking the family for a vacation along the coast—or really want to impress your partner—consider renting a furnished home at the Sea Ranch, one of the most beautiful seaside communities around. All of the low-swept buildings on the ranch are designed to blend in with the surrounding forest, meadows, and ocean bluffs; many have outdoor hot tubs, and almost all have wood-burning fireplaces or stoves. About 300 homes are available as rentals with prices starting at about $150 per night. Rentals also include use of the community's three outdoor heated swimming pools, tennis courts, and recreation center. The Sea Ranch also has a Scottish-style 18-hole public course, a fine-dining restaurant, and private access to 10 miles of coastline and several secluded beaches. For more information, log on to www.sea ranchvillage.com or call **Sea Ranch Rentals** at © **888/732-7262.**

36601 Calif. 1 (P.O. Box 523), Gualala, CA 95445. © **707/884-3303.** Fax 707/884-1840. www.saintorres. com. 8 units (sharing 3 bathrooms), 13 cottages. $80–$95 double; cottage $110–$235 double. Rates include full breakfast. MC, V. **Amenities:** Restaurant; bar; nearby golf course; Jacuzzi; sauna; bike rental; in-room massage; babysitting. *In room:* Kitchenette in some units, fridge, coffeemaker, hair dryer, iron.

Whale Watch Inn By the Sea 🐋🐋   This inn has one of the best vantage points along the Northern Coast to contemplate ocean vistas. Perched 90 feet above the water in five contemporary buildings on 2 cliff-side acres, private guest rooms at the Whale Watch all have ocean views, decks, and fireplaces. Room styles range from traditional bed-and-breakfast to French Provincial to contemporary casual, so check out the pictures on the website before you make your reservation. For a closer encounter with nature, a private stairway leads to a half-mile long beach with tidal pools. If you and your friends want to form your own pod, the Whale Watch building has a common room with a circular fireplace, floor-to-ceiling windows, and a wraparound deck for prime—what else?—whale-watching.

35100 Hwy. 1, Gualala, CA 95445. © **800/942-5342** or 707/884-3667. Fax 707/884-3667. www.whale-watch. com. 18 units. $180–$300 double. Rates include full breakfast delivered to room at prearranged time. AE, MC, V. **Amenities:** Nearby golf course. *In room:* Kitchen, fridge, and coffeemaker in some units; hair dryer, phone upon request.

WHERE TO DINE
The Food Company (Value) DELI   If the St. Orres restaurant (see below) is out of your price range, you'll be happy to know you can have an equally romantic lunch or dinner down the road for a fraction of the price. Place your order at the deli counter, grab a bottle of wine from the rack, then head to the adjacent garden and have a seat at one of the picnic tables. The menu offers a dizzying array of specials from around the globe—corn tamales, Greek moussaka, lamb curry, quiche Lorraine, pasta puttanesca—as well as fresh-baked breads, pastries, and sandwiches. Better yet, order it all to go and head for the beach.

38411 Calif. 1 (at Robinsons Reef Rd.), Gualala. © **707/884-1800.** Most items $7–$12. MC, V. Thurs–Mon 11am–7pm (closing hours flexible).

St. Orres Restaurant 🍽️🍽️ NORTH COAST CUISINE   Self-taught chef Rosemary Campiformio has been wowing fans and food writers for years with her version of North Coast cuisine, which favors local organic meats and produce along with wild game in dark, fruity sauces. Every day fishermen and farmers deliver their best goods to Rosemary's kitchen door, so you never know what will be on her prix-fixe dinner menu, but it'll probably go something like this: an appetizer of pheasant and venison pâté with a huckleberry glaze and Rosemary's mustard, followed by a garden-fresh salad and an entree of grilled veal chop with garlic mashed potatoes, foie gras, and truffle Madeira sauce (it's either that or the pan-roasted fresh wild salmon with zucchini cakes and wasabi lime and ginger). For dessert it's a tossup between the bread pudding with homemade nutmeg ice cream and caramel sauce, or the freshly baked individual apple pie with St. Orres cinnamon ice cream. The wine cellar stores a suitable selection of reds that pair well with the hearty entrees. If you're staying at the St. Orres Inn (see review above), it's a short walk from your cabin to this rustically romantic restaurant situated under the main lodge's distinctive onion dome.

36601 Hwy. 1 (St. Orres Inn), Gualala. ⓒ 707/884-3335. www.saintorres.com. Reservations recommended. Prix-fixe dinner menu $40; appetizers and desserts a la carte. Beer and wine only. MC, V. Checks accepted. Dinner daily 6–9:30pm (winter schedule varies).

NORTH FROM POINT ARENA
Driving north from Point Arena, you'll pass Elk (a good place to stop for lunch), Manchester, Albion, and Little River on your way to Mendocino.

WHERE TO STAY
Greenwood Pier Inn & Cafe ⚿   Perched on the edge of a dramatic bluff, the Greenwood Pier Inn is an eclectic, New Age kind of place. It's the unique domain of Kendrick Petty, who owns and operates this quartet of cafe, country store, garden shop, and accommodations. Kendrick is an artist and gardener whose collages, tiles, and marble work can be seen in the interiors of several of the buildings in the complex and also outside in the gardens. Of the accommodations, which are in various buildings in addition to the main inn, the Cliffhouse is my top choice: a seaside redwood cabin with a fireplace, a large deck, and an upper-level bathtub with ocean views. All the rooms have private decks, fireplaces or wood burners, and lie within 100 feet of the cliff edge. A beautiful building called The Tower has three levels: a two-person Jacuzzi at the bottom, a deck overlooking the ocean on the second level, and, up a library ladder, there's a full-size bed facing an ocean view. A continental breakfast is delivered to your room; breakfast, lunch, and dinner—roast pork loin, grilled rack of lamb, grilled Chilean sea bass—are served daily in the Greenwood Pier Cafe.

5928 Calif. 1 (P.O. Box 336), Elk, CA 95432. ⓒ 707/877-9997. Fax 707/877-3439. www.greenwoodpierinn. com. 12 units. $130–$300 double. Rates include continental breakfast. AE, MC, V. Pets accepted in some units for $15 per night. **Amenities:** Restaurant; nearby golf course; oceanview Jacuzzi; in-room massage. *In room:* Fridge, coffeemaker, hair dryer in some units, no phone.

Harbor House Inn & Restaurant ⚿⚿   While the Greenwood Pier Inn is New Age, the beautiful, redwood-sided, two-story Harbor House is traditional. Built in 1916 by the president of the Goodyear Redwood Lumber Co. as a hideaway for corporate executives, it's not a hotel but an upscale inn offering 3 acres of gardens, access to a private beach, and views overlooking the Pacific. None of the units has a TV or phone, and that's how guests like it. Five of the rooms in the main building have their own fireplaces, many are furnished with antiques purchased by the lumber executives, and all have private bathrooms. The four cottages tend to be small but have fireplaces and private decks. Set dinners, included in the rates, change nightly and feature California and Pacific Northwest cuisines, making use of seafood harvested from local waters, local herbs, freshly baked breads, and vegetables from the inn's gardens.

5600 S. Calif. 1 (P.O. Box 369), Elk, CA 95432. © **800/720-7474** or 707/877-3203. Fax 707/877-3452. www.theharborhouseinn.com. 10 units. $295–$470 double (winter rates are considerably less). Extra person $100. Rates include full breakfast and 4-course dinner. AE, MC, V. **Amenities:** Restaurant; nearby golf course; in-room massage. In room: A/C, coffeemaker, hair dryer, iron in cottages, no phone.

KOA Kamping Kabins (Kids) "What? You expect me to stay at a Kampgrounds of America?!" You bet. Once you see these neat little log "kabins," you can't help but admit that this is one great way to spend a weekend on the coast. The cabins have one or two bedrooms with log-frame double beds or bunk beds for the kids and sleep four to six people, respectively. Rustic is the key word: Mattresses, a heater, and a light bulb are your standard amenities. Beyond that, you're on your own, but all you need is some bedding or a sleeping bag, cooking and eating utensils, and a bag of charcoal for the barbecue in front. Enjoy your meal at the picnic table or on the front porch in the log porch swing. If this is a little too spartan for you, opt for one of the fully furnished "kottages," both decked out with private bathrooms, fireplaces, comfy beds, and other creature comforts. Hot showers, bathrooms, laundry facilities, a small store, and a swimming pool are a short walk away, as is Manchester Beach. It's kid heaven.

On Kinney Rd. (off Calif. 1, 5 miles north of Point Arena). © **800/562-4188** or 707/882-2375. Fax 707/882-3104. www.manchesterbeachkoa.com. 24 cabins, 2 cottages. $52–$72 cabin (up to 6 people); $135–$165 cottage (up to 4 people). AE, DISC, MC, V. **Amenities:** Heated outdoor pool (seasonal); spa; children's center and playground; coin-op laundry. In room: TV and kitchenette in cottages, no phone.

WHERE TO DINE

Ledford House Restaurant ⊛ NEW AMERICAN If James Beard were alive today, he'd feel right at home at this innovative but simply decorated restaurant overlooking the pounding surf of the Pacific from a bluff above. The kitchen offers self-styled "New American cuisine," experimenting with the bounty of the Golden State to fashion rich combinations and harmonious flavors. One part of the menu is reserved primarily for the pastas and hearty stews suitable to this far-northern setting, such as their award-winning Antoine's cassoulet, a jumble of pork, lamb, garlic sausage, and duck confit slowly cooked with white beans. Although the menu changes seasonally, for a taste of California, try the salmon primavera with lemon-caper butter, or the crisp-roasted duckling with wild-huckleberry sauce. Evenings bring live jazz in the cocktail lounge.

3000 N. Calif. 1, Albion. © **707/937-0282.** www.ledfordhouse.com. Reservations recommended. Main courses $22–$26. AE, MC, V. Wed–Sun 5–9pm.

3 Mendocino ⊛⊛⊛

166 miles N of San Francisco

Mendocino is, to my mind, *the* premier destination on California's northern coast. Despite (or because of) its relative isolation, it emerged as one of Northern California's major centers for the arts in the 1950s. It's easy to see why artists were—and still are—attracted to this idyllic community, a cluster of New England–style captains' homes and stores on headlands overlooking the ocean.

At the height of the logging boom, Mendocino was an important and active port. Its population was about 3,500, and eight hotels were built, along with 17 saloons and more than a dozen bordellos. Today it has only about 1,000 residents, most of whom reside on the north end of town. On summer weekends the population seems more like 10,000, as hordes of tourists drive up from the Bay Area—but despite the crowds, Mendocino still manages to retain its charm.

ESSENTIALS

GETTING THERE   The fastest route from San Francisco is via U.S. 101 north to Cloverdale. Then take Calif. 128 west to Calif. 1, and then go north along the coast. It's about a 4-hour drive. (You could also take U.S. 101 all the way to Ukiah or Willits, and cut over to the west from there.) The most scenic route, if you have the time and your stomach doesn't mind the twists and turns, is to take Calif. 1 north along the coast the entire way; it's at least a 5- to 6-hour drive.

VISITOR INFORMATION   You can stock up on lots of free brochures and maps at the **Fort Bragg/Mendocino Coast Chamber of Commerce,** 332 N. Main St. (P.O. Box 1141), Fort Bragg, CA 95437 (© **800/726-2780** or 707/ 961-6300; www.mendocinocoast.com). Pick up a copy of the center's monthly magazine, *Arts and Entertainment,* which lists upcoming events throughout Mendocino. It's available at numerous stores and cafes, including the Mendocino Bakery, Gallery Bookshop, and Mendocino Art Center.

EXPLORING THE TOWN

Stroll through town, enjoy the architecture, and browse through the dozens of galleries and shops. My favorites include the **Highlight Gallery,** 45052 Main St. (© **707/937-3132**), for its handmade furniture, pottery, and other craft work; and the **Gallery Bookshop & Bookwinkle's Children's Books,** at Main and Kasten streets (© **707/937-2665;** www.gallerybooks.com), one of the best independent bookstores in Northern California, with a wonderful selection of books for children and adults. Another popular stop is **Mendocino Jams & Preserves,** 440 Main St. (© **800/708-1196** or 707/937-1037; www.mendojams.com), which offers free tastings of its natural, locally made gourmet wares on little bread chips.

After exploring the town, walk out on the headlands that wrap around the town and constitute **Mendocino Headlands State Park** ⋆. (The visitor center for the park is in the Ford House on Main St.; © **707/937-5397.**) Three miles of trails wind through the park, giving visitors panoramic views of sea arches and hidden grottoes. If you're here at the right time of year, the area will be blanketed with wildflowers; when I last stopped by, I could pick fresh blackberries beside the trails. The headlands are home to many unique species of birds, including black oystercatchers. Behind the Mendocino Presbyterian Church on Main Street is a trail leading to stairs that take you down to the beach, a small but picturesque stretch of sand where driftwood formations have washed ashore.

On the south side of town, **Big River Beach** is accessible from Calif. 1; it's good for picnicking, walking, and sunbathing.

In town, stop by the **Mendocino Art Center,** 45200 Little Lake St. (© **707/ 937-5818;** www.mendocinoartcenter.org), the town's unofficial cultural headquarters. It's also known for its gardens, galleries, and shops that display and sell local fine arts and crafts. Admission is free; open daily from 10am to 5pm.

After a day of hiking, head to **Sweetwater Spa & Inn,** 955 Ukiah St. (© **800/ 300-4140** or 707/937-4140; www.sweetwaterspa.com), which offers group and private saunas and hot-tub soaks by the hour. Additional services include Swedish or deep-tissue massages. Reservations are recommended. Private tub prices are $12 per person per half-hour, $16 per person per hour. Group tub prices are $10 per person with no time limit. Special discounts are available on Wednesdays. The spa is open Monday through Thursday from 1 to 10pm, Friday and Sunday from noon to 10pm, and Saturday and holidays from noon to 11pm.

OUTDOOR PURSUITS

Explore the Big River by renting a canoe, kayak, or outrigger from **Catch a Canoe & Bicycles Too** (© **707/937-0273;** www.stanfordinn.com), open daily from 9am to sunset and located on the grounds of the Stanford Inn by the Sea (see "Where to Stay" below). If you're lucky, you'll see some osprey, blue herons, harbor seals, deer, and wood ducks. These same folks will also rent you a mountain bike (of much better quality than your usual bike rental), so you can head up Calif. 1 and explore the nearby state parks on two wheels.

Horseback riding (both English and western) on the beach and into the woods is offered by **Ricochet Ridge Ranch,** 24201 N. Calif. 1, Fort Bragg (© **888/873-5777** or 707/964-PONY; www.horse-vacation.com). Prices range from $40 for a 1½-hour beach ride to $205 for an all-day beach-and-redwoods trail ride.

In addition to Mendocino Headlands State Park (see "Exploring the Town" above), there are several other state parks near Mendocino, all within an easy drive or bike ride, which make for a good day's outing. Information on all the parks' features, including maps of each one, is found in the brochure *Mendocino Coast State Parks,* available from the visitor center in Fort Bragg. These areas include **Manchester State Park,** located where the San Andreas Fault sweeps to the sea; **Jughandle State Reserve;** and **Van Damme State Park** ⊛, with a sheltered, easily accessible beach.

My favorite, on Calif. 1 just north of Mendocino, is **Russian Gulch State Park** ⊛⊛. It's one of the region's most spectacular parks, where waves crash against the cliffs that protect the park's California coastal redwoods. The most popular attraction is the **Punch Bowl,** a collapsed sea cave that forms a tunnel through which waves crash, creating throaty echoes. Inland, there's a scenic paved bike path, and visitors can also hike along miles of trails, including a gentle, well-marked 3-mile **Waterfall Loop** that winds past tall redwoods and damp green foliage to a 36-foot-high waterfall. Admission is $2 and camping is $12 per night. Call © **800/444-7275** for reservations; for general state park information, call © **707/937-5804** or visit www.cal-parks.ca.gov.

Fort Bragg is just a short distance up the coast; deep-sea fishing charters are available from its harbor.

WHERE TO STAY
EXPENSIVE
Stanford Inn by the Sea ⊛⊛   Just south of Mendocino, this rustic but sumptuous lodge is on 11 acres of land abutting the Big River. The grounds are captivating, with tiers of gardens, a pond for ducks and geese, and fenced pastures containing horses, llamas, and old gnarled apple trees. The solarium-style indoor hot tub and pool surrounded by tropical plants are gorgeous. The luxurious rooms come with special touches such as thick robes, down comforters, fresh flowers, and works by local artists. All have fireplaces or stoves and private decks from which you can gaze on the Pacific. Second honeymooners should inquire about the romantic River Cottage; families will want the big renovated barn. Pets are welcome and receive the royal treatment. The inn also has a small massage studio, individual and group yoga lessons, and **The Raven's Restaurant,** the only totally vegetarian restaurant on the Mendocino coast, which has become a big hit with both guests and locals.

N. Calif. 1 and Comptche Ukiah Rd. (P.O. Box 487), Mendocino, CA 95460. © **800/331-8884** or 707/937-5615. Fax 707/937-0305. www.stanfordinn.com. 33 units. $235–$295 double; $310–$720 suite. Rates include breakfast. AE, DC, DISC, MC, V. Pets accepted with $25 fee. **Amenities:** Vegetarian restaurant, nearby golf

Tips Mendocino Nightlife

Typical of a small town, the nightlife scene in Mendocino is like molasses in winter. There are only three options for the visitor: 1) have a casual cocktail in the elegant bar and lounge at the **Mendocino Hotel** (see review below); 2) knock down a few Buds with the locals at **Dick's Place** (45080 Main St.; ⓒ **707/937-5643**), the town's oldest bar; or 3) get in the car and head up Highway 1 a bit to the **Caspar Inn,** the best nightclub on the North Coast. Everything from rock and jazz to reggae and blues is played live Thursday through Saturday nights starting at 9:30pm. Check their website calendar for upcoming shows and bring a designated dancer and driver. It's located at 14957 Caspar Rd. (take the Caspar Rd. exit off Hwy. 1, a quarter mile north of Mendocino; ⓒ**707/964-5565;**www.casparinn.com).

---

course; solarium-style pool, spa, and sauna; exercise room; kayak and canoe rental; complimentary bikes; concierge; courtesy car; business center; secretarial services; evening room service; in-room massage. *In room:* TV/VCR w/pay movies, dataport, kitchenette and minibar in some units, fridge, coffeemaker, hair dryer, iron.

MODERATE

Agate Cove Inn ⓡⓡ   Good luck trying to find an accommodation with a more beautiful coastal setting than Agate Cove Inn's. Words can barely convey the splendor of the view from the inn's front lawn, a sweeping, unfettered vista of the sea and its surging waves crashing onto the bluffs. Situate yourself on one of the Adirondack chairs with a good book, and you'll never want to leave. The inn consists of a main house trimmed in blue and white, surrounded by a bevy of single and duplex cottages. All but 1 of the 10 spacious units have views of the ocean, king- or queen-size beds, down comforters, fireplaces, and private decks. In the morning, a fantastic country breakfast is served in the main house's enclosed porch (yes, with the same ocean view).

11201 N. Lansing St. (P.O. Box 1150), Mendocino, CA 95460. ⓒ 800/527-3111 or 707/937-0551. Fax 707/ 937-0550. www.agatecove.com. 10 units. $119–$269 double. Rates include full breakfast. AE, MC, V. **Amenities:** Nearby golf course; concierge; activities desk; in-room massage. *In room:* TV/VCR w/complimentary videos, iron, hair dryer, no phone, CD player.

Brewery Gulch Inn ⓡⓡ   You don't have to be a connoisseur of redwood to enjoy a stay at the Brewery Gulch Inn, but it sure helps. I've never met anyone as passionate about the intricacies of virgin redwood than Dr. Arky Ciancutti, the owner, builder, and visionary behind the Brewery Gulch Inn, a beautiful three-story inn set high on a bluff overlooking Mendocino's Smuggler's Cove. A "self-confessed wood freak," Arky salvaged more than 100,000 board feet of century-old redwood logs that were embedded in the silty bottom of Mendocino's Big River, then carefully milled the 12-foot-thick trunks to obtain the finest cuts of redwood lumber for building his dream inn.

The first thing you notice when you enter the inn, however, isn't the wood or soaring cathedral ceiling—it's the massive steel and glass fireplace that is the centerpiece of the inn. Like a moth to flame, you can't help but walk over and stare into the glowing embers. Spend a few minutes talking wood with Arky and you too will be marveling at the subtle red, purple, and blond tones that swirl throughout the redwood beams, doors, decks, and details that make this inn unique. Built in a clean-lined Arts and Crafts style, the inn's 10 soundproofed guest rooms are luxuriously appointed with down comforters, gas-lit fireplaces, hardwood furnishings, leather club chairs, CD players, and private bathrooms with heated flooring; most have Jacuzzis or soaking tubs for two, as well as private decks with expansive views of the ocean and hundreds of acres of unoccupied meadow and forest. A gourmet organic country breakfast is prepared by the in-house chef using eggs from Arky's chicken coop and herbs and fruit from the inn's gardens and orchards; hors d'oeuvres and Mendocino wines are offered in the evening as well. *Tip:* Check the inn's website for tempting package deals such as the "Marry Me!" and "Ocean Kayaking."

9401 Coast Hwy. 1 N., Mendocino, CA 95460. © **800/578-4454** or 707/937-4753. Fax 707/937-1279. www. brewerygulchinn.com. 10 units. $150–$350. Rates include organic gourmet country breakfast and evening wine tasting with hors d'oeuvres. AE, MC, V. **Amenities:** Concierge service; gift shop; telescope; daily newspaper and turndown service; common room with fireplace; library with wide selection of books, CDs and videos. *In room:* TV/VCR, phone with dataport, hair dryer, CD player, fireplace, fresh-cut flowers, private deck, soaking tub for 2, robes.

Joshua Grindle Inn ☆☆ When it was built in 1879, this stately Victorian was one of the most impressive houses in Mendocino, owned by the town's wealthiest banker. Now the oldest B&B in Mendocino, it features redwood siding, a wraparound porch, and emerald lawns. From its prettily planted gardens, there's a view across the village to the distant bay. There are five rooms in the main house, two in the cottage, and three in the water tower. All have well-lit, comfortably arranged sitting areas; some offer fireplaces, three have deep-soak tubs, and three have whirlpool tubs. Each is individually decorated: The Library room has a New England feel with its four-poster pine bed, floor-to-ceiling bookcase, and 19th-century tiles around the fireplace depicting Aesop's fables. Sherry, sweets, and tea are served in the parlor in front of the fireplace; breakfast is in the dining room. In addition to the inn, the proprietors also have a beautiful two-bedroom, two-bathroom oceanview rental home with floor-to-ceiling windows, a large kitchen, and a wood-burning fireplace. It's a few minutes north of Mendocino, and rates range from $245 to $375, depending on occupancy.

44800 Little Lake Rd. (P.O. Box 647), Mendocino, CA 95460. © **800/GRINDLE** or 707/937-4143. www.joshgrin. com. 10 units. June–Oct $130–$245 double; Nov–May Mon–Thurs $115–$195 double, Fri–Sun $130–$245 double. Rates include full breakfast, afternoon tea, and wine. MC, V. **Amenities:** Nearby golf course; concierge. *In room:* TV/DVD in some units, hair dryer, no phone.

MacCallum House Inn & Restaurant ☆☆ A historic 1882 gingerbread Victorian mansion, MacCallum House is one of Mendocino's top accommodations. Originally owned by local matriarch Daisy MacCallum, the house still bears the imprint of this daughter of the town's richest lumber baron. It remained in the family until 1974, when it was turned into a B&B. Now owned by Melanie and Joe Redding, the home has been preserved with all of its original furnishings and contents—right down to Daisy's Christmas cards and books of pressed flowers. Boasting the occasional Tiffany lamp or Persian carpet, each uniquely decorated guest room is furnished with many original pieces—a Franklin stove, a handmade quilt, a cushioned rocking chair, or a child's cradle. All have private bathrooms, many equipped with claw-foot or spa tubs for two. The luxurious barn suite, complete with a stone fireplace, can accommodate up to six adults. The popular dinner restaurant on the premises serves sophisticated North Coast cuisine ranging from pan-seared Sonoma duck breast with huckleberry-honey vinegar sauce, to roasted Pacific salmon with saffron-pistachio risotto and arugula pesto.

45020 Albion St. (P.O. Box 206), Mendocino, CA 95460. © **800/609-0492** or 707/937-0289. Fax 707/964-2243. www.maccallumhouse.com. 19 units. $120–$195 double. Extra person $15. AE, MC, V. **Amenities:** Restaurant; cafe; bar; concierge. *In room:* Fridge, coffeemaker in some units.

Mendocino Hotel & Garden Suites ☆ In the heart of town, this 1878 hotel evokes California's Gold Rush days. Beveled-glass doors open into a Victorian-style lobby and parlor. The hotel's decor combines antiques and reproductions, like the oak reception desk from a demolished Kansas bank. Remington paintings, stained-glass lamps, and Persian carpets contribute to the Wild West aura. Guest rooms feature hand-painted French porcelain sinks with floral designs, quaint wallpaper, old-fashioned beds and armoires, and photographs and memorabilia of historic Mendocino. About half the rooms are located in four handsome small buildings behind the main house. Many of the deluxe rooms have fireplaces, as well as modern bathrooms and good views. Suites have an additional parlor, as well as a fireplace or balcony.

45080 Main St. (P.O. Box 587), Mendocino, CA 95460. ℂ 800/548-0513 or 707/937-0511. Fax 707/937-0513. www.mendocinohotel.com. 51 units, 37 with private bathroom. $95 double with shared bathroom, $120–$215 double with private bathroom; $275 suite. Extra person $20. AE, MC, V. **Amenities:** 2 restaurants; 2 bars; nearby golf course; access to nearby health club ($5); room service. *In room:* TV, hair dryer.

INEXPENSIVE

Mendocino Village Inn & Spa ☆ This historic Victorian inn is across the street from the headlands, overlooking the ocean and the Big River beach. A garden of flowers, plants, and frog ponds fronts the blue-and-white guesthouse, which was built in 1882 by a doctor and later occupied by famed local artist Emmy Lou Packard. Each room is individually decorated, and many have fireplaces and Jacuzzi tubs. The Queen Anne Room features a four-poster canopy bed and other Victorian furnishings, and the sentimental Madge's Room is named for a child who etched her name in the window glass almost a century ago (you can still see it). Except for two attic units, all have private bathrooms, and four rooms have private outside entrances. Complimentary beverages are served in the evening, and all guests have spa privileges at the nearby Sweetwater Spa.

44860 Main St. (P.O. Box 626), Mendocino, CA 95460. ℂ 800/882-7029 or 707/937-0246. www.mendocino inn.com. 12 units, 10 with private bathroom. $85–$95 double with shared bathroom; $125–$195 double with private bathroom; $165 Water Tower suite. Winter midweek discounts. Rates include full breakfast and evening refreshments. MC, V. **Amenities:** Spa privileges and massage discount at adjacent Sweetwater Spa.

IN NEARBY ALBION & LITTLE RIVER

Albion River Inn and Restaurant ☆☆ A quarter-mile north of Albion (or 6 miles south of Mendocino), this modern, beautiful inn overlooks the mouth of the Albion River from a bluff some 90 feet above the Pacific. The view is, of course, spectacular. A plaintive harbor horn in the area adds to the seaside atmosphere. (If you are a light sleeper, earplugs are provided.) The rooms are decorated in a contemporary style with comfortable furnishings; all have ocean views, and most have decks. You'll find wingbacks placed in front of the fireplaces, down comforters on the queen- and king-size beds, well-lit desks, binoculars for wildlife viewing, and bathrobes. *Insider tip:* If you really want to impress your sweetie, reserve one of the rooms with a spa tub for two, which has a picture window offering dazzling views of the coast. The cuisine at the inn's restaurant changes daily, featuring fresh local produce whenever possible, but the view from the tables remains the same: stellar. The award-winning wine list is also impressive. Evenings, soft piano music adds to the romantic atmosphere.

3790 N. Calif. 1 (P.O. Box 100), Albion, CA 95410. ℂ 800/479-7944 or 707/937-1919. Fax 707/937-2604. www.albionriverinn.com. 20 units. $200–$250 double; $290–$310 spa suite. Rates include full breakfast. AE, DC, DISC, MC, V. **Amenities:** Restaurant. *In room:* Fridge, coffeemaker, hair dryer, iron, CD player.

Glendeven ★★ Named 1 of the 12 best inns in America by *Country Inns* magazine, this 1867 farmhouse has been converted into a place of exceptional style and comfort. Accommodations are spread across 2½ acres that encompass the main house, the Carriage House Suite, and an addition known as Stevenscroft. Each room is individually decorated with a well-balanced mixture of antiques and contemporary pieces and original art. Most have ocean views, fireplaces, and porches. Etta's Suite in the Farmhouse includes an antique walnut bed, while the Eastlin and Carriage House suites are furnished with king-size feather beds. The four rooms in the Stevenscroft annex are also spacious and beautifully furnished. A vacation rental house, La Bella Vista, has two bedrooms, two bathrooms, a kitchen, Jacuzzi, and its namesake beautiful view of the ocean and surrounding gardens. Adjacent to the inn are the numerous fern-lined canyon trails to the ocean and beaches of Van Damme State Park.

8205 N. Hwy. 1, Little River, CA 95456. © **800/822-4536** or 707/937-0083. Fax 707/937-6108. www. glendeven.com. 10 units. Weekend and summer rates $145–$250. Ask about off-season midweek specials. Rates include full breakfast. AE, DISC, MC, V. **Amenities:** In-room massage (with notice). *In room:* Hair dryer, no phone.

Heritage House Inn & Restaurant ★★ Famous as the site of the movie *Same Time, Next Year*, most of the rooms at this country-club-style property have great views of the ocean and coastline. Thirty-seven seafront acres of lush gardens house a variety of accommodations ranging from the attractive to frankly lush. Only three guest rooms are located in the ivy-covered New England–style main building; the others are in cottages grouped two to four under one common roof. Rooms are individually decorated with original antiques and locally made furnishings, with every kind of amenity, including bathrobes, umbrellas, wine splits, and newspaper delivery. Most have wood-burning fireplaces or stoves, private decks, sitting areas, and ocean views; several suites have wet bars and Jacuzzis. Wooded trails wind along the coastline, offering spectacular scenery. The Heritage House dining room is in a magnificent setting overlooking the ocean, features a seasonal menu, and has a highly touted wine cellar.

5200 N. Calif. 1, Little River, CA 95456. © **800/235-5885** or 707/937-5885. Fax 707/937-0318. www.heritage houseinn.com. 66 units. Summer $150–$500 double; winter $150–$425 double. Extra person $20. Rates include a full breakfast for 2. AE, MC, V. **Amenities:** Restaurant; concierge; tour and activities desk; in-room massage. *In room:* Fax, dataport, fridge, coffeemaker, hair dryer, iron, no phone.

WHERE TO DINE

In addition to the following, see "Where to Stay," above, for hotel restaurants.

EXPENSIVE

Café Beaujolais ★★ AMERICAN/FRENCH This is one of Mendocino's top dining choices and was, for a time, one of the most celebrated restaurants in Northern California and a pioneer in using locally grown organic produce, meat from humanely raised animals, and fresh locally caught seafood. Though Café Beaujolais started out as a breakfast-and-lunch place, it's strictly a dinner house now. The French country–style tavern is set in an early 1900s house; rose-colored carnival-glass chandeliers add a burnish to the oak floors and the heavy oak tables adorned with flowers. The menu changes weekly and usually lists about five main courses. A typical dinner may start with a warm free-range duck confit salad in raspberry vinaigrette with fresh raspberries and toasted walnuts on mixed greens, followed by a Washington sturgeon filet, pan-roasted with truffle emulsion sauce and served with house-made tagliatelle, wild mushrooms, beets, and snap peas. For dessert, order the lemon-glazed persimmon cake with

---

(Fun Fact   Bread Winner

Few tourists know that Café Beaujolais's renowned "brickery breads" are sold daily from 11am to around 5pm at their Brickery bakery on Ukiah Street, just east of the restaurant.

---

vanilla-bean panna cotta and red-currant sauce. On warm summer nights, request a table at the enclosed deck overlooking the gardens. *Note:* The restaurant usually closes for a winter vacation for most of December.

961 Ukiah St. ⓒ 707/937-5614. Fax 707/937-3656. www.cafebeaujolais.com. Reservations recommended. Main courses $21–$28. AE, DISC, MC, V. Daily 5:30–9pm.

The 955 Ukiah Street Restaurant ⋆⋆ NORTH COAST CUISINE Shortly after this building's construction in the 1960s, the region's most famous painter, Emmy Lou Packard, commandeered its premises as an art studio for the creation of a series of giant murals. Today it's a large but surprisingly cozy restaurant, accented with railway ties and vaulted ceilings. Ask for a window table overlooking the gardens. The cuisine is creative and reasonably priced, a worthy alternative to the perpetually booked Café Beaujolais next door. It's hard to pick a favorite dish, although the phyllo-wrapped red snapper with pesto and lime has a zesty tang, while the crispy duck with ginger, apples, and a Calvados sauce would earn enthusiastic friends in Normandy.

955 Ukiah St. ⓒ 707/937-1955. www.955restaurant.com. Reservations recommended. Main courses $12–$26. MC, V. Wed–Sun 6–10pm.

MODERATE

Bay View Café ⋆ AMERICAN   This reasonably priced cafe is one of the most popular in town. From the second-floor dining area of the cafe, there's a sweeping view of the Pacific and faraway headlands; to reach it, climb a flight of stairs running up the outside of the town's antique water tower, then detour sideways. Surrounded by dozens of ferns suspended from the ceiling, you'll find a menu with Southwestern selections (the marinated chicken breast is very popular), a good array of sandwiches (my favorite is the hot crabmeat with avocado slices), fish and chips, and the fresh catch of the day. Breakfast ranges from the basic bacon 'n' eggs to eggs Florentine and honey-wheat pancakes.

45040 Main St. ⓒ 707/937-4197. Reservations not accepted. Main courses $6–$15. No credit cards. Summer daily 8am–9pm; winter Mon–Thurs 8am–3pm, Fri–Sun 8am–9pm.

The Moosse Café ⋆ CALIFORNIA BISTRO   This petite cafe in a New England–style home is another of the most popular restaurants in Mendocino. In 1995 the place was gutted and redone with an attractive, modern interior. The menu, which changes seasonally, boasts many local items such as organic herbs and vegetables, as in the outstanding Caesar salad. I also enjoyed the roast chicken with garlic mashed potatoes and the swordfish special, which came with a pile of fresh vegetables. Other popular entrees are the mixed seafood cakes over basmati rice with a roasted red pepper rémoulade, and the lavender-smoked double-thick pork chop served with roasted yam and apple purée. Service is friendly; my only complaint is that the tables are a bit too close together, especially if it's crowded.

390 Kasten St. (at Albion St.). ⓒ 707/937-4323. Reservations recommended for dinner. Main courses $13–$19. MC, V. Daily 11:30am–3:30pm; Sun–Thurs 5:30–9pm; Fri–Sat and holidays 5:30–10pm.

INEXPENSIVE

You'd be surprised what $5 will get you for lunch if you know where to go. **Tote Fete Bakery** (© 707/937-3140) has a wonderful carryout booth at the corner of Albion and Lansing streets. I like the foil-wrapped barbecued-chicken sandwiches, but the pizza, focaccia bread, and twice-baked potatoes are also good choices. Dine at the stand-up counter, or opt for a picnic at the headlands down the street.

Regardless of preference—beef, chicken, turkey, or veggie—burger lovers won't be let down at **Mendo Burgers** (© 707/937-1111), arguably the best burger joint on the Northern Coast. A side of thick, fresh-cut fries is mandatory, as is a pile of napkins. Hidden behind the Mendocino Bakery and Café at 10483 Lansing St., it's a little hard to find, but well worth searching out.

In the back of the **Little River Market** (© 707/937-5133), located directly across from the Little River Inn on Calif. 1, is a trio of small tables overlooking the beautiful Mendocino coastline. Order a tamale, sandwich, or whatever else is on the menu at the tiny deli inside the market, or buy a loaf of Café Beaujolais bread sold at the front counter and your favorite spread.

4 Fort Bragg

10 miles N of Mendocino; 176 miles N of San Francisco

As the Mendocino coast's commercial center—hence the site of most of the area's fast-food restaurants and supermarkets—Fort Bragg is far more down-to-earth than Mendocino. Inexpensive motels and cheap eats used to be its only attractions, but over the past few years, gentrification has spread throughout the town as the logging and fishing industries have continued to decline. With no room left to open new shops in Mendocino, many gallery, boutique, and restaurant owners have moved up the road. The result is a huge increase in Fort Bragg's tourist trade, particularly during the Whale Festival in March and Paul Bunyan Days over Labor Day weekend.

To explore the town properly, get a free walking-tour map from the **Fort Bragg/ Mendocino Coast Chamber of Commerce,** 332 N. Main St. (P.O. Box 1141), Fort Bragg, CA 95437 (© 800/726-2780 or 707/961-6300; www.mendocino coast.com). The friendly staff can answer any questions about Mendocino, Fort Bragg, and the surrounding region.

SHOPPING & EXPLORING THE AREA

The town doesn't boast as many well-coiffed stores and galleries as its dainty cousin to the south, but it does have some worthwhile shopping spots. **Antiques shops** line Franklin Street between Laurel and Redwood (aka Antiques Row), and several boutiques are housed within the newly refurbished **Union Lumber Company Store,** an impressive edifice built almost entirely with handcrafted redwoods (on the corner of Main and Redwood sts.).

For the Shell of It, 344 N. Main St. (© 707/961-0461), stocks handmade jewelry, chimes, and collectibles made of shells or designed around a nautical theme, as well as rocks, gems, minerals, and fossils. The **Hot Pepper Jelly Company,** 330 N. Main St. (© 707/961-1899; www.hotpepperjelly.com), is famous for its assortment of Mendocino food products—dozens of varieties of pepper jelly, plus local mustards, syrups, and biscotti along with hand-painted porcelain bowls, baskets, and more. The **Mendocino Chocolate Company,** 542 N. Main St. (© 707/964-8800), makes and sells homemade chocolates and truffles, which it ships all over the world. Painters, jewelers, sculptors, weavers, potters, woodworkers, and other local artists display their works at **Northcoast Artists,** 362 N. Main St. (© 707/964-8266). At **Windsong,** 324 N. Main St. (© 707/ 964-2050), predominantly a nice used-book store, you'll also find a clutter of colorful kites, cards, candles, records, and other gifts.

Fort Bragg is also the home of the **Mendocino Coast Botanical Gardens,** 18220 N. Calif. 1 (© 707/964-4352; www.gardenbythesea.org), about 7 miles north of Mendocino. This cliff-top public garden, set among the pines along the coast, nurtures rhododendrons, fuchsias, azaleas, and a multitude of flowering shrubs. The area has bridges, streams, canyons, dells, picnic areas, and trails for easy walking. Admission is $7.50 for adults, $6 for seniors ages 60 and over, $3 for children 13 to 17, $1 for children 6 to 12, and free for 5 and under. (Children under 18 must be accompanied by an adult.) Open March through October daily from 9am to 5pm, November through February daily from 9am to 4pm.

From Fort Bragg, the **Skunk Train** ☆ (© 800/866-1690 or 707/964-6371; www.skunktrain.com) gives riders a fine tour of the area's redwoods. Locals have always said of the logging trains, "You can smell 'em before you can see 'em," which explains the nickname. The trains, which can be boarded at the Fort Bragg Depot at the foot of Laurel Avenue in Fort Bragg (2 blocks from the Grey Whale Inn), travel inland along Pudding Creek to Northspur. It's a scenic route through the forest, crossing bridges and trestles and cutting through a 1,100-foot tunnel. The trains run trips daily from May 1 to December 31, but call for times as schedules vary. During the summer it's a good idea to make advance reservations. Tickets cost $35 to $45 for a half-day trip, depending on whether you ride the steam or diesel engine; children ages 3 to 11 board for $20. Serious train buffs can ride in the locomotive cab with the engineer for $100. Family packages are also available.

Also worth checking out is the **North Coast Brewing Company,** 455 N. Main St. (© 707/964-2739; www.northcoastbrewing.com), which offers free tours of the brewery Monday through Friday at 1pm. Across the street is the Brewing Company's pub, open for lunch and dinner (see "Where to Dine" below).

OUTDOOR PURSUITS

Fort Bragg is the county's sport-fishing center. Just south of town, **Noyo Fishing Center,** 32440 N. Harbor, Noyo (© 707/964-3000; www.fortbraggfishing. com), is a good place to buy tackle and the best source of information on local fishing boats. Lots of party boats leave from the town's harbor, as do whale-watching tours.

Lost Coast Kayaking, located in Van Damme State Park (© 707/937-2434; www.lostcoastkayaking.com), offers guided kayak tours of the coastline's numerous sea caves. All the necessary equipment is provided; all you need to bring is a bathing suit and $45 for the 2-hour tour (closed during the winter).

Three miles north of Fort Bragg, off Calif. 1, lies **MacKerricher State Park** (© 707/937-5804), a popular place for biking, hiking, and horseback riding. This 1,700-acre park has 142 campsites and 8 miles of shoreline. For a true biking or hiking venture, travel the 8-mile-long "Haul Road," an old logging road (partly washed out, but safe) that provides fine ocean vistas all the way to Ten Mile River. Harbor seals make their home at the park's Laguna Point Seal Watching Station.

WHERE TO STAY

Beachcomber Motel _Value_   If the room rates in Mendocino have you reconsidering a visit to the coast, the Beachcomber Motel may be just what you're looking for. Granted, the plain guest rooms lack the antique and lace you'll find at most B&Bs in the area, but they are spacious, comfortable, and equipped with the necessities. None of this matters, though, since you'll be spending most of your time on the huge back deck that overlooks the Pacific and gorgeous sunsets. Better yet, directly across from the motel are MacKerricher State Park's miles of beaches and dunes. If you really want to save a bundle, get a room with a kitchenette, stock up on groceries, and make use of the large barbecue area. Low-end rates are for a standard room with no ocean view, and the top rate is for the deluxe suite with king bed, Jacuzzi, fireplace, and ocean view. Three units here are wheelchair accessible.

1111 N. Main St., Fort Bragg, CA 95437. © 800/400-7873 or 707/964-2402. Fax 707/964-8925. www.the beachcombermotel.com. 75 units. $79–$250 double. Rates include continental breakfast. AE, DC, DISC, MC, V. Pets accepted with $10 fee. **Amenities:** Exercise room. *In room:* TV/VCR, dataport, kitchenette in suites, fridge, coffeemaker.

Colombi Motel *(Value*   Considering a room here costs about a quarter of the average room rate in Mendocino, the Colombi Motel is a real score. For only 50 bones, you get a lot for your money at this little motel just off Fort Bragg's main strip: It's clean and neat, has all the essentials (including kitchens in some rooms), and you even get your own carport. Families will want to reserve one of the two-bedroom units that sleep up to six. Across the street is a laundromat, a cafe serving good Mexican food, and the Colombi Market, which is where the motel's guests check in and where you can get free ice and coffee.

600 E. Oak St., Fort Bragg, CA 95437. © 707/964-5773 or 707/964-8015. Fax 707/964-5627. 22 units. Winter $35–$85 double; summer $40–$95 double. MC, V. *In room:* TV, kitchen in some units, fridge.

Grey Whale Inn *(Kids*   In downtown Fort Bragg and a short walk from the beach, this B&B was built as a hospital in 1915, hence the wide hallways and large guest rooms. The redwood building is now a well-run, relaxed inn, furnished with antiques, handmade quilts, and plenty of local art. Each room is unique: Two have ocean views, four have fireplaces, one has a whirlpool tub, three have private decks, and one offers a shower with wheelchair access. My favorite is the spacious, elegant Campbell Suite, which comes with a king bed, TV with VCR, and marble gas-log fireplace. The buffet breakfast, served in the Craftsman-style breakfast room (with trays for carrying your food back to bed, if you prefer) includes a hot entree, homemade bread or coffee cake, and fresh fruit. Kids will appreciate the game room with a pool table and foosball table.

615 N. Main St., Fort Bragg, CA 95437. © 800/382-7244 or 707/964-0640. Fax 707/964-4408. www.grey whaleinn.com. 14 units. $130–$230 double. Discounted winter rates available midweek Nov–Mar. Rates include buffet breakfast. AE, MC, V. **Amenities:** Access to nearby health club; game room; in-room massage. *In room:* TV, some units w/VCR, kitchenette, fridge, hair dryer, iron.

WHERE TO DINE

North Coast Brewing Company *(AMERICAN   Since it opened in 1988, this homey brewpub has been the most happening place in town, especially at happy hour, when the bar and dark-wood tables are occupied by boisterous locals. The brewery's proudest achievement was being ranked "1 of the 10 best breweries in the world" in 1998 by the Beverage Testing Institute. The building that houses the pub is a century-old redwood structure, which in previous lives has functioned as a mortuary, an annex to the local Presbyterian church, an art studio, and administration offices for the College of the Redwoods. Nine types of beer are available (to go, even) year-round, in addition to seasonal brews. Standard fare such as burgers and barbecued-chicken sandwiches are supplemented by more substantial dishes, ranging from beef Romanov made with braised sirloin tips, fresh mushrooms, and Russian Imperial Stout, to genuine Carolina barbe-cued pork served with corn cakes and slaw, and a roast Cornish game hen with a raspberry-balsamic glaze. After your meal, browse the shop or take a free tour of the brewery (see "Shopping & Exploring the Area," above).

455 N. Main St. © 707/964-3400. www.northcoastbrewing.com. Reservations accepted for large parties only. Main courses $7–$22. DISC, MC, V. Daily 11:30am–11pm.

The Restaurant *(Kids* PACIFIC NORTHWEST/CALIFORNIA   One of the oldest family-run restaurants on the coast, this unpretentious Fort Bragg land-mark is known for its good dinners and Sunday brunches. The eclectic menu offers dishes from just about every corner of the planet: New York strip steak, a Provençal-style seafood stew, and a few less expensive options like the Asian noo-dle bowl filled with bay shrimp and fresh vegetables. My favorite is the super-fresh blackened rockfish. There are also a few vegetarian specialties, including grilled polenta with melted mozzarella and sautéed mushrooms, topped with tomato-herb sauce and Parmesan cheese. A nicely priced kids' menu is available as well. The booth section is the best place to sit if you want to keep an eye on the entertainment—courtesy of ebullient chef Jim Larsen—in the kitchen.

418 N. Main St. © 707/964-9800. www.therestaurantfortbragg.com. Reservations recommended. Dinner $13–$22; Sun brunch $5–$10. MC, V. Thurs–Tues 5–9pm; Sun brunch 10am–1pm.

Viraporn's Thai Café THAI   Born in northern Thailand, Viraporn Lobell attended cooking school and apprenticed in restaurants there before coming to the United States. After working at Mendocino's Café Beaujolais, she opened her own restaurant in Fort Bragg in 1991, giving local Thai-food fans good reason to cheer. Viraporn works wonders with Thai mainstays such as pad Thai, lemon-grass soup, spring rolls, and satays, all of which have a balance of the five tradi-tional Thai flavors of tart, bitter, hot, sweet, and salty. Viraporn also whips up good curry dishes, best washed down with a cool, supersweet Thai iced tea.

500 S. Main St. (across from PayLess drugstore off Calif. 1). © 707/964-7931. Main courses $3.95–$9.95. No credit cards. Wed–Mon 11:30am–2:30pm and 5–9pm.

5 The Avenue of the Giants (★ (★

From Fort Bragg, Calif. 1 continues north along the shoreline for about 30 miles before turning inland to Leggett and the Redwood Highway (U.S. 101), which runs north to Garberville. Six miles beyond Garberville, the **Avenue of the Giants** (Calif. 254) begins around Phillipsville. The Avenue of the Giants is one of the most spectacular routes in the West, cutting along the Eel River through the 51,000-acre Humboldt Redwoods State Park. It roughly parallels U.S. 101, and there are about a half-dozen interchanges between the two roads if you don't want to drive the whole thing. The avenue ends just south of Scotia; from here, it's only about 10 miles to the turnoff to Ferndale, about 5 miles west of U.S. 101.

For more information or a detailed map of the area, go to the **Humboldt Redwoods State Park Visitor Center** in Weott (© 707/946-2263; www. humboldtredwoods.org), in the center of the Avenue of the Giants.

TOURING THE AVENUE

Thirty-three miles long, the Avenue of the Giants was left intact for sightseers when the freeway was built. The giants are the majestic coast redwoods *(Sequoia sempervirens);* more than 50,000 acres of them make up the most outstanding display in the redwood belt. Their rough-bark columns climb 100 feet or more without a branch and soar to a total height of more than 340 feet. With their fire-resistant bark and immunity to insects, they have survived for thousands of years. The oldest dated coast redwood is more than 2,200 years old.

Sadly, the route has several tacky attractions that attempt to turn the trees into some kind of freak show. My suggestion is to skip these and appreciate the trees by taking advantage of the trails and the campgrounds off the beaten path. As you drive along, you'll see many parking areas with short loop trails leading into the forest. From south to north, the first of these "attractions" is the **Chimney Tree,** where J. R. R. Tolkien's Hobbit is rumored to reside. This living, hollow redwood is more than 1,500 years old. Nearby are a gift shop and a burger place. Then there's the **One-Log House,** a small apartment-like house built inside a log. At Myers Flat midway along the avenue, you can also drive your car through a living redwood at the **Shrine Drive-Thru Tree.**

A few miles north of Weott is **Founders Grove,** named in honor of those who established the Save the Redwoods League in 1918. Farther north, close to the end of the avenue, stands the 950-year-old **Immortal Tree,** just north of Redcrest. Near Pepperwood at the end of the avenue, the **Drury Trail** and the **Percy French Trail** are two good short hikes. The park itself is also good for mountain biking. Ask the rangers for details. For more information, contact Humboldt Redwoods State Park (© **707/946-2409;** www.humboldtredwoods.org).

The state park has three **campgrounds** with 248 campsites: Hidden Springs, half a mile south of Myers Flat; Burlington, 2 miles south of Weott, near park headquarters; and Albee Creek State Campground, 5 miles west of U.S. 101 on the Mattole Road north of Weott. Reservations are advised in the summer months; you can make them online via **ReserveAmerica** at www.reserveamerica. com or call © **800/444-7275.** Remaining sites are on a first-come, first-served basis. You'll also come across picnic and swimming facilities, motels, resorts, restaurants, and numerous rest and parking areas.

WHERE TO STAY & DINE NEAR THE SOUTHERN ENTRANCE

Benbow Inn This elegant National Historic Landmark, overlooking the Eel River and surrounded by gardens, has housed such notables as Eleanor Roosevelt, Herbert Hoover, and Charles Laughton. Constructed in 1926 in a mock-Tudor style, it's named after the family who built it. Guests enter through a grand hall and into the lobby with its huge fireplace surrounded by cushy sofas, grandfather clocks, Oriental carpets, and cherrywood wainscoting. Rooms vary in size and amenities, though all are decorated with period antiques; the deluxe units have fireplaces, Jacuzzis, private entrances, and patios. The Honeymoon Cottage is the most popular accommodation, with its vaulted ceilings, canopy bed, wood-burning fireplace, and private patio overlooking the river. A comfortable annex with elegant woodwork was added in the 1980s. Beautiful Benbow Lake State Park is right out the front door. Complimentary afternoon tea and scones are served in the lobby at 3pm, hors d'oeuvres in the lounge at 5pm, and port wine at 9pm—all very proper, of course. The dramatic high-ceilinged dining room opens onto a spacious terrace and offers internationally inspired (and expensive) main courses. *Tip:* Be sure to request that the housekeeping staff goes light on the "air freshener," which doesn't smell anything like fresh air.

445 Lake Benbow Dr., Garberville, CA 95542. © 800/355-3301 or 707/923-2124. Fax 707/923-2122. www. benbowinn.com. 55 units. $130–$275 double; $350 cottage. AE, DISC, MC, V. **Amenities:** Restaurant; bar; nearby golf course; complimentary bikes; guided day hikes; courtesy car; babysitting (with advance notice). *In room:* A/C, coffeemaker, hair dryer, iron; some units with TV/VCR, minibar, fridge.

FERNDALE ⚐

The village of Ferndale, beyond the Avenue of the Giants and west of U.S. 101, has been declared a National Historic Landmark because of its Victorian homes and storefronts (which include a smithy and a saddlery). About 5 miles inland from the coast and close to the redwood belt, Ferndale is one of the best-preserved Victorian hamlets in Northern California. Despite its unbearably cute shops, it is nonetheless a vital part of the northern coastal tourist circuit.

What's less known about this small town is that it has a number of artists in residence and is home to one of California's oddest happenings, the **World Championship Great Arcata to Ferndale Cross-Country Kinetic Sculpture Race,** a 3-day event held every Memorial Day weekend. The race, which draws more than 10,000 spectators, is run 38 miles over land, sand, mud, and water in whimsically designed, handmade, people-powered vehicles that have to be seen to be believed—dragons, Christmas trees, flying saucers, pyramids to mention but a few. Awards range from Best Art to Best Engineering to Best Bribe, and as the Grand Prizes are worth about $15, inspired madness is the only incentive. Stop in at the museum at 780 Main St. if you want to see a few past race entries, although they're poor, pale facsimiles of the contrivances in glorious action.

WHERE TO STAY

Gingerbread Mansion ⚐⚐ This peach-and-yellow structure with stained glass and other fine details is one of Ferndale's most frequently photographed Victorians. Built in 1899 as the home of a doctor and his family and now run by Ken Torbert, it's beautifully furnished with antiques. Some of the large guest rooms have two old-fashioned claw-foot tubs for bubble baths for two, and others offer fireplaces. My favorite is the attic-level Empire Suite, a spare-no-expense blowout with Ionic columns, massage-jet shower, two fireplaces, and a king-size bed draped with Royal Sateen fabric. The ultraluxurious Veneto Room is also impressive. Bathrobes and thick, extra-large towels are provided. Beds are turned down for the night, and you'll find hand-dipped chocolates on the nightstand. When you rise, there's morning coffee or tea outside your door, enough to sustain you until your breakfast of fruit, cheese, muffins, breads, cakes, and a baked egg dish. Afternoon tea with sandwiches, pastries, and fresh fruit are also served. *Tip:* Even if you're not staying in Ferndale, it's worth stopping by for a tour, scheduled from noon to 4pm daily.

400 Berding St. (P.O. Box 40), Ferndale, CA 95536. ℂ **800/952-4136** or 707/786-4000. Fax 707/786-4381. www.gingerbread-mansion.com. 11 units. $150–$210 double; $170–$385 suite. Extra person $40. Rates include full breakfast and afternoon tea. AE, MC, V. **Amenities:** Concierge; activities desk. *In room:* Hair dryer, no phone.

Shaw House Inn Bed and Breakfast ⚐⚐ Modeled after the titular manse of Hawthorne's House of the Seven Gables, this gorgeous B&B is the oldest structure in Ferndale, the oldest B&B in California, and one of the prettiest Victorian homes I've ever seen (and I've seen a *lot* of B&Bs). It was built in 1854 by Ferndale founder Seth Louis Shaw, who obviously had a penchant for jutting gables, bay windows, balconies, and gazebos. Each of the eight individually decorated guest rooms is handsomely furnished with period antiques, plush fabrics, and—rare for a 19th-century B&B—private bathrooms. Four rooms have private entrances, and three have private balconies overlooking the cottage garden. My favorite is the romantic Fountain Suite, which has its own fireplace (I'm a sucker for a fireplace), parlor, and claw-foot tub. The immaculate flower-filled lawns and fish pond are shaded by 25 varieties of majestic trees, and the restaurants and shops along Main Street are a short walk away.

703 Main St., Ferndale, CA 95536. ℭ 800/557-SHAW or 707/786-9958. Fax 707/786-9758. www.shawhouse. com. 8 units. $85–$225 Nov–Mar; $100–$245 Apr–Oct. Rates include breakfast and afternoon tea. DISC, MC, V. Checks accepted. **Amenities:** 1-acre garden; gift shop; game table. *In room:* Private bathroom, antique furnishings, wireless Internet access.

WHERE TO DINE

Curley's Grill ✿ CALIFORNIA GRILL   This bright and lively restaurant specializes in California-inspired grilled foods, but don't think for a moment that the menu is limited to steaks, prime rib, and fall-off-the-bone baby back ribs. Owner Curley Tait also grills up such items as portobello-mushroom towers, pork loin with caramelized onion sauce, polenta with a sausage-tomato sauce, crab cakes, and some of the freshest seafood and vegetables on the California coast. Curley has added homemade breads and desserts to the menu as well. Curley's also offers an interesting selection of California wines, and has a Victorian-style full bar area. On sunny afternoons, request a seat on the shaded back patio.

400 Ocean St., inside the Victorian Inn. ℭ 707/786-9696. www.restaurant.com/curleysgrill. Main courses $9–$18. DISC, MC, V. Daily 11:30am–9pm; breakfast Sat–Sun 8–11am.

6 Eureka & Environs ✿

296 miles N of San Francisco

EUREKA

On first glance, Eureka (pop. 27,000) doesn't look very appealing: Fast-food restaurants, cheap motels, and shopping malls predominate on the main thoroughfare. But if you turn west off U.S. 101 anywhere between A and M streets, you'll discover **Old Town Eureka** along the waterfront, which is worth exploring. It has a large number of Victorian buildings, a museum, and some good-quality stores and restaurants.

The city's newest development is a waterfront boardwalk between C and F streets, adjacent to the Old Town historic district. The boardwalk opens a section of the waterfront that was previously closed to the public, offering sweeping views of the harbor and bay.

For more visitor information, contact or visit the **Eureka/Humboldt County Convention and Visitors Bureau,** 1034 Second St., Eureka, CA 95501 (ℭ **800/ 346-3482** or 707/443-5097; www.redwoodvisitor.org), or the **Eureka Chamber of Commerce,** 2112 Broadway, Eureka, CA 95501 (ℭ **800/356-6381** or 707/442-3738; www.eurekachamber.com).

WHAT TO SEE & DO

The **Clarke Memorial Museum,** 240 E St. (ℭ **707/443-1947**), has a fine collection of Native American baskets and other artifacts. The other popular attraction is the architectural gem, the **Carson Mansion** ✿ (on the corner of Second and M sts.), built from 1884 to 1886 for lumber baron William Carson. A three-story conglomeration of ornamentation, its design is a mélange of styles—Queen Anne, Italianate, Stick, and Eastlake. It took 100 men over 2 years to build. Today it's a private club, so you can only marvel at the exterior of this 18-room mansion—said to be the most photographed Victorian home in the United States. Across the street stands the **Pink Lady,** designed for William Carson as a wedding present for his son. Both testify to the wealth that was once made in Eureka's lumber trade. As early as 1856, there were seven sawmills producing 2 million board feet of lumber every month. A meticulously restored building now houses the **Morris Graves Museum of Art,** 636 F St. (ℭ **707/442-0278;**

www.thepalette.com), with four galleries showcasing local artists as well as traveling exhibitions.

If you're in need of a good read, drop in at the **Booklegger,** 402 Second St., at E St. (© 707/445-1344), a fantastic bookstore in Old Town with thousands of used paperbacks (especially mysteries, westerns, and science fiction), children's books, and cookbooks.

Humboldt Bay, where the town stands, was discovered by settlers in 1850. In 1853, Fort Humboldt was established to protect them from local Native American communities. Ulysses S. Grant was stationed here for 5 months until he resigned after disputes with his commanding officer about his drinking. The fort was abandoned in 1870. Today there's a self-guided trail past a series of logging exhibits, plus a reconstructed surgeon's quarters and a restored fort hospital, used today as a museum housing Native American artifacts and military and pioneer paraphernalia. **Fort Humboldt State Historic Park** is located at 3431 Fort Ave. (© 707/445-6567). Admission is free; it's open daily from 8am to 5pm.

OUTDOOR PURSUITS

Humboldt Bay supplies a large portion of California's fish, and Eureka has a fishing fleet of about 200 boats. To get a better view (and perspective) of the bay and surrounding waters, you can board skipper Leroy Zerlang's *Madaket*—a state historic landmark and the oldest passenger-carrying vessel in continuous service in the United States—for a 75-minute narrated **Humboldt Bay Harbor Cruise,** departing from the foot of L Street in downtown Eureka daily at 1 and 2:30pm. Tickets are about $10 per person, free for children ages 4 and under. The *Madaket* also has the smallest licensed bar in California, and to celebrate this fact, there's an hour-long casual cocktail cruise Tuesday through Saturday at 5:30pm and a Sunday Champagne Brunch Cruise. Call © 707/445-1910 for a recorded departure schedule.

For more active water recreation, kayaks, canoes, and sailboats can be rented from **Hum Boats** Friday through Monday from 9am to 5pm at the foot of F Street (© 707/443-5157; www.humboats.com). Tours and lessons are available as well.

Humboldt County is suitable for biking because it's relatively uncongested. Bikes can be rented from **Pro Sport Center,** 508 Myrtle Ave. (© 707/443-6328). Fishing, diving, biking, and hiking information are also available here.

Humboldt Bay is an important stopover point along the Pacific Flyway and is the winter home for thousands of migratory birds. South of town, the **Humboldt Bay National Wildlife Refuge** ⚐, 1020 Ranch Rd., Loleta (© 707/733-5406), provides an opportunity to see many of the 200 or so species that live in the marshes and willow groves—including Pacific black brant, western sandpiper, northern harrier, great blue heron, and green-winged teal. The egret rookery on the bay, best viewed from Woodley Island Marina across the bay, is spectacular. Peak viewing for most species of water birds and raptors is between September and March. The refuge's entrance is off U.S. 101 north at the Hookton Road exit. Cross the overpass and turn right onto Ranch Road.

WHERE TO STAY

Abigail's Elegant Victorian Mansion Bed & Breakfast ⚐   For anyone interested in Victorian history and design, this is a special experience; those who just want comfort, service, a gourmet breakfast, and a beautiful garden will also find this lodging ideal. The 1888 house, a National Historic Landmark, is the labor of love of owners Doug and Lily Vieyra, who have combed the country for the fabrics and designs that provide the most authentic Victorian atmosphere I have encountered in the U.S. The wallpapers are extraordinary—brilliant blues, golds, jades, and reds in patterns that feature peacocks and mythological figures. Doug pays attention to every detail, from the butler who greets you in morning dress to the silent movies and period music on the phonograph. Each unit is individually furnished: The Van Gogh room contains the Belgian bedroom suite of Lily's mother. The Lily Langtry room, named after the actress and king's mistress who stayed here when she performed locally, features a four-poster bed and Langtry memorabilia. Guests can play croquet on the manicured lawn, where ice-cream sodas and lemonade are served in the afternoon.

1406 C St. (at 14th St.), Eureka, CA 95501. (C) 707/444-3144. Fax 707/442-3295. www.eureka-california. com. 4 units. $95–$215 double. Additional person $40–$50. Rates include breakfast. MC, V. **Amenities:** Sauna; complimentary bikes; massage; laundry service. In room: A/C.

Hotel Carter, Carter House, Bell Cottage, and Carter Cottage ★★★

At the north end of Eureka's Old Town is the building that launched Carter's renowned hostelry empire: the Carter House. Copied from an 1884 San Francisco Victorian, it was built by Mark Carter as a family home in 1982. Soon afterwards, Mark and his wife, Christi Carter, began taking guests, and before long they built a stately hotel across the street, the Hotel Carter. Later, the pretty Victorian Bell Cottage was acquired, and most recently the ultraluxurious Carter Cottage.

The 23 rooms in the large, full-service Hotel Carter have beautiful modern furnishings and pine four-posters. The suites have such luxury appointments as fireplaces and Jacuzzis, and distant views of the waterfront can be seen from the tubs. There are seven rooms in the original Carter House, which is furnished with antiques, Oriental rugs, and modern artwork. The Bell Cottage's rooms are also individually decorated in grand Victorian fashion. If you really want to splurge, reserve the Carter Cottage, a small home that's been converted into one of the most luxurious lodgings in Northern California, a minimansion with a chef's kitchen, two fireplaces, a grand bathroom with a whirlpool tub for two, a private deck, and a wine cellar. The foursome of inn, hotel, and two cottages offers a contrasting array of luxury accommodations, ranging from classic Victorian in the house and cottage to a softer, brighter, more contemporary look in the hotel. On the ground level of the Hotel Carter is one of Eureka's finest restaurants, **Restaurant 301** (see "Where to Dine" below), where a full breakfast—included in the room rate—is served each morning.

301 L St., Eureka, CA 95501. (C) 800/404-1390 or 707/444-8062. Fax 707/444-8067. www.carterhouse.com. 32 units. $125–$187 double; $297–$326 suite; $497 Carter Cottage. Packages available. AE, DC, DISC, MC, V. From U.S. 101 N., turn left onto L St. and go to Third St. **Amenities:** Restaurant; nearby golf course; activities desk; in-room massage; babysitting; laundry service; wine shop. In room: A/C, TV/VCR w/pay movies, kitchen in some units, hair dryer, iron.

WHERE TO DINE

Ramone's Bakery & Cafe _Value_ BAKERY   Ramone's combines a bakery on one side with a small dining room on the other. The baked items are extraordinary: croissants, Danishes, cinnamon rolls, truffles, muffins—all made from scratch every morning without preservatives or dough conditioners. The bakery also prepares soups, salads, and huge sandwiches, plus a few lunch specials such as lasagna and quiche. At any time of the day, it's a great place to stop in for a light, inexpensive meal and cup of coffee. There's a second bakery location at 2223 Harrison St., in Eureka, as well as one in Arcata at 747 13th St., at Wildberries Marketplace.

209 E St. (in Old Town). ℭ 707/445-2923. www.ramonesbakery.com. Main courses $4–$6. No credit cards.
Mon–Sat 7am–6pm; Sun 7am–4pm.

Restaurant 301 ℛℛℛ CALIFORNIA The large, light, and airy dining
room adjacent to the hotel's lobby has tall windows looking out on the waterfront. It's the best restaurant in the area, with most of the herbs and many of the
vegetables picked fresh from the hotel's organic gardens across the street. At dinner, diners may order either a la carte or off the Discovery Menu, a highly recommended prix-fixe five-course menu that pairs each course with suggested
wines by the glass. A typical dinner might begin with an artichoke, green lentil,
and fennel salad, followed by a warm chèvre cake appetizer, then on to a grilled
duck breast served with a seasonal fruit and zinfandel sauce. The cuisine also displays Asian accents, as in the chicken with spicy peanut sauce and the tiger
prawns with sesame, ginger, and soy. If you're an oyster lover, start with a few
Humboldt Bay oysters roasted with barbecue sauce. There's an excellent and
extensive wine list (a Grand Award recipient from *Wine Spectator* magazine),
courtesy of the 301 Wine Shop within the hotel, and a wine bar.

In the Hotel Carter, 301 L St. ℭ 800/404-1390 or 707/444-8062. Reservations recommended. Main courses
$18–$26. AE, DC, DISC, MC, V. Breakfast daily 7:30–10am; dinner daily 6–9pm.

Samoa Cookhouse ℛ *Finds* AMERICAN During the lumber industry's heyday, cookhouses (like this one dating from 1885) were common, serving as community centers. Here the mill men and longshoremen came to chow down on
three hot meals before, during, and after their 12-hour workday. The food is still
hearty—though not necessarily healthy by today's standards—and served family-style at long tables covered with red-checkered cloths. Nobody leaves hungry.
The price includes soup, salad, fresh-baked bread, the main course, and dessert
(usually pie). The lunch-and-dinner menu still features a different dish each
day—roast beef, fried or barbecued chicken, ham, or pork chops. Breakfast typically includes eggs, potatoes, sausage, bacon, pancakes, and all the orange juice
and coffee you can drink. Adjacent to the dining room is a small museum featuring memorabilia from the lumbering era. This is the last cookhouse in the
West, so bring the kids before it vanishes into history.

Cookhouse Rd., Samoa. ℭ 707/442-1659. www.humboldtdining.com/cookhouse. Reservations accepted
for large groups only. Main courses $7.45–$12. AE, DISC, MC, V. Mon–Sat 7am–3:30pm and 5–10pm; Sun
7am–10pm (closes 1 hr. earlier in winter). From U.S. 101, take Samoa Bridge to the end and turn left on Samoa
Rd., then take the 1st left.

ARCATA ℛ

From Eureka it's only 7 miles to Arcata, one of my favorite towns on the Northern Coast. Sort of a cross between Mayberry and Berkeley, it has an undeniable
small-town flavor—right down to the bucolic town square—yet it possesses that
intellectual and environmentally conscious esprit de corps so characteristic of
university towns (Arcata is the home of Humboldt State University).

There are loads of family-type things to do. On Wednesday, Friday, and Saturday evenings between June and July, Arcata's semi-pro baseball team, the
Humboldt Crabs, play at Arcata Ballpark (ℭ 707/822-3619), at Ninth and F
streets. Also worth a stop: the kid-friendly **Humboldt State University Natural
History Museum,** 1315 G St. (ℭ 707/826-4479), which is open Tuesday
through Saturday from 10am to 5pm; **Tin Can Mailman,** at 10th and H streets
(ℭ 707/822-1307), a used-book store with more than 130,000 titles; **Redwood Park** (east end of 11th St.), which has an outstanding playground for kids
and miles of forested hiking trails; and the **Humboldt Brewing Company,** 10th

and I streets (© **707/826-BREW;** www.humbrew.com), creators of the heavenly Red Nectar Ale (call for tour information).

Some 40 miles east of Eureka and a few miles north of the town of Willow Creek lies the Hoopa Indian Reservation. In the Hoopa Shopping Center, the **Hoopa Tribal Museum** (© **530/625-4110**) archives the culture and history of the native people of Northern California, including their ceremonial regalia, basketry, canoes, and tools. Guided tours of Hoopa Valley's historic sites, including the traditional village of Takimildiñ, are available through the museum by appointment. Hours are Monday through Friday from 8am to noon and 1 to 5pm year-round, and in summer on Saturday from 10am to noon and 1 to 4pm.

OUTDOOR PURSUITS

The **Arcata Marsh and Wildlife Sanctuary** ℱ, at the foot of South I Street (© **707/826-2359**), is a thought-provoking excursion. The 154-acre sanctuary—which doubles as Arcata's integrated wetland wastewater treatment plant—is a stopover for marsh wrens, egrets, and other waterfowl, including the rare Arctic loon. Every Saturday at 8:30am and 2pm, there are free 1-hour guided tours starting at the cul-de-sac at the foot of South I Street. Or just pick up a free self-guided walking tour map of the preserve, available at the Arcata Chamber of Commerce, 1062 G St., at 11th St. (© **707/822-3619**). The town populace is proud of its wastewater solution, boasting "Arcata Residents Flush with Pride."

Heading east from Arcata, Calif. 299 leads to the Trinity River in **Six Rivers National Forest.** Willow Creek and Somes Bar are the recreational centers for the area. Visitors can sign up for canoeing, rafting, and kayaking trips with such outfitters as **Aurora River Adventures,** in Willow Creek (© **800/562-8475** or 530/629-3843), which offers some offbeat, educationally oriented excursions that are great for kids, as well as gnarly Class V trips for the more daring. They also rent equipment for self-guided adventures.

WHERE TO STAY

Hotel Arcata *Value*   This is the town's most prominent hotel, and many guests are parents visiting their offspring at Humboldt State University. If you're not inclined to stay at the fancier Lady Anne B&B (see review below), this is definitely the next best choice. Located at the northeast corner of the town plaza, the Hotel Arcata consists of a handsome early-1900s brick facade and an appealing lobby. The individually decorated rooms range from small, inexpensive singles to large executive suites that overlook the plaza. The minisuites are the quietest, and a bargain at about $90. On the premises, under different management, is a Japanese restaurant called **Tomo.**

708 Ninth St., Arcata, CA 95521. © 800/344-1221 or 707/826-0217. Fax 707/826-1737. www.hotelarcata. com. 32 units. $66–$110 double; $116–$138 executive suite. Rates include continental breakfast. AE, DC, DISC, MC, V. Pets accepted with $5-a-day fee and $50 deposit. **Amenities:** Restaurant; free passes to nearby indoor pool and health club; salon; executive suites. *In room:* TV, dataport, coffeemaker.

The Lady Anne ℱ   Easily Arcata's finest lodging, this Queen Anne–style bed-and-breakfast is kept in top-notch condition by innkeepers Sharon Ferrett and Sam Pennisi, who also served a term as Arcata's mayor. The large, cozy guest rooms are individually decorated with antiques, lace curtains, Oriental rugs, and English stained glass. For second honeymooners, there's the Lady Sarah Angela Room with its four-poster bed and bay view. Breakfast (request the Belgian waffles) is served in the grand dining room, warmed on winter mornings by a toasty fire. On summer afternoons you can lounge on the veranda with a book or play a game of croquet on the front lawn. Several good dining options are only a few blocks away at Arcata Plaza.

902 14th St., Arcata, CA 95521. © 707/822-2797. www.arcataplaza.com/lodging. 5 units. $100–$120 double. Rates include breakfast. MC, V. *In room:* Hair dryer, iron, no phone.

WHERE TO DINE

Abruzzi ⊛ ITALIAN   The best way to review your dining options in Arcata is to stroll to Jacoby's Storehouse, a mid-19th-century brick warehouse at the southwest corner of the town plaza, and ponder the menus posted outside the Abruzzi and Plaza Grill (see below). Abruzzi—named after a region of central Italy—is generally acknowledged as the best Italian restaurant in town (it certainly smells good when you walk in). It's a romantic setting, replete with dark woods and dim lighting. Meals begin with a basket of warm bread sticks, focaccia and a baguette from a local bakery. Specialties include range-fed veal piccata and sea scallops with langostinos tossed with cheese tortellini. Well-seasoned filet steaks are available as well. The standout dessert is the chocolate paradiso, a dense chocolate cake set in a pool of champagne mousseline.

Jacoby's Storehouse (at the corner of Eighth and H sts.). © 707/826-2345. www.abruzzicatering.com. Reservations recommended. Main courses $9–$22. AE, DISC, MC, V. Daily 5:30–9pm.

Folie Douce ⊛ BISTRO   Humboldt Hip meets Cuisine Chic at Folie Douce, the most energized and inventive restaurant in town. Designer wood-oven-fired pizza is its mainstay, like the grilled duck sausage fennel, chèvre, and sun-dried tomato pizza, or the spicy shrimp with fontina, mozzarella, and scallion combo. The appetizers and entrees are equally intriguing. The highlight of your vacation may well be the artichoke-heart cheesecake appetizer, followed by a plate of grilled wild-rice polenta in a light cream sauce. Other heartier menu items range from brandy-flambéed filet mignon topped with Roquefort cheese and green peppercorns, to the rosemary and mustard grilled lamb chops topped with a roasted garlic and red-wine demi-glace. The restaurant has a serious wine list. This small, festive eatery is extremely popular, so be sure to make reservations.

1551 G St. (between 15th and 16th sts.). © 707/822-1042. www.holyfolie.com. Reservations recommended. Main courses $9–$27. AE, DISC, MC, V. Tues–Thurs 5:30–9pm; Fri–Sat 5:30–10pm.

Plaza Grill *(Kids* AMERICAN   If the prices at Abruzzi are a bit more than you care to spend, consider the Plaza Grill, directly above Abruzzi. Despite efforts to make it more upscale, it can't seem to shake its image as a college-student burger joint, albeit a nice one. The menu is more substantial than you'd think, with a choice of salads, sandwiches, burgers, fish platters, chicken specialties, steaks, and all kinds of coffee drinks. There's a very reasonably priced children's menu.

Jacoby's Storehouse (at the corner of Eighth and H sts.). © 707/826-0860. Main courses $7–$17. AE, DISC, MC, V. Sun–Thurs 5–8:30pm; Fri 5–11pm; Sat 5–10:30pm.

TRINIDAD & PATRICK'S POINT STATE PARK ⊛

Back on U.S. 101 north of Arcata, you'll come to **Trinidad,** a tiny coastal fishing village of 400 people. One of the smallest incorporated cities in California, it's on a peninsula 25 miles north of Eureka. If you're not into fishing, there's little to do in town except poke around at the handful of shops, walk along the busy pier, and wish you owned a house here.

Five miles north of Trinidad takes you to the 640-acre **Patrick's Point State Park** ⊛, 4150 Patrick's Point Dr. (© **707/677-3570**), which has one of the finest ocean access points in the north at **Agate Beach.** It's suitable for driftwood picking, rockhounding, and camping on a sheltered bluff. The park contains a re-creation of a Sumeg village, which is used by the Yurok people and neigh-boring tribes. A self-guided tour takes you to replicas of family homes and sweat houses.

WHERE TO STAY

The Lost Whale Bed & Breakfast Inn ★★ *(Kids)*   This modern version of a blue-and-gray Cape Cod–style house is on 4 acres of seafront studded with firs, alders, spruces, and redwoods. Its very friendly owners welcome children (there's a playground and playhouse on the lawn) as well as romantically inclined cou-ples (on the back deck there's a very inviting Jacuzzi with a view of the sea), and they claim it's the only hotel in the state of California with its own private beach with tide pools and sea lions. Five of the inn's eight soundproof rooms have pri-vate balconies or sitting alcoves with views of the Pacific, two rooms have sepa-rate sleeping lofts, and all have private bathrooms and queen-size beds. In the morning you'll marvel at the huge breakfasts prepared by the resident cook: casseroles, quiches, home-baked muffins, fresh fruit, and locally smoked salmon.

3452 Patrick's Point Dr., Trinidad, CA 95570. (℃) **800/677-7859** or 707/677-3425. Fax 707/677-0284. www. lostwhaleinn.com. 8 units. Summer $170–$200 double; winter $140–$170 double. Rates include country breakfast and afternoon tea. AE, DISC, MC, V. **Amenities:** Oceanview Jacuzzi; children's playground and play-house; game room; business center. *In room:* No phone.

Trinidad Bay Bed & Breakfast ★   Set 175 feet above the ocean, all the rooms at this Cape Cod–style home have sweeping views of Trinidad Bay. On a clear day you can see up to 65 miles of the rugged coastline. Your hosts are Cor-lene and Don Blue (Cordon Blue to their friends), two innkeepers who have cre-ated what many visitors think is the most charming inn around. Rare for an older B&B, all the rooms have private bathrooms. Decor throughout is an eclec-tic mix of New England–style antiques and a collection of antique clocks. If it's available, opt for the Mauve Fireplace Suite, with its wraparound window, wood-burning fireplace, king-size bed, and private entrance. A full breakfast is served at 8:30am and features entrees such as French toast puff and Italian egg pie served with fresh and baked fruit and homemade breads. *Note:* The inn is open daily March through November, weekends and for special events only December through February.

560 Edwards St. (P.O. Box 849), Trinidad, CA 95570-0849. (℃) **707/677-0840.** Fax 707/677-9245. www. trinidadbaybnb.com. 4 units. Summer $150–$180 double; winter $135–$165 double. Rates include breakfast. MC, V. *In room:* Fridge, coffeemaker, hair dryer, iron, no phone.

Trinidad Inn *(Value)*   There's a bevy of inexpensive motels in these parts, but the Trinidad Inn is the best of the lot. It's 2 miles north of Trinidad on a serene stretch of road ensconced by a towering cadre of redwoods. Both the motel's exte-rior—trimmed in shades of white and blue—and guest rooms are impeccably maintained. Each room is unique: Some are family units that hold up to four per-sons, while others offer a comfortable queen bed and private bathroom for as lit-tle as $70 per night (access to the adjoining kitchen is an extra $10). A good room for couples is no. 10, an adorable little cottage complete with a full kitchen, liv-ing room, private bathroom, bedroom, and small patio. Each morning fresh cof-fee, tea, and homemade raspberry scones and muffins are served under the gazebo in the flower-filled garden. Guests are free to use the picnic table and barbecue, or wander through the adjacent forest to the beaches a short stroll away.

1170 Patrick's Point Dr., Trinidad, CA 95570. (℃) **707/677-3349.** www.trinidadinn.com. 10 units. $70–$130 double. Rates include continental breakfast. AE, DC, DISC, MC, V. From U.S. 101, take the Trinidad exit and head 2 miles north on Patrick's Point Dr. Pets accepted with $10 fee and $20 deposit. *In room:* TV, no phone.

WHERE TO DINE

Larrupin Café 👉👉 AMERICAN   On a quiet country road 2 miles north of Trinidad, this popular and beautifully decorated restaurant sports an eclectic blend of Indonesian and African artifacts mingled with colorful urns full of exotic flowers and candlelit tables. The patio with a reflecting pool and bamboo fencing is a charmer, and the wood-burning fireplace gives off welcome warmth in the winter. Dinner starts with an appetizer board stocked with gravlax, pâté, dark pumpernickel, apple slices, and sauce, followed by a red- and green-leaf salad tossed with a Gorgonzola vinaigrette. Many menu items are barbecued over mesquite fires, such as a hefty cut of halibut basted with lemon butter and served with mustard-flavored dill sauce, and pork ribs served with a side of sweet-and-spicy barbecue sauce. Another recommended dish is the barbecued Cornish game hen with an orange-and-brandy glaze. For appetizers, go with the barbecued oysters, and for dessert it's either a slice of pecan-chocolate pie topped with hot buttered rum sauce, or the sinfully good triple-layer chocolate cake layered with caramel and whipped cream. *Note:* They don't take credit cards and the hours tend to vary seasonally, so be sure to call ahead and bring plenty of cash.

1658 Patrick's Point Dr. ⓒ 707/677-0230. Reservations recommended. Main courses $15–$22. No credit cards. Thurs–Mon 10am–2pm (coffee and light dishes only) and 5–9pm.

The Seascape Restaurant *(Finds)* CALIFORNIA   Established in the 1940s, this is an unpretentious cross between a cafe and a diner, with three dining rooms, ocean views, overworked but cheerful waitresses, and a nostalgic aura. Folks pop in for coffee or snacks from early morning until after sundown, but by far the biggest seller here is the Trinidad Bay Platter ($18). Heaped with halibut, scallops, and shrimp, and accompanied by salad and rice pilaf, it's even more popular than the excellent prawn brochette. How fresh is the fish? As the menu states, "Availability of seafood depends on Season, Weather conditions, Regulations and Luck." Halibut, rock cod, sole, and other local catches can be prepared in six different styles, including charbroiled and sautéed in garlic, onions, and mushrooms. For you late-risers, breakfast is served until 4pm.

Beside the pier at the foot of Bay St. ⓒ 707/677-3762. Full dinners $9.50–$22. DISC, MC, V. Daily 7am–9pm.

ORICK

From Trinidad, it's about another 15 miles to Orick. You can't miss it: Just look for the dozens of burl stands alongside the road. Carved with chisels and chain saws, these former redwood logs have been transformed into just about every creature you can imagine—perhaps a gift for your mother-in-law?

At the south end of Orick is the **Redwood National Park Information Center** 👉 (ⓒ **707/464-6101,** ext. 5265; www.nps.gov/redw). If you plan to spend any amount of time in the park, stop here and pick up a free map; the displays of fauna and wildlife aren't bad, either. It's open daily from 9am to 5pm.

The first of the parks that make up Redwood National Park, Prairie Creek, is 6 miles north of Orick. About 14 miles farther on is the mouth of the **Klamath River,** famous for its salmon, trout, and steelhead. Tours aboard a jet boat take visitors upriver from the estuary to view bear, deer, elk, osprey, hawks, otters, and more along the riverbanks. Rates for the 30-mile scenic trip (offered May 1–Oct 30) are $25 for adults, $12 for children ages 4 to 11, and free for kids under 4. For more information and reservations, contact **Klamath River Jet Boat Tours,** Klamath (ⓒ **800/887-JETS** or 707/482-5822; www.jetboattours.com).

A more serene alternative to exploring the Klamath is taking a ranger-led **kayak tour.** Offered only during the summer months (and only if they have enough money in their budget), the trip costs about $50 and includes all the requisite kayak gear. For more information, call the Redwood National Park Information Center at the phone number listed above.

From Klamath, it's another 20 miles to Crescent City, gateway to the other parks that make up Redwood National Park.

7 Crescent City

79 miles N of Eureka; 375 miles N of San Francisco

Crescent City itself has little to offer, but it makes a good base for exploring Redwood National Park and the Smith River, one of the great recreational rivers of the West. The **Battery Point Lighthouse,** at the foot of A Street (© **707/464-3089;** www.lighthousefriends.com), which is accessible on foot only at low tide, houses a museum with exhibits on the coast's history. Tours of the lighthouse ($2 for adults, 50¢ for children 12 and under) are offered Wednesday through Sunday from 10am to 4pm, tides permitting, April through September.

Another draw is the **Smith River National Recreation Area** ☆, east of Jedediah Smith State Park and part of Six Rivers National Forest. The Area Headquarters is at 10600 U.S. 199, Gasquet (© **707/457-3131**), reached via U.S. 199 from Crescent City (about a 30-min. drive). You can get maps of the forest at the Supervisor's Office in Eureka, or at either of the Redwood National Park centers in Orick and Crescent City.

The 300,000-plus acres of wilderness offer camping at five modest-size campgrounds (all with fewer than 50 sites) along the Smith River. Sixteen trails attract hikers from across the country. The easiest short trail is the **McClendon Ford,** which is 2 miles long and drops from 1,000 to 800 feet in elevation to the south fork of the river. Other activities include mountain biking, white-water rafting, kayaking, and fishing for salmon and trout.

For information, contact the **Crescent City–Del Norte County Chamber of Commerce,** 1001 Front St., Crescent City, CA 95531 (© **800/343-8300** or 707/464-3174; www.northerncalifornia.net).

WHERE TO STAY

Crescent Beach Motel *(Value*   Crescent City doesn't have any fancy hotels or bed-and-breakfasts, but it does have lots of modestly priced motels, the best of which is the Crescent Beach Motel. Near the highway, about a mile south of town, this single-story structure is the only local motel on the beach. The freshly remodeled and refurbished rooms are clean and simple. Four of the units face the highway; try to get one of the others, all of which have sliding glass doors to decks and a small lawn area overlooking the bay. One of the city's most popular restaurants, the **Beachcomber** (see "Where to Dine" below), is next door.

1455 Redwood Hwy. S. (U.S. 101), Crescent City, CA 95531. © 707/464-5436. www.crescentbeachmotel. com. 27 units. Summer $73–$85 double; winter $50–$59 double. AE, DISC, MC, V. *In room:* TV, no phone.

Curly Redwood Lodge *(Value*   This is a blast from the past, the kind of place you might have stayed at as a kid during a cross-country vacation in the family station wagon. It was built in 1957 on grasslands across from the harbor, and is trimmed with lumber from a single ancient redwood. Although they're not full of high-tech gadgets, the bedrooms are among the largest and best-soundproofed in town, and certainly the most evocative of a bygone age. In winter about a third of the rooms (the ones upstairs) are locked and sealed. Overall, the aura is more akin to Oregon than what you might imagine in California. I still prefer the on-the-beach rooms at the Crescent Beach Motel, but the Curly is a solid bet for a clean, comfortable, and inexpensive hotel room.

701 Redwood Hwy. S. (U.S. 101), Crescent City, CA 95531. ℂ 707/464-2137. Fax 707/464-1655. www.curly redwoodlodge.com. 36 units. Summer $60–$86 double; winter $39–$68 double. Winter rates include break-fast. AE, DC, MC, V. *In room:* TV.

WHERE TO DINE

Beachcomber SEAFOOD   The decor is as nautical as the name implies: rough-cut planking and a scattering of driftwood, fishnets, and buoys dangling above a dimly lit space. The restaurant is beside the beach, 2 miles south of Crescent City's center. The cuisine is a joy to fish lovers who prefer not to mask the flavor of their seafood with complicated sauces. Most of the dishes are grilled over madrone-wood barbecue pits, a technique perfected since this place was established in 1975. Freshly harvested Pacific salmon, halibut, lingcod, shark, sturgeon, Pacific snapper, oysters, and steamer clams have visitors lining up, especially on weekends. The Beachcomber also serves great flame-broiled steaks; thick cuts of prime rib are the special every Saturday and Sunday.

1400 U.S. 101. ℂ 707/464-2205. Reservations recommended. Main courses $6–$15. MC, V. Thurs–Tues 5–9pm. Closed Dec–Jan and part of Feb.

Harbor View Grotto Restaurant & Lounge SEAFOOD/STEAKS   This friendly local restaurant has been specializing in fresh seafood at market prices since 1961. Its food's not as good as the Beachcomber's, but it's a little less expensive, it's open for lunch, and it's far less crowded on weekend nights. The "light eaters" menu includes a choice of a cup of white chowder (made fresh daily) or salad, a main course, and vegetables; heartier appetites can choose from among three different cuts of prime rib. Menu items include fresh, locally caught fish like Pacific snapper and salmon. Crab or shrimp Louis, as well as crabmeat or shrimp sandwiches, are popular in season.

150 Starfish Way. ℂ 707/464-3815. Reservations recommended. Main courses $4–$9 lunch, $6–$20 din-ner. DISC, MC, V. Daily 11:30am–9pm, later in the summer months.

8 Redwood National & State Parks ⭑⭑

40 miles N of Eureka; 336 miles N of San Francisco

It's impossible to explain the feeling you get in the old-growth forests of Redwood National and State Parks without resorting to Alice-in-Wonderland comparisons. Like a tropical rainforest, the redwood forest is a multistoried affair, the tall trees just the top layer. Everything seems big, misty, and primeval—flowering bushes cover the ground, 10-foot-tall ferns line the creeks, and the smells are rich and musty. It's so *Jurassic Park* you half expect to turn the corner and see a dinosaur.

When Archibald Menzies first noted the botanical existence of the coast red-wood in 1794, more than 2 million acres of redwood forest carpeted California and Oregon. By 1965, heavy logging had reduced that to 300,000 acres, and it was obvious something had to be done if any were to survive. The state created several parks around individual groves in the 1920s, and in 1968 the federal gov-ernment created Redwood National Park. In May 1994 the National Park Service and the California Department of Parks and Recreation signed an agreement to manage these four redwood parks cooperatively, hence the Redwood National *and* State Parks.

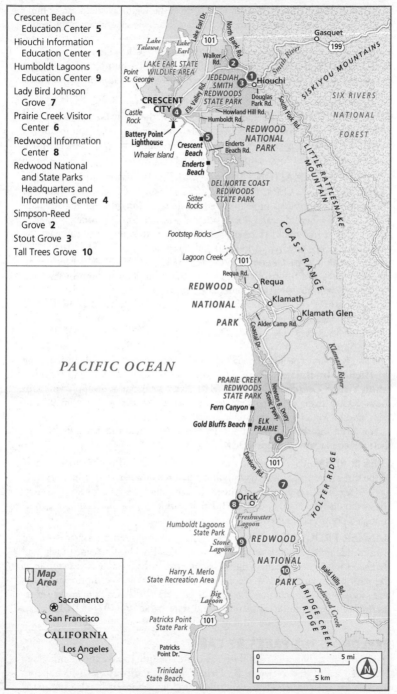

Redwood National & State Parks

Gasquet

Lake
Talawa

Lake
Earl

101

Walker
Rd.

2

Smith River

199

North Bank Rd.

Lake Earl Dr.

*LAKE EARL STATE
WILDLIFE AREA*

Point
St. George

1 Hiouchi

3

Douglas
Park Rd.

*JEDEDIAH
SMITH
REDWOODS
STATE PARK*

**CRESCENT
CITY**

*Castle
Rock*

**Battery Point
Lighthouse**

Whaler Island

Elk Valley Rd.

4

Howland Hill Rd.

Humboldt Rd.

5

*Crescent
Beach*

Enderts
Beach Rd.

*Enderts
Beach*

South Fork Rd.

SISKIYOU MOUNTAINS

SIX RIVERS

NATIONAL

FOREST

*REDWOOD
NATIONAL
PARK*

*LITTLE RATTLESNAKE
MOUNTAIN*

*Sister
Rocks*

*DEL NORTE COAST
REDWOODS
STATE PARK*

Footstep Rocks

COAST RANGE

Lagoon Creek

101

Requa Rd.

Requa

REDWOOD

NATIONAL

PARK

Klamath

Klamath Glen

Coastal Dr.

Alder Camp Rd.

Klamath River

PACIFIC OCEAN

*PRARIE CREEK
REDWOODS
STATE PARK*

Fern Canyon ■

Gold Bluffs Beach ■

*ELK
PRAIRIE*

6

Newton B. Drury Scenic Pkwy.

Dawson Rd.

101

7

HOLTER RIDGE

8

Orick

*Freshwater
Lagoon*

*Humboldt Lagoons
State Park*

*Stone
Lagoon*

9

REDWOOD

NATIONAL

10

PARK

Bald Hills Rd.

Redwood Creek

BRIDGE CREEK RIDGE

*Harry A. Merlo
State Recreation Area*

*Big
Lagoon*

*Patricks Point
State Park*

101

Patricks
Point Dr.

*Trinidad
State Beach*

**Map
Area**

Sacramento

San Francisco

CALIFORNIA

Los Angeles

0		5 mi
0		5 km

N

Although logging of old-growth redwoods in the region is still a major bone of contention among the government, private landowners, and environmentalists, it's an auspicious sign that contention even exists, a sign that perhaps we have all learned to see the forest *and* the trees for what they are—the monarchs of all living things, a link to the age of dinosaurs, and a humble reminder that the age of mankind is but a hiccup in time to the venerable *Sequoia sempervirens*.

ESSENTIALS

GETTING THERE   The southern gateway to the Redwood National and State Parks is the town of Orick. U.S. 101 runs right through the middle of town. The northern gateway to the park is Crescent City, your best bet for a cheap motel, gas, fast food, and outdoor supplies.

VISITOR INFORMATION   In Orick you'll find the **Redwood Information Center,** P.O. Box 7, Orick, CA 95555 (© **707/464-6101,** ext. 5265), one of California's rare examples of well-placed tax dollars (though some may dispute this because it's located near a floodplain and within a tsunami zone). Stop here and pick up a free map; it's open daily from 9am to 5pm. If you missed the Orick center, don't worry: About 10 miles farther north on U.S. 101 is the **Prairie Creek Visitor Center** (© **707/464-6101,** ext. 5300), which carries all the same maps and information. It's open daily from 9am to 5pm in summer, daily from 10am to 4pm (sometimes later) in winter.

Before touring the park, pick up a free guide at the **Redwood National and State Parks Headquarters and Information Center,** 1111 Second St. (at K St.), Crescent City, CA 95531 (© **707/464-6101,** ext. 5064). It's open daily from 9am to 5pm.

If you happen to be arriving via U.S. 199 from Oregon, the rangers manning the **Hiouchi Information Station** (© 707/464-6101, ext. 5067) and **Jedediah Smith Visitor Center** (© 707/464-6101, ext. 5113) can also supply you with the necessary maps and advice. Both are open daily in summer from 9am to 5pm, and in winter when staffing is available.

For more information about the Redwood National and State Parks, visit their website at **www.nps.gov/redw.**

FEES & PERMITS   Admission to the national park is free, but to enter any of the three state parks (which contain the best redwood groves), you'll pay a $2 day-use fee, which is good at all three. The camping fee is $12 for drive-in sites. (Reservations are highly recommended in summer.) Walk-in sites are free, though a permit is required.

RANGER PROGRAMS   The park service runs interpretive programs—from trees to tide pools, legends to landforms—at the Hiouchi, Crescent Beach, and Redwood information centers during summer months, as well as year-round at the park headquarters in Crescent City. State rangers lead campfire programs and numerous other activities throughout the year as well. Call the **Parks Information** service for both the national and state parks (© **707/464-6101,** ext. 5265) to get information on current schedules and events.

EXPLORING THE PARKS BY CAR

If you're approaching the park from the south, be sure to take the detour along U.S. 101 called the **Newton B. Drury Scenic Parkway** ✿, which passes through groves of redwoods and elk-filled meadows before leading back onto the highway 8 miles later. Another spectacular route is the **Coastal Drive** ✿, which winds through stands of redwoods and offers grand views of the Pacific.

The most amazing car-friendly trail in the Redwood National and State Parks is the hidden, well-maintained gravel **Howland Hill Road** 🎄🎄 that winds for about 12 miles through Jedediah Smith Redwoods State Park. It's an unforgettable journey through a spectacular old-growth redwood forest—considered by many to be one of the most beautiful areas in the world. To get here from U.S. 101, keep an eye out for the 76 gas station at the south end of Crescent City; just before the station, turn right on Elk Valley Road, and follow it to Howland Hill Road, which will be on your right. After driving through the park, you'll end up at U.S. 199 near Hiouchi, and from here it's a short jaunt west to get back to U.S. 101. Plan at least 2 to 3 hours for the 45-mile round-trip, or all day if you want to do some hiking or mountain biking. This drive is not recommended for trailers and RVs.

SPORTS & OUTDOOR PURSUITS

BEACHES, WHALE-WATCHING & BIRD-WATCHING The park's beaches vary from long white-sand strands to cobblestone pocket coves. The water temperature is in the high 40s to low 50s (low 10s Celsius) year-round; it's often rough, so swimmers and surfers should be prepared for adverse conditions.

Crescent Beach is a long sandy beach 2 miles south of Crescent City that's popular with beachcombers, surf fishermen, and surfers. Just south of Crescent Beach is **Endert's Beach,** a protected spot with a hike-in campground and tide pools at the southern end of the beach.

High coastal overlooks (such as Klamath and Crescent Beach overlooks) make great whale-watching outposts during the southern migration in December and January and the return migration in March and April. The northern sea cliffs also provide valuable nesting sites for marine birds like auklets, puffins, murres, and cormorants. Birders will thrill at the park's freshwater lagoons as well. These coastal lagoons are some of the most pristine shorebird and waterfowl habitats left, and are chock-full of hundreds of different species.

HIKING The park's official map and guide, available at any of the information centers, provides a fairly good layout of hiking trails within the park. Regardless of how short or long your hike may be, dress warmly and bring plenty of water and sunscreen. Pets are prohibited on all of the park's trails.

The most popular walk is the short, heavily traveled **Fern Canyon Trail** 🎄, which leads to a lush grotto of lady, deer, chain, sword, five-finger, and maidenhair ferns clinging to 50-foot-high vertical walls divided by a brook. It's only about a 1.5-mile walk from Gold Bluffs Beach, but be prepared to scramble across the creek several times on your way via small footbridges.

The **Lady Bird Johnson Grove Loop** 🎄 is an easy, 1-hour self-guided tour that loops 1 mile around a glorious lush grove of mature redwoods. It's the site at which the national park was dedicated by Mrs. Johnson in 1968. Also an easy trek is the **Yurok Loop Nature Trail** at Lagoon Creek. The 1-mile self-guided trail gradually climbs to the top of a rugged sea bluff (with wonderful panoramic views of the Pacific) before looping back to the parking lot. If someone's willing to act as shuttle driver, have him or her meet you at the Requa Trailhead and take the 4-mile coastal trail to the mouth of the Klamath. And for the whiner in your group, there's **Big Tree Trail,** a quarter-mile paved trail leading to a big tree.

Tall Trees Trail leads to one of the world's tallest trees—perhaps 365 feet tall, 14 feet in diameter, and more than 600 years old. This was once touted as the tallest tree in the world, but new candidates keep popping up and this proud giant has also lost a couple of feet. Now, who knows? It's still worth it to see the contender. You'll have to go to the Redwood Information Center near Orick (see

"Essentials," above) to obtain a free map and permit to drive to the trail head of Tall Trees Grove. Only 50 permits are issued per day on a first-come, first-served basis. After driving to the trail head, you have to walk a steep 1.33 miles down into the grove. The trail is 3.25 miles round-trip.

WILDLIFE VIEWING One of the most striking aspects of Prairie Creek Redwood State Park is its 200- to 300-strong herd of **Roosevelt elk** 🦌, usually found in the appropriately named Elk Prairie in the southern end of the park. These beasts can weigh 1,000 pounds, and the bulls carry huge antlers from spring to fall. Elk are also sometimes found at Gold Bluffs Beach—it's an incredible rush to come upon them out of the fog or after a turn in the trail. Nearly a hundred **black bears** also call the park home but are seldom seen. Unlike those at Yosemite and Yellowstone, these are still afraid of people. Keep them that way by giving them a wide berth, observing food-storage etiquette while camping, and disposing of garbage properly.

WHERE TO STAY

Five small campgrounds are in the national park proper. Four of the walk-in (more like backpack-in) camps—Little Bald Hills, Nickel Creek, Flint Ridge, and Butler Creek—are free, and only one (the Redwood Creek Gravel Bar) requires a permit from the visitor center in advance.

Most car campsites are in the **Prairie Creek** and **Jedediah Smith state parks,** which lie entirely inside the national park. Prairie Creek has two campgrounds, at Elk Prairie and Gold Bluffs Beach. Sites are $12 per night and can be reserved by calling the ReserveAmerica reservations system (© **800/444-7275;** www. reserveamerica.com). It helps if you know what campground and if possible which site you would like.

If the camping areas above are filled, try the **Mill Creek Campground,** in Del Norte Coast Redwoods State Park (part of RNSP), 7 miles south of Crescent City on U.S. 101, which has 145 tent or RV sites. The walk-in tent sites are quite nice, situated amidst the forest. Fees are $12 per night. The ReserveAmerica system (see above) handles reservations for this campground as well.

A number of bed-and-breakfasts and funky roadside motels are available in the surrounding communities of Crescent City, Orick, and Klamath. The **Crescent City/Del Norte Chamber of Commerce** (© **800/343-8300**) can probably steer you toward the proper match.

Hostelling International—Redwood National Park (Value) The only lodging actually within the park, this settler's homestead was remodeled in 1987 to accommodate 30 guests dormitory-style (that is, bunks and shared bathrooms) from March through December. The location is perfect, a mere 100 yards from the beach, and surrounded by hiking trails leading along the Redwood Coast (the staff leads nature walks and is well versed in local history). A couple's room is available for an additional $10, with advance notice, and the hostel even takes reservations by credit card (strongly recommended in the summer). The nightly rate includes use of the showers, common room with VCR and videos, redwood deck, help-yourself common kitchen, laundry room, dining room, pellet stove, and bicycle storage.

14480 U.S. 101 (at U.S. 101 and Wilson Creek Rd., across from False Klamath Cove), Klamath, CA 95548. © **800/909-4776,** ext. 74, or 707/482-8265. Fax 707/482-4665. www.norcalhostels.org. 30 bunks, 1 couple's room ($42). Closed daily 10am–5pm. Closed Dec–Feb, except for groups of 15 or more. $16 adults, $8 children ($3 additional for non-AYH/HI members). MC, V. **Amenities:** On-site parking; information desk; baggage check; groceries/snacks available.

The Far North: Lake Tahoe, the Shasta Cascades & Lassen Volcanic National Park

by Matthew Richard Poole

Dominated by the eternally snow-capped Mount Shasta—visible for 100 miles on a clear day—California's upper northern territory is among the least-visited parts of the state. Often referred to as "the Far North," this region stretches from the rice fields north of Sacramento to the Oregon border. The area is so immense that the state of Ohio would fit comfortably within its borders.

The Far North is an outdoor playground for the adventurous traveler, offering myriad inexpensive recreational activities like hiking, climbing, skiing, white-water rafting, and mountain biking. Other attractions, both artificial and natural, range from the amazing Shasta Dam to Lava Beds National Monument, which has dozens of caves to explore, and Lassen Volcanic National Park, a towering laboratory of volcanic phenomena.

South of the Cascade Range is one of the most popular recreational regions in the Golden State: Lake Tahoe. At 6,225 feet above sea level in the Sierra Nevada, it straddles the border between Nevada and California. Although the lake has been marred by overdevelopment—particularly along the casino-riddled southern shore—the western and eastern coastlines still provide quiet havens for hiking and cycling. The surrounding mountains offer some of the best skiing in the United States at more than a dozen resorts.

1 Lake Tahoe ★★★

107 miles E of Sacramento; 192 miles E of San Francisco; 45 miles SW of Reno, NV

Lake Tahoe is one of America's national treasures. It's stunningly beautiful, the air is crisp and clear, and the sun shines 80% of the time. In summer you can enjoy boating and watersports, sandy beaches, bicycling, golf, tennis, hiking, camping, ballooning, horseback riding, rock climbing, bungee jumping, parasailing, skating—the possibilities are endless. In winter, with an average snowfall of 409 inches, Lake Tahoe is one of the nation's premier ski destinations, offering 15 downhill resorts and 10 cross-country ski centers. There's also snowboarding, ice-skating, snowshoeing, snowmobiling, sleigh riding, sledding, and snow play. Year-round activities include fishing, Vegas-style gambling, and big-name entertainment in the casinos.

Then there's the lake. It's hard to imagine any lake view as captivating. When Mark Twain first saw it, he declared it "the fairest picture the whole earth affords." Famed for its crystal-clear water (a white dinner plate at the depth of 75 ft. would be visible from the surface) and its size, 22 miles long and 12 miles

---

Tips **A Tale of Two Shores**

Before you visit Tahoe for the first time, it's important to know that there's a huge difference between the North and the South shores. Don't let the "City" in North Shore's "Tahoe City" fool you: The town can be driven through in a couple of minutes, whereas South Lake Tahoe is brimming with high-rise casinos, motels, and minimalls. Where you choose to stay is important because driving from one end of the lake to the other takes an hour or more in summer and can be downright treacherous in the winter.

So which side is for you? If you're here for gambling or entertainment, stay south: The selection of casinos is better and there's more action. If it's the outdoors you're after, or a relaxing retreat, head north. The North Shore offers a better selection of quality resorts and vacation rentals, while the South Shore offers more lodging options, often at better rates. The woodsy West Shore has the most camping spots, while the East Shore has been protected from development and has no commercial activity.

Wherever you stay, you'll find no shortage of water and mountain sports. The lake is crowded during the summer and ski seasons, so plan far ahead. It's much easier to get reservations for the spring and fall, and the rates are significantly lower. There are also numerous vacation homes and condominiums available to rent; call the visitor-center bureaus or visit the websites listed below under "Visitor Information" for a list of rental agents.

---

wide, it is the largest alpine lake in North America. Its average depth is 989 feet, with the deepest point being 1,645 feet, containing enough water to cover the entire state of California to a depth of 14½ inches. Surrounded by the majestic peaks of the Sierra Nevada, its waters seem to soak up the colors of the sky and the mountains, creating a kaleidoscope of sparkling blues, greens, and purples. It's a sight that will lure you back year after year.

ESSENTIALS

GETTING THERE   It's a 4-hour drive from San Francisco; take I-80 east to Sacramento, then U.S. 50 to the South Shore, or I-80 east to Calif. 89 or Calif. 267 to the North Shore. Be prepared for snow in the winter. During heavy storms, you won't be permitted to pass the CHP (California Highway Patrol) checkpoints without four-wheel-drive or chains. From Los Angeles, it's a 9-hour drive; take I-5 through the Central Valley to Sacramento, and then follow the directions above.

Reno-Tahoe International Airport (45 min. to North Shore, 90 min. to South Shore; www.renoairport.com) offers regular service by 10 major airlines, including **American** (© 800/433-7300), **Delta** (© 800/221-1212), and **United** (© 800/241-6522). Rent a car or take a shuttle up to the lake: **No Stress Express** (© 888/4-SHUTTLE; www.nostressexpress.com) serves the North and West shores; **Tahoe Casino Express** (© 800/446-6128; www.tahoe casinoexpress.com) serves the South Shore (1-day advance reservations recommended). To get to the lake, take U.S. 395 South to Route 431 for the North

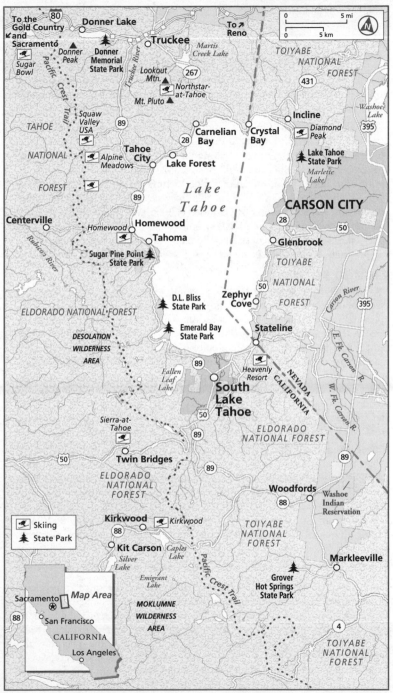

Lake Tahoe & Environs

To the Gold Country and Sacramento

80

Donner Lake

Donner Peak

Sugar Bowl

Donner Memorial State Park

Truckee

To Reno

Martis Creek Lake

TOIYABE NATIONAL FOREST

267

431

Lookout Mtn.

Northstar-at-Tahoe

Mt. Pluto

Washoe Lake

395

TAHOE

Squaw Valley USA

89

Carnelian Bay

Crystal Bay

Incline

Diamond Peak

28

NATIONAL

Alpine Meadows

Tahoe City

Lake Forest

Lake Tahoe State Park

Marlette Lake

FOREST

89

Lake Tahoe

CARSON CITY

28

50

Centerville

Homewood

Homewood

Glenbrook

Rubicon River

Tahoma

Sugar Pine Point State Park

TOIYABE

ELDORADO NATIONAL FOREST

D.L. Bliss State Park

Zephyr Cove

50

NATIONAL

FOREST

Carson River

395

DESOLATION WILDERNESS AREA

Emerald Bay State Park

Stateline

Fallen Leaf Lake

89

Heavenly Resort

NEVADA

CALIFORNIA

E. Fk. Carson R.

South Lake Tahoe

50

W. Fk. Carson R.

Sierra-at-Tahoe

89

ELDORADO NATIONAL FOREST

50

89

89

Twin Bridges

ELDORADO NATIONAL FOREST

89

Woodfords

Washoe Indian Reservation

88

Kirkwood

Kirkwood

TOIYABE NATIONAL FOREST

88

Kit Carson

Caples Lake

Markleeville

Silver Lake

Emigrant Lake

Pacific Crest Trail

Grover Hot Springs State Park

4

TOIYABE NATIONAL FOREST

Skiing

State Park

Sacramento

Map Area

88

San Francisco

CALIFORNIA

Los Angeles

MOKLUMNE WILDERNESS AREA

0   5 mi
0   5 km

Pacific Crest Trail

Truckee River

245

Shore or U.S. 50 for the South Shore. While all of the roads leading to the lake are scenic, the panorama as you descend into the Lake Tahoe Basin from Route 431 is spectacular. Pull into the overlook and enjoy the view.

Amtrak (© 800/USA-RAIL; www.amtrak.com) stops in Truckee, 10 miles north of the lake. Public transportation (TART or Truce Trolley) is available from the train depot, or you can take a taxi to the North Shore. **Greyhound Bus Lines** (© 800/229-9424; www.greyhound.com) serves both Truckee and South Lake Tahoe with daily arrivals from San Francisco and Sacramento.

VISITOR INFORMATION   In Tahoe City, stop by the **Visitor Service Center,** 245 North Lake Blvd. (© 888/434-1262 or 530/583-3494; www.tahoefun. org). In Incline Village, go to the **Incline Village/Crystal Bay Visitors Center,** 969 Tahoe Blvd. (© 800/468-2463 or 775/832-1606; www.gotahoe.com). In South Lake Tahoe, go to the **Lake Tahoe Visitors Authority,** 1156 Ski Run Blvd. (© 800/288-2463 or 530/544-5050; www.virtualtahoe.com), or to the **South Lake Tahoe Chamber of Commerce,** 3066 Lake Tahoe Blvd. (© 530/ 541-5255; www.tahoeinfo.com). Many other websites offer information about Lake Tahoe, including www.skilaketahoe.com, www.laketahoeconcierge.com, and www.tahoevacationguide.com.

WHAT TO SEE & DO
SKIING & SNOWBOARDING

With the largest concentration of ski resorts in North America, Lake Tahoe offers California's best skiing. The ski season typically lasts from November to May and frequently extends into the summer. Lift tickets last winter ranged from $40 to $70 per day for adults, and from free to $35 for children, with special rates for teens and seniors. Ticket prices go up every year, but bargains are available, particularly midweek. Many resorts, hotels, and motels offer ski packages. Contact the visitor centers or visit the websites listed under "Visitor Information" above to look for these values. The resorts offer instruction for adults and children, equipment rental, special courses for snowboarding, and restaurants. Most have free shuttles.

Alpine Meadows 🎿🎿 (Kids)   With more than 100 runs over 2,400 acres, Alpine has something for everyone: kids' programs and a family ski zone, as well as its "wild side" for the double black diamond crowd. In addition to its 14 lifts, this low-key resort also has a beginner surface lift designed especially for children, novice skiers, and snowboarders. You can get a great bargain through its Bed and Board package, which provides lift tickets and lodging (© 800/949-3296). Alpine also offers ski and snowboard instruction for all ages, excellent snowboarding-terrain parks, snowshoe rentals, and snow play areas.

2600 Alpine Meadows Rd., Tahoe City, CA 96145. © 800/441-4423 or 530/583-4232. www.skialpine.com.

Diamond Peak 🎿 (Kids) (Value)   This smaller, less expensive resort has spectacular lake views and is a premier destination for families. Whether your child chooses to ski or snowboard, there will be something available, including a snow play program for the younger ones who aren't quite ready to learn to ski yet. Kids love the snowboard park and sledding area. In the heart of the quiet, upscale community of Incline Village, this is a great choice for a low-key, less crowded, beautiful skiing adventure. The Diamond Peak Cross Country and Snowshoe Center (same telephone number), east of Incline Village on NV Route 431, is gorgeous and even allows dogs to share in the fun in the afternoon.

1210 Ski Way, Incline Village, NV 89451. © 775/832-1177 or 775/831-3249. www.diamondpeak.com.

Heavenly Resort *★★* *(Kids)* This hugely popular resort—and the only one on the South Shore—has the highest elevation (10,067 ft.) of any resort at the lake. Skiers and snowboarders of all levels will find something to challenge them, including three snowboard parks, 4,800 skiable acres, 30 lifts (including a 50-passenger aerial tram), and 86 runs. Heavenly is also the only resort that offers day care for infants as young as 6 weeks up through 6 years old, child care and ski combinations for ages 3 to 5, and full-day programs for older kids. With the nearby arcades, recreation centers, bowling alleys, and movie theaters, it's a great choice if you have teenagers or if you want to visit the big casinos at night. The latest addition to the resort is the $20-million **Heavenly Gondola,** featuring state-of-the-art cars holding up to eight people that can take you from the South Shore casino area up to an observation deck at 9,200 feet on Heavenly Mountain—a 2½-mile journey. The resort also recently invested nearly $30 million in on-mountain improvements including two new high-speed lifts and a new 15-acre beginner's area

P.O. Box 2180 (on Ski Run Blvd.), Stateline, NV 89449. © **775/586-7000.** www.skiheavenly.com.

Homewood Mountain Resort *★* *(Kids)* *(Value)* Homewood is one of my favorite small ski areas, a homey little resort with 1,260 acres, 56 runs, 8 lifts, and spectacular lake views. It's a good family resort with child care for ages 2 to 6 and ski schools for ages 4 to 12. Lift tickets were only $44 last winter, and children under 10 skied free when accompanied by an adult.

5145 W. Lake Blvd., Homewood, CA 96141 (6 miles south of Tahoe City and 19 miles north of South Lake Tahoe on Calif. 89). © **530/525-2992.** www.skihomewood.com.

Kirkwood *★★* *(Kids)* Kirkwood's only drawback is that it's 30 miles south of South Lake Tahoe; otherwise, it's one of the top ski areas in Tahoe, with lots of snow and excellent spring skiing. It has 2,300 skiable acres, 12 lifts, and 65 trails. Many programs are offered for children, including child care for the younger ones (ages 2–6). The **Cross Country Ski Center** (© **209/258-7248**) is one of the best around, offering lessons for all ages, and spectacular scenery. Kirkwood is also ideal for summertime hiking, horseback riding, mountain biking, and rock climbing. With ample lodging (© **800/967-7500**) and dining options, this is a year-round destination. There's free shuttle service to South Lake Tahoe.

Off Hwy. 88 at Carson Pass (P.O. Box 1), Kirkwood, CA 95646. © **209/258-6000.** www.kirkwood.com.

Northstar-at-Tahoe *★★* *(Kids)* With 70 runs covering 2,420 acres on two mountains, Northstar is consistently rated among the top Western resorts. Its sophisticated series of lifts, including an express gondola, insure speedy access to the slopes and short lift lines. Whatever age or experience level, you'll find what you're looking for here. Backcountry terrain on Saw Tooth Ridge will test the skills of expert skiers and snowboarders on 200 acres of ungroomed, out-of-boundary terrain. The Learning Center offers coaching in skiing, snowboarding, cross-country, and the new snow toys. Child care (ages 2–6) is provided, as well as instruction, including the "magic carpet" lift and special "Paw Parks," Northstar's pint-size obstacle courses. Other outdoor fun includes cross-country, telemarking, snowshoeing, sleigh rides, tubing, and, now, ice-skating in the heart of Northstar's new Village. Check out the snow toys such as the snowscoot, the ski-fox, the snowbike, and the snowskate, a skateboard deck without wheels. See p. 260 for a full review of Northstar-at-Tahoe Resort.

P.O. Box 129, Truckee, CA 96160 (6 miles north of Kings Beach). © **800/466-6784** or 530/562-1010. www. northstarattahoe.com.

Sierra-at-Tahoe ★ *Kids*   Tahoe's third-largest ski area is a great all-around resort, offering a slightly better price than most comparable places in the area. There are more than 2,000 acres of slopes ranging from bunny to expert. What I really like about this ski area is that the runs are very wide and well groomed, giving skiers plenty of room to fly down the mountain. On a powder day, the trees are a must-ski. There are also four terrain parks for both boarders and skiers and 200 acres of backcountry terrain for steeps and deeps. If you're staying on the South Shore, it's a good alternative to Heavenly Ski Resort. Free ski shuttle service is provided from about 40 locations in South Lake Tahoe.

1111 Sierra at Tahoe Rd., Twin Bridges, CA 95735 (off Hwy. 50, 12 miles west of South Lake Tahoe). ℂ 530/659-7453. www.SierraAtTahoe.com.

Squaw Valley USA ★★★ *Kids*   Site of the 1960 Olympic Winter Games, Squaw is one of the world's finest year-round resorts. Skiing is spread across six peaks with one of the most advanced lift systems in the world providing access to over 4,000 acres of skiable terrain—70% geared toward beginners and intermediates and 30% for the advanced, expert, and/or insane. Children's World offers child care (reservations required; call ℂ **530/581-7280** 1–4pm) and snow school. For nonskiers and skiers alike, High Camp, at the top of the cable car, has the Olympic Ice Pavilion (year-round ice-skating), a swimming lagoon and spa (spring and summer), snow tubing, snowboarding school, bungee jumping, restaurants, and bars. Squaw also has an arcade, cinema, climbing wall, and Central Park (a snowboarder's dream). The Cross-Country Ski Center (ℂ **530/583-6300**) has 400 acres of groomed trails. For those who can't get enough of a good thing, Squaw offers free night skiing with the purchase of a full-day lift ticket. Children ages 12 and under ski for only $5. See p. 261 for a full review of The Resort at Squaw Creek.

Olympic Valley, CA 96146 (6 miles north of Tahoe City). ℂ **800/545-4350** or 530/583-6985. www.squaw.com.

Sugar Bowl ★★ *Kids*   If you are driving from the Bay Area or Sacramento on I-80 and don't want to drive all the way to Tahoe, Sugar Bowl is an excellent place to ski. This medium-size resort (13 lifts, 1,500 skiable acres) offers child care, ski school, snowboard parks, and lodging at the foot of the mountains. It was a popular getaway for the Hollywood set in the 1940s and 1950s.

P.O. Box 5, Norden, CA 95724 (3 miles east of the Soda Springs/Norden exit of I-80). ℂ **530/426-9000.** www.sugarbowl.com.

MORE WINTER FUN

CROSS-COUNTRY SKIING   In addition to the major resorts, here are some other excellent choices: **Royal Gorge Cross-Country Ski Resort** ★★★, Soda Springs, near Sugar Bowl (ℂ **800/666-3871;** www.royalgorge.com), has 90 trails, including 28 novice trails and four ski lifts, and is one of the largest and best cross-country resorts anywhere. **Tahoe Cross Country Ski Area** ★, 925 Country Club Dr., Tahoe City (ℂ **530/583-5475;** www.tahoexc.org), is a small (14 trails), full-service ski center run by a nonprofit community group and is easy and convenient to North Shore visitors. **Spooner Lake Cross Country Ski Area** ★, near the intersection of Highway 28 and U.S. 50 on the East Shore (ℂ **888/858-8844;** www.spoonerlake.com), is a quiet, full-service ski center off the beaten path, but it offers some of the most scenic skiing at the lake.

ICE-SKATING   Accessible only by a tram ride (included in the admission fee of $20 for adults, $10 for children under 12), **Squaw Valley's High Camp** ★★

(© 530/583-6985) has one of the world's most beautiful and unusual ice rinks. It's open daily from 11am to 9pm (11am–4pm Apr 14–June 22).

SNOWMOBILING   Snowmobile rental and tours are available at several locations in the Lake Tahoe Area. Call ahead for reservations and directions. The **Zephyr Cove Snowmobile Center** ☀, 760 U.S. 50, about 4 miles northeast of the casinos (© 775/589-4908), offers several exciting tours daily for all experience levels (really, they're loads of fun, especially if you've never been on a snowmobile in your life). The cost for a 2-hour tour is about $94 for a single rider, $139 for two. **Snowmobiling Unlimited** (© 530/583-7192; www.snowmobiling unlimited.com) offers 2-hour backcountry tours from Brockway Summit, about 3 miles north of Kings Beach on Calif. 267; prices are $90 for one, $120 for two. **TC Snomos**, 205 River Rd., Tahoe City (© 530/581-3906; www.snowmobile laketahoe.com), starts its tours in Tahoe City, and charges $80 for one and $110 for two.

SNOW PLAY   For snow play other than at the big resorts, try the **North Tahoe Regional Park**, at the top of National Avenue off Highway 28, Tahoe Vista (© 530/546-0605). This ultimate snow play hill has a $5 fee that includes a choice of sled, tube, or saucer. **Taylor Creek Snow Park** off Calif. 89 in South Lake Tahoe is run by the U.S. Forest Service. Bring your own equipment for sledding and tubing. For information about all the California Sno Park locations, call the **Sno Park Hot Line** at © 916/324-1222.

SUMMER ACTIVITIES

BALLOONING   See the lake and mountains from 8,000 to 10,000 feet above with **Lake Tahoe Balloons** (© 800/872-9294; www.laketahoeballoons.com) in South Lake Tahoe. A 1-hour tour and brunch costs about $195 per person.

BEACHES   Here are a few popular spots around the lake. All have sandy beaches, picnic areas, and restrooms; many have playgrounds. Remember that this is an alpine lake so the water is *very* cold.

- **Baldwin Beach:** Calif. 89, 4 miles north of South Lake Tahoe
- **Commons Beach Park:** Downtown Tahoe City, free movie (Fri at dusk)
- **Connolly Beach:** U.S. 50 at Timber Cove Lodge; boat launches
- **D. L. Bliss State Park:** South of Meeks Bay on Calif. 89; camping, trails
- **El Dorado Beach:** Between Rufus Allen and Lakeview in South Lake Tahoe
- **Kings Beach State Recreation Center:** Highway 28 in Kings Beach
- **Pope Beach:** Calif. 89, 2 miles north of South Lake Tahoe
- **Sand Harbor:** 4 miles south of Incline Village on Highway 28; lifeguards
- **Sugar Pine Point:** Calif. 89, just south of Tahoma; camping, trails, pier
- **Zephyr Cove Beach:** U.S. 50 at Zephyr Cove

BICYCLING   There are miles of paved bicycle paths around the lake. Incline Village has a scenic, easy 2½-mile path along Lakeshore Boulevard. This is a safe choice for younger children. In Tahoe City you can follow the path in three directions. The one that follows Truckee River is a relaxing, beautiful ride. On the South Shore, the Pope-Baldwin bike path runs parallel to Calif. 89 through Camp Richardson and the Tallac Historic Site. Nearby in South Lake Tahoe, a paved pathway runs from El Dorado Beach along the lake, paralleling U.S. 50. The Tahoe City trails are my personal favorites, especially the Truckee River section. You can rent a bicycle from any of the shops listed below.

Mountain biking is big at Lake Tahoe. For serious bikers, there is a dizzying choice of trails. At both **Northstar-at-Tahoe Resort** (© 530/562-1010; p.260) and **Squaw Valley USA** (© **530/583-6985;** p. 248), you can take the cable car (Squaw) or chairlift (Northstar) up with your bike and ride the trails all the way down. For other trails, check with one of the bicycle-rental shops for maps and information. In North Tahoe, try **The Back Country,** 255 N. Lake Blvd., Tahoe City (© 530/581-5861); **Olympic Bike Shop,** 620 N. Lake Blvd., Tahoe City (© 530/581-2500); **Tahoe Bike & Ski,** 8499 N. Lake Blvd., Kings Beach (© 530/546-7437); or **Porter's Sports Shop,** 885 Tahoe Blvd., Incline Village (© 775/831-3500). In South Tahoe, try **Anderson's Bike Rental,** 645 Emerald Bay Rd. (© 530/541-0500), or **Lakeview Sports,** 3131 Hwy. 50 at El Dorado Beach (© 530/544-0183).

Another great choice is **Cyclepaths Mountain Bike Adventures,** 1785 W. Lake Blvd. in Tahoe Park, a few miles south of Tahoe City (© **800/780-BIKE;** www.cyclepaths.com), where you can arrange a guided off-road tour. Whether you're into hard-core downhill single track or easy-going scenic outings, the expert guides will provide you with all the necessary equipment, food, and transportation. They offer day tours ($29 and up), weekenders ($199), and 3- and 5-day adventure camps (rates vary).

BOATING, WATERSPORTS & PARASAILING   Nothing beats actually getting out on the water. Take a guided tour, go off on your own, or just paddle around. Here are a few reliable choices: **Zephyr Cove Marina** (© **775/588-3833;** www.tahoedixie2.com) is the lake's largest marina. It's the home of the paddle-wheeler MS *Dixie II* and the catamaran *Woodwind II.* Here you can parasail (© **775/588-3530**), charter sport-fishing trips (© **775/586-9338**), or take guided tours. You can also rent motorized boats, pedal boats, kayaks, canoes, water-ski equipment, and jet skis. **Tahoe City Marina** (© **530/583-1039**), 700 N. Lake Blvd., Tahoe City, rents motorized boats, sailboats, and fishing boats. Sailboat cruises are available. This is also the location for **Lake Tahoe Parasailing** (© **530/583-7245**).

Lighthouse Water Sports, 950 N. Lake Blvd., Tahoe (© **530/583-6000**), rents jet skis, paddleboats, and canoes. **Tahoe Paddle and Oar,** North Lake Beach Center, 7860 N. Lake Blvd., Kings Beach (© **530/581-3029**), is a good place to rent kayaks, canoes, pedal boats, and windsurfing equipment. Paddling around in the clear waters of Crystal Bay is great fun. **Action Water Sports** has two locations: 3411 Lake Tahoe Blvd. at Timber Cove Marina, South Lake Tahoe (© **530/544-2942**); and across from the Hyatt in Incline Village (© **775/831-4386**). You can rent boats, kayaks, jet skis, paddleboats, and other water toys here; parasailing and guided tours are also available. **Camp Richardson Marina,** 1900 Jameson Beach Rd., off Calif. 89 on the South Shore (© **530/542-6570**), on a long sandy beach, rents power- and ski boats, jet skis, kayaks, and paddleboats. It also offers fishing charters, ski school, cruises on the *Woodwind I* sailboat, and raft and kayak tours to Emerald Bay. **SunSports,** 3564 Lake Tahoe Blvd., South Lake Tahoe (© **530/541-6000**), provides rentals, tours, and lessons for kayaking, rafting, sailing, and scuba diving.

CAMPING   If you have an appetite for the great outdoors, here are a few of the many good campgrounds at Tahoe:

D. L. Bliss State Park, on the western shore (© **530/525-7277**), has 168 campsites, fine beaches, and hiking trails.

Sugar Pine Point State Park, also on the western shore (© **530/525-7982**), offers 175 campsites, a picnic area, a beach, a nature center, and cross-country skiing, and is open year-round.

Campground by the Lake, 1150 Rufus Allen Blvd., South Lake Tahoe (© 530/542-6096), features 170 campsites, a boat ramp, a gym, and a history museum.

Zephyr Cove RV Park and Campground, located at Zephyr Cove Resort on U.S. 50 (© 775/589-4907), has a beach, a marina, and complete facilities.

FISHING   The cold, clear waters of Lake Tahoe are home to kokanee salmon and rainbow, brown, and Mackinaw trout. With lots of hiding places in the deep water, fishing here is a challenge, and many anglers opt to use a guide or charter boat. There are dozens of charter companies offering daily excursions. Rates run about $65 for a half day to $95 for a whole day (bait, tackle, fish cleaning, and food included). On the North Shore, try **Mickey's Big Mack Charters** at the Sierra Boat Company in Carnelian Bay (© 530/546-4444; www.mickeys bigmack.com); or **Reel Deal Sportfishing,** Tahoe City (© 530/581-0924). On the South Shore, try **Avid Fisherman,** Zephyr Cove (© 775/588-7675); **Blue Ribbon Fishing Charters,** Tahoe Keys Marina (© 530/541-8801); or **Tahoe Sportfishing,** 900 Ski Run Blvd. (© 800/696-7797 or 530/541-5448).

FITNESS CENTERS & SPAS   The **Incline Recreation Center,** 980 Incline Way, Incline Village (© 775/832-1310), is a gorgeous facility with a heated indoor Olympic-size swimming pool, aerobics, basketball, cardiovascular fitness room, lounge, fireplace, and on-site child care. The fee is $13 for adults and $8 for children.

GOLF   With its world class golf courses, mild summer weather, and magnificent scenery, Lake Tahoe is a golfer's paradise. All of the following courses are very busy in the summer so call *far* in advance for tee times. For more information about Tahoe-area golf courses, log on to **www.tahoesbest.com/Golf**.

Starting at the north end of the lake, there are four highly rated courses: **Incline Village Championship Course,** 955 Fairway Blvd., and the smaller **Incline Village Mountain (Executive) Course,** 690 Wilson Way (© 775/832-1144 for both); **Northstar-at-Tahoe Resort** (© 530/562-2490; p. 260); and **The Resort at Squaw Creek** (© 800/327-3353; p. 261).

In the south, there's **Edgewood,** U.S. 50 at Lake Parkway, Stateline, Nevada (© 775/588-3566), home of the Celebrity Golf Championship; and **Lake Tahoe Golf Course,** 2500 Emerald Bay Rd., South Lake Tahoe, California (© 530/577-0788). There are also some good 9-hole municipal courses: **Old Brockway Golf Course,** 7900 N. Lake Blvd., Kings Beach (© 530/546-9909); **Tahoe City Golf Course,** 251 N. Lake Blvd., Tahoe City (© 530/583-1516); and **Bijou Municipal Golf Course,** 3436 Fairway Ave., South Lake Tahoe (© 530/542-6097).

HIKING   The mountains surrounding Lake Tahoe are crisscrossed with hiking trails for all levels of experience. Before setting out, you may wish to contact the local visitor centers or sporting-goods shops for a map and more in-depth information on particular trails, or hire a guide. Try **Tahoe Trips & Trails** (© 530/583-4506; www.tahoetrips.com) for short and long guided hikes. Everything is provided: food, drinks, transportation, and information about the lake. Going on your own? Some of the most popular short hikes in the area are:

Eagle Falls/Eagle Lake: This moderately easy trail is well marked and begins at Eagle Picnic Area, directly across Calif. 89 from Emerald Bay. It's only about a third of a mile to the steel footbridge overlooking the falls and 2 miles roundtrip (1½–2 hr.) to Eagle Lake. Be sure to sign in at the self-registration station at the trail head.

Emerald Bay/Vikingsholm: The trail starts at the parking area on the north side of Emerald Bay, on Highway 89. It's a wide, well-maintained trail but fairly steep, about 2.5 miles round-trip. At the bottom of the trail is a picnic area, as well as world-famous Vikingsholm, a replica of a Scandinavian castle.

Nevada Shoreline: Begin at the paved parking lot on the west side of Highway 28, 3 miles south of Sand Harbor. The trail drops to the beach and follows the shoreline, passing Chimney Beach, Secret Harbor, and Whale Beach. The trail eventually connects to a service road that can be followed back up to the parking area. It's an easy 4-mile hike, with a vertical climb of only 300 feet.

Shirley Lake: This trail leads to Shirley Lake, then down to Shirley Canyon. Take the tram at Squaw Valley up to High Camp and hike down, or vice-versa. The trail begins at the end of Squaw Creek Road, next to the cable-car building. It's a 4-mile hike, easy to moderate in difficulty, with some steep sections.

HORSEBACK RIDING Most stables offer a variety of guided trail rides and lessons for individuals, families, and groups. Choose the one that appeals to your sense of adventure: 1- to 2-hour trail rides; breakfast, lunch, or dinner rides; half-day, full-day, overnight, and extended pack trips. Expect to pay $20 to $25 for a 1-hour ride, $6 for a half-hour pony ride. Saddle up and savor the scenery. Try **Alpine Meadows Stables,** Alpine Meadows Road, Tahoe City (© 530/583-3905); **Northstar Stables,** Highway 267, 6 miles north of Kings Beach (© 530/562-2480); **Squaw Valley Stables,** 1525 Squaw Valley Rd., north of Tahoe City (© 530/583-7433); **Camp Richardson Corral,** Calif. 89, South Lake Tahoe (© 530/541-3113); or **Zephyr Cove Stables,** Zephyr Cove Resort, U.S. 50 at Zephyr Cove (© 775/588-5664).

RIVER RAFTING For a swift but gentle ride down the Truckee River (the lake's only outlet), try **Truckee River Raft Rental,** 185 River Rd., Tahoe City (© **530/583-0123;** www.truckeeriverraft.com). Only available in the summer, the rates are $25 for adults and $20 for children (12 and under).

TENNIS The mild summer weather at Lake Tahoe is perfect for great tennis. If you want to sharpen your skills, **Northstar-at-Tahoe Resort** (© **530/562-0321;** p. 260) offers several excellent tennis packages for its guests only. **Squaw Creek** (© **530/581-6694;** p. 261) tennis courts are open to the public for $12 an hour. **Kirkwood** (p. 247), **Caesars Tahoe** (p. 255), and **Harveys Casino Resort** (p. 256) all feature tennis courts for a fee.

Budget-minded players looking for good local courts should visit Tahoe Lake School on Grove Street in Tahoe City, or Tahoe Regional Park, at the end of National Avenue in Tahoe Vista. South Tahoe Intermediate School on Lyons Avenue has eight lighted courts and charges a manageable $3 per hour. South Tahoe High School, 1735 Lake Tahoe Blvd., has free courts.

LAKE CRUISES

If you can possibly fit a cruise into your vacation plans, you won't regret it. It's one of the best ways to see the lake.

MS *Dixie II*, Zephyr Cove Marina, 4 miles north of the casinos on U.S. 50 (© **800/238-2463;** www.zephyrcove.com), is a 570-passenger vessel with bars, a dance floor, and a full dining room. Emerald Bay scenic cruises cost $26 for adults, $9 for children. They also have champagne-brunch and breakfast cruises ($30), dinner cruises ($44), and sunset dinner-dance cruises ($55).

Hornblower's *Tahoe Queen* (© **800/238-2463** or 530/541-3364; www.hornblower.com), departing from the Marina Village at Ski Run Boulevard in

South Lake Tahoe, is an authentic paddle-wheeler with a capacity of 500. It offers Emerald Bay sightseeing tours ($26 adults, $9 children) and dinner/dance cruises ($53 adults, $29 children), as well as full-service charters. Live music, buffet breakfast, dinner, and appetizers are all available onboard. The **Hornblower Ski Shuttle** ($129, including lift ticket, snacks, and ground transportation) is the world's only waterborne ski shuttle. On the way to Squaw Valley, you can have a breakfast buffet, and on the way home, enjoy an après-ski party. This ski shuttle allows skiers staying on the South Shore an opportunity to ski on the North Shore without having to drive over. Buses pick up passengers from their hotels in the morning and drop them off at night.

The *Tahoe Gal* (© 800/218-2464 or 530/583-0141; www.tahoegal.com), departing from the Lighthouse Marina (behind Safeway) in Tahoe City, is the only cruise boat on the North Shore. Cruises include Scenic Shoreline ($21 adults, $10 children), Emerald Bay ($26 adults, $14 children), Happy Hour (4:30–6pm; $22 for two adults, $8 children), and Sunset Dinner ($22 adults, $12 children). *Note:* Prices are for the cruise only; food and beverages cost extra.

Woodwind Sailing Cruises (© 888/867-6394; www.sailwoodwind.com) specializes in daily sightseeing cruises ($26 adults, $23 seniors, $12 children 3–12), sunset champagne cruises ($32), weddings, and charters. The Woodwind fleet includes the *Woodwind I,* a 30-passenger Searunner trimaran sailing to Emerald Bay from Camp Richardson Marina in South Lake Tahoe, and the *Woodwind II,* a 50-passenger Searunner catamaran sailing from Zephyr Cove Marina.

A DRIVE AROUND THE LAKE

Overwhelmed by the choices? Get in your car and take a leisurely drive around the lake. It's only 72 miles, but plan on taking several hours, even in the best of weather. In the worst of weather, don't try it! Parts of the road, if not closed, can be icy and dangerous. On a mild day, it will be a memorable experience. If your car has a tape deck, consider buying *Drive Around the Lake,* a drive-along audio cassette that contains facts, legends, places of interest, and just about everything else you might want to know about the lake. It's available at many gift shops or at the **South Lake Tahoe Chamber of Commerce,** 3066 Lake Tahoe Blvd. (© 530/541-5255; www.tahoeinfo.com), which is closed on Sundays.

We'll start at the California-Nevada border in South Lake Tahoe and loop around the western shore on Calif. 89 to Tahoe City and beyond. U.S. 50, which runs along the South Shore, is an ugly, overdeveloped strip that obliterates any view of the lake. Keep heading west and you will be free of this boring stretch.

First stop is the **Tallac Historic Site,** site of the former Tallac Resort and a cluster of 100-year-old mansions that provide a fascinating glimpse into Tahoe's past. In its heyday, the resort included two large hotels, a casino, and numerous outbuildings. Throughout the summer the **Valhalla Festival of Arts and Music** (© 888/632-5859 or 530/541-4975; www.valhalla-tallac.com) showcases jazz, bluegrass, rock, mariachi, and classical music. Summer highlights include June's Valhalla Renaissance Festival, July's Native American Fine Arts Festival, and August's Great Gatsby Festival.

From here the highway winds north along the shore until you reach **Cascade Lake** on the left and **Emerald Bay** 🌴🌴 on the right. The Emerald Bay Lookout is a spectacular picture-taking spot. Emerald Bay's deep green water is the site of the only island in Lake Tahoe, Fannette Island. The small structure atop the island is the teahouse, built by Ms. Lora Knight, who also constructed **Vikingsholm** 🌴 (© 530/541-3030), a 38-room Scandinavian Castle built in 1929, located at the head of Emerald Bay. Tours of this unique structure are available from mid-June to Labor Day every half-hour from 10am to 4pm. Even if you don't want to take the tour, it's a pleasant walk from the parking area down to the beach and the mansion's grounds. Just remember that you have to walk back up. Across the highway, there's another parking area. From here, it's a short, steep .25-mile hike to a footbridge above **Eagle Falls.** Then it's about a mile farther up to **Eagle Lake.**

Continuing on, it's only about 2 miles to **D. L. Bliss State Park** (© 530/ 525-7982), where you'll find one of the lake's best beaches. It gets crowded in the summer, so arrive early to get a parking place. The park also contains 168 campsites and several trails, including one along the shoreline.

In about 7 miles you will reach **Sugar Pine State Park** (© 530/525-7232), the largest (2,000 acres) of the lake's parks and also the only one that has year-round camping. In summer you can visit its beaches, plus a nature center and miles of trails; in winter there's cross-country skiing on well-maintained trails.

Continuing on through the town of **Homewood** (site of the ski resort), **Sunnyside,** on the right, is a pleasant place to stop for a lakeside lunch. Or, if you feel like taking a stroll, drive on to Tahoe City where there is a beautiful paved path along the Truckee River. Check out the big trout at **Fanny Bridge** 🏖 first. If you would like to see **Squaw Valley** and **Alpine Meadows,** take a left at Calif. 89. A ride on the Squaw Valley cable car (© 530/583-6985) will reward you with incredible vistas from 2,000 feet above the valley floor. It operates year-round and costs $17 for adults, $14 for seniors, and $5 for children under 13. Back on Calif. 28, as you leave **Tahoe City,** you will pass a string of small malls at 700 through 850 North Lake Blvd. If you enjoy just wandering around, this is a good area to stop and eat, watch the activity at the **Tahoe City Marina** (parasailing, cruises on the *Tahoe Gal,* and boat rental), or visit the shops.

Continuing around the lake on Calif. 28, you'll reach Carnelian Bay, Tahoe Vista, and Kings Beach before crossing the state line into Nevada. **Kings Beach State Recreation Area** 🏖 (© 530/546-7248) is a long, wide beach and picnic area. It is jammed in the summer with sunbathers and swimmers. As you approach **Crystal Bay,** you will immediately know you have crossed the state line by the string of small casinos that suddenly appear. The **Cal-Neva Resort, Spa & Casino** (p. 261) on the right was once owned by Frank Sinatra and has a very colorful, celebrity-filled history. The state line goes right through the lodge, and gambling is allowed only on the Nevada side. This is worth stopping to see.

Your journey next takes you to woodsy Incline Village, arguably the most beautiful community on the lake. Take a right on Lakeshore Boulevard to view the elegant estates. Lunch or dinner time? The **Lone Eagle Grille** (p. 260), at the Hyatt Regency Lake Tahoe, offers panoramic lake views as well as superb food.

The east shore of the lake is largely undeveloped and very scenic. Drive about 4 miles south of Incline Village to **Sand Harbor** 🏖 (© 775/831-0494), one of the lake's best-loved beaches, and home to the very popular **Lake Tahoe Shakespeare Festival** (© 800/747-4697; www.tahoebard.com) every mid-July through August. In addition to turquoise blue water dotted with big boulders and a wide sandy beach, you'll find nature trails, picnic areas, and boating.

Going south you will come to an outcropping called **Cave Rock** where the highway passes through 25 yards of solid stone. Farther along is **Zephyr Cove**

(Moments) Gondola to Heaven

If you want a preview of what it's like to be in heaven, take a ride on the Heavenly Valley Ski Resort gondola. At a cost of a mere $20 million, the gondola consists of state-of-the-art "cars" that whisk you from South Shore's downtown area up the mountain to Heavenly Resort's 14,000-square-foot observation deck. Each car holds up to eight people. The 2½-mile ride rises to an elevation of 9,123 feet, offering passengers shore-to-shore views of Lake Tahoe, Carson Valley to the east, and Desolation Wilderness to the west (all best seen at sunset).

The gondola is a half block west of Stateline, an easy walk from the downtown hotels. It's open year-round Monday through Friday from 10am to sunset, and Saturday and Sunday from 9am to sunset. Tickets are $20 for adults, $12 for children ages 6 to 12, and free for kids 5 and under.

Resort and Marina, home to the MS *Dixie II* and a beehive of watersports activity. You'll then return to Stateline and South Lake Tahoe, your original starting point.

WHERE TO STAY
SOUTH SHORE & SOUTH LAKE TAHOE
Expensive

Black Bear Inn Bed & Breakfast 🐾🐾   Within a wooded acre near Heavenly Ski Resort, this beautiful neo-rustic lodge offers luxury accommodations in a tranquil setting and convenient location (though not the prettiest in town). The great room, with its beamed ceilings, grand piano, early American antiques, three-story rock fireplace, and complimentary evening hors d'oeuvres, offers a relaxing environment after a long day of outdoor activities. Or better yet, soak your tired body in the sheltered Jacuzzi. Breakfast—included in the room rate—is an event in itself, with fresh-baked muffins, eggs Benedict, omelets, and other hearty fare. Each of the spacious guest rooms has an artful blend of modern and authentic Old West furnishings, including a king-size bed, private bathroom, and gas fireplace. For additional privacy, request one of the three cabins behind the inn, and ask for breakfast to be delivered to your door.

1202 Ski Run Blvd., South Lake Tahoe, CA 96150. ⓒ 877/232-7466 or 530/544-4451. www.tahoeblack bear.com. 5 lodge rooms, 3 cabins. $205–$245 lodge rooms; $265–$475 cabins. Rates include full breakfast. MC, V. **Amenities:** Nearby golf course; Jacuzzi. *In room:* A/C; TV/VCR; dataport; kitchenette, fridge, and coffeemaker; in cabins, hair dryer.

Caesars Tahoe 🐾   This 16-story hotel, built in the early 1980s, has the same glitter, glitz, and campy references to Roman mythology that Caesars Palace in Las Vegas has perfected. The guest rooms, many of which offer beautiful views of the lake, are furnished with contemporary hardwood pieces and equipped with extralarge tubs (Roman-style, of course). There's also a variety of suites, ranging from executive-style to lavishly appointed themed suites with Roman tubs (kinky, baby!). Highlights include a full casino with sports booking, the Circus Maximus showroom featuring top-name entertainment, and a lagoon-style indoor pool, plus indoor and outdoor wedding chapels. If you feel like gettin' jiggy with it,

Club Nero has live music and the biggest dance floor around. You can even indulge yourself in Caesars' full-service spa.

55 U.S. 50 (P.O. Box 5800), Lake Tahoe, NV 89449. ℂ 800/648-3353 or 775/588-3515. www.caesars.com. 440 units. $79–$300 double; $370–$950 suite. Packages available. AE, DC, MC, V. **Amenities:** 6 restaurants; 4 lounges; indoor pool; 3 outdoor tennis courts; health club; spa; Jacuzzi; sauna; ski rental; bike rental; video arcade; activities desk; car-rental desk; business center; shopping arcade; salon; 24-hr. room service; in-room massage; babysitting; dry cleaning; executive-level rooms. *In room:* A/C, TV, dataport, kitchenette and mini-bar in suites, fridge upon request, hair dryer, iron, safe.

Embassy Suites Resort 🌟 *Kids*   Perched on the edge of the state line and just steps away from Heavenly's gondola, this is the only major noncasino hotel on Tahoe's south shore, earning its keep by luring the upscale gambling crowd and the convention business with its uncommonly large suites. A nine-story château-style hotel, the roofline is pierced with a double layer of dormers; equally impressive is the massive inner atrium filled with plants. The one- and two-bedroom suites all have a separate living room with sofa bed, armchair, a well-lit dining/work table, a microwave, and a wet bar. Complimentary cooked-to-order breakfasts are served in a garden atrium. The resort's fine-dining restaurant, **Echo,** serves superb New American cuisine developed by award-winning chef Roy Choi. **Turtles Sports Bar & Dance Emporium,** which opens onto an outdoor deck, serves great pizzas during the day and turns into a dance club later in the evening. In the summer all guests have access to a private beach, and family skiers fill up the place in winter, partly because kids 18 and under stay free.

4130 Lake Tahoe Blvd., South Lake Tahoe, CA 96150. ℂ 800/362-2779 or 530/544-5400. Fax 530/544-4900. www.embassy-suites.com. 400 suites. $149–$359 double. Rates include full breakfast and evening cocktail reception. Special packages available. Children 18 and under stay free in parent's room. AE, DC, DISC, MC, V. **Amenities:** Restaurant; pizzeria; sports bar; indoor pool; outdoor sun deck; health club; spa; Jacuzzi; dry sauna; watersports equipment rental; concierge; car-rental desk; limited room service; in-room massage; babysitting; same-day dry cleaning; executive-level rooms. *In room:* A/C, TV/VCR, dataport, minibar, fridge, coffeemaker, hair dryer, iron.

Harrah's Casino Hotel 🌟 *Kids*   Understatement is not a word that comes to mind when you visit Harrah's, the most luxurious and glitzy of Tahoe's cadre of casinos. Harrah's takes great pride in its special blend of luxury, beauty, unparalleled guest service, and casino entertainment. The large rooms have two bathrooms, each with its own TV and telephone so you won't miss anything while bathing, and those thick, fluffy, white towels Sinatra always demanded. Most have bay windows overlooking the lake or the mountains. With families in mind, the casino has an enormous fun center with the latest in video and arcade games, virtual reality, and an indoor "playscape" for young children. Weddings and parties can be arranged aboard the private yacht, the *Tahoe Star*. The legendary **South Shore Room** features showbiz stars, and, in case you've forgotten what you're there for, the casino is a gambler's dream.

P.O. Box 8, Stateline, NV 89449. ℂ 800/427-7247 or 775/586-6607. Fax 775/586-6601. www.harrahstahoe. com. 525 units. $109–$229 double; $229–$399 suite. Packages available. AE, DC, DISC, MC, V. **Amenities:** 3 restaurants; cafe; deli; coffeehouse; indoor pool; full-service health club/spa; family fun center; game room; shopping arcade; salon; 24-hr. room service; in-room massage; same-day dry cleaning. *In room:* A/C, TV/VCR, coffeemaker, hair dryer, iron, safe.

Harveys Casino Resort, Lake Tahoe *Kids*   With its two massive towers and 740 rooms, Harveys is the largest (and possibly the ugliest) hotel in Tahoe. It features an 88,000-square-foot casino, eight restaurants (including a Hard Rock Cafe), and a cabaret with some of the most glittering, bespangled entertainment in town. More than a hotel, Harveys is like a city unto itself. There's a children's day camp, beauty and barber shops, and even a wedding chapel should you get the urge. Heck, you never have to see the real world again. *Tip:* Try to get a room between the 15th and 19th floors in the Lake Tower, where every unit has a view of both Lake Tahoe and the surrounding Sierra.

U.S. 50 at Stateline Ave. (P.O. Box 128), Stateline, NV 89449. © 800/HARVEYS or 775/588-2411. Fax 775/588-6643. www.harveystahoe.com. 740 units. $89–$299 double; $299–$699 suite. AE, DC, DISC, MC, V. **Amenities:** 8 restaurants; 10 bars; outdoor heated pool; nearby golf course; health club; spa; Jacuzzi; sauna; watersports equipment rental; children's day camp; video arcade; concierge; car-rental desk; business center; shopping arcade; salon; 24-hr. room service; in-room massage; laundry service; same-day dry cleaning. *In room:* A/C, TV w/pay movies, dataport, minibar, coffeemaker, hair dryer, iron, safe.

Tahoe Seasons Resort   Big, modern, and loaded with luxuries, the Tahoe Seasons lies in a relatively uncongested residential neighborhood at the base of the Heavenly Valley Ski Resort, 2 miles from Tahoe's casinos. Every unit here is a spacious, attractive suite, sleeping up to four in the smaller one and six in the larger one. Most have gas fireplaces, and all have huge whirlpool spas complete with shoji screens (just in case you plan on losing your shirt in more ways than one). Skiing isn't the only activity around here: Play a round of tennis on the roof or hop aboard the free casino shuttles.

3901 Saddle Rd., off Ski Run Blvd. (P.O. Box 5656), South Lake Tahoe, CA 96157. © 800/540-4874 or 530/541-6700. Fax 530/541-7342. www.tahoeseasons.com. 160 suites. Summer $170–$240 double; winter $180–$250 double; spring and fall $122–$200 double. Seasonal packages available. AE, MC, V. **Amenities:** Restaurant; pub; outdoor heated pool; nearby golf course; 2 rooftop tennis courts; complimentary use of health club at Harveys Resort; game room; concierge; tour and activities desk; courtesy car; room service; in-room massage; same-day dry cleaning. *In room:* A/C, TV/VCR, dataport, fridge, coffeemaker, hair dryer on request, iron.

Moderate

Best Western Station House Inn *Value*   Ensconced amid towering pine trees but just 3 blocks from the casinos, the Best Western Station House Inn was built

---

Village People

That sprawling "alpine village" that wasn't next to the casinos last year is the new 464-room **Marriott's Timber Lodge & Grand Residence Club** (4100 Lake Tahoe Blvd; © 800/845-5279; www.marriottvillarentals.com). It's the first phase of a massive redevelopment project slated for Stateline that will level most of the old, inexpensive motels that house the nickel-slotters and replace them with that expensive corporate faux-village thing that's taking over the world's tourist destinations. The two adjacent vacation ownership resorts also sell rooms on a per-night basis, but it's only a good deal if your family takes full advantage of the resort amenities: restaurants, bars, an ice-skating rink, two pools, a movie theater, a ski gondola, an arcade, and an alpine-style minimall of small retail shops. A silver lining to all this redevelopment is that the new building codes are fiercely pro-environment. Holding and treatment ponds are now required to prevent polluted snowmelt and rainwater from dumping straight into the lake, and the central ski gondola and a high-tech bus system are two new eco-friendly modes of luring people away from their SUVs.

in the late 1970s and is one of the few hotels in town that still has its own private "gated" beach on the lake. Okay, so it's not a particularly exciting hotel (the decor is corporate dull), but the location is ideal, the large swimming pool and hot tub are a huge bonus, and it even has its own *Wine Spectator*–award-winning restaurant, **LewMarNel's.** The complimentary cooked-to-order breakfast and free shuttle service make staying here a particularly good value.

901 Park Ave., South Lake Tahoe, CA 96150. 🕐 **800/822-5953** or 530/542-1101. Fax 530/542-1714. www.stationhouseinn.com. 100 units. $98–$138 double; $135–$165 suite; $200–$300 cabin. Rates include full breakfast. Packages available. AE, DC, DISC, MC, V. **Amenities:** Restaurant; heated outdoor pool; Jacuzzi; babysitting. *In room:* A/C, TV, coffeemaker, hair dryer.

Camp Richardson Resort 🕐🕐 *Kids*

If you are planning a family vacation, a reunion, or just a weekend getaway, Camp Richardson has it all (really, I love this place). Located on a long sandy beach on the southwest shore, this rustic, woodsy resort offers a wide array of activities as well as several lodging and dining choices. Its two restaurants offer lakeside dining, but there are also more-informal dining options, plus a general store, a candy store, and an ice-cream parlor. The sports center rents all the seasonal equipment you'll need. You can ski right along the shore here, or try scaling the rock-climbing wall. The full-service marina rents power- and ski boats, jet skis, kayaks, and paddleboats, and also offers guided tours, cruises, and chartered fishing trips. There's even a stable for horseback riding. Lodging options include a hotel, cabins, a beachside inn, a marina duplex, tent campgrounds, and an RV park. The children will fall into bed exhausted at night with all of the available organized activities. Cabins are only rented by the week in the summer and fill up quickly, so plan early. *Tip:* Be sure to check their website for seasonal money-saving packages.

Jameson Beach Rd. (P.O. Box 9028), South Lake Tahoe, CA, 96158. 🕐 **800/544-1801** or 530/541-1801. Fax 530/541-1802. www.camprichardson.com. $65–$175 hotel; $90–170 cabins per day, $565–$1,625 per week in summer. Camping or RV hookup $17–$26 per day. DISC, MC, V. **Amenities:** 2 restaurants; deli; cafe; Jacuzzi; sports center with bike, snowshoe, and ski rental; children's program; tour and activities desk; marina. *In room:* Coffeemaker. Inn has TV; duplex has TV, kitchen; cabin has kitchen. Hotel and cabin units have no phone.

Horizon Casino Resort *Value*

This massive resort hotel stands next to the even larger Harveys, and though it's not as well known as the other casinos, it charges less for basically the same facilities. The lobby is a cheesy sea of white marble and mirrors, and the standard rooms are decorated in typical bland yet inoffensive style (the suites, however, are far racier). The upper floors of the two towers naturally open onto the best views of mountains and the lake. Besides the 42,000-square-foot gaming room, the resort has a multiplex movie theater, cabaret, lounge, nightclub, the largest outdoor pool in Tahoe, and restaurants ranging from buffet to gourmet.

U.S. 50 (P.O. Box C), Lake Tahoe, NV 89449. 🕐 **800/648-3322** or 775/588-6211. Fax 775/588-0349. www.horizoncasino.com. 539 units. Summer $119–$169 double; winter $99–$169 double; $250–$500 suite. Children 11 and under stay free in parent's room. Packages available. AE, DC, DISC, MC, V. **Amenities:** 3 restaurants; large heated outdoor pool; nearby golf course; health club; bike and ski rental; video arcade; concierge; car-rental desk; business center; shopping arcade; salon; 24-hr. room service; in-room massage; babysitting; laundry service; same-day dry cleaning; executive-level rooms. *In room:* A/C, TV w/pay movies, dataport, minibar, fridge, coffeemaker, hair dryer, iron in suites.

Lakeland Village Beach & Mountain Resort 🕐 *Kids*

This condominium resort is a good choice for families. Clustered on 19 lightly forested acres of shoreline property, the half residential condo/half holiday resort complex was built in the 1970s. The layout is a labyrinth of redwood buildings that blend into the surrounding landscape. The only drawback is the proximity to traffic headed into Lake Tahoe, although some units are quieter than those in the main lodge, which lies adjacent to the road. The units, ranging from studios to four-bedroom lakeside apartments, have streamlined California architecture, and many have upstairs sleeping lofts. All rooms come with fully equipped kitchens and fireplaces. Perks include a large private beach opening directly onto the lake, access to a boat dock, and free shuttle service to Heavenly and the casinos.

3535 Lake Tahoe Blvd., South Lake Tahoe, CA 96150. ✆ 800/822-5969 or 530/544-1685. Fax 530/541-6278. www.lakeland-village.com. 212 condo units. $88–$290 double; $135–$975 for a 1 to 4-bedroom town house. Children stay free in parent's room. AE, DISC, MC, V. **Amenities:** 2 heated outdoor pools; nearby golf course; 2 outdoor tennis courts; 2 Jacuzzis; sauna; children's play area and wading pool; seasonal concierge; room service; laundry service; same-day dry cleaning. *In room:* TV/VCR, dataport, kitchen, fridge, coffeemaker, hair dryer, iron.

Inexpensive

Viking Motor Lodge *Value* You get a lot for your money here: agreeable accommodations, access to a private beach, and an easy walk to the casinos and the Heavenly gondola. Nothing fancy, but the rooms are clean and pleasant, and have all the standard conveniences. If you're traveling with kids, you may want one of the units with a kitchen. Be sure to inquire about the ski and golf packages.

4083 Cedar Ave., South Lake Tahoe, CA 96150. ✆ 800/288-4083 or 530/541-5155. Fax 530/541-5643. www.tahoeviking.com. 76 units. $49–$110 double. Children 11 and under stay free in parent's room. Rates include continental breakfast. Packages available. AE, DC, DISC, MC, V. **Amenities:** Outdoor heated pool; nearby golf course; Jacuzzi. *In room:* TV/VCR, dataport, fridge on request, coffeemaker, kitchen in 14 units, hair dryer, iron.

Zephyr Cove 🌟 *Kids* *Value* There are two places you want to bring the family to in Lake Tahoe: the Historic Camp Richardson Resort (see review above) and this lakeside bargain, Zephyr Cove. Amid a shady grove of tall pines about 4 miles from the casinos, this Nevada-side resort has everything you need for a relaxing vacation: a beautiful gold-sand beach, volleyball courts, a beachside bar serving strong mai tais, and water toys for rent: pedal boats, kayaks, canoes, and ski boats. Zephyr Cove's pier is also the launching point for cruises on the MS *Dixie II* paddle-wheeler and the *Woodwind II* catamaran. The resort's 28 cabins range in size from studios and cottages to four-bedroom cabins sleeping up to 10. The decor is low Levitz, but all units are very clean and come with well-equipped kitchens and a front porch with patio furniture (you'll be on the beach most of the time anyway). Even in the winter it's fun to stay here—the resort's snowmobile tours are fantastic, and the Heavenly ski resort is only a 10-minute drive away. The **Zephyr Cove Restaurant** serves hearty American fare for breakfast, lunch, and dinner daily, and there's free shuttle service to the restaurants and casinos down the road.

Hwy. 50 at Zephyr Cove, Nevada 89448. ✆ 775/589-4907. www.zephyrcove.com. 28 cabins. $119–$469 summer; $69–$399 off season. AE, DISC, MC, V. Pets are allowed with a $15 charge per pet, per night. **Amenities:** Restaurant; bar; gift shop; beach; volleyball court; watersports; sailing; horseback riding; snowmobiling. *In room:* TV w/cable and HBO; kitchen with refrigerator, oven, microwave, coffeemaker, cookware, dishes, and utensils; private bathroom; telephone; Internet access.

NORTH SHORE/TAHOE CITY
Expensive

Hyatt Regency Lake Tahoe 🌟 *Kids* If you like to gamble but hate gauche, glitzy casinos, you'll like the Hyatt in Incline Village. Located amid towering pines and mountains on the lake's pristine northeast shore, it's far, far classier and quieter than the casino hotels you'll find along Stateline. The resort's private beach, loaded with water toys—catamaran cruises, boat rentals, jet skis, parasailing—is available only to guests. The adjoining Lakeside Cottages are a wee bit o' heaven for families or honeymooners who want beachfront access and large, comfortable rooms with unobstructed panoramas of the lake. A bonus for families is the popular Camp Hyatt, which lets kids ages 3 to 12 get a break from their parents for the day. In addition to its other restaurants, the **Lone Eagle Grille** is one of the most beautiful restaurants on the lake. Be sure to take a walk (or a jog) down Lakeshore Boulevard to see the magnificent estates fronting the lake. The latest addition is a 15,000-square-foot spa facility with a multitiered swimming pool and an entire 150-room wing of "Spa Terrace" guest rooms.

Country Club at Lakeshore, 111 Country Club Dr., Incline Village, NV 89451. ℂ **888/899-5019** or 775/832-1234. Fax 775/831-7508. www.laketahoehyatt.com. 405 units, 24 cottages. $160–$330 double; $405–$1,385 cottage. Packages available. AE, DC, DISC, MC, V. **Amenities:** 4 restaurants; 4 lounges; nearby golf course; watersports equipment rental; bike rental; children's program; video arcade; concierge; tour and activities desk; car-rental desk; business center; room service; in-room massage; laundry service; same-day dry cleaning; executive-level rooms. *In room:* A/C, TV w/pay movies, dataport, minibar, fridge, coffeemaker, hair dryer, iron, safe.

Northstar-at-Tahoe Resort ★★★ (Kids)

The folks at Northstar continue to come up with even more ways to have fun year-round—the list of activities is mind-boggling. Priding itself on being the ultimate self-contained family destination, Northstar is about to get even better as it embarks on Phase I of the new Village, scheduled to be complete by December 2005. When it's finished, the Village will include seven new buildings in all, with 213 new luxury ski-in, ski-out condominium residences, stylish boutiques, outdoor restaurants, an ice rink, and a pedestrian plaza. The Northstar Village and Lodge will be surrounded by a honeycomb of fully equipped redwood condos and vacation homes, all nestled among the pines. Lodging options range from a hotel room in the lodge to a five-bedroom house, with every size in between. Summer activities include golf, swimming, tennis, mountain biking, hiking, fly-fishing, rock climbing, rope courses, and horseback riding. See "Skiing & Snowboarding," earlier in this chapter, for winter activities.

Off Hwy. 267, Box 129, Northstar-at-Tahoe, CA 96160. ℂ **800/466-6784** or 530/562-1010. Fax 530/562-2215. www.NorthstarAtTahoe.com. 100 new condominiums plus 262 existing units. $209–$349 double in lodge; $178–$989 condos, homes. Packages available. AE, DISC, MC, V. **Amenities:** Restaurants; cafe; deli; bars; outdoor heated pool; heated lap pool year-round; children's pool; golf course; 10 tennis courts; health club; 3 outdoor Jacuzzis; sauna; ice rink; bike rental; children and teen center; game room/video arcade; tour and activities desk; business center; babysitting; laundry facilities. *In room:* TV/VCR, kitchen in condos, coffeemaker, hair dryer, iron.

PlumpJack Squaw Valley Inn ★★★

Part ski chalet, part boutique hotel, PlumpJack Squaw Valley Inn is one of Tahoe's most refined and elegant hotels. Granted, it lacks the fancy toys offered by its competitor across the valley, The Resort at Squaw Creek (see below), but the PlumpJack is unquestionably more genteel, a tribute to the melding of artistry and hostelry. The hotel is draped in muted, earthy tones; swirling sconces and sculpted metal accents are candy for the eyes, while the rest of your body parts are enveloped in thick hooded robes, terry-cloth slippers, and down comforters atop expensive mattresses. Each room has mountain views for your pampered body to contemplate. The inn's equally fine restaurant, **PlumpJack Café**, is reviewed on p. 266.

1920 Squaw Valley Rd. (P.O. Box 2407), Olympic Valley, CA 96146. ℂ **800/323-7666** or 530/583-1576. Fax 530/583-1734. www.plumpjack.com. 61 units. Summer $145–$370; winter $175–$545. Rates include continental breakfast. AE, DISC, MC, V. **Amenities:** Restaurant; bar; heated outdoor pool (seasonal); nearby golf course; 2 Jacuzzis; bike rental; concierge; room service; in-room massage; laundry service; same-day dry cleaning; executive-level rooms. *In room:* TV w/pay movies, dataport, 1 unit available with kitchenette, minibar, fridge, coffeemaker in suites, hair dryer.

The Resort at Squaw Creek ★★★ *Kids* The most deluxe resort on the lake is the $130-million Resort at Squaw Creek, a paradise for skiers, golfers, and tennis players. It's ranked among the top 50 resorts in North America by *Conde Nast Traveler.* You can't beat the resort's ski-in/ski-out access to Squaw Valley skiing—in fact, a chairlift lands just outside the door. Don't ski? Don't worry. There are lots of other sports facilities to keep active travelers happy, including 20 miles of groomed cross-country skiing trails (marked for hiking and biking in the summer), sleigh and dogsled rides, an ice-skating rink, and, in summer, a world-class golf course and an equestrian center with riding stables. Particularly good for families, trained counselors lead a "Mountain Buddies" program for kids ages 4 to 13, offering different activities every day. While the standard guest rooms are not particularly spacious, they're well equipped with attractive furnishings, original artwork, and even windows with beautiful views that open to let in the mountain air. Suites come in all different sizes and configurations. *Tip:* Be sure to ask about the money-saving midweek package deals.

400 Squaw Creek Rd., Olympic Valley, CA 96146. © 800/403-4434 or 530/583-6300. Fax 530/581-6632. www.squawcreek.com. 403 units. $250–$395 double; $450–$1,900 suite. Packages available. AE, DC, DISC, MC, V. Valet parking $15; free self-parking. **Amenities:** 4 restaurants; deli; 4 bars; 3 pools (1 heated); golf course; 2 outdoor tennis courts; health club; region's largest spa; indoor and outdoor Jacuzzis; dry saunas; bike rental; children's program; video arcade; concierge; activities desk, courtesy car; business center; secretarial services; shopping arcade; salon; room service; in-room massage; babysitting; laundry service; same-day dry cleaning. *In room:* A/C, TV w/pay movies, dataport, minibar, coffeemaker, kitchen in some units, hair dryer, iron.

The Shore House ★★ This romantic little bed-and-breakfast inn, right on the lake, is a real charmer. Each individually decorated room has its own entrance, handmade log furniture, knotty-pine walls, a gas-log fireplace, and a blissfully comfortable feather bed. Guests have access to a private beach and landscaped lawn that overlook the lake, as well as to an in-house spa. Boat owners can even make use of its six buoys and private dock. If you're planning on tying the knot, the charming hosts will provide everything you need for a beautiful wedding ceremony, including an outdoor lakeside setting and a honeymoon cottage with a two-person spa tub.

7170 N. Lake Blvd. (P.O. Box 499), Tahoe Vista, CA 96148. © 800/207-5160 or 530/546-7270. Fax 530/546-7130. www.shorehouselaketahoe.com. 8 units, 1 cottage. $160–$240 double; $225–$285 cottage. Rates include full breakfast. DISC, MC, V. **Amenities:** Jacuzzi; massage. *In room:* A/C, fridge, hair dryer, no phone.

Moderate

Cal-Neva Resort, Spa & Casino ★ You might guess from its name that the state line literally runs right through this hotel, but you could never imagine its colorful, sometimes scandalous history. Ownership has been passed around by names like "Pretty Boy," "Babyface," and Sinatra, who built the famed Celebrity Room where many big names sang for their supper. It's here that Marilyn Monroe is alleged to have had her rendezvous with John F. Kennedy (you can even see the secret tunnel). Respectability, however, has laid claim to the Cal-Neva, and it is now a popular (and reputable) lakeside resort. Almost all of the rooms in the lodge have lake views and are quite elegantly decorated. Besides the casino (on the Nevada side of the hotel, of course), the Cal-Neva offers the full array of sport and spa options, a complete wedding-planning service, and two wedding chapels. Even if you don't stay here, stop by and take a look.

2 Stateline Rd. (Box 368), Crystal Bay, NV 89402-0368. © 800/225-6382 or 775/832-4000. Fax 775/831-9007. www.calnevaresort.com. 188 units, 9 chalets, 3 bungalows. $79–$189 double; $179–$269 suite, chalet, or bungalow. Packages available. AE, DC, DISC, MC, V. **Amenities:** Lake-view restaurant; heated outdoor pool; nearby golf course; 2 outdoor tennis courts; full-service European health spa; Jacuzzi; large video arcade; concierge; business center; salon; room service. *In room:* A/C, TV, fax, dataport, coffeemaker, hair dryer, iron.

Meeks Bay Resort 🐾 Located 10 miles south of Tahoe City, rustic Meeks Bay Resort is one of the oldest hostelries on the lake and something of a historical landmark. Opened as a public campground in 1920, its sweeping lakefront location boasts one of the finest beaches on the lake. During the next 50 years, the resort grew to include cabins and other improvements, and attracted many celebrities from Southern California. Acquired by the U.S. Forest Service in 1974, the property is open during summers only. Most rentals are on a weekly basis and consist of motel lodging or modest wood cabins perched near the lake. Facilities include a full marina with boat rentals, a campground with RV access ($20 a night, 4-night minimum), a beachfront snack bar, a playground, and a visitor center with a cultural display, coffee bar, and retail store. The Kehlet House, set on a rock that juts out into the lake, is the resort's prime accommodation. Owned at one time by William Hewlett, co-founder of the Hewlett-Packard Corporation, and later the summer residence of billionaire Gordon Getty, it has seven bedrooms, three bathrooms, a large kitchen, a living room, and water on three sides. The entire house is rented by the week, sleeps a dozen, and costs $3,850. Make all reservations here early.

P.O. Box 787, Tahoma, CA 96142 ✆ 877/326-3357 or 530/525-6946. Fax 530/525-4028. www.meeksbay resort.com. 21 units, 28 campsites. $85–$195 double per night; $770–$1,650 per week. AE, MC, V. Open May–Nov only. **Amenities:** Watersports equipment rental. *In room:* Kitchen in log cabins.

River Ranch Lodge & Restaurant 🐾🐾 The River Ranch Lodge has long been one of my favorite places to stay in Lake Tahoe. Situated alongside the Truckee River, the lodge is mere minutes away from Alpine Meadows and Squaw Valley ski resorts, and a short drive (or ride along the bike path) into Tahoe City. The best rooms in this rustic lodge have balconies that overlook the river. All have a handsome mountain-home decor, lodgepole-pine furniture, and down comforters. Room nos. 9 and 10, the farthest from the road, are my top choices. In summer, guests relax under umbrellas on the huge patio overlooking the river, working down burgers and beer while watching the rafters float by. During the ski season, the River Ranch's spectacular circular cocktail lounge and dining area, which cantilevers over the river, is a popular après-ski hangout. Also a big hit is the handsome **River Ranch Lodge Restaurant,** which serves fresh seafood, thick steaks, rack of lamb, and more exotic meats such as wood-oven roasted Montana elk loin with a dried-cherry/port sauce.

On Calif. 89, at Alpine Meadows Rd. (P.O. Box 197), Tahoe City, CA 96145. ✆ 800/535-9900 or 530/583-4264. Fax 530/583-7237. www.riverranchlodge.com. 19 units. $100–$160 double. Rates include continental breakfast. Packages available. AE, MC, V. **Amenities:** Restaurant; bar; golf course nearby; concierge. *In room:* TV, dataport, iron.

Sunnyside Lodge 🐾🐾 Built as a private home in 1908, this hotel and restaurant is one of the few grand old lodges still left on the lake. Located 2 miles south of Tahoe City, it looks very much like a giant wood cabin, complete with dormers, steep pitched roofs, and natural-wood siding—rustic looking but fairly sophisticated. Stretching across the building, a large deck fronts a tiny marina and gravel beach. The Lakefront rooms (suites 30 and 31 and rooms 32 to 39) are the most desirable and go for about $20 more than the others—well worth the added expense. Five units have rock fireplaces. Most of the lodge's ground floor is dominated by the popular **Sunnyside Restaurant** (p. 267).

1850 W. Lake Blvd. (P.O. Box 5969), Tahoe City, CA 96145. ✆ 800/822-2754 or 530/583-7200. Fax 530/583-2551. www.sunnysideresort.com. 23 units. $100–$250 double. Rates include continental breakfast. Packages available. AE, MC, V. **Amenities:** Restaurant; bar; nearby golf course; watersports equipment rental; room service. *In room:* TV/VCR, fridge in some units, hair dryer, iron.

Tahoma Meadows Bed & Breakfast *Kids*   Nothing glitzy about this historic bed-and-breakfast, just some cute red cabins nestled on a gentle forest slope surrounded by flowers and sugar pines. The units are individually decorated with paintings of bucolic settings, a private bathroom, and a comfy king- or queen-size bed; four units have gas-log fireplaces. The largest cabins, Treehouse and Sugar Pine, sleep up to six and are ideal for families. In the main lodge is the highly recommended **Stoneyridge Café,** serving breakfast daily (included in the room rate) and dinner Thursday through Saturday. Nearby activities include skiing at Ski Homewood (including shuttle service) and sunbathing at the lakeshore across the street. The friendly owners, Ulli and Dick White, will happily give advice on the best hiking and fishing spots (Dick's an avid fly-fisherman).

6821 W. Lake Blvd. (P.O. Box 810), Homewood, CA 96141. © **800/355-1596** or 530/525-1553. www.tahomameadows.com. 14 units. $95–$295 double. Rates include full breakfast. AE, DISC, MC, V. 8½ miles from Tahoe City; Pets accepted in some units with $25 fee. **Amenities:** Cafe; nearby golf course. *In room:* TV/VCR, kitchen in some units, no phone.

Inexpensive

Ferrari's Crown Resort *Value*   If you're looking for convenient, lakefront accommodations at a reasonable price, this family-operated motel is a great choice. The Ferrari family has proudly offered a warm family atmosphere to its guests since 1957. Family suites are completely equipped with kitchenettes and gas fireplaces and can sleep up to seven. Nothing fancy here, but this place is well run, the rooms are very inviting, and you can't beat the location. Plan a trip during the off season to take advantage of their great bargain rates.

8200 N. Lake Blvd. (P.O. Box 845), Kings Beach, CA 96143. © **800/645-2260** or 530/546-3388. Fax 530/546-3851. www.tahoecrown.com. 45 units. $45–$95 double; $70–$210 2-bedroom suites or lakefront rooms. Packages available. AE, DISC, MC, V. **Amenities:** Heated outdoor pool (seasonal); nearby golf course; free passes to nearby health club; Jacuzzi. *In room:* A/C, TV, stocked kitchenette, fridge, coffeemaker, hair dryer, iron in some units.

Lake of the Sky Motor Inn   This remodeled 1960s-style A-frame motel in the heart of Tahoe City offers clean, quiet, inexpensive accommodations in a central location—only steps away from shops and restaurants and a main stop for the ski shuttles. Just the basics here—TV, phone, bathroom—so plan on spending most of your time outdoors. Some rooms have lake views, and there's an attractively landscaped picnic-and-barbecue area.

955 N. Lake Blvd. (P.O. Box 227), Tahoe City, CA 96145. © **530/583-3305.** Fax 530/583-7621. www.lakeoftheskyinn.com. 23 units. $59–$129 double. Children 11 and under stay free in parent's room. Rates include continental breakfast. AE, DC, DISC, MC, V. **Amenities:** Heated outdoor pool (seasonal); nearby golf course. *In room:* TV, dataport, fridge in some units.

North Lake Lodge *Value*   Sure, the private lakeside cabins at North Lake Lodge are a little on the funky side, but for as little as $60 a night, most people are willing to put up with a few blemishes here and there. This is truly a great deal: Each unit, some dating from the 1920s, has its own bathroom, deck, and picnic facilities, and many have fully equipped kitchens and views of the lake (units without kitchens have refrigerators, coffeemakers, and microwaves). The cabins are the popular first choice. There's a public beach nearby (as well as a boat ramp), and in the winter free shuttle buses from Alpine Meadows, Squaw, and Northstar swing by. Be sure to bring a bag of charcoal for the lodge's barbecue pits, and some chump change for the nearby casinos.

8716 N. Lake Blvd. (P.O. Box 955), Kings Beach, CA 96143. © **888/923-5253** or 530/546-2731. Fax 530/546-5130. www.northlakelodge.com. 20 units, 4 bungalows, 5 cabins. $85–$105 double. AE, DC, DISC, MC, V. **Amenities:** Spa. *In room:* TV, fridge, coffeemaker.

Tamarack Lodge ✿   One of the oldest lodges on the North Shore—so old it was a favorite haunt of Clark Gable and Gary Cooper—is now one of the best bets for the frugal traveler. Hidden among a 4-acre cadre of pines just east of Tahoe City, the Tamarack Lodge consists of a few old cabins, five "poker rooms," and a modern (and far less nostalgic) motel unit. The rooms in the motel unit are the least appealing but are certainly clean and comfortable. The cabins all have kitchenettes and can hold up to four guests, but the most popular rooms by far are the original poker rooms (where Gable and Cooper used to play cards) lined with gleaming knotty pine. Complimentary coffee and tea are served in the lobby, and rollaway beds are available for only $5 extra. Though the beach is within walking distance, you'll need a car to make forays into town.

2311 N. Lake Blvd. (P.O. Box 859), Tahoe City, CA 96145. ✆ **888/824-6323** or 530/583-3350. Fax 530/583-3531. www.tamarackattahoe.com. 17 units, 4 cabins. $54–$145 double. DISC, MC, V. *In room:* TV.

WHERE TO DINE
SOUTH SHORE & SOUTH LAKE TAHOE
Expensive

Evan's American Gourmet Café ✿✿ AMERICAN/CONTINENTAL After a dinner at Evan's, you'll feel you've had not just a good meal but a great dining experience. The restaurant's impeccable service, award-winning wine list, and unyielding attention to detail serve as a perfect backdrop for the creative culinary artistry of Candice or Evan Williams. The philosophy here is to use only the finest, freshest ingredients and not overwhelm them with heavy sauces or overstylized culinary technique. The cuisine is an original blend of styles from around the world, with each dish being an artistic creation. For appetizers, typical choices are sautéed Dungeness crab cakes on roasted red-pepper purée with crème fraîche or seared Sonoma foie gras with curried ice cream and roast pineapple. Entrees might include house-smoked-duck-breast salad with microgreens and papaya vinaigrette, or roast Cevena venison with balsamic roast cherries, fresh tarragon, and lacquered root vegetables. If you have room, the desserts are luscious as well as beautiful. Seats are limited in this cozy little restaurant so be sure to call ahead for reservations.

536 Emerald Bay Rd., South Lake Tahoe. ✆ **530/542-1990.** www.evanstahoe.com. Reservations required (must confirm by 4pm). Main courses $18–$25. DISC, MC, V. Daily 5:30–9:30pm.

Fresh Ketch ✿ SEAFOOD   Ensconced in a small marina at the foot of Tahoe Keys Boulevard, Fresh Ketch has long been regarded as South Lake's premier seafood restaurant. Try to get a window table so you can watch the marina activities. For starters, I always order half a dozen oysters and the seared *ahi* tuna with ponzu and wasabi dipping sauces. Then it's on to the sautéed sea bass encrusted with pistachio, herbs, and garlic, or the big ol' Alaskan king crab, steamed in the shell and served with the requisite drawn butter. There's also a modest selection of meat and poultry dishes, including a great surf and turf of petite mignon and lobster. For dessert, the calorie fest continues with a big slice of Kimo's Hula Pie. Prices are a bit steep, but you can always join the locals at the bar and order from the extensive bar menu, which offers everything from blackened mahimahi to fresh-fish tacos and fish and chips, all for under $10. There's also live music Friday and Saturday evenings.

2433 Venice Dr. ✆ **530/541-5683.** Reservations recommended. Main courses $17–$24; market price for crab and lobster. AE, DC, DISC, MC, V. Daily 11:30am–10pm (bar open until 10pm).

Moderate

Cantina Bar & Grill *★* MEXICAN   The Cantina Bar & Grill is a favorite local hangout and serves the best Mexican food in South Lake. With friendly service, sports on three TVs, and 30 kinds of beer, joviality reigns. The menu is well priced and extensive, offering Cal-Mex specialties such as tacos, burritos, and enchiladas along with a half-dozen Southwestern dishes such as smoked chicken polenta and grilled pork chops with jalapeño mashed potatoes. The steak fajitas get a thumbs-up, as do the barbecued baby back ribs. To demonstrate their sense of whimsy and eclectic ethnic appeal, they offer an Oriental chicken salad and a Southwestern Reuben sandwich, as well as a few vegetarian selections.

765 Emerald Bay Rd. © 530/544-1233. www.cantinatahoe.com. Main courses $8–$15. MC, V. Daily 11:30am–10:30pm (bar open until midnight).

Ivano's *★★* *Finds* ITALIAN   Although Ivano Costantini is well known among South Lake's connoisseurs of authentic Italian cuisine, his bistro is easy to miss. On Nevada's southeastern shoreline, it's recessed into a tiny business complex off the highway. But follow the hunger-inducing aromas of garlic, olive oil, and fresh basil and you'll soon find the front door. Ivano, the charismatic owner and maitre d', is usually there to greet guests and escort them to his intimate dining room adorned with crisp white tablecloths, fresh flowers, and framed paintings of Italian coastal towns. Entrees range from reasonably priced pasta standards such as *tortellini di Parma,* linguine puttanesca, and *fettuccini al Bolognese,* to well-prepared *secondi* classics. My favorite dish is the *filetto di Giovanni,* thinly sliced tenderloin marinated in olive oil, vinegar, and rosemary, then quickly seared to lock in the juices (no fusion confusion at this restaurant). The *scaloppine parmigiana* (veal with fresh tomato sauce, prosciutto, and mozzarella) is also quite good. The lengthy wine list offers more than 100 wines from Italy and California.

605 Hwy. 50, #4, Zephyr Cove. © 775/586-1070. Reservations recommended. Entrees $10–$19. AE, DISC, MC, V. Daily 5–10pm.

The Naked Fish *★★* SUSHI   I exist to eat sushi, so believe me when I tell you that The Naked Fish in South Lake is the best sushi bar in Tahoe. I can never understand a word the Japanese chefs are saying to me, but I'm not paying much attention—the warm-butter-soft *hamachi nigiri* (yellowtail) has made my toes curl again. The colorful aquamarine theme with mermaids floating across the walls adds to the laid-back atmosphere of this locally owned Japanese restaurant. Before you open the menu, read the "specials" board above the sushi bar—this is the *really* fresh stuff, such as the deftly shelled live scallop sashimi that's still moving as the chef carves it into edible art. In the spirit of a true sushi bar, the chefs are friendly and talkative, particularly if you buy them a beer. Wimps can order cooked dinners such as sesame-crusted halibut and teriyaki chicken, but it's the flavorful rolls, tender cuts of nigiri, and festive bar that true sushi hounds will appreciate.

3940 Lake Tahoe Blvd. (at the junction of Hwy. 50 and Pioneer Trail). © 530/541-3474. Reservations recommended for parties of 6 or more. Main courses $14–$23; sushi $4–$11. AE, DC, DIS, MC, V. Lunch Sat–Sun 11:30am–2pm; dinner daily 5–9pm.

Inexpensive

Sprouts Natural Foods Café *Value* HEALTH FOOD/JUICES   Sprouts owner Tyler Cannon has filled a much-needed niche in South Lake, serving wholesome food that looks good, tastes good, and *is* good. Most everything is made in-house, including the soups, smoothies, and fresh-squeezed juices. Menu items range from rice bowls to sandwiches (try the Real Tahoe Turkey), huge burritos, coffee drinks, muffins, fresh-fruit smoothies, and a marvelous mayo-free tuna sandwich made with yogurt and packed with fresh veggies. Order from the counter, then scramble for a vacant seat (outdoor tables are coveted). This is also an excellent place to pack a picnic lunch.

3123 Harrison Ave. (at U.S. 50 and Alameda St., next to Lakeview Sports). (✆ **530/541-6969.** Meals $4.50–$6.75. No credit cards. Daily 8am–9pm.

Yellow Sub *Value* SANDWICHES   When it comes to picnic supplies, there's stiff competition in South Lake Tahoe: three sandwich shops on this block alone. Still, my favorite is Yellow Sub, voted best deli sandwich shop by readers of the *Tahoe Daily Tribune* for 8 years straight. It offers 21 versions of overstuffed subs—made in 6-inch and 12-inch varieties—as well as several kinds of wraps. The shop is in a small shopping center across from the El Dorado Campground.

983 Tallac Ave. (at U.S. 50). (✆ **530/541-8808.** Sandwiches and wraps $3.20–$7.15. No credit cards. Daily 10:30am–10pm.

NORTH SHORE/TAHOE CITY
Expensive

PlumpJack Café ★★ MODERN AMERICAN   Squaw Valley's investors have spent oodles of money trying to turn the ski resort into a world-class destination, and one major step in the right direction is the sleek, sexy PlumpJack Café. Although dinner prices have dropped slightly (guests balked at the original rates), none of PlumpJack's standards have diminished. Expect impeccable service regardless of your attire (this is, after all, a ski resort). Menu choices range from spicy Maine soft-shell crab with pickled ginger vinaigrette and chili tobiko to milk-brined double-cut pork chop with Yorkshire pudding and summer vegetables, plus a fabulous dish of braised oxtail paired with horseradish mashed potatoes and carrots. Those familiar with PlumpJack in San Francisco know that the reasonably priced wine list is among the nation's best.

In the PlumpJack Squaw Valley Inn, 1920 Squaw Valley Rd., Squaw Valley. (✆ **530/583-1576.** www.plump jack.com. Reservations recommended. Main courses $17–$20. AE, MC, V. Daily 7–10am, 11:30am–2:30pm, and 6–10pm.

Wild Goose ★★★ CONTEMPORARY AMERICAN   Without question, Wild Goose is the finest restaurant in Lake Tahoe and one of my favorites in all of California. It offers the best of everything: a panoramic view of the lake, sleek yet warmly textured modern design elements, and contemporary American cuisine on par with the Bay Area's finest. The restaurant is fashioned after those classic lake cruisers of the 1920s with a profusion of finely polished mahogany and metal; large picture windows overlook a terraced patio dining area with a postcard view. The beautifully arranged presentations are expertly prepared and presented by a well-trained staff. A recent meal started with a fried squash blossom appetizer stuffed with herbed goat cheese, followed by curried blue claw crab with mango crème fraîche. The main courses we ordered were superb: wild-mushroom-crusted halibut with purslane salad and creamy mashed potatoes, and hoisin-barbecued salmon with braised bok choy and shiitake mushrooms, topped with a coconut–green curry sauce. In the winter, request a table near the custom-built fireplace, and be sure to arrive before the sun sets.

7320 N. Lake Blvd, Tahoe Vista. (✆ **530/546-3640.** www.wildgoosetahoe.com. Reservations recommended. Entrees $10–$29. AE, DISC, MC, V. Daily 5–10pm.

Wolfdale's ★★ CALIFORNIA/JAPANESE   Wolfdale's has long been one of Tahoe's finest restaurants, where everything from focaccia to sausages, smoked fish, and desserts is prepared in-house. Chef-owner Douglas Dale knows how to put an international spin on regional ingredients, fusing flavors and textures of the East and the West for a "cuisine unique" experience. Although the menu changes frequently, dinner might begin with soft-shell crab tempura, vegetable spring roll with a Thai curry-ginger sauce, or spinach salad tossed with smoked local trout, olives, and grated eggs. Main courses are equally inventive, such as roasted quail stuffed with fennel sausage and onions served on a bed of kale, or grilled Columbia River sturgeon with mushroom duxelles and tomato coulis. I prefer to dine at the small bar, but if it's nice out, request a table on the outdoor deck.

640 N. Lake Blvd., Tahoe City. ✆ 530/583-5700. www.wolfdales.com. Reservations recommended. Main courses $18–$24. DISC, MC, V. Wed–Mon 6–10pm (open daily July–Aug).

Moderate

Café 333 ☆☆ ECLECTIC AMERICAN   The cuisine at this chic little cafe has been described as contemporary French country style with a San Francisco flair. Whatever you call it, the food is outstanding. If you're tired of the same old breakfasts, you'll love your choices here. Try the Breakfast Strata ("bread pudding" baked with prosciutto, spinach, tomato, basil, mascarpone, Parmesan, and cream), the chicken hash, or the caramelized-apple French toast. Gourmet coffees and creative omelets also grace the menu. For lunch you can't go wrong with any of their tasty salads, sandwiches, or pastas. The dinner menu might include grilled vegetable risotto or salmon with fresh herbed gnocchi and Gorgonzola sauce. The desserts are made in-house and include such tempters as crème brûlée, caramel chocolate pecan pie, and berry shortcake. They need more room to accommodate their enthusiastic guests, but the ambience is so cheerful that somehow you don't mind sometimes rubbing elbows.

333 Village Blvd., Incline Village. ✆ 775/832-7333. Breakfast $7–$9; lunch $8–$12; dinner $15–$24. MC, V. Daily 7am–3pm and 5:30–9pm.

Gar Woods Grill & Pier ☆ AMERICAN   Named after the builder of those beautiful mahogany race boats that used to grace the lake in the 1930s and 1940s, Gar Woods attempts to capture the nostalgia and atmosphere of that old wooden boat era. Whether folks are watching *Monday Night Football* or drinking a famous "Wet Woody," it seems like there's always something going on in the bar. And on a sunny day, it's great fun to sit out on the lakeside deck to enjoy the good food and good cheer. The menu is wide-ranging, covering everything from a shrimp-and-lobster bisque to a pepper-and-garlic turkey burger with curly fries. Appetizers go from beer-battered coconut prawns to sashimi. Dinner entrees include nothing out of the ordinary, but the preparation is good and the service is friendly. Try the sumptuous Sunday brunch—it's more food than you could ever imagine for $26.

5000 N. Lake Blvd., Carnelian Bay. ✆ 800/BY-TAHOE or 530/546-3366. www.garwoods.com. Lunch $9–$14; dinner $14–$27; brunch $26. AE, DISC, MC, V. Mon–Sat 11:30am–10pm; Sun 10:30am–10pm.

Sunnyside Restaurant ☆ CALIFORNIA   In summer when the sun's shining, there's no more highly coveted table in Tahoe than one on Sunnyside's lakeside veranda. Guests can also dine in the lodge's more traditional Chris Craft Dining Room with its 1930s aura. Nothing out of the ordinary here: The lunch menu has fresh pastas, burgers, chicken, and fish sandwiches, together with a variety of soups and salads. Dinners are fancier, with such main courses as Australian lobster tail, lamb chops with roasted-garlic chutney butter, and fresh salmon oven-baked on a cedar plank. In the winter the bar has a lively après-ski scene where both tourists and locals come to watch ski flicks on the big screen and refuel on inexpensive appetizers.

At the Sunnyside Lodge, 1850 W. Lake Blvd., Tahoe City. © **800/822-2754** or 530/583-7200. www.sunnyside resort.com. Main courses $14–$24. AE, DISC, MC, V. Oct–June daily 4–9:30pm; July–Sept Sun–Thurs 11am–9:30pm, Fri–Sat 11am–10pm; year-round Sun brunch 9:30am–2pm.

Inexpensive

Bridgetender Tavern and Grill *Value* PUB GRUB Although it's located in one of the most popular tourist areas in North Lake, the Bridgetender is a locals' hangout through and through. Still, they're surprisingly tolerant of out-of-town-ers, who come for the cheap grub and huge selection of draft beers. Big burgers, salads, pork ribs, fish and chips, and such round out the menu, all very filling and inexpensive. In summer, dine at the patio among the pines.

65 W. Lake Blvd. (at Fanny Bridge), Tahoe City. © **530/583-3342**. Burgers, salads, and ribs $5–$8. DISC, MC, V. Daily 11am–2am.

Fire Sign Café *Value* AMERICAN Choosing a place to have breakfast in North Tahoe is a no-brainer. Since the late 1970s, the Fire Sign Café has been the locals' choice—which explains the lines out the door on weekends. Just about everything is made from scratch, such as the delicious coffee cake that accompanies the big plates of bacon and eggs or blackberry-buckwheat pan-cakes. Even the salmon for chef and owner Bob Young's legendary salmon omelet is smoked in-house. Lunch—burgers, salads, sandwiches, burritos, and more—is also quite popular, particularly when the outdoor patio is open.

1785 W. Lake Blvd., Tahoe City. © **530/583-0871**. Breakfast and lunch $4–$9. MC, V. Daily 7am–3pm.

TAHOE AFTER DARK

Tahoe is not particularly known for its nightlife, although there's always some-thing going on in the showrooms of the major casinos on the South Shore. Call **Harrah's** (© 775/588-6611), **Harveys** (© 775/588-2411), **Caesars** (© 775/588-3515), and the **Horizon** (© 775/588-6211) for current show schedules and prices. Most cocktail shows cost $15 to $45. On the North Shore, there's usually live music nightly in **Bullwhackers Pub,** at the Resort at Squaw Creek (© 530/583-6617; p. 261). The **Pierce Street Annex,** 850 N. Lake Blvd. (© 530/583-5800), behind the Safeway in Tahoe City, has pool tables, shuffle-board, and DJ dancing every night. It's one of the livelier places around. If it's just a casual cocktail you're after, my favorite spot is the cozy fireside lounge at **River Ranch Lodge,** which cantilevers over a turbulent stretch of the Truckee River, on Calif. 89 at the entrance to Alpine Meadows (© **530/583-4264**).

2 Mount Shasta & the Cascades ★★

274 miles N of San Francisco

Chances are, your first glimpse of Mount Shasta's majestic, snowcapped peak will result in a twang of awe. A dormant volcano with a 17-mile-diameter base, it stands in virtual isolation 14,162 feet above the sea. When John Muir first saw Shasta from 50 miles away in 1874, he wrote: "[I] was alone and weary. Yet my blood turned to wine, and I have not been weary since." He went on to describe it as "the pole star of the landscape," which indeed it is.

Keep in mind, however, that dining and lodging in these parts lean more toward sustenance than indulgence: It's the fresh air, not fresh fish, that lures vis-itors this far north. You can leave the dinner jacket at home—all that's really

Redding/Mount Shasta Area

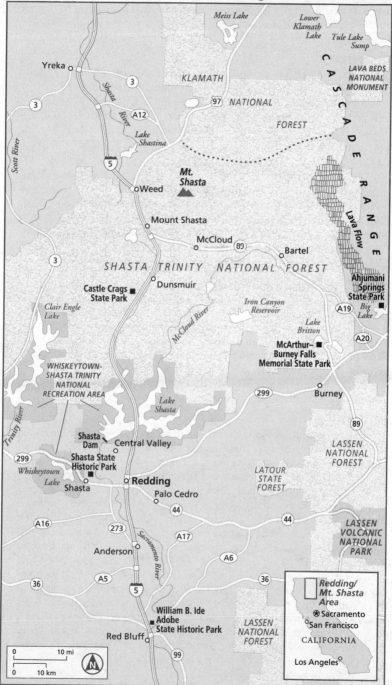

Yreka

Meiss Lake

Lower Klamath Lake

Tule Lake Sump

3

3

A12

Shasta River

Scott River

5

Lake Shastina

KLAMATH

97

NATIONAL

FOREST

C A S C A D E

LAVA BEDS NATIONAL MONUMENT

Mt. Shasta

Weed

Mount Shasta

McCloud

80

Bartel

R A N G E

Lava Flow

SHASTA TRINITY NATIONAL FOREST

3

Castle Crags State Park

Dunsmuir

McCloud River

Iron Canyon Reservoir

Lake Britton

Ahjumani Springs State Park

A19

Big Lake

A20

Clair Engle Lake

WHISKEYTOWN-SHASTA TRINITY NATIONAL RECREATION AREA

Lake Shasta

McArthur–Burney Falls Memorial State Park

Trinity River

299

Burney

89

Shasta Dam

Central Valley

LASSEN NATIONAL FOREST

299

Whiskeytown Lake

Shasta State Historic Park

Shasta

Redding

Palo Cedro

LATOUR STATE FOREST

44

44

A16

273

Sacramento River

A17

A6

LASSEN VOLCANIC NATIONAL PARK

Anderson

36

A5

5

36

William B. Ide Adobe State Historic Park

Red Bluff

99

LASSEN NATIONAL FOREST

Redding/ Mt. Shasta Area

⊗ Sacramento

San Francisco

CALIFORNIA

Los Angeles

0   10 mi
0   10 km

N

269

required when visiting the Far North are a pair of broken-in hiking boots, binoculars (the bald eagle is a common sight in these parts), some warm clothing, and an adventurous spirit.

ESSENTIALS

GETTING THERE   From San Francisco, take I-80 to I-505 to I-5 to Redding. From the coast, pick up Calif. 299 East north of Arcata, to Redding.

Redding Municipal Airport, 6751 Woodrum Circle (© 530/224-4321), is serviced by **United Express** (© 800/241-6522) and **Horizon Air** (© 800/547-9308). **Amtrak** (© 800/USA-RAIL) stops in Dunsmuir and Redding.

VISITOR INFORMATION   Regional information can be obtained from the following organizations: **Shasta Cascade Wonderland Association,** 1699 Calif. 273, Anderson, CA 96007 (© 800/474-2782 or 530/365-7500; www.shasta cascade.org); **Mount Shasta Visitors Bureau,** 300 Pine St., Mount Shasta, CA 96067 (© 800/926-4865 or 530/926-4865; www.mtshastachamber.com); **Redding Convention & Visitors Bureau,** 777 Auditorium Dr., Redding, CA 96001 (© 800/874-7562 or 530/225-4100; www.visitredding.org); and **Trinity County Chamber of Commerce,** 210 N. Main St., P.O. Box 517, Weaverville, CA 96093 (© 800/487-4648 or 530/623-6101; www.trinitycounty.com).

THE REPUBLIC OF CALIFORNIA

En route to Mount Shasta from the south, you may want to stop near Red Bluff at **William B. Ide Adobe State Historic Park,** 21659 Adobe Rd. (© **530/529-8599**), for a picnic along the Sacramento River and a visit to an adobe home dating back to 1852. The 4-acre park commemorates William B. Ide, the Republic of California's first and only president. The Republic of California was proclaimed on June 14, 1846, following the Bear Flag Rebellion and lasted only 3 weeks. In summer the park is open from 8am to sunset, the house from noon to 4pm; call ahead in winter. Parking costs $3 per vehicle.

REDDING

The major town and gateway to the region is Redding, the hub of the panoramic Shasta-Cascade region, at the top of the Sacramento Valley. From here, you can turn westward into the wilderness forest of Trinity and the Klamath Mountains, or north and east into the Cascades and Shasta Trinity National Forest.

In Redding, with its fast-food joints, gas stations, and cheap motels, summer heat generally hovers around 100°F (38°C). A city of some 80,000, Redding is the transportation hub of the upper reaches of Northern California. It has little of interest; it's mainly useful as a base for exploring the natural wonders nearby. Information is available from the **Redding Convention & Visitors Bureau,** 777 Auditorium Dr., Redding, CA 96001 (© **800/874-7562** or 530/225-4100; www.visitredding.org), west of I-5 on Calif. 299. It's open Monday through Friday from 8am to 5pm. Ahead and northeast, Mount Shasta rises to a height of more than 14,000 feet. From Redding, I-5 cuts north over the Pit River Bridge, crossing Lake Shasta and leading eventually to the mount itself. Before striking north, however, you may want to explore **Lake Shasta** and see **Shasta Dam.** Another option is to take a detour west of Redding to Weaverville, Whiskeytown–Shasta Trinity National Recreation Area, and Trinity Lake (see "Whiskeytown National Recreation Area" below).

About 3 miles west, stop at the old mining town of **Shasta,** which has been converted into a state historic park (© **530/243-8194**). Shasta was founded on gold and was the "Queen City" of the northern mines in the Klamath Range. Its

---

Tips **Shasta vs. Mount Shasta**

Don't confuse the old mining town, Shasta, located a few miles west of Redding, with the much larger community, Mount Shasta, a major tourist destination located on Interstate 5 near the base of Mount Shasta.

---

life was short, and it expired in 1872 when the Central Pacific Railroad bypassed it in favor of Redding. Today the business district is a ghost town, complete with a restored general store and a Masonic hall. The **1861 courthouse** has been converted into a museum where you can view the jail and a gallows out back, as well as a remarkable collection of California art assembled by Mae Helen Bacon Boggs. The collection includes works by Maynard Dixon, Grace Hudson, and many others. It's open Wednesday through Sunday from 10am to 5pm. Admission is $2 for adults; children visit for free.

Continue along Calif. 299 west to Calif. 3 north, which will take you to Weaverville and then to the west side of the lake and Trinity Center.

WHERE TO STAY

In addition to Tiffany House (see below), Redding has a **Red Lion Hotel,** 1830 Hilltop Drive, Redding (© **800/733-5466** or 530/221-8700; www.redlion.com) and a **La Quinta Inn,** 2180 Hilltop Drive, Redding (© **800/NU-ROOMS** or 530/221-8200; www.laquinta.com). Both are fine choices.

Tiffany House Bed and Breakfast Inn   Perched on a hill above town is this beautifully refurbished Cape Cod–style inn. A sweeping view of the Lassen Mountain Range is visible from every guest room and cottage, as well as from the oversize deck, which seems to float above the garden in back. There's also a Music Room with piano and a Victorian Parlor with fireplace, games, and puzzles. Each guest room is appointed with a queen-size bed and antique furnishings, and all have private bathrooms and soft robes. Top choice is the secluded Lavinia's Cottage, which has a 7-foot spa tub, sitting area, and magnificent laurel-wreath iron bed.

1510 Barbara Rd., Redding, CA 96003. © **530/244-3225.** www.sylvia.com/tiffany.htm. 4 units. $90–$110 double; $140 cottage. Rates include full breakfast. AE, DISC, MC, V. **Amenities:** Outdoor pool; nearby golf courses; Jacuzzi; game room. In room: A/C, hair dryer, no phone.

WHERE TO DINE

Buz's Crab Stand ★★ (Finds) SEAFOOD   Don't let the Naugahyde booths and Formica tables fool you: This funky fish joint is one of the best roadside seafood stands in Northern California. What's been drawing fans here from all over California for over 30 years are the "seafood baskets," which come packed with crisp potato rounds, fresh-baked sourdough bread, and whatever's in season: could be prawns, oysters, scallops, clam strips, calamari, catfish, or even Cajun halibut. The fish and chips are excellent as well. From December to May, crab's the hot ticket, served freshly boiled from the crab pots on the patio and served with drawn butter and cocktail sauce. **Tip:** Log on to Buz's website and print the fantastic cioppino recipe—I've slayed 'em at dinner parties with this one.

2159 East St., at Cypress Ave. © **530/243-2120.** www.buzscrab.com. Main courses $2.50–$10. MC, V. Daily 11am–9pm.

Jack's Grill ★ STEAKHOUSE   This building was originally constructed in 1835 as a secondhand-clothing store. The second floor served as a brothel in the late 1930s, and an entrepreneur named Jack Young set up the main floor as a steakhouse (his establishment serviced all of a body's needs, you might say). Today it's a local favorite. Waiting for a table over drinks in the bar is part of the fun. Good old-fashioned red meat—thick 1-pound steaks, tender brochettes, fat steak sandwiches—is supplemented by a couple of seafood dishes, such as deep-fried jumbo prawns and ocean scallops. It's a very fetching spot, with good, honest tavern food and a jovial crowd. Be prepared to wait on weekends.

1743 California St. ✆ 530/241-9705. www.jacksgrillredding.com. Reservations not accepted. Main courses $9.15–$22. AE, DISC, MC, V. Mon–Sat 4–11pm.

WEAVERVILLE

Weaverville was a gold mining town in the 1850s, and part of the history of the place is captured at the **Jake Jackson Memorial Museum–Trinity County Historical Park,** 508 Main St. (✆ 530/623-5211). The collection of memorabilia, from firearms to household items, is interesting for what it reveals about the residents—Native Americans, miners, pioneers, and especially the Chinese. In the Gold Rush era, the town was half Chinese, with a Chinatown of about 2,500 residents. Admission is free, but a donation of $1 is suggested.

Across the parking lot, you can view the oldest continuously used Taoist temple in California at the **Joss House State Historic Park** (✆ 530/623-5284). This well-preserved temple was built by immigrant Chinese miners in 1874. Admission is $2 for adults, free for children ages 16 and under.

WHERE TO DINE

LaGrange Café ★★ *Finds* CREATIVE TRADITIONAL CUISINE Weaverville isn't exactly a star in the culinary firmament, but there is one bright spot, far and away the best food in town. Heck, it would be considered really good in Redding, Sacramento, or Tahoe. It's located in Weaverville's historic district; two adjoining buildings were combined and stripped down to the original old brick walls to make a spacious, attractive dining area with a sit-down bar. Chef and owner Sharon Heryford's menu includes the local favorite—chicken enchiladas with marinated tri-tip—plus seasonal items such as the local rabbit braised with mushrooms, fresh herbs, and white wine. The tender Duane's Chicken served with wheat pilaf is also popular. The interesting menu includes other things like buffalo steaks, venison bratwurst, and wild-boar sausages. Heryford's buffalo ragout won third place in a national contest. The 135-plus selections on the wine list make it one of the strongest in Northern California. Desserts, like a sinfully rich banana cream pie and that quintessential comfort food, bread pudding, are all made on the premises.

226 Main St. ✆ 530/623-5325. Main courses $10–$25. AE, DISC, MC, V. Mon–Thurs 11am–9pm; Fri–Sun 11am–10pm.

THE TRINITY ALPS

West of Weaverville stretch the Trinity Alps, with Thompson Peak rising to more than 9,000 feet. The second-largest wilderness area in the state lies between the Trinity and Salmon rivers and contains more than 55 lakes and streams. Its alpine scenery makes it popular with hikers and backpackers. You can access the **Pacific Crest Trail** west of Mount Shasta at Parks Creek, South Fork Road, or Whalen Road, and also from Castle Crags State Park. For trail and other information, contact the forest service at Weaverville (✆ 530/623-2121).

The Fifth Season, 300 N. Mount Shasta Blvd. (✆ 530/926-3606; www.the fifthseason.com), offers mountaineering and backpack rentals and will provide trail maps and other information concerning Shasta's outdoor activities.

Living Waters Recreation (© 800/994-RAFT or 530/926-5446; www.living watersrec.com) offers half-day to 2-day rafting trips on the Upper Sacramento, Klamath, Trinity, and Salmon rivers. **Trinity River Rafting Company,** on Calif. 299W in Big Flat (© **800/30-RIVER** or 530/623-3033), also operates local white-water trips.

For additional outfitters and information, contact the **Trinity County Chamber of Commerce,** 210 N. Main St. (P.O. Box 517), Weaverville, CA 96093 (© **800/487-4648** or 530/623-6101; www.trinitycounty.com).

WHISKEYTOWN NATIONAL RECREATION AREA

In adjacent Shasta County, Whiskeytown National Recreation Area is on the eastern shore of Trinity Lake, a quiet and relatively uncrowded lake with 157 miles of shoreline. When this reservoir was created, it was named Clair Engle, after the politician who created it. But locals insist on calling it Trinity after the river that used to rush through the region past the towns of Minersville, String-town, and an earlier Whiskeytown. All of these were destroyed when the river was dammed. They now lie submerged under the lake's glassy surface.

Both Trinity Lake and the Whiskeytown National Recreation Area are in the Shasta Trinity National Forest, 1.3 million acres of wilderness with 1,269 miles of hiking trails. For information on trails, contact **Shasta Trinity National Forest** (© **530/244-2978;** www.fs.fed.us/r5/shastatrinity).

LAKE SHASTA

Heading north on I-5 from Redding, travel about 12 miles and take the Shasta Dam Boulevard exit to the **Shasta Dam and Power Plant** ⚡ (© **530/275-4463;** www.shastalake.com/shastadam), which has an overflow spillway that is three times higher than Niagara Falls. The huge dam—3,460 feet long, 602 feet high, and 883 feet thick at its base—holds back the waters of the Sacramento, Pit, and McCloud rivers. A dramatic sight indeed, it is a vital component of the Central Valley water project. At the visitor center is a series of photographs and displays covering the dam's construction period. You can either walk or drive over the dam, but far more interesting are the **free 1-hour tours** given daily from 9am to 5pm on the hour in the summer, and at 10am, noon, and 2pm Labor Day to Memorial Day. The guided tour takes you deep within the dam's many chilly corridors (not a good place for claustrophobes) and below the spill-way. It's an entertaining way to beat the summer heat. *Note:* Tours may be canceled due to security reasons, so call ahead first.

Lake Shasta has 370 miles of shoreline and attracts anglers (bass, trout, and king salmon), water-skiers, and other boating enthusiasts—two million, in fact, in summer. The best way to enjoy the lake is aboard a houseboat; they can be rented from several companies, including **Antlers Resort & Marina,** P.O. Box 140, Antlers Road, Lakehead, CA 96051 (© **800/238-3924** or 530/238-2553; www.shastalakevacations.com); and **Packers Bay Marina,** 16814 Packers Bay Rd., Lakehead, CA 96051 (© **800/331-3137** or 530/275-5570; www.packers bay.com). There is a 1-week minimum during the summer, and a 3- to 4-day minimum during the off season.

While you're here, you can visit **Lake Shasta Caverns** (© **800/795-CAVE** or 530/238-2341; www.lakeshastacaverns.com). These caves contain 20-foot-high stalactite and stalagmite formations—60-foot-wide curtains of them in the great Cathedral Room. To see the caves, drive about 15 miles north of Redding on I-5 to the O'Brien/Shasta Caverns exit. A ferry will take you across the lake and a short bus ride will follow to the cave entrance for a 2-hour-long tour. Admission is $18 for adults, $9 for children ages 4 to 12, and free for kids under 4. The caverns are open daily from 9am to 3pm year-round.

For information about the Lake Shasta region, contact the **Redding Convention & Visitors Bureau,** 777 Auditorium Dr., Redding, CA 96001 (© **800/ 874-7562** or 530/225-4100; www.visitredding.org), west of 1-5 on Calif. 299. It's open Monday through Friday from 8am to 5pm.

MOUNT SHASTA 𝒜𝒜𝒜

A volcanic mountain with eight glaciers, **Mount Shasta** is a towering peak of legend and lore. It stands alone, always snowcapped, unshadowed by other mountains—visible from 125 miles away. Although it's been dormant since 1786, eruptions cannot be ruled out, and indeed, hot sulfur springs bubble at the summit. The springs saved John Muir on his third ascent of the mountain in 1875. Caught in a severe snowstorm, he and his partner took turns submersing themselves in the hot mud to survive.

Many New Agers are convinced that Mount Shasta is the center of an incredible energy vortex. These devotees flock to the foot of the mountain. In 1987, the foothills were host to the worldwide Harmonic Convergence, calling for a planetary union and a new phase of universal harmony. Yoga, massage, meditation, and metaphysics are all the rage here. These New Agers seem to coexist harmoniously with those whose metaphysical leanings begin and end with Dolly Parton song lyrics.

Those who don't want to climb can drive up to about 7,900 feet. From the town of Mount Shasta, drive 14 miles up the Everitt Memorial Highway to the end of the road near Panther Meadow. At the **Everitt Vista Turnout,** you'll be able to stop and see the Sacramento River Canyon, the Eddy Mountains to the west, and glimpses of Mount Lassen to the south. You can also take the short hike through the forests to a lava outcrop overlooking the McCloud area.

Continue on to **Bunny Flat,** a major access point for climbing in summer and also for cross-country skiing and sledding in winter. The highway ends at the Old Ski Bowl Vista, providing panoramic views of Mount Lassen, Castle Crags, and the Trinity Mountains.

While in Mount Shasta, visit the **Fish Hatchery** at 3 N. Old State Rd. (© **530/926-2215**), which was built in 1888. Here you can observe rainbow and brown trout being hatched to stock rivers and streams statewide—millions are born here annually. You can feed them via coin-operated food dispensers, and observe the spawning process on certain Tuesdays during the fall and winter. Admission is free; hours are daily from 8am to sunset. Adjacent to the hatchery is the **Sisson Museum** (© **530/926-5508**), which displays a smattering of local-history exhibits. It's open daily year-round, from 10am to 4pm in summer, from 1 to 4pm in winter; admission is free.

OUTDOOR PURSUITS

GOLF & TENNIS   Golfers should head for the 27-hole Robert Trent Jones, Jr., golf course at **Lake Shastina Golf Resort,** 5925 Country Club Dr., Weed (© **800/358-4653** or 530/938-3205; www.shastinagolf.com), or the 18-hole course at **Mount Shasta Resort,** 1000 Siskiyou Lake Blvd., Mount Shasta (© **800/958-3363** or 530/926-3030; www.mountshastaresort.com). The Mount Shasta resort also has tennis courts.

MOUNTAIN CLIMBING   Mount Shasta attracts thousands of hikers from around the world each year, from timid first-timers to serious mountaineers who search for the most difficult paths up. The hike isn't technically difficult, but it's a demanding ascent that takes about 8 hours of continuous exertion, particularly when the snow softens up. (*Tip:* Start early, while the snow is still firm.) Before setting out, hikers must secure a permit by signing in at the trail head or at the **Mount Shasta Ranger District** office, which also gives out plenty of good advice for amateur climbers. The office is at 204 W. Alma St., off North Mount Shasta Boulevard in Mount Shasta (© **530/926-4511**). Be sure to wear good hiking shoes and carry crampons and an ice ax, a first-aid kit, a quart of water per person, and a flashlight in case it takes longer than anticipated. Sunblock is an absolute necessity. All the requisite equipment can be rented at **The Fifth Season,** 300 N. Mount Shasta Blvd. (© **530/926-3606;** www.thefifthseason. com). (By the way, for those mere mortals who just want to hike and don't feel compelled to summit, there are lots of low-elevation trails.)

Weather can be extremely unpredictable, and every year hikers die on this dormant volcano, usually from making stupid mistakes. For **weather and climbing conditions,** call © **530/926-5555** for recorded information. Traditionally, climbers make the ascent from the Sierra Lodge at Horse Camp, which can be reached from the town of Mount Shasta via Alma Street and the Everitt Memorial Highway or from Bunny Flat.

For more information as well as supervised trips, contact **Shasta Mountain Guides,** 1938 Hill Rd. (© **530/926-3117;** www.shastaguides.com). This outfitter offers a 2-day climb that follows the traditional John Muir route and costs $395. It also offers a glacier climb and rock climbing in Castle Crags State Park, backpacking trips, plus cross-country and telemark skiing. You can take its basic rock-climbing course for $120, mountaineering course for $100, or one of its 3-day ski and snowboard descents for $495.

Also nearby is **Castle Crags State Park** (© **530/235-2684**), a 4,300-acre park with 64 campsites and 28 miles of hiking trails. Here, granite crags that were formed 225 million years ago tower more than 6,500 feet above the Sacramento River. The park is filled with dogwood, oak, cedar, and pine as well as tiger lilies, azaleas, and orchids in summer. You can walk the 1-mile Indian Creek nature trail or take the easy 1-mile Root Creek Trail. The entrance fee is $4 per vehicle per day. Castle Crags is off I-5, about 50 miles north of Redding.

OTHER WARM-WEATHER ACTIVITIES Mount Shasta offers some excellent **mountain biking.** In the summer, ride the chairlifts to the top of Mount Shasta Ski Park and bike down the trails. An all-day chairlift pass is $15 (© **530/926-8600;** www.skipark.com). Another good source for renting mountain bikes and getting trail information is **Shasta Cycling** (© **530/938-3002**).

For fishing information or guided trips, call **Jack Trout Flyfishing Guide** (© **530/926-4540**). Two other recommended sources are **Mount Shasta Fly Fishing** (© **530/926-6648**) and **Hart's Guide Service** (© **530/926-2431**).

SKIING In winter, visitors can ski at **Mount Shasta Board & Ski Park,** 104 Siskiyou Ave., Mount Shasta (© **800/SKI-SHASTA** or 530/926-8610; www. skipark.com), which has 31 runs with 80% snowmaking, three triple chairlifts, and a surface lift. Lift tickets are $35. There's also a Nordic ski center with 16 miles of groomed trails, as well as a Terrain Park that's geared toward snowboarders. The Learning Center offers instruction for adults and children. In summer you can ride the chairlifts to scenic views, mountain-bike down the trails (an all-day pass costs $15), or practice on the two-story climbing wall. Access to the park is 10 miles east of Mount Shasta (the town) on Calif. 89.

WATERSPORTS   The source of the headwaters of the Sacramento River accumulates in **Lake Siskiyou,** a popular spot for boating, swimming, and fishing—and a great vantage point for photographs of Mount Shasta and its reflection. Water-skiing and jet-skiing are not allowed, but windsurfing is, and boat rentals are offered at **Lake Siskiyou Camp Resort,** 4239 W. A. Barr Rd., Mount Shasta (ⓒ **888/926-2618** or 530/926-2618; www.lakesis.com).

WHERE TO STAY

Best Western Tree House   Just off the main highway, this motor inn is one of the better places to stay in the town of Mount Shasta, and it keeps its prices low. The lobby and refurbished rooms, some with decks and fridges, are pleasant enough, plus there's a huge indoor pool, usually deserted, making this a family favorite. Downhill and cross-country ski areas are 10 miles away.

111 Morgan Way (at I-5 and Lake St.), Mount Shasta, CA 96067. ⓒ 800/780-7234 or 530/926-3101. Fax 530/926-3542. www.bestwestern.com. 95 units. $82–$125 double. AE, DC, DISC, MC, V. **Amenities:** Restaurant; bar; indoor pool; nearby golf course; exercise room; Jacuzzi; video arcade; business center; secretarial services. In room: A/C, TV, fridge, coffeemaker, hair dryer, iron.

Mount Shasta Ranch B&B ⚡ (Kids)   Mount Shasta Ranch was conceived and built in 1923 by one of the country's most famous horse trainers and racing tycoons, H. D. ("Curley") Brown, as the centerpiece of a private retreat and thoroughbred-horse ranch. Despite the encroachment of nearby buildings, the main two-story house and its annex are still available as a cozy B&B with touches of nostalgia, the occasional antique, and spectacular views of Mount Shasta. Four bedrooms (the ones with private bathrooms) are in the main house; the remaining five share two bathrooms in the carriage house. It's a 3-minute trek to the shores of nearby Lake Siskiyou (15 min. to the ski slopes), or you could stay here to enjoy the Jacuzzi, Ping-Pong tables, pool table, darts, and horseshoes. And unlike most B&Bs, kids are welcome

1008 W. A. Barr Rd., Mount Shasta, CA 96067. ⓒ 530/926-3870. Fax 530/926-6882. www.stayinshasta. com. 10 units, 5 with private bathroom; 1 cottage. $60–$80 double with shared bathroom; $110 double with private bathroom; $115 cottage for 2. Rates include country breakfast (except cottage). AE, DISC, MC, V. Take Central Mount Shasta exit off I-5 to W. A. Barr Rd. Pets accepted with $10 fee. **Amenities:** Nearby golf course; game room. In room: A/C, TV, kitchen in 2 units, no phone.

Railroad Park Resort (Kids)   Lying a quarter of a mile from the Sacramento River, this is an offbeat place that kids will enjoy. It's at the foot of Castle Crags and contains a campground and RV park, four rustic cabins, and the Caboose Motel. Railroad cabooses from the Southern Pacific, Santa Fe, and Great Northern Railroads have been converted into rooms, leaving their pipes, ladders, and lofts in place. Located around the fenced-in kidney-shaped pool, they're furnished with modern king- or queen-size brass beds, table and chairs, and dressers; most have with small bay windows or rooftop cupolas. The restaurant and lounge are also in vintage railroad cars.

100 Railroad Park Rd., Dunsmuir, CA 96025. ⓒ 530/235-4440. Fax 530/235-4470. www.rrpark.com. 27 units. $75–$100 double. $10 less off season. Extra person $10. AE, DISC, MC, V. Take Railroad Park exit off I-5, 1 mile south of Dunsmuir. Pets accepted with $10 fee. **Amenities:** Restaurant; lounge; outdoor pool; Jacuzzi; game room; coin-op laundry. In room: A/C, TV, fridge, coffeemaker; minibar and microwave in some units.

Stewart Mineral Springs Resort (Finds)   Stewart Mineral Springs is one of the most unusual health spas in California, loaded with lore and legends. It lies above cold-water springs that Native Americans valued for their healing powers. Don't expect anything approaching a European spa or big-city luxury here. Everything is deliberately rustic, with as few intrusions from the urban world as possible. Designed in a somewhat haphazard compound of about a dozen build-ings, 4 miles west of the town of Weed, it occupies a 37-acre site of sloping, forested land accented with ponds, gazebos, and decorative bridges and is rid-dled with hiking and nature trails, freshwater streams, and a swimming hole.

Activities revolve around hiking, nature-watching, and taking the healing waters of the legendary springs. The bathhouse is the curative headquarters of the resort and contains 13 private rooms where water from the springs is heated and run into tubs for soaking. A staff member will describe the rituals for you: A 20-minute soak is followed by a visit to a nearby sauna and an immersion in the chilly waters of Parks Creek, just outside the bathhouse. Other feel-good options include massages ($30 per 30-min. session). On Saturdays, medicine man Walking Eagle guides guests on a spiritual journey within the Native Amer-ican Purification Sweat Lodge. Heck, they even have a juice bar. If you opt for treatment and R&R here, you won't be alone. Despite its rusticity, the place has been discovered by young Hollywood, including many soap actors, San Fran-cisco 49ers football players, and local newscasters.

4617 Stewart Springs Rd., Weed, CA 96094. © 530/938-2222. Fax 530/938-4283. www.stewartmineral springs.com. 6 tepees (for up to 4 persons), 4 motel rooms, 6 apt units, 5 cabins with kitchens, and a large A-frame house (suitable for 10 persons). $24 double tepee; $45–$79 double in motel, apts, and cabins; $375 for house. $5 for each extra person. DISC, MC, V. Leashed pets accepted with $3-per-day fee. **Amenities:** Restaurant (closed in winter); spa; sauna; massage. *In room:* Kitchen and coffeemaker in cabins and some units, no phone.

WHERE TO DINE

Café Maddalena 🎖🎖 *(Finds)* WORLD CUISINE   The smells wafting from this place will draw you into the refurbished old railroad quarter of Dunsmuir. The seasonal menu offers authentic dishes from southern France, Spain, and North Africa: couscous with a tangine of yam, carrots, and prunes; *zarzuela* (a Spanish shellfish stew in a tomato-saffron broth); herb-roasted lamb rack with ratatouille. Everything is made fresh, including the breads and desserts. During the summer months, request a table outside under the grape arbor.

5801 Sacramento Ave., Dunsmuir. © **530/235-2725.** Reservations recommended. Main courses $10–$19. MC, V. Thurs–Sun 5–10pm. Closed mid-Dec to mid-May.

Lily's 🎖 WORLD CUISINE   Set in a white-clapboard, early 1900s house in a residential neighborhood south of the town center, this friendly little restau-rant has a front porch, a picket fence, a back garden, and dining in two rooms inside and two patios out. It's popular for breakfast, when chunky breads, omelets, and cheesy polenta fritters start the morning off right. Lunch and din-ner dishes—tamale pie, chicken curry, *scampi al roma,* and Kung Pao shrimp salad—span the globe. Popular dishes are the enchiladas *suizas* stuffed with shrimp, crab, and fresh spinach, and Chicken Rosie, a tender breast of chicken simmered with raspberries, hazelnut liqueur, and cream.

1013 S. Mount Shasta Blvd., Mount Shasta. © **530/926-3372.** www.lilysrestaurant.com. Reservations rec-ommended. Breakfast $7–$11; lunch $8–$12; dinner $14–$23. AE, DISC, MC, V. Mon–Fri 7am–9pm; Sat–Sun 7am–9:30pm.

MCARTHUR–BURNEY FALLS MEMORIAL STATE PARK 🎖

On its way to Lassen Volcanic National Park (see below) from Mount Shasta, Calif. 89 east loops back south to **McArthur–Burney Falls Memorial State Park** (© 530/335-2777). One of the most spectacular features of this 910-acre park is **Burney Falls** 🎖🎖, an absolutely gorgeous waterfall that cascades over a 129-foot cliff. Theodore Roosevelt once called the falls "the eighth wonder of the world." Giant springs a few hundred yards upstream feed the falls and keep them flowing—100 million gallons every day—even during California's legendary dry spells.

The half-mile **Headwater Trail** will take you to a good vantage point above the falls. If you're lucky, you can observe the black swifts that nest in the mossy crevices behind the cascade. Other birds to look for include barn and great horned owls, the belted kingfisher, the common flicker, and even the Oregon junco. The year-round park also has 5 miles of nature trails, 128 campsites, picnicking grounds, and good fishing for bass, crappie, and brown, rainbow, and brook trout. For **camping reservations,** call © **800/444-PARK** (7275).

From here, Lassen Volcanic National Park lies about 40 miles south.

3 Lassen Volcanic National Park ⟨★

45 miles E of Redding; 255 miles NE of San Francisco

Stashed away in the far northeastern corner of California, Lassen Volcanic National Park is a remarkable reminder that North America is still forming, and that the ground below is alive with the forces of creation and, sometimes, destruction. Lassen Peak is the southernmost peak in a chain of volcanoes (including Mount Saint Helens) that stretches all the way from British Columbia.

Although it's dormant, 10,457-foot **Lassen Peak** is still very much alive. It last awakened in May 1914, beginning a cycle of eruptions that spit lava, steam, and ash until 1921. The eruption climaxed in 1915 when Lassen blew its top, sending a cloud of ash 7 miles high that could be seen from hundreds of miles away. The peak has been dormant for nearly three-quarters of a century now, but the area still boils with a ferocious intensity: Hot springs, fumaroles, geysers, and mud pots are all indicators that Lassen hasn't had its last word. Monitoring of geothermal features in the park shows that they are getting hotter, not cooler, and some scientists take this as a sign that the next big eruption in the Cascades is likely to happen here.

Until then, the park gives visitors an interesting chance to watch a landscape recover from the massive destruction brought on by an eruption. To the north of Lassen Peak is the aptly named **Devastated Area,** a huge swath of volcanic destruction steadily repopulating with conifer forests. Forest botanists have revised their earlier theories that forests must be preceded by herbaceous growth after watching the Devastated Area immediately revegetate with a diverse mix of eight different conifer species, four more than were present before the blast.

The 108,000-acre park is a place of great beauty. The flora and fauna are an interesting mix of species from the Cascade Range, which stretches north from Lassen, and species from the Sierra Nevada Range, which stretches south. The blend accounts for an enormous diversity of plants: 715 species have been identified in the park. Although it is snowbound in winter, Lassen is a summer feeding ground for transient herds of mule deer and numerous black bears.

In addition to the volcano and all its geothermal features, Lassen Volcanic National Park includes miles of hiking trails, 50 beautiful alpine lakes, large meadows, cinder cones, lush forests, cross-country skiing, and great backcountry camping. In fact, three-quarters of the park is designated wilderness.

And crowds? Forget it. Lassen is one of the least-visited national parks in the lower 48 states, so crowd control isn't as big a consideration here as in other places. Unless you're here on the Fourth of July or Labor Day weekend, you won't encounter anything that could rightly be called a crowd. Even then, you

Lassen Volcanic National Park

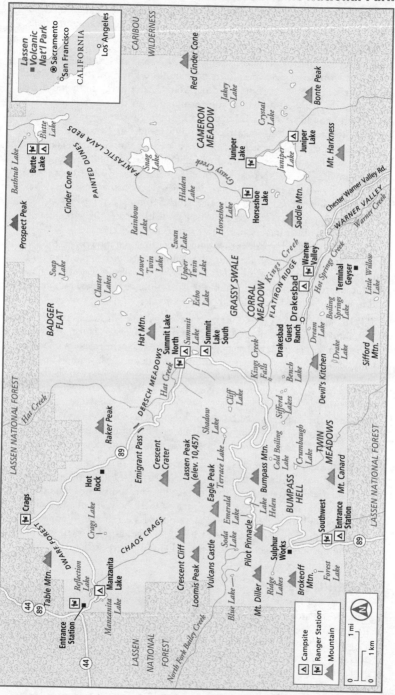

can escape the hordes simply by skipping the popular sites like Bumpass Hell or the Sulphur Works and heading a few miles down any of the backcountry trails.

ESSENTIALS

GETTING THERE   One of the reasons Lassen Volcanic National Park is one of the least visited national parks is its remote location. The most foolproof route here is to take Calif. 44 east from Redding, which leads directly to the northern gateway to the park. A shortcut if you're coming from the south along I-5 is Calif. 36 in Red Bluff, which leads to the park's southern gateway. If you're arriving from the east via I-80, take the U.S. 395 turnoff at Reno and head to Susanville. Depending on which end of the park you're shooting for, take either Calif. 44 (to the northwest entrance) or Calif. 36 (to the southwest entrance) from Susanville. The $10-per-car entrance fee, valid for a week, comes with a copy of the *Lassen Park Guide,* a handy little newsletter listing activities, hikes, and points of interest. Camping fees range from $10 to $16.

Only one major road, Calif. 89 (aka the Park Rd.), crosses the park, in a 39-mile half-circle with entrances and visitor centers at either end.

Most visitors enter the park at the southwest entrance station, drive through the park, and leave through the northwest entrance, or vice versa. Two other entrances lead to remote portions of the park. Warner Valley is reached from the south on the road from Chester. The Butte Lake entrance is reached by a cut-off road from Calif. 44 between Calif. 89 and Susanville.

VISITOR INFORMATION   **Ranger stations** are clustered near each entrance and provide the full spectrum of interpretive displays, ranger-led walks, informational leaflets, and emergency help. The largest **visitor center** is located just inside the northwest entrance station at the Loomis Museum. The park information number for all requests is (C) **530/595-4444,** or you can visit www.nps.gov/lavo or write Lassen Volcanic National Park, P.O. Box 100, Mineral, CA 96063-0100.

Because of the dangers posed by the park's thermal features, rangers ask that you remain on trails at all times. Fires are allowed in campgrounds only; please make sure they're dead before leaving. Mountain bikes are prohibited on all trails.

WEATHER   Lassen Volcanic National Park is in one of the coldest places in California. Winter begins in late October and doesn't release its grip until June. Even in the summer, you should plan for possible rain and snow. Temperatures at night can drop below freezing at any time. Winter, however, shows a different and beautiful side of Lassen that more people are starting to appreciate. Since most of the park is over a mile high and the highest point is 10,457 feet, snow accumulates in incredible quantities. Don't be surprised to find snow banks lining the Park Road into July.

EXPLORING THE PARK

The highlight of Lassen is, of course, the volcano and all of its offshoots: boiling springs, fumaroles, mud pots, and more. You can see many of the most interesting sites in a day, making it possible to visit Lassen as a short detour from I-5 or U.S. 395 on the way to or from Oregon. Available at park visitor centers, the *Road Guide to Lassen Park* is a great traveling companion that will explain a lot of the features you'll see as you traverse the park.

Bumpass Hell ⚑, a 1.5-mile walk off the Park Road in the southern part of the park, is the largest single geothermal site in the park—16 acres of bubbling mud pots cloaked in a stench of rotten-egg-smelling sulfur. The hike leads you through a quiet and peaceful meadow of wildflowers and chirping birds before arriving at the geothermal site. The name comes from an early Lassen traveler, Bumpass, who lost a leg after he took a shortcut through the area while hunting and plunged into a boiling pool. Stay on the wooden catwalks that safely guide visitors past the pyrite pools, steam vents, and noisy fumaroles and you won't suffer Bumpass's fate.

Sulphur Works ⚑ is another stinky, steamy example of Lassen's residual heat. Two miles from the southwest park exit, the ground roars with seething gases escaping from the ground.

Boiling Springs Lake and **Devil's Kitchen** are two of the more remote geothermal sites; they're located in the Warner Valley section of the park, which can be reached by hiking from the main road or entering the park through Warner Valley Road from the small town of Chester.

OUTDOOR PURSUITS

In addition to the activities below, free naturalist programs are offered daily in the summer, highlighting everything from flora and fauna to geologic history and volcanic processes. For more information, call the **park headquarters** at C 530/595-4444.

CANOEING & KAYAKING   Paddlers can take canoes, rowboats, and kayaks on any of the park lakes except Reflection, Emerald, Helen, and Boiling Springs. Motors, including electric motors, are strictly prohibited on all park waters. Park lakes are full of trout, and fishing is popular. You must have a current California fishing license, which you can obtain in Red Bluff at **Lassen Ranch and Home Store,** 22660 Antelope Rd. (C **530/527-6960**).

CROSS-COUNTRY SKIING   The park road usually closes due to snow in November, and most years it doesn't open until June, so cross-country skiers have their run of the park. Snowmobiles were once allowed but are now forbidden. Marked trails of all skill levels leave from Manzanita Lake at the north end of the park and Lassen Chalet at the south. Most visitors come to the southwest entrance, where the ski chalet offers lessons, rental gear, and a warm place to stay. Popular trips are the beginners' trails to Lake Helen or Summit Lake. More advanced skiers can make the trek into Bumpass Hell, a steaming valley of sulfuric mud pots and fumaroles.

You can also ski the popular 30-mile course of the Park Road in an overnight trek, but doing this involves a long car shuttle. For safety reasons, the park requires all skiers to register at the ranger stations before heading into the backcountry, whether for an overnight or just the day. For more information, contact the **park headquarters** at C **530/595-4444**.

HIKING   Most Lassen visitors drive through in a day or two, see the geothermal hot spots, and move on. That leaves 150 miles of trails and expanses of backcountry to the few who take the time to get off-road. The *Lassen Trails* booklet available at the visitor centers gives good descriptions of some of the most popular hikes and backpacking destinations. Anyone spending the night in the backcountry must have a wilderness permit issued at the ranger stations. And don't forget to bring plenty of water, sunscreen, and warm clothing.

The most popular hike in the park is the **Lassen Peak Trail** ⚑, a 2.5-mile climb from the Park Road to the top of the peak. The trail may sound short, but it's steep and generally covered with snow until late summer. At an elevation of 10,457 feet, though, you'll get a view of the surrounding wilderness that's worth every step of the way. On clear days, you can see south all the way to Sutter Buttes near Yuba City and north into the Cascades. The round-trip takes about 4 to 5 hours.

Running a close second in popularity is **Bumpass Hell Trail.** This 1.5-mile walk off the Park Road in the southern part of the park deposits you right in the middle of the largest single geothermal site in the park. (See "Exploring the Park," above.)

The **Cinder Cone Trail,** located in the northeast corner of the park, is another worthy hike, best reached from Butte Lake Campground at the far northeast corner of the park. If 4 miles seems too short, you can extend the hike (and shorten the drive) by walking in about 8 miles from Summit Lake on the Park Road. Now dormant, Cinder Cone is generally accepted as the source of mysterious flashing lights that were seen by early settlers to the area in the 1850s. Black and charred-looking, Cinder Cone is bare of any sort of life and surrounded by dunes of multihued volcanic ash.

SNOWSHOEING   From January to March, park naturalists give free 2-hour eco-adventure snowshoe hikes across Lassen's snowpacked hills. The tours take place on Saturdays at 1:30pm at the Lassen Chalet, located at the park's southwestern entrance. You must be at least 8 years old, be warmly dressed, and be wearing boots. Snowshoes are provided free of charge on a first-come, first-served basis, although a $1 donation is requested for upkeep. For more details, call park headquarters (© **530/595-4444,** ext. 5133).

CAMPING

Car campers have their choice of seven park campgrounds with 375 sites, more than enough to handle the trickle of visitors who come to Lassen every summer. In fact, so few people camp in Lassen that there is no reservations system except at the **Lost Creek Group Campground,** and stays are granted a generous 14-day limit. Sites do fill up on weekends, so get to the park early on Friday to secure a place to stay. If the park is packed, there are 43 campgrounds in surrounding Lassen National Forest, so you're bound to find a site somewhere.

By far the most "civilized" campground in the park is at **Manzanita Lake,** where you can find hot showers, electrical hookups, flush toilets, and a camper store. When Manzanita fills up, rangers open the **Crags Campground** overflow camp, about 5 miles away and much more basic. Further within the park along Calif. 89 is **Summit Lake Campgrounds,** located on the north and south ends of Summit Lake. It's a pretty spot, often frequented by deer, and it's a launching point for some excellent day hikes.

On the southern end of the park, you'll find **Southwest Campground,** a walk-in camp directly adjacent to the Lassen Chalet parking lot.

The two remote entrances to Lassen and Warner Valley have their own primitive campgrounds with pit toilets and no water, but the price is right—free.

Backcountry camping is allowed almost everywhere, and traffic is light. Ask about closed areas when you get your wilderness permit, which are issued at the ranger stations and required for anyone spending the night in the backcountry.

WHERE TO STAY
INSIDE THE PARK

Drakesbad Guest Ranch 🌟🌟🌟   The only lodge operating within Lassen Park is Drakesbad Guest Ranch, hidden in a high mountain valley inside the park and surrounded by meadows, lakes, and streams. It's famous for its rustic cabins, lodge, and steaming thermal swimming pool (where they offer massage service), fed by a natural hot spring and open 24 hours a day. Drakesbad is as deluxe as a place with some electricity and no phones can be, with handmade quilts on every bed and kerosene lamps to read by. Full meal service is available—and it's very good. Since the lodge is very popular and only open from June to mid-October, reservations are booked as far as 2 years in advance (although May or June are good times to call to take advantage of cancellations).

c/o California Guest Services, 2150 N. Main St., no. 5, Red Bluff, CA 96080. © 530/529-1512. Fax 530/529-4511. www.drakesbad.com. 19 units. $115–$140 per person, double occupancy. Rates include meals. DISC, MC, V. **Amenities:** Restaurant; hot-spring-fed pool; children's center. *In room:* No phone.

NEAR THE PARK

The Bidwell House Bed and Breakfast Inn ★★ *(Kids)* In 1901 General John Bidwell, a California senator who made three unsuccessful bids for the U.S. presidency, built a country retreat and summer home for his beloved young wife, Annie. After her death, when Chester had developed into a prosperous logging hamlet, the building, with its farmhouse-style design and spacious veranda, was converted into the headquarters for a local ranch. Today it's one of the most charming B&Bs in the region, fronted by a yard of aspens and cottonwoods with sprawling views of mountain meadows and pretty Lake Almanor. The 14 individually decorated guest rooms are furnished with antiques; most have private bathrooms, a few have wood-burning stoves, and seven units are equipped with Jacuzzi tubs. A cottage that sleeps up to six is ideal for families. Breakfast is presented with fanfare and many gourmet touches, including home-baked breads (the inn's manager is a creative pastry chef) and delicious omelets.

1 Main St. (P.O. Box 1790), Chester, CA 96020. © 530/258-3338. www.bidwellhouse.com. 14 units, 12 with private bathroom. $75–$150 double; $165 for cabin (sleeps 6). Rates include full breakfast. MC, V. **Amenities:** Nearby golf course. *In room:* TV.

Lassen Mineral Lodge *(Kids)* A mere 9 miles south of Lassen Volcanic National Park's southern entrance, the Lassen Mineral Lodge offers 20 motel-style accommodations in a forested setting. In summer the lodge is almost always bustling with guests and customers who venture into the gift shop, ski shop, general store, and full-service restaurant and bar. This is probably the best lodging option for families in the Lassen area.

On Hwy. 36E (P.O. Box 160), Mineral, CA 96063. © 530/595-4422. Fax 530/595-4452. www.minerallodge.com. 20 units. $65–$85 double. AE, DISC, MC, V. **Amenities:** Restaurant; saloon; coin-op laundry. *In room:* Kitchens in some units, no phone.

Mill Creek Resort ★ Set deep within the forest next to ol' Mill Creek, the Mill Creek Resort is that rustic mountain retreat you've always dreamed of while slaving away in the office. A homey country general store and coffee shop serve as the resort's center, a good place to stock up on food while exploring Lassen Volcanic National Park. Nine housekeeping cabins, available on a daily or weekly basis, are clean, cute, and outfitted with vintage 1930s and 1940s furniture, including kitchens (a good thing, since restaurants are scarce in this region). Pets are welcome, too.

1 Calif. 172 (3 miles south of Calif. 36), Mill Creek, CA 96061. © 888/595-4449 or 530/595-4449. www.millcreekresort.net. 9 units. $75–$100 per cabin. No credit cards. Pets accepted. **Amenities:** Bike rental; coin-op laundry (open May–Oct.). *In room:* Kitchen, coffeemaker, no phone.

WHERE TO DINE
INSIDE THE PARK

The only restaurant within Lassen Volcanic National Park (besides the Drakesbad Guest Ranch; see above) is the **Summer Chalet Café** (© **530/595-3376**), which serves inexpensive, basic breakfasts, as well as sandwiches and burgers for lunch. Located at the park's south entrance, it's open daily from 8am to 6pm (grill closes at 4pm, however) from mid-May to mid-October, weather permitting.

NEAR THE PARK

When you're this far into the wilderness, the question isn't *which* restaurant to choose, but *if* there is a restaurant to choose. If bacon and eggs, sandwiches, steaks, chicken, burgers, pizza, and salads aren't part of your diet, you're in big trouble unless you packed your own grub.

Deciding where you're going to eat near Lassen Volcanic National Park depends mostly on which side you're on, north or south. At the south entrance to the park, the closest restaurant is the **Lassen Mineral Lodge** (see "Where to Stay" above) in the town of Mineral, which serves the usual uninspired American fare. The best approach, however, is to stay at a B&B or lodge that offers meals to its guests—such as the **Bidwell House** or **Drakesbad Guest Ranch**— or at least provides a kitchen to cook your own meals, such as the **Mill Creek Resort** (see above). Food and camping supplies are available at the **Manzanita Lake Camper Store** (© 530/335-7557; open mid-May to mid-Oct), located at the north entrance to the park, or **Lassen Mineral Lodge,** on Calif. 36 in Mineral, at the southern end of the park (© **530/595-4422**). They also sell or rent just about every outdoor toy you'd ever want to play with in Lassen Park, including cross-country and alpine ski equipment.

4 Lava Beds National Monument

324 miles NE of San Francisco; 50 miles NE of Mount Shasta

Lava Beds takes a while to grow on you. It's a seemingly desolate place with high plateaus, cinder cones, and rolling hills covered with lava cinders, sagebrush, and twisted junipers. Miles of land just like it cover most of this corner of California. So why, asks the first-time visitor, is this a national monument? The answer lies underground.

The earth here is like Swiss cheese, so porous in places that it actually makes a hollow sound. When lava pours from a shield volcano, it doesn't cool all at once; the outer edges cool first and the core keeps flowing, forming underground tunnels like a giant pipeline system.

More than 330 lava-tube caves lace the earth at Lava Beds—caves that are open to the public to explore on their own or with park rangers. Whereas most caves lend themselves to a fear of getting lost with their huge chambers, multiple entrances, and bizarre topography, these are simple, relatively easy-to-follow tunnels with little room to go wrong. Once inside, you'll feel that this would be a great place for a game of hide-and-seek.

ESSENTIALS

GETTING THERE   The best access to the park is from Highway 139, 4 miles south of Tulelake.

VISITOR INFORMATION   Call the **Lava Beds National Monument** headquarters (© **530/667-2282;** www.nps.gov/labe) for information on ranger-led hikes, cave trips, and campfire programs. The visitor center is located at the southern end of the park.

ENTRY FEES   The entry fee is $10 per vehicle for 7 days, $5 per bike or walk-in, and camping costs $10 a day.

WHEN TO GO   Park elevations range from 4,000 to 5,700 feet, and this part of California can get cold any time of year. Summer is the best time to visit, with average temperatures in the 70s (20s Celsius); winter temperatures plunge down to about 40°F (4°C) in the day and as low as 20°F (–7°C) by night. Summer is also the best time to participate in ranger-led hikes, cave trips, and campfire programs.

EXPLORING THE PARK

A hike to **Schonchin Butte** (.75 miles each way) will give you a good perspective on the stark beauty of the monument and nearby Tule Lake Valley. Wildlife lovers should keep their eyes peeled for terrestrial animals like mule deer, coyote, marmots, and squirrels, while watching overhead for bald eagles, 24 species of hawks, and enormous flocks of ducks and geese headed to the Klamath Basin, one of the largest waterfowl wintering grounds in the Lower 48. Sometimes the sky goes dark with ducks and geese during the peak migrations.

The caves at **Lava Beds** are open to the public with little restriction. All you need to see most of them are a good flashlight or headlamp, sturdy walking shoes, and a sense of adventure. Many of the caves are entered by ladders or stairs, others still, by holes in the side of a hill. Once inside, walk far enough to round a corner, and then shut off your light—a chilling experience, to say the least.

One-way **Cave Loop Road,** just southwest of the visitor center, is where you'll find many of the best cave hikes. About 15 lava tubes have been marked and made accessible. Two are ice caves, where the air temperature remains below freezing year-round and ice crystals form on the walls. If exploring on your own gives you the creeps, check out **Mushpot Cave.** Almost adjacent to the visitor center, this cave has been outfitted with lights and a smooth walkway; you'll have plenty of company.

Hardened spelunkers will find enough remote and relatively unexplored caves to keep themselves busy. Many caves require specialized climbing gear.

Above ground, several trails crisscross the monument. The longest of these, the **Lyons Trail** (8.25 miles one-way), spans the wildest part of the monument, where you are likely to see plenty of animals. The **Whitney Butte Trail** (3 miles one-way) leads from Merill Cave along the shoulder of 5,000-foot Whitney Butte to the edge of the Callahan Lava Flow and monument boundary.

PICNICKING, CAMPING & ACCOMMODATIONS

The 43-unit **Indian Well Campground** near the visitor center has spaces for tents and small RVs year-round, with water available only during the summer. The rest of the year, you'll have to carry water from the nearby visitor center.

Two **picnic grounds,** Fleener Chimneys and Captain Jacks Stronghold, have tables but no water; open fires are prohibited.

There are no hotels or lodges in the monument, but numerous services are available in nearby Tulelake and Klamath Falls. For more information, call or write **Lava Beds National Monument,** P.O. Box 867, Tulelake, CA 96134 (℃ 530/667-2282).

The High Sierra: Yosemite, Mammoth Lakes & Sequoia/Kings Canyon

by Matthew Richard Poole

The national parks of California's Sierra are meccas for travelers from around the globe. The big attraction is Yosemite, of course, but the entire region is packed with natural wonders and adventures.

It was in Yosemite that naturalist John Muir found "the most songful streams in the world . . . the noblest forests, the loftiest granite domes, the deepest ice-sculpted canyons." Even today, few visitors would disagree with Muir's early impressions as they explore this land of towering cliffs, alpine lakes, river beaches, and dazzling fields of snow in winter. Yosemite Valley, lush with waterfalls and dramatic peaks reaching toward the sky, is the most central and accessible part of the park, stretching for some 7 miles from Wawona Tunnel in the west to Curry Village in the east. If you visit during spring or early fall, you'll encounter fewer problems with crowds and have more opportunities to see the park's splendor the way it was meant to be seen.

Across the heart of the Sierra Nevada, in east-central California, Sequoia and Kings Canyon National Parks comprise a vast, mountainous region that stretches some 1,300 square miles, taking in the giant sequoias for which they're fabled. This is a land of alpine lakes, granite peaks, and deep canyons. At 14,495 feet, Mount Whitney is the highest point in the lower 48 states.

Another big attraction is Mammoth Lakes, one of the major playgrounds of California, where you can enjoy recreational activities in a setting of lakes, streams, waterfalls, and meadows. Glaciers carved out much of this panoramic region.

Because of the vast popularity of the parks, facilities can be strained at peak visiting times. Always make your reservations in advance if possible (and that definitely includes camping).

1 Yosemite's Gateways

The good news: Towns on each gateway's periphery are virtually built around the tourism industry. They offer plenty of places to stay and eat and have natural wonders of their own. The bad news: If you stay here, reaching any point within the park requires at least a half-hour drive (usually closer to 1 hr.), which is especially frustrating during high season, when motor homes and congestion cause traffic to move at a snail's pace. A new, controversial park plan is being debated that would cut the number of day-use parking places in the park from 1,600 to 550, encourage bus and shuttle usage, reduce lodging rooms from

1,260 to 981, restore 180 acres to their natural state, and eliminate a 3¼-mile section of road to be replaced with a foot-and-bike trail.

In the meantime, there's no shortage of options to encourage you to help the park by leaving your car at your lodging or a parking area and entering on convenient, inexpensive buses (and then moving around the valley floor on free shuttles). The **Yosemite Area Regional Transit System** (YARTS) (© **877/989-2787;** www.yarts.com) provides round-trip transit from communities within Mariposa, Merced, and Mono counties to Yosemite. The Merced route along Highway 140 operates year-round, although the winter schedule is limited. Fares for riding YARTS vary, but generally range from $7 to $15 round-trip for adults, including entrance to the park, with discounts for children and seniors. Summer routes originate at Coulterville, Mammoth Lake and Lee Vining, and Wawona. For information on the Highway 120 east service (Mammoth Lakes to Yosemite Valley) call © **800/427-7623** from May until it snows (typically Sept or Oct).

Should you need to reserve accommodations outside the park, make a choice based on which gate offers you easiest access. The following selections are grouped by the three most popular entrances: The west entrances are Big Oak Flat (via Calif. 120), which is 88 miles east of Manteca and accommodates traffic from San Francisco; and Arch Rock (via Calif. 140), 75 miles northeast of Merced, is the easiest route from central California. The South Entrance is Wawona (via Calif. 41), which is 64 miles north of Fresno and the passage leading from Southern California.

BIG OAK FLAT ENTRANCE

The Big Oak Flat entrance is 150 miles east of San Francisco and 130 miles southeast of Sacramento. Among the string of small communities along the way is **Groveland** (24 miles from the park's entrance), a throwback to gold-mining days, complete with rednecks, the oldest saloon in the state, and at least some semblance of a real town. It'll take around an hour to reach the park entrance from Groveland, but at least there's some extracurricular activity if you're planning to stay in the area awhile. Big Oak Flat has a few hotels as well, but no town. Call the visitor information number below for details.

GETTING THERE   If you're driving from San Francisco, take I-580 (which turns into I-205) to Manteca, then Calif. 120 east.

VISITOR INFORMATION   Contact the **Highway 120 Chamber of Commerce** (© **800/449-9120;** www.groveland.org) for an exhaustive list of hotels, motels, cabins, RV parks, and campsites in the area.

WHERE TO STAY & DINE

Besides the places mentioned below, there are not a lot of great dining options. Ask anyone in town and they'll point you to more offerings.

Evergreen Lodge ★★ *Kids*   If you are looking for *the* classic Yosemite experience, you'll want to book a cabin at the Evergreen Lodge. This idyllic, affordable, and crowd-free hideaway—40 minutes east of Groveland right next to Yosemite—has it all: quaint cabins in the woods, a beautiful old bar, excellent food, a wonderful recreation center and library, and guided trips, as well as evening programs including campfires, movies, music and slide shows. The 65 cabins, scattered throughout groves of towering pines, come with private bathrooms, private decks, sitting areas, and cozy quilted beds. In the evenings you can enjoy a pitcher of beer and a game of Ping-Pong in the beer garden, sit

---

(*Fun Fact*   **Burgers & Bullets at the Iron Door Saloon**

Walk through the English iron doors that were shipped around the Horn and you'll step into a saloon that's been serving shots of whiskey to thirsty travelers for more than 150 years. Built from solid blocks of granite, the Iron Door Saloon is a must-stop on your way to Yosemite, if only to gawk at the thousands of $1 bills tacked to the ceiling (ask the bartender for a tack and the trick to getting them up there). They say the infamous Black Bart enjoyed a tumbler here now and again, and even put a few bullet holes in the walls to keep the locals jumpy (keep looking). A stuffed buffalo's head hangs on the wall to remind guests of the house special—a thick, juicy, charbroiled buffalo burger served with a side of pickles, tomato, onions, and house-made coleslaw. Espressos, cappuccinos, and lattes are available as well in case you need a boost from the long drive. Located at 18763 Main St. in downtown Groveland, it's open daily for lunch and dinner and for breakfast Friday through Sunday (© **209/962-6244;** www.iron-door-saloon.com). Live music acts (with both local and national names) regularly play at the saloon, a connection from the days when the owners used to work for concert promoter Bill Graham.

---

around the campfire telling stories and roasting marshmallows, or research your next day's outing in the recreation center. During the day, you have easy access to all parts of Yosemite, and there are hiking and biking trails near the lodge (as well as beautiful swimming holes). In summer there's access to tennis courts, a pool, and horseback riding right next door at Camp Mather. "Evergreen Dan" Braun, an Evergreen owner and one of the leading Yosemite experts, is in charge of the outdoor programs and just might be your guide. You can plan to join one of the Evergreen's daily hiking, fishing, or snowshoeing trips, or hire your own guide to show you the wonders of Yosemite.

33160 Evergreen Rd. (at Calif. 120), Groveland, CA 95321. © **800/935-6343** or 209/379-2606. Fax 209/379-2607. www.evergreenlodge.com. 65 units. Open year-round. Rates vary with season and cabin size: $79–189 for 1- and 2-bedroom cabins. AE, DISC, MC, V. From San Francisco, take I-580 E. (which turns into I-205) to Manteca; take Calif. 120 E. through Groveland; turn left at Hetch Hetchy/Evergreen Rd. **Amenities:** Restaurant; bar; beer garden; general store; recreation center; meeting hall; campfire area; group tent campground and heated outdoor pool; lake and tennis courts at neighboring Camp Mather for day-use fee (summer only). *In room:* Minifridge, CD player, fans.

The Groveland Hotel ✫   Constructed in1849 out of adobe, this charming historic hotel is one of the oldest buildings in the region and loaded with 19th-century character. The guest rooms are cozily appointed with down comforters, private bathrooms, and attractive European antiques. The best rooms are the two-room suites equipped with spa tubs and fireplaces. Along with an authentic Gold Rush–era saloon, the hotel has a restaurant offering baby back ribs, rack of lamb, fresh fish, and pasta, and a wine list that's a recipient of *Wine Spectator*'s Award of Excellence. Be sure to visit the hotel's website for money-saving package deals.

18767 Main St. (P.O. Box 289), Groveland, CA 95321. © **800/273-3314** or 209/962-4000. Fax 209/962-6674. www.groveland.com. 17 units. $145–$175 double; $225–$275 suite. Rates include extended continental breakfast. AE, DC, DISC, MC, V. Pets accepted with $10-per–night fee. **Amenities:** Restaurant; nearby golf course; small game room; concierge; business center; secretarial services; limited room service; babysitting; laundry service. *In room:* A/C, TV/VCR in some units, dataport, minibar, coffeemaker, hair dryer, iron.

Hotel Charlotte *(Kids) (Value)*   A less expensive alternative to The Groveland Hotel is the two-story Hotel Charlotte, built in 1921 and listed on the National Register of Historic Places. The new owners have made a lot of sorely needed improvements, adding fresh paint, carpets, wallpaper, linens, wainscoting, and furniture. The individually decorated guest quarters are upstairs and have a cheery vibe, with colorful floral prints, cast-iron beds, and lots of sunlight; many are adjoining, which is a plus for families. Prices are a flashback, too, and rates even include a breakfast buffet—hotcakes, waffles, oatmeal, fresh fruit—served from 7:30 to 10:30am. There's even a well-stocked game room that'll keep the kids entertained. Another plus: The in-house restaurant, **Cafe Charlotte,** offers a wide array of dinnertime classics—calamari, Greek salad, lasagna, Hawaiian chicken, filet mignon—Thursday through Sunday from 5 to 9pm.

18736 Main St. (Calif. 120), Groveland, CA 95321. ((**c**)) **800/961-7799** or 209/962-6455. Fax 209/962-6254. www.hotelcharlotte.com. 10 units. $83 double. Rates include buffet breakfast. Extra person $20. AE, DISC, MC, V. Pets accepted with $10 fee. **Amenities:** Restaurant; full bar; Internet access; game room.

ARCH ROCK ENTRANCE

This is the most heavily used park entrance, offering easy access to the valley.

GETTING THERE   Arch Rock is 75 miles northeast of Merced. If you're driving from central California, take I-5 to Calif. 99 to Merced, then Calif. 140 east through El Portal.

Greyhound ((**c**) **800/229-9424;** www.greyhound.com) and **Amtrak** ((**c**) **800/ USA-RAIL;** www.amtrak.com) have routes to Fresno from many cities. **VIA Adventures** ((**c**) **800/VIA-LINE** or 209/384-1315; www.via-adventures.com) offers service from Merced Amtrak Passenger Station to Yosemite Valley Visitor Center and Yosemite Lodge. Coaches, which can be wheelchair-lift equipped with advance notice, provide several round-trips daily between Merced and Yosemite.

WHERE TO STAY

The Yosemite Bug Lodge *(R) (Kids)*   Located 25 miles from Yosemite Valley, the Bug is sort of a cross between a mountain lodge and summer camp, complete with a big ol' sun deck, a killer swimming hole, and a festive atmosphere. The accommodations are simply but pleasantly furnished (even the tent cabins have real beds and linens) and come in multiple configurations: antique-filled private cabins with bathrooms, B&B-style private rooms with shared bathrooms in the main lodge, Yosemite-style wood-frame tent cabins, and campsites. The on-site **Cafe at the Bug** serves good California-American fare—seared yellowtail tuna with a sesame crust, roast pork with almonds and cilantro—along with beer, wine, vegan dishes, and box lunches to go. The cafe also doubles as the lodge's communal lounge. Other perks include hiking trails on the property, a game room with a pool table, a kitchen for hostel guests, and organized outings.

6979 Calif. 140 (P.O. Box 81), Midpines, CA 95345. ((**c**)) **209/966-6666.** Fax 209/966-6667. www.yosemitebug. com. Private rooms with private bathroom $55–$115; family and private rooms with semiprivate bathroom $40–$70; dorm beds with semiprivate bathrooms $16. Tent cabins $30–$50. 2 campsites $17 with grill and table. DISC, MC, V. **Amenities:** Restaurant; bike rentals; coin-op laundry; game room. *In room:* A/C, no phone.

Yosemite View Lodge   Once you've come this far, you're practically at the gate, so it's shocking to drive onto this gargantuan compound amidst the otherwise awesome natural surroundings. But the busloads of tourists need to stay somewhere, and this 279-room megamotel under perpetual construction is scheduled to eventually offer around 500 rooms. The motel-style units include fridges, microwaves, and HBO; some offer kitchenettes, river views, balconies, and fireplaces. The indoor pool is popular with kids. There's also a general store. The restaurant provides okay food, but it would be pricey for a family. If this place is booked, they also represent other properties in the vicinity, although they're not nearly as close to the entrance. Call ahead for information or check out the website, which also provides weather and road conditions.

11136 Hwy. 140 (P.O. Box D), El Portal, CA 95318. (℃ 888/742-4371 or 209/379-2681. Fax 209/379-2704. www.yosemite-motels.com. 279 units. Apr–Oct $125–$155 double; Nov–Mar $82–$155 double. 2-night minimum during holidays. MC, V. Pets accepted with $10-per–night fee. **Amenities:** Restaurant; pizza parlor; lounge; indoor and outdoor heated pools; 4 Jacuzzis; tour and activities desk. *In room:* A/C, TV, kitchenette in some units, fridge.

SOUTH ENTRANCE

The South Entrance is 332 miles north of Los Angeles, 190 miles east of San Francisco, 59 miles north of Fresno, and 33 miles south of Yosemite Valley. Fish Camp and Oakhurst are the closest towns to the South Entrance at Wawona. This entrance to the valley leads through the Wawona Tunnel to the **Tunnel View** where you must stop to admire the panorama. If you've never been to Yosemite before, I promise you this is a view you'll never forget.

GETTING THERE   If you're driving from Los Angeles, take I-5 to Calif. 99 north, then Calif. 41 north. Fresno-Yosemite International Airport, in nearby Fresno, is 93 miles south of Yosemite Village. The airport is served by Alaska Airlines, America West, American, Continental, Delta, Horizon, and United; all major car-rental companies are represented at the airport. From the airport, take Calif. 41 north to the South Entrance.

VISITOR INFORMATION   Ask the **Yosemite Sierra Visitors Bureau,** 40637 Calif. 41, Oakhurst, CA 93644 (℃ 559/683-4636; www.go2yosemite.net), for a helpful brochure on the area, and be sure to check out its excellent online guide.

WHERE TO STAY & DINE

If you can't afford to eat at the opulent Erna's Elderberry House in Oakhurst (see below), try the pleasant **Three Sisters Café,** 40291 Junction Dr., Suite 3, off Highway 49 (℃ 559/642-2253), for breakfast, lunch, or dinner. For more dining and lodging options, contact the visitors bureau (see above).

Big Creek Inn 🐾🐾   A mere 2 miles from the south entrance to Yosemite National Park is this shiny new B&B run by owner/innkeeper Pamela Salisbury. Near the banks of Big Creek, this immaculate B&B has everything you could want from a mountain lodging: easy access to Yosemite, great fishing right outside the front door, a balcony for reading, sounds of the creek from every room, a telescope for stargazing, an outdoor spa tub overlooking the creek, complimentary sunset wine and hors d'oeuvres, and even spa services—facials, body wraps, foot care—offered in the privacy of your own room (after climbing Half Dome, you'll need a massage!). There's even a game room filled with books, maps, and board games, free Internet access, and more than 300 movies available for in-room viewing. The three guest rooms all have private balconies with French doors and forest views, large bathrooms with Neutrogena bath products, and cozy comforters; two come with gas fireplaces and bistro-style dining tables. A hearty homemade breakfast is served in the dining room or, if you're getting up early for a hike, Pamela will deliver a continental breakfast to your room.

1221 Hwy. 41 (P.O. Box 39), Fish Camp, CA 93623. (℃ 559/641-2828. Fax 559/641-2727. www.bigcreekinn. com. 3 units. $110–$180 double. Rates include continental breakfast, wine, and hors d'oeuvres. AE, DC, DISC,

MC, V. **Amenities:** Nearby golf course and ski areas; game room with refreshments; state-of-the-art robotic telescope; Internet access. *In room:* TV/VCR/DVD, CD player, ceiling fan, private balcony, complimentary local calls.

Château du Sureau ✿✿✿   Its kudos say it all: five diamonds, five stars, hailed by Zagat as one of the top three small hotels in the United States. The domain of Vienna-born Erna Kubin-Clanin, the Elderberries estate (*sureau* is French for elderberry) is the sine qua non of luxurious lodging, decadent dining, and exclusivity. The château—"built to look old"—dates from 1991 and is set back off the road on a hill. From the renowned restaurant, a pathway leads through gardens to the house, which resembles a French château, with turret and terra-cotta-tile roof. The interior is exquisitely furnished with antiques, rugs, and fabrics. Each individually decorated room has a wood-burning fireplace and a wrought-iron balcony. Canopy beds are covered in Italian linens and goose-down comforters; several rooms have whirlpool tubs. Celebrities fleeing Los Angeles are fond of the $2,800-per-night Villa Sureau ($2,500 without the butler), a two-bedroom, two-bathroom luxury villa with a library, full kitchen, and 24-hour butler service. The restaurant, **Erna's Elderberry House** (✆ 559/683-6800), is famous in its own right, offering impeccable food, ambience, and service. The six-course prix-fixe menu changes daily.

48688 Victoria Lane (P.O. Box 577), Oakhurst, CA 93644. ✆ 559/683-6860. Fax 559/683-0800. www.chateaudusureau.com. 10 units. $375–$550 double. Rates include full European breakfast. Extra person $75. AE, DISC, MC, V. **Amenities:** Restaurant; bar; outdoor pool; nearby golf course; spa services; concierge; activities desk; 24-hr. room service; in-room massage; laundry service; same-day dry cleaning. *In room:* A/C, TV/VCR on request, hair dryer, CD player.

Hound's Tooth Inn ✿   This immaculate bed-and-breakfast is in a great location, 12 miles from Yosemite's southern entrance. It has comfortable, pretty rooms (some with spas or fireplaces), which are individually decorated in a Victorian style with a mix of reproductions and antiques, wallpaper, lace valances, and original art. My favorite rooms are the Hound's Tooth, with a king bed, fireplace, and view of the Sierra; and the Victorian Tower, with a romantic decor complete with white sheer netting, rattan chairs, and a spa. Kids are welcome by prior arrangement (rooms are set up for two people, so additional bedding must be brought in). The private garden area below is the ideal spot for a relaxing read.

42071 Hwy. 41, Oakhurst, CA 93644. ✆ 888/642-6610 or 559/642-6600. Fax 559/658-2946. www.houndstoothinn.com. 12 units, 1 cottage. $95–$175 double; $225 cottage. Extra person $20. Rates include full breakfast. AE, DC, DISC, MC, V. *In room:* A/C, TV/VCR, hair dryer, iron; kitchenette, minibar, fridge, and coffeemaker in some units.

The Narrow Gauge Inn   If you want to stay in a place that celebrates the mountain atmosphere, book a room at this friendly inn, 4 miles south of the park entrance. All of the motel-style units have a rustic cabin feel, complete with A-frame ceilings, little balconies or decks, antiques, quilts, and lace curtains; some have wood-paneled walls. The higher the price of the room, the cuter it gets. (Nos. 16–26 are the best and most secluded; they look directly into forest.) There are hiking trails on the property, as well as a wonderfully old-fashioned, lodge-style restaurant and buffalo bar serving "Old California Rancho Cuisine" that's open daily (though seasonally) from 5:30 to 9pm.

48571 Calif. 41, Fish Camp, CA 93623. ✆ 888/644-9050 or 559/683-7720. Fax 559/683-2139. www.narrowgaugeinn.com. 26 units. Apr–Oct $129–$229 double; Nov–Mar $79–$99 double. Extra person $10. Children under 6 stay free in parent's room. Rates include continental breakfast. DISC, MC, V. Pets accepted with $25 fee. **Amenities:** Restaurant (seasonal); bar; outdoor heated pool (seasonal); Jacuzzi (seasonal). *In room:* TV, dataport, coffeemaker.

Moments   White-Water Rafting on the Tuolumne

One of the most depressing facts about Yosemite tourism is that few folks do more than get out of their car, take a brief walk around the valley floor, "ooh" and "ah," snap some photos, and go back to their hotel. But if you really want to experience the wonders of the outdoors, contact **Ahwahnee Whitewater**, P.O. Box 1161, Columbia, CA 95310 (*C* **800/359-9790** or 209/533-1401; www.ahwahnee.com). Its rafting trips offer one of the best ways to truly interact with nature—especially if you're not the type to throw on a backpack and hoof it. The 1- to 3-day trips are ideal for white-water rebels in the spring (when the melting snow makes the ride most exciting) and for families later in the season. Although the trip doesn't go through the park, it's still an all-wilderness adventure—except they make the arrangements, provide and cook the food (gourmet by camping standards), steer the rafts, and practically hand you an experience you'll never forget. All you need to do is reserve well in advance, and if you're going on an overnight trip (highly recommended!), bring a tent, sleeping bag, and a few other camping accouterments—and get ready for a great time.

Tenaya Lodge ⭐⭐ *Kids*   Tenaya Lodge is a large full-service resort outside the southern entrance to Yosemite and is particularly idyllic for families. The three- and four-story complex is set on 35 acres of forested land a few miles outside the park. Inside, the decor is a cross between an Adirondack hunting lodge and a Southwestern pueblo, with a lobby dominated by a massive river-rock fireplace rising three stories. The modern guest rooms are done in a tasteful Southwestern decor with quality furnishings and roomy, well-appointed bathrooms. At the lodge's Guest Experience Center, you can sign up for tours of Yosemite, white-water rafting, mountain-bike rentals, rock climbing, horseback riding, and other outdoor activities. The lodge's Camp Tenaya for Kids program offers nature hikes, arts and crafts, games, and music 7 days a week Memorial Day to Labor Day. It's available Friday and Saturday evenings year-round, excepting outdoor activities precluded by winter conditions.

1122 Calif. 41, Fish Camp, CA 93623. *C* **888/514-2167** or 559/683-6555. Fax 559/683-8684. www.tenaya lodge.com. 244 units. Winter from $169 double; summer from $259 double. Buffet breakfast $15 per person. Children 17 and under stay free in parent's room. AE, DC, DISC, MC, V. **Amenities:** 2 restaurants; deli; indoor and outdoor pools; 2 nearby golf courses; exercise room; full-service spa; indoor and outdoor Jacuzzis; bike rental; children's program; game room; video arcade; activities desk; business center; secretarial services; 24-hr. room service; massage; babysitting; laundry service; dry cleaning. *In room:* A/C, TV w/pay movies, dataport, minibar, fridge on request, coffeemaker, hair dryer, iron, safe.

2 Yosemite National Park ⭐⭐⭐

Yosemite is a place of record-setting statistics: the highest waterfall in North America and 3 of the world's 10 tallest waterfalls (Upper Yosemite Fall, Ribbon Fall, and Sentinel Falls); the tallest and largest single granite monolith in the world (El Capitan); the most recognizable mountain (Half Dome); one of the world's largest trees (the Grizzly Giant in the Mariposa Grove); and thousands of rare plant and animal species. But trying to explain its majesty is impossible: This is a place you simply must experience firsthand.

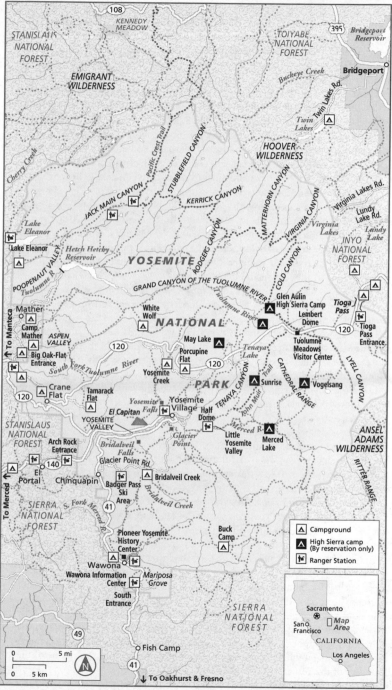

Yosemite National Park

STANISLAUS NATIONAL FOREST

EMIGRANT WILDERNESS

KENNEDY MEADOW

108

TOIYABE NATIONAL FOREST

395

Bridgeport Reservoir

Bridgeport

Buckeye Creek

Twin Lakes Rd.

Twin Lakes

HOOVER WILDERNESS

Cherry Creek

Pacific Crest Trail

JACK MAIN CANYON

STUBBLEFIELD CANYON

KERRICK CANYON

RODGERS CANYON

MATTERHORN CANYON

VIRGINIA CANYON

COLD CANYON

Virginia Lakes Rd.

Virginia Lakes

Lundy Lake Rd.

Lundy Lake

INYO NATIONAL FOREST

Lake Eleanor

Lake Eleanor

Hetch Hetchy Reservoir

POOPENAUT VALLEY

Tuolumne R.

YOSEMITE

GRAND CANYON OF THE TUOLUMNE RIVER

Tuolumne River

Glen Aulin High Sierra Camp

Lembert Dome

Tioga Pass

120

Tioga Pass Entrance

Mather

Camp Mather

ASPEN VALLEY

To Manteca

White Wolf

NATIONAL

120

May Lake

Porcupine Flat

Tuolumne Meadows Visitor Center

Tenaya Lake

LYELL CANYON

Big Oak-Flat Entrance

South Fork Tuolumne River

Yosemite Creek

120

Sunrise

TENAYA CANYON

John Muir Trail

CATHEDRAL RANGE

Vogelsang

Crane Flat

Tamarack Flat

Yosemite Falls

Yosemite Village

PARK

Merced R.

ANSEL ADAMS WILDERNESS

120

El Capitan

Half Dome

Merced Lake

STANISLAUS NATIONAL FOREST

Arch Rock Entrance

YOSEMITE VALLEY

Glacier Point

Little Yosemite Valley

Merced Lake

RITTER RANGE

140

El Portal

Chinquapin

Bridalveil Falls

Glacier Point Rd.

Bridalveil Creek

To Merced

SIERRA NATIONAL FOREST

S. Fork Merced R.

Badger Pass Ski Area

Bridalveil Creek

41

Buck Camp

Pioneer Yosemite History Center

Wawona

Wawona Information Center

Mariposa Grove

South Entrance

SIERRA NATIONAL FOREST

49

	Campground
	High Sierra camp (By reservation only)
	Ranger Station

CALIFORNIA

Sacramento

San Francisco

Map Area

Los Angeles

0   5 mi

0   5 km

N

Fish Camp

41

↓ To Oakhurst & Fresno

What sets the valley apart is its incredible geology. The Sierra Nevada was formed between 10 million and 80 million years ago, when a tremendous geological uplift pushed layers of granite lying under the ocean up into a mountain range. Cracks and rifts in the rock gave erosion a start at carving canyons and valleys. During the last ice age, at least three glaciers flowed through the valley, shearing vertical faces of stone and hauling away the rubble. The last glacier retreated 10,000 to 15,000 years ago, but left its legacy in the incredible number and size of the waterfalls pouring into the valley from hanging side canyons. From the 4,000-foot-high valley floor, the 8,000-foot tops of El Capitan, Half Dome, and Glacier Point look like the top of the world, but they're small in comparison to the highest mountains in the park, some of which reach over 13,000 feet. The 7-square-mile valley is really a huge bathtub drain for the combined runoff of hundreds of square miles of snow-covered peaks (which explains why the valley flooded during the great storm of 1997).

High-country creeks flush with snowmelt catapult over the abyss left by the glaciers and form an outrageous variety of falls, from tiny ribbons that never reach the ground to the torrents of Nevada and Vernal falls. Combined with the shadows and lighting of the deep valley, the effect of all this falling water is mesmerizing. All that vertical stone gets put to use by hundreds who flock to the park for some of the finest climbing anywhere.

The valley is also home to beautiful meadows and the Merced River. When the last glacier retreated, its debris dammed the Merced and formed a lake. Eventually, sediment from the river filled the lake and created the rich and level valley floor we see today. Tiny Mirror Lake was created later by rockfall that dammed up Tenaya Creek; the addition of a man-made dam in 1890 made it more of a lake than a pond. Rafters and inner-tubers enjoy the slow-moving Merced during the heat of summer.

Deer and **coyote** frequent the valley, often causing vehicular mayhem as one heavy-footed tourist slams on brakes to whip out the camera while another rubbernecker, also mesmerized, drives right into him. Metal crunches, tempers flare, and the deer daintily hops away.

Bears, too, are at home in the valley. Grizzlies are gone from the park now, but black bears are plentiful—and hungry for your food. Bears will rip into cars that have even the smallest treats inside, including things you think are safe inside your trunk. Each year as many as 500 bear-eats-car incidents occur, and several bears have had to be killed when they became too aggressive and destructive. If that doesn't deter you, you should know there is a fine of up to $5,000 for feeding park animals and your car can be impounded. There are food storage lockers throughout the park—please use them.

In the middle of the valley's thickest urban cluster is the **Yosemite Valley Visitor Center** (℃ **209/372-0200;** www.nps.gov/yose), with exhibits about glacial geology, history, and the park's flora and fauna. Check out the **Yosemite Museum** next door for insight into what life in the park was once like. Excellent exhibits highlight the Miwok and Paiute cultures that thrived here. The **Ansel Adams Gallery** (℃ **209/372-4413;** www.adamsgallery.com) displays the famous photographer's prints as well as other artists' works. You'll also find much history and memorabilia from the career of nature writer John Muir, one of the founders of the conservation movement.

While it's easy to let the beauty of the valley monopolize your attention, remember that 95% of Yosemite is wilderness. Of the four million visitors who come to the park each year, few ever venture more than a mile from their cars.

That leaves most of Yosemite's 750,000 acres open for anyone adventurous enough to hike a few miles. Even though the valley is the hands-down winner for dramatic freak-of-nature displays, the high country offers a more subtle kind of beauty: glacial lakes, rivers, and miles of granite spires and domes. In the park's southwest corner, the Mariposa Grove is a forest of rare sequoias, the world's largest trees, as well as several meadows and the south fork of the Merced River.

Tenaya Lake and Tuolumne Meadows are two of the most popular high-country destinations, as well as starting points for many trails to the backcountry. Since this area is under snow November through June, summer is really more like spring. From snowmelt to the first snowfall, the high country explodes with wildflowers and wildlife trying to make the most of the short season.

ESSENTIALS

ENTRY POINTS   There are four main entrances to the park. Most valley visitors enter through the **Arch Rock Entrance** on Calif. 140. The best entrance for Wawona is the **South Entrance** on Calif. 41 from Oakhurst. If you're going to the high country, you'll save a lot of time by coming in through the **Big Oak Flat Entrance,** which puts you straight onto Tioga Road without forcing you to deal with the congested valley. The **Tioga Pass Entrance** is open only in summer and is only really relevant if you're coming from the east side of the Sierra (in which case it's your only choice). A fifth, little-used entrance is the **Hetch Hetchy Entrance** in the euphonious Poopenaut Valley, on a dead-end road.

FEES   It costs $20 per car per week to enter the park or $10 per person per week. Annual Yosemite Passes are a steal at only $40. Wilderness permits are free, but reserving them requires a $5 fee per person. If you are 62 or older and you haven't purchased a lifetime Golden Age Passport for $10, what are you waiting for? You can apply for this passport here (or at any other national park or national forest), and you must show reasonable proof of age.

GAS   There are no gas stations in Yosemite Valley, so fill up before entering.

VISITOR CENTERS & INFORMATION   There's a central, 24-hour recorded information line for the park (✆ **209/372-0200;** www.nps.gov/yose). All visitor-related service lines, including hotels and information, can be accessed by touch-tone phone at ✆ **209/372-1000,** or at www.yosemitepark.com.

The biggest visitor center is the **Valley Visitor Center** (✆ **209/372-0200**). The **Wawona Information Station** (✆ **209/375-9501**) gives general park information (closed in winter). For biological and geological displays about the High Sierra, as well as trail advice, the **Tuolumne Meadows Visitor Center** (✆ **209/372-0263**) is great (closed in winter). All can provide you with maps, plus more newspapers, books, and photocopied leaflets than you'll ever read.

REGULATIONS   Rangers in the Yosemite Valley spend more time being cops than rangers. They even have their own jail, so don't do anything you wouldn't do in your hometown. Despite the pressure, park regulations are pretty simple: Permits are required for overnight backpacking trips; fishing licenses are required; utilize proper food-storage methods in bear country; don't collect firewood in the valley; no off-road bicycle riding; dogs are allowed in the park but must be leashed and are forbidden from trails; and *don't feed the animals.*

SEASONS   Winter is my favorite time to visit the valley. It isn't crowded as it is in summer, and a dusting of snow provides a stark contrast to all that granite. To see the waterfalls at their best, come in spring when snowmelt is at its peak.

Fall can be cool, but it's beautiful and much less crowded than summer. Sunshine seekers will love summer—if they can tolerate the crowds.

The high country is under about 20 feet of snow November through May, so unless you're snow camping, summer is pretty much the only season to pitch a tent. Even in summer, thundershowers are a frequent occurrence, sometimes with a magnificent lightning show. Mosquitoes can be a plague during the peak of summer, but the situation improves after the first freeze.

RANGER PROGRAMS Even though they're overworked just trying to keep the peace, Yosemite's wonderful rangers also take time to lead a number of educational and interpretive programs ranging from backcountry hikes to fireside talks to snow-country survival clinics. Call the main park information number with specific requests for the season and park area you'll be visiting. Also a great service are the free painting, drawing, and photography classes offered spring to fall at the Art Activity Center next to the Yosemite Museum Gallery in the valley.

AVOIDING THE CROWDS Popularity isn't always the greatest thing for wild places. Over the last 20 years, Yosemite Valley has set records for the worst crowding, noise, crime, and traffic in any California national park.

The park covers more than 1,000 square miles, but most visitors flock to the floor of Yosemite Valley, the 1-mile-wide, 7-mile-long glacial scouring that tore a deep and steep valley from the solid granite of the Sierra Nevada. It becomes a total zoo between Memorial Day and Labor Day. Cars line up bumper to bumper on almost any busy weekend. In 1995, Yosemite's superintendent closed the entrances to the park 11 times between Memorial Day and mid-August when the number of visitors reached the park's quota; she turned away 10,000 vehicles.

Our best advice is to try to come before Memorial Day or after Labor Day. If you must go in summer, do your part to help out. It's not so much the numbers of people that are ruining the valley but their insistence on driving from attraction to attraction. Once you're here, park your car, then bike, hike, or ride the shuttle buses. You can rent bicycles at **Curry Village** (© **209/372-8319**) and **Yosemite Lodge** (© **209/372-1208**) in summer. It may take longer to get from point A to point B, but you're in one of the most gorgeous places on earth—so why hurry?

EXPLORING THE PARK
THE VALLEY

First-time visitors are often dumbstruck as they enter the valley from the west. The first two things you'll see are the delicate and beautiful **Bridalveil Fall** 🌟🌟 and the immense face of **El Capitan** 🌟🌟, a stunning 3,593-foot-tall solid-granite rock. A short trail leads to the base of Bridalveil, which at 620 feet tall is only a medium-size fall by park standards, but one of the prettiest.

This is a perfect chance to get those knee-jerk tourist impulses under control early: Resist the temptation to rush around to see everything. Instead, take your time and look around. One of the best things about the valley is that many of its most famous features are visible from all over. Instead of rushing to the base of every waterfall or famous rock face and getting a crick in your neck from staring straight up, go to the visitor center and spend a half-hour learning something about the features of the valley. Buy the excellent *Map and Guide to Yosemite Valley* for $2.50; it describes many hikes and short nature walks. Then go take a look. Walking and biking are the best ways to get around. To cover longer distances, the park shuttles run frequently around the east end of the valley.

If you absolutely must see it all and want to have someone tell you what you're seeing, the **Valley Floor Tour** is a 2-hour narrated bus or open-air tram tour (depending on the season) that provides an introduction to the valley's natural history, geology, and human culture. Fees are $21 for adults, $16 for kids ages 5 to 12, and kids under 5 tour for free, although they may have to sit on a parent's lap. Purchase tickets at valley hotels or call ☎ **209/372-1240** for reservations.

Three-quarters of a mile from the visitor center is **The Ahwahnee Hotel** (p. 302). Unlike the rest of the hotel accommodations in the park, the Ahwahnee lives up to its surroundings. The native granite-and-timber lodge was built in 1927 and reflects an era when grand hotels were, well, grand. Fireplaces bigger than most Manhattan studio apartments warm the immense common rooms. Parlors and halls are filled with antique Native American rugs. Don't worry about what you're wearing unless you're going to dinner—this is Yosemite, after all.

The best view in the valley is from **Sentinel Bridge** 😊 over the Merced River. At sunset, Half Dome's face functions as a projection screen for all the sinking sun's hues from yellow to pink to dark purple, and the river reflects it all. Ansel Adams took one of his most famous photographs from this very spot.

The **Nature Center at Happy Isles** 😊 has great hands-on nature exhibits for kids, plus a wheelchair-accessible path along the banks of the Merced River.

VALLEY WALKS & HIKES   Yosemite Falls is within a short stroll of the visitor center. You can see it better elsewhere in the valley, but it's really impressive to stand at the base of all that falling water. The wind, noise, and spray generated when millions of gallons catapult 2,425 feet through space onto the rocks below are sometimes so overwhelming you can barely stand on the bridge.

If you want more, the **Upper Yosemite Fall Trail** 😊 zigzags 3½ miles from Sunnyside Campground to the top of Upper Yosemite Fall. This trail gives you an inkling of the weird, vertically oriented world climbers enter when they head up Yosemite's sheer walls. As you climb this narrow switchback trail, the valley floor drops away until people below look like ants, but the top doesn't appear any closer. It's a little unnerving at first, but braving it promises great rewards. Plan on spending all day on this 7-mile round-trip trail because of the incredibly steep climb.

A mile-long trail leads from the Valley Stables (take the shuttle; no car parking) to **Mirror Lake** 😊. The already tiny lake is gradually becoming a meadow as it fills with silt, but the reflections of the valley walls and sky on its surface remain one of the park's most unforgettable sights.

Also accessible from the Valley Stables or nearby Happy Isles is the best valley hike of all—the **John Muir Trail** 😊😊 to Vernal and Nevada falls. It follows the Sierra crest 200 miles south to Mount Whitney, but you only need go 1.5 miles round-trip to get a great view of 317-foot Vernal Fall. Add another 1.5 miles and 1,000 vertical feet for the climb to the top of Vernal Fall on the **Mist Trail** 😊, where you'll get wet as you climb alongside the falls. On top of Vernal and before the base of Nevada Fall is a beautiful valley and deep pool. For a truly outrageous view of the valley and one heck of a workout, continue on up the Mist Trail to the top of Nevada Fall. From 2,000 feet above Happy Isles where you began, it's a dizzying view straight down the face of the fall. To the east is an interesting profile perspective of Half Dome. Return either by the Mist Trail or the slightly easier John Muir Trail for a 7-mile round-trip hike.

Half Dome 😊😊😊 may look insurmountable to anyone but an expert rock climber, yet thousands take the strenuous-but-popular cable route up the backside every year. It's almost 17 miles round-trip and a 4,900-foot elevation gain from Happy Isle on the John Muir Trail. Many do it in a day, starting at first light and rushing home to beat nightfall. A more relaxed strategy is to camp in the back-packing campground in Little Yosemite Valley just past Nevada Fall. From here, the summit is within easy striking distance of the base of Half Dome. If you plan to spend the night, you need a Wilderness Pass (see "Camping" below). You must climb up a very steep granite face using steel cables installed by the park service. In summer, boards are installed as crossbeams, but they're still far apart. Wear shoes with lots of traction and bring your own leather gloves for the cables (your hands will thank you). If there's any chance of a thunderstorm, the trail is closed—that cable turns into a lighting rod. The view from the top is an unbeatable vista of the high country, Tenaya Canyon, Glacier Point, and the awe-inspiring abyss of the valley below. When you shuffle up to the overhanging lip for a look down the face, be extremely careful not to kick rocks or anything else onto the climbers below, who are earning this view the hard way.

THE SOUTHWEST CORNER

This corner of the park is densely forested and gently sculpted in comparison to the stark granite that makes up so much of Yosemite. Coming from the valley, Calif. 41 takes you to **Tunnel View** ✦✦✦, site of a famous Ansel Adams pho-tograph, and the best scenic outlook of the valley accessible by car. Virtually the whole valley is laid out below: Half Dome and Yosemite Falls straight ahead in the distance, Bridalveil to the right, and El Capitan to the left.

A few miles past the tunnel, Glacier Point Road turns off to the east. Closed in winter, this winding road leads to a picnic area at **Glacier Point** ✦✦, site of another fabulous view of the valley, this time 3,000 feet below. Schedule at least an hour to drive here from the valley and an hour or two to absorb the view. This is a good place to study the glacial scouring of the valley below; the Glac-ier Point perspective makes it easy to picture the valley filled with sheets of ice.

Some 30 miles south of the valley on Calif. 41 are the **Wawona Hotel** (p. 302) and the **Pioneer Yosemite History Center.** The Wawona was built in 1879 and is the oldest hotel in the park. Its Victorian architecture evokes a time when trav-elers spent days in horse-drawn wagons to get here. The Pioneer Center is a col-lection of early homesteading log buildings across the river from the Wawona.

One of the primary reasons Yosemite was set aside as a park was the **Mariposa Grove** ✦ of giant sequoias. (Many trails lead through the grove.) These huge trees have personalities that match their gargantuan size. Single limbs on the biggest tree in the grove, the Grizzly Giant, are 10 feet thick. The tree itself is 209 feet tall, 32 feet in diameter, and more than 2,700 years old. Totally out of proportion with the size of the trees are the tiny cones of the sequoia. Smaller than a baseball and tightly closed, the cones won't release their cargo of seeds until opened by fire.

THE HIGH COUNTRY ✦✦✦

The high country of Yosemite is stunning. Dome after dome of crystalline gran-ite reflects the sunlight above deep-green meadows and icy-cold rivers.

Tioga Pass is the gateway to the high country. At times, it clings to the side of steep rock faces; in other places, it weaves through canyon bottoms. Several good campgrounds make it a pleasing overnight alternative to fighting summer-time crowds in the valley, although use is increasing here, too. **Tenaya Lake** ✦ is a popular windsurfing, fishing, canoeing, sailing, and swimming spot. The water is very chilly. Many good hikes lead into the high country from here, and the granite domes surrounding the lake are popular with climbers. Fishing here varies greatly from year to year.

Near the top of Tioga Pass is **Tuolumne Meadows** ★★. This meadow covering several square miles is bordered by the Tuolumne River on one side and granite peaks on the other. The meadow is cut by many streams full of trout, and herds of mule deer are almost always present. The **Tuolumne Meadows Lodge** and store are a welcome counterpoint to the overdeveloped valley. In winter the canvas roofs are removed and the buildings fill with snow. You can buy last-minute backpacking supplies here, and there's a burgers-and-fries cafe.

TUOLUMNE MEADOWS HIKES & WALKS   So many hikes lead from here into the backcountry that it's impossible to do them justice. A good trail passes an icy-cold spring and traverses several meadows.

On the far bank of the Tuolumne from the meadow, a trail leads downriver, eventually passing through the grand canyon of the Tuolumne and exiting at Hetch Hetchy. Shorter hikes will take you downriver past rapids and cascades.

An interesting geological quirk is the **Soda Springs** on the far side of Tuolumne Meadow from the road. This bubbling spring gushes carbonated water from a hole in the ground; a small log cabin marks its site.

For a selection of Yosemite high-country hikes and backpacking trips, consult some of the guidebooks to the area. Two of the best are published by Wilderness Press: *Tuolumne Meadows,* a hiking guide by Jeffrey B. Shaffer and Thomas Winnett; and *Yosemite National Park,* by Thomas Winnett and Jason Winnett.

SPORTS & OUTDOOR PURSUITS

BICYCLING   With 10 miles of bike paths in addition to the valley roads, biking is the perfect way to go. You can rent them at the **Yosemite Lodge** (© 209/372-1208) or **Curry Village** (© 209/372-8319) for $5.25 per hour or $20 per day. You can also rent bike trailers for little kids at $11 an hour or $33 a day. All trails in the park are closed to mountain bikes.

FISHING   The Merced River from Happy Isles downstream to the Pohono Bridge is catch-and-release only for native rainbow trout, and barbless hooks are required. Brown-trout limits are 5 fish per day and 10 in possession. Trout season begins on the last Saturday in April and continues through November 15. A California license is required and must be displayed by everyone 16 years old and over. Get **licenses** at the Yosemite Village Sport Shop (© 209/372-1286).

HORSEBACK RIDING   Three stables offer day rides and multi-day excursions in the park. **Yosemite Valley Stables** (© 209/372-8348) is open spring through fall. The other two—**Wawona** (© 209/375-6502) and **Tuolumne Stables** (© 209/372-8427)—operate only in summer. Day rides run from $51 to $94, depending on length. Multi-day backcountry trips cost roughly $100 per day and must be booked almost a year in advance. The park wranglers can also be hired to make resupply drops at any of the High Sierra Camps if you plan an extended trip. Log on to www.yosemiteparktours.com (click on "Summer Activities") for more information.

ICE-SKATING   In winter the **Curry Village Ice Rink** (© 209/372-8341) is a lot of fun. It's outdoors and melts quickly when the weather warms up. Rates are $6.50 for adults and $5 for children under 12. Skate rentals are available for $3.25.

ROCK CLIMBING   Much of the most technical advancement in rock climbing came out of the highly competitive Yosemite Valley climbing scene of the

1970s and 1980s. Though other places have taken some of the limelight, Yosemite is still one of the most desirable climbing destinations in the world.

The **Yosemite Mountaineering School** (© 209/372-8344 or 209/372-8444; www.yosemitemountaineering.com) runs classes for beginning through advanced climbers. Considered one of the best climbing schools in the world, it offers private lessons for $170 per person per day, $90 for two people per day, $70 for three or more people per day, that will teach you basic body moves and rappelling, and will take you on a single-pitch climb. Classes run from early spring to early October in the valley, and during summer in Tuolumne Meadows.

SKIING & SNOWSHOEING   Opened in 1935, **Badger Pass** (© 209/372-8430; www.yosemitepark.com) is the oldest operating ski area in California. It's nice for families. Four chairs and one rope tow cover a compact mountain of beginner and intermediate runs. At $31 for adults and $16 for children under 12, it's a great place to learn how to ski or snowboard. There are naturalist-led winter children's programs and even babysitting.

Yosemite is also a popular destination for cross-country skiers and snowshoers. Both the Badger Pass ski school and the mountaineering school run trips and lessons for all abilities, ranging from basic technique to trans-Sierra crossings. There are two ski huts available on guided cross-country tours, including the spiffy **Glacier Point Hut** with its massive stone fireplace, beamed ceilings, and bunk beds; for information, call © **209/372-8444.** Then there's the **Ostrander Hut** (© **209/372-0740**) with 25 bunks, and you have to pack in your own supplies. If you're on your own, Crane Flat is a good place to go, as is the groomed track up to Glacier Point, a 20-mile round-trip self-guided tour.

CAMPING

Campgrounds in Yosemite can be reserved up to 5 months in advance through the **National Park Reservation Service** (© **800/436-7275;** http://reservations. nps.gov). During the busy season, all valley campsites sell out within hours of becoming available on the service.

Backpacking into the wilderness and camping is the least crowded option and takes less planning than reserving a campground. If you plan to camp in the wilderness, you must get a free **Wilderness Pass** (and pay the park entrance fee). At least 40% of each trail-head quota is allocated up to 24 hours in advance; the rest is available by mail. Write to the Wilderness Center, P.O. Box 545, Yosemite, CA 95389, specify the dates and trail heads of entry and exit, destination, number of people, and any accompanying animals; include a $5 per person advance-registration fee. You may also call © **209/372-0740** for a pass.

VALLEY CAMPGROUNDS

Until January 1997, the park had five car campgrounds that were always full except in the dead of winter. Now the park has half the number of campsites, and getting a reservation on short notice takes a minor miracle. (Yosemite Valley lost almost half of its 900 camping spaces in a freak winter storm that washed several campsites downstream and buried hundreds more beneath a foot of silt.)

The two-and-a-half campgrounds that remain—**North Pines, Upper Pines,** and half of **Lower Pines**—charge $18 per night. All have drinking water, flush toilets, pay phones, fire pits, and a heavy ranger presence. Showers are available for a small fee at Curry Village. Upper Pines, North Pines, and Lower Pines allow small RVs (less than 40 ft. long). If you're expecting a real nature experience, skip camping in the valley unless you like doing so with 4,000 strangers.

> ⌐**Tips** **Securing Accommodations**
>
> All hotel reservations can be made exactly 366 days in advance. Call
> **Yosemite Concessions Services** at ℭ **559/252-4848** in the morning 366
> days before your intended arrival for the best chance of securing your
> reservation. If you don't plan far in advance, it's good to call anyway—
> cancellations may leave new openings. Online reservations may be
> booked through **www.yosemitepark.com**. Keep in mind that reservations
> held without deposit must be confirmed on the scheduled day of arrival
> by 4pm. Otherwise, you'll lose your reservation.

Camp 4 (previously named Sunnyside campground) is a year-round, walk-in
campground in the valley and fills up with climbers since it's only $5 per night.
Hard-core climbers used to live here for months at a time, but the park service
has cracked down on that. It still has a much more bohemian atmosphere than
any of the other campgrounds.

CAMPGROUNDS ELSEWHERE IN THE PARK

Outside the valley, things start looking up for campers. Two car campgrounds
near the South Entrance of the park, **Wawona** and **Bridalveil Creek,** offer a
total of 210 sites with all the amenities. Wawona is open year-round, and reservations are required May through September; otherwise, it's first-come, first-
served. Family sites at Wawona are $18 per night, and group sites, which hold
up to 30 people, are $40 per night. Because it sits well above the snow line at
more than 7,000 feet, Bridalveil is open in summer only. Its rates are $12 per
night for first-come, first-served sites, and $40 for group sites.

Crane Flat, Hodgdon Meadow, and Tamarack Flat are all in the western corner of the park near the Big Oak Flat Entrance. **Crane Flat** is the nearest to the
valley, about a half-hour drive away, with 166 sites, water, flush toilets, and fire
pits. Its rates are $18 per night, and it's open June through September. **Hodg-
don Meadow** is directly adjacent to the Big Oak Flat Entrance at 4,800 feet elevation. It's open year-round, charges $18 per night, and requires reservations
May through September through the National Park Reservation Service. Facilities include flush toilets, running water, a ranger station, and pay phones. It's
one of the least crowded low-elevation car campgrounds, but there's not a lot to
do here. **Tamarack Flat** is a waterless, 52-site campground with pit toilets.
Open June through October, it's a bargain at $8 per night.

Tuolumne Meadows, White Wolf, Yosemite Creek, and Porcupine Flat are all
above 8,000 feet and open in summer only. **Tuolumne Meadows** ℛ is the
largest campground in the park, with more than 300 spaces, but it absorbs the
crowd well and has all the amenities, including campfire programs and slide
shows in the outdoor amphitheater. You will, however, feel sardine-packed
between hundreds of other visitors. Half of the sites are reserved in advance; the
rest are set aside on a first-come, first-served basis. Rates are $15 per night.

White Wolf, west of Tuolumne Meadows, is the other full-service campground in the high country, with 87 sites available for $18 per night for family
sites, $40 for group sites. It offers a drier climate than the meadow and doesn't
fill up as quickly. Sites are available on a first-come, first-served basis.

Two primitive camps, **Porcupine Flat** and **Yosemite Creek,** are the last to fill
up in the park. Both have pit toilets but no running water, and charge $8 per
night on a first-come, first-served basis.

WHERE TO STAY IN THE PARK

Yosemite Concessions Services, 5410 E. Home Ave., Fresno, CA 93727 (© **559/252-4848**), operates all accommodations within the park and accepts all major credit cards. The reservations office is open Monday through Friday from 7am to 6pm, Saturday and Sunday from 8am to 5pm (PST). For more lodging options and information or to make an online reservation request, visit its website at **www.yosemitepark.com**.

An option that bridges the gap between backpacking and staying in a hotel is staying in one of Yosemite's five backcountry **High Sierra Camps** (© **559/253-5674**). The camps—Glen Aulin, May Lake, Sunrise, Merced Lake, and Vogelsang—are good individual destinations. Or you can link several together, because they're arranged in a loose loop about a 10-mile hike from one another. Guests bunk dormitory-style in canvas tents; each camp has bathrooms and showers. Unguided stays cost $112 per night, per person; guided hikes are $625 for 4 nights (rates include breakfast and dinner). Due to the enormous popularity of these camps, reservations are booked by lottery. Applications are accepted from October 15 to November 30. The lottery is then held in December and the winning applicants are notified by the end of March.

The Ahwahnee Hotel ✦✦✦   A National Historic Landmark noted for its granite-and-redwood architecture, the six-story Ahwahnee is one of the most romantic and beautiful hotels in California, with a VIP guest list that ranges from Winston Churchill and John F. Kennedy to Greta Garbo and Queen Elizabeth. With its soaring lobby, cathedral-like dining room, outstanding views, and steep prices, it's definitely a special-occasion sort of affair. Try to reserve one of the more spacious cottages, which cost the same as rooms in the main hotel. For the price you're paying, the hotel's guest rooms, although pleasant in warm woods and Indian motif fabrics, may seem simple to the point of austerity. On the other hand, where else in the world can you look out your window and see Half Dome, Yosemite Falls, or Glacier Point? The **Ahwahnee Restaurant** is a colossal and impressive chamber highlighted by 50-foot-tall, floor-to-ceiling leaded windows. However, it's more noteworthy for its ambience than for its expensive cuisine.

© **559/252-4848.** Fax 559/456-0542. www.yosemitepark.com. 99 units, 24 cottages. $366–$665 double. Children 12 and under stay free in parent's room. Extra person $21. AE, DC, DISC, MC, V. Pets not accepted, but there is a kennel at the park stables. **Amenities:** Restaurant and lounge; heated outdoor pool; nearby golf course; 2 tennis courts; Jacuzzi; concierge; tour desk; room service; babysitting (need 2 weeks notice; child must be potty-trained and at least 2 years old). *In room:* A/C (ceiling fan in cottages), TV, fridge in cottages, coffeemaker, hair dryer, iron.

Curry Village 🄺🄸🄳🅂   Accommodations at Curry Village, which celebrates its 106th birthday in 2005, range from a few motel-type rooms or heated wood cabins with private bathrooms to canvas tent cabins with central bathrooms. Ironically, the older wood cabins are the nicest. The tent cabins have wood floors and canvas walls. Without a real wall to stop noise, they lack any sort of privacy, but they're fun in that summer-camp sort of way. You'll have to sustain yourself with fast food, as no cooking is allowed in the rooms.

© **559/252-4848.** Fax 559/456-0542. www.yosemitepark.com. 628 units. $63–$112 double. Children 12 and under stay free in parent's room. Extra person $9–$11, tent cabins $4. AE, DC, DISC, MC, V. **Amenities:** Buffet-style dining from spring to fall; fast-food court; heated outdoor pool; nearby golf course; bike rental; tour/activities desk. *In room:* No phone.

Wawona Hotel ✦   If the Ahwahnee doesn't fit your plans or your pocketbook, the Wawona is the next best thing. Also a National Historic Landmark—and the oldest resort hotel in the state—the Wawona is a romantic throwback to simpler times. A pair of century-old white buildings face an expansive manicured lawn, giving the Wawona the look of an antebellum mansion. However, old-world charm has its ups and downs. Private bathrooms were not a necessity in the 19th century, rooms were small to hold in heat, there were no TVs or telephones, and walls were thin—and all of the above still applies today. Still, the Wawona is less commercial than other accommodations on the valley floor, and even has its own 9-hole golf course. *Note:* Nonguests can attend the Saturday-evening summer lawn barbecues or Sunday brunch.

(C) 559/252-4848. www.yosemitepark.com. 104 units, 52 with private bathroom. $112 double without private bathroom; $167 double with private bathroom. Children 12 and under stay free in parent's room. Extra person $16. AE, DC, DISC, MC, V. **Amenities:** Restaurant; outdoor pool; golf course; tennis court. *In room:* Iron, no phone.

Yosemite Lodge   The next step down in valley accommodations, Yosemite Lodge is not actually a lodge but a large, more modern complex with two types of accommodations. The larger "Lodge" rooms with outdoor balconies have striking views of Yosemite Falls. Indeed the largest bonus—and curse—is that every room's front yard is the valley floor, which means you're near glorious larger-than-life natural attractions and equally gargantuan crowds.

(C) 559/252-4848. www.yosemitepark.com. 245 units. $115–$146 double. Children 12 and under stay free in parent's room. Extra person $10–$12. AE, DC, DISC, MC, V. **Amenities:** 2 restaurants; bar; food court; heated outdoor pool; nearby golf course; bike rental; tour/activities desk; babysitting.

3 Mammoth Lakes ★★

40 miles E of Yosemite; 319 miles E of San Francisco; 325 miles NE of Los Angeles

High in the Sierra, just southeast of Yosemite, Mammoth Lakes is surrounded by glacier-carved, pine-covered peaks that soar up from flower-filled meadows. It's an alpine region of sweeping beauty and one of California's favorite playgrounds for hiking, biking, horseback riding, skiing, and more. It's also home to one of the top-rated ski resorts in the world. At an elevation of 11,053 feet, Mammoth Mountain is higher than either Squaw or Heavenly so the snow stays firm longer in the year for spring skiing. You won't find the long lift lines that you find at Tahoe, either—there's more mountain and fewer people.

ESSENTIALS
GETTING THERE   It's a 6-hour drive from San Francisco via Calif. 120 over the Tioga Pass in Yosemite (closed in winter); 5 hours north of Los Angeles via Calif. 14 and U.S. 395; and 3 hours south of Reno, Nevada, via U.S. 395. In winter, Mammoth is accessible via U.S. 395 from the north or the south.

   Mammoth Air Charter (C) 760/934-4279) offers charter flights to the area. It services Mammoth Lakes Airport on U.S. 395. The closest international airport is Reno-Tahoe Airport (C) 775/328-6400). See "Lake Tahoe" in chapter 8 for airlines that service the Reno-Tahoe Airport.

VISITOR INFORMATION   Contact the **Mammoth Lakes Visitors Bureau,** Calif. 203 (P.O. Box 48), Mammoth Lakes, CA 93546 (C) **888/466-2666** or 760/934-2712; www.visitmammoth.com).

OUTDOOR PURSUITS
Mammoth Lakes is at the heart of several wilderness areas and is cut through by the San Joaquin and Owens rivers. Mammoth Mountain overlooks the Ansel Adams Wilderness Area to the west and the John Muir Wilderness Area to the

southeast, and beyond to the Inyo National Forest and the Sierra National Forest.

The **Mammoth Mountain Ski Area** 🌟🌟 (© **888/462-6668** or 760/934-2571; www.mammothmountain.com) is the central focus for both summer and winter activities. Visitors can ride the lifts to see panoramic vistas; those who want an active adventure have many options. If you do hit the slopes in winter, you can use the free **Mammoth Area Shuttle (MAS;** www.mammothweb.com/shuttlemap) or **Mammoth Sierra Express** taxi service (© **760/934-TAXI**) for transportation between the town and the ski area. The shuttle makes stops throughout town and eliminates the long wait you may encounter if you take your own car.

The park's state-of-the-art **Panorama Gondola** provides great viewing every day, winter or summer, weather permitting. Tickets are $17 for adults, $13 for seniors, $9 for children ages 7 to 12; kids under 7 ride free. The gondola carries eight passengers and stops midway up the mountain and at the summit with 360-degree views. In summer you can use the gondola to gain access to the hiking and biking trails on the mountain.

In addition to the activities below, golfers can play at **Snowcreek Golf Course,** Old Mammoth Road (© 760/934-6633). Adventurers can also go hot-air ballooning with **Mammoth Balloon Adventures** (© 760/937-UPUP; www.mammothballoonadventures.com).

HIKING   Trails abound in the Mammoth Lakes Basin area. They include the .5-mile-long **Panorama Dome Trail,** just past the turnoff to Twin Lakes on Lake Mary Road, leading to the top of a plateau that provides a view of the Owens Valley and Lakes Basin. Another trail is the 5-mile **Duck Lake Trail,** starting at the end of the Coldwater Creek parking lot with switchbacks across Duck Pass past several lakes to Duck Lake. The head of the **Inyo Craters Trail** is reached via a gravel road, off the Mammoth Scenic Loop Road. This trail takes you to the edge of these craters and a sign that explains how they were created.

For additional trail information and maps, contact the **Mammoth Ranger Station** (© 760/924-5500). For equipment and maps, go to **Footloose Sports Center,** at the corner of Canyon and Minaret (© 760/934-2400; www.footloosesports.com), which also rents in-line skates and mountain bikes.

HORSEPACKING TRIPS   The region is also great for people who love to ride horses, and numerous outfitters offer pack trips. Among them are **Red's Meadows Pack Station,** Red's Meadows, past Minaret Vista (© 800/292-7758 or 760/934-2345); **Mammoth Lakes Pack Outfit,** Lake Mary Road, past Twin Lakes (© 760/934-2434), which offers 1- to 6-day riding trips and semiannual horse drives, plus other wilderness workshops; and **McGee Creek Pack Station,** McGee Creek Road, Crowley Lake (© 760/935-4324).

KAYAKING   Kayaks are available at Crowley Lake from **Caldera Kayaks** (© 760/935-4942; www.calderakayak.com), starting at $30 a day. This outfitter also offers tours on Crowley and Mono lakes and provides instruction as well.

MOUNTAIN BIKING   In summer the mountain becomes one huge bike park and climbing playground. The bike park is famous for its **Kamikaze Downhill Trail,** an obstacle arena and slalom course where riders can test their balance and skill. Of course, there are also lots of trails for gentler folk who just want to commune with nature and get a little exercise. Bike shuttles will haul you and your bike to the lower mountain trails if you want to skip the uphill part, or the gondola will take you to the summit and you get down any way you

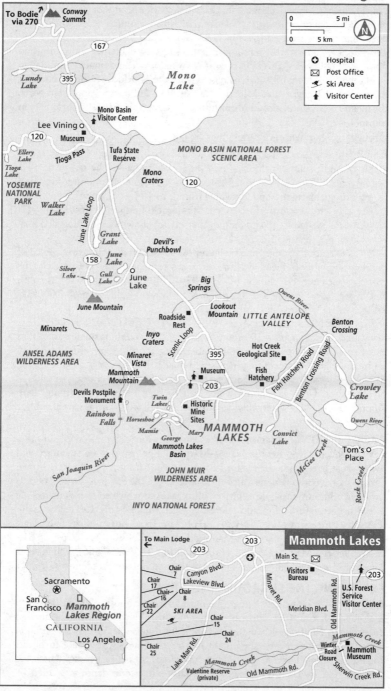

Mammoth Lakes Region

To Bodie via 270
Conway Summit

167

Lundy Lake

395

Mono Lake

Mono Basin Visitor Center

Lee Vining
120
Museum

Ellery Lake

Tioga Lake

Tioga Pass

Tufa State Reserve

MONO BASIN NATIONAL FOREST SCENIC AREA

Mono Craters

120

YOSEMITE NATIONAL PARK

Walker Lake

June Lake Loop

Grant Lake

Devil's Punchbowl

158
June Lake

Silver Lake
Gull Lake
June Lake

June Mountain

Big Springs

Lookout Mountain

LITTLE ANTELOPE VALLEY

Owens River

Benton Crossing

Minarets

Roadside Rest

Inyo Craters

Scenic Loop

ANSEL ADAMS WILDERNESS AREA

Minaret Vista

Mammoth Mountain

395

Museum

Hot Creek Geological Site

Fish Hatchery

Fish Hatchery Road

Benton Crossing Road

203

Devils Postpile Monument

Rainbow Falls

Twin Lakes

Horseshoe

Mamie

George   *Mary*

Mammoth Lakes Basin

Historic Mine Sites

MAMMOTH LAKES

Convict Lake

Crowley Lake

Owens River

Tom's Place

McGee Creek

Rock Creek

San Joaquin River

JOHN MUIR WILDERNESS AREA

INYO NATIONAL FOREST

Map Legend
- ⊕ Hospital
- ⊠ Post Office
- 🎿 Ski Area
- 🚶 Visitor Center

0 — 5 mi
0 — 5 km
N

Sacramento
San Francisco
Mammoth Lakes Region
CALIFORNIA
Los Angeles

Mammoth Lakes

To Main Lodge

203

Chair 7
Canyon Blvd.
Lakeview Blvd.
Chair 17
Chair 16
Chair 8
Chair 22

SKI AREA

Chair 15
Chair 24
Chair 25

Lake Mary Rd.

Main St.

Visitors Bureau

Minaret Rd.

Meridian Blvd.

U.S. Forest Service Visitor Center

203

Old Mammoth Rd.

Winter Road Closure

Mammoth Creek

Mammoth Museum

Sherwin Creek Rd.

Valentine Reserve (private)

Old Mammoth Rd.

can. There's also an area designed for kids. The park operates daily from 9am to 6pm, during summer months. A 1-day pass with unlimited access to the gondola, bike shuttle, and trail system is $28 for adults, $14 for kids ages 12 and under. There's a variety of rent-and-ride packages available; for more information, call ℂ **800/MAMMOTH** or visit www.mammothmountain.com.

In town, mountain bikes can be rented from the **Footloose Sports Center,** at the corner of Canyon and Minaret (ℂ **760/934-2400;** www.footloosesports. com). The **NORBA National Mountain Bike Championships** are held here in summer.

SKIING & SNOWBOARDING   In winter Mammoth Mountain has more than 3,500 skiable acres, a 3,100-foot vertical drop, 150 trails (32 with snow-making), and 30 lifts, including seven high-speed quads. The terrain is 30% beginner, 40% intermediate, and 30% advanced. It's known for power sun, ideal spring skiing conditions, and anywhere from 8 to 12 feet of snow.

There's a cross-country ski center at **Tamarack Lodge** (ℂ **760/934-2442;** www.tamaracklodge.com), and for nonskiers there's snowmobiling, dog-sledding, snowshoeing, and sleigh rides.

If you're renting equipment, you'll save money if you do it in town instead of the resort. Two recommended rental shops are **Footloose Sports Center,** at the corner of Canyon and Minaret (ℂ **760/934-2400;** www.footloosesports.com); and **Wave Rave Snowboard Shop,** on Main Street (Calif. 203; ℂ **760/934-2471**), for snowboards and accessories.

The **June Mountain Ski Area** ✿ (ℂ **888/JUNEMTN** or 760/648-7733; www.junemountain.com), 20 minutes north of Mammoth, is smaller and offers many summer activities. It has 500 skiable acres, a 2,590-foot vertical drop, 35 trails, and eight lifts, including high-speed quads. The terrain is 35% beginner, 45% intermediate, and 20% advanced. It's at the center of a chain of lakes—Grant, Silver, Gull, and June—which can be seen on a scenic driving loop around Calif. 158. It's especially beautiful in the fall when the aspens are ablaze with gold.

TROUT FISHING   Mammoth Lakes Basin sits in a canyon a couple of miles west of town. Here are the lakes—Mary, Mamie, Horseshoe, George, and Twin—that have made the region known for trout fishing. Southeast of town, Crowley Lake is also famous for trout fishing, as are the San Joaquin and Owens rivers. In addition, there are plenty of other lakes in which to spin your reel.

For fishing information and guides, contact **Rick's Sport Center,** at Calif. 203 and Center Street (ℂ **760/934-3416**); **The Trout Fitter,** in the Shell Mart Center at Main Street and Old Mammoth Road (ℂ **760/924-3676**); or **Kittredge Sports,** Main Street and Forest Trail (ℂ **760/934-7566**), which rents equipment, supplies guides, teaches fly-fishing, and offers backcountry trips.

EXPLORING THE SURROUNDING AREA

Bodie ✿ (www.bodie.net), one of the most authentic ghost towns in the West, is about an hour's drive north of Mammoth, past the Tioga Pass entrance to Yosemite. In 1870 more than 10,000 people lived in Bodie, mining $32 million in gold; today it's an eerie shell that's full of ghost stories. En route to Bodie, you'll pass **Mono Lake** ✿ (pronounced *Mow*-no), near Lee Vining, which has startling tufa towers arising from its surface—limestone deposits formed by underground springs. It's a major bird-watching area—about 300 species nest or stop here during their migrations. Right off Highway 395 is the **Mono Basin Scenic Area Visitors Center** (ℂ **760/647-3044;** www.monolake.org; open

> ## (Tips Winter Driving in the Sierra
>
> Winter driving in the Sierra Nevada Range can be dangerous. While the most hazardous roads are often closed, others are negotiable by vehicles with four-wheel-drive or with tire chains. Be prepared for sudden blizzards, and protect yourself by taking these important pre-trip precautions:
>
> - Check road conditions before setting out by calling ② 800/427-7623.
> - Let the rental-car company know you're planning to drive in snow, and ask whether the antifreeze is prepared for cold climates.
> - Make sure your heater and defroster work.
> - Always carry chains. If there's a blizzard, the police will not allow vehicles without chains on some highways. If you don't know how to put them on, you'll have to pay about $40 to have someone "chain up" your car at the side of the road.
> - Recommended items include an ice scraper, a small shovel, sand or burlap for traction if you get stuck, warm blankets, and an extra car key (motorists tend to lock their keys in the car while chaining up).
> - Don't think winter ends in March. At the end of last April, snow was up to 7 feet high on the sides of the roads leading to the valley, and cold temperatures made more snowfall a very real possibility.

every day in summer, Thurs–Mon in winter), which offers scheduled guided tours and has a terrific environmental and historical display of this hauntingly beautiful 60-square-mile desert salt lake. After touring the visitors center, head for the **South Tufa Area** at the southern end of the lake and get a closer look at the tufa formations and briny water. FYI, mono means "flies" in the language of the Yokuts, the Native Americans who live south of this region—get to the lake's edge and you'll see why they chose such as a suitable moniker.

WHERE TO STAY

If you stay at the resort, you'll be steps from the lifts. If you opt for the town, you're closer to the restaurants and nightlife. Regardless, they're within a 5-minute drive, so whatever you choose, you're never too far from the action.

There are more than 700 campsites in the area. These open on varying dates in June, depending on the weather. The largest campgrounds are at Twin Lakes and Cold Water (both in the Mammoth Lakes Basin), Convict Lake, and Red's Meadow. For additional information, call the **Mammoth Ranger Station** (② 760/924-5500).

Fern Creek Lodge *(Value* You'll have to drive about 25 miles north of Mammoth to get the best lodging deal in the region. Less than a mile from the June Mountain ski areas is the Fern Creek Lodge, a spread of simple, fully furnished cabins on the sunrise side of the Eastern High Sierra. Built in 1927, it has seen its ups and downs, but thanks to the latest owners—the Hart family—the year-round fishing and skiing resort is better than ever. The least expensive cabins are small, with just enough room for a bed, a table and chairs, and a bathroom. All have fully equipped kitchens, and most have fireplaces. The units are all so different that your best bet is to call and tell them what you're looking for. There are no phones in rooms, but there is a pay phone on the premises.

4628 Hwy. 158, June Lake, CA 93529. © 800/621-9146 or 760/648-7722. www.ferncreeklodge.com. 10 cabins, 4 apts. $65 cabin for 2; $80–$150 cabin for 4; $235 cabin for 8; $90 apt for 4. Extra person $10. AE, DISC, MC, V. "Certain pets" allowed ($10 extra). **Amenities:** Common BBQ area; full kitchen; grocery and sporting-goods store. *In room:* TV w/HBO.

Holiday Inn ⟨🐕⟩ This faux alpine lodge is Mammoth's newest hotel. A woodsy exterior with a river-rock base gives the three-story hotel a rustic appeal, while the interior boasts a more contemporary atmosphere. The generically decorated guest rooms contain all the comfort and amenities you could want, and come in variety of configurations, including a King/Kid suite with bunk beds. The suites offer a little extra room and Jacuzzi tubs. A spacious honeymoon suite caters to those who want romance in the great outdoors.

3236 Main St. (behind the Chevron station), Mammoth Lakes, CA 93546. © 800/HOLIDAY or 760/924-1234. Fax 760/934-3626. www.holiday-inn.com. 72 units. $129–$349 double and suite. Packages available. AE, DC, DISC, MC, V. **Amenities:** Cafe; bar; indoor heated pool; nearby golf course; exercise room; Jacuzzi; room service; coin-op laundry. *In room:* A/C, TV (VCR in some units), dataport, kitchenette in some units, fridge, coffeemaker, hair dryer, iron.

Mammoth Mountain Inn ⟨🐕⟩ *Kids* Located opposite the ski lodge at the base of the ski resort, the inn started out in 1954 as only one building, but was expanded a decade later into a larger, glossier complex. Though it was remodeled in the early 1990s, it retains the rustic charm you'd expect from a mountain resort. The guest rooms, which were recently upgraded with new carpets and furnishings, are well equipped and pleasantly furnished. The best are the junior suites with a view of the ski area. Families love this place for its large condo units, day-care activities, cribs ($10 one-time charge), playground, box lunches and picnic tables, and game room. There's also an array of sports facilities, including bicycles, fishing or hiking guides, downhill or cross-country skiing, sleighing, horseback riding, and hay-wagon rides. Extras include free airport transportation and occasional entertainment. The only downside is the 10-minute drive into town, but if you're here to ski, you can't get any closer to the slopes.

Minaret Rd. (P.O. Box 353), Mammoth Lakes, CA 93546. © 800/228-4947 or 760/934-2581. Fax 760/934-0701. www.mammothmountain.com. 173 units, 40 condos (some suitable for up to 13 people). Winter $125–$225 double, from $220–$535 condo; summer $99–$150 double, from $150 condo. Ski and mountain-biking packages available. AE, MC, V. **Amenities:** Restaurant; bar; heated outdoor pool; nearby golf course; 2 indoor and an outdoor whirlpool spas; mountain-bike rental; day-care center; game room; video arcade; concierge; 24-hr. room service; babysitting; coin-op laundry; executive-level rooms. *In room:* TV (VCR in 1- and 2-bedroom units), dataport, coffeemaker, kitchen in some units, hair dryer, iron.

Motel 6 *Value* The rooms may be small, but accommodations here are the nicest around in this price range. Although quarters are a bit more cramped than some other options, factor in the pool, vending machines, and free coffee in the lobby and you've got all you really need to set up camp.

3372 Main St. (P.O. Box 1260), Mammoth Lakes, CA 93546. © 800/4-MOTEL6 or 760/934-6660. Fax 760/934-6989. www.motel6.com. 151 units. Winter $62–$86 double; summer from $55 double. Extra person $6. AARP discounts. AE, DC, DISC, MC, V. Pets accepted (1 pet per room). **Amenities:** Heated outdoor pool (summer only); coin-op laundry. *In room:* A/C, TV, dataport.

Sherwin Villas *Value* Just outside the center of town on Old Mammoth Road is this cluster of woodsy condos, perfect for families or groups of friends traveling together. You'll find one- to four-bedroom units, each with a fully stocked kitchen, fireplace, linens, and access to a free ski shuttle that will take you to the slopes (a 5-min. drive away). Considering how many people you can pack into these apartments—and if you stay 4 weekday nights, the fifth night is free—it's a good deal. When making reservations, specify exactly what you're looking for: Each condo is independently owned and varies dramatically in both decor and quality (you can see a few photos of each condo on their website).

362 Old Mammoth Rd. (P.O. Box 2249), Mammoth Lakes, CA 93546. © 800/228-5291 or 760/934-4773. www.sherwinvillas.com. 70 condos. 1-bedroom unit for up to 4 people $100–$120 winter, from $95 summer; 2-bedroom loft for up to 6 people $140–$190 winter, from $115 summer; 3-bedroom unit for up to 8 people $155–$220 winter, from $135 summer; 4-bedroom unit for up to 10 people $195–$260 winter, from $155 summer. Extra person $10. MC, V. **Amenities:** Outdoor pool; tennis courts; 2 Jacuzzis; Finnish sauna; game room. *In room:* TV, kitchen, phone on request.

Sierra Lodge *(Value)* In the heart of Mammoth Lakes, this two-story inn offers contemporary lodgings without a trace of rusticity. The large guest rooms are pleasantly decorated with framed blond-wood furnishings, modern prints, track lighting, big beds, kitchenettes, and small patios or balconies with partial mountain views. The two-bedroom suite—equipped with two queen beds and a full-size pull-out sofa—is ideal for groups or families. Facilities include an outdoor Jacuzzi and a fireside room for relaxing. Other perks include ski lockers, free covered parking, continental breakfast, free shuttle service right out front, and a short walk to Mammoth's best restaurant, Nevados (see review below).

3540 Main St. (Calif. 203; P.O. Box 9228), Mammoth Lakes, CA 93546. © 800/356-5711 or 760/934-8881. Fax 760/934-7231. www.sierralodge.com. 36 units. $85–$159 double. Rates include continental breakfast. AE, DISC, MC, V. Pets accepted for $10 per night with $100 deposit. **Amenities:** Nearby golf course; outdoor Jacuzzi. *In room:* TV, dataport, kitchenette, fridge, hair dryer.

Tamarack Lodge & Resort The lodge and cabin accommodations at this rustic lakeside retreat are nothing fancy, but that's exactly what's kept guests coming here since the 1920s. The cabins, which can accommodate two to nine people, are dotted around the 6-acre property and offer a variety of configurations, from studios with wood-burning stoves and showers to two-bedroom/two-bathroom accommodations with fireplaces. The best units are the lakefront cabins, so be sure to request one with a lake view. The least expensive rooms are in the main lodge and come with private or shared bathrooms. The rustic Lakefront Restaurant offers a romantic dinner setting and a seasonally changing menu with entrees ranging from grilled medallions of elk filet to seared sea scallops and fresh Hawaiian *ahi* (tuna) flown in daily. In the winter the lodge opens its popular cross-country ski center with over 25 miles of trails and skating lanes, ski rentals, and a ski school. Boat and canoe rentals are also available.

Twin Lakes Rd., off Lake Mary Rd. (P.O. Box 69), Mammoth Lakes, CA 93546. © 800/MAMMOTH or 760/ 934-2442. Fax 760/934-2281. www.tamaracklodge.com. 11 units, 6 with private bathroom; 27 cabins. $84–$230 double; $120–$350 cabin. AE, MC, V. **Amenities:** Restaurant; nearby golf course. *In room:* Fax, kitchen in cabins, fridge, coffeemaker, iron.

WHERE TO DINE

Berger's Restaurant *(Kids)* *(Value)* AMERICAN If after a full day's skiing you're in need of a big, hearty American meal at a fair price, head down the mountain to Berger's. Its cabinlike interior, with local photographs on the wooden walls, fits its surroundings. Portions are huge and include an array of burgers, steak, ribs, chicken, and sandwiches. There are even a few hefty salads to satisfy a more health-conscious hunger. Entrees include salad, garlic bread, and either fries or a baked potato. Sandwiches, which cost up to $8 and come with salad and fries, will also easily fill you up without emptying your wallet. The children's menu is the ultimate bargain, offering a selection of kid-friendly feasts for under $6. The daily lunch specials are most coveted by locals, but if you want to try one, come early—they almost always sell out.

6118 Minaret Rd. ℭ 760/934-6622. Reservations recommended. Main courses $8.25–$15. MC, V. Daily 11am–9:30pm.

Grumpy's Saloon and Eatery ⭐ *Kids* AMERICAN   More than just a sports bar, for more than 2 decades, Grumpy's has been Mammoth's main "sports restaurant," a log building replete with TVs (35 of 'em), pool tables, pinball machines, video games, and foosball tables. The bar serves a great selection of beers on tap, and the hearty, affordable grub features burgers (go for the Grumpy Burger), tasty barbecued ribs, homemade chili, a handful of Mexican items, and the famous quarter-pound Dogger, an unbelievably enormous hot dog. Everything on the menu comes with a choice of fries, coleslaw, or barbecued baked beans, just to make certain that nobody leaves hungry. Stop by for happy hour, when there's usually a free buffet of hors d'oeuvres that may include Buffalo wings, cheese and crackers, or miniquesadillas.

361 Mammoth Rd. ℭ 760/934-8587. www.grumpysmammoth.com. Main courses $6.25–$16. AE, MC, V. Mon–Sun 11am–10pm; bar stays open until 2am.

Nevados ⭐⭐ EUROPEAN/CALIFORNIA   Nevados is one of Mammoth Lakes' best restaurants and a longtime favorite with the locals and Los Angelenos on their annual ski or summer holiday. Owner/host Tim Dawson is usually on hand nightly to ensure that everyone's satisfied with the innovative cuisine and house-baked breads. Most everyone orders the prix-fixe three-course meal, which consists of a first course such as a strudel appetizer of wild mushrooms and rabbit with roasted shallots and grilled scallions; a main course (perhaps braised Provimi veal shank with roasted tomatoes and garlic mashed potatoes); and for dessert a fantastic warm pear-and-almond tart sweetened with caramel sauce and vanilla-bean ice cream. Throw in the casual-but-sweet ambience (white tablecloths, candles, and French country murals) and the extensive selection of wines, single-malt scotches, and single-batch bourbons, and it's no wonder this is the hangout for ski instructors and race coaches.

Main St. (at Minaret Rd.). ℭ 760/934-4466. Reservations recommended. Main courses $19–$25; fixed-price meal $40. AE, DC, DISC, MC, V. Daily 5:30–9:30pm.

The Restaurant at Convict Lake ⭐⭐ CONTINENTAL/FRENCH   For years this rustic restaurant on the edge of Convict Lake was a local secret, but when it was featured in *Wine Spectator* magazine, the gig was up. Now you'd better make reservations if you want to enjoy a meal within this plank-sided cabin with its open-beam ceiling, wood floors, copper-hooded free-standing fireplace, and mountain views. Located 5 miles south of Mammoth Lakes, it's well worth the drive to spend a romantic evening feasting on duck confit flavored with sun-dried cherry sauce, Chilean sea bass with mango-pineapple-cilantro relish, or lamb loin in a hazelnut-and-rosemary sauce. Linger a bit longer to savor the bananas Foster flambé or meringue topped with kiwi fruit and whipped cream.

Convict Lake Rd. ℭ 760/934-3803. Reservations recommended. Main courses $15–$30. AE, MC, V. Summer daily 11am–2pm; year-round daily 5:30–9:30pm.

Shogun ⭐ JAPANESE   Sushi and tempura in an alpine setting may seem out of context, but this authentic Japanese restaurant, located on the second floor of a strip mall, consistently packs in both tourists and locals. Diners at the eight-seat sushi bar sup on sashimi, hand rolls, and a variety of sushi creations. Delicate tempura, sweet and tangy teriyaki dishes, and grilled yakitori skewers are offered individually or as combination dinners. Those with hearty appetites can order the Boat Dinner, which includes beef and chicken teriyaki, tempura, tonkatsu, sashimi or salmon, and dessert for $21 per person (minimum two people). Sake, beer, and cocktails are also available.

Old Mammoth Rd. (in the Sierra Center Mall). © 760/934-3970. Reservations recommended. Main courses $8.95–$18. AE, DC, DISC, MC, V. Mon–Sun 5–9:30pm.

Skadi ✦✦ ECLECTIC Suitably named after the Viking goddess of skiing and hunting, Skadi is the domain of chef-owner Ian Algerøenof, a former chef at Nevados who felt a need to open his own restaurant. It's the perfect place to drop by for an après-ski cocktail at the 14-seat bar, a snack from the substantial selection of appetizers and desserts, or a full dinner. The decor has a big-city postmodern aura that's a welcome change after all that local alpine rusticity. Main courses are self-proclaimed "Alpine cuisine" and include such dishes as pan-roasted crispy-skin salmon served with mashed potatoes and roasted beets, or braised lamb shanks with rosemary-garlic mashed potatoes and a side of garlic confit. Finish the evening with the wild-honey-roasted strawberries or house-made chocolates.

587 Old Mammoth Rd. (in the Sherwin Plaza III shopping mall). © 760/934-3902. Reservations recommended. Main courses $22–$28. AE, MC, V. Wed–Sun 5:30–10pm.

Whiskey Creek ✦ AMERICAN If you favor surf-and-turf fare combined with alpine atmosphere and a swinging nightlife scene, you'll want to make a reservation here. Whiskey Creek's wraparound windows encompass a pretty view of the snow-clad mountains, and the menu is known for its excellent South Carolina pork chops, bacon-wrapped meatloaf, and barbecued pork spareribs, all served with a heaping side of roasted garlic mashed potatoes (don't worry, you'll burn it off on the slopes tomorrow). Although the dining room may offer a peaceful experience, the upper-level brewpub is a different world. If you're not too stuffed, head upstairs to hear live music every night from 9pm until at least 1am, making it the number one spot in town to hear cheesy pickup lines.

24 Lake Mary Rd. (at Minaret Rd.). © 760/934-2555. Reservations recommended. Main courses $16–$25. AE, DC, DISC, MC, V. Daily 5–10pm (summer 5:30pm); bar stays open until 2am.

4 Devils Postpile National Monument ✦

10 miles W of Mammoth; 50 miles E of Yosemite's eastern boundary

Just a few miles outside the town of Mammoth Lakes, Devils Postpile National Monument is home to one of nature's most curious geological spectacles. Formed when molten lava cracked as it cooled, the 60-foot-high, blue-gray basalt columns that form the postpile look more like some sort of enormous eerie pipe organ or a jumble of string cheese than anything you'd expect to see made from stone. The mostly six-sided columns formed underground and were exposed when glaciers scoured this valley in the last ice age, some 10,000 years ago. Similar examples of columnar basalt are found in Ireland and Scotland.

Because of its high elevation (7,900 ft.) and heavy snowfall, the monument is open only from summer until early fall. The weather in summer is usually clear and warm, but afternoon thundershowers can soak the unprepared. Nights are still cold, so bring good tents and sleeping bags if you'll be camping. The Mammoth Lakes region is famous for its beautiful lakes—but unfortunately all that water also means lots of mosquitoes. Plan for them.

GETTING THERE

From late June to early September, cars are prohibited in the monument between 7:30am and 5:30pm because of the small roads' inability to handle the traffic. Visitors must take a shuttle bus to and from locations in the monument. While it takes some planning, the resulting peace and quiet are well worth the trouble and make you wonder why the park service hasn't implemented similar programs at Yosemite Valley and other traffic hot spots.

VISITOR INFORMATION　For information before you go, call © 760/934-2289 during open season, or © 760/872-4881 from November to May. You'll also find plenty of info at **www.nps.gov/depo/depomain.htm**.

HIKING

There's more to Devils Postpile than a bunch of rocks, no matter how impressive they might be. Located on the banks of the San Joaquin River in the heart of a landscape of granite peaks and crystalline mountain lakes, the 800-acre park is a gateway to a hiker's paradise. Short paths lead from here to the top of the postpile and to **Soda Springs,** a spring of cold carbonated water.

A longer hike (about 1.25 miles) from the separate Rainbow Falls Trailhead will take you to spectacular **Rainbow Falls** ⚘, where the middle fork of the San Joaquin plunges 101 feet from a lava cliff. From the trail, a stairway and short trail lead to the base of the falls and swimming holes below.

The **John Muir Trail,** which connects Yosemite National Park with Kings Canyon and Sequoia National Parks, and the **Pacific Crest Trail** run through here. Named after the conservationist and author who is largely credited with saving Yosemite and popularizing the Sierra Nevada as a place worth preserving, the 211-mile John Muir Trail traverses some of the most rugged, remote parts of the Sierra. There are two accesses to it in Devils Postpile, one via the ranger station, the other from the Rainbow Falls Trailhead. From here, you can hike as far as your feet will take you north or south. *Note:* Mountain bikes are not permitted on trails.

CAMPING

While most visitors stay in or around Mammoth Lakes, the monument does maintain a 21-site campground with piped water, flush toilets, fire pits, and picnic tables on a first-come, first-served basis. Rates are $8 per night. Bears are common in the park, so take proper food-storage measures. Leashed pets are permitted on trails and in camp. Call the **National Park Service** (© **760/934-2289,** or 760/872-4881 Nov–May; www.nps.gov/depo/depomain.htm) for details. There are several other U.S. Forest Service campgrounds nearby, including **Red's Meadow** and **Upper Soda Springs.**

5 En Route to Sequoia & Kings Canyon

Though **Visalia** is the official "gateway" and the city closest to Sequoia and Kings Canyon National Parks, it's still 40 minutes to the park entrance. Much closer is the small town of **Three Rivers,** which until recently had a few mediocre restaurants, coffee shops, and motels to offer visitors. That's changing with the opening of the **Shoshone Inn,** which has added 60 more hotel rooms in Visalia in addition to its two restaurants.

ESSENTIALS

GETTING THERE　If you're driving from San Francisco, take I-580 east to I-5 south to Calif. 198 east. The trip takes about 5 hours.

Amtrak (© 800/USA-RAIL; www.amtrak.com) stops at nearby Hanford, and there's a shuttle from there to Visalia.

VISITOR INFORMATION   Contact the **Visalia Chamber of Commerce,** 720 W. Mineral King Rd., Visalia, CA 93291 (© **559/734-5876;** www.visalia chamber.org).

WHERE TO STAY

In Three Rivers try the **Holiday Inn Express,** 40820 Sierra Dr. (Calif. 198), Three Rivers, CA 93271 (© **800/HOLIDAY** or 559/561-9000), which has an outpost here. For other options, contact **The Reservation Centre** (© **559/561-0410;** www.rescentre.com).

Ben Maddox House ★   Set on a residential street of Victorian homes 4 blocks from the town's main street, the Ben Maddox House is an impressive sight. Its triangular gable is punctuated with a round window and two tall palm trees looming over the front yard. The house, built in 1876, is constructed of redwood, and its rooms retain their original dark-oak trim and white-oak floors. The six guest rooms contain 18th- and 19th-century furnishings, and the two front rooms have French doors leading to two small porch/sitting areas. A full made-to-order breakfast is part of the experience.

601 N. Encina St., Visalia, CA 93291. © 800/401-9800 or 559/739-0721. Fax 559/625-0420. www.ben maddoxhouse.com. 6 units. $85–$100 single; $100–$120 double. Rates include breakfast. AE, DISC, MC, V. **Amenities:** Outdoor pool; nearby golf course. *In room:* A/C, TV w/free movies, dataport, fridge, hair dryer, iron.

Radisson Hotel   Seven blocks from the town center, the eight-story Radisson is the largest hotel in Visalia and a favorite for those en route to Sequoia and Kings Canyon National Parks. Some of the attractive rooms open onto balconies. This is not the most glamorous Radisson in California, but it's serviceable in every way. The restaurant serves breakfast, lunch, and dinner, with last seating at 10pm. The local bar provides entertainment on Friday and Saturday nights.

300 S. Court St., Visalia, CA 93291. © 800/333-3333 or 559/636-1111. Fax 559/636-8224. www.radisson. com/visaliaca. 201 units. $90–$168 double; $239–$469 suite. Extra person $10. Cribs provided free. AE, DC, MC, V. **Amenities:** Restaurant; bar; large pool; complete fitness center; Jacuzzi; bike rental; room service (until 2am); executive-level rooms. *In room:* A/C, TV/VCR w/pay movies, dataport, coffeemaker, iron.

WHERE TO DINE

The Vintage Press ★★ AMERICAN/CONTINENTAL   This has long been the best restaurant within a 100-mile radius, a culinary stopover of widely acknowledged merit in the gastronomic wasteland between Los Angeles and San Francisco. The design is reminiscent of a *fin de siècle* gin mill in Gold Rush San Francisco, with a bar imported from that city manufactured by the Brunswick Company (of bowling-alley fame), lots of antiques bought at local auctions, and glittering panels of leaded glass and mirrors. The place is big enough (250 seats) to feed a boatload of Gold Rush hopefuls and has a bustling bar and lounge where a pianist presents live music Thursday through Saturday from 5:30 to 9pm.

The menu is supplemented by daily specials—a zesty rack of lamb roasted in a cabernet sauce with rosemary and pistachios, for example. The regular menu offers about a dozen meat and fish dishes, with steaks as well as such choices as red snapper with lemon, almonds, and capers, or pork tenderloin with Dijon mustard, red chile, and honey. To start, I recommend farm-raised fresh oysters on the half shell or the wild mushrooms with cognac in puff pastry.

216 N. Willis St. © 559/733-3033. Reservations recommended. Main courses $18–$30. AE, DC, MC, V. Mon–Sat 11:30am–2pm and 5:30-10pm; Sun 10am–2pm and 5–9pm.

6 Sequoia & Kings Canyon National Parks ⭑⭑

30 miles E of Visalia

Only 200 road miles separate Yosemite from Sequoia and Kings Canyon national parks, but they're worlds apart. While the National Park Service has taken every opportunity to modernize, accessorize, and urbanize Yosemite, resulting in a frenetic tourist scene, at Sequoia and Kings Canyon, they've treated the wilderness beauty of the parks with respect and care. Only one road, the Generals Highway, loops through the area, and no road traverses the Sierra here. The park service recommends that vehicles over 22 feet long avoid the steep and windy stretch between Potwisha Campground and the Giant Forest in Sequoia National Park. Generally speaking, the park is much less accessible by car than most, but spectacular for those willing to head out on foot.

The Sierra Nevada tilts upward as it runs south. **Mount Whitney,** at 14,494 feet (the highest point in the lower 48 states), is just one of many high peaks in Sequoia and Kings Canyon. The **Pacific Crest Trail** also reaches its highest point here, crossing north to south through both parks. In addition to snow-covered peaks, Sequoia and Kings Canyon are home to the largest groves of giant sequoias in the Sierra Nevada, as well as the headwaters of the Kern, Kaweah, and Kings rivers. A few high-country lakes are home to some of the only remaining pure-strain golden trout. Bears, deer, and numerous smaller animals and birds depend on the parks' miles of wild habitat for year-round breeding and feeding grounds.

Technically two separate parks, Sequoia and Kings Canyon are contiguous and managed jointly from the park headquarters at Ash Mountain, just past the entrance on Calif. 198 east of Visalia.

⟨Tips⟩ National Parks vs. National Forests: What You Don't Know Can Cost You

Sierra, Inyo, and Sequoia national forests surround Kings Canyon and Sequoia national parks. What's the difference between a national park and a national forest? National parks are intended to preserve natural and historic features, in addition to providing areas of easy-on-the-land recreation. National forests, on the other hand, operate under a multiple-use concept, sometimes including the harvesting of commodities such as lumber and minerals. National parks and national forests have different rules, and you should know them. An activity that's legal in a forest can earn you a fine in a park.

Parks forbid hunting; forests usually allow it. Dogs can be taken on forest trails, but not in parks. You can only camp in numbered sites in designated areas in parks; in the forest it's either campgrounds or, unless posted otherwise, near roadsides. You can ride your bike on a forest trail; in parks you must stay on the roads and helmets are required for persons 18 and younger. To protect the ecosystem in parks, you can't disturb anything—plants, pinecones, or rocks. In the forest, collecting a few things for personal use is permitted.

For more information, contact the **National Park Service** at ℂ 559/565-3341, or the **Forest Service** at ℂ 559/784-1500.

Sequoia & Kings Canyon National Parks

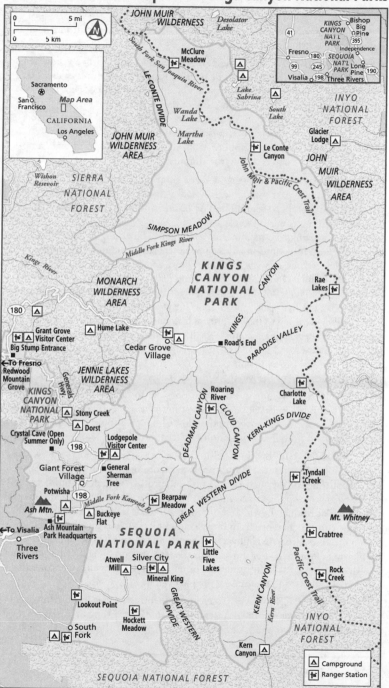

ESSENTIALS

Most visitors make a loop through the parks by entering at Grant Grove and leaving through Ash Mountain, or vice versa.

VISITOR INFORMATION   The **Lodgepole** and **Grant Grove** visitor centers are the largest, with a selection of park information and displays about the history, biology, and geology of this incredible place. Some time spent here will pay off by letting you decide which parts of the parks you want to concentrate on. For information before you go, log on to www.nps.gov/seki, www.sequoia-kingscanyon.com, or www.visitsequoia.com, or call ✆ **559/565-3341.**

Park rangers offer hikes, campfire talks, and slide shows at several campgrounds and visitor centers during the summer.

FEES & PERMITS   A $10-per-car fee is good for 7 days' entry at any park entrance. An annual pass costs $20; the Golden Age pass offers lifetime access for seniors 62 and over for $10; and blind or visitors with permanent disabilities get free entry with the Golden Access pass.

Wilderness permits are required for overnight backpacking in the parks. You can reserve the $10 permits in advance by downloading an application from the national park website at www.fs.fed.us/r5/inyo and mailing or faxing it to the Wilderness Permit Office, 351 Pacu Lane, Suite 200, Bishop, CA 93514 (✆ **760/873-2485;** fax 760/873-2484). There's also a phone reservation system at ✆ **760/873-2483.** It's open 8am to 4pm 7 days a week from June 1 to October 1, and weekdays the rest of the year. If you plan on climbing Mount Whitney, you must enter a lottery to get a permit. You'll need to fill out an application, which can be downloaded and printed from the park website (www.fs.fed.us/r5/inyo). Send it to the Wilderness Permit Office, 351 Pacu Lane, Suite 200, Bishop, CA 93514. Applications for the Mount Whitney trail are $15 a person.

REGULATIONS   Mountain bikes and dogs are forbidden on all park trails (dogs are permitted in developed areas but must be leashed). The park service allows firewood gathering at campgrounds, although supplies can be scarce. Removing wood from living or standing trees is forbidden.

THE SEASONS   In the high altitudes, where most Sequoia and Kings Canyon visitors are headed, the summers are short and the winters cold. Snow in July and August, although rare, is not unheard of. At midelevations, where the sequoias grow, spring can come as early as April or as late as June. Afternoon showers are occasional. In winter, only the main roads into the parks are usually open; the climate can range from bitter cold to pleasant and can change minute by minute. The Generals Highway between Sequoia and Kings Canyon closes for plowing during and after snowstorms. Be ready for anything if you head into the backcountry on skis. In summer, poison oak and rattlesnakes are common in lower elevations, and mosquitoes are plentiful in all wet areas.

AVOIDING THE CROWDS   To escape the crowds and see less-used areas of the parks, enter on one of the dead-end roads to Mineral King or Cedar Grove (both open only in summer), or South Fork. The lack of through traffic makes

---

⌒Tips Fill 'Er Up

Note that there are no gas stations in the parks, so be sure to fill up your gas tank before you enter.

these parts of the parks incredibly peaceful even at full capacity, and they're gateways to some of the best hiking.

EXPLORING THE PARKS

There are some 75 groves of giant sequoias in the parks, but the easiest places to see the trees are **Grant Grove** ✿, in Kings Canyon near the park entrance on Calif. 180 from Fresno, or **Giant Forest** ✿, a huge grove of trees containing 40 miles of footpaths, located 16 miles from the entrance to Sequoia National Park on Calif. 198. Saving the sequoias was one of the reasons Sequoia National Park was created in 1890 at the request of San Joaquin Valley residents, making it the second-oldest national park in the United States.

The 2-mile **Congress Trail** loop in Giant Forest starts at the base of the **General Sherman Tree** ✿, the largest living thing in the world. Single branches of this monster are more than 7 feet thick. Each year it grows enough wood to make a 60-foot-tall tree of normal dimensions. Other trees in the grove are nearly as large, and many of the peaceful-looking trees have also been saddled with militaristic and political monikers like General Lee and Lincoln. Longer trails lead to remote reaches of the grove and nearby meadows.

Unlike the coast redwoods, which reproduce by sprouting or by seeds, giant sequoias only reproduce by seed. Adult sequoias rarely die of diseases and are protected from most fire by thick bark. The huge trees have surprisingly shallow roots, and most die from toppling when their roots are damaged and can no longer support them. These groves, like the ones in Yosemite, were explored by conservationist and nature writer John Muir, who named the Giant Forest.

Besides the sequoia groves, Sequoia and Kings Canyon are home to the most pristine wilderness in the Sierra Nevada. At **Road's End** on the Kings Canyon Highway (open late May to early Nov), you can stand by the banks of the Kings River and stare up at granite walls rising thousands of feet above the river, the deepest canyon in the United States.

Near Giant Forest Village, **Moro Rock** is a 6,725-foot-tall granite dome formed by exfoliation of layers of the rock. A quarter-mile trail scales the dome for a spectacular view of the adjacent Canyon of the Middle Fork of the Kaweah. The trail gains 300 feet in 400 yards, so be ready for a climb.

Crystal Cave ✿ is located 15 miles from the Calif. 198 park entrance and an additional 7 miles to cave parking. Here you can take a 50-minute tour of Crystal's beautiful marble interior. The tour is $8 for adults, $6 for seniors, $4 for children ages 6 to 12, and free for kids 6 and under. Tickets are not sold at the cave and must be purchased at the Lodgepole or Foothills visitor centers at least 1½ hours in advance. Be sure to wear sturdy shoes and bring a jacket. For information, call © **559/565-3759** or log on to www.sequoiahistory.org. The cave is open mid-May to late September daily from 11am to 4pm.

Boyden Cavern, on Calif. 180 in neighboring Sequoia National Forest, is a cave where you can take a 45-minute tour to see stalactites and stalagmites. A fee is charged; call © **209/736-2708** for details or visit www.caverntours.com. The cave is open April through October daily from 10am to 5pm.

HIKING THE PARKS

Hiking and backpacking are what these parks are really all about. Some 700 miles of trails connect canyons, lakes, and high alpine meadows and snowfields.

When traveling overnight inside the parks' boundaries, overnight and/or day-use permits are required. If you want to do serious overnight backpacking, see "Fees & Permits" under "Essentials" above.

Some of the park's most impressive hikes start in the **Mineral King** section in the southern end of Sequoia. Beginning at 7,800 feet, trails lead onward and upward to destinations like Sawtooth Pass, Crystal Lake, and the old White Chief Trail to the now-defunct White Chief Mine. Once an unsuccessful silver-mining town in the 1870s, Mineral King was the center of a battle in the late 1970s when developers sought to build a huge ski resort. They were defeated when Congress added Mineral King to Sequoia National Park, and the wilderness remains.

The **John Muir Trail,** which begins in Yosemite Valley, ends at Mount Whitney. For many miles it coincides with the **Pacific Crest Trail** as it skirts the highest peaks in the park. This is the most difficult part of the Pacific Crest, above 10,000 feet most of the time and crossing 12,000-foot-tall passes.

Other hikers like to explore the northern part of Kings Canyon from **Cedar Grove** and **Road's End.** The **Paradise Valley Trail,** leading to beautiful Mist Falls, is a fairly easy day trip by park standards. The **Copper Creek Trail** immediately rises into the high wilderness around Granite Pass at 10,673 feet, one of the most strenuous day hikes in the parks.

If the altitude and steepness are too much for you at these trail heads, try some of the longer hikes in **Giant Forest** or **Grant Grove.** These forests are woven with interlocking loops that allow you to take as short or as long a hike as you want. The 6-mile **Trail of the Sequoias** in Giant Forest will take you to the grove's far-eastern end, where you'll find some of the finest trees. In Grant Grove, a 100-foot walk through the hollow trunk of the **Fallen Monarch** makes a fascinating side trip. The tree has been used for shelter for more than 100 years and is tall enough inside that you can walk through without bending over.

Perhaps the most traversed trail to the park is the **Whitney Portal Trail.** It runs from east of Sequoia near Lone Pine, through Inyo National Forest, to Sequoia's boundary, the summit of Mount Whitney. Though it's a straightforward walk to the summit and it's possible to do it in a long day hike, you'd better be in really good shape before attempting it. Almost half the people who attempt Whitney, including those who camp partway up, don't reach the summit. Weather, altitude, and fatigue can stop even the most prepared party. For more information, contact the **Mount Whitney Ranger Station** at © **760/876-6200.** For wilderness permits, see "Fees & Permits" at the beginning of this section.

The official park map and guide has good road maps for the parks, but for serious hiking you'll want to check out *Sierra South: 100 Back-Country Trips,* by Thomas Winnett and Jason Winnett (Wilderness Press). Another good guide is *Kings Canyon Country,* a hiking handbook by Ginny and Lew Clark. The Grant Grove, Lodgepole, Cedar Grove, Foothills, and Mineral King visitor centers sell a complete selection of maps and guidebooks to the parks. Books and maps are also available by mail through the **Sequoia Natural History Association** (© **559/565-3759;** www.sequoiahistory.org).

OTHER OUTDOOR PURSUITS

FISHING   Trout fishing in the lower altitudes is limited; most fishing takes place along the banks of the Kings and Kaweah rivers. A few high-country lakes are refuges for trout and are not stocked with hatchery fish. Before venturing into the high country, inquire at a ranger station to find out about closures or specific regulations. A California fishing license is required for everyone over 16 years old. Tackle and licenses are available at several park stores.

RAFTING & KAYAKING   Only fairly recently have professional outfitters begun taking experienced rafters and kayakers down the Class IV and V Kaweah and Upper Kings rivers outside the parks. Check **The Reservation Center** website at **www.rescentre.com/rafting.htm** for a good list of companies running trips. Rafting and kayaking here are only for the very adventurous.

SKIING & SNOWSHOEING   **Wolverton,** 2 miles north of the General Sherman tree, has a snow-play and cross-country ski area. You can rent skis and snowshoes at the Lodgepole Market. In the **Giant Forest** and **Grant Grove** areas, there are about 50 miles of marked cross-country trails. Rangers offer naturalist talks and snowshoe walks some weekends. Rental equipment (including snowshoes) and lessons are available at the Grant Grove Market. For more information on cross-country skiing, sledding, or snowshoeing at Grant Grove, call the park service at © **559/335-5500;** for Wolverton, call © **559/565-3435.** Kids can sled and play in the snow play areas near Wolverton and at Big Stump, Columbine, and Azalea in Grant Grove.

The Sequoia Natural History Association operates the **Pear Lake Ski Hut** for snowshoers and cross-country skiers, which can accommodate up to 10 people. Use of the facility is by lottery. For further information, call © **559/565-3759.**

CAMPING

There are 13 campgrounds in the parks, offering the most convenient and economical accommodations, although none have hookups. Only two accept reservations: **Lodgepole Campground** and **Dorst Campground** in Sequoia (© **800/ 365-2267).** Both are close to Giant Forest. Lodgepole is within a short stroll of a restaurant, market, showers, laundry, and visitor center. With more than 200 sites each, they tend to be the noisiest campgrounds in Sequoia. Lodgepole charges $20 per night and Dorst charges $20 per night. Other campgrounds are first-come, first-served, and often fill up on weekends. Three campgrounds— Azalea, Lodgepole, and Potwisha—are open year-round. The rest are open from snowmelt through September. Call © **559/565-3341** for information. Even in summer, campers should prepare for rain and cold temperatures. Bring a good tent and warm sleeping bags. *Note:* Due to bears, proper food storage is required.

Smaller and more peaceful are **South Fork, Potwisha, Buckeye Flat, Atwell Mill,** and **Cold Springs.** Atwell Mill and Cold Springs have pit toilets and cost $12 per night. Potwisha and Buckeye Flat, with flush toilets and sinks, charge $18. South Fork, with pit toilets and no drinking water, charges $12.

Campers in the remote Cedar Grove area of Kings Canyon National Park in the Kings River gorge can choose from **Moraine, Sentinel, Sheep Creek,** and **Canyon View,** which also has a group camp. All four have flush toilets and are convenient to some of the parks' best hiking. Sites cost $18. Nearby, the small **Cedar Grove Village** offers a restaurant, motel, showers, and store.

Three campgrounds in the Grant Grove area will put you near the sequoias without the noise and crowds of Giant Forest Village. All three—**Sunset, Azalea,** and **Crystal Springs**—have flush toilets and phones.

WHERE TO STAY IN THE PARKS

Lodging in the parks ranges from rustic cabins with no bathrooms or heat to brand-new rooms with all the modern comforts (well, maybe not all—hot tubs aren't mentioned anywhere). New structures are increasing the numbers of rooms and the comfort level. There are a dizzying array of types of accommodations with prices that change seasonally. Your best bet is to check online for the location and accommodation that suits your needs, and call for the current price. **Lodging** in Kings Canyon is operated by the park concessionaire, Kings

Canyon Park Services Co., P.O. Box 909, Kings Canyon National Park, CA 93633 (© **559/335-5500** for information and reservations; www.sequoia-kings canyon.com).

Cedar Grove Lodge on the Kings River in the eastern section of Kings Canyon in Cedar Grove Village has 18 motel-style rooms and is open from early May to early October. Each room has two queen-size beds and a private bathroom. Grant Grove Village, on Calif. 180, 30 miles northwest of Giant Forest, offers a variety of cabins with private or shared bathrooms and tent cabins. The newest lodge in Kings Canyon is named after John Muir, and has 30 rooms, each with two queen beds and a private bathroom. The lodge features an extensive collection of Muir's writings, and paintings and photographs of his journeys decorate the walls.

Sequoia National Park is in the process of eliminating the old lodgings at Giant Forest and replacing them with new facilities. The **Wuksachi Village & Lodge** ⚐, 64740 Wuksachi Way in Lodgepole (© **888/252-5757** or 559/565-4070; www.visitsequoia.com), is Sequoia's most recent addition. It's open year-round, offering 102 rooms in the park from $86 to $123 off season, and from $150 to $219 during peak season (Apr 1–Nov 30). Each room in the cedar-and-stone, mountain-themed lodge has two queens or a king and a sofa bed. Children under 12 can stay free in their parent's room. The Wuksachi Lodge dining room serves good lunches and dinners, including a kids' menu. The lodge offers winter ski promotions such as cross-country skis or snowshoes for two adults as part of the room rates. Unfortunately, you have to leave your pets at home.

10

Sacramento, the Gold Country & the Central Valley

by Matthew Richard Poole

On the morning of January 24, 1848, carpenter James Marshall was working on John Sutter's mill in Coloma when he stumbled upon a gold nugget on the south fork of the American River. Despite Sutter's wishes to keep it a secret, word leaked out—a word that would change the fate of California almost overnight: *Gold!*

The news spread like wildfire, and a frenzy seized the nation: The Gold Rush was on. Within 3 years, the population of the state grew from 15,000 to more than 265,000. Most of these newcomers were single men under the age of 40, and not far behind were the merchants, bankers, and women who made their fortunes catering to the miners, most of whom went bust in their search for wealth.

Sacramento quickly grew as a supply town at the base of the goldfields. The Gold Country boom lasted less than a decade; the supply was quickly exhausted, and many towns shrank or disappeared. Sacramento, however, continued to grow as the fertile Central Valley south of it exploited another source of wealth, becoming the vegetable-and-fruit garden of the nation.

A trip along Calif. 49 from the northern mines to the southern mines will give visitors a sense of what life might have been like on the mining frontier. Many of the towns along this route seem frozen in time, down to Main Street with its raised wooden sidewalks, double-porched buildings, saloons, and Victorian storefronts. Each town tells a similar story of sudden wealth and explosive growth, yet each has also left behind its own unique imprint. Any fan of movie westerns will recognize the setting—hundreds, perhaps even thousands, of films have been shot in these parts.

At the base of the Gold Country's rolling hills is the sprawling, flat Central Valley. Some 240 miles long and 50 miles wide, it's California's agricultural breadbasket, the source of much of the bounty shipped across the nation and overseas. A lot of California history has revolved around the struggle for control of the water used to irrigate the valley and make this inland desert bloom. Despite the scarcity of water (it receives less than 10 in. of rainfall per year), a breathtaking panorama of orange and pistachio groves, grapevines, and strawberry fields stretches uninterrupted for miles.

1 Sacramento ✸

90 miles E of San Francisco; 383 miles N of Los Angeles

Sacramento, with a metro-area population of nearly 1.7 million, is one of the state's fastest-growing areas. In addition to being the state capital, it is a thriving shipping and processing center for the fruit, vegetables, rice, wheat, and dairy goods produced in the Central Valley. In the past decade, it's also become an area of high-tech spillover from Silicon Valley, and more recently, a suburb for Bay Area workers seeking affordable homes. The quantity and quality of downtown restaurants—such as the Esquire Grill and The Waterboy—have improved as well. This prosperous and politically charged city has broad, tree-shaded streets lined with some impressive Victorians and well-crafted bungalows. At its heart sits the capitol—Sacramento's most visible attraction—in a large park replete with flower gardens, memorial statuary, and curious squirrels.

Sacramento is far from a tourist town, but it does have its share of touristy activities. Visitors and locals alike enjoy spending the day walking through Old Sacramento, floating down the American River, or biking the shady paths along the Sacramento and American rivers. Locals fondly refer to their water-bordered town as "River City." And did I mention that in summer the weather is seriously hot? So much so that San Franciscans drive to Sacramento just to thaw out.

ESSENTIALS

GETTING THERE If you're driving from San Francisco, Sacramento is about 90 miles east on I-80. From Los Angeles, take I-5 through the Central Valley directly into Sacramento. From North Lake Tahoe, get on I-80 west, and from South Lake Tahoe take U.S. 50.

Sacramento International Airport (© **916/929-5411**), 12 miles northwest of downtown Sacramento, is served by about a dozen airlines, including Alaska Airlines, American, America West, Continental, Delta, Northwest, Southwest, and United. **Taxi and Shuttle Service** (© **916/362-5525**) will get you from the airport to downtown; it charges a flat rate of $15 to the capital, a bargain compared to the $25 a conventional taxi would cost.

Amtrak (© **800/USA-RAIL;** www.amtrak.com) trains serve Sacramento daily. The Greyhound terminal is at Seventh and L streets.

VISITOR INFORMATION The **Sacramento Convention and Visitors Bureau,** 1303 J St., Sacramento, CA 95814 (© **916/264-7777;** www.sacramentocvb.org), provides plenty of information for travelers. It's open Monday through Friday from 8am to 5pm. Once in the city, you can also stop by the **Old Sacramento Visitor Center,** 1101 Second St. (© **916/442-7644**), in Old Sacramento; it's usually open daily from 10am to 5pm. The city's major daily paper is the *Sacramento Bee* (www.sacbee.com).

ORIENTATION Suburbia sprawls around Sacramento, but its downtown area is relatively compact. Getting around the city is made easy by a gridlike pattern of streets that are designated by numbers or letters. The capitol, on 10th Street between N and L streets, is the key landmark. From the front of the capitol, M Street—which is at this point called Capitol Mall—runs 10 straight blocks to Old Sacramento, the oldest section of the city.

WHAT TO SEE & DO

In town, you'll want to stroll around **Old Sacramento** ✮, 4 square blocks at the foot of the downtown area that have become a major tourist attraction. These blocks contain more than 100 restored buildings (California's largest restoration project), including restaurants and shops. Although the area has cobblestone streets, wooden sidewalks, and authentic Gold Rush–era architecture, the high concentration of T-shirt shops and other gimmicky stores has turned it into a sort of historical amusement park. Nonetheless, there are interesting things to see, such as where the Pony Express ended and the transcontinental railroad—and the

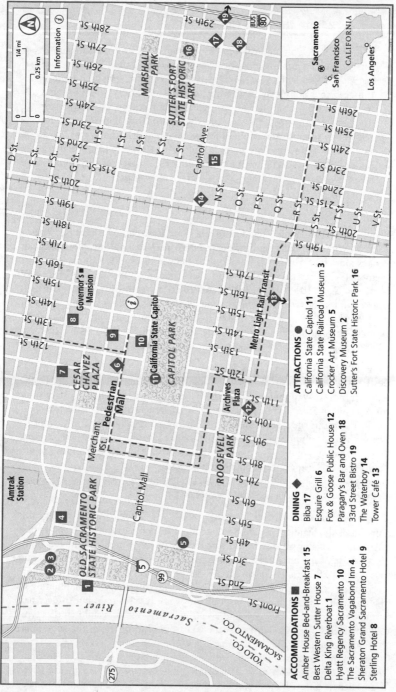

Downtown Sacramento

ACCOMMODATIONS ■
Amber House Bed-and-Breakfast **15**
Best Western Sutter House **7**
Delta King Riverboat **1**
Hyatt Regency Sacramento **10**
The Sacramento Vagabond Inn **4**
Sheraton Grand Sacramento Hotel **9**
Sterling Hotel **8**

DINING ◆
Biba **17**
Esquire Grill **6**
Fox & Goose Public House **12**
Paragary's Bar and Oven **18**
33rd Street Bistro **19**
The Waterboy **14**
Tower Café **13**

ATTRACTIONS ●
California State Capitol **11**
California State Railroad Museum **3**
Crocker Art Museum **5**
Discovery Museum **2**
Sutter's Fort State Historic Park **16**

(Kids) Where the Wild Things Are

The best place to take little kids to let them tear around on a sunny afternoon is **Fairytale Town,** at William Land Park, Land Park Drive and Sutterville Road ((C) **916/264-5233**). Although the slides and other climbing toys are pretty basic and showing their age, little ones seem to think it's the best place in the world. After you've explored every nook and cranny, cross the street to the **Sacramento Zoo** ((C) **916/264-5885**), buy some cotton candy, and see the animals. Adjacent to Fairytale Town, there's also the small but pleasant **Funderland** amusement park ((C) **916/456-0115**) with kid-size rides, open all week in summer months and on spring and fall weekends, weather permitting.

Republican Party—began. The **California State Railroad Museum** (see below) is loved by railroad buffs, and the **Sacramento Jazz Festival,** mostly Dixieland, attracts more than 100 bands from around the world for 4 days of madness over Memorial Day weekend. While you're meandering, stop at the **Discovery Museum** (G) at 101 I St. ((C) **916/264-7057;** www.thediscovery.org), which houses exhibits of California's history, highlighting the valley's agricultural Gold Rush as well as the real one in 1849. It's open Tuesday through Sunday from 10am to 5pm. Admission is $5 for adults, $4 for seniors over 60, $4 for kids ages 13 to 17, $3 for kids 4 to 12, and free for kids under 3.

THE MAIN ATTRACTIONS

California State Capitol (G)(G)(G)   Closely resembling a scale model of the U.S. Capitol in Washington, D.C., the beautiful, domed California state capitol was built in 1869 and renovated in 1976. Sacramento's most distinctive landmark, the capitol has been the stage of many political dramas in California history. The 1-hour guided tours provide insight into the building's architecture and the workings of the government it houses. *Note:* Security will ask you to put your purse or backpack through a metal detector.

10th St. (between N and L sts.). (C) 916/324-0333. Free admission. Daily 9am–5pm. Tours offered every hour on the hour until 4pm. Closed Thanksgiving, Dec 25, and Jan 1.

California State Railroad Museum (G)(G)(G) (Kids)   Well worth visiting, this museum is the highlight of Old Sacramento. You won't miss much if you bypass the memorabilia displays and head straight for the museum's 105 shiny locomotives and rail cars, beautiful antiques that are true works of art. Afterward, you can watch a 20-minute film on the history of the Western railroads that's quite good, then peruse related exhibits that tell the amazing story of the building of the transcontinental railroad. This museum is not just for train buffs: Over half a million people visit each year, and even the hordes of schoolchildren that typically mob this place shouldn't dissuade you from visiting one of the largest and best railroad museums in the country. Allow about 2 hours to see it all.

From April to September, on weekends and holidays from 11am to 5pm, **steam locomotive rides** carry passengers 6 miles along the Sacramento River. Trains depart on the hour from the Central Pacific Freight Depot in Old Sacramento, at K and Front streets. Fares are $6 for adults and children ages 13 and older, $3 for children 6 to 12, and free for children under 6.

125 I St. (at Second St.). ✆ **916/445-6645.** Fax 916/327-5655. www.californiastaterailroadmuseum.org. Admission $4 adults 17 and older, free for children 16 and under. Daily 10am–5pm. Closed Thanksgiving, Dec 25, and Jan 1.

Crocker Art Museum ★ This museum houses an outstanding collection of California art, as well as changing exhibits from around the world. It's in an imposing century-old Italianate building, with an ornate interior of carved and inlaid woods. The Crocker Mansion Wing, the museum's most recent addition, is modeled after the Crocker family home and contains works by Northern California artists from 1945 to the present. Plan to spend about an hour here.

216 O St. (at Third St.). ✆ **916/264-5423.** www.crockerartmuseum.org. Admission $6 adults, $4 seniors 65 and over, $3 students with ID, free for children 6 and under. Free for all every Sun 10am–1pm. Tues–Wed and Fri–Sun 10am–5pm; Thurs 10am–9pm. Closed major holidays.

Sutter's Fort State Historic Park ★ John Sutter established this outpost in 1839, and the park, restored to its 1846 appearance, aims to recapture the spirit of 19th-century California. Exhibits include a blacksmith's forge, cooperage, bakery, and jail—and a self-guided audio tour is available. Demonstrations and reenactments in costume are staged daily Memorial Day to Labor Day, when admissions are bumped to $4 for adults and $1 for children 6 to 16.

2701 L St. ✆ **916/445-4422.** Admission $2 adults, free for children 16 and under. Daily 10am–5pm.

OUTDOOR PURSUITS

BICYCLING One good thing about a town that's as flat as a tortilla: It's perfect for exploring on a bike. One of the best places to ride is through Old Sacramento and along the 22-mile American River Parkway, which runs right through it. If you didn't bring your own wheels, the friendly guys at **City Bicycle Works,** 2419 K St., at 24th Street (✆ **916/447-2453**), will rent you one for about $15 a day and point you in the right direction.

RIVER RAFTING Sacramento lies at the confluence of the American and Sacramento rivers, and rafting on the clear blue water of the American is popular, especially on warm weekends. Several Sacramento-area outfitters rent rafts for 4 to 15 persons, along with life jackets and paddles for about $10 to $15 per person. Their shuttles drop you and your entourage upstream and meet you 3 to 4 hours later at a predetermined point downstream. A recommended outfitter is **American River Raft Rentals,** 11257 S. Bridge St. (at Sunrise Ave.), Rancho Cordova (✆ **888/338-RAFT** or 916/635-6400; www.raftrentals.com).

WHERE TO STAY

EXPENSIVE

Amber House Bed-and-Breakfast ★★ Just 8 blocks from the Capitol on a quiet street, Amber House offers lovely, individually decorated rooms possessing all the amenities you could wish for. Named for famous artists, musicians, and writers, accommodations are located in adjacent historic houses: the Poet's Refuge, a 1905 home with five rooms, and the Artist's Retreat, a Mediterranean-style house built in 1913. A third house—an old colonial revival home called the Musician's Manor—is across the street, and its Mozart Room is the B&B's best, with a four-poster queen bed, a heart-shaped Jacuzzi, a private patio, and three bay windows overlooking the tree-shaded street. A living room and library are available for guests' use. A fourth large, turreted home is currently being remodeled. It will be called The Library, featuring room decor with French, English, Southern plantation, and safari themes named after authors Christie, Hemingway, Fitzgerald, and Twain. A full breakfast is served at the time and location you request—either in your room, in the large dining room, or outside on the veranda. Coffee and a newspaper are brought to your door each morning, as are freshly baked cookies and wine or champagne every evening.

1315 22nd St., Sacramento, CA 95816. © **800/755-6526** or 916/444-8085. Fax 916/552-6529. www.amber house.com. 18 units. $149–$319 double. Rates include breakfast. AE, DC, DISC, MC, V. **Amenities:** Complimentary bike use; concierge; in-room massage; laundry service; same-day dry cleaning. *In room:* A/C, TV/VCR, dataport, hair dryer, iron.

Hyatt Regency Sacramento &&

Sacramento's top hotel stands right in the heart of downtown, across from the State Capitol and adjacent to the convention center. It's the high-status address for visiting politicos and is popular with conventioneers as well, as its facilities and services are unmatched in the city. While the rooms themselves are not terribly distinctive, they conform to a high standard and come with all the amenities you expect from Hyatt. The best are the corner units with views facing the State Capitol.

1209 L St., Sacramento, CA 95814. © **800/233-1234** or 916/443-1234. Fax 916/321-3799. www.sacramento. hyatt.com. 503 units. $220–$260 double; from $375 suite. AE, DC, DISC, MC, V. Self-parking $12; valet parking $18. **Amenities:** 2 restaurants; bar; heated outdoor pool; nearby golf course; health club; Jacuzzi; concierge; car-rental desk; business center; full-service salon; room service; in-room massage; babysitting; laundry service; same-day dry cleaning; executive-level rooms. *In room:* A/C, TV w/pay movies, dataport, minibar, fridge upon request, coffeemaker, hair dryer, iron.

Sheraton Grand Sacramento Hotel &

This convention hotel opened in 2001 and is praised for its high-tech amenities, a million-dollar public art collection, and the preservation of a beloved landmark. The hotel's 504 rooms are in a shiny, 26-story building adjoining a three-story building that was originally Sacramento's public market from 1920 to the 1960s. This historic structure, designed by Julia Morgan, architect for Hearst Castle, was a favorite gathering place for three generations of Sacramentans. Now housing the lobby, bar, and two restaurants, the site is again a downtown focal point for residents and travelers alike. The accommodations are convention-type hotel rooms—a mite anonymous, but not unpleasant.

1230 J St., Sacramento, CA 95814. © **800/325-3535** or 916/447-1700. Fax 916/477-1701. www.sheraton. com. 504 units. $119–$275 double; from $350 suite. AE, DC, DISC, MC, V. Self-parking $12; valet parking $21. **Amenities:** 2 restaurants; bar; heated outdoor pool; health club; concierge; car-rental desk; business center; full-service salon; room service; in-room massage; babysitting; laundry service; same-day dry cleaning; club-level rooms. *In room:* A/C, TV w/pay movies, dataport, minibar, coffeemaker, hair dryer, iron.

MODERATE

Delta King Riverboat &

The *Delta King* carried passengers between San Francisco and Sacramento in the 1930s. Permanently moored in Sacramento since 1984, the riverboat is now a somewhat gimmicky but charming hotel. Staying here can be a novelty, but the staterooms in a boat are not ultra-cozy and may bother landlubbers, especially if you're planning to spend a lot of time in your room. All units are nearly identical and have private bathrooms and low ceilings. The captain's quarters, a pricey suite, is a unique, mahogany-paneled stateroom, complete with an observation platform and private deck.

The **Pilothouse Restaurant** is popular for local office parties. When the weather is nice, there's dining on outside decks with views of Old Sacramento. Live entertainment is presented below decks in two venues on Friday and Saturday nights. In the Mark Twain Lounge, "Suspect's Murder Mystery Dinner Theatre," an interactive whodunit, challenges the audience to reveal the true murderer, played by actors in period dress. It's $35 per person to attend, but that includes dinner, tax, and gratuity. Drinks are extra. Or for $14 a person, you can see a local production of a Broadway play in the 75-seat Delta King Theatre.

1000 Front St., Old Sacramento, CA 95814. © 800/825-5464 or 916/444-5464. www.deltaking.com. 44 units. Sun–Thurs $119–$139 double; $400 captain's quarters; Fri–Sat $169 double, $400 captain's quarters. Riverside rooms are $15 extra. Rates include continental breakfast. AE, DC, DISC, MC, V. **Amenities:** Restaurant; lounge; laundry service; same-day dry cleaning. *In room:* A/C, TV, dataport, hair dryer, iron.

Sterling Hotel ★★ In the heart of Sacramento, 3 blocks from the capitol, this inn occupies a white-fronted Victorian mansion built in the 1890s and heavily renovated in 1995. The Sterling has all the charm of a small, well-managed, sophisticated inn, with a carefully tended flowering yard, tasteful decor, designer furnishings, Italian marble, and a Jacuzzi in every room. **The Chanterelle,** which serves well-prepared California regional cuisine in a dignified setting, is one of Sacramento's better restaurants.

1300 H St., Sacramento, CA 95814. © **800/365-7660** or 916/448-1300. Fax 916/448-8066. www.sterling hotel.com. 17 units. Sun–Thurs $179–$199 double; $325 suite. Fri–Sat $199–$249 double; $325 suite. Rates include continental breakfast. AE, DC, MC, V. **Amenities:** Restaurant; Jacuzzi; room service. *In room:* A/C, TV w/pay movies, dataport, fridge in most units, hair dryer, iron.

INEXPENSIVE

Best Western Sutter House *Value* You would never know from the plain, motel-like exterior that this is one of the best values in Sacramento. Rooms here are as up-to-date as any offered by upscale hotels such as the Hilton or the Hyatt, including well-coordinated furnishings and lots of amenities. There's a pool in the courtyard, guest passes to a nearby fitness center, free covered parking, and complimentary coffee and pastries are served each morning in the lobby.

1100 H St., Sacramento, CA 95814. © **800/830-1314** or 916/441-1314. Fax 916/441-5961. www.bestwestern. com. 98 units. $85–$160 double. Rates include continental breakfast. AE, DC, DISC, MC, V. **Amenities:** Solar-heated outdoor pool; access to fitness center; room service; same-day dry cleaning; executive-level rooms. *In room:* A/C, TV, fax, dataport, fridge, coffeemaker, hair dryer, iron.

The Sacramento Vagabond Inn *Value* A reliable choice within walking distance of the State Capitol, the Vagabond Inn has a host of free features, including local phone calls, weekday newspapers, and continental breakfast. Bedrooms are clean and comfortable but not exceptional—it's the economical rates and the convenient location that make it worth your while. There's an adjoining 24-hour Denny's restaurant as well.

909 Third St., Sacramento, CA 95814. © **800/522-1555** or 916/446-1481. Fax 916/448-0364. www. vagabondinns.com. 108 units. $85 double. Extra person $10. Children 18 and under stay free in parent's room. Rates include continental breakfast. AE, DC, DISC, MC, V. **Amenities:** Restaurant; heated pool; nearby golf course; laundry service; same-day dry cleaning. *In room:* A/C, TV, fridge in some units, coffeemaker, hair dryer, iron.

WHERE TO DINE
EXPENSIVE

Biba ★★★ ITALIAN Locals flock to this neo–Art Deco restaurant to sample the classical Italian cuisine of Bologna-born owner Biba Caggiano, who has published nine cookbooks. Although the menu changes seasonally, you can expect to find about 10 pastas and an equal number of main courses. There might be a delicate pappardelle with a fresh-seafood sauce, or a more pungent spaghetti alla Siciliana, which combines eggplant, tomatoes, capers, garlic, and anchovies. For a main course, the classic *osso buco* Milanese served with a soft, creamy polenta is excellent, but save room for the double-chocolate trifle made with dark and white chocolate, Grand Marnier–soaked pound cake, and raspberry purée.

2801 Capitol Ave. ℂ 916/455-2422. www.biba-restaurant.com. Reservations recommended. Main courses $18–$28. AE, DC, MC, V. Mon–Fri 11:30am–2:30pm; Mon–Thurs 5:30–9:30pm; Fri–Sat 5:30–10:30pm.

MODERATE

Esquire Grill ⛄ AMERICAN GRILL   Next door to Sacramento's convention center and a short walk from the capitol, Sheraton Grand, and the Hyatt Regency, the Esquire Grill was a hit as soon as it opened its handsome doors. The Michael Guthrie architectural group designed the restaurant using rich woods and warm colors. Sacramento has been struggling for years to revive its downtown area and this urbane place is one giant step toward creating the revitalized scene the city planners are hoping for. The bar is always lively with well-dressed folks sipping martinis and Cosmopolitans, and the restaurant's food is classic American grill. Dinner specialties might include a mixed fry of calamari, fennel, and onions; or spit-roasted pork chops with buttermilk onion rings and house-made applesauce. Some folks come just for the onion rings.

1221 K St. ℂ 916/448-8900. Main courses $15–$46 ($46 for porterhouse steak for 2). AE, DC, DISC, MC, V. Mon–Fri 11am–2:30pm; Sun–Thurs 4:30–10:30pm; Fri–Sat 4:30–11:30pm. Limited menu Mon–Fri 2:30–4:30pm.

Paragary's Bar and Oven ⛄⛄ MEDITERRANEAN   Occupying two dining rooms across the street from Twenty Eight, Paragary's is widely considered the best moderately priced restaurant downtown. In good weather the best seats are outside amid the gorgeous fountains and plantings of the courtyard; other seating options include the formal fireplace room and the brightly lit cafe. The same menu is served no matter where you sit, with some of the best dishes coming from the kitchen's wood-burning pizza oven. But this is more than a gourmet pizza parlor, as evidenced by the grilled rib-eye steak with mashed potatoes, portobello mushrooms, and grilled leeks, or the hand-cut rosemary noodles with seared chicken, pancetta, artichokes, leeks, and garlic.

1401 28th St. ℂ 916/457-5737. Main courses $12–$20. AE, DC, DISC, MC, V. Mon–Thurs 11:30am–11pm; Fri 11:30am–midnight; Sat 4:30pm–midnight; Sun 4:30–10pm.

33rd Street Bistro ⛄ BISTRO   Seattle transplants Fred Haynes (chef) and his brother Matt (manager) have taken an old brick building and transformed it into a hugely successful bistro. It's popular for all the right reasons—the food is good (and priced right), the staff is friendly, and the ambience is cheerful. Selections include a variety of Italian grilled sandwiches and house favorites such as wood-roasted vegetables with sun-dried tomatoes and goat-cheese crostini, Uncle Bum's jerk ribs with Jamaican barbecue sauce and Key lime crème fraîche, and wood-roasted pork loin with ancho-chile butter and linguisa risotto.

3301 Folsom Blvd. (at 33rd St.). ℂ 916/455-2282. Main courses $8–$19. AE, MC, V. Sun–Thurs 8am–10pm; Fri–Sat 8am–11pm.

The Waterboy ⛄⛄ COUNTRY FRENCH/CALIFORNIA   Until recently, Sacramento had a slim list of really good restaurants, but now it has achieved hard-to-choose-where-to-go status. At the top of everybody's list is The Waterboy. It's got everything going for it: an appealing, airy but unpretentious atmosphere, friendly and knowledgeable servers, and, best of all, outstanding food cooked perfectly. Chef/owner Rick Mahan uses Niman Ranch naturally raised meats and local organic produce, and he offers a particularly fine selection of wines. Main courses change every 5 weeks but include dishes such as saffron risotto, cassoulet, grilled duck breast, or pan-roasted pork chops.

> ### (Value) An Insider's Guide to Sacramento's Budget Dining Bests
>
> I used to live in Sacramento as a starving writer, so I'm well acquainted with the city's best dining deals. Here are five of my favorites that you won't find in any other travel guide:
>
> - **Best Burger: Willie's Burgers,** 2415 16th St., between Broadway and X Street (℃ 916/444-2006), slathers everything in so much chili and cheese that heavy-duty paper towel dispensers are mandatory. Open late most nights.
> - **Best Coffee Joint:** A tough one, but **Java City** (℃ 916/444-5282), at the corner of Capitol Avenue and 18th Street, has been popular forever. Sure, there are a few street people around, but at least they keep the yuppies at bay.
> - **Best Mexican: Taco Loco Taqueria,** 2326 J St., at 24th Street (℃ 916/447-0711). Try the charbroiled black-tip shark taco, a big ole shrimp burrito, or snapper ceviche tostada, all so fresh the restaurant doesn't even own a freezer. Wash it all down with a Los Cabos Margarita while soaking up the sun on the front patio.
> - **Best Breakfast:** At the **Cornerstone Restaurant,** 2330 J. St., at 24th Street (℃ 916/441-0948), the choices are all standard American, but the servings are huge, the service is friendly, and the price is right. A four-egg omelet with home fries, toast, and fruit costs less than $6. My dad eats here once a week.
> - **Best Brewery:** The **Rubicon Brewing Company,** 2004 Capitol Ave., at 20th Street (℃ 916/448-7032), still remains my favorite hangout. A pitcher of India Pale and a side of fries is de rigueur.

20th St. and Capitol Ave. ℃ 916/498-9891. Main courses $14–$20. AE, DC, DISC, MC, V. Tues–Fri 11:30am–2:20pm; Sun and Tues–Thurs 5–9pm; Fri–Sat 5–10pm.

INEXPENSIVE

Fox & Goose Public House ★★ (Value) ENGLISH PUB The Fox is your classic British pub, down to the dartboard, picture of the queen, and numerous beers from across the pond. The soups at lunch are excellent, and the specials often include bangers and mash, Welsh rarebit, and Cornish pasties. The burnt cream dessert is famous. Arrive early for lunch or be prepared for a wait, as locals love this place (no reservations taken and they won't even seat you until all the members of your party have arrived). Equally popular breakfasts include kippers, grilled tomatoes, and crumpets, as well as waffles, omelets, and French toast. There's live entertainment by local bands 6 nights a week, as well as pub grub like fish and chips and hamburgers Monday through Friday from 5:30 to 9:30pm.

1001 R St. (at 10th St.). ℃ 916/443-8825. Reservations not accepted. Main courses $4–$7. AE, MC, V. Mon–Fri 7am–2pm; Sat–Sun 8am–1pm. Bar stays open until midnight Mon–Thurs, until 2am Fri–Sat.

Tower Café INTERNATIONAL The Tower Café gets its name from the building in which it's located: a grand old 1939 movie house with a tall Art Deco spire. The restaurant occupies the same space where a small mom-and-pop music store once stood. The former resident, Tower Records, has since grown

---

Tips **Nightlife in Sacramento**

If you're in need of some nocturnal entertainment in Sacramento, do what the locals do: Pick up a free copy of the *Sacramento News & Review (SN&R)*. You'll find it in red boxes or racks at most major entertainment venues and shopping malls, as well as bookstores, coffee shops, music stores, and convenience stores throughout the downtown area. You can also peruse online at **www.newsreview.com/sacto**.

---

into America's second-largest record retailer. While it's unlikely that Tower Café will share the phenomenal success of its predecessor, it's popular with locals. The multicultural decor—kind of Art Deco meets *National Geographic*—is a feast for the eyes. Dishes reflect a variety of international flavors, from the Jamaican jerk chicken to Shanghai chow mein. Usually the food is good, especially the desserts, but once in a while you get something that makes you wonder what's going on in the kitchen. On warm days it seems as if everyone in the city is lunching here on the large outdoor deck (past patrons have included serious foodie Bill Clinton), so people-watching can be a real treat. The movie house typically shows good foreign films, and Tower Records is just across the street. These are all great places to round out a lazy River City afternoon.

1518 Broadway. © 916/441-0222. Main courses $8–$14. AE, MC, V. Sun–Thurs 8am–10pm; Fri–Sat 8am–10:30pm, with dessert and drinks only until 11:30pm.

2 The Gold Country ★★

Cutting a serpentine swath for nearly 350 miles along the aptly numbered Calif. 49, the Gold Country stretches from Sierra City to the foothills of Yosemite. Much of this rugged region still retains its '49er ambience: Mining sites, horse ranches, and Wild West saloons are common sights in these parts. Along with its numerous ghost towns and Gold Rush–era architecture, it's enough to make Gene Autry or Roy Rogers feel right at home.

The town of Placerville, 44 miles east of Sacramento at the intersection of U.S. 50 and Calif. 49, is in the approximate center of the Gold Country. To the north are the old mining towns of Grass Valley and Nevada City, while in the central and southern Gold Country are such well-preserved towns as Amador City, Sutter Creek, Columbia, and Jamestown, to name a few.

In fact, the Gold Country is so immense that it would take weeks to thoroughly explore. But rather than provide an exhaustive list of every town, I have narrowed my coverage to include three of my favorite regions, each of which can be explored in just 2 or 3 days: the charismatic side-by-side towns of Nevada City and Grass Valley to the north; the well-preserved Gold Rush communities of Amador City, Sutter Creek, and Jackson in the central Gold Country; and at the southern end of the Gold Country, the wonderfully authentic neighboring mining towns of Angels Camp, Murphys, Columbia, Sonora, and Jamestown.

Any of these regions will provide an excellent base for exploring and experiencing the Gold Country, whether you're intent on panning for gold, exploring old mines and caverns, or rafting the area's many white-water rivers. In fact, the Gold Country is one of the most underrated and least congested tourist destinations in California, a winning combination of Old West ambience, adorable (and affordable) bed-and-breakfasts, and outdoor adventures galore.

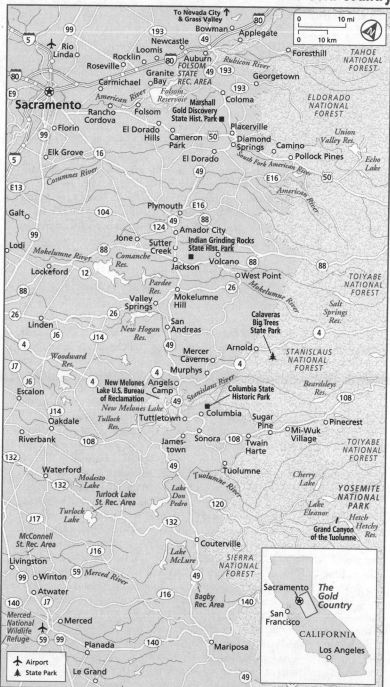

The Gold Country

To Nevada City
& Grass Valley ↑

0 ——— 10 mi
0 ——— 10 km

Sacramento

TAHOE NATIONAL FOREST

ELDORADO NATIONAL FOREST

TOIYABE NATIONAL FOREST

STANISLAUS NATIONAL FOREST

TOIYABE NATIONAL FOREST

YOSEMITE NATIONAL PARK

SIERRA NATIONAL FOREST

Bowman
Applegate
Newcastle
Loomis
Rio Linda
Rocklin
Auburn
FOLSOM STATE REC. AREA
Roseville
Carmichael
Granite Bay
Foresthill
Rubicon River
Georgetown
Folsom Reservoir
American River
Coloma
Marshall Gold Discovery State Hist. Park
Rancho Cordova
Folsom
Placerville
Union Valley Res.
Florin
El Dorado Hills
Cameron Park
Diamond Springs
Camino
Pollock Pines
Echo Lake
Elk Grove
El Dorado
South Fork American River
American River
Cosumnes River
Galt
Plymouth
Amador City
Lodi
Ione
Sutter Creek
Indian Grinding Rocks State Hist. Park
Mokelumne River
Comanche Res.
Jackson
Volcano
West Point
Lockeford
Pardee Res.
Mokelumne Hill
Mokelumne River
Salt Springs Res.
Linden
Valley Springs
San Andreas
Calaveras Big Trees State Park
New Hogan Res.
Mercer Caverns
Arnold
Woodward Res.
Murphys
Beardsleys Res.
Escalon
New Melones Lake U.S. Bureau of Reclamation
Angels Camp
Stanislaus River
Columbia State Historic Park
Oakdale
New Melones Lake
Tuttletown
Columbia
Sugar Pine
Pinecrest
Tulloch Res.
Mi-Wuk Village
Riverbank
James-town
Sonora
Twain Harte
Waterford
Tuolumne
Cherry Lake
Modesto Lake
Turlock Lake St. Rec. Area
Lake Don Pedro
Tuolumne River
Turlock Lake
Lake Eleanor
Hetch Hetchy Res.
McConnell St. Rec. Area
Couterville
Grand Canyon of the Tuolumne
Livingston
Lake McLure
Winton
Merced River
Atwater
Bagby Rec. Area
Merced National Wildlife Refuge
Merced
Planada
Mariposa
Le Grand

✈ Airport
🌲 State Park

Inset map

Sacramento
San Francisco
The Gold Country
CALIFORNIA
Los Angeles

THE NORTHERN GOLD COUNTRY:
NEVADA CITY & GRASS VALLEY

About 60 miles northeast of Sacramento, Nevada City and Grass Valley are far and away the top tourist destinations of the northern Gold Country.

These two historic towns were at the center of the hard-rock mining fields of Northern California. Grass Valley was California's richest mining town, producing more than a billion dollars worth of gold. Both are attractive, although I usually spend most of my time in smaller Nevada City. Its wealth of Victorian homes and storefronts makes it one of the most appealing small towns in California, particularly in the fall when the maple trees are ablaze with color. (In fact, its entire downtown has been designated a National Historic Landmark.)

It's easy to get here. If you're driving from San Francisco, take I-80 to the Calif. 49 turnoff in Auburn and follow the signs heading north. For information about the area, contact the **Grass Valley & Nevada County Chamber of Commerce,** 248 Mill St., Grass Valley (© **800/655-4667** in California or 530/273-4667; www.grassvalleychamber.com), or the **Nevada City Chamber of Commerce,** 132 Main St., Nevada City (© **800/655-NJOY** or 530/265-2692; www.nevada citychamber.com).

NEVADA CITY 🐾🐾

Rumors of miners pulling a pound of gold a day out of Deer Creek brought thousands of fortune seekers to the area in 1849. Within a year, Nevada City was a boisterous town of 10,000, the third-largest city in California. In its heyday, everyone who was anyone visited this rollicking Western outpost with its busy red-light district. Mark Twain lectured here in 1866, telling the audience about his trips to the Sandwich Islands (Hawaii). Former president Herbert Hoover also lived and worked here as a gold miner.

Pick up a walking-tour map at the **Chamber of Commerce,** 132 Main St., and stroll the streets lined with impressive Victorian buildings, including the **Firehouse Number 1 Museum,** 214 Main St. (© **530/265-5468**), with bell tower, gingerbread decoration, a small museum that displays mementos from the Donner Party, a Maidu Indian basket collection, and an altar from a temple originally located in the Chinese section of Grass Valley. Admission is free. It's open in summer daily from 11am to 4pm; from November 1 to May 1 hours are Thursday through Sunday from 11:30am to 4pm. The **National Hotel** (built 1854–56) is here (I always stop in at the Gold Rush–era bar for a spicy Bloody Mary), as is the **Nevada Theatre** (1865), one of the oldest theaters in the nation still operating as such. Today it's home to the Foothill Theatre Company.

If you want to see the source of much of the city's wealth, visit **Malakoff Diggins State Historic Park** 🐾, 23579 N. Bloomfield Rd. (© **530/265-2740**), 28 miles northeast of Nevada City. Once the world's largest hydraulic gold mine, it's an awesome (some might say disturbing) spectacle of hydraulic mining— nearly half a mountain has been washed away by powerful jets of water, leaving behind a 600-foot-deep canyon of exposed rock. In the 1870s, North Bloomfield, then located in the middle of this park, had a population of 1,500. Some of the buildings have been reconstructed and refurnished to show what life was like then. The 3,000-acre park also offers several hiking trails, swimming at Blair Lake, and 30 campsites that can be reserved through **ReserveAmerica** (© **800/ 444-7275;** www.reserveamerica.com). The museum is open daily in summer from 10am to 5pm, in winter on weekends only from 10am to 4pm. To reach the park, take Calif. 49 toward Downieville for 11 miles. Turn right onto Tyler-Foote Crossing Road for 17 miles. The name will change to Curzon Grade and then to Backbone. Turn right onto Derbec Road and into the park. The fee is $2 per car.

Another 6 miles up Calif. 49 from the Malakoff Diggins turnoff will bring you to Pleasant Valley Road, the exit that will take you (in about 7 miles) to one of the most impressive **covered bridges** in the country. Built in 1862, it's 225 feet long and was crossed by many a stagecoach (in autumn, it makes for a spectacular photo opportunity).

Where to Stay

Deer Creek Inn Bed & Breakfast ⚜   An 1860 three-floor Victorian overlooking Deer Creek and within walking distance of downtown Nevada City, this inn feels like a warm home-away-from-home. The individually decorated rooms, most with private verandas facing the creek or town, are furnished with antiques and four-poster or canopy beds with down comforters. Most bathrooms have claw-foot tubs. A full breakfast is served either on the deck or in the formal dining room. Guests are invited to try a little panning, fish, play croquet, or simply relax and enjoy the lawn and landscaped rose gardens along the creek.

116 Nevada St., Nevada City, CA 95959. ✆ 800/655-0363 or 530/265-0363. Fax 530/265-0980. www.deer creekinn.com. 5 units. $110–$185 double. Rates include breakfast. AE, MC, V. **Amenities:** Nearby golf course; bike rental. *In room:* A/C, phone on request.

Emma Nevada House ⚜⚜   One of the finest—and prettiest—B&Bs in the Gold Country, Emma Nevada House is a picture-perfect Victorian that was the childhood home of 19th-century opera star Emma Nevada. You'll like everything about it: the quiet location, sun-drenched decks, wraparound porch, understated decor, and breakfast, which is served in the hexagonal Sun Room. The guest rooms range from small and intimate to large and luxurious; all have private bathrooms and queen-size beds. Top choice for honeymooners is the Empress's Chamber, with its wall of windows, ivory and burgundy tones, and—of course—the Jacuzzi tub for two. You'll also like the fact that the shops and restaurants of Nevada City's Historic District are only a short walk away.

528 E. Broad St., Nevada City, CA 95959. ✆ 800/916-EMMA or 530/265-4416. Fax 530/265-4416. www. emmanevadahouse.com. 6 units. $115–$180 double. Rates include breakfast. AE, MC, V. **Amenities:** Concierge. *In room:* A/C, hair dryer, iron, phone on request.

National Hotel   You can't miss this classic three-story Victorian, the oldest hotel in continuous operation west of the Rocky Mountains, and it shows its age. Some folks feel this makes it more historic and authentic; others may opt for more upscale and restored lodgings. It's near what was once the center of the town's red-light district. The lobby is full of mementos from that era, hence the grandfather clock and early square piano. The suites are replete with Gold Rush–era antiques and large, cozy beds. Most rooms have private bathrooms, and some come with canopy beds and romantic love seats. A definite bonus during typically sweltering summers is the swimming pool filled with cool mountain water.

The hotel's Victorian dining room and bar, which serves traditional items such as prime rib, steaks, lobster tails, and homemade desserts, also has a Gold Rush atmosphere; tables, for example, are lit with coal-oil lamps. The hotel provides live entertainment on Friday and Saturday nights. There's also a popular Sunday brunch, one of the best in the county.

211 Broad St., Nevada City, CA 95959. ✆ 530/265-4551. Fax 530/265-2445. www.thenationalhotel.com. 42 units, 30 with private bathroom. $80–$100 double without bathroom; $100–$120 double with bathroom; $120–$130 suite with bathroom. AE, MC, V. **Amenities:** Restaurant; bar; outdoor pool; business center; room service. *In room:* A/C, TV, dataport.

Nevada City Inn *(Value)*   Surely no Forty-Niner had it this good: his own cabin-like motel room cooled by the shade of a small tree-lined park equipped with barbecues, picnic tables, and a horseshoe pit. Granted, the rooms are small and simple at this restored 1940s motor lodge, but considering that you get all the standard amenities for a really low price, the cash-conscious traveler could hardly ask for more. The inn also rents seven fully furnished cottages with kitchens, popular with families and groups. They're a good deal for such a prime location, about a half mile from Nevada City's historic district.

760 Zion St., Nevada City, CA 95959. ℂ 800/977-8884 or 530/265-2253. www.nevadacityinn.com. Fax 530/265-3310. 27 units. $59–$99 double room; $115–$189 cottage. Rates include continental breakfast. AE, DC, DISC, MC, V. *In room:* A/C, TV, fridge.

Red Castle Inn Historic Lodgings *(★)*   This elegant, comfortable hillside inn occupies a four-story Gothic Revival brick house built in 1860 in a secluded spot with a panoramic view of the town. The house retains its original woodwork, plaster moldings, ceiling medallions, and much of the handmade glass. It lacks modern intrusions like TVs and phones. Guests enjoy five-course buffet breakfasts and relax on the verandas that encircle the first two floors of the house and overlook the rose gardens. My favorite rooms are the Garden Room, with a canopy bed and French doors leading into the gardens, and the three-room garret suite tucked under the eaves, with sleigh beds and Gothic arched windows.

109 Prospect St., Nevada City, CA 95959. ℂ 800/761-4766 or 530/265-5135. www.historic-lodgings.com. 7 units. $110–$165 double. Rates include breakfast. MC, V. *In room:* A/C, no phone.

Where to Dine

Citronée Bistro & Wine Bar *(★★)* REGIONAL AMERICAN/INTERNATIONAL   With few serious restaurants in town for some years, Nevada City has taken a leap forward with two notable temples to fine cuisine—Citronée and New Moon (see below). It took a review by the *New York Times* to get California foodies to turn their appetites from Napa and San Francisco to Citronée. And owner/chef Robert Perez's restaurant is worth exploring. For example, at lunch the barbecued-brisket sandwich topped with white cheddar cheese on chipotle focaccia served with cayenne-dusted waffle potato chips is a must. The evening menu ranges from oven-roasted Maui onion stuffed with sautéed wild mushrooms on a bed of creamy polenta with a thyme lavender honey sauce, to the highly acclaimed rare seared ahi tuna with a crust of black and white sesame seeds served with a soy chile vinaigrette and wasabi crème fraîche. And if that isn't enough, ask for the menu *gastronomique*, a five-course surprise menu specially chosen each night.

320 Broad St. ℂ 530/265-5697. Reservations recommended. Main courses $13–$25. AE, MC, V. Mon–Thurs 5:30–9:30 or 10:30pm; Fri–Sat 5–10pm.

Country Rose Café *(★)* COUNTRY FRENCH   The flowery country-French atmosphere of this popular Nevada City restaurant belies a serious (and seriously priced) menu put together by owner and chef Michael Johns. Dinner selections, written on a huge board that's lugged over to your table after you've been seated, are mostly French with a dash of Italian, Mexican, and American dishes. Skip the typical pastas and head straight for John's specialty—fresh fish prepared in a myriad of classic styles such as filet of sole doré, swordfish Oskar, and sea bass with garlic-basil sauce. Other regular menu items include filet mignon, lobster, rack of lamb, and roast game hen, all served with soup or salad. Both lunch and dinner are served on the pretty walled-in patio in the summer, so be sure to request alfresco seating when making a reservation.

300 Commercial St. ⓒ 530/265-6252. Reservations recommended. Main courses $14–$31. AE, DC, MC, V. Daily 11am–2:30pm; Sun–Thurs 5–9pm; Fri–Sat 5–10pm; Sun brunch 11am–2:30pm.

New Moon Café ⭐⭐ AMERICAN/INTERNATIONAL Nevada City's favorite chef, Peter Selaya, offers a menu of imaginatively prepared items that feature free-range and antibiotic-free meats and poultry, house-baked breads, house-made pastas using organic flours and grains, and local organic vegetables when available—which is regularly in this hotbed of natural foodstuffs. So not only is the food healthy, it tastes great. Dinner entrees include the likes of a Niman Ranch top sirloin cap grilled with a roast garlic zinfandel and rosemary sauce, or fresh line-caught wild salmon pan-seared with julienne vegetables and a beurre blanc verjus. The raviolis are made fresh daily, as are the desserts. The fresh strawberry Napoleons we had were beyond delicious. Nevada City's balmy climate makes the front deck a great place to dine and people-watch.

203 York St. ⓒ 530/265-6399. Reservations recommended. Main courses $15–$21. DC, MC, V. Tues–Fri 11:30am–2pm; Tues–Sun 5–8pm (or later).

GRASS VALLEY ⭐

In contrast to Nevada City's "tourist town" image, Grass Valley is the commercial and retail center of the region. The **Empire Mine State Historic Park** ⭐, 10791 E. Empire St., Grass Valley (ⓒ 530/273-8522), the largest and richest gold mine in California, is just outside of town. This mine, which once had 367 miles of shafts, produced an estimated 5.8 million ounces of gold between 1850 and 1956. You can look down the shaft of the mine, walk around the mine yard, and stroll through the owner's gardens. From March to November, tours are given daily, and a mining movie is shown. You can also enjoy picnicking, cycling, mountain biking, or hiking in the 784-acre park. It's open year-round except for Thanksgiving, Christmas, and New Year's Day. Admission to the park, tour, and museum costs $1 for adults and children, and dogs are free.

In town, visitors can pick up a walking-tour map at the **Chamber of Commerce,** 248 Mill St. (ⓒ 530/273-4667; www. grassvalleychamber.com), and explore the historic downtown area along Mill and Main streets. There are also a few museums that California-history and gold-mining buffs will want to visit: the **Grass Valley Museum,** 410 S. Church St., adjacent to St. Joseph's Cultural Center (ⓒ 530/273-5509); the **North Star Mining Museum,** at the south end of Mill Street at Allison Ranch Road (ⓒ 530/273-4255; open May–Oct); and the **Video History Museum,** in the center of Memorial Park off Calif. 174 (ⓒ 530/274-1126; open May–Oct), which houses a collection of old films of the region from the 1920s.

Grass Valley was, for a time, the home of **Lola Montez,** singer, dancer, and paramour of the rich and famous. A fully restored home that she bought and occupied in 1853 can be viewed at 248 Mill St., now the site of Grass Valley's chamber of commerce. **Lotta Crabtree,** Montez's famous protégé, lived down the street at 238 Mill St., now an apartment house. Also pop into the **Holbrooke Hotel,** 212 Main St., to see the signature of Mark Twain, who stayed here, as did five U.S. presidents. The saloon has been in continuous use since 1852, and it's the place to meet the locals and have a tall cold one.

The surrounding region offers many recreational opportunities on its rivers and lakes and in the Tahoe National Forest. You can enjoy fishing, swimming, and boating at **Scotts Flat Lake** near Nevada City (east on Calif. 20) and at **Rollins Lake** on Calif. 174, between Grass Valley and Colfax. White-water rafting is available on several rivers. **Tributary Whitewater Tours,** 20480 Woodbury

Dr., Grass Valley, CA 95949 (© **800/672-3846** or 530/346-6812; www.white watertours.com), offers half- to 3-day trips March through October. The region is also ideal for mountain biking. The chambers of commerce publish a trail guide, but there's nowhere to rent a bike in Nevada City or Grass Valley, so bring your own wheels. For regional hiking information, contact **Tahoe National Forest Headquarters,** at Coyote Street and Calif. 49 in Nevada City (© **530/265-4531;** www.r5.fs.fed.us/tahoe).

Where to Stay

Holbrooke Hotel 🖈 This Victorian-era white-clapboard building was a saloon during the Gold Rush days, and then evolved into a place for miners to "rack out." The oldest and most historic hotel in town, it's hosted a number of legendary figures: Mark Twain and presidents Ulysses Grant, Benjamin Harrison, and Grover Cleveland, among others. Seventeen of the rooms lie within the main building. The remainder are in an adjacent annex, a house occupied long ago by the hotel's owner. Each guest room is decorated with an eclectic collection of Gold Rush–era furniture and antiques. All have cable TVs tucked away in armoires, and most bathrooms have claw-foot tubs. If you can, reserve one of the larger Veranda rooms that face Main Street and have access to the balconies; it's well worth the few extra dollars. A continental breakfast is served in the library.

212 W. Main St., Grass Valley, CA 95945. © **800/933-7077** or 530/273-1353. Fax 530/273-0434. www. holbrooke.com. 28 units. $58–$115 double; $100–$155 suite. Rates include breakfast. AE, DC, DISC, MC, V. **Amenities:** Restaurant; saloon; business center; salon. *In room:* A/C, TV.

Holiday Lodge *Value* Anyone who loves to lounge poolside with a good book will appreciate the Holiday Lodge. Located just outside downtown Grass Valley, the motel is a short drive away from the historic Old Town of Nevada City and Grass Valley, and across the street from a 9-hole golf course. The rooms are your typical ordinary motel style, with queen beds. The real bonus, however, is the central sauna (open 24 hr.) and swimming pool, the perfect place to rest your tired, sweaty bones after a hard day's shopping.

1221 E. Main St., Grass Valley, CA 95945. © **800/742-7125** or 530/273-4406. www.holidaylodge.biz. 36 units. $60–$80 double. Rates include continental breakfast. AE, DC, DISC, MC, V. **Amenities:** Outdoor heated pool; sauna; coin-op laundry. *In room:* A/C, TV, dataport, fridge, coffeemaker.

Where to Dine

Tofanelli's *Value* INTERNATIONAL If a diet of meat and potatoes isn't your cup of tea, head to Tofanelli's, which specializes in good—and good for you— entrees for brunch, lunch, and dinner. You'll like the setting—a bright, cheery trio of dining areas (atrium, outdoor patio, and dining room) separated by exposed brick walls and decorated with beautiful prints and paintings. Specials on the menu, such as Gorgonzola ravioli topped with garlic cream sauce, or pad Thai noodles with fresh ginger and marinated beef, change weekly, but you can always rely on Tofanelli's classics like Linda's famous vegetarian lasagna and the popular veggie burger. And yes, they serve good ol' New York steak, too. Don't you dare depart without a slice of Katherine's chocolate cake.

302 W. Main St. (across from the Holbrooke Hotel). © **530/272-1468.** Main courses $7–$15. AE, MC, V. Mon–Fri 7am–8:30pm; Sat brunch 8:30am–3pm, dinner 5–9pm; Sun brunch 8:30am–3pm, dinner 5–8:30pm.

212 Bistro at the Holbrooke AMERICAN This elegant hotel dining room is the most formal place in town—an ironic twist, given its past life as a Gold Rush saloon and a flophouse for drunken miners. In its way, it's the most authentic and nostalgic restaurant in a town filled with worthy competitors.

Items on the ever-changing menu range from mesquite-smoked prime rib, Cajun-rubbed New York steak, and seared salmon filet encrusted with a cashew-coconut herb and lime-hibiscus sauce. For lunch try the tri-tip sandwich, Holbrooke hamburger, or the Chinese chicken salad.

212 W. Main St. (in the Holbrooke Hotel). © 530/273-1353. www.holbrooke.com. Reservations recommended Fri–Sat nights. Main courses $15–$25. AE, DC, DISC, MC, V. Mon–Sat 11:30am–2pm and 5:30–9pm; Sun 10am–2pm and 5–8:30pm.

THE CENTRAL GOLD COUNTRY: AMADOR CITY, SUTTER CREEK & JACKSON

Though Placerville is technically the center of the Gold Country, it's the small trio of towns a few miles to the south—Amador City, Sutter Creek, and Jackson—that are far and away the most appealing destination in this region of rolling hills, dotted with solitary oaks and granite outcroppings. When the mining boom went bust, most of the towns were abandoned; nowadays, most of these restored Gold Rush towns rely solely on tourism (hence the conversion of many Victorian homes into B&Bs), though a few mines have reopened recently.

One of the advantages of staying in this area, 55 miles southeast of Sacramento, is that both the northern and southern regions of the Gold Country are only a few hours' drive away (via very winding roads, however). If you're intent on seeing as much of the Gold Country as possible in a few days' time, any one of these three towns will suffice as a good home base.

To reach Amador City, Sutter Creek, or Jackson from Placerville, head south along Calif. 49 past Plymouth and Drytown. If you're coming straight here from Sacramento, take U.S. 50 to Placerville and head south on Calif. 49; Calif. 16 from Sacramento is another option, but only slightly faster. For more information about any of these towns, contact the **Amador County Chamber of**

(*Fun Fact*   **Poor But Proud**

Three miles south of Placerville is the funky little town of El Dorado, whose claim to fame is gold of another kind—Galliano liqueur. Legend has it that, long ago, one of the town's locals became the proud owner of a gold-colored Cadillac. To celebrate his purchase, he went to the town saloon, Poor Red's, and asked the bartender to whip him up a commemorative drink, preferably something to match the color of his Caddy. Grabbing the only golden-hued elixir he could find, the bartender mixed a little of this with a jigger of that and presto! The Golden Cadillac cocktail was born. Word got around quickly about how great the drink was, and soon people from all over the *world* were lining up for a glass of Poor Red's finest.

What? You don't believe me? Right then, go see for yourself. At the end of the bar in a glass showcase is a plaque—sent directly from the Galliano company in Italy—that honors Poor Red's as the largest user of Galliano liqueur in North America. And while you're there, try their barbecued chicken, ham, steak, and pork ribs—all of which are served big and priced small. **Poor Red's,** 6221 Pleasant Valley Rd., in El Dorado (© 530/622-2901), is open for lunch Monday through Friday and daily for dinner.

Commerce, 125 Peek St., Jackson (© **209/223-0350;** www.amadorcounty chamber.com).

AMADOR CITY ☆

Once a bustling mining town, Amador City is now devoted mostly to dredging up tourist dollars. Although Amador City sounds impressive, it is so tiny that it is the smallest incorporated city in California. Local merchants have made the most of a refurbished block-long boardwalk, converting the historic false-fronted buildings into a gallery of sorts; the stores sell everything from early 1900s antiques and folk art to handcrafted furniture, Gold Rush memorabilia, rare books, and Native American crafts. Parking can be difficult, however, especially in summer.

Where to Stay & Dine

Imperial Hotel ☆☆   located at the foot of Main Street overlooking Amador City, this stately 1879 brick hotel and restaurant has been beautifully restored and successfully manages to be both elegant and whimsical. For example, the centerpiece of the Oasis Bar is a fresco of a Saharan oasis complete with palm trees, belly dancers, and camels. The individually decorated rooms, all with private bathrooms, are furnished with brass, iron, or pine beds and numerous antiques; two come with private balconies. Room no. 6 is the quietest, but room no. 1—with its high ceiling, hand-painted queen-size canopy bed, Art Deco appointments, and French doors that open onto a private balcony overlooking Main Street—is the most requested. Breakfast is served downstairs, in your room, or on the patio or balcony. The Imperial Hotel restaurant, serving Mediterranean/California cuisine—smoked pork chop with fig-and-onion confit, pan-broiled rib-eye with a Provençal herb crust, lemon-baked sea bass wrapped in parchment—has a sterling reputation, and hotel guests can take advantage of room service when it's open from 5 to 9pm. The restaurant is worth a detour, even if you aren't staying here.

Main St. (Calif. 49), P.O. Box 195, Amador City, CA 95601-0195. © 209/267-9172. Fax 209/267-9249. www. imperialamador.com. 6 units. $85–$115 double. Rates include breakfast. AE, DISC, MC, V. **Amenities:** Restaurant; bar; room service; in-room massage. *In room:* A/C, hair dryer, no phone.

SUTTER CREEK ☆

The self-proclaimed "nicest little town in the Mother Lode," Sutter Creek was named after sawmill owner John Sutter, employer of James Marshall (whose discovery of gold triggered the 1849 Gold Rush). Railroad baron Leland Stanford made his fortune at Sutter Creek's Lincoln Mine, and then invested his millions to both build the transcontinental railroad and to fund his successful campaign to become governor of California.

The town is a charmer, lined with beautiful 19th-century buildings in pristine condition, including **Downs Mansion,** the former home of the foreman at Stanford's mine (now a private residence on Spanish St., across from the Immaculate Conception Church), and the landmark **Knight's Foundry,** 81 Eureka St., off Main Street, the last water-powered foundry and machine shop in the nation. There are also numerous shops and galleries along Main Street, though finding a free parking space can be a real challenge on summer weekends.

Where to Stay

The Foxes ☆☆   This 1857 clapboard house is Sutter Creek's most elegant hostelry. The seven rooms are all unique, each with a queen-size bed and down comforters. Five rooms, including the Garden Room and the Fox Den, have

---

Tips **A Modern Gold Mine Tour**

One of the most entertaining and educational attractions in the Gold Country is the **Sutter Gold Mine Tours'** hour-long excursion into the bowels of a modern hard-rock gold mine. With an emphasis on authenticity, the tour starts with a ride on a mining shuttle to the mine, where you'll have to "tag in" and go through the safety training room, just as if you were one of the miners. Wearing your hardhat, you'll proceed deep into the mine, learning about geology and the history of mining while marveling at the gemstones and gold deposits embedded in the quartz of the Comet Vein (you'll even learn to spot the difference between real gold and "fool's gold").

After the tour, be sure to buy a bag of mining ore—about $5 per bag—head over to the wood sluice, grab one of the gold pans or sluice boxes, and pan for real gold. Each bag is guaranteed to hold either gold or gemstones (emeralds, amethysts, topaz, and many other birthstones), and there's always an assistant on hand to show you how it's done. The kids get a real kick out of this. Other diversions include the Company Store gift shop filled with a huge assortment of inexpensive semiprecious gems and minerals, and a small movie theater that offers a 1-hour documentary about the Gold Rush and a half-hour movie about modern gold mining (a heavy-machinery flick that kids will love). And if you're truly a gold-mine enthusiast, there's also a 3- to 4-hour "Deep Mine Experience" that really goes deep into the mine, but it's by reservation only.

The **Sutter Gold Mine** (© **866/762-2837** or 209/736-2708; www.suttergold.com) is open daily year-round from 9am to 5pm in the summer and 10am to 4pm October through May. The 1-hour Family Tour is $15 for adults and children ages 14 and older, $13 for AAA members and seniors 55 and older, and $10 for kids 4 to 13; kids under 4 are not allowed on the tour. The Family Tours take place on the hour and reservations are not necessary. The mine is located at 13660 Hwy. 49, about half a mile south of Amador City, just north of Sutter Creek.

---

gas-burning fireplaces. The Fox Den also has a little library of its own, while the Anniversary room features a 9-foot-tall Renaissance Revival bed and a separate sitting room. All have private bathrooms. Breakfast, cooked to order and delivered on silver service along with the morning paper, can be served in your room or in the gazebo in the flower-filled garden. Located on Main Street, the inn is only steps away from Sutter Creek's shops and restaurants.

77 Main St. (P.O. Box 159), Sutter Creek, CA 95685. © **800/987-3344** or 209/267-5882. Fax 209/267-0712. www.foxesinn.com. 7 units. $140–$215 double. Rates include breakfast. AE, DISC, MC, V. *In room:* A/C, TV/VCR, fridge, hair dryer, no phone.

Grey Gables Inn 🐾   The Grey Gables Inn is a postcard-perfect replica of a Victorian manor. The two-story B&B is surrounded by terraces of gardens and embellished with fountains and vine-covered arbors. Each of the plushly carpeted guest rooms is named after a British poet; the Byron Room features hues of deep green and burgundy, dark-wood furnishings, and a Renaissance Revival bed. All rooms have queen or king beds, gas-log fireplaces, armoires, and private bathrooms (a few with claw-foot tubs). Breakfast, delivered on English bone china, is served in the formal dining room adjacent to the Victorian parlor or in your room. The only flaw is the bit-too-close proximity to heavily traveled Calif. 49, but once inside, you'll hardly notice. The shops and restaurants of Sutter Creek are within walking distance.

Fun Fact Coloma: Where the Gold Rush Began

On Calif. 49 between Auburn and Placerville, the town of **Coloma** 🌟 is so small and unpretentious it's hard to imagine the significant role it played in the rapid development of California and the West. It was here that James Marshall first discovered that there was gold aplenty in the foothills of California. Over the next 50 years, 125 *million* ounces of gold were taken from the Sierra foothills, an amount worth a staggering $50 billion today.

Although Marshall and Sutter tried to keep the discovery secret, word soon leaked out. Sam Brannan, who ran a general store at Fort Sutter, secured some gold samples himself—as well as significant amounts of choice Coloma real estate—and then headed for San Francisco, where he ran through the streets shouting, "Gold! Gold! Gold! From the American River!" San Francisco rapidly emptied as men rushed off to seek their fortunes at the mines (and make Sam Brannan's as well).

Coloma was quickly mined out, but its boom brought 10,000 people to the settlement and lasted long enough for residents to build a schoolhouse, a gunsmith, a general store, and a tin-roofed post office. The miners also planted oak and mimosa trees that shade the street during hot summers. About 70% of this quiet, pretty town lies in the **Marshall Gold Discovery State Historic Park** (📞 530/622-3470; www.coloma.com/gold), which preserves the spot where James Wilson Marshall discovered gold along the banks of the south fork of the American River.

Farther up Main Street is a replica of the mill Marshall was building when he made his discovery. The largest building in town, the mill is powered by electricity during the summer. Other attractions include the **Gold Discovery Museum,** which relates the story of the Gold Rush, and a number of Chinese stores, all that remain of the once-sizable local Chinese community. The park also has three picnic areas, four trails, recreational gold panning, and a number of buildings and exhibits relating the way of life that prevailed here in the 19th century. Admission is $5 per vehicle; hours are daily from 10am to 5pm, except on major holidays.

Folks also come here for white-water thrills on the American River. (Coloma is a popular launching point.) **White Water Connection,** in Coloma (📞 530/622-6446; www.whitewaterconnection.com), offers half- to 2-day trips down the frothy forks of the American River. It's great fun and one of the Gold Country's best outdoor attractions.

161 Hanford St., Sutter Creek, CA 95685. ⓒ 800/473-9422 or 209/267-1039. Fax 209/267-0998. www.grey gables.com. 8 units. $110–$200 double. AE, DC, DISC, MC, V. *In room:* A/C, hair dryer, no phone.

Where to Dine

Zinfandels 👌👌 CALIFORNIA   Greg West's Zinfandels has received kudos since it first opened in 1996. Greg, a 6-year veteran of Greens (San Francisco's most famous vegetarian restaurant), makes and bakes just about everything in-house, including the breads and pastries. Though the emphasis is on low-fat vegetarian fare such as butternut-squash risotto with pancetta, leeks, crimini mushrooms, and spinach, West also offers a trio of fresh fish, chicken, and beef dishes ranging from cannelloni filled with lamb sausage, chard, and smoked mozzarella to Petrale sole with a citrus-ginger beurre blanc. The menu changes monthly to take advantage of seasonal produce from local farms, and even the wines—paired with each dish—are provided by local wineries such as Sobon and Karly. An appealing alternative to a full sit-down dinner is the wine bar/appetizer/dessert room downstairs.

51 Hanford St. ⓒ 209/267-5008. www.zinfood.com. Reservations recommended. Main courses $17–$25. AE, DISC, MC, V. Thurs–Sun 5:30–9:30pm.

JACKSON 👌

Jackson, the county seat of Amador County, is far livelier than its neighboring towns to the north. (It was the last place in California to outlaw prostitution.) Be sure to stroll through the center of town, browsing in the stores and admiring the Victorian architecture. Although the Kennedy and Argonaut mines ultimately produced more than $140 million in gold, Jackson initially earned its place in the Gold Rush as a supply center. That history is apparent in the town's wide Main Street, lined by tall buildings adorned with intricate iron railings.

Make no mistake: This is not a ghost town, but rather a modern minicity that has worked to preserve its pre-Victorian influence. At the southern end of the street is the **National Hotel,** 2 Water St., at Main Street (ⓒ 209/223-0500; www.national-hotel.com), one of California's oldest continuously operating hotels since 1862. Will Rogers, John Wayne, Leland Stanford, and many other celebrities and big-time politicos once stayed here. Today the hotel's **Louisiana House Bar**—a cool, dark establishment where weary travelers can rest while a honky-tonk pianist beats out ragtime tunes and classic oldies—does a brisk business (alas, the guest rooms aren't nearly as enjoyable).

The **Amador County Museum,** a huge brick building at 225 Church St. (ⓒ 209/223-6386), is where Will Rogers filmed *Boys Will Be Boys* in 1920. Today the former home of Armistead Calvin Brown and his 11 children is filled with mining memorabilia and information on two local mines, the Kennedy and the Argonaut, that were among the deepest and richest in the nation. Within the museum is a working large-scale model of the Kennedy. The museum is open Wednesday through Sunday from 10am to 4pm; admission is by a contribution of any amount. Tours of the museum cost $2 and are offered Saturday and Sunday on the hour from 11am to 3pm.

If you would rather see the real thing, head to the **Kennedy Tailing Wheels Park,** site of the Kennedy and Argonaut mines, the deepest in the Mother Lode. The mines have been closed for years, but the tailing wheels and head frames, used to convey debris over the hills to a settling pond, remain. To reach the park, take Main Street to Jackson Gate Road, just north of Jackson (no phone).

A few miles south of Jackson on Calif. 49 is one of the most evocative towns of the region: **Mokelumne Hill** 👌. The town consists of one street overlooking a valley with a few old buildings, and somehow its sad, abandoned air has the mark of authenticity. At one time, the hill was dotted with tents and wood-and-tar paper shacks, and the town housed a population of 15,000, including an old French quarter and a Chinatown. But now many of its former residents are memorialized in the town's Protestant, Jewish, and Catholic cemeteries.

Where to Stay & Dine

Court Street Inn ☆ Two blocks from Main Street, this Victorian beauty—listed on the National Register of Historic Places—was built around 1870 and is brimming with elegant details such as eyelash shutters, embossed ceilings, and a marble fireplace. My favorite room is Burgundy Court, with its oak-mantled fireplace and four-poster king-size bed. Romantics will like the Bordeaux Court's sitting room and sleigh bed, or the separate and secluded Chablis Court with its own terrace, skylight, and corner fireplace. The guest rooms are nicely decorated; all have down bedding and gas or electric fireplaces, and some have whirlpool or claw-foot tubs. The separate two-story/two-bedroom Indian House cottage can accommodate up to four guests. There's a porch where guests can relax outside, and an outdoor Jacuzzi that's ideal for stargazing. A full homemade breakfast (served outside on the terrace on sunny days) and complimentary evening refreshments are included in the room rate.

215 Court St., Jackson, CA 95642. © 800/200-0416 or 209/223-0416. Fax 209/223-5429. www.courtstreet inn.com. 6 units, 1 cottage. $115–$155 double; $175–$225 cottage. Rates include breakfast. AE, DISC, MC, V. **Amenities:** Jacuzzi. *In room:* A/C, TV on request, iron, no phone.

Mel and Faye's Diner ⓥ*alue* AMERICAN How can anybody not love a classic old roadside diner? In business since 1956, Mel and Faye have been cranking out the best diner food in the Gold Country for so long that it's okay not to feel guilty for salivating over the thought of a sloppy double Moo Burger smothered with onions and special sauce and washed down with a chocolate shake. And could you please add a large side of fries with that? And how much is a slice of pie? It's a time-honored Jackson tradition, so forget about your diet.

205 Calif. 49 (at Main St.). © 209/223-0853. Menu items $4–$8. DISC, MC, V. Daily 4:45am–10pm.

Upstairs Restaurant & Streetside Bistro ☆ INTERNATIONAL This adorable little restaurant offers a limited menu that changes weekly, but you might stumble on some true culinary gems, such as pasta puttanesca with tomato-basil fettuccine and fresh Roma tomatoes, or julienned duck served with a blackberry-ginger sauce. Layne McCollum, a graduate of California's Culinary Academy, is known as the town's finest and most sophisticated chef, with a reputation for imaginative, innovative cuisine. Crisp white linens, bowls of fresh flowers, and background music provide a romantic backdrop to the restaurant's 12 candlelit tables. Lunch—quiche, soups, salads, and gourmet sandwiches such as smoked pork loin with red-chile pesto on chipotle—is served until about 2:30pm in the bright, cheery Streetside Bistro, which is tastefully outfitted with wrought-iron furniture, tile flooring, and colorful oil paintings.

164 Main St. © 209/223-3342. Reservations recommended. Main courses $16–$30. AE, DISC, MC, V. Wed–Fri 11:30am–2:30pm; Sat–Sun 11:30am–3:30pm; Wed–Sun 5:30–9pm.

THE SOUTHERN GOLD COUNTRY: ANGELS CAMP, MURPHYS, COLUMBIA, SONORA & JAMESTOWN

No other region in the Gold Country offers more to see and do than these towns in the south, 86 miles southeast of Sacramento. From exploring caverns to riding in the stagecoach and panning for gold, the neighboring towns of Angels Camp,

Finds   A Visit to Volcano

About a dozen miles east of Jackson on Calif. 88 is the enchantingly decrepit town of **Volcano** 🔍, one of the most authentic ghost towns in the central Sierra. The town got its name in 1848, after miners mistook the origins of the craggy boulders that lie in the center of town. The dark rock and the blind window frames of a few backless, ivy-covered buildings give the town's main thoroughfare a haunted look. Sprinkled between boarded-up buildings, about 100 residents do business in the same sagging storefronts that a population of 8,000 frequented nearly 150 years ago.

The tiny, now-quiet burg has a rich history: Not only was this boomtown once home to 17 hotels, courts of quick justice, and the state's first lending library and astronomical observatory, but Volcano gold also supported the Union during the Civil War. Residents smuggled a huge cannon to the front lines in a hearse (it was never used). The story goes that had the enthusiastic blues actually fired it, it was so overcharged that "Old Abe" would have exploded. The cannon sits in the town center today, under a rusting weather vane.

Looming over the small buildings is the stately **St. George Hotel** 🔍 (© 209/296-4458; www.stgeorgehotel.com), a three-story, balconied building that testifies to the $90 million in gold mined in and around the town. Its ivy-covered brick and shuttered windows will remind you of colonial New England. In 1998 new owners took over the run-down 20-room hotel and have totally turned it around. The restaurant serves brunch on Sunday, and dinner Thursday through Sunday. Even if you're not hungry, stop in for a libation at the classic old bar, the Whiskey Flat Saloon.

In summer the **Volcano Theatre Company** performs at the town's outdoor amphitheater, hidden behind stone facades on Main Street, a block north of the St. George Hotel. It's a wonderful Gold Country experience. For information on performances, call © 209/296-2525 or visit www.volcanotheatre.org. And in early spring, people come from all around to picnic amid the nearly half-million daffodils in bloom on **Daffodil Hill,** a 4-acre ranch 3 miles north of Volcano (follow the sign on Ram's Horn Grade).

Murphys, Columbia, Sonora, and Jamestown offer a cornucopia of Gold Rush–related sites, museums, and activities. It's a great place to bring the family (kids love roaming around the dusty car-free streets of Columbia), and the region offers some of the best lodgings and restaurants in the Gold Country. In short, if you're the Type A sort who needs to stay active, the southern Gold Country is for you. For information about lodging, dining, events, and the arts and entertainment in the area, contact the **Tuolumne County Visitors Bureau,** P.O. Box 4020, Sonora, California 95370; (© **800/446-1333** or 209/533-4420; www.the greatunfenced.com).

To reach any of these towns from Sacramento, head south on Calif. 99 to Stockton, then take Calif. 4 east into Angels Camp. (From here, it's a short, scenic drive to the other towns.) For a longer but more scenic route, take U.S. 50 east to Placerville and head south on Calif. 49, which takes you to Angels Camp.

ANGELS CAMP &

You've probably heard of Angels Camp, the town that inspired Mark Twain to pen "The Celebrated Jumping Frog of Calaveras County." This pretty, peaceful community is built on hills honeycombed with tunnels. In the 1880s and 1890s, five mines were located along Main Street—Sultana, Angel's, Lightner, Utica, and Stickle—and the town echoed with noise as more than 200 stamps crushed the ore. Between 1886 and 1910, the mines generated close to $20 million.

But a far-more lasting legacy than the town's gold production is the **Jumping Frog Jubilee,** started in 1928 to mark the paving of the town's streets. The rib-biting competition takes place every third weekend in May. The record, 21 feet 5¾ inches, was set in 1986 by "Rosie the Ribbiter," beating the old record by 4½ inches. Livestock exhibitions, pageants, cook-offs, arm-wrestling tournaments, live music, carnival rides, a rodeo, and plenty of beer and wine keep the thousands of spectators entertained between jump-offs. (You can even rent a frog if you forgot to pack one.) For more information and entry forms (around $5 per frog), call the Jumping Frog Jubilee headquarters at © 209/736-2561 or log on to their website at www.frogtown.org.

Where to Stay

Cooper House Bed & Breakfast Inn & Once the home and office of a prominent physician, Dr. George P. Cooper, the Cooper House is now Angels Camp's only B&B. This small Arts and Crafts home is positioned well away from the hustle and bustle of the town's Main Street. Owner and innkeeper Kathy Reese maintains three units, all with private bathrooms. The Zinfandel Suite has its own private entrance and deck, and the Chardonnay Suite has a king-size bed, antique claw-foot bathtub, and a private deck. The third bedroom, the Cabernet Suite, is midsize, with a queen bed, adjoining sunroom, and pretty garden view.

1184 Church St. (P.O. Box 1388), Angels Camp, CA 95222. © 800/225-3764, ext. 326, or 209/736-2145. 3 units. $125 double. Rate includes breakfast. MC, V. *In room:* A/C.

Where to Dine

Camps && *Kids* CALIFORNIAN Located on the edge of a golf resort on the western fringes of Angels Camp is Camps, the culinary feather in the cap of Greenhorn Creek golf resort. The restaurant's architects have integrated the building into its natural surroundings by constructing the outer walls with locally mined rhyolite and painting it in natural earth tones. The interior is fur-nished with leather armchairs, wicker, and antique woods. The best seats in the house are on the veranda overlooking the golf course, particularly on warm sum-mer nights. Though the menu changes seasonally, a typical dinner may start with house salad with field greens, toasted pistachios, julienned red onions, and a raspberry vinaigrette, followed by macadamia-crusted halibut with a mandarin orange beurre blanc or crisp roasted duck with kumquat and sun-dried toma-toes. The lengthy wine list has been given *Wine Spectator*'s Award of Excellence for 4 years running. The restaurant also offers kids' meals for about $5.

676 McCauley Ranch Rd. (½ mile west of Calif. 4/Calif. 49 junction off Angel Oaks Dr.). © 209/736-8181. www.greenhorncreek.com. Reservations recommended. Main courses $15–$24. AE, MC, V. Wed–Sun 5:30–9pm; Sat–Sun brunch 10am–2pm.

Crusco's Ristorante & ITALIAN The sign at the entrance says it all: RELAX AND ENJOY. THIS IS NOT FAST FOOD. The point being that the overall experience is as important as the cuisine at Crusco's, a family-run restaurant headed by Celeste Lusher, the amiable chef/owner who oversees the kitchen along with her daughter Sarah, while her husband and son-in-law cater to their customers. In the heart of old-town Angels Camp, the restaurant's decor is an attractive balance of 19th-century Gold Rush architecture—wood beams, 1½-foot-thick stone walls, dark-wood furnishings—and old-world Mediterranean *objets d'art* such as faux columns and bas-relief sculptures. It's an apropos setting for Lusher's classic Italian menu, made from scratch using generations of family recipes. Each meal begins with house-made focaccia served with olive oil and balsamic vinegar; then come the tough choices: grilled tenderloin of lamb with rosemary and garlic, the creamy polenta, or the popular penne rigate. For lunch, Celeste recommends the New York steak sandwich on focaccia. Sampling a few of the house-made desserts is highly advised as well.

1240 S. Main St. ⓒ **209/736-1440.** www.goldrush.com/~ciao. Reservations recommended. Main courses $14–$20. DISC, MC, V. Thurs–Mon 11:30am–3pm and 5–9pm (possibly closed in spring—call ahead).

MURPHYS ⚜

From Angels Camp, a 20-minute drive east along Calif. 4 takes you to Murphys, one of my favorite Gold Country towns. Legend has it Murphys started as a former trading post set up by brothers Dan and John Murphy in cooperation with local Indians (John married the chief's daughter). These days, its peaceful community is made up of gingerbread Victorians shaded by tall locust trees bordering narrow streets. Be sure to take a stroll down Main Street, stopping in **Grounds** (p. 346) for a bite to eat and perhaps a cool draft of Murphys Red—direct from **Murphys Brewing Company**—at the rustic saloon within Murphys Historic Hotel and Lodge at 457 Main St.

While you're here, you might also want to check out **Ironstone Vineyards,** 1894 Six Mile Rd., 1 mile south of downtown Murphys (ⓒ **209/728-1251;** www.ironstonevineyards.com), a veritable wine theme park built by the Kautz family. It boasts an enormous tasting room, jewelry shop, museum housing the largest crystalline gold piece in existence, gallery, theater, music room, caverns, park and gardens, and even a culinary center. It's open daily from 10am to 6pm.

Also in the vicinity—just off Calif. 4, 1 mile north of Murphys off Sheep Ranch Road—are the **Mercer Caverns** (ⓒ **209/728-2101;** www.mercercaverns. com). These caverns, discovered in 1885 by Walter Mercer, contain a variety of geological formations—stalactites and stalagmites—in a series of chambers. Tours of the well-lit caverns take nearly an hour. From Memorial Day to September, hours are Sunday through Thursday from 9am to 6pm, Friday and Saturday from 9am to 8pm; from October to late May, Sunday through Thursday from 10am to 4:30pm, Friday and Saturday from 10am to 6pm. Admission is $9 for adults, $5 for children ages 5 to 12, and free for children under 5.

Fifteen miles east of Murphys up Calif. 4 is **Calaveras Big Trees State Park** ⚜ (ⓒ **209/795-2334;** www.bigtrees.org), where you can see giant sequoias that are among the biggest and oldest living things on earth. It's a popular summer retreat that offers camping, swimming, hiking, and fishing along the Stanislaus River. It's open daily; admission is $2 per car for day use.

Where to Stay

Dunbar House, 1880 ⚜⚜   This Italianate home, built in 1880 for the bride of a local businessman, is one of the finest B&Bs in the Gold Country. The front porch, which overlooks the exquisite gardens, is decorated with wicker furniture and hanging baskets of ivy. Inside, the emphasis is on comfort and elegance. The guest rooms are furnished with quality antiques and equipped with every possible amenity. Beds have lace-trimmed linens and down comforters, and each room has a wood-burning stove and fridge stocked with mineral water and a complimentary bottle of wine. My favorite room, the Cedar, is a fabulous two-room suite with a private sun porch, whirlpool tub, and complimentary champagne. I also like the Sugar Pine suite, with its private balcony in the trees. Lemonade and cookies are offered in the afternoon, appetizers and wine in the early evening. Breakfast is served in your room, the dining room, or the garden.

271 Jones St., Murphys, CA 95247. ℂ 800/692-6006 or 209/728-2897. Fax 209/728-1451. www.dunbar house.com. 5 units. $175–$225 double. Rates include breakfast and afternoon appetizers. AE, MC, V. *In room:* A/C, TV/VCR, hair dryer, iron.

Where to Dine

Firewood ⭐ *Value* AMERICAN   Local restaurateur River Klass opened this order-at-the-counter cafe just down the street from his Grounds restaurant (see below). The open-air establishment specializes in fast, inexpensive, and darn good dishes such as Baja-style fish tacos, drippingly juicy "not healthy" burgers, baby back ribs with house-made barbecue sauce, and superb gourmet pizzas baked in a wood-burning oven (the prosciutto and arugula, shrimp and feta, and sausage and pepperoni versions are all big hits). Good micro-beer and local wine selections are available as well.

420 Main St. ℂ 209/728-3248. Reservations not accepted. Main courses $5–$10. MC, V. Wed–Fri 11am–8pm; Sat–Sun 11am–9pm.

Grounds ⭐⭐ ECLECTIC   When River Klass moved here from the East Coast to open his own place, Murphys's restaurant-challenged residents heaved a sigh of relief. Its nickname is the "Rude Boy Cafe," after Klass's acerbic wit, but you'll find happy smiles and friendly service. The majority of Grounds's business is with the locals, who have become addicted to the potato pancakes that come with every made-to-order omelet. For lunch, try the sausage sandwich on house-baked bread or the grilled eggplant sandwich stuffed with smoked mozzarella and fresh basil. Although the menus change twice a week, typical dinner choices include fettuccine topped with sautéed shrimp, halibut, and mussels in a garlic cream sauce; grilled halibut served with rock shrimp and spinach dumplings; and a big, fat Angus rib-eye served with fresh grilled vegetables and garlic mashed potatoes. The wine list is impressive (and reasonably priced). The long, narrow dining rooms are bright and airy with pine-wood furnishings, wood floors, and an open kitchen. On sunny days, request a table on the back patio.

402 Main St. ℂ 209/728-8663. Reservations recommended. Main courses $7.50–$16. AE, DISC, MC, V. Mon–Tues 7am–4pm; Wed–Sat 7am–9pm; Sun 8am–9pm.

COLUMBIA

Though a little hokey, **Columbia State Historic Park** ⭐⭐ (ℂ **209/532-4301** for the museum and tours; www.columbiacalifornia.com) is the best-maintained Gold Rush town in the Mother Lode (as well as one of the most popular, so expect crowds in the summer). At one point, this boisterous mining town was the state's second-largest city (and only two votes shy of becoming the state capital). When gold mining no longer panned out in the late 1850s, most of the town's 15,000 residents departed, leaving much of the mining equipment and buildings in place. In 1945 the entire town was turned into a Historic Park.

As a result, Columbia has been preserved and functions much as it did in the 1850s, with stagecoach rides, Western-style Victorian hotels and saloons, a newspaper office, a blacksmith's forge, a Wells Fargo express office, and numerous other relics of California's early mining days. Cars are banned from its streets, giving the shady town an authentic feel. Merchants still do business behind some storefronts, as horse, stagecoach, and pedestrian traffic wanders by.

If Columbia's heat and dust get to you, pull up a stool at the **Jack Douglass Saloon** on Main Street (no phone), open daily from 10am to 5pm. Inside the swinging doors of the classic Western bar, you can sample homemade sarsaparilla and wild cherry, drinks the saloon has been serving since 1857. The storefront's large shuttered windows open onto a dusty main street, so put up your boots, relax awhile, and watch the stagecoach go by.

Historical tours of the park depart from the Main Museum daily at 11am and 1:30pm. The 45-minute, $2 stroll takes you down Main Street and into dusty old structures that are off-limits to the general public.

Where to Stay & Dine

City Hotel ⊛ *Kids*   Established in 1856, the City Hotel was restored in 1975 by the State of California, the nonprofit City Hotel Corporation, and Columbia College, and is now run as a sort of on-the-job training center for hospitality-management students (hence the eager-to-please staff). It's a big, beautiful building, complete with a stately parlor furnished with Victorian sofas, antiques, and Oriental rugs. The largest guest rooms have two balconies overlooking Main Street; the units off the parlor are also spacious. The hallway rooms are smaller but still nicely furnished with Renaissance Revival beds and antiques. Each room has a sink and toilet, but the shower rooms are separate. A buffet breakfast is served in the dining room. The hotel also runs a fine-dining restaurant serving classic Continental cuisine (roast rack of lamb, grilled salmon, and smoked duck breast) Tuesday through Sunday, as well as the What Cheer saloon. Noise from the saloon, though perhaps not as loud as when the customers packed pistolas, does travel upstairs, so if you're a light sleeper, bring earplugs.

Main St. (P.O. Box 1870), Columbia State Park, CA 95310. © 800/532-1479 or 209/532-1479. Fax 209/532-7027. www.cityhotel.com. 10 units (all with shared shower rooms). $105–$125 double. Rates include breakfast. DISC, MC, V. **Amenities:** Restaurant (open Tues–Sun); saloon; nearby golf course. *In room:* A/C, no phone.

Fallon Hotel ⊛ *Kids*   Opened in 1857, this hotel has been restored and decorated to evoke the 1890s. The two-story building retains many of its original antiques and furniture. The largest rooms are those along the front upper balcony. Only one unit has a full bathroom; the rest have a private sink and toilet, and showers are down the hall. Rooms are furnished with high-backed Victorian beds, marble-topped dressers, rockers, and similar oak pieces. A full breakfast is served in the downstairs parlor.

Washington St. (P.O. Box 1870), Columbia State Park, CA 95310. © 800/532-1479 or 209/532-1470. Fax 209/532-7027. www.cityhotel.com. 14 units, 13 with shared bathroom. $60–$125 double. Rates include breakfast. DISC, MC, V. **Amenities:** Ice-cream parlor; nearby golf course. *In room:* A/C, no phone.

SONORA

A few miles south of Columbia, Sonora is the largest town in the southern Gold Country. (You'll know you've arrived when traffic starts to crawl.) In Gold Rush days, Sonora and Columbia were the two richest towns in the Mother Lode. Dozens of stores and cafes line the main thoroughfare. If you can find a parking space, it's worth your while to spend an hour or two checking out the sites, like the 19th-century **St. James Episcopal Church,** at the top of Washington Street, and the **Tuolumne County Museum and History Center,** 158 W. Bradford Ave. (© 209/532-1317), in the 1857 County Jail. Admission is free, and it's open daily year-round from 10am to 4pm, closed some holidays.

Fun Fact **How to Pan for Gold**

Find a gold pan, ideally a 12- to 15-inch steel pan. Place the pan over an oven burner, or better yet, in a campfire. This will darken the pan, making it easier to see any flakes of placer gold (many gold pans come already blackened). Find some gravel, sand, or dirt in a stream that looks promising or feels lucky. Scoop dirt into the pan until it's nearly full, then place it under water and keep it there while you break up the clumps of mud and clay and toss out any stones. Then grasp the pan with both hands. Holding it level, rotate it in swirling motions. This will cause the heavier gold to loosen and settle to the bottom of the pan. Drain off the dirty water and loose stuff. Keep doing this until gold and heavier minerals called "black sand" are left in the pan. Carefully inspect the black sand for nuggets or speck traces of gold. Who knows? You just might get lucky.

If this all seems too much to try on your own, you can sign up for a lesson with Jamestown's **Gold Prospecting Adventures** (© **800/596-0009** or 209/984-4653; www.goldprospecting.com). The hour-long class costs about $15, and yes, you get to keep any gold you might find.

Where to Stay

Gunn House Hotel ★ *Value* Built in 1850 by Dr. Lewis C. Gunn, the Gunn House was the first two-story adobe structure in Sonora, built to house his family, who sailed around Cape Horn from the East Coast to join him in the Gold Rush. Painstakingly restored, it's now one of the best moderately priced hotels in the Gold Country. It's easy to catch the Forty-Niner spirit here, as the entire hotel and grounds are brimming with quality antiques and turn-of-the-20th-century artifacts. Rare for a building this old, each guest room has a private bathroom and air-conditioning. What really makes the Gunn House one of my favorites, though, is the hotel's beautiful pool and patio, surrounded by lush vegetation and admirable stonework. It's in a convenient location as well, right in downtown Sonora.

286 S. Washington St., Sonora, CA 95370. © **209/532-3421**. 20 units. $69–$109 double. Rates include continental breakfast. AE, DISC, MC, V. **Amenities:** Outdoor heated pool. *In room:* A/C, TV, fridge.

Where to Dine

Diamondback Grill *Value* AMERICAN For more than a decade, this modest family-owned diner has whipped up the Gold Country's best burger: the Diamondback—a grilled-to-order half-pounder that comes with the works, including fries. There are about a dozen other burgers, as well as gourmet sandwiches (go for the grilled eggplant with fresh tomato and mozzarella), house-made soups and pecan pies, a zesty black-bean-and-steak chili, and great daily specials listed. There's also a good selection of beer and wine by the glass.

110 S. Washington St. © **209/532-6661**. Main courses $5–$10. No credit cards. Mon–Sat 11am–9pm; Sun 11am–5pm.

JAMESTOWN ★

About 4 miles southwest of Sonora on Calif. 49 is Jamestown, a 4-block-long town of old-fashioned storefronts and two rustic turn-of-the-20th-century hotels. Yes, there's gold in these parts, too, as the marker commemorating the discovery of a 75-pound nugget will attest (panning nearby Woods Creek is a popular pastime among both locals and tourists). If Jamestown looks eerily familiar to you, that's probably because you've seen it in the movies or on television. It's one of Hollywood's favorite Western movie sets; scenes from such films as *Butch Cassidy and the Sundance Kid* were shot here.

Jamestown's most popular attraction is the **Railtown 1897 State Historic Park** ⚘, a train buff's paradise featuring three Sierra steam locomotives. These great machines were used in many a movie and television show, including *High Noon, Little House on the Prairie, Bonanza*, and *My Little Chickadee*. The trains at the roundhouse are on display daily year-round. Call for information on weekend rides and guided tours. The Depot Store and Museum are open daily from 9:30am to 4:30pm. The park is located near the center of town, on Fifth Avenue at Reservoir Road (ⓒ **209/984-3953**; www.csrmf.org/railtown).

Where to Stay & Dine

Jamestown Hotel & Restaurant ⚘

The most worked-over building in town, the Jamestown was originally built in 1858; it burned down and was rebuilt twice before 1915. To achieve the old-fashioned, brick-fronted Victorian look it sports today, a lot of stucco and Spanish-revival paraphernalia had to be removed. Most of the lower floor is devoted to the front office, bar, and restaurant. The second floor contains a cadre of cozy bedrooms outfitted with antiques. All of the spacious rooms are loaded with nostalgic charm; a few have sitting rooms and TVs with VCRs, and all have private bathrooms (some with claw-foot tubs). The most popular has its own balcony. The street-level rooms are the most luxurious, outfitted with whirlpool tubs, private patios, and individual heat and air-conditioning controls. The dining room serves upscale American dishes such as salmon steak poached in white wine, bacon-wrapped filet mignon, prime rib, and charbroiled rib-eye. If you're staying for the weekend, be sure to attend the hotel's popular Sunday champagne brunch

18153 Main St. (P.O. Box 539), Jamestown, CA 95327. ⓒ 800/205-4901 or 209/984-3902. Fax 209/984-4149. www.jamestownhotel.com. 11 units. $105–$195 double. Rates include full breakfast. AE, DC, DISC, MC, V. **Amenities:** Restaurant; bar; activities desk; business center. *In room:* A/C, TV/VCR in some units, hair dryer, iron.

National Hotel & Restaurant ⚘

In the center of town, this two-story classic Western hotel has been operating since 1859, making it one of the 10 oldest continuously operating hotels in the state. The saloon has its original 19th-century redwood bar, and you can imagine what it must have been like when miners traded gold dust for drinks. The guestrooms blend 19th-century details (handmade quilts, oak furnishings, lace curtains, brass beds) with 20th-century comforts such as private bathrooms. All guests have access to the authentic "Soaking Room," a private room equipped with a sort of 1800s claw-foot Jacuzzi for two (when cowboys longed for a good, hot soak). Brunch, lunch, and dinner are served to the public in the handsome old-fashioned dining room or pretty garden courtyard. Dishes range from steak and prime rib to chicken, seafood, pasta dishes, and house-made desserts.

77 Main St. (P.O. Box 502), Jamestown, CA 95327. ⓒ 800/894-3446 or 209/984-3446. Fax 209/984-5620. www.national-hotel.com. 9 units. $90–$130 double. Rates include buffet breakfast. AE, DC, DISC, MC, V. Pets accepted with $10-per-night fee. **Amenities:** Restaurant; saloon; nearby golf course; concierge; tour/activities desk; business center; secretarial services; room service; in-room massage. *In room:* A/C, TV, dataport, coffeemaker, hair dryer.

3 The Central Valley & Sierra National Forest

The Central Valley (also known as the San Joaquin Valley) is about as far as you can get from California's glamorous movie-stars-in-stretch-limos image. This hot, flat strip of farms, dairies, fast-food joints, cheap motels, and truck stops stretches for some 225 miles from Bakersfield to Redding. The 18,000-square-mile valley is central to the economy of the Golden State, in part because of its cultivated and irrigated fields, orchards, pastures, and vineyards.

The major traffic arteries through the valley are Calif. 99 and I-5. Calif. 99 links the agricultural communities, while I-5 provides access routes to the attractions in the valley. Rivers cutting through the valley offer fishing, boating, houseboating on the delta, and whitewater rafting on the rapids. And once you get off the freeways, the valley's spectacular landscapes provide unrivaled natural beauty. Many visitors drive through in spring just to view the orchards in bloom.

The Central Valley also stands on the doorstep of some of America's greatest attractions, the most well known being Yosemite National Park. See chapter 9 for coverage of two Central Valley towns, Merced and Visalia, which are good gateways to Yosemite, Sequoia, and Kings Canyon, respectively.

Fresno, although not much in itself, is on the doorstep of the Sierra National Forest and nearby attractions like the Millerton Lake State Recreation Area.

FRESNO

The running joke in California is that Fresno is the "gateway to Bakersfield." For most visitors, Fresno, 185 miles southeast of San Francisco, is just a place to pass through en route to the state parks; it can, however, be a good place to stop for food and lodging, and it makes a good base for exploring the Sierra National Forest (see below).

Founded in 1874 in the geographic center of the state, Fresno is in the heart of the Central Valley and has experienced incredible growth in recent years. Like most growing cities, it has seen increases in crime, drugs, and urban sprawl.

As the seat of Fresno County, the city handles more than $3 billion annually in agricultural production. It also contains Sun Maid, the world's largest dried-fruit packing plant, and Guild, one of the country's largest wineries.

If you have any reason at all to be in Fresno, try to visit between late February and late March so you can drive the **Fresno County Blossom Trail** ☆. This 62-mile, self-guided tour takes in the beauty of California's agrarian bounty at its peak. The trail courses through fruit orchards in full bloom and citrus groves with lovely orange blossoms and a heady natural perfume. The **Fresno Convention and Visitors Bureau,** 847 M St., third floor, in Fresno (℡ **800/788-0836** or 559/233-0836; www.fresnocvb.org), supplies full details, including a map.

WHERE TO STAY

San Joaquin ☆   On the northern edge of Fresno, this full-service hotel was conceived as an apartment complex in the 1970s. Around 1985 a lobby was added, the floor plans were adjusted, and the place was reconfigured as an all-suite hotel. Suites range from junior one-bedroom suites to three-bedroom suites with kitchens, and each is outfitted in a slightly different style, with light, contemporary colors and furniture. Room service is available from a restaurant down the street.

1309 W. Shaw Ave., Fresno, CA 93711. ℡ **800/775-1309** or 559/225-1309. Fax 559/225-6021. www.sjhotel. com. 68 suites. $99–$205 suite. Rates include continental breakfast. AE, DC, DISC, MC, V. **Amenities:** Outdoor pool; Jacuzzi; business center; limited room service; laundry service. *In room:* A/C, TV/VCR, dataport, kitchen, fridge, coffeemaker, hair dryer, iron.

WHERE TO DINE

Veni, Vidi, Vici ⍟ CALIFORNIA CUISINE   The most innovative and creative restaurant in Fresno occupies a prominent position about 6 miles south of the commercial center, in a funky neighborhood known as the Tower District. The place's rustic exterior strikes an interesting contrast to the polished and artful interior on the other side of the 15-foot doors, where the decor is accented with exposed-brick walls, mirrors, and chandeliers fashioned from twisted wire and metal leaves. The menu changes often but might include roasted loin of pork with Chinese black beans and citrus-flavored glaze, served with grilled portobello mushrooms, sun-dried tomatoes, risotto, and red-pepper coulis; or a wild-mushroom lasagna with preserved tomato sauce. There are also fresh-fish specials nightly. This is the only restaurant in Fresno that makes its own ice cream (the flavor of the day when I arrived was Technicolor lime sorbet). Have a scoop or two with the restaurant's perennial dessert favorite: bittersweet chocolate cake.

1116 N. Fulton St. ⓒ 559/266-5510. Reservations recommended. Main courses $19–$26. AE, DC, DISC, MC, V. Tues–Sun 5–10pm (late-night menu Fri–Sat 10pm–midnight).

SIERRA NATIONAL FOREST ⍟⍟

Leaving Fresno's taco joints, used-car lots, and tract houses behind, an hour's drive and 45 miles northeast gets you to the Sierra National Forest, a land of lakes and coniferous forests between Yosemite, Sequoia, and Kings Canyon national parks. The entire eastern portion of the park is unspoiled wilderness protected by the government. Development—some of it, unfortunately, beside the bigger lakes and reservoirs—is confined to the western side.

The 1.3-million-acre forest contains 528,000 acres of wilderness. The Sierra's five wilderness areas include Ansel Adams, Dinkey Lakes, John Muir, Kaiser, and Monarch (see below). The forest offers plenty of opportunities for fishing, swimming, sailing, boating, camping, water-skiing, whitewater rafting, kayaking, and horseback riding, all regulated by certain guidelines. Downhill and cross-country skiing, as well as hunting, are also available, depending on the season. Backpackers looking to retreat to the wilderness will find solace here, as some 1,100 miles of forest hiking trails traverse the park.

ESSENTIALS

GETTING THERE   After visiting the ranger station at Oakhurst, take Calif. 41 to Calif. 49, the major road into the northern part of the national forest. This is more convenient for visitors approaching the park from Northern California. Calif. 168 via Clovis is the primary route from Fresno if you're headed for Shaver Lake. There is no approach road from the eastern Sierra, only from the west.

VISITOR INFORMATION & PERMITS   To learn about hiking, camping, or other activities, or to get the fire and wilderness permits, visit one of the ranger stations in the park's western section. These include **Mariposa and Minarets Ranger Station,** 57003 North Fork (ⓒ 559/877-2218); and the **Pineridge Ranger Station,** 29688 Auberry Rd., Prather (ⓒ 559/855-5360).

SUPPLIES   Shaver Lake is one place where you can stock up on goods and supplies if you're going into the wilderness, but stores in Fresno carry much of the same stuff at lower prices. Cheaper supplies are also available in Clovis, outside Fresno (which you must pass through en route to the forest), at the **Peacock Market,** at Tollhouse Road (Third St.) and Sunnyside Avenue (ⓒ 559/299-6627).

WEATHER   In the lower elevations, summer temperatures can frequently reach 100°F (38°C), but in the higher elevations, more comfortable temperatures in the 70s and 80s (20s Celsius) are the norm.

THE MAJOR WILDERNESS & RECREATION AREAS

ANSEL ADAMS WILDERNESS   Divided between the Sierra and Inyo national forests, this wilderness area covers 228,500 acres. Elevations range from 3,500 to 13,157 feet. The frost-free period extends from mid-July to August, the best time for a visit to the park's upper altitudes.

Ansel Adams is dotted with alpine vistas, including steep-walled gorges and granite peaks. There are several glaciers in the north and some large lakes on the eastern slope of the Ritter Range. This wilderness has excellent stream and lake fishing, especially for rainbow, golden, and brook trout, and offers challenging mountain climbing on the Minarets Range. The wilderness is accessed by the Tioga Pass Road in the north, U.S. 395 and Reds Meadow Road in the east, the Minarets Highway in the west, and Calif. 168 to High Sierra in the south.

DINKEY LAKES WILDERNESS   The 30,000-acre Dinkey Lakes area was created in 1984 and occupies the western slope of the Sierra Nevada, southeast of Huntington Lake and northwest of Courtright Reservoir. Most of the timbered, rolling terrain here is 8,000 feet above sea level, reaching its highest point (10,619 ft.) at Three Sisters Peak. Sixteen lakes are clustered in the west-central region. You can reach the area on Kaiser Pass Road (north), Red/Coyote Jeep Road (west), Rock Creek Road (southwest), or Courtright Reservoir (southeast), generally from mid-June to late October.

JOHN MUIR WILDERNESS   Occupying 584,000 acres in the Sierra and Inyo national forests, John Muir Wilderness—named after the naturalist—extends southeast from Mammoth Lakes along the crest of the Sierra Nevada for 30 miles before forking around the boundary of Kings Canyon National Park to Crown Valley and Mount Whitney. Elevations range from 4,000 to 14,496 feet at Mount Whitney, with many of the area's peaks surpassing 12,000 feet. The wilderness can be accessed from numerous points west of U.S. 395 between Mammoth Lake and Independence.

Split by deep canyons, the wilderness is also a land of meadows (especially beautiful when wildflowers bloom), lakes, and streams. The south and middle forks of the San Joaquin River, the north fork of Kings River, and many creeks draining into Owens Valley originate in the John Muir Wilderness. Mountain hemlock, red and white fir, and white-bark and western pine dot the park's landscape. Temperatures vary wildly throughout any 24-hour period: Summer temperatures range from 25° to 85°F (−4° to 29°C), and the only really frost-free period is between mid-July and August. The higher elevations are marked by barren expanses of granite splashed with many glacially carved lakes.

KAISER WILDERNESS   North of Huntington Lake and 70 miles northeast of Fresno, Kaiser is a 22,700-acre forest tract commanding a view of the central Sierra Nevada. It was named after Kaiser Ridge, which divides the area into two different regions. Four trail heads provide access to the wilderness, but the northern half is much more open than the forested southern half; the primary point of entry is the Sample Meadow Campground. All other lakes are approached cross-country. Winter storms begin to blow in late October, and the grounds are generally snow-covered until early June.

MONARCH WILDERNESS   Monarch is at the southern end of the John Muir Wilderness, on the western border of Sequoia and Kings Canyon National

Parks, 65 miles east of Fresno via Calif. 180. The area extends across 45,000 acres in the Sierra and Sequoia national forests. The Sierra National Forest portion of the region—about 21,000 acres—is rugged and hard to traverse. Steep slopes climb from the middle and main forks of Kings River, with elevations increasing from 2,400 to more than 10,000 feet. Rock outcroppings are found throughout Monarch, and most of the lower elevations are chaparral covered with pine stands near the tops of the higher peaks. Monarch is located at the southern end of the John Muir Wilderness, on the western border of Sequoia and Kings Canyon National Parks, approximately 65 miles east of Fresno via Calif. 180.

HUNTINGTON LAKE RECREATION AREA At 7,000 feet, this area is a 2-hour drive east of Fresno via Calif. 168. The lake is one of the reservoirs in the Big Creek Hydroelectric System and has 14 miles of shoreline. It's a popular recreational area, offering camping, hiking, picnicking, sailing, swimming, windsurfing, fishing, and horseback riding—or you can just appreciate the beauty. The main summer season stretches from Memorial Day to Labor Day. There are seven campgrounds and four picnic areas in the Huntington Lake Basin, plus numerous hiking and riding trails.

NEIDER GROVE OF GIANT SEQUOIAS 🌲 This 1,540-acre tract in the Sierra National Forest contains 101 mature giant sequoias in the center of the Sequoia Range, south of Yosemite National Park. A **visitor center** stands near the Neider Grove Campground, with historical relics and displays, including two restored log cabins. The Bull Buck Tree—at one time thought to be the largest in the world—is 246 feet high and has a circumference at ground level of 99 feet. There's a mile-long, self-guided walk along the "Shadow of the Giants" National Recreational Trail in the southwest corner of the grove.

OUTDOOR PURSUITS

CAMPING The Sierra National Forest seems like one vast campsite. Options range from primitive wilderness camps to developed and often crowded camp-grounds with snack bars, flush toilets, bathhouses, and RV hookups. For infor-mation and reservations, call the **National Recreation Reservation Service** toll-free at © 877/444-6777, or visit its website at www.reserveusa.com.

The major campgrounds are the Shaver Lake area; the Huntington Lake area (which has seven family campgrounds open from the end of June to Labor Day that must be reserved in advance); the Florence and Edison Lake area (first-come, first-served); the Dinkey Creek area (family and group camping); the Wishon and Courtright area (four campgrounds; first-come, first-served); the Pine Flat Reservoir (in the Sierra foothills, with two first-come, first-served campgrounds); and Upper Kings River, east of Pine Flat Reservoir (family camp-grounds; first-come, first-served).

FISHING The many streams of the Sierra are home to rainbow, golden, brown, and brook trout. The best freshwater angling is in the Pineridge and Kings River Rangers District. At the lower elevations, Shaver Lake, Bass Lake, and Pine Flat Reservoirs are known for their black-bass fishing. Questions about fishing in the national forest can be directed to the **California Department of Fish and Game,** 1234 E. Shaw Ave., Fresno, CA 93710 (© 559/243-4005).

SKIING Lying 65 miles northeast of Fresno on Calif. 168 in the Sierra National Forest, the **Sierra Summit Ski Area** offers mildly challenging alpine skiing, as well as marked trails for cross-country skiing and snowmobiling. The resort area has two triple and three double chairlifts, plus four surface lifts and

30 runs, the longest of which extends for 2¼ miles. There's a vertical drop off of 1,600 feet. Other facilities include a lodge, snack bar, cafeteria, restaurant, and bar, all open daily from mid-November until mid-April. For resort information or a ski report, call © **559/893-3311.**

The **Pineridge Ranger Station** (© **559/855-5360**) maintains several marked cross-country trails along Calif. 168, ranging from a 1-mile tour for beginners to a 6-mile trail for more advanced skiers.

WHITE-WATER RAFTING   The Upper Kings River, east of Pine Flat Reservoir, offers a 10-mile rafting run through Garnet Dike to Kirch Flat Campground. Rafting season is from late April to mid-July, with the highest waters in late May and early June. To get there, take Belmont Avenue in Fresno east (toward Pine Flat Reservoir) for about 63 miles. For more information about guided rafting trips on the Kings River, call **Kings River Expeditions** (© **559/ 233-4881;** www.kingsriver.com).

11

The Monterey Peninsula & the Big Sur Coast

by Matthew Richard Poole

The Monterey Peninsula and the Big Sur coast comprise one of the world's most spectacular shorelines, skirted with cypress trees, rugged shores, and crescent-shaped bays. Monterey reels in visitors with its world-class aquarium and array of outdoor activities. Pacific Grove is so peaceful that the butterflies choose it as their yearly mating ground. Pebble Beach attracts the golfing elite, and although packed with tourists who come for the beaches, shops, and restaurants, tiny Carmel-by-the-Sea somehow remains romantic and sweet. Big Sur's dramatic and majestic coast, backed by pristine redwood forests and rolling hills, is one of the most breathtaking and tranquil environments on earth. If you're traveling on Calif. 1 (which you should be), the coastline will guide you all the way through the region.

This chapter begins with Santa Cruz, at the northwestern end of Monterey Bay. It's one of my favorite coastal destinations and home of the Santa Cruz Beach Boardwalk. Across Monterey Bay at the northern tip of the Monterey Peninsula are the seaside communities of Monterey and Pacific Grove, while Pebble Beach and Carmel-by-the-Sea hug the peninsula's south coast along Carmel Bay. Between the north and south coasts, which are only about 5 miles apart, are many golf courses, some of the state's most stunning homes and hotels, and the 17-Mile Drive, one of the most scenic coastal roads in the world.

Inland lies Carmel Valley, with its elegant inns and resorts, golf courses, and guaranteed sunshine, even when the coast is socked in with fog. Farther down the coast along Calif. 1 is Big Sur, a stunning 90-mile stretch of coast south of the Monterey Peninsula and west of the Santa Lucia Mountains.

1 Santa Cruz ★★

77 miles SE of San Francisco

For a small bayside city, Santa Cruz has a lot to offer. The main show, of course, is the Beach Boardwalk, the West Coast's only seaside amusement park, which attracts millions of visitors each year. But past the arcades and cotton candy is a surprisingly diverse and energetic city that has a little something for everyone. Shopping, hiking, mountain biking, sailing, fishing, kayaking, surfing, wine tasting, golfing, whale-watching—the list of things to do here is almost endless, making Santa Cruz one of the premier family destinations on the California coast.

ESSENTIALS

GETTING THERE   Santa Cruz is 77 miles southeast of San Francisco. The most scenic route to Santa Cruz is along Calif. 1 from San Francisco, which, aside from the "you fall, you die" stretch called Devil's Slide, allows you to cruise at a steady 50 mph. Faster but less romantic is Calif. 17, which is accessed near San Jose from I-280, I-880, or U.S. 101, and ends at the foot of the boardwalk. The exception to this rule is on weekend mornings, when Calif. 17 tends to log-jam with beachgoers while Calif. 1 remains relatively uncrowded.

VISITOR INFORMATION For information, contact the **Santa Cruz County Conference and Visitors Council,** 1211 Ocean St., Santa Cruz, CA 95060 (© **800/833-3494** or 831/425-1234; www.santacruzca.org), open Monday through Saturday from 9am to 5pm, Sunday from 10am to 4pm.

SPECIAL EVENTS Special events include **Shakespeare Santa Cruz** in July and August (© **831/459-2121**), and the **Cabrillo Music Festival** in August (© **831/426-6966**).

WHAT TO SEE & DO
BEACHES, HIKING, FISHING & MORE IN SANTA CRUZ
One of the few ol' fashioned amusement parks left in the world, the **Santa Cruz Beach Boardwalk** ★★ (© **831/426-7433**) draws more than three million visitors a year to its 30 rides and arcades, shops, and restaurants. The park has two national landmarks—a 1924 wooden Giant Dipper roller coaster and a 1911 carousel with hand-carved wooden horses and a 342-pipe organ band. It's open daily in the summer (from Memorial Day weekend to Labor Day) and on weekends and holidays throughout the spring and fall, from 11am (noon sometimes in winter). Admission to the boardwalk is free, but an all-day "unlimited rides" pass will set you back $26. Check the boardwalk calendar (© **831/423-5590**; www.beachboardwalk.com) for discounts, concerts and events, and up-to-date info on hours, which can often vary.

Here, too, is **Neptune's Kingdom,** 400 Beach St. (© **831/426-7433**; www.beachboardwalk.com), an enormous indoor family recreation center whose main feature is a two-story miniature golf course. Also on Beach Street is the **Municipal Wharf** (© **831/420-6025**), lined with shops and restaurants—a beachfront strip that is serenaded by the sea lions below. You can also crab and fish from here. Most shops are open daily from 7am to 9pm, the wharf daily from 5am to 2am. **Stagnaro's** (© **831/427-2334**; www.stagnaros.com) operates fishing and whale-watching trips from the wharf year-round, as well as hour-long narrated bay cruises for a mere $10 for adults, $5 for kids under 14.

Farther down on West Cliff Drive, you'll come to a favorite surfing spot, **Steamer Lane,** where you can watch pro surfers shredding the waves. If you want to find out more about this local sport that's been practiced here for more than 100 years, go to the **Santa Cruz Surfing Museum,** at the lighthouse (© **831/420-6289**; www.santacruzparksandrec.com), open Wednesday through Monday from noon to 4pm. Antique surfboards, videos, photographs, and other memorabilia depict the history and evolution of surfing around the world.

Continue along West Cliff and you'll reach **Natural Bridges State Beach,** 2531 W. Cliff Dr. (© **831/423-4609**; www.scparkfriends.org), a large sandy beach with nearby tide pools and hiking trails. It's also home to a large colony of monarch butterflies that cluster and mate in the nearby eucalyptus grove.

Other Santa Cruz beaches worth noting are **Bonny Doon,** at Bonny Doon Road and Calif. 1, an uncrowded sandy beach and a major surfing spot accessible by a steep walkway; **Pleasure Point Beach,** East Cliff Drive at Pleasure Point Drive; and **Twin Lakes State Beach,** which is ideal for sunning and also provides access to Schwann Lagoon, a bird sanctuary.

In addition to hosting many cultural and sporting events, the University of California at Santa Cruz also features the **Seymour Marine Discovery Center** at the Long Marine Laboratory, 100 Shaffer Rd., at the northwest end of Delaware Avenue (© **831/459-3800;** www2.ucsc.edu/seymourcenter), where you can observe the activities of marine scientists and the species in tide-pool touch tanks and aquariums. Visitors get to learn how marine research aids in the conservation of the world's oceans. Hours are Tuesday through Saturday from 10am to 5pm, and Sunday from noon to 5pm; admission is $5 for adults, $3 children ages 6 to 16, and free for kids under 6 (free admission for the first Tues of each month).

The **Santa Cruz Harbor,** 135 Fifth Ave. (© **831/475-6161;** www.santa cruzharbor.org), is the place to head for boat rentals, open-boat fishing (cod, shark, and salmon), and whale-watching trips. Operators include **Santa Cruz Sportfishing Inc.** (© **831/426-4690;** www.santacruzsportfishing.com) and **Shamrock Charters,** 2210 E. Cliff Dr. (© **831/476-2648**). Even if you're not into fishing, it's worth a walk down the harbor to browse through the numerous shops and restaurants.

Bikes—mountain, kids', tandem, hybrid—are available by the hour, day, or week from various bike-rental shops in convenient locations around the city. For a list of shops, call the **Santa Cruz Visitors Council** at © **800/833-3494,** or check the website at www.santacruzca.org. Figure on paying $25 a day, which includes helmets, locks, and packs.

There are several public golf courses, the best being the **Pasatiempo Golf Club,** at 18 Clubhouse Rd. (© **831/459-9155;** www.pasatiempo.com), which is rated among the top 100 courses in the United States. Greens fees are $135 Monday through Friday, $150 Saturday, Sunday, and holidays.

Kayaking is also an option. Outfitters include **Kayak Connection,** 413 Lake Ave. No. 4 (© **831/479-1121;** www.kayakconnection.com), and **Venture Quest Kayaking** (© **831/427-2267;** www.kayaksantacruz.com), which rent single, double, and triple kayaks at Building No. 2 on the wharf and at 125 Beach St. Classes, wildlife tours, and moonlight paddles are also available.

Surfing equipment can be rented at the **Cowell's Beach 'n' Bikini Surf Shop,** 109 Beach St. (© **831/427-2355**), and from the **Club Ed Surf School** (© **800/ 287-SURF** or 831/459-6664; www.club-ed.com), on Cowell Beach in front of the West Coast Santa Cruz Hotel (formerly the Dream Inn). Both offer surf lessons: Club Ed's rates are $85 for a 2-hour group session, $95 for private lessons (equipment included), and $950 for a 7-day surf camp; Cowell's costs $70 for a 2-hour group lesson and includes the use of a board and wet suit.

IN NEARBY CAPITOLA & APTOS

South along the coast lies the small, attractive community of **Capitola** ✦ at the mouth of the Soquel Creek, which is a spawning ground for steelhead and salmon. You can fish without a license from the **Capitola Wharf,** 1400 Wharf Rd., or you can rent a fishing boat from **Capitola Boat and Bait** (© **831/ 462-2208;** www.santacruzboatrentals.net).

Capitola Beach fronts the bustling Esplanade. Surf fishing and clamming are popular pastimes at Capitola's **New Brighton State Beach,** 1500 State Park Dr. (© **831/464-6330**), where camping is allowed. Another popular activity is **antiquing** in the stores along Soquel Drive between 41st and Capitola avenues.

Still farther south around the bay is **Aptos** ✦, home to the 10,000-acre **Forest of Nisene Marks State Park** (© **831/763-7063**), which has hiking trails that wind through redwoods and past abandoned mining camps. Mountain bikers and leashed dogs are also welcome. This was the infamous epicenter of the 1989 earthquake. It's located at the end of Aptos Creek Road off Soquel Drive and is open year-round from sunrise to sunset.

In the redwood-forested mountains behind Santa Cruz, there are quite a few **wineries,** although visitors may not be familiar with the labels because the output is small and consumed locally. Most are clustered around Boulder Creek and Felton or around Capitola. All offer tours by appointment; some feature tastings, including the **Bargetto Winery,** 3535 N. Main, Soquel (© **800/422-7438** or 831/475-2258; www.bargetto.com), which has a courtyard wine-tasting area overlooking the creek. For information, contact the **Santa Cruz Mountains Winegrowers' Association** (© **831/479-WINE;** www.scmwa.com).

WHERE TO STAY
IN SANTA CRUZ

Two **Travelodges** (© **800/578-7878;** www.travelodge.com), two **Best Westerns** (© **800/528-1234;** www.bestwestern.com), two **Super 8s** (© **800/800-8000;** www.super8.com), and an **Econo Lodge** (© **800/553-2666;** www.hotel choice.com) provide moderate- and budget-priced accommodations in addition to the more individual choices below.

Babbling Brook Bed & Breakfast Inn ⭐⭐   With charm to spare, the rooms in this popular inn are like treehouses perched over and around a brook running through an acre of gardens, pines, and redwoods. Although it's on a busy street, what you hear from your room is running water cascading over waterfalls and a large waterwheel. The romantic guest rooms are decorated in tasteful, simple style with lots of windows, skylights, open beam ceilings, balconies, and decks; most have gas fireplaces. The inn is within a mile of the beach and the boardwalk and a short walk to the attractions of downtown Santa Cruz, a great place to browse and have dinner. Breakfast is served in the comfortable lobby, and wine and snacks are also served there from 5:30 to 7:30pm.

1025 Laurel St., Santa Cruz, CA 95060. © **800/866-1131** or 831/427-2456. Fax 831/427-2457. www.bab-blingbrookinn.com. 13 units. $179–$265 double. Rates include full country-breakfast buffet. AE, DISC, MC, V. **Amenities:** Nearby golf. *In room:* TV, VCR in some units.

Casa Blanca Inn   Across from the wharf in a heavily trafficked area, this motel along the waterfront was once the Mediterranean-style Cerf Mansion, dating from 1918. Other motel-style accommodations have grown up around the main building. Originally the home of a federal judge, it offers individually decorated bedrooms, some with brass beds and velvet draperies. Some units contain fireplaces and terraces, and all have microwaves. Most of the rooms have views of the ocean. Casa Blanca Restaurant serves California-Continental cuisine in a romantic oceanview setting.

101 Main St. (at the corner of Beach St.), Santa Cruz, CA 95060. © **800/644-1570** or 831/423-1570. Fax 831/423-0235. www.casablanca-santacruz.com. 39 units. High season (summer) $96–$300 double; low season $78–$295 double. AE, DC, DISC, MC, V. **Amenities:** Restaurant; bar; nearby golf course; room service; laundry service. *In room:* TV, dataport, kitchen in some units, minibar, fridge, coffeemaker, hair dryer, iron, safe.

Darling House ⭐   This stately Spanish-style house, designed in 1910 by William Weeks (architect of Santa Cruz's Coconut Grove), has a panoramic view of the Pacific Ocean and is in a residential area within walking distance of the boardwalk and lighthouse. The gardens are fragrant with citrus and orchids, and contain some palms as well. From the tiled front veranda, guests enter an elegant interior, the focal point of which is the dining room handcrafted from tiger oak. The house boasts fine architectural features, such as beveled glass, antiques, and handsome fireplaces. Each of the eight rooms is individually decorated; although all have sinks, only two come with private bathrooms. The Pacific Ocean room, decorated like a captain's quarters, features a fireplace, telescope, and one of the finest ocean views in Santa Cruz. Breakfast includes fresh breads and pastries, fruit, and granola made with walnuts from the Darling's own farm.

314 W. Cliff Dr., Santa Cruz, CA 95060. ℂ 831/458-1958. www.darlinghouse.com. 8 units, 2 with bathroom. $95 double without bathroom; $260 double with bathroom. Rates include breakfast. AE, DISC, MC, V. **Amenities:** Concierge.

Edgewater Beach Motel   If the other three inns listed here are booked, consider the Edgewater Beach Motel. It looks like a time capsule from the 1960s, which, oddly enough, makes it all the more appealing (how they kept the furnishings in such prime condition is a mystery). The motel offers a range of accommodations, from family suites with kitchens to rooms with fireplaces; most have microwaves. The Edgewater also sports a nice pool, sun deck, and barbecue area, but the bonus is the location—the Santa Cruz Beach Boardwalk is a block away. *Tip:* Inquire about the Edgewater's off-season minivacation packages, which can save you a bundle. Smoking is not permitted in any of the rooms.

525 Second St., Santa Cruz, CA 95060. ℂ 888/809-6767 or 831/423-0440. www.edgewaterbeach motel.com. 17 units. Winter $85–$219 double; summer $139–$299 double. AE, DC, DISC, MC, V. **Amenities:** Outdoor heated pool. *In room:* TV/VCR, fully equipped kitchen in suites, fridge, coffeemaker.

Fern River Resort 𝕽 *Finds*   Few tourists know about this nifty mountain retreat, located 4 miles from Santa Cruz down a curvy redwood-lined road. The "resort" consists of 13 furnished and equipped cabins on 4 forested acres with lawn, garden, or river views. There you will find a gaggle of outdoor toys to keep you amused, including badminton, Ping-Pong, tetherball, horseshoes, 20 miles of hiking and mountain-biking trails in nearby Henry Cowell Park. There's even a private beach on the San Lorenzo River for sunning, swimming, and fishing. To sweeten the deal they've also added an enclosed spa tub. The cabins range in size from studios to some that sleep up to six and have equipped kitchens, but if you plan on cooking, you might want to bring some pots and pans.

5250 Hwy. 9, Felton, CA, 95018. ℂ 831/335-4412. www.fernriver.com. 13 units. High season $80–$135 double; low season $60–$105 double. AE, MC, V. **Amenities:** Jacuzzi. *In room:* TV.

IN NEARBY CAPITOLA

The Inn at Depot Hill 𝕽𝕽𝕽   A few blocks from the bay front, this converted 1910-era railroad station has been beautifully designed and decorated with great attention to detail—which explains why Martha Stewart chose to stay here during her coastal tour a few years ago. Sporting fine fabrics and linens, all rooms and suites have wood-burning fireplaces, stereos, bathrobes, two-person showers, and full bathrooms. Most have private patios with private Jacuzzis (guests in the other rooms share a common Jacuzzi, and sign up for times). Perhaps you'll check into the Portofino Room, patterned after an Italian villa right down to the frescoes and stone cherub, or the Stratford-on-Avon, a replica of an English cottage. The evening wine and hors d'oeuvres and the breakfast are of similar prime quality, and can be enjoyed either in your room or out back in the garden courtyard on wrought-iron tables shaded by market umbrellas.

250 Monterey Ave. (near Park Ave.), Capitola, CA 95010. ℂ 800/572-2632 or 831/462-3376. Fax 831/462-3697. www.innatdepothill.com. 12 units. $235–$355 double. Rates include breakfast, afternoon tea or wine, hors d'oeuvres, and after-dinner dessert. AE, DC, DISC, MC, V. **Amenities:** Jacuzzi; room service. *In room:* A/C, TV/VCR, fax, dataport, hair dryer.

WHERE TO DINE
IN SANTA CRUZ

The Crepe Place *Value* CREPES/ECLECTIC   Beloved by locals—particularly as a late-night hangout—The Crepe Place has been in business for more than a quarter of a century. Choose from 15 styles of crepes (the Spinach Supreme, Salsa, and Jambalaya are the local favorites, or create your own combination), then sit your booty in the wood-paneled dining room or outdoor garden area. Other menu items include soups, salads (good clam chowder), oven-baked whole-wheat honey bread, and a popular dessert called a Tunisian Doughnut, a yeasty concoction cooked to order with your choice of toppings. On weekends, all kinds of egg dishes are served at brunch in addition to the regular menu.

1134 Soquel Ave. (at Seabright Ave.) ℂ 831/429-6994. Main courses $5–$12. AE, MC, V, local checks only. Mon–Thurs 11am–midnight; Fri–Sun 10am–1am.

O'Mei ⭐⭐ PROVINCIAL SZECHUAN   O'Mei's (pronounced "Oh-*may*") minimall location may not be very inviting, but the fantastic food more than makes up for it. Named after a mountain in the Sichuan province of China, O'Mei's menu features some unusual specialties such as Chengdu-bean curd sea bass in a spicy *dou-ban* sauce (a rich, velvety wine-chile sauce), apricot-almond chicken, and lichee *pi-pa* bean-curd balls, along with more familiar dishes like chicken with cashews or beef with asparagus. The most popular dish is *gang pung chicken*—battered chicken with wood ear mushrooms, ginger, and cilantro, served with a sweet and slightly spicy sauce, but I usually order the rock cod in black-bean-and-sweet-pepper sauce. Dinner starts with a dim sum–style tray of exotic vegetarian offerings such as sesame-cilantro-eggplant salad or pan-roasted peppers with feta cheese. Cool things off with a bowl of black-sesame ice cream.

2316 Mission St. (where Calif. 1 turns into Mission St.). ℂ 831/425-8458. Reservations recommended. Main courses $9.25–$19. AE, MC, V. Mon–Fri 11:30am–2pm; Sun–Thurs 5–9pm; Fri–Sat 5–10pm.

Rosa's Rosticeria ⭐ *Finds* CUBAN   Rosa's, my friends, rocks. The first person to greet you as you enter the cafe is one cheery muchacho in a T-shirt and shorts standing behind a well-used blender. "Margarita?" Oh yeah. The Black Margarita, made with raw sugar, is the house specialty, best enjoyed at the outdoor dining area overlooking the harbor. The thumping Latin music gets you in the festive mood, and the aroma of grilled meats from the open kitchen puts the urge on your appetite. The menu is crammed with exotic examples of Cuban cuisine. One of my favorites is the Havana-style Cuban Barbecue—pork and ham slow-cooked on the grill and topped with sweet salsa, black beans, rice, and fried plantains. As you'd expect, all the meats are rotisserie-grilled, and the fresh seafood—particularly the scallop tacos—is superb. Make sure you start off the feast with Two Fisherman Arguing Squid: crispy fried tentacles and tequila-marinated tubes sautéed in bell peppers and chili pasilla and served with black beans and polenta. For parties of four or more, the Mambo Combo is a great deal: a big platter of chicken, ribs, rice, beans, polenta, and tortillas for only $23. Darn good $8 tri-tip sandwich as well. Really, you'll love this place.

439 Lake Ave. (at the Santa Cruz Yacht Harbor). ℂ 831/479-3536. Main courses $6–$17. DISC, MC, V. Daily 11am–10pm.

IN NEARBY CAPITOLA & APTOS

Bittersweet Bistro ⭐⭐ CALIFORNIA   What started out as a tiny operation in a small strip development has grown into one of the most popular restaurants in the Santa Cruz region. Its relocation to bigger digs in Rio Del Mar hasn't tarnished chef and owner Thomas Vinolus's reputation for serving exceptional cuisine. The menu offers a wide array of carefully crafted dishes, ranging from pizzas from the wood-fired oven to grilled lamb porterhouse in a sun-dried-cranberry demiglace. Fresh fish is Vinolus's forte, however, such as the Monterey Bay halibut, baked in parchment over fresh vegetables, or the roasted Chelis River wild sturgeon finished with an exotic mushroom sauce. Co-proprietor and wine director Elizabeth Vinolus has put together an exceptional wine list and often hosts winemaker dinners. "Bistro Hour" is from 3 to 6pm every afternoon, featuring half-price specials on gourmet pizzettas and special pricing on all wines by the glass, beer, and spirits.

787 Rio Del Mar Blvd., Aptos (about 10 miles southeast of Santa Cruz on Calif. 1). © 831/662-9799. www.bittersweetbistro.com. Reservations recommended. Main courses $18–$24. AE, MC, V. Daily "bistro" lunch 3–6pm; dinner 5:30–10pm; Sun brunch 10am–2pm.

Shadowbrook ⍟ AMERICAN/CONTINENTAL Shadowbrook, one of Capitola's most venerable and romantic restaurants, occupies a serene setting above Soquel Creek. To reach it, diners have to take the cable-driven "hillavator" down or walk the long, steep steps beside a running waterfall. At the bottom is a log cabin built in the 1920s, which has been enlarged and now contains a series of dining rooms on different levels: the wood-paneled Wine Cellar, the airy Garden Room, the Fireplace Room, and the creek-side Greenhouse.

The menu doesn't hold many surprises, featuring thick-cut prime rib and steaks along with seafood such as scampi and grilled trout, plus pasta dishes including shellfish linguine and porcini ravioli. Prawn cocktail, deep-fried artichoke hearts, and baked brie are among the appetizers. Standout desserts are the mud pie and chocolate torte with raspberry sauce. If you don't have the time, appetite, or budget for a big dinner, grab a seat in the lounge and nosh on appetizers and light entrees prepared in the restaurant's wood-fired oven.

1750 Wharf Rd., Capitola. © 831/475-1511. Fax 831/475-7664. www.shadowbrook-capitola.com. Reservations recommended. Main courses $13–$24. AE, DC, DISC, MC, V. Mon–Fri 11:30am–9:30pm; Sat 4:30–10:30pm; Sun 10am–2:30pm and 4:30–9pm.

A SIDE TRIP TO MISSION SAN JUAN BAUTISTA

On U.S. 101, **San Juan Bautista** ⍟ is a charming mission town that works hard to honor its pioneer heritage by retaining the flavor of a 19th-century village. The mission complex is perched in a picturesque farming valley, surrounded by the restored buildings of the original city plaza.

From U.S. 101, take Calif. 156 east (south) to the center of town to the mission itself, which was founded in 1797. Here you'll see the largest church in the mission chain and the only one in continuous service since its founding. The padres here inspired many Native Americans to convert, creating one of the largest congregations in all of California. The small museum contains many musical instruments and transcriptions, evidence of the mission's musical focus—it once boasted a formidable Native American boys' choir. Mission San Juan Bautista is open daily year-round from 9:30am to 4:45pm. Suggested donation is $1 per person. For further information, call © 831/623-4528 or check www.oldmissionsjb.org or www.san-juan-bautista.ca.us.

East of the church, perched at the edge of an abrupt drop created by the movement of the San Andreas Fault, is a marker pointing out the path of the old **El Camino Real.** Accompanying the marker are seismographic measuring equipment and an earthquake science exhibit.

In addition to the mission, there's much to see on the restored city plaza. Be sure to visit the **San Juan Bautista State Historic Park.** The park is comprised of not only the old Plaza Hotel with its frontier barroom and furnished rooms, but also the Plaza Hall, its adjoining stables and blacksmith shop, and the Castro House, where the Breen family lived after traveling here with the ill-fated Donner Party in 1846. Allow 1½ to 2 hours to see the entire plaza. Admission to the park buildings is $2 for adults, $1 for children ages 6 to 12 (separate from your charge to the mission). Hours are daily from 10am to 4:30pm. For further information (including event schedules), call © 831/623-4526.

2 Monterey ⟨★⟨★

45 miles S of Santa Cruz; 116 miles S of San Francisco; 335 miles N of Los Angeles

Settled in 1770, Monterey was one of the West Coast's first European outposts, and the capital of California under the Spanish, Mexican, and American flags. California's constitution was drafted here in 1849, paving the way for admission to the Union a year later. In fact, many buildings from the early colonial era still stand. A major whaling center in the 1800s, Monterey eventually became the sardine capital of the Western Hemisphere when the first packing plant was built in 1900. By 1913 the boats were bringing in 25 tons of sardines a night to the 18 canneries. The gritty lives of the mostly working-class residents were captured by local hero John Steinbeck in his 1945 novel *Cannery Row.*

After the sardines disappeared, Monterey was forced to fish for tourist dollars instead; hence, an array of boutiques, knickknack stores, and theme restaurants now reside in converted sardine factories along the bay. Granted, plenty of history and heritage remains along Cannery Row, but you'll have to weed through the tourist schlock to find them. Its saving grace is the world-class aquarium and beautiful Monterey Bay, where sea lions and otters still frolic in abundance.

As you distance yourself from the Row, however, you'll soon discover that Monterey is a pleasant seaside community, replete with magnificent vistas, historic architecture, stately Victorians, and a number of quality lodgings and restaurants. More important, Monterey is only a short drive from Pacific Grove, Carmel, Pebble Beach, and Big Sur, and the lodgings here are far less expensive, which makes it a great place to set up base while exploring the Monterey coast.

ESSENTIALS

GETTING THERE   The region's most convenient runway, at the **Monterey Peninsula Airport** (© **831/648-7000**), is 3 miles east of Monterey on Calif. 68. American Eagle, Northwest, United, and US Airways offer daily flights in and out of Monterey.

Many area hotels offer free airport shuttle service. If you take a taxi, it will cost about $10 to $15 to get to a peninsula hotel. Several national car-rental companies have airport locations, including **Dollar** (© **800/800-3665;** www.dollar.com) and **Hertz** (© **800/654-3131;** www.hertz.com).

VISITOR INFORMATION   The **Monterey Peninsula Visitors and Convention Bureau** (© **888/221-1010** or 831/649-1770; www.montereyinfo.org) has two visitor centers: one located in the lobby of the Maritime Museum at Custom House Plaza near Fisherman's Wharf, and the other at Lake El Estero on Camino El Estero. Both locations, open daily, offer an array of good maps, as well as free pamphlets and publications, including an excellent visitors' guide and the magazine *Coast Weekly.* Two other good sources for Monterey information are the **Monterey Peninsula On-Line Guide** at www.monterey.com and **Monterey-Carmel.com** (www.monterey-carmel.com).

GETTING AROUND   The **Waterfront Area Visitor Express (WAVE)** shuttle operates each year from Memorial Day weekend to Labor Day and takes passengers to and from the aquarium and other waterfront attractions. The free shuttle departs from the downtown parking garages at Tyler Street and Del Monte Avenue every 10 to 12 minutes and operates all day between 9am and 6pm. Other WAVE stops include many hotels and motels in Monterey and Pacific Grove, which eliminates the stress of parking in crowded downtown. For further information, call **Monterey Salinas Transit** at (C) **831/899-2555.**

WHAT TO SEE & DO

The **National Steinbeck Center** (%) is not in town, but if you're a fan of this unique American writer, you can make the 20-mile drive northeast from Monterey on Calif. 68 to 1 Main St. in Salinas ((C) **831/796-3833;** www.steinbeck.org). An $11-million, 37,000-square-foot museum, opened in 1998, it features walk-through interactive exhibits, a changing exhibition gallery, an orientation theater presenting a short video on Steinbeck's life, educational programs, a gift shop, and a cafe. Admission is $11 for adults, $8.95 for seniors over 62, $7.95 for children ages 13 to 17, $5.95 for children 6 to 12, and free for children under 6. Hours are daily from 10am to 5pm.

If you're traipsing through Monterey on a Tuesday afternoon, check out the **Old Monterey Marketplace** on Alvarado Street, from Pearl to Del Monte streets ((C) **831/655-8070;** www.oldmonterey.org), open from 4 to 8pm (until 7pm in winter). More than 100 vendors participate in this farmers market, bringing food, music, crafts, and entertainment together for an afternoon of festivities.

Cannery Row *(Overrated)*   Once the center for an industrial sardine-packing operation immortalized by John Steinbeck as "a poem, a stink, a grating noise, a quality of light, a tone, a habit, a nostalgia, a dream," this area today is better described as a strip congested with tourists, tacky gift shops, overpriced seafood restaurants, and an overall parking nightmare. What changed it so dramatically? The silver sardines suddenly disappeared from Monterey's waters in 1948 as a result of overfishing, changing currents, and pollution. Fishermen left, canneries closed, and the Row fell into disrepair. But curious tourists continued to visit Steinbeck's fabled area, and where there are tourists, there are capitalists.

After visiting Cannery Row in the 1960s, Steinbeck wrote, "The beaches are clean where they once festered with fish guts and flies. The canneries that once put up a sickening stench are gone, their places filled with restaurants, antique shops, and the like. They fish for tourists now, not pilchards, and that species they are not likely to wipe out." And I couldn't put it any better.

Between David and Drake aves. (C) 831/373-1902.

Fisherman's Wharf   Just like San Francisco's Fisherman's Wharf, this wooden pier is jam-packed with crafts and gift shops, boating and fishing operations, fish markets, and seafood restaurants—all trawling for tourist dollars. But Monterey's wharf does have redeeming qualities: The natural surroundings are so beautiful that if you cast your view toward the bobbing boats and surfacing sea lions, you might not even notice the hordes of tourists around you. Grab some clam chowder in a sourdough-bread bowl and find a seaside perch along the pier. Or, when the wind picks up, find a bay-front seat at one of the seafood restaurants (see "Where to Dine" later in this section).

If the seaside sights have got you itching to set sail, boats depart regularly from Fisherman's Wharf and will lead you on a number of ocean adventures. See "Outdoor Pursuits" below for details on some of the offerings.

99 Pacific St. (C) 831/649-6544.

The Monterey Peninsula

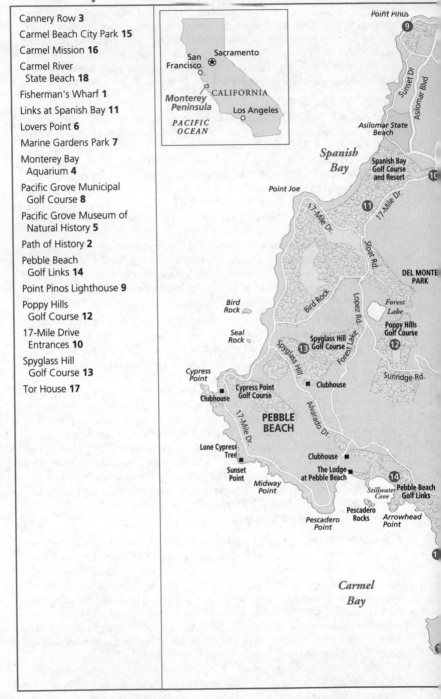

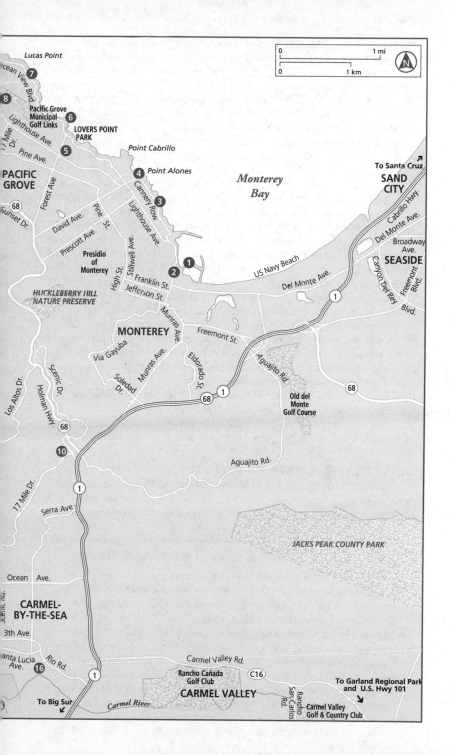

Lucas Point

7

8

Pacific Grove
Municipal
Golf Links **6**

LOVERS POINT
PARK

Lighthouse Ave.

5

Point Cabrillo

Pine Ave.

4 Point Alones

3

Canning Row

Monterey
Bay

To Santa Cruz

SAND
CITY

Cabrillo Hwy.

Del Monte Ave.

Broadway
Ave.

SEASIDE

Canyon Del Rey

Freemont Blvd.

Blvd.

PACIFIC
GROVE

68

Sunset Dr.

Forest Ave.

David Ave.

Pine St.

Prescott Ave.

Presidio
of
Monterey

HUCKLEBERRY HILL
NATURE PRESERVE

Stillwell Ave.

High St.

Lighthouse Ave.

Franklin St.

Jefferson St.

US Navy Beach

Del Monte Ave.

1

2 **1**

MONTEREY

Via Gayuba

Munras Ave.

Soledad
Dr.

Munras Ave.

Freemont St.

Eldorado St.

Aguajito Rd.

1

68 1

68

Old del
Monte
Golf Course

Los Altos Dr.

Scenic Dr.

Holman Hwy.

68

10

1

17 Mile Dr.

Serra Ave.

Aguajito Rd.

JACKS PEAK COUNTY PARK

Ocean Ave.

CARMEL-
BY-THE-SEA

3th Ave.

anta Lucia
Ave.

16

Rio Rd.

To Big Sur

Carmel River

1

Carmel Valley Rd.

Rancho Cañada
Golf Club

CARMEL VALLEY

C16

Rancho
San Carlos
Rd.

To Garland Regional Park
and U.S. Hwy 101

Carmel Valley
Golf & Country Club

Monterey Bay Aquarium ★★★ *Kids*   Attracting nearly two million visitors each year, the site of one of the world's most spectacular aquariums was not chosen at random. It sits on the border of one of the largest underwater canyons on earth (wider and deeper than the Grand Canyon) and is surrounded by incredibly diverse marine life. The Monterey Bay Aquarium is one of the best exhibit aquariums in the world, and one of the largest—home to more than 350,000 marine animals and plants. One of the main exhibits is a three-story, 335,000-gallon tank with clear acrylic walls that offers a stunning view of leopard sharks, sardines, anchovies, and other sea creatures swimming through a towering kelp forest. The outstanding Outer Bay exhibit features creatures that inhabit the open ocean. This tank—holding a million gallons of water—houses yellowfin tuna, large green sea turtles, barracuda, sharks, the very cool giant ocean sunfish, and schools of bonito. The Outer Bay's jellyfish exhibit is guaranteed to amaze, and kids will love Flippers, Flukes, and Fun, a learning area for families.

The newest exhibit is "Sharks: Myth and Mystery," which features nearly two dozen species of beautiful sharks and rays from around the world. The Splash Zone exhibit (designed for families with kids up to 9 years old) features daily programs and exhibits of black-footed penguins, invertebrates, and fish whose habitats are coral reefs and the cooler waters and rocky shores of Northern California. Additional exhibits re-create other undersea habitats found in Monterey Bay. Everyone falls in love with the sea otters playing in their two-story exhibit. There are also coastal streams, tidal pools, a sand beach, and a petting pool, where you can touch living bat rays and handle sea stars. Visitors can also watch a live video link that transmits from a deep-sea research submarine thousands of feet below the surface of Monterey Bay.

Tip: You can avoid lines at the gate by calling ℂ **800/756-3737** (or 831/648-4888 outside California) and ordering tickets in advance.

886 Cannery Row. ℂ **800/756-3737** or 831/648-4800. Fax 831/648-4810. www.montereybayaquarium.org. Admission $20 adults, $16 students, $18 seniors 65 and over, $8.95 visitors with disabilities and children 3–12, free for children under 3. AE, MC, V. Daily 10am–6pm.

FOLLOWING THE PATH OF HISTORY

The dozen or so historic buildings around Fisherman's Wharf and the adjacent town collectively comprise the "Path of History," a tour that examines 1800s architecture and lifestyle. Many of the buildings are a part of the **Monterey State**

Finds The Otters, Seals & Birds of the Elkhorn Slough

One of my favorite stops along the coast is Moss Landing, which is 25 minutes north of Monterey on Calif. 1. Along the one-street town are a few down-home restaurants and antiques shops. But what really attracts me is Captain Yohn Gideon's **Elkhorn Slough Safari**. For $26 for adults or $19 for children 3 to 14, friendly Cap'n Gideon loads guests onto a 27-foot pontoon boat (safe for old and young) and embarks on a 2-hour tour of the Elkhorn Slough Wildlife Reserve, which is like jumping into a *National Geographic* special. It's not uncommon to see a "raft" of up to 50 otters feet-up and sunning themselves, an abundance of harbor seals, and hundreds of species of waterfowl and migratory shorebirds. An onboard naturalist answers questions, Cap'n Gideon educates on the surroundings, and binoculars are available. For reservations and information, call ℂ **831/633-5555** or check out www.elkhornslough.com.

Historic Park ⚲, 20 Custom House Plaza (© **831/649-7118**). Highlights include the **Custom House,** built around 1827 and the oldest government building in California, and the **Maritime Museum of Monterey,** 5 Custom House Plaza (© **831/372-2608**), which showcases ship models and other collections that relate the area's seafaring history, including a two-story-high, 10,000-pound Fresnel lens, used for nearly 80 years at the Point Sur lighthouse. Admission is $5 for adults, $2.50 for seniors and children ages 13 to 18, and free for children 12 and under; it's open Tuesday through Sunday from 11am to 5pm.

You can go the self-guided route by picking up a free tour booklet at the Monterey Peninsula Visitors and Convention Bureau (see above), the Cooper-Molera Adobe (at the corner of Polk and Munras sts.), and various other locations. You may also opt to take the free guided tour, which departs several times daily. Call © **831/649-7118** for exact schedule information, or visit the **State Park Visitor Center** at Stanton Center, 5 Custom House Plaza. A free film on the history of Monterey is shown here every 20 minutes.

MONTEREY WINE COUNTRY

The congestion and price of Napa and Sonoma vineyards and the increasingly lucrative and romantic occupation of winemaking have forced newcomers to plant their grapes elsewhere. Fortunately, much of the California coast offers perfect growing conditions. Nowadays, if you visit any area between Monterey and Santa Barbara, there's easy access to new appellations and a variety of boutique vintners making respectable wines. Stop by **A Taste of Monterey,** 700 Cannery Row (© **831/646-5446;** www.tastemonterey.com), daily between 11am and 6pm to learn about and taste local wines in front of huge bay-front windows. This is also the place to get a map and winery touring information.

OUTDOOR PURSUITS

Along with excellent scuba diving, the waters off Monterey are teeming with game fish. Among the public fishing boats are **Chris' Fishing Trips,** 48 Fisherman's Wharf (© **831/375-5951;** www.chrissfishing.com), which offers party boats. Cod and salmon are the main catches, with separate boats leaving daily. Call or log on to the website for a price list and departure schedule. Check-in is 45 minutes prior to departure, and equipment rental costs a bit extra.

Several outfitters rent kayaks for a spin around the bay. Contact **Monterey Bay Kayaks,** 693 Del Monte Ave. (© **800/649-5357** or 831/373-5357; www.montereykayaks.com), on Del Monte Beach north of Fisherman's Wharf, which offers instruction as well as natural-history tours that introduce visitors to the Monterey Bay National Marine Sanctuary and nearby Elkhorn Slough, one of the last remaining estuaries in California (see "The Otters, Seals & Birds of the Elkhorn Slough" on p. 366). Prices start at $55 for the tours, from $30 for rentals.

For bikes and in-line skates, as well as kayak tours and rentals, contact **Adventures by the Sea,** 299 Cannery Row (© **831/372-1807;** www.adventuresbythesea.com). Bikes cost $6 per hour or $24 per day; kayaks are $30 per person or $50 for a 2½-hour tour; and skates are $12 for 2 hours, $24 for a day. Adventures by the Sea also has another location at 201 Alvarado Mall (© **831/648-7235**), at the Doubletree Hotel.

Experienced scuba divers can contact **Monterey Bay Dive Center,** 225 Cannery Row (© **800/60-SCUBA** or 831/656-0454; www.mbdc.to), which arranges personal dives with a dive master and has scheduled weekend dives. **Aquarius Dive Shop,** 2040 Del Monte Ave. (© **831/375-1933;** www.aquariusdivers.com), also has regularly scheduled trips and dive masters. Certification cards are required.

If the kids need to let off some steam, take them to the **Dennis the Menace Playground** 𝄞 at Camino El Estero and Del Monte Avenue, near Lake Estero (© **831/646-3860**), an old-fashioned playground created by Pacific Grove resident and cartoonist Hank Ketcham. It has bridges, tunnels, and an authentic Southern Pacific Railroad engine teeming with wannabe conductors. There's also a hot-dog-and-burger stand, and a big lake where you can rent paddleboats or feed the ducks. The park is open daily from 10am to sunset.

WHERE TO STAY

There are three types of accommodations in Monterey: lace-and-flowers B&Bs, large corporate hotels with only a slight beachy feel (if even that), or run-of-the-mill motel digs. Consider which area you'd like to be in—beach, Cannery Row, wharf, secluded, central, and so forth—as well as how much you want to spend, then check out the options below or contact these two reservations services: **Resort 2 Me** (© **800/757-5646;** www.resort2me.com), a local reservations service that offers free recommendations of Monterey Bay–area hotels in all price ranges; and **Monterey Land and See** (© **877/MONTEREY**), which represents numerous lodging facilities in Monterey, Carmel, and Pacific Grove.

EXPENSIVE

In addition to the choices below, there are two chain hotels near Fisherman's Wharf: The **Monterey Marriott,** 350 Calle Principal, at Del Monte Boulevard (© **800/228-9290** or 831/649-4234; www.marriott.com), offers some rooms with bay views, an outdoor pool, health club, Jacuzzi, and saunas. There's also the **Doubletree Hotel at Fisherman's Wharf,** 2 Portola Plaza (© **800/222-8733** or 831/649-4511; www.doubletree.com). Less centrally located but great for families and golfers is the **Hyatt Regency Monterey** resort, 1 Old Golf Course Rd. (© **800/233-1234** or 831/372-1234; www.hyatt.com). It adjoins the Del Monte Golf Course and has three pools, two Jacuzzis, a gym, tennis courts, and two restaurants. These are popular with business travelers and conventioneers.

Hotel Pacific 𝄞𝄞 Although the Hotel Pacific isn't even remotely waterfront (it's close to the wharf and across the street from the Monterey Conference Center), it's still my favorite upscale choice in Monterey. Beyond the Spanish-Mediterranean architecture of the common areas, each unit is in 1 of 16 buildings clustered around courtyards and compact gardens complete with spas and fountains. The junior suites have down comforters atop four-poster feather beds (for the full effect, request a canopied bed), stylish Southwestern decor, terra-cotta-tiled floors, fireplaces surrounded by cushy couches and seats, and private patios or terraces overlooking the gardens. *Tip:* Ask for a room on the fourth level with a panoramic view of the bay.

300 Pacific St., Monterey, CA 93940. © 800/554-5542 or 831/373-5700. Fax 831/373-6921. www.hotel pacific.com. 105 suites. $229–$409 suite for 2. Rates include continental breakfast and afternoon tea. AE, DC, DISC, MC, V. **Amenities:** Nearby golf course; 2 Jacuzzis; room service; in-room massage; laundry service; same-day dry cleaning. *In room:* TV/VCR, dataport, minibar, coffeemaker, hair dryer, iron.

Monterey Plaza Hotel and Spa 𝄞𝄞 One of the most formal hotels in town, the Monterey Plaza is comprised of three buildings—two on the water and one across the street—that are connected by a second-story enclosed "skywalk." The public areas are elegantly decorated with marble, Brazilian teak, and attractive artwork. The bedrooms are more upscale-corporate than most around town and have double or king beds, decor reminiscent of 19th-century Biedermeier, and Italian marble bathrooms. Many have balconies overlooking the water (sea otters included in the view). The least desirable rooms are across the street from the ocean. There's also a 11,000-square-foot European-style spa, the **Duck Club Restaurant** serving American regional cuisine at a romantic seaside setting, and the adjacent **Schooner's Bistro,** which serves lighter fare.

400 Cannery Row, Monterey, CA 93940. ℂ 800/334-3999 in California, 800/631-1339 outside of California, or 831/646-1700. Fax 831/646-5937. www.woodsidehotels.com. 290 units. $185–$505 double; $510–$2,500 suite. Children 17 and under stay free in parent's room. Packages available. AE, DC, DISC, MC, V. Parking $14 per day. From Calif. 1, take the Soledad Dr. exit and follow the signs to Cannery Row. **Amenities:** 2 restaurants; nearby golf course; full fitness center; full-service European-style spa; Jacuzzi; dry sauna; concierge; tour desk; business center; secretarial services; shopping arcade; 24-hr. room service; in-room massage; laundry service; same-day dry cleaning; executive-level rooms. *In room:* TV w/pay movies, dataport, fully stocked minibar, fridge, coffeemaker, hair dryer, iron.

Old Monterey Inn ✦✦   Proprietors Ann and Gene Swett did a masterful job of converting their three-story family home into a vine-covered Tudor-style country inn. Although it's away from the surf, it's a perfect choice for romantics, with rose gardens, a bubbling brook, and brick-and-flagstone walkways shaded by a panoply of oaks. All but one guest room enjoy garden views and cozy beds with goose-down comforters and pillows. Most units also have feather beds and wood burning fireplaces, and two open onto private patios. The guest rooms are all charmingly furnished and unique; two of my favorites are the Library and the Serengeti Room. Special touches are evident, including fresh fruit, flowers, and candies, sachets by the pillow, and books and magazines. The private cottage out back has an English country look and comes with a double Jacuzzi, linen-and-lace-draped king-size bed, wood-burning fireplace, sitting area, and private patio.

Breakfast, prepared by Gene, is stellar, consisting of perhaps orange French toast, soufflé, or Belgian waffles. It's served in your room, the dining room, or the rose garden. The Swetts will also provide blankets and towels for the beach. At 5pm, guests retire to the living room for wine and hors d'oeuvres in front of a blazing fire.

500 Martin St. (off Pacific Ave.), Monterey, CA 93940. ℂ 800/350-2344 or 831/375-8284. Fax 831/375-6730. www.oldmontereyinn.com. 9 units, 1 cottage. $240–$390 double; from $450 cottage. Rates include full breakfast and evening wine and hors d'oeuvres. MC, V. Free parking. From Calif. 1, take the Soledad Dr. exit and turn right onto Pacific Ave., then left onto Martin St. **Amenities:** Nearby golf course; passes to nearby health club; Jacuzzi; concierge; tour desk; in-room massage. *In room:* TV/VCR, dataport, hair dryer, iron.

Spindrift Inn ✦   Down in the middle of honky-tonk Cannery Row, along a narrow stretch of beach, this four-story hotel is an island of Continental style in a sea of commercialism. It's elegant and well-maintained, and the rooms are decorated with feather beds (a few with canopies), hardwood floors, wood-burning fireplaces, and cushioned window seats or private balconies. The bathrooms are adorned with marble and brass fixtures. Extras include terry robes and two phones. The ocean views are worth the additional cost, particularly from one of the corner rooms with their cushioned window seats and breathtaking ocean views.

652 Cannery Row, Monterey, CA 93940. ℂ 800/841-1879 or 831/646-8900. Fax 831/646-5342. www.spindriftinn.com. 42 units. $199–$329 double with Cannery Row view; $329–$459 double with ocean view. Rates include continental breakfast delivered to your room and afternoon wine and cheese. AE, DC, DISC, MC, V. Parking $14. **Amenities:** 2 restaurants; bar; nearby golf course; room service; in-room massage; same-day dry cleaning. *In room:* TV/VCR, fully stocked minibar, hair dryer.

MODERATE

Munras Avenue and northern Fremont Avenue are lined with moderate and inexpensive family-style motels, some independently owned and some chains. They're not as central as the downtown options, and atmosphere is seriously lacking on Fremont Avenue, but if transportation's not an issue, you can save a bundle by staying in one of these areas. If the selections below are full, try calling **Best Western** (© 800/528-1234) for several other options. There's also the **Cypress Gardens Inn,** 1150 Munras Ave. (© 831/373-2761), with a pool, Jacuzzi, free movie channels, and continental breakfast; dogs are welcome.

Casa Munras Garden Hotel Casa Munras was built around the original hacienda of Don Esteban Munras, the last Spanish diplomat to California. Accommodations are scattered among 11 one- and two-story buildings along the 4.5-acre landscaped property. Each is decorated with an armoire, comfy furnishings, and sweet window shutters. All guests have access to the outdoor pool, and there's an on-site restaurant called the **Casa Café & Bar** that's a good place to have breakfast. *Tip:* Spend a few extra bucks and get a room with a gas fireplace—it gets chilly at night in Monterey.

700 Munras Ave., Monterey, CA 93940. © 800/222-2558 in the U.S. except California, 800/222-2446 in California, or 831/375-2411. Fax 831/375-1365. www.casamunras-hotel.com. 166 units. $139–$209 double. AAA and entertainment discounts available. AE, DC, MC, V. **Amenities:** Outdoor pool; access to nearby health club. *In room:* TV, dataport, iron.

The Jabberwock Bed & Breakfast 🐸 One of the better B&Bs in the area, the Jabberwock (named after a poem in Lewis Carroll's *Through the Looking Glass*) is 4 blocks from Cannery Row. Although centrally located, the property is tranquil, and its half-acre garden with waterfalls offers a welcome respite from the downtown crowds. The seven rooms are individually furnished, some more elegantly than others; all have goose-down comforters and pillows, and three are outfitted with Jacuzzi tubs for two, fireplaces, and king beds. The Toves Room has a huge walnut Victorian bed, the Borogrove has a fireplace and a view of Monterey Bay, the Mimsey has a fine ocean view from its window seat, and the Wabe has an Austrian carved bed. A full breakfast is served in the dining room or in your room. Evening hors d'oeuvres are offered on the veranda, and a Vorpal rabbit tucks each guest in with cookies and milk.

598 Laine St., Monterey, CA 93940. © 888/428-7253 or 831/372-4777. Fax 831/655-2946. www.jabberwockinn.com. 7 units, 5 with bathroom. $115 double without private bathroom; $155–$265 double with private bathroom. Rates include full breakfast, afternoon aperitifs, and bedtime cookies. MC, V. **Amenities:** Nearby golf course; Jacuzzi; concierge; activities desk; in-room massage. *In room:* Hair dryer, no phone.

Monterey Fireside Lodge Location is the primary advantage of this newly remodeled hotel near Fisherman's Wharf and downtown. The room furnishings are relatively standard but make an attempt at coziness with wicker chairs set around the gas-heated brick fireplace. Families on a budget will appreciate the kitchen facilities, plus the continental breakfast served daily in the hotel's lobby will ease the food bill, too.

1131 10th St., Monterey, CA 93940. © 800/722-2624 in California, or 831/373-4172. Fax 831/655-5640. www.montereyfireside.com. 24 units. $69–$399 double. Rates include continental breakfast. AE, DC, DISC, MC, V. Pets accepted with $10 (under 20 lb.) or $20 (over 20 lb.) fee. **Amenities:** Nearby golf course; Jacuzzi. *In room:* TV, dataport, kitchenette, fridge.

INEXPENSIVE

Opt for a motel to get the best rates in town. Some reliable options are **Motel 6** (© 800/4-MOTEL6), **Super 8** (© 800/800-8000), and **Best Western** (© 800/528-1234).

Cypress Tree Inn *Value* Although it's 2 miles from downtown, if you're on a budget and have transportation, you won't be sorry if you stay here. The staff is friendly, the large rooms are spotless, and all but one has a combination tub/shower. Nine rooms even have Jacuzzis. There are no designer soaps or other in-room treats (other than the taffy left by the maid), but the hostelry does have a handy coin-op laundry. RV spaces are also available.

2227 N. Fremont St., Monterey, CA 93940. ℂ 800/446-8303 or 831/372-7586. Fax 831/372-2940. www.cypresstreeinn.com. 55 units. $52–$129 double. Rates include continental breakfast. AE, DC, DISC, MC, V. **Amenities:** Nearby golf course; Jacuzzi; sauna; coin-op laundry. *In room:* TV, dataport, kitchen or kitchenette in some units, fridge, hair dryer, iron.

WHERE TO DINE

Bubba Gump Shrimp Co. Restaurant & Market *(Overrated* AMERICAN Culinary cognoscenti will flee at the sight of this tourist haven, but the fact is, lots of folks love this place. It could be the location—near the aquarium and offering a million-dollar unobstructed bay-front view—or the old boatyard decor that attracts visitors in droves. But it's more likely the entertainment value: Gump's (as in *Forrest Gump*) is packed with movie gimmicks and memorabilia. The food is far less exciting. As the roll of paper towels at each table suggests, you're guaranteed a go with grease, likely to arrive in the form of fried and buttered-up seafood. The "Bucket of Boat Trash," for example, is shrimp and lobster tails cooked and served in a bucket with a side of fries and coleslaw. There are also pork chops, a veggie dish, salads, and burgers. The "market" referred to in the moniker is a gift shop packed with T-shirts, caps, and, of course, boxes of chocolate.

720 Cannery Row (at Prescott). ℂ **831/373-1884.** Fax 831/373-1139. www.bubbagump.com. Main courses $7.95–$25. AE, DC, DISC, MC, V. Sun–Thurs 11am–10pm; Fri–Sat 11am–11pm.

Cafe Fina ℛ ITALIAN/SEAFOOD While other pier-side restaurants lure tourists with little more than a sea view, Cafe Fina's mesquite-grilled meats, well-prepared fresh fish, brick-oven pizzas, and an array of delicious salads and pastas give even locals a reason to head here. Hidden behind the facade of a to-go pizza counter, the specialties at this little jewel are the seafood and pasta dishes, but anything that comes out of the wood broiler or wood-fired brick oven is a winner. Be sure to request a table by the back window to watch the sea otters and sea lions playing in the kelp.

47 Fisherman's Wharf. ℂ **831/372-5200.** Fax 831/3725209. www.cafefina.com. Reservations recommended. Main courses $14–$19. AE, DC, DISC, MC, V. Mon–Fri 11:30am–2:30pm; Sat–Sun 11:30am–3pm; daily 5–9:30pm.

Montrio ℛℛ AMERICAN BISTRO Big-city sophistication meets old Monterey at this converted 1910 firehouse. The enormous dining room is the sharpest in town, a playfully chic expanse with clouds hanging from the ceiling and curvaceous walls. Anything cooked in the open kitchen's oak-fired rotisserie grill is what you want to order, such as the crispy Dungeness crab cakes with spicy rémoulade; succulent grilled pork chops with apple, pear, and currant

---

Tips Monterey's Best Seafood Buffet

Even if I had all the money in the world (and I don't), I'd still have lunch the same way every day in Monterey. I'd walk down **Old Fisherman's Wharf** and snack on all those small cups of fresh seafood offered at the numerous faux fish markets. Priced at a couple of bucks each, I can dine alfresco on fresh mussels, octopus, shrimp, crab, oysters, ceviche, and clam chowder for a fraction of what I'd pay at a sit-down restaurant. You can either dine on foot as you head down the wharf, or make a picnic of it by carting your cups to the benches at the end of the pier (just to the left of Rappa's restaurant).

compote; or a roasted portobello mushroom with polenta and ragout of vegeta bles. The wine list, which received *Wine Spectator* magazine's Award of Excellence, includes numerous vintages by the glass. Finish the evening with the white nectarine pecan crisp with vanilla-bean ice cream.

414 Calle Principal (at Franklin). ℂ 831/648-8880. www.montrio.com. Reservations recommended. Main courses $12–$25. AE, DISC, MC, V. Sun–Thurs 5–10pm; Fri–Sat 5–11pm.

Rosine's *Value* AMERICAN

Everything served at Rosine's is mighty filling and fairly priced, which explains why this local favorite is always busy. Aside from the large, airy window seats, the place has an upscale cafeteria feel, but its menu, filled with standard entrees, aims to please all tastes. Lunch features an extensive list of salads and sandwiches, and dinner offers an array of pastas, burgers, and more expensive items such as charbroiled pork chops with applesauce and mashed potatoes ($15) and prime rib ($17, Fri–Sat only). Other than steak and seafood, most entrees hover around $8 and include side salads and/or potatoes. Sugar fiends will appreciate the huge cakes behind glass as you walk in the front door (yes, you can buy them by the slice).

434 Alvarado St. (at Franklin St.). ℂ 831/375-1400. www.rosinesmonterey.com. Breakfast $3.50–$8.25; lunch $5.50–$7.95; most dinner dishes $5.75–$8.50. AE, DC, DISC, MC, V. Sun–Thurs 8am–9pm; Fri–Sat 8am–10pm; Sun 8am–9pm.

Stokes Restaurant and Bar *★★* CALIFORNIA/MEDITERRANEAN

This historic adobe and board-and-batten house, built in 1833 for the town doctor, has been converted into one of Monterey's finest restaurants. It's a handsome establishment, consisting of a bar and several large dining rooms, all outfitted with terra-cotta floors, bleached-wood-plank ceilings, and Southwestern-style wood chairs and tables. It's the perfect rustic-yet-contemporary showcase for chef Brandon Miller's California-Mediterranean fare: butternut squash soup with apple cider and maple crème fraîche; cassoulet of duck confit and homemade currant sausage with chestnut beans. Everything from Miller's wood-burning oven—chicken, fish, pizza, clams—is recommended. Desserts are dreamy, and the wine list is excellent.

500 Hartnell St. (at Madison St.). ℂ 831/373-1110. Fax 831/373-1202. www.stokesrestaurant.com. Reservations recommended. Main courses $12–$23. AE, DC, DISC, MC, V. Mon–Thurs 11:30am–10pm; Fri–Sat 11:30am–10:30pm; Sun 4–10pm.

Tarpy's Roadhouse *★★* AMERICAN

A mandatory stop when I'm passing through Monterey is this lively Southwestern-style restaurant a few miles east of downtown (worth the detour). The handsome dining room has stylish yet soothingly rustic decor. On sunny afternoons, patrons relax under market umbrellas on the outdoor patio, sipping margaritas and munching on Tarpy's legendary Caesar salad. Come nightfall, the place fills with tourists and locals who pile in for the hefty plate of bourbon-molasses pork chops or Dijon-crusted lamb loin. There's also a modest selection of fresh fish, shellfish, and vegetable dishes, but it's the good ol' meat 'n' potato mainstays that sell the best. (The juicy meatloaf with garlic mashers and fresh veggies is a bargain at $13.)

2999 Monterey-Salinas Hwy. (at Calif. 68 and Canyon del Rey near the Monterey Airport). ℂ 831/647-1444. Fax 831/647-1103. www.tarpys.com. Reservations recommended for dinner. Most main courses $14–$30. AE, DISC, MC, V. Daily 11:30am–10pm.

Wharfside Restaurant & Lounge SEAFOOD

While the fresh seafood is okay, the real attraction is the Wharfside's casual upstairs dining room, which offers a nautical decor and a great view from the end of Fisherman's Wharf (there's also downstairs and upper-deck outdoor seating). Choose from six varieties of ravioli (made on the premises), such specialties as a combination bouillabaisse, and any of the house-made desserts. Daily specials usually include fresh seasonal fish, beef, and pasta. Clam chowder, sandwiches (including hot crab), and pizzas are on the regular menu.

60 Fisherman's Wharf, Monterey. (C) 831/375-3956. Fax 831/375-2967. www.wharfsiderestaurant.com. Reservations recommended. Main courses $11–$20. AE, DC, DISC, MC, V. Daily 11am–10pm. Closed Dec 1–10.

3 Pacific Grove ⟨★⟨★

42 miles S of Santa Cruz; 113 miles S of San Francisco; 338 miles N of Los Angeles

Some compare 2½-square-mile Pacific Grove—the locals call it "PG"—to Carmel as it was 20 years ago. Although tourists wind their way through here on oceanfront trails and dining excursions, the town remains quaint and peaceful—amazing considering that Monterey is a stone's throw away (a quarter of the Monterey Bay Aquarium is actually in Pacific Grove). While neighboring Monterey is comparatively congested and cosmopolitan, Pacific Grove is a community sprinkled with historic homes, flowers, and the kind of tranquillity that inspires butterflies to flutter about and deer to meander fearlessly across the road in search of another garden to graze.

ESSENTIALS

VISITOR INFORMATION   Although the town is small, there is a **Pacific Grove Chamber of Commerce,** at the corner of Forest and Central avenues (© **800/656-6650** or 831/373-3304; www.pacificgrove.org).

ORIENTATION   Lighthouse Avenue is the Grove's principal thoroughfare, running from Monterey to the lighthouse at the point of the peninsula. Lighthouse Avenue is bisected by Forest Avenue, which runs from Calif. 1 (where it's called Holman Hwy., or Calif. 68) to Lover's Point, an extension of land that sticks out into the bay in the middle of Pacific Grove.

WHAT TO SEE & DO

Pacific Grove is a town to be strolled, so park the car, put on your walking shoes, and make an afternoon of it. Meander around George Washington Park and along the waterfront around the point.

The **Point Pinos Lighthouse** ★, at the tip of the peninsula on Ocean View Boulevard (© **831/648-5716**), is the oldest working lighthouse on the West Coast. Its 50,000-candlepower beacon has illuminated the rocky shores since 1855, when Pacific Grove was little more than a pine forest. The museum and grounds are open, free to visitors, Thursday through Sunday from 1 to 4pm.

Marine Gardens Park ★, a stretch of shoreline along Ocean View Boulevard on Monterey Bay and the Pacific, is renowned not only for its ocean views and colorful flowers, but also for its tide-pool seaweed beds. Walk out to **Lover's Point** (named after Lovers of Jesus, not groping teenagers) and watch the sea otters playing in the kelp beds and cracking open an occasional abalone.

An excellent shorter alternative, or complement, to the 17-Mile Drive (see "Pebble Beach & the 17-Mile Drive" below) is the scenic drive or bike ride along Pacific Grove's **Ocean View Boulevard** ★. This coastal stretch starts near Monterey's Cannery Row and follows the Pacific around to the lighthouse point. Here it turns into Sunset Drive, which runs along secluded **Asilomar State Beach** ★ (© **831/648-3130**). Park on Sunset and explore the trails, dunes, and tide pools of this sandy stretch of shore. You might find purple shore crabs, green anemone, sea bats, starfish, and limpets, as well as all kinds of kelp and algae. The 11 buildings of the conference center established here by the YWCA in 1913 are landmarks that were designed by noted architect Julia Morgan. If you follow this route during winter, a furious sea rages and crashes against the rocks.

To learn more about the marine and other natural life of the region, stop in at the **Pacific Grove Museum of Natural History,** 165 Forest Ave. (© **831/648-5716;** www.pgmuseum.org). It has displays on monarch butterflies and their migration, stuffed examples of the local birds and mammals, and temporary exhibits and special events. Admission is free; hours are Tuesday through Sunday from 10am to 5pm.

Pacific Grove is widely known as "Butterfly Town, USA," a reference to the thousands of **monarch butterflies** that migrate here from November to February, traveling from as far away as Alaska. Many settle in the Monarch Grove sanctuary, a eucalyptus stand on Grove Acre Avenue off Lighthouse Avenue. George Washington Park, at Pine Avenue and Alder Street, is also famous for its "butterfly trees." To reach these sites, the butterflies may travel as far as 2,000 miles, covering 100 miles a day at an altitude of 10,000 feet. Collectors beware: The town imposes strict fines for disturbing the butterflies.

Just as Ocean View Boulevard serves as an alternative to the 17-Mile Drive, the **Pacific Grove Municipal Golf Course,** 77 Asilomar Ave. (© **831/648-5777**), serves as a reasonable alternative to the high-priced courses at Pebble Beach. The back 9 of this 5,500-yard, par-70 course overlooks the sea and offers the added challenge of coping with the winds. Views are panoramic, and the fairways and greens are better maintained than most semiprivate courses. There's a restaurant, pro shop, and driving range. Eighteen holes start at $32 Monday through Thursday and $38 Friday through Sunday and holidays; twilight rates are available. Optional carts cost $28.

The **American Tin Cannery Factory Premium Outlets,** 125 Ocean View Blvd., around the corner from the Monterey Bay Aquarium (© **831/372-1442;** www.premiumoutlets.com), is a converted warehouse housing 40 factory-outlet shops, including Bass Shoes, OshKosh B'Gosh, Samsonite, and Izod. It's open Monday through Saturday from 10am to 7pm, Sunday from 10am to 6pm.

WHERE TO STAY

If you're having trouble finding a vacancy, try calling **Resort 2 Me** (© **800/ 757-5646;** www.resort2me.com), a local reservations service that offers free recommendations of Monterey Bay–area hotels in all price ranges.

EXPENSIVE

Martine Inn ⓖⓖ   One glance at the lavish Victorian interior and the bay views and you'll know why this Mediterranean-style inn is one of the best B&Bs in the area. Built in 1899 for James and Laura Parke (of Parke-Davis Pharmaceuticals fame), each room has a view of the ocean or the garden courtyard; most have wood-burning fireplaces. Request a room with a bathtub if it matters to you; some have only a shower. The inn also maintains an adjacent Victorian cottage, which has been converted into a luxury suite. A full breakfast is served at lace-covered tables in the front room; hors d'oeuvres are served in the evening. Guests also have access to two additional common rooms: a room downstairs overlooking the ocean and a larger room with shelves of books.

255 Ocean View Blvd., Pacific Grove, CA 93950. (© **800/852-5588** or 831/373-3388. Fax 831/373-3896. www.martineinn.com. 24 units. $170–$300 double. Rates include full breakfast and evening hors d'oeuvres. AE, DISC, MC, V. **Amenities:** Nearby golf course; Jacuzzi; game room; concierge; tour desk; room service; in-room massage; babysitting. *In room:* Fridge, hair dryer.

Seven Gables Inn ★★★ This is one of the most opulent B&Bs I've ever seen. Named after the seven gables that cap the inn, the compound of Victorian buildings was built in 1886 by the Chase family (as in Chase Manhattan Bank). Outside is the coast road overlooking the sea; inside is a collection of mostly European antiques. Everything here is luxurious and gilded, including the oceanview rooms, which are scattered among the main house, cottages (including a two-bedroom option), and the guesthouse. The accommodations are linked by gardens filled with roses and marble sculpture. If the hotel's booked, ask about the Grand View Inn, a slightly less ornate but comparable B&B next door that's run by the same owners.

555 Ocean View Blvd., Pacific Grove, CA 93950. ② 831/372-4341. www.pginns.com. 14 units. $175–$385 double. Rates include breakfast and afternoon tea. 2-night minimum on weekends. MC, V. **Amenities:** Nearby golf course. *In room:* Kitchenette in 1 unit, fridge in some units, hair dryer, no phone.

MODERATE

Butterfly Grove Inn (Kids) Despite the name, this place is more like a motor lodge than an inn. Located right at the very tip of the Monterey Peninsula, accommodations here are run-of-the-mill, but the amenities are not; some rooms come with refrigerators, kitchenettes, Jacuzzi tubs, and/or fireplaces, and guests have access to the property's pool, spa, Jacuzzi, and shuffleboard, croquet, and volleyball courts. Folks traveling with the family should opt for one of the six family units tucked into a Victorian house. The hotel is located in one of the quieter parts of Pacific Grove, so just meander out your door and you're likely to see a soiree of butterflies (during winter), who migrate here each year, as well as deer who frequently wander the streets.

1073 Lighthouse Ave., Pacific Grove, CA 93950. ② 800/337-9244 or 831/373-4921. Fax 831/373-7596. www.butterflygroveinn.com. 31 units. Summer $99–$299 double; winter $79–$249 double. Children under 18 stay free in parent's room. AE, DISC, MC, V. **Amenities:** Outdoor pool; Jacuzzi. *In room:* TV/VCR, dataport, fridge, microwave, coffeemaker, hair dryer, iron.

Centrella Inn ★ A couple blocks from the waterfront and from Lover's Point Beach, the two-story Centrella is a turreted Victorian built as a boardinghouse in 1889. Today the rooms are decorated in Victorian style, but they're somewhat plain—iron beds, side table, floor lamp, and armoire—although the bathrooms do have claw-foot tubs. In the back, connected to the house by walkways, are several cottages and suites with fireplaces, and separate bedrooms and bathrooms. Two have private decks; the others offer decks facing the rose garden and patio, which is set with umbrella tables and chairs.

612 Central Ave., Pacific Grove, CA 93950. ② 800/233-3372 or 831/372-3372. Fax 831/372-2036. www.centrellainn.com. 26 units. $119–$249 double; $189–$300 suites and cottages. Rates include buffet breakfast and evening hors d'oeuvres. AE, DISC, MC, V. **Amenities:** Nearby golf course. *In room:* TV in cottages, fridge, hair dryer, iron.

Gosby House ★ Originally a boardinghouse for Methodist ministers, this Victorian was built in 1888, 3 blocks from the bay. It's still one of the most charming Victorians in town, with individually decorated rooms, floral-print wallpapers, lacy pillows, and antique furnishings. Twelve guest rooms have fireplaces, and all come with the inn's trademark teddy bears. Especially noteworthy are the two Carriage House rooms, which come with TV/VCR, a fridge and coffeemaker, fireplace, balcony, and bathroom with spa tub. The house has a separate dining room and parlor, where guests gather for breakfast and complimentary wine and hors d'oeuvres in the afternoon. Other amenities include complimentary newspaper, twice-daily maid service, and bicycles.

643 Lighthouse Ave., Pacific Grove, CA 93950. ℂ 800/527-8828 or 831/375-1287. Fax 831/655-9621. www.foursisters.com. 22 units, 20 with bathroom. $115 double without bathroom; $95–$170 double with bathroom. Rates include full breakfast and afternoon wine and hors d'oeuvres. AE, DC, MC, V. From Calif. 1, take Calif. 68 to Pacific Grove, where it turns into Forest Ave.; continue on Forest to Lighthouse Ave., turn left, and go 3 blocks. **Amenities:** Nearby golf course; complimentary bike use. *In room:* Hair dryer.

Green Gables Inn ⚶ This 1888 Queen Anne–style mansion, decorated like an English country inn, forgoes opulence (and in some cases private bathrooms) to allow for reasonable rates and less formal accommodations. The rooms are divided between the main building and the carriage houses behind it. The Carriage House rooms, which are better for families, have large private bathrooms with Jacuzzi tubs. All accommodations are individually decorated with period furnishings, including some antiques and an occasional poster bed. Most rooms in the original home have ocean views and share two immaculate bathrooms. There's an antique carousel horse in the comfortable parlor, where complimentary wine, tea, and hors d'oeuvres are served each afternoon.

301 Ocean View Blvd., Pacific Grove, CA 93950. ℂ 800/722-1774 or 831/375-2095. Fax 831/375-5437. www.foursisters.com. 11 units, 7 with bathroom. $120–$155 double without bathroom; $170–$200 double with bathroom; $200–$260 suite. Rates include full breakfast and afternoon wine and hors d'oeuvres. AE, MC, V. From Calif. 1, take the Pacific Grove exit (Calif. 68) and continue to the Pacific Ocean; turn right on Ocean View Blvd. and drive ½ mile to Fifth St. **Amenities:** Complimentary bike use. *In room:* Iron.

Pacific Grove Inn Five blocks from the beach, this 1904 Queen Anne–style mansion is one of the town's bevy of painted ladies. Despite heavy Victorian embellishments, the accommodations feel light and airy. Rooms come with fireplaces and queen- or king-size beds. Afternoon tea is served in the parlor.

581 Pine Ave., Pacific Grove, CA 93950. ℂ 800/732-2825 or 831/375-2825. Fax 831/375-0752. www.paci ficgrove-inn.com. 16 units. $99–$239 double; $119–$279 suite. Rates include buffet breakfast and afternoon tea. AE, DC, DISC, MC, V. From Calif. 1, take the Pacific Grove exit (Calif. 68) to the corner of Pine and Forest aves. **Amenities:** Nearby golf course. *In room:* TV/VCR, fridge, safe.

INEXPENSIVE

The Wilkies Inn *(Value)* This motel consistently charges less than the other hotels in town, gets an A+ for service, and is on a tree-lined street with a resident deer who often drops by for breakfast. The motel boasts well-kept furnishings and carpets, and stylish bedspreads. All the squeaky-clean rooms come with free HBO and local calls; some have partial ocean views. Putting up with occasionally noisy plumbing and thin walls might be worth the money saved.

1038 Lighthouse Ave., Pacific Grove, CA 93950. ℂ 866/372-5960 or 831/372-5960. Fax 831/655-1681. 24 units. $49–$210 double. Extra person $10. 2-night minimum on weekends. Rates include continental breakfast. Packages available. AE, DISC, MC, V. **Amenities:** Nearby golf course. *In room:* TV/VCR, dataport, coffeemaker, hair dryer, iron.

WHERE TO DINE
EXPENSIVE

Fandango ⚶⚶ MEDITERRANEAN Provincial Mediterranean specialties from Spain to Greece to North Africa spice up the menu with such offerings as seafood paella with North African couscous (the recipe has been in the owner's family for almost 200 years), cassoulet maison, cannelloni niçoise, and a Greek-style lamb shank. You'll feel transported to Europe in one of the five upstairs and downstairs dining rooms, cozied by roaring fires, wood tables, and antiqued walls. There's an award-winning international wine list with 450 options and a dessert menu that includes a Grand Marnier soufflé with fresh raspberry purée sauce and profiteroles. In winter ask to be seated in the fireplace dining room, and in summer request the terrace room—but whenever you come, expect everything here to be lively and colorful, from the decor to the owner himself.

223 17th St. ℂ 831/372-3456. Fax 831/372-2673. www.fandangorestaurant.com. Reservations recommended. Main courses $11–$24. AE, DC, DISC, MC, V. Mon–Sat 11:30am–2:30pm; Sun 10am–2pm; daily 5–9:30pm. From Calif. 1, take the Pacific Grove exit (Calif. 68), turn left on Lighthouse Ave., and continue a block to 17th St.

Joe Rombi's ⭐ ITALIAN   In an area where most restaurants pack 'em in, Joe Rombi's offers a refreshingly intimate dining room with dimmed lights and antique French posters. The food here is very fresh (lasagnas and pastas are made that day). Once seated at 1 of the 11 tables, you'll immediately be served a basket of fresh house-made focaccia to munch on while you peruse the limited menu of appetizers, soups, salads, pastas, and four main courses (some of which come with soup and salad). Go with the fish of the day—I had a halibut dish that any upscale San Francisco restaurant would be proud to serve.

208 17th St. (at Lighthouse Ave.). ℂ **831/373-2416.** Fax 831/373-2106. Reservations recommended. Main courses $12–$21. AE, MC, V. Wed–Sun 5–10pm.

The Old Bath House ⭐ CONTINENTAL   Romance is in the air at this restored Victorian restaurant, on the edge of the earth overlooking Lover's Point. It may be pricey and frequented by tourists, but dinner here is a stately affair with knockout bay views, superb service, and competently prepared cuisine. A popular starter is the grilled prawns and wild-boar sausage appetizer. Main courses range from oak-grilled filet mignon to scallops on lemon risotto. The signature dish is the duck merlot, served with a dried cherry-merlot reduction and risotto. End your decadent dinner with a plate of hot pecan ice cream fritters.

620 Ocean View Blvd. ℂ **831/375-5195.** Fax 831/375-5379. www.oldbathhouse.com. Reservations required. Main courses $20–$40. AE, DC, DISC, MC, V. Mon–Fri 5–11pm; Sat–Sun 4–11pm.

MODERATE

The Fishwife at Asilomar Beach ⭐ _Kids_ SEAFOOD   The Fishwife is the ideal dining spot for anyone looking for a casual, affordable, and quality meal. The restaurant dates from the 1830s, when a sailor's wife started a small food market that became famous for its Boston clam chowder. Today locals still return for the soup as well as some of the finest seafood in Pacific Grove. Two bestsellers are calamari steak sautéed with shallots, garlic, tomatoes, and white wine; and prawns Belize, served sizzling with red onions, tomatoes, fresh Serrano chiles, jicama, lime juice, and cashews. Steak and pasta dishes are also available, and all main courses come with vegetables, bread, black beans, and rice or potatoes. Kids get their own menu, which has smaller portions for less than $6.

1996½ Sunset Dr. (at Asilomar Beach). ℂ **831/375-7107.** www.fishwife.com. Main courses $8.95–$15. AE, DISC, MC, V. Mon–Sat 11am–10pm; Sun 10am–10pm. From Calif. 1, take the Pacific Grove exit (Calif. 68) and stay left until it becomes Sunset Dr.; the restaurant will be on your left about 1 mile ahead as you approach Asilomar Beach.

Peppers Mexicali Café ⭐ MEXICAN/LATIN AMERICAN   Peppers is a casual, festive place serving good food at reasonable prices. The inviting dining room has wooden floors and tables, pepper art visible from every vantage point, and a perpetual crowd who come to suck up beers and savor spicy specialties such as well-balanced seafood tacos and fajitas or house-made tamales and chiles rellenos. Other fire-starters include the snapper Yucatán, which is cooked with chiles, citrus cilantro, and tomatoes; and grilled prawns with lime-cilantro dressing. More than a dozen daily specials are offered as well, such as Mexican seafood paella and grilled mahimahi tacos. Add a substantial selection of cervezas, an addicting compilation of chips and salsa, and a friendly staff, and your taste buds are bound to bellow *"Olé!"*

170 Forest Ave. ✆ **831/373-6892.** Fax 831/373-5467. Reservations recommended. Main courses $7–$15. AE, DC, DISC, MC, V. Mon and Wed–Thurs 11:30am–1pm; Fri–Sat 11:30am–10:30pm; Sun 4–10pm.

INEXPENSIVE

First Awakenings 🐟 *Value* AMERICAN   What was once a dank canning factory is now a bright, huge, open restaurant offering one of the cheapest and healthiest breakfasts in the area. Eye-openers include eight varieties of omelets; granola with nuts, fruit, and yogurt; walnut and wheat pancakes; "gourmet" pancakes; and raisin French toast. At lunch there's a fine choice of salads and a slew of sandwiches ranging from albacore to zucchini. On sunny days, take advantage of the outdoor patio tables.

In the American Tin Cannery, 125 Ocean View Blvd. ✆ **831/372-1125.** Reservations not accepted. Breakfast $3–$7; lunch $5–$7. AE, DISC, MC, V. Daily 7am–2:30pm. From Calif. 1, take the Pacific Grove exit (Calif. 68) and turn right onto Lighthouse Ave.; after a mile, turn left onto Eardley Ave., and take it to the corner of Ocean View.

Thai Bistro 🐟 THAI   One of the most popular Thai restaurants in the area is this small white house with blue trim. Inside you'll find a modern, congenial dining room that's usually filled with locals. The menu is a minimanifesto, with more than 60 options. Some of the most popular dishes are the Panang curry (a heavenly blend of spices and coconut milk with your choice of meat or seafood), Tom kha Gai soup (chicken in coconut milk), and pad Thai. There's a full vegetarian menu as well. It's all accompanied by local wines and French desserts.

159 Central Ave. (between David Ave. and Eardley St.). ✆ **831/372-8700.** Reservations recommended on weekends. Most main courses $8–$12. AE, DISC, MC, V. Daily 11:30am–9:30pm.

Toastie's Cafe AMERICAN   While most restaurants' success depends not only on food but also on clever decor and elaborate presentation, Toastie's shrugs its traditional-style shoulders and continues to pack 'em in. What's the attraction? A good old-fashioned meal served in a no-frills casual dining room. Some rave about the eggs Benedict (with roasted potatoes), while others swear by the hefty, sinful waffles. One thing's for sure: This place serves up what everyone wants from breakfast—lots of selections, good service, endless coffee refills, and heaping plates of food. Weekend dinner is an equally homey affair and includes chicken and prawn Marsala, teriyaki steak, seafood pasta, and stuffed chicken.

702 Lighthouse Dr. ✆ **831/373-7543.** Breakfast and lunch dishes $5.95–$7.25; dinner main courses $9–$12. MC, V. Mon–Sat 6am–3pm; Sun 7am–2pm; Fri–Sat 5–8pm.

4 Pebble Beach & the 17-Mile Drive 🐟🐟🐟

Pebble Beach is a world unto itself. Polo shirts, golf shoes, and big bankrolls are standard, and if you have to ask how much accommodations and greens fees are, you definitely can't afford them. In this elite golfers' paradise, endless grassy fairways are interrupted only by luxury resorts and cliffs where the ocean meets the land. In winter it's also the site of the AT&T Pebble Beach National Pro-Am, a celebrity tournament originally launched in 1937 by crooner Bing Crosby.

THE 17-MILE DRIVE 🐟🐟

The beautiful 17-Mile Drive demands a leisurely afternoon. Pack a picnic, fork over $8 to enter the drive, and prepare to see some of the most exclusive coastal real estate in California.

The drive can be entered from any of five gates: two from Pacific Grove to the north, one from Carmel to the south, or two from Monterey to the east. The most convenient entrance from Calif. 1 is off the main road at the Holman Highway exit. You may beat traffic by entering at the Carmel Gate and doing the tour backwards.

Admission to the drive includes an informative map that lists 26 points of interest. Aside from homes of the ultrarich, highlights include **Seal and Bird Rocks,** where you can see countless gulls, cormorants, and other offshore birds as well as seals and sea lions; and **Cypress Point Lookout,** which affords a 20-mile view all the way to the Big Sur Lighthouse on a clear day. Also visible is the famous **Lone Cypress** tree, inspiration to so many artists and photographers, which you can admire from afar but to which you can no longer walk. The drive also traverses the **Del Monte Forest,** thick with tame black-tailed deer and often described as some "billionaire's private game preserve."

One of the best ways to see 17-Mile Drive is by bike, but the ride toward Carmel is all downhill, so unless you're in great shape, arrange for a ride back. For further information, call the Pebble Beach Resort at ✆ **831/624-3811** or visit www.pebblebeach.com/17miledrive.html.

GREAT GOLF COURSES

Locals tell me it's almost impossible to get a tee time unless you're staying at the golf resort. If you're one of the lucky few, you can choose from several famous courses along the 17-Mile Drive.

PEBBLE BEACH GOLF LINKS ✸✸✸   The most famous course is Pebble Beach Golf Links (✆ **800/654-9300**) at The Lodge at Pebble Beach (p. 380). It's home each year to the AT&T Pebble Beach National Pro-Am, a celebrity-laden tournament televised around the world. Jack Nicklaus has claimed, "If I could play only one course for the rest of my life, this would be it." He should know: He won the 1961 U.S. Amateur and the 1972 U.S. Open here. Indeed, 10 national championships have been decided here. Herbert Warren Wind, dean of 20th-century golf writers, said, "There is no finer seaside golf course in creation"—and that includes the Old Course at St. Andrews. Built in 1919, this 18-hole course is 6,799 yards and par 72. It's precariously perched over a rugged ocean. Greens fees are a staggering $395 plus cart fee.

SPYGLASS HILL GOLF COURSE ✸✸   Also frequented by celebrities is this course at Stevenson Drive and Spyglass Hill Road (✆ **800/654-9300**). Its slope rating of 143 means that it's one of the toughest courses in California. It's justi-fiably famous at 6,859 yards and par 72 with five oceanfront holes. The rest reach deep into the Del Monte Forest. Greens fees are $275 plus cart. Reserva-tions for nonguests should be made a month in advance. The excellent Grill Room is on the grounds.

POPPY HILLS ✸✸   This 18-hole, 6,219-yard course on 17-Mile Drive (✆ **831/625-2035**) was named one of the world's top 20 by *Golf Digest*. It was designed by Robert Trent Jones, Jr., in 1986. One golf pro said the course is "long and tough on short hitters." Greens fees are $115 Monday through Thurs-day and $130 Friday through Sunday, plus $15 per player for the cart rental. You can make reservations 30 days in advance.

THE LINKS AT SPANISH BAY ✸✸   Lying on the north end of 17-Mile Drive at the Pebble Beach Resort and Inn at Spanish Bay (✆ **800/654-9300**), this is the most easily booked course. Serious golfers say it's the most challeng-ing of the Pebble Beach links. Robert Trent Jones, Jr., Tom Watson, and Frank

Tatum (former USGA president) designed it to duplicate a Scottish links course. Its fescue grasses and natural fairways lead to rolls and unexpected bounces for your ball. Greens fees are $215. Cart rental is an additional $25. Reservations can be made 60 days in advance.

DEL MONTE GOLF COURSE ☆   At 1300 Sylvan Rd. (© 831/373-2700) lies the oldest course west of the Mississippi, charging some of the most "reasonable" greens fees: $95 per player, plus a cart rental of $20. The course, often cited in magazines for its "grace and charm," is relatively short—only 6,339 yards. This seldom-advertised course, located at the Hyatt east of Monterey, is part of the Pebble Beach complex, but is not along the 17-Mile Drive.

WHERE TO STAY & DINE

Casa Palmero Resort ☆☆☆   The Casa Palmero is a small, ultraluxury resort on the first tee of the Pebble Beach Golf Links. The two-story villa is the newest gem in the sister properties, which include the Inn at Spanish Bay and The Lodge at Pebble Beach. The most intimate and private of the three, Casa Palmero is fashioned as a European villa with stucco walls, window boxes dripping bougainvillea, every modern comfort, and a staff to anticipate your every wish. It has 24 cottages and suites with amenities that include French doors opening onto private garden spas, oversize window-box sofas, wood-burning fireplaces, and soaking tubs that open to the main room. "Convivial" areas, places where you can hang out, include a trellised patio, library, billiards parlor, living room, private dining room, executive boardroom and small conference room, intimate courtyards with fountains, and lavish outdoor pool pavilion.

1518 Cypress Dr. (on 17-Mile Dr.), Pebble Beach, CA 93953. © 800/654-9300 or 831/622-6650. Fax 831/622-6655. www.pebblebeach.com. 24 units. $625–$1,950 cottage or suite. $20 gratuity added. Rates include continental breakfast and evening hors d'oeuvres and cocktails. AE, MC, V. From Calif. 1 S., turn west onto Calif. 68 and south onto 17-Mile Dr., and follow the coastal road to the hotel. **Amenities:** 3 restaurants; outdoor heated pool; golf course; 12 tennis courts; health club; full-service spa; Jacuzzi; sauna; bike rental; concierge; 24-hr. room service; in-room massage; babysitting; laundry service; same-day dry cleaning; executive-level rooms. *In room:* TV/VCR w/pay movies, dataport, minibar, fridge, coffeemaker, hair dryer, iron, safe.

The Inn at Spanish Bay ☆☆☆   Surrounded by the renowned Links at Spanish Bay golf course, the Inn at Spanish Bay is a plush three- and four-story low-rise on 236 manicured acres 10 miles north of The Lodge at Pebble Beach. Approximately half the rooms face the ocean and are more expensive than their counterparts, which overlook the forest. Each unit contains about 600 square feet of floor space and has a private fireplace and either an outdoor deck or a patio. The bathrooms are finished in Italian marble; the custom-made furnishings include four-poster beds with down comforters. My favorite time here is dusk, when a bagpiper strolls the terrace with a skirling tribute to Scotland.

2700 17-Mile Dr., Pebble Beach, CA 93953. © 800/654-9300 or 831/647-7500. Fax 831/644-7960. www.pebblebeach.com. 270 units. $450–$650 double; $1,750–$2,165 2-bedroom suite. $20 gratuity added. AE, DC, MC, V. From Calif. 1 S., turn west onto Calif. 68 and south onto 17-Mile Dr.; the hotel is on your right, just past the toll plaza. **Amenities:** 3 restaurants; bar/lounge; heated outdoor pool; golf course; 8 outdoor tennis courts (2 night-lit); health club; full-service spa; Jacuzzi; sauna; bike rental; concierge; tour desk; business center; shopping arcade; 24-hr. room service; in-room massage; babysitting; laundry service; same-day dry cleaning; executive-level rooms. *In room:* TV/VCR w/pay movies, dataport, minibar, fridge, coffeemaker, hair dryer, iron, safe in most units.

The Lodge at Pebble Beach ☆☆   For the combined cost of greens fees and a room here, you could easily create a professional putting green in your own backyard—and still have money left over. But even if you're a dedicated hacker, you've got to play here at least once. Look on the bright side—at least you can expect ultraplush rooms equipped with every conceivable amenity, including wood-burning fireplaces. Most are in two-story cottage clusters, with anywhere from 8 to 12 units in each. Those opening onto the ocean have the highest prices.

1700 17-Mile Dr., Pebble Beach, CA 93953. (© 800/654-9300 or 831/624-3811. Fax 831/625-8598. www.pebblebeach.com. 161 units. $500–$800 double; from $1,350 suite. $15 gratuity added. AE, MC, V. From Calif. 1 S., turn west on Calif. 68, turn south onto 17-Mile Dr., and follow the coastal road to the hotel. **Amenities:** 4 restaurants; bar/lounge; heated outdoor pool; golf course; 12 tennis courts; health club; full-service spa; Jacuzzi; sauna; bike rental; concierge; business center; shopping arcade; 24-hr. room service; in-room massage; babysitting; laundry service; same-day dry cleaning. *In room:* TV/VCR w/pay movies, dataport, minibar, fridge, coffeemaker, hair dryer, iron, safe in most units.

5 Carmel-by-the-Sea ★★

5 miles S of Monterey; 121 miles S of San Francisco; 33 miles N of Big Sur

Carmel began as a seaside artists' colony that attracted such luminaries as Robinson Jeffers, Sinclair Lewis, Robert Louis Stevenson, and Ansel Adams. It was a peaceful and intellectually inspiring enclave where residents resisted assigned street numbers and lighting (they carried lanterns, which they considered more romantic). Although it's still intimate enough that there's no need for street numbers—Carmel's inns, restaurants, boutiques, and art galleries all identify their locations only by cross streets—the charmingly ragtag bohemian village of yesteryear is long gone. It's now a tourist hot spot where weekend traffic can be intolerable and the lodging rates grossly inflated. But, oddly enough, nobody ever seems to mind: The village's thousands of annual visitors are so enamored by the eclectic dwellings, pricey boutiques, quaint cafes, majestic cypress trees, and silky white beaches that they really don't mind a few inconveniences.

ESSENTIALS

The **Carmel Business Association,** P.O. Box 4444, Carmel (© **831/624-2522;** www.carmelcalifornia.org), is on San Carlos Street between 5th and 6th streets. It distributes local maps, brochures, and publications. Pick up the *Guide to Carmel* and a schedule of events. Hours are Monday through Friday from 9am to 5pm. On weekends, an information booth is set up from 11am to 3pm at Carmel Plaza, on Ocean Avenue between Junipero and San Carlos streets.

WHAT TO SEE & DO

A wonderful stretch of white sand backed by cypress trees, **Carmel Beach City Park** ★★ is a bit o' heaven on earth (though the jammed parking lot can feel more like a visit to a car rally). There's room for families, surfers, and dogs with their owners (yes, pooches are allowed to run off-leash). If the parking lot is full, there are some spaces on Ocean Avenue, but take heed: They're generally good for 90-minute parking, and you will get a ticket if you park for the day.

Farther south around the promontory, **Carmel River State Beach** ★ is a less crowded option, with white sand and dunes, plus a bird sanctuary where brown pelicans, black oystercatchers, cormorants, gulls, curlews, godwits, and sanderlings make their home.

The **Mission San Carlos Borromeo del Río Carmelo** ★★, on Basilica Rio Road at Lasuen Drive, off Calif. 1 (© **831/624-3600;** www.carmelmission.org), is the burial ground of Father Junípero Serra and the second-oldest of the 21 Spanish missions he established. Founded in 1771 on a site overlooking the Carmel River, it remains one of the largest and most interesting of California's

---

(*Tips* **Carmel Walking Tours**

The main tourist activity in Carmel is walking around town, so you might as well do it with the pros: **Carmel Walks.** The tour company offers 2-hour guided walks through Carmel's gardens, hidden pathways, fairytale-like cottages and homes of famous writers, artists, and washed-up movie stars. During the walk you'll learn about Carmel's seemingly endless spirits, unusual customs, and juicy gossip. For $20 it's a good deal for such an entertaining outing. The tours are offered every Saturday at 10am and 2pm, and Tuesday through Friday at 10am. For reservations, call © **831/ 642-2700** or visit their website at www.carmelwalks.com.

---

missions. The stone church, with its curving walls and Moorish bell tower, was begun in 1793. Its walls are covered with a lime plaster made of burnt seashells. The mission kitchen, the first library in California, the high altar, and the flower gardens are all worth visiting. More than 3,000 Native Americans are buried in the adjacent cemetery; their graves are decorated with seashells. The mission is open June through August, Monday through Saturday from 9:30am to 7:30pm, Sunday from 10:30am to 7:30pm; in other months, Monday through Saturday from 9:30am to 4:30pm, Sunday from 10:30am to 4:30pm. A $2 donation is requested.

One of Carmel's prettiest homes and gardens is **Tor House** (𝒦, 26304 Ocean View Ave. (© **831/624-1813;** www.torhouse.org), built by poet Robinson Jeffers. Standing on Carmel Point, the house dates from 1918 and includes a 40-foot tower containing stones from around the world embedded in the walls (there's even one from the Great Wall of China). Inside, an old porthole is reputed to have come from the ship on which Napoleon escaped from Elba in 1815. No photography is allowed. Admission is by guided tour only, and reservations are requested. It's $7 for adults, $4 for college students, and $2 for high-school students (no children under 12). Open on Friday and Saturday from 10am to 3pm.

If the tourists aren't lying on the beach in Carmel, then they're probably **shopping**—the sine qua non of Carmel activities. You'll be surprised at the number of shops packed into this small town—more than 500 boutiques offering unique fashions, baskets, housewares, imported goods, and a veritable cornucopia of art galleries. Most of the commercial action is packed along the small stretch of Ocean Avenue between Junipero and San Antonio avenues.

If you want to tour the **galleries,** pick up a copy of the *Carmel Gallery Guide* from the Carmel Business Association (see "Essentials," above).

Serious shoppers should also head south a few miles to the **Crossroads Shopping Center** (from Calif. 1 south, take the Rio Rd. exit west for 1 block and turn right onto Crossroads Blvd.). As far as malls go, this is a great one, with oodles of shopping and a few good restaurants.

WHERE TO STAY

Most Carmel lodgings are booked solid from May to October, so make your reservations as far in advance as possible. If you're traveling with pets, your best bet is **The Cypress Inn,** Lincoln and Seventh (P.O. Box Y), Carmel-by-the-Sea, CA 93921 (© **800/443-7443** or 831/624-3871; www.cypress-inn.com), which is a moderately priced option run by owner and actress Doris Day.

EXPENSIVE

Carriage House Inn ☆☆   The luxurious atmosphere and pampering make this one of my top picks in the "downtown" area. Each room comes with a wood-burning fireplace and king-size bed with down comforter. Most of the second-floor rooms have sunken tubs and vaulted beam ceilings; first-floor rooms have single whirlpool tubs. Not only is breakfast delivered to guests' rooms, but there's also wine and hors d'oeuvres served in the afternoon and cappuccino, wine, and cheese in the evening. While almost all choices in the area are frill-and-lace, the Carriage House is a more mature, formal, yet cozy environment.

Junipero St., between Seventh and Eighth aves. (P.O. Box 1900), Carmel, CA 93921. ✆ **800/433-4732** or 831/625-2585. Fax 831/624-0974. www.ibts-carriagehouse.com. 13 units. $229–$375 double; $279–$415 suite. Rates include continental breakfast and afternoon wine and hors d'oeuvres. AE, DISC, MC, V. Free parking. From Calif. 1, exit onto Ocean Ave. and turn left onto Junipero St. **Amenities:** Nearby golf course; concierge. *In room:* TV/VCR, minibar, coffeemaker, fridge, hair dryer, iron, safe.

Highlands Inn, Park Hyatt Carmel ☆☆   Four miles south of Carmel on a 12-acre cliff overlooking Point Lobos, this one- and two-story inn has attracted everyone from celebrities—Madonna, Sammy Hagar, Walt Disney, Marlon Brando—to honeymooners and business executives. It's rustic yet luxurious, with wildflowers gracing its pathways, plenty of character, and a rather exclusive atmosphere. The old-style main lounge dates from 1916 and has panoramic coastal vistas. The guest rooms are distributed throughout a cluster of buildings terraced into the hillside; most units have decks or balconies and wood-burning fireplaces. The suites come with Jacuzzi tubs and fully equipped kitchens; four rooms have showers only.

120 Highlands Dr., Carmel, CA 93923. ✆ **800/682-4811** or 831/620-1234. Fax 831/626-8105. 142 units. $205 double; $260–$695 spa suite; $485–$1,025 2-bedroom, full oceanview spa suite. AE, DC, DISC, MC, V. **Amenities:** 2 restaurants; lounge; outdoor heated pool; nearby golf course; exercise room; 3 outdoor Jacuzzis; complimentary bike use; concierge; tour/activities desk; business center; secretarial services; room service; in-room massage; babysitting; laundry service; same-day dry cleaning. *In room:* TV w/pay movies, VCR on request, CD player, fridge, coffeemaker, kitchen in suites, hair dryer, iron, safe.

La Playa ☆   Only 2 blocks from the beach and within walking distance of town, the four-story La Playa is a romantic, Mediterranean-style villa built in 1904. Norwegian artist Christopher Jorgensen ordered its construction for his bride, an heiress of the Ghirardelli chocolate dynasty. The stylish lobby sets the elegant tone with its terra-cotta floors, Oriental rugs, and white marble fireplace. In the courtyard, walkways lead through beautifully landscaped grounds that surround a heated pool. Compared to the splendor of the lobby and grounds, the standard guest rooms are a bit of a disappointment. The walls are thin and the furnishings perfunctory. The luxury cottages are an improvement—all have kitchens, wet bars, garden patios, and limited room service, and most have wood-burning fireplaces—but yes, they're expensive.

Camino Real and Eighth Ave. (P.O. Box 900), Carmel, CA 93921. ✆ **800/582-8900** or 831/624-6476. Fax 831/624-7966. www.laplayahotel.com. 80 units. $160–$315 double; $315–$625 suite or cottage. Complimentary valet parking. AE, DC, MC, V. **Amenities:** Restaurant; bar; outdoor heated pool; nearby golf course; bike rental; concierge; business center; room service; babysitting; same-day dry cleaning. *In room:* TV, fridge, hair dryer, iron.

Mission Ranch ☆☆   If you want to stay a bit off the beaten track, consider this converted 1850s dairy farm, which was purchased and restored by Clint Eastwood to preserve the vista of the nearby wetlands stretching out to the bay. The ranch's accommodations are scattered amid different structures, both old and new, and surrounded by wetlands and grazing sheep. Guest rooms range from "regulars" in the main barn (which are less desirable) to meadow-view units, each with a vista across the fields to the bay. As befits a ranch, rooms are decorated in a provincial style, with carved wooden beds bedecked with hand-made quilts. Most are equipped with whirlpool baths, fireplaces, and decks or patios. The Martin Family farmhouse contains six units, all arranged around a central parlor, while the Bunkhouse (the oldest structure on the property) con-tains separate living and dining areas, bedrooms, and a fridge. Even if you're not staying here, call for a table at **The Restaurant at Mission Ranch** (p. 387).

26270 Dolores St., Carmel, CA 93923. © **800/538-8221** or 831/624-6436. Fax 831/626-4163. 31 units. $100–$280 double. Rates include continental breakfast. AE, MC, V. **Amenities:** Restaurant; 6 tennis courts; exercise room; babysitting; laundry service; dry cleaning. In room: TV, dataport, fridge in some units, cof-feemaker, hair dryer, iron.

MODERATE

Carmel Sands Lodge ℛ   The Sands is a motor lodge, but it's decorated bet-ter than most and is on a quiet street in Carmel. The modern rooms have pretty bedspreads and updated furnishings; some have fireplaces and wet bars. There's a small pool, but it's practically in the center courtyard parking lot. Several restaurants are nearby. I like the quiet location here better than that of the com-parable Carmel Village Inn (see below).

San Carlos and Fifth (P.O. Box 951), Carmel, CA 93921. © **800/252-1255** or 831/624-1255. Fax 831/624-2576. www.carmelsandslodge.com. 38 units. July–Oct $98–$169 double; Nov–June $79–$149 dou-ble. AE, DC, DISC, MC, V. From Ocean Ave., take a right onto San Carlos and go 2 blocks. **Amenities:** Restau-rant; heated pool (seasonal); nearby golf course. In room: TV; minibar, fridge, coffeemaker, and hair dryer in some units.

Carmel Village Inn   Well run and centrally located, the Village Inn is a motor lodge. The rooms, arranged around a courtyard and parking lot lined with pot-ted geraniums, are outfitted with bland but functional decor. Breakfast, accom-panied by the morning newspaper, is served in the downstairs lounge.

Ocean Ave. and Junipero St. (P.O. Box 5275), Carmel, CA 93921. © **800/346-3864** or 831/624-3864. Fax 831/626-6763. www.carmelvillageinn.com. 48 units. $69–$190 double; $89–$380 triple or quad; from $108 suite. Rates include continental breakfast. AE, MC, V. From Calif. 1, exit onto Ocean Ave. and continue straight to Junipero St. **Amenities:** Babysitting. In room: Fax, kitchenette, fridge.

Cobblestone Inn ℛ   The Cobblestone may not be Victorian like other prop-erties owned by the Four Sisters Inns, but it's just as flowery, well kept, and cute, with hand-stenciled wall decorations, fireplaces, and a trademark abundance of teddy bears. The first floor is built of stones taken from the Carmel River (hence the inn's name), and the rooms encircle a slate courtyard; some look out onto the brick patio where breakfast is occasionally served. The guest rooms vary in size; some can be small, and only the Honeymoon suite comes with a bathtub and VCR, but the largest units include a wet bar, sofa, and separate bedroom. Guests have the use of a comfortable living room with a large stone fireplace. Extras include daily maid and turndown service and morning newspaper.

Junipero St. (between Seventh and Eighth aves., 1½ blocks from Ocean Ave.; P.O. Box 3185), Carmel, CA 93921. © **800/833-8836** or 831/625-5222. Fax 831/625-0478. www.foursisters.com. 24 units. $125–$200 double; from $250 suite. Rates include full breakfast and afternoon wine and hors d'oeuvres. AE, DC, MC, V. **Amenities:** Complimentary bike use. In room: TV, dataport, fridge, hair dryer.

Normandy Inn ℛ   Three blocks from the beach, this French Provincial–style hotel is like something out of a storybook, with an array of colorful flowers that brighten up the property. Some of the guest rooms are showing their age a lit-tle, but they're well appointed with French country decor, feather beds, and down comforters. Some have fireplaces and/or kitchenettes. The tiny heated pool is banked by a flower garden. The three large family-style units are an especially good deal and accommodate up to eight; each has three bedrooms, two bathrooms, a fully equipped kitchen, a dining room, a living room with a fireplace, and a back porch. Reserve well in advance, especially in summer.

Ocean Ave., between Monte Verde and Casanova sts. (P.O. Box 1706), Carmel, CA 93921. © 800/343-3825 or 831/624-3825. Fax 831/624-4614. www.normandyinncarmel.com. 48 units. $99–$279 double; $169–$500 suite or cottage. Rates include continental breakfast. Extra person $10. AE, DC, MC, V. From Calif. 1, exit onto Ocean Ave. and continue straight for 5 blocks past Junipero St. **Amenities:** Outdoor pool (seasonal); nearby golf course. *In room:* TV, kitchenette in some units, coffeemaker, hair dryer, iron.

Pine Inn Hotel   The three-story historic Pine Inn, which was built in 1889 and claims to be the oldest hotel in Carmel, looks like a set out of *Wild, Wild West.* The ornate deep-red and mahogany lobby and library (with fireplace) is a fun departure from the beachy alternatives (think turn-of-the-20th-century bordello meets the Far East). The most affordable (doubles) are also very small; pay a bit more to secure a larger room with a half-canopy. It's in a good location, just a few blocks from the beach on Carmel's main strolling street. Room service hails from adjoining Il Fornaio from 7am to 10:30pm. One big bummer: no elevators.

Ocean Ave., between Monte Verde and Lincoln (P.O. Box 250), Carmel-by-the-Sea, CA 93921. © 800/228-3851 or 831/624-3851. Fax 831/624-3030. www.pine-inn.com. 49 units. $135–$260 double. AE, DC, DISC, MC, V. **Amenities:** Restaurant. *In room:* TV.

Sandpiper Inn by the Sea ℛ   A garden of flowers welcomes visitors to this quiet, relaxing, midscale Carmel standby that's been in business for more than 60 years. The inn's rooms, from which you can hear the surf, offer a range of well-kept accommodations. The highest priced are corner rooms with four-poster beds and plenty of windows framing the ocean view. All are decorated with handsome country antiques and fresh flowers that are changed daily; three have fireplaces. Carmel's fabled white-sand beaches are a mere 100 yards away.

2408 Bay View Ave., Carmel, CA 93923. © 800/633-6433 or 831/624-6433. Fax 831/624-5964. www.sandpiper-inn.com. 17 units. $110–$285 double. Rates include extended continental breakfast and afternoon sherry/tea. AE, DISC, MC, V. **Amenities:** Nearby golf course; concierge; tour desk. *In room:* No phone.

Vagabond House ℛ   In typical Carmel style, oodles of attention have been paid to every element of this English Tudor inn—from the lobby adorned with knickknack antiques and a welcoming decanter of sherry to the wonderfully lush garden courtyard that's draped with greenery and dotted with blooms. Each room is warm and homey, decorated in country decor, and has a private entrance; all have wood-burning fireplaces except two, which means the least expensive rooms book quickly, so call ahead if you want one. Guests are welcomed with a basket of fruit, and the extended continental breakfast is delivered to your room, but you'll most likely prefer to enjoy it on the garden patio.

Fourth and Dolores (P.O. Box 2747), Carmel-by-the-Sea, CA 93921. © 800/262-1262, 800/221-1262 in Canada, or 831/624-7738. Fax 831/626-1243. www.vagabondshouseinn.com. 12 units. $125–$255 double. Rates include continental breakfast. 2-night minimum on weekends. AE, DISC, MC, V. Pets allowed for a fee. *In room:* TV, dataport, fridge, coffeemaker, hair dryer, iron.

WHERE TO DINE
EXPENSIVE
Anton & Michel ℛ CONTINENTAL   This elegant restaurant, across from Carmel Plaza, serves traditional French cuisine in one of the most formal rooms in town. During the day, it's best to dine fountain-side on the patio or encased in the glass-wrapped terrace. The view is equally alluring in the evening, when the

courtyard is lit and the fountain's water sparkles. Decorated with French chandelier lamps and oil paintings, the main dining room is a formal affair—but, as in most restaurants in town, patrons' attire need not match it. Appetizers include crab cakes with cilantro-pesto aioli or delicate ravioli filled with ricotta cheese and spinach. Specialties include rack of lamb with an herb-Dijon mustard au jus and more eclectic items such as a chicken breast Jerusalem, sautéed with olive oil, white wine, cream, and artichoke hearts. The wine list is impressive.

At Court of the Fountain, Mission St. (between Ocean and Seventh aves.). (C) **831/624-2406.** www.carmels best.com. Reservations recommended. Main courses $17–$33. AE, DC, DISC, MC, V. Daily 11:30am–3pm and 5:30–9:30pm.

Casanova (F) NORTHERN ITALIAN/COUNTRY FRENCH It's the engaging European ambience that has drawn locals and tourists to Casanova for over a quarter of a century. The building, which once belonged to Charlie Chaplin's cook, is divided into three Belgian chalet–style dining rooms that serve as the perfect setting for leaning over a bottle of red wine and creating vacation memories. More festive folk step back to the old-world-style covered patio where it's bustling and crowded. Because all dinner entrees include antipasto and a choice of appetizers (such as baked stuffed eggplant with rice, herbs, cheese, and tomatoes), prices here are not a bad deal (at least in overpriced Carmel). The menu features typical Mediterranean cuisine: paella, homemade pastas, meats, and fish. Casanova also boasts a *Wine Spectator* award–winning wine cellar featuring more than 1,600 French, California, German, and Italian wines.

Fifth Ave. (between San Carlos and Mission sts.). (C) **831/625-0501.** www.casanovarestaurant.com. Reservations recommended. 3-course dinner $22–$43. MC, V. Mon–Sat 11:30am–3pm; Sun 10am–3pm; Sun–Thurs 5–10pm; Fri–Sat 5–10:30pm. From Calif. 1, take the Ocean Ave. exit and turn right on Mission, then left onto Fifth Ave.

Flying Fish Grill (F)(F) PACIFIC RIM/SEAFOOD I always feel more confident when a restaurant's kitchen is run by its owner—and a dinner here will confirm that chef/proprietor Kenny Fukumoto is in the house. Dark, romantic, and Asian-influenced, the dining room has an intimate atmosphere with redwood booths (built by Kenny) and fish hanging (flying?) from the ceiling. The cuisine features fresh seafood with exquisite Japanese accents. Start with sushi, tempura, or any of the other exotic, tantalizing taste teasers. Main-course favorites include a rare peppered *ahi* (tuna), blackened and served with mustard-and sesame-soy vinaigrette and angel-hair pasta; a pan-fried almond sea bass with whipped potatoes, Chinese cabbage, and rock shrimp stir-fry.

In Carmel Plaza, Mission St. (between Ocean and Seventh aves.). (C) **831/625-1962.** Reservations recommended. Main courses $15–$24. AE, DISC, MC, V. Wed–Mon 5–10pm.

Grasing's Coastal Cuisine (F) CALIFORNIA When chef Kurt Grasing and renowned Bay Area restaurateur Narsai David teamed to open Grasing's Coastal Cuisine, the result was one of Carmel's best restaurants. The bright, split-room dining area is simple yet stylish, with buttercup yellow walls, beaded lamps, and colorful artwork. Grasing's menu also reflects a stylish simplicity; ultrafresh ingredients gleaned from California's coast and Central Valley are displayed in a modest fashion that belie an intense combination of textures and flavors. The warm Napa Salad, for example, appears ordinary enough, but "when I took it off the menu," says Grasing, "I still made 30 a night." Two other dishes that have generated such interest are the lobster risotto made with pearl pasta (rather than arborio rice, for a smoother texture) and the Bronzed Salmon served in a garlic cream sauce. Even the bread, which comes fresh from Gail's Bakery in Aptos, is fantastic. When the sun's out, request a table at the dog-friendly patio, and be sure to inquire about the very reasonable prix-fixe meal.

Sixth St. (at Mission St.). © **831/624-6562.** www.grasings.com. Reservations recommended. Main courses $17–$26. AE, MC, V. Daily 11am–4pm and 5–10pm.

The Restaurant at Mission Ranch 🎔🎔 AMERICAN   Clint Eastwood bought this rustic property in 1986 and restored the ranch-style building to its original integrity, and although the chance of seeing him brings in some folks, it's the views, quality food, and merry atmosphere that really make the place special. The wooden building is encased with large windows that accentuate the wonderful view of the marshlands, grazing sheep, and bay beyond. Warm days make patio dining the prime choice, but the key time to come is at sunset, when the sky is transforming and happy hour is in full swing (you'll find some of the cheapest drinks around, and Clint often stops by when he's in town). As you'd expect from the ranch motif, meat is king here: Burgers are freshly ground on-site, and prime rib with twice-baked potato and vegetables is the favored dish. There are, of course, wonderful seafood, chicken, and vegetarian options as well; and all dinners include soup or salad. Entertainment is provided at the piano bar, where locals and tourists have been known to croon their favorites. The Sunday buffet brunch with live jazz piano is also hugely popular; be sure to reserve a table.

At Mission Ranch, 26270 Dolores St. © **831/625-9040.** Fax 831/625-5502. Reservations recommended. Most main courses $17–$29. DC, MC, V. Sat 11am–2:30pm; Sun 9:30am–1:30pm; daily 4:30–9:30pm; bar stays open until midnight.

MODERATE

Caffè Napoli 🎔 *Value* ITALIAN   The decor here is so quintessentially Italiana, with flags, gingham tablecloths, garlic, and baskets overhead, that I expected a flour-coated pot-bellied Padrino Napoli to emerge from the kitchen, embrace me wholeheartedly, and exclaim *"Mangia! Mangia!"* as he slapped down a bowl overflowing with sauce-drenched pasta. Of course, there is no Padrino here, and I received no welcoming hug, but I did indulge in the fine Italian fare that keeps locals coming back for more.

Ocean Ave. (between Dolores and Lincoln). © **831/625-4033.** Reservations recommended. Main courses $10–$20. MC, V. Daily 11:30am–9pm.

Club Jalapeño 🎔🎔 MEXICAN   Follow the divine aroma wafting down San Carlos Avenue and you'll end up at Club J, tearing into in a plate of Oaxacan enchiladas drizzled with rich mole sauce. Authentic Mexican is this lively restaurant's claim and nobody's arguing. The fried and battered Baja fish tacos are just like the ones in Tijuana (love that salsa and lime-cilantro dressing). For something truly different, try the coconut-encrusted fish that's lightly fried then topped with spicy chipotle sauce and fruit salsa. A righteous meal for two is Club J's spicy shrimp fajitas served with a side of fresh-fruit salsa. You'll like the decor as well—faux-hacienda-rustic with dark-wood flooring, exposed beams, iron furnishings, textured walls, soft lighting, dried hanging chilies, and a sexy little corner bar serving soothing shots of pure agave tequila.

San Carlos (between Fifth and Sixth in the courtyard). ©**831/626-1997.** www.clubjalapeno.com. Main courses $10–$18. AE, MC, V. Daily noon–10pm.

The Hog's Breath Inn AMERICAN   Clint Eastwood's involvement with this restaurant made it famous, but it's a rare day that he pays a visit (better odds are at the Mission Ranch restaurant). No matter: The patio with tree-trunk tables and plastic chairs is ideal for drinking a pint or two and chowing down on good ol' American standbys—that is, if you don't mind the usual wait. (Tables in the wood-paneled dark-and-rustic dining room fill up, too, though they're not as lively as outdoor seats.) The food—burgers, nachos, and the like—is decidedly unremarkable, but the small dark bar with sports on the tube is the best place to pull up a stool and kick back on a rainy day (or a sunny one for that matter). Come for lunch—it's more affordable.

San Carlos St. (between Fifth and Sixth aves.). ℂ **831/625-1044.** www.hogsbreathinn.net. Reservations not accepted. Main courses $9.50–$23. AE, DC, MC, V. Daily 11:30am–10pm. From Calif. 1, take the Ocean Ave. exit and turn right onto San Carlos St.

La Bohème ✿ FRENCH COUNTRY   Like a set from Disney's "It's a Small World," La Bohème mimics a French street with cartoony asymmetrical shingled house facades and a painted blue sky overhead. Thankfully, the similarity stops with the decor, and there are no singing dolls. Dinner here is romantic French cuisine, served at cramped tables set with floral-print cloths in bright colors, hand-painted dinnerware, and vibrant bouquets. Dinner is a three-course, fixed-price feast consisting of a large salad, a tureen of soup, and a main dish (perhaps roast breast of duckling with green-peppercorn sauce). Vegetarian specials are also available. Homemade desserts and fresh coffee are sold separately, and are usually worth the extra expense.

Dolores St. and Seventh Ave. ℂ **831/624-7500.** www.laboheme.com. Reservations not accepted. Prix-fixe 3-course dinner $24. MC, V. Daily 5:30–10pm. From Calif. 1, exit onto Ocean Ave. and turn left onto Dolores St.

Rio Grill ✿✿ AMERICAN   Both the food and the festive atmosphere (a cartoon mural of famous locals such as Clint Eastwood and the late Bing Crosby, plus playful sculpture, cacti, and other vibrant art) have kept this place popular for the past several years. The whimsical nature of the modern Santa Fe–style dining room belies the kitchen's serious preparations, which include homemade soups; a rich quesadilla with almonds, cheeses, and smoked-tomato salsa; barbecued baby back ribs from a wood-burning oven; and fresh fish from an open oak grill. The restaurant's good selection of wines includes some rare California vintages and covers a broad price range.

Crossroads Shopping Center, 101 Crossroads Blvd. ℂ **831/625-5436.** www.riogrill.com. Reservations recommended. Main courses $8–$25. AE, DISC, MC, V. Sun–Thurs 11:30am–10pm; Fri–Sat 11:30am–11pm. From Calif. 1, take the Rio Rd. exit west for 1 block and turn right onto Crossroads Blvd.

Tommy's Wok ✿✿ (Value CHINESE   Far be it for Carmel to have just an ordinary Chinese restaurant. Instead, chef/owner Tommy Mao has eschewed the typical flaming-red-and-gold color scheme for a far more subdued—almost Japanese in its austerity—decor at this Carmel newcomer. The small 12-table restaurant—with its soothing pastel hues, rice-paper posters, semiopen kitchen, and glossy wood floor—is an apt setting for Mao's stylish presentations and unique combinations of Szechuan, Hunan, and Mandarin dishes. Mao's make-it-all-from-scratch philosophy is evident in all his dishes: potstickers made with fresh Napa cabbage, mu shu vegetables with house-made pancakes, tea-smoked duck marinated for 48 hours. All these dishes are proven winners, as are the Hot & Spicy String Beans, Pinenut Chicken, marinated Lover's Prawns, and Mongolian Lamb (okay, now I'm hungry). The combo lunch plates are a real bargain, and a modest dim sum menu is offered for lunch as well.

Mission (between Ocean and Seventh, next to the Wells Fargo ATM). ℂ **831/624-8518.** Main courses $7–$14. AE, DISC, MC, V. Tues–Sun 11:30am–2:30pm and 4:30–9:30pm.

INEXPENSIVE
Little Swiss Cafe CONTINENTAL   This quirky little spot is designed to look like a Swiss cottage. Kids may love the decor (old-fashioned Grandma cute) but the grown-ups come for the best homemade blintzes and pancakes in town. Breakfast is served all day. Lunch is affordable and features sandwiches, which are served with potato salad, mixed green salad, or soup ($5–$7); salads; and an array of unusual entrees such as Swiss sausage with smothered onions, calves' liver sauté, and fillet of red snapper with a rémoulade sauce.

Sixth (between Lincoln and Mission). (C) 831/624-5007. Reservations not accepted. $5–$9. No credit cards. Mon–Sat 7:30am–3pm; Sun 8am–2pm.

Neilsen Brothers Market DELI   Why bother burning away precious midday vacation minutes indoors when you can dine alfresco on the sands of Carmel Beach? Duck a few blocks off the main drag to Neilsen Brothers market and you'll find everything you could want to fill your picnic basket, including sandwiches, barbecued chicken and ribs, pasta salads, and a vast selection of cheeses. You can even get french fries and veggie and meat burgers (noon–6pm), but expect a 10-minute wait—they cook to order. Call and order over the phone or drop in.

San Carlos (at Seventh). (C) 831/624-6263 (deli), or 831/624-6441 (market). Picnic items $3–$5. MC, V. Mon–Sat 8am–8pm; Sun 10am–7pm.

6 Carmel Valley
3 miles SE of Carmel-by-the-Sea

Inland from Carmel stretches Carmel Valley, where wealthy folks retreat beyond the reach of the coastal fog and mist. It's a scenic and perpetually sunny valley of rolling hills dotted with manicured golf courses and many a tony pony ranch.

Hike the trails in **Garland Regional Park,** 8 miles east of Carmel on Carmel Valley Road (dogs are welcome off-leash). The sun really bakes you out here, so bring lots of water. You could also sign up for a trail ride or riding lesson at **The Holman Ranch,** 60 Holman Rd. ((C) **831/659-2640;** www.theholmanranch. com), 12 miles east of Calif. 1.

Golf is offered at several resorts and courses in the valley, notably at **Quail Lodge,** 8205 Valley Green Dr. ((C) **800/538-9516** or 831/620-8858; www.quaillodge.com), and **Rancho Cañada Golf Club,** Carmel Valley Road ((C) **800/536-9459** or 831/624-0111; www.ranchocanada.com).

While you're in the valley, taste the wines at the **Château Julien Winery,** 8940 Carmel Valley Rd. ((C) **831/624-2600;** www.chateaujulien.com), which is open Monday through Friday from 8am to 5pm, Saturday and Sunday from 11am to 5pm. Tours are available by reservation.

WHERE TO STAY
Quail Lodge Resort and Golf Club 𝒜𝒜   In the foothills of the Santa Lucia Range, Quail Lodge has received Mobil's five-star ratings for more than 20 years. Its pastoral setting encompasses more than 850 acres of lakes, woodlands, meadows, an 18-hole championship golf course, and a full-service spa. The guest rooms are in two-story balconied wings, with terraces overlooking the pool or 1 of the 10 man-made lakes, or in cottages holding five units each. Executive villas are the most expensive and luxurious digs. The guest rooms are decorated in earth tones jazzed up with striped and checkered patterns. Higher-priced accommodations, on the upper floors, have cathedral ceilings. Every room has a separate dressing area and French doors opening to an ample balcony; some have

fireplaces and wet bars. All units have coffeemakers, supplied with freshly ground beans; a fresh-fruit plate is delivered to each room daily as well.

8205 Valley Greens Dr., Carmel, CA 93923. © 888/828-8787 or 831/624-2888. Fax 831/624-3726. www.quaillodge.com. 97 units. Apr–Nov $270–$390 double; $435–$685 suite. Extra person $35. Call for winter specials. Packages available. AE, DC, DISC, MC, V. From Calif. 1 N., past the Carmel exits (after which the highway narrows to 2 lanes), turn east on Carmel Valley Rd. and continue 3½ miles to Valley Greens Dr. Pets accepted with $100 fee per stay; $25 fee per extra pet. Pet amenities and doggie treats included. **Amenities:** 3 restaurants; 2 bars; 2 outdoor pools (1 heated); golf course; 4 tennis courts; exercise room; full spa services; Jacuzzi; bike rental; concierge; business center; room service; in-room massage; babysitting; laundry service; same-day dry cleaning; executive-level rooms. *In room:* TV w/pay movies, dataport, minibar, coffeemaker, hair dryer.

7 The Big Sur Coast ★★★

3 miles S of Carmel-by-the-Sea; 123 miles S of San Francisco; 87 miles N of Hearst Castle

Big Sur is more than a drive along one of the most dramatic coastlines on earth or a peaceful repose amid a forest of California redwoods. It's a stretch of wilderness so overwhelmingly beautiful—especially when the fog glows in the moonlight—that it enchants everyone who visits. It's also home to a particular breed of nature lover who prefers a rustic lifestyle to the rest of California's offerings. When the 1997 and 1998 El Niño storms caused landslides and major road damage, cutting the area off from civilization for months, reports from Big Sur were unusual: Some residents fled, vowing never to return. The remaining residents rejoiced in the temporary solitude; Post Ranch, the area's ultimate luxury resort, shared the impromptu intimacy with deep-pocketed guests by flying them in via helicopter (for an extra fee, of course). Such is the price paid for living amid the California wilderness. The reopened roads are packed again, and driving through the region is slow; rubberneckers admiring the view and nervous Nellies fearing the cliffs drive with their foot on the brakes.

Although there is an actual Big Sur Village 25 miles south of Carmel, "Big Sur" refers to the entire 90-mile stretch of coastline between Carmel and San Simeon, blessed on one side by the majestic Santa Lucia Range and on the other by the rocky Pacific coastline. It's one of the most romantic and relaxing places in California, and if you need respite from the rat race, I can recommend no better place to find it (although Yosemite, if you hike past the crowds, is equally rejuvenating). There's little more to do than explore the mountains and beaches, or just perch yourself atop the cliffs and take in the California sea air—but spend a few days here and you'll find that you need nothing else.

ESSENTIALS

VISITOR INFORMATION Contact the **Big Sur Chamber of Commerce** (© 831/667-2100; www.bigsurcalifornia.org) for specialized information on places and events in Big Sur.

ORIENTATION Most of this stretch is state park, and Calif. 1 runs its entire length, hugging the ocean the whole way. Restaurants, hotels, and sights are easy to spot—most are situated directly on the highway—but without major towns as reference points, their addresses can be obscure. For the purposes of orientation, I'll use the River Inn as a mileage guide. Located 29 miles south of Monterey on Calif. 1, the inn is generally considered to mark the northern end of Big Sur.

EXPLORING THE BIG SUR COAST

Big Sur offers visitors tranquillity and natural beauty—ideal for hiking, picnicking, camping, fishing, and beachcombing.

The Big Sur Coast

The first settlers arrived here only a century ago, and the present highway was built in 1937, making the area accessible by car. (Electricity arrived only in the 1950s, and it's still not available in the remote inland mountains.) Big Sur's mysterious, misty beauty has inspired several modern spiritual movements (the Esalen Institute was the birthplace of the human potential movement). Even the tourist bureau bills the area as a place in which "to slow down . . . to meditate . . . to catch up with your soul." Take the board's advice and take your time.

The region affords a bounty of wilderness adventure opportunities. The inland **Ventana Wilderness,** maintained by the U.S. Forest Service, contains 167,323 acres straddling the Santa Lucia Mountains and is characterized by steep ridges separated by V-shaped valleys. The streams that cascade through the area are marked by waterfalls, deep pools, and thermal springs. The wilderness offers 237 miles of hiking trails that lead to 55 designated trail camps—a backpacker's paradise. One of the easiest trails to access is the **Pine Ridge Trail** at Big Sur station (℗ **831/667-2315**).

From Carmel, the first stop along Calif. 1 is **Point Lobos State Reserve** ✸✸ (℗ **831/624-4909**; www.pt-lobos.parks.state.ca.us), 3 miles south of Carmel. Sea lions, harbor seals, sea otters, and thousands of seabirds reside in this 1,276-acre reserve. Between December and May you can also spot migrating California gray whales offshore. Trails follow the shoreline and lead to hidden coves. Note that parking is limited; on weekends especially, you need to arrive early to secure a place.

From here, cross the Soberanes Creek, passing **Garrapata State Park** (© **831/624-4909**), a 2,879-acre preserve with 4 miles of coastline. It's unmarked and undeveloped, though the trails are maintained. To explore them, you'll need to park at one of the turnouts on Calif. 1 near Soberanes Point and hike in.

Ten miles south of Carmel, you'll find North Abalone Cove. From here, Palo Colorado Road leads back into the wilderness to the first of the Forest Service camping areas at **Bottchers Gap** ($12 to camp, $5 to park overnight; © **805/434-9199;** www.campone.com).

Continuing south, about 13 miles from Carmel, you'll cross the **Bixby Bridge** and see the **Point Sur Lighthouse** off in the distance. The Bixby Bridge, one of the world's highest single-span concrete bridges, towers nearly 270 feet above Bixby Creek Canyon, and offers canyon and ocean views from observation alcoves at intervals along the bridge. The lighthouse, which sits 361 feet above the surf on a volcanic rock promontory, was built in 1889, when only a horse trail provided access to this part of the world. Tours, which take 2 to 3 hours and involve a steep half-mile hike each way, are scheduled on most weekends. For information, call © **831/625-4419,** or visit www.pointsur.org. Admission is $5 for adults, $3 for youths ages 13 to 18, $2 for children 5 to 12, and free for kids under 5.

About 3 miles south of the lighthouse is **Andrew Molera State Park** (© **831/667-2315;** www.bigsurcalifornia.org), the largest state park on the Big Sur coast at 4,800 acres. It's much less crowded than Pfeiffer–Big Sur (see below). Miles of trails meander through meadows and along beaches and bluffs. Hikers and cyclists use the primitive trail camp about a third of a mile from the parking area. The 2½-mile-long beach, sheltered from the wind by a bluff, is accessible via a mile-long path flanked in spring by wildflowers, and offers excellent tide-pooling. You can walk the entire length of the beach at low tide; otherwise, take the bluff trail above the beach. There are trails through the park for horseback riders of all levels. **Molera Big Sur Trail Rides** (© **800/942-5486** or 831/625-5486; www.molerahorsebacktours.com) offers coastal trail rides daily from April to December, or until the rains come. The cost varies but starts at about $25 for a 1-hour ride along the beach. The park also has campgrounds.

Back on Calif. 1, you'll soon reach the village of Big Sur, where commercial services are available.

About 26 miles south of Carmel is **Big Sur Station** (© **831/667-2315**), where you can pick up maps and information about the region. It's a quarter mile past the entrance to **Pfeiffer–Big Sur State Park** 🐾 (© **831/667-2315;** www.bigsurcalifornia.org), an 810-acre park that offers 218 camping sites along the Big Sur River (call © **800/444-7275** for camping reservations), picnicking, fishing, and hiking. It's a scenic park of redwoods, conifers, oaks, and meadows, and it gets very crowded. The Big Sur Lodge in the park has cabins with fireplaces and other facilities (see p. 395 and the "Camping in Big Sur" box below). Admission is $5 per car, and it's open daily from dawn to dusk.

Just over a mile south of the entrance to Pfeiffer–Big Sur State Park is the turnoff to Sycamore Canyon Road (unmarked), which will take you 2 winding miles down to beautiful **Pfeiffer Beach** 🐾, a great place to soak in the sun on the wide expanse of golden sand. It's open for day-use only, there's no fee, and it's the only beach accessible by car (but not motor homes).

Back on Calif. 1, the road travels 11 miles past Sea Lion Cove to Julia Pfeiffer Burns State Park. High above the ocean is the famous **Nepenthe** restaurant (p. 397), the retreat bought by Orson Welles for Rita Hayworth in 1944. A few miles farther south is the **Coast Gallery** (© **831/667-2301**), the premier local art gallery, which displays lithographs of works by the late writer and, yes, artist Henry Miller. The gallery's Coast Cafe offers simple serve-yourself lunches of soup, sandwiches, baked goods, and coffee. Miller fans will also want to stop at the **Henry Miller Memorial Library** (© 831/667-2574; www.henrymiller.org) on Calif. 1, 30 miles south of Carmel and a quarter mile south of Nepenthe restaurant. The library displays and sells books and artwork by Miller and houses a permanent collection of first editions. It also serves as a community art center, hosting concerts, readings, and art exhibitions (check for upcoming events on the website). The rear gallery room is a video-viewing space where films about Henry Miller can be seen. There's a sculpture garden, plus tables on the adjacent lawn where visitors can rest and enjoy the surroundings. Admission is free; hours are Wednesday through Monday from 11am to 6pm.

Julia Pfeiffer Burns State Park 𝔎𝔎 (© 831/667-2315; www.bigsurcalifornia. org) encompasses some of Big Sur's most spectacular coastline. To get a closer look, take the trail from the parking area at McWay Canyon, which leads under the highway to a bluff overlooking the 80-foot-high McWay Waterfall dropping directly into the ocean. It's less crowded here than at Pfeiffer–Big Sur, and there are miles of trails to explore in the 3,580-acre park. Scuba divers can apply for permits to explore the 1,680-acre underwater reserve.

From here, the road skirts the Ventana Wilderness, passing Anderson and Marble Peaks and the Esalen Institute before crossing the Big Creek Bridge to Lucia and several campgrounds farther south. **Kirk Creek Campground** 𝔎, about 3 miles north of Pacific Valley, offers camping with ocean views and beach access. Beyond Pacific Valley, the **Sand Dollar Beach** 𝔎 picnic area is a good place to stop and enjoy the coastal view and take a stroll. A half-mile trail leads down to the sheltered beach, from which there's a fine view of Cone Peak, one of the coast's highest mountains. Two miles south of Sand Dollar is **Jade Cove,** a popular spot for rockhounds. From here, it's about another 27 miles past the Piedras Blancas Light Station to San Simeon.

WHERE TO STAY

Only a handful of Big Sur's accommodations offer the kind of pampering and luxury you'd expect in a fine urban hotel; even direct-dial phones and TVs (often considered gauche in these parts) are rare. Big Sur hotels are especially busy in summer, when advance reservations are required. There are more accommodations than those listed here, so if you're having trouble securing a room or a site, contact the chamber of commerce (listed in the "Essentials" section earlier in this chapter) for other options.

Big Sur Lodge (Kids) A family-friendly place, the Big Sur Lodge—sheltered by towering redwoods, sycamores, and broad-leafed maples—is situated in the enormous state park. The rustic motel-style cabins are huge, with high peaked cedar- and redwood-beamed ceilings. They're clean and heated, and have private bathrooms and reserved parking spaces. Some have fireplaces. All offer porches or decks with views of the redwoods or the Santa Lucia Range. An advantage to staying here is that you're entitled to free use of all the facilities of the park, including hiking, barbecue pits, and picnic areas. In addition, the lodge has its own grocery store and laundry facilities.

In Pfeiffer–Big Sur State Park, Calif. 1 (P.O. Box 190), Big Sur, CA 93920. © 800/424-4787 or 831/667-3100. Fax 831/667-3110. www.bigsurlodge.com. 61 cottages. $89–$149 cottage for 2; $119–$219 cottage with kitchen or fireplace; $139–$239 cabin with kitchen and fireplace. Rates include park entrance fees. AE, MC, V. From Carmel, take Calif. 1 south 26 miles. **Amenities:** Restaurant; heated outdoor pool (seasonal); coin-op laundry. *In room:* Coffeemaker, kitchen in some units, no phone.

Deetjen's Big Sur Inn ☆   In the 1930s, before Calif. 1 was built, this homestead was an overnight stopping place on the coastal wagon road. Located in a redwood canyon, it was begun by Norwegian homesteader Helmuth Deetjen, who built several units from hand-hewn logs and lumber. Folks either love or hate the accommodations, set in a redwood canyon. They're rustic, cozy, and adorable with their old-fashioned furnishings and down-home feel (the hand-hewn doors don't even have locks). But those who want extensive creature comforts should go elsewhere, or at least reserve a cabin with a private bathroom. Single-wall construction means that the rooms are far from soundproof, so children under 12 are allowed only if families reserve both rooms of a two-room building. There's no insulation, so prepare to crank up the fire or wood-burning stove. *Tip:* The cabins near the river offer the most privacy, and if you stay in one of the two-story units, be sure to request the quieter upstairs rooms. The **restaurant** (p. 397) is a local favorite and consists of four intimate, English country inn–style rooms lit by candlelight.

Calif. 1, Big Sur, CA 93920. **(**℃**) 831/667-2377.** www.deetjens.com. 20 units, 15 with bathroom. $75–$180 double with shared bathroom; $110–$195 double with private bathroom. MC, V. **Amenities:** Restaurant. *In room:* No phone.

Post Ranch Inn ☆☆☆   This is one of my very favorite places to stay on the planet. Perched on 98 acres of seaside ridges 1,200 feet above the Pacific, this romantic resort opened in 1992 and was instantly declared one of the world's finest retreats. What's the big deal? The Post Ranch doesn't attempt to beat its stunning natural surroundings, but to join them. The wood-and-glass guest cottages are built around existing trees—some are elevated to avoid damaging the delicate redwood root structures—and the ultraprivate Ocean and Coast cottages are so close to the edge of the earth, you get the impression that you've joined the clouds (imagine that from your private spa tub). Other cottages face the woodlands and are as impressive in design. Each room has a fireplace, terrace, massage table, and wet bar filled with complimentary goodies. The bathrooms, fashioned out of slate and granite, feature spa tubs. Also on the premises are the best Jacuzzi I've ever encountered (it's on a cliff and seems to join the sky), an infinity pool, and sun decks. The only drawback is that the vibe can be stuffy, which is due more to the clientele than the staff (my Subaru was sneered at). The **Sierra Mar** restaurant is open to guests-only for continental breakfast, and to the public for dinner. It, too, has floor-to-ceiling views of the ocean.

Calif. 1 (P.O. Box 219), Big Sur, CA 93920. **(**℃**) 800/527-2200** or 831/667-2200. Fax 831/667-2824. www.post ranchinn.com. 30 units. $485–$935 double. Rates include continental breakfast. AE, MC, V. **Amenities:** Restaurant; bar/lounge; outdoor heated pool; exercise room; spa services; cliff-side Jacuzzi; game room; concierge; activities desk; room service; in-room massage. *In room:* A/C, CD player, minibar, coffeemaker, hair dryer, iron, safe.

Ventana Inn and Spa ☆☆☆   Luxuriously rustic and utterly romantic, Ventana has been a popular wilderness outpost for more than 20 years, and with good reason. Located on 243 mountainous oceanfront acres, Ventana has an elegance that's atypical of the region, and has attracted famous guests such as Barbra Streisand, Goldie Hawn, and Francis Ford Coppola since opening in 1975.

The accommodations, in 12 one- and two-story natural-wood buildings along winding wildflower-flanked paths, blend in with the magical Big Sur countryside. The extensive grounds are dotted with hammocks and hand-carved benches, strategically located under shady trees and at vista points. The guest rooms are divinely decorated in warm, cozy luxury, with private terraces or balconies overlooking the ocean or forest. Most rooms offer wood-burning fireplaces, and some have Jacuzzis and cathedral ceilings. A small fitness center

(Tips) Camping in Big Sur

Big Sur is one of the most spectacular places in the state for camping. One of the most glorious settings is at **Pfeiffer–Big Sur State Park**, on Calif. 1, 26 miles south of Carmel (© **831/667-2315**). The 810-acre state park offers hundreds of secluded sites on hundreds of acres of redwood forest. Hiking trails, streams, and the river are steps away from your sleeping bag, and the most modern amenities are the 25¢ showers (for 3 min.). Water faucets are located between sites, and each spot has its own picnic table and fire pit. There are no RV hookups or electricity. Riverfront sites are most coveted, but others promise more seclusion among the shaded hillsides. Campfire programs and nature walks are also offered. At the entrance are a store, gift shop, restaurant, and cafe. There's a total of 218 sites (fees are $14 for regular sites, $26 for group sites); call © **800/ 444-7275** or log on to www.reserveamerica.com for reservations. Senior discounts are available, and leashed dogs permitted ($1 per night extra).

The entrance to the **Ventana Campground**, on Calif. 1, 28 miles south of Carmel and 4¼ miles south of the River Inn (© **831/667-2712;** www. ventanawildernesscampground.com), is adjacent to the entrance to the resort of the same name, but the comparison stops there. This is pure rusticity. The 80 campsites, on 40 acres of a redwood canyon, are set along a hillside and spaced well apart. Each is shaded by towering trees and has a picnic table and fire ring but offers no electricity, RV hookups, or river access. There are, however, three bathhouses with hot showers (25¢ fee), which are conveniently located. To reserve a space, call and charge on a credit card (MasterCard or Visa) 1 night's deposit. Or you can mail a check for the deposit along with the dates you'd like to stay and a stamped, self-addressed envelope at least 2 weeks in advance (earlier during peak months). Rates are $27 for a site for two with one vehicle; $35 per night weekends. An additional person is $4 extra, and it'll cost you $5 to bring Fido. Rates include entrance fee for your car. Open April through October.

Big Sur Campground and Cabins is on Calif. 1, 26 miles south of Carmel (½ mile south of the River Inn; © **831/667-2322;** www.bigsurcali fornia.org/camping.html). The sites are cramped, so the feel is more like a camping village than an intimate retreat. However, it's very well maintained and perfect for families, who love the playground, river swimming, and inner-tube rentals. Each campsite has its own wood-burning fire pit, picnic table, and freshwater faucet within 25 feet of the pitching area. There are also RV water and electric hookups. Facilities include bathhouses with hot showers, laundry facilities, an aged volleyball/basketball court, and a grocery store. There are 81 tent sites (30 RV-ready with electricity and water hookup), plus 13 cabins (all with shower). The all-wood cabins are adorable, with stylish country furnishings, wood-burning ovens, patios, and full kitchens. Rates are $27 for a tent site for two or an RV hookup (plus $4 extra for electricity and water), $57 for a tent cabin (bed, but no heat or plumbing) for two, or $105 to $221 for a cabin for two. Rates include entrance for your car. MasterCard and Visa are accepted. Pets cost $4 for campsites and $12 for tent cabins; pets are not allowed in the other cabins. Open year-round.

offers the basics—but you'll be more inspired to hike the grounds, where you'll not only find plenty of pastoral respite, but also a pool, a rustic library, and clothing-optional tanning decks and spa tubs. This, along with Post Ranch, is one of the best retreats in the region, if not the state. But I can't say which is better. I prefer the rooms at Post Ranch but the laid-back energy and the grounds at Ventana. *Families take heed:* Children are permitted but not exactly embraced. Ventana's restaurant, **Cielo** (p. 397), is a romantic and first-rate dining experience.

Calif. 1, Big Sur, CA 93920. © 800/628-6500 or 831/667-2331. Fax 831/667-2287. www.ventanainn.com. 62 units. $340–$975 double; from $575 suite. Rates include continental breakfast and afternoon wine and cheese. AE, DC, DISC, MC, V. **Amenities:** Restaurant; 2 heated outdoor pools; exercise room; full spa with 2 Japanese hot baths; sauna; concierge; room service; in-room massage; laundry service; executive-level rooms. *In room:* A/C, TV/VCR, minibar, fridge, coffeemaker, hair dryer, iron, safe.

WHERE TO DINE

In addition to the following choices, you should try the **Big Sur Bakery and Restaurant** on Calif. 1, just past the post office and a mile south of Pfeiffer–Big Sur State Park (© **831/667-0520**). It offers friendly service and healthy fare, ranging from wood-fired pizzas and portobello mushroom burgers at lunch to salmon, tuna, and chicken selections at dinner. All the pastries are freshly baked on the premises, along with hearth-baked breads. It's open Tuesday through Sunday from 8am to 10pm; they close early on Monday.

Big Sur River Inn CALIFORNIA/AMERICAN   Popular with everyone from families to bikers, the River Inn is an unpretentious, rustic, down-home restaurant that's got something for all tastes. Trying to seat a small army? No problem. Want to watch sports on TV at a local bar? Pull up a stool. Looking to snag a few rays from a deck right beside the Big Sur River? Break out the suntan lotion. In winter the wooden dining room is the prime spot; on summer days, some folks grab their patio chairs and cocktails and hang out literally midstream. Along with the local color, attractions include a full bar and good ol' American breakfasts (steak and eggs, omelets, pancakes, and so on, plus espresso, with most dishes for around $6), lunches (an array of salads, sandwiches, and baby back ribs, or fish and chips), and dinners (fresh catch, pastas, burgers, or ribs). I usually order the Black Angus Burger with a side of beer-battered onion rings, or a big platter of the Roadhouse Ribs served with cowboy beans.

On Calif. 1, 2 miles north of Pfeiffer–Big Sur State Park. © **831/667-2700.** Fax 831/667-2743. www.bigsur riverinn.com. Main courses $8.75–$15 lunch, $8.95–$28 dinner. AE, DC, MC, V. Daily 8am–10pm; 8am–9pm in winter.

Café Kevah SOUTHWEST/CALIFORNIA   One level below Nepenthe (see below), Café Kevah offers the same celestial view at a fraction of the price, a more casual environment, and—depending on your taste—better food. Seating is entirely outdoors—a downside when the biting fog rolls in, but perfect on a clear day. You can order breakfast (served all day) or lunch from the shack of a kitchen, then grab an umbrella-shaded table, and enjoy the feast for your eyes and taste buds. Fare here is more eclectic than Nepenthe's, with such choices as homemade granola, baby greens with broiled salmon and papaya, chicken brochettes, omelets, and new-potato hash. It ain't cheap, but innovative cuisine, the view, and a decent mocha make it worthwhile. Don't forget to bring a coat.

On Calif. 1, 29 miles south of Carmel (5 miles south of the River Inn). © **831/667-2345.** www.nepenthe-bigsur.com. Appetizers $6.25–$12; main courses $11–$18. AE, MC, V. Daily 9am–4pm; closes when it rains.

Tips **Where to Stock Up for a Big Sur Picnic**

Talk about one-stop shopping: **The Big Sur Center Deli** not only sells fresh-baked goods, a variety of salads, wine, and beer, it also carries a slew of more substantial options such as fettuccine, calzones, enchiladas, and barbecued chicken—all made on the premises. You can even rent videos and do your grocery shopping here. Sandwiches are made to order, or you can grab a ready-made hoagie or vegetarian portobello mushroom on a roll. Sugary treats and coffee drinks are available. It's on Highway 1, 26½ miles south of Carmel, next to the Big Sur Post Office, and is open daily from 7:30am to 8:30pm; ℂ 831/667-2225.

Cielo Restaurant 🌟🌟 NEW AMERICAN   Like the resort, Ventana's "heaven" restaurant is woodsy but extravagant, and is an excellent place to dine alfresco at lunch or for a romantic dinner. The airy cedar interior is divided into two spaces: the lounge, where a wooden bar and cocktail tables look onto a roaring fire and through picturesque windows; and the dining room, which overlooks the mountains and/or the ocean. But in summer it's the outdoor patio, with its views of the ocean expanse and 50 miles of Big Sur coast, that's the coveted lunch spot. Unlike some costly restaurants in the area, a meal here is as gratifying as the surroundings. Lunch offers sandwiches, burgers, and an array of gourmet salads, as well as main courses such as grilled Atlantic salmon; dinner includes stellar starters like a perfectly dressed Caesar salad and a well-balanced chanterelle-mushroom risotto, and main courses such as oak-grilled Kansas City steak au poivre, caramelized Maine Diver scallops in a red Thai curry coconut milk broth, and summer vegetable risotto with English peas and summer squash.

At Ventana Inn and Spa, Calif. 1, Big Sur. ℂ 831/667-4242. Fax 831/667-2287. www.ventanainn.com. Reservations recommended for dinner. Main courses $11–$17 lunch, $23–$32 dinner. AE, DC, DISC, MC, V. Daily noon–3:30pm and 6–9pm.

Deetjen's Big Sur Inn Restaurant 🌟 AMERICAN   With the feel of an English farmhouse—white painted wood walls, wood-burning stove, dimly lit old-fashioned lamps, country antiques—this cozy, country setting is the perfect venue for the delicious comfort food and friendly service you'll find here. Mornings start off with a cup of the strong coffee, and breakfast offers all the basics: omelets, eggs Benedict, pancakes, and granola, most of which come piled high with breakfast potatoes. Dinner is highly regarded by locals, and might include grilled chicken with mushrooms and a garlic Marsala sauce; roasted rack of lamb with a panko crust; prime New York steak with macadamia-nut risotto; and roast duckling with brandy, peppercorn, and molasses sauce.

On Calif. 1. ℂ 831/667-2377. www.deetjens.com. Reservations recommended. Main courses $4.25–$12 breakfast, $15–$33 dinner. MC, V. Daily 8am–noon and 6–9pm.

Nepenthe AMERICAN   Stop by Nepenthe if only to admire the view. At 808 feet above sea level along the cliffs overlooking the ocean, the view from your table is naturally celestial—especially when fog lingers above the water. On a warm day, join the crowds on the terrace. On colder days, go the indoor route: The redwood-and-adobe structure offers a warmer and equally magical view, and with its wood-burning fireplace, redwood ceilings, and bay-front windows, the atmosphere is something you can't find anywhere else. Unfortunately, that's not been my experience with the fare. I would scoff at an $11 burger (without fries!), $16 swordfish sandwich, and a $4 draft Budweiser anywhere else—but I'd cough up the cash all over again for an afternoon here. (Think of it as nominal admission to dine at heights only angels usually enjoy.) Lunch is adequate and basic: burgers, sandwiches, and salads. Dinner main courses include steak, broiled chicken, and fresh fish prepared any number of ways, though I suggest you come for lunch and spend big dinner bucks elsewhere.

Calif. 1, 29 miles south of Carmel (5 miles south of the River Inn). © **831/667-2345.** Fax 831/667-2394. www.nepenthebigsur.com. Reservations accepted only for parties of 5 or more. Main courses $9–$25. AE, MC, V. Daily 11:30am–10pm.

8 Pinnacles National Monument ★

58 miles SE of Monterey

Once a little-known outpost, the 24,000-acre Pinnacles National Monument has become one of the most popular weekend climbing destinations in central California over the past decade. The mild winter climate and plentiful routes make this a perfect off-season training ground for climbers. It's also a popular haven for campers, hikers, and nature lovers. One of the most unique chaparral ecosystems in the world supports a community of plant and animal life, including one of California's largest breeding populations of raptors.

The Pinnacles themselves—hundreds of towering crags, spires, and hoodoos—are seemingly out of place in the rolling hills of the coast range. And they are, in fact, out of place, part of the eroded remains of a volcano formed 23 million years ago, 195 miles south in the middle of the Mojave Desert. The movement of the San Andreas Fault, which runs just east of the park, carried them here. (The other half of the volcano remains in the Mojave.)

You could spend days here, but it's possible to cover the most interesting features in a weekend. With a single hike, you can go from the oak woodland around the Bear Gulch Visitor Center to the dry, desolate crags of the high peaks, then back down through a half-mile-long cave with underground waterfalls.

ESSENTIALS

GETTING THERE   Two entrances lead to the park: The **West Entrance** from Soledad and U.S. 101 is a dusty, winding single-lane road (not suitable for trailers) with the best drive-up view. It doesn't connect with the east side.

The alternative route is via the **East Entrance.** Unless you're coming from nearby, take the longer drive on Calif. 25 to enter through the east. Because most of the peaks of the Pinnacles face east and the watershed drains east, most of the interesting hikes and geologic features are on this side. No road crosses the park.

FEES   Park entrance fees, good for 7 days, are $2 per person or $5 per car.

VISITOR CENTER   The first place you should go when entering from the east is the **Bear Gulch Visitor Center** (© **831/389-4485**), open daily from 9am to 5pm. This small center is rich with exhibits on the park's history, wildlife, and geology, and also has a great selection of nature handbooks and climbing guides for the Pinnacles. Climbers should check with rangers about closures and other information before heading out: Many routes are closed during hawk- and falcon-nesting season, and rangers like to know how many climbers are in the park.

Adjacent to the visitor center, the Bear Gulch picnic ground is a great place to fuel up before setting out on a hike or, if you're not planning to leave your car, one of the best places to gaze up at dramatic spires of the high peaks (the ultimate spot is from the west side).

For more information, log on to the park's website at **www.nps.gov/pinn**.

REGULATIONS & WARNINGS   Beware of poison oak, particularly in Bear Gulch. Rattlesnakes are common but rarely seen. Bikes and dogs are prohibited on all trails, and no backcountry camping is allowed in the park.

Hiking through this variety of landscapes demands versatility. Come prepared with a good pair of hiking shoes, snacks, lots of water, and a flashlight.

Daytime temperatures often exceed 100°F (38°C) in summer, so the best time of year to visit is spring, when the wildflowers are blooming, or in the fall. Crowds are common during spring weekends.

HIKING & EXPLORING THE PARK

To see most of the park in a single, moderately strenuous morning, take the **Condor Gulch Trail** from the visitor center. As you climb out of the parking area, the Pinnacles' wind-sculpted spires seem to grow taller. In less than 2 miles, you're among them, and Condor Gulch intersects with the **High Peaks Trail.** The view from the top spans miles: the Salinas Valley to your west, the Pinnacles below, and miles of coast to the east. After traversing the high peaks (including stretches of footholds carved in steep rock faces) for about a mile, the trail drops back toward the visitor center via a valley filled with eerie-looking hoodoos.

In another 1.5 miles you'll reach the reservoir marking the top of **Bear Gulch Cave,** which closes occasionally; in 1998 it closed due both to storm damage and to accommodate migrating Townsend bats, who in the past several years have come here to have their babies. It's usually open, but if you want to explore, you'll need your flashlight and you might get wet; still, this half-mile-long talus cave is a thrill. From the end of the cave, you're just a short walk (through the most popular climbing area of the park) away from the visitor center. It's also possible to hike just Bear Gulch and the cave, then return via the **Moses Spring Trail.** It's about 2 miles round-trip, but you'll miss the view from the top.

If you're coming from the West Entrance, the **Juniper Canyon Trail** is a short (1.25 miles), but very steep, blast to the top of the high peaks. You'll definitely earn the view. Otherwise, try the short **Balconies Trail** to the monument's other talus cave, **Balconies Cave.** Flashlights are required here, too.

CAMPING

The park's campground on the west side was demolished by El Niño storms in 1997 and 1998 and is not scheduled for repair. Now the only campground is the privately run **Pinnacles Campground, Inc.,** on the east side (© **831/389-4462; www.pinncamp.com**), which charges $7 per person. It's just outside the park (off Calif. 25, 32 miles south of Hollister), with lots of privacy and space between sites, plus showers, a store, and a large swimming pool. It's close enough so you can hike into the park from the campground, though it will add a few miles to your outing. Though private campgrounds are often overdeveloped, the management here saw the benefits of leaving the surroundings natural. Dogs are not recommended, but you can bring them if you're willing to pay a $10 leash deposit. *Note:* No other animals are allowed at Pinnacles.

12

The Central Coast

by Matthew Richard Poole

California's Central Coast—a gorgeous amalgam of beaches, lakes, and mountains—is the state's most diverse region. The narrow strip that runs for more than 100 miles from San Simeon to Ventura spans several climate zones and is home to an eclectic mix of students, middle-class workers, retirees, farmers, immigrant labor, computer techies, and fishermen. The ride along Calif. 1, which follows the ocean cliffs, is almost always packed with rental cars, RVs, and bicycles. Traffic may give your brakes a workout, but it also allows you to take longer looks at one of the spectacular vistas in the world.

Whether you're driving up from Los Angeles or down from San Francisco, Calif. 1 is the most scenic and leisurely route. (U.S. 101 gets you there faster but is less picturesque.) Most bicyclists pedal from north to south, the direction of the prevailing winds. Those in cars may prefer to drive south to north so they can get a better look at the coastline as it unfolds toward the west. No matter which direction you drive, break out the camera—you're about to experience unparalleled beauty, California-style.

1 San Simeon: Hearst Castle ★★★

205 miles S of San Francisco (via Calif. 1); 254 miles NW of Los Angeles

Few buildings on earth are as elaborate as **Hearst Castle.** The 165-room estate of publishing magnate William Randolph Hearst, high above the village of San Simeon atop a hill he called La Cuesta Encantada ("the Enchanted Hill"), is an ego trip *par excellence.* One of the last great estates of America's Gilded Age, it's an over-the-top monument to wealth—and to the power that money brings.

Hearst Castle is a sprawling compound, constructed over 28 years in a Mediterranean Revival style, in magical surroundings. The focal point of the estate is the you-have-to-see-it-to-believe-it **Casa Grande,** a 100-plus-room mansion filled with art and antiques. Hearst acquired most of his collection via New York auction houses, where he bought entire rooms (including walls, ceilings, and floors) and shipped them here. The result is an old-world-style castle done in a mix-and-match style. You'll see 400-year-old Spanish and Italian ceilings, 500-year-old mantels, 16th-century Florentine bedsteads, Renaissance paintings, Flemish tapestries, and innumerable other treasures.

Three opulent "guesthouses" also contain magnificent works of art. A lavish private movie theater was used to screen first-run films twice nightly—once for employees, and again for the guests and host.

And then there are the swimming pools. The Roman-inspired indoor pool has intricate mosaic work, Carrara-marble replicas of Greek gods and goddesses, and alabaster globe lamps that create the illusion of moonlight. The breathtaking

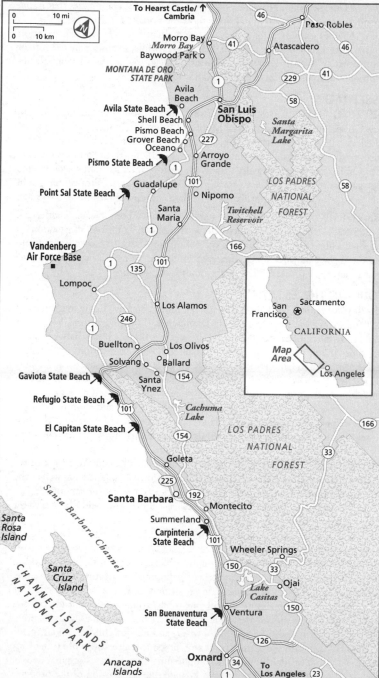

The Central Coast

outdoor Greco-Roman Neptune pool, flanked by marble colonnades that frame the distant sea, is one of the mansion's most memorable features.

In 1957, in exchange for a massive tax write-off, the Hearst Corporation donated the estate to the state of California (while retaining ownership of approximately 80,000 acres). The California Department of Parks and Recreation now administers it as a State Historic Monument.

ESSENTIALS

GETTING THERE   Hearst Castle is on Calif. 1, about 42 miles north of San Luis Obispo and 94 miles south of Monterey. From San Francisco or Monterey, take U.S. 101 south to Paso Robles, then Calif. 46 west to Calif. 1, and Calif. 1 north to the castle. From Los Angeles, take U.S. 101 north to San Luis Obispo, then Calif. 1 north to the castle. Park in the visitor center lot; a bus takes guided tour guests up the hill to the estate. The movie theater and visitor center adjoin the parking lot and are easily accessible without heading up to the actual estate.

VISITOR INFORMATION   To get information about Hearst Castle, call ℂ 805/927-2020 or log on to **www.hearstcastle.org**. For more information on nearby Cambria (see below), check out **www.cambria-online.com** or stop into the **Cambria Chamber of Commerce**'s visitor center at 767 Main St., in the west village (ℂ **805/927-3624;** www.cambriachamber.org).

TOURING THE ESTATE

Hearst Castle can be visited only by guided tours, conducted daily beginning at 8:20am, except on New Year's Day, Thanksgiving, and Christmas. Two to six tours leave every hour, depending on the season. Allow 2 hours between starting times if you plan on taking more than one tour. Reservations are strongly recommended and can be made up to 8 weeks in advance. Tickets can be purchased by phone or online at **California Reservations** (ℂ **800/444-4445;** www.hearstcastle.org). Four different daytime tours are offered on a daily basis, each lasting 1 hour 45 minutes, including the bus ride to and from the castle.

The **Experience Tour (Tour 1)** is ideal for first-time visitors and is the first to get filled up. In addition to the swimming pools, this tour visits several rooms on the ground floor of Casa Grande, including Hearst's private theater, where you'll see some home movies taken during the castle's heyday. You'll get to see the sculptures and flowers in the gardens and the formal esplanade, as well as the largest guesthouse, Casa del Sol. This tour includes a ticket for the film *Hearst Castle: Building the Dream* (see below). The price for the tour and film is $18 for adults, $9 for kids 6 to 17, and free for children under 6.

Tour 2 focuses on Casa Grande's upper floors, including Hearst's opulent library, private suite of rooms, and lots of fabulous bathrooms. Ongoing efforts are made to lend a lived-in look to the house; examples are the lifelike food in the kitchen and pantry, and vintage sewing equipment in Marion Davies's suite. Although Tour 1 is recommended for first-timers, Tour 2 is a perfectly fine choice if you're only planning to take one tour, particularly if your interest lies more in the home's private areas. The price for Tour 2 (as well as tours 3 and 4, below) is $12 for adults, $7 for kids 6 to 17, and free for children under 6.

Tour 3 delves into the construction and subsequent alterations of Hearst Castle. You'll visit Casa del Monte, a guesthouse unaltered from its original design, then head to the North Wing of Casa Grande, the last portion of the property to be completed, to see the contrast in styles. A short video, which uses film and photographs from the 1920s and 1930s to depict the construction process, is shown. Tour 3 is fascinating for architecture buffs and detail hounds, but it shouldn't be the first and only tour if you've never visited the castle before.

Tour 4 is dedicated to the estate's gardens, terraces, and walkways, and is offered from April to October. You'll also tour the Casa del Mar guesthouse, the wine cellar of Casa Grande, and the dressing rooms at the Neptune Pool. Like Tour 3, this one is best taken after you've seen some of the more essential areas of the estate.

Evening tours are held most Friday and Saturday nights during spring and fall. These last about 30 minutes longer than the daytime tours, and visit highlights of the main house, the largest and most elaborate guesthouse, and the estate's pools and gardens, which are illuminated by hundreds of restored light fixtures. The pools in particular are most breathtaking when seen this way. The entire living-history experience is enhanced by docents dressed in period costume assuming a variety of roles. The evening tour is $24 for adults, $12 for kids 6 to 17, and free for children under 6.

Tip: Because these are walking tours, be sure to wear comfortable shoes—you'll be walking about a half mile per tour, which includes between 150 and 400 steps to climb or descend. (Wheelchair tours are available by calling © **805/927-2020** at least 10 days in advance.)

The latest addition to the estate is the giant-screen **Hearst Castle National Geographic Theater,** which you can visit regardless of whether you take a tour. The main attraction is *Hearst Castle: Building the Dream* and is included in the Experience Tour package. For current information, call © **805/927-6811** or visit their website at www.ngtheater.com. The Hearst film shows every 45 minutes, and tickets cost $8 for adults and $6 for kids 17 and under.

WHAT TO SEE & DO IN NEARBY CAMBRIA ✿

After driving for close to an hour without passing anything but lush green hills and nature at its most glorious (especially from Calif. 46 off U.S. 101), it's a quaint surprise to roll into the adorable coastal minitown of Cambria, 6 miles south of San Simeon. Cambria, known as an artists' colony, is so charming that the town itself is reason enough to make the drive. With little more than 3 blocks worth of shops, restaurants, and a handful of B&Bs, Cambria is the perfect place to escape the everyday, enjoy the endless expanses of pristine coastal terrain, and meander through little shops selling local artwork and antiques.

An overnight stay in Cambia also allows visitors to see the area's "new" attraction: **elephant seals.** Once thought to be extinct, since 1990 these 3,000-pound mammals have returned to Piedras Blancas, a shoreline 12 miles north of Cambria—today more than 2,000 of these magnificent, prehistoric-looking beasts are counted here annually. Breeding takes place here December through March; molting occurs August through September. Keep your distance from the elephant seals: They're a protected species and can be dangerous if approached. There is a parking lot, and docents are usually on hand to answer questions. The beaches and coves are also wonderful places for humans to frolic as well.

SHOPPING

Shopping is a major pastime in the village. Boutique owners are hyper-savvy about keeping their merchandise current—and priced just a hair lower than L.A. or San Francisco. This close-knit community has always attracted artists and artisans. For the finest handcrafted glass artworks, from affordable jewelry to investment-scale sculpture, head to **Seekers Collection & Gallery,** 4090 Burton Dr. (© **805/927-4352;** www.seekersglass.com). Nearby, at **Moonstones Gallery,** 4070 Burton Dr. (© **805/927-3447**), you'll find a selection of works

Fun Fact **Weekends at the Ranch: William Randolph Hearst & the Legacy of Hearst Castle**

The lavish palace that William Randolph Hearst always referred to simply as "the ranch" took root in 1919. William Randolph ("W.R." to his friends) had inherited 275,000 acres from his father, mining baron George Hearst, and was well on his way to building a formidable media empire. He often escaped to a spot known as "Camp Hill" on his lands in the Santa Lucia Mountains above the village of San Simeon, the site of boyhood family outings. Complaining that "I get tired of going up there and camping in tents," Hearst hired architect Julia Morgan to design the retreat that would become one of the most famous private homes in the world.

An art collector with indiscriminate taste and inexhaustible funds, Hearst overwhelmed Morgan with interiors and furnishings from the ancestral collections of Europe. Each week, railroad cars carrying fragments of Roman temples, lavish doors and carved ceilings from Italian monasteries, Flemish tapestries, hastily rolled paintings by the old masters, ancient Persian rugs, and antique French furniture arrived—5 tons at a time—in San Simeon. Orson Welles's 1941 masterpiece *Citizen Kane*, which depicts a Hearst-like mogul with a similarly excessive estate called Xanadu, has a memorable scene of hoarded priceless treasures warehoused in dusty piles, stretching as far as the eye can see. Like Kane, Hearst, once described as a man with an "edifice complex," purchased so much that only a fraction of what he bought was ever installed in the estate.

In 1925 Hearst separated from his wife and began to spend time in Los Angeles overseeing his movie company, Cosmopolitan Pictures. His principal actress, Marion Davies, became W.R.'s constant companion and hostess at Hearst Castle; this would be her main role for the rest of his life. The ranch soon became a playground for the Hollywood crowd as well as for dignitaries like Winston Churchill and playwright

ranging from woven crafts to jewelry and an exceptional collection of woodcarvings and other crafts. If a visit to the nearby Paso Robles wine country has inspired you, **Fermentations,** 4056 Burton Dr. (© **805/927-7141;** www.fermentations.com), has wines, wine accessories, and gifts, plus wine country gourmet goodies open for tasting. Women who appreciate casual style and ease of care mustn't miss **Leslie Mark,** 801 Main St. (© **805/927-1434;** www.lesliemark.com), and her deceptively simple line of versatile cotton and rayon separates. Nearby, **Heart's Ease,** 4101 Burton Dr. (© **800/266-4372** or 805/927-5224), is inside a quaint historic cottage and is packed with an abundance of garden delights, apothecary herbs, and custom-blended potpourris.

If Cambria has tickled your artistic instincts, a few miles south is another charming, tiny artists colony, **Harmony.**

WHERE TO STAY

Cambria's popularity in summertime and on holiday weekends makes advance planning a necessity. If my favorites are full, try one of these alternatives: **Captain's**

George Bernard Shaw, who is said to have wryly remarked of the estate, "This is the way God would have done it if He had the money."

Despite its opulence, Hearst promoted "the ranch" as a casual weekend home. He regularly laid the massive refectory table in the dining room with paper napkins and bottled ketchup and pickles to evoke a rustic camplike atmosphere. In Hearst's beautiful library, his priceless collection of ancient Greek pottery—one of the greatest collections of its kind in the world—is arranged casually among the rare volumes, like knickknacks.

The Hollywood crowd would take Hearst's private railway car from Los Angeles to San Luis Obispo, where a fleet of limousines waited to transport them to San Simeon. Those who didn't come by train were treated to a flight on Hearst's private plane from the Burbank airport (MGM head Irving Thalberg and his wife, Norma Shearer, preferred this mode of transportation). Hearst, an avid aviator, had a landing strip built; Charles Lindbergh used it when he flew up for a visit in the summer of 1928.

Oh, if the walls could talk . . . Atop one of the castle's towers are the hexagonal Celestial Suites. One was a favorite of Clark Gable and Carole Lombard, who would be startled out of their romantic slumber by the clamor of 18 carillon bells overhead. David Niven, a frequent guest, was one of the unknown number who defied Hearst's edict against liquor in private rooms: Niven was called upon more than once to explain the "empties" under the bed (which Cardinal Richelieu once owned) in his customary suite.

W. R. Hearst and Marion Davies hosted frequent costume parties at the ranch, which were as intricately planned as a movie production. The most legendary, the Circus Party, was held to celebrate W.R.'s 75th birthday on April 29, 1938. Much of Hollywood attended to honor the tycoon, including grande dame Bette Davis—dressed as a bearded lady.

Cove Inn, 6454 Moonstone Beach Dr. (© **800/781-COVE** or 805/927-8581; www.captainscoveinn.com), is a small beachfront B&B whose motel-style exterior belies the array of creature comforts provided by the family owners. The **Ragged Point Inn,** 19019 Hwy. 1 (© **805/927-5708;** fax 805/927-8862; www.ragged pointinn.com), is 21 miles north of Cambria and offers sweeping ocean views from every room. One mile north is **San Simeon State Beach** (© **800/444-7275** or 805/927-2020), a 133-site beachfront campground.

Best Western Cavalier Oceanfront Resort ⚓ *(Kids)* Of the dozen or so budget and midrange motels along Highway 1 near Hearst Castle, this surprisingly nice chain is the only one that's actually oceanfront. Sprawled across a gentle slope, the hotel invites guests to huddle around cliff-side bonfires each evening. Every room—whether you choose a basic double or opt for extras such as a fireplace, ocean view, wet bar, or oceanfront terrace—features an array of amenities (tape rentals for the VCR are conveniently next door). The Cavalier is top-notch in its class, and a terrific choice for Castle-bound families.

9415 Hearst Dr. (Calif. 1), San Simeon, CA 93452. ℭ 800/826-8168 or 805/927-4688. Fax 805/927-6472. www.cavalierresort.com. 90 units. $119–$259 double. AE, DC, DISC, MC, V. Pets accepted. **Amenities:** Restaurant; 2 outdoor heated pools; Jacuzzi; exercise room; concierge; room service (7am–9pm); coin-op laundry. *In room:* TV/VCR, dataport, minibar, coffeemaker, hair dryer, iron.

Cambria Pines Lodge 🏵

On a mountain just above town on 25 acres of mostly landscaped grounds dotted with Monterey pines, the Cambria Pines is equal parts vacation lodge and summer camp. Accommodations are in 31 different buildings, and range from rustic, secluded cabins to contemporary hotel-style units. At the heart is the main lodge, a re-creation of the original 1927 building that sports a communal welcome. Nearly all the rooms have fireplaces; dedicated bargain hunters can snag the lowest rates by choosing an older cabin without one. Bonus points for the awesome, nearly Olympic-size pool.

2905 Burton Dr., Cambria, CA 93428. ℭ 800/445-6868 or 805/927-4200. Fax 805/927-4016. www.cambria pineslodge.com. 125 units. $99–$299 double. Rates include buffet breakfast. AE, DC, DISC, MC, V. **Amenities:** Restaurant; large heated pool; Jacuzzi; massage. *In room:* A/C, TV, fridge, coffeemaker, hair dryer, iron.

FogCatcher Inn 🏵 *Value*

You'll spot the FogCatcher by its faux English architecture (though a contemporary hotel), that fits right in with the mishmash of styles on funky Moonstone Beach. The U-shaped building is situated so many rooms have unencumbered views of the crashing waves across the street; some gaze oceanward over a sea of parked cars, and others are hopelessly land-locked—be sure to inquire when reserving. Though rates vary wildly according to view, each room interior sports identical amenities and comforts. Immaculately maintained and furnished in a comfy cottage style with pine furniture, each room is made cozier by a gas fireplace and also has a microwave oven. Unlike many comparably priced Moonstone Beach lodgings, the FogCatcher has a heated swimming pool and Jacuzzi. Stop by the breakfast room in the morning for basic coffee, juice, and muffins to start the day.

6400 Moonstone Beach Dr., Cambria, CA 93428. ℭ 800/425-4121 or 805/927-1400. www.fog catcherinn.com. Fax 805/927-0204. 60 units. $189–$269 double; from $359 suites. Rates include continental breakfast. AE, DISC, MC, V. Pets accepted in select rooms with $25 fee per night. **Amenities:** Outdoor heated pool; Jacuzzi. *In room:* TV, fireplace, minibar, fridge, coffeemaker, hair dryer, iron.

J. Patrick House 🏵

Hidden in a pine-filled neighborhood overlooking Cambria's village, this picture-perfect B&B is cozy, elegant, and welcoming. The main house is a two-story log cabin, where each afternoon innkeepers Ann and John host wine and hors d'oeuvres next to the living room fireplace, and each morning serve breakfast by windows overlooking a hummingbird-filled garden. Most guest rooms are in the adjacent carriage house and feature wood-burning fireplaces, feather duvets, bedtime milk and cookies, and country elements like knotty pine, bent-twig furniture, calico prints, and hand-stitched quilts. Amenities like phone, fax, and guest fridge are available in the common area.

2990 Burton Dr., Cambria, CA 93428. ℭ 800/341-5258 or 805/927-3812. Fax 805/927-6759. www.jpatrick house.com. 8 units. $155–$195 double. Rates include full breakfast, afternoon wine/hors d'oeuvres, and evening milk and cookies. Seasonal discounts and packages available. DISC, MC, V. *In room:* Hair dryer, iron available upon request, no phone.

Olallieberry Inn 🏵🏵

This 1873 Greek Revival house is my favorite B&B in the area. The grounds are manicured but bloom whimsically. In the afternoon the aromas of baked brie and homemade bread (served during the wine hour) waft through the main house, and the staff does everything imaginable to make your stay special. They also have a passion for cooking and gardening, but the decor doesn't fall by the wayside: A countrified berry motif reigns, and the guest rooms are lovingly and individually appointed. Each has its own private bathroom, although some are across or down the hall. Rooms in an adjoining building overlook a creek; they're charming and have a fireplace and private deck. The full breakfast—accompanied by olallieberry jam, of course—is gourmet all the way. Amenities like phone, fax, and guest fridge are available in the common area.

2476 Main St., Cambria, CA 93428. ℂ 888/927-3222 or 805/927-3222. Fax 805/927-0202. www.olallieberry.com. 9 units. $127–$207 double. Rates include full breakfast and evening wine and hors d'oeuvres. AE, MC, V. **Amenities:** Massage. *In room:* Hair dryer, iron available upon request, no phone.

WHERE TO DINE

Tiny Cambria boasts an unusual concentration of superb restaurants. (The town's eateries dominate Zagat's mere two pages of Central Coast listings.) In addition to the restaurants listed below, consider **Moonstone Beach Bar & Grill,** 6550 Moonstone Beach Dr. (ℂ **805/927-3859**), whose incredible view must be what accounts for prices on the expensive side for this tasty but casual restaurant—stick to breakfast or lunch; or local institution **Linn's Main Binn,** 2277 Main St. (ℂ **805/927-0371**), a casual all-day diner featuring homemade potpies, fresh-from-the-farm salads, breakfast treats, and Linn's famous fruit pies.

Bistro Solé ⭐ ECLECTIC   In an old house surrounded by ivy gardens in the town's east village, this is one of the most sophisticated and contemporary places to eat in town. The cozy California bungalow and the tree-filled back garden are the ideal settings for to-die-for oysters Rockefeller, tasty wontons with baked yam and goat cheese, lobster bisque, fresh salads, and an eclectic selection of main courses. When I last dined here, the nut-crusted pork loin was a bit dry, but the charbroiled New Zealand rack of lamb in a cabernet reduction was on the money. The 20 or so main courses include a handful of pastas balanced with a selection of chicken and daily seafood specials. Lunch plates range from fish and chips to wild-mushroom fettuccine, artichoke risotto, and the great Bistro Burger.

1980 Main St., Cambria. ℂ **805/927-0887.** Reservations recommended. Main courses $9–$11 at lunch, $12–$18 at dinner; obligatory 20% gratuity for parties of 6 or more. MC, V. Daily 11:30am–10pm.

Robin's ⭐ ECLECTIC   Robin's is a restaurant with something for everyone, from exotic dishes from Mexico, Thailand, India, and beyond to more straightforward preparations like a tasty salad, a juicy steak, and a nightly vegetarian dish, along with tofu and tempeh specials. Offerings include a salmon bisque appetizer; artichoke and Gorgonzola ravioli in a spinach-cream sauce; and other combinations such as tandoori prawns with basmati brown rice, fruit chutney, and chapati; and *roghan josh,* Indian lamb curry topped with yogurt, almonds, and toasted coconut. Don't miss dessert—try the espresso-soaked cake with Mascarpone mousse and shaved chocolate or vanilla-custard bread pudding.

4095 Burton Dr., Cambria. ℂ **805/927-5007.** www.robinsrestaurant.com. Reservations recommended. Main courses $7–$13 lunch, $11–$18 dinner. MC, V. Daily 11am–9pm (open late in summer).

Sea Chest Oyster Bar ⭐ SEAFOOD   Feeling like a dozen other seaside old-salt hangouts, the strangely familiar Sea Chest is a must for seafood lovers. Sporting nautical kitsch and warm, welcoming atmosphere, this gray clapboard cottage even has a game-filled lounge complete with cribbage, checkers, and chess to keep you amused during the inevitable wait for a table. Oysters are the main attraction: on the half shell, oyster stew, oysters Casino, oysters Rockefeller, or "devils on horseback" (with wine, garlic, and bacon). The menu is also filled with very fresh seafood from local and worldwide waters: steamed New Zealand green-lipped mussels, clams in several preparations, halibut, salmon, lobster, scampi, plus whatever looked good off the boats that morning. There's a respectable list of microbrewed and imported beers, along with a selection of Central Coast wines. *Note:* If you don't enjoy seafood, stay away—there's not even a token steak on this menu!

6216 Moonstone Beach Dr. (𝒞 805/927-4514. Reservations not accepted. Main courses $11–$22. No credit cards. Wed–Mon 5:30–9pm (open Tues May–Sept only).

Sow's Ear Café 𝒦𝒦 AMERICAN/SEAFOOD   This tiny old cottage at the center of the village has been transformed into a warm, romantic hideaway. The best tables are in the fireside front room, lit just enough to highlight its rustic wood-and-brick decor. Pigs appear everywhere, in oil paintings, as ceramic or cast-iron models, and the logo is a woodcut sow. Though the menu features plenty of contemporary California cuisine, the most popular dishes are American favorites given a contemporary lift; these include a warmly satisfying chicken-fried steak with gravy, chicken and dumplings, and zesty baby pork ribs. Other standouts are parchment-wrapped salmon, and pork loin glazed with chunky olallieberry chutney. Every meal begins with the restaurant's signature marbled bread baked in terra-cotta flowerpots, and the wine list is among the area's best. *Tip:* Early birds (5–6pm nightly) choose from six dinners from $11 to $14.

2248 Main St. (𝒞 805/927-4865. Reservations recommended. Main courses $14–$23. DISC, MC, V. Daily 5–9pm (open later in summer).

2 Morro Bay

124 miles S of Monterey; 235 miles S of San Francisco (via Calif. 1); 220 miles N of L.A.

Morro Bay is separated from the ocean by a long peninsula of towering sand dunes. It's best known for dramatic **Morro Rock,** an enormous egg-shaped monolith that juts out of the water just offshore. Across from the rock, a huge oceanfront electrical plant mars the visual appeal of the otherwise pristine bay, which is filled with birds, sea mammals, and calm water offering plenty of recreational activities.

Other than gawking at the "Gibraltar of the Pacific," there's not all that much to see in the town itself. Motels, shops, and restaurants line the waterfront Embarcadero and adjacent blocks, but the town's best feature is its setting: The beaches and wildlife sanctuaries can be quite peaceful and wondrous.

ESSENTIALS

Morro Bay is on U.S. 101 (itself only four lanes on this stretch). The **Morro Bay Chamber of Commerce,** 880 Main St., Morro Bay, CA 93442 (𝒞 **800/231-0592** or 805/772-4467; www.morrobay.com), offers lots of information. It's open Monday through Friday from 8:30am to 5pm and Saturday from 10am to 3pm.

EXPLORING THE AREA

Most visitors come to Morro Bay to ogle the 576-foot **Morro Rock,** the much-photographed Central Coast icon that anchors the mouth of the waterway. This ancient landmark, whose name comes from the Spanish word for a Moorish turban, is a volcanic remnant inhabited by the peregrine falcon and other migratory birds.

BEACHES   Popular **Atascadero State Beach,** just north of Morro Rock, has gentle waves and lovely views. Restrooms, showers, and dressing rooms are available. Just north of Atascadero is **Morro Strand State Beach,** a long, sandy stretch with normally gentle surf. Restrooms and picnic tables are available. Morro Strand has its own campgrounds; for information, call 𝒞 **805/772-2560,** or reserve through **Park-Net** (𝒞 **800/444-7275;** www.reserveamerica.com).

STATE PARKS   Cabrillo Peak, in the **Morro Bay State Park** (© 805/
772-7434), makes a terrific day hike and offers 360-degree views from its summit. There's a zigzagging trail, but the best way to reach the top is by bush-
whacking straight up the gentle slope—a hike that takes about 2 hours
round-trip. To reach the trail head, take Calif. 1 south and turn left at the Morro
Bay State Park/Montana de Oro State Park exit. Follow South Bay Boulevard for
three-quarters of a mile, then take the left fork another half a mile to the
Cabrillo Peak dirt parking lot on your left. The park also offers camping and
the beautiful **Morro Bay Golf Course,** which charges $32 to $40 for greens fees
(© 805/782-8060).

South of Morro Bay in Los Osos is **Montana de Oro State Park** ("Mountain
of Gold"), known as "petite Big Sur" because of its stony cliffs and rugged terrain. There's great swimming at Spooner's Cove and lots of easy hiking trails,
including some that lead to coastal vistas or forest streams. The Hazard Reef
Trail will take you up on the Morro Bay Sandspit dunes. The park's campground
is in the trees, across from the beach, and is worth the detour, if you have a reservation in summer. For information, call the park rangers (© 805/528-0513), or
reserve a spot through **Park-Net** (© 800/444-7275; www.reserveamerica.com).

ON THE WATER   You can take a kayak tour with **Kayak Horizons of Morro
Bay,** 551 Embarcadero (© 805/772-1119). If you've always yearned for sailing
lessons, call ahead to the **Sailing Center of Morro Bay** (© 805/772-9463). It's
next to Morro Bay Yacht Club and offers everything from 1-day intro classes to
weeklong series and scheduled sunset sails.

IN TOWN   The Embarcadero is also home to the **Giant Chessboard,** whose
3-foot-tall redwood pieces were inspired by open-air boards in Germany. Nearby
is the **Morro Bay Aquarium,** 595 Embarcadero (© 805/772-7647), a modest
operation notable for the injured or abandoned sea otters, seals, and sea lions it
rescues and rehabilitates. During their stay, all the animals learn to perform tricks
for a morsel of fishy food (admission is $2 for adults, $1 for children 5–11).

WHERE TO STAY

Baywood Bed & Breakfast Inn *(Finds)*   South of Morro Bay in Baywood Park,
facing out onto Morro's "back bay," this two-story gray inn is a 1970s garden-
style office building with B&B suites, each furnished in a distinctive (over-the-
top) theme and Grandma-style flair. Every room has a private entrance, gas
fireplace, and microwave (plus a fridge stocked with complimentary sodas and
snacks); all but a few have bay views. Included in your stay is a full breakfast each
morning and a late-afternoon wine-and-cheese reception highlighted by a room
tour. If you're looking for solitude, Baywood Park fits the bill. There are a couple of decent restaurants on the block, and pretty Montana de Oro is close by.

1370 Second St. (2½ blocks south of Santa Ysabel Ave.), Baywood Park, CA 93042. © 805/528-8888. Fax
805/528-8887. www.baywoodinn.com. 18 units. $130–$170 double; from $150 suite. Extra person $15. Rates
include full breakfast and afternoon wine and cheese. MC, V. *In room:* TV/VCR, kitchenette, minibar, fridge,
coffeemaker, hair dryer.

The Inn at Morro Bay   This comfortable and moderately priced resort is
smart enough to let its splendid natural surroundings be the focus of attention—
beach cruisers and mountain bikes are loaned out to guests. Situated right on the
water, the inn's two-story Cape Cod–style buildings have contemporary interiors
amid a quiet garden setting. The inn has been enhancing itself with a spa ambience; features include an on-site massage center and private balcony Jacuzzis for
some guest quarters. Rates vary according to view, with the best rooms enjoying

unobstructed views of Morro Rock plus access to a bay-front sun deck; those in back face the swimming pool, gardens, and eucalyptus-forested golf course at Morro Bay State Park (see above). The hotel has a romantic bay side lounge and California/Mediterranean restaurant.

60 State Park Rd., Morro Bay, CA 93442. ✆ **800/321-9566** or 805/772-5651. Fax 805/772-4779. www.innat morrobay.com. 98 units. $159–$379 double. Midweek and seasonal discounts available. AE, DISC, MC, V. Take Main St. south, past park entrance. **Amenities:** Restaurant; lounge; outdoor heated pool; full-service spa; nearby golf and water recreation; complimentary bikes; room service (7am–10pm); massage; babysitting. *In room:* TV, dataport, fridge, coffeemaker, hair dryer, iron, CD player.

WHERE TO DINE

Hofbrau *Value* *Kids* GERMAN/AMERICAN   When you're hungry in Morro Bay and want something other than fish and chips, Hofbrau is the place. Although they do serve the standard wharfside fare, the star here is the roast beef French Dip (their strategically placed carving station ensures its popularity). Those in the know order the minisandwich, which is a dollar less and just an inch shorter. As the name would suggest, they have a nice selection of beers as well as a kids' menu with six choices at $3.50.

901 Embarcadero. ✆ 805/772-2411. Reservations not accepted. Most items $4.25–$8.75. AE, DISC, MC, V. Daily 11am–9pm.

Windows on the Water 🦆 CALIFORNIA   If you're looking for a special meal in town, you'll find Morro Bay's best at this restaurant that takes full advantage of prime waterfront views with its airy, high-ceilinged, multilevel space. But the cuisine—a California/French/Mediterranean hybrid incorporating local fresh seafood and produce—is the main attraction. On a given evening, the menu might include seared halibut in a Dijon crust offset by sweet-tangy orange marmalade and tequila sauce, shellfish braised in champagne and tossed with house-made fettuccine, or pheasant breast enveloped in prosciutto and brie atop a Riesling reduction sauce. The first-rate wine list is composed of choice Central Coast vintages and select French bottles. Live jazz on Friday and Saturday evenings adds to the celebratory ambience.

699 Embarcadero (in Marina Sq.). ✆ 805/772-0677. www.windowsonthewater.net. Reservations recommended. Main courses $17–$27. AE, DC, DISC, MC, V. Daily 5–10pm.

3 San Luis Obispo 🦆

38 miles S of Cambria; 226 miles S of San Francisco; 198 miles N of L.A.

Because the town of San Luis Obispo is not visible from U.S. 101, even many Californians don't know that it's more than another fast-food-and-gasoline stopover on the highway. But its "secret" location is part of what helps this relaxed yet vital college town keep its charm and character intact—it has much of the appeal that defined Santa Barbara a few decades ago.

San Luis Obispo (SLO to locals) is tucked into the mountains about halfway between San Francisco and Los Angeles. It's surrounded by green, pristine mountain ranges and filled with a mix of college kids (Cal Poly), big-city transplants, dotcom entrepreneurs, and agricultural folk.

The town grew up around an 18th-century mission, and its dozens of historic landmarks, Victorian homes, shops, and restaurants are its primary attractions for visitors. Today it's still quaint, almost undiscovered, and best ventured around on foot. It also makes a good base for exploration of the region as a whole. To the west of town, a short drive away, are some of the state's prettiest swimming beaches; to the north and south you'll find the Central Coast's wine country, home to dozens of respectable wineries and bucolic scenery.

ESSENTIALS

GETTING THERE   U.S. 101, one of the state's primary north-south roadways, runs through San Luis Obispo; it's the fastest land route here from anywhere. If you're driving down along the coast, Calif. 1 is the way to go for its natural beauty and oceanfront cliffs. If you're entering the city from the east, take Calif. 46 or 41 to U.S. 101, then go south. **Amtrak** (© **800/USA-RAIL;** www.amtrak.com) offers daily service into SLO from Oakland and Los Angeles.

VISITOR INFORMATION   The **San Luis Obispo Visitors Center,** 1039 Chorro St. (© 805/781-2777; www.visitslo.com), is downtown, between Monterey and Higuera streets. It offers a colorful, comprehensive *Visitors Guide* and the self-guided *Points of Interest Walking Tour.* The center is open Sunday and Monday from 10am to 5pm, Tuesday and Wednesday from 8am to 5pm, Thursday and Friday from 8am to 8pm, and Saturday from 10am to 8pm.

ORIENTATION   San Luis Obispo is about 10 miles inland, at the junction of Calif. 1 and U.S. 101. The downtown is laid out in a grid, roughly centered on the historic mission and its Mission Plaza (see below). Most of the main tourist sights are around the mission, within the small triangle created by U.S. 101 and Santa Rosa and Marsh streets.

EXPLORING THE TOWN

Before heading downtown, make a pit stop at the perpetually pink **Madonna Inn,** 100 Madonna Rd., off U.S. 101 (© **805/543-3000**), if for no other reason than to use its unique public restrooms (the men's has a waterfall urinal; the women's is a barrage of crimson and pink). Every over-the-top inch of this place is an exercise in excess, from the dining room, complete with pink leather booths, pink table linens, and colored sugar that's—you guessed it—piquantly pink, to the rock-walled, cavelike guest rooms (see p. 413 for a complete review).

   Once downtown, you can ride the free trolley that does a repeat loop through the downtown area daily from noon to 5pm. (Stops are well marked.)

Ah Louis Store *(Finds*   Mr. Ah Louis was a Cantonese immigrant who was lured to California by gold fever in 1856. Emerging from the mines empty-handed, he began a lucrative career as a labor contractor, hiring and organizing Chinese crews that built the railroad. In 1874 he opened this store. Today the store is rarely open, but if it is, you can browse the clutter of Asian merchandise. Don't be afraid to call—this is a worthwhile gem!

800 Palm St. (at Chorro St.). © 805/543-4332. Hours vary; serious shoppers phone in advance.

Farmers Market *(*   If you're lucky enough to be in town on a Thursday, take an evening stroll down Higuera Street, when the county's largest weekly street fair fills 4 downtown city blocks. You'll find much more here than fresh-picked produce—there's an ever-changing array of street entertainment, open-pit barbecues, food stands, and market stalls selling fresh flowers, cider, and other seasonal goodies. Surrounding stores stay open until 9pm.

Higuera St. (between Osos and Nipomo sts.). © 805/781-2777. Thurs 6–9pm (weather permitting).

Mission San Luis Obispo de Tolosa   Founded by Father Junípero Serra in 1772, California's fifth mission was built with adobe bricks by Native American Chumash people. It remains one of the prettiest and most interesting structures in the Franciscan chain. Serra chose this valley for the site of his fifth mission based on tales of friendly natives and bountiful food (including grizzly bears). Here the traditional red-tile roof was first used atop a California mission, after the original thatched tule roofs repeatedly fell to hostile Native Americans' burning arrows. The former padres' quarters are now an excellent museum chronicling both Native American and missionary life through all eras of the mission's use. Allow about 30 to 45 minutes to tour the mission and its grounds.

Mission Plaza, a garden with brick paths and park benches fronting a creek in which children love to wade, still functions as San Luis Obispo's town square. It's the focal point for local festivities and activities, from live concerts to poetry readings and dance and theater productions. Check at the visitor center (see "Essentials," above) to find out what's on when you're in town.

At the south end of Mission Plaza, you'll find the **San Luis Obispo Art Center** (© 805/543-8562), whose three galleries display and sell an array of California-made art. Admission is free; hours are 11am to 5pm Wednesday through Monday (open daily July–Aug).

751 Palm St. © 805/781-8220. www.missionsanluisobispo.org. Free admission ($2 donation requested). Summer daily 9am–5pm (sometimes later); winter daily 9am–4pm.

San Luis Obispo Children's Museum _Kids_   This children's museum features a playhouse for toddlers, a reproduction of a Native American Chumash cave dwelling, a music room, a computer corner, a pint-size bank and post office, and over 20 interactive exhibits. Special events like mask making, singalongs, and stage makeup classes are held regularly; call for a list of events.

1010 Nipomo St. (at Monterey St.). © 805/544-KIDS. Admission $5 adults and children 2 and older, free for children under 2. Tues–Sat 11am–5pm; Sun noon–4pm; open some Mon holidays.

SHOPPING

You'll find SLO resembles a smaller version of Santa Barbara, where unique boutiques and specialty shops are interspersed with recognized names and finer chains. With an influx of new residents, big-name businesses have been popping up all over the place: Look for the Gap, Barnes & Noble, Victoria's Secret, and Starbucks on SLO's tree-lined streets. The best place to exercise your credit cards is on the downtown streets surrounding the mission, specifically the 5 blocks of **Higuera Street** from Nipomo to Osos streets, as well as a short stretch of **Monterey Street** between Chorro and Osos streets.

Check out **Hands Gallery,** 777 Higuera St. (© 805/543-1921), which has a playful, bright collection of local and international art. Trinkets range from glass candies to vases, jewelry, and ceramics and can be examined Monday through Wednesday from 10am to 6pm, Thursday and Friday from 10am to 8pm, Saturday 10am to 7pm, and Sunday from 11am to 5pm (extended hours in summer).

ATTRACTIONS OUTSIDE OF TOWN

There are dozens of **wineries** in the area that offer tastings and tours daily and make for a fun diversion. See "The Central Coast Wine Country: Paso Robles & the Santa Ynez Valley," later in this chapter for further details. If you don't have time to tour the wineries or would like more information before heading out to taste, you can visit **Central Coast Wines,** 712 Higuera St. in downtown SLO (© 805/784-9463), a wine shop specializing in central coast wines, and offering daily wine tastings and weekly winemaker pourings.

WHERE TO STAY

In addition to what's listed below, there's a pristine branch of **Holiday Inn Express** (© **800/465-4329** or 805/544-8600), and a reliable **Motel 6** (© **800/ 4-MOTEL-6** or 805/541-6992).

Apple Farm Inn 🍎🍎   Ultrapopular, the Apple Farm Inn is a peaceful getaway in a Disney-plantation kind of way. Every square inch of the immaculate Victorian-style farmhouse is cheek-pinchingly cute with floral wallpaper, fresh flowers, and sugar-sweet colorful touches. No two rooms are alike; although each has a gas fireplace, large well-equipped bathroom, pine antiques, lavish country decor, and either a canopy four-poster or brass bed. Some bedrooms open onto cozy turreted sitting areas with romantic window seats; others have bay windows and a view of San Luis Creek, where a working mill spins its huge wheel to power an apple press. The outstanding service here includes nightly turndown and a morning wake-up knock, delivered with complimentary coffee or tea and a newspaper. Other features include complimentary cribs and train and airport shuttle service. Cider is always on hand in the lobby. The hotel shares a name with their on-site restaurant, one of Highway 101's best-loved pit stops.

Those who want the bang without the requisite bucks can opt for the adjoining motel-style **Apple Farm Trellis Court,** which shares the inn's wonderful grounds. Rooms are smaller, but are well decorated and have gas fireplaces. Rates include a continental breakfast and cost much less than the inn, $139 to $239.

2015 Monterey St., San Luis Obispo, CA 93401. © **800/255-2040** or 805/544-2040. Fax 805/546-9495. www.applefarm.com. 69 units. $219–$359 double. Rates include complimentary morning coffee/tea and afternoon wine reception. AE, DISC, MC, V. **Amenities:** Restaurant; outdoor heated pool; Jacuzzi; room service (6am–11pm); laundry service; dry cleaning. *In room:* A/C, TV w/pay movies, dataport, hair dryer, iron.

Garden Street Inn 🍎   SLO's prettiest (and most-polished) bed-and-breakfast is this gracious Italianate/Queen Anne downtown. Built in 1887 and restored in 1990, the house is a monument to gentility and to the good taste of owners Dan and Kathy Smith. Each bedroom and suite is decorated with well-chosen antique armoires, fabric or paper wall coverings, and vintage memorabilia. Choose one with a claw-foot tub, fireplace, whirlpool tub, or private deck—whatever suits your fancy. Breakfast is served in the stained-glass morning room, and each evening wine and cheese are laid out for guests. A well-stocked library is always available.

1212 Garden St. (between Marsh and Pacific), San Luis Obispo, CA 93401. © **800/488-2045** or 805/545-9802. Fax 805/545-9403. www.gardenstreetinn.com. 13 units. $130–$190 double. Rates include full breakfast and evening wine and cheese. AE, MC, V. *In room:* A/C, dataport.

Madonna Inn 🍎   This one you've got to see for yourself. The creative imaginations of owners Alex and Phyllis Madonna gave birth to the wildest—and most superfluously garish—fantasy world this side of Graceland. The only decor consistency throughout the hotel is its color scheme, which is perpetual pink. Beyond that, it's a free-for-all. Although tongue-in-cheek, this place can seem tired and tacky, and some of the rooms could use updating. However, the lobby men's room with its rock-waterfall urinal and clamshell sinks is a must-see. One guest room features a trapezoidal bed—it's 5 feet long on one side and 6 feet long on the other. "Rock" rooms with zebra- or tiger-patterned bedspreads and stonelike showers and fireplaces conjure up thoughts of a Flintstones's Playboy palace. There are also blue rooms, red rooms, and over-the-top Spanish, Italian, Irish, Alps, Currier and Ives, Native American, Swiss, and hunting rooms. The cocktail lounges are also outlandishly ornate. Even if you don't stay here, stop by and check it out. *One caveat:* The Madonna Inn, surprisingly, lacks a swimming pool.

100 Madonna Rd. (off U.S. 101), San Luis Obispo, CA 93405. © **800/543-9666** or 805/543-3000. Fax 805/543-1800. www.madonnainn.com. 109 units. $147–$248 double; from $210 suite. AE, DISC, MC, V. **Amenities:** Restaurant; coffee shop; 2 lounges. *In room:* A/C, TV, coffeemaker, hair dryer, iron.

Petit Soleil Bed et Breakfast   Formerly known as the Adobe Inn, new owners John and Dianne Conner have taken this old motor inn and renovated it in a French country atmosphere. Each room is individually decorated, with quirky additions such as painted cupboards or a window-side reading nook; all have private bathrooms and phones for free local calls. Breakfast is served in a dining area that faces the street, but coffee snobs will delight in the strong, locally roasted blend, and hot offerings like quiche or caramel-apple French toast are a treat.

1473 Monterey St., San Luis Obispo, CA 93401. © **800/676-1588** or 805/549-0321. Fax 805/549-0383. www.petitsoleilslo.com. 15 units. $125–$179 double. Rates include breakfast. Extra person $10. AE, DISC, MC, V. **Amenities:** Complimentary bikes. *In room:* TV, dataport, coffeemaker, hair dryer, iron, CD player.

WHERE TO DINE

Big Sky Cafe 🦋 AMERICAN   The folk-artsy fervor of San Luis shines at this Southwestern mirage, where local art and a blue, star-studded ceiling surround diners who come for fresh, healthy food. The menu is self-classified "modern food," a category that here means a dizzying international selection including Caribbean shrimp tacos with chipotle-lime yogurt, Thai curry pasta tossed with sautéed tiger shrimp, chilled sesame ginger noodles, and breakfast's red-flannel turkey hash—a beet-fortified ragout topped with basil-Parmesan-glazed eggs. Big Sky's owner also runs L.A.'s funky Gumbo Pot, whose Cajun-Creole influences spice up the menu at every turn. In fact, this might be the only Central Coast outlet for decent jambalaya, gumbo, or authentically airy beignets.

1121 Broad St. © 805/545-5401. www.bigskycafe.com. Main courses $10–$17; lunch $6–$11; breakfast $5–$10. AE, MC, V. Mon–Sat 7am–10pm; Sun 8am–9pm.

Buona Tavola 🦋🦋 NORTHERN ITALIAN   While most choices in town are burger-and-sandwich casual, Buona Tavola offers well-prepared Italian food in a more upscale setting. You can stroll in wearing jeans, but the dining room, with checkerboard floors and original artwork, is warmer and more intimate than other spots in town. There's also a backyard terrace where you can enjoy your meal surrounded by magnolias, ficus, and grapevines. The menu boasts a number of salads on the antipasti list. Favorite pastas include *agnolotti de scampi allo zafferano,* house-made pockets filled with scampi, then served in a cream-saffron sauce; *linguini fra diavolo* served with Manila clams, mussels, and river shrimp in a spicy tomato sauce; or the classic *timballo di parma,* a vegetarian delight baked with two cheeses. Don't worry—once you've gotten past trying to pronounce your desired dish, the rest of the evening should be both relaxing and satisfying.

1037 Monterey St. © 805/545-8000. Reservations recommended. Main courses $12–$23. AE, DISC, MC, V. Mon–Fri 11:30am–2:30pm; Sun–Thurs 5:30–9:30pm; Fri–Sat 5:30–10pm.

Mondéo Pronto *(Value (Kids* INTERNATIONAL   Mondéo Pronto provides patrons an affordable bite of international fillings in a burrito-type wrap. But unlike most "wrap" restaurants in California, this place goes a step beyond by paying attention to detail with presentation and freshness. Choices range from American versions like the Mardi Gras (a tomato tortilla with Cajun sausage, rock shrimp, Creole veggies, and jambalaya sauce) to Mediterranean selections like the Sicilian, with grilled portobello mushrooms, herb polenta, veggies, goat cheese, olives, capers, and sun-dried tomato pesto. "Fusion bowls" satisfy nonwrappers with such combinations as basil scampi, a shrimp dish over bowtie pasta with pesto, marinara, pine nuts, and herbs. Everything on the kids' menu is under $3, and as the menu states, "Substitutions and sides are no problem."

893 Higuera St. (in the plaza). © 805/544-2956. Most items $5–$7. MC, V. Sun–Wed 11am–9pm; Thurs–Sat 11am–10pm.

Mo's Smokehouse BBQ ★★ BARBECUE   Just about everyone in SLO is a devotee of this place, whose reputation and great barbecue belie its humble ambience. It's not fancy, but you name it, it's here—pork or baby back ribs, barbecued beef, and chicken in either a mild or hot sauce, all accompanied by baked beans, bread, potato salad, or coleslaw. To top off this delectable deal, practically everything on the menu is under $10.

970 Higuera St. (at Osos St.). © 805/544-6193. Most items $4.95–$13. AE, MC, V. Sun–Wed 11am–9pm; Thurs–Sat 11am–10pm.

Thai-rrific THAI   Although it's located on Higuera Street, Thai-rrific is a bit removed from the downtown action—but once you step inside this cute, ivy-covered building, the aroma will convince you you've made a worthy diversion. Fine examples of authentic Bangkok-style cuisine are the ginger beef, garlic noodles, and my favorite, lemon grass chicken (grilled chicken breasts topped with lemon-grass cream sauce, roasted chiles, and peanuts). Don't overlook the great array of tasty appetizers and salads, including the grilled shrimp or beef with cucumber, lime, and chili. An impressive wine list rounds out the offerings. Prices here are a little higher than at most Thai restaurants, but well worth it.

208 Higuera St. © 805/541-THAI. Reservations not accepted. Most dishes $7–$13. MC, V. Mon–Fri 11:30am–2pm; Mon–Sat 5–9pm.

4 Pismo Beach

13 miles S of San Luis Obispo

Just outside San Luis Obispo, on Pismo's 23-mile stretch of prime beachfront, flip-flops are the shoes of choice and surf wear is the dominant fashion. It's all about beach life here, so bring your bathing suit, your board, and a good book.

If building sand castles or tanning isn't your idea of a tantalizing time, you can explore isolated dunes, cliff-sheltered tide pools, and old pirate coves. Bring your dog (Fido's welcome here) and play an endless game of fetch. Or go fishing—it's permitted from Pismo Beach Pier, which also offers arcade entertainment, bowling, and billiards. Pismo is also the only beach in the area that allows all-terrain vehicles on the dunes.

Because the town itself consists of little more than tourist shops and surf-and-turf restaurants, nearby San Luis Obispo is a far more charming place to stay. But if all you want are a few lazy days on a beautiful beach at half the price of an oceanfront room in Santa Barbara, Pismo is the perfect choice.

ESSENTIALS

The **Pismo Beach Chamber of Commerce and Visitors Bureau,** 581 Dolliver St., Pismo Beach, CA 93449 (© **800/443-7778** or 805/773-4382; www.pismo chamber.com), offers free brochures and information on local attractions, lodging, and dining. The office is open Monday through Saturday from 9am to 5pm and Sunday from 10am to 4pm. You can peruse their tourist information online at **www.classiccalifornia.com**.

WHAT TO SEE & DO

Beaches in Pismo are exceptionally wide, making them some of the best in the state for sunning and playing. The beach north of Grand Avenue is popular with families and joggers. North of Wadsworth Street, the coast becomes dramatically rugged as it rambles northward to Shell Beach and Pirates Cove.

Pismo Beach was once one of the most famous places in America for **clamming,** but the famed "Pismo clam" reached near-extinction in the mid-1980s due to overharvesting. If you'd like to get your feet wet digging for bivalves, you'll need to obtain a license and follow strict guidelines. Or come for the annual **Clam Festival:** Held at the pier each October since 1946, the celebration features a chowder cook-off, sand-sculpture contest, and Miss Pismo Beach pageant.

If **fishing** is more your style, you'll be pleased to know that no license is required to fish from Pismo Beach Pier. Catches here are largely bottom fish like red snapper and lingcod. There's a bait-and-tackle shop on the pier.

Livery Stables, 1207 Silver Spur Place (© **805/489-8100**), in Oceano (about 5 min. south of Pismo Beach), is one of the few places in the state that rents horses for riding on the beach. Horses go for $20 per hour and can be ridden at your own pace, or you can opt for a guided ride.

You can hike along the **Guadalupe-Nipomo Dunes** year-round. This 18-mile strip of coastline 20 minutes south of Pismo has the highest beach dunes in the West. It's a great place for observing native plants and birds, including the California brown pelican, one of 200 species that migrate here each year.

From late November to February, thousands of migrating **monarch butterflies** take up residence in the area's eucalyptus and Monterey-pine-tree groves. The butterflies form dense clusters on the trees, each hanging with its wings over the one below it, providing warmth and shelter for the entire group. During the monarchs' stay, naturalists at Pismo State Beach conduct 45-minute narrated walks every Saturday and Sunday at 11am and 2pm (call © **805/772-2694** for tour information). The Butterfly Grove is located on Highway 1, between Pismo Beach and Grover Beach, to the south.

WHERE TO STAY

Cottage Inn by the Sea 🌴   One of Pismo Beach's newest cliff-side lodgings, the Cottage Inn is a good, moderately priced choice for couples and families. With its thatched roofs and Laura Ashley–style decor, the country charm is evident inside and out. Rooms, refreshingly clean and spacious, range both in price and style from traditional to oceanview. All come with the amenities of a romantic inn (including fireplaces) as well as modern conveniences (like in-room microwaves). This seaside retreat is one of the best in town.

2351 Price St., Pismo Beach, CA 93449. © **888/440-8400** or 805/773-4617. Fax 805/773-8336. www.cottage-inn.com. 80 units. $169–$269 double. Rates include deluxe continental breakfast. Extra person $10. AE, DC, DISC, MC, V. Pets accepted with $10-per–night fee. **Amenities:** Oceanfront heated pool and Jacuzzi. *In room:* TV w/pay movies and Nintendo, fridge, coffeemaker, hair dryer, iron, safe.

Kon Tiki Inn *Value*   The over-the-top Polynesian architecture of this three-story gem is easy to spot from the freeway, and upon closer examination evokes memories of 1960s Waikiki hotels. Rooms are modest, small, and simply furnished with unremarkable faux bamboo furniture, yet each has an oceanfront balcony or patio. Outside, vast lawns slope gently toward the cliffs, broken only by the shielded, kidney-shaped swimming pool flanked by twin Jacuzzis. This humble hotel—which is privately owned and does no advertising—has a sandy beach with stairway access, and lacks the highway noise that plagues many neighbors. Note that all rooms are nonsmoking.

1621 Price St., Pismo Beach, CA 93449. ⓒ **888/KON-TIKI** or 805/773-4833. Fax 805/773-6541. www.kontiki-inn.com. 86 units. $92–$142 double. Extra person $16. AE, DISC, MC, V. **Amenities:** Outdoor heated pool; 2 Jacuzzis; access to adjacent health club; laundry service. *In room:* TV w/pay movies, dataport, fridge, coffeemaker.

The Sea Venture Resort ⭐ If luxury accommodations overlooking the beach and an outdoor spa on your private deck sound like heaven to you, head for Sea Venture, a resort providing the most luxurious accommodations in Pismo. Once in your room, you need only drag your tired feet through the thick forest-green carpeting and past the white country furnishings and feather bed, and turn on your gas fireplace to begin a relaxing stay. Rent a movie from the video library, schedule a massage, or bathe your weary bones in your own outdoor hydrotherapy spa tub. With the beach right outside your door, there's not much more you could ask for—although there is, in fact, more provided: plush robes, a wet bar, continental breakfast delivered to your room, and a restaurant on the premises with a lovely tapas bar and Sunday brunch. Most rooms have ocean views and many have a private balcony overlooking the beach.

100 Ocean View Ave., Pismo Beach, CA 93449. ⓒ **800/760-0664** or 805/773-4994. Fax 805/773-0924. www.seaventure.com. 50 units. $179–$349 double. Rates include continental breakfast. AE, DC, DISC, MC, V. Take U.S. 101 to the Price St. exit, turn west onto Ocean View (at the beach). **Amenities:** Restaurant; outdoor heated pool; massage center; complimentary bikes; room service (5–9pm); laundry service; dry cleaning. *In room:* TV/VCR, dataport, minibar, coffeemaker, hair dryer, iron.

WHERE TO DINE

Local icon **F. McLintocks** has a lock on Pismo with two crowd-pleasing ocean-view eateries: **F. McLintocks Saloon & Dining House,** 750 Mattie Rd. (across Hwy. 101; ⓒ **805/773-1892**), for stick-to-your-ribs, ranch-style meals in an Old West setting; and **Steamers of Pismo,** 1601 Price St. (ⓒ **805/773-4711**), a warehouse-style space with "Miles of Clams" and plenty for landlubbers.

Giuseppe's Cucina Italiana ⭐ SOUTHERN ITALIAN   This is the region's best southern Italian restaurant—would you believe owner Giuseppe DiFronza started it as his senior project at Cal Poly University? It's true, and DiFronza's love of (and expertise at) cuisine from the Pugliese region (an Adriatic seaport) continues to bring diners a taste of the Italian countryside. Along with the homemade bread baked in a wood-burning oven imported from Italy, Giuseppe's fare uses authentic recipes, imported ingredients, and organically grown produce; the large menu of antipasti, salads, pizzas, pastas, fish, and steak makes it easy to find something you like. Highlights of the meal included linguine with shrimp, scallops, pancetta, and garlic in a vodka cream sauce, and seared *ahi* (tuna) with a peppercorn crust and garlic-caper aioli.

891 Price St. ⓒ **805/773-2870.** www.giuseppesrestaurant.com. Reservations not accepted. Main courses $7–$14 lunch, $9.50–$24 dinner. AE, DISC, MC, V. Nightly 4:30–10pm (till 11pm Fri–Sat); Mon–Fri 11:30am–3pm.

Splash Cafe AMERICAN   This beachy burger stand, with a short menu and a few tables, gets high marks for its award-winning clam chowder in a sourdough bread bowl—10,000 gallons a year are served! Fish and chips, burgers, hot dogs, and grilled ahi sandwiches are also available. Far-flung aficionados know that Splash ships its chowder frozen, overnight, anywhere in the U.S. (sourdough loaves, too). There's often a line, but it usually moves quickly.

197 Pomeroy St. (near Pismo Beach Pier). ⓒ **805/773-4653.** www.splashcafe.com. Most items $3–$7. MC, V. Daily 10am–8pm.

5 The Central Coast Wine Country: Paso Robles & the Santa Ynez Valley

Paso Robles: 29 miles N of San Luis Obispo; Solvang: 60 miles S of San Luis Obispo

When people talk about California wines, we usually assume they mean those from the Napa and Sonoma regions north of San Francisco. But here in California, and increasingly across the country, wine lovers are becoming more aware of vintages coming from California's Central Coast wineries in the green hills and sun-kissed valleys of San Luis Obispo and Santa Barbara counties. The Central Coast is coming into its own as a wine region, and offers another excuse to visit some of the state's most scenic countryside. Wine snobs might tell you that Central Coast wines cannot compare to those from the northern appellations, where vintages can age to sublime flavor and astronomical price, but if you're in the market for bottles in the $20-to-$30 range that are ready to drink within a couple of years, then trust us—you'll love what this up-and-comer has to offer.

PASO ROBLES

Welcome to Paso Robles—"pass of the oaks"—so named for the clusters of oak trees scattered throughout the rolling hills of this inland region. The town has a faintly checkered past: It was established in 1870 by Drury James, uncle of outlaw Jesse James (who reportedly hid out in tunnels under the original Paso Robles Inn). In 1913, pianist Ignace Paderewski came to live in Paso Robles, where he brought zinfandel vines for his ranch—Paderewski played often in the Paso Robles Inn, which today maintains a small exhibit in his honor in the lobby. He really wasn't here for long, returning to Poland after World War I, but the town today treats Paderewski like a native son.

ESSENTIALS

GETTING THERE/ORIENTATION Paso Robles is on U.S. 101; there's an exit for the town's main thoroughfare, Spring Street. Calif. 46 intersects, and briefly joins, U.S. 101. **Amtrak** (© **800/USA-RAIL;** www.amtrak.com) offers daily service to Paso Robles from Oakland and Los Angeles.

Many wineries are located on the winding roads off Calif. 46 on either side—try to cluster your visit according to this destination, visiting one side and then the other. You'll be able to feel how the weather on the western side, which is cooler due to higher elevations and frequent coastal fog, differs from the hotter east side, on a flat plain leading inland; winemakers bicker constantly over which conditions are better for growing wine grapes.

VISITOR INFORMATION For a list of area wineries, tasting rooms, and seasonal events, contact the **Paso Robles Vintners and Growers Association,** 744 Oak St., Paso Robles, CA 93446 (© **800/549-WINE** or 805/239-8463; fax 805/237-6439; www.pasowine.com). Additional information on the area is offered by the **Paso Robles Chamber of Commerce and Visitors & Conference Bureau,** 1225 Park St., Paso Robles, CA 93446 (© **800/406-4040** or 805/238-0506; fax 805/238-0527; www.pasorobleschamber.com).

TOURING THE LOCAL WINERIES

They've been tending vines in Paso Robles's fertile foothills since the turn of the century—the 19th century, that is. For decades, wine aficionados overlooked the area, even though in 1983 it was granted its own "Paso Robles" appellation (the official government designation of a recognized wine-producing region; "Napa Valley" and "Sonoma County" are probably more familiar). But somewhere around 1992, wine grapes surpassed lettuce as San Luis Obispo County's primary cash crop, and there are now at least 70 wineries and more than 100 vineyards (which grow grapes but do not produce their own wine from them).

Wine touring in Paso Robles is reminiscent of another, unhurried time. Because not all wine enthusiasts are wine experts, an advantage of the area is its friendly attitude and small crowds, which make it easy to learn more about the winemaking process as you go along. Enjoy the relaxed rural atmosphere along two-lane country roads, driving leisurely from winery to winery and, more often than not, chatting with the winemaker while tasting his/her product.

Eberle Winery   Owner Gary Eberle, who's been making Paso Robles wine since 1973, is sometimes called the "grandfather of Paso Robles's Wine Country," because many of the new vintners in the area honed their craft working under his tutelage. A visit to Eberle Winery includes a tour through its underground caves, where hundreds of aging barrels share space with the Wild Boar Room, site of Eberle's monthly winemaker dinners featuring guest chefs from around the country (always held on Sat nights; the prix-fixe meal is around $110, including wine). Call for a current events schedule.

Hwy. 46 E. (3½ miles east of U.S. 101). ℂ 805/238-9607. www.eberlewinery.com. Complimentary tastings daily 10am–5pm (until 6pm in summer).

EOS Estate Winery at Arciero Vineyards   Follow the checkered flag to the 700 acres of wine grapes owned by former race-car driver Frank Arciero, Sr. Arciero was drawn to the area by its resemblance to his native Italy; he passed through on his way to Laguna Seca, a racetrack near Salinas. (Trivia buffs know it as James Dean's intended destination in 1955, when he was killed in nearby Cholame while driving his Porsche.) The label specializes in Italian varietals *(nebbiolo, sangiovese)* and blends. The facility includes a self-guided tour, a race-car exhibit, rose gardens, a Mediterranean marketplace, and picnic area.

Hwy. 46 E. (6 miles east of U.S. 101). ℂ 805/239-2562. www.eosvintage.com. Complimentary tastings daily 10am–5pm (until 6pm summer weekends).

Justin Vineyards & Winery 🐗🐗🐗   At the end of a scenic country road lies Justin and Deborah Baldwin's boutique winery, and even a casual glance shows how much love and dedication the ex–Los Angelenos have put into their operation. The tasting room, dining room, offices, and even winemaking barns have a stylish Tuscan flair. Justin's flagship wine is Isosceles, a Bordeaux-style blend that—at about $55 a bottle—is pricier than most area wines but exudes sophistication—and earns *Wine Spectator* raves. Also worth a try is their port-style dessert wine, called Obtuse.

Finds **Gourmet Picnics, Paso Robles–Style**

You'll find everything you need for a snack or sophisticated picnic at Paso Robles's **Odyssey Culinary Provisions**, 1214 Pine St. (ℂ **805/237-7516**). A sandwich board features gourmet deli selections on focaccia and other fresh-baked breads, and refrigerated cases yield up salads, cheeses, salami, olives, and other goodies. Mustards, crackers, chocolates, and pastries line the shelves, along with baskets and knapsacks to hold your feast. Odyssey is also the place to come for fresh-brewed coffee and espresso. It's open Monday through Thursday from 7:30am to 8:30pm, Friday through Sunday from 7:30am to 9pm.

For a special treat, the winery has a three-suite B&B called the **JUST Inn.** Impeccably outfitted, the inn has an undeniable serenity, and you can even have a gourmet dinner prepared for you with advance notice. Room rates are $245 to $295—and worth every penny. *Tip:* When space permits, Justin's private dining room is also open to the public; if you're celebrating—or just want to have the best meal of your trip—call for advance reservations.

11680 Chimney Rock Rd. (15 miles west of U.S. 101). © 800/726-0049 or 805/237-4149. www.justin wine.com. Tastings daily 10am–5pm. Tasting fee $4, includes souvenir glass.

Meridian Vineyards 🕊   The local vintner with the largest profile is also the Central Coast's best-known label, producing more cases each year than all the other Paso wineries combined. Veteran winemaker Chuck Ortman brought a respected Napa Valley pedigree to Meridian; as a result, here's where you'll get the most Napa-like tasting experience. In addition to a grand tasting room, there's a man-made lake surrounded by rolling lawns, where picnicking is encouraged.

Hwy. 46 E. (7 miles east of U.S. 101). © 805/237-6000. www.meridianvineyards.com. Complimentary tastings daily 10am–5pm.

Summerwood Winery & Inn 🕊🕊   There's a spit and polish about this sleek player in the Paso wine game. The former Treana Winery's elegant tasting room (Treana's still in business, crafting wonderful red blends at a different location with no public tastings) now features a gourmet deli for picnickers, plush fireside chairs for relaxed sipping, and the luxurious Summerwood Inn bed-and-breakfast set among the vines (p. 421). With the help of internationally experienced winemaker Scott Hawley, Summerwood is turning out some of the best reds around, including cabernet and syrah from pedigreed estate vineyards.

2175 Arbor Rd. (at Hwy. 46 W., 1 mile west of U.S. 101). © 805/227-1365. www.summerwoodwine.com. Complimentary tastings daily 10am–5pm (till 6pm in summer).

Tobin James Cellars 🕊🕊   Winemaker Tobin James is a walking contradiction. A lifelong wine expert who claims to wear the same pair of khaki shorts every day, Toby has patterned his winery in the spirit of local bad boys, the James Gang. The tasting room has a Wild West theme, a 100-year-old saloon bar, and plays country music, all serving to dispel the wine-snob atmosphere that prevails at so many other wineries. Tobin James's expertise lies in the production of a "user-friendly" zinfandel; the late-harvest dessert wine from zinfandel grapes is smooth and spicy.

8950 Union Rd. (at Hwy. 46 E., 8 miles east of U.S. 101). © 805/239-2204. www.tobinjames.com. Complimentary tastings daily 10am–6pm.

York Mountain Winery *(Finds)*   If you're impressed by "firsts" and "onlys," don't miss York Mountain. It was the first winery in the area (begun in 1882 by Andrew York, on land originally deeded by Pres. Ulysses S. Grant) and is the oldest continuously operating vintner, as well as the only producer in the "York Mountain" viticulture appellation. In the 100-year-old stone tasting room, look for a dry chardonnay with a complex, spicy aroma, and award-winning cabernet sauvignons, the best of which are the reserve bottlings from hand-chosen grapes.

7505 York Mountain Rd. (off Hwy. 46 W., 7 miles west of U.S. 101). © 805/238-3925. www.yorkmountain winery.com. Tasting fee $1. Tastings daily 10am–5pm.

OTHER DIVERSIONS IN THE PASO ROBLES AREA

The fragrance emanating from **Sycamore Farms,** Highway 46 West, several miles west of U.S. 101 (© 800/576-5288 or 805/238-5288; www.sycamore farms.com), is that of hundreds of herbs, grown for culinary, medicinal, and decorative purposes. Learn about them at the farm's walkthrough garden; it also sells fresh-cut and dried herbs, seedlings to transplant at home, and a bevy of herbal vinegars, olive oils, mustards, herbal soaps, and potpourri. Hours are daily from 10am to 5pm; tours (by appointment) are $2 per person.

WHERE TO STAY

Adelaide Inn *Value*   Tended with loving care that's rare among lower-priced accommodations, the Adelaide Inn stands out from other motels. Although it's adjacent to gas stations and coffee shops, attention has been paid to isolate this quiet, lushly landscaped property from its surroundings. The rooms are clean and comfortable with extra warmth, and the motel has a welcoming ambience. Unexpected comforts include complimentary newspaper and fruit and muffins. Facilities include summertime water diversions and even a putting green.

1215 Ysabel Ave., Paso Robles, CA 93446. © 800/549-PASO or 805/238-2770. Fax 805/238-3497. www.adelaideinn.com. 67 units. $55–$86 double. Extra person $6. Rates include morning coffee and muffins. AE, DC, DISC, MC, V. From U.S. 101, exit Hwy. 46 E. Turn west at 24th St.; the hotel is just west of the freeway. **Amenities:** Heated outdoor pool; Jacuzzi; sauna; coin-op laundry and laundry service; dry cleaning. *In room:* A/C, TV w/pay movies, dataport, fridge, coffeemaker, hair dryer, iron.

Paso Robles Inn   This Mission Revival–style inn was built to replace the 1891 Stanford White masterpiece, El Paso De Robles Hotel, that burned in 1940. Photos of the landmark in its heyday line the Spanish-tiled lobby and adjacent dining room and cocktail lounge. A creek meanders through the oak-shaded property, and two-story motel units are scattered across the tranquil grounds. Well shielded from street noise, these rooms are simple but boast creature comforts (shiny bathrooms, gas fireplaces, and microwaves in many rooms) added in a 2000 update that, unfortunately, removed much of their nostalgic charm. The best rooms are worth the extra bucks: "Spa Rooms" with fireplaces and shielded outdoor Jacuzzis supplied by the property's mineral springs. Carports are located behind each building. Skip the overpriced Hot Springs Grill in favor of the retro-flavored **Coffee Shop**, both served by the same kitchen. *Tip:* Avoid room numbers beginning with 1 or 2—they're too close to the street.

1103 Spring St., Paso Robles, CA 93446. © 800/676-1713 or 805/238-2660. www.pasoroblesinn.com. 100 units. $145–$165; spa room $235. Extra person $10. AE, DC, DISC, MC, V. **Amenities:** 2 restaurants; lounge; outdoor heated pool; Jacuzzi; business center; room service (6am–9pm); laundry service; dry cleaning. *In room:* A/C, TV w/pay movies, dataport, fridge, coffeemaker, hair dryer, iron.

The Summerwood Inn *☆*   The guest book at this elegant B&B sports more than its share of honeymooners drawn by the splendid setting and luxurious treatment. Located at Summerwood Winery (p. 420), this three-story clapboard house looks like a cross between Queen Anne and Southern-plantation styles, but is furnished in formal English country. It's a contemporary building throughout, so rooms are spacious and bathrooms ultramodern; the main floor (including two guest rooms) is wheelchair accessible. Every room has a private balcony overlooking the vineyards, plus a gas fireplace, fresh flowers, and terry robes; morning coffee is left discreetly outside your door in insulated carafes.

2130 Arbor Rd. (P.O. Box 3260), Paso Robles, CA 93447. © 805/227-1111. www.summerwoodinn.com. 9 units. $245–$295 double; $345 suite. Extra person $65. Rates include full breakfast, afternoon wine and hors d'oeuvres, and evening cookies. MC, V. From U.S. 101, exit Hwy. 46 W. Continue 1 mile to Arbor Rd. *In room:* A/C, TV, hair dryer.

WHERE TO DINE

You should also consider Paso's branch of the San Luis Obispo favorite, **Buona Tavola,** 943 Spring St. (© **805/237-0600**), whose house-made pastas and fresh-from-the-fields northern Italian cuisine are a welcome addition to town.

Bistro Laurent *⋆* FRENCH/CALIFORNIA   Executive chef/owner Laurent Grangien's sophisticated bistro caused quite a stir in this town unaccustomed to such innovations as a chef's tasting menu. But once the dust settled, everyone kept returning for the unpretentious neighborhood atmosphere, delicious recipes, and reasonable (by L.A. or San Francisco standards) prices. Whet your appetite with a complimentary teaser of hors d'oeuvres (goat cheese toasts, for example) before plunging into dishes like rosemary-garlic chicken, pork loin bathed in peppercorn sauce, or ahi tuna in red-wine reduction. "Twilight dinners" are served nightly until 6:30pm.

1202 Pine St., Paso Robles. ℂ 805/226-8191. Reservations recommended. Main courses $5–$12 lunch, $15–$23 dinner. MC, V. Mon–Sat 11:30am–2:30pm and 5:30–10pm.

Busi's on the Park CALIFORNIA ECLECTIC   The name may sound snooty and scenic, but Busi's is neither. It's a comfortable, tavernlike joint across the street from downtown's City Park, but the offerings draw a big local crowd. A short seasonal menu highlights fresh local ingredients; eclectic offerings include pan-roasted salmon with oriental salsa; roasted loin of pork with a peach reduction sauce; and seafood ravioli with fresh crab and shrimp. Weekend brunch runs the gamut from French toast or a Spanish frittata to Thai noodle salad or saffron mussels. Whenever you come, try to nab one of the spaces on the pretty outdoor patio.

1122 Pine St., Paso Robles. ℂ 805/238-1390. Main courses $15–$24. AE, MC, V. Sat–Sun 10am–2pm; daily 5–9pm.

McPhee's Grill *⋆⋆* (Kids) CALIFORNIA GRILL   When Ian McPhee left Ian's Restaurant in Cambria and launched this one, it didn't take long for word to get out. McPhee's is worth the short drive to the historic town of Templeton. The converted old saloon features contemporary country decor, an open kitchen, and indoor and outdoor dining. The menu offers half a dozen appetizers such as a duck *carnitas* quesadilla, and seared ahi tuna on crispy sesame won-ton crackers with wasabi cream and pickled ginger. Gourmet pizza, pasta, an amazing macadamia-crusted Alaskan halibut, and four varieties of tender, juicy steaks cooked to perfection round out the Americana-with-a-twist-style menu. Especially impressive are the prices—it's rare that a restaurant "dedicated to great food and great service" offers the majority of its dishes for under $20. A champagne buffet brunch is offered on Sundays. McPhee's is one of the very best in the region, and families will appreciate the economical kids' menu.

416 Main St., Templeton. ℂ 805/434-3204. www.mcphees.com. Reservations recommended. Main courses $9–$12 lunch, $15–$34 dinner; brunch $19 adults, $9 for kids under 10. MC, V. Mon–Sat 8–10:30am; daily 11:30am–2pm and 5–9pm; Sun 10am–2pm.

THE SANTA YNEZ VALLEY

Welcome to the Santa Ynez Valley, an idyllic domain of oak-covered hills and uncrowded roads set against a mountain backdrop. This is beautiful country, where the clear blue sky achieves a brilliance unheard of in the smog-clogged cities. In the Santa Ynez Valley, the pace is a little slower, and the locals a little friendlier. Don't expect to find yokels gnawing on hay—this is gentleman-farmer country, where some of the nicest ranches are gated and have video surveillance, and even Disney's Davy Crockett is a respected winemaker. This balance of old-fashioned living and modern sophistication is what makes the area enjoyable: You can wallow in simple pleasures one day and go wine tasting the next.

Los Olivos is a good, ol' fashioned country town in the middle of the Central Coast Wine Country. There's a flagpole in the center of the town's intersection, and stretches of boardwalk stand in for sidewalk here and there, giving the town a Wild West air. If you saw TV's *Return to Mayberry,* that was Los Olivos standing in for Andy Griffith's sentimental Southern hamlet. But these days, the town's storefronts feature art galleries, stylish cafes, and wine-tasting rooms; you'll see more Land Rovers than John Deeres in this upscale retreat.

Just minutes away from one another, Los Olivos, Santa Ynez, Ballard, Solvang, and Buellton each make an excellent base for touring the wineries of this fertile area.

ESSENTIALS

GETTING THERE   From U.S. 101, take Calif. 246 east 4 miles to reach Solvang, Santa Ynez, and Ballard. Los Olivos is on Calif. 154 a couple of miles from U.S. 101. Lake Cachuma is also on Calif. 154, traveling southeast toward Santa Barbara.

VISITOR INFORMATION   Contact the **Santa Ynez Valley Visitors Association,** P.O. Box 1918, Santa Ynez, CA 93460 (✆ **800/742-2843;** www.syvva. com), for general visitors information. Or try the **Santa Barbara County Vintners' Association,** 3669 Sagunto St., Unit 101 (P.O. Box 1558), Santa Ynez, CA 93460 (✆ **800/218-0881** or 805/688-0881; www.sbcountywines.com), for its *Winery Touring Map.* Hours are Monday through Friday from 9am to 5pm. The **Solvang Conference & Visitors Bureau,** 1511 Mission Dr., at Fifth Street (P.O. Box 70), Solvang, CA 93464 (✆ **800/GO-SOLVANG** or 805/688-6144; www.solvangusa.com), has additional information on the Santa Ynez Valley. It's open daily from 10am to 4pm.

ORIENTATION   U.S. 101, Calif. 246, and Calif. 154 form a triangle enclosing the towns of the Santa Ynez Valley. Calif. 246 becomes Mission Drive within Solvang city limits, then continues east past the mission toward Santa Ynez. Alamo Pintado Road connects Solvang with Los Olivos, whose commercial stretch is along 3 blocks of Grand Avenue. Foxen Canyon Road continues north from downtown Los Olivos.

TOURING THE LOCAL WINERIES

Santa Barbara County has a 200-year tradition of growing grapes and making wine—an art originally practiced by Franciscan friars at the area's missions—but only in the past 20 to 30 years have wine grape fields begun to approach the size of other crops that do so well in these fertile inland valleys.

Geography makes the area well suited for vineyards: The Santa Ynez and San Rafael mountain ranges are transverse (east-west) ranges, which allows ocean breezes to flow through, keeping the climate temperate. Variations in temperature and humidity within the valley create many microclimates, and vintners have learned how to cultivate nearly all the classic grape varietals. But it's the chardonnay, pinot noir, and syrah that draw the most acclaim, and you'll find more than 50 wineries in the Santa Ynez Valley area, most of which have tasting rooms—a few offer tours as well. If you'd like to start with a winery tour to acquaint yourself with viticulture, Gainey Vineyard or Firestone Vineyard are good bets (see below). And if you'd like to sample wines without driving around, head to **Los Olivos Tasting Room & Wine Shop,** 2905 Grand Ave. (✆ 805/688-7406), in the heart of town, or **Los Olivos Wine & Spirits Emporium,** 2531 Grand Ave. (✆ **805/688-4409;** www.sbwines.com), a friendly barn in a field half a mile away. Both offer a wide selection of vintners, including those—such as Au Bon Climat and Qupé—who don't have their own tasting rooms.

The Brander Vineyard   Winemaker Fred Brander has been making a name for himself since 1976; although the winery's production is small, his is a name you'll frequently see on local wine lists. Brander is among the valley's most pleasant wineries, with a friendly family of staff. The best bets are Cuvée Nicolas, which is a 100% sauvignon blanc from low-yielding vines; or choose a high-density cabernet from the cellar for full-bodied perfection.

2401 Refugio Rd., Los Olivos. ℰ 800/970-9979 or 805/688-2455. www.brander.com. Tastings daily 10am–4pm (till 5pm in summer). Tasting fee of $3 includes souvenir glass and is applied toward any purchase.

Fess Parker Winery & Vineyard ℰ You loved him as a child, now see what Hollywood's Davy Crockett/Daniel Boone is up to. Fess Parker has made a name for himself in Santa Barbara County, with resort hotels, cattle ranches, and now an eponymous winery that's turning out some critically acclaimed syrahs, among other varietals. Look for the syrah and chardonnay American Tradition Reserve vintages in the tasting room. Parker's grandiose complex, shaded by the largest oak tree I've ever seen, also features picnic tables on a terrace and an extensive gift shop where you can even buy (you guessed it!) coonskin caps.

6200 Foxen Canyon Rd., Los Olivos. ℰ 800/841-1104 or 805/688-1545. www.fessparker.com. Tastings daily 10am–5pm; tours daily at 11am, 1pm, and 3pm. Tasting fee $7, includes souvenir glass.

Firestone Vineyard Probably the largest producers in Santa Barbara County, this operation started by Brooks Firestone (of tire-manufacturing fame, and yes, the father of TV's "The Bachelor" Andrew Firestone) now includes two "second" labels. Its wines are affordable and reasonably good, and it's started experimenting with Chilean-grown grapes, some of which can be excellent. Firestone's tasting room and gift shop are a three-ring circus of merchandise, but it offers a quick, worthwhile tour six times a day.

5000 Zaca Station Rd., Los Olivos. ℰ 805/688-3940. www.firestonewine.com. Tastings daily 10am–5pm; $7, includes souvenir glass. Free tours hourly.

The Gainey Vineyard ℰ This slick operation is one of the most visited wineries in the valley, thanks to its prime location on Calif. 246 and its in-depth tours, offered daily. It has every hallmark of a visitor-oriented winery: a terra-cotta-tiled tasting room, plenty of logo merchandise, and a deli case for impromptu lunches at the picnic tables in a secluded vineyard garden. It bottles the most popular varietals—chardonnay, cabernet sauvignon, pinot noir, sauvignon blanc—and offers them at moderate prices.

3950 E. Calif. 246, Santa Ynez. ℰ 888/424-6398. www.gaineyvineyard.com. Tastings daily 10am–5pm; tours daily 11am and 1, 2, and 3pm. Tasting fee $5, includes souvenir glass.

Sunstone Vineyards and Winery ℰℰℰ Take a rambling drive down to this locally known winery, whose wisteria-wrapped stone tasting room belies the dirt road you take to reach it. Sunstone is nestled in an oak grove overlooking the river, boasting a splendid view from the lavender-fringed picnic courtyard. Inside, try its flagship merlot or treasured reserve vintages; there's also a fine selection of gourmet foods, logo ware, and cigars. The lovely setting and attractive tasting room, combined with excellent products, make this a quintessentially enjoyable wine-touring experience.

125 Refugio Rd., Santa Ynez. ℰ 800/313-WINE or 805/688-WINE. www.sunstonewinery.com. Tastings daily 10am–4pm. Tasting fee $5, includes souvenir glass.

Zaca Mesa Winery ℰℰ One of the region's old-timers, Zaca Mesa has been in business since 1972, so we can forgive the hippie/New Age mumbo-jumbo pleasantly interwoven with the well-honed vintages. Situated on a unique plateau that the Spanish named *la zaca mesa* (the restful place), this winery's 750 acres are uniquely beautiful—a fact it celebrates with two easy nature trails for visitors. You'll also find picnic tables and a giant lawn chessboard. Inside, look for the usual syrah and chardonnay offerings jazzed up with experimental Rhône varietals like *grenache, roussanne,* and *voignier.*

6905 Foxen Canyon Rd., Los Olivos. © 800/350-7972 or 805/688-9339. www.zacamesa.com. Complimentary tastings daily 10am–4pm; call for tour schedule.

A TASTE OF DENMARK: SOLVANG

The valley's largest town is also one of the state's most popular tourist stops, and Solvang takes a lot of flack for being a Disneyfied version of its founders' vision. Everything here that *can* be Danish *is* Danish: You've never seen so many windmills, cobblestone streets, wooden shoes, and so much gingerbread trim—even the trash cans look like little Danish farmhouses with pitched-roof lids.

To reach Solvang from U.S. 101 south, turn east (left) onto Calif. 246 at Buellton. It's a well-marked 20-minute drive along an extremely scenic two-lane road. From Santa Barbara, take U.S. 101 north to Calif. 154, a truly breathtaking 45-minute drive over San Marcos Pass. For a destination guide or hotel information, contact the **Solvang Conference & Visitors Bureau** (© **800/GO-SOLVANG** or 805/688-6144; www.solvangusa.com).

One way to weed through the unabashed tourism for a little authentic history is to visit the **Elverhøj Museum,** 1624 Elverhoy Way (© **805/686-1211**), a warm, welcoming place devoted to Danish culture and Solvang history. Set in a handcrafted Scandinavian-style home, and featuring many original old-world furnishings, this museum can be fully appreciated in 30 minutes or less. Hours are Wednesday through Sunday from 1 to 4pm; a $2 donation is suggested.

Old Mission Santa Inés   On the edge of town, and one of the few buildings without a windmill or other Scandinavian fanfare, this Spanish mission was founded by Franciscan friars in 1804 and is still in use for daily services. Most of the original structure, painstakingly constructed of adobe by Native Americans, has been destroyed. The reconstruction features the ornately tiled and painted chapel typical of the Spanish missions, and an extensive museum display of mission artifacts and Franciscan vestments.

1760 Mission Dr., Solvang. © 805/688-4815. $3 donation requested, free for children under 16. Summer Mon–Fri 9am–7pm, Sat 9am–4pm, Sun 1:30–5:30pm; winter Sun–Fri 9am–5:30pm, Sat 9am–4pm. From downtown Solvang, take Calif. 246 1 mile east to Mission Dr.

CACHUMA LAKE: A BALD-EAGLE HABITAT

Created in 1953 by damming the Santa Ynez River, this picturesque reservoir running along Calif. 154 is the primary water source for Santa Barbara County. It's also the centerpiece of a 6,600-acre county park with a flourishing wildlife population and well-developed recreational facilities. Cachuma has, through both agreeable climate and diligent ranger efforts, become a notable habitat for resident and migratory birds, including rarely sighted bald eagles, which migrate south from as far as Alaska in search of food.

One of the best ways to appreciate this fine-feathered bounty is to take one of the naturalist-led **Eagle Cruises** of the lake, offered between November and February. The 48-foot *Osprey* was specially designed for wildlife observation, with unobstructed views from nearly every seat. During the rest of the year, rangers lead **Wildlife Cruises** around the lake, helping you spot resident waterfowl, deer, and the elusive bobcats and mountain lions that live here. Eagle Cruises depart Wednesday through Sunday at 10am, with additional cruises Friday and Saturday at 2pm. Wildlife Cruises run Friday and Saturday at 3pm, and

Saturday and Sunday at 10am. All cruises are 2 hours long. In addition to the park day-use fee of $5 per car, the fare is $15 for adults and $7 for children 12 and under. Reservations are recommended; call the **Santa Barbara County Parks Department** (© 805/686-5050; www.sbparks.com).

The recreational opportunities also offer campers, boaters, and fishermen abundant facilities. Contact the **Lake Cachuma Recreation Area** (© 805/686-5054) for recorded information.

WHERE TO STAY

Ballard Inn ⭐⭐ This two-story inn may look 100 years old, but it's actually of modern construction, offering both contemporary comforts and charming country details like wicker rockers on a wraparound porch. The entry and parlors are tastefully furnished with a comfortable mix of antiques and reproductions. Sumptuous wallpaper and fabrics lend a cozy touch, and hand-hooked rugs, bent-twig furniture, and vintage accessories lend character to the house. The guest rooms upstairs are unique—some have fireplaces and/or private balconies, and all have well-stocked bathrooms, many featuring a separate antique washbasin in the bedroom. The best (and most expensive) unit is the Mountain Room, a minisuite decorated in rich forest green and outfitted with a fireplace and private balcony. In addition to cooked-to-order breakfast and a wine-and-hors d'oeuvres reception, you'll be treated to evening coffee and tea, plus addictive chocolate cookies on your nightstand at bedtime.

The inn's restaurant, **Cafe Chardonnay,** is tucked into a cozy room downstairs by a crackling fire. The California-style seasonal menu can include grilled meats, seafood pastas, and catch-of-the-day specials. *Note:* The inn staff doesn't accept gratuities; instead, a 10% service charge is added at checkout.

2436 Baseline Ave., Ballard, CA 93463. © 800/638-2466 or 805/688-7770. Fax 805/688-9560. www. ballardinn.com. 15 units. $195–$275 double. Rates include full breakfast, afternoon wine and hors d'oeuvres, and evening coffee and tea. AE, MC, V. Take Alamo Pintado Rd. to Baseline; the inn is half a block east of the intersection. **Amenities:** Restaurant; bike rental; activities desk; in-room massage. *In room:* A/C, hair dryer, iron.

Inn at Petersen Village ⭐ If you think every hotel in Solvang has a kitschy, Danish theme, then step into this quiet, tasteful, and affordable hotel. Rooms are decorated in a European country motif, with print wallpaper, canopy beds, and mahogany-hued furniture. But it's the little touches that impress the most, like lighted magnifying mirrors, bathroom lights controlled by dimmers, free coffee and tea service to your room, and the complimentary food that's nearly always laid out in the hotel's friendly piano lounge. Some rooms overlook a bustling courtyard of shops, while others face Solvang's scenic hills. All are designed so everyone's happy: Smaller units have private balconies, those with noisier views are more spacious, and so on.

1576 Mission Dr., Solvang, CA 93463. © 800/321-8985 or 805/688-3121. Fax 805/688-5732. www.petersen inn.com. 42 units. $195–$350 double. Extra person $25. Rates include full dinner and breakfast buffet. AE, MC, V. **Amenities:** Restaurant; piano/wine bar; room service (7am–11pm). *In room:* A/C, TV, dataport, hair dryer, iron.

Royal Scandinavian Inn If you're looking for a traditional, full-service hotel, this attractive and comfortable mainstay in Solvang is away from the congested main drag. Popular with conventions and leisure groups, the Royal Scandinavian has an all-day restaurant and cocktail lounge and is within walking distance of downtown Solvang; the championship Alisal River Golf Course is next door. The remodel means rooms are spiffed up nicely. Ask for a room overlooking the courtyard—the view extends to the foothills beyond. The hotel's restaurant,

Meadows, is one of the better options in the area, with an attractive patio for dining—equipped with heaters for cool nights and misters for hot days.

400 Alisal Rd. (P.O. Box 30), Solvang, CA 93464. (*C*) 800/624-5572 or 805/688-8000. Fax 805/688-0761. www.royalscandinavianinn.com. 133 units. $104–$204 double; from $219 suite. Extra person $15. AE, DC, DISC, MC, V. **Amenities:** Restaurant; lounge; outdoor pool; nearby golf; fitness room; Jacuzzi; business center; room service (7am–10pm); laundry service; dry cleaning. *In room:* A/C, TV w/pay movies, fax, fridge, coffeemaker, hair dryer, iron.

WHERE TO DINE

If you're looking for traditional Danish fare, head for **Bit o' Denmark,** 473 Alisal Rd. ((*C*) 805/688-5426). Its smorgasbord may not be the largest in town, but it's the freshest and highest quality; you can also order from the regular menu. It's open daily from 11:30am to 9pm; the smorgasbord costs $10 at lunch, $13 at dinner. **The Hitching Post,** 406 E. Hwy. 246, Buellton ((*C*) 805/688-0676), is the valley's mecca for meat lovers. Within these Western-themed surroundings, steaks are grilled to perfection over an oak-wood pit, and—fittingly—the house label wine is better than you'd expect.

Brothers Restaurant at Mattei's Tavern *&* AMERICAN/CONTINENTAL Mattei's is proud of its stagecoach past, and this rambling white Victorian submerged in wisteria has successfully retained its historic charm. Rumors abound of high-stakes poker games in Mattei's back room, where many an early rancher literally "lost the farm." The restaurant is known throughout the county for its signature reduction sauces and house-made ice cream. You'll find thick steaks on the menu, along with Australian lobster tail, seared diver scallops, grilled veal chop, and fresh trout. Bust a pant button with the sinful fudge brownie sundae with banana ice cream.

Calif. 154, Los Olivos. (*C*) 805/688-4820. Reservations recommended on weekends. Dinner $15–$35. MC, V. Daily 5–9pm; Sat–Sun noon–2:30pm.

Paula's Pancake House *(Kids* AMERICAN/DANISH Morning means one thing in Solvang, and that's Paula's three-page menu of *just breakfast!* There are wafer-thin Danish pancakes, served plain and simple, sweet and fruity, or with sausage and eggs; buttermilk pancakes, whole-wheat/honey pancakes, waffles, sourdough French toast, and every omelet and egg dish imaginable, including some south-of-the-border salsafied specials. Paula's is friendly and casual, in the heart of town where patio diners can watch the world go by.

1531 Mission Dr., Solvang. (*C*) 805/688-2867. Most menu items under $7. AE, DISC, MC, V. Daily 6am–3pm.

(Tips) Picnicking in the Santa Ynez Valley

You can assemble a picnic at the **Los Olivos Grocery,** on Calif. 154 about a mile east of Los Olivos ((*C*) 805/688-5115), where a deli counter prepares simple sandwiches and side salads. With a little advance notice, they'll prepare box lunches that include a sandwich, chips, a piece of fruit, and a cookie. The market is open daily from 7am to 9pm.

Los Olivos offers easy-to-carry, eat-at-room-temperature goodies packed up with all the necessary utensils. At **Panino,** 2900 Grand Ave. ((*C*) 805/688-9304), choose from 31 gourmet sandwiches, all served on Panino's fresh-baked, Italian-style bread; varieties include grilled chicken with sun-dried tomatoes, fresh basil, and provolone, or English Stilton with Asian pear on fresh walnut bread. It's open Monday through Friday from 10am to 4pm, Saturday and Sunday from 9am to 5pm.

6 Santa Barbara ★★★

45 miles S of Solvang; 105 miles S of San Luis Obispo; 92 miles NW of L.A.

Santa Barbara is nestled between palm-lined Pacific beaches and the foothills of the Santa Ynez Mountains. This resort community presents a mosaic of white-washed stucco and red tile roofs and a gracious, relaxed attitude that has earned it the sobriquet "American Riviera." It's ideal for kicking back on white-sand beaches, prowling the shops and galleries that line the village's historic streets, and relaxing over a meal in one of many top-notch cafes and restaurants.

Downtown Santa Barbara is distinctive for its Spanish-Mediterranean architecture. But it wasn't always this way. Santa Barbara had a thriving Native American Chumash population for hundreds, if not thousands, of years. The European era began in the late 18th century, around a Spanish *presidio* (fort) that's been reconstructed in its original spot. The earliest architectural hodge-podge was destroyed in 1925 by a powerful earthquake that leveled the business district. Out of the rubble rose the Spanish-Mediterranean town of today, a stylish planned community that continues to enforce strict building codes.

Visit Santa Barbara's waterfront on a Sunday and you're sure to see the weekly **Waterfront Arts and Crafts Show,** one of the city's best-loved traditions. Since 1965, artists, craftspeople, and street performers have been lining grassy Chase Palm Park, along Cabrillo Boulevard.

ESSENTIALS

GETTING THERE   By car, U.S. 101 runs right through Santa Barbara. It's the fastest and most direct route from north or south (1½ hr. from L.A., 6 hr. from San Francisco).

The **Santa Barbara Municipal Airport** (✆ 805/683-4011) is in Goleta, about 10 minutes north of downtown Santa Barbara. Airlines serving Santa Barbara include **American Eagle** (✆ 800/433-7300), **AmericaWest Airlines** (✆ 800/235-9292), **Delta** (✆ 800/221-1212), and **United** (✆ 800/241-6522). **Yellow Cab** (✆ 805/965-5111) and other metered taxis line up outside the terminal; the fare is about $24 (without tip) to downtown.

By train, **Amtrak** (✆ **800/USA-RAIL;** www.amtrak.com) offers daily service to Santa Barbara (five daily from L.A., one a day from Oakland and the Bay Area). Trains arrive and depart from the **Santa Barbara Rail Station,** 209 State St. (✆ **805/963-1015**). Fares can be as low as $34 (round-trip) from Los Angeles.

VISITOR INFORMATION   Stop by the **Santa Barbara Visitor Information Center,** at 1 Garden St., Santa Barbara, CA 93101 (✆ **805/965-3021;** www.sbchamber.org). The center distributes maps, brochures, an events calendar, and information. It's open Monday through Saturday from 9am to 4pm and Sunday from 10am to 4pm. The **Santa Barbara Conference & Visitors Bureau and Film Commission,** 1601 Anacapa St., Santa Barbara, CA 93101 (✆ **800/ 676-1266** or 805/965-3021; www.santabarbaraca.com), does not offer a walk-up facility, but will send out a visitors guide in advance of your visit; request it through ✆ 800/927-4688.

Pick up a copy of the *Independent,* Santa Barbara's free weekly, for events listings; the local daily newspaper is the *Santa Barbara New-Press.* Two good online sources for events listings are the *Independent*'s website, www.independent.com, and **SantaBarbara.com** (www.santabarbara.com).

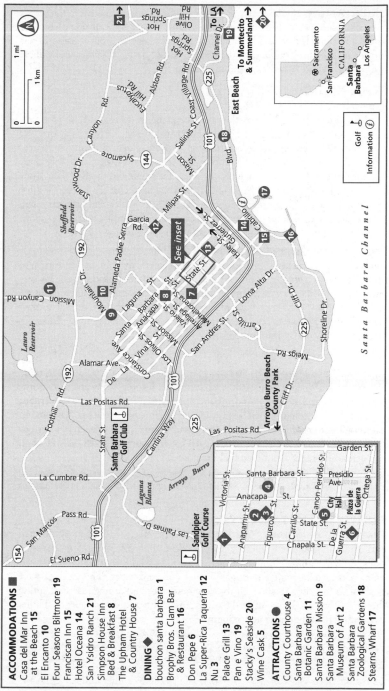

Santa Barbara

CALIFORNIA

Sacramento
San Francisco
Santa Barbara
Los Angeles

Santa Barbara Channel

To LA
To Montecito & Summerland
East Beach

Golf ⛳
Information ⓘ

See inset

Santa Barbara Golf Club

Sandpiper Golf Course

Arroyo Burro Beach County Park

Inset map
Garden St.
Santa Barbara St.
Presidio Ave.
Anacapa St.
Victoria St.
Anapamu St.
Figueroa St.
Carrillo St.
Canon Perdido St.
City Hall
Plaza de la Guerra
Ortega St.
State St.
De la Guerra St.
Chapala St.

ORIENTATION   State Street, the city's primary commercial thoroughfare, is the geographic center of town. It ends at Stearns Wharf and Cabrillo Street; the latter runs along the ocean and separates the city's beaches from touristy hotels and restaurants. Electric shuttles (25¢ fare) provide frequent service along these two routes if you'd rather leave the car behind.

EXPLORING THE TOWN
HISTORIC DOWNTOWN
Following a devastating 1925 earthquake, city planners decreed that all new construction would follow codes of Spanish and Mission-style architecture. In time, the adobe-textured walls, rounded archways, artfully glazed tile work, and terra-cotta rooftops would come to symbolize the Mediterranean ambience that characterizes Santa Barbara. The architecture also gave a name to the **Red Tile Tour,** a self-guided walking tour of historic downtown. The visitor center (see "Visitor Information" above) has a map and guide of the tour, which can take anywhere from 1 to 3 hours, including time to visit some of the buildings, and covers about 12 blocks. Some of the highlights are destinations in their own right.

Santa Barbara County Courthouse ⋒   Built in 1929, this grand "palace" is considered the local flagship of Spanish Colonial Revival architecture (you've undoubtedly seen its facade on TV during the Michael Jackson trial). It's certainly the most flamboyant example, with impressive facades, beamed ceilings, striking murals, an 85-foot-high observation clock tower, and formal sunken gardens. Free guided tours are offered on Monday, Tuesday, and Friday at 10:30am and Monday through Saturday at 2pm.

1100 Anacapa St. ⓒ **805/962-6464.** Mon–Fri 8am–4:45pm; Sat–Sun and holidays 10am–4:45pm.

Santa Barbara Museum of Art ⋒   This little jewel of a museum feels more like the private gallery of a wealthy collector. Its leaning is toward early-20th-century Western American paintings and 19th- and 20th-century Asian art, but the best displays might be the antiquities and Chinese ceramics collections. In addition, there are often visiting exhibits featuring small but excellent collections from other establishments. Free docent-led gallery tours are given daily at 1pm, and exhibition tours are offered daily at noon.

1130 State St. ⓒ **805/963-4364.** www.sbmuseart.org. Admission $7 adults, $5 seniors, $4 students and children 6–17, free for children under 6; free for all Thurs and the 1st Sun of each month. Tues–Sun 11am–5pm.

ELSEWHERE IN THE CITY
Santa Barbara Botanic Garden ⟅Finds⟆   The Botanic Garden is devoted entirely to indigenous California plants. More than 5½ miles of meandering trails on 65 acres offer glimpses of cacti, redwoods, wildflowers, and much more, many arranged in representational habitats or landscapes. The gardens were established in 1926. You'll catch the very best color and aroma just after spring showers. Docent tours are offered daily at 2pm, with additional tours on Thursday, Saturday, and Sunday at 10:30am.

1212 Mission Canyon Rd. (a short drive uphill from the mission). ⓒ **805/682-4726.** www.santabarbarab-otanicgarden.org. Admission $6 adults, $4 seniors, $3 children 13–18 and seniors over 60, $1 children 5–12, free for children under 5. Mon–Fri 9am–5pm; Sat–Sun 9am–6pm (closing time 1 hr. earlier Nov–Feb).

Santa Barbara Mission ⋒⋒   Established in 1786 by Father Junípero Serra and built by the Chumash Indians, this is a rare example in physical form of the blending of Indian and Hispanic spirituality. The hilltop structure is called the "Queen of the Missions" for its twin bell towers and graceful beauty. It overlooks the town and the Channel Islands. Brochures are available in six languages, and docent-guided tours can be arranged in advance ($1 extra per person).

Laguna and Los Olivos sts. (**C** 805/682-4149. www.sbmission.org. Admission $4, free for children under 12. Daily 9am–5pm.

Santa Barbara Zoological Gardens (*Kids*   When you're driving around the bend on Cabrillo Boulevard, look up—you might spot the head of a giraffe poking up through the palms. This zoo is a thoroughly charming, pint-size place, where all 600 animals can be seen in about 30 minutes. Most of the animals live in natural, open settings. There are also a children's Discovery Area, a miniature train ride, and a small carousel. The picnic areas (complete with barbecue pits) are underutilized and especially recommended.

500 Ninos Dr. (**C** 805/962-5339, or 805/962-6310 for a recording. www.santabarbarazoo.org. Admission $9 adults, $7 seniors and children 2–12, free for children under 2. Parking $3. Daily 10am–5pm; last admission 1 hr. prior to closing. Closed Thanksgiving and Dec 25.

Stearns Wharf   California's oldest working wharf attracts visitors for strolling, shopping, and snacking. There's also a Sea Center with aquariums, an outdoor touch-tank, and other exhibits. The wharf has a family-friendly atmosphere, and it's not as touristy as San Francisco's Fisherman's Wharf. Although the wharf no longer functions for passenger and freight shipping as it did when built in 1872 by local lumberman John C. Stearns, you might still see local fishing boats unloading their daily catch. You could also take a narrated sunset harbor cruise aboard the *Harbour Queen* at **Captain Don's** (**C** 805/969-5217). Public parking is available on the wharf; it's free with merchant validation.

At the end of State St.

BEACHES

East Beach is Santa Barbara's favorite beach, stretching from the Zoological Gardens to Chase Palm Park and the wharf. Nearer the pier you can enjoy manicured lawns, tall palms, and abundant facilities; to the east are many volleyball courts, plus the Cabrillo Pavilion, a recreational center, bathhouse, and architectural landmark dating from 1925. Picnic areas with barbecue grills, showers, and clean, well-patrolled sands make this beach a good choice for everyone. **West Beach,** between the wharf and the harbor, has recently been dredged to create a kid-friendly water-play lagoon, conveniently located across the street from some of Santa Barbara's best family-choice hotels.

On the other side of Santa Barbara Harbor is **Leadbetter Beach,** less sheltered than those to the south, and thus popular with surfers. It's reached by following Cabrillo Boulevard after it turns into Shoreline Drive. This beach is also a great place to watch pleasure boats entering or leaving the harbor. Leadbetter has basic facilities, including restrooms, picnic areas, and a metered parking lot. Two miles west of Leadbetter is the secluded but popular **Arroyo Burro Beach County Park,** also known as "Hendry's Beach." This gem has a grassy park beneath the cliffs and a white crescent beach with great waves for surfing and bodysurfing. There are volleyball nets, picnic areas, restrooms, and a free parking lot.

OUTDOOR ACTIVITIES

BIKING & SURREY CYCLING   A relatively flat, palm-lined 2-mile coastal pathway, perfect for biking, runs along the beach. More adventurous riders can pedal through town (where painted bike lanes line many major routes, including one up to the mission). These routes and many more are outlined in the *Santa*

Barbara County Bike Map, a free and comprehensive resource available at the visitor center (see "Essentials," above) or by calling © **805/963-7283.**

Wheel Fun Rentals, 22 State St., just off Cabrillo Boulevard (© **805/ 966-6733;** www.wheelfunrentals.com), rents well-maintained beach cruisers, mountain bikes, tandem bikes, and an Italian four-wheel Surrey that seats three adults; rates vary. It's open daily from 8am to 8pm.

BOATING The **Santa Barbara Sailing Center,** in Santa Barbara Harbor (© **800/350-9090** or 805/962-2826; www.sbsail.com), rents sailboats from 21 to 50 feet in length. Both skippered and bareboat charters are available by the day or hour. Sailing instruction for all levels of experience is also available. Coastal, island, whale-watching, dinner-cruise, and adventure tours are offered on the 50-foot sailing catamaran *Double Dolphin.* Open daily 9am to 6pm.

GOLF At the **Santa Barbara Golf Club,** 3500 McCaw Ave., at Las Positas Road (© **805/687-7087**), there is a great 6,009-yard, 18-hole course with a driving range. Unlike many municipal courses, the Santa Barbara Golf Course is well maintained and presents a moderate challenge for the average golfer. Greens fees are $30 weekdays and $40 on weekends, twilight rates available after 1pm.

The 18-hole, 7,000-yard course **Sandpiper,** at 7925 Hollister Ave. (© **805/ 968-1541;** www.sandpipergolf.com), a breathtakingly scenic ocean-side course, has a pro shop and driving range. Greens fees are $135, or $150 with a cart, twilight rates available.

HIKING The foothill trails in the Santa Ynez Mountains above Santa Barbara are perfect for day hikes. In general, they aren't overly strenuous. Trail maps are available at **Pacific Travelers Supply,** 12 W. Anapamu St. (© **888/PAC-TRAV** or 805/963-4438), at the visitor center (see "Essentials," above), and from **Traffic Solutions** (© **805/963-7283**).

One of the most popular hikes is the **Seven Falls/Inspiration Point Trail,** an easy trek that begins on Tunnel Road, past the mission, and skirts the edge of Santa Barbara's Botanic Garden (which contains some pleasant hiking trails itself). The hike takes about 4 hours if you go all the way to Inspiration Point.

SKATING The paved beach path that runs along Santa Barbara's waterfront is perfect for rollerblading. **Wheel Fun Rentals,** 22 State St., just off Cabrillo Blvd (© **805/966-6733;** www.wheelfunrentals.com), rents Rollerblades and all the requisite protective gear. It's open daily from 8am to 8pm.

WHALE-WATCHING Whale-watching cruises are offered between late December and late March, when Pacific gray whales pass by on migratory journeys from Baja California, Mexico, to their Alaskan feeding grounds. **Shoreline Park,** west of the harbor, has high bluffs ideal for land-based whale-spotting. Sea excursions are offered by both **Captain Don's Harbor Tours** (© **805/969-5217;** www.captdon.com), on Stearns Wharf, and **The Condor** (© **888/77-WHALE** or 805/963-3564; www.condorcruises.com), located at 301 W. Cabrillo Blvd. in the Santa Barbara Harbor.

SHOPPING

State Street from the beach to Victoria Street is the city's main thoroughfare and has the largest concentration of shops. Many specialize in T-shirts and postcards, but there are a number of boutiques as well. If you get tired of strolling, hop on one of the electric shuttle buses (25¢ fare) that run up and down State Street.

Also check out **Brinkerhoff Avenue** (off Cota St., between Chapala and De La Vina sts.), Santa Barbara's "antiques alley." Most shops here are open Tuesday

---

⌒Finds Lotusland: Montecito's Hidden, Magical Garden

For many Southern Californians, it's the stuff of legends: a secret, lavishly landscaped estate—open only to a select few visitors—renowned for exotic plants and mysterious garden paths. But it's easier than you might expect to gain entry to **Ganna Walska Lotusland,** 695 Ashley Rd. (© 805/ 969-9990; www.lotusland.org), as long as you're able to plan ahead.

Named for the estate's vivacious European-born mistress and the romantic, lotus-filled ponds that many associate with her gardens, the late Madame Walska's Montecito estate reflects both her eccentricity and the skill of her prestigious gardeners. She was especially fond of succulents and cacti, interspersing them artistically among native plants and decorative objects. Assembled when money was no object and import regulations were lenient (primarily in the 1940s), the garden contains priceless rare specimens, and even prehistoric plants that are extinct in the wild.

Montecito is a 5-minute freeway drive south of downtown Santa Barbara. Two-hour guided tours are conducted from mid-February to mid-November Wednesday through Saturday at 10am and 1:30pm. The tax-deductible admission fee is $15 for adults and $8 for children 2 to 10. Reservations are suggested as much as 6 months in advance.

---

through Sunday from 11am to 5pm. **El Paseo,** 814 State St., is a shopping arcade reminiscent of an old Spanish street. It was built around an 1827 adobe home and is lined with shops and art galleries. **Paseo Nuevo,** on the other side of State Street, is an equally charming modern outdoor mall, featuring chain stores and inviting cafes, and anchored by a branch of Nordstrom's department store.

WHERE TO STAY

Before you even begin calling around for reservations, keep in mind that Santa Barbara's accommodations are expensive—especially in summer. Then decide whether you'd like to stay beachside (even more expensive) or downtown. Santa Barbara is small, but not small enough to happily stroll between the two areas.

The Convention and Visitors Bureau's reservations service, **Hot Spots** (© **800/793-7666** or 805/564-1637; www.hotspotsusa.com), keeps an updated list of availability for about 90% of the area's hotels, motels, inns, and B&Bs. The service will have the latest information on who might be looking to fill last-minute vacancies at reduced rates. Reservationists are available Monday through Saturday from 9am to 9pm and Sunday from 9am to 4pm at no charge.

VERY EXPENSIVE

Four Seasons Biltmore ⋆⋆⋆   This gem of the "American Riviera" manages to adhere to the most elegant standards of hospitality without making anyone feel unwelcome. It's easy to sense the ghosts of golden-age Hollywood celebs like Greta Garbo, Errol Flynn, and Bing Crosby, who used to play croquet or practice putting on the hotel's perfectly manicured lawns and then head over to the private Coral Casino Beach & Cabana Club—because that's exactly what today's privileged guests are *still* doing! The Four Seasons company acquired this Spanish-style hacienda (ca. 1927) in 1987 and restored the 20-acre property without spoiling a bit of its historic charm. Rooms have an airy feel, heightened by white plantation shutters, light-wood furnishings, and full marble bathrooms with all the modern amenities. Guests can amuse themselves with a putting green, shuffleboard courts, and croquet lawn. In addition to two acclaimed dining rooms, the Biltmore offers a no-holds-barred Sunday brunch that draws folks from 100 miles away. The hotel's most recent addition is **The Spa,** a multimillion-dollar, 10,000-square-foot Spanish-style annex that houses numerous treatment rooms, a swimming pool and two huge whirlpool baths, a state-of-the-art fitness center, and for the big spenders, 10 oceanview deluxe suites with fireplaces, in-room bars, changing rooms, and twin massage tables (essentially your own private treatment room).

1260 Channel Dr. (at the end of Olive Mill Rd.), Santa Barbara, CA 93108. ℂ 800/332-3442 or 805/969-2261. Fax 805/565-8323. www.fourseasons.com. 213 units. $430–$540 double; from $1,180 suite. Children 18 and under stay free in parent's room. AE, DC, DISC, MC, V. Valet parking $20; free self-parking. **Amenities:** 3 restaurants; lounge; 2 outdoor heated pools; 3 lit tennis courts; fitness center; spa; Jacuzzi; complimentary bikes; salon; 24-hr. room service; laundry service; dry cleaning. *In room:* A/C, TV w/pay movies, dataport, minibar, hair dryer, iron.

San Ysidro Ranch 𝍐𝍐𝍐   Considered one of the most romantic destinations in the world and a legendary hideaway for the rich and famous, the San Ysidro Ranch is best known as the honeymoon retreat for John and Jackie Kennedy. Set on 500 rolling acres at the base of the Santa Ynez Mountains, the first thing you notice as you enter this ranch-style retreat are the aromas of orange blossoms, eucalyptus, and bougainvillea. As you walk past terraced gardens and secluded cottages, you can't help but feel the tensions ease away; eventually you start to realize that you're going to regret having to leave this special place.

You could write a book on the history of the ranch, from the early days when shoeing a guest's horse cost $1.50 and cottages let for $30 a week, to a historic who's-who guest list that includes Sir Laurence Olivier, Katharine Hepburn, Groucho Marx, Bing Crosby, John Steinbeck, and Jean Harlow. Today's Hollywood stars are still lured to this tranquil low-profile estate, more for what it isn't—slick, trendy, elite, fashionable—than what it is: a humble, friendly lodging where everyone is treated like a sorely missed friend. Case in point: The ranch's hugely popular bistro doesn't take reservations, so no matter how wealthy or famous you are, you still have to wait for a table (I *love* that).

The 38 guest rooms and cottages are individually decorated in French country style, and each has a private terrace, fireplace or wood-burning oven, and king-size beds with Frette linens and goose-down comforters. Premium cottages come with freshly drawn hot tubs and private outdoor decks. The most requested unit is the Kennedy Suite (yes, where John and Jackie stayed), a lavish two-bedroom stone cottage with three fireplaces and a large deck with distant views of the Channel Islands. **The Stonehouse Restaurant** offers formal dining (and takes reservations), whereas the **Plow & Angel Bistro** is far more casual and typically filled with regulars from the very upscale Montecito neighborhood that surrounds the ranch; both serve excellent cuisine. There's a small pool, fitness room, two tennis courts, and an outdoor jungle gym on the property, as well as 17 miles of hiking trails. In-room spa treatments are available upon request.

900 San Ysidro Lane, Santa Barbara, CA 93108. ℂ 800/368-6788 or 805/969-5046. Fax 805/565-1995. www.sanysidroranch.com. 38 units. $399–$4,100 double. AE, DISC, MC, V. Pets are welcome in free-standing cottages. **Amenities:** 2 restaurants with outdoor seating; heated pool; 2 outdoor tennis courts; children's outdoor jungle gym; fitness center; 24-hr. room service; dry cleaning/laundry service; newspaper delivery; private outdoor decks and wood-burning fireplaces. *In room:* A/C, TV/VCR and DVD, minibar, hair dryer, iron, personal safe, CD player, high-speed Internet access.

Tips It's a Dog's Life

The San Ysidro Ranch in Montecito not only welcomes dogs, they give them the royal treatment. After checking in, each dog receives a welcome bone, cedar-stuffed fleece bedding, a luxury doggie pillow, a 2-liter bottle of *Pawier* vitamin-enriched water, and an amenity package that includes a tennis ball, a water dish, a chew toy, and a doggie bagel. And after a day of hiking, surely Fifi will want to indulge in a half-hour in-room massage while placing an order from the doggie in-room dining menu, which includes Petite New York steak ($17.95), ravioli, baked salmon, and cheeseburgers. The cost? $100 per pet per stay.

EXPENSIVE

El Encanto Hotel & Garden Villas This romantic hillside retreat, whose very name means "enchantment," was built in 1915 and is made up of charming Craftsman cottages and Spanish bungalows. Uphill from the mission and surrounded by an exclusive older residential community, El Encanto features a spectacular view, secluded nooks, peaceful gardens and lily ponds, and lush landscaping. The hotel's discreetly attentive service has made it a favorite among privacy-minded celebs. The spacious rooms are tastefully decorated in a European country style, and many have fireplaces, balconies, or patios.

1900 Lasuen Rd., Santa Barbara, CA 93103. © 800/346-7039 or 805/687-5000. Fax 805/687-3903. www.elencantohotel.com. 84 units. $239–$259 double; from $469 suite. AE, DC, MC, V. Valet parking $10. **Amenities:** Restaurant; lounge; outdoor heated pool; outdoor tennis court; access to nearby health club; concierge; business center; room service (6am–10pm); in-room massage; babysitting; laundry service; dry cleaning. *In room:* TV, dataport, minibar, coffeemaker, hair dryer, iron.

Simpson House Inn Bed & Breakfast Simpson House is truly something special. Rooms within the 1874 Historic Landmark main house are decorated to Victorian perfection, with extras ranging from a claw-foot tub and antique brass shower to skylight and French doors opening to the manicured gardens; romantic cottages are nestled throughout the grounds. The rooms have everything you could possibly need, but most impressive are the extras: the gourmet Mediterranean hors d'oeuvres and Santa Barbara wines served each afternoon; the enormous video library; and the full gourmet breakfast (delivered, for detached cottages, on delicate china). Fact is, the Simpson House goes the distance—and then some—to create the perfect stay. Although this property is packed into a relatively small space, it still manages an ambience of country elegance and exclusivity—especially if you book one of the cottages.

121 E. Arrellaga St. (between Santa Barbara and Anacapa sts.), Santa Barbara, CA 93101. © 800/676-1280 or 805/963-7067. Fax 805/564-4811. www.simpsonhouseinn.com. 14 units. $255–$455 double; from $555 suite/cottage. Rates include full gourmet breakfast and evening wine and hors d'oeuvres. AE, DISC, MC, V. Free parking. **Amenities:** Complimentary bikes; croquet; concierge; in-room massage; laundry service; dry cleaning. *In room:* A/C, TV/VCR, dataport, coffeemaker, minibar, hair dryer, iron.

MODERATE

Casa del Mar Inn at the Beach *Value* A half block from the beach (sorry, no views), Casa del Mar is an excellent-value Spanish-architecture motel with one- and two-room suites. The largish rooms have relatively new furnishings, with plenty of pastels. The flower-sprinkled grounds are well maintained, with an attractive sun deck (but no swimming pool), and the staff is eager to please.

Many rooms have kitchenettes, and a dozen different room configurations guarantee something to suit your needs (especially families). Guests get discounts at a nearby day spa, and golf packages can be arranged. *Tip:* Despite the hotel's multitude of rates, rooms can often be an unexpected bargain. Also check the website for Internet-only specials.

18 Bath St., Santa Barbara, CA 93101. ℭ 800/433-3097 or 805/963-4418. Fax 805/966-4240. www. casadelmar.com. 21 units. $194–$234 double; from $249 suite. Rates include continental breakfast and wine-and-cheese social. Extra person $10. AE, DC, DISC, MC, V. Free parking. From northbound U.S. 101, exit at Cabrillo, turn left onto Cabrillo, and head toward the beach; Bath is the 2nd street on the right after the wharf. From southbound U.S. 101, take the Castillo exit and turn right on Castillo, left on Cabrillo, and left on Bath. Pets accepted with $10 fee. **Amenities:** Jacuzzi; in-room massage; laundry service; dry cleaning. *In room:* TV, fridge and kitchen or kitchenette in some units, coffeemaker, hair dryer, iron.

Hotel Oceana ℛ If you're going to vacation in Santa Barbara, you might as well stay in style and on the beach. Ergo, the Hotel Oceana, a "beach chic" hotel with an oceanfront setting and an L.A. makeover. The 2½-acre Spanish Mission–style property consists of four adjacent motels built in the 1940s that have been merged and renovated into one sprawling hotel. The result is a wide range of charmingly old-school accommodations—everything from apartments with real day beds (great for families) to inexpensive courtyard rooms and deluxe oceanview suites—with modern furnishings. Each guest room, decorated by renowned interior designer Kathryn Ireland, is smartly appointed with soft Frette linens, down comforters (the beds are fantastic), ceiling fans, CD players, cozy duvets, and Aveda bath products. Along with the size and location of your room, you also get to choose between color schemes—soothing blue or green, racy red, and a cheery yellow. The beach and jogging path are right across the street, and there's a huge lawn area that's perfect for picnic lunches.

202 W. Cabrillo Blvd., Santa Barbara, CA 93101. ℭ 800/965-9776 or 805/965-4577. Fax 805/965-9937. www.hoteloceana.com. 122 units. $250–$350 double. AE, DISC, MC, V. Parking $6. **Amenities:** Breakfast room; 2 outdoor pools; Jacuzzi; spa and fitness center; room service (11:30am–9pm); laundry/dry cleaning service. *In room:* TV w/pay movies, dataport, minibar, hair dryer, iron, CD player.

The Upham Hotel and Country House This conveniently located inn combines the intimacy of a B&B with the service of a small hotel. Built in 1871, the Upham is the oldest continuously operating hostelry in Southern California. At some point the management made time for upgrades, though, because guest accommodations are complete with all modern comforts. My favorites are the charming cottage rooms, each with a private garden entrance and cozy fireplace. The hotel is constructed of redwood, with sweeping verandas and a Victorian cupola on top. It has a warm lobby and a cozy restaurant.

1404 De La Vina St. (at Sola St.), Santa Barbara, CA 93101. ℭ 800/727-0876 or 805/962-0058. Fax 805/963-2825. www.uphamhotel.com. 50 units. $165–$235 double; from $275 suite/cottage. Rates include continental breakfast and afternoon wine and cheese. Additional guest $10. AE, DC, MC, V. Free parking. **Amenities:** Restaurant; laundry service; dry cleaning. *In room:* TV, hair dryer, iron.

INEXPENSIVE

All the best buys fill up fast in the summer months, so be sure to reserve your room in advance—even if you're just planning to stay at the decent, reliable **Motel 6** (ℭ 800/466-8356 or 805/564-1392) near the beach.

Franciscan Inn ℛ *Value* The Franciscan is nestled in a quiet neighborhood a block from the beach, near Stearns Wharf. This privately owned and meticulously maintained hotel is an affordable retreat with enough frills that you'll still feel pampered. The small but comfy rooms feature a country-tinged decor and finely tiled bathrooms. Services include morning newspaper and free local calls. Most second-floor rooms have unobstructed mountain views, and some suites feature fully equipped kitchenettes. All in all, the inn stacks up as a great family choice that's classy enough for a romantic weekend, too.

109 Bath St. (at Mason St.), Santa Barbara, CA 93101. © 805/963-8845. Fax 805/564-3295. www.franciscaninn.com. 53 units. $125–$170 double; from $195 suite. Extra person $8. Rates include continental breakfast and afternoon refreshments. AE, DC, MC, V. Free parking. **Amenities:** Heated outdoor pool; Jacuzzi; coin-op laundry; laundry service; dry cleaning. *In room:* A/C, TV/VCR, dataport, kitchenette in some suites, coffeemaker, hair dryer, iron.

WHERE TO DINE
EXPENSIVE

bouchon santa barbara 🏯🏯 CALIFORNIA   You can tell this warm and inviting restaurant is passionate about wine just from the name—*bouchon* is the French word for "wine cork." And not just any wines, but those of Santa Barbara County. There are 50 different Central Coast wines available by the glass; have some fun by enhancing each course with a glass (or half-glass) of wine—knowledgeable servers help make the perfect match. The seasonally composed—and regionally inspired—menu has included dishes such as smoked Santa Barbara albacore "carpaccio," arranged with a tangy vinaigrette and shaved Parmesan; luscious sweetbread and chanterelle ragout cradled in a potato-leek basket; local venison sliced and laid atop cumin spaetzle in a shallow pond of green peppercorn-Madeira demiglace; or monkfish saddle fragrant with fresh herbs and accompanied by a creamy fennel-Gruyère gratin. Request a table on the heated front patio, and don't miss the signature chocolate soufflé for dessert.

9 W. Victoria St. © 805/730-1160. www.bouchonsantabarbara.com. Reservations recommended. Main courses $24–$32. AE, DC, MC, V. Daily 5:30–9:30pm.

Nu 🏯🏯 CALIFORNIA CUISINE   *Nu* is French for naked, which explains why the entire staff here works totally naked. Just kidding! Proprietor and executive chef David Cecchini picked the name to convey that his restaurant "strips away" any preconceived notions you may have about dining in Santa Barbara. Metaphors aside, I love everything about Nu, from its pleasant, woodsy neo-Tuscan decor to the exceptional service, plant-filled courtyard seating, and weekend jazz sessions. But the food is really the thing here. You might want to start with lobster risotto, featuring a carrot-infused crème fraîche and orange demiglace, or the yellowfin tuna tartare, then move on to a citrus-spiced swordfish, served with beet-infused toasted quinoa, cabbage fondue, shiitake mushrooms, and saffron nage. If all this sounds slightly fussy, it is; yet it works, and beautifully. *Tip:* If you're not in the mood for a full sit-down dinner, the cocktail lounge has its own menu of appetizers, including great pizzas made in a wood-burning oven.

1129 State St., Santa Barbara. © 805/965-1500. www.restaurantnu.com. Main courses $10–$11 lunch, $22–$28 dinner. AE, DC, DISC, MC, V. Mon–Thurs and Sun 5:30–10pm; Fri–Sat 5:30–11pm.

Wine Cask 🏯 CALIFORNIA/ITALIAN   Take a venerable wine shop, a large 1920s landmark dining room with a big stone fireplace, and outstanding Italian fare, and mix them with an attractive staff and clientele, and you've got the Wine Cask—the most popular upscale dining spot in Santa Barbara. Here you'll be treated to such heavenly creations as braised oxtail with crème fraîche mashed potatoes and roasted seasonal vegetables. Other options include potato and prosciutto-wrapped local halibut in cioppino sauce, Niman Ranch pork cheek ravioli, and butternut squash risotto with a fig glaze and Parmesan crisp. The wine list reads like a novel, with more than 2,500 wines (ranging from $26 to the impossible), and has deservedly received the *Wine Spectator* award for excellence. There's also a happy hour at the beautiful maple bar from 4 to 6pm daily.

In El Paseo Center, 813 Anacapa St. ⓒ **805/966-9463.** Reservations recommended. Main courses $13–$20 lunch, $22–$34 dinner. AE, DC, MC, V. Mon–Fri 11:30am–2:30pm; nightly 5:30–10pm (till 11pm Fri–Sat).

MODERATE

Brophy Bros. Clam Bar & Restaurant ⚘ SEAFOOD   This place is most known for its unbeatable view of the marina, but the dependable fresh seafood keeps tourists and locals coming back. Dress is casual, portions are huge, and favorites include New England clam chowder, cioppino, and any one of an assortment of seafood salads. The scampi and garlic-baked clams are consistently good, as is all the fresh fish, which comes with soup or salad, coleslaw, and pilaf or french fries. A great deal is the hot-and-cold shellfish combo platter for $13. Ask for a table on the narrow deck overlooking the harbor. *Be forewarned:* The wait at this small place can be up to 2 hours on a weekend night.

119 Harbor Way (off Cabrillo Blvd. in the Waterfront Center). ⓒ **805/966-4418.** Reservations not accepted. Main courses $8–$17. AE, MC, V. Sun–Thurs 11am–10pm; Fri–Sat 11am–11pm.

Palace Grill CAJUN/CREOLE   Strolling by this restaurant, a stone's throw from State Street, you'll see why descriptions like "rollicking" and "atmosphere as hot as the food" are applied to the Palace Grill. The scene extends to the sidewalk, where waiting diners thirst after Mason-jar Cajun martinis and Caribbean rum punch. Once inside, you'll find yourself part of the loud and fun atmosphere; this is not the place for meaningful conversation. Try a platter of spicy blackened steak and seafood, crawfish étouffée, or Creole jambalaya pasta. Be sure to save room for the renowned Southern desserts, including sweet potato-pecan pie, Florida Key lime pie, and the superstar Louisiana bread-pudding soufflé, laced with Grand Marnier and accompanied by whiskey cream sauce.

8 E. Cota St. ⓒ **805/963-5000.** www.palacegrill.com. Reservations recommended (but not accepted Fri–Sat for after 5:30pm). Main courses $5–$13 lunch, $9–$25 dinner. AE, MC, V. Daily 11am–3pm; Sun–Thurs 5:30–10pm; Fri–Sat 5:30–11pm.

Pan e Vino ⚘ ITALIAN   This perfect Italian trattoria offers food as authentic as you'd find in Rome. The simplest spaghetti topped with basil-tomato sauce is so delicious it's hard to understand why diners would want to occupy their taste buds with more complicated concoctions. But this kitchen is capable of almost anything. Pasta puttanesca, with tomatoes, anchovies, black olives, and capers, is always tops. Pan e Vino also gets high marks for its reasonable prices, service, and casual atmosphere. Although many diners prefer to eat outside on the patio, some of the best tables are in the charming, cluttered dining room.

1482 E. Valley Rd., Montecito (a 5-min. drive south of downtown Santa Barbara). ⓒ **805/969-9274.** Reservations required. Main courses $10–$22. AE, MC, V. Mon–Thurs 11:30am–9pm; Fri–Sat 11:30am–9:30pm; Sun 5–9pm.

INEXPENSIVE

Don Pepe (Value) MEXICAN   Don't be put off by the simplicity of this seeming taco stand—the *mariscos* (seafood) here is fresh and fabulous, and comes at a fraction of fancy-restaurant prices. Staples like *carne asada* (grilled marinated beef) and *carnitas* (roasted marinated pork) are also among the best in town, but you'll want to go for the "love octopus" (with mayo, onions, cilantro, sour cream, cheese, and white whine [*sic*]) or the shrimp Veracruz style (deep-fried and served with tomato sauce, bell and yellow peppers, Talapia-style olives, and white "whine"). Orthography aside, this modest stand turns out some of the most wonderful seafood in town, all at a dream price.

701 Chapala St., Santa Barbara ℂ 805/730-1612. Main courses $4–$9. No credit cards. Daily 9am–9pm.

La Super-Rica Taquería ★★ *(Value* MEXICAN   Looking at this humble street-corner shack, you'd never guess it's blessed with an endorsement by Julia Child. The tacos here are authentic and no-nonsense, with generous portions of filling piled onto fresh, grainy corn tortillas. My favorites are the *adobado* (marinated pork), *gorditas* (thick corn *masa* pockets filled with spicy beans), and the flank steak. A dollop of house-made salsa and green or red hot sauce is the only adornment required. (It wasn't unusual to catch the late, great Julia Child lining up for Sunday's special, *pozole,* a stew of pork and hominy in red chili sauce.) On Friday and Saturday the specialty is freshly made tamales (if the Dover-sole tamales are one of the specials, order them: They're incredible). *Tip:* Always check the daily specials first—those pieces of paper taped to the glass partition—and be sure to ask for extra tortillas no matter what you order.

622 N. Milpas St. (between Cota and Ortega sts.). ℂ 805/963-4940. Most menu items $3–$6. No credit cards. Sun–Thurs 11am–9pm; Fri–Sat 11am–9:30pm.

Stacky's Seaside *(Value* SANDWICHES   This ivy-covered shack filled with fishnets, surfboards, and local memorabilia has been a local favorite for years. A classic seafood dive, its menu of sandwiches is enormous, as are most of their pita pockets, hoagies, and club sandwiches. A sign proudly proclaims HALF OF ANY SANDWICH, HALF PRICE—NO PROBLEM, and Stacky's has made a lot of friends because of it. Choices include the Santa Barbaran (roasted tri-tip and melted jack cheese on sourdough), the Rincon pita (jack and cheddar cheeses, green Ortega chiles, onions, and ranch dressing), and a hot pastrami hoagie with Swiss cheese, mustard, and onions. Heck, they even serve a PB&J for $2.99. And if you like fish and chips, they nail it here. Stacky's also serves breakfast, featuring scrambled-egg sandwiches and south-of-the-border egg dishes. An order of crispy fries is enough for two.

2315 Lillie Ave., Summerland (5 min. on the freeway from Santa Barbara). ℂ 805/969-9908. Most menu items under $6. AE, DISC, MC, V. Mon–Fri 6:30am–7:30pm; Sat–Sun 7am–7:30pm.

SANTA BARBARA AFTER DARK

To find out what's going on while you're in town, check the free weekly *Independent,* or call the following venues: the **Center Stage Theater,** upstairs at the Paseo Nuevo Shopping Center, Chapala and De La Guerra streets (ℂ 805/963-0408); the **Lobero Theater,** 33 E. Canon Perdido St. (ℂ 805/963-0761); the **Arlington Theater,** 1317 State St. (ℂ 805/963-4408); and the **Earl Warren Showgrounds,** at Las Positas Road and U.S. 101 (ℂ 805/687-0766).

Unlike most American towns of its size, Santa Barbara has an active after-dark street life, which centers entirely along State Street. College kids are out in force, of course, but you can find folk of all ages promenading after dinner and beyond. If you're in the mood to barhop, you'll want to try the **Blue Agave,** 20 E. Cota St. (ℂ 805/899-4694), a favorite among an upscale 20-something crowd; **Wildcat Lounge,** 15 W. Ortega St. (ℂ 805/962-7970), one of the hippest watering holes in town; or **Firebird Café,** 14 E. Cota St. (ℂ 805/899-3400), with a Moroccan-style motif. Gay and lesbian visitors may want to check out **Hades,** 235 W. Montecito St. (ℂ 805/962-2754), at present the city's only gay spot.

7 The Ojai Valley ⟨⋆⟩

35 miles E of Santa Barbara; 88 miles NW of L.A.

In a crescent-shaped valley between Santa Barbara and Ventura, surrounded by mountain peaks, lies Ojai (pronounced "*Oh*-hi"). It's a magical place, selected by Frank Capra as Shangri-La, the legendary utopia of his 1936 classic *Lost Horizon*. The spectacularly tranquil setting has made Ojai a mecca for artists and a large population of New Age spiritualists, drawn by the area's mystical beauty.

Life is low-key in the Ojai Valley. Perhaps the most excitement generated all year happens during the first week of June when the **Ojai Music Festival** draws world-renowned classical artists to perform in the Libbey Bowl amphitheater (for more information, call ⓒ **805/646-2094** or visit www.ojaifestival.org).

While in Ojai, you're bound to hear folks wax poetically about something called the "pink moment." It's a phenomenon first noticed by the earliest Native American valley dwellers, when the brilliant sunset over the nearby Pacific is reflected onto the mountainside, creating an eerie and beautiful pink glow.

ESSENTIALS

GETTING THERE   The 45-minute drive south from Santa Barbara to Ojai is along two-lane Calif. 150, a road that's as curvaceous as it is stunning. From Los Angeles, take U.S. 101 north to Calif. 33, which winds through eucalyptus groves to meet Calif. 150—the trip takes about 90 minutes. Calif. 150 is called Ojai Avenue in the town center and is the village's primary thoroughfare.

VISITOR INFORMATION   The **Ojai Valley Chamber of Commerce & Visitors Bureau,** 150 W. Ojai Ave., Ojai, CA 93023 (ⓒ **805/646-8126;** www.the-ojai.org), distributes free area maps, brochures, and the *Visitor's Guide to the Ojai Valley,* which lists galleries and events. It's open Monday through Friday from 9:30am to 4:30pm, Saturday and Sunday from 10am to 4pm.

EXPLORING THE TOWN & VALLEY

Ojai is home to more than 35 artists working in a variety of media; most have home studios and are represented in one of several galleries in town. The best for jewelry and smaller pieces is **HumanArts,** 310 E. Ojai Ave. (ⓒ **805/646-1525**). It also has a home-accessories annex, **HumanArts Home,** 246 E. Ojai Ave. (ⓒ **805/646-8245**). Artisans band together each October for an organized **Artists' Studio Tour** (ⓒ **805/646-8126** for information). It's fun to drive from studio to studio at your own pace, meeting artists and perhaps purchasing some of their work. Ojai's most famous artist was world-renowned Beatrice Wood, who worked until her death in 1998 at 104. Her whimsical sculpture and luminous pottery are internationally acclaimed, and her spirit is still a driving force in Ojai.

Strolling the Spanish arcade shops downtown and the surrounding area will yield a treasure trove, including open-air **Bart's Books,** Matilija Street at Canada Street (ⓒ **805/646-3755**), an Ojai fixture for many years. Antiques hounds head for **Treasures of Ojai,** 110 N. Signal St. (ⓒ **805/646-2852**), an indoor antiques mall packed to the rafters with treasures, trash, and everything in between.

Residents of the Ojai Valley *love* their equine companions—miles of bridle paths are painstakingly maintained, and HORSE CROSSING signs are everywhere. If you'd like to explore the equestrian way, call the **Ojai Valley Inn's Ranch & Stables** (ⓒ **805/646-5511**).

Ojai has long been a haven for several esoteric sects of metaphysical and philosophical beliefs. The **Krotona Institute and School of Theosophy,** Calif. 33

and Calif. 150 at Hermosa Road (📞 **805/646-2653**), has been in the valley since 1926, and visitors are welcome at their library and bookstore.

In the **Lake Casitas Recreation Area** (📞 **805/649-2233** for visitor information), the beautiful Lake Casitas boasts nearly 32 miles of shoreline and was the site of the 1984 Olympic canoeing and rowing events. You can rent rowboats and small powerboats year-round from the **boathouse** (📞 **805/649-2043**) or enjoy picnicking and camping by the lakeside. Because the lake serves as a domestic water supply, swimming is not allowed. From Calif. 150, turn left onto Santa Ana Road, and then follow the signs to the recreation area.

When Ronald Coleman saw Shangri-La in *Lost Horizon,* he was really admiring the Ojai Valley. To visit the spot where Coleman stood for his view of **Shangri-La,** drive east on Ojai Avenue, up the hill, and stop at the stone bench near the top—the view is spectacular.

WHERE TO STAY

Blue Iguana Inn 🏆 *(Kids)* *(Value)* The Mission-style architecture, colorful Southwestern decor, and artwork by local artists (most of which are for sale) are just a few of the highlights of this small, charming hotel. The double rooms at the Blue Iguana are reasonably priced, and the fact that they are also equipped with clean, modern kitchens makes the inn an even bigger value for cook-at-home types. There's even a detached, private two-bedroom bungalow with one-and-a-half bathrooms and a full kitchen starting at $180. Kids can play croquet on the large open lawn while parents take a breather under the shady oaks; on hot summer days it's straight to the pool for everyone. The icing on the cake is the friendly, helpful staff, which makes the Blue Iguana an excellent all-around choice. Heck, they even offer spa treatments. *Tip:* Be sure to visit their website for package deals.

11794 N. Ventura Ave., Ojai, CA 93023. 📞 **805/646-5277.** www.blueiguanainn.com. 23 units. Rates $95–$145 double; $139–$209 suite; $179–$229 cottage. AE, DC, DISC, MC, V. **Amenities:** Pool; spa services. *In room:* A/C, TV, kitchen, fridge, coffeemaker.

The Moon's Nest Inn 🏆 Just a block off Ojai Avenue, this comfortable clapboard B&B was built as a schoolhouse in 1874 and is Ojai's oldest building, reborn in 1997 as a charming bed-and-breakfast. The innkeepers have preserved, replaced, or complemented the inn's historic details, and the building now boasts every modern comfort, including four private balconies. Throughout the house, from a cozy fireplace parlor to the sunny breakfast room, dramatically painted walls highlight architectural features like crown molding, and the entire inn is furnished with a mix of antiques and high-quality contemporary pieces. A once-neglected side lawn has been transformed into a restful, tree-shaded garden retreat, complete with rock-lined pond and large trellised veranda (where breakfast is served on pleasant days).

210 E. Matilija, Ojai, CA 93023. 📞 **805/646-6635.** Fax 805/646-5665. www.moonsnestinn.com. 7 units, 5 with private bathroom. $115–$175 double. Rates include breakfast and evening wine and cheese. AE, MC, V. Small pets accepted with $25-per-night fee. **Amenities:** Nearby health club; bike rental; in-room massage. *In room:* A/C, no phone.

Ojai Valley Inn & Spa 🏆🏆 In 1923, Hollywood architect Wallace Neff designed the clubhouse that's now the focal point of this quintessentially Californian, Spanish Colonial–style resort. The inn has carefully kept a sprawling Mediterranean estate ambience while providing gracious, elegant service and amenities, along with an oak-studded Senior PGA Tour golf course. Next to the golf course, the jewel of the resort is Spa Ojai, where stylish spa treatments—some modeled after Native American traditions—are administered inside a beautifully designed and exquisitely tiled Spanish-Moorish complex. Mind- and body-fitness classes, art classes, nifty workout machines, and a sparkling outdoor pool complete the relaxation choices. Many guest rooms have fireplaces, and most have sofas, writing desks, and secluded terraces or balconies that open onto expansive views of the valley and the mountains. Take advantage of the scenery with wooded jogging trails and available horseback riding.

905 Country Club Rd. (off Calif. 33), Ojai, CA 93023. ℂ 800/422-OJAI or 805/646-5511. Fax 805/646-7969. www.ojairesort.com. 207 units. $195 double; from $425 suite. AE, DC, DISC, MC, V. Free self- and valet parking. Pets accepted with $35-per-night fee and advance notice. **Amenities:** Restaurant; outdoor heated 60-ft. lap pool; championship golf course; 4 tennis courts; fitness center; full-service spa; Jacuzzi; complimentary bikes; concierge; in-room massage; laundry service; dry cleaning. *In room:* A/C, TV w/pay movies and Nintendo, fax, dataport, minibar, coffeemaker, hair dryer, iron, safe.

Rose Garden Inn This classic ranch-style motel has been well maintained and presents a low-key alternative to the pricey country club around the corner. A few blocks from the heart of town, with rose-filled gardens that border the Ojai equestrian and walking trail, this inn has a lazy, nostalgic feel. Rooms are small but have kitchen alcoves and brand-new beds. A mismatch of functional furniture reflects this place's rustic and inexpensive nature. The Rose Garden's best feature is hidden behind hedges: an enormous heated swimming pool (and Jacuzzi) next to a tree-shaded yard complete with hammock. There's even a two-person redwood sauna in a minispa facility. Check for seasonal specials. *Note:* The rooms and cottages in back tend to be quieter than the front rooms near the street.

615 W. Ojai Ave. (at Country Club Dr.), Ojai, CA 93023. ℂ **800/799-1881** or 805/646-1434. Fax 805/640-8455. www.rosegardeninnofojai.com. 18 units. $94–$137 double; $179–$219 cottage. Extra person $10. Rate includes continental breakfast and afternoon snacks. AE, DISC, MC, V. **Amenities:** Heated outdoor pool; Jacuzzi; sauna. *In room:* A/C, TV, fridge, hair dryer.

WHERE TO DINE
EXPENSIVE

In addition to the choices below, check out **Deer Lodge,** 2261 Maricopa Hwy. (ℂ **805/646-4256**), the latest incarnation of Ojai's favorite hippie-biker hangout on Highway 33, a few minutes north of Ojai. Nestled in the valley's gorgeous foothills, the building dates back to the Depression, when it served as a country store with bait and hunting supplies for local sportsmen, but new owners have been busy sprucing the place up and expanding to include a live stage in the bar, enclosed outdoor dining, and a hearty lodge menu with enough contemporary touches to bring in an upscale—yet adventuresome—clientele.

L'Auberge ✸✸ FRENCH/BELGIAN Possibly the most romantic restaurant in the Ojai Valley, L'Auberge is in a 1910 mansion with a fireplace, chandeliers, and a terrace with an excellent view of Ojai's famous sunset "pink moment." The dinner menu is traditional, featuring scampi, frogs' legs, trout filet, tournedos of beef, sweetbreads, and duckling a l'orange. The weekend brunch menu offers a selection of crepes. Service is expert and friendly, and this elegant house is an easy walk from downtown.

314 El Paseo (at Rincon St.). ℂ 805/646-2288. Reservations recommended. Main courses $18–$27. AE, MC, V. Sat–Sun 11am–2:30pm; daily 5:30–9pm.

The Ranch House ✸✸✸ CALIFORNIA This restaurant has been placing an emphasis on the freshest vegetables, fruits, and herbs since opening its doors in 1965, long before this practice became a national craze. Freshly snipped sprigs from the restaurant's lush herb garden will aromatically transform your simple meat, fish, or game dish into a work of art. From an appetizer of cognac-laced liver pâté served with its own chewy rye bread to desserts such as fresh raspberries with sweet Chambord cream, the ingredients always shine through. And you'll dine in a magical setting, for the Ranch House offers alfresco dining year-round on the wooden porch facing the scenic valley, as well as in the romantic garden amid twinkling lights and stone fountains.

S. Lomita Ave. © **805/646-2360.** www.theranchhouse.com. Reservations recommended. Main courses $20–$32; Sun brunch $21. AE, DC, DISC, MC, V. Tues–Sat 5:30–8:30pm; Sun 11am–7:30pm. From downtown Ojai, take Hwy. 33 north to El Roblar Dr. Turn left, then left again at Lomita Ave.

Suzanne's Cuisine 🏵🏵 CONTEMPORARY EUROPEAN   Enjoy a great meal in a comfortably sophisticated setting at this local fave, where every little touch bespeaks a preoccupation with quality details. Ask for a table on the covered outdoor patio, where lush greenery frames a casual setting warmed by a fireplace; when it rains, a plastic curtain descends to keep water out without losing that airy garden feel. Favorites from a seasonal menu include the lunch-only Southwest salad (wild, brown, and jasmine rice tossed with smoked turkey, feta cheese, veggies, and green chiles) and pepper-and-sesame encrusted ahi, served at dinner sautéed or seared (your choice). From seafood specialties to Italian recipes from chef and owner Suzanne Roll's family, everything is fresh and natural. Veggies are crisply al dente, and even the occasional cream sauce tastes light and healthy. Don't skip dessert.

502 W. Ojai Ave. © **805/640-1961.** www.suzannescuisine.com. Reservations recommended. Main courses $8–$16 lunch, $15–$28 dinner. MC, V. Wed–Mon 11:30am–3pm and 5:30–8:30pm.

MODERATE

Boccali's 🏵 ITALIAN   This small, wood-frame restaurant among citrus groves is a pastoral spot where patrons eat at picnic tables under umbrellas and oak trees, or inside at tables covered with red-and-white checked oilcloths. Pizza is the main dish served, topped California-style with the likes of crab, garlic, shrimp, and chicken. I think Boccali's lasagna (served piping hot *en casserole*) would win a statewide contest hands down. Fresh lemonade, from fruit plucked from local trees, is the drink of choice. Come hungry, and plan on sharing.

3277 Ojai–Santa Paula Rd. © **805/646-6116.** Reservations recommended for dinner. Pizza $9–$23; pasta $7–$16. No credit cards. Mon–Tues 4–9pm; Wed–Sun 11:45am–9pm.

Oak Pit BBQ *(Kids)* BARBECUE   This stick-to-your-ribs joint on the road between Ojai and Ventura is worth building up an appetite for. The rust-colored shack doesn't have much going for it—just some gingham curtains, a few tables indoors and out, and stacks of wood for firing up the barbecue—but generous portions of slowly oak-smoked meats will have dedicated carnivores coming back for more. Barbecue tri-tip brisket, ham, pork, Cajun sausage, and chicken—they're all served up in sandwiches or full dinners, with available sides of coleslaw, potato salad, fries, baked beans, and corn on the cob.

820 N. Ventura Ave. (Calif. 33), Oak View. © **805/649-9903.** Reservations not accepted. Sandwiches $6; main courses $9–$13. AE, DISC, MC, V. Tues–Thurs and Sun 11:30am–8:30pm; Fri–Sat 11am–9pm.

8 En Route to Los Angeles: Ventura

15 miles SW of Ojai; 74 miles NW of L.A.

Nestled between rolling foothills and the sparkling blue Pacific Ocean, Ventura may not have the cultural and gastronomic appeal of Los Angeles or even Santa Barbara, but it does boast the picturesque setting and clean sea breezes typical of California coastal towns. Southland antiques hounds have long reveled in Ventura's quirky collectible markets, but trendy home-decor shops, coffeehouses, wine bars, and fashionable restaurants are providing another lure for time-pressed vacationers who zip up from L.A. to charming bed-and-breakfasts. Ventura is also the headquarters and main point of embarkation for Channel Islands National Park (see below).

Most travelers don't bother exiting U.S. 101 for a closer look. But think about stopping to while away a few hours around lunchtime. Sleepy Ventura's charm might even convince you to spend a night.

ESSENTIALS

GETTING THERE   If you're traveling northbound on U.S. 101, exit at California Street; southbound, take the Main Street exit. If you're coming west on Calif. 33 from Ojai, there's also a Main Street exit. By the way, don't let the directions throw you off; because of the curve of the coastline, the ocean is not always to the west, but often southward.

VISITOR INFORMATION   For a visitor's guide and genial answers to any questions you might have, stop in at the **Ventura Visitors & Convention Bureau,** 89-C S. California St., Ventura, CA 93001 (© **800/333-2989** or 805/648-2075; www.ventura-usa.com).

EXPLORING THE TOWN

Much of Ventura's recent development has taken place along the charming seaside **Main Street,** the town's historic center, which grew outward from the Spanish mission of San Buenaventura (see below). The best section for strolling is between the mission (to the north) and Fir Street (to the south). Although many of the antiques stores and thrift stores are no more, you'll find plenty of window-shopping opportunities in the revitalized downtown.

Although Ventura stretches south to one of California's most picturesque harbors (the jumping-off point for the Channel Islands; see section 9, below), the town has its own **pier** at the end of California Street. Well maintained and favored by area fishers, the charming wooden pier is the longest of its kind in the state.

Mission San Buenaventura   Founded in 1782 (current buildings date from 1815) and still in use for daily services, this whitewashed and red-tile church lent its style to the contemporary civic buildings across the street. Step back in time by touring the mission's inside garden, where you can examine the antique water pump and olive press once essential to daily life here. The mission is small and near the rest of Ventura's action. Pick up a self-guided tour brochure in the adjacent gift shop for the modest donation of $1 per adult, 50¢ per child.

225 E. Main St. © **805/643-4318.** Free admission; donations appreciated. Mon–Sat 10am–5pm; Sun 10am–4pm.

San Buenaventura City Hall   This majestic neoclassical building was built in 1912 to serve as the Ventura County Courthouse. It sits on the hillside, overlooking old downtown and the ocean. To either side on Poli Street are some of Ventura's best-preserved and most ornate late-19th- and early-20th-century houses. Full of architectural detail (like the carved heads of Franciscan friars adorning the facade) inside and out, City Hall can be explored by escorted tour.

501 Poli St. © **805/658-4726.** Guided tours $7 adults, free for children 6 and under. 1-hr. tours given May–Sept Sat 11am–1pm.

Ventura County Museum of History & Art   This museum is worth visiting for its Native American Room, filled with Chumash treasures, and its Pioneer Room, which contains a collection of artifacts from the Mexican-American War (1846–48). The art gallery features exhibits of local painters and photographers, and the museum has an enormous archive (20,000 and counting) of photos of Ventura County from its origins to the present. There is also a small archaeological museum across Main Street from the main building. Allow 1 to 2 hours for your visit.

100 E. Main St. ℂ 805/653-0323. www.vcmha.org. Admission $4 adults, $3 seniors 62 and over, $1 kids 6–17, free for children under 6. Tues–Sun 10am–5pm.

WHERE TO STAY

Bella Maggiore Inn The Bella Maggiore is an intimate Italian-style small hotel whose simply furnished rooms (some with fireplaces, balconies, or bay-window seats) overlook a romantic courtyard or roof garden. The style is Mediterranean casual, with shuttered windows, ceiling fans, and fresh flowers in every room. An open-air center courtyard is the inn's focal point, with stone fountains and flowering trees. Complimentary breakfast is served downstairs at Nona's Courtyard Cafe, which also offers dinner and weekday lunches and a wine bar. A kind of European elegance pervades all but the reasonable rates here.

67 S. California St. (½ block south of Main St.), Ventura, CA 93001. ℂ 800/523-8479 or 805/652-0277. 24 units. $75–$135 double; $175 suite. Extra person $10. Rates include full breakfast and afternoon refreshments and appetizers. AE, DISC, MC, V. **Amenities:** Restaurant; wine bar; laundry service; dry cleaning. *In room:* TV, dataport.

Holiday Inn Ventura *(Kids)* One of the nicer Holiday Inns I've seen, this waterfront high-rise enjoys spectacular views courtesy of its 12 stories. Because there's little else around as tall, nearly every room has a panoramic view of the sea or Ventura's pretty foothills—or both! Situated on the boardwalk that runs between the pier and the fairgrounds, the hotel is also within walking distance of historic downtown Ventura. There's excellent beach access, a heated outdoor pool facing the ocean, a couple of nearby restaurants in addition to the hotel's coffee shop, plus bike and surrey rentals outside the front door. Ride up to the top floor and check out the hotel's circular ballroom; its adjacent cocktail lounge is oh-so-perfect for sunset gazing. Guest rooms are decent but unremarkable. At press time, a connection to the Crowne Plaza chain was in the works.

450 E. Harbor Blvd. (at California St.), Ventura, CA 93001. ℂ 800/HOLIDAY or 805/648-7731. Fax 805/653-6202. www.venturaca.holiday-inn.com. 260 units. $139–$159 double; from $200 suite. AE, DC, DISC, MC, V. **Amenities:** Restaurant; 3 lounges; heated outdoor pool; exercise room; bike rental; game room; business center; room service; coin-op laundry and laundry service; dry cleaning. *In room:* A/C, TV w/pay movies, dataport, hair dryer, iron.

La Mer European Bed & Breakfast *(★)* Perfect for a romantic getaway, La Mer is an 1890 Cape Cod–style home with a great view of the ocean from the parlor and two of the five guest rooms, each of which is furnished in a different international style. Whether you choose the "Santa Barbara" Victorian chamber with wood-burning stove, the turn-of-the-20th-century "Anacapa" hideaway with sunken bathtub, or one of three other rooms, you'll love this cozy little cottage. The owners arrange gourmet candlelit dinners, cruises to the Channel Islands, country carriage rides, therapeutic massages, and more.

411 Poli St. (west of City Hall), Ventura, CA 93001. ℂ 805/643-3600. Fax 805/653-7329. www.lamerbnb.com. 5 units (4 with private entrance). $115–$205 double. Rates include full breakfast and complimentary wine in room. AE, DISC, MC, V. No children accepted. **Amenities:** In-room massage. *In room:* No phone.

WHERE TO DINE

Deco *(★)* CALIFORNIA/CONTINENTAL CUISINE Deco is a sterling addition to Ventura's gastronomic scene. The dining room, bedecked with modern painting and sculpture, is like a million other midsize restaurants of recent vintage, but you'll spend most of your time looking at your plate: The contemporary California/Continental specialties are first-rate. The crab cakes, served with wasabe and a delightful Asian-influenced cabbage salad, are among the best I've had; the San Francisco–style cioppino is perfectly spiced; and the pinot noir–braised lamb shank is just, well, beyond. If the charbroiled lambburger is available at lunch, don't pass it up—the perfectly spiced grilled meat is first-rate.

394 E. Main St. © 805/667-2120. Main courses $7–$10 lunch, $14–$25 dinner. AE, MC, V. Mon–Fri 11:30am–2pm and 5:30–9:30pm; Sat 5:30–10pm.

Eric Ericsson's SEAFOOD/AMERICAN   Having already established a reputation in Ventura for crowd-pleasing seafood, Ericsson's moved to this pier-top spot in 1997. Here scruffy beachgoers mingle with suited business folk at lunch, sports fans and 20-somethings scarf down appetizers at cocktail hour, families come early for generous dinners, and couples on dates linger at window tables until closing. The staggering array of seafood includes clams, oysters, mussels, shrimp, scallops, cod, halibut, lobster, and calamari. Add specialties like Mexican cioppino or traditional clambake, plus plenty of nonfish and vegetarian dishes, and there's something for every taste on this menu.

668 Harbor Blvd. (on the Ventura Pier). © 805/643-4783. Reservations suggested on weekends. Main courses $7–$15 lunch; most full dinners $12–$28. AE, MC, V. Sun–Thurs 11am–10pm; Fri–Sat 11am–11pm.

71 Palm Restaurant COUNTRY FRENCH   Situated in a beautifully restored 1910 Craftsman, this country-French restaurant is a pleasant change of pace. Upstairs tables have an ocean view, while downstairs a crackling fire warms diners. Chef Didier Poirier of Le Mans takes an earnest approach to traditional specialties like steak au poivre with *pommes frites,* roast escolar over spinach with a garlic-cream sauce, New Zealand rack of lamb Provençal style, or homemade pâté served with crusty bread and tangy cornichons. But Poirier also dabbles with vegetarian dishes and pastas, and every night the cuisine of a different region of France is highlighted—his cooking classes (first Sat of the month) are a treat. Don't miss the antiques-filled original restrooms.

71 N. Palm St. (between Main and Poli sts.). © 805/653-7222. www.71palm.com. Reservations recommended. Main courses $11–$23; lunch $5-12. AE, DC, DISC, MC, V. Mon–Fri 11:30am–2pm; Mon–Sat 5–9pm.

Taquería Vallarta ⋆ MEXICAN   There's no better place to find a snapshot of Ventura than at the Taquería Vallarta, where young, old, rich, poor, Anglo, and Chicano come for *muy*-delicious Mexican food. There's nothing fancy here—it's your standard order-at-the-counter then slide-into-your-Formica-booth kinda of joint, but that's no problemo. The carnitas are among the best you'll find anywhere, perfect in a burrito, and the *carne asada* stars in the enchiladas of your dreams. Don't forget to dress up your dishes with the fresh salsas, limes, and chile peppers available at the condiment bar. For fans of great, cheap Mexican food, Taquería Vallarta's a must.

278 E. Main St. © 805/643-3037. Main courses $4–$8. No credit cards. Mon–Sun 8am–9pm.

9 Channel Islands National Park ⋆

Approximately 40 miles W (offshore) of Ventura

There's nothing like a visit to the Channel Islands for discovering the sense of awe explorers must have felt more than 400 years ago. It's miraculous what 25 miles of ocean can do, for compared to the mainland, this is wild and empty land, and only 55,000 visitors a year come to the islands. Whether you approach them by sea or air, you'll be bowled over by how untrammeled they remain despite neighboring Southern California's teeming masses.

Channel Islands National Park encompasses the five northernmost islands of the eight-island chain: Santa Barbara, Anacapa, Santa Cruz, Santa Rosa, and San Miguel. The park also protects the ocean 1 nautical mile offshore from each island, thereby prohibiting oil drilling, shipping, and other industrial uses.

The islands are the meeting point of two distinct marine ecosystems: The cold waters of Northern California and the warmer currents of Southern California swirl together here, creating an awesome array of marine life. On land, the isolation from mainland influences has allowed distinct species—including the island fox and the night lizard—to evolve and survive here. The islands are also the most important seabird-nesting area in Southern California and home to one of the biggest seal- and sea-lion-breeding colonies in the United States.

ESSENTIALS

VISITOR INFORMATION   Each of the five islands is distinct and takes some forethought to reach. Odds are, you're only going to visit one island on a given trip, so it's a good idea to study your options before going. Visit the **Channel Islands National Park Headquarters and Visitor Center,** 1901 Spinnaker Dr., Ventura, CA 93001 (© **805/658-5730;** www.nps.gov/chis), to get acquainted with the programs and individual personalities of the islands through maps and displays. Rangers run interpretive programs both on the islands and at the center year-round.

GETTING THERE   **Island Packers,** near the visitor center at 1691 Spinnaker Dr. (© **805/642-7688** for recorded information, 805/642-1393 for reservations; www.islandpackers.com), is the park's main concessionaire for boat transportation to and from the islands. Daylong tours are offered daily year-round to Anacapa and Santa Cruz; the price to Anacapa is $37 for adults, $34 for seniors, and $20 for children ages 3 to 12 (Santa Cruz is slightly higher). A half-day trip is also offered to Anacapa on Saturdays. Trips to Santa Rosa and San Miguel operate weekly May through October; boats to Santa Barbara Island are less frequent. Boats to Anacapa leave from the Channel Islands Harbor in Oxnard, 15 minutes south of Ventura. Also see Santa Barbara–based **Truth Aquatics,** under "Diving" below.

Another option, for visiting Santa Rosa Island only, is **Channel Islands Aviation,** 305 Durley Ave., Camarillo (© **805/987-1301;** www.flycia.com), which flies nine-passenger, fixed-wing aircraft. Day trips are scheduled every Saturday and every other Sunday (year-round, weather permitting); flying time to Santa Rosa is 25 minutes. The fare is $130 per person, which includes a guided island tour with a ranger via four-wheel-drive. Campers (that is, people camping) are flown over for $162 round-trip (these flights scheduled on demand).

THE WEATHER   While the climate is mild, with little variation in temperature year-round, the weather in the islands is always unpredictable. Thirty-mph winds can blow for days, or sometimes a fog bank will settle in and smother the islands for weeks. Winter rains can turn island trails into mud baths. In general, plan on wind, lots of sun (bring sunscreen), cool nights, and the possibility of hot days. Water temperatures are in the 50s and 60s (10s–20s Celsius) year-round. If you're camping, bring a good tent—if you don't know the difference between a good and a bad tent, the island wind will gladly demonstrate it for you.

CAMPING   Camping is permitted on all the park-owned islands but is limited to a certain number of campers per night, depending on the island. Fires and pets are prohibited on all the islands. You must bring everything you'll need;

there are no supplies on any of the islands. To reserve camping permits for any of the islands, call ✆ **800/365-CAMP** or log on to http://reservations.nps.gov. The rate is $10 per night, per site.

EXPLORING THE ISLANDS

ANACAPA Most people who visit the park come to Anacapa. It's 14 nautical miles from Ventura, an easy day trip—it takes about an hour to reach by boat. At only 1¼ square miles, Anacapa—actually three small islets divided by narrow stretches of ocean—is only marginally larger than Santa Barbara and, consequently, not a place for those who need a lot of space. Only East Anacapa is open to visitors, as the other two islets are important brown-pelican breeding areas. Several trails on the island will take you to beautiful overlooks of clear-watered coves and wild ocean. **Arch Rock,** a natural land bridge, is visible from the landing cove, where you'll clamber up 154 stairs to the island's flat top.

Camping is allowed on East Anacapa year-round, but don't bring more than you can carry the half mile from the landing cove. Bring earplugs and steer clear of the foghorn, which can cause permanent hearing damage. Most of the waters around the island, including the landing cove, are protected as a National Marine Preserve, where divers can look but not take anything. Pack a good wet suit, mask, fins, and snorkel; you can dive right off the landing-cove dock.

SANTA CRUZ By far the biggest of the islands—nearly 100 square miles— Santa Cruz is also the most diverse. It has huge canyons, year-round streams, beaches, cliffs, the highest mountain in the Channel Islands (2,450 ft.), now-defunct early cattle and sheep ranches, and Native American Chumash village sites—2,000 Chumash were probably living on the island when Cabrillo first visited in 1542. The island also hosts seemingly endless displays of flora and fauna, including 680 species of plants, 45 of which are multi-island endemics and 8 of which are single-island endemics; 140 land-bird species; and a small group of other land animals, including the island fox.

Most of the island is still privately owned: The Nature Conservancy holds the western three-quarters. When the park service took over the eastern end from the Gherini family, who had owned a sheep ranch here, it eliminated the island's formerly exorbitant landing and camping fees, but also eliminated the Channel Islands' only noncamping overnight options. The ranch house and adobe bunkhouse at Scorpion Ranch are currently used by the Gherini family under a special-use-and-occupancy permit.

Valdez Cave (aka Painted Cave for its colorful rock types, lichens, and algae) is one of the largest and deepest known sea caves in the world. The huge cave stretches nearly a quarter of a mile into the island and is nearly 100 feet wide. The entrance ceiling rises 160 feet, and in the spring, a waterfall tumbles over the opening. Located on the northwest end of the island, the cave can only be entered via dinghy or kayak.

SANTA ROSA The second-largest of the chain, windy Santa Rosa also has a ranching past—one that ended in 1998 in a storm of controversy that pitted the National Park Service against both environmental groups and the 97-year-old Vail & Vickers cattle ranch. The cows are all gone now, taking with them a slice of California history. In the meantime, the island's native vegetation has begun to recover. Santa Rosa is home to a large concentration of endangered plant species, 34 of which occur only on the islands. And like Santa Cruz, Santa Rosa is home to the diminutive island fox, a tiny cousin of the gray fox that has become nearly fearless as it has evolved in the predator-free island environment.

They'll walk right through your camp if you let them. Santa Rosa also has great beaches, a benefit somewhat outweighed by the nearly constant winds.

SAN MIGUEL   People often argue about what's the wildest place left in the lower 48 states. They bat around names like Montana, Colorado, and Idaho. Curiously, no one ever thinks to consider San Miguel, 55 miles off Ventura. They should, for this 9,325-acre island is a wild, wild place. The wind blows constantly, and the island can be shrouded in fog for days at a time. Human presence is definitely not the status quo here.

Visitors land at Cuyler Harbor, a half-moon-shaped cove on the island's east end. Arriving here is like arriving on earth the day it was made: perfect water, perfect sand, outrageously blue water. Seals bask on the offshore rocks. The island's two most interesting features are the **Caliche Forest,** a sort of petrified forest left when the wind exposed sandstone casts of trees that once stood on the island, and **Point Bennett,** the outrageous-sounding (and smelling) breeding ground of four separate species of seals and sea lions. In winter as many as 50,000 pinnipeds carpet the beach; their barking is deafening.

The waters around San Miguel are the richest and most dangerous of all the islands. The island's 27 miles of rocky coastline is exposed to wave action from all sides—many ships have sunk here. A 3-foot-tall stone cross stands in memory of Juan Rodríguez Cabrillo, the Spanish explorer credited with discovering the Channel Islands in 1542. Although his grave has never been found, Cabrillo is believed to be buried at sea, near Catalina Island.

SANTA BARBARA   As you come upon Santa Barbara Island after a typical 3-hour crossing, you'll think that someone took a single, medium-size, grassy hill, ringed it with cliffs, and plunked it down in the middle of the ocean. When you drop anchor, you'll realize that your initial perception is basically on target. Landwise, there's just not a lot here. But the upside is that, of all the islands, Santa Barbara gives you the best sense of what it's like to be stranded on a desert isle. Being on Santa Barbara, far enough out to sea that the mainland is almost invisible, gives you an idea of just how immense the Pacific really is.

Other than the landing cove, there's no access to the water's edge. The snorkeling in the chilly cove is great. You can hike the entire 639-acre island in a few hours; then it's time to stare out to sea. You won't be let down. The cliffs and rocks are home to elephant seals, sea lions, and swarms of seabirds such as you'll never see on the mainland. There's also a small campground, pit toilets, and a tiny museum chronicling island history.

THE EXTRA MILE: EXPLORING THE COASTLINE & WATERS OFF THE CHANNEL ISLANDS

DIVING   A good portion of Channel Islands National Park is underwater. In fact, almost as many visitors come to dive the waters as ever set foot *on* the islands. Divers come from all over to explore stunning kelp forests, pinnacles, and underwater caves, all with the best visibility in California. Everything from sea snails and urchins to orcas and great white sharks call these waters home.

Truth Aquatics, in Santa Barbara (© 805/962-1127; www.truthaquatics.com), is the best provider of single- and multi-day dive trips to all the islands. They also offer single- and multi-day hiking, kayaking, and fishing tours. **Ventura Dive & Sport** (© 805/650-6500) also leads trips, including a "Discover Program" that allows novice and uncertified divers to explore the waters accompanied by an instructor. **Channel Islands Scuba** in Thousand Oaks (© 805/644-3483; www.channelislandsscuba.com) and **Pacific Scuba** in Oxnard (© 805/984-2566;

www.pacificscuba.com) also lead regular trips, as do boats from San Pedro and other Southern California ports.

SEA KAYAKING   One of the best ways to explore the fascinating coastline of the islands is by sea kayak. The excursions allow you to explore sea caves and rock gardens. Fares generally run about $175 per person for full-day trips; channel crossing by charter boat, equipment, and brief lessons are included. Two- and 3-day adventures to Santa Rosa—campsite, camp gear, and guide included—are offered for $265 to $330 (you'll need to bring your own food, sleeping bag, and tent). **Aquasports** (© **800/773-2309** or 805/968-7231; www.islandkayaking.com) operates most trips out of Ventura Harbor, and **Paddle Sports of Santa Barbara** (© **888/254-2094** or 805/899-4925; www.kayaksb.com) leads similar excursions.

Los Angeles

by Matthew Richard Poole

Like Las Vegas, the allure of L.A.—for better or for worse—is undeniable. Los Angelenos know their city will never have the sophisticated style of Paris or the historical riches of London, but they cheerfully lay claim to living in the most entertaining city in the country, if not the world. It really is warm and sunny most days, movie stars do live and dine amongst the commoners, and you can't swing a cellphone without hitting a rollerblading blond in Venice Beach.

This part of the L.A. mystique—however exaggerated it may be—truly does exist, and it's not hard to find. In fact, it's fitting that L.A. is home to

the world's first amusement park, because it feels like one, as the line between fantasy and reality is often obscured. From the unattainable, anachronistic glamour of Beverly Hills to the vibrant street energy of Venice, each of the city's neighborhoods is like a mini–theme park, offering its own kind of adventure. Drive down Sunset Boulevard and you'll see what I mean: The billboards are racier, the fashions trendier, the cars fancier, the bodies sexier, the sun brighter, and the energy higher than anyplace you've ever been. Darlin', you ain't in Kansas anymore—you're in LA-LA land. Let's go play.

1 Orientation

ARRIVING
BY PLANE
LAX & the Other Los Angeles–Area Airports

There are five airports in the Los Angeles area. Most visitors fly into **Los Angeles International Airport** (© 310/646-5252; www.lawa.org/lax), better known as LAX. This behemoth—which handles about 57 million passengers each year—is on the ocean, between Marina del Rey and Manhattan Beach. LAX is a convenient place to land; it's located within minutes of Santa Monica and the beaches, and not more than a half-hour from downtown, Hollywood, and the Westside. Despite its size, the eight-terminal airport has a straightforward, easy-to-understand design. Free blue, green, and white **shuttle buses** connect the terminals and stop in front of each ticket building. Special minibuses accessible to travelers with disabilities are also available. **Travelers Aid of Los Angeles** (© 310/646-2270; www.travelersaid.org) operates booths in each terminal. You can find extensive information about LAX—including maps, parking and shuttle-van information, and links to weather forecasts—online at **www.lawa.org**. All car-rental agencies are in the neighborhood surrounding LAX, within a few minutes' drive; each provides a complimentary shuttle to and from the airport.

For some travelers, one of the area's smaller airports might be more convenient than LAX. **Burbank-Glendale-Pasadena Airport,** 2627 N. Hollywood Way, Burbank (© 818/840-8840; www.burbankairport.com), is the best place

Southern California at a Glance

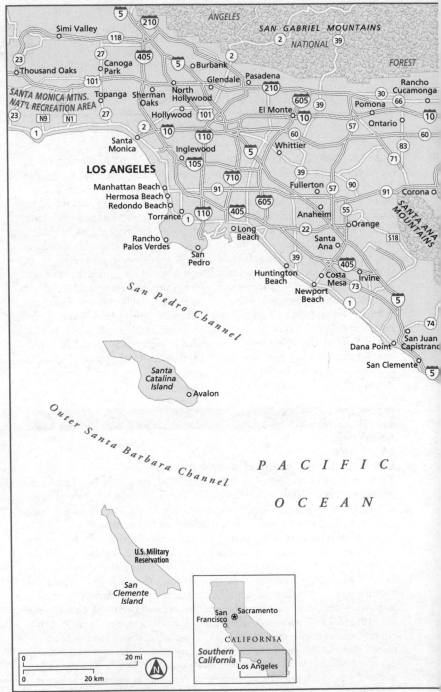

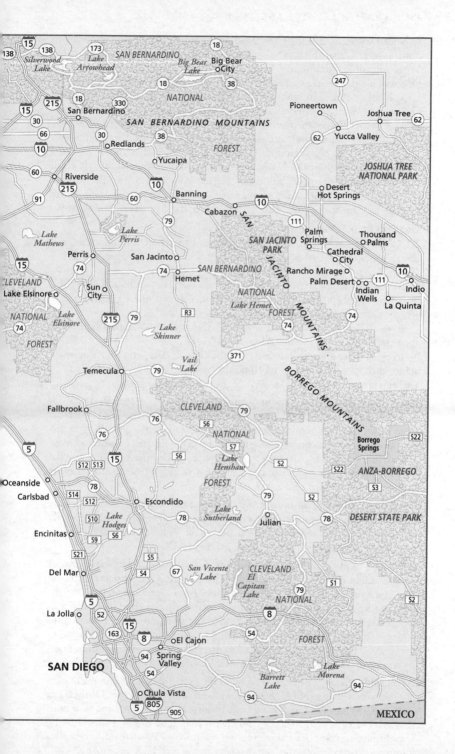

to land if you're headed for Hollywood or the valleys—and it's even closer to downtown L.A. than LAX. The small airport has especially good links to Las Vegas and other southwestern cities. **Long Beach Municipal Airport,** 4100 Donald Douglas Dr., Long Beach (℘ **562/570-2600;** www.lgb.org), south of LAX, is the best place to land if you're visiting Long Beach or northern Orange County and want to avoid L.A. (JetBlue also offers excellent fares to Long Beach.) **John Wayne Airport,** 19051 Airport Way N., Anaheim (℘ **949/ 252-5200;** www.ocair.com), is closest to Disneyland, Knott's Berry Farm, and other Orange County attractions. **Ontario International Airport,** Terminal Way, Ontario (℘ **909/937-2700;** www.lawa.org/ont/ontframe.html), is not a popular airport for tourists; businesspeople use it to head to San Bernardino, Riverside, and other inland communities. However, it's convenient if you're heading to Palm Springs, and also a viable choice if you're staying in Pasadena.

Getting into Town from LAX

BY CAR   To reach Santa Monica and other northern beach communities, exit the airport, take Sepulveda Boulevard north, and follow the signs to Calif. 1 (Pacific Coast Hwy., or PCH) north.

To reach Redondo, Hermosa, Newport, and the other southern beach communities, take Sepulveda Boulevard south, then follow the signs to Calif. 1 (Pacific Coast Hwy., or PCH) south.

To reach Beverly Hills or Hollywood, exit the airport via Century Boulevard, then take I-405 north to Santa Monica Boulevard east.

To reach downtown or Pasadena, exit the airport, take Sepulveda Boulevard south, then take I-105 east to I-110 north.

BY SHUTTLE   Many city hotels provide free shuttles for their guests; ask when you make reservations. **SuperShuttle** (℘ **800/258-3826** or 310/782-6600; www.supershuttle.com) offers regularly scheduled minivans from LAX to any location in the city. The fare can range from about $15 to $35 per person, depending on your destination. Reservations aren't needed for your arrival, but required for a return to the airport. It's cheaper to cab it to most places if you're a group of three or more, but you might have to stop at other passengers' destinations before you reach your own.

BY TAXI   Taxis line up outside each terminal on the lower level. Rides are metered. Expect to pay about $35 to Hollywood and downtown, $25 to Beverly Hills, $20 to Santa Monica, and $45 to $60 to the Valley and Pasadena, *including* a $2.50 service charge for rides originating at LAX.

BY RAIL   Budget-minded travelers heading to downtown, Universal City, or Long Beach can take L.A.'s Metro Rail service from LAX. An airport shuttle can take you to the Green Line light-rail station; from there, connections on the Blue and Red Lines can get you where you're headed; it's a good idea to contact your hotel for advice on the closest station. The service operates from 5am to midnight and the combined fare is under $2—but you should be prepared to spend 1 to 2 hours in transit. Call the **Los Angeles County Metropolitan Transit Authority (MTA)** at ℘ **800/COMMUTE** (www.mta.net) for information.

BY PUBLIC BUS   The city's MTA buses also go between LAX and many parts of the city. Phone **MTA Airport Information** (℘ **800/COMMUTE;** www.mta.net) for the schedules and fares. If you're arriving at LAX and your hotel is in Santa Monica, you can hop aboard the city's **Big Blue Bus** (℘310/451-5444; www.bigbluebus.com). It's a slow ride, but the price—75¢—is hard to beat. Bus information is available in the baggage-claim area of each LAX terminal.

BY CAR

Los Angeles is well connected to the rest of the United States by several major highways. Among them are Interstate 5, which enters the state from the north; Interstate 10, which originates in Jacksonville, Florida, and terminates in Los Angeles; and U.S. 101, a scenic route that follows the western seaboard from Los Angeles north to the Oregon state line.

If you're driving **from the north,** you have two choices: the quick route, along I-5 through the middle of the state, or the scenic route along the coast. Heading south along I-5, you'll pass a small town called Grapevine. This marks the start of the mountain pass with the same name. Once you've reached the southern end of the pass, you'll be in the San Fernando Valley, which is the start of Los Angeles County. To reach the beach communities and L.A.'s Westside, take I-405 south; to get to Hollywood, take Calif. 170 south to U.S. 101 south (this route is called the Hollywood Fwy. the entire way); I-5 will take you along the eastern edge of downtown and into Orange County.

If you're taking the **scenic coastal route** from the north, take U.S. 101 to I-405 or I-5, or stay on U.S. 101, following the instructions above to your destination.

If you're approaching **from the east,** you'll be coming in on I-10. For Orange County, take Calif. 57 south. I-10 continues through downtown and terminates at the beach. If you're heading to the Westside, take I-405 north. To get to the beaches, take Calif. 1 (PCH) north or south, depending on your destination.

From the south, head north on I-5. At the southern end of Orange County, I-405 splits off to the west; take this road to the Westside and beach communities. Stay on I-5 to reach downtown and Hollywood.

Here are some **driving times** if you're on one of those see-the-USA car trips: From Phoenix, it's about 350 miles, or 6 hours (okay, 7 if you drive the speed limit) to Los Angeles via I-10. Las Vegas is 265 miles northeast of Los Angeles (about a 4- or 5-hr. drive). San Francisco is 390 miles north of Los Angeles on I-5 (6–7 hr.), and San Diego is 115 miles south (about 2 hr.).

BY TRAIN

Amtrak (© **800/USA-RAIL;** www.amtrak.com) connects Los Angeles with about 500 American cities. As with plane travel along popular routes, fares fluctuate depending on the season and special promotions. As a general rule, heavily restricted advance tickets are competitive with similar airfares. Remember, however, those low fares are for coach travel in reclining seats; private sleeping accommodations cost substantially more.

The L.A. train terminus is **Union Station,** 800 N. Alameda (© **213/ 617-0111**), on downtown's northern edge. Completed in 1939, this was the last of America's great train depots—a unique blend of Spanish Revival and Streamline Moderne architecture. From the station, you can take one of the taxis that line up outside, board the Metro Red Line to Hollywood or Universal City, or the Metro Blue Line to Long Beach. If you're headed to the San Fernando Valley or Anaheim, Metrolink commuter trains leave from Union Station; call © **800/371-LINK** (www.metrolinktrains.com).

BY BUS

Bus travel is an inexpensive and often-flexible option. **Greyhound** (© **800/ 229-9424;** www.greyhound.com) can get you to L.A. from anywhere in the U.S. and offers several money-saving multi-day passes. The main station for arriving buses is downtown at 1716 E. Seventh St., east of Alameda.

VISITOR INFORMATION
INFORMATION CENTERS

The **Los Angeles Convention and Visitors Bureau** (aka LA Inc.) (© **800/ 366-6116** or 213/689-8822; www.visitLAnow.com) is the city's main source for information. In addition to its informative website, answering phone inquiries, and sending free visitors kits, the bureau provides a **walk-in visitor center** at 685 S. Figueroa St., downtown (open Mon–Fri 8am–5pm, Sat 8:30am–5pm).

Many Los Angeles–area communities also have their own information centers, and often maintain detailed and colorful websites that are loaded with timely information. These include:

Beverly Hills Visitors Bureau, 239 S. Beverly Dr. (© **800/345-2210** or 310/248-1015; www.beverlyhillscvb.com), is open Monday through Friday from 8:30am to 5pm.

Hollywood Arts Council, P.O. Box 931056, Dept. 1995, Hollywood, CA 90093 (© **323/462-2355;** www.discoverhollywood.com), distributes the magazine *Discover Hollywood* for a $2 postage-and-handling fee. This biannual publication contains listings and schedules for the area's many theaters, galleries, music venues, and comedy clubs; the current issue is always available online. You can also load up on visitor information at the **Hollywood Visitor Center,** 6801 Hollywood Blvd., Suite 237 (© **800/228-2452;** www.visitLAnow.org), on the second level of the Hollywood & Highland mall (between Babylon Court and Awards Walk).

West Hollywood Convention and Visitors Bureau, 8687 Melrose Ave., M-26, West Hollywood, CA 90096 (© **800/368-6020** or 310/289-2525; www.visitwest hollywood.com), is located in the Pacific Design Center and is open Monday through Friday from 8am to 6pm.

Santa Monica Convention and Visitors Bureau (© **800/544-5319** or 310/393-7593; www.santamonica.com), is the best source for information about Santa Monica. Their Palisades Park walk-up center is located near the Santa Monica Pier, at 1400 Ocean Ave. (between Santa Monica Blvd. and Broadway), and is open daily from 10am to 4pm. Also check out **www. malibu.org** for information about Malibu to the northwest.

Pasadena Convention and Visitors Bureau, 171 S. Los Robles Ave. (© **626/795-9311;** www.pasadenacal.com), is open Monday through Friday from 8am to 5pm and Saturday from 10am to 4pm.

OTHER INFORMATION SOURCES

Local tourist boards are great for information regarding attractions and special events, but they often fail to keep a finger on the pulse of what's "in" in L.A., especially with regard to dining, culture, and nightlife. Several city-oriented newspapers and magazines offer more up-to-date info. *L.A. Weekly* (www.laweekly.com), a free listings magazine, is packed with information on current events around town. It's available from sidewalk news racks and in many stores and restaurants around the city; it also has a lively website.

The *Los Angeles Times* **"Calendar"** section of the Sunday paper, an excellent guide to the world of entertainment in and around L.A., includes listings of what's doing and where to do it. The *Times* also maintains a comprehensive website at **www.calendarlive.com**; once there you can find departments with names like "Southland Scenes," "Tourist Tips," "Family & Kids," and "Recreation & Fitness." Information is culled from the newspaper's many departments and is always up-to-date. If you want to check out L.A.'s most immediate news, the *Times*'s main website is **www.latimes.com**.

Los Angeles magazine (**www.lamag.com**) is a glossy city-based monthly full of real news and gossip, plus guides to L.A.'s art, music, and food scenes. Its calendar of events, which has been getting better lately, gives an excellent overview of goings-on at museums, art galleries, musical venues, and other places. The magazine is available at newsstands and in other major U.S. cities; you can also access stories and listings from the current issue on the Internet. Cybersurfers should visit **At L.A.**'s website, **www.at-la.com**; its exceptional search engine (one of our favorite tools) provides links to more than 23,000 sites relating to the L.A. area, including many destinations covered in chapter 14, "Side Trips from Los Angeles."

CITY LAYOUT

Los Angeles isn't a single compact city like San Francisco but a sprawling suburbia comprising dozens of disparate communities located either on the ocean or the flatlands of a huge desert basin. Ocean breezes push the city's infamous smog inland and through mountain passes into the sprawl of the San Fernando and San Gabriel valleys. Downtown Los Angeles is in the center of the basin, about 12 miles east of the Pacific Ocean. Most visitors spend the bulk of their time either along the coastline or on the city's ever-trendy Westside.

MAIN ARTERIES & STREETS

L.A.'s extensive system of toll-free, high-speed freeways connects the city's patchwork of communities. The system works well to get you where you need to be, although rush-hour (roughly 7–9am and 4–6pm) traffic can be bumper-to-bumper. Here's an overview (best read with an L.A. map in hand):

U.S. 101, called the "Ventura Freeway" in the San Fernando Valley and the "Hollywood Freeway" in the city, runs across L.A. in a roughly northwest-southeast direction, from the San Fernando Valley to the center of downtown. Heavy rush-hour traffic.

Calif. 134 continues as the "Ventura Freeway" after U.S. 101 turns into the city and becomes the Hollywood Freeway. This branch of the Ventura Freeway continues directly east, through the valley towns of Burbank and Glendale, to I-210 (the "Foothill Freeway"), which takes you through Pasadena and out toward the eastern edge of Los Angeles County.

I-5, otherwise known as the "Golden State Freeway" north of I-10 and the "Santa Ana Freeway" south of I-10, bisects downtown on its way from Sacramento to San Diego.

I-10, labeled the "Santa Monica Freeway" west of I-5 and the "San Bernardino Freeway" east of I-5, is the city's major east-west freeway, connecting the San Gabriel Valley with downtown and Santa Monica.

I-405, known as the "San Diego Freeway," runs north-south through L.A.'s Westside, connecting the San Fernando Valley with LAX and southern beach areas. *Tip:* This is one of the area's busiest freeways—avoid it as much as possible and like the plague during rush hour.

⸜Tips⸝ Stay Away from Santa Monica Boulevard

If you're driving to or from Santa Monica and the Westside communities—Beverly Hills, West Hollywood, Century City—try to avoid Santa Monica Boulevard, which is almost always jammed and in terrible condition. Both Wilshire and Pico boulevards parallel Santa Monica Boulevard and are usually less congested and far smoother (Pico Blvd. is my savior).

I-105, Los Angeles's newest freeway—called the "Century Freeway"—extends from LAX east to I-605.

I-110, commonly known as the "Harbor Freeway," starts in Pasadena as Calif. 110 (the "Pasadena Freeway"); it becomes an interstate in downtown Los Angeles and runs directly south, where it dead-ends in San Pedro. The section that is now the Pasadena Freeway was Los Angeles's first freeway, known as the Arroyo Seco when it opened in 1940.

I-710, aka the "Long Beach Freeway," runs in a north-south direction through East Los Angeles and dead-ends at Long Beach. Crammed with big rigs leaving the port in San Pedro, this is the ugliest, most dangerous freeway in California.

I-605, the "San Gabriel River Freeway," runs parallel to the I-710 farther east, through the cities of Hawthorne and Lynwood and into the San Gabriel Valley.

Calif. 1—called "Highway 1," the "Pacific Coast Highway," or simply "PCH"—is really more of a scenic parkway than a freeway. It skirts the ocean, linking all of L.A.'s beach communities, from Malibu to the Orange Coast. It's often slow-going due to all the stoplights but far more scenic than the freeways.

A complex web of surface streets complements the freeways. From north to south, the major east-west thoroughfares connecting downtown to the beaches are **Sunset Boulevard, Santa Monica Boulevard, Wilshire Boulevard,** and **Olympic, Pico,** and **Venice boulevards.**

NEIGHBORHOODS IN BRIEF

Los Angeles is a very confusing city to newcomers in that "downtown" isn't the center point of the city. Rather, it's more of a juxtaposition of disparate communities that loosely form a metropolis (67 suburbs searching for a city, so they say). The best way to grasp the geography of L.A. is to break it into six regions: Santa Monica and the beach communities, L.A.'s Westside and Beverly Hills, Hollywood and West Hollywood, downtown, Pasadena, and—on the other side of the Hollywood Hills—the San Fernando Valley (just "The Valley" to locals). Each encompasses a more-or-less distinctive patchwork of city neighborhoods and independently incorporated communities.

Santa Monica & the Beaches

These are nearly everyone's favorite L.A. communities and get my highest recommendation as the premier place to book a hotel during your vacation. The 60-mile beachfront stretching from Malibu to the Palos Verdes Peninsula has milder weather and less smog than the inland communities, and traffic is lighter, except on summer weekends. The towns along the coast all have a distinct mood and charm, and most are connected via a walk/bike path. They're listed below from north to south.

Malibu At the northern border of Los Angeles County, 25 miles from downtown, was once a privately owned ranch—purchased in 1857 for 10¢ an acre and now the most

expensive real estate in L.A. Today, its 27 miles of wide beaches, beachfront cliffs, sparsely populated hills and relative remoteness from the inner city make it popular with rich recluses such as Johnny Carson and Barbra Streisand. Indeed, the resident lists of Malibu Colony and nearby Broad Beach—oceanfront strips of closely packed mansions—read like a who's who in Hollywood. With plenty of green space and rocky outcroppings, Malibu's rural beauty is unsurpassed in L.A. and surfers flock to "The 'Bu" for great, if crowded, waves.

Santa Monica Los Angeles's premier beach community is known for its festive ocean pier, stylish (and expensive) oceanfront hotels, artsy atmosphere, and somewhat wacky residents. Shopping is king here, especially along the Third Street Promenade, a pedestrian-only outdoor mall lined with shops and restaurants.

Venice Beach My favorite L.A. neighborhood, was created by tobacco mogul Abbot Kinney, who set out in 1904 to transform a worthless marsh into a resort town modeled after Venice, Italy. Hence, the series of canals connected by one-lane bridges that you'll see as you explore this refreshingly eclectic community. It was once infested with grime and crime, but regentrification has brought scores of restaurants, boutiques, and rising property values for the canal-side homes and apartment duplexes. Even the movie stars are moving in: Dennis Hopper, Anjelica Huston, Nicolas Cage, and Julia Roberts reside in this pseudo-bohemian community. Some of L.A.'s most innovative and interesting architecture lines Main Street. But without question, Venice Beach is best known for its Ocean Front Walk, a Mardi Gras of thong-wearing skaters, vendors, fortunetellers, street musicians, and poseurs of all ages, colors, types, and sizes.

Marina del Rey Just south of Venice is a quieter, more upscale waterside community best known for its man-made small-craft harbor, the largest of its kind in the world.

Manhattan, Hermosa, and **Redondo beaches** These are laidback, mainly residential neighborhoods with modest homes (except for oceanfront real estate), mild weather, and residents happy to have fled the L.A. hubbub. There are excellent beaches for volleyball, surfing, and tanning here, but when it comes to cultural activities, pickings can be slim. The restaurant scene, while limited, has been improving steadily and some great new bars and clubs have opened near their respective piers.

L.A.'s Westside & Beverly Hills

The Westside Sandwiched between Hollywood and the city's coastal communities, this prime real estate includes some of Los Angeles's most prestigious neighborhoods, virtually all with names you're sure to recognize:

Beverly Hills Politically distinct from the rest of Los Angeles, this famous enclave is best known for its palm-tree-lined streets of palatial homes, famous residents (Jack Nicholson, Warren Beatty and Annette Bening), and high-priced shops. But it's not all glitz and glamour; the healthy mix of filthy rich, wannabes, and tourists that peoples downtown Beverly Hills creates a unique—and often snobby-surreal—atmosphere.

West Hollywood This is a key-shaped community whose epicenter is the intersection of Santa Monica and La Cienega boulevards. Nestled between Beverly Hills and Hollywood, this politically independent—and blissfully fast-food free—town is home to some of the area's best restaurants, clubs, shops, and art galleries. WeHo, as it's come to be known, is also the center of L.A.'s gay community—you'll know you've arrived when you see the billboards. Encompassing about 2 square miles, it's a pedestrian-friendly place with plenty of metered parking. Highlights include the 1½ miles of Sunset Boulevard known as Sunset Strip, the chic Sunset Plaza retail strip, and the liveliest stretch of Santa Monica Boulevard.

Bel Air and **Holmby Hills** In the hills north of Westwood and west of Beverly Hills are old-money residential areas featured on maps to the stars' homes.

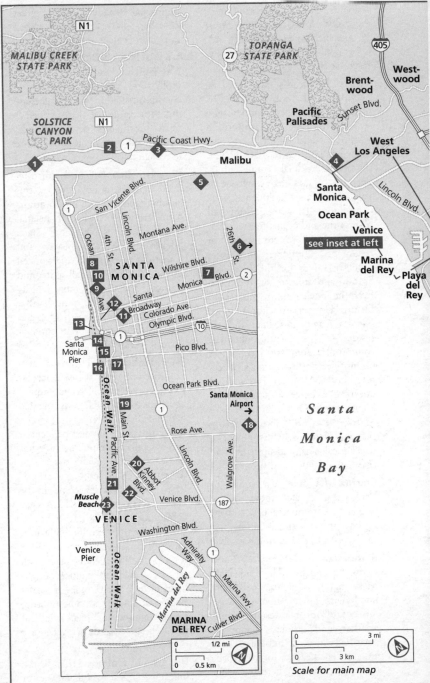

MALIBU CREEK
STATE PARK

N1

SOLSTICE
CANYON
PARK

N1

27

TOPANGA
STATE PARK

405

West-
wood

Brent-
wood

Pacific
Palisades

Sunset Blvd.

Pacific Coast Hwy.

Malibu

West
Los Angeles

Lincoln Blvd.

Santa
Monica

Ocean Park

Venice

see inset at left

Marina
del Rey

Playa
del
Rey

1

2

3

4

5

San Vicente Blvd.

Montana Ave.

Lincoln Blvd.

Ocean Ave.

4th St.

26th St.

SANTA
MONICA

Wilshire Blvd.

Monica   Blvd.

2

6

7

8

10

9

Santa

Broadway

Colorado Ave.

Olympic Blvd.

Pico Blvd.

12

11

13

14

15

16

17

Santa
Monica Pier

Ocean Walk

Main St.

Pacific Ave.

Ocean Park Blvd.

Santa Monica
Airport

Rose Ave.

Lincoln Blvd.

Walgrove Ave.

19

18

20

Abbot
Kinney
Blvd.

21

22

Muscle
Beach 23

VENICE

Venice Blvd.

187

Washington Blvd.

Venice Pier

Ocean Walk

Admiralty
Way

Marina del Rey

MARINA
DEL REY

Culver Blvd.

Marina Fwy.

1

Santa

Monica

Bay

0   1/2 mi
0   0.5 km

0   3 mi
0   3 km

Scale for main map

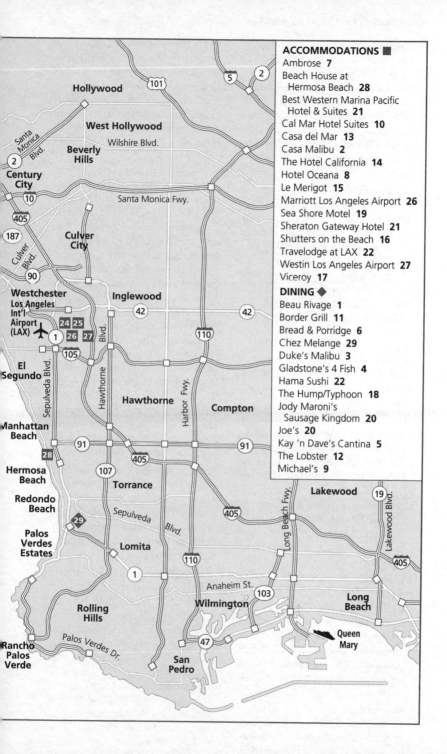

ACCOMMODATIONS ■

Ambrose **7**
Beach House at
  Hermosa Beach **28**
Best Western Marina Pacific
  Hotel & Suites **21**
Cal Mar Hotel Suites **10**
Casa del Mar **13**
Casa Malibu **2**
The Hotel California **14**
Hotel Oceana **8**
Le Merigot **15**
Marriott Los Angeles Airport **26**
Sea Shore Motel **19**
Sheraton Gateway Hotel **21**
Shutters on the Beach **16**
Travelodge at LAX **22**
Westin Los Angeles Airport **27**
Viceroy **17**

DINING ◆

Beau Rivage **1**
Border Grill **11**
Bread & Porridge **6**
Chez Melange **29**
Duke's Malibu **3**
Gladstone's 4 Fish **4**
Hama Sushi **22**
The Hump/Typhoon **18**
Jody Maroni's
  Sausage Kingdom **20**
Joe's **20**
Kay 'n Dave's Cantina **5**
The Lobster **12**
Michael's **9**

Brentwood This is the community best known as the famous backdrop to the O. J. Simpson melodrama. If Starbucks ever designed a neighborhood, this is what it would look like—a quiet, relatively upscale mix of homes, restaurants, and strip malls. The Getty Center looms over Brentwood from its hilltop perch next to I-405.

Westwood An urban village founded in 1929 and home to the University of California at Los Angeles (UCLA), this used to be a hot destination for a night on the town, but lost much of its appeal in the past decade due to overcrowding and even some minor street violence. Although Westwood is unlikely to regain its old charm, the vibrant new culinary scene has brought new life to the village. Combined with the high concentration of movie theaters, it's now the premiere L.A. destination for dinner and a flick.

Century City A compact and rather bland high-rise area sandwiched between West Los Angeles and Beverly Hills, the primary draws here are the 20th Century Fox studios, Shubert Theatre, and the Westside Pavilion, a huge open-air mall. Century City's three main thoroughfares are Century Park East, Avenue of the Stars, and Century Park West.

West Los Angeles This title is nothing more than a label that applies to everything that isn't one of the other Westside neighborhoods. It's the area south of Santa Monica Boulevard, north of Venice Boulevard, east of Santa Monica and Venice, and west and south of Century City.

Hollywood

Yes, they still come to the birthplace of the film business—young hopefuls with stars in their eyes gravitate to this historic heart of L.A.'s movie production like moths fluttering to the glare of neon lights. But today's Hollywood is more illusion than industry. Many of the neighborhood's former movie studios have moved to more spacious venues in Burbank, the Westside, and other parts of the city.

Despite the downturn, visitors continue to flock to Hollywood's landmark attractions such as the star-studded Walk of Fame and Grauman's Chinese Theatre. And now that the city's $1-billion, 30-year revitalization project is in full swing, Hollywood Boulevard is, for the first time in decades, showing signs of rising out of a seedy slump, with refurbished movie houses and stylish restaurants and clubs making a comeback. The centerpiece "Hollywood & Highland" complex anchors the neighborhood, with shopping, entertainment, and a luxury hotel built around the Kodak Theatre, which is designed specifically to host the Academy Awards (really, you'll want to poke your head into this gorgeous theater).

Melrose Avenue Scruffy but fun, this is the city's funkiest shopping district, with secondhand and avant-garde clothing shops. Though it may cater to often-raucous youth, there are also several good restaurants worth visiting.

Mid-Wilshire district, or **Miracle Mile** This area, referring to the stretch of Wilshire Boulevard running through the southern part of Hollywood, is lined with tall, contemporary apartment houses and office buildings. The section just east of Fairfax Avenue, known as Museum Row, is home to almost a dozen museums, including the Los Angeles County Museum of Art, the La Brea Tar Pits, and that shrine to L.A. car culture, the Petersen Automotive Museum.

L.A.'s Westside & Beverly Hills

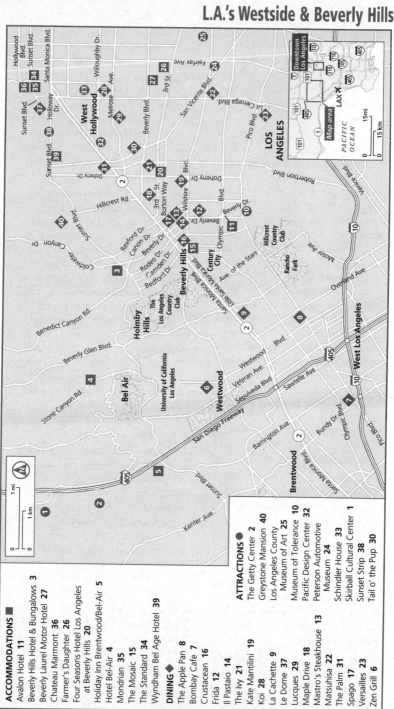

Griffith Park Up Western Avenue in the northernmost part of Hollywood is one of the country's largest urban parks, home to the Los Angeles Zoo, Griffith Observatory, and the outdoor Greek Theater.

Downtown

Despite the recent construction of numerous cultural centers (such as the Walt Disney Concert Hall and Cathedral of Our Lady of the Angels) and a handful of trendy restaurants, L.A.'s downtown isn't the tourist hub that it would be in most cities. When it comes to entertaining visitors, the Westside, Hollywood, and beach communities are all far more popular.

Easily recognized by the tight cluster of high-rise offices—skyscrapers bolstered by earthquake-proof technology—the business center of the city is eerily vacant on weekends and evenings, but the outlying residential communities such as Koreatown, Little Tokyo, Chinatown, and Los Feliz are enticingly ethnic and vibrant. If you want a tan, head to Santa Monica, but if you want a refreshing dose of non-90210 culture, come here.

El Pueblo de Los Angeles Historic District This 44-acre ode to the city's early years is worth a visit.

Chinatown Small and touristy, this section of the city can be plenty of fun for souvenir-hunting or dim sum.

Little Tokyo A genuine gathering place for the Southland's Japanese population, this community has a wide array of shops and restaurants with an authentic flair.

Silver Lake A residential neighborhood north of downtown, and adjacent to **Los Feliz,** just to the west, it has arty areas with unique cafes, theaters, graffiti, and art galleries—all in equally plentiful

proportions. The local music scene has been burgeoning of late.

Exposition Park South and west of downtown is an area home to the Los Angeles Memorial Coliseum and the L.A. Sports Arena, as well as the Natural History Museum, African-American Museum, and the California Science Center. The University of Southern California (USC) is next door.

East and **South-Central L.A.** Just east and south of downtown are the city's large barrios. This is where the 1992 L.A. riots were centered. It was here, at Florence and Normandie avenues, that a news station's reporter, hovering above in a helicopter, videotaped Reginald Denny being pulled from the cab of his truck and beaten. These neighborhoods are, without question, quite unique, though they contain few tourist sites (the Watts Towers being a notable exception). This can be a rough part of town, so avoid looking like a tourist if you decide to visit, particularly at night.

The San Fernando Valley

The San Fernando Valley, known locally as "The Valley," was nationally popularized in the 1980s by the mall-loving "Valley Girl" stereotype. Sandwiched between the Santa Monica and the San Gabriel mountain ranges, most of the Valley is residential and commercial and off the beaten track for tourists. But some of its attractions are bound to draw you over the hill.

Universal City West of Griffith Park between U.S. 101 and Calif. 134 is Universal Studios Hollywood and the supersize shopping and entertainment complex CityWalk.

Burbank About the only reason to go west of these other suburbs and north of Universal City to Burbank is to see one of your favorite TV

Hollywood

Information ⓘ

RUNYAN CANYON PARK

HOLLYWOOD

To Griffith Park

Franklin Ave.
Franklin Ave.
Hollywood Blvd.

Sunset Blvd.
DeLongpre Ave.
Fountain Ave.

Santa Monica Blvd.
Romaine St.
Willoughby Ave.
Melrose Ave.
Rosewood Ave.

Oakwood Ave.

Beverly Blvd.

CBS Television City
PAN PACIFIC PARK

PARK LA BREA

HANCOCK PARK

San Vicente Blvd.

Olympic Blvd.

Pico Blvd.

Crescent Heights Blvd.
Fairfax Ave.
Gardner St.
Martell Ave.
La Brea Ave.
Sycamore Ave.
Alta Vista Blvd.
Highland Ave.
Cahuenga Blvd.
Wilcox Ave.
Vine St.
Gower St.
Western Ave.

HOLLYWOOD CEMETERY (HOLLYWOOD FOREVER)

Rosewood Ave.

The Wilshire Country Club

1st St.
2nd St.
3rd St.

Gower St.
Larchmont Blvd.
Rossmore Ave.
Van Ness Ave.
Western Ave.

Mid-Wilshire

6th St.
Wilshire Blvd.

Hauser Blvd.
Cochran Ave.

101

Map area

Downtown Los Angeles

PACIFIC OCEAN

LAX

0   1/2 mi
0   0.5 km

0   15mi
0   15 km

ACCOMMODATIONS ■
Best Western
  Hollywood Hills Hotel **4**
Days Inn Hollywood/
  Universal Studios **12**
Roosevelt Hotel,
  Hollywood **11**
Magic Castle Hotel **9**
Renaissance Hollywood
  Hotel **13**

DINING ◆
Ca'Brea **23**
Campanile **28**
El Cholo **29**
Paladar **15**

Pink's Hot Dogs **18**
Roscoe's House of
  Chicken 'n' Waffles **6**
Sofi **22**
Swingers **19**
Toi on Sunset **16**

ATTRACTIONS ●
Capitol Records Building **5**
Craft & Folk Art Museum **26**
The Egyptian Theatre **14**
Farmers Market
  & the Grove **21**
Freeman House **8**
Griffith Observatory **1**
The "Hollywood" Sign **3**

Hollywood Walk of Fame **7**
Los Angeles County
  Museum of Art **25**
Los Angeles Zoo **2**
Grauman's
  Chinese Theatre **10**
Museum of the
  American West **1**
Paramount Pictures **17**
Petersen Automotive
  Museum **24**
Rancho La Brea Tar Pits **27**
Sunset Ranch
  Hollywood Stables **3**

Downtown Los Angeles

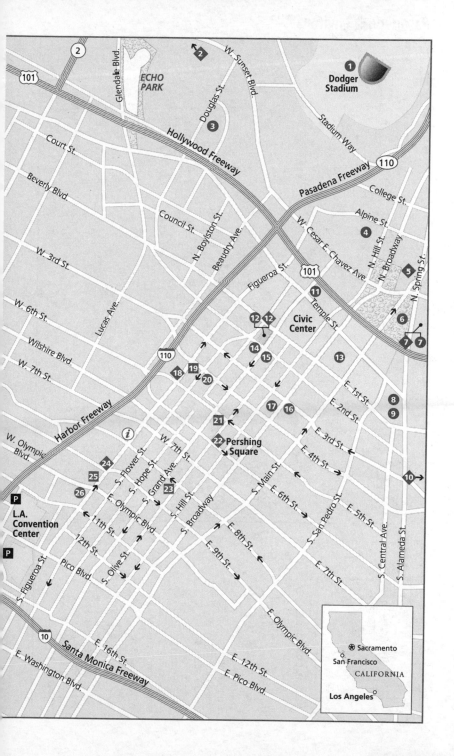

Pasadena & Environs

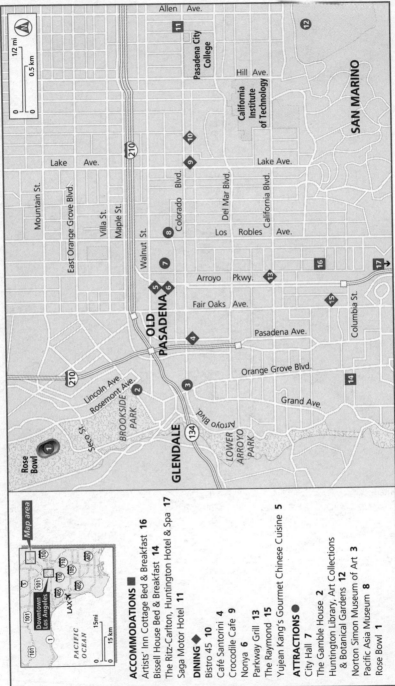

Allen Ave.

11

12

Pasadena City College

Hill Ave.

California Institute of Technology

SAN MARINO

10

9

Lake Ave.

Colorado Blvd.

Del Mar Blvd.

California Blvd.

Mountain St.

East Orange Grove Blvd.

Lake Ave.

Villa St.

Maple St.

8

Walnut St.

Los Robles Ave.

7

16

17

Arroyo Pkwy.

13

OLD PASADENA

5

6

Fair Oaks Ave.

15

Columbia St.

4

Pasadena Ave.

Orange Grove Blvd.

Lincoln Ave.

Rosemont Ave.

2

BROOKSIDE PARK

3

134

14

Grand Ave.

Seco St.

Arroyo Blvd.

GLENDALE

LOWER ARROYO PARK

Rose Bowl

1

210

Map area

10

710

405

105

Downtown Los Angeles

101

LAX

110

405

101

1

PACIFIC OCEAN

15mi

15km

ACCOMMODATIONS ■
Artists' Inn Cottage Bed & Breakfast **16**
Bissell House Bed & Breakfast **14**
The Ritz-Carlton, Huntington Hotel & Spa **17**
Saga Motor Hotel **11**

DINING ◆
Bistro 45 **10**
Café Santorini **4**
Crocodile Cafe **9**
Nonya **6**
Parkway Grill **13**
The Raymond **15**
Yujean Kang's Gourmet Chinese Cuisine **5**

ATTRACTIONS ●
City Hall **7**
The Gamble House **2**
Huntington Library, Art Collections & Botanical Gardens **12**
Norton Simon Museum of Art **3**
Pacific Asia Museum **8**
Rose Bowl **1**

shows being filmed at NBC or Warner Brothers Studios. There are also a few good restaurants and shops along Ventura Boulevard, in and around Studio City.

Glendale This is a largely residential community north of downtown between the Valley and Pasadena. Here you'll find Forest Lawn, the city's best cemetery for very retired movie stars.

Pasadena & Environs

Best known as the site of the Tournament of Roses Parade each New Year's Day, **Pasadena** was spared from the tear-down epidemic that swept L.A. so it has a refreshing old-time feel. Once upon a time, Pasadena was every Angeleno's best-kept secret—a quiet community whose slow and careful regentrification meant nonchain restaurants and boutique shopping without the crowds, in a revitalized downtown respectful of its old brick and stone commercial buildings. Although the area's natural and architectural beauty still shines through—so much so that Pasadena remains Hollywood's favorite backyard location

for countless movies and TV shows—Old Town has become a pedestrian mall similar to Santa Monica's Third Street Promenade, complete with huge crowds, midrange chain eateries, and standard-issue mall stores. It still gets our vote as a scenic alternative to the congestion of central L.A., but it has lost much of its small-town charm.

Pasadena is also home to the famous California Institute of Technology (Caltech), which boasts 22 Nobel Prize winners among its alumni. The Caltech-operated Jet Propulsion Laboratory was the birthplace of America's space program, and Caltech scientists were the first to report earthquake activity worldwide.

The neighborhoods in Pasadena and its adjacent communities—**Arcadia, La Cañada–Flintridge, San Marino,** and **South Pasadena**—are renowned for well-preserved historic homes, from humble bungalows to lavish mansions. These areas feature public gardens, historic neighborhoods, house museums, and quiet bed-and-breakfast inns.

2 Getting Around

BY CAR

Need we tell you that Los Angeles is a car-crazed city? You're really going to need one to easily get around (there *is* public transportation in L.A., but you really don't want to rely on it). An elaborate network of well-maintained freeways connects this urban sprawl, but you have to learn how to make sense of the system and cultivate some patience for dealing with the traffic—purchasing one of those plastic-covered fold-out maps is a smart investment. The golden rule of driving in Los Angeles is this: Always allow more time to get to your destination than you think you might need, especially during morning and evening rush hours (40 min. of leeway usually suffices). For an explanation of the city layout and details on the freeway system, see "Orientation" earlier in this chapter and the tear-out map tucked inside the back cover.

RENTALS Los Angeles is one of the cheaper places in America to rent a car. Major national car-rental companies usually rent economy- and compact-class cars for about $35 per day and $120 per week with unlimited mileage.

All the major car-rental agencies have offices at the airport and in the larger hotels. If you're thinking of splurging on a dig-me road machine such as Maserati, Ferrari, Rolls Royce, Lamborghini, or Hummer, the place to call is either **Budget Beverly Hills Car Collection,** 9815 Wilshire Blvd. (℗ **800/ 227-7117** or 310/881-2335; www.budgetbeverlyhills.com), or **Beverly Hills Rent-A-Car,** 9732 Little Santa Monica Blvd., Beverly Hills (℗ **800/479-5996** or 310/274-6969; www.bhrentacar.com). Both car-rental companies have additional locations in Santa Monica, LAX, Orange County, and Newport Beach, and both offer complimentary delivery to local hotels or pickup service at LAX.

BY PUBLIC TRANSPORTATION

There are visitors who successfully tour Los Angeles entirely by public transportation (I've met them both), but we can't honestly recommend that plan for most readers. L.A. is a metropolis that's grown up around—and is best traversed by—the automobile, and many areas are inaccessible without one. As a result, an overwhelming number of visitors rent a car for their stay. Still, if you're in the city for only a short time, are on a very tight budget, or don't expect to be moving around a lot, public transport might be for you.

The city's trains and buses are operated by the **Los Angeles County Metropolitan Transit Authority** (MTA; ℗ **213/922-2000;** www.mta.net), and MTA brochures and schedules are available at every area visitor center.

BY BUS OR SHUTTLE

Spread-out stops, sluggish service, and frequent transfers make extensive touring by bus impractical. For short hops and occasional jaunts, however, buses are economical and environmentally correct. However, we don't recommend riding buses late at night.

The basic bus fare is $1.25 for all local lines, with transfers costing 25¢. Express buses, which travel along the freeways, and buses on intercounty routes charge higher fares; phone for information.

The **Downtown Area Short Hop (DASH)** shuttle system operates buses throughout downtown, Hollywood, and the Westside of L.A. Service runs every 5 to 20 minutes, depending on the time of day, and costs just 25¢. Contact the Department of Transportation (℗ **213/808-2273;** www.ladottransit.com) for schedules and route information (it's pretty confusing—you'll definitely need a weekday *and* weekend map).

The **Cityline** shuttle is a great way to get around West Hollywood on weekdays (9am–4pm) and Saturday (10am–7:30pm). For 50¢ it'll take you to most of the major shops and restaurants throughout WeHo (very handy if you park your car in a flat-fee lot). For more information call ℗ **800/447-2189.**

BY RAIL & SUBWAY

The 62-station **MetroRail** system is a sore subject around town. For years the MTA has been digging up the city's streets, sucking huge amounts of tax money, and pushing exhaust vents up through peaceful parkland—and for what? Let's face it, L.A. will never have New York's subway or San Francisco's BART. Today the system is still in its infancy, mainly popular with commuters from outlying suburbs. Here's an overview of what's currently in place:

The **Metro Blue Line,** an aboveground rail line, connects downtown Los Angeles with Long Beach. Trains operate daily from 6am to 9pm; the fare is $1.35.

The **Metro Red Line,** L.A.'s first subway, has been growing since 1993 and opened a highly publicized Hollywood–Universal City extension in 2000. The line begins at Union Station, the city's main train depot, and travels west underneath Wilshire Boulevard, looping north into Hollywood and the San Fernando Valley. The fare is $1.35; discount tokens are available at Metro service centers and many area convenience stores.

The **Metro Green Line,** opened in 1995, runs for 20 miles along the center of the new I-105, the Glenn Anderson (Century) Freeway, and connects Norwalk in eastern Los Angeles County to LAX. A connection with the Blue Line offers visitors access from LAX to downtown L.A. or Long Beach. The fare is $1.35.

The **Metro Gold Line,** which opened in July 2003, is a 13¾-mile link between Pasadena and Union Station in downtown L.A. Stops include Old Pasadena, the Southwest Museum, and Chinatown. The fare is $1.35.

Weekly Metro passes are available for $14 at Metro Customer Centers and local convenience and grocery stores. For more information on public transportation—including construction updates and details on purchasing tokens or passes—call **MTA** at ✆ **213/922-2000** or, better yet, log on to their handy website at www.mta.net.

BY TAXI

Distances are long in Los Angeles, and cab fares are high; even a short trip can cost $10 or more. Taxis currently charge $1.90 at the flag drop, plus $1.60 per mile, but it will probably go up by the time you read this. A service charge is added to fares originating at LAX.

Except in the heart of downtown, cabs will usually not pull over when hailed. Cabstands are located at airports, at downtown's Union Station, and major hotels. To ensure a ride, order a taxi in advance from **Checker Cab** (✆ **323/654-8400**), **L.A. Taxi** (✆ **213/627-7000**), or **United Taxi** (✆ **213/483-7604**).

FAST FACTS: Los Angeles

American Express In addition to those at 327 N. Beverly Dr., Beverly Hills (✆ **310/274-8277**), and at the Beverly Connection, 8493 W. Third St., Los Angeles (✆ **310/659-1682**), offices are located throughout the city. To locate one nearest you, call ✆ **800/221-7282**.

Area Codes Within the past 20 years, L.A. has gone from having a single (213) area code to a whopping seven. Even residents can't keep up. Here's the basic layout: Those areas west of La Cienega Boulevard, including Beverly Hills and the city's beach communities, use the **310** area code. Portions of Los Angeles county east and south of the city, including Long Beach, are in the **562** area. The San Fernando Valley has the **818** area code, while points east—including parts of Burbank, Glendale, and Pasadena—use the newly created **626** code. What happened to 213, you ask? The downtown business area still uses **213**. All other numbers, including Griffith Park, Hollywood, and parts of West Hollywood (east of La Cienega Blvd.) now use the new area code **323**. If it's all too much to remember, just call directory assistance at ✆ **411**.

Babysitters If you're staying at one of the larger hotels, the concierge can usually recommend a reliable babysitter. If not, contact the **Baby-Sitters Guild** in Glendale (✆ **310/837-1800** or 818/552-2229), L.A.'s oldest and largest babysitting service.

Camera Repair On-site repairs are the specialty at family-owned **General Camera Repair**, 2218 E. Colorado Blvd., Pasadena (© **626/449-4533**); they opened in 1964 at this spot on the Rose Parade route.

Dentists For a recommendation in the area, call the **Dental Referral Service** (© **800/422-8338**).

Emergencies For police, fire, or highway patrol, or in case of medical emergencies, dial © **911**. No coins are needed when dialing from a payphone.

Hospital The centrally located (and world-famous) **Cedars-Sinai Medical Center**, 8700 Beverly Blvd., Los Angeles (© **310/423-3277**), has a 24-hour emergency room staffed by some of the country's finest MDs.

Liquor Laws Liquor and grocery stores can sell packaged alcoholic beverages between 6am and 2am. Most restaurants, nightclubs, and bars are licensed to serve alcoholic drinks during the same hours. The legal age for purchase and consumption is 21; proof of age is required.

Newspapers & Magazines **World Book & News Co.**, at 1652 N. Cahuenga Blvd. (© **323/465-4352**), near Hollywood and Vine and Grauman's Chinese Theatre, stocks out-of-town and foreign papers and magazines. No one minds if you browse through the magazines, but you'll be reprimanded for thumbing through newspapers. It's open 24 hours.

Pharmacies **Horton & Converse** has locations around L.A., including 2001 Santa Monica Blvd., Santa Monica (© **310/829-3401**); 9201 Sunset Blvd., Beverly Hills (© **323/272-0488**); and 11600 Wilshire Blvd., West Los Angeles (© **310/478-0801**). Hours vary, but the West L.A. location is open until 2am. Chances are good that there's either a **Walgreen's** (www.walgreens.com) or **Rite Aid** (www.riteaid.com) within a mile of where your staying.

Police In an emergency, dial © **911**. For nonemergency police matters, call © **213/485-2121**; in Beverly Hills, dial © **310/550-4951**.

Post Office Call © **800/ASK-USPS** to find the one closest to you.

Taxes The combined Los Angeles County and California state sales taxes amount to 8.25%; hotel taxes add 12% to 17% to room tariffs.

Taxis See "Getting Around" earlier in this chapter.

Time Zone Los Angeles is in the Pacific time zone, which is 8 hours behind Greenwich Mean Time and 3 hours behind Eastern time.

Weather Call **Los Angeles Weather Information** (© **213/554-1212**) for the daily forecast. For beach conditions, call the **Zuma Beach Lifeguard** recorded information (© **310/457-9701**).

3 Where to Stay

Due to space considerations, I've had to limit the number of hotels included here. If you'd like a larger selection, check out *Frommer's Los Angeles 2005*, which lists dozens of additional lodging options.

CHOOSING A LOCATION   In sprawling Los Angeles, location is everything. The neighborhood you choose as a base can make or break your vacation. If you plan to spend your days at the beach but stay downtown, for example, you're going to lose a lot of valuable relaxation time on the freeway. For business travelers, choosing a location is easy: Pick a hotel near your work—don't commute if you don't have to. For vacationers, though, the decision about where to stay is more difficult. Consider where you want to spend your time before you commit yourself to a base. But wherever you stay, count on doing a good deal of driving—no hotel in Los Angeles is convenient to everything.

The relatively smog-free beach communities such as **Santa Monica** and **Venice** are understandably popular with visitors—just about everybody loves to stay at the beach. Book ahead, because hotels fill up quickly, especially in summer.

If they're not at one of the beach communities, most visitors stay on the city's **Westside,** a short drive from the beach and close to most of L.A.'s colorful sights. The city's most elegant and expensive accommodations are in **Beverly Hills** and **Bel Air;** a few of the hotels in these neighborhoods, such as the **Beverly Hills Hotel & Bungalows,** have become visitor attractions unto themselves. The focal point of L.A. nightlife, **West Hollywood** is home to the greatest range and breadth of hotels, from $300-plus-per-night boutiques to affordably priced motels.

There are fewer hotels in **Hollywood** than you might expect. Accommodations are generally moderately priced and well maintained but unspectacular. Centrally located between downtown and Beverly Hills, just a stone's throw from Universal Studios, Hollywood makes a convenient base if you're planning to do a lot of exploring, but it has more tourists and is less visually appealing than some other neighborhoods.

Downtown hotels are generally business-oriented, but thanks to direct Metro (L.A.'s subway) connections to Hollywood and Universal Studios, the demographic has begun to shift. The top hotels offer excellent deals on weekend packages. But chances are good that downtown doesn't embody the picture of L.A. you've been dreaming of; you need a coastal or Westside base for that.

Families might want to head to the **Universal City** to be near Universal Studios, or straight to **Anaheim and Disneyland** (see chapter 14). **Pasadena** offers historic charm, small-town ambience, easy access to downtown L.A., and picture-postcard beauty, but driving to the beach can take forever.

To locate the hotels reviewed below, see the individual neighborhood maps in section 1, "Orientation."

RATES   The **rates** quoted in the listings that follow are the rack rates—the maximum rates that a hotel charges for rooms. But rack rates are only guidelines, and there are often many ways around them. *Always* check each hotel's website for package deals and special Internet rates. The hotels listed in this chapter have provided their best estimates for 2005, and all rates were correct at press time. **Be aware that rates can change at any time,** and are subject to availability, seasonal fluctuations, and plain old increases.

SANTA MONICA & THE BEACHES
VERY EXPENSIVE

Casa del Mar ✸✸✸   Housed in a former 1920s Renaissance Revival beach club, this Art Deco stunner is a real dream of a resort hotel, equal in every respect to big sister Shutters down the beach (see below). Which one you prefer depends on your personal style. While Shutters is outfitted like a chic contemporary beach house, this impeccable, U-shaped villalike structure radiates period glamour. The building's shape awards ocean views to most of the guest rooms; unfortunately, windows don't open more than an inch or two (which gives Shutters, whose rooms have floor-to-ceiling windows and balconies, a slight advantage). You're unlikely to be too disappointed thanks to the summery European-inspired decor in golds and sea-grass hues, plus abundant luxuries that include sumptuously dressed beds and big Italian marble bathrooms with extralarge whirlpool tubs and separate showers. Rooms are laid out for relaxation, not business, so travelers with work on their minds should stay elsewhere.

Downstairs you'll find a big, elegant living room with ocean views, a stylish lounge, and the **Oceanfront** restaurant, which has earned kudos (and more than a few celebrity fans) for its beautiful setting, great service, and seafood-heavy California cuisine. Outdoors, the Mediterranean-evocative Palm Terrace boasts a gorgeous Roman-style pool and Jacuzzi with spectacular ocean views.

1910 Ocean Way (next to the Santa Monica Pier), Santa Monica, CA 90405. ✆ **800/898-6999** or 310/581-5533. Fax 310/581-5503. www.hotelcasadelmar.com. 129 units. $345–$625 double; from $875 suite. AE, DC, DISC, MC, V. Valet parking $21. **Amenities:** Oceanfront restaurant; lobby lounge for cocktails and light fare; alfresco cafe for daytime dining; heated outdoor Roman-style pool; plunge pool; Jacuzzi overlooking Santa Monica Beach; state-of-the-art health club with spa services; 24-hr. concierge; business center; 24-hr. room service; dry-cleaning/laundry service. *In room:* A/C, TV/VCR, dataport, minibar, hair dryer, iron, CD player, laptop-size safe.

Hotel Oceana ★★ *(Kids)* Right across the street from the ocean, this all-suite hotel sits alongside low-rise, high-rent condos on a gorgeous stretch of Ocean Avenue, several blocks north of the Santa Monica hubbub. With their bright Matisse-style interiors and cushy IKEA-ish furniture, the wonderful apartment-like suites are colorful, modern, and amenity laden: Goodies run the gamut from comfy robes, multiple TVs, and CD players to full gourmet kitchens stocked with Wolfgang Puck microwavable pizzas, Häagen-Dazs pints, and bottles of California merlot. The enormous size of the suites—even the studios are huge—makes the Oceana terrific for families or shares. Oceanview suites feature balconies and two-person whirlpool tubs in the mammoth bathrooms, but don't feel the need to stretch your budget for a view, as all units sit garden-style around the courtyard with its cushiony chaises and boomerang-shaped pool. Everything is fresh, welcoming, and noninstitutional—the primary colors and playful modern style suits the beach location perfectly, and service is excellent—so it's no wonder advertising execs and others who could stay anywhere make the Oceana their choice for long-term stays.

849 Ocean Ave. (south of Montana Ave.), Santa Monica, CA 90403. ✆ **800/777-0758** or 310/393-0486. Fax 310/458-1182. www.hoteloceana.com. 63 units. $380 studio suite; $390–$500 1-bedroom suite; $750–$800 2-bedroom suite. AE, DC, DISC, MC, V. Valet parking $21. **Amenities:** Outdoor heated pool; exercise room; access to nearby health club; watersports equipment; concierge; business center; 24-hr. room service; room service from Wolfgang Puck Cafe (7am–10pm); in-room massage; babysitting; dry-cleaning/laundry service. *In room:* A/C; TV/VCR w/pay movies; dataport; kitchen with minibar, fridge, coffeemaker, and microwave; hair dryer; iron; safe; video games; Internet access; CD player.

Shutters on the Beach ★★★ This Cape Cod–style luxury hotel enjoys one of the city's most prized locations: on the beach, a block from Santa Monica Pier. Only relative newcomer Casa del Mar (above) can compete, but Shutters bests the Casa by attaching alfresco balconies to every guest room. The beach-cottage rooms overlooking the sand are more desirable and no more expensive than those in the towers. The views and sounds of the ocean are the most outstanding qualities of the spacious, luxuriously outfitted rooms, some of which have fireplaces and/or whirlpool tubs; all have floor-to-ceiling windows that open. The marble bathrooms come with generous counter space and welcome whimsies that include waterproof radios and toy whales. A relaxed ambience pervades the contemporary art-filled public spaces, which feel like the common areas of a deluxe Montauk beach house. The small swimming pool and the sunny lobby lounge overlooking the sand are two great perches for spotting the celebrities who swear by Shutters as an alternative hangout to smoggy Hollywood. **One Pico,** the hotel's premier restaurant, serves modern American cuisine in a seaside setting; the best meals at the more casual **Pedals Cafe** come from the wood-burning grill.

1 Pico Blvd., Santa Monica, CA 90405. ℭ **800/334-9000** or 310/458-0030. Fax 310/458-4589. www. shuttersonthebeach.com. 198 units. $380–$615 double; from $895 suite. AE, DC, DISC, MC, V. Valet parking $22. **Amenities:** Restaurant; cafe; lobby lounge; outdoor heated pool and Jacuzzi; health club with spa services; sauna; extensive beach-equipment rentals; concierge; activities desk; courtesy car; business center with secretarial services; 24-hr. room service; babysitting; dry-cleaning/laundry service; video library. *In room:* A/C, TV/VCR, CD, dataport, hair dryer, iron, laptop-size safe, private mini–wine cellar.

EXPENSIVE

Beach House at Hermosa Beach 🖈🖈 *Finds*   Sporting a Cape Cod style that suits the on-the-sand location, this luxurious, romantic inn is comprised of beautifully designed and outfitted split-level studio suites. Every bright, sunny unit comes with a plush, furnished living room with wood-burning fireplace (Duraflame logs provided) and entertainment center; a micro-kitchen with china and flatware for four; an elevated sleeping niche with a down-dressed king bed, a second TV, and a generous work area; an extralarge bathroom with extradeep soaking tub, a separate shower, cotton robes, and Aveda products; and a furnished balcony, many of which overlook the beach (believe me—it's worth the extra money to score a beachfront room). While sofas convert into second beds, the unit configuration is best suited to couples rather than families; more than three is too many. Despite the summertime carnival atmosphere of The Strand, the Beach House keeps serene with double-paned windows and noise-insulated walls. An excellent light breakfast is served in the sunny breakfast room overlooking The Strand. The attentive staff has an easygoing attitude that suits the property perfectly. While L.A.'s city center is at least a half-hour's drive away, Hermosa is airport-convenient and ideal for a beach getaway.

1300 The Strand, Hermosa Beach, CA 90254. ℭ **888/895-4559** or 310/374-3001. Fax 310/372-2115. www.beach-house.com. 96 units. $209–$349 double. Rates include continental breakfast. AE, DC, DISC, MC, V. Valet parking $17. **Amenities:** Concierge; room service from nearby restaurant; dry-cleaning/laundry service. *In room:* A/C; 2 TVs; dataport; stocked kitchenette with microwave, coffeemaker, stovetop, and fridge; hair dryer; iron; menu of spa services; stereo with 5-disc CD changer.

Le Merigot 🖈🖈   If you're accustomed to hotels that are roomier and more contemporary than the historic Georgian, yet not as pricey and prestigious as the Shutters or Casa del Mar properties, the porridge that's just right is Le Merigot, a low-key luxury hotel and spa that doesn't try to be anything other than a comfortable place to spend your seaside vacation. Ideally situated on the sandy side of Ocean Avenue in the heart of Santa Monica's beach scene, the 175-room hotel is essentially a business hotel that doubles as a resort, complete with a well-regarded French-California restaurant called **Cézanne** and the 5,500-square-foot **SPA Merigot,** which offers a full range of services along with an outdoor pool and a state-of-the-art fitness center. Most of the contemporary-style guest rooms offer ocean views, and all are plushly furnished with thick carpeting, marble-tiled bathrooms, oversize lounge chairs, and "Cloud Nine" beds topped with Frette linens, down comforters, and feather pillows. What I really like about this hotel are the clever package deals, such as the "California Dreamin'," which includes your choice of a convertible Porsche Boxster or a BMW Z4 Roadster rental car, or the "California Surfin' Safari," a deluxe package that includes a full breakfast for two, a 2-hour surf lesson, a rejuvenating full-session Swedish massage, and celebratory Blue Crush graduation martinis (how very L.A.).

1740 Ocean Ave., Santa Monica, CA 90401. ℭ **800/228-9290** or 310/395-9700. Fax 310/395-9200. www. lemerigothotel.com. 175 units. $299–$499 double; from $800 suite. AE, DISC, MC, V. Valet parking $28. **Amenities:**

Full-service restaurant; lobby bar; outdoor pool; fitness facilities and spa; gift shop; concierge; business services; 24-hr. in-room dining; choice of morning newspaper. *In room:* A/C, cable TV, fax machine upon request, minibar, iron and ironing board, laptop safe, 3 dual-line phones with voice mail, high-speed Internet access.

Viceroy ⋆⋆   Currently at the top of L.A.'s coveted "in" list is this new über-chic hotel on the sea side of Santa Monica. Of course, part of being "in" is breaking new ground, and that's certainly what designer Kelly Wearstler has achieved with her "Modern Colonialism" makeover. It's the startling color scheme that first grabs your attention as you enter the lobby—a rather unorthodox blend of parrot green, charcoal gray, and glossy white with chrome, silver, and ebony highlights. Then there's the dish thing: hundreds of custom-made china arranged in symmetrical patterns throughout the hotel and guest rooms (Where's The Who when you really need them?). The array of white patent-leather chaises in the lobby seem more for form than function; most guests prefer more conventional seating in the Cameo bar, Whist restaurant, and private poolside cabanas. The edgy-English theme is applied to each guest room as well, along with an array of high-tech toys (27-in. flat-screen TV, another flat-screen TV in the marble-laden bathrooms, a CD/DVD player, and T-1 Internet access), custom-made furnishings, and luxuries such as Frette linens and bathrobes, Molton Brown products, and down comforters and pillows. You'll enjoy the location as well—a short walk to the beach and in the thick of the shopping, entertainment, and restaurant scene. *Tip:* Splurge for an oceanview room; your only other choice is the hotel parking lot.

1819 Ocean Ave., Santa Monica, CA 90401. ℭ **800/622-8711** or 310/260-7500. Fax 310/260-7518. www.viceroysantamonica.com. 170 units. $249–$339 double; from $689 suite. AE, DC, DISC, MC, V. Valet parking $24. **Amenities:** Restaurant; bar; lounge; 2 heated outdoor pools; fitness center, concierge; 24-hr. room service; in-room massage; dry-cleaning/laundry service; newspaper delivery; videos available. *In room:* TV w/pay movies and video games, dataport and high-speed connection, minibar, hair dryer, safe, CD/DVD player.

MODERATE

The Ambrose ⋆⋆ (Value)   If being within walking distance of the ocean isn't crucial but a soothing, peaceful environment is, I've found your hotel. Located in a residential Santa Monica neighborhood, the new 77-room Ambrose is quickly becoming a favorite boutique hideaway for CEOs who are tired of the megahotel experience and just want a relaxing place to hang their coats (repeat guests are given their own fitness-room locker) and unwind. The Ambrose's unique architecture blends the Arts and Crafts movement with soothing Asian influences—a tranquil Japanese garden, a koi pond, fountains, beautiful artwork, and a profusion of dark woods and mossy palates. The majority of the guest rooms are on the small side—if you're not satisfied with the elbow room, feel free to ask for another—but are luxuriously appointed with Matteo Italian bedding, Frette cotton kimonos and bath linens, oversize goose-down pillows, and surround-sound CD-DVD music systems. Studio rooms are the largest and come with a private deck with a fireplace and partial ocean views. It's the many complimentary amenities that really sold me on the Ambrose, though (a strategy I wish more hotels would follow): underground parking with direct elevator access, wireless Internet access, access to the community computer, breakfast provided by local gourmet Celestino Drago, a 24-hour fitness room filled with top-of-the-line equipment, and shuttle service around Santa Monica via the hotel's cute-as-all-get-out London taxi. Other perks include a 24-hour in-room dining menu (again, from Drago), Aveda bath products, organic minibar offerings, and one-on-one Pilates training available on-call. With rack rates starting at a very reasonable $165, book a room fast while it's still a bargain.

1255 20th St. (at Arizona), Santa Monica, CA 90404. (C) **877/262-7673** or 310/315-1555. Fax 310/315-1556. www.ambrosehotel.com. 77 units. $165–$300 double. AE, DC, DISC, MC, V. Valet parking free. **Amenities:** Restaurant; 2 heated outdoor pools; 24-hr. fitness center; 24-hr. room service; in-room massage; complimentary local transportation and continental breakfast. *In room:* TV/VCR, free dataport and wireless high-speed connection, minibar, hair dryer, safe, CD/DVD surround sound.

The Hotel California *Finds*   Situated on enviable real estate along Ocean Avenue—right next door to the behemoth Loews—this welcoming hacienda-style beachfront motel embodies the surfer/sun-worshiper ambience you'd expect from a Santa Monica lodging. The well-tended complex sits above and across an alley from the beach but offers excellent views and direct access to the sand via a stepped path. The inn offers small, comfortable rooms with modern furnishings—including beds with down comforters and surfboard headboards—hardwood floors, and tiled bathrooms. Five one-bedroom suites also have kitchenettes and pullout sofas that make them great for families or longer stays; all rooms have minifridges and ceiling fans. A handful of rooms have only showers in the bathrooms, so be sure to request a room with a tub from the friendly front-desk staff if it matters to you. *Tip:* Pay a few bucks extra for a courtyard view, as the cheapest rooms face the parking lot and noisy Ocean Avenue.

1670 Ocean Ave. (south of Colorado Ave.), Santa Monica, CA 90401. (C) **866/571-0000** or 310/393-2363. Fax 310/393-1063. www.hotelca.com. 26 units. $169–$279 double or suite. AE, DISC, MC, V. Self-parking $9. **Amenities:** Jacuzzi; activities desk; discount car-rental desk; high-speed Internet access, fax/copier, and coffeemaker in front office. *In room:* TV/VCR, dataport, fridge, hair dryer, iron.

INEXPENSIVE

Best Western Marina Pacific Hotel & Suites *Kids*   This bright four-story hotel is a haven of smart value. Located just off the newly renovated Venice Boardwalk and 200 feet from the beach, the hotel's spacious rooms are brightened with beachy colors and dutifully equipped with chain-standard furnishings, fridges, and two-line phones. The one-bedroom suites are terrific for families, offering master bedrooms with king-size beds, fully outfitted kitchens with microwave and dishwasher, dining areas, queen-size sofa sleepers, balconies, and fireplaces. Photos of local scenes and rock 'n' roll legends along with works by local artists give the public spaces a cool L.A. vibe, and many rooms have at least partial ocean views. Additional incentives include complimentary upscale continental breakfast, free local shuttle service, and secured indoor parking. Stay elsewhere if you need a lot in the way of service or if you don't relish the party-hearty human carnival of Venice Beach (Santa Monica is generally quieter and more refined).

1697 Pacific Ave. (at 17th Ave.), Venice, CA 90291. (C) **800/786-7789** or 310/452-1111. Fax 310/452-5479. www.mphotel.com or www.bestwestern.com. 88 units. $109–$159 double; $169–$269 suite. Rates include continental breakfast. Extra person $10. Children 12 and under stay free in parent's room. Ask about AAA, senior, and other discounts; weekly and monthly rates also available. AE, DC, DISC, MC, V. Self-parking $9. **Amenities:** Free shuttle to Santa Monica and Marina del Rey; dry-cleaning/laundry service; continental breakfast; coin laundry. *In room:* A/C, cable TV w/HBO, free high-speed dataport, fridge, coffeemaker, hair dryer, iron and ironing board.

Cal Mar Hotel Suites *Value*   Tucked away in a residential neighborhood 2 blocks from the ocean, this garden apartment complex delivers a lot of bang for your vacation buck. Each unit is an apartment-style suite with a living room and pullout sofa, a full-size kitchen with utensils, and a separate bedroom; most are spacious enough to accommodate four in comfort. The building was constructed in the 1950s with an eye for quality (attractive tile work, large closets). While the furnishings aren't luxurious, they're all modern, very clean, and everything is well kept. It's easy to be comfortable here for stays of a week or more, especially since it's so well located—a mere bock from the Third Street shopping promenade and a short walk to the beach—and parking is free. The staff is attentive and courteous, which helps account for the high rate of repeat guests. The garden courtyard has an inviting swimming pool and plenty of chaises for lounging. *Tip:* Request a room on the second floor to avoid the sound of stomping feet.

220 California Ave., Santa Monica, CA 90403. © 800/776-6007 or 310/395-5555. Fax 310/451-1111. www.calmarhotel.com. 36 units. $109–$169 suite. Extra person $10. Children under 10 stay free in parent's room. AE, DC, DISC, MC, V. Free parking. **Amenities:** Heated outdoor pool; coin-op laundry. *In room:* TV, full kitchen with fridge and coffeemaker, CD sound system, hair dryer, iron.

Casa Malibu ★★ *(Finds)*

Sitting right on its very own beach, this leftover jewel from Malibu's golden age doesn't try to play the sleek resort game (and what a refreshing exception). Instead, the modest, low-rise inn has a traditional California-beach-cottage look that's cozy and timeless.

Wrapped around a palm-studded inner courtyard brightened with well-tended flower beds and climbing *cuppa d'oro* vines, the 21 rooms are comfortable and thoughtfully outfitted. Many have been upgraded with tile bathrooms, air-conditioning (almost never needed on the coast), and VCRs or DVDs, but even the older ones are in great shape and boast top-quality bedding and bathrobes. Depending on which you choose, you might also find a fireplace, a kitchenette (in a half dozen or so), a CD player (in suites), a tub (instead of shower only), and/or a private deck over the sand. The upstairs Catalina Suite (Lana Turner's old hideout) has the best view, while the gorgeous Malibu Suite—the best room in the house, and, like the Beachfront rooms, located right on the beach—offers state-of-the-art pampering. More than half have ocean views, but even those facing the courtyard are quiet and offer easy beach access via wooden stairs to the private stretch of beach, which is raked smooth each morning. There's also a handsome, wind-shielded brick sun deck, which extends directly over the sand, allowing everyone to enjoy the blue Pacific even in cool months. Book well ahead for summer—this one's a favorite of locals and visitors alike.

22752 Pacific Coast Hwy. (about ¼ mile south of Malibu Pier), Malibu, CA 90265. © 800/831-0858 or 310/456-2219. Fax 310/456-5418. 21 units. $99–$189 garden- or oceanview double; $229–$249 beachfront double; $229–$379 suite. Rates include continental breakfast. Extra person $15. AE, MC, V. Free parking. **Amenities:** Private beach; access to nearby private health club; room service for lunch and dinner; in-room massage; dry-cleaning/laundry service; hotel-wide wireless access. *In room:* TV, 2-line telephone with dataport, fridge, coffeemaker, hair dryer, iron.

Sea Shore Motel ★★ *(Finds)*

Located in the heart of Santa Monica's best dining and shopping action, this small, friendly, family-run motel is the bargain of the beach. The Sea Shore is such a well-kept secret that most denizens of stylish Main Street are unaware of the incredible value in their midst. Arranged around a parking courtyard, rooms are small and unremarkable, but the conscientious management has done a nice job with them, installing attractive terra-cotta floor tiles, granite countertops, and conveniences like voice mail and data-jack phones. Complete with a sitting room and microwave, the suite is a phenomenal deal; book it as far in advance as possible. With a full slate of restaurants out the front door and the Santa Monica Pier and beach just a couple of blocks away, it's a terrific bargain base for exploring the sandy side of the city.

2637 Main St. (south of Ocean Park Blvd.), Santa Monica, CA 90405. © 310/392-2787. Fax 310/392-5167. www.seashoremotel.com. 20 units. $75–$95 double; $110–$135 suite. Extra person $5. Children under 12 stay free in parent's room. Midweek discounts available. AE, DISC, MC, V. Free parking. Pets accepted for $10-per-night fee. **Amenities:** Deli; coin-op laundry; sun deck. *In room:* TV, coffeemaker, dataport, fridge, iron.

NEAR LAX

If you have an early-morning flight and you need an airport hotel, the **Westin Los Angeles Airport,** 5400 W. Century Blvd. (© **800/WESTIN-1** or 310/216-5858; www.westin.com/losangelesairport), is a cut above the rest, with its patented Westin Heavenly Beds. Two good, moderately priced choices are the **Sheraton Gateway Hotel,** 6101 W. Century Blvd., near Sepulveda Boulevard (© **800/325-3535** or 310/642-1111; www.sheraton.com), a comfortable, California-style hotel that literally overlooks the runway; and the **Marriott Los Angeles Airport,** 5855 Century Blvd. (© **800/228-9290** or 310/641-5700; www.marriott.com), a reliable choice for on-the-fly travelers.

If you're looking for an inexpensive option, try the **Travelodge at LAX,** 5547 W. Century Blvd. (© **800/421-3939** or 310/649-4000; www.travelodgelax. com), an otherwise standard member of the reliable chain with a surprisingly beautiful tropical garden surrounding the pool area.

L.A.'S WESTSIDE & BEVERLY HILLS
VERY EXPENSIVE

Beverly Hills Hotel and Bungalows ✿✿✿   Behind the famous facade (Remember the Eagles' *Hotel California* album?) lies this star-studded haven where legends were, and still are, made: The "Pink Palace" was center stage for both deal- and star-making in Hollywood's golden days. Today, stars and industry hotshots, or as one member of the staff joked, "all the current rulers of the universe," can still be found lounging around the Olympic-size pool (into which Katharine Hepburn once dove fully clothed) and digging into Dutch apple pancakes in the iconic **Polo Lounge,** where Hunter S. Thompson kicked off his adventure to Las Vegas, and where Ozzy Osbourne has been known to take afternoon tea. I had the pleasure of staying here recently and was so impressed with the entire experience that the Beverly Hills Hotel has become my new favorite among every other hotel in Los Angeles.

Following a $100-million restoration a few years ago, the hotel's grand lobby and impeccably landscaped grounds retain their over-the-top glory, while the guest rooms—each uniquely decorated in a subdued palate of pinks, greens, apricots, and yellows—boast every state-of-the-art luxury, including extralarge bathrooms with double Grecian marble sinks and TVs. The management has assembled a refreshingly unpretentious, service-oriented staff bent on guest comfort, and the best original touches have been retained, like butler service at the touch of a button. Many rooms feature private patios, Jacuzzi tubs, kitchens, and/or dining rooms. The 21 bungalows are more luxurious than ever, and the lush grounds are brimming with exotic trees and flowers that emit divine aromas. Even the outdoor pathways are carpeted to keep noise to a minimum. *Tip:* The inexpensive and informal **Fountain Coffee Shop,** open daily for 7am to 7pm, is a great excuse to visit the hotel for an hour, and you never know who might be sitting on the stool next to you slurping down a chocolate malt.

9641 Sunset Blvd. (at Rodeo Dr.), Beverly Hills, CA 90210. © 800/283-8885 or 310/276-2251. Fax 310/887-2887. www.beverlyhillshotel.com. 203 units. $345–$375 double; from $745 suite or bungalow. AE, DC, MC, V. Parking $23. Pets accepted in bungalows only. **Amenities:** 3 restaurants (Polo Lounge, Fountain Coffee Shop, alfresco Cabana Club Cafe); 2 lounges (Sunset Lounge for high tea and cocktails, bar in Polo Lounge); Olympic-size outdoor heated pool; 2 outdoor tennis courts (lit for night play); fitness center; whirlpool; concierge; car-rental desk; courtesy limo; business center with computers; salon services; 24-hr. room service; in-room or poolside massage; babysitting; dry-cleaning/laundry service; video rentals. *In room:* A/C, TV/VCR, DSL dataport, fax/copier/scanner, minibar, hair dryer, safe, CD player.

Four Seasons Hotel Los Angeles at Beverly Hills ⋆⋆   This intimate-feeling 16-story hotel attracts a mix of A-list jet-setters loyal to the Four Seasons brand and an L.A. showbiz crowd who cherish the hotel as an après-event gathering place. The small marbled lobby is anchored by an always-stunning floral extravaganza, and lush gardens will help you forget you're in the heart of the city. Four Seasons operates terrific hotels, with a concierge that's famously well connected and service that goes the distance. Guest rooms are sumptuously furnished in traditional style and pastel hues. Luxuries include custom extrastuffed Sealy mattresses with heavenly linens and pillows, marble bathrooms with vanity TVs, and French doors leading to private balconies. Room rates rise with the elevator, so bargain hunters need to sacrifice the view; ask for a corner room to get extra space at no additional cost.

Since you're already in for a penny, get the pounding as well: a "California Sunset Massage" at one of the private poolside cabanas. Along with a full-service spa, the view-endowed fourth-floor deck features a lap pool, poolside grill, and glass-walled fitness center. **Gardens** is a refined and excellent California-French restaurant often overlooked by locals.

300 S. Doheny Dr. (at Burton Way), Los Angeles, CA 90048. ⓒ **800/819-5053**, 800/332-3442, or 310/273-2222. Fax 310/859-3824. www.fourseasons.com/losangeles. 285 units. $370–$470 double; from $600 suite. AE, DC, DISC, MC, V. Valet parking $21; free self-parking. Pets under 15 lb. welcome (no charge). **Amenities:** Restaurant and lounge; poolside grill; rooftop heated pool; exercise room; full-service spa; Jacuzzi; children's program; concierge; courtesy limo within 5-mile radius; business center; 24-hr. room service; in-room massage; dry-cleaning/laundry service. *In room:* A/C, TV/VCR w/pay movies (suites have DVD), dataport, minibar, hair dryer, iron, safe, CD player.

Hotel Bel-Air ⋆⋆⋆   Spread over 12 luxuriant garden acres, this stunning Mission-style hotel is one of the most beautiful, romantic, exclusive, and all-around impressive hotels not just in L.A. but in all of California. This early-20th-century castle wins a never-ending stream of praise for its faultless service, luxurious accommodations, and ambience. The parklike grounds—rich with ancient trees, fragrant flowers, bubbling fountains, playful statuary, and swan-dotted ponds—are enchanting, and the welcoming, richly traditional public rooms are filled with fine antiques. Rooms, villas, and garden suites are individually decorated but equally stunning; some have Jacuzzis, many have private patios and wood-burning fireplaces, but all feature romantic country French decor.

The hotel is a natural for honeymooners and other celebrants, but families might be put off by the Bel-Air's relative formality, which is geared to the jet set, CEO types, and ladies who lunch. Even if you don't stay here, you might consider brunch, lunch, or dinner at the highly regarded and ultraromantic restaurant or on the woodsy outdoor terrace, or drinks at the cozy bar.

701 Stone Canyon Rd. (north of Sunset Blvd.), Los Angeles, CA 90077. ⓒ **800/648-4097** or 310/472-1211. Fax 310/476-5890. www.hotelbelair.com. 92 units. $465–$555 double; $700–$3,500 suite. AE, DC, DISC, MC, V. Parking $20. **Amenities:** Indoor/outdoor restaurant; lounge with pianist nightly; outdoor heated pool; exercise room; concierge; business center; 24-hr. room service; in-room massage; babysitting; dry-cleaning/laundry service; video library. *In room:* A/C, digital TV/VCR w/pay movies, fax, dataport and high-speed connection, minibar, hair dryer, laptop-size safe, CD player.

Mondrian ⋆⋆   Theatrical, coveted, sophisticated—this is the kind of place superhotelier Ian Schrager has created from a once-drab apartment building. Working with his regular partner, *enfant terrible* French designer Philippe Starck (as he successfully did at Miami's Delano and Manhattan properties like the Royalton and Hudson), Schrager used the Mondrian's breathtaking views (from every room) as the starting point for his vision of a "hotel in the clouds." Purposely underlit hallways lead to bright, clean rooms done in shades of white, beige, and pale gray and outfitted with simple furniture casually slip-covered in white; about three-quarters of the rooms and suites have fully outfitted kitch-enettes. Truthfully, the accommodations themselves are only secondary—stay here if you want to be part of a superhip, star-studded scene. Set poolside and in a magical treehouse, **Skybar** is still one of L.A.'s hottest watering holes, and booking a room guarantees admission. (Soundproof windows on the entire south side of the building have already dealt with a troublesome noise problem in rooms overlooking the raucous late-night scene.) In addition to its ter-rific—and ultrahip—Asian-Latin fusion restaurant **Asia de Cuba,** light meals and sushi are served at a quirky communal table in the lobby. The beautiful-peo-ple staff isn't strong on service, but so what? They look great.

8440 Sunset Blvd., West Hollywood, CA 90069. ✆ 800/525-8029 or 323/650-8999. Fax 323/650-5215. www.mondrianhotel.com and www.ianschragerhotels.com. 238 units. $310–$560 double; from $385 suite. Weekend rates available. AE, DC, DISC, MC, V. Valet parking $23. **Amenities:** Asia de Cuba restaurant; Seabar for sushi in lobby; Skybar alfresco bar; Agua Spa; outdoor pool; exercise room with sauna and Jacuzzi; concierge; business center; 24-hr. room service; in-room massage; dry-cleaning/laundry service; video, DVD, and CD libraries. In room: A/C, TV/VCR, dataport, minibar, coffeemaker, hair dryer, iron, safe, CD player.

EXPENSIVE

Avalon Hotel ★★ *Finds* The first style-conscious boutique hotel on the L.A. scene, this mid-twentieth-inspired gem in the heart of Beverly Hills still leads the pack. With a sherbet-hued palette and Atomic Age furnishings—Eames cabinets, Heywood-Wakefield chairs, Nelson bubble lamps—mixed with smart custom designs, every room looks as if it could star in a *Metropolitan Home* photo spread. But fashion doesn't forsake function at this beautifully designed hotel, which offers enough luxury comforts and amenities to please design-blind travelers, too.

The property is comprised of the former Beverly-Carlton (seen on *I Love Lucy* and once home to Marilyn Monroe and Mae West) as well as two neighboring 1950s-era apartment houses. The main building is the hub of a chic but low-key scene, but I prefer the quieter Canon building, where many of the units have kitchenettes and/or furnished terraces. No matter which you end up in, you'll find a gorgeous, restful cocoon with terry bathrobes and Frette linens. You'll also have access to the sunny courtyard with its retro-hip amoeba-shaped pool, the fit-ness room, and the *Jetsons*-style restaurant and bar, which shakes a terrific green apple martini. Service is friendlier than you'll find in other style-minded hotels.

9400 W. Olympic Blvd. (at Beverly Dr.), Beverly Hills, CA 90212. ✆ 800/535-4715 or 310/277-5221. Fax 310/277-4928. www.avalonbeverlyhills.com. 88 units. $199–$289 double; from $249 junior or 1-bedroom suite. Extra person $25. AE, DC, MC, V. Valet parking $17. **Amenities:** Restaurant and lounge; courtyard pool; concierge; 24-hr. room service; in-room spa and massage; dry-cleaning/laundry service. In room: A/C, TV/VCR w/pay movies and video games, fax, dataport, minibar, coffeemaker, hair dryer, iron, safe, CD player.

Chateau Marmont ★★ Perched secretively in a curve above the Sunset Strip, the château modeled after a Loire Valley castle is a landmark from 1920s-era Hollywood; step inside and you expect to find John Barrymore or Errol Flynn holding inebriated court in the baronial living room (some say it's actu-ally haunted). Greta Garbo regularly checked in as "Harriet Brown," and Jim Morrison was one of many celebrities to call this home in later years. This land-mark built its reputation on exclusivity and privacy, which was shattered when John Belushi overdosed in Bungalow No. 2. Now under the guiding hand of boutique hotelier Andre Balazs (also lord of The Standard; see below), the funky luxury oasis revels in its lore-filled past, yet it's hipper and more exclusive than ever. No two of the antiques-filled accommodations—standard rooms, suites, cottages, and bungalows—are alike: The poolside Spanish-style garden cottages are outfitted in Arts and Crafts style, while suites and bungalows may get a '50s look or a Gothic style. Many units have fireplaces and CD stereos, and all but 11 have kitchenettes or full kitchens.

The Chateau Marmont is beautifully kept, eternally chic, faultlessly service-oriented, and overflowing with Hollywood and rock 'n' roll lore (not to mention a look-at-me/don't-look-at-me clientele), but it's not for everybody. This is a place where quirkiness rules, so don't expect traditional luxuries. It's best for those with left-of-center attitudes and a penchant for Hollywood romanticism. If that's you, don't stay anywhere else—this will be the highlight of your vacation.

8221 Sunset Blvd. (between La Cienega and Crescent Heights boulevards), West Hollywood, CA 90046. ⓒ 800/242-8328 or 323/656-1010. Fax 323/655-5311. www.chateaumarmont.com. 63 units. $250–$325 double; from $375 suite; from $400 cottage; from $875 bungalow. AE, DC, MC, V. Valet parking $21. Pets accepted with $100-per-pet fee. **Amenities:** Restaurant (serves in lobby, garden, and dining room); Bar Marmont; outdoor heated pool with brick sun deck; exercise room; access to nearby health club; 24-hr. concierge; business center; secretarial services; 24-hr. room service; in-room massage; babysitting; same-day laundry and dry-cleaning; CD library. *In room:* A/C, TV/VCR, dataport, minibar, fridge, coffeemaker, hair dryer, iron, laptop-size safe, CD player.

The Mosaic ⋆⋆⋆ *Finds* I've seen hundreds of hotel renovations, but none have impressed me as much as this boutique Beverly Hills hotel. Formerly the Beverly Hills Inn, the new owners pumped $3 million into renovating the entire hotel and the result is spectacular. The lobby is a showcase of functional art, with tile mosaics, fabrics in deep, rich tones, and a profusion of artfully arranged orchids. Continuing a recent trend that I'm all for, a wall has been removed to allow direct access from the check-in desk to the bar and lounge, where guests are encouraged to sample the house special—a Mosaic Sake Martini. The guest rooms are equally impressive, done in soothing earth tones with 300-count Frette linens, goose-down comforters and piles of pillows, windows that open onto the neighborhood street or garden courtyard, minibars stocked with Wolfgang Puck snacks and libations, and sparkling bathrooms with Bvlgari bath products and huge Rain Forest showerheads. Other perks include free high-speed Internet access, poolside cabanas, CD players, DVD players in the suites, late room service from the hotel's small cafe, a fitness room, and covered parking. *Tip:* The corner deluxe rooms are worth the extra $15.

125 S. Spalding Dr., Beverly Hills, CA 90212. ⓒ 800/463-4466 or 310/278-0303. Fax 310/278-1728. www.innatbeverlyhills.com. 49 units. $225–$450 double; from $600 2-bedroom suite. AE, DC, MC, V. Parking $15. Small pets accepted. **Amenities:** Restaurant; full bar; heated outdoor pool; exercise room with sauna; tour desk; business services; full room service menu until 10pm; dry-cleaning/laundry service. *In room:* A/C, TV, high-speed dataport, fridge, hair dryer, iron, cordless phone, CD player.

Wyndham Bel Age Hotel ⋆⋆ *Kids* *Value* This high-rise all-suite hotel is one of West Hollywood's best. The Bel Age has it all: huge, amenity-laden suites, excellent service, terrific rooftop sun deck with pool and Jacuzzi, and A-1 location just half a block off the Sunset Strip but removed from the congestion and noise. What's more, thanks to an excellent art collection (assembled by the hotel's original owners) that fills the public spaces and guest rooms, the hotel has far more personality than your average chain hotel.

Accommodations hardly get better for the money. The monster-size suites offer contemporary decor with a few classic touches and a soothing palette of navy, burgundy, and gray. Selected to suit every need—including those of families and business travelers—luxuries include pillow-top mattresses with cushioned headboards and plush bedding, a sleeper sofa in the living area that opens into a queen bed, plus an excellent work desk with an ergonomically correct Herman Miller desk chair. The bathrooms come with generous counter space and robes. The best rooms face south; on a clear day, you can see all the way to the Pacific. Be sure to make reservations before you leave home for a special meal at the hotel's Franco-Russian **Diaghilev** restaurant.

1020 N. San Vicente Blvd. (between Sunset and Santa Monica boulevards), West Hollywood, CA 90069. © 800/WYNDHAM or 310/854-1111. Fax 310/854-0926. www.wyndham.com. 200 units. $199–$339 suite (accommodates up to 4 at no extra charge). Ask about weekend rates, holiday specials, and discounts on longer stays. AE, DC, DISC, MC, V. Valet parking $18. **Amenities:** Restaurant; bar and grill with live entertainment; rooftop outdoor heated pool and Jacuzzi; exercise room; concierge; salon; room service (6am–2am); dry-cleaning/laundry service. *In room:* A/C; TV/VCR w/pay movies, PlayStation, and onscreen Internet access; dataport and high-speed connection; minibar; coffeemaker; hair dryer; iron; CD player.

MODERATE

Holiday Inn Brentwood/Bel-Air   This L.A. landmark is the last of a vanishing breed of circular hotels from the 1960s and 1970s. It's perched beside the city's busiest freeway a short hop from the popular Getty Center and centrally located between the beaches, Beverly Hills, and the San Fernando Valley. Completely refurbished in 2000, each pie-shaped room boasts a private balcony and double-paned glass to keep the noise out; little extras like Nintendo games, in-room bottled water, and great views add panache to otherwise-unremarkable chain-style accommodations. You'll also enjoy a million-dollar 360-degree view from the hotel's top-floor **West** restaurant, which serves a casual, please-all cuisine; the adjoining cocktail lounge features live piano nightly. Popular with older travelers and museum groups, the hotel provides complimentary pickup and drop-off service to the Getty Center and Westwood.

170 N. Church Lane (at intersection of Sunset Blvd. and I-405), Los Angeles, CA 90049. © 800/HOLIDAY or 310/476-6411. Fax 310/472-1157. www.holiday-inn.com/brentwood-bel. 211 units. $149–$189 double; from $275 suite. Inquire about AAA and AARP discounts, breakfast packages, and "Great Rates," often as low as $119. AE, DC, DISC, MC, V. Valet parking $11; self-parking $8. Small pets accepted for $50-per-pet nonrefundable fee. **Amenities:** Rooftop restaurant and lounge; heated outdoor pool and Jacuzzi; exercise room; concierge; activities desk; free shuttle to Getty Center and within a 3-mile radius; room service (6am–10pm); coin-op laundry; dry-cleaning/laundry service. *In room:* A/C; TV w/pay movies and Nintendo, dataport, coffeemaker, hair dryer, iron.

The Standard 🎭🎭   If Andy Warhol had gone into the hotel business (which he no doubt would have, if he had arrived on the scene a few decades later), The Standard would've been the end result. Designed to appeal to the under-35 It-crowd, Andre Balazs's swank West Hollywood neo-motel is sometimes absurd, sometimes brilliant, and always provocative (not to mention crowded!). It's a scene worthy of its Sunset Strip location: Shag carpeting on the lobby ceiling, blue Astroturf around the swimming pool, a DJ spinning ambient sounds while a performance artist showing more skin than talent poses in a display case behind the check-in desk—this place is definitely left of center.

The good news is that The Standard is more than just an attitude. Look past the retro clutter and often-raucous party scene and you'll find a level of service more often associated with hotels costing twice as much. Constructed from the bones of a vintage 1962 motel, it boasts comfortable size rooms outfitted with cobalt-blue indoor-outdoor carpeting, silver beanbag chairs, safety-orange tiles in the bathrooms, and Warhol's Poppy-print curtains, plus private balconies, and minibars whose contents include goodies like sake, condoms, and animal crackers. On the downside, the cheapest rooms face noisy Sunset Boulevard, and the relentless scene can get tiring if you're not into it. The Standard's trendy new full-service **NestSpa** offers so-L.A.-style treatments such as Touch Thyself, Jet Lag Therapy, and Hangover Helper.

Note: A 12-story **Downtown Standard**, 550 S. Flower St. (© 213/892-8080), brings a similar dose of retro-future style and attitude to downtown. The Cheap

Rooms—yes, that's what they call them—run about $100 on weekends. It's worth visiting just to check out the rooftop bar with its vibrating waterbed pleasure pods, movies projected onto neighboring buildings, and hot waitresses.

8300 Sunset Blvd. (at Sweetzer Ave.), West Hollywood, CA 90069. ℂ **323/650-9090.** Fax 323/650-2820. www.standardhotel.com. 139 units. $99–$225 double; from $450 suite. AE, DC, DISC, MC, V. Valet parking $18. Pets under 30 lb. accepted for $100-per-pet fee. **Amenities:** 24-hr. coffee shop; poolside cafe; bar/lounge; outdoor heated pool; access to nearby health club; concierge; business center; barbershop; 24-hr. room service; in-room massage; babysitting; dry-cleaning/laundry service. *In room:* A/C, TV/VCR w/pay movies, dataport and high-speed connection, minibar, CD player.

INEXPENSIVE

Beverly Laurel Motor Hotel *(Value* Touted by the *New York Times* for its Gen-X appeal and value, the Beverly Laurel is a great choice for wallet-watching travelers who want a central location and a room with more style than your average motel. Overlooking the parking lot, the budget-basic but well-kept rooms are smartened up with diamond-print spreads and eye-catching artwork; other features include a minifridge, microwave, and ample closet space, and a large kitchenette for an extra 10-spot. The postage-stamp-size outdoor pool is a little public for carefree sunbathing but does the job on hot summer days. Best of all is the motel's own excellent coffee shop, **Swingers** (p. 571)—nobody serves burgers and malts better, and you may even spot your favorite alt-rocker tucking into a 3pm breakfast in the vinyl booth next to yours.

8018 Beverly Blvd. (between La Cienega Blvd. and Fairfax Ave.), Los Angeles, CA 90048. ℂ **800/962-3824** or 323/651-2441. Fax 323/651-5225. 52 units. $79–$84 double; $89 double with kitchen. AAA and senior discounts may be available. AE, DC, MC, V. Free parking. **Amenities:** Heated outdoor pool; access to nearby health club; car-rental desk; laundry service. *In room:* A/C, TV, dataport, minifridge, microwave, hair dryer.

Farmer's Daughter *(Value* Most people end up at the Farmer's Daughter hotel fortuitously because they're waiting to be the next contestant on *The Price is Right*. The CBS Studios across the street recommend the budget motel to its game show fans, but I'm recommending it just because I dig this chic little lodge. It's cheery from the moment you walk in the lobby. Bright yellows and cool blues mix well with the country-kitsch theme: rooster wallpaper, faded barn-wood paneling, denim bedspreads, cow-skin rugs, and a parade of inflatable animals that float around the pool. It's obvious that someone with smart fashion sense and a little money turned a dumpy motel into an oasis of stylish affordability for people like me who drive Jettas and wear flip-flops in the winter. Money-saving perks include free Internet hookup, free parking, free DVD library, and across-the-street access to an entire farmers market of inexpensive foodstuffs and entertainment. *Tip:* Request a room facing the alley—the view sucks but you don't get the 24-hour road noise off Fairfax Avenue.

115 S. Fairfax Ave. (between Beverly Dr. and Third), Los Angeles, CA 90036. ℂ **800/334-1658** or 323/937-3930. Fax 323/932-1608. www.farmersdaughterhotel.com. 65 units. $115–$135 double; from $159 suite. AE, DISC, MC, V. Free on-site parking. **Amenities:** Restaurant and bar; swimming pool; concierge services; daily laundry/dry cleaning; morning coffee and tea service. *In room:* A/C, TV w/DVD player and complimentary DVD library, telephone with voice mail, minifridge, coffeemaker, personal safe, free high-speed Internet access, CD player.

HOLLYWOOD
EXPENSIVE

Renaissance Hollywood Hotel Part of the $615-million Hollywood & Highland project to restore Hollywood to the glory of its heyday, the Renaissance Hollywood opened in late 2001. The hotel now serves as Oscar-night headquarters for the frenzy of participants and paparazzi attending the Academy Awards at

(Kids) Family-Friendly Hotels

Best Western Marina Pacific Hotel & Suites (p. 477) gives families a place to stay just off the carnival-like Venice Boardwalk. The suites are a terrific choice for the brood: Each features a full kitchen, dining area, pullout sofa, and connecting door to an adjoining room that lets you form an affordable two-bedroom, two-bathroom suite.

Beverly Garland's Holiday Inn (p. 489) is a terrific choice for wallet-watching families: Rates are low, the North Hollywood location is close to Universal Studios (a free shuttle ride away), and kids stay and eat free.

The **Roosevelt Hotel, Hollywood** (p. 486) welcomes kids under 18 free with a parent. The heart-of-gentrified-Hollywood location makes an excellent base for families who want easy access to the touristy but fun Walk of Fame.

Hotel Oceana (p. 474) offers big apartment-style suites outfitted with all the conveniences of home. Kids will love the bright colors, the cushy furniture, the video games, and the location—across the street from the beach.

Magic Castle Hotel (p. 487) is a good budget choice, with roomy apartment-style suites and proximity to Hollywood Boulevard's family-friendly attractions.

Sheraton Universal Hotel (p. 490) enjoys a terrifically kid-friendly location, adjacent to Universal Studios and the fun CityWalk mall. Babysitting services are available, and there's a game room on the premises.

Wyndham Bel Age Hotel (p. 482) is a terrific all-suite hotel whose megasize suites feature everything a family requires, including a king-size sleeper sofa in the living area, VCR and PlayStation, and a wet bar with fridge that allows for easy prep of morning cereal. There's no extra-person charge for kids (rates include up to four per unit).

the Kodak Theatre next door. Despite its high profile, the hotel is principally a convention property and not quite as elite or elegant as the media hype might have you believe. Nonetheless, its commitment to the history of the area infuse it with far more personality than most chain hotels. Wood-paneled headboards and Technicolor furniture (think: *The Jetsons* meets Ikea) paint guest rooms as swinging '50s bachelor pads. Rooms on the seventh floor and up offer truly impressive views. One-third look toward the Pacific Ocean, one-third face the skyline of downtown L.A., and one-third take in the lush Hollywood Hills (yes, you can see the sign).

The hotel's location makes getting around on foot unusually easy in a town where most destinations require navigating L.A.'s notorious freeway system. Sightseeing is virtually unavoidable since the hotel shares the same block as two of the city's most famous landmarks—the Hollywood Walk of Fame and Grauman's Chinese Theatre. The Hollywood Bowl is less than a mile away (check with the concierge about shuttle service), and the subway stops under the complex, offering access to Universal Studios and destinations farther afield.

1775 N. Highland Ave., Hollywood, CA 90028. (C) **800/HOTELS-1** (Marriott) or 323/856-1200. Fax 323/856-1205. www.renaissancehollywood.com. 637 units. $249 double; $279 executive bedroom; $299

1-bedroom suite; other suites from $300 and way up. Discount rates and packages available. AE, DC, DISC, MC, V. Valet parking $22. **Amenities:** Restaurant; 2 bars (lobby and poolside); outdoor pool; small fitness room; concierge; business center; shopping complex; 24-hr. room service; dry cleaning. *In room:* A/C, TV w/pay movies, dataport, minibar, coffeemaker, hair dryer, iron, safe, robes, high-speed Internet access, CD player, 2-line cordless phone.

MODERATE

Roosevelt Hotel, Hollywood ★★ *Kids* This 12-story Hollywood landmark is located on an unabashedly touristy but no longer seedy section of Hollywood Boulevard—across from Grauman's Chinese Theatre and along the Walk of Fame. Host to the first Academy Awards in 1929—not to mention a few famous-name ghosts—this national landmark is Hollywood's only historic hotel still in operation today, and celebrated its 75th anniversary with a $15-million renovation that has harmoniously melded the Roosevelt's historical highlights with modern hotel luxuries. Much of the 1927 Spanish-influenced sunken lobby remains the same—the handcrafted columns and dramatic arches are magnificent—but the guest rooms have been completely—and tastefully—renovated with extralarge bathrooms, dark-wood platform beds with Frette linens, and all the latest hi-tech accessories. Rooms on the upper floors have unbeatable skyline views, while cabana rooms have a balcony or patio overlooking the Olympic-size pool, whose mural was originally painted by David Hockney. **Theodore's Restaurant** serves breakfast, lunch, and dinner daily, and the poolside **Tropicana Bar** is your new best friend, offering refreshing cocktails and great brick-oven pizzas. Also here is **Feinstein's at the Cinegrill,** a cool, dark, tier-leveled supper club hosted by celebrity performer Michael Feinstein. *Tip:* Request the "Steven Spielberg" room on the ninth floor—the view of Hollywood Boulevard is fantastic.

7000 Hollywood Blvd., Hollywood, CA 90028. © **800/950-7667** or 323/466-7000. Fax 323/462-8056. www.hollywoodroosevelt.com. 305 units. $179–$279 double; from $289 suite. Ask about AAA, senior, business, government, and other discounted rates (as low as $149 at press time). Children under 18 stay free in parent's room. AE, DC, DISC, MC, V. Valet parking $18. **Amenities:** Asian-fusion restaurant; cocktail lounge; Feinstein's at the Cinegrill cabaret and nightclub; outdoor pool and Jacuzzi; spa and fitness center; concierge; activities desk; room service (6am–11pm); babysitting; dry-cleaning/laundry service; executive-level rooms. *In room:* A/C, TV w/pay movies, high-speed dataport, minibar, coffeemaker, hair dryer, video games.

INEXPENSIVE

Best Western Hollywood Hills Hotel ★ Location is a big selling point for this family-owned (since 1948) member of the Best Western chain: It's just off U.S. 101 (the Hollywood Fwy.); a Metro Line stop just 3 blocks away means easy car-free access to Universal Studios, and Hollywood and Vine is just a 5-minute walk away. The walls showcase images from the golden age of movies, and the front desk offers an endless variety of arranged tours. Rooms are plain and clean but lack warmth—outer walls are painted cinder block, and closets are hidden behind metal accordion doors. Still, management is constantly striving to improve the hotel, and all rooms have a refrigerator, coffeemaker, microwave, and free movies. Rooms in the back building are my favorites, as they sit well back from busy Franklin Avenue, face the gleaming blue-tiled, heated outdoor pool, and have an attractive view of the neighboring hillside. A major convenience is the **101 Hills Coffee Shop** located off the lower lobby.

6141 Franklin Ave. (between Vine and Gower sts.), Hollywood, CA 90028. © **800/780-7234** or 800/287-1700 (in California only), or 323/464-5181. Fax 323/962-0536. www.bestwestern.com/hollywoodhillshotel. 86 units. $79–$129 double. AAA and AARP discounts available. AE, DISC, MC, V. Free covered parking. Small pets accepted with $25-per-night fee. **Amenities:** Coffee shop; heated outdoor pool; access to nearby health club; tour desk; coin-op laundry. *In room:* A/C, TV, dataport, fridge, coffeemaker, hair dryer, iron, microwave.

Days Inn Hollywood/Universal Studios   While it's east of the prime Sunset Strip action, this freshly renovated motel is safe and convenient, and extras like free underground parking and continental breakfast make it an especially good value. Rooms with two double beds are large enough for families. Some rooms have microwaves, fridges, and coffeemakers; if yours doesn't have a hair dryer or an iron, they're available at the front desk. It's usually easy to snare an under–$100 rate; for maximum bang for your buck, ask for a room overlooking the pool.

7023 Sunset Blvd. (between Highland and La Brea aves.), Hollywood, CA 90028. © 800/329-7466 or 323/464-8344. Fax 323/962-9748. www.daysinn.com. 72 units. $82–$160 double; $125–$200 Jacuzzi suite. Rates include continental breakfast. Ask about AAA, AARP, and other discounted rates (as low as $73 at press time). AE, DC, DISC, MC, V. Free secured parking. **Amenities:** Heated outdoor pool; dry-cleaning/laundry service. *In room:* A/C, TV.

Magic Castle Hotel *(Kids (Value*   Located a stone's throw from Hollywood Boulevard's attractions, this garden-style hotel/motel at the base of the Hollywood Hills offers L.A.'s best cheap sleeps. You won't see the Magic Castle Hotel in a shelter mag spread—the rooms are done in high Levitz style—but the newly refurbished units are spacious, comfortable, and well kept. Named for the Magic Castle, the illusionist club just uphill, the hotel was once an apartment building; it still feels private and insulated from Franklin Avenue's constant stream of traffic. The units are situated around a swimming-pool courtyard ensconced with trees. Most are full, extralarge apartments, with fully equipped kitchens with microwave and coffeemaker (grocery shopping service is available as well). Several units have balconies overlooking the large heated pool. Ideal for wallet-watching families or long-term stays.

7025 Franklin Ave. (between La Brea and Highland), Hollywood, CA 90028. © 800/741-4915 or 323/851-0800. Fax 323/851-4926. www.magiccastlehotel.com. 49 units. $99 double; $129–$219 suite. Extra person $10. Off-season and other discounts available. AE, DC, DISC, MC, V. Free secured parking. **Amenities:** Outdoor heated pool; full-service or coin-op laundry. *In room:* A/C, TV, dataport, coffeemaker, hair dryer, iron, safe.

DOWNTOWN
EXPENSIVE/MODERATE

How much you'll pay at any of the following hotels largely depends on when you visit. All become quite affordable once the business travelers go home; more often than not, rooms go for a relative song over holidays and weekends. Some even offer good-value weekday rates to leisure travelers during periods when rooms would otherwise sit empty.

Millennium Biltmore Hotel Los Angeles *本本*   The Biltmore is one of those hotels that's worth a visit even if you're not staying here. Built in 1923 and encompassing an entire square block, this Italian-Spanish Renaissance landmark is the grande dame of L.A.'s hotels. Chances are you've seen it in many movies, including *The Fabulous Baker Boys, Chinatown, Ghostbusters, Bugsy, Beverly Hills Cop,* and Barbra Streisand's *A Star Is Born.* The hotel lobby—JFK's campaign headquarters during the 1960 Democratic National Convention—appeared upside-down in *The Poseidon Adventure.* Always in fine shape and host to world leaders and luminaries, the former Regal Biltmore is now under the guiding hand of the Millennium Hotels and Resorts group, and the sense of refinement and graciousness endures. The "wow" factor ends at the guest rooms, however, which are a little on the small side (common for older hotels) and aren't quite as eye-popping as the public spaces, but they've recently been redecorated in a style that meshes well with the hotel's vibe. Bathrooms are on the small side as well, but peach-toned marble adds a luxurious edge.

A range of dining and cocktail outlets includes **Sai Sai** for Japanese cuisine. Pretty, casual **Smeraldi's Bistro** serves homemade pastas and lighter California fare. Off the lobby is the stunning **Gallery Bar,** named by *Los Angeles* magazine as one of the sexiest cocktail lounges in L.A. Afternoon tea and cocktails are served in the **Rendezvous Court,** which used to be the hotel's original lobby and resembles the interior of a Spanish cathedral, complete with a Moorish ceiling of carved beams and an altarlike baroque doorway. Spend the few bucks to appreciate the Art Deco health club, with its gorgeous Roman-style pool.

506 S. Grand Ave. (between Fifth and Sixth sts.), Los Angeles, CA 90071. ℭ 800/245-8673 or 213/624-1011. Fax 213/612-1545. www.millennium-hotels.com. 683 units. $174–$319 double; from $459 suite. Weekend discount packages available. AE, DC, DISC, MC, V. Parking $22. **Amenities:** 3 restaurants; 2 lounges; health club with original 1923 inlaid pool, Jacuzzi, steam, sauna; concierge; Enterprise car-rental desk; courtesy car; business center; salon; 24-hr. room service; in-room massage; babysitting; dry-cleaning/laundry service; executive-level rooms. *In room:* A/C, TV w/pay movies, dataport, minibar, hair dryer, laptop-size safe.

Westin Bonaventure Hotel & Suites 🏠🏠 This 35-story, 1,354-room monolith is the hotel that locals love to hate. The truth is that the Bonaventure is a terrific hotel. It's certainly not for travelers who want intimacy or personality in their accommodations—but with more than 20 restaurants and bars, a full-service spa, a monster health club, a Kinko's-size business center, and much more on hand, you'll be hard-pressed to want for anything here (except maybe some individualized attention). And with a $35-million renovation recently completed, this convention favorite has never looked better or felt fresher.

The hotel's five gleaming glass silos encompass an entire square block and form one of downtown's most distinctive landmarks. The six-story lobby houses fountains and trees (and, surprise, a Starbucks). A tangle of concrete ramps and 12 high-speed glass elevators lead to the extensive array of shops and services. Among the highlights are the rooftop **L.A. Prime Steak House** and revolving **BonaVista lounge,** both offering unparalleled views; and even a **Krispy Kreme Donut Stand** (Well that settles it!).

The pie-shaped guest rooms are on the small side, but a wall of windows offering great views, and Westin's unparalleled Heavenly Bed—the ultimate in hotel-bed comfort—make for a very comfortable cocoon. With an executive workstation, fax, and wet bar, guest office suites are great for business travelers, while tower suites—with a living room, an extra half-bathroom, minifridge, microwave, and two TVs—are ideal for families.

404 S. Figueroa St. (between 4th and 5th sts.), Los Angeles, CA 90071. ℭ 800/WESTIN-1 or 213/624-1000. Fax 213/612-4800. www.starwood.com/westin. 1,354 units. $227–$279 double; from $287 suite. Ask about theater packages. AE, DC, DISC, MC, V. Valet parking $19. **Amenities:** 17 restaurants and fast-food outlets; 5 bars and lounges; outdoor heated lap pool; 15,000-sq.-ft. full-service spa with exercise room, running track, and access to adjacent 85,000-sq.-ft. health club; Westin Kids Club; concierge; tour desk; Dollar Rent-a-Car desk; full-service business and copy center; shops; salon; 24-hr. room service; babysitting; dry-cleaning/laundry service; executive-club level. *In room:* A/C, TV w/pay movies and video games, high-speed Internet dataport, coffeemaker, hair dryer, iron, laptop-size safe.

INEXPENSIVE

Figueroa Hotel 🏠🏠 *(Finds)* With an artistic eye and a heartfelt commitment to budget travelers—particularly from Europe and Japan—owner Uno Thimansson has transformed a 1925-vintage former YWCA residence into L.A.'s best budget hotel. This enchanting 12-story property sits in an increasingly gentrified corner of downtown, within shouting distance of the Staples Center and a block from the Original Pantry Cafe, the landmark 24-hour breakfast house.

The big, airy lobby exudes a romantic Spanish colonial–Gothic vibe with beamed ceilings and soaring columns, tile flooring, ceiling fans, Moroccan chandeliers, and medievalist furnishings such as big floor pillows made of Kurdish grain sacks, Persian kilims, and exotic fabrics draped from the ceiling. Elevators lead to equally artistic guest rooms, which, though a bit dark and small, are very comfortable. Each comes with a firm, well-made bed with a wrought-iron headboard or canopy and a Georgia O'Keeffe–reminiscent spread, a Mexican-tiled bathroom, and Indian fabrics that double as blackout drapes. My favorite is no. 1130, a large double-queen with a Spanish terra cotta-print chaise, but you can't go wrong with any room. The Casablanca Suite is a Moroccan pleasure den, ideal for romance. Out back you'll find a gorgeous desert-garden deck with mosaic-tiled pool and Jacuzzi, and the **Verandah Bar,** the poolside place to go on warm Southern California nights for a minty *mojito,* that innocent-tasting Cuban-born libation of mint, lime juice, sugar and rum.

939 S. Figueroa St. (at Olympic Blvd.), Los Angeles, CA 90015. ℂ 800/421-9092 or 213/627-8971. Fax 213/689-0305. www.figueroahotel.com. 285 units. $94–$124 double; $195 Casablanca suite. AE, DC, MC, V. Parking $8. **Amenities:** Restaurant; bar; outdoor pool area with lounge chairs and Jacuzzi; dry-cleaning/laundry service. *In room:* A/C, TV, dataport, minifridge.

Hotel Stillwell   The Stillwell is far from fancy, but its modestly priced rooms are a good option in a generally pricey neighborhood. Built in 1906, this once-elegant 250-room hotel is conveniently located near the Staples Center, the Civic Center, and the Museum of Contemporary Art. Rooms are clean, basic, and simply decorated with decent furnishings; much-needed new paint and carpeting were added in 2000. The hotel is quiet, though, and hallways feature East Indian artwork. That said, I much prefer the Hotel Figueroa, but this is a less eccentric and perfectly reasonable choice. The lobby-level Indian restaurant is a popular lunch spot for downtown office workers; other options include a casual Mexican restaurant and so-old-it's-retro **Hanks Cocktail Lounge.**

838 S. Grand Ave. (between 8th and 9th sts.), Los Angeles, CA 90017. ℂ 800/553-4774 or 213/627-1151. www.hotelstillwell.com. Fax 213/622-8940. 250 units. $59 double; $75–$95 suite. AE, DC, DISC, MC, V. Parking $4.50. **Amenities:** 2 restaurants; lounge; activities desk; business center; coin-op laundry; dry-cleaning/laundry service. *In room:* A/C, TV, fax, fridge, iron.

SAN FERNANDO VALLEY & UNIVERSAL CITY
MODERATE

Beverly Garland's Holiday Inn (Kids)   The "Beverly Garland" in this 258-room hotel's name is the actress who played Fred MacMurray's wife on *My Three Sons.* Grassy areas and greenery abound at this North Hollywood Holiday Inn, a virtual oasis in the concrete jungle. The Mission-influenced buildings are a bit dated, but if you grew up with *Brady Bunch* reruns, this only adds to the charm—the spread looks like something Mike Brady would have designed. Southwestern-themed fabrics complement the natural-pine furnishings in the spacious guest rooms, attracting your attention away from the painted cinder-block walls. On the upside, all of the well-outfitted rooms have balconies overlooking the pleasant grounds, which include a pool and two lighted tennis courts. With Universal Studios just down the street and a free shuttle to the park, the location can't be beat for families. Since proximity to the 101 and 134 freeways also means the constant buzz of traffic, ask for a room facing Vineland Avenue for maximum quiet. *Tip:* If you're bringing the kids along, be sure to inquire about the "KidSuites"—an adjoining room designed just for kids.

4222 Vineland Ave., North Hollywood, CA 91602. ℂ 800/BEVERLY or 818/980-8000. Fax 818/766-0112. www.beverlygarland.com. 255 units. $149–$179 double; from $209 suite. Ask about AAA, AARP, corporate, military, Great Rates, weekend, and other discounted rates (from $109 at press time). Kids 12 and under stay free in parent's room and eat free. AE, DC, DISC, MC, V. Free parking. **Amenities:** Restaurant; heated outdoor pool; lighted tennis courts; sauna; car-rental desk; complimentary shuttle to Universal Studios. *In room:* A/C, TV, coffeemaker, hair dryer, iron.

Sheraton Universal Hotel ⭐ *Kids*   Despite the addition of the sleekly modern Hilton just uphill, the 21-story Sheraton is still considered "the" Universal City hotel of choice for tourists, businesspeople, and industry folks visiting the studios' production offices. Located on the back lot of Universal Studios, it has a spacious 1960s feel, with updated styling and amenities. Although the Sheraton does its share of convention/event business, the hotel feels more leisure-oriented than the Hilton next door (an outdoor elevator connects the two properties). Choose a Lanai room for balconies that overlook the lushly planted pool area, or a Tower room for stunning views and solitude. The hotel is very close to the Hollywood Bowl, and you can practically roll out of bed and into the theme park (via a continuous complimentary shuttle). An extra $35 per night buys a Club Level room—worth the money for the extra in-room amenities, plus free continental breakfast and afternoon hors d'oeuvres; business rooms also feature a movable workstation and a fax/copier/printer.

333 Universal Hollywood Dr., Universal City, CA 91608. © 800/325-3535 or 818/980-1212. Fax 818/985-4980. www.sheraton.com/universal. 436 units. $149–$219 double; from $350 suite. Children stay free in parent's room. Ask about AAA, AARP, and corporate discounts; also inquire about packages that include theme-park admission. AE, DC, DISC, MC, V. Valet parking $16; self-parking $11. **Amenities:** Casual indoor/outdoor restaurant; lobby lounge with pianist; Starbucks coffee cart in lobby; outdoor pool and whirlpool; health club; game room; concierge; free shuttle to Universal Studios every 15 min.; business center; room service (6am–midnight); babysitting; dry-cleaning/laundry service; executive-level rooms. *In room:* A/C, TV w/pay movies and video games, dataport, minibar, hair dryer and iron in club-level rooms, safe.

INEXPENSIVE

Best Western Mikado Hotel   This Asian-flavored garden hotel has been a Valley fixture for 40-plus years. A 1999 renovation muted but didn't obliterate the kitsch value, which extends from the pagoda-style exterior to the sushi bar (the Valley's oldest) across the driveway. Two-story motel buildings face two well-maintained courtyards, one with a koi pond and wooden footbridge, the other with a shimmering blue-tiled pool and hot tub. The face-lift stripped most of the Asian vibe from guest rooms, which are suitably comfortable and well outfitted. Furnished in 1970s-era chic (leather sofas, earth tones), the one-bedroom apartment is a steal, with enormous rooms and a full-size kitchen.

12600 Riverside Dr. (between Whitsett and Coldwater Canyon), North Hollywood, CA 91607. © 800/780-7234 or 800/433-2239 in California, or 818/763-9141. Fax 818/752-1045. www.bestwestern.com/mikadohotel. 58 units. $129–$139 double; $175 1-bedroom apt. Rates include full breakfast. Ask about AAA, senior, and other discounted rates (as low as $98 at press time). Extra person $10. Children under 12 stay free in parent's room. Rates include full American breakfast. AE, DC, DISC, MC, V. Free parking. **Amenities:** Japanese restaurant and sushi bar; cocktail lounge; outdoor pool and Jacuzzi; fax and copying services at front desk. *In room:* A/C, TV, dataport, coffeemaker, hair dryer, iron.

Safari Inn ⭐ *Finds*   This 1957-vintage motel is so retro that it—and its landmark neon sign—have starred in such films as *Apollo 13* and *True Romance*. Located just down the street from Universal Studios, the hotel's exterior is still gloriously intact (note the groovy wrought-iron railings and the floating stone fireplace in the lobby), while the interiors have been upgraded with a smart, colorful SoCal look and all the modern comforts. Everything within is 21st-century new, including the attractive IKEA-style furniture, the bright contemporary textiles and wall prints, and the modern bathrooms; about 10 rooms also have microkitchens (basically wet bars) with a microwave. *Attention families:* Book now to snare one of the two suites, which have pullout sofas, huge closets, full kitchens, and a second TV. Other amenities that elevate the Safari above the motel standard include an exercise room, room service from the modest but sur-prisingly good restaurant at the Anabelle Hotel (the Safari's sister property) next door, and valet service as well as self-serve laundry.

1911 W. Olive Ave., Burbank, CA 91506. ℂ **800/663-1144** or 818/845-8586. Fax 818/845-0054. www.safariburbank.com. 55 units. $109–$119 double; $168 suite. AAA and corporate rate $95. Extra person $10. AE, DC, DISC, MC, V. Free parking. Pets accepted with $100 deposit. **Amenities:** Restaurant and martini bar (in hotel next door); heated outdoor pool; exercise room; limited room service; coin-op laundry; dry-clean-ing/laundry service; sun deck. *In room:* TV w/pay movies, dataport, fridge, coffeemaker, hair dryer, iron.

PASADENA & ENVIRONS
VERY EXPENSIVE

The Ritz-Carlton, Huntington Hotel & Spa 🏨🏨🏨   Originally built in 1906, the opulent Huntington Hotel was one of America's grandest hotels, but not the most earthquake-proof. No matter—the hotel was rebuilt and opened on the same spot in 1991, and the astonishing authenticity (including reinstallation of many decorative features) even fools patrons from the resort's early days. This Spanish-Mediterranean beauty sits on 23 spectacularly landscaped acres that seem a world apart from L.A., though downtown is only 20 minutes away. Each oversize guest room is dressed in elegant Ritz-Carlton style, softened by English garden textiles and a beautiful palette of celadon, cream, and butter yellow. Lux-uries include beds dressed in Frette linens, marble bathrooms, thick carpets, and terry robes. You might consider spending a few extra dollars on a club-level room, which also features featherbeds, down comforters, CD players, coffee delivered with your wake-up call, and access to the club lounge with dedicated concierge and complimentary gourmet spreads all day (including breakfast).

The 12,000-square-foot full-service Ritz-Carlton Spa makes the Huntington an ideal place for a pampering getaway. Guests and locals enjoy dining in the casual elegance of **The Dining Room,** but I prefer the more casual California-style **Terrace Restaurant,** which also serves at umbrella-covered tables by the Olympic-size pool. High tea is served in the **Lobby Lounge.**

1401 S. Oak Knoll Ave., Pasadena, CA 91106. ℂ **800/241-3333** or 626/568-3900. Fax 626/568-3700. www.ritzcarlton.com. 392 units. $310–$420 double; from $415 suite. Discount packages always available. AE, DC, MC, V. Valet parking $21. Pets accepted. **Amenities:** 2 restaurants; 2 lounges (bar, Lobby Lounge for high tea); Olympic-size heated outdoor pool and Jacuzzi; 3 lighted tennis courts; full-service spa with whirlpool, sauna, and steam room; fitness center, concierge; business center; salon; 24-hr. room service; in-room mas-sage; babysitting; dry-cleaning/laundry service. *In room:* A/C, TV w/pay movies, dataport and high-speed con-nection, minibar, hair dryer, iron, laptop-size safe, CD player.

MODERATE

Artists' Inn & Cottage Bed & Breakfast   Pleasantly unpretentious and furnished with wicker throughout, this yellow-shingled Victorian-style inn was built in 1895 as a farmhouse and expanded to include a neighboring 1909 home. Each of the 10 rooms is decorated to reflect the style of a particular artist or period. Among the artistically inspired choices are the country-cozy New England–style Grandma Moses room; the soft, pastel-hued Degas suite; and the bold-lined, primary-hued Expressionist suite, a nod to such artists as Picasso and Dufy. Every room is thoughtfully arranged and features a private bathroom (many with period fixtures, three with Jacuzzi tubs), phone, fresh roses from the front garden, port wine, and chocolates. Most rooms have TVs; if yours doesn't, the innkeeper will provide one if you want it. The quiet residential location is just 5 minutes from the heart of Old Town Pasadena.

1038 Magnolia St., South Pasadena, CA 91030. ℂ **888/799-5668** or 626/799-5668. Fax 626/799-3678. www.artistsinns.com. 10 units. $120–$205 double. Rates include full breakfast and afternoon tea. Check for mid-week specials. Extra person $20. AE, MC, V. Free parking. *In room:* A/C, TV (upon request), dataport, hair dryer.

Bissell House Bed & Breakfast ✦   If you enjoy the true B&B experience, you'll love the Bissell House. Hidden behind hedges that isolate it from busy Orange Grove Avenue, this antiques-filled 1887 gingerbread Victorian—the former home of the vacuum heiress and now owned by hosts Russell and Leonore Butcher—offers a unique taste of life on what was once Pasadena's "Millionaire's Row." Outfitted in a traditional chintz-and-cabbage roses style, all individually decorated rooms have private bathrooms (one with an antique claw-foot, one with a whirlpool tub, two with shower only), individual heating and air-conditioning (a B&B rarity), Internet access, and comfortable beds. If you don't mind stairs, request one of the more spacious top-floor rooms. The modern world doesn't interfere with the mood in these romantic sanctuaries, but the downstairs library features a TV with VCR and a telephone/fax machine for guests' use. The landscaped grounds boast an inviting pool, Jacuzzi, and deck with lounge chairs. Included in the room rate is an elaborately prepared breakfast served in the large dining room, as well as an afternoon tea, cookies, and wine service.

201 Orange Grove Ave. (at Columbia St.), South Pasadena, CA 91030. ✆ 800/441-3530 or 626/441-3535. Fax 626/441-3671. www.bissellhouse.com. 6 units. $125–$185 double. Rates include full breakfast. AE, MC, V. Free parking. **Amenities:** Outdoor pool and Jacuzzi; CD and video libraries. *In room:* A/C, hair dryer, iron.

INEXPENSIVE

Saga Motor Hotel (Value   This 1950s relic of old Route 66 has far more character than most other motels in its price range. The rooms are small, clean, and simply furnished with the basics. The rooms with two double beds are spacious enough for shares, but budget-minded families will prefer the extralarge configuration dedicated to them, which has a king and two doubles. The best rooms are in the front building surrounding the gated swimming pool, shielded from the street and inviting in warm weather. The grounds are attractive and well kept, if you don't count the Astroturf "lawn" on the pool deck. The location is very quiet and very good, just off the Foothill (210) Freeway about a mile from the Huntington Library and within 10 minutes of both the Rose Bowl and Old Pasadena.

1633 E. Colorado Blvd. (between Allen and Sierra Bonita aves.), Pasadena, CA 91106. ✆ 800/793-7242 or 626/795-0431. Fax 626/792-0559. www.thesagamotorhotel.com. 70 units. $74–$92 double; $110–$130 family suite. Rates include continental breakfast. AE, DC, DISC, MC, V. Free parking. **Amenities:** Outdoor heated pool; free self-serve laundromat; dry-cleaning/laundry service. *In room:* A/C, TV, dataport.

4 Where to Dine

All cities are defined by their restaurants, and as one of the world's cultural crossroads, Los Angeles is an international atlas of exotic cuisines. Afghan, Argentinean, Armenian, Burmese, Cajun, Cambodian, Caribbean, Cuban, Ethiopian, Indian, Jewish, Korean, Lebanese, Moroccan, Oaxacan, Peruvian, Persian, Spanish, Thai, Vietnamese . . . well, you get the point. Whatever you're in the mood for, this town has it covered, and all you need to join the dinner party is an adventurous palate, because half the fun of visiting Los Angeles is experiencing worldly dishes that only a major metropolis can provide. And since it's L.A., there's always the added bonus of spotting celebrities.

Although it's those famous celebrity chef and celebrity-owned restaurants that attract most of the limelight, the majority of L.A.'s best dining experiences are at its neighborhood haunts and minimalls, the kind you'll never find unless someone lets you in on the city's dining secrets, and this section is full of them. However, limited space forced me to make tough choices; for a greater selection of reviews, pick up a copy of *Frommer's Los Angeles 2005,* also by yours truly. For additional late-night dining options, see "Late-Night Bites" under "Los Angeles After Dark," later in this chapter. To locate the restaurants reviewed below, see the individual neighborhood maps in section 1, "Orientation."

SANTA MONICA & THE BEACHES
EXPENSIVE

The Lobster 🦞🦞 SEAFOOD   There's been a seafood shack called The Lobster on the Santa Monica Pier since 1923—almost as long as the pier's been standing—but 2000's revival brings a new sophistication to the old favorite. The interior is completely rebuilt, but still accentuates a seaside ambience and a million-dollar ocean view; the menu has been revamped by chef Allyson Thurber, who brings an impressive culinary pedigree (including downtown's Water Grill) to the kitchen. Although the namesake crustacean from Maine is a great choice, the menu consistently presents a multitude of ultrafresh fish with thoughtful and creative preparation. Specialties range from spicy Louisiana prawns with dirty rice to Jumbo Lump Crab Cakes and an excellent sautéed North Carolina black bass luxuriating in white truffle sauce accompanied by lobster salad. Creative appetizers include *ahi* (tuna) carpaccio with tangy tobiko wasabi, steamed mussels and Manila clams with apple-wood bacon, and oysters plain or fancy. For something truly decadent, try the Kasu Marinated Seabass and pick a bottle of dry chardonnay from the well-stocked cellar. The menu offers a couple of fine steaks for landlubbers, and there's a practiced bar that serves lots of Bloody Marys garnished with jumbo shrimp to dedicated locals. For dessert, the strawberry shortcake and devil's food cake are terrific. *Tip:* Request a table on the deck and enjoy the 180-degree panoramic view of the Pacific.

1602 Ocean Ave. (at Colorado). 📞 310/458-9294. www.thelobster.com. Reservations recommended. Main courses $15–$32. AE, DC, DISC, MC, V. Mon–Thurs 11:30am–3pm and 5–10pm; Fri–Sat 11:30am–3pm and 5–11pm. Self-parking $3–$6.

Michael's 🦞🦞 CALIFORNIA   Owner Michael McCarty, L.A.'s answer to Alice Waters, is considered by many to be the father of California cuisine. Since Michael's opened in 1979 (when McCarty was only 25), several top L.A. restaurants have caught up to it, but this fetching Santa Monica venue remains one of the city's best. The dining room is filled with contemporary art by Michael's wife, Kim McCarty, and the restaurant's garden is Santa Monica's most romantic setting for always-inventive menu choices like Baqueta sea bass with a chanterelle-mushroom ragout and fresh Provençal herbs, seared Hawaiian ahi accented with braised enoki mushrooms and earthy-tangy sesame wasabi ponzu sauce, or grilled pork chop sweetened with sweet-potato purée and anise–pinot noir sauce. Don't miss Michael's famous warm mushroom salad, tossed with crumbled goat cheese, watercress, caramelized onion, and mustard-sage vinaigrette. The dry-aged New York strip is also fantastic, as are the steak *frites*.

1147 Third St. (north of Wilshire Blvd.), Santa Monica. 📞 310/451-0843. www.michaelssantamonica.com. Reservations recommended. Dinner main courses $28–$39; lunch $14–$23. AE, DC, DISC, MC, V. Mon–Fri noon–2:30pm and 6–10:30pm; Sat 5:30–10:30pm. Valet parking $5.50.

MODERATE

Border Grill 🦞🦞 MEXICAN   Before Mary Sue Milliken and Susan Feniger spiced up cable TV as "Too Hot Tamales," they started this restaurant in West Hollywood. Now Border Grill has moved to a boldly painted, cavernous (read: loud) space in Santa Monica, and the gals aren't in the kitchen very much at all (though cookbooks and paraphernalia from their Food Network show are

Finds L.A.'s Best Sushi & Stir-Fried Crickets

If you want to start a heated argument with L.A.'s foodies, just claim that you know where the best sushi in the city is served. Well, let the tongue-fu begin, because I'm claiming that **The Hump** ✮✮✮ (© **310/ 313-0977**; www.typhoon-restaurant.com) serves L.A.'s best sushi. If I'm ever on death row, I want my last meal to be a giant plate of sushi prepared by these master chefs. Much of the seafood here is flown in daily from Tokyo's Tsukijii and Fukuoka fish markets in oxygen-filled containers and is so fresh that the management had to put a sign at the entrance to warn the faint-of-heart from sitting at the sushi bar. Why? Because much of what they slice is still moving (when they cut the tails off the feisty giant sweet shrimp, they line up the flailing torsos conga-line style—it's like a macabre death dance).

Alongside Santa Monica Airport's runway, this small wedge-shaped Japanese restaurant bears the nickname aviators gave to the Himalayas. It's ranked among the top sushi restaurants in America but only has nine tables, so make a reservation a few days in advance. The specialties here are the *dengaku* (stuffed eggplant and avocado with seafood and miso sauce), live baby squid, live whitefish served in martini grass with a vinegary broth, hairy crab, live red snapper, and the most tender, flavorful baby hamachi I've ever had (and I live for hamachi). If you want to dine Ozzie-style, order the $220 snapping turtle (the blood goes well with a rich cabernet or port), the snake saki (yes, there's a snake in the bottle), and the blowfish (it's to die for). If the menu's all Greek to you, say *"omakase"* and get ready for a chef's choice seven-course seafood adventure. Skip the rolls—they're so huge you'll look like an idiot trying to eat one and they fill you up too fast—and don't be surprised if you spot a celebrity: Regulars include Harrison Ford, Calista Flockhart, Kurt Russell, Goldie Hawn, Dustin Hoffman, Meryl Streep, and Phil Jackson.

Directly below The Hump is the much larger **Typhoon** ✮✮ (© **310/ 390-6565**; www.typhoon-restaurant.com), a popular and high-energy Pan-Asian restaurant where stir-fried Taiwanese spicy crickets, dried Manchurian ants, and Thai-style crispy white sea worms punctuate a family-style menu filled with less exotic fare from throughout Southeast Asia. The huge open kitchen serves everything from Burma-style chicken wings (really hot!) to Filipino fried squid, Vietnamese pho soup, Mongolian lamb, and Thai-style garlic short ribs and deep-fried frogs' legs. Most items are in the $7 to $12 range. The well-stocked bar even offers a Chinese herb-infused vodka reputed to have aphrodisiac qualities. Both restaurants are on the second and third floors of the airport's administration building at 3221 Donald Douglas Loop Rd. in Santa Monica. Call, or visit their two-restaurants-for-one website for directions and hours.

displayed prominently for sale). But their influence on the menu is enough to maintain the cantina's popularity with folks who swear by the authentic flavor of Yucatan fish tacos, rock shrimp with ancho chilies, green corn tamales, and meaty *ropa vieja,* the traditional Latin stew. The best meatless dish is *mulitas de hongos,* a layering of portobello mushrooms, poblano chilies, black beans, cheese, and guacamole, spiced up with roasted garlic and seared red chard. The plantain empanadas with chipotle salsa and Mexican *crema* are also *muy bueno.* Distracting desserts are displayed near the entrance, so you may spend the meal fantasizing about the Aztec chocolate cake, coconut flan, or Key lime cheesecake. *Note:* A second location, Border Grill Pasadena, is at the Paseo Colorado shopping complex in Pasadena (260 E. Colorado Blvd.; © **626/844-8988**).

1445 Fourth St. (between Broadway and Santa Monica Blvd.), Santa Monica. © **310/451-1655.** www.bordergrill.com. Reservations recommended. Main courses $13–$25. AE, DC, DISC, MC, V. Mon 5–10pm; Tues–Thurs and Sun 11:30am–10pm; Fri–Sat 11:30am–11pm. Metered parking lots; valet parking $4.

Chez Melange ★★ BREAKFAST/CALIFORNIA   Located inside the modest Palos Verdes Inn, this "Spago of Redondo Beach" brasserie has been presenting artful California cuisine so long it's become a South Bay institution. Though the menu is no longer cutting-edge, it does seem to get more and more eclectic, moving seamlessly from Japanese to Cajun, Italian to Chinese, and keeping up-to-date with premium vodkas and a crowded oyster-and-seafood bar. The decor has a dated, late-1980s feel, but the conservative, moneyed crowd here doesn't mind. Each meal begins with a basket of irresistible breads before moving on to international dishes like shrimp and chicken in orange vindaloo curry over basmati rice with sweet, chunky chutney; rosemary-laced pork tenderloin and shallot-sherry cream sauce; Parmesan-crusted albacore with Greek feta salad and tabbouleh; or spicy blackened halibut sauced with horseradish and served with seafood gumbo. Spa-cuisine selections are available at every meal.

1716 Pacific Coast Hwy. (between Palos Verdes Blvd. and Prospect Ave.), Redondo Beach. © **310/540-1222.** www.chezmelange.com. Reservations recommended. Dinner main courses $13–$19; lunch $8–$13. AE, DISC, MC, V. Sun–Thurs 8am–9:30pm; Fri–Sat 8am–10pm. Free parking.

Hama Sushi ★★ *(Finds)*   It's called a sushi "bar" for a reason—a place where people gather to socialize, drink, and have a good time. Unfortunately, too many sushi bars in California focus more on presentation than salutation. So imagine my surprise when I walked into Hama Sushi for the first time and was greeted with a chorus of *"Heeeeeyyyyy!"* from the six jolly chefs behind the bar (along with a few well-juiced regulars). Because at Hama Sushi everybody's a somebody, and it's only a matter of time before you too are cheering newcomers and buying those madcap chefs another round of Sapporos. Located in Venice at the town's only roundabout, the restaurant is usually packed each night with regulars, so expect to wait a bit before diving into Hama's melt-in-your-mouth (literally) yellowtail, albacore, unagi, and specialty rolls. Standard Japanese hot plates such as chicken teriyaki and grilled Chilean sea bass are available as well (the grilled marinated squid is excellent), along with a wide selection of premium chilled sake. If it's your first visit, pass on the outside patio dining area and request a stool at the sushi bar to get the full Hama effect. *Tip:* Stay long enough to close the place down and you'll be in for a singing surprise.

213 Windward Ave., at Main St., Venice. © **310/396-8783.** Main courses $6–$13. AE, DC, DISC, MC, V. Mon–Fri 11:30am–2:30pm; Mon–Thurs 6–10:30pm; Fri–Sat 5:30–11pm; Sun 5–10pm. Valet parking $3.

Joe's Restaurant ★★ *Value* AMERICAN ECLECTIC   This is one of L.A.'s best dining bargains. Chef/owner Joeseph Miller excels in simple New American cuisine, particularly grilled fish and roasted meats accented with piquant herbs. Formerly a tiny, quirky storefront with humble elbow room, Joe gutted and completely remodeled the entire restaurant, adding a far more spacious dining room and display wine room (though the best tables are still tucked away on the trellised outdoor patio complete with a gurgling waterfall). But don't let the upscale additions dissuade your budgeted appetite—Joe's remains a hidden treasure for those with a champagne palate but a seltzer pocketbook. Case in point: For lunch an autumn vegetable platter of butternut squash purée, braised greens, grilled portobello mushrooms, and Brussels sprout leaves wilted with truffle oil and wild mushrooms goes for a mere $12. And this *includes* a fresh mixed green salad or one of Miller's exquisite soups. Dinner entrees are equally sophisticated: beet risotto with grilled asparagus, fallow deer wrapped in bacon (served in a black-currant sauce with a side of roasted root vegetables), monk-fish in a saffron broth, wild striped bass with curried cauliflower coulis. A double whammy is Joe's grilled ahi tuna *and* Hudson Valley foie gras appetizer served with rösti potatoes and a red-wine herb sauce, and the desserts are equally fantastic. *Tip:* Joe's four-course prix-fixe menu is a real bargain for under $40.

1023 Abbot Kinney Blvd., Venice. © 310/399-5811. www.joesrestaurant.com. Reservations required. Dinner main courses $18–$25; lunch $8–$15. AF, MC, V. Tues–Thurs noon–2:30pm and 6–10pm; Fri noon–2:30pm and 6–11pm; Sat 11am–2:30pm and 6–11pm; Sun 11:30am–2:30pm and 6–10pm. Free street parking or valet parking in rear of building.

INEXPENSIVE

Bread & Porridge ★ INTERNATIONAL/BREAKFAST   A dozen tables are all that compose this neighborhood cafe, but steady streams of locals mill outside, reading their newspapers and waiting for a vacant seat. Once inside, surrounded by the vintage fruit-crate labels adorning the walls and tabletops, you can sample the delicious breakfasts, fresh salads and sandwiches, and superaffordable entrees. There's a vaguely international twist to the menu, which leaps from breakfast quesadillas and omelets—all served with black beans and salsa—to the southern comfort of Cajun crab cakes and coleslaw to typical Italian pastas adorned with Roma tomatoes and plenty of garlic. All menu items are cheap—truck-stop cheap—but with an inventive elegance that truly makes this a best-kept secret. Get a short stack of one of five varieties of pancakes with any meal; this place thoughtfully serves breakfast all day.

2315 Wilshire Blvd. (3 blocks west of 26th St.), Santa Monica. © 310/453-4941. Main courses $6–$9. AE, MC, V. Mon–Fri 7am–2pm; Sat–Sun 7am–3pm. Metered street parking.

Jody Maroni's Sausage Kingdom ★ *Finds* SANDWICHES   Your cardiologist might not approve, but Jody Maroni's all-natural, preservative-free "haut dogs" are some of the best wieners served anywhere. The grungy walk-up (or in-line skate-up) counter looks fairly foreboding—you wouldn't know there was gourmet fare behind that aging hot-dog-stand facade, from which at least 14 different grilled-sausage sandwiches are served up. Bypass the traditional hot Italian and try the Toulouse garlic, Bombay curried lamb, all-chicken apple, or orange-garlic-cumin. Each is served on a freshly baked onion roll and smothered with onions and peppers. Burgers, BLTs, and rotisserie chicken are also served, but why bother?

Other locations include the Valley's Universal CityWalk (© **818/622-5639**), and inside LAX Terminals 3, 4, and 6, where you can pick up some last-minute vacuum-packed sausages for home. Having elevated sausage-worship to an art form, Jody's now boasts a helpful and humorous cookbook, plus its own website offering franchising opportunities.

2011 Ocean Front Walk (north of Venice Blvd.), Venice. ✆ 310/822-5639. www.maroni.com. Sandwiches $4–$6. No credit cards. Daily 10am–sunset.

Kay 'n Dave's Cantina *Kids* BREAKFAST/MEXICAN   A beach community favorite for "really big portions of really good food at really low prices," Kay 'n Dave's cooks with no lard and has a vegetarian-friendly menu with plenty of meat items, too. Come early (and be prepared to wait) for breakfast, as local devotees line up for five kinds of fluffy pancakes, zesty omelets, or one of the best breakfast burritos in town. Grilled tuna Veracruz, spinach and chicken enchiladas in tomatillo salsa, seafood fajitas tostada, vegetable-filled corn tamales, and other Mexican specialties are served in huge portions, making this mostly locals minichain a great choice to energize for (or reenergize after) an action-packed day of sightseeing. Bring the family—there's a kids' menu and crayons on every table.

262 26th St. (south of San Vicente Blvd.), Santa Monica. ✆ 310/260-1355. Reservations not accepted. Main courses $5–$10. AE, MC, V. Mon–Thurs 11am–9:30pm; Fri 11am–10pm; Sat 8:30am–10pm; Sun 8:30am–9:30pm. Metered street parking.

L.A.'S WESTSIDE & BEVERLY HILLS
EXPENSIVE

Crustacean *★★* SEAFOOD/VIETNAMESE   It's an amazing story how this Beverly Hills restaurant came to be. Helene An, matriarch and executive chef of the An family restaurants, is by title a Vietnamese princess, great-granddaughter of the vice-king of Vietnam. When she and her family fled from Saigon penniless in 1975, they relocated to San Francisco, purchased a small deli, and introduced the city to their now-legendary recipe: An Family's Famous Roast Crab and Garlic Noodles. From this single dish spawned a Horatio Alger story and a family restaurant dynasty. The Beverly Hills location is pure drama from the moment you walk in: You're immediately scrutinized by the patrons to see 1) if you're a somebody and 2) what you're wearing; but, you're too busy admiring the Indochina-themed decor—curvaceous copper bar, balcony seating, bamboo garden, waterfall, and an 80-foot-long "stream" topped with glass and filled with exotic koi—to notice. What you won't see is the Secret Kitchen (literally, it's off-limits to most of the staff), where the An family's signature dishes such as tiger prawns with garlic noodles, roasted lobster in tamarind sauce, and roast Dungeness crab are prepared. Although all these dishes are quite good, they're also heavy on the butter—I prefer the lighter sea-bass dish with ginger and garlic–black bean sauce. On weekend nights Helene (a real sweetheart and timeless beauty) is often holding court, making sure your dining experience is flawless.

9646 Little Santa Monica Blvd. (at Bedford St.), Beverly Hills. ✆ 310/205-8990. www.anfamily.com. Reservations recommended. Main courses $19–$26. AE, DC, DISC, MC, V. Mon–Fri 11:30am–2:30pm; Mon–Thurs 5:30–10:30pm; Fri–Sat 5:30–11:30pm. Valet parking $4.50.

The Ivy *★★* NEW AMERICAN   If you're willing to pay lots for a perfect meal, and willing to endure the cold shoulder to ogle L.A.'s celebrities, The Ivy can be enjoyable. This snobby place attracts one of the most industry-heavy crowds in the city, and treats celebrities and nobodies as differently as Brahmans and untouchables. Just past the cool reception lie two disarmingly countrified dining rooms filled with rustic antiques, comfortably worn chintz, and hanging

(Moments Sea Breezes & Sunsets: Oceanview Dining in Malibu

Gladstone's 4 Fish, 17300 Pacific Coast Hwy., at Sunset Boulevard (© 310/454-3474; www.gladstones.com). A local tradition, Gladstone's is immersed in the Malibu scene. It shares a parking lot with a public beach, so the wood deck has a constant view of surfers, bikini-clad sunbathers, and other beachgoers. At busy times, Gladstone's even sets up picnic-style tables on the sand. Prices are moderate, and the atmosphere is casual. The menu offers several pages of fresh fish and seafood, augmented by a few salads and other meals for landlubbers—it's mostly fried tourist food, but the large portions get the job done. Gladstone's is popular for afternoon/evening drinking and offers nearly 20 seafood appetizer platters; it's also known for decadent chocolate dessert, the Mile High Chocolate Cake, large enough for the whole table. Open Monday through Thursday from 11am to 11pm, Friday from 11am to midnight, Saturday from 7am to midnight, and Sunday from 7am to 11pm. Parking is $3.50.

Duke's Malibu ✿, 21150 Pacific Coast Hwy., at Las Flores Canyon (© 310/317-0777; www.dukesmalibu.com). Lovers of Hawaii and all things Polynesian will thrive in this outpost of the Hawaiian chain. Imagine a South Pacific T.G.I. Fridays where the food is secondary to the decor, then add a rocky perch atop breaking waves, and you have this surfing-themed crowd-pleaser. It's worth a visit for the memorabilia alone—the place is named for Hawaiian surf legend "Duke" Kahanamoku. Duke's offers up pretty good food at inflated, but not outrageous, prices. You'll find plenty of fresh fish prepared in the Hawaiian regional style, hearty surf and turf, a smattering of chicken and pasta dishes, and plenty of pupus to accompany Duke's Day-Glo tropical cocktails. Open Monday through Thursday from 11:30am to 10pm, Friday and Saturday from 11:30am to 10:30pm, and Sunday from 10am to 10pm. Valet parking $2 (dinner and weekends only, otherwise free self-parking).

Beau Rivage, 26025 Pacific Coast Hwy., at Corral Canyon (© 310/456-5733; www.beaurivagerestaurant.com). Though it's my only pick located on the *other* side of PCH from the beach, this romantic Mediterranean restaurant (whose name means "beautiful shore") has nearly unobstructed ocean views. The baby-pink villa and its flagstone dining patio are overgrown with flowering vines. The place is prettiest at sunset; romantic lighting takes over after dark. The menu is composed of country French and Italian dishes with plenty of moderately priced pastas, many with seafood. Other main courses are more expensive; they include chicken, duck, rabbit, and lamb, all traditionally prepared. An older, nicely dressed crowd dines at this special-occasion place. Open Monday through Saturday from 5 to 11pm, Sunday from 11am to 11pm. Valet parking $4 (Fri–Sat only, otherwise free self-parking). *Tip:* Sunday's brunch menu, which isn't limited to breakfast dishes, is a less pricey alternative to dinner.

baskets of fragrant flowers. Huge roses bloom everywhere, including out on the charming brick patio (where the highest-profile patrons are seated). The food is excellent. The Ivy's Caesar salad is perfect, as are the plump and crispy crab cakes. Recommended dishes include spinach linguine with a peppery tomato-basil sauce, prime rib dusted with Cajun spices, and tender lime-marinated grilled chicken. There's even a great burger. The wine list is notable, and there's always a terrific variety of desserts (pink boxes are on hand for chocolate-chip cookies to go).

113 N. Robertson Blvd. (between Third St. and Beverly Blvd.), West Hollywood. © **310/274-8303.** Reservations recommended on weekends. Dinner main courses $22–$38; lunch $10–$25. AE, DC, DISC, MC, V. Mon–Sat 11:30am–3pm; Sun 11am–3pm and 5:30–10:30pm; Mon–Thurs 6–11pm; Fri–Sat 6–11:30pm. Valet parking $4.50.

La Cachette 🐨🐨🐨 FRENCH   Widely considered one of the most influential French chefs in America, Jean Francois Meteigner literally wrote the book on *Cuisine Naturelle,* a revolutionary approach to fine French cuisine that eschews heavy creams, butter, and complex recipes in favor of dishes that are simple, light, full of flavor, and 90% free of cream and butter. Meteigner began his career as a chef in France, moved to Los Angeles in 1980 to serve as executive chef at L'Orangerie, then opened La Cachette ("The Hideaway") in 1994. On the edge of a residential neighborhood in Century City, the elegant, romantic white-on-white dining room is bit hard to find—you have to access it from an alley off Little Santa Monica Boulevard—but it only adds to the restaurant's charm. As a fan of rich lobster bisque, I found Meteigner's dairy-free crab and lobster bisque to be flavorful but lacking the richness that only cream can provide (cream is an option, however), and the escargot was bland, but all was forgiven as I devoured my entree: braised Kurobuta black pork shank with braised baby back ribs and Banyul vinegar sauce, with a side of roasted apples and Yukon mashed potatoes (it took effort not to lick the plate). Matching the right wine isn't a problem, as the wine list has earned the *Wine Spectator* Award of Excellence. The warm fruit tart is a fitting finale—light and flavorful.

10506 Santa Monica Blvd. (between Beverly Glen Blvd. and Overland Ave.), Century City. © **310/470-4992.** www.lacachetterestaurant.com. Reservations recommended. Dinner main courses $26–$35; lunch $15–$32. AE, DC, MC, V. Mon–Thurs 11:30am–2:30pm and 6–10pm; Fri–Sat 5:30–10:30pm; Sun 5:30–9pm. Valet parking $3.50.

Le Dôme 🐨🐨 WORLD CUISINE   For more than 25 years, Le Dôme was the place where eye-popping starlets hung out by the circular bar, hoping to be noticed by regulars such as Frank Sinatra, Kirk Douglas, Gregory Peck, Sly Stallone, and Richard Gere. But when the menu and decor started to get tired, it was closed in 2002 for a year-long $2-million makeover by designer *du moment* Dodd Mitchell and executive chef Sam Marvin. The result is a hybrid of old and new elements—both design (Tuscan-Gothic?) and dinner menu—and the word about town is that Le Dôme is back on again. That explains why Kobe Bryant was seated nearby, and why the lunch crowd is almost a sure bet for spotting a somebody dining at the outdoor terrace. Marvin's eclectic and enticing menu is still a work-in-progress, offering Le Dôme classics—Mediterranean fish soup, pasta with vodka and caviar, steamed mussels Belgian-style—along with trendier plates such as Japanese black pig baby back ribs, Kumamoto oysters, and "Vegetarian Ecstasy" (imagine The Chairman ordering *that*). Dishes I've tried and give the thumbs-up to are the grilled giant tiger prawns, the baby back ribs, the filet mignon steak tartare on walnut toast, the Maine diver scallops with asparagus risotto, and the rack of Colorado lamb rubbed with a minty Moroccan oil and served with couscous and Barolo wine sauce. The Harlequin chocolate soufflé with Grand Marnier sauce and Chantilly cream had me crooning.

8720 Sunset Blvd. (at N. Sherbourne Dr.), West Hollywood. ℂ 310/659-6919. Reservations recommended. Dinner main courses $22–$60; lunch $16–$26. AE, DC, MC, V. Mon–Thurs noon–3pm and 5:30–10:30pm; Fri–Sat 6:30–11:30pm; closed Sun. Valet parking $5.

Lucques ⭐⭐ FRANCO-MEDITERRANEAN Once Los Angeles became accustomed to this restaurant's unusual name—"Lucques" is a variety of French olive, pronounced "Luke"—local foodies fell hard for this quietly and comfortably sophisticated home of former Campanile chef Suzanne Goin. The old brick building, once silent star Harold Lloyd's carriage house, is decorated in mute, clubby colors with subdued lighting that extends to the handsome enclosed patio. Goin cooks with bold flavors, fresh-from-the-farm produce, and an instinctive feel for the food of the Mediterranean. The short and oft-changed menu makes the most of unusual ingredients like salt cod and oxtails. Standout dishes include Tuscan bean soup with tangy greens and pistou, grilled chicken served alongside spinach sautéed with pancetta and shallots, braised beef short ribs with potato purée and horseradish cream, and a perfect vanilla *pòt de crème* for dessert. Lucques's bar menu, featuring steak *frites* béarnaise, omelets, and tantalizing hors d'oeuvres (olives, warm almonds, sea salt, chewy bread), is a godsend for late-night diners, and the bartenders make a mean vodka Collins. *Insider Tip:* On Sunday Lucques offers a bargain $35 prix-fixe three-course dinner from a weekly changing menu.

8474 Melrose Ave. (east of La Cienega), West Hollywood. ℂ 323/655-6277. www.lucques.com. Reservations recommended. Main courses $18–$30. AE, DC, MC, V. Mon 6–11pm; Tues–Sat noon–2:30pm and 6pm–midnight; Sun 5:30–10pm. Closed the last 2 weeks of Aug. Metered street parking or valet ($3.50).

Maple Drive ⭐⭐ NEW AMERICAN Located in a quiet Beverly Hills neighborhood, Maple Drive is well known for attracting the big celebrities: Barbra, Elton, Arnold, and their ilk usually enter through a second, more discreet, door and sit in secluded booths in back of the multilevel dining room. Although the Maple Drive classics—meatloaf, Caesar salad, "Kick Ass Chili"—are still available, the eclectic menu has an entirely new look since chef Eric Klein quit his executive sous chef position at Spago to remake this Beverly Hills landmark in August 2003. You're bound to meet the beefy Alsatian and his wife, Tori, as they both work the dining room several times nightly to greet guests. About the only thing stronger than Klein's handshakes are his sauces, which, unfortunately, severely overpowered the sashimi of diver scallops appetizer I ordered. The flavorful Hunan skirt steak, however, benefited from Klein's rich, dark sauce and a glass of David Bruce zinfandel. Be sure to start with a family-style order of the thin-crusted tarte flambé with wild mushrooms, followed by the superb heirloom beet salad. On warm nights the best seats are out on the patio, and the live jazz trio and provocative photography by Aleta Ashley certainly enhance the cool dinner vibe. *Tip:* For a really different dining experience, request seating for two at the open kitchen's stainless-steel counter—it's a front-row seat to the best cooking show in Beverly Hills.

345 N. Maple Dr. (at Alden Dr.), Beverly Hills. ℂ 310/274-9800. www.mapledriverestaurant.com. Reservations recommended. Dinner main courses $15–$42; lunch $12–$22. AE, DC, MC, V. Mon–Fri 11:30am–2:45pm; Mon–Sat 6–10pm. Limited street parking. Valet $4.

Mastro's Steakhouse ⭐⭐⭐ STEAKS/SEAFOOD Down the street from Spago—so you know it's expensive—is one of the best steakhouses in Southern

California: Mastro's. Typical of an upscale steakhouse, the dimly lit dining room on the first floor has a dark, leathery, serious men's club feel to it, so be sure to request a table on the second floor where the bar, live music, and cool vibe are located. Slide into a black leather booth, order a Mastro dry ice martini (which come with the shaker, so it only takes one to get a groove on), and start the feast off with an Iced Seafood Tower—a massive pyramid of crab legs, lobster, shrimp, clams, and oysters the size of your palm. Oh, and I've found the beef: Fred Flint-stone–size slabs of hand-cut USDA beef served on sizzling plates heated to 400°F (204°C) so your steak stays warm and juicy throughout the meal. Forget the greens—the only side you need is the Mastro Mash, a big bowl of creamy mashed potatoes mixed with sour cream, chives, bacon, and butter. ("I'll have a Diet Coke with that."). The bad news is that a bone-in rib-eye runs about $50; the good news is that one will feed three normal-size people. The white-jacketed waiters are friendly and attentive, and be sure to say hello to the manager, Jin Yu—he's got some stories to tell about this celebrity-filled joint.

246 N. Canon Dr. (between Dayton Way and Wilshire Blvd.), Beverly Hills. © 310/888-8782. www. mastrossteakhouse.com. Reservations recommended. Dinner main courses $26–$84. AE, DC, MC, V. Mon–Thurs 11am–1pm and 5–11pm; Fri–Sat 5pm–midnight; Sun 5–11pm. Valet parking $7.

Matsuhisa ✿✿✿ JAPANESE/PERUVIAN   Japanese chef/owner Nobuyuki Matsuhisa arrived in Los Angeles via Peru in 1987 and opened what may be the most creative restaurant in the city. A true master of fish cookery, Matsuhisa creates unusual dishes by combining Japanese flavors with South American spices and salsas (he was the first to introduce Americans to yellowtail sashimi with sliced jalapeños). Broiled sea bass with black truffles, miso-flavored black cod, sautéed squid with garlic and soy, tempura sea urchin in a shiso leaf, and Dungeness crab tossed with chilies and cream are just a few examples of the masterfully prepared dishes that are available in addition to thickly sliced nigiri and creative sushi rolls. Matsuhisa is perennially popular with celebrities and hardcore foodies, so reserve well in advance for those hard-to-get tables. The small, crowded main dining room suffers from poor lighting and precious lack of privacy; many big names are ushered through to private dining rooms. Expect a bit of attitude from the staff as well. *Tip:* If you're feeling adventurous, ask for *omakase* and the chef will personally compose a selection of eccentric dishes.

129 N. La Cienega Blvd. (north of Wilshire Blvd.), Beverly Hills. © 310/659-9639. www.nobumatsuhisa.com. Reservations recommended. Main courses $15–$50; sushi $4–$13 per order; full omakase dinner from $65. AE, DC, MC, V. Mon–Fri 11:45am–2:15pm; daily 5:30–10:15pm. Valet parking $3.50.

The Palm ✿✿ STEAKS/LOBSTER   Every great American city has a renowned steakhouse; in Los Angeles it's The Palm. The child of the famous New York restaurant of the same name, The Palm is widely regarded by local foodies as one of the best traditional American eateries in the city. The glitterati seem to agree, as stars and their handlers are regularly in attendance. In both food and ambience, this West Coast apple hasn't fallen far from the proverbial tree. The restaurant is brightly lit, bustling with energy, and playfully decorated with dozens of celebrity caricatures on the walls. Live Nova Scotia lobsters are flown in almost daily, then broiled over charcoal and served with big bowls of melted butter. Most are an enormous 3 to 7 pounds and, although they're obscenely expensive, can be shared. The steaks and swordfish are similarly sized, perfectly grilled to order, and served a la carte by cheeky white-jacketed waiters who have been around since the Nixon administration. Diners also swear by the creamed spinach and celebrated Gigi Salad—a mixture of lettuce, shrimp,

> **Tips** **The ABCs of Grading Restaurant Cleanliness**
>
> There's something far more valuable to Wolfgang Puck than having movie stars dine at his world-famous Spago restaurant. If he doesn't earn an "A" by the city's health department, then he might as well "86" his hoity-toity Beverly Hills business. Here's the scoop: The L.A. County Department of Health Services started issuing report cards on restaurants' cleanliness and food-handling practices in the late 1990s, and now all of L.A.'s 37,000 retail food establishments are required to post their letter grades prominently or face closure. Anything less than a big blue "A" means bad business for a restaurant owner, since only about one in four residents will dine at a "B" restaurant (I've never even seen a "C" placard). Inevitably, those "A" placards have become a hot commodity, so much so that restaurateurs with "B" or "C" grades are stealing the "A" (which is why you'll usually see tape around those "A" signs). Offenses include hair in food, chipped dishware, and waitstaff with dirty fingernails. The program has been so effective in improving restaurant standards that other major cities around the world are looking into similar programs.

bacon, green beans, pimento, and avocado. For dessert, stick with The Palm's perfect New York cheesecake, flown in straight from the Bronx.

9001 Santa Monica Blvd. (between Doheny Dr. and Robertson Blvd.), West Hollywood. ℂ 310/550-8811. www.thepalm.com. Reservations recommended. Dinner main courses $17–$41; lobsters $18 per lb.; lunch $10–$19. AE, DC, MC, V. Mon–Fri noon–10:30pm; Sat 5–10:30pm; Sun 5–9:30pm. Valet parking $4.

Spago Beverly Hills ★★★ CALIFORNIA Wolfgang Puck is more than a great chef, he's also a masterful businessman and publicist who has made Spago one of the best-known restaurants in the United States. Despite all the hoopla—and 23 years of stiff competition—Spago remains one of L.A.'s top-rated restaurants. Talented Puck henchman Lee Hefter presides over the kitchen, delivering the culinary sophistication demanded by an upscale Beverly Hills crowd. This high-style indoor/outdoor space glows with the aura of big bucks, celebrities, and the perfectly honed California cuisine that can honestly take credit for setting the standard. Spago is also one of the last places in L.A. where men will feel most comfortable in jacket and tie (suggested, but not required). All eyes may be on the romantically twinkle-lit outdoor patio (the most coveted tables), but the food takes center stage. You simply can't make a wrong choice—highlights include the appetizer of foie gras "three ways," crawfish salad, savory duck either honey-lacquered and topped with foie gras or Cantonese-style with a citrus tang, slow-roasted Sonoma lamb with braised greens, and rich Austrian dishes from "Wolfie's" childhood, like spicy beef goulash or perfect veal schnitzel.

176 N. Canon Dr. (north of Wilshire). ℂ 310/385-0880. www.wolfgangpuck.com. Reservations required. Jacket and tie advised for men. Main courses $18–$34; tasting menu $85. AE, DC, DISC, MC, V. Mon–Sat 11:30am–2:30pm; Sun–Thurs 6–10:30pm; Fri–Sat 5:30–10:30pm. Valet parking $4.50.

MODERATE

Bombay Café ★★ INDIAN This friendly sleeper may be L.A.'s best Indian spot, serving excellent curries and kurmas typical of South Indian street food. Once seated, immediately order *sev puri* for the table; these crispy little chips topped with chopped potatoes, onions, cilantro, and chutneys are the perfect accompaniment to what's sure to be an extended menu-reading session. Also recommended are the burrito-like "frankies," juicy little bread rolls stuffed with lamb, chicken, or cauliflower. The best dishes come from the tandoor and include spicy yogurt-marinated swordfish, lamb, and chicken. While some dishes are authentically spicy, plenty of others have a mellow flavor for less incendiary palates. This restaurant is phenomenally popular and gets its share of celebrities.

12021 W. Pico Blvd. (at Bundy Dr.), Los Angeles, CA 90064. ✆ 310/473-3388. Reservations recommended for dinner. Main courses $9–$17. MC, V. Mon–Fri 11:30am–3pm; Sun–Thurs 5–10pm; Fri–Sat 5–11pm. Metered street parking (lunch); valet parking $3.50 (dinner).

Frida 🌟🌟 *Finds* MEXICAN   The last time I had Mexican food this good I was living on the shores of Lake Chapala near Guadalajara. Made from recipes handed down by the owner's ancestors, the Mexican cuisine at Frida is as traditional and authentic as it gets on this side of the border. It's the kind of food you find when you're so far south of Tijuana that the culture appears more Mayan than Mexican. Both the friendly owner and waiters are justly proud of the dishes they present as patrons tuck into handmade soft tacos brimming with sautéed shrimp bathed in a dark, tangy *pasilla*-orange sauce (fantastic), or generous portions of *carnitas* in an annatto-seed sauce topped with onion-habanero relish and served over fresh corn tortillas. And we've only started. Ceviches, sopas, ensalads, moles, pescados, carnes—there's so many choices of dishes you've probably never heard of that it helps to enlist the advice of the waitstaff. Trust me on a couple, though: the dark, rich chicken mole simmered in ground-pumpkin-seed sauce, and the *Filete Tentacion:* charbroiled filet mignon on a bed of dry chile and Mexican truffle sauce *(cuitlacoche),* topped with goat cheese and jalapeño sauce, and served with a side of grilled chayote squash. The wide selection of margaritas are the perfect accompaniment to the spicy dishes. Even the velvety refried beans were the best I've ever had. I claim some expertise here, since I grew up eating my Mexican neighbor Anna's hand-mashed frijoles. If you like authentic Mexican cuisine, *Ay! Chiwawa!* will you love Frida.

236 S. Beverly Dr. (between Charleville Blvd. and Gregory Way), Beverly Hills, CA 90212. ✆ **310/278-7666.** Fax 310/278-9699. www.fridarestaurant.com. Reservations recommended. Dinner main courses $6–$27; lunch $6–$32. AE, DC, MC, V. Mon–Sat 11am–10:30pm; Sun 2–9pm. Valet parking $5.

Il Pastaio 🌟🌟 NORTHERN ITALIAN   Sicilian-born chef Giacomino Drago (scion of L.A.'s well-known Drago restaurateur family) hit the jackpot with this successful, value-priced cafe, on a busy corner in the shopping district of Beverly Hills. All day long Giacomino's fans take a break from work or shopping and converse over glasses of chianti and plates of oh-so-authentic pasta. With 57 menu items to choose from, I haven't come close to trying everything, but I can tell you with certainty that you will swoon over the *arancini,* breaded rice cones that are filled with mozzarella cheese and peas then fried crispy brown (highly addictive); the pumpkin tortelloni in a light sage and cream sauce; the *arrabbiata,* a simple penne pasta dish in a fantastic spicy tomato-and-garlic sauce; and for dessert the panna cotta (the silkiest in the south). There's almost always a wait—and not much room to wait in—but by meal's end it always seems worth it.

400 N. Canon Dr. (at Brighton Way), Beverly Hills. ✆ 310/205-5444. Dinner main courses $16–$25; lunch $8–$14. AE, DC, MC, V. Mon–Sat 11:30am–11pm; Sun 5–10pm.

Koi Restaurant 🌟🌟 ASIAN-FUSION   If your goal is to spot Hollywood's A-list of celebrities, make a reservation at Koi, the current fave of L.A.'s glam scene: George Clooney, Jennifer Garner, the Osbournes, Madonna, Demi and Ashton, Jessica and Nick, Liv Tyler, J-Lo, Martin Lawrence—they're all spotted here with regularity. Or just make a reservation because the food is so damn good. Either way, you won't be disappointed. Incorporating feng shui elements of trickling water, votive candles, open-air patios, and soft lighting, the minimalist earthen-hued interior has a calming ambience that is a relief from the hectic Melrose scene outside the ornately carved gates. Exec chef Stephane Chevet's brilliant fusions of Japanese and California cuisine accounts for the repeat clientele. Start with the cucumber sunomono tower flavored with sweet vinegar and edible flowers, followed by baked crab roll with edible rice paper, the tuna tartare and avocado on crispy won tons, the yellowtail carpaccio delicately flavored with grape-seed oil, and the house specialty, black cod bronzed with miso that's warm-butter soft and exploding with sweet flavor. *Tip:* Request one of the horseshoe booths on the back patio amid Buddha statues and candlelight.

730 N. La Cienega Blvd. (between Melrose Ave. and Santa Monica Blvd.), West Hollywood. ℂ 310/659-9449. www.koirestaurant.com. Reservations recommended. Dinner main courses and lunch $13–$27. AE, DC, DISC, MC, V. Mon–Thurs 11:30am–2:30pm and 6:30–11pm; Fri–Sat 6:30pm–midnight; Sun 6:30–10pm. Valet parking $5.

Zen Grill & Sake Lounge 🎏🎏 PAN ASIAN   L.A.'s rising star of interior design, Dodd Mitchell, has wowed 'em again with his elements-of-the-earth approach to restaurant design at this new Westwood Village hot spot. Bathed in a soothing amber glow, it takes a few moments for the eye to take in all of Mitchell's Asian-inspired design elements: dark ebony woods, lacquered cement walls, enigmatic images of Buddhist temples and koi ponds, and a sweeping staircase with Chinese abacus railings—it's like dining in the world's hippest opium den. Befitting the decor is a pan-Asian menu with Thai, Indian, Japanese, Korean, and Chinese influences. Dishes are served family-style; recommended starters are the minced-chicken-and-lettuce cups with Hoisen sauce, shrimp dumplings, tuna rice tower, Mongolian lamb with jasmine rice, and my favorite dish, Chilean sea bass simmered in a light caramelized sauce. It took a couple of Happy Buddhas—a refreshing cocktail made with schochu Japanese vodka, cranberry, pineapple juice, and herbal tonic—to awaken my inner self, but nobody's in a hurry to leave this Asian oasis. After a dessert of sautéed bananas topped with ice cream and drizzled with chocolate and caramel sauce, head upstairs to the sake loft and order a sweet/strong glass of unfiltered nigori.

1051 Broxton Ave. at Weyburn, Westwood Village. ℂ 310/209-1994. Fax 310/209-1984. www.zengrill sakelounge.com. Reservations recommended. Dinner main courses $8–$26; lunch $8–$10. AE, DC, MC, V. Mon–Fri 11:30am–2:30pm and 5–10:30pm; Fri–Sat 5–11:30pm. Free parking.

INEXPENSIVE

The Apple Pan 🎏 SANDWICHES/AMERICAN   There are no tables, just a U-shaped counter, at this classic American burger shack and hugely popular L.A. landmark. Open since 1947, the Apple Pan is a diner that looks—and acts—the part. It's famous for juicy burgers, speedy service, and an authentic frills-free atmosphere. The hickory burger is best, though the tuna sandwich also has its share of fans. Ham, egg-salad, and Swiss-cheese sandwiches round out the menu. Definitely order fries and, if you're in the mood, the house-baked apple pie, too. Expect to wait a bit during the lunch rush.

10801 Pico Blvd. (east of Westwood Blvd.). ℂ 310/475-3585. www.applepan.com. Most menu items under $6. No credit cards. Tues–Thurs and Sun 11am–midnight; Fri–Sat 11am–1am. Free parking.

Versailles 🎏 *Value* CARIBBEAN/CUBAN   Outfitted with Formica tabletops and looking something like an ethnic IHOP, Versailles feels much like any number of Miami restaurants that cater to the Cuban community. The menu reads like a veritable survey of Havana-style cookery and includes specialties like

---

Tips   Stars in Your Eyes

If you're searching for incognito celebrities dining among us common folk, around 1pm casually stroll past the elevated sidewalk patio at **The Ivy**, 113 N. Robertson Blvd. (between Third St. and Beverly Blvd.), West Hollywood. On a sunny day, the odds are good (though the goods may be odd). If that doesn't pan out, walk over to **The Palm**, 9001 Santa Monica Blvd. (between Doheny Dr. and Robertson Blvd.), West Hollywood, and order a Coke at the bar, followed by a long, leisurely trip to the risqué bathroom.

"Moors and Christians" (black beans with white rice), *ropa vieja* (a stringy beef stew), *eastin lechón* (suckling pig with sliced onions), and fried whole fish (usually sea bass). Anybody who's eaten here will tell you the same thing: "Order the shredded roast pork." Tossed with the restaurant's trademark garlic-citrus sauce, it's highly addictive. Equally as fetching is the chicken—succulent, slow roasted, smothered in onions and either garlic-citrus sauce or barbecue sauce. Almost everything is served with black beans and rice; wine and beer are available. Because meals are good, bountiful, and cheap, there's often a wait.

Another Versailles restaurant is in Culver City at 10319 Venice Blvd. (© **310/ 558-3168**).

1415 S. La Cienega Blvd. (south of Pico Blvd.). © 310/289-0392. Main courses $5–$11. AE, MC, V. Daily 11am–10pm. Free parking.

HOLLYWOOD
EXPENSIVE
Campanile   ★★★   BREAKFAST/CALIFORNIA-MEDITERRANEAN
Built as Charlie Chaplin's private offices in 1928, this Tuscan-style building has a multilevel layout with flower-bedecked interior balconies, a fountain, and a skylight through which diners can see the campanile (bell tower). The kitchen, headed by Spago alumnus chef/co-owner Mark Peel, gets a giant leg up from pastry chef/co-owner (and wife) Nancy Silverton, who also runs the now-legendary La Brea Bakery next door. Consistently ranked as one of L.A.'s finest restaurants, a meal here might begin with fried zucchini flowers drizzled with melted mozzarella or lamb carpaccio surrounded by artichoke leaves—a dish that arrives looking like one of van Gogh's sunflowers. Chef Peel is known for his grills and roasts; try the wood-grilled prime rib smeared with black-olive tapenade or pappardelle with braised rabbit, roasted tomato, and collard greens; or the rosemary-charred lamb with artichokes and fava beans. The cedar-smoked trout with fennel salad is also excellent. And don't skip desserts: Nancy's many fans have turned her dessert book into a bestseller (the sour-cherry brioche is fabulous). The weekend brunch is a surprising crowd-pleaser and a terrific way to appreciate this beautiful space on a budget.

624 S. La Brea Ave. (north of Wilshire Blvd.). © 323/938-1447. www.campanilerestaurant.com. Reservations required. Main courses $26–$38. AE, DC, DISC, MC, V. Mon–Fri 11:30am–2:30pm; Sat–Sun 9:30am–1:30pm; Mon–Thurs 6–10pm; Fri–Sat 5:30–11pm. Valet parking $3.50.

MODERATE
Ca' Brea ★★ NORTHERN ITALIAN   When Ca' Brea opened in 1990, its talented chef/owner, Antonio Tommasi, was catapulted into a spotlight shared by only a handful of L.A. chefs—Wolfgang Puck, Michel Richard, and Joachim Splichal. Since then, Tommasi has opened two other celebrated restaurants,

Locanda Veneta in Hollywood and **Ca' Del Sole** in the Valley, but, for many, Ca' Brea remains tops. The Venetian-style trattoria's refreshingly bright two-story dining room is a cheerful place, hung with colorful, oversize contemporary paintings and backed by an open prep-kitchen where you can watch as your seafood cakes are sautéed and your Napa cabbage braised. Booths are the most coveted seats, but with only 20 tables in all, just be thankful you're sitting any-where. Detractors might complain that Ca' Brea isn't what it used to be since Tommasi began splitting his time between three restaurants, but Tommasi stops in daily and keeps a very close watch over his handpicked staff. Consistently excellent dishes include the roasted pork sausage, the butter squash–stuffed ravi-oli, and a different risotto each day—always rich, creamy, and indulgent.

346 S. La Brea Ave. (north of Wilshire Blvd.). 𝄢 323/938-2863. www.cabrearestaurant.com. Reservations recommended. Dinner main courses $9–$21; lunch $7–$20. AE, DC, MC, V. Mon–Fri 11:30am–2:30pm; Sun–Thurs 5:30–10:30pm; Fri–Sat 5:30–11pm. Valet parking $3.50.

Paladar 𝄐𝄐 CUBAN   In Cuba *paladares* are small, privately owned restau-rants in people's homes that offer authentic, home-cooked meals at affordable prices. This explains Paladar's unique "room-within-a-room" design using ornate steel-grill partitions, a stylish illusion meant to make guests feel as if they're din-ing in different parts of a house. Currently one of L.A.'s most "in" restaurants, this hot spot is all about *Nuevo Cubano*—from the unique plaster-and-tobacco-leaf wallpaper to chef Joe Herreros's Afro-Cuban-American menu. If you like pork chops, you're in luck: Their specialty is an 1½-inch thick grilled chop topped with mango/quince chutney and served with a side of boniato sweet-potato mash. Other standouts are the boiled Yucca salad with spiced onion and a citrus mojo vinaigrette, the oxtail soup, and the grilled octopus served over a plantain-and-cranberry bean salsa. Some of Herreros's arrangements work better than others, but the experience is worth the pesos (a sure bet is the roasted jerk chicken, marinated and served with roasted garlic mash). All entrees come with sides such as plantains, yucca mash, and rice and beans. *Tip:* After dinner, head to the bar in the back and warm your chichis with a few Key lime *mojitos*.

1651 Wilcox Ave., at Hollywood Blvd., Hollywood. 𝄢 323/465-7500. Main courses $8–$13. AE, DC, DISC, MC, V. Mon–Fri 11:30am–midnight; Sat–Sun 6pm–midnight. Valet parking $4.50.

Sofi 𝄐 *Finds* GREEK   Look for the simple black awning over the narrow pas-sageway that leads from the street to this hidden Aegean treasure. Be sure to ask for a table on the romantic patio amid twinkling lights, and immediately order a plate of their thick, satisfying *tsatziki* (yogurt-cucumber-garlic spread) accompanied by a basket of warm pita for dipping. Other specialties (recipes courtesy of Sofi's

---

Tips **Hallelujah! A Brunch Worth Singing About**

Have mercy and say Hallelujah! for the Gospel Brunch at the **House of Blues.** For more than a decade, it's been a Sunday tradition at the HOB to feed both the body and soul with gospel performances and heaping plates of all-you-can-eat Southern home cookin'. Every week different gospel groups from around the region perform uplifting and energetic music that gets the crowd on their feet and raising the roof. Seatings are every Sun-day at 10am and 1pm. Tickets are $33 including tax and gratuity and are available through the HOB Sunset Strip box office; call 𝄢 323/848-5100. 8430 Sunset Blvd., West Hollywood. www.hob.com.

old-world grandmother) include herbed rack of lamb with rice, fried calamari salad, *saganaki* (kasseri cheese flamed with ouzo), and other hearty taverna favorites. Sofi's odd, off-street setting, near the Farmers Market in a popular part of town, has made it an insiders' secret.

8030¾ W. Third St. (between Fairfax Ave. and Crescent Heights Blvd.). ℰ 323/651-0346. Reservations recommended. Main courses $7–$14. AE, DC, MC, V. Mon–Sat 11:30am–3pm; daily 5:30–11pm. Metered street parking or valet parking $3.

INEXPENSIVE

El Cholo ℛ MEXICAN   L.A.'s oldest Mexican restaurant, El Cholo has been serving up authentic Mexican cuisine in this pink adobe hacienda since 1927, even though the once-outlying mid-Wilshire neighborhood around them has since turned into Koreatown. El Cholo's expertly blended margaritas, invitingly messy nachos, and classic combination dinners don't break new ground, but the kitchen has perfected these standards over 70 years (I wish they bottled their rich enchilada sauce). Other specialties include seasonally available green-corn tamales and creative sizzling vegetarian fajitas that go way beyond just eliminating the meat. The atmosphere is festive, as people from all parts of town dine happily in the many rambling rooms that compose the restaurant. There's valet parking as well as a free self-park lot directly across the street.

Westsiders head to El Cholo's Santa Monica branch at 1025 Wilshire Blvd. (ℰ 310/899-1106); the Pasadena branch is at 958 S. Fair Oaks Blvd. (ℰ 626/441-4353)

1121 S. Western Ave. (south of Olympic Blvd.). ℰ 323/734-2773. www.elcholo.com. Reservations suggested. Main courses $8–$14. AE, DC, DISC, MC, V. Mon–Thurs 11am–10pm; Fri–Sat 11am–11pm; Sun 11am–9pm. Free self-parking or valet parking $3.

Pink's Hot Dogs ℛ *Kids* SANDWICHES/BURGERS/HOT DOGS   Pink's isn't your usual guidebook recommendation, but then again, this crusty corner stand isn't your typical hot-dog shack either. Name another hot-dog stand that has its own valet who deftly parks the stream of Rolls-Royces and Mercedes that pull up regularly. This L.A. icon grew around the late Paul and Betty Pink, who opened for business in 1939 selling 10¢ wieners from a used hot-dog cart. Now 2,000 of them are served every day on Pink's soft, steamed rolls. There are 24 varieties of dogs available, many of the them coined by the celebrities who order them. Martha Stewart once stopped her caravan to order a 10-incher with mustard, relish, onions, chopped tomatoes, sauerkraut, bacon, and sour cream, and now you too can order a "Martha Stewart" dog. The heartburn-inducing chili dogs (made from Betty's "secret chili formula" that's still a secret) are craved by even the most upstanding, health-conscious Angelenos. There's lots of folklore emanating from this wiener shack as well: Bruce Willis reportedly proposed to Demi Moore in the parking lot, and Orson Welles holds the record for the most hot dogs consumed in one sitting (18). Even though the dogs are churned out every 30 seconds, expect to wait in line even at midnight—you'll invariably meet a true crossroads of Los Angeles cultures. Pray that greedy developers spare this little nugget of Americana.

709 N. La Brea Ave. (at Melrose Ave.). ℰ 323/931-4223. www.pinkshollywood.com. Hot dogs $2.10. No credit cards. Sun–Thurs 9:30am–2am; Fri–Sat 9:30am–3am.

Roscoe's House of Chicken 'n' Waffles ℛ BREAKFAST/SOUTHERN It sounds like a bad joke—fried chicken and waffles on the same plate. But Roscoe's is one of those places that you have to visit at least once to see how it works (and judging by the wait, it definitely works). This Hollywood institution's proximity to CBS Television City has turned this restaurant into a kind of de facto commissary for the network. A chicken-and-cheese omelet isn't everyone's ideal way to begin the day, but it's de rigueur at Roscoe's. At lunch, few calorie-unconscious diners (and they come in all colors here) can resist the juicy fried chicken smothered in gravy and onions, a house specialty that's served with waffles or grits and biscuits. Large chicken-salad bowls and chicken sandwiches also provide plenty of cluck for the buck. Homemade corn bread, sweet-potato pie, homemade potato salad, and corn on the cob are available as side orders. Granted, the waffles are of Eggo quality and come with enough whipped butter to stop your heart, but the Southern-fried chicken is addictive.

1514 N. Gower St. (at Sunset Blvd.). (C) 323/466-7453. Main courses $4–$11. No credit cards. Sun–Thurs 9am–midnight; Fri–Sat 9am–4am. Metered street parking.

Swingers ⋇ AMERICAN/TRADITIONAL/BREAKFAST Resurrected from a motel coffee shop, Swingers was transformed by a couple of L.A. hipster nightclub owners into a 1990s version of comfy Americana. The interior seems like a slice of the 1950s until you notice the plaid upholstery and Warhol-esque graphics, which contrast nicely with the retro red-white-and-blue "Swingers" logo adorning *everything*. Guests at the attached Beverly Laurel Motor Hotel chow down alongside body-pierced industry hounds from nearby record companies, while a soundtrack that runs the gamut from punk rock to "Schoolhouse Rock" plays in the background. It's not all attitude, though—you'll enjoy a menu of high-quality diner favorites with trendy crowd-pleasers: Steel-cut Irish oatmeal, challah French toast, grilled Jamaican jerk chicken, and a selection of tofu-enhanced vegetarian dishes are just a few of the eclectic offerings. Sometimes I just swinger by for a malt or milkshake to go—they're among the best in town. *Note:* There's a second location in Santa Monica at 802 Broadway at Lincoln Ave. ((C) **310/393-9793**).

8020 Beverly Blvd. (west of Fairfax Ave.). (C) 323/653-5858. www.swingersdiner.com. Most items less than $8. AE, DISC, MC, V. Sun–Thurs 6am–2am; Fri–Sat 9am–4am. Metered street parking.

Toi on Sunset ⋇ *Value* THAI Because they're open *really* late, Toi has become an instant fave of Hollywood hipsters like Sean Penn and Woody Harrelson, who make post-clubbing excursions to this rock 'n' roll eatery a few blocks from the Sunset Strip. After all the hype, I was surprised to find possibly L.A.'s best bargain Thai food, authentically prepared and served in portions so generous the word "enormous" seems inadequate. Menu highlights include hot-and-sour chicken, coconut soup, and the house specialty: chicken curry *somen*, a spicy dish with green curry and mint sauce spooned over thin Japanese rice noodles. Vegetarians will be pleased with the vast selection of meat-free items like *pad kee mao*, rice noodles served spicy with tofu, mint, onions, peppers, and chili. The interior is a noisy amalgam of cultish movie posters, rock 'n' roll memorabilia, and haphazardly placed industrial-issue dinette sets; and the plates, flatware, and drinking glasses are cheap coffee-shop issue. In other words, it's all about the food and the scene—neither will disappoint.

Westsiders can opt for Toi on Wilshire, 1120 Wilshire Blvd., Santa Monica ((C) **310/394-7804**), open daily from 11am to 3am; or Toi on Vine, 1360 N. Vine St., Hollywood ((C) **323/467-8378**).

7505½ Sunset Blvd. (at Gardner). (C) 323/874-8062. www.toirockinthaifood.com. Reservations accepted only for parties of 6 or more. Main courses $6–$11. AE, DISC, MC, V. Daily 11am–4am.

DOWNTOWN
EXPENSIVE

Patina ☆☆☆ FRENCH   When celebrity L.A. restaurateur Joachim Splichal moved his flagship Patina restaurant from Melrose Avenue to the new Walt Disney Concert Hall, it raised one pertinent question: "Is it as good as the old Patina?" If you arrived after a performance ended, you wouldn't hear the answer anyway. Billowing walls of laser-cut walnut and floor-to-ceiling glass panels only augment the hubbub as droves of smartly clad fans of the performing arts dine on Splichal's signature dishes of wild game and the de rigueur ahi tuna appetizer. The après-show performances continue when a trio of carts—mounds of caviar, giant rib-eye steaks for two, and expensive cheeses—crisscross the dining room. My dinner started when soft, thinly sliced hamachi matched with green-apple granite and mango met it's match with the seared foie gras atop caramel-poached apples, and segued into an entree of crispy skinned yellowtail snapper served on a bed of fava-bean purée. Dishes I reluctantly passed on included a puff pastry–encrusted grouse with caramelized endive-and-black-olive reduction sauce, sautéed black truffled Brussels sprouts with a sweet-potato purée, and roasted venison loin with porcini–foie gras polenta. Vegetarian dishes and wine pairing are also available, as are prix-fixe theater menus. Jackets are suggested but not required for dinner, and valet service is recommended as it's a bit of a hike from the nearest pay lot. *Tip:* If you want a quiet, romantic dinner, ask the hostess to schedule it at the *start* of a performance.

141 S. Grand Ave. (near First St.), Los Angeles. ℭ 213/972-3331. Reservations recommended. Dinner main courses $31–$39; lunch $15–$29. AE, DC, MC, V. Daily 11:30am–2pm and 5–11pm. Valet parking $8.

Water Grill ☆☆☆ SEAFOOD   Widely considered by L.A. foodies to be the best seafood house in the city, Water Grill is popular with the suit-and-tie crowd at lunch and with concertgoers en route to the Music Center at night. The dining room is a stylish and sophisticated fusion of wood, leather, and brass, but gets a lighthearted lift from cavorting papier-mâché fish that play against an aquamarine ceiling painted with bubbles. The restaurant is known for its shellfish; among the appetizers are a dozen different oysters, Nantucket Bay scallops with Queensland blue pumpkin, and crispy sweetbreads with crayfish, chanterelles, and roasted asparagus. Main courses are imaginative dishes influenced by the cuisines of Hawaii, the Pacific Northwest, New Orleans, and New England. A good start to the feast is the appetizer seafood platter, a mouthwatering assortment served with well-made aioli. Other selections from the menu may range from Santa Barbara spot prawns paired with fingerling potato salad, to line-caught pan-roasted Alaskan halibut with Niman Ranch bacon and sweet-pea tendril juice. For dessert, try the mascarpone with figs and cherries or the chocolate bread pudding. Better yet, splurge on the $85 seven-course tasting menu.

544 S. Grand Ave. (between 5th and 6th sts.). ℭ 213/891-0900. www.watergrill.com. Reservations recommended. Main courses $19–$31. AE, DC, DISC, MC, V. Mon–Tues 11:30am–9pm; Wed–Fri 11:30am–10pm; Sat 5–10pm; Sun 4:30–9pm. Valet parking $4.

MODERATE

Ciudad ☆☆ LATIN   The latest L.A. venture of celebrity chefs Susan Feniger and Mary Sue Milliken is this intriguing restaurant in the heart of downtown. Ciudad means "city" in Spanish and is a nod to the partners' long-ago venture City Restaurant. Here, amid juicy sherbet pastel walls and 1950s geometric abstract designs, crowds gather to revel in a menu that brings together cuisines from the world's great Latin urban centers: Havana, Rio de Janeiro, Barcelona, and so on. Standout dishes include the tortilla soup, Honduran ceviche (presented in a martini glass and accented with tropical coconut and pineapple), Argentine empanadas, Swiss chard with tomatillo sauce, citrus-roasted Cuban-style chicken (served with Puerto Rican rice and fried plantains), and a Brazilian *moqueca*—shrimp, mussels, and other seafood in a coconut-lime broth over coconut rice. Between 3 and 6:30pm on weekdays, Ciudad presents *cuchifrito*, traditional Latin snacks served at the bar; it's easy to make a meal of several, choosing from sweet-savory pork-stuffed green tamales, *papas rellenos* (mashed-potato fritters stuffed with oxtail stew), plantain gnocchi in tomatillo sauce, and more. As with the pair's Border Grill, desserts are worth saving room for and large enough to share. *Tip:* Ciudad provides free shuttle service to the Music Center, Walt Disney Concert hall, and to selected Staples Center events.

445 S. Figueroa St. ℂ 213/486-5171. www.millikenandfeniger.com. Reservations recommended. Main courses $12–$23; *cuchifrito* $5–$8. AE, MC, V. Mon–Thurs 11:30am–9pm; Fri 11:30am–10:30pm; Sat 5–11pm; Sun 5–9pm. Day parking $2 with validation; valet parking (after 5pm) $5.

R23 𝔸𝔸 *Finds* JAPANESE/SUSHI   This gallery-like space in downtown's out-of-the-way warehouse/artist loft district has been the secret of sushi connoisseurs since 1991 and consistently ranked as one of the city's top sushi restaurants. At the back of R23's single, large exposed-brick dining room, the 12-seat sushi bar shines like a beacon; what appear at first to be ceramic wall ornaments are really stylish sushi platters hanging in wait for large orders. More functional art reveals itself in the corrugated-cardboard chairs designed by renowned architect Frank Gehry—they're funky yet far more comfortable than wood. Genial sushi wizards stand in wait, cases of the finest fish before them. Salmon, yellowtail, shrimp, tuna, and scallops are among the always-fresh selections; an excellent and unusual offering is seared *toro*, where the rich belly tuna absorbs a faint and delectable smoky flavor from the grill. Though R23's sublimely perfect sushi is the star, the short but inventive menu also includes pungent red miso soup, creamy baked scallops, finely sliced beef "sashimi," and several other choices. Browse among a wide selection of premium wines and sakes (try the addictively sweet nigori).

923 E. Second St. (between Alameda St. and Santa Fe Ave.). ℂ 213/687-7178. www.r23.com. Reservations recommended. Main courses $12–$20; sushi $4–$8. AE, DC, DISC, MC, V. Mon–Fri 11:45am–2pm; Mon–Sat 5:45–10pm. Free parking.

Tantra 𝔸𝔸 INDIAN   In typical L.A. over-the-top fashion, Tantra owner Navraj Singh hired a studio design company to create an Indian restaurant unlike any you've ever seen. Hammered copper doors, iron and silk light fixtures, curtains of oxidized metals, murals of gender-fused beings, and black-and-white Ballywood movies shown on a giant plasma screen are just a few of the unorthodox props that vie for your attention. Part restaurant and nightclub, Tantra is one of L.A.'s current "in" destinations, both for its scene and the cuisine. The gym-size building is equally divided: Veer right at the foyer and join the eclectic Silver Lake hipsters sipping too-cool cocktails such as Tears of Ganesha and Shiva's Revenge while the DJ spins vinyl; veer left and behold Lord Ganesha, God of Prosperity, perched high above the temple-style dining room. Just about all of the curries, stir-fries, masalas, and kabobs are expertly prepared, but two standout dishes are the coconut-curry shrimp flavored with *ajwain* (caraway seeds) and stir-fried with palm vinegar, red onions, and peppers, then finished with tomato coconut broth; and the *mumbai* crepes—chickpea-and-corn crepes with a tangy cream cheese filling and topped with mango sauce.

3705 W. Sunset Blvd., Silver Lake. ℂ 323/663-8268. Reservations for parties of 6 or more. Main courses $11–$16. AE, MC, V. Tues–Sun 11:30am–3pm and 6–11pm (bar open until 2pm). Valet parking $3.50.

INEXPENSIVE

The Original Pantry *Value* AMERICAN/BREAKFAST   An L.A. institution if there ever was one, this place has been serving huge portions of comfort food around the clock since 1924. In fact, there isn't even a key to the front door. Owned by former L.A. mayor and botched governor contender Richard Riordan, the Pantry is popular with politicos, who come here for weekday lunches, and with conference-goers en route to the nearby L.A. Convention Center. The well-worn restaurant is also a welcoming beacon to clubbers after hours, when downtown becomes a virtual ghost town. A bowl of celery stalks, carrot sticks, and whole radishes greets you at your Formica table, and creamy coleslaw and sourdough bread come free with every meal. Famous for quantity rather than quality, the Pantry serves huge T-bone steaks, densely packed meatloaf, macaroni and cheese, and other American favorites. A typical breakfast (served all day) might consist of a huge stack of hotcakes, a big slab of sweet cured ham, home fries, and coffee.

877 S. Figueroa St. (at Ninth St.). ℂ 213/972-9279. Main courses $6–$11. No credit cards. Daily 24 hr. Free parking with validation.

Philippe the Original BREAKFAST/SANDWICHES   Good old-fashioned value is what this legendary landmark cafeteria is all about. Popular with both South Central project residents and Beverly Hills elite, Philippe's unspectacular dining room with sawdust floors is one of the few places in L.A. where everyone can get along. Philippe's claims to have invented the French-dipped sandwich at this location in 1908; it remains the most popular menu item. Patrons push trays along the counter and watch while their choice of beef, pork, ham, turkey, or lamb is sliced and layered onto crusty French bread that's been dipped in meat juices. Other menu items include house-made beef stew, navy bean soup, chili, and pickled pigs' feet. A hearty breakfast, served daily until 10:30am, is worthwhile if only for Philippe's uncommonly good cinnamon-dipped French toast. Beer and wine are available. For added entertainment, request a booth in the Train Room, which houses the nifty Model Train Museum.

1001 N. Alameda St. (at Ord St.). ℂ 213/628-3781. www.philippes.com. Most menu items under $7. No credit cards. Daily 6am–10pm. Free parking.

SAN FERNANDO VALLEY & UNIVERSAL CITY
EXPENSIVE

Pinot Bistro ★★ *Kids* CALIFORNIA/FRENCH   When the Valley crowd doesn't want to make the drive to Patina, they pack into Pinot Bistro, one of Joachim Splichal's other successful restaurants. The Valley's only great bistro is designed with dark woods, etched glass, and cream-colored walls that scream "trendy French" almost as loudly as the rich, straightforward cooking. The menu, a symphony of California and Continental elements, includes a beautiful

---

Value **Budget Brew**

The price of a regular coffee at **Philippe the Original** is the same as it was when the diner opened in 1924: 9¢. That explains why the restaurant serves more than 20,000 cups per week.

warm potato tart with smoked whitefish, and baby lobster tails with creamy polenta—both studies in culinary perfection. The most popular dish here is the Frenchified Tuscan bean soup, infused with oven-dried tomatoes and roasted garlic and served over crusty ciabatta bread. The generously portioned main dishes continue the gourmet theme: baby lobster risotto, braised oxtail with parsley gnocchi, and puff pastry stuffed with bay scallops, Manila clams, and roast duck. The service is good, attentive, and unobtrusive. Many regulars prefer Pinot Bistro at lunch, when a less expensive menu is served to a more easygoing crowd.

12969 Ventura Blvd. (west of Coldwater Canyon Ave.), Studio City. © **818/990-0500.** www. patinagroup.com. Reservations required. Dinner main courses $16–$22; lunch $7–$13. AE, DC, DISC, MC, V. Mon–Fri noon–2pm; Mon–Thurs 6–10pm; Fri 6–10:30pm; Sat 5:30–10:30pm; Sun 5:30–9:30pm. Valet parking $3.50.

MODERATE

Jerry's Famous Deli ✿ *Kids* BREAKFAST/DELICATESSEN   Here's a simple yet sizable deli where all the Valley's hipsters go to relieve their late-night munchies. This place probably has one of the largest menus in America—a tome that spans cultures and continents, from Central America to China to New York. From salads to sandwiches to steak-and-seafood platters, everything—including breakfast—is served all day. Jerry's is consistently good at lox and eggs, pastrami sandwiches, potato pancakes, and all the deli staples. It's also an integral part of L.A.'s cultural landscape and a favorite of the show-business types who populate the adjacent foothill neighborhoods. It even has a full bar.

12655 Ventura Blvd. (just east of Coldwater Canyon Ave.), Studio City. © **818/980-4245.** www.jerrys famousdeli.com. Dinner main courses $9–$14; breakfast $2–$11; sandwiches and salads $4–$12. AE, MC, V. Daily 24 hr. Free parking.

Miceli's *Kids* TRADITIONAL ITALIAN   Mostaccioli marinara, lasagna, thin-crust pizza, and eggplant parmigiana are indicative of the Sicilian-style fare at this cavernous, stained-glass-windowed Italian restaurant adjacent to Universal City. The waitstaff sings show tunes or opera favorites in between serving dinner (and sometimes instead of); make sure you have enough chianti to get into the spirit of it all. This is a great place for kids, but too rollicking for romance.

3655 Cahuenga Blvd. (east of Lankershim), Los Angeles. © **323/851-3344.** www.micelisrestaurant.com. Main courses $7–$12; pizza $9–$15. AE, DC, MC, V. Mon–Thurs 11:30am–midnight; Fri 11:30am–1am; Sat 4pm–1am; Sun 4–11pm. Parking $2.50.

INEXPENSIVE

Du-par's Restaurant & Bakery ✿ AMERICAN/TRADITIONAL/BREAKFAST   It's been called a "culinary wax museum," the last of a dying breed, the kind of coffee shop Donna Reed took the family to for blue-plate specials. This isn't a trendy new theme place, it's the real deal—and that motherly waitress who calls everyone under 60 "hon" has probably been slinging hash here for 20 or 30 years. Du-par's is popular among old-timers who made it part of their daily routine decades ago, show business denizens who eschew the industry watering holes, a new generation that appreciates a tasty, cheap meal . . . well, everyone, really. It's common knowledge that Du-par's makes the best buttermilk pancakes in town, though some prefer the eggy, perfect French toast (extra crispy around the edges, please). Mouthwatering pies (blueberry cream cheese, coconut cream, and others) line the front display case and can be had for a song.

12036 Ventura Blvd. (1 block east of Laurel Canyon Blvd.), Studio City. © **818/766-4437.** www.dupars.com. All items under $11. AE, DC, DISC, MC, V. Sun–Thurs 6am–1am; Fri–Sat 6am–4am. Free parking.

PASADENA & ENVIRONS
EXPENSIVE

Bistro 45 ★★ CALIFORNIA-FRENCH   All class, yet never stuffy, Bistro 45 is a favorite among Pasadena's old guard and nouvelle riche. The restaurant's warm, light ambience and gallery-like decor are an unexpected surprise after the ornately historic Art Deco exterior (the building is a former bank), and provides a romantic backdrop for owner Robert Simon's award-winning cuisine. The seasonally inspired menu changes frequently; dishes might include salmon and tuna tartares flavored with cilantro, rock shrimp risotto with saffron, panroasted monkfish with garlic polenta, roasted veal loin filled with Roquefort, Fanny Bay oyster salad, and Nebraska pork with figs. For dessert, try the "chocolate soup," a creamy soufflé served with chocolate-kirsch sauce and vanilla ice cream. The knowledgeable waitstaff can answer questions about the excellent wine list; Bistro 45 appears regularly on *Wine Spectator*'s "Best of" lists, and hosts special-event wine dinners.

45 S. Mentor Ave. (between Colorado and Green), Pasadena. ✆ 626/795-2478. www.bistro45.com. Reservations recommended. Dinner main courses $17–$27; lunch $11–$16. AE, DC, MC, V. Tues–Fri 11:30am–2:30pm; Tues–Thurs 6–9pm; Fri–Sat 6–9:30pm; Sun 5–9pm. Valet parking $4.

Parkway Grill ★★ CALIFORNIA   This vibrant, quintessentially Southern California restaurant has been one of the L.A. area's top-rated spots since 1985, gaining a reputation for avant-garde flavor combinations and gourmet pizzas to rival Spago's. Although some critics find many dishes too fussy, others thrill to appetizer innovations like lobster-stuffed cocoa crepes or Dungeness crab cakes with ginger cream and two salsas. Take my advice and start with the hot cheese-pear-walnut flatbread and the roasted beet salad, followed by any main dish from the iron mesquite grill. The richly sweet and substantial desserts can easily satiate two appetites. Located where the old Arroyo Seco Parkway glides into an ordinary city street, the Parkway Grill is within a couple of minutes' drive from Old Pasadena and thoughtfully offers free valet parking.

510 S. Arroyo Pkwy. (at California Blvd.), Pasadena. ✆ 626/795-1001. Reservations recommended. Main courses $8–$27. AE, DC, MC, V. Mon–Fri 11:30am–2pm; Sun–Thurs 5–10pm; Fri–Sat 5:30–11pm. Free valet parking.

The Raymond ★★ NEW AMERICAN/CONTINENTAL   With its easy-to-miss setting in a sleepy part of Pasadena, the Raymond is a jewel not even many locals know about. This Craftsman cottage was once the caretaker's house for a Victorian hotel called The Raymond. Though the city has grown to surround it, the place maintains an enchanting air of seclusion, romance, and serenity. Chef/owner Suzanne Bourg brings a romantic sensibility and impeccable culinary instincts to dishes that are mostly haute American—with an occasional European flair. The menu changes weekly. One night a grilled rack of lamb is sauced with orange, Grand Marnier, and peppercorns; another night it comes with a creamy white-wine-and-chèvre sauce with dried cherries. Bourg's soups are always heavenly (the restaurant gladly gives out the recipes), and desserts are inspired. Tables are scattered throughout the house and in the lush English garden, and there's plenty of free, nonvalet parking (you wouldn't find *that* on the Westside).

1250 S. Fair Oaks Ave. (at Columbia St.), Pasadena. ✆ 626/441-3136. www.theraymond.com. Reservations required. Dinner main courses $30–$34; 4-course dinner $45–$49; prix-fixe 3-course dinner $36 (including wine); lunch $13–$20. AE, DC, DISC, MC, V. Tues–Fri 11:30am–2:30pm; Tues–Thurs 6–9:30pm; Fri–Sat 5:45–10pm; Sat 11am–2:30pm; Sun 10am–2:30pm and 4:30–8pm; afternoon tea Tues–Sun noon–4pm. Free parking.

MODERATE

Café Santorini *Greek* **GREEK**   Located in the heart of Pasadena's crowded Old Town shopping mecca, this second-story gem has a secluded Mediterranean ambience, due in part to its historic brick building with patio tables overlooking, but insulated from, the plaza below. In the evening, lighting is subdued and romantic, but ambience is casual; many diners are coming from or going to an adjacent movie-theater complex. The food is terrific and affordable, featuring grilled meats and kabobs, pizzas, fresh and tangy hummus, plenty of warm pita, and other staples of Greek cuisine. The menu includes regional flavors like lamb, feta cheese, spinach, or Armenian sausage; the vegetarian baked butternut squash is filled with fluffy rice and smoky roast vegetables.

64-70 W. Union St. (main entrance at the shopping plaza at the corner of Fair Oaks and Colorado), Pasadena. ⓒ 626/564-4200. www.cafesantorini.com. Reservations recommended on weekends. Main courses $9–$22. AE, DC, DISC, MC, V. Daily 11am–11pm (until midnight Fri–Sat). Valet or self-parking $4.

Nonya *Finds* CHINESE/MALAYSIAN/PERANAKAN   It's a rare day in a travel writer's career when he enjoys a cuisine he's never even heard of. Peranakan cuisine (aka Nonya) was developed in the 15th century by Peranakans, a people whose heritage stems from the intermarriage between Chinese settlers of Singapore and the local Malaysians. It's a complex and sophisticated style of cooking, involving exotic ingredients and a layering of flavors, and there are only a few chefs in the Western world—including Nonya's executive chef Tony Pat, a Hong Kong native—who know the authentic techniques to make it. Pungent roots such as ginger, turmeric, and galangal are used liberally along with aromatic and often spicy seasonings to an eclectic and wondrous effect. Case in point: It's a sure bet you haven't had a *mangga ikan* salad—a light yet flavorful dish made with fresh mango, tender halibut, thinly sliced red onions, and a lemon grass-lime vinaigrette. Nor are you familiar with *khaj panggang*, thin slices of chicken breast marinated in chili and grilled in banana leaves. The seafood dishes are equally enticing: red snapper spiced with turmeric and tamarind, cooked in banana leaves and served with house-pickled vegetables; whole Dungeness crab sautéed with curry leaves and black pepper. Owner Simon Tong, who owned Asian restaurants in London for 25 years until recently settling in Pasadena, hired designer Dodd Mitchell to create a gorgeous dining room, replete with glimmering hardwoods, metals, and lush foliage that surround a tranquil elevated pond (it's both sexy and soothing, the perfect date place).

61 N. Raymond St. (at Union St.), Pasadena. ⓒ 626/583-8398. www.nonyarestaurant.com. Reservations recommended. Main courses $9–$42. AE, MC, V. Mon–Fri 11:30am–2:30pm; Mon–Wed 5–10pm; Thurs 5–11pm; Fri–Sat 5pm–midnight; Sun 1–10pm. Valet parking $4.

Yujean Kang's Gourmet Chinese Cuisine *Finds* CHINESE   Many Chinese restaurants put the word *gourmet* in their name, but few really mean it—or deserve it. Not so at Yujean Kang's, where Chinese cuisine is taken to an entirely new level. A master of "fusion" cuisine, the eponymous chef/owner snatches bits of techniques and flavors from both China and the West, commingling them in an entirely fresh way. Can you resist such provocative dishes as "Ants on Tree" (beef sautéed with glass noodles in chile and black sesame seeds), or lobster with caviar and fava beans, or Chilean sea bass in passion-fruit sauce? Kang is also a wine aficionado and has assembled a magnificent cellar of California, French, and particularly German wines. Try pairing a German Spätlese with tea-smoked duck salad. The red-wrapped dining room is less subtle than the food, but just as elegant.

67 N. Raymond Ave. (between Walnut St. and Colorado Blvd.), Pasadena. ⓒ 626/585-0855. Reservations recommended. Main courses $8–$19. AE, MC, V. Daily 11:30am–2:30pm and 5–10pm. Street parking.

INEXPENSIVE

Crocodile Cafe AMERICAN/TRADITIONAL/INTERNATIONAL   Casual and colorful, this offshoot of Pasadena's groundbreaking Parkway Grill builds a menu around simple crowd-pleasers (pizza, pasta, burgers, salads) prepared with fresh ingredients and jazzed up with creative marinades, vinaigrettes, and salsas. It's a formula that works; this Lake Avenue branch is the original location, but siblings have sprung up throughout the San Fernando and San Gabriel valleys—even as far away as Santa Monica. Popular selections include the oak-wood-grilled burger with curly french fries, the Croc's signature blue corn chicken tostada with warm black beans and fresh guacamole, wood-grilled gourmet pizzas in the California Pizza Kitchen style, excellent chili, zesty tortilla soup, and ooey-gooey desserts.

Other branches include Old Town Pasadena, 88 W. Colorado Blvd. (© **626/568-9310**); Glendale, 626 N. Central Ave. (© **818/241-1114**); and Santa Monica, 101 Santa Monica Blvd. (© **310/394-4783**).

140 S. Lake Ave., Pasadena. © **626/449-9900**. www.crocodilecafe.com. Main courses $8–$18. AE, MC, V. Daily 11am–10pm (till midnight Fri–Sat). Free self-parking.

5 L.A.'s Top Attractions

Farmers Market & The Grove 🌟 *Kids*   The original market was little more than a field with stands set up by farmers during the Depression so they could sell directly to city dwellers. Eventually, permanent buildings grew up, including the trademark shingled 10-story clock tower. Today the place has evolved into a sprawling marketplace with a carnival atmosphere, a kind of "turf" version of San Francisco's Fisherman's Wharf. About 100 restaurants, shops, and grocers cater to a mix of workers from the CBS Television City complex, locals, and tourists, brought here by the busload. Retailers sell greeting cards, kitchen implements, candles, and souvenirs, but everyone comes for the food stands, which offer oysters, hot donuts, Cajun gumbo, fresh-squeezed orange juice, corned-beef sandwiches, fresh-pressed peanut butter, and all kinds of international fast foods. You can still buy produce here—it's no longer a farm-fresh bargain, but the selection's better than at the grocery store. Don't miss **Kokomo** (© **323/933-0773**), a "gourmet" outdoor coffee shop that has become a power breakfast spot for showbiz types. Red turkey hash and sweet-potato fries are the dishes that keep them coming back. The seafood gumbo and gumbo ya ya at the **Gumbo Pot** (© **323/933-0358**) are also very popular.

At the eastern end of the Farmers Market is **The Grove,** a massive 575,000-square-foot Vegas-style retail complex composed of various architectural styles ranging from Art Deco to Italian Renaissance. Miniature streets link The Grove to the market via a double-deck electric trolley. Granted, it's all a bit Disney-gaudy, but the locals love it. Where else can you power-shop until noon, check all your bags at a drop-off station, get a spa treatment at **Amadeus Spa** (© **323/297-0311**), see a movie at the 14-screen **Grove Theatre,** have an early dinner at **Maggiano's Little Italy** (© **323/965-9665**), and be home by 7pm?

6333 W. Third St. (at Fairfax Ave.), Hollywood. © **323/933-9211**. www.farmersmarketla.com or www.the-grovela.com. Mon–Fri 9am–9pm; Sat 9am–8pm; Sun 10am–7pm.

Grauman's Chinese Theatre 🌟   This is one of the world's great movie palaces and one of Hollywood's finest landmarks. The theater was opened in 1927 by Sid Grauman, a brilliant promoter who's credited with originating the idea of the paparazzi-packed movie "premiere." Outrageously conceived, with both authentic and simulated Chinese embellishments, Grauman's theater was designed to impress. Original Chinese heavenly doves top the facade, and two of the theater's columns once propped up a Ming dynasty temple.

Visitors by the millions flock to the theater for its famous entry court, where stars like Elizabeth Taylor, Paul Newman, Ginger Rogers, Humphrey Bogart, Frank Sinatra, Marilyn Monroe, and about 160 others set their signatures and hand/footprints in concrete (a tradition started when actress Norma Talmadge accidentally stepped in wet cement during the premiere of Cecil B. DeMille's *King of Kings*). It's not always hands and feet: Betty Grable's shapely leg; the hoof prints of Gene Autry's horse, Champion; Jimmy Durante's and Bob Hope's trademark noses; Whoopi Goldberg's dreadlocks; George Burns's cigar; and even R2D2's wheels.

6925 Hollywood Blvd. (between Highland and La Brea Ave.). **(℃ 323/464-MANN** or 323/461-3331. www.manntheaters.com. Movie tickets $10. Call for show times.

Griffith Observatory   Made world-famous in the film *Rebel Without a Cause,* Griffith Observatory's bronze domes have been Hollywood Hills landmarks since 1935. Most visitors don't actually go inside; they come to this spot on the south slope of Mount Hollywood for unparalleled city views. On warm nights, with the lights twinkling below, this is one of the most romantic places in L.A.

The main dome houses a **planetarium,** where narrated projection shows reveal the stars and planets that are hidden from the naked eye by the city's lights and smog. Other shows take you on excursions into space to search for extraterrestrial life, or examine the causes of earthquakes and moonquakes.

The adjacent **Hall of Science** holds exhibits on galaxies, meteorites, and other cosmic objects, including a telescope trained on the sun, a Foucault pendulum, and earth and moon globes 6 feet in diameter. On clear nights you can gaze at the heavens through the powerful 12-inch telescope.

Please note: The entire Griffith Observatory area is closed for a major renovation and expansion and will not reopen until late 2005 (possibly even later, according to rumor). However, a temporary "Griffith Observatory Satellite," located just south of the Los Angeles Zoo at 4800 Western Heritage Way, hosts planetarium shows, a modest display of astronomy exhibits, and a telescope to view the moon and planets at night; public access is free. It's open from 1 to 10pm Tuesday through Friday and 10am to 10pm on Saturday and Sunday. Call **(℃ 323/664-1181** for more information.

2800 E. Observatory Rd. (in Griffith Park, at the end of Vermont Ave.). **(℃ 323/664-1191,** or 323/663-8171 for the Sky Report, a recorded message on current planet positions and celestial events. www.griffithobs.org.

The "Hollywood" Sign ℛ   These famous 50-foot-high white sheet-metal letters have come to symbolize the movie industry and the city itself. The sign was erected on Mount Lee in 1923 for $21,000 as an advertisement for a real-estate development. The full text originally read HOLLYWOODLAND and was lined with thousands of 20-watt bulbs around the letters (changed periodically by a caretaker who lived in a small house behind the sign). The sign gained dubious notoriety when actress Peg Entwistle leapt to her death from the "H" in 1932. The LAND section was damaged by a landslide, and the entire sign fell into major disrepair until the Hollywood Chamber of Commerce spearheaded a campaign to repair it (Hugh Hefner, Alice Cooper, Gene Autry, and Andy Williams were all major contributors). Officially completed in 1978, the 450-foot-long installation is now protected by a fence and motion detectors. The best view is from down below, at the corner of Sunset Boulevard and Bronson Avenue. *Tip:* It may look like it on a map, but Beachwood Drive does not lead to the sign. If you want to reach the sign on foot, it requires a rather arduous 5-mile round-trip hike on the Brush Canyon Trail in Griffith Park—the trail head is at the end of Canyon Drive. For more information, call the Griffith Park headquarters at © **323/913-4688.**

Hollywood Walk of Fame ★ *Kids*   When the Hollywood honchos realized how limited the footprint space was at the Grauman's Chinese Theatre, they came up with another way to pay tribute to the stars. Since 1960, more than 2,000 celebrities have been honored along the world's most famous sidewalk. Each bronze medallion, set into the center of a terrazzo star, pays homage to a television, film, radio, theater, or recording personality. Although about a third of them are no longer household names—their fame simply hasn't withstood the test of time—millions of visitors are thrilled by the sight of famous names like **James Dean** (1719 Vine St.), **John Lennon** (1750 Vine St.), **Marlon Brando** (1765 Vine St.), **Rudolph Valentino** (6164 Hollywood Blvd.), **Marilyn Monroe** (6744 Hollywood Blvd.), **Elvis Presley** (6777 Hollywood Blvd.), **Greta Garbo** (6901 Hollywood Blvd.), **Louis Armstrong** (7000 Hollywood Blvd.), **Barbra Streisand** (6925 Hollywood Blvd.), and **Eddie Murphy** (7000 Hollywood Blvd.). **Gene Autry**'s all over the place: The singing cowboy earned five different stars (a sidewalk record), one in each category.

The sight of bikers, metalheads, homeless wanderers, and hordes of tourists all treading on memorials to Hollywood's greats makes for a bizarre and somewhat tacky tribute. But the Hollywood Chamber of Commerce has been doing a terrific job sprucing up the pedestrian experience with filmstrip crosswalks, swaying palms, and more. And at least one weekend a month, a group of fans calling themselves Star Polishers busy themselves scrubbing tarnished medallions.

The legendary sidewalk is continually adding new names, such as Muhammad Ali in front of the Kodak Theatre. The public is invited to attend dedication ceremonies; the honoree—who pays a whopping $15,000 for the eternal upkeep—is usually in attendance. Contact the **Hollywood Chamber of Commerce,** 6255 Sunset Blvd., Suite 911, Hollywood, CA 90028 (© **323/469-8311**), for information on who's being honored this week.

Hollywood Blvd., between Gower St. and La Brea Ave.; and Vine St., between Yucca St. and Sunset Blvd. © 323/469-8311. www.hollywoodchamber.net.

J. Paul Getty Museum at the Getty Center ★★ *Kids*   Since opening in 1997, the Richard Meier–designed Getty Center has quickly assumed its place in the L.A. landscape (literally and figuratively) as the city's cultural acropolis and international mecca. Headquarters for the Getty Trust's research, education, and conservation concerns, the postmodernist complex—perched on a hillside in the Santa Monica Mountains and swathed in Italian travertine marble—is most frequently visited for the museum galleries displaying collector J. Paul Getty's enormous collection of art. Always known for antiquities, expanded galleries now allow the display of Impressionist paintings, truckloads of glimmering French furniture and decorative arts, fine illuminated manuscripts, contemporary photography, and previously overlooked graphic arts. The area that's open to the public consists of five two-story pavilions set around an open courtyard, and each gallery within is specially designed to complement the works on display. A sophisticated system of programmable window louvers allows many works (particularly paintings) to be displayed in the natural light they were created in for the first time in the modern era. One of these is van Gogh's *Irises,* one of the museum's finest and most popular holdings. Trivia buffs will enjoy knowing that the museum spent $53.9 million to acquire this paint-ing; it's displayed in a complex that cost roughly $1 *billion* to construct.

Visitors to the center park at the base of the hill and ascend via a cable-driven electric tram. On clear days, the sensation is of being in the clouds, gazing across Los Angeles and the Pacific Ocean (and into a few chic Brentwood backyards). If you're like me and don't remember a thing from your college art appreciation class, plunk down $3 for a self-guided audio tour that gives a brief overview of the 250-plus works in the collection. The 45-minute architectural tours, offered throughout the day, are also worth looking into. Dining options include several espresso/snack carts, a cafeteria, a self-service cafe, and the elegant (though infor-mal) "Restaurant" offering table service for lunch (Tues–Sun) and dinner (Fri–Sat) with breathtaking views overlooking the ocean and mountains (reser-vations are recommended, though walk-ins are accepted; call ℭ 310/440-7300 or make reservations online at www.getty.edu).

Realizing that fine-art museums are usually dreadfully boring for kids, the center provides several clever programs for kids, including: exploratory games such as *Perplexing Paintings* and *The Getty Art Detective;* a Family Room filled with puzzles, computers, picture books, and games; mythical storytelling ses-sions on weekends at 11am, noon, and 1pm; weekend family workshops; and self-guided audio tours made specifically for families.

Entrance to the Getty Center is free—they don't need your money—but parking reservations are required weekdays (though we've heard of people get-ting in without one on slow days). College students with current IDs and those arriving by public transportation, motorcycle, or bicycle do not require reserva-tions. Reservations are not required after 4pm, or all day Saturday and Sunday. Cameras and video cams are permitted but only if you use existing light (flash units are verboten).

1200 Getty Center Dr., Los Angeles. ℭ 310/440-7300. www.getty.edu. Free admission. Tues–Thurs and Sun 10am–6pm; Fri–Sat 10am–9pm. Closed major holidays. Parking $5; reservations required weekdays (see above).

La Brea Tar Pits 𝕽𝕽 *Kids*   An odorous swamp of gooey asphalt oozes to the earth's surface in the middle of Los Angeles. No, it's not a low-budget horror-movie set—it's the La Brea Tar Pits, a bizarre primal pool on Museum Row where hot tar has been bubbling from the earth for more than 40,000 years. The bubbling pools may look like a fake Disney set, but they're the real thing and have enticed thirsty animals throughout history. Nearly 400 species of mam-mals, birds, amphibians, and fish—many of which are now extinct—walked, crawled, landed, swam, or slithered into the sticky sludge, got stuck in the worst way, and stayed forever. In 1906 scientists began a systematic removal and clas-sification of entombed specimens, including ground sloths, giant vultures, mastodons, camels, bears, lizards, a Starbucks, and even prehistoric relatives of today's super-rats. Today it's one of the world's richest excavation sites for Ice Age fossils. The best finds are on display in the adjacent **Page Museum at the La Brea Tar Pits,** which houses the largest and most diverse collection of Ice Age plants and animals in the world. Archaeological work is ongoing; you can watch as scientists clean, identify, and catalog new finds in the Paleontology Labora-tory. An entertaining 15-minute film documenting the recoveries is also shown.

5801 Wilshire Blvd. (east of Fairfax Ave.), Los Angeles. ℭ 323/934-PAGE. www.tarpits.org. Admission $7 adults, $4.50 seniors 62 and older and students with ID, $2 children ages 5–12, free for kids under 5; free for everyone the 1st Tues of every month. Mon–Fri 9:30am–5pm; Sat–Sun 10am–5pm (museum).

Stargazing in L.A.: Top Spots for Sighting Celebrities

Celebrities pop up everywhere in L.A. If you spend enough time here, you'll surely bump into a few of them. If you're in the city for only a short time, however, it's best to go on the offensive.

Restaurants are your surest bet. Dining out is such a popular recreation among Hollywood's elite that you sometimes wonder whether frequently sighted folks like Johnny Depp, Nicole Kidman, Kobe Bryant, Bridget Fonda, Harrison Ford, Nicolas Cage, Brad and Jennifer, or Cindy Crawford ever actually eat at home. **Matsuhisa, The Ivy, The Palm, Le Dôme, Koi Restaurant, Paladar, Spago Beverly Hills,** and **Maple Drive** can almost guarantee sightings any night of the week. The city's stylish hotels can also be good bets—the poolside cabanas at the **Viceroy** in Santa Monica are a possibility, **Mondrian** draws stars galore to its dining room **Asia de Cuba,** as well as the elite **Skybar; Shutters'** lobby lounge is the rendezvous of choice for famous faces heading to dinner at the hotel's **One Pico** restaurant; and spotting stars at the **Beverly Hills Hotel & Bungalows** is almost too easy. A couple of cocktails will run you about $26, but a late-afternoon visit to the outdoor cocktail lounge at **Chateau Marmont** is almost a sure thing. The trendiest clubs and bars—**Whiskey Bar, House of Blues, Viper Room,** and **Skybar**—are all good for star sighting, but cover charges can be astronomical and the velvet-rope gauntlet oppressive. And it's not always Mick and Quentin and Madonna; a recent night on the town turned up only Yanni, Ralph Macchio, and Dr. Ruth.

Often, the best places to see members of the A-list aren't as obvious as a back-alley stage door or the front room of Spago. Shops along Sunset Boulevard, like **Tower Records** and the **Virgin Megastore,** are often star-heavy, as are chichi shops within the **Beverly Center** mall. **Book Soup,** that browser's paradise across the street from Tower, is usually good for a star or two. A midafternoon stroll along **Melrose Avenue** might also produce a familiar face, likewise the chic European-style shops of **Sunset Plaza** or the **Beverly Center.**

Or you can seek out the celebrities on the job. It's not uncommon for star-studded movie productions to use L.A.'s diverse cultural landscape for **location shots**; in fact, it's such a regular occurrence that locals are usually less impressed with an A-list presence than perturbed about the precious parking spaces lost to all those equipment trucks and dressing-room trailers. On-the-street movie shoots are part of what makes L.A. unique, and onlookers gather wherever hastily scrawled production signs point to a hot site. This isn't some word-of-mouth groupie posting—it's a strictly legit online listing of every filming permit applied for within the city limits. Entries are classified by type (commercial advertisement, feature film, student film, TV program) and working title, and the site lists production hours and exact street addresses.

If you're really intent on seeing as many stars as possible, log on to www.seeing-stars.com, a website that keeps tabs on where all the stars shop, eat, stay, and play in L.A.

Mulholland Drive ⨍ Los Angeles is the only major city in the world divided by a mountain range, and the road on top of this range is the famous Mulholland Drive. It travels 21 miles along the peaks and canyons of Hollywood Hills and the Santa Monica mountains, separating the Los Angeles basin from the San Fernando Valley. The winding road provides amazing views of the city (particularly at night) and offers many opportunities to pull over and enjoy the view 1,400 feet above sea level.

Completed in 1924, it's named after William Mulholland, the engineer of the aqueduct connecting L.A. and the Valley. Yes, there are celebrities up in them thar hills—Warren Beatty and Annette Bening, Kevin Costner, and Jack Nicholson, to name a few—but you'll never find them, as most of the mansions are well hidden. You don't need to drive the whole road to get the full effect. From Cahuenga Boulevard (near the Hollywood Bowl) take the Mulholland Drive turnoff heading west. After a few miles you'll see a "scenic view" area on your left. Park at the small paved parking lot (which closes at sunset), ooh and aah over the view of the L.A. basin, then drive a few miles further west until you spot the other scenic view area on your right (dirt this time) overlooking the Valley. The whole trip should take you less than an hour. *Tip:* Don't drive here after 3pm on weekdays—the rush-hour traffic in this area is horrible. Also, no matter what your map says, there is no Mulholland Drive exit off of U.S. 101; you have to get on Cahuenga Boulevard.

Between Coldwater Canyon Dr. and U.S. 101.

Santa Monica Pier ⨍⨍ *Kids* Piers have been a tradition in Southern California since the area's 19th-century seaside resort days. Many have long since disappeared (like Pacific Ocean Park, an entire amusement park perched on offshore pilings), and others have been shortened by battering storms and are now mere shadows (or stumps) of their former selves, but you can still get a chance to experience those halcyon days of yesteryear at world-famous Santa Monica Pier.

Built in 1908 for passenger and cargo ships, the Santa Monica Pier does a pretty good job of recapturing the glory days of Southern California. The wooden wharf is now home to seafood restaurants and snack shacks, a touristy Mexican cantina, and a gaily colored turn-of-the-20th-century indoor wooden carousel (which Paul Newman operated in *The Sting*). Summer evening concerts, which are free and range from big band to Miami-style Latin, draw crowds, as does the small amusement area perched halfway down. Its name, **Pacific Park** (② 310/260-8744; www.pacpark.com), hearkens back to the granddaddy pier amusement park in California, Pacific Ocean Park; this updated version has a Ferris wheel, roller coaster, and other rides, plus a high-tech arcade shoot-out. But anglers still head to the end to fish, and nostalgia buffs to view the photographic display of the pier's history. This is the last of the great pleasure piers, offering rides, romance, and perfect panoramic views of the bay and mountains.

The pier is about a mile up Ocean Front Walk from Venice; it's a great round-trip stroll. Parking is available for $6 to $8 on both the Pier Deck and the Beachfront nearby. Limited short-term parking is also available. For information on twilight concerts (generally held Thurs between mid-June and the end of Aug), call ② 310/458-8900 or visit www.santamonicapier.org.

Ocean Ave. at the end of Colorado Blvd., Santa Monica.

Six Flags California (Magic Mountain and Hurricane Harbor) 🎢🎢 (Kids)

What started as a countrified little amusement park with a couple of relatively tame roller coasters in 1971 has been transformed by Six Flags into a thrill-a-minute daredevil's paradise called "The Xtreme Park." Located about 20 to 30 minutes north of Universal Studios, Six Flags Magic Mountain is one of the only ones out of the 38 Six Flags parks that is open year-round. The 16 world-class roller coasters (more than any other place in the world) make it enormously popular with teenagers and young adults, and the children's playland—Bugs Bunny World—creates excitement for the pint-size set (kids that are under 48 in. tall.) Bring an iron constitution: Rides with names like Goliath, Déjà Vu, Ninja, Viper, Colossus, and Psyclone will have your cheeks flapping with G-force intensity, and queasy expressions are common at the exit. Some rides are themed to action-film characters (like Superman The Escape and The Riddler's Revenge); others are loosely tied to their themed surroundings, like a Far East pagoda or gold rush mining town. The newest thrill rides are Scream!, where riders are strapped into a "flying chair" and raced upside down seven times at 65 mph, and X, the world's first and only roller coaster where riders rotate 360 degrees forward and backwards. Arcade games and summer-only entertainment (stunt shows, animal shows, and parades) round out the park's attractions.

Hurricane Harbor is Six Flags' tropical paradise, which is located right next door to Magic Mountain and is open May through September. You really can't see both in 1 day—combo tickets allow you to return sometime before the end of the season. Bring your own swimsuit; the park has changing rooms with showers and lockers. Like Magic Mountain, areas have themes like a tropical lagoon or an African river (complete with ancient temple ruins). The primary activities are swimming, water slides, rafting, volleyball, and lounging; many areas are designed especially for the little "buccaneer."

Magic Mountain Pkwy. (off Golden State Fwy. [I-5] north), Valencia. © **661/255-4500** or 818/367-5965. www.sixflags.com. Magic Mountain $47 adults, $30 seniors 55 and older and children age 2 to 48 in. high, free for kids under 2; Hurricane Harbor $24 adults $17 seniors and children; combo ticket $57. Magic Mountain: daily Apr to Labor Day and weekends and holidays the rest of the year. Hurricane Harbor: daily Memorial Day to Labor Day; weekends May and Sept; closed Oct–Apr. Both parks open at 10am; closing hours vary between 6pm–midnight. Parking $9. All prices and hours are subject to change without notice so please call before you arrive.

Sunset Boulevard & The Sunset Strip 🎢🎢

Unless you were raised in a cave, you've undoubtedly heard of L.A.'s Sunset Boulevard. The most famous of the city's many legendary boulevards, it winds dozens of miles over prime real estate as it travels from downtown to the beach, taking its travelers on both a historic and microcosmic journey that defines Los Angeles as a whole—from tacky strip malls and historic movie studios to infamous strip clubs and some of the most coveted zip codes on earth. In fact, driving the stretch from U.S. 101 to the Pacific should be a prerequisite for all first-time visitors because it provides so perfectly what L.A. is all about: instant gratification.

Bam! From the start you'll see the original **CBS Studios** where *The Jack Benny Show* emanated; the **Hollywood Palladium** where Lawrence Welk and the Dorsey Brothers performed; the **Sahara Hotel** of many a movie shoot; the Guitar Center's **Hollywood RockWalk** where superstars like Chuck Berry, Little Richard, Santana, and the Van Halen brothers left handprints or signatures; the **"Riot Hyatt"** where The Doors, Led Zeppelin, and Guns n' Roses crashed and smashed from the 1960s through the 1980s; and **Chateau Marmont** where Greta Garbo lived and John Belushi died.

Phew! And you've barely even started. Once you pass the Chateau Marmont, you're officially cruising the **Sunset Strip**—a 1¾-mile stretch of Sunset Boulevard from Crescent Heights Boulevard to Doheny Drive. The tour continues with: **The Comedy Store** where Rosanne, Robin Williams, and David Lettermen rose to stardom; Dan Aykroyd's **House of Blues** where the rock stars still show up for impromptu shows; **Tower Records,** the largest record store in the world; the **Argyle Hotel** where Clark Gable, Marilyn Monroe, and John Wayne once lived; the ultraexclusive **Skybar** within the Mondrian hotel; Johnny Depp's **Viper Room** where River Phoenix overdosed in '93; **Whisky A Go-Go** where The Doors where once a house band; and the **Rainbow Bar & Grill** where Jimi Hendrix, Bruce Springsteen, and Bob Marley became legends.

Once you emerge from the strip, things calm down considerably as you drive through the tony neighborhoods of **Beverly Hills, Bel Air, Brentwood,** and **Pacific Palisades.** By the time you've reached the ocean, you'll have seen a vivid cross-section of the city and a pretty good idea of what L.A. is all about.

Universal Studios Hollywood & CityWalk 🎞🎞 *Kids* Believing that film-making itself is a bona fide attraction, Universal Studios began offering tours to the public in 1964. The concept worked: Today Universal is more than just one of the largest movie studios in the world—it's one of the largest amusement parks as well. By integrating shows and rides with behind-the-scenes presentations on moviemaking, Universal created a new genre of theme park, stimulating a number of clone and competitor parks.

The main attraction continues to be the **Studio Tour,** a 1-hour guided tram ride around the company's 420 acres. En route you pass stars' dressing rooms and production offices before visiting famous back-lot sets that include an eerily familiar Old West town, a clean New York City street, the famous town square from the *Back to the Future* films, and newer sets such as *Curse of the Mummy's Tomb, Jurassic Park III,* and *The Grinch.* Along the way the tram encounters several staged "disasters," which I won't divulge here lest I ruin the surprise (they're all very tame). Though the wait to board might appear long, don't be discouraged—each tram carries several hundred people and departures are frequent, so the line moves quickly.

Other attractions are more typical of high-tech theme-park fare, but all have a film-oriented slant. The newest ride, **Revenge of the Mummy,** is a high-tech indoor rollercoaster that's enhanced with animatronics, motion picture technology, and lots of creepy Warrior Mummies that drop down and scare the bejeezus out of you. **Back to the Future** is a virtual-reality ride within a bucking simulation chamber (similar to Star Tours at Disneyland). You're a guest in Doc Brown's lab and get caught up in a high-speed chase in a time-traveling DeLorean through a million years (try to count how many times Biff says "butthead"). **Jurassic Park—The Ride** is short in duration but long on dinosaur animatronics; riders in jungle boats float through a world of five-story-tall T-rexes and airborne raptors that culminates in a pitch-dark vertical drop with a splash ending. **Terminator 2: 3-D** is a cyberwar show that combines live action along with triple-screen 3-D technology, explosions, spraying mists, and laser fire (Arnold prevails, of course). **Shrek 4-D** is one of the park's best attractions, a multisensory animated show that combines 3-D effects, a humorous storyline, and "surprise" special effects—the flying dragon chase is wild.

There are also several live shows performing daily. **Waterworld** is an entertaining, fast-paced outdoor theater presentation (and far better than the film that inspired it) featuring stunts and special effects performed on and around a small man-made lagoon (most performances are sold out, so arrive at the theater

Moments **Topanga Canyon: Nature's Solution to L.A.'s Noise Pollution**

When you've had enough of cellphones, cement, and Mercedes, it's time to take the short drive from L.A. to Topanga Canyon to bargain-shop, drink margaritas, and play cowgirl for a day. Here's the game plan: Call **Escape on Horseback** (see "Horseback Riding" below) and make a reservation for a guided horseback ride in the late afternoon. Next, take the winding drive up Topanga Canyon Boulevard to tiny **Topanga,** one of the last art communities left in Southern California and the perfect antidote to the dig-me L.A. scene. Spend an hour or so picking through the treasure trove of vintage clothes, accessories, and antiques at **Hidden Treasures** (154 S. Topanga Canyon Blvd; © 310/455-2998), one of the funkiest little shops I've ever seen (the custom-made sea-theme toilet seat lids are mesmerizing). After the scenic horseback ride through the boulder-strewn Topanga canyons lined with oaks, sycamores, chaparral, and sage, finish off your relaxing day with a leisurely dinner in Topanga at **Abuelitas** (137 S. Topanga Canyon Rd.; © 310/455-8788), a popular Mexican restaurant, or the romantic **Inn of the Seventh Ray** (128 Old Topanga Canyon Rd.; © 310/455-1311; www.innoftheseventhray.com).

at least 15 min. before the show time listed in the handout park map). In **Backdraft,** guests move from theater to theater amidst realistic ruptured fuel lines, melting metal, and scorching warehouse scenes. **Spider-Man Rocks!** is a high-energy rock 'n' roll musical with lots of song, dance, acrobatics, loud noises, and pyrotechnics. **Animal Planet Live!** stars trained monkeys, pigs, hawks, and other animals doing various entertaining tricks (well, most of the time). *Tip:* Straight ahead of the park's main entrance on Main Street is the **TV Audience Ticket Booth,** where you can obtain free tickets to join the audience for any TV shows that are taping during your visit (subject to availability).

Universal Studios is an exciting place for kids and teens, but just as in any theme park, lines can be brutally long; the wait for a 5-minute ride can sometimes last more than an hour. In summer the Valley heat can dog you all day. To avoid the crowds, try not to visit on weekends, school vacations, and Japanese holidays. If you're willing to pay extra to save the hassle of standing in line, the park offers a "Front of Line" pass with—obviously—front-of-the-line privileges, as well as VIP passes (essentially private tours). You can also save time by purchasing and printing your tickets online. Log on to the website for more information.

Located just outside the gate of Universal Studios Hollywood is **Universal CityWalk** (© 818/622-4455; www.citywalkhollywood.com), Universal Studio's version of Downtown Disney, complete with throngs of bored-looking teens. If you have any money left from the amusement park, you can spend it at this 3-block-long pedestrian promenade crammed thick with flashy name-brand stores (Billabong, Fossil, Skechers, Vans), dorky nightclubs (Blues at B. B. King's, Howl at the Moon dueling piano bar, Rumba Room Latin dance club), chain restaurants (Hard Rock Cafe, Daily Grill, Jerry's Famous Deli), a six-story 3-D IMAX theater, 18-screen cinema, 6,200-seat amphitheater, NASCAR virtual racing, and even a bowling alley (Take *that,* Disney!). Entrance to CityWalk is free; it's open until 9pm on weekdays and until midnight Friday and Saturday. *Tip:* The sushi at the Wasabi at CityWalk restaurant (© 818/622-7224) was surprisingly good and very reasonably priced.

Hollywood Fwy. (Universal Center Dr. or Lankershim Blvd. exits), Universal City. © 818/662-3801. www. universalstudioshollywood.com. Admission $50 adults, $40 children under 48 in. tall. Parking $8. Weekdays 10am–6pm; weekends 9am–7pm.

Venice Beach's Ocean Front Walk ⭐⭐⭐ *Kids*   This has long been one of L.A.'s most colorful areas and a must-visit for any first-time tourist. Founded at the turn of the last century, Venice was a development inspired by its Italian namesake. Authentic gondolas plied miles of inland waterways lined with rococo palaces. In the 1950s, Venice became the stomping grounds of Jack Kerouac, Allen Ginsberg, William S. Burroughs, and other Beats. In the 1960s, this was the epicenter of L.A.'s hippie scene.

Today Venice is still one of the world's most engaging bohemian locales. It's not an exaggeration to say that no visit to L.A. would be complete without a stroll along the famous paved beach path, an almost surreal assemblage of every L.A. stereotype—and then some. Among stalls and stands selling cheap sunglasses, Mexican blankets, and "herbal ecstasy" pills swirls a carnival of humanity that includes bikini-clad in-line skaters, tattooed bikers, tan hunks pumping iron at Muscle Beach, panhandling vets, beautiful wannabes, and plenty of tourists and gawkers. On any given day, you're bound to come across all kinds of performers: mimes, break-dancers, seriously stoned drummers, chain-saw jugglers, talking parrots, and the occasional apocalyptic evangelist.

On the beach, between Venice Blvd. and Rose Ave., Venice. www.venicebeach.com.

Walt Disney Concert Hall ⭐⭐⭐   The strikingly beautiful Walt Disney Concert Hall isn't just the new home of the Los Angeles Philharmonic, it's a key element in an urban revitalization effort now underway downtown. The Walt Disney family insisted on the best and, with an initial gift of $50 million to build a world-class performance venue, that's what they got: a masterpiece of design by world-renowned architect Frank Gehry, and an acoustical quality that equals or surpasses the best concert halls in the world. Similar to Gehry's most famous architectural masterpiece, the Guggenheim Museum in Bilbao, the concert hall's dramatic stainless-steel exterior consists of a series of undulating curved surfaces that partially envelop the entire building, presenting multiple glimmering facades to the surrounding neighborhood. Within is a dazzling 2,273-seat auditorium replete with curved woods and a dazzling array of organ pipes (also designed by Gehry), as well as a Joachim Splichal's Patina restaurant, the hip Concert Hall Cafe, a bookstore, and a gift shop.

The 3½-acre Concert Hall is open to the public for viewing, but to witness it in its full glory, do whatever it takes to attend a concert by the world-class Los Angeles Philharmonic (p. 564). Also highly recommended are the $10 audio tours, which lead visitors through the Concert Hall's history from conception to creation. The 45-minute self-guided tour is narrated by actor John Lithgow and includes interviews with Frank Gehry, Los Angeles Philharmonic music director Esa-Pekka Salonen, and acoustician Yasuhisa Toyota, among others. One big caveat is that you see just about everything except the auditorium: There's almost always a rehearsal in progress and the acoustics are so good that there's no discreet way to sneak a peak. The audio tours are available on nonmatinee days from 9am to 3pm and matinee days from 9 to 10:30am.

111 S. Grand Ave. (at First St.). © 213/972-4399 or 323/850-2000. www.musiccenter.org or www.laphil.com.

6 Exploring the City

To locate the attractions discussed below, see the individual neighborhood maps in section 1, "Orientation."

MUSEUMS & GALLERIES
L.A.'S WESTSIDE & BEVERLY HILLS

Museum of Tolerance   The Museum of Tolerance is designed to expose prejudices, bigotry, and inhumanity while teaching racial and cultural tolerance. Since its opening in 1993, it's hosted 3.5 million visitors from around the world, including King Hussein of Jordan and the Dalai Lama. It's located in the Simon Wiesenthal Center, an institute founded by the legendary Nazi-hunter. While the Holocaust figures prominently here, this is not just a Jewish museum—it's an academy that broadly campaigns for a live-and-let-live world. Tolerance is an abstract idea that's hard to display, so most of this $50-million museum's exhibits are high-tech and conceptual in nature. Fast-paced interactive displays are designed to touch the heart as well as the mind, and engage everyone from heads of state to the MTV generation.

9786 W. Pico Blvd. (at Roxbury Dr.). 🕐 310/553-8403. www.museumoftolerance.com. Admission $10 adults, $8 seniors 62 and over, $7 students with ID, $7 children ages 3–12, free for children age 2 and under. Advance purchase recommended; photo ID required for admission. Mon–Thurs 11:30am–4pm; Fri 11:30am–3pm (to 1pm Nov–Mar); Sun 11am–5pm. Closed Sat and many Jewish and secular holidays; call for schedule.

UCLA Hammer Museum   Created by the former chairman and CEO of Occidental Petroleum, the Hammer Museum has had a hard time winning the respect of critics and the public. Barbs are aimed at both the museum's relatively flat collection and its patron's tremendous ego. The Hammer is ensconced in a two-story Carrara marble building attached to the oil company's offices. It's better known for its high profile and often provocative visiting exhibits, such as the opulent prerevolution treasures of Russian ruler Catherine the Great. In conjunction with UCLA's Wight Gallery, a feisty gallery with a reputation for championing contemporary political and experimental art, the Hammer continues to present often daring and usually popular special exhibits, and it's definitely worth calling ahead to find out what will be there during your visit to L.A. The permanent collection (Armand Hammer's personal collection) consists mostly of traditional Western European and Anglo-American art, and contains noteworthy paintings by Toulouse-Lautrec, Rembrandt, Degas, and van Gogh. A $25-million renovation and expansion—including four new galleries, a restaurant, and a 288-seat theater—should be completed by the time you're reading this.

10899 Wilshire Blvd. (at Westwood Blvd.). 🕐 310/443-7000. www.hammer.ucla.edu. Admission $5 adults, $3 students and seniors 55 and over, free for kids age 17 and under; free for everyone Thurs. Tues–Wed and Fri–Sat 11am–7pm; Thurs 11am–9pm; Sun 11am–5pm. Parking $2.75 for 1st 3 hr. with validation.

HOLLYWOOD

Craft & Folk Art Museum   This gallery, in a prominent Museum Row building, has grown into one of the city's largest. "craft and folk art" encompasses everything from clothing, tools, religious artifacts, and everyday objects to wood carvings, papier-mâché, weaving, and metalwork. The museum displays folk objects from around the world, but its strongest collection is masks from India, America, Mexico, Japan, and China. The museum is also known for its annual International Festival of Masks, held each October in Hancock Park, across the street. Be sure to stop in the funky, eclectic Museum Shop (🕐 323/857-4677) to peruse the wearable art, books, and handmade crafts.

5814 Wilshire Blvd. (between Fairfax and La Brea aves). ℂ 323/937-4230. www.cafam.org. Admission $3.50 adults, $2.50 seniors and students, free for children under age 12, free to all the 1st Wed of each month. Museum exhibits Wed–Sun 11am–5pm; Museum Shop Tues–Sun 11am–5pm.

Los Angeles County Museum of Art ℛℛ

For more than 50 years, the LACMA has been one of the finest art museums in the nation, housing a 110,000-piece collection that includes works by Degas, Rembrandt, Hockney, and Monet. The huge complex—it's the largest visual-arts museum west of the Mississippi—was designed by three very different architects over a span of 30 years, and though the architectural fusion can be migraine inducing, this city landmark is well worth delving into.

The **Japanese Pavilion** has exterior walls made of Kalwall, a translucent material that, like shoji screens, permits the entry of soft natural light. Inside is a collection of Japanese Edo paintings that's rivaled only by the holdings of the emperor of Japan. The **Anderson Building,** the museum's contemporary wing, is home to 20th-century painting and sculpture. Here you'll find works by Matisse, Magritte, and a good number of Dada artists. The **Ahmanson Building** houses the rest of the museum's permanent collections. You'll find everything from 2,000-year-old pre-Columbian Mexican ceramics to 19th-century portraiture to a unique glass collection spanning the centuries. Other displays include one of the nation's largest holdings of costumes and textiles, and an important Indian and Southeast Asian art collection. The **Hammer Building** is primarily used for major special-loan exhibitions. Free guided tours covering the museum's highlights depart on a regular basis from here. Also, be sure to visit the museum's website to see what special exhibits are currently on display.

5905 Wilshire Blvd. ℂ 323/857-6000. www.lacma.org. Admission $9 adults, $5 students and seniors age 62 and over, $1 children ages 6–17, free for kids age 5 and under; regular exhibitions free for everyone the 2nd Tues of each month. Mon–Tues and Thurs noon–8pm; Fri noon–9pm; Sat–Sun 11am–8pm. Parking $5

Museum of the American West ℛℛ

Located north of downtown in Griffith Park, this is one of the country's finest and most comprehensive museums of the American West. More than 78,000 artifacts showcasing the history of the region west of the Mississippi River are intelligently displayed. Evocative exhibits illustrate the everyday lives of early pioneers, not only with antique firearms, tools, saddles, and the like, but with many hands-on displays that successfully stir the imagination and the heart. You'll find footage from Buffalo Bill's Wild West Show, movie clips from the silent days, contemporary films, the works of Wild West artists, and plenty of memorabilia from Gene "The Singing Cowboy" Autry's film and TV projects. The "Hall of Merchandising" displays Roy Rogers bedspreads, Hopalong Cassidy radios, and other items from the collective consciousness—and material collections—of baby boomers. Provocative visiting exhibits (whose banners are visible from Interstate 5) usually focus on cultural or domestic regional history. Docent-led tours are generally scheduled on Saturdays at 11am and noon. *Tip:* You can purchase a $12 two-site ticket that includes entry into the Southwest Museum; it's valid for 3 months.

4700 Western Heritage Way (in Griffith Park). ℂ 323/667-2000. www.museumoftheamericanwest.org. Admission $7.50 adults, $5 seniors 60 and over and students ages 13–18, $3 children ages 2–12, free for kids under age 2; free to all Thurs after 4pm. Tues–Sun 10am–5pm (Thurs until 8pm). Parking is free.

Petersen Automotive Museum ℛ *Kids*

When the Petersen opened in 1994, many locals were surprised that it had taken this long for the city of freeways to salute its most important shaper. Indeed, this museum says more about the city than probably any other in L.A. Named for Robert Petersen, the publisher responsible for *Hot Rod* and *Motor Trend* magazines, the four-story museum displays more than 200 cars and motorcycles, from the historic to the futuristic. Cars on the first floor are exhibited chronologically in period settings. Other floors are devoted to frequently changing shows of race cars, early motorcycles, famous movie vehicles, and celebrity wheels such as Jack Benny's old Chrysler Imperial. On the third floor is the Discovery Center, a 6,500-square-foot interactive "hands-on" learning center that teaches the basic scientific principles of how a car works. Past shows have included a comprehensive exhibit of "woodies" and surf culture, Hollywood "star cars," and the world's fastest and most valuable cars.

6060 Wilshire Blvd. (at Fairfax Ave.). (C) **323/930-CARS**. www.petersen.org. Admission $10 adults, $5 seniors and students, $3 children ages 5–12, free for kids age 4 and under. Tues–Sun 10am–6pm. Parking $6.

DOWNTOWN

California Science Center ★★ *Kids*   A $130-million renovation—reinvention, actually—has turned the former Museum of Science and Industry into Exposition Park's newest attraction. Using high-tech sleight-of-hand, the center stimulates kids of all ages with questions, answers, and lessons about the world. One of the museum's highlights is Tess, a 50-foot animatronic woman whose muscles, bones, organs, and blood vessels are revealed, demonstrating how the body reacts to a variety of external conditions and activities. (Appropriate for children of all ages, Tess doesn't possess reproductive organs.) Another highlight is the new **Air and Space Gallery,** a seven-story space where real air- and spacecraft are suspended overhead.

There are nominal fees, ranging from $2 to $5, to enjoy the science center's more thrilling attractions. You can pedal a bicycle across a high wire suspended 43 feet above the ground (demonstrating the principle of gravity and counterweights) or get strapped into the Space Docking Simulator for a virtual-reality taste of zero gravity. There's plenty more, and plans for expansion are always in the works. The IMAX theater boasts a screen seven stories high and 90 feet wide, with state-of-the-art surround sound and 3-D technology. Films are screened throughout the day until 9pm and are nearly always breathtaking, even the two-dimensional ones.

700 State Dr., Exposition Park. (C) **323/724-3623**. IMAX theater (C) **213/744-7400**. www.casciencectr.org. Free admission to the museum; IMAX theater $7.50 adults, $4.50 ages 4–12, $5.50 seniors over 60 and children ages 13–17. Multishow discounts available. Daily 10am–5pm. Closed Thanksgiving, Christmas, and New Year's Day. Parking $6.

Japanese American National Museum ★ *Finds*   Located in an architecturally acclaimed modern building in Little Tokyo, this soaring 85,000-square-foot pavilion—designed by renowned architect Gyo Obata—is a private nonprofit institute created to document and celebrate the history of the Japanese in America. The permanent and rotating exhibits chronicle Japanese life in the United States, highlighting distinctive aspects of Japanese-American culture ranging from the internment camp experience during the early years of World War II to the lives of Japanese-Americans in Hawaii. The experience is made even more poignant by the personal accounts of the docents, many of whom are elderly Japanese-American citizens who were imprisoned in these camps during the war. It's a very popular museum, attracting more than 150,000 annual visitors. *Tip:* Don't miss the museum store, which carries excellent gift items ranging from hand-fired sake sets to mini-Zen gardening kits.

369 E. First St. (at Central Ave.). (C) **213/625-0414**. www.janm.org. Admission $6 adults, $5 seniors, $3 students and kids 6–17, free for kids age 5 and under; free to all the 3rd Thurs of each month, and every Thurs after 5pm. Tues–Sun 10am–5pm (Thurs till 8pm).

Museum of Contemporary Art/Geffen Contemporary at MOCA 🕸🕸
MOCA is Los Angeles's only institution devoted to art from 1940 to the present. Displaying works in a variety of media, it's strong in works by Cy Twombly, Jasper Johns, and Mark Rothko, and shows are often superb. For many experts, MOCA's collections are too spotty to be considered world-class, and the conservative museum board blushes when offered controversial shows (they passed on a Whitney exhibit that included photographs by Robert Mapplethorpe). Nevertheless, I've seen some excellent exhibitions here.

MOCA is housed in three buildings: The Grand Avenue main building (250 S. Grand Ave., Los Angeles) is a contemporary red-sandstone structure by renowned Japanese architect Arata Isozaki. The museum restaurant, **Patinette** (Mon, Wed, and Fri 11am–5pm, Thurs 11am–8pm, Sat–Sun 11am–6pm; 🕾 213/ 626-1178), located here, is the casual-dining creation of celebrity chef Joachim Splichal (see Patina, p. 509). The museum's second space, on Central Avenue in Little Tokyo (152 N. Central Ave., Los Angeles), was the "temporary" Contemporary while the Grand structure was being built, and now houses a superior permanent collection in a warehouse-type space that's been renamed for entertainment mogul and art collector David Geffen. An added feature is a timeline corresponding to the progression of works. Unless there's a visiting exhibit of great interest at the main museum, I recommend you start at the Geffen building—where it's also easier to park. The third gallery is at the Pacific Design Center (8687 Melrose Ave., West Hollywood)—it's the compact building next to the Pacific Design Center. Unlike the other two, admission to this gallery is only $3, and emphasis is on contemporary architecture and design, as well as new work by emerging and established artists.

Main MOCA information line: 🕾 213/626-6222. www.moca-la.org. Admission $8 adults, $5 seniors 65 and over and students, free for children age 11 and under; free admission to all MOCA galleries every Thurs. Mon and Fri 11am–5pm; Thurs 11am–8pm; Sat–Sun 11am–6pm.

Natural History Museum of Los Angeles County 🕸🕸 The "Fighting Dinosaurs" are not a high school football team but the trademark symbol of this massive museum: *Tyrannosaurus rex* and triceratops skeletons poised in a stance so realistic that every kid feels inspired to imitate their *Jurassic Park* bellows. Opened in 1913 in a beautiful domed Spanish Renaissance building, this massive museum—it's the largest natural and historical museum in the western United States—is a 35-hall warehouse of Earth's history, chronicling the planet and its inhabitants from 600 million years ago to the present day and housing more than 33 million specimens and artifacts. There's a mind-numbing number of exhibits of prehistoric fossils, bird and marine life, gems and minerals, and North American mammals. The kid-friendly Discovery Center entertains children via hands-on, interactive exhibits: kids can make fossil rubbings, dig for fossils, and view live animals such as snakes and lizards. The best permanent displays include the world's rarest shark, a walk-through vault of priceless gems (including the largest collection of gold in the United States), and an Insect Zoo.

The Dinosaur Shop sells ant farms and exploding volcano and model kits, the Ethnic Arts Shop has one-of-a-kind folk art and jewelry, and the bookstore has an extensive selection of scientific titles and hobbyists' field guides.

900 Exposition Blvd., Exposition Park. 🕾 213/763-DINO. www.nhm.org. Admission $9 adults; $6.50 children ages 13–17, seniors, and students with ID; $2 children ages 5–12; free for kids under 5; free for everyone the 1st Tues of each month. Mon–Fri 9:30am–5pm; Sat–Sun 10am–5pm.

SANTA MONICA & THE BEACHES

Bergamot Arts Station & Santa Monica Museum of Art ★★   One of L.A.'s primary cultural destinations is the Bergamot Arts Station. Home to the **Santa Monica Museum of Art,** this campuslike complex is a hugely popular destination for visitors from around the world. The location dates from 1875 when it was a stop for the Red Line trolley and retains its industrial, rustic look. Filled with 20 galleries, the unique installations on display here range from photography and sculpture to interactive pieces that are both eclectic and cutting edge. Its central location allows visitors to park and spend the day seeing art rather than driving from one gallery to the next, and many pieces are available for purchase. A must-see for the arts lover.

2525 Michigan Ave., Santa Monica. ℭ 310/829-5854. www.bergamotstation.com. Free admission. Most galleries open Tues–Sat 11am–6pm.

PASADENA & ENVIRONS

Norton Simon Museum of Art ★★ *Finds*   Named for a food-packing king and financier who reorganized the failing Pasadena Museum of Modern Art, the Norton Simon displays one of the finest private collections of European, American, and Asian art in the world (and yet another feather in the cap of architect Frank Gehry, who redesigned the interior space). Comprehensive collections of masterpieces by Degas, Picasso, Rembrandt, and Goya are augmented by sculptures by Henry Moore and Auguste Rodin, including *The Burghers of Calais,* which greets you at the gates. The "Blue Four" collection of works by Kandinsky, Jawlensky, Klee, and Feininger is impressive, as is a superb collection of Southeast Asian sculpture. *Still Life with Lemons, Oranges, and a Rose* (1633), an oil by Francisco de Zurbarán, is one of the museum's most important holdings. Perhaps the most popular piece is *The Flower Vendor/Girl with Lilies* by Diego Rivera, followed by Goya's *Disasters of War.* The collection of paintings, sculptures, pastels, and prints by French Impressionist Edgar Degas are among the best in the world. **Tip:** Unless you're an art expert, you'll probably want to take the "Acoustiguide" audio tour—it's $3 well spent.

411 W. Colorado Blvd., Pasadena. ℭ 626/449-6840. www.nortonsimon.org. Admission $6 adults, $3 seniors, free for students and kids 17 and under; free for everyone the 1st Fri of each month 6–9pm. Wed–Mon noon–6pm (Fri till 9pm). Free parking.

Pacific Asia Museum   The most striking aspect of this museum is the building itself. Designed in the 1920s in Chinese Imperial Palace style, it's rivaled in flamboyance only by Grauman's Chinese Theatre in Hollywood (see "L.A.'s Top Attractions," earlier in this chapter). Rotating exhibits of 14,000 rare Asian and Pacific Islands art and artifacts span the centuries, from 100 B.C. to the current day. This manageably sized museum is worth a visit, particularly if you're an adherent of Buddhism.

46 N. Los Robles Ave., Pasadena. ℭ 626/449-2742, ext. 10. www.pacificasiamuseum.org. Admission $7 adults, $5 students and seniors, free for children under 12; free for everyone the 3rd Sat of each month. Wed–Thurs and Sat–Sun 10am–5pm; Fri 10am–8pm. Free parking.

ARCHITECTURAL HIGHLIGHTS

Los Angeles is a veritable Disneyland of architecture (and not too far from the real Disneyland). The city is home to an amalgam of styles, from Art Deco to Spanish Revival to coffee-shop kitsch to suburban ranch to postmodern—and much more. Cutting-edge, over-the-top styles that would be out of place in

---

Moments   Greystone Mansion

If you've seen *The Witches of Eastwick* or *War and Remembrance*, then you know how beautiful and opulent the Greystone Mansion and surrounding gardens are. Situated on a slope overlooking Beverly Hills, the 18½-acre park is a prime filming location where dozens of TV episodes, movies *(Spiderman, X-Men, Batman, Ghostbusters, The Bodyguard)*, commercials, and music videos are filmed annually. It's worth a visit just to admire the matriarch of Beverly Hills mansions and the meticulously groomed gardens. A self-guided tour takes you through the Formal Gardens, Mansion Gardens, and Lower Ground Estate. Picnics are welcome in designated areas (as are dogs), and **Afternoon Tea on the Terrace** is offered one Saturday per month from May through August at 4pm. The price is $34 for nonresidents and includes musical entertainment and a tour of the mansion's first floor. Tickets must be purchased in advance by calling Ⓒ **310/550-4796.** The park is at 905 Loma Vista Dr., just off Doheny, and is open daily from 10am to sunset. Admission is free. For more information, log on to www.beverlyhills.org.

---

other cities, from the oversize hot dog that is Tail o' the Pup to the mansions lining the streets of Beverly Hills, are perfectly at home. The newest gem on the scene is the Frank Gehry–designed **Walt Disney Concert Hall,** located at the intersection of First Street and Grand Avenue in the historic Bunker Hill area (see p. 524 for information on tickets and tours of the state-of-the-art facility.)

SANTA MONICA & THE BEACHES
When you're strolling the historic canals and streets of Venice, be sure to check out the **Chiat/Day** offices at 340 Main St. What would otherwise be an unspectacular contemporary office building is made fantastic by a **three-story pair of binoculars** that frames the entrance. The sculpture is modeled after a design created by Claes Oldenburg and Coosje van Bruggen.

When you're on your way in or out of LAX, be sure to stop for a moment to admire the **Control Tower** and **Theme Building.** The spacey *Jetsons*-style Theme Building, which has always loomed over LAX, has been joined by a more recent silhouette. The main control tower, designed by local architect Kate Diamond to evoke a stylized palm tree, is tailored to present Southern California in its best light. You can go inside to enjoy the view from the Theme Building's observation deck, or have a space-age cocktail at the Technicolor bachelor pad that is the **Encounter at LAX** restaurant.

L.A.'S WESTSIDE & BEVERLY HILLS
In addition to the sights below, don't miss the **Beverly Hills Hotel & Bungalows** (p. 479), and be sure to wind your way through the streets of Beverly Hills off Sunset Boulevard.

Pacific Design Center   The bold architecture and overwhelming scale of the Pacific Design Center, designed by Argentinean architect Cesar Pelli, aroused controversy when it was erected in 1975. Sheathed in gently curving cobalt-blue glass, the seven-story building houses more than 750,000 square feet of wholesale interior-design showrooms and is known to locals as "the blue whale." When the property for the design center was acquired in the 1970s, almost all of the small businesses that lined this stretch of Melrose Avenue were demolished. Only Hugo's Plating, which still stands in front of the center, successfully resisted the wrecking ball. In 1988 a second boxlike structure, dressed in equally dramatic Kelly green, was added to the design center and surrounded by a protected outdoor plaza.

8687 Melrose Ave., West Hollywood. © 310/657-0800. www.pacificdesigncenter.com.

Schindler House ☆ A protégé of Frank Lloyd Wright and contemporary of Richard Neutra, Austrian architect Rudolph Schindler designed this innovative modern house for himself in 1921–22. It's now home to the Los Angeles arm of Austria's Museum of Applied Arts (MAK). The house is noted for its complicated interlocking spaces; the interpenetration of indoors and out; simple, unadorned materials; and technological innovations. Docent-guided tours are conducted at no additional charge on weekends only.

The MAK Center offers guides to L.A.-area buildings by Schindler and other Austrian architects, and presents visiting related exhibitions and creative arts programming. Call for schedules.

835 N. Kings Rd. (north of Melrose Ave.), West Hollywood. © 323/651-1510. www.makcenter.com. Admission $5 adults, free to children age 12 and under; free to all every Fri after 4pm, Sept 10 (Schindler's birthday), May 24 (International Museum Day), and Dec 1. Wed–Sun 11am–6pm.

Tail o' the Pup At first glance, you might not think twice about this hot-dog-shaped bit of kitsch across from the Beverly Center. But locals adored this closet-size wiener dispensary so much that when it was threatened by the developer's bulldozer, they spoke out en masse to save it. One of the last remaining examples of 1950s representational architecture, the "little dog that could" serves up an "only in L.A." experience to go with its great Baseball Special.

329 N. San Vicente Blvd. (between Beverly Blvd. and Melrose Ave.), West Hollywood. © 310/652-4517.

HOLLYWOOD

In addition to the buildings listed below, don't miss the **Griffith Observatory** (p. 516), **Grauman's Chinese Theatre** (p. 515), and the **Roosevelt Hotel, Hollywood** (p. 486).

Capitol Records Building Opened in 1956, this 13-story tower, just north of the legendary intersection of Hollywood and Vine, is one of the city's most recognizable buildings. The world's first circular office building is often incorrectly said to have been made to resemble a stack of 45s under a turntable stylus (it kinda does, though). Nat "King" Cole, songwriter Johnny Mercer, and other 1950s Capitol artists populate a giant exterior mural. Look down and you'll see the sidewalk stars of Capitol's recording artists (including John Lennon). In the lobby numerous gold albums are on display as well.

1750 Vine St. © 323/462-6252.

The Egyptian Theatre Conceived by grandiose impresario Sid Grauman, the Egyptian Theatre is just down the street from his better-known Chinese Theatre, but it remains less altered from its original design, which was based on the

---

(Fun Fact **Not quite S.O.S., but . . .**

The light on the rooftop spire of the Capitol Records building flashes "H-O-L-L-Y-W-O-O-D" in Morse code. Really, it does.

Stargazing in L.A., Part II: The Less-Than-Lively Set

Almost everybody who visits L.A. hopes to see a celebrity—they are, after all, our most common export. But celebrities usually don't cooperate, failing to gather in readily viewable herds. There is, however, an absolutely guaranteed method to approach within 6 feet of many famous stars. Cemeteries are *the* place for star (or at least headstone) gazing: The star is always available, and you're going to get a lot more up close and personal than you probably would to anyone who's actually alive. Here is a guide to the most fruitful cemeteries, listed in order of their friendliness to stargazers.

Weathered Victorian and Art Deco memorials add to the decaying charm of **Hollywood Forever** (formerly Hollywood Memorial Park), 6000 Santa Monica Blvd., Hollywood (*©* **323/469-1181**). Fittingly, there's a terrific view of the Hollywood sign over the graves, as many of the founders of the community rest here. The most notable tenant is Rudolph Valentino, who rests in an interior crypt. Outside are Tyrone Power, Jr.; Douglas Fairbanks, Sr.; Cecil B. DeMille (facing Paramount, his old studio); Carl "Alfalfa" Spitzer from *The Little Rascals* (the dog on his grave is not Petey); Hearst mistress Marion Davies; John Huston; and a headstone for Jayne Mansfield (she's really buried in Pennsylvania with her family). In 2000 Douglas Fairbanks, Jr., joined his dad at Hollywood Forever.

Catholic **Holy Cross Cemetery**, 5835 W. Slauson Ave., Culver City (*©* **310/670-7697**), hands out maps to the stars' graves. In one area, within mere feet of each other, lie Bing Crosby, Bela Lugosi (buried in his Dracula cape), and Sharon Tate; not far away are Rita Hayworth and Jimmy Durante. Also here are "Tin Man" Jack Haley and "Scarecrow" Ray Bolger, Mary Astor, John Ford, and Gloria Morgan Vanderbilt. More recent arrivals include John Candy and Audrey Meadows.

The front office at **Hillside Memorial Park**, 6001 Centinela Ave., Baldwin Hills (*©* **310/641-0707**), can provide a guide to this Jewish cemetery, which has an L.A. landmark: the behemoth tomb of Al Jolson. His rotunda, complete with a bronze reproduction of Jolson and cascading fountain, is visible from I-405. Also on hand are Jack Benny, Eddie Cantor, Vic Morrow, and Michael Landon.

You just know developers get stomachaches looking at **Westwood Village Memorial Park**, 1218 Glendon Ave., Westwood (*©* **310/474-1579**; the staff can direct you around), smack-dab in the middle of some of L.A.'s priciest real estate (behind the AVCO office building south of

then-headline-news discovery of hidden treasures in Pharaohs' tombs—hence the hieroglyphic murals and enormous scarab decoration above the stage. Hollywood's first movie premiere, *Robin Hood* starring Douglas Fairbanks, was shown here in 1922, followed by the premiere of *The Ten Commandments* in 1923. The building recently underwent a sensitive restoration by American Cinematheque, which now screens rare, classic, and independent films here.

6712 Hollywood Blvd. *©* **323/466-FILM**. www.egyptiantheatre.com.

Wilshire Blvd.). But it's not going anywhere, especially when you consider its most famous resident: Marilyn Monroe (entombed in a simple wall crypt, number 24). It's also got Truman Capote, Roy Orbison, John Cassavetes, Armand Hammer, Donna Reed, and Natalie Wood. Walter Matthau and Jack Lemmon are buried here as well, a fitting ending for the Odd Couple.

Forest Lawn Glendale, 1712 S. Glendale Ave. ((*C*) **323/254-3131**), likes to pretend it has no celebrities. The most prominent of L.A. cemeteries, it's also the most humorless. The place is full of bad art, all part of the vision of founder Huburt Eaton, who thought cemeteries should be "happy" places. So he banished those gloomy upright tombstones and monuments in favor of flat, pleasant, character-free, flush-to-the-ground slabs. Contrary to urban legend, Walt Disney was *not* frozen and placed under Cinderella's castle at Disneyland. His cremated remains are in a little garden to the left of the Freedom Mausoleum. Turn around, and just behind you are Errol Flynn and Spencer Tracy. In the Freedom Mausoleum itself are Nat "King" Cole, Chico Marx, Gummo Marx, and Gracie Allen—finally joined by George Burns. In a columbarium near the Mystery of Life is Humphrey Bogart. Unfortunately, some of the best celebs—such as Clark Gable, Carole Lombard, and Jean Harlow—are in the Great Mausoleum, which you often can't get into unless you're visiting a relative.

You'd think a place that encourages people to visit for fun would understand what the attraction is. But no—Forest Lawn Glendale won't tell you where any of their illustrious guests are, so don't ask. This place is immense—and, frankly, dull in comparison to the other cemeteries, unless you appreciate the kitsch value of the Forest Lawn approach to art.

Forest Lawn Hollywood Hills, 6300 Forest Lawn Dr. ((*C*) **800/204-3131**), is slightly less anal than the Glendale branch, but the same basic attitude prevails. On the right lawn, near the statue of George Washington, is Buster Keaton. In the Courts of Remembrance are Lucille Ball, Charles Laughton, and the not-quite-gaudy-enough tomb of Liberace. Outside, in a vault on the Ascension Road side, is Andy Gibb. Bette Davis's sarcophagus is in front of the wall, to the left of the entrance to the Courts. Gene Autry is also buried here, almost within earshot of the museum that bears his name.

Freeman House   Frank Lloyd Wright's Freeman House, built in 1924, was designed as a prototype for mass-produced affordable housing. The home's richly patterned "textile-block" exterior was Wright's invention and is the most famous aspect of the home's design. On a dramatic site overlooking Hollywood, Freeman House is built with the world's first glass-to-glass corner windows. Dancer Martha Graham, bandleader Xavier Cugat, art collector Galka Sheye, photographer Edward Weston, and architects Philip Johnson and Richard Neutra all lived or spent time at this house, which became known as an avant-garde salon. The house is currently closed for restoration; call ahead to see if it's been reopened.

1962 Glencoe Way (off Hillcrest, near Highland and Franklin aves.). ℂ 323/851-0671.

DOWNTOWN

For a taste of what downtown's Bunker Hill was like before the bulldozers, visit the residential neighborhood of **Angelino Heights,** near Echo Park. Entire streets are still filled with stately gingerbread Victorian homes; most still enjoy the beautiful views that led early L.A.'s elite to build here. The 1300 block of Carroll Avenue is the best preserved. Don't be surprised if a film crew is scouting locations while you're there—these blocks appear often on the silver screen.

The Bradbury Building This National Historic Landmark, built in 1893 and designed by George Wyman, is Los Angeles's oldest commercial building and one of the city's most revered architectural achievements. Legend has it that an inexperienced draftsman named George Wyman accepted the $125,000 commission after communicating with his dead brother through a Ouija board. Capped by a five-story skylight, Bradbury's courtyard combines glazed brick, ornate Mexican tile floors, Belgian marble, Art Nouveau grillwork, handsome oak paneling, and lacelike wrought-iron railings—it's one of the great interior spaces of the 19th century. The glass-topped atrium is often used as a movie and TV set; you've probably seen it before in *Chinatown* and *Blade Runner.*

304 S. Broadway (at Third St.). ℂ 213/626-1893. Mon–Fri 9am–6pm; Sat–Sun 9am–5pm.

Cathedral of Our Lady of the Angels ℛ Completed in September 2002 at a cost of $163 million and built to last 500 years, this ultracontemporary cathedral is one of L.A.'s newest architectural treasures and the third-largest cathedral in the world. It was designed by award-winning Spanish architect Jose Rafael Moneo and features a 20,000-square-foot plaza, more than 6,000 crypts and niches (making it the largest crypt mausoleum in the U.S.), Mission-style colonnades, biblically inspired gardens, and numerous works of art created by world-acclaimed artists. While most Angelenos admit that the exterior of this austere, sand-colored structure is rather uninspiring and uninviting (the church doors don't face the street but rather a private plaza in back surrounded by fortresslike walls), the view from the inside is breathtaking: soaring heights, 12,000 panes of translucent alabaster, and larger-than-life tapestries lining the walls create an awe-inspiring sense of magnificence and serenity. The bronze doors, created by sculptor Robert Graham, pay homage to Ghiberti's bronze baptistery door in Florence. The cathedral now serves as the Mother Church of the Archdiocese of L.A.

555 W. Temple St. (at Grand Ave.), Los Angeles. ℂ 213/680-5200. www.olacathedral.org.

Moments Divine Vibrations

Every Wednesday from 12:45 to 1:15pm, the Cathedral of Our Lady of the Angels—the city's new $163-million architectural jewel—hosts an **organ recital** that is open to the public and free of charge. The power of the 42-ton organ's 6,019 pipes makes the cathedral vibrate, enabling you to not only hear the music but also feel it, making the experience physically poignant well as emotionally moving. See p. 534 for directions.

Central Library 𝒜𝒜 This is one of L.A.'s early architectural achievements and the third-largest library in the U.S. The city rallied to save the library when arson nearly destroyed it in 1986; the triumphant restoration has returned much of its original splendor. Working in the early 1920s, architect Bertram G. Goodhue employed the Egyptian motifs and materials popularized by the discovery of King Tut's tomb, and combined them with a more modern use of concrete block to great effect. Walking tours are the best way to explore this old beauty; they're lead Monday through Friday at 12:30pm, Saturday at 11am and 2pm, and Sunday at 2pm. *Warning:* Parking in this area can involve a heroic effort. Try visiting on the weekend and using the Flower Street parking entrance; the library will validate your ticket and you can escape for only $2.

630 W. Fifth St. (between Flower St. and Grand Ave.). © **213/228-7000.** www.lapl.org.

City Hall Built in 1928, the 27-story triangular Los Angeles City Hall was the tallest building in the city for more than 30 years. The structure's distinctive ziggurat roof was featured in the film *War of the Worlds,* but it is probably best known as the headquarters of the *Daily Planet* in the *Superman* TV series. When it was built, City Hall was the sole exception to an ordinance outlawing buildings taller than 150 feet. On a clear day (yeah, right), the top-floor observation deck offers views to Mount Wilson, 15 miles away.

200 N. Spring St. © **213/485-2121.** www.lacityhall.org. Observation deck open Mon–Fri 10am–4pm.

El Alisal 𝒜 El Alisal is a small, two-story "castle," built between 1889 and 1910 from large rocks and telephone poles purchased from the Santa Fe Railroad. The architect and creator was Charles F. Lummis, a Harvard graduate, archaeologist, and writer, who walked from Ohio to California and coined the slogan "See America First." A fan of Native American culture, Lummis is credited with popularizing the concept of the "Southwest," referring to New Mexico and Arizona. He often lived the lifestyle of the Indians, and he founded the Southwest Museum, a repository of Indian artifacts. Lummis held fabulous parties for the theatrical, political, and artistic elite; his guest list often included Will Rogers and Theodore Roosevelt. The outstanding feature of his house is the fireplace, which was carved by Mount Rushmore creator Gutzon Borglum. The lawn has been turned into an experimental garden of water-conserving plants.

200 E. Ave. 43, Highland Park. © **323/222-0546.** www.socalhistory.org. Free admission. Fri–Sun noon–4pm.

Union Station 𝒜 Union Station, completed in 1939, is one of the finest examples of California Mission-style architecture and one of the last of America's great rail stations. It was built with the opulence and attention to detail that characterize 1930s WPA projects. The cathedral-size, richly paneled ticket lobby and waiting area of this cream-colored structure stand sadly empty most of the time, but the MTA does use Union Station for Blue Line commuter trains. When you're strolling through these grand historic halls, it's easy to imagine the glamorous movie stars who once boarded *The City of Los Angeles* and *The Super Chief* to journey back east during the glory days of rail travel; it's also easy to picture the many joyous reunions between returning soldiers and loved ones following the victorious end to World War II, in the station's heyday. Movies shot here include *Bugsy* and *Blade Runner.* There's always been a restaurant in the station; the latest to occupy this unusually beautiful setting is **Traxx.**

800 N. Alameda St. (at Cesar E. Chavez Ave.).

US Bank Tower (aka Library Tower) Designed by renowned architect I M. Pei, L.A.'s most distinctive skyscraper (it's the round one) is the tallest building between Chicago and Singapore. Built in 1989 at a cost of $450 million, the 76-story monolith is both square and rectangular, rising from its Fifth Street base in a series of overlapping spirals and cubes. The Bunker Hill Steps wrapping around the west side of the building were inspired by Rome's Spanish Steps. Gee Whiz Fact: The glass crown at the top—illuminated at night—is the highest helipad in the world.

633 W. Fifth St. at S. Grand Ave.

Watts Towers & Art Center Watts became notorious as the site of riots in the summer of 1965, during which 34 people were killed and more than 1,000 injured. Today a visit to Watts is a lesson in inner-city life. It's a high-density land of gray strip malls, well-guarded check-cashing shops, and fast-food restaurants; but it's also a neighborhood of hardworking families struggling to survive in the midst of gangland. Although there's not much for the casual tourist here, the Watts Towers are truly a unique attraction, and the adjoining art gallery illustrates the fierce determination of area residents to maintain cultural integrity.

The Towers—the largest piece of folk art created by a single person—are colorful, 99-foot-tall cement and steel sculptures ornamented with mosaics of bottles, seashells, cups, plates, pottery, and ceramic tiles. They were completed in 1955 by folk artist Simon Rodia, an immigrant Italian tile-setter who worked on them for 33 years in his spare time. True fans of decorative ceramics will enjoy the fact that Rodia's day job was at the legendary Malibu Potteries (are those fragments of valuable Malibu tile encrusting the Towers?). Closed since 1994 due to earthquake damage, the towers were triumphantly reopened in 2001 and now attract 20,000 visitors annually. Tours are offered every half-hour on a first-come, first-served basis.

Note: Next to these designated Cultural Landmarks is the Art Center, which has an interesting collection of ethnic musical instruments as well as several visiting art exhibits throughout the year.

1727 E. 107th St., Los Angeles. ℂ **213/847-4646.** www.wattstowers.net. Gallery open Tues–Sat 10am–4pm; Sun noon–4pm.

PASADENA & ENVIRONS
For a quick but profound architectural fix, stroll past Pasadena's grandiose and baroque **City Hall,** 100 N. Garfield Ave., 2 blocks north of Colorado Boulevard. Closer inspection will reveal its classical colonnaded courtyard, formal gardens, and spectacular tiled dome.

The Gamble House ✿✿ The huge two-story Gamble House, built in 1908 as a California vacation home for the wealthy family of Procter and Gamble fame, is a sublime example of Arts and Crafts architecture. The interior, designed by the famous Pasadena-based Greene and Greene architectural team, abounds with handcraftsmanship, including intricately carved teak cornices, custom-designed furnishings, elaborate carpets, and a fantastic Tiffany glass door. No detail was overlooked. Every oak wedge, downspout, air vent, and switch plate contributes to the unified design. Admission is by 1-hour guided tour only, which departs every 15 minutes. Tickets go on sale on tour days in the bookstore at 10am. No reservations are necessary, but tours are often sold out, especially on weekends by 2pm.

If you can't fit the tour into your schedule but have an affection for Crafts-man design, visit the well-stocked bookstore and museum shop in the former garage (you can also see the exterior and grounds of the house this way). The bookstore is open Tuesday through Saturday from 10am to 5pm, Sunday 11:30am to 5pm.

Additional elegant Greene & Greene creations (still privately owned) abound 2 blocks away along **Arroyo Terrace,** including **nos. 368, 370, 400, 408, 424,** and **440.** The Gamble House bookstore can give you a walking-tour map and also conducts guided neighborhood tours by appointment.

4 Westmoreland Place (in the 300 block of N. Orange Grove Blvd.), Pasadena. ℂ 626/793-3334. www. gamblehouse.org. Tours $8 adults, $5 students and seniors 65 and over, free for children under 12. Tours Thurs–Sun noon–3pm. Closed holidays.

PARKS & GARDENS

In addition to the two examples of urban parkland below, check out **Pan Pacific Park,** a hilly retreat near the Farmers Market and CBS Studios, named for the Art Deco auditorium that unfortunately no longer stands at its edge.

Griffith Park 👁👁 (Kids)   Mining tycoon Colonel Griffith J. Griffith donated these 4,107 acres to the city in 1896 as a Christmas gift. Today Griffith Park is the largest urban park in America. There's a lot to do here, including 53 miles of hiking trails (the prettiest is the Fern Dell trail near the Western Ave. entrance, a shady hideaway cooled by waterfalls and ferns), horseback riding, golfing, swim-ming, biking, and picnicking (see "Outdoor Pursuits" later in this chapter). For a general overview of the park, drive the mountainous loop road that winds from the top of Western Avenue, past Griffith Observatory, and down to Vermont Avenue. For a more extensive foray, turn north at the loop road's midsection, onto Mt. Hollywood Drive. To reach the golf courses, the **Museum of the American West** (p. 526), or **Los Angeles Zoo** (p. 538), take Los Feliz Boulevard to Riverside Drive, which runs along the park's western edge.

Near the zoo, in a particularly dusty corner of the park, you can find the **Travel Town Transportation Museum,** 5200 Zoo Dr. (ℂ **323/662-5874**), a little-known outdoor museum with a small collection of vintage locomotives and old airplanes. Kids love the miniature train ride that circles the perimeter of the museum. The museum is open Monday through Friday from 10am to 4pm, Sat-urday and Sunday from 10am to 5pm; admission is free. Griffith Park entrances are along Los Feliz Boulevard, at Riverside Drive, Vermont Avenue, and Western Avenue (Hollywood; ℂ **323/913-4688;** www.laparks.org/grifmet/griffith.htm). Park admission is free.

Huntington Library, Art Collections & Botanical Gardens 👁👁   The Huntington Library is the jewel in Pasadena's crown. The 207-acre hilltop estate was once home to industrialist and railroad magnate Henry E. Huntington (1850–1927), who bought books on the same massive scale on which he acquired businesses. The continually expanding collection includes dozens of Shakespeare's first editions, Benjamin Franklin's handwritten autobiography, a Gutenberg Bible from the 1450s, and the earliest known manuscript of Chaucer's *Canterbury Tales.* Although some rare works are available only to vis-iting scholars, the library has a regularly changing (and always excellent) exhibit showcasing different items in the collection.

If you prefer canvas to parchment, Huntington also put together a terrific 18th-century British and French art collection. The most celebrated paintings are Gainsborough's *The Blue Boy,* and *Pinkie,* a companion piece by Sir Thomas

Lawrence depicting the youthful aunt of Elizabeth Barrett Browning. These and other works are displayed in the stately Italianate mansion on the crest of this hillside estate, so you can also get a glimpse of its splendid furnishings. American art and Renaissance paintings are exhibited in two additional galleries.

But it's the **botanical gardens** that draw most locals to the Huntington. The Japanese Garden comes complete with a traditional open-air Japanese house, koi-filled stream, and serene Zen garden. The cactus garden is exotic, the jungle garden is intriguing, the lily ponds are soothing—and there are many benches scattered about so you can sit and enjoy the surroundings.

Because the Huntington surprises many with its size and wealth of activities to choose from, first-timers might want to start with a tour. One-hour garden tours are offered daily; no reservations or additional fees required. Times vary, so check at the information desk on arrival. I also recommend that you tailor your visit to include the popular English high tea served Tuesday through Friday from noon to 4:30pm, and Saturday and Sunday from 10:45am to 4:30pm (last seating at 3:30pm). The **tearoom** overlooks the Rose Garden (home to 1,000 varieties displayed in chronological order of their breeding), and since the finger sandwiches and desserts are served buffet-style, it's a genteel bargain even for hearty appetites at $15 per person (please note that museum admission is a separate required cost). Phone ✆ **626/683-8131** for tearoom reservations, which are required and should be made at least 2 weeks in advance.

1151 Oxford Rd., San Marino. ✆ 626/405-2100. www.huntington.org. Admission $13 adults, $10 seniors 65 and over, $8.50 students and children age 12 and over, $5 children age 5–11, free for children under age 5; free to all 1st Thurs of each month. Sept–May Tues–Fri noon–4:30pm, Sat–Sun 10:30am–4:30pm; June–Aug Tues–Sun 10:30am–4:30pm. Closed major holidays.

Will Rogers State Historic Park

Will Rogers State Historic Park was once Will Rogers's private ranch and grounds. Willed to the state of California in 1944, the 168-acre estate is now both a park and a historic site, supervised by the Department of Parks and Recreation. Visitors may explore the grounds, the former stables, and the 31-room house filled with the original furnishings, including a porch swing in the living room and many Native American rugs and baskets. Charles Lindbergh and his wife, Anne Morrow Lindbergh, hid out here in the 1930s during part of the craze that followed the kidnap and murder of their first son. There are picnic tables, but no food is sold.

Who's Will Rogers you ask? He was born in Oklahoma in 1879 and became a cowboy in the Texas Panhandle before drifting into a Wild West show as a folksy, speechifying roper. The "cracker-barrel philosopher" performed lariat tricks while carrying on a humorous deadpan monologue on current events. The showman moved to Los Angeles in 1919, where he become a movie actor as well as the author of numerous books detailing his down-home "cowboy philosophy."

1501 Will Rogers State Park Rd., Pacific Palisades (between Santa Monica and Malibu). ✆ 310/454-8212. Park entrance $6 per vehicle. Daily 8am–sunset. House opens daily 10am–5pm; guided tours can be arranged for groups of 10 or more. From Santa Monica, take the Pacific Coast Hwy. (Calif. 1) north, turn right onto Sunset Blvd., and continue to the park entrance.

THE ZOO

Los Angeles Zoo 🅐 *(Kids)* The L.A. Zoo, which shares its parking lot with the Museum of the American West, has been welcoming visitors and busloads of school kids since 1966. In 1982 the zoo inaugurated a display of cuddly koalas, still one of its biggest attractions. Although it's smaller than the world-famous San Diego Zoo, the L.A. Zoo is surprisingly enjoyable and easy to fully explore. As much an arboretum as a zoo, the grounds are thick with mature shade trees

Value Free Culture

To beef up attendance and give indigent folk like us travel writers a break, almost all of L.A.'s art galleries and museums are open free to the public 1 day of the week or month (or both), and several charge no admission at all. Use the following list to plan your week around the museums' free-day schedules; refer to the individual attractions listings in this chapter for more information on most of these museums.

Free Every Day
- J. Paul Getty Museum at the Getty Center
- Museum of Television and Radio (donation suggested)
- Frederick's of Hollywood Lingerie Museum
- Los Angeles County Museum of Art *after* 5pm.
- California African American Museum
- California Science Center
- Bergamot Arts Station & Santa Monica Museum of Art

Free Every Thursday
- Museum of Contemporary Art (MOCA) from 11am to 8pm
- Museum of the American West from 4 to 8pm
- UCLA Hammer Museum from 11am to 9pm
- Japanese American National Museum from 5 to 8pm
- Geffen Contemporary at MOCA from 5 to 8pm

Free Every Friday
- Schindler House from 4 to 6pm

Free Every First Tuesday
- Natural History Museum of Los Angeles County from 9:30am to 5pm
- Page Museum at La Brea Tar Pits from 9:30am to 5pm

Free Every First Wednesday
- Craft & Folk Art Museum from 11am to 5pm

Free Every First Thursday
- Huntington Library, Art Collections & Botanical Gardens from noon to 4:30pm

Free Every First Friday
- Norton Simon Museum of Art from 6 to 9pm

Free Every Second Tuesday
- Museum of the American West from 10am to 5pm
- Los Angeles County Museum of Art from noon to 8pm

Free Every Third Saturday
- Pacific Asia Museum from 10am to 5pm

Free Every Third Tuesday
- Arboretum of Los Angeles County from 9am to 4:30pm
- Japanese American National Museum from 10am to 8pm

from around the world that help cool the once-barren grounds, and new habitats are light-years ahead of the cruel concrete roundhouses originally used to exhibit animals (though you can't help feeling that, despite the fancy digs, all the creatures would rather be in their natural habitats). Highlights include the

Chimpanzees of the Mahale Mountains habitat, where visitors can see plenty of primate activity; **the Red Ape Rain Forest,** a natural orangutan habitat; the entertaining **World of Birds** show; the **Pachyderm Forest** (climate-controlled digs for the elephants and hippos complete with an underwater viewing area); the new mandrills exhibit (the world's largest and most colorful baboons); and the **silverback gorilla exhibit.** The gargantuan Andean condor had me enthralled as well (the facility is renowned in zoological circles for the successful breeding and releasing of California condors, and occasionally it has some of these majestic and endangered birds on exhibit).

The zoo's latest attraction (and one they're rightfully proud of) is the **Winnick Family Children's Zoo,** a fantastic and forward-thinking children's zoo that contains a petting area, exhibition animal care center, "Adventure Theater" storytelling and puppet show, and other kid-hip exhibits and activities. *Tip:* To avoid the busloads of rambunctious school kids, arrive after noon.

5333 Zoo Dr., Griffith Park. © 323/644-4200. www.lazoo.org. Admission $9 adults, $4 kids ages 2–12, $6 seniors 62 and over, free to children under age 2. Daily 10am–5pm (till 6pm July 1 to Labor Day). Closed Christmas Day. Free parking.

ORGANIZED TOURS
STUDIO TOURS

NBC Studios *(Kids* According to a security guard, John Wayne and Redd Foxx once got into a fight here after Wayne refused to ride in the same limo as Foxx, who called the movie star a "redneck." Well, your NBC tour will probably be a bit more docile than that. The guided 70-minute indoor tour, which departs every half-hour, includes a behind-the-scenes unstaged look at *The Tonight Show with Jay Leno* set (see p. 543 on how to get free tickets); wardrobe, makeup, and set-building departments; and several sound studios. In fact, NBC is the only TV studio that offers the public a behind-the-scenes look at the inner workings of its television operation, and it's a lot less expensive than the competition's studio tours. It doesn't have the cachet of a major-motion-picture studio tour, but it's entertaining nonetheless. *Note:* Tours are sold on a first-come, first-served basis and sell out early during peak vacation season, so arrive early. Also, this is one of the few studio tours that doesn't have a minimum age requirement.

3000 W. Alameda Ave., Burbank. © 818/840-3537. www.studioaudiences.com/tvstudios. Tours $7.50 adults, $6 seniors 60 and over, $4.25 children 5–12, free for ciildren under 5. Mon–Fri 9am–3pm (open weekends and extended hours during summer and holiday season—call for current schedule).

Paramount Pictures *(★★* Paramount is the only major studio still located in Hollywood, which makes the 2-hour walking tour around its Hollywood headquarters far more historically enriching than the modern studios in Burbank (even the wrought-iron gates Gloria Swanson motored through in *Sunset Boulevard* are still there). The tour is both a historical ode to filmmaking and a real-life behind-the-scenes look at working movie and television facilities in day-to-day operation; ergo, no two tours are alike, and chances of spotting a celebrity are pretty good. Visits typically include a walk through the soundstages of TV shows or feature films, though you can't enter while taping is taking place. Tours depart every half-hour on a first-come, first-served basis; the itinerary varies, depending on what productions are in progress. Certain age restrictions apply, and cameras and recording equipment are verboten. *Tip:* After the tour, have lunch at the Paramount Studios' world-famous Commissary; you never know who might drop in for a bite and the food's pretty darn good.

5555 Melrose Ave. © 323/956-1777. www.paramount.com. Tours $15 per person. Mon–Fri 9am–2pm.

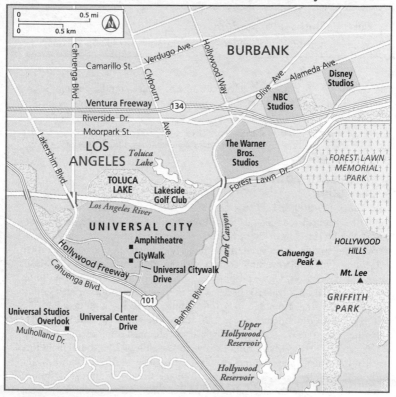

Universal Studios 🎬 Universal offers daily tram tours of their studio lot every day as part of the general admission price to their amusement park. See listing on p. 522 for more information.

Warner Brothers Studios 🎬🎬 Warner Brothers offers the most comprehensive—and the least theme-park-like—of the studio tours. The tour takes visitors on a 2¼-hour informational drive-and-walk jaunt around the studio's faux streets. After a brief introductory film, you'll pile into glorified golf carts and cruise past parking spaces marked "Clint Eastwood," "Michael Douglas," and "Sharon Stone," then walk through active film and television sets such as *ER* and *The West Wing*. Whether it's an orchestra scoring a film or a TV show being taped or edited, you'll get a glimpse of how it's done (nothing is staged for the tour). Stops include the wardrobe department or the mills where sets are made. Whenever possible, you can also visit working sets to watch actors filming actual productions. Reservations are required; children under 8 are not admitted. Bring valid photo ID.

WB Studio Gate 3, 4301 W. Olive Ave. (at Hollywood Way), Burbank. © **818/972-TOUR.** www.wbstudio tour.com. Advance reservations recommended. Tours $32 per person, departing every 20 min. Mon–Fri 8am–4pm (9am–3pm winter).

Sony Pictures Studio Tour Although it doesn't have quite the historical cachet as Warner Brothers or Paramount, a lot of movie history was made at this Culver City lot. The 2-hour walking tour includes stops at classic stage scenes such as the Yellow Brick Road winding through Munchkinland, sets from modern

---

Fun Fact **That's a lot of Popcorn!**

L.A.'s motion picture industry generates more than $31 billion annually.

---

thrillers like *Men in Black,* and an opportunity to drop in on the *Jeopardy!* set to test your trivia prowess. But the main reason for the tour is the chance to catch a glimpse at the stars who work here (it's one of the busiest studio lots in the world). Sony Picture Studios, 10202 W. Washington Blvd., Culver City. ② **323/520-TOUR.** www.sonypictures studios.com. Advance reservations required; children under 12 are not admitted. Tours $20 per person, departing Mon–Fri 9am–3pm. Photo ID required.

SIGHTSEEING TOURS
Bus/Van Tours
L.A. Tours (② **800/881-7715** or 323/460-6490; www.latours.net) operates regularly scheduled tours of the city. Plush shuttle buses (27 passengers maximum) pick up riders from major hotels for morning or afternoon tours of Sunset Strip, the studios, Farmers Market, Hollywood, homes of the stars, and other attractions. Different itineraries are available, from downtown and the Music Center to Disneyland, Universal Studios, or Six Flags Magic Mountain. Tours vary in length from a half-day Beached & Shopping tour to a full-day Grand City Tour, and range from $36 to $76 for adults. Reservations are required.

The other major tour company in L.A. is **Starline Tours** (② **800/959-3131;** www.starlinetours.com)—you'll see their air-conditioned minibuses all over the city. Since 1935 they've been offering a wide selection of L.A. tours, including the first-ever Movie Stars' Homes. Their most popular tour, the 2-hour neighborhood jaunt, departs every half-hour from the front of Grauman's Chinese Theatre between 9:30am and 5:30pm (you'll see the Starline kiosk to the right of the theater entrance at 6925 Hollywood Blvd.). If you really like driving tours, sign up for the *pièce de résistance:* the 5½-hour Grand Tour of L.A. Check out their website for more tour information.

Walking Tours
If you want the classic Hollywood walking tour, **Red Line Tours** (② **323/402-1074;** www.redlinetours.com) offers daily sightseeing expeditions to all the famous (and infamous) landmarks in Hollywood. Their unique "live-audio" system allows customers to hear the tour guide even over the city noise. Customers wear an audio headset receiver while the tour guide wears a headset microphone transmitter (pretty clever, actually). Trips depart from the Stella Adler Academy & Theatres (6773 Hollywood Blvd.) at 10am, noon, 2pm, and 4pm 7 days a week. Rates are $20 for adults, $18 for students and seniors, and $15 for children ages 9 to 15. Many other tours throughout L.A. are offered as well—visit the Red Line Tour website for more information.

The **L.A. Conservancy** (② **213/623-2489;** www.laconservancy.org) conducts about a dozen entertaining walking tours of historic downtown L.A. In Pasadena, **Pasadena Heritage** (② **626/441-6333;** www.pasadenaheritage.org) offers a walking tour of Old Pasadena.

The free **Beverly Hills Public Art Walking Tour** takes place at 1pm on the first Saturday of the month from May through September. The 60-minute docent-led tour departs from the front of City Hall (450 Crescent Dr.). Highlights include the Municipal Gallery, City Hall, the Beverly Gardens Park, and several galleries. For more information, call ② **310/288-2202** or log on to www.beverlyhills.org.

Bicycle Tours

For a refreshingly aerobic way to see L.A., stop in at **Hollywood Pro Bicycles,** 6731 Hollywood Blvd., Hollywood (© **888/775-BIKE** or 323/466-5890; www.hollywoodprobicycles.com), and rent a bicycle for the day. With your rental you'll receive a free tour map along with plenty of advice and tips from the staff. It's a great way to spend a leisurely day tooling around Hollywood or Beverly Hills (very flat), plus longer excursions to the Getty Center, Venice Beach, and Griffith Park. Rates are from $25 for a 24-hour period, and $15 for each additional day. Every rental comes with a safety helmet, a bike lock, and a handlebar bag for storage. Reservations are encouraged for all rentals. Another good choice if you're staying in the Santa Monica/Venice Beach area is **Blazing Saddles Bike Rentals** (© **310/393-9778**) at the Santa Monica Pier, which rents bikes for about $30 a day but gives away nifty self-guided tour maps for free.

Jogging Tours

Off 'N Running Tours (© **310/246-1418**) combines sporting with sightseeing, taking joggers on guided runs through Los Angeles. The themed tours are customized to take in the most entertaining areas around the city and can accommodate any skill level for 4 to 12 miles. One of the most popular routes is up to Holmby Hills, past the Playboy Mansion and Aaron and Candy Spelling's massive estate. It's a fun way to get the most out of your morning jog. Tours cost about $45 and include a T-shirt, bagel, snacks, and plenty of water.

Beverly Hills Trolley Tours

The city of Beverly Hills offers two inexpensive trolley tours that detail the city's history as well as little-known facts and celebrity tidbits. The **Sites and Scenes Trolley Tour** takes visitors on a 40-minute docent-led tour through the tony avenues of Beverly Hills, including Rodeo Drive and the Golden Triangle. The summer schedule is Tuesday through Saturday on the hour from noon to 5pm (call for winter schedule). The 50-minute docent-led **Art and Architecture Trolley Tour** visits Beverly Hills' architectural highlights, including the Creative Artists Agency, Museum of Television & Radio, and the Gagosian Art Gallery. It runs May through December on Saturdays at 11am. Fares for both tours are $5 and both depart at the Trolley Stop at the intersection of Rodeo Drive and Dayton Way. For more information, call © **310/285-2438** or log on to www.beverlyhills.org.

7 TV Tapings

Being part of the audience for the taping of a television show might be the quintessential L.A. experience. This is a great way to see Hollywood at work, to find out how your favorite sitcom or talk show is made, and to catch a glimpse of your favorite TV personalities. Timing is important—remember that most series go on hiatus between March and July. And tickets to the top shows are in greater demand than others, so getting your hands on them takes advance planning—and possibly some waiting in line.

Request tickets as far in advance as possible. Several episodes may be shot on a single day, so you may be required to remain in the theater for up to 4 hours (in addition to the recommended 1-hr. early check-in). If you phone at the last moment, you may luck into tickets for your top choice. More likely, however, you'll be given a list of shows that are currently filming, and you won't recognize many of the titles; studios are always taping pilots, few of which end up on the air. But you never know who may be starring in them—look at all the famous faces that have launched new sitcoms in the past couple of years. Tickets are always free, usually limited to two per person, and are distributed on a first-come, first-served basis. Many shows don't admit children under the age of 10; in some cases no one under the age of 18 is admitted.

Tickets are sometimes given away to the public outside popular tourist sites like Grauman's Chinese Theatre in Hollywood and Universal Studios in the Valley; L.A.'s visitor information centers in downtown and Hollywood often have tickets as well. But if you're determined to see a particular show, contact the following suppliers:

Audiences Unlimited, Inc. (© 818/753-3470; www.tvtickets.com) is a good place to start. It distributes tickets for most of the top sitcoms, including *That '70s Show, Will & Grace,* and many more. This service is organized and informative (as is their website), and sanctioned by production companies and networks. ABC, for example, no longer handles ticket distribution directly, but refers all inquiries to Audiences Unlimited, Inc. **TVTIX.COM** (© 323/653-4105; www.tvtix.com) also distributes tickets for numerous talk and game shows, including *Jeopardy!*

You also may want to contact the networks for information on a specific show, including some whose tickets are not available at the above agencies. At **ABC,** all ticket inquiries are referred to Audiences Unlimited (see above), but you may want to check out ABC's website at **www.abc.com** for a colorful look at their lineup and links to specific shows' sites.

For **CBS Television City,** 7800 Beverly Blvd., Los Angeles, CA 90036, call © 323/575-2458 between Monday and Friday from 9am to 5pm to see what's being filmed while you're in town. Tickets for CBS tapings are distributed on a first-come, first-served basis; you can write in advance to reserve them or pick them up at the studio up to an hour before taping. Tickets for many CBS sitcoms are also available from Audiences Unlimited (see above). For tickets to *The Price Is Right,* call the 24-hour ticket hot line at © 323/575-2449 or log on to www.cbs.com/daytime/price/tickets.

For **NBC,** 3000 W. Alameda Ave., Burbank, CA 91523 (© 818/840-3537), call to see what's on while you're in L.A. Tickets for NBC tapings, including *The Tonight Show with Jay Leno* (minimum age to attend is 16), can be obtained in two ways: Pick them up at the NBC ticket counter on the day of the show (they're distributed on a first-come, first-served basis at the ticket counter off California Ave.), or, at least 6 weeks before your visit, send a self-addressed, stamped envelope with your ticket request to the address above. Be sure to include show name, number of tickets (four per request), and dates desired. All the NBC shows are represented online at either www.nbc.com or www.tvtickets.com.

Paramount Studios also offers free tickets to their live-audience shows. All you need to do is call one of the friendly employees at Paramount Guest Relations (© 323/956-1777) between 9am and 6pm on weekdays, find out which shows are being filmed or taped while you're in town, and make a reservation (you might want to log on to www.paramount.com to see what shows they're currently taping; click on "The Studio" link). **Universal Studios** (© 800/UNIVERSAL; www.universalstudios.com) also offers free tickets to their live-audience shows. At the amusement park's **TV Audience Ticket Booth,** you can obtain free tickets to join the audience for any TV shows that are taping during your visit (subject to availability).

8 Beaches

Los Angeles County's 72-mile coastline sports more than 30 miles of beaches, most of which are operated by the **Department of Beaches & Harbors,** 13837 Fiji Way, Marina del Rey (© **310/305-9503**). County-run beaches usually charge for parking ($4–$8). Alcohol, bonfires, and pets are prohibited. For recorded **surf conditions** (and coastal weather forecast), call © **310/457-9701.** The following are the county's best beaches, listed from north to south.

EL PESCADOR, LA PIEDRA & EL MATADOR BEACHES *Finds*   These rugged and isolated beaches front a 2-mile stretch of the Pacific Coast Highway (Calif. 1) between Broad Beach and Decker Canyon roads, a 10-minute drive from the Malibu Pier. Picturesque coves with unusual rock formations are great for sunbathing and picnicking, but swim with caution as there are no lifeguards. The beaches can be difficult to find; only small signs on the highway mark them. There are a limited number of parking spots atop the bluffs. Descend to the beach via stairs that cling to the cliffs.

ZUMA BEACH COUNTY PARK ⚶   Jam-packed on warm weekends, L.A. County's largest beach park is located off the Pacific Coast Highway (Calif. 1), a mile past Kanan Dume Road. While it can't claim to be the most scenic beach in the Southland, Zuma has the most comprehensive facilities: plenty of rest-rooms, lifeguards, playgrounds, volleyball courts, and snack bars. The southern stretch, toward Point Dume, is Westward Beach, separated from the noisy high-way by sandstone cliffs. A trail leads over the point's headlands to Pirate's Cove, once a popular nude beach.

PARADISE COVE   This private beach in the 28000 block of the Pacific Coast Highway (Calif. 1) charges $15 to park and $5 per person if you walk in. Changing rooms and showers are included in the price. The beach is often full by noon on weekends.

MALIBU LAGOON STATE BEACH ⚶⚶   Not just a pretty white-sand beach but an estuary and wetlands area as well, Malibu Lagoon is the historic home of the Chumash Indians. The entrance is on the Pacific Coast Highway (Calif. 1) south of Cross Creek Road, and there's a small admission charge. Marine life and shorebirds teem where the creek empties into the sea, and the waves are always mild. The historic **Adamson House** is here, a showplace of Malibu tile now operating as a museum.

SURFRIDER BEACH   Without a doubt, L.A.'s best waves roll ashore here. One of the city's most popular surfing spots, this beach is between the Malibu Pier and the lagoon. In surf lingo, few "locals-only" wave wars are ever fought here—surfing is not as territorial here as it can be in other areas, where out-of-towners can be made to feel unwelcome. Surfrider is surrounded by all of Malibu's hustle and bus-tle; don't come here for peace and quiet as the surf is always crowded.

TOPANGA STATE BEACH   Highway noise prevents solitude at this short, narrow strip of sand located where Topanga Canyon Boulevard emerges from the mountains. Why go? Ask the surfers who wait in line to catch Topanga's excellent right point breaks. There are restrooms and lifeguard services here, and across the street you'll find one of the best fresh-fish restaurants around.

WILL ROGERS STATE BEACH   Three miles along the Pacific Coast High-way (Calif. 1), between Sunset Boulevard and the Santa Monica border, are named for the American humorist whose ranch-turned-state-historic-park (see

L.A.'s Beaches & Coastal Attractions

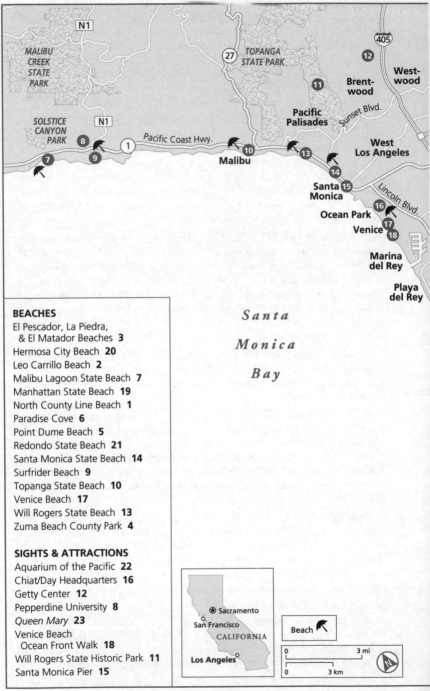

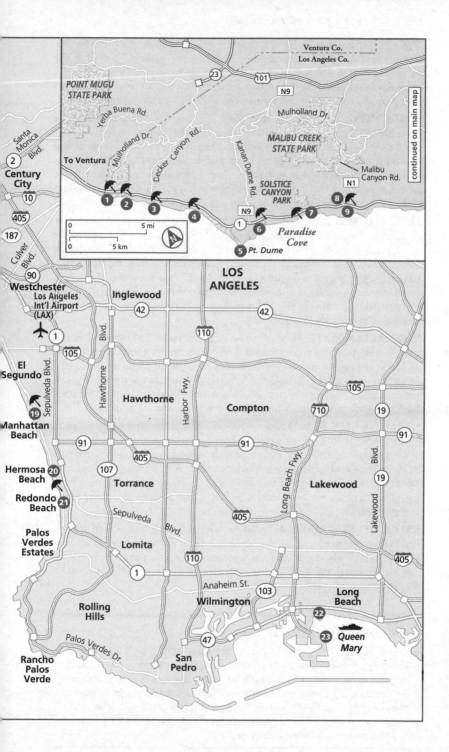

continued on main map

Ventura Co.
Los Angeles Co.

POINT MUGU
STATE PARK

Yerba Buena Rd.

Mulholland Dr.

N9

Mulholland Dr.

MALIBU CREEK
STATE PARK

To Ventura

Decker Canyon Rd.

Kanan Dume Rd.

SOLSTICE
CANYON PARK

Malibu
Canyon Rd.

N1

Santa
Monica
Blvd.

2

Century
City

10

405

187

Culver
Blvd.

90

Westchester
Los Angeles
Int'l Airport
(LAX)

El
Segundo

19
Manhattan
Beach

Hermosa
Beach

20

Redondo
Beach

21

Palos
Verdes
Estates

Inglewood

42

110

Hawthorne

Sepulveda Blvd.

Hawthorne Blvd.

Harbor Fwy.

105

91

107

405

Sepulveda Blvd.

Torrance

Lomita

1

110

LOS
ANGELES

42

Compton

105

710

91

405

Long Beach Fwy.

Lakewood

Lakewood Blvd.

19

19

91

405

Rolling
Hills

Palos Verdes Dr.

Rancho
Palos
Verde

San
Pedro

47

Anaheim St.

Wilmington

103

Long
Beach

22

23 Queen
Mary

1
2
3
4
5 Pt. Dume
6
7
8
9

N9

1

Paradise
Cove

0   5 mi
0   5 km

547

"Parks & Gardens," earlier in this chapter) is nestled above the palisades that provide the backdrop for this popular beach. A pay parking lot extends the entire length of Will Rogers, and facilities include restrooms, lifeguards, and a snack hut in season. While the surfing is not the best, the waves are friendly for swimmers and there are always competitive volleyball games to be found.

SANTA MONICA STATE BEACH *Kids* The beaches on either side of the Santa Monica Pier (see "L.A.'s Top Attractions," earlier in this chapter) are popular for their white sands and accessibility. There are big parking lots, cafes, and well-maintained restrooms. A paved beach path runs along here, allowing you to walk, bike, or skate to Venice and points south. Colorado Boulevard leads to the pier; turn north on the Pacific Coast Highway (Calif. 1) below the coastline's bluffs, or south along Ocean Avenue; you can find parking in both directions.

VENICE BEACH *★★* Moving south from the city of Santa Monica, the paved pedestrian Promenade becomes Ocean Front Walk and gets progressively weirder until it reaches an apex at Washington Boulevard and the Venice fishing pier. Although there are people who swim and sunbathe, Venice Beach's character is defined by the sea of humanity on the Ocean Front Walk, plus the bevy of boardwalk vendors and old-fashioned pedestrian streets a block away (see "L.A.'s Top Attractions," earlier in this chapter). Park on the side streets or in the plentiful lots west of Pacific Avenue.

MANHATTAN STATE BEACH The Beach Boys used to hang out at this wide, friendly beach backed by beautiful oceanview homes. Plenty of parking on 36 blocks of side streets (between Rosecrans Ave. and the Hermosa Beach border) draws weekend crowds from the L.A. area. Manhattan has some of the best surfing around, restrooms, lifeguards, and volleyball courts. Manhattan Beach Boulevard leads west to the fishing pier and adjacent seafood restaurants.

HERMOSA CITY BEACH *★★* This very wide white-sand beach is one of the best in Southern California and my favorite. Hermosa extends to either side of the pier and includes "The Strand," a wide, smooth pedestrian lane that runs its entire length. Main access is at the foot of Pier Avenue, which is lined with interesting shops and cafes with outdoor seating. There's plenty of street parking, as well as restrooms, lifeguards, volleyball courts, a fishing pier, playgrounds, and good surfing.

REDONDO STATE BEACH Popular with surfers, bicyclists, and joggers, Redondo's white sand and ice-plant-carpeted dunes are just south of tiny King Harbor, along "The Esplanade" (S. Esplanade Dr.). Get there via the Pacific Coast Highway (Calif. 1) or Torrance Boulevard. Facilities include restrooms, lifeguards, and volleyball courts.

Moments A Break by the Beach

One of my favorite places in L.A. to get away from it all is a tiny, little-known park in Marina del Rey that overlooks the mouth of the harbor. You can sit on a bench all day long and enjoy the cool breeze as a never-ending parade of beautiful yachts and sailboats slowly works its way to the ocean or back to the harbor. To reach this relaxing oasis, drive to the south end of Pacific Avenue, turn left on Via Marina, and park in one of the metered spaces (bring quarters).

9 Outdoor Pursuits

Bisected by the Santa Monica Mountains and fronted by long stretches of beach, Los Angeles is one of the best cities in the world for nature and sports lovers. Where else can you hike in the mountains, in-line-skate along the beach, swim in the ocean, enjoy a gourmet meal, and then take in a basketball, ice-hockey, or baseball game—all in the same day?

BICYCLING Los Angeles is great for biking. If you're into distance pedaling, you can do no better than the flat 22-mile paved **Ocean Front Walk** that runs along the sand from Pacific Palisades in the north to Torrance in the south. The path attracts all levels of riders and gets pretty busy on weekends. For information on this and other city bike routes, phone the **Los Angeles Dept. of Transportation** (© 213/485-9957).

The best place to mountain-bike is along the trails of **Malibu Creek State Park** (© 818/880-0367), in the Santa Monica Mountains between Malibu and the San Fernando Valley in Calabasas. Fifteen miles of trails rise to a maximum of 3,000 feet and are appropriate for intermediate to advanced bikers. Pick up a trail map at the park entrance, 4 miles south of U.S. 101 off Las Virgenes Road, just north of Mulholland Highway. Park admission is $5 per car.

Spokes 'N Stuff Bike Rental has two locations: 4175 Admiralty Way, Marina del Rey (© 310/306-3332), open on weekends only, and 1715 Oceanfront Walk, behind Loews Hotel, Santa Monica (© 310/395-4748), which is open every day. They rent 10-speed cruisers for $7 per hour and $16 per day; 15-speed mountain bikes rent for $8 per hour and $20 per day. Another good Santa Monica rental shop is **Blazing Saddles Bike Rentals** (Santa Monica Pier; © 310/393-9778). The rates are about the same as at Spokes 'N Stuff. Be sure to ask for a free **self-guided tour map** (it's really handy).

In Hollywood, **Hollywood Pro Bicycles** (6731 Hollywood Blvd.; © 888/775-BIKE or 323/466-5890; www.hollywoodprobicycles.com) rents mountain bikes at $25 for a 24-hour period, and $15 for each additional day. Every rental comes with a free tour map, a safety helmet, a bike lock, and a handlebar bag for storage.

In the South Bay, bike rentals—including tandem bikes—are available 1 block from The Strand at **Hermosa Cyclery,** 20 13th St. (© 310/374-7816; www.hermosacyclery.com). Cruisers are $7 per hour, tandems $13 per hour. FYI, The Strand is an excellent car-free path that's tailor-made for a leisurely bike ride.

FISHING **Del Rey Sport Fishing,** 13759 Fiji Way, Marina del Rey (© 310/822-3625; www.marinadelreysportfishing.com), has three deep-sea boats departing daily on half- and full-day ocean-fishing trips. Of course, it depends on what's running when you're out, but bass, barracuda, halibut, and yellowtail are the most common catches on these party boats. Excursions cost from $28 to $40; tackle rental is available. Phone for reservations.

No permit is required to cast from shore or drop a line from a pier. Local anglers will hate me for giving away their secret spot, but the **best saltwater fishing spot** in all of L.A. is at the foot of Torrance Boulevard in Redondo Beach.

GOLF The greater Los Angeles area has more than 100 golf courses, which vary in quality from abysmal to superb. Most of the city's public courses are administered by the Department of Recreation and Parks, which follows a complicated registration/reservation system for tee times. While visitors cannot reserve start times in advance, you're welcome to play any of the courses by showing up and getting on the call sheet. Expect to wait for the most popular tee times, but try to use your flexible vacationer status to your advantage by avoiding the early-morning rush.

Of the city's seven 18-hole and three 9-hole courses, you can't get more central than the **Rancho Park Golf Course,** 10460 W. Pico Blvd. (© **310/ 838-7373;** www.rpgc.org), located smack-dab in the middle of L.A.'s Westside. The par-71 course has lots of tall trees, but not enough to blot out the towering Century City buildings next door. Rancho also has a 9-hole, par-3 course.

For a genuinely woodsy experience, try one of the three courses inside Griffith Park, northeast of Hollywood (see "Parks & Gardens," earlier in this chapter). The courses are extremely well maintained, challenging without being frustrating, and (despite some holes alongside I-5) a great way to leave the city behind. Bucolic pleasures abound, particularly on the 9-hole **Roosevelt,** on Vermont Avenue across from the Greek Theatre; early-morning wildlife often includes deer, rabbits, raccoons, and skunks (fore!). **Wilson** and **Harding** are each 18 holes and start from the main clubhouse off Riverside Drive, the park's main entrance.

Greens fees on all city courses are $22 Monday through Friday, and $29 on weekends and holidays; 9-hole courses cost $13 weekdays, $17 on weekends and holidays. For details on other city courses, or to contact the starter directly by phone, call the Department of Recreation and Parks at © **888/527-2757** or log on to the city's parks website at www.laparks.org.

Industry Hills Golf Club, 1 Industry Hills Pkwy., City of Industry (© **626/ 810-4653**), has two 18-hole courses designed by William Bell. Together they encompass 8 lakes, 160 bunkers, and many long fairways. The Eisenhower Course, ranked among *Golf Digest*'s top 25 public courses, has extralarge undulating greens and the challenge of thick Kikuyu rough. An adjacent driving range is lit for night use. Greens fees are $63 Monday through Thursday and $93 Friday through Sunday, including cart; call in advance for tee times.

For more information on regional golf courses, log on to www.golfcalifornia.com.

HIKING   The **Santa Monica Mountains,** a small range that runs only 50 miles from Griffith Park to Point Mugu, on the coast north of Malibu, makes Los Angeles a great place for hiking. The mountains, which peak at 3,111 feet, are part of the Santa Monica Mountains National Recreation Area, a contiguous conglomeration of 350 public parks and 65,000 acres. Many animals live in this area, including deer, coyote, rabbit, skunk, rattlesnake, fox, hawk, and quail. The hills are also home to almost 1,000 drought-resistant plant species, including live oak and coastal sage.

Hiking is best after spring rains, when the hills are green, flowers are in bloom, and the air is clear. Summers can be very hot; hikers should always carry fresh water. Beware of poison oak, a hearty shrub that's common on the West Coast. Usually found among oak trees, poison oak has leaves in groups of three, with waxy surfaces and prominent veins. If you come into contact with this itch-producing plant, you'll end up with a California souvenir that you'll soon regret.

For trail maps and more information, contact the **National Parks Service** (© **818/597-1036**), or stop by its visitor center at 30401 Agoura Rd., Suite 100, in Agoura Hills. It's open Monday through Friday from 8am to 5pm, and Saturday and Sunday from 9am to 5pm. Some areas are administered by the **California Department of Parks** (© **800/275-8777**); the offices are located in Calabasas at 1925 Las Virgenes Rd.

⟨Tips⟩ Spectator Sports

The **Los Angeles Dodgers** (© 323/224-1448; www.dodgers.com), winners of eight National League championships and five World Series, play at Dodger Stadium, 1000 Elysian Park, near Sunset Boulevard. The team's slick, interactive website offers everything from game schedules to souvenir merchandise online. The 2002 World Series champion **Anaheim Angels** (© 888/796-HALO; www.angels.mlb.com) play American League ball at Anaheim Stadium, 2000 S. State College Blvd. (near Katella Ave.), in Anaheim, about 30 minutes from downtown L.A. The regular Major League baseball season runs from April to October.

Los Angeles has two NBA franchises: the **L.A. Lakers** (www.lakers.com), who have won 14 NBA titles, and the hapless **L.A. Clippers** (www.clippers.com), who haven't even made the playoffs. Both teams play in **Staples Center** in downtown L.A., 1111 S. Figueroa St. (© 310/426-6031; www.staplescenter.com). Celebrity fans like Jack Nicholson, Leonardo DiCaprio, Heather Locklear, and Dyan Cannon have the best tickets, but this 20,000-seater should have room for you—that is, if you have the big bucks for a Lakers ticket or the interest in watching a Clippers game. The season runs from October to April with 2 months of playoffs following.

The **L.A. Sparks** (© 310/426-6031; www.lasparks.com) of the WNBA play at the Staples Center May through August. The Sparks are especially proud of star center, Olympic gold-medalist Lisa Leslie.

The National Hockey League's **L.A. Kings** (© 888/546-4752; www.lakings.com) also call the Staples Center home (see above) and down the road in Orange County, the **Mighty Ducks** (© 714/940-2900; www.mightyducks.com) play at the Arrowhead Pond in Anaheim. The hockey season runs from October through mid-April with playoffs following.

Los Angeles suffers from an absence of major-league football, but it gets by just fine with two popular college teams and an Arena League team. The college season runs September through November; if you're interested in checking out a game, contact **UCLA Bruins Football** (© 310/825-2101; www.uclabruins.com) or **USC Trojan Football** (© 213/740-2311; www.usctrojans.com)

Since its inaugural season in 1996, the **Los Angeles Galaxy** (© 310/630-2200; www.lagalaxy.com) have already won the Major League Soccer Cup of 2002 and earned a reputation as a major force in MLS. Visitors can catch a game at the new Home Depot stadium at 18400 Avalon Blvd. in Carson.

Santa Ynez Canyon, in Pacific Palisades, is a long, difficult climb that rises steadily for about 3 miles. At the top, hikers are rewarded with fantastic views over the Pacific. At the top is **Trippet Ranch,** a public facility providing water, restrooms, and picnic tables. From Santa Monica, take Pacific Coast Highway (Calif. 1) north. Turn right onto Sunset Boulevard, then left onto Palisades Drive. Then continue for 2½ miles, turn left onto Verenda de la Montura, and park at the cul-de-sac at the end of the street, where you can find the trail head.

Polo Anyone?

Back in 1930, cowboy humorist Will Rogers got a hankerin' to play some polo, so he cleared the field in front of his Pacific Palisades home for a friendly match with his ponies and celebrity pals. Shortly after, he started his famed **Will Rogers Polo Club,** and of the 25 polo organizations that existed at the time, his polo field is the only one that remains. Matches are held on weekends from mid-April through early October, and the setting of wide green fields, whitewashed fences, and majestic oaks is ideal for a picnic lunch and a bit of respite from the city. The polo field is at 1501 Will Rogers State Park Rd. in Pacific Palisades, off West Sunset Boulevard. For more information, call the club at ℂ 310/573-5000 or visit www.willrogerspolo.org (there's a great feature on "How to Watch a Polo Game").

Temescal Canyon, in Pacific Palisades, is far easier than the Santa Ynez trail and far more popular, especially among locals. This is one of the quickest routes into the wilderness. Hikes here are anywhere from 1 to 5 miles. From Santa Monica, take Pacific Coast Highway (Calif. 1) north; turn right onto Temescal Canyon Road and follow it to the end. Sign in with the gatekeeper, who can also answer your questions.

Will Rogers State Historic Park, Pacific Palisades, is also a terrific place for hiking. An intermediate-level hike from the park's entrance ends at Inspiration Point, a plateau from which you can see a good portion of L.A.'s Westside. See "Parks & Gardens," earlier in this chapter for complete information.

HORSEBACK RIDING   The **Griffith Park Livery Stable,** 480 Riverside Dr. (in the Los Angeles Equestrian Center), Burbank (ℂ **818/840-9036;** www.la-equestriancenter.com), rents horses by the hour for Western or English riding through Griffith Park's hills. There's a 200-pound weight limit, and children have to be at least 6 and at least 4 feet tall. Horse rental costs about $20 per hour; maximum rental is 2 hours. You can also arrange for private 1-hour lessons by calling ℂ **818/569-3666.** The stables are open daily from 8am to 5pm, and cash is required for payment.

Another popular horseback-riding outfit is **Sunset Ranch,** located at 3400 Beachwood Dr., off of Franklin Avenue., just under the HOLLYWOOD sign. Horse rentals are offered daily from 9am to 5pm for all levels of riders. The ranch is on the edge of Griffith Park with access to 52 miles of trails. Also available are private night rides (very romantic), Dinner Rides (see the "Sunset Margarita Horse Rides" box above), and riding lessons. Rates are $20 per hour with a $10 deposit. No reservations are required. For more information, call ℂ **323/ 469-5450** or log on to their website at www.sunsetranchhollywood.com.

Closer to the ocean in the Topanga Canyon is **Escape on Horseback,** 2623 Old Topanga Canyon Rd., Topanga (ℂ **818/591-2032;** www.topangahorses.com), a small, friendly outfit that offers guided Western-style trail rides for beginning to advanced riders. It's situated at the top of a 1,800-foot ridgeline—about a 25-minute drive from Santa Monica—with panoramic views of the ocean and San Fernando Valley (best seen on one of their sunset rides). What I like about this outfit is that if the guide feels that the group is experienced enough, she'll pick up the pace to a canter. Although same-day reservations are sometimes possible, try to book at least 3 days in advance. Kids 7 and older are welcome, and kids under 16 must wear helmets (bring a bike helmet if possible). Prices are about $55 for a guided 70-minute ride, plus tip; 3-hour canyon rides are available as well.

SEA KAYAKING   Sea kayaking is all the rage in Southern California, a simple and serene way to explore the southern coastline. **Southwind Kayak Center,** 17855 Skypark Circle, Irvine (© **800/768-8494** or 949/261-0200; www.southwindkayaks. com), rents sit-on-top sea kayaks for use in the bay or open ocean at rates of $40 per day; instructional classes are available on weekends only. The center also conducts several easy-going guided outings, including a $55 "Back to Nature" trip that highlights the marine life around Dana Point. Visit their website for more details.

SKATING   The 22-mile-long Ocean Front Walk that runs from Pacific Palisades to Torrance is one of the premier skating spots in the country. In-line skating is especially popular, but conventional roller skates are often seen here, too. Skating is allowed just about everywhere bicycling is, but be advised that cyclists have the right of way. **Spokes 'N Stuff,** 4175 Admiralty Way, Marina del Rey (© **310/306-3332;** open weekends only), is just one of many places to rent wheels near the Venice portion of Ocean Front Walk. In the South Bay, in-line-skate rentals are available 1 block from The Strand at **Hermosa Cyclery,** 20 13th St. (© **310/374-7816;** www.hermosacyclery.com). Skates cost $6 per hour ($18 max); kneepads and wrist guards come with every rental. *Tip:* A 10% discount coupon is available at their website.

SURFING   Surfing was invented by the Polynesians; Captain Cook made note of it in Oahu in 1778. George Freeth (1883–1918), who first surfed Redondo Beach in 1907, is widely credited with introducing the sport to California. But surfing didn't catch on until the 1950s, when Cal Tech graduate Bob Simmons invented a more maneuverable lightweight fiberglass board. The Beach Boys and other surf-music groups popularized Southern California in the minds of beach babes and dudes everywhere, and the rest, as they say, is history. You'll also find some great surf an hour or two down the coast in the Huntington Beach and Newport areas of Orange County.

(Moments **Sunset Margarita Horse Rides**

This is so cool! Every Friday night the Sunset Ranch Hollywood Stables company hosts **Friday Night Dinner Rides.** They saddle you up on a big ol' horse, then y'all take a scenic 1½-hour ride through Griffith Park—with the city lights shining far below—to the Viva Fresh Mexican restaurant in Burbank. After dinner and a few tasty margaritas, you mount up and ride back to the ranch, arriving at about 11pm. Is that cool or what? Anyone under 250 pounds can go, and no reservations are required—it's strictly first-come, first-served. The ride costs $45, not including dinner and drinks (they just get you there, they don't serve you). Sign-up begins at 5pm and the ride leaves at 6pm. Consider yourself warned, however: Many a sore derriere has wished it hadn't been subjected to 180 minutes in the saddle. The ranch is located at the very end of Beachwood Drive off of Franklin Avenue, just under the HOLLYWOOD sign. For more information, call © **323/469-5450** or 323/464-9612, or log on to their website at www.sunsetranchhollywood.com.

If you're a first-timer eager to learn the sport, contact **Pure Surfing Experience** (© 310/546-4451; www.puresurfingexperience.com) in Manhattan Beach. This highly respected school features a team of experienced instructors and will supply all necessary equipment. Single lessons are $80, but subsequent follow-ups are deeply discounted. Call for reservations, but don't expect anyone to answer the phone if the waves are good.

Boards are available for rent at shops near all top surfing beaches in the L.A. area. **Zuma Jay Surfboards,** 22775 Pacific Coast Hwy., Malibu (© 310/456-8044), Malibu's oldest surf shop, is about a quarter mile south of Malibu Pier. Rentals are about $20 per day, plus $8 for wet suits in winter.

TENNIS   While soft-surface courts are more popular on the East Coast, hard surfaces are most common in California. If your hotel doesn't have a court and can't suggest any courts nearby, try the well-maintained, well-lit **Griffith Park Tennis Courts,** on Commonwealth Road, just east of Vermont Avenue (© 323/662-7772). Call or log on to the website of the **City of Los Angeles Department of Recreation and Parks** (© 888/527-2757; www.laparks.org) to see a long list of free tennis courts or make a reservation at a municipal court near you. *Tip:* Spectators can watch free collegiate matches at the UCLA campus's L.A. Tennis Center from October through May. For a schedule of tournaments, call © 310/206-6831.

10 Shopping

Here's a rundown of the primary shopping areas, along with descriptions of a few of their best stores. The sales tax in Los Angeles is 8.25%, but savvy out-of-state shoppers know how to have more expensive items shipped directly home, thereby avoiding the tax.

L.A.'S WESTSIDE & BEVERLY HILLS

BEVERLY BOULEVARD (from Robertson Blvd. to La Brea Ave.) ⭐   Beverly is L.A.'s premier boulevard for mid-twentieth-century furnishings; expensive showrooms line the street, but the one that started it all is **Modernica,** 7366 Beverly Blvd. (© 323/933-0383). You can still find vintage Stickley and Noguchi pieces, but Modernica has become best known for the authentic—and more affordable—replicas they offer (Eames storage units are one popular item).

Every Picture Tells a Story, 7525 Beverly Blvd. (© 323/932-6070), a gallery devoted to the art of children's literature, displays antique children's books as well as the works of more than 100 illustrators, including lithos of Curious George, Eloise, and *Charlotte's Web.* Across the street from Cedars-Sinai Medical Center, the **Mysterious Bookshop,** 8375 W. Third St. (© 323/655-0575; www.travelbooks.com), carries more than 20,000 used, rare, and out-of-print titles in the field of mystery, espionage, detective stories, and thrillers. Author appearances and other special events are regularly scheduled. If you can name more than three tenors, then pleasantly cluttered **Opera Shop of Los Angeles,** 8384 Beverly Blvd. (3 blocks east of La Cienega Blvd.; © 323/658-5811), is for you. Everything imaginable with an opera theme is available: musical motif jewelry, stationery, T-shirts, opera glasses, and tapes, videos, and CDs of your favorite productions.

If you complain that they just don't make 'em like they used to . . . well, they do at **Re-Mix,** 7605½ Beverly Blvd. (between Fairfax and La Brea aves.; © 323/936-6210). This shop sells only vintage (1940s–70s)—but brand-new (as in unworn)—shoes for men and women, such as wingtips, Hush Puppies, Joan

Tips Window-Shopping—L.A.-Style

The gorgeous Bvlgari jewelry store at the corner of Rodeo Drive and
Wilshire Boulevard—former home of the Brown Derby restaurant—
displays many of the priceless (literally) jewels worn by the stars at the
big awards ceremonies. Look wealthy and they might even invite you
upstairs for an espresso.

Crawford pumps, and 1970s platforms. It's more like a shoe-store museum. A
rack of unworn vintage socks all display their original tags and stickers, and the
prices are downright reasonable. Celebrity hipsters and hep cats from Madonna
to Roseanne are often spotted here.

Other vintage wares are found at **Second Time Around Watch Co.,** 8840
Beverly Blvd. (west of Robertson Blvd.; © 310/271-6615). The city's best selection of collectible timepieces includes dozens of classic Tiffanys, Cartiers,
Piagets, and Rolexes, plus rare pocket watches. Priced for collectors, but a fascinating browse for the Swatch crowd, too.

LA BREA AVENUE (north of Wilshire Blvd.) This is L.A.'s artiest shopping strip. La Brea is anchored by the giant **American Rag, Cie** alterna-com-
plex, 148 S. La Brea St. (© 323/935-3154), and is also home to lots of great
urban antiques stores dealing in Art Deco, Arts and Crafts, 1950s modern, and
the like. You'll also find vintage clothiers, furniture galleries, and other ware-
house-size stores, as well as some of the city's hippest restaurants, such as Campanile (see p. 505 for a compete listing).

Bargain hunters find flea-market furnishings at **Nick Metropolis,** 100 S. La
Brea Ave. (© 323/934-3700), while more upscale seekers of home decor head
to **Mortise & Tenon,** 446 S. La Brea Ave. (© 323/937-7654), where handcrafted wood pieces sit next to overstuffed velvet-upholstered sofas and even vintage steel desks. The best place for a snack is Nancy Silverton's **La Brea Bakery,**
624 S. La Brea Ave. (© 323/939-6813; www.labreabakery.com), which foodies
know from gourmet markets and the attached Campanile restaurant.

Stuffed to the rafters with hardware and fixtures of the past 100 years, **Liz's
Antique Hardware,** 453 S. La Brea Ave. (© 323/939-4403; www.lahard
ware.com), thoughtfully keeps a canister of wet wipes at the register—believe us,
you'll need one after sifting through bags and crates of doorknobs, latches,
finials, and any other home hardware you can imagine. Perfect sets of Bakelite
drawer pulls and antique ceramic bathroom fixtures are some of the more
intriguing items. Be prepared to browse for hours, whether you're redecorating
or not. There's also a respectable collection of coordinatingly trendy clothing for
men and women. Souvenir seekers know to visit **Moletown,** 900 N. La Brea
Ave. (© 323/851-0111; www.moletown.com), for studio merchandise featuring logo graphics from new blockbuster movies.

RODEO DRIVE & BEVERLY HILLS' GOLDEN TRIANGLE (between
Santa Monica Blvd., Wilshire Blvd., and Crescent Dr., Beverly Hills)
Everyone knows about Rodeo Drive, the city's most famous shopping street.
Couture shops from high fashion's Old Guard are located along these 3 hallowed
blocks, along with plenty of newer high-end labels. And there are two examples
of the Beverly Hills version of minimalls, albeit more insular and attractive—the
Rodeo Collection, 421 N. Rodeo Dr, a contemporary center with towering

palms; and **2 Rodeo,** a cobblestoned Italianate piazza at Wilshire Boulevard. The 16-square-block area surrounding Rodeo Drive is known as the "Golden Triangle." Shops off Rodeo are generally not as name-conscious as those on the strip (and you might actually be able to afford something), but they're nevertheless plenty upscale. Little Santa Monica Boulevard has a particularly colorful line of specialty stores, and Brighton Way is as young and hip as relatively staid Beverly Hills gets. Parking is a bargain, with nine city-run lots offering 2 hours of free parking and a flat fee of $2 after 2pm.

The big names to look for here are **Bvlgari,** 201 N. Rodeo Dr. (② **310/ 858-9216**); **Giorgio Beverly Hills,** 327 N. Rodeo Dr. (② **800/GIORGIO**); **Gucci,** 347 N. Rodeo Dr. (② **310/278-3451**); **Hermès,** 434 N. Rodeo Dr. (② **310/278-6440**); **Louis Vuitton,** 295 N. Rodeo Dr. (② **310/859-0457**); **Polo/Ralph Lauren,** 444 N. Rodeo Dr. (② **310/281-7200**); and **Tiffany & Co.,** 210 N. Rodeo Dr. (② **310/273-8880**). The newest arrivals are the ultra-chic clothiers **Dolce & Gabbana,** 312 N. Rodeo Dr. (② **310/888-8701**), and **Badgley Mischka,** 202 Rodeo Dr. (② **310/248-3750**), British plaid palace **Burberry Limited,** 9560 Wilshire Blvd. (② **310/550-4500**), and **NikeTown** on the corner of Wilshire Boulevard and Rodeo Drive (② **310/275-9998**), a behemoth shrine to the reigning athletic-gear king.

Wilshire Boulevard is also home to New York–style department stores (each in spectacular landmark buildings) like **Saks Fifth Avenue,** 9600 Wilshire Blvd. (② **310/275-4211**), **Barneys New York,** 9570 Wilshire Blvd. (② **310/ 276-4400**), and **Neiman Marcus,** 9700 Wilshire Blvd. (② **310/550-5900**).

THE SUNSET STRIP (between La Cienega Blvd. and Doheny Dr., West Hollywood)   The monster-size billboards advertising the latest rock god make it clear this is rock 'n' roll territory. So it makes sense that you'll find legendary **Tower Records,** 8811 W. Sunset Blvd. (② **310/657-7300;** www.tower-records.com), in the heart of the action. Tower insists that it has L.A.'s largest selection of compact discs (more than 125,000 titles)—despite the Virgin Megastore's contrary claim—and it's open 365 days a year. At the east end of the strip sits the gigantic **Virgin Megastore,** 8000 Sunset Blvd. (② **323/650-8666;** www.virginrecords.com). Some 100 CD "listening posts" and an in-store "radio station" make this place a music-lover's paradise. Virgin claims to stock 150,000 titles, including an extensive collection of hard-to-find artists.

The "Strip" is lined with trendy restaurants, industry-oriented hotels, and dozens of shops offering outrageous fashions and stage accessories. One anomaly is Sunset Plaza, an upscale cluster of Georgian-style shops resembling Beverly Hills at its snootiest. You'll find **Billy Martin's,** 8605 Sunset Blvd. (② **310/ 289-5000**), founded by the legendary Yankees manager in 1978. This chic men's Western shop—complete with fireplace and leather sofa—stocks hand-forged silver and gold belt buckles, Lucchese and Liberty boots, and stable staples like flannel shirts. Next door is the fine-jewelry store, **Philip Press, Inc.,** 8601 Sunset Blvd. (② **310/360-1180**), which specializes in platinum and diamonds, handcrafted to evoke ornate estate jewelry. If you want to commemorate a special occasion or want the best selection, this is the place to go. **Book Soup,** 8818 Sunset Blvd. (② **310/659-3110;** www.booksoup.com), has long been one of L.A.'s most celebrated bookshops, selling mainstream and small-press books and hosting book signings and readings.

WEST THIRD STREET (between Fairfax and Robertson boulevards) ⭐   You can shop till you drop on this trendy strip, anchored on the east end by the **Farmers Market & The Grove** (see "L.A.'s Top Attractions," above). Many of

Melrose Avenue's shops have relocated here, along with terrific up-and-comers. "Fun" is more the catchword here than "funky," and the shops (including the vintage-clothing stores) are a bit more refined than those along Melrose. **The Cook's Library,** 11975 San Vicente Blvd. (© 310/476-6263; www.duttonsbrentwood.com), is where the city's top chefs find classic and offbeat cookbooks, wine guides, and other food-oriented tomes. Browsing is welcomed, even encouraged, with tea, tasty treats, and rocking chairs. **Traveler's Bookcase,** 8375 W. Third St. (© 323/655-0575; www.travelbooks.com), is one of the best travel bookshops in the West, stocking a huge selection of guidebooks and travel literature, as well as maps and travel accessories. Nearby **Memory Lane,** 8387 W. Third St. (© 323/655-4571), is filled with 1940s, 1950s, and 1960s collectibles.

There's lots more to see along this always-growing street. Refuel at **Chado Tea Room,** 8422 W. Third St. (© 323/655-2056), a temple for tea lovers. Chado is designed with a nod to Paris's renowned Mariage Frères tea purveyor; one wall is lined with nooks whose recognizable brown tins are filled with more than 250 different varieties of tea from around the world. Among the choices are 15 kinds of Darjeeling, Indian teas blended with rose petals, and ceremonial Chinese and Japanese blends. You can also get tea meals here, featuring delightful sandwiches and individual pots of any loose tea in the store.

HOLLYWOOD

HOLLYWOOD BOULEVARD (between Gower St. and La Brea Ave.)   One of Los Angeles's most famous streets is, for the most part, a cheesy tourist strip. But along the Walk of Fame, between the T-shirt shops and greasy pizza parlors, you'll find some excellent poster shops, souvenir stores, and Hollywood-memorabilia dealers worth getting out of your car for—especially if there's a chance of getting your hands on that long-sought-after Ethel Merman autograph or *200 Motels* poster.

Some long-standing purveyors of memorabilia include **Book City Collectibles,** 6627 Hollywood Blvd. (© 323/466-2525), which has more than 70,000 color prints of past and present stars, along with a good selection of famous autographs. **Hollywood Book and Poster Company,** 6562 Hollywood Blvd. (© 323/465-8764; www.hollywoodbookandposter.com), has an excellent collection of posters (from about $15 each), strong in horror and exploitation flicks. Photocopies of about 5,000 movie and television scripts are sold for $10 to $15 each—*Pulp Fiction* is just as good in print, by the way—and the store carries music posters and photos. The **Collector's Book Store,** 6225 Hollywood Blvd. (© 323/467-3296), is a movie buff's dream, with enough printed memorabilia for an afternoon of browsing; vintage copies of *Photoplay* and other fan mags cost $2 to $5, and the selection of biographies is outstanding.

LARCHMONT BOULEVARD (between Beverly Blvd. and Second St.) Neighbors congregate on this old-fashioned street just east of busy Vine Avenue. As the surrounding Hancock Park homes become increasingly popular with artists and young industry types, the shops and cafes lining Larchmont get more stylish. Sure, chains like Jamba Juice and The Coffee Bean are infiltrating this formerly mom-and-pop terrain, but plenty of unique shopping awaits amidst charming elements like diagonal parking, shady trees, and sidewalk bistro tables.

One of L.A.'s landmark independent bookstores is **Chevalier's Books,** 126 N. Larchmont Blvd. (© 323/465-1334), a 60-year Larchmont tradition. If your walking shoes are letting you down, stop into **Village Footwear,** 240 N. Larchmont Blvd. (© 323/461-3619), which specializes in comfort lines like Josef Siebel.

MELROSE AVENUE (between Fairfax and La Brea aves.)★★ It's showing some wear—some stretches have become downright ugly—but this is still one of the most exciting shopping streets in the country for cutting-edge fashions (and some eye-popping people-watching to boot). Melrose is always an entertaining stroll, dotted with plenty of hip restaurants and funky shops selling the latest in clothes, gifts, jewelry, and accessories that are sure to shock. Where else could you find green patent-leather cowboy boots, a working 19th-century pocket watch, an inflatable girlfriend, and glow-in-the-dark condoms on the same block? From east to west, here are some highlights:

l.a. Eyeworks, 7407 Melrose Ave. (© **323/653-8255**), revolutionized eyeglass designs from medical supply to stylish accessory, and now their brand is nationwide. **Retail Slut,** 7308 Melrose Ave. (© **323/934-1339**), is a rock 'n' roll shop carrying new clothing and accessories for men and women. The unique designs are for a select crowd (the name says it all), so don't expect to find anything for your next PTA meeting here. **Betsey Johnson Boutique,** 8050 Melrose Ave. (© **323/852-1534;** www.betseyjohnson.com), is a favorite among the young and pencil-thin; the New York–based designer has brought to L.A. her brand of fashion—trendy, cutesy, body-conscious women's wear in colorful prints and faddish fabrics. Across the street, **Off the Wall,** 7325 Melrose Ave. (© **323/930-1185**), is filled with neon-flashing, bells-and-whistles kitsch collectibles, from vintage Wurlitzer jukeboxes to life-size fiberglass cows. The L.A. branch of a Bay Area hipster hangout, **Wasteland,** 7248 Melrose Ave. (© **323/653-3028**), has an enormous steel-sculpted facade. There's a lot of leather and denim, and some classic vintage—but mostly funky 1970s-style garb, both vintage and contemporary. More racks of vintage treasures (and trash) are found at **Aardvark's Odd Ark,** 85 Market St. (© **310/392-2996**), which stocks everything, from suits and dresses to neckties, hats, handbags, and jewelry. This place also manages to anticipate some of the hottest new street fashions.

SANTA MONICA & THE BEACHES

MAIN STREET (between Pacific St. and Rose Ave., Santa Monica and Venice boulevards)★ An excellent street for strolling, Main Street is crammed with a combination of mall standards as well as upscale, left-of-center individual boutiques. You can also find plenty of casually hip cafes and restaurants. The primary strip connecting Santa Monica and Venice, Main Street has a relaxed, beach-community vibe that sets it apart from similar strips. The stores here straddle the fashion fence between upscale trendy and beach bum edgy. Highlights include **Obsolete,** 222 Main St. (near Rose Ave.; © **310/399-0024**), the most hip antiques store I've ever seen. Collectibles range from antique carnival curios to 19th-century anatomical charts from Belgium (you'd be amazed at how much some of that junk in your attic is worth). **CP Shades,** 2937 Main St. (between Ashland and Pier sts.; © **310/392-0949**), is a San Francisco ladies' clothier whose loose and comfy cotton-and-linen line is carried by many department stores and boutiques. **Horizons West,** 2011 Main St. (south of Pico Blvd.;

Tips **Cinderella Complex: Custom Shoes**

If you're still searching for The Perfect Pair of Shoes, why not have them custom-made just for your feet? **Stanners & Kent,** a tiny shoe shop at 800 B 14th St., at Montana Ave. (© **310/656-2720**), creates custom-designed shoes in whatever style you desire. Prices start at about $200.

© 310/392-1122), sells brand-name surfboards, wet suits, leashes, magazines, waxes, lotions, and everything else you need to catch the perfect wave. If you're looking for some truly sophisticated, finely crafted eyewear, friendly **Optical Shop of Aspen,** 2904 Main St. (between Ashland and Pier sts.; © **310/ 392-0633**), is for you. Ask for frames by cutting-edge L.A. designers Bada and Koh Sakai. For aromatherapy nirvana, it's **Cloud's,** 2719 Main St. (© **310/ 399-2059**), where Jill Cloud (happily assisted by her lovely mom) carries the most heavenly scented candles. Then there's **Arts & Letters,** 2665 Main St. (© **310/314-7345**), a stationery haven that includes invitations by the owner herself, Marilyn Golin. Outdoors types will get lost in 5,600-square-foot **Patagonia,** 2936 Main St. (© **310/314-1776;** www.patagonia.com), where climbers, surfers, skiers, and hikers can gear up in the functional, colorful duds that put this environmentally friendly firm on the map.

MONTANA AVENUE (between 17th and 7th sts., Santa Monica; www. montanaave.com)   This breezy stretch of slow-traffic Montana has gotten a lot more pricey than in the late 1970s when tailors and laundromats ruled the roost, but the specialty shops still outnumber the chains. Look around and you can see upscale moms with strollers and cellphones shopping for designer fashions, country home decor, and gourmet takeout.

Montana is still original enough for residents from across town to make a special trip here, seeking out distinctive shops like **Shabby Chic,** 1013 Montana Ave. (© **310/394-1975**), a much-copied purveyor of slip-covered sofas and flea-market furnishings, while clotheshorses shop for designer wear at minimalist **Savannah,** 706 Montana Ave. (© **310/458-2095**); ultrahip **Jill Roberts,** 920 Montana Ave. (© **310/260-1966**); and sleekly professional **Weathervane,** 1209 Montana Ave. (© **310/393-5344**). For more grown-up style, head to **Ponte Vecchio,** 702 Montana Ave. (© **310/394-0989**), which sells Italian hand-painted dishes and urns, or to **Cinzia,** 1129 Montana Ave. (© **310/393-7751**), which features a smattering of both Tuscan and English home accessories. If Valentine's Day is approaching, duck into **Only Hearts,** 1407 Montana Ave. (© **310/393-3088**), for heart-themed gifts and seductively comfortable intimate apparel. And don't forget the one-of-a-kind shops such as **Sun Precautions,** 1600 Montana Ave. (© **310/451-5858**), specializing in 100% UV protection apparel, and the second-largest **Kiehl's** store outside of NYC, 1515 Montana Ave. (© **310/255-0055**). Enjoy a meal at the local favorite, **Café Montana,** 1534 Montana Ave. (© **310/829-3990**), for great people-watching through its floor-to-ceiling glass windows.

THIRD STREET PROMENADE *(Overrated* (Third St. from Broadway to Wilshire Blvd., Santa Monica; www.downtownsm.com)   Packed with those ubiquitous corporate chain stores, restaurants, and cafes (gee, *another* Starbucks), Santa Monica's pedestrians-only section of Third Street is the most popular shopping area in the city and certainly the least original (picture a suburban shopping mall without a roof and you've got it). The promenade bustles all day and well into the evening with a seemingly endless assortment of street performers, shoppers, bored teens, and homeless drifters.

There are, however, a few shopping gems squeezed between the Abercrombie & Fitches and Old Navies. You can easily browse for hours at **Hennessey & Ingalls,** 214 Wilshire Blvd. (© **310/458-9074;** www.hennesseyingalls.com), a bookstore devoted to art and architecture. **Restoration Hardware,** 1221 Third Street Promenade (© **310/458-7992**), is still the retro-current leader for reproduction home furnishings and accessories. **Puzzle Zoo,** 1413 Third Street

Finds **GR8 Finds in West L.A.'s J-Town**

What started off as a magazine has now spawned two of L.A.'s most talked-about new stores: **GR2**, 2062 Sawtelle Blvd. (© **310/445-9276**) and **Giant Robot**, 2015 Sawtelle Blvd. (© **310/478-1819**). Located across the street from each other in West L.A.'s Japantown (at Sawtelle and Olympic boulevards), both specialize in Asian-American pop culture items ranging from T-shirts and books to music, stationery, toys (you *must* get a Kubrick doll), and art. There are several other cool shops and restaurants along this 1½-block stretch as well. One of my favorite stores is **Happy Six**, 2115 Sawtelle Blvd. (© **310/479-5363**), which looks like Hello Kitty on acid and sells playful apparel and accessories for men and women. If you're hungry, my favorites along Sawtelle are **Manpuku**, 2125 Sawtelle Blvd. (© **310/ 473-0580**), **Sawtelle Kitchen**, 2024 Sawtelle Blvd. (© **310/445-9288**), and **Hurry Curry**, 2131 Sawtelle Blvd. (© **310/473-1640**). Or you can pop into **Nijiya Market**, 2130 Sawtelle Blvd. (© **310/575-3300**), and grab a bento (Japanese boxed lunch) to go.

Promenade (© **310/393-9201**), voted "Best in L.A." by *Los Angeles* magazine, is where you'll find the double-sided World's Most Difficult Puzzle, the Puzzle in a Bottle, and many other brain-teasing challenges. Music lovers can get CDs and vinyl at **Hear Music**, 1429 Third Street Promenade (© **310/319-9527**). Stores stay open late (often till 1 or 2am on the weekends) for the moviegoing crowds, and there's plenty of metered parking in six structures along Second and Fourth streets between Broadway and Wilshire Boulevard, so bring lots of quarters.

DOWNTOWN

Since the late, lamented Bullock's department store closed in 1993 (its Art Deco masterpiece salons rescued to house the Southwestern Law School's library), downtown has become less of a shopping destination than ever. Although many of the once-splendid streets are lined with cut-rate luggage and electronics stores, shopping here can be a rewarding—albeit gritty—experience for the adventuresome.

Savvy Angelenos still go for bargains in the garment and fabric districts, florists and bargain hunters arrive at the vast Flower Mart before dawn for the city's best selection of fresh blooms, and families of all ethnicities stroll the **Grand Central Market** ★★, 317 S. Broadway (between 3rd and 4th sts.; © **213/624-2378;** www.grandcentralsquare.com). Opened in 1917, this bustling market has watched the face of downtown L.A. change while changing little. Today its sawdust-covered aisles serve Latino families, enterprising restaurateurs, and cooks in search of unusual ingredients—stuffed goat heads, mole paste, plantains, deep-fried smelt, Mexican cane alcohol—and bargain-priced produce. On weekends you'll be greeted by a mariachi band at the Hill Street entrance, near my favorite market feature, the fruit-juice counter, which dispenses 20 fresh varieties from wall spigots, and blends the tastiest, healthiest "shakes" in town. Farther into the market you'll find produce sellers and prepared-food counters, spice vendors who seem straight out of a Turkish bazaar, and a grain-and-bean seller who'll scoop out dozens of exotic rices and dried legumes. It's open 9am to 6pm daily.

Another of my favorite downtown shopping zones is **Olvera Street** ★ (© **213/628-1274;** www.olvera-street.com), a lively brick pedestrian lane near Union Station that's been lined with stalls selling Mexican wares since the 1930s.

Abbot Kinney Boulevard: the Anti-Rodeo Drive

When you're finally fed up with the Rodeo Drive attitude and megamall conformity, it's time to drive to Venice and stroll the eclectic shops along **Abbot Kinney Boulevard.** This refreshingly antiestablishment stretch of street has the most diverse array of shops, galleries, and restaurants in Los Angeles (locals still cheer that there are no franchises in the neighborhood). You can easily spend the entire afternoon here pouring over vintage clothing, antique furniture, vintage Vespas, local art, and amusing gifts. For one-of-a-kind designed jewelry, check out **Nagual,** 1326 Abbott Kinney Blvd. (© **310/396-8500**), whose "metals with an edge" designs have caught the eye of many celebrities. Or if you're looking for a unique gift, you'll want to walk into the shop of **Strange Invisible Perfumes,** 1209 Abbot Kinney Blvd. (© **310/314-1505**), where they can custom-make a scent to match your musk. Then there's **Firefly,** 1413 Abbot Kinney Blvd. (© **310/450-6288**), a local favorite. It's that one store you can go into and find a great baby gift, stationery, books, quirky handbags, and cool clothing. When you're ready to sit down and look over your loot, take a break to eat at one of the boulevard's many restaurants, including **Joe's** (the best California cuisine in L.A.; see p. 496), **Primitivo, Axe, Lilly's, Massimo's, Jin's Patisserie, French Market Café,** and, of course, **Hal's Bar & Grill,** with it's live jazz music. Heck, there's even 2 hours of free street parking.

Everything that's sold south of the border is available here, including custom leather accessories, huarache sandals, maracas, and—but of course—freshly baked churros. On weekends you're bound to see strolling bolero musicians, mariachis music, folk dancers, and performances by Aztec Indians. It's open daily from 10am to about 7pm.

11 Los Angeles After Dark

Your best bet for current entertainment info is the *L.A. Weekly* (**www.la weekly.com**), a free weekly paper available at sidewalk stands, shops, and restaurants. It has all the most up-to-date news on what's happening in Los Angeles's playhouses, cinemas, museums, and live-music venues. The Sunday "**Calendar**" and Thursday "**Weekend**" sections of the *Los Angeles Times* (**www.calendar live.com**) are also a good source of information on what's going on throughout the city. **Ticketmaster** (© **213/480-3232;** www.ticketmaster.com) is L.A.'s major charge-by-phone ticket agency, selling tickets to concerts, sporting events, plays, and special events, but beware of the absurdly high processing fees.

THEATER

Tickets for most plays usually cost $10 to $35, although big-name shows at the major theaters can fetch up to $75 for the best seats. **Theatre League Alliance** (© **213/614-0556;** www.TheatreLA.org), an association of live theaters and producers in Los Angeles—they also put on the yearly Ovation Awards, L.A.'s theater awards—offers same-day, half-price tickets via **Web Tix,** an Internet-only service at www.TheatreLA.org. Tickets are available Tuesday through Saturday from 4 to 11pm; purchase them online with a credit card and they'll be waiting for you at the box office. The site features a frequently updated list of shows and availability; you can also sign up for e-mail alerts. If you didn't bring your computer, log on at any public library, Internet cafe, or office service store.

MAJOR THEATERS & COMPANIES

The all-purpose **Music Center of Los Angeles County,** 135 N. Grand Ave., downtown, houses the city's top two playhouses—the **Ahmanson Theatre** and **Mark Taper Forum.** They're both home to the Center Theater Group (www. taperahmanson.com), as well as traveling productions (often Broadway- or London-bred). Each season the Ahmanson Theatre (© 213/628-2772) hosts a handful of high-profile shows, such as Andrew Lloyd Webber's *Phantom of the Opera,* the Royal National Theatre's production of Ibsen's *Enemy of the People* starring Sir Ian McKellan, and the Adventures in Motion Pictures presentation of Matthew Bourne's *Cinderella. Tip:* The best seats in the theater are in the mezzanine section.

The Mark Taper Forum (© 213/628-2772; www.marktaperforum.com) is a more intimate theater with a thrust stage—where the audience is seated on three sides of the acting area—that performs contemporary works by international and local playwrights. Neil Simon's humorous and poignant *The Dinner Party* and Tom Stoppard's witty and eclectic *Arcadia* are among the more popular productions performed on this internationally recognized stage, which has won three Pulitzer Prizes and 18 Tony Awards.

One of L.A.'s most venerable landmarks, the **Orpheum Theatre,** 842 S. Broadway at Ninth St. (© 213/749-5171; www.laorpheum.com), has recently reopened after a 75-year hiatus. Built in 1926, this renowned venue has hosted an array of theatrical productions, concerts, film festivals, and movie shoots—from Judy Garland's 1933 vaudeville performance to *Ally McBeal.* The 2,000-seat theater is home to the Mighty Wurlitzer, one of three original theater organs still existing in Southern California theaters.

Across town, the moderately sized **Geffen Playhouse,** 10886 Le Conte Ave., Westwood (© 310/208-5454; www.geffenplayhouse.com), presents dramatic and comedic works by prominent and emerging writers. UCLA purchased the theater—which was originally built as a Masonic temple in 1929 and later served as the Westwood Playhouse—back in 1995 with a little help from philanthropic entertainment mogul David Geffen. This striking venue is often the West Coast choice of many acclaimed off-Broadway shows, and also attracts locally based TV and movie actors eager for the immediacy of stage work. One recent production featured Annette Bening in Ibsen's *Hedda Gabler.* Always audience-friendly, the Playhouse prices tickets in the $28 to $43 range.

You've probably already heard of the **Kodak Theatre,** 6834 Hollywood Blvd. (© 323/308-6300; www.kodaktheater.com), home of the Academy Awards. The crown jewel of the Hollywood & Highlands entertainment complex, this

---

Finds Free Morning Music at Hollywood Bowl

It's not widely known, but the Bowl's morning rehearsals are open to the public and absolutely free. On Tuesday, Thursday, and Friday from 9:30am to 12:30pm, you can see the program scheduled for that evening. So bring some coffee and doughnuts (the concession stands aren't open) and enjoy the best seats in the house (© 323/850-2000; www.hollywoodbowl.org).

Tips **Great Theater, Cheap Tickets**

Two hours before curtain time, the Ahmanson Theatre and Mark Taper Forum offers specially priced $12 tickets, which must be purchased in person at the box office with cash. All performances are subject to availability with restrictions.

---

modern beauty hosts a wide range of international performances, musicals, and concerts ranging from Prince and Elvis Costello to the Moscow Stanislavski Ballet and *Grease* starring Frankie Avalon. Guided tours are given 7 days a week from 10:30am to 2:30pm.

The recently restored **Pantages Theatre,** 6233 Hollywood Blvd., between Vine and Argyle (© **323/463-4367**), reflects the full Art Deco glory of L.A.'s theater scene. Opened in 1930, this historical and cultural landmark was the first Art Deco movie palace in the U.S. and site of the Academy Awards from 1949 to 1959. The theater recently presented the run of Disney's *The Lion King* and Mel Brooks's smash hit, *The Producers* with Jason Alexander and Martin Short.

At the foot of the Hollywood Hills, the 1,245-seat outdoor **John Anson Ford Amphitheatre** (© **213/974-1343;** www.lacountyarts.org/ford.html) is located in a county regional park and is set against a backdrop of cypress trees and chaparral. It is an intimate setting with no patron more than 96 feet away from the stage. Music, dance, film, theater, and family events run from May through September. The indoor theater space, a cozy 87-seat space that was extensively renovated in November 1998 and renamed **[Inside] The Ford,** features live music and theater year-round.

One of the most highly acclaimed professional theaters in L.A., the **Pasadena Playhouse,** 39 S. El Molino Ave., near Colorado Boulevard, Pasadena (© **626/ 356-7529;** www.pasadenaplayhouse.org), is a registered historic landmark that has served as the training ground for many theatrical, film, and TV stars, including William Holden and Gene Hackman. Productions are mounted on the main theater's elaborate Spanish Colonial revival stage.

For a schedule at any of the above theaters, check the listings in *Los Angeles* magazine (www.lamag.com), available at most area newsstands, or the "Calendar" section of the Sunday *Los Angeles Times* (www.calendarlive.com), or call the box offices at the numbers listed above.

SMALLER PLAYHOUSES & COMPANIES

On any given night, there's more live theater to choose from in Los Angeles than in New York City, due in part to the surfeit of ready actors and writers chomping at the bit to make it in Tinseltown. Many of today's familiar faces from film and TV spent plenty of time cutting their teeth on L.A.'s busy theater circuit, which is home to nearly 200 small- and medium-size theaters and theater companies, ranging from the 'round-the-corner, neighborhood variety to high-profile, polished troupes of veteran actors. With so many options, navigating the scene to find the best work can be a monumental task. A good bet is to choose one of the theaters listed below, which have established excellent reputations for their consistently high-quality productions; otherwise, consult the *L.A. Weekly* (www.laweekly.com), which advertises most current productions, or call **Theatre LA** (© **213/614-0556**) for up-to-date performance listings.

The **Colony Studio Theatre,** 555 N. Third St., Burbank (ⓒ **818/558-7000,** www.colonytheatre.org), was formed in 1975 and has developed from a part-time ensemble of TV actors longing for their theatrical roots into a nationally recognized company. The company produces plays in all genres at the 276-seat Burbank Center Stage, which is shared with other performing-arts groups.

Actors Circle Theater, 7313 Santa Monica Blvd., West Hollywood (ⓒ **323/ 882-8043**), is a 47-seater that's as acclaimed as it's tiny. Look for original contemporary works throughout the year.

The **Actor's Gang Theater,** 6201 Santa Monica Blvd., Hollywood (ⓒ **323/ 465-0566**), is not one to shy from irreverence. Back in 1997 the in-house company, a group of UCLA alums, presented *Bat Boy: The Musical,* based on a story in the bizarre tabloid *Weekly World News.*

Founded in 1965, **East West Players,** 120 N. Judge John Aiso St., Los Angeles (ⓒ **213/625-7000;** www.eastwestplayers.org), is the oldest Asian American theater company in the United States. It's been so successful that the company moved from a 99-seat venue to the 200-seat David Henry Hwang Theater in downtown L.A.'s Little Tokyo.

The 25-year-old **L.A. Theatre Works** (ⓒ **310/827-0889**) is renowned for its marriage of media and theater and has performed more than 200 plays and logged more than 350 hours of on-air programming. Performances are held at the Skirball Cultural Center, nestled in the Sepulveda Pass near the Getty Center. In the past, personalities such as Richard Dreyfuss, Julia Louis-Dreyfus, Jason Robards, Annette Bening, and John Lithgow have given award-winning performances of plays by Arthur Miller, Neil Simon, Joyce Carol Oates, and others. For nearly a decade the group has performed simultaneously for viewing and listening audiences in its radio theater series. Tickets are usually around $35; a full performance schedule can be found online at www.skirball.org.

Founded in 1981, **West Coast Ensemble Theater,** 522 N. La Brea Ave., between Melrose and Beverly, Hollywood (ⓒ **323/876-8723;** www.wcensemble. org), is a nonprofit multiethnic assemblage of professional actors, writers, and directors. The ensemble has collected accolades from local critics, as well as many awards for its excellent production quality. Expect to see well-written, well-directed, and socially relevant plays performed by a talented and professional cast. Ticket prices range from $15 to $22.

CLASSICAL MUSIC & OPERA

While L.A. is best known for its pop entertainment realms, other types of music here consist of top-flight orchestras and companies—both local and visiting—to fulfill the most demanding classical music appetites; scan the papers to find out who's performing while you're in the city.

The world-class **Los Angeles Philharmonic** (ⓒ **323/850-2000;** www.laphil. org) is the only major classical-music company in Los Angeles, and it's just gotten a whole lot more popular with the completion of its incredible new home—the **Walt Disney Concert Hall,** located at the intersection of First Street and Grand Avenue in the historic Bunker Hill area (p. 534). Designed by world-renowned architect Frank O. Gehry, this exciting addition to the Music Center of L.A. includes a breathtaking 2,265-seat concert hall, outdoor park, restaurant, cafe, bookstore, and gift shop.

The philharmonic's Finnish-born music director, Esa-Pekka Salonen, concentrates on contemporary compositions; despite complaints from traditionalists, he does an excellent job attracting younger audiences. Tickets can be hard to come by when celebrity players like Itzhak Perlman, Isaac Stern, Emanuel Ax, and Yo Yo Ma are in town. In addition to performances at the Walt Disney Concert Hall, the philharmonic also plays a summer season at the **Hollywood Bowl** (see "Concerts Under the Stars," below), and a chamber-music series at the **Skirball Cultural Center.**

Slowly but surely, the **Los Angeles Opera** (© 213/972-8001; www.losangeles opera.com), which performs at the **Dorothy Chandler Pavilion,** is gaining respect and popularity with inventive stagings of classic pieces, modern operas, visiting divas, and the contributions from high-profile artistic director Plácido Domingo. The 120-voice **Los Angeles Master Chorale** sings a varied repertoire that includes classical and pop compositions. Concerts are held at the **Walt Disney Concert Hall** (© 213/972-7200) October through June.

The **UCLA Center for the Performing Arts** (© 310/825-2101; www. performingarts.ucla.edu) has presented music, dance, and theatrical performances of unparalleled quality for more than 60 years and continues to be a major presence in the local and national cultural landscape. Presentations occur at several different theaters around Los Angeles, both on and off campus. UCLA's **Royce Hall** is the center's pride; it has even been compared to New York's Carnegie Hall. Recent standouts from the center's busy calendar included the famous Gyuto Monks Tibetan Tantric Choir and the Cinderella story *Cendrillon* with an original score by Sergei Prokofiev.

CONCERTS UNDER THE STARS

Hollywood Bowl ★★★ *Moments*   Built in the early 1920s, the Hollywood Bowl is an elegant Greek-style natural outdoor amphitheater cradled in a small mountain canyon. It's the summer home of the Los Angeles Philharmonic and Hollywood Bowl orchestras, and often hosts internationally known conductors and soloists on Tuesday and Thursday nights. Friday and Saturday concerts typically feature orchestral swing or pops concerts. The summer season also includes a jazz series; past performers have included Natalie Cole, Dionne Warwick, and Chick Corea. Other events, from standard rock 'n' roll acts like Radiohead to Garrison Keillor programs, summer fireworks galas, and the annual Mariachi Festival, are often on the season's schedule.

To round out an evening at the Bowl, many concertgoers use the occasion to enjoy a picnic dinner and a bottle of wine—it's one of L.A.'s grandest traditions. You can prepare your own, or order a picnic basket with a choice of hot and cold dishes and a selection of wines and desserts from Patina's on-site catering department, which also provides delivery to box seats: Call © 323/850-1885 by 4pm the day before you go to place your food order.

2301 N. Highland Ave. (at Pat Moore Way), Hollywood. © 323/850-2000. www.hollywoodbowl.org.

THE CLUB & MUSIC SCENE

Los Angeles is more or less the center of the entertainment industry, so on any given night, finding something to satisfy any musical taste can be a snap. From acoustic rock to jazz fusion, from Judas Priest cover bands to Latin funk, from the up-and-coming to the already gone, L.A. has something for everyone. For a listing of shows, check the websites of the *LA Weekly* (www.laweekly.com) and the *Los Angeles Times* "Calendar" section (www.calendarlive.com).

The Avalon Hollywood   Formerly known as The Palace, this 1,200-capacity theater and nightclub—just across Vine from the famed Capitol Records tower—was the site of numerous significant alternative-rock shows throughout

---

Finds Supper & a Show at the Cinegrill

If you enjoy the Hollywood scene, the supper club experience, and Gershwin classics, have we got a treat for you. Michael Feinstein, one of the top interpreters of the popular American song, recently opened his West Coast club in the historic Roosevelt Hotel in the heart of Hollywood. Appropriately dim, curvaceously cozy, and equipped with state-of-the-art audio and visual systems, the tier-leveled supper club serves excellent Asian-fusion cuisine along with top talent performing Monday through Saturday. For show times and reservations, call ✆ **323/769-7269** or log on to www.hollywoodroosevelt.com. 7000 Hollywood Blvd., between Highland and La Brea avenues.

---

the late 1990s and has been given a much-needed makeover. Its lounge, the Spider Club, acts as the VIP room/late-night oasis and makes for an excellent place to see and be seen, imbibe, dance, and cavort until the wee hours of the morning. Club nights feature famous DJs like Paul Oakenfeld. 1735 N. Vine St., Hollywood. ✆ **323/462-8900.** www.avalonhollywood.com.

Babe's & Ricky's Inn ✮ *Finds*   In South Central L.A.'s up-and-coming Leimert Park, this blues club stands out as an original, a place where we can imagine B. B. King himself would have played before he became famous. Mama Laura Gross is the Cultivator of the fabulous, endangered sound and the house Goddess of this intimate bar. Great guitarists are the rule, not the exception here. 4339 Leimert Blvd., Leimert Park. ✆ **323/295-9112.**

B. B. King's Blues Club   Nestled in Universal CityWalk's commercial plaza, this three-level club/restaurant—the ribs alone are worth the trip—hosts plenty of great local and touring blues acts and is a testament to the establishment's venerable namesake. There's no shortage of good seating, but if you find yourself on the top two levels, it's best to grab a table adjacent to the railing to get an ideal view of the stage. CityWalk, Universal City. ✆ **818/622-5464.**

Forty Deuce   Owner Ivan Kane has just reopened this suave nightclub, formerly known as Kane. Designed as "back-alley, striptease lounge," the low bar, lounge chair seating, vintage brass registers, and cocktail tables with chic lamps all chip in to create a sexy, burlesque-esque vibe. Models use the bar as a runway, so watch your cocktail. 5574 Melrose Ave., Hollywood. ✆ **323/466-6263.** www.fortydeuce.com.

House of Blues ✮   With three great bars, cutting-edge Southern art, and a key Sunset Strip location, there are plenty of reasons music fans and industry types keep coming back to House of Blues. Night after night, audiences are dazzled by performances from nationally and internationally acclaimed acts as diverse as Duran Duran, B. B. King, and Queensryche. The food in the upstairs restaurant can be great (reservations are a must), and the Sunday gospel brunch, though a bit pricey, puts a mean raise on the roof. 8430 Sunset Blvd., West Hollywood. ✆ **323/848-5100.** www.hob.com.

The Knitting Factory   Straight from the New York City legend, a West Coast branch of the famous Knitting Factory has arrived in the redeveloping Hollywood Boulevard nightlife district. The Main Stage was inaugurated by a Posies performance and sees such diverse bookings as Kristin Hersh, Pere Ubu, and Jonathan Richman; a secondary AlterKnit stage has sporadic shows. The Factory is totally wired for digital, including interactive online computer stations throughout the club. 7021 Hollywood Blvd., Hollywood. ℭ 323/463-0204. www.knittingfactory.com.

Roxy   Veteran record producer/executive Lou Adler opened this Sunset Strip club in the mid-1970s with concerts by Neil Young and a lengthy run of the premovie *Rocky Horror Show*. Since then, it's remained among the top showcase venues in Hollywood—although the revitalized Troubadour and such new entries as the House of Blues challenge its preeminence among cozy clubs, you can still find national acts that will pop in as well as great local bands. 9009 Sunset Blvd. ℭ 310/276-2222.

Spaceland ⚡   The wall-to-wall mirrors and shiny brass posts decorating the interior create the feeling that, in a past life, Spaceland must've been a seedy strip joint, but the club's current personality offers something entirely different. Having hosted countless performances by cutting-edge artists such as Pavement, Mary Lou Lord, the late Elliot Smith, and the Eels, this hot spot on the fringe of east Hollywood has become one of the most important clubs on the L.A. circuit. 1717 Silver Lake Blvd., Silver Lake. ℭ 323/661-4380. www.clubspaceland.com.

The Troubadour   This West Hollywood mainstay radiates rock history— from the 1960s to the 1990s, the Troub really has seen 'em all. Audiences are consistently treated to memorable shows from the already-established or young-and-promising acts that take the Troubadour's stage. But bring your earplugs—this beer- and sweat-soaked club likes it loud. 9081 Santa Monica Blvd., West Hollywood. ℭ 310/276-6168. www.troubadour.com. All ages.

Viper Room   This world-famous club on the Strip has been king of the hill since it was first opened by actor Johnny Depp and co-owner Sal Jenco back in 1993. With an intensely electric and often star-filled scene, the intimate club is also known for unforgettable late-night surprise performances from such powerhouses as the late Johnny Cash, Iggy Pop, Tom Petty, Slash, and Trapt (to name but a few) after headline gigs elsewhere in town. 8852 Sunset Blvd., West Hollywood. ℭ 310/358-1881. www.viperroom.com.

Whisky A Go-Go ⚡   This legendary bi-level venue personifies L.A. rock 'n' roll, from Jim Morrison and X to Guns N' Roses and Beck. Every trend has passed through this club, and it continues to be the most vital venue of its kind. With the hiring of an in-house booker a few years ago, the Whisky began showcasing local talent on free-admission Monday nights. 8901 Sunset Blvd., West Hollywood. ℭ 310/652-4202. www.whiskyagogo.com. All ages.

DANCE CLUBS

The Conga Room   Attracting such Latin-music luminaries as Pucho & The Latin Soul Brothers, this one-time health club on the Miracle Mile has quickly become *the* nightspot for live salsa and merengue. Break up the evening of heart-melting, sexy Latin dancing with a trip to the dining room, where the chef serves up savory Cuban fare in a setting that conjures the romance of pre-Castro Cuba, or indulge yourself in the Conga Room's stylish cigar lounge. 5364 Wilshire Blvd., Los Angeles. ℭ 323/938-1696. www.congaroom.com.

The Derby   This class-A east-of-Hollywood club has been at the core of the swing revival since the very beginning. Located at a former Brown Derby site, the club was restored to its original luster and detailed with a heavy 1940s edge. With Big Bad Voodoo Daddy as the onetime house band and regular visits from Royal Crown Revue, hep guys and dolls knew that The Derby was money even before *Swingers* transformed it into one of the city's most happenin' hangs. But if you come on the weekends, expect a wait to get in, and once you're inside, dance space is at a premium. 4500 Los Feliz Blvd., Los Feliz. ℂ 323/663-8979. www.the-derby.com. Cover $7–$10.

El Floridita *(Finds)* This tiny Cuban restaurant-and-salsa club is hot, hot, hot. Despite its modest strip-lot locale, it draws the likes of Jennifer Lopez, Sandra Bullock, Jimmy Smits, and Jack Nicholson in addition to a festive crowd of Latin-dance devotees who groove well into the night. The hippest nights continue to be Mondays, when Johnny Polanco and his swinging New York–flavored salsa band get the dance floor jumpin'. 1253 N. Vine St., Hollywood. ℂ 323/871-8612. Cover $10.

Hollywood Athletic Club Built in 1924, this pool hall, restaurant, and nightclub is home to some groovin' dance clubs. Saturdays feature a lively mix of progressive house music spun by DJs Drew Down and Dave Audé. On Sundays the sounds of Latin house, merengue, hip-hop, and salsa fill the air. Hollywood Athletic Club also hosts concerts from internationally known DJs and bands as diverse as Mono and the Wu Tang Clan. 6525 Sunset Blvd., Hollywood. ℂ 323/462-6262 or 323/957-0722. Cover $10–$20.

Nacional *(𝓡)* Quickly becoming Hollywood's most desirable dance floor, you'll find a hip and gorgeous crowd here engaging in an orgiastic celebration of youth. It also has a well-designed balcony where you can watch all the flirting among a lively outdoor smoking area. So grab a *mojito* and mingle among the young, beautiful, and unshakably self-assured, and remember, even the rest of us can have fun here. 1645 Wilcox Ave., Hollywood. ℂ 323/962-7712.

BARS & COCKTAIL LOUNGES

Beauty Bar It's a proven concept in New York and San Francisco, a cocktail lounge/beauty salon. Decorated with vintage salon gear and sporting a hip-retro vibe, the Beauty Bar is campy, fun, and trendy all at once. Where else can you actually get a manicure while sipping cocktails with names like Blue Rinse (made with blue Curaçao) or Prell (their version of a grasshopper)? 1638 N. Cahuenga Blvd., Hollywood. ℂ 323/464-7676. www.beautybar.com.

The Dresden Room *(𝓡)* Hugely popular with L.A. hipsters because of its longevity, location, often-overlooked cuisine, and elegant ambience, "The Den" was pushed into the mainstream of L.A. nightlife thanks to its inclusion in the movie *Swingers*. But it's the timeless lounge act of Marty and Elayne (the couple has been performing there up to 5 nights a week since 1982) that has proven that fad or no fad, this place is always cool. Sidle up to the bar for a blue glass of the house classic, Blood and Sand—a space-age margarita of sorts. 1760 N. Vermont Ave., Hollywood. ℂ 323/665-4294.

Good Luck Bar Until they installed a flashing neon sign outside, only locals and hipsters knew about this *Kung Fu*–themed room in the Los Feliz/Silver Lake area. The dark red windowless interior boasts Oriental ceiling tiles, fringed Chinese paper lanterns, sweet-but-deadly drinks like the "Yee Mee Loo" (translated as "blue drink"), and a jukebox with selections ranging from Thelonius Monk to Cher's "Half Breed." The spacious sitting room, furnished with mismatched sofas, armchairs, and banquettes, provides a great atmosphere for conversation or romance. Arrive early to avoid the throngs of L.A. scenesters. 1514 Hillhurst Ave. (between Hollywood and Sunset boulevards), Los Angeles. ℂ 323/666-3524.

Hank's Bar ⓖ Although the original grand old man behind the bar, Henry "Hank" Holzer, is no longer with us, his legacy endures at this classic downtown watering hole. Its battered booths and well-liquored patrons who have been elbowing up to the bar here for a decade, mingle nicely with the drop-in customers currently infusing the new surge in downtown L.A.'s recently reinvigorated night life (the ground floor of the Stillwell Hotel). 840 S. Grand Ave., Los Angeles. ⓒ **213/396-7718.**

Skybar, at Mondrian Hotel *(Overrated* Since its opening in hotelier Ian Schrager's refurbished Sunset Strip hotel, Skybar has been a favorite among L.A.'s most fashionable of the fashionable set. This place is so hot that even the agents to the stars need agents to get in. (Rumor has it that one agent was so desperate to get in he promised one of the servers a contract.) Nevertheless, a little image consulting—affect the right look, strike the right pose, and look properly disinterested—might get you in to rub elbows with some of the faces that regularly appear on the cover of *People* (but please don't stare). 8440 W. Sunset Blvd., West Hollywood. ⓒ **323/848-6025.**

The Standard Downtown ⓖⓖ This rooftop bar, located atop the Standard Hotel in downtown L.A. (formerly Superior Oil Headquarters) is surrounded by high office towers and helipads, and the view is magnificent. The skyscrapers act like strangely glowing lava lamps amongst the night sky as exotic ladies sip exotic cocktails amid waterbeds and bent-plastic loungers. 550 S. Flower St.ⓒ **213/892-8080.**

360 This 19th-story, penthouse-perched restaurant and lounge is a perfect place to romance your special someone. It's all about the view here—all 360 degrees of it. The understated and softly lit sleek interior emphasizes the scene outside the plentiful windows, including a spectacular vista of the famed HOLLYWOOD sign. 6290 Sunset Blvd., Hollywood. ⓒ **323/871-2995.** www.360hollywood.com.

COMEDY CLUBS

Comedy Store ⓖ You can't go wrong here: New comics develop their material, and established ones work out their kinks, at this landmark owned by Mitzi Shore (Pauly's mom). The **Best of the Comedy Store Room,** which seats 400, features professional stand-ups continuously on Friday and Saturday nights. Several comedians are always featured, each doing about a 15-minute stint. The talent is always first-rate and includes comics who appear on *The Tonight Show* and other shows. The **Original Room** features a dozen or so comedians back-to-back nightly. Sunday night is amateur night: Anyone with enough guts can take the stage for 3 minutes—Lord only knows what you'll get. 8433 Sunset Blvd., West Hollywood. ⓒ **323/650-6268.** www.comedystore.com.

Groundling Theater ⓖ L.A.'s answer to Chicago's Second City has been around for more than 25 years, yet it remains the most innovative and funny group in town. The skits change every year or so, but they take new improvisational twists every night and the satire is often savage. The Groundlings were the springboard to fame for Pee-Wee Herman, Elvira, and former *Saturday Night Live* stars Jon Lovitz, Phil Hartman, and Julia "It's Pat" Sweeney. Phone for show times and reservations. 7307 Melrose Ave., Los Angeles. ⓒ **323/934-9700.** www. groundlings.com. Tickets $11–$20.

The Improv A showcase for top stand-ups since 1975, the Improv offers something different each night. Although it used to have a fairly active music schedule, the place is now mostly doing what it does best—showcasing comedy.

Owner Budd Freedman's buddies—like Jay Leno, Billy Crystal, and Robin Williams—hone their skills here more often than you would expect. But even if the comedians on the bill are all unknowns, they won't be for long. Shows are at 8pm Sunday and Thursday, at 8:30 and 10:30pm Friday and Saturday. 8162 Melrose Ave., West Hollywood. ✆ 323/651-2583. www.improvclubs.com.

LATE-NIGHT BITES

The Apple Pan 🟊🟊   This classic American burger shack, an L.A. landmark, hasn't changed much since 1947—and its burgers and pies continue to hit the spot. Open until 1am Friday and Saturday, until midnight other nights; closed Monday. See p. 504 for a full review. 10801 W. Pico Blvd., West L.A. ✆ 310/475-3585.

Canter's Fairfax Restaurant, Delicatessen & Bakery   This 24-hour Jewish deli has been a winner with late-nighters since it opened more than 65 years ago. If you show up after the clubs close, you're sure to spot a bleary-eyed celebrity or two alongside the rest of the after-hours crowd, chowing down on a giant pastrami sandwich, matzo-ball soup, potato pancakes, or other deli favorites. Try a potato knish with a side of brown gravy—trust us, you'll love it. 419 N. Fairfax Ave., West Hollywood ✆ 323/651-2030.

Dolores's   One of L.A.'s oldest surviving coffee shops, Dolores's offers just what you might expect: Naugahyde, laminated counters, lots of linoleum, and comforting predictability. Expect the usual coffee-shop fare of pancakes, burgers, and eggs at this 24-hour joint. 11407 Santa Monica Blvd., Los Angeles. ✆ 310/477-1061.

Du-par's Restaurant & Bakery 🟊   During the week, this popular Valley coffee shop serves up blue-plate specials until 1am; come the weekend, they're slingin' hash until 4am. See p. 512 for a full review. 12036 Ventura Blvd. (1 block east of Laurel Canyon), Studio City. ✆ 818/766-4437.

Fred 62   Silver Lake/Los Feliz hipsters hankering for a slightly demented take on classic American comfort grub skulk into Fred around the clock. 1850 N. Vermont, Los Angeles. ✆ 323/667-0062.

Jerry's Famous Deli 🟊   Valley hipsters head to 24-hour Jerry's to satiate the late-night munchies. See p. 512 for a full review. 12655 Ventura Blvd. (east of Coldwater Canyon Ave.), Studio City. ✆ 818/980-4245.

Kate Mantilini 🟊   Kate's serves stylish nouveau comfort food in a striking setting. It's open until midnight Sunday and Monday, Tuesday through Friday until 1am, and Saturday until 2am. 9101 Wilshire Blvd. (at Doheny Dr.), Beverly Hills. ✆ 310/278-3699.

Mel's Drive-in   Straight from an episode of *Happy Days*, this 24-hour 1950s diner on the Sunset Strip attracts customers ranging from chic shoppers during the day to rock 'n' rollers at night. The fries and shakes here are among the best in town. 8585 Sunset Blvd. (west of La Cienega), West Hollywood. ✆ 310/854-7200.

101 Coffee Shop   A retro coffee shop right out of the early '60's, with rock walls, funky colored tiles, comfy booths, and cool light fixtures, all pulled together nicely in a hip yet subdued fashion. Count on tasty grinds until 3am (try the breakfast burritos). 6145 Franklin Ave., Hollywood. ✆ 323/467-1175.

Original Pantry Cafe   Owned by former Los Angeles mayor Richard Riordan, this downtown diner has been serving huge portions of comfort food around the clock for more than 60 years; in fact, they don't even have a key to the front door. 877 S. Figueroa St. (at Ninth St.), downtown. ✆ 213/972-9279.

Pink's Hot Dogs   Many a woozy hipster has awakened with the telltale signs of a post-cocktailing trip to this greasy street-side hot-dog stand—the oniony morning-after breath and chili stains on your shirt are dead giveaways. Open Friday and Saturday until 3am, all other nights until 2am. 709 N. La Brea Ave., Los Angeles. ✆ 323/931-4223.

Swingers ⍟   This hip coffee shop keeps L.A. scene-stealers happy with its retro comfort food. Open Tuesday until 2am, all other nights until 4am. See p. 508 for a full review. Two locations: 8020 Beverly Blvd. (west of Fairfax Ave.; ✆ 323/653-5858) in Hollywood, and 802 Broadway (at Lincoln Ave.; ✆ 310/393-9793) in Santa Monica.

Toi on Sunset ⍟   Those requiring a little more *oomph* from their late-night snack should come here. At this colorful and *loud* hangout, garbled pop culture metaphors mingle with the tastes and aromas of "rockin' Thai" cuisine in delicious ways, until 4am nightly. See p. 508 for a full review. 7505 Sunset Blvd. (at Gardner), Hollywood. ✆ 323/874-8062.

MOVIES

This being L.A., it's saturated with megaplexes catering to high-budget, high-profile flicks featuring the usual big-ticket lures such as Hanks, Willis, and Leonardo. But there are times when those polished Hollywood-studio stories just won't do. Below are some nonmainstream options that play movies from bygone eras or those with an indie bent. Consult the *L.A. Weekly* (www.laweekly.com) to see what's playing when you're in town.

Film festivals are another great way to explore the other side of contemporary movies. Aside from AFI's yearly October fete, the **Los Angeles Film Festival** (✆ 888/ETM-TIXS or 310/432-1200) looks at what's new in American indies, short films, and music videos during a weeklong event in April. Each July since 1982, the **Gay and Lesbian Film Festival** (✆ 213/480-7088; www.outfest.org), also known as "Outfest," has aimed to bring high-quality gay, lesbian, bi, and transgender films to a wider public awareness. In 1998 the festival became Los Angeles's largest, with 31,000 audience members.

Promoting moving pictures as this country's great art form, **The American Cinematheque** in Hollywood (✆ 323/466-3456; www.egyptiantheatre.com) presents not-readily-seen videos and films, ranging from the wildly arty to the old classics. Since relocating to the historic and beautifully refurbished 1923 **Egyptian Theatre** (6712 Hollywood Blvd., Hollywood), American Cinematheque has hosted several film events, including a celebration of contemporary flicks from Spain, a tribute to the femme fatales of film noir, and a retrospective of the films of William Friedkin. Events highlighting a specific individual are usually accompanied by at least one in-theater audience Q&A session with the honoree.

The **Leo S. Bing Theater** at the **L.A. County Museum of Art,** 5905 Wilshire Blvd., Los Angeles (✆ 323/857-6010), presents a themed film series each month. Past subjects have ranged from 1930s blonde-bombshell films to Cold War propaganda flicks and contemporary British satire (complete with a 3-day *Monty Python's Flying Circus* marathon).

Laemmle's Sunset 5, 8000 Sunset Blvd., West Hollywood (✆ 323/848-3500; www.laemmle.com), despite being a multiplex in a bright outdoor mall, features films that most theaters of its ilk won't even touch. This is the place to come to see independent art films. There's often a selection of gay-themed movies.

The **Nuart Theater,** 11272 Santa Monica Blvd., Los Angeles (✆ 310/478-6379), digs deep into its archives for real classics, ranging from campy to cool. They also feature frequent in-person appearances and Q&A sessions from

The World's Most Private Public Theater

Part of the culture of L.A. is to avoid standing in line because you're *far* too important and busy. So it was only a matter of time before someone came up with the idea of treating everyone like a VIP at the movie theater. **ArcLight Cinemas** (© **323/464-4226;** www.arclightcinemas.com) is specifically designed for anyone who abhors rude patrons (ushers keep it quiet), late arrivals (forbidden), searching for seats (reserved in advance by customer preference), uncomfortable chairs (think La-Z-Boy), neck strain (the first rows start 25 ft. from the screen), pimply teenage employees (most of the staff are struggling actors or film students), crappy popcorn (real butter and freshly made caramel popcorn), and paying for parking (4 free hr. are included in the ticket price). And it only gets better: There's a full bar and groovy lounge where themed cocktails such as the "Mordor" are served with appetizers.

The ArcLight shows a mix of indie and Hollywood films, and ticket prices—as you would expect—are higher than average: $11 for an afternoon show and $14 on weekend nights. But the rewards are worth the occasional splurge. The sound and picture quality are so good that filmmakers come here to host Q&A sessions (George Clooney on *Confession of a Dangerous Mind,* James Cameron on *Terminator 3*), and celebrities such as Brad Pitt and Leonardo DiCaprio prefer the ArcLight's reserved seating system. Check the "Now Playing" and "Coming Soon" sections at the ArcLight's website to see what movies and Q&A sessions are scheduled. It's at 6360 W. Sunset Blvd., between Vine and Ivar streets.

stars and filmmakers, and screen *The Rocky Horror Picture Show* (yes, still!) every Saturday at midnight.

It's only open for social events and once-a-month movies when the new owner fancies, but fans of silent-movie classics will still appreciate the **Silent Movie Theatre,** 611 N. Fairfax Ave. (½ block south of Melrose), near the Miracle Mile (© **323/655-2520** for recorded program information, or 323/655-2510 for main office; www.silentmovietheatre.com). Tickets are $8 ($6 for kids and seniors).

If TV's more your thing, the **Museum of Television and Radio,** 465 N. Beverly Dr., Beverly Hills (© **310/786-1000**), celebrates this country's long relationship with the tube. The museum often features a movie of the month, and it also shows free selections from past television programs.

Side Trips from Los Angeles

by Matthew Richard Poole

The area within a 100-mile radius of Los Angeles is one of the most diverse regions in the world. Here, you can find arid deserts, rugged mountains, historic towns, alpine lakes, and even an island paradise. In the following pages, I've included a variety of the best attractions outside of Los Angeles County, such as the smog-free mountain communities of Big Bear and Lake Arrowhead, the world-famous Disneyland and Knott's Berry Farm amusement parks, SoCal beach towns like Newport and Huntington Beach, and the ultimate L.A. weekend getaway, Catalina Island. From L.A., you can reach most of these scenic side trips in less than an hour by car or boat—an easy and refreshing diversion from the big-city scene.

1 Long Beach & the *Queen Mary*

21 miles S of downtown L.A.

The fifth-largest city in California, Long Beach is best known as the permanent home of the former cruise liner *Queen Mary* and the Long Beach Grand Prix, whose star-studded warm-up race sends hipster Jason Priestly and perennial racer Paul Newman burning rubber through the streets of the city in mid-April.

ESSENTIALS

GETTING THERE   See chapter 2 for airport and airline information. Driving from Los Angeles, take either I-5 or I-405 to I-710 south, which leads directly to both downtown Long Beach and the *Queen Mary* Seaport.

ORIENTATION   Downtown Long Beach is at the eastern end of the vast Port of Los Angeles; Pine Avenue is the central restaurant-and-shopping street, which extends south to Shoreline Park and the Aquarium of the Pacific. The *Queen Mary* is docked just across the waterway, gazing south toward tiny Long Beach marina and Naples Island.

VISITOR INFORMATION   Contact the **Long Beach Area Convention & Visitors Bureau,** One World Trade Center, Suite 300 (© **800/452-7829** or 562/436-3645; www.golongbeach.org). For information on the **Long Beach Grand Prix,** call © **562/981-2600** or check out www.longbeachgp.com.

THE MAJOR ATTRACTIONS

The *Queen Mary* ✛   It's easy to dismiss this old cruise ship/museum as a barnacle-laden tourist trap, but it's the only surviving example of this particular kind of 20th-century elegance and excess. From the staterooms paneled lavishly in now-extinct tropical hardwoods to the perfectly preserved crew quarters and the miles of hallway handrails made of once-pedestrian Bakelite, wonders never cease aboard this 81,237-ton Art Deco luxury liner. Stroll the teakwood decks with just a bit of imagination and you're back in 1936 on the maiden voyage

---

Tips **Saving Money**

If you plan on visiting the *Queen Mary* and the aquarium in the same day, you can purchase a combined ticket package at either venue for $34 ($19 for kids 3-11). You'll save about $10 (hey, that's a free lunch).

---

from Southampton, England. Don't miss the streamlined modern observation lounge, featured often in period motion pictures, and have drinks and listen to some live jazz. Kiosk displays of photographs and memorabilia are everywhere—following the success of the movie *Titanic,* the *Queen Mary* even hosted an exhibit of artifacts from its less fortunate cousin. The Cold War–era Soviet submarine *Scorpion* resides alongside; separate admission is required to tour the sub. *Tip:* Buy a "First Class Passage" ticket to both the sub and the ship and you'll also get a behind-the-scenes guided tour, peppered with worthwhile anecdotes and details—well worth the extra $5.

1126 Queen's Hwy. (end of I-710), Long Beach. ✆ 562/435-3511. www.queenmary.com. Admission $23 adults, $20 seniors age 55 and over and military, $12 children ages 5–11, free for kids under 5. First Class Passage admission $28 adults, $25 seniors age 55 and over and military, $17 children ages 5–11, free for kids under 5. Daily 10am–6pm (last entry at 5:30pm), with extended summer hours. Parking $8.

Aquarium of the Pacific *Ⓡ* *Ⓚₐ* This enormous aquarium—one of the largest in the U.S.—is the cornerstone of Long Beach's ever-changing waterfront. Figuring that what stimulated flagging economies in Monterey and Baltimore would work in Long Beach, planners gave their all to this project, creating a crowd-pleasing attraction across the harbor from Long Beach's other mainstay, the *Queen Mary.* The vast facility—it has enough exhibit space to fill three football fields—re-creates three areas of the Pacific: the warm Baja and Southern California regions, the Bering Sea and chilly northern Pacific, and faraway tropical climes, including re-creations of a lagoon and barrier reef. There are more than 12,500 creatures in all, including 150 sharks (some you can touch, some you can't) prowling a 90,000-gallon home, a habitat for sea horses, moon jellies, and, above sea level, gaggles of tropical birds within the Lorikeet Forest. Learn little-known aquatic facts at the many educational exhibits, or come nose-to-nose with sea lions, moray eels, and other inhabitants of giant, three-story-high tanks.

100 Aquarium Way, off Shoreline Dr., Long Beach. ✆ 562/590-3100. www.aquariumofpacific.org. Admission $19 adults, $15 seniors age 60 and over, $11 ages 3–11, free for kids under age 3. Daily 9am–6pm. Closed Christmas Day and Toyota Grand Prix weekend (mid-Apr). Parking $7 maximum.

WHERE TO STAY

Hotel Queen Mary *Ⓡ* *Ⓕᵢₙds* The *Queen Mary* isn't only a piece of maritime history, it's also a hotel. But although the historic ocean liner is considered the most luxurious vessel ever to sail the Atlantic, with some of the largest rooms built aboard a ship, the quarters aren't exceptional when compared to those on terra firma today, nor are the amenities. The idea is to enjoy the novelty and charm of features like the original bathtub watercocks ("cold salt," "cold fresh," "hot salt," "hot fresh"). The beautifully carved interior is a feast for the eye and fun to explore, and the weekday rates are hard to beat. Three onboard restaurants are overpriced but convenient, and the shopping arcade has a decidedly British feel (one shop sells great *Queen Mary* souvenirs). An elegant Sunday champagne brunch—complete with ice sculpture and harpist—is served in the ship's Grand Salon, and it's always worth having a cocktail in the Art Deco Observation Bar. If you're too young to have traveled on the old luxury liners, this is the perfect opportunity to experience the romance of an Atlantic crossing—with no seasickness or cabin fever.

1126 Queen's Hwy. (end of I-710), Long Beach, CA 90802-6390. © 800/437-2934 or 562/435-3511. Fax 562/437-4531. www.queenmary.com. 365 units. From $119 inside cabin; from $179 deluxe cabin; from $460 suite. Many packages available. AE, DC, MC, V. Valet parking $12; self-parking $8. **Amenities:** 3 restaurants; spa; shopping arcade. *In room:* A/C, TV.

WHERE TO DINE

The Sky Room 🏵🏵   It takes a 40-minute drive from Los Angeles to Long Beach to get a sense of what fine dining must have been like during Hollywood's golden age. The Sky Room is more than just another retro supper club, it's a bit of a time warp from the moment the valet opens your car door. Spiffily dressed doormen in top hats and coattails escort arriving diners up a private elevator to the penthouse level of the stately Breakers building, situated between the harbor and downtown Long Beach. Built in 1926 and meticulously restored by proprietor Bernard Rosenson, the restaurant's Art Deco–period design inspires oohs and aahs among first-time guests. Awash in brilliant white, the interior's massive pillars, curvaceous ramps, glimmering brass, elevated maple-and-ebony dance floor, and classic jazz band playing enticing dance tunes all combine to create the illusion of dining on a luxury ocean liner (the beautiful view of the stately *Queen Mary* certainly enhances the effect). Opulence continues with white Frette linens, custom black-rimmed china, Villeroy and Boch tableware, and a Wine Spectator Award–winning wine list. The Californian/French menu offers a pleasing presentation of the classics: grilled chicken breast in a chanterelle au jus, line-caught salmon with goat-cheese pesto, New York steak on a grilled onion brioche. Nothing groundbreaking here, but that's not what The Sky Room is about. I highly recommend you take the advice of the experienced waitstaff and sommelier—our duo handled the task flawlessly. A night of dinner, drinking, dancing, and romance—what's not to like?

40 S. Locust Ave. (at Ocean Blvd.), Long Beach, CA 90802. © 562/983-2703. Fax 562/983-2738. www. theskyroom.com. Reservations recommended. Dinner main courses $24–$41. AE, DC, DISC, MC, V. Mon–Thurs 5:30am–10:30pm and 6–10pm; Fri–Sat 5:30pm–midnight. Valet parking $6.

Yard House 🏵 AMERICAN ECLECTIC   Not only does it have one of the best outdoor dining venues in Long Beach, the Yard House also features one of the *world's* largest selections of draft beers. The keg room houses more than 1,000 gallons of beer, all visible through a glass door where you can see the golden liquids transported to a signature oval bar via miles of nylon tubing to the dozens of taps. The restaurant takes its name from the early Colonial tradition of serving beer in 36-inch-tall glasses—or yards—to weary stagecoach drivers. Customers are encouraged to partake in this tradition and can drink from the glass yards, as well as half-yards and traditional pint glasses. Signature dishes range from the tortelike California Roll to the crab-cake hoagie and an impressive selection of steaks and chops. There's also an extensive list of appetizers—perfect for a tapas-style meal—salads, pasta, and rice dishes, as well as sandwiches and individual pizzas (the Thai chicken pizza is excellent, as are the crab cakes and coconut-encrusted shrimp). On sunny days be sure to request a table on the deck overlooking the picturesque harbor.

401 Shoreline Village Dr., Long Beach. © 562/628-0455. www.yardhouse.com. Reservations not accepted. Main courses $10–$30. AE, DC, MC, V. Mon–Thurs 11:30am–midnight; Fri–Sat 11am–2am; Sun 11am–midnight.

2 Santa Catalina Island

22 miles W of mainland Los Angeles

by Trisha Clayton

After an unhealthy dose of the mainland's soupy smog and freeway gridlock, you'll appreciate an excursion to Santa Catalina Island with its clean air, crystal-clear water, and the blissful absence of traffic. In fact, there isn't a single traffic light on the entire island. Conditions like these can fool you into thinking that you're miles away from the hustle and bustle of the city, but the reality is that you're only 22 miles off the Southern California coast and *still* in L.A. County.

Because of its relative isolation, out-of-state tourists tend to ignore Santa Catalina—which everyone calls simply Catalina—but those who do make the crossing have plenty of elbow room to boat, fish, swim, scuba, and snorkel. There are also miles of hiking and biking trails, plus golf, tennis, and horseback riding, but the main sport here seems to be barhopping.

Catalina is so different from the mainland that it almost seems like a different country, remote and unspoiled. In 1915 the island was purchased by William Wrigley, Jr., the chewing-gum magnate, who had plans to develop it into a fashionable pleasure resort. To publicize the new vacation land, Wrigley brought big-name bands to the Avalon Ballroom and moved the Chicago Cubs, which he owned, to the island for spring training. His marketing efforts succeeded and Catalina soon became a world-renowned playground, luring such celebrities as Laurel and Hardy, Cecil B. DeMille, John Wayne, and even Winston Churchill.

In 1975 the Santa Catalina Island Conservancy—a nonprofit operating foundation organized to preserve and protect the island's natural habitat—acquired about 88% of Catalina Island, protecting virtually all of the hilly acreage and rugged coastline that make up what is known as the interior. In fact, some of the most spectacular outlying areas can only be reached by arranged tour (see "Exploring the Island," below).

ESSENTIALS

GETTING THERE   The most common way to get to and from the island is via the **Catalina Express** ferryboat (© **800/481-3470;** www.catalinaexpress.com), which operates up to 30 daily departures year-round from San Pedro and Long Beach. The trip takes about an hour. Round-trip fares are $42 for adults, $38 for seniors 55 and over, $33 for children ages 2 to 11, and $3 for infants. In San Pedro the Catalina Express departs from the **Sea/Air Terminal,** Berth 95; take the Harbor Freeway (I-110) south to the Harbor Boulevard exit, then follow signs to the terminal. In Long Beach, boats leave from the **Catalina Landing;** take the 710 Freeway south into Long Beach. Stay to the left, follow the signs to downtown,

---

⎛Fun Fact Cart Culture

One of the first things you'll notice when you arrive in Avalon is the abundance of golf carts in a comical array of styles and colors. Since Avalon is the only city in California authorized by the state legislature to regulate the number of vehicles allowed to drive on city streets, there are no rental cars and only a handful of privately owned vehicles.

Santa Catalina Island

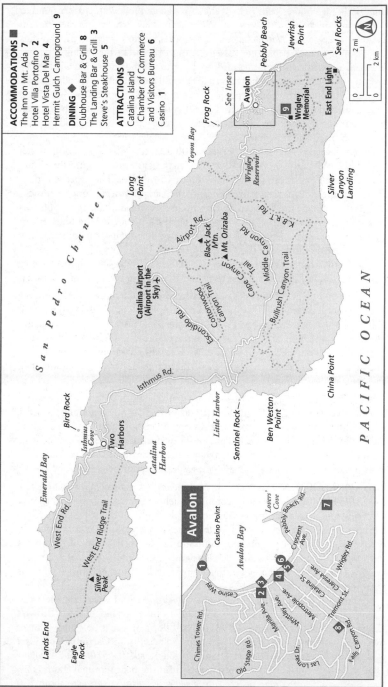

See Inset

Avalon

Pebbly Beach

Jewfish Point

Seal Rocks

East End Light

Wrigley Memorial

9

Frog Rock

Toyon Bay

Wrigley Reservoir

Silver Canyon Landing

Long Point

Airport Rd.

Black Jack Mtn.

Mt. Orizaba

K.B.R.T. Rd.

Middle Canyon Rd.

Cape Canyon Trail

Catalina Airport
(Airport in the Sky) ✈

Cottonwood Canyon Trail

Escondido Rd.

Bullrush Canyon Trail

China Point

S a n   P e d r o   C h a n n e l

Isthmus Rd.

Little Harbor

Sentinel Rock

Ben Weston Point

P A C I F I C   O C E A N

Bird Rock

Isthmus Cove

Two Harbors

Catalina Harbor

Emerald Bay

West End Rd.

West End Ridge Trail

Lands End

Eagle Rock

Silver Peak

2 mi

2 km

0

0

Avalon

Casino Point

Lovers' Cove

Pebbly Beach Rd.

7

Crescent Ave.

Avalon Bay

1

6

5

4

2 3

Wrigley Rd.

Catalina St.

Clarissa Ave.

Metropole Ave.

Whitley Ave.

Marilla Ave.

Tremont St.

Las Lomas Dr.

8

Falls Canyon Rd.

Casino Way

Chimes Tower Rd.

Old Stage Rd.

and exit Golden Shore. Turn right at the stop sign and follow the road around to the terminal on the right. There's parking in the parking structure on the left. Call ahead for reservations. *Note:* Check-in at the ticket window is required and begins 1 hour prior to each departure. Passengers must be checked-in, holding tickets, and ready to board at 15 minutes prior to departure or the reservation will be canceled and the credit card will be charged for the full amount of the round-trip fare. Luggage is limited to 70 pounds per person; reservations are necessary for bicycles, surfboards, and dive tanks; and there are restrictions on transporting pets. You can leave your car at designated lots at each departure terminal; the parking fee is around $8 per 24-hour period.

Island Express Helicopter Service, 900 Queens Way Dr., Long Beach (© **800/2-AVALON** or 310/510-2525; www.islandexpress.com), flies from Long Beach or San Pedro to Avalon in about 15 minutes. The expense is definitely worth the thrill and convenience, particularly if you're prone to seasickness. It flies on demand between 8am and sunset year-round, charging $66 plus tax each way. The weight limit for luggage, however, is a mere 25 pounds. It also offers brief air tours over the island; prices vary. The heliport is located a few hundred yards southwest of the *Queen Mary.*

Tip: **Elite Airport Transportation** (© **310/831-1369**) offers shuttle service from LAX to the Catalina Express ferry and Island Express Helicopter Service.

VISITOR INFORMATION The **Catalina Island Chamber of Commerce and Visitors Bureau,** P.O. Box 217, Avalon, CA 90704 (© **310/510-1520;** fax 310/510-7606), located on the Green Pleasure Pier, distributes brochures and information on island activities, hotels, and transportation. Call for a free 100-page visitors guide. Its colorful website, **www.catalina.com**, offers current news from the *Catalina Islander* newspaper in addition to updated activities, events, and general information.

ORIENTATION The town of **Avalon** is both the port of entry for the island and the island's only city. From the ferry dock, you can wander along Crescent Avenue, the main road along the beachfront, and explore adjacent side streets.

Northwest of Avalon is the village of **Two Harbors,** accessible by boat or shuttle bus. Its twin bays are favored by pleasure yachts from L.A.'s various marinas, so there's more camaraderie and a less touristy ambience overall.

GETTING AROUND Once in Avalon, call **Catalina Cab Company** (© **310/510-0025**) to take a taxi from the heliport or dock to your hotel and enjoy the quick, colorful trip through town (don't blink or you'll miss it). Only a limited number of cars are permitted on the island; visitors are not allowed to drive cars, and most residents motor around in golf carts (many of the homes only have golf-cart-size driveways). Don't worry, though—you'll be able to get everywhere you want to go by renting a cart yourself or just hoofing it, which is what most visitors do.

If you want to explore the area around Avalon beyond where your feet can comfortably carry you, try renting a mountain bike or tandem from **Brown's Bikes,** 107 Pebbly Beach Rd. (© **310/510-0986**). If you'll be doing a lot of exploring, you'll want to rent a gas-powered golf cart from **Cartopia Golf Cart Rentals** on Crescent Avenue at Pebbly Beach Road (© **310/510-2493**), or **Island Rentals** (© **310/510-1456**) across from the boat terminal. Both companies offer a detailed map of town for a self-guided tour. Rates are about $30 per hour.

Fun Fact **Avalon's Abundance**

The 1-square-mile town of Avalon is populated by about 3,200 full-time residents, but on sunny summer weekends, the body count nearly triples to more than 10,000.

EXPLORING THE ISLAND

ORGANIZED TOURS The Santa Catalina Island Company's **Discovery Tours** (© **800/626-1496** or 310/510-TOUR; www.scico.com) has a ticket and information office on Crescent Avenue across from the Green Pier. It offers the greatest variety of excursions from Avalon; many last just a couple of hours, so you don't have to tie up your whole day. Tours are available in money-saving combo packs; inquire when you call.

Noteworthy excursions include the **Undersea Tour,** a leisurely 45-minute cruise of Lover's Cove Marine Preserve in a semisubmerged boat that allows you to sit 5 feet under the water in a climate-controlled cabin where you comfortably observe Catalina's kelp forests by day or night ($32 for adults and $16 for kids); the **Casino Tour,** a fascinating 1-hour look at the style and inventive engineering of this elegant ballroom (see the "Catalina's Grand Casino" sidebar below; $13 adults, $6.50 kids); nighttime **Flying Fish Boat Trips,** a 50-minute Catalina tradition in searchlight-equipped open boats ($20 adults, $9.75 kids); and the **Inland Motor Tour,** a 32-mile, 4-hour jaunt through the island's rugged interior, including a stop at the **Airport-in-the-Sky, Little Harbor,** on Catalina's west coast (our favorite locale for camping, hiking, and swimming), and Wrigley's **El Rancho Escondido,** a working ranch where some of America's finest Arabian horses are raised and trained ($47 adults, $24 kids).

VISITING TWO HARBORS If you want to get a better look at the rugged natural beauty of Catalina and escape the throngs of beachgoers, head over to Two Harbors, the quarter-mile "neck" at the island's northwest end that gets its name from the "twin harbors" on each side, known as the Isthmus and Cat harbors. An excellent starting point for campers and hikers, Two Harbors also offers just enough civilization for the less-intrepid traveler.

The **Banning House Lodge** (© **310/510-2800**) is an 11-room bed-and-breakfast overlooking the Isthmus. The clapboard house was built in 1910 for Catalina's pre-Wrigley owners, and has seen duty as on-location lodging for movie stars like Errol Flynn and Dorothy Lamour. Peaceful and isolated, the simply furnished but comfortable lodge has spectacular views of both Isthmus harbors. Rates range from $161 to $230 (Apr–Oct), and they'll even give you a lift from the pier.

Everyone eats at **The Harbor Reef Restaurant** (© **310/510-4233**), on the beach. This nautical- and tropical-themed saloon/restaurant serves breakfast, lunch, and dinner, the latter consisting of steaks, ribs, swordfish, chicken teriyaki, and buffalo burgers in summer. The house drink is sweet "buffalo milk," a potent concoction of vodka, crème de cacao, banana liqueur, milk, and whipped cream.

WHAT TO SEE & DO IN AVALON Walk along horseshoe-shaped Crescent Avenue, past private yachting and fishing clubs, toward the landmark **Casino** building. You can see the Art Deco **theater** for the price of a movie ticket any

---

Catalina's Grand Casino

No trip to Catalina is complete without taking the **Casino Tour** (see "Organized Tours" above). The Casino Building, Avalon's world-famous Art Deco landmark, is not—and never was—a place to gamble your vacation money away (*casino* is an Italian word for a place of entertainment or gathering). Rather, the incredibly ornate structure (the craftsmanship inside and out is spectacular) is home to the island's only movie theater and the world's largest circular ballroom. Virtually every big band in the '30s and '40s played in the 158-foot-diameter ballroom, carried over CBS radio since its grand opening in May 1929. Today it's a coveted venue for elaborate weddings, dances, gala dinners, and the Catalina Jazz Festival. The 3-week **JazzTrax Festival** (© **888/330-5252;** www.jazztrax.com) takes place every October. This music fest is extremely popular and makes finding hotel rooms nearly impossible. To experience the festival, be sure to book your tickets and accommodations as far in advance as possible.

---

night. Also on the ground floor is the **Catalina Island Museum** (© **310/510-2414**), which features exhibits on island history, archaeology, and natural history. The museum has a contour relief map of the island that's helpful to hikers. Admission is $1.50 for adults, 50¢ for kids; it's included in the price of Discovery's Casino Tour (see above).

Around the point from the Casino lies **Descanso Beach Club** (© **310/510-7410**), a mini–Club Med in a private cove. While you can get on the beach year-round, the club's facilities (including showers, restaurant/bar, volleyball lawns, and thatched beach umbrellas) are only open from Easter to September 30. Admission is $1.50.

About 1½ miles from downtown Avalon is the **Wrigley Memorial and Botanical Garden** (© **310/510-2288**), an invigorating walk or short taxi ride. The specialized gardens, a project of Ada Wrigley, showcase plants endemic to California's coastal islands. Open daily from 8am to 5pm; admission is $1.

DIVING, SNORKELING & SEA KAYAKING 🌲

Snorkeling, scuba diving, and sea kayaking are among the main reasons mainlanders head to Catalina. Catalina Island's naturally clean water and giant kelp forests teeming with marine life have made it a renowned diving destination that attracts experts and beginning divers alike. **Casino Point Marine Park,** Southern California's first city-designated underwater park established in 1965, is located behind the Casino. Due to its convenient location, it can get outrageously crowded in the summer (just like everything else at that time of year).

Catalina Divers Supply (© **800/353-0330** or 310/510-0330; www.catalina diverssupply.com) runs two full-service dive shops: one from a trailer behind the Casino at the edge of Avalon's underwater park—where they offer guided snorkeling tours and intro scuba dives—another at the Green Pier, where they launch boat dives aboard the Scuba Cat. The three best locations for snorkeling are **Lover's Cove Marine Preserve, Casino Point Marine Park,** and **Descanso**

Beach Club. Catalina Snorkeling Adventures, at Lover's Cove (© 877/ SNORKEL), offers snorkel gear rental. Snorkeling trips that take you outside of Avalon depart from **Joe's Rent-a-Boat** (© 310/510-0455) on the Green Pier.

At Two Harbors, stop by **West End Dive Center** (© 310/510-2800). Excursions range from half-day introductory dives to complete certification courses to multi-day dive packages. It also rents snorkel gear and offers kayak rental, instruction, and excursions.

HIKING & BIKING

When the summer crowds become overwhelming it's time to head on foot for the peacefulness of the interior, where secluded coves and barren rolling hills soothe frayed nerves. Visitors can obtain a free **hiking permit** at the Conservancy Office (125 Claressa Ave.; © 310/510-2595; www.catalinaconservancy. org), where you'll find maps, wildlife information, and friendly assistance from conservancy staffers who love to share their knowledge of the interior. It's open daily from 9am to 5pm, closed for lunch on weekends. Among the sights you may see are the many giant buffalo roaming the hills, scions of movie extras that were left behind in 1929 and have since flourished.

Mountain biking is allowed on the island's designated dirt roads, but requires a $50-per-person permit ($75 family) that must be purchased in person at the Conservancy Office.

BEACHES

Unfortunately, Avalon's beaches leave much to be desired. The town's central beach, off Crescent Avenue, is small and completely congested in the busy season. Be sure to claim your spot early in the morning before it's full. **Descanso Beach Club** offers the best beach in town but also gets crowded very quickly. Your best bet is to kayak to a secluded cove where you have the beach virtually to yourself.

WHERE TO STAY

If you plan to stay overnight, be sure to reserve a room in advance, because most places fill up quickly during the summer and holiday seasons. There are only a handful of hotels whose accommodations and amenities justify the rates that they charge. Some are downright scary, so be sure to book as far in advance as possible to get a room that makes the trip worthwhile. Don't stress too much over your accommodations, as you'll probably spend most of your time outdoors. The best time to visit is in September or October when the water is warm,

---

(Tips Instant Massaging

After a full day of island activity, why not pamper yourself with a relaxing professional massage in your hotel room? Make a reservation with **Massage by Michelle** and she'll tote her table and oils to your hotel room. Michelle specializes in sports, deep tissue, Swedish, Thai, Swede-Thai combo, and pregnancy massage. Other treatments include aromatherapy wraps, sugar glow, body polishing, foot scrubs, peppermint scalp massage, and lavender or honey facial massages. Michelle works in 50- to 80-minute increments, and if you're just visiting for the day, she offers her own pampering facility for you to visit. Prices range from $75 to $120. Call © 310/ 510-8920 for an appointment.

the crowds have somewhat subsided, and hotel occupancy is easier to find. If you're having trouble finding a vacancy, try calling the **Convention and Visitors Bureau** (✆ **310/510-1520**); they keep tabs on last-minute cancellations. **Catalina Island Accommodations** (✆ **310/510-3000**) might be able to help you out in a pinch; it's a reservations service with updated information on the whole island. When booking, ask the hotel agent about money-saving packages that offer discounted room rates, boat or helicopter fare, and tours.

EXPENSIVE

The Inn on Mt. Ada 🕃🕃

When William Wrigley, Jr., purchased Catalina Island in 1921, he built this hilltop Georgian colonial mansion as his summer vacation home; it's now one of the finest small hotels in California. The opulent inn—considered to be the best in town for its luxury accommodations and views—has several ground-floor salons, a club room with fireplace, a deep-seated formal library, and a wickered sunroom where tea, cookies, and fruit are always available. The best guest room is the Grand Suite, fitted with a fireplace and a large private patio. Amenities include bathrobes and the use of a golf cart during your stay. TVs are available on request, but there are no phones in the rooms. A hearty full breakfast, a light deli-style lunch, appetizers, fresh fruit, freshly baked cookies, soft drinks, beers, wines, and champagne are included in the rate. **Tip:** Even if you find that they're sold out or too pricey to fit your budget, make a lunch reservation and enjoy amazing views from the inn's spectacular balcony.

398 Wrigley Rd. (P.O. Box 2560), Avalon, CA 90704. ✆ **800/608-7669** or 310/510-2030. Fax 310/510-2237. www.catalina.com/mtada. 6 units. Nov–May Mon–Thurs $300–$450 double, $530 suite; June–Oct and Fri–Sun year-round $340–$530 double, $640 suite. Rates include 2 meals daily. DC, MC, V. **Amenities:** Courtesy car. *In room:* TV, hair dryer, iron, no phone.

MODERATE

Hotel Villa Portofino 🕃

Enjoy European elegance on the oceanfront from your courtyard room or harbor-view suite after a warm welcome from the hotel's efficient and friendly staff. The hotel boasts recently renovated rooms and well-appointed bathrooms, some with Alacante-colored Spanish marble, and fantastic views overlooking the bay. There's also a spacious rooftop deck that's perfect for people-watching, sunbathing, and cocktail sipping. Some rooms have luxurious touches like fireplaces, deep soaking tubs, and separate showers. Just outside the front door is all of Avalon Bay's activity.

111 Crescent Ave. (PO Box 127), Avalon, CA 90704. ✆ **310/510-0555.** Fax 310/510-0839. www.hotelvilla portofino.com. 35 units. May–Oct $125–$320 double, from $325 suite; winter $65–$270 double, from $225 suite. Rates include continental breakfast, beach towels, and chairs. AE, DC, MC, V. **Amenities:** Award-winning restaurant; adjacent art gallery. *In room:* A/C, TV, fridge, coffeemaker, hair dryer, iron and ironing board.

Hotel Vista Del Mar

Located smack dab in the middle of town, its recently renovated open-air atrium garden courtyard, gigantic fish tank, freshly baked cookies and milk each evening, and friendly staff make it an island favorite for families and couples alike. The oceanview suites are fantastic but hard to secure, as there are only two and they're booked by regulars almost year-round.

417 Crescent Ave. (P.O. Box 1979), Avalon, CA 90704. ✆ **310/510-1452.** www.hotel-vistadelmar.com. 15 units. May–Oct $125–$350 double; Nov–Apr $105–$300 double. Winter discounts and midweek rates available. Rates include continental breakfast and freshly baked cookies and milk in the evening. AE, DISC, MC, V. **Amenities:** Garden atrium courtyard with sitting area and balcony with a huge fish tank and views of the harbor. *In room:* A/C, cable TV w/VCR, wet bar with refrigerator, coffeemaker, Jacuzzi, fireplace.

Tips **For Travelers Who Use Wheelchairs**
Visitors who use wheelchairs should request a room at **Hotel Metropole** (© **800/541-8528** or 310/510-1884). One of the most modern properties in Avalon, it has an elevator, a large sun deck that overlooks Avalon Bay, a shopping complex, and a convenient location in the heart of Avalon.

INEXPENSIVE

Our recommended choices for inexpensive lodgings are: the **Pavilion Lodge** (© **800/414-2754** or 310/510-2500), which recently completed an extensive renovation on all guest rooms. Rooms are basic but affordable and clean (a great alternative when budgets and availability are tight). **Hotel Catalina** (© **800/ 540-0184** or 310/510-0027) is a well-maintained Victorian-style hotel just a half block from the beach with tons of charm, family cottages, a courtyard with beautiful stained glass, and large verandas with bay views. **Zane Grey** (© **310/ 510-0966**), a Hopi-style pueblo built in 1926 and former home of American author Zane Grey, is situated above town and equipped with a cozy living room with fireplace and piano, free shuttle service, and a swimming pool. **Hermit Gulch Campground** (© **310/510-7254**), Avalon's only campground, can be crowded and noisy in peak season. Campsites can be tough to secure, especially when hotels are booked, so it's a good idea to make reservations in advance. The walk to town and back can be draining, so hop on the green-and-white tram that runs you back and forth to town for a dollar each way.

WHERE TO DINE

Along with the choices below, recommended options include **The Busy Bee** on Crescent Avenue (© **310/510-1983**), an always-crowded waterfront diner with a heated and wind-protected patio. On the Two Harbors side of the island, **The Harbor Reef Restaurant** is the place to eat; see "Exploring the Island," above.

EXPENSIVE

Clubhouse Bar & Grille ⊛ CALIFORNIA   You'll find some of Avalon's most elegant meals at the landmark Catalina Country Club, whose stylish Spanish-Mediterranean clubhouse was built by William Wrigley, Jr., during the 1920s. Recently restored, it exudes a chic and historic atmosphere; the menu is peppered with archival photos and vintage celebrity anecdotes. Sit outdoors in an elegant tiled courtyard, or inside the intimate, clubby dining room. Much of the menu is served throughout the afternoon, including gourmet pizzas, international appetizer samplers, and soups (fisherman's bisque or French onion, both available in a sourdough bowl). Dinner offerings follow a fusion style, such as New Zealand lamb accented with a piquant mango-mint chutney; cioppino and pad Thai both appear on the menu. The club is a few blocks uphill, so shuttle service is available from Island Plaza (on Sumner Ave.) on weekends.

1 Country Club Dr. (above Sumner Ave.). © **310/510-7404**. Reservations recommended. Main courses $10–$30. AE, DISC, MC, V. Daily 11:30am–2:30pm and 5–9pm (closing hours will vary seasonally).

MODERATE

The Landing Bar and Grill AMERICAN   With a secluded deck overlooking the harbor, The Landing is generally agreed to be the most romantic dining spot in Avalon. It boasts Spanish-style architecture in the historical El Encanto

Center that manages to attract as many jeans-clad vacationers as dressed-up islanders. The menu is enticing, with local seafood offerings, pasta, Mexican cuisine, and gourmet pizzas that can be delivered to your hotel room if you wish.

Intersection of Crescent and Marilla. (𝒞 310/510-1474. Reservations recommended. Main courses $11–$22. AE, DISC, MC, V. Lunch daily 11am–3pm; dinner daily from 4–10pm year-round (subject to changes in winter).

Steve's Steakhouse AMERICAN   Step up above the busy bayside promenade into a fantastic collage of museum-quality photos capturing the Avalon of old. This setting overlooking Avalon Bay feels just right for the hearty menu of steaks, seafood, and pasta. Catalina swordfish is their specialty along with excellent cuts of meat. You can also make a respectable repast from the many appetizer selections, especially the fresh oysters and sashimi.

417 Crescent Ave. (directly across from the Green Pier, upstairs). (𝒞 310/510-0333. Reservations recommended on weekends. Main courses $7–$15 lunch; $15–$25 dinner. AE, DISC, MC, V. Lunch daily 11am–3pm; dinner daily 5–10pm. Full bar.

INEXPENSIVE

Note: Street addresses are pretty much useless in a town as small as Avalon, so they are not listed here. All these restaurants are within a stone's throw of each other on the main strip.

Our three favorite places for a low-bucks meal in Avalon are: **Rosie's Fish and Chips** (𝒞 310/510-0197), an Avalon classic located on the Green Pier that serves fresh seafood favorites like fish and chips and seafood cocktails; **Casino Dock Café** (𝒞 310/510-2755), because nothing beats the cafe's live summertime entertainment, marina views from the sun-drenched deck, and delicious breakfast burritos loaded with homemade salsa and a Bloody Mary (or wait till the outdoor bar opens and the lunch menu rolls out with fresh burgers and addictive fish tacos); and **Lori's Good Stuff** (𝒞 310/510-2489), a tiny restaurant that serves the best sandwiches, smoothies, and milkshakes around. Their fresh and healthy fare is a nice alternative to the heavy burgers, burritos, and pizza offered elsewhere.

BARHOPPING

Note: Since there are no listed street addresses in Avalon, they are not listed here. Not that it matters, as all these bars are within stumbling distance of each other.

Avalon's bar scene offers a slew of watering holes to choose from, most with good food and live entertainment. The **Chi Chi Club** (𝒞 310/510-2828), the "noisy bar in Avalon" referred to in Crosby, Stills, and Nash's song "Southern Cross," is the island's only dance club and quite a scene on summer weekend evenings—the DJ spins an eclectic mixture of dance tunes for the islanders and tourists to get their mai tai cocktail groove on. **Luau Larry's** (𝒞 310/510-1919) is Avalon's signature bar that everyone must visit; its tacky Tiki theme kicks you into island mode as soon as you step inside and stumble out. Many a tourist has gotten his "Wicky Wacked" (the bar's signature drink) in Luau's famous cave. Don't leave without the straw hat sitting lopsided on your head and a Wicky Wacker bumper sticker proudly affixed. Go where the locals go and swill beers at **The Marlin Club** (𝒞 310/510-0044), Avalon's oldest drinking hole, catch the Dodgers game at **J.L.'s Locker Room** (𝒞 310/510-0258), and recover from your hangover with a spicy Bloody Mary at the rustic bar inside **The Busy Bee** (𝒞 310/510-1983).

SHOPPING

Don't worry—you won't have any trouble finding that must-have Catalina key chain or refrigerator magnet, as Crescent Avenue is lined with a myriad of souvenir shops. There are, however, a few stores that do offer unique and tasteful items. **CC Gallagher** (© 310/510-1278) carries high-end gifts as well as a flower and coffee shop; they're best for finding beautiful art, music, and jewelry created by local artists. For handmade pottery, stop by **Chet's Hardware** (© 310/510-0990) in The Arcade—an arched shopping annex that connects Sumner and Metropole avenues. **Latitude 33** (© 310/510-0802) is the place to get your vintage aloha shirts, shorts, hats, and sandals. **Buoys and Gulls** (© 310/510-0416) offers men's and women's wear such as Nautica, Reyn Spooner islander shirts, Hurley, and Billabong. **The Steamer Trunk** (© 310/510-2600) is loaded with gifts to take home to the dog-sitter or neighbor who collected your mail. **Leo's Drugstore** (© 310/510-0189) is the spot to pick up the sunscreen that you forgot to pack. **Von's,** located on Metropole Avenue in the center of town, is Avalon's main grocery store, where you'll find all your food staples.

3 Big Bear Lake & Lake Arrowhead

100 miles NE of L.A.

These two deep-blue lakes lie close to each other in the San Bernardino mountains and have long been favorite year-round alpine playgrounds for city-weary Angelenos.

Big Bear Lake has always been popular with skiers as well as boaters (it's much larger than Arrowhead, and equipment rentals abound), and in the past decade the area has been given a much-needed face-lift. Big Bear Boulevard was widened to handle high-season traffic, and downtown Big Bear Lake (the "Village") was spiffed up without losing its woodsy charm. In addition to two excellent ski slopes less than 5 minutes from town, you can enjoy the comforts of a real supermarket and several video-rental shops, all especially convenient if you're staying in a cabin. Most people choose Big Bear over Arrowhead because there's so much more to do, from boating, fishing, and hiking to snow sports, mountain biking, and horseback riding. The weather is nearly always perfect at this 7,000-foot-plus elevation: If you want proof, ask Caltech, which operates a solar observatory here to take advantage of nearly 300 days of sunshine per year.

Lake Arrowhead has always been privately owned, as is apparent from the affluence of the surrounding homes, many of which are gated estates rather than rustic mountain cabins. The lake and the private docks lining its shores are reserved for the exclusive use of homeowners, but visitors can enjoy Lake Arrowhead by boat tour or use of the summer-season beach clubs, a privilege included in nearly all private-home rentals. Reasons to choose a vacation at Lake Arrowhead? The roads up are less grueling than the winding ascent to Big Bear Lake and, being at a lower elevation, Arrowhead gets little snow (you can forget those pesky tire chains). It's very easy and cost effective to rent a luxurious house from which to enjoy the spectacular scenery, crisp mountain air, and relaxed resort atmosphere—and if you do ski, the slopes are only a half-hour away.

ESSENTIALS

GETTING THERE   Lake Arrowhead is reached by taking Calif. 18 from San Bernardino. The last segment of this route takes you along the aptly named **Rim of the World Highway,** offering a breathtaking view over the valley below on clear days. Calif. 18 then continues east to Big Bear Lake, but to get to Big Bear Lake, it's quicker to bypass Arrowhead by taking Calif. 330 from Redlands, which meets Calif. 18 in Running Springs. During heavy-traffic periods, it can be worthwhile to take scenic Calif. 38, which winds up from Redlands through mountain passes and valleys to approach Big Bear from the other side.

Note: Nostalgia lovers can revisit legendary **Route 66** on the way from Los Angeles to the mountain resorts, substituting scenic motor courts and other relics of the "Mother Road" in place of impersonal I-10. For a complete driving tour, see "Get Your Kicks on Historic Route 66" in chapter 15.

VISITOR INFORMATION National ski tours, mountain-bike races, and one of Southern California's largest Oktoberfest gatherings are just some of the events held year-round—which may either entice or discourage you from visiting when they're on. Contact the **Big Bear Lake Resort Association,** 630 Bartlett Rd., Big Bear Lake Village (© **800/4BIG-BEAR** or 909/866-7000; www.bigbearinfo.com), for schedules and information. They also provide information on sightseeing and lodging and will send you a free visitors guide.

In Lake Arrowhead, contact the **Lake Arrowhead Communities Chamber of Commerce** (© **800/337-3716** for the Lodging Information Line, or 909/337-3715; www.lakearrowhead.net). The visitor center is located in the Lake Arrowhead Village lower shopping center.

ORIENTATION The south shore of Big Bear Lake was the first resort area to be developed here and remains the most densely populated. Calif. 18 passes first through the city of Big Bear Lake and its downtown village; then, as Big Bear Boulevard, it continues east to Big Bear City, which is more residential and suburban. Calif. 38 traverses the north shore, home to pristine national forest and great hiking trails, as well as a couple of small marinas and a lakefront bed-and-breakfast inn (see the Windy Point Inn on p. 591).

Arrowhead's main town is Lake Arrowhead Village, located on the south shore at the end of Calif. 173. The village's commercial center is home to factory-outlet stores, about 40 chain and specialty shops, and the Lake Arrowhead Resort (p. 592). Minutes away is the town of Blue Jay (along Calif. 189), where the Blue Jay Ice Castle skating rink is located (see "Winter Fun" below).

ENJOYING THE OUTDOORS

In addition to the activities described below, there's a great recreation spot for families near the heart of Big Bear Lake: **Magic Mountain,** on Calif. 18/Big Bear Boulevard (© **909/866-4626;** www.bigbear.com), has a year-round bobsled-style Alpine Slide, a splashy double water slide open from mid-June to mid-September, and bunny slopes for snow tubing from November to Easter. The dry Alpine Slide is $4 a ride, the water slide is $1 (or $12 for a day pass), and snow play costs $18 per day including tube and rope tow.

WATERSPORTS

BOATING You can rent all kinds of boats—including speedboats, rowboats, paddleboats, pontoons, sailboats, and canoes—at a number of Big Bear Lake marinas. Rates vary only slightly from place to place: A 14-foot dinghy with an outboard runs around $15 per hour or $35 for a half day; pontoon (patio) boats that can hold large groups range in size and price from $50 to $60 per hour or $110 to $130 for a half day. **Pine Knot Landing** (© **909/866-BOAT;** www.pineknotlanding.com) is the most centrally located marina, behind the post office at the foot of Pine Knot Boulevard in Big Bear Lake. **Big Bear Marina,**

Big Bear Lake & Lake Arrowhead

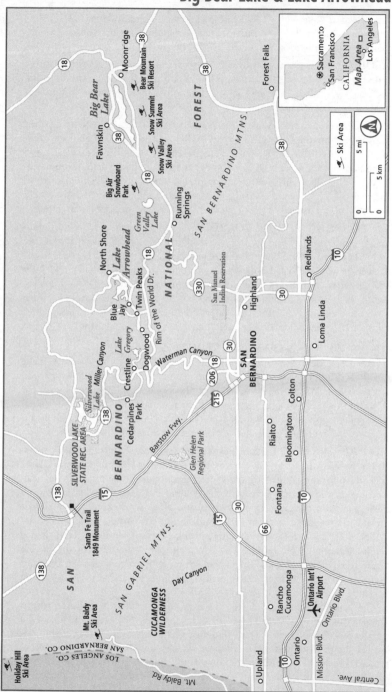

Paine Road at Lakeview (℃ **909/866-3218;** www.bigbearmarina.com), is close to Big Bear Lake Village and provides take-along dinners when you rent a pontoon boat for a sunset cruise.

FISHING   Big Bear Lake brims with rainbow trout, bass, and catfish in spring and summer, the best fishing seasons. Pine Knot Landing, Gray's Landing, and Big Bear Marina (see "Boating" above) all rent fishing boats and have bait-and-tackle shops that sell licenses.

JET-SKIING   Personal Water Craft (PWCs) are available for rent at **Big Bear Marina** (see "Boating" above) and **Pleasure Point Landing,** 603 Landlock Landing Rd. (℃ **909/866-2455**), where you can rent a single-rider Sea-Doo for $35 an hour, or opt for a two-seat WaveRunner at $55 per hour. **North Shore Landing,** on Calif. 38, 2 miles west of Fawnskin (℃ **909/878-4-FUN**), rents jet skis and two- and three-person WaveRunners at rates ranging from $55 to $65 per hour. Call ahead to reserve your craft and check age and deposit requirements.

WATER-SKIING & WAKE BOARDING   Big Bear Lake, Pine Knot Landing, North Shore Landing, and Big Bear Marina (see above) all offer water-ski and wake-board lessons and speedboat rentals. Lake Arrowhead is home to the **McKenzie Water Ski School,** dockside in Lake Arrowhead Village (℃ **909/ 337-3814;** www.mckenzieskischool.com), famous for teaching Kirk Douglas, George Hamilton, and other Hollywood stars to ski. It's open from Memorial Day to the end of September and offers group lessons for $45 per hour, short pulls for $35, and boat charters (including driver) for $135 an hour.

OTHER WARM-WEATHER ACTIVITIES
GOLF   The **Bear Mountain Golf Course,** Goldmine Drive, Big Bear Lake (℃ **909/585-8002;** www.bigbearmountainresorts.com), is a 9-hole, par-35, links-style course that winds through a gently sloping meadow at the base of the Bear Mountain Ski Resort. The course is open daily April through November. Weekend greens fees are $28 and $40 for 9 and 18 holes, respectively. Both riding carts and pull carts are available. Call ahead for tee times.

HIKING   Hikers love the **San Bernardino National Forest.** The gray squirrel is a popular native so you may see them scurrying around gathering acorns or material for their nests. You can sometimes spot deer, coyotes, and American bald eagles, which come here with their young in winter. The black-crowned Steller's jay and the talkative red, white, and black acorn woodpecker are the most common of the great variety of birds in this pine forest.

The best choice for a short mountain hike is the **Woodland Trail,** which begins near the ranger station. The best long hike is a section of the **Pacific Crest Trail,** which travels 39 miles through the mountains above Big Bear and Arrowhead lakes. The most convenient trail head is located at Cougar Crest, a half mile west of the Big Bear Ranger Station.

The best place to begin a hike in Lake Arrowhead is at the **Arrowhead Ranger Station** (℃ **909/337-2444**), in the town of Skyforest on Calif. 18 a quarter mile east of the Lake Arrowhead turnoff (Calif. 173). The staff will provide you with maps and information on the best area trails, which range from easy to difficult. The **Enchanted Loop Trail,** near the town of Blue Jay, is an easy half-hour hike. The **Heaps Peak Arboretum Trail** winds through a grove of redwoods; the trail head is on the north side of Calif. 18, at an auxiliary ranger kiosk west of Running Springs.

The area is home to a **National Children's Forest,** a 20-acre area developed so that children, people in wheelchairs, and the visually impaired can enjoy nature. To get to the Children's Forest from Lake Arrowhead, take Calif. 330 to Calif. 18 east, past Deer Lick Station; when you reach a road marked IN96 (open only in summer), turn right and go 3 miles.

HORSEBACK RIDING Baldwin Lake Stables, southeast of Big Bear City (© 909/585-6482; www.baldwinlakestables.com), conducts hourly, lunch, and sunset rides along a wide variety of terrains and trails—all with spectacular vistas—including the Pacific Crest Trail, which includes expansive views of the Mojave Desert. It's open year-round.

MOUNTAIN BIKING Big Bear Lake has become a mountain-biking center, with most of the action around the Snow Summit ski area (see "Winter Fun," below), where a $10 lift ticket will take you and your bike to a web of trails, fire roads, and meadows at about 8,000 feet. Call its **Summer Activities Hot Line** (© 909/866-4621). The lake's north shore is also a popular destination; the forest-service ranger stations (see "Hiking," above) have maps to the historic Gold Rush–era Holcomb Valley and the 2-mile Alpine Pedal Path (an easy lake-side ride).

Big Bear Bikes, 41810 Big Bear Blvd. (© 909/866-6588), rents quality mountain bikes for about $9 an hour or $50 a day, as does **Bear Valley Bikes,** 40298 Big Bear Blvd. (© 909/866-8000; www.bearvalleybikes.com). **Team Big Bear** is located at the base of Snow Summit (© 909/866-4565; www.team bigbear.com); it rents bicycles and provides detailed maps and guides for all Big Bear–area trails.

At Lake Arrowhead, bikes are permitted on all hiking trails and back roads except the Pacific Crest Trail. See the local ranger station for an area map. Gear can be rented from the **Lake Arrowhead Resort** (© 909/336-1511) or **Above & Beyond Sports,** 32877 Calif. 18, Running Springs (© 909/867-5517).

WINTER FUN
SKIING & SNOWBOARDING When the L.A. basin gets wintertime rain, skiers rejoice, for they know snow is falling up in the mountains. The last few seasons have seen abundant natural snowfall at Big Bear, augmented by snow-making equipment. While the slopes can't compare with those in Utah or Colorado, they do offer diversity, difficulty, and convenience.

Snow Summit at Big Bear Lake (© 909/866-5766; www.bigbearmountain-resorts.com) is the skiers' choice, especially because it installed its second high-speed quad express from the 7,000-foot base to the 8,200-foot summit. There are also green (easy) runs, even from the summit, so beginners can also enjoy the Summit Haus lodge and breathtaking lake views from the top. Advanced risk-takers will appreciate three double black-diamond runs. Lift tickets range from $37 to $50. The resort offers midweek, beginner, half-day, night, and family specials, as well as ski and snowboard instruction. You can even ski free on your birthday here! Other helpful Snow Summit phone numbers include advance lift-ticket sales (© 909/866-5841), the ski school (© 909/866-4546), and a snow report (© 888/SUMMIT-1).

The **Bear Mountain Resort** at Big Bear Lake (© 800/BEAR-MTN or 909/585-2519; www.bigbearmountainresorts.com) has the largest beginner area, but experts flock to the double-black-diamond "Geronimo" run from the 8,805-foot Bear Peak. Natural-terrain skiers and snowboarders will enjoy legal access to off-trail canyons, but the limited beginner slopes and kids' areas get pretty crowded in season. One of two high-speed quad expresses rises from the 7,140-foot base to 8,440-foot Goldmine Mountain; most runs from here are intermediate. Bear Mountain has a ski-and-snowboard school, abundant dining facilities, and a well-stocked ski shop.

The **Snow Valley Ski Resort** in Arrowbear, midway between Arrowhead and Big Bear (© **800/680-SNOW** or 909/867-2751; www.snow-valley.com), has improved its snowmaking and facilities to be competitive with the other two major ski areas, and is the primary choice of skiers staying at Arrowhead. From a base elevation of 6,800 feet, Snow Valley's 13 chairlifts (including 5 triples) can take you from the beginner runs all the way up to black-diamond challenges at the 7,898-foot peak. Lift tickets cost $29 to $43 for adults; children's programs, night skiing, and lesson packages are available.

ICE-SKATING   The **Blue Jay Ice Castle,** at North Bay Road and Calif. 189 (© **909/337-0802;** www.ice-castle.com), near Lake Arrowhead Village, is a training site for world champion Michelle Kwan and boasts Olympic gold medalist Robin Cousins on its staff. Several public sessions each day—as well as hockey, broomball, group lessons, and book-in-advance private parties—give nonpros a chance to enjoy this impeccably groomed "outdoor" rink (it's open on three sides to the scenery and fresh air).

ORGANIZED TOURS

LAKE TOURS   The *Big Bear Queen* (© **909/866-3218;** www.bigbear marina.com), a midget Mississippi-style paddle-wheeler, cruises Big Bear Lake on 90-minute tours daily from late April to the end of November. The boat departs from Big Bear Marina (at the end of Paine Ave.). Tours are $11 for adults, $10 for seniors 65 and older and children ages 3 to 12, and free for kids under 3. Call for reservations and information on the special Sunday brunch, champagne sunset, and dinner cruises.

Fifty-minute tours of Lake Arrowhead are offered year-round on the *Arrowhead Queen* (© **909/336-6992**), a sister ship that departs hourly each day between 10am and 6pm from Lake Arrowhead Village. Tours are $12 for adults, $10 for seniors, $7.50 for children 2 to 12, and free for kids under 2. It's about the only way to really see this alpine jewel, unless you know a resident with a boat.

WHERE TO STAY
BIG BEAR LAKE

Vacation rentals are plentiful in the area, from cabins to condos to private homes. Some can accommodate up to 20 people and can be rented on a weekly or monthly basis. For a wide range of rental properties, all pictured in detail online, contact **Big Bear Mountain Rentals** (© **909/878-2233;** www.bigbear mountainrentals.com). The **Village Reservation Service** (© **909/866-8583;** www.bigbear.com) can arrange for everything from condos to lakefront homes, or call the **Big Bear Lake Resort Association** (© **909/866-7000**) for information and referrals on all types of lodgings.

Besides the places below, other choices I recommend are **Apples Bed & Breakfast Inn,** 42430 Moonridge Rd. (© **909/866-0903;** www.applesbedand breakfast.com), a crabapple-red New England–style clapboard that blends hotel-like professionalism with B&B amenities (and lots of frilly touches); and **Gold Mountain Manor,** 1117 Anita Ave. (© **800/509-2604** or 909/585-6997; www.goldmountainmanor.com), a woodsy 1920s lodge that's now an ultracozy (and affordable) B&B.

Grey Squirrel Resort *(Kids*   This is the most attractive of the many cabin-cluster-type motels near the city of Big Bear Lake, offering a wide range of rustic cabins, most with fireplace and kitchen. They're adequately, if not attractively, furnished—the appeal is the flexibility and privacy afforded large or long-term parties. Facilities include a heated pool that's enclosed in winter, a fire pit and barbecues, volleyball and basketball courts, and completely equipped kitchens.

39372 Big Bear Blvd., Big Bear Lake, CA 92315. ✆ **800/381-5569** or 909/866-4335. Fax 909/866-6271. www. greysquirrel.com. 18 cabins. $85–$115 1-bedroom cabin; $115–$145 2-bedroom cabin; $155–$275 3-bedroom cabin. Value rates available. Higher rates on holidays. AE, DISC, MC, V. Pets accepted with $10-per-day fee. **Amenities:** Heated indoor/outdoor pool; Jacuzzi; coin-op laundry. *In room:* TV/VCR, kitchen in some units.

Holiday Inn Big Bear Chateau *(Kids*   This European-flavored property is one of only two traditional full-service hotels in Big Bear. Its location—just off Big Bear Boulevard at the base of the road to Bear Mountain—makes the Chateau a popular choice for skiers and families (kids 17 and under stay free in their parent's room, and there are also children's activities). The rooms are modern but more charming than your average Holiday Inn, with tapestries, brass beds, antique furniture, gas fireplaces, and marble bathrooms with heated towel racks and many with whirlpool tubs. The compound is surrounded by tall forest. The restaurant (which provides room service) is advertised as "casually elegant," which means you can enjoy upscale Continental/American cuisine in après-ski duds.

42200 Moonridge Rd. (P.O. Box 1814), Big Bear Lake, CA 92315. ✆ **800/232-7466** or 909/866-6666. Fax 909/866-8988. www.bigbearlake.holiday-inn.com. 80 units. Winter $99–$180 double; summer $79–$160 double. Children 17 and under stay free in parent's room. Extra person $10. Winter-ski and summer-fun packages available. AE, DISC, MC, V. **Amenities:** Restaurant; lounge; heated outdoor pool; Jacuzzi; children's activities; limited room service. *In room:* A/C, TV, dataport, coffeemaker, hair dryer, iron.

Knickerbocker Mansion Country Inn *(★*   Innkeepers Thomas Bicanic and Stan Miller faced quite a task reviving this landmark log house; when they moved in, it was empty of all furnishings and suffered from years of neglect. But Knickerbocker Mansion has risen to become the most charming and sophisticated inn on the lake's south side; chef Bicanic, who honed his craft in L.A.'s culinary temple Patina restaurant, even has plans to begin serving intimate gourmet dinners. The pair scoured antiques stores in Big Bear and Los Angeles for vintage furnishings, creating a warm and relaxing ambience in the grand-yet-quirky, house of legendary local character Bill Knickerbocker, who assembled it by hand almost 90 years ago. Today's guest rooms are a cedar-paneled dream, with luxury bed linens, cozy bathrobes, modern marble bathrooms with deluxe Australian showerheads, and refreshing mountain views. After Bicanic's stunning breakfast, you can spend the day relaxing on veranda rockers or garden hammocks; Big Bear's village is also an easy walk away.

869 Knickerbocker Rd. (P.O. Box 1907), Big Bear Lake, CA 92315. ✆ **877/423-1180** or 909/878-9190. Fax 909/878-4248. www.knickerbockermansion.com. 11 units. $110–$155 double; $200–$225 suite. Rates include full gourmet breakfast and all-day refreshments and snacks. AE, DISC, MC, V. *In room:* TV/VCR, dataport, iron, hair dryer.

Windy Point Inn *(★★*   A contemporary architectural showpiece on the scenic north shore, the Windy Point is the only shorefront B&B in Big Bear; ergo, all guest rooms have a view of the lake. Hosts Val and Kent Kessler's attention to detail is impeccable—if you're tired of knotty pine and Victorian frills, here's a grown-up place for you, with plenty of romance and all the pampering you can stand. Every room has a wood-burning fireplace, feather bed, private deck, and DVD player (borrow DVDs from the inn's plentiful collection); some also feature whirlpool tubs and luxurious state-of-the-art bathrooms. The welcoming great room features a casual sunken fireplace nook with floor-to-ceiling windows overlooking the lake, a telescope for stargazing, a baby grand, and up-to-date menus for every local eatery. You might not want to leave the cocoon of your room after Kent's custom gourmet breakfast, but if you do, you'll find a winter-time bald-eagle habitat just up the road, and the city of Big Bear Lake is only a 10-minute drive around the lake.

39015 N. Shore Dr., Fawnskin, CA 92333. © **909/866-2746.** Fax 909/866-1593. www.windypointinn.com. 5 units. $135–$255 double. Rates include welcome cookies, lavish full breakfast, and afternoon hors d'oeuvres. Midweek discounts available. AE, DISC, MC, V. *In room:* TV/DVD, fridge, coffeemaker, hair dryer, CD player in some units, no phone.

LAKE ARROWHEAD

There are far more private homes than tourist accommodations in Arrowhead, but rental properties abound, from cozy cottages to mansions; many can be eco-nomical for families or other groups. Two of the largest agencies are **Arrowhead Cabin Rentals** (© **800/244-5138** or 909/337-2403; www.arrowheadrent.com) and **Arrowhead Mountain Resorts Rentals** (© **800/743-0865** or 909/337-4413; www.lakearrowheadrentals.com). Overnight guests in rentals enjoy some resident lake privileges—ask when you reserve.

Two other options are **Chateau du Lac,** 911 Hospital Rd. (© **800/601-8722** or 909/337-6488; www.chateau-du-lac.com), an elegant and contemporary five-room B&B with stunning views of the lake; and the **Saddleback Inn,** 300 S. Calif. 173 (© **800/858-3334** or 909/336-3571; www.saddlebackinn.com), an inn and restaurant that still boasts historic charm while offering up-to-date amenities, all at a prime location in the center of the village.

Bracken Fern Manor 𝔊 *Finds*   Billing itself as a "House of Now Fine Repute," this off-the-beaten-path inn boasts a registered historical marker as well as a check-ered past. The present owners work hard at evoking its 1930s heyday: They've pre-served the downstairs public rooms, along with many well-maintained antiques, and named each guest room for one of the "girls." There are many quiet corners for relaxing, including a game room, hidden library, whirlpool gazebo, and wood-lined sauna. Rooms are decorated in a fresh country style and have private bath-rooms, a feature not originally included in the house. A detached cottage sleeps four and rents for $380 for 2 nights.

815 Arrowhead Villas Rd. (P.O. Box 1006), Lake Arrowhead, CA 92352. © **888/244-5612** or 909/337-8557. Fax 909/337-3323. www.brackenfernmanor.com. 10 units. $80–$185 double. Rates include full breakfast. MC, V. Located ½ mile north of Calif. 18. **Amenities:** Jacuzzi; sauna. *In room:* No phone.

Lake Arrowhead Resort *Kids*   This sprawling resort has been upgraded some-what since it was part of the Hilton chain, but location is still its most outstand-ing feature, coupled with unparalleled (for the mountains) service and facilities. Situated on the lakeshore adjacent to Lake Arrowhead Village, the hotel has its own beach, plus docks that are ideal for fishing. The rooms are fitted with good-quality, bulk-purchased contemporary furnishings, and most have balconies, king-size beds, and fireplaces. The suites, some in private cottages, are equipped with full kitchens and whirlpool tubs.

The hotel caters primarily to groups, and sports a businesslike ambience dur-ing the week. A full program of supervised children's activities, ranging from nature hikes to T-shirt painting, is offered on weekends year-round.

27984 Hwy. 189, Lake Arrowhead, CA 92352. © **800/800-6792** or 909/336-1511. Fax 909/336-1378. www.lakearrowheadresort.com. 177 units. $109–$229 double; $325–$475 suite. Inquire about auto-club discounts. AE, DC, DISC, MC, V. **Amenities:** 2 restaurants; outdoor pool (summer only); 2 lit rooftop tennis courts; health club; Jacuzzi; children's programs; video arcade; business center; salon; babysitting; laundry service; dry cleaning. *In room:* A/C, TV w/pay movies, dataport, minibar, coffeemaker, hair dryer.

Pine Rose Cabins *(Kids*   Pine Rose Cabins is a good choice for families. Situated on 5 forested acres about 3 miles from the lake, the wonderful free-standing cabins offer lots of privacy. Innkeeper Tricia Dufour has 15 cabins, ranging in size from romantic studios to a large five-bedroom lodge, each decorated in a different theme: The Indian cabin has a tepeelike bed; the bed in Wild Bill's cabin is covered like a wagon. Multibedroom units have fully stocked kitchens and separate living areas; for all cottages, daily maid service is available at an additional charge. There are plenty of fun and games on the premises, including swing sets, croquet, tetherball, and Ping-Pong.

25994 Calif. 189 (P.O. Box 31), Twin Peaks, CA 92391. © 800/429-PINE or 909/337-2341. Fax 909/337-0258. www.lakearrowheadcabins.com. 17 units. $59–$179 studio for 2; $69–$179 1-, 2-, and 3-bedroom cabins for up to 10 people; $395–$450 large-group lodges. Ski packages available. AE, DISC, MC, V. Pets accepted with $10 fee per night and $100 refundable deposit. **Amenities:** Outdoor heated pool; Jacuzzi. *In room:* TV/VCR, kitchen, coffeemaker.

WHERE TO DINE
BIG BEAR LAKE

A reliable option for all-day dining is **Stillwell's,** 40650 Village Dr. (© **909/866-3121,** ext. 3). You might otherwise pass right by, because Stillwell's is the dining room for convention-friendly Northwoods Resort at the edge of the village; despite the unmistakable hotel feel, though, its something-for-everyone American/Continental menu is surprisingly good, with noted attention to detail and fair prices (rare in this mountain resort town).

The Captain's Anchorage STEAK/SEAFOOD   Historic and rustic, this knotty-pine restaurant has been serving fine steaks, prime rib, seafood, and lobster since 1947. Inside, the dark, nautical decor and fire-warmed bar are just right on blustery winter nights. It's got one of those mile-long soup-and-salad bars, plus some great early-bird and weeknight specials.

Moonridge Way at Big Bear Blvd., Big Bear Lake. © 909/866-3997. Reservations recommended. Full dinners $15–$29. AE, MC, V. Sun–Thurs 4:30–9pm; Fri–Sat 4:30–10pm.

Madlon's AMERICAN/CONTINENTAL   One of the few non-retro-fare dining rooms at the mountain resorts, Madlon's brings a bit of European flair to this fairytale cottage. A variety of creative croissant sandwiches at lunch are complemented by dinner selections like black-pepper filet mignon with mushroom-and-brandy sauce, and lemon-pepper-marinated chicken breast over pasta, all of which are prepared with a sophisticated touch.

829 W. Big Bear Blvd., Big Bear City. © 909/585-3762. Reservations recommended. Main courses $12–$25. DC, DISC, MC, V. Sat–Sun 8am–1:30pm; Tues–Fri 11am–1:30pm; Tues–Sun 5–9pm.

Old Country Inn DINER/GERMAN   The Old Country Inn has long been a favorite for hearty pre-ski breakfasts and stick-to-your-ribs dinners. The restaurant is casual and welcoming, and the adjacent cocktail lounge is raucous on weekends. At breakfast, enjoy German apple pancakes or colossal omelets, while lunch choices include salads, sandwiches, and burgers. At lunch or dinner, feast on Wiener schnitzel, sauerbraten, and other gravy-topped German standards, along with grilled steaks and chicken.

41126 Big Bear Blvd., Big Bear Lake. © 909/866-5600. Main courses $6–$28. AE, DC, DISC, MC, V. Sun–Thurs 8am–9pm; Fri–Sat 8am–10pm.

LAKE ARROWHEAD

For an affluent residential community, there are surprisingly few dining options around Lake Arrowhead. But not surprisingly, what there is tends to run toward pricey elegance—elegant for a rustic mountain resort, that is. Although there are both a California/Continental restaurant and a casual family eatery in the Lake Arrowhead Resort (p. 592), you might want to venture out to some of the locals' choices. These include the **Chef's Inn & Tavern,** 29020 Oak Terrace, Cedar Glen (© **909/336-4488**), a moderate to expensive Continental restaurant in a former bordello; the **Antler's Inn,** 26125 Calif. 189, Twin Peaks (© **909/ 337-4020**), serving prime rib, seafood, and buffalo in a log lodge; the **Royal Oak,** 27187 Calif. 189, Blue Jay Village (© **909/337-6018**), an expensive American/Continental steakhouse with a pub; and **Belgian Waffle Works,** dockside at Lake Arrowhead Village (© **909/337-5222**), an inexpensive coffee shop with Victorian decor, known for its crispy waffles with tasty toppings.

4 The Disneyland Resort ★★★

30 miles SE of downtown L.A.

There are newer and larger Disneyland parks in Florida, Tokyo, and even France, but the original and inspiration for all of them still opens its gates in Anaheim, California, every day, proudly proclaiming itself "The Happiest Place on Earth." Smaller than Walt Disney World, Disneyland—which opened in 1955 on a 107-acre tract surrounded almost exclusively by orange groves—has always capitalized on being the world's first family-oriented mega–theme park. Nostalgia is a big part of the original park's appeal, and despite many advancements, changes, and expansions over the years, Disneyland remains true to the vision of founder Walt Disney.

In 2001 Disney unveiled a brand-new theme park (Disney's California Adventure), a new shopping/dining/entertainment district (Downtown Disney), and a third on-site hotel (Disney's Grand Californian Hotel). They also revamped their name to "The Disneyland Resort," reflecting an expanded array of entertainment options. There's lots of new stuff to check out, and we'll give you the lowdown on the best of the new, as well as the classic Disneyland experience.

ESSENTIALS

GETTING THERE   To reach the Disneyland Resort by car from LAX, take I-105 east to I-605 north, then I-5 south. From Los Angeles, take I-5 south until you see signs for Disneyland. Off-ramps from I-5 lead to into the attraction's parking lots and surrounding streets (follow the THEME PARKS signs). The drive from LAX takes approximately 40 minutes with no traffic (yeah, right).

If Anaheim is your first—or only—destination, and you want to avoid L.A., consider flying into **John Wayne Airport** in Santa Ana (© **949/252-5200;** www.ocair.com), Orange County's largest airport. It's about 15 miles from Disneyland at the intersection of I-405 and Calif. 55. Check to see if your hotel has a free shuttle to and from either airport (some will pick you up at LAX), or call one of the following commercial shuttle services (fares are generally $12 one-way from John Wayne): **Xpress** (© **800/427-7483;** www.xpressshuttle.com), **Prime Time** (© **800/733-8267;** primetimeshuttle.com), or **SuperShuttle** (© **800/258-3826;** www.supershuttle.com). Car-rental agencies at the airport include **Budget** (© **800/527-0700;** www.budget.com) and **Hertz** (© **800/ 654-3131;** www.hertz.com). To reach Anaheim from the airport, take Calif. 55 north to I-5 north, then take the Harbor Boulevard exit and follow signs leading to "Theme Parks." You can also catch a ride with **American Taxi** (© 888/ 482-9466), whose cabs queue up at the Ground Transportation Center on the lower level; reservations are not necessary. Expect the fare to Disneyland to cost about $30.

VISITOR INFORMATION   For information on **The Disneyland Resort,** including show schedules and ride closures that apply to the specific day(s) of your visit, call © 714/781-4565 for automated information or © 714/781-7290 to speak to Guest Relations (but expect a long wait). Better yet, log on to the Disneyland Resort's official website at **www.disneyland.com**.

For general information on the entire Anaheim region, contact the **Anaheim/Orange County Visitor and Convention Bureau,** 800 W. Katella Ave., inside the Anaheim Convention Center (© 714/765-8888; www.anaheim oc.org). It's open Monday to Friday from 8:30am to 5:30pm. They can fill you in on area activities and shopping, as well as send you their *Official Visitors Guide* and the AdventureCard, which offers discounts at dozens of local attractions, hotels, restaurants, and shops.

You can find out everything you need to know about the Disneyland Resort online, beginning with the official site, **www.disneyland.com**, which contains the latest information on park improvements and additions, plus special offers (sometimes on airfare or reduced admission) and an interactive trip planner that lets you build a custom Disney vacation package.

There are numerous unofficial Disney websites as well, which provide very detailed—and often judgmental—information about the Disneyland Resort. The best we've found are: **IntercotWest.com**, an active and friendly website filled with detailed information on every corner of the Disneyland Resort; **LaughingPlace.com** and **MouseInfo.com** both feature daily updated headlines and columns on all things Disney; **Mouseplanet.com**, a comprehensive Disneyland information resource that offers features and reviews by guest writers; and **MouseSavers.com**, which offers in-depth information on Disney theme parks and helps users save money on lodging and admissions.

ADMISSION, HOURS & INFORMATION   Admission to *either* Disneyland or Disney's California Adventure, including unlimited rides and all festivities and entertainment, is $50 for adults and children over 9, $40 for children 3 to 9, and free for children under 3. Parking is $8. Two-day Park Hopper tickets, which allow you to go back and forth as much as you'd like each day, are $99 for adults and children over 9, $79 for children 3 to 9. Other multi-day, multi-park combination passes are available as well. In addition, many area accommodations offer lodging packages that include admission for one or more days. Be sure to check the Disney website, www.disneyland.com, for seasonal ticket specials.

If you plan on arriving during a busy time (when the gates open in the morning, or between 11am and 2pm), purchase your tickets in advance and get a jump on the crowds at the ticket counters. Advance tickets may be purchased through Disneyland's website (www.disneyland.com), at Disney stores in the United States, or by calling the ticket mail-order line (© 714/781-4043).

Disneyland and Disney's California Adventure are open every day of the year, but operating hours vary, so be sure to call for information that applies to the specific day(s) of your visit (© 714/781-7290). The same information, including ride closures and show schedules, can be found online at **www.disneyland.com**. Generally speaking, the parks are open from 9 or 10am to 6 or 7pm on weekdays, fall to spring; and from 8 or 9am to midnight or 1am on weekends, holidays, and

---

(Value The Art of the (Package) Deal

If you intend to spend 2 or more nights in Disney territory, it pays to investigate the bevy of packaged vacation options. Start by logging on to www.disneyland.com and clicking on "Parks & Hotels" to peruse their standard package offers, take a virtual tour of Disney hotel properties, and get online price quotes for customized, date-specific packages including airline tickets. Their packages are value-packed time-savers with abundant flexibility. Rates are highly competitive, considering each package includes multi-day and multi-park admission, plus keepsake souvenirs, preferred seating at Disney shows, Disney pocket guides, and coupon books. If you're staying in a non-Disney hotel (even those in Los Angeles or San Diego), ask whether they sell Disneyland admission packages—many hotels offer inclusive vacation packages that include Disneyland and Disney's California Adventure (and other attractions). To make sure you're getting the absolute best deal, call the official Disney travel agency, **Walt Disney Travel Co.** (© 877/700-DISNEY or 714/520-5050), and compare their package deals with the ones you've already been quoted.

---

during winter, spring, or summer vacation periods. *Tip:* The park's operating hours can give you some idea of what kinds of crowds to expect: The later the parks close, the more people that will be there.

WHEN TO GO   The Disneyland Resort is busiest in summer (between Memorial Day and Labor Day), on holidays (Thanksgiving week, Christmas week, Presidents' Day weekend, Easter week, and Japan's "Golden Week" in early May), plus weekends year-round. All other periods are considered "off season." Peak hours are from noon to 5pm; visit the most popular rides before and after these hours and you'll cut your waiting times substantially. If you plan to arrive during a busy time, buy your tickets in advance and get a jump on the crowds at the ticket counters. Advance tickets may be purchased through Disneyland's website (www.disneyland.com), at Disney stores in the United States, or by calling the ticket mail-order line (© 714/781-4043).

Attendance falls dramatically during the winter, so the park offers discounted (about 25% off) admission to Southern California residents, who may buy up to five tickets per zip code verification. If you'll be visiting the park with someone who lives here, be sure to take advantage of this "Resident Salutes" promotion.

Once in the park, many visitors tackle Disneyland (or Disney's California Adventure) systematically, beginning at the entrance and working their way clockwise around the park. My advice: Arrive early and run to the most popular rides—the Indiana Jones Adventure, Star Tours, Big Thunder Mountain Railroad, Splash Mountain, the Haunted Mansion, and Pirates of the Caribbean rides in Disneyland; and Twilight Zone Tower of Terror, Soarin' Over California, California Screamin', Grizzly River Run, and It's Tough to be a Bug rides in Disney's California Adventure. Waits for these rides can last an hour or more in the middle of the day.

This time-honored plan of attack may eventually become obsolete, thanks to the **Disney's FASTPASS** system. Here's how it works: Say you want to ride

Space Mountain, but the line is long—*so* long the wait sign indicates a 75-minute standstill. Now you can head to the Automated FASTPASS ticket dispensers, which allow you to swipe the magnetic strip of your Disneyland entrance ticket, get a free FASTPASS for later that day, and return to use the reduced-wait FASTPASS entrance (to the envy of everyone in the slowpoke line). At press time, more than a dozen Disneyland rides were equipped with FASTPASS; several more will be added by the time you read this. The hottest features at Disney's California Adventure had FASTPASS built in from the start; for a complete list for each park, check your official map/guide when you enter. *Note:* You can only obtain a FASTPASS for one attraction at a time. Also, the FASTPASS system doesn't eliminate the need to arrive at the theme park early because there's only a limited supply of FASTPASSes available for each attraction on a given day. So, if you don't show up until the middle of the afternoon, you might find that all the FASTPASSes have been distributed.

DISNEYLAND 🐭🐭🐭

Disneyland is divided into eight subareas or "lands" arranged around a central hub, each of which has a number of rides and attractions that are, more or less, related to that land's theme. Be sure to pick up a free park map on the way in or you'll probably get lost almost immediately.

MAIN STREET U.S.A.   At the park's entrance is Main Street U.S.A., an idealized version of a turn-of-the-20th-century American small-town street inspired by Marceline, Missouri (Walt Disney's childhood home), and built on a 7/8 scale. Many visitors are surprised to discover that all the buildings are real. Attention to detail here is exceptional—interiors, furnishings, and fixtures conform to the period. As with any real Main Street, the Disney version is a collection of shops and eating places, with a city hall, a fire station, and an old-time silent cinema. Live performances include piano playing at the Carnation ice-cream parlor and the Dapper Dan's barbershop quartet along the street. A mixed-media attraction combines a presentation on the life of Walt Disney (*The Walt Disney Story*) with a patriotic remembrance of Abraham Lincoln. Horse-drawn trolleys, fire engines, and horseless carriages give rides along Main Street and transport visitors to the central hub (properly known as the Central Plaza).

Because there are no major rides, it's best to tour Main Street during the afternoon, when lines for rides are longest, and in the evening, when walkways can be packed with visitors viewing Disneyland's parades and shows. There's always something happening on Main Street; stop in at the information booth to the left of the Main Entrance for a schedule of the day's events.

ADVENTURELAND   Inspired by the most exotic regions of Asia, Africa, India, and the South Pacific, Adventureland is home to several popular rides. Here's where you can cavort inside **Tarzan's Treehouse,** a climb-around attraction based on the animated film. Its African-themed neighbor is the **Jungle Cruise,** where passengers board a large authentic-looking Mississippi River paddleboat and float along an Amazon-like river; a spear's throw away is the **Enchanted Tiki Room,** one of the most sedate attractions in Adventureland. Inside, you can sit down and watch a 20-minute musical comedy featuring electronically animated tropical birds, flowers, and "Tiki gods."

The **Indiana Jones Adventure** is Adventureland's star ride. Based on the Steven Spielberg films, this ride takes adventurers into the Temple of the Forbidden Eye, in joltingly realistic all-terrain vehicles. Riders follow Indy and experience the perils of bubbling lava pits, whizzing arrows, fire-breathing serpents, collapsing bridges, and the familiar cinematic tumbling boulder (an effect that's very realistic in the front seats).

NEW ORLEANS SQUARE   A large, grassy green dotted with gas lamps, New Orleans Square is home to the **Haunted Mansion,** where the dated effects are more funny than scary. Even more fanciful is **Pirates of the Caribbean,** one of Disneyland's most popular rides. Visitors float on boats through mock underground caves, entering an enchanting world of swashbuckling, rum-running, and buried treasure. Even in the middle of the afternoon you can dine by the cool moonlight and to the sound of crickets in the **Blue Bayou** restaurant, situated in the middle of the ride itself.

CRITTER COUNTRY   An ode to the backwoods, Critter Country is a sort of Frontierland without those pesky settlers. Older kids and grown-ups head straight for **Splash Mountain,** one of the largest water flume rides in the world. Loosely based on the Disney movie *Song of the South,* the ride is lined with about 100 characters that won't stop singing "Zip-A-Dee-Doo-Dah." Be prepared to get wet, especially if someone sizable is in the front seat of your log-shaped boat. **The Many Adventures of Winnie the Pooh** is a new children's attraction based on Winnie the Pooh and his friends from the Hundred-Acre Wood—Tigger, Eeyore, Piglet, and the rest of the familiar gang. The attraction is of the a kindler, gentler sort, where you board "hunny bee-hives" and take a slow-moving journey through the Hundred-Acre Wood on an endless pursuit of hunny. The high-tech gadgetry and illusions are spellbinding for kids and mildly entertaining for adults. (*Tip:* It's a very popular attraction, so be sure to arrive early or make use of FASTPASS.) While it may not be the fastest ride in the park, **Davy Crockett's Explorer Canoes** allows folks to row around Tom Sawyer Island. It's the only ride where you actively control your boat (no underwater rails!). Hop into replica canoes, grab a paddle, and away you go.

FRONTIERLAND   Inspired by 19th-century America, Frontierland features a raft to **Tom Sawyer's Island,** a do-it-yourself play area with balancing rocks, caves, and a rope bridge. You'll also find the **Big Thunder Mountain Railroad,** a runaway roller coaster that races through a deserted 1870s gold mine. Children will dig the petting zoo and there's an Abe Lincoln–style log cabin; both are great for exploring with the little ones. This is also where you board one of two large-capacity riverboats—*Mark Twain* and the *Sailing Ship Columbia*—that navigate the waters around Tom Sawyer Island and Fort Wilderness. A beautiful craft, the Riverboat provides a lofty perch from which to see Frontierland and New Orleans Square. The Sailing Ship Columbia, however, has far more historic and aesthetic appeal. As with the other river craft, the Riverboat suspends operations at dusk.

When it's showing (it's a seasonal presentation), head to Frontierland's **Rivers of America** after dark to see the FANTASMIC! show. It mixes magic, music, live performers, and sensational special effects. Just as he did in *The Sorcerer's Apprentice,* Mickey Mouse appears and uses his magical powers to create giant water fountains, enormous flowers, and fantasy creatures. There's plenty of pyrotechnics, lasers, and fog, as well as a 45-foot-tall dragon that breathes fire and sets the water of the Rivers of America aflame.

MICKEY'S TOONTOWN   This is a colorful, whimsical world inspired by the "Roger Rabbit" films—a wacky, gag-filled land populated by 'toons. It even looks like a cartoon come to life, a trippy, smile-inducing world without a straight line or right angle in sight. In addition to serving as a place where guests can be certain of finding Disney characters at any time during the day, Mickey's Toontown also serves as an elaborate interactive playground where it's okay for the kids to run, climb, and let off steam. There are several rides and play areas, including **Roger Rabbit's CarToonSpin, Donald's Boat, Chip 'n' Dale's Treehouse, Gadget's Go Coaster, Goofy's Bounce House,** and **Mickey's House & Minnie's House.** *Tip:* Because of its popularity with families, Toontown is most crowded during the day but often deserted after dinnertime.

FANTASYLAND With a storybook theme, this is the catchall "land" for stuff that doesn't quite fit anywhere else. Most of the rides are geared to the under-6 set, including the **King Arthur Carousel, Mad Tea Party, Dumbo the Flying Elephant Ride,** and the **Casey Jr. Circus Train.** Some, like **Mr. Toad's Wild Ride** and **Peter Pan's Flight,** appeal to grownups as well. You'll also find **Alice in Wonderland, Snow White's Scary Adventures, Pinocchio's Daring Journey,** and more.

The most lauded attraction is **"it's a small world,"** a slow-moving indoor river ride through a saccharine nightmare of all the world's children singing the song everybody loves to hate. (Perhaps the ride would be more entertaining if each person got four softballs on the way in?) For a different kind of thrill, try the **Matterhorn Bobsleds,** a zippy roller coaster through chilled caverns and drifting fog banks. It's one of the park's most popular rides.

TOMORROWLAND Conceived as an optimistic look at the future, Tomorrowland employs an angular, metallic look popularized by futurists like Jules Verne. Longtime Tomorrowland favorites include **Space Mountain** (a pitch-black indoor roller coaster that assaults your equilibrium and ears), and **Star Tours,** the original Disney–George Lucas joint venture. It's a 40-passenger StarSpeeder that encounters a space-load of misadventures on the way to the Moon of Endor, achieved with wired seats and video effects—not for the queasy.

Other Tomorrowland attractions include: **"Honey, I Shrunk the Audience,"** an interactive 3-D movie based on the popular movie series featuring Rick Moranis in the role of Wayne Szalinski; the **Disneyland Monorail,** a "futuristic" transportation ride that affords the only practical opportunity for escaping the park during the crowded lunch period and early afternoon; and **Innoventions,** a huge, busy collection of industry-sponsored hands-on exhibits. Exhibits, many of which change each year, demonstrate such products as virtual-reality games, high-definition TV, voice-activated appliances, and various CD-ROM applications, among others.

DISNEY'S CALIFORNIA ADVENTURE ★★
The Walt Disney Company's newest theme park, Disney's California Adventure, held its grand opening on February 8, 2001. With a grand entrance designed to resemble one of those "wish you were here" scenic postcards, the 55-acre park starts out with a bang. Beneath a scale model of the Golden Gate Bridge (watch carefully, the monorail passes overhead) are handcrafted mosaic tiles depicting scenes of Northern and Southern California on each side. Just inside, **Sunshine Plaza** is anchored by a perpetual wave fountain and an enormous gold titanium "sun" that shines all day, illuminated by computerized heliostats that follow the real sun's path. From this point, visitors can head into four themed "districts," each containing rides, interactive attractions, live-action shows, and plenty of dining, snacking, and shopping opportunities.

THE GOLDEN STATE This multidimensional area represents California's history, heritage, and physical attributes. Sound boring? Actually, the park's splashiest attractions are here. "Condor Flats" is a tribute to daring aviators; inside a weathered corrugated test-pilots' hangar is **Soarin' Over California,** the ride that immediately rose to the top of everyone's "ride first" list (it's equipped with FASTPASS and I highly recommend using it). It uses cool cutting-edge technology to combine suspended seats with a spectacular IMAX-style surround-movie—so riders literally "soar" over California's scenic lands.

Nearby, California Adventure's iconic "Grizzly Peak" towers over the **Grizzly River Run,** a splashy Gold Country ride through caverns, mine shafts, and water slides; it culminates with a wet plunge into a spouting geyser. Kids can cavort nearby on the **Redwood Creek Challenge Trail,** a forest playground with smoke-jumper cable slides, net climbing, and swaying bridges.

Pacific Wharf was inspired by Monterey's Cannery Row and features mouth-watering demonstration attractions by **Boudin Sourdough Bakery, Mission Tortillas,** and **Lucky Fortune Cookies.** If you get hungry, each has a food counter where you can enjoy soup-in-a-sourdough-bowl; tacos, burritos, and enchiladas; and teriyaki bowls, egg rolls, and wonton soup.

PARADISE PIER　Journey back to the glory days of California's beachfront amusement piers—remember Santa Monica, Santa Cruz, Belmont Park?—on this fantasy boardwalk. Highlights include **California Screamin',** a classic roller coaster that replicates the whitewashed wooden white-knucklers of the past—but with state-of-the-art steel construction and a smooth, computerized ride. There's also the **Maliboomer,** a trio of towers (giant strongman sledgehammer tests) that catapult riders to the tip-top bell, then lets them down bungee-style with dangling feet; the **Orange Stinger,** a whooshing swing ride inside an enormous orange, complete with orange scent piped in; **Mulholland Madness,** a wacky wild-trip along L.A.'s precarious hilltop street; and the **Sun Wheel Carousel,** featuring unique zigzagging cars that bring a new twist to the familiar ride.

There are all the familiar boardwalk games (complete with stuffed prizes), guilty pleasure fast foods like pizza, corn dogs, and burritos, plus a full-service over-water restaurant called **Ariel's Grotto.**

HOLLYWOOD PICTURES BACKLOT　If you've visited Disney World in Florida, you might recognize many elements of this *trompe l'oeil* re-creation of a Hollywood movie studio lot. Pass through a classic studio archway flanked by gigantic golden elephants and you'll find yourself on a surprisingly realistic "Hollywood Boulevard." The resort's hottest new attraction is **Twilight Zone Tower of Terror.** Brand-spooking new for 2004, this truly scary ride has been a huge hit since its debut at Walt Disney World. Legend has it that during a violent storm on Halloween night 1939, lightning struck the Hollywood Tower Hotel, causing an entire wing and an elevator full of people to disappear—and you're about to meet them in person as you become the star in a special Disney episode of . . . *The Twilight Zone.*

The Backlot's other main attraction is **Playhouse Disney—Live on Stage!** starring the characters from the popular "Playhouse Disney" kids' program on the Disney Channel. It's a hugely popular high-energy show where Bear in the Big Blue House, Rolie Polie Olie, Stanley, and other television characters entertain kids with songs, music, and stories. Another popular show is **Jim Henson's MuppetVision 3D,** an onscreen comedy romp featuring Kermit, Miss Piggy, Gonzo, Fozzie Bear—and even hecklers Waldorf and Statler. Although it's not nearly as entertaining as **"It's Tough to Be a Bug,"** it has its moments and won't scare the bejeezus out of little kids.

At the end of the street, the replica movie palace **Hyperion Theater** presents Broadway-caliber live-action shows of classic Disney films such as **"Aladdin—A Musical Spectacular."** Also here is **"Who Wants to Be a Millionaire—Play It!,"** an interactive, high-energy mockup of the game show. It's re-created to look and feel as it does on television, complete with the dramatic lighting and high-tech set. In the **Disney Animation** building, visitors can participate in six different interactive galleries and learn how stories become animated features.

A BUG'S LAND   The new bug-themed **"a bug's land"** encompasses **It's Tough to Be a Bug, Flik's Fun Fair,** and **Bountiful Valley Farm.** Inspired by the movie *A Bug's Life,* It's Tough to Be a Bug uses 3-D technology to lead the audience on an underground romp with bees, termites, grasshoppers, stink bugs, spiders, and a few surprises that keep everyone hopping, ducking, and laughing along (I could see how little kids might find the show rather terrifying, however). The **Flik's Fun Fair** area features bug-themed rides and a water playground designed for little ones from 4 to 7—but sized so their parents can ride along too—whereas **Bountiful Farm** pays tribute to California's agriculture (a real ho-hum if you're Californian). Exhibits include a demonstration vineyard, Mission-style "aging room" (with a presentation on the art of winemaking), wine bars, and the park's most upscale eatery, **Vineyard Room.**

DOWNTOWN DISNEY ⚑

Borrowing a page from central Florida's successful Disney compound, **Downtown Disney** is a colorful (and very sanitized) "street scene" filled with restaurants, shops, and entertainment for all ages. Options abound: window-shop with kids in tow, have an upscale dinner for two, or party into the night. The promenade begins at the amusement park gates and stretches toward the Disneyland Hotel; there are nearly 20 shops and boutiques, and a dozen-plus restaurants, live-music venues, and entertainment options.

Highlights include **House of Blues,** the blues-jazz restaurant/club that features Delta-inspired cuisine and big-name music; **Ralph Brennan's Jazz Kitchen,** a spicy mix of New Orleans traditional foods and live jazz; **ESPN Zone,** the ultimate sports dining and entertainment experience, including an interactive game room; and **World of Disney,** one of the biggest Disney shopping experiences anywhere, with a vast and diverse range of toys, souvenirs, and collectibles. There is also a 12-screen multiplex, LEGO Imagination Center, Sephora cosmetics store, and much more.

WHERE TO STAY
VERY EXPENSIVE

Disney's Grand Californian Hotel ✯✯✯ *Kids*   Disney didn't miss the details when constructing this enormous version of an Arts and Crafts–era lodge (think Yosemite's Ahwhanee, Pasadena's Gamble House), hiring craftspeople throughout the state to contribute one-of-a-kind tiles, furniture, sculptures, and artwork. Taking inspiration from California's redwood forests, Mission pioneers, and plein-air painters, designers managed to create a nostalgic yet state-of-the-art high-rise hotel.

Enter through subtle (where's the door?) stained-glass sliding panels to the hotel's centerpiece, a six-story "living room" with a William Morris–designed marble "carpet," angled skylight seen through exposed support beams, display cases of Craftsman treasures, and a three-story walk-in "hearth" whose fire warms Stickley-style rockers and plush leather armchairs.

Guest rooms are spacious and smartly designed, carrying through the Arts and Crafts theme surprisingly well considering the hotel's grand scale. The best ones overlook the park, but you'll pay for that view. Despite the sophisticated air of the Grand Californian, this is a hotel that truly caters to families, with a bevy of room configurations including one with a double bed plus bunk beds with trundle. Since the hotel provides sleeping bags (rather than rollaways) for kids, this standard-size room will sleep a family of six—but you have to share the bathroom. *Tip:* Ask for a free upgrade to a room with a view of the park when you check in—they're pretty generous about this.

The hotel's two main restaurants are the upscale **Napa Rose** and the **Story-tellers Cafe,** a "character dining" restaurant that's always bustling with excited kids who pay more attention to Chip and Dale than their eggs and bacon (be sure to make a breakfast reservation).

1600 S. Disneyland Dr., Anaheim, CA 92802. © **714/956-MICKEY** (central reservations) or 714/635-2300. Fax 714/956-6099. www.disneyland.com. 745 units. $205–$335 double; from $345 suite. AE, DC, DISC, MC, V. Free self-parking; valet $6. **Amenities:** 3 restaurants; lounge; 2 outdoor pools; health club with massage therapy; whirlpool; children's center; game room/arcade; concierge; business center; 24-hr. room service; laundry/dry-cleaning service; concierge-level rooms. *In room:* A/C, TV, dataport, minibar, coffeemaker, hair dryer, iron, safe, bathrobes, portable crib.

EXPENSIVE

The Disneyland Hotel ★★ *Kids*   The holy grail of Disney-goers has always been this, the "Official Hotel of the Magic Kingdom." A monorail connection via Downtown Disney means you'll be able to return to your room anytime, whether to take a much-needed nap or to change your soaked shorts after riding Splash Mountain. The theme hotel is an attraction unto itself, and the best choice for families with small children. The rooms aren't fancy, but they're comfortably furnished and all have balconies. In-room amenities include movie channels (with free Disney Channel, naturally) and even Disney-themed toiletries and accessories. This all-inclusive resort offers several restaurants (see below for a full review of **Goofy's Kitchen**), snack bars, and cocktail lounges; every kind of service desk imaginable; the Never Land Pool Complex themed after Peter Pan and Captain Hook (complete with a white-sand beach); and video-game center.

1150 W. Magic Way, Anaheim, CA 92802. © **714/956-MICKEY.** Reservations fax 714/956-6582. www.disneyland.com. 990 units. $170–$310 double; from $265 suite. AE, MC, V. Parking $10. **Amenities:** 4 restaurants; 3 lounges; 3 outdoor pools; health club; whirlpool; children's programs; game room; concierge; shopping arcade; room service; babysitting; laundry/dry-cleaning service. *In room:* A/C, TV, dataport, minibar, coffeemaker, hair dryer, safe.

Paradise Pier Hotel ★ *Kids*   The whimsical beach boardwalk theme of this 15-story, 65-acre resort hotel ties in with the Paradise Pier section of Disney's California Adventure park across the street—it even has it's own private entrance to California Adventure via your Paradise Pier Hotel room key (though you have to cross the street to get there). We only recommend this smallest Disney property if the other two are booked—it's not as "magical" as the original Disneyland Hotel and is soundly trounced by the superlative Grand Californian. It's also not as centrally located as the other two hotels, which could be a problem if you're not fond of walking. It does, however, have excellent programs for kids, including breakfast with Minnie & Friends—featuring songs, storytelling, and table-side visits—at the hotel's **PCH Grill.** Kids even get to make their own pizzas. As a guest you also have full access to the pools and other perks at the other two

Disney hotels. *Tip:* Request a room that either overlooks the Paradise Pier section of California Adventure or has direct access to the poolside cabanas.

1717 S. Disneyland Dr., Anaheim, CA 92802. ⓒ **714/956-MICKEY**. Reservations fax 714/956-6582. www. disneyland.com. 489 units. $170–$310 double; from $265 suite. AE, MC, V. Parking $10. **Amenities:** 2 restaurants; lounge; outdoor pool; fitness center; whirlpool; children's programs; game room; concierge; shopping arcade; room service; babysitting; laundry/dry-cleaning service. *In room:* A/C, TV w/pay movies, dataport, minibar, coffeemaker, hair dryer, safe.

Sheraton Anaheim Hotel ⚔   This hotel rises to the festive theme-park occasion with its fanciful English Tudor architecture; it's a castle that lures business conventions, Disney-bound families, and local high school proms. The public areas are quiet and elegant—intimate gardens with fountains and koi ponds, plush lobby and lounges—which can be a pleasing touch after a frantic day at the amusement park. The rooms are modern and unusually spacious but otherwise not distinctive. A large swimming pool sits in the center of the complex, surrounded by attractive landscaping. Don't be put off by the high rack rates; rooms commonly go for $100 to $130, even on busy summer weekends.

900 S. Disneyland Dr. (at I-5), Anaheim, CA 92802. ⓒ **800/331-7251** in California, 800/325-3535 in the U.S., or 714/778-1700. Fax 714/535-3889. www.sheratonanaheim.com. 489 units. $190–$225 double; $290–$360 suite. AE, DC, MC, V. Parking $10; free Disneyland shuttle. **Amenities:** 2 restaurants; lounge; outdoor pool; fitness center; whirlpool; concierge; 24-hr. room service; coin-op laundry; laundry/dry-cleaning service. *In room:* A/C, TV w/pay movies, dataport, minibar, coffeemaker, hair dryer, iron.

MODERATE

The Anabella Hotel ⚔   Uniting several formerly independent low-rise hotels across the street from Disney's California Adventure, the Anabella started from scratch, gutting each building to create carefully planned rooms for park-bound families and business travelers alike. The new complex features a vaguely Mission-style facade of whitewashed walls and red-tiled roofs, though guestroom interiors are strictly contemporary in style and modern in appointments. Bathrooms are generously sized and outfitted in honey-toned granite; most have a tub/shower combo—just a few are shower-only. Though parking areas dot the grounds, you'll also find a pleasant garden around the central swimming pool and whirlpool; a separate adult pool hides out next to the street-side fitness room. Business travelers will appreciate the in-room executive desks with high-speed Internet access, while families can take advantage of "kids suites" complete with bunk beds and separate bedrooms. There's a pleasant indoor-outdoor all-day restaurant, and the hotel is a stop on both the Disney and Convention Center shuttle routes. *Note:* Rooms and rates vary wildly in terms of room size, layout, and occupancy limits; extra time spent at the hotel's website and with the reservationist will pay off in the most comfortable room for your needs.

1030 W. Katella Ave., Anaheim, CA 92802. ⓒ **800/863-4888** or 714/905-1050. Fax 714/905-1054. www. anabellahotel.com. 360 units. $79–$299 double. AE, DC, DISC, MC, V. Free parking. **Amenities:** Restaurant; lounge; 2 outdoor heated pools; whirlpool; exercise room; nail salon; concierge; activities desk; business center; room service (7am–11pm); dry cleaning/laundry; self-service laundromat. *In room:* A/C; TV w/pay movies, Web TV, and PlayStation; dataport; fridge; coffeemaker; hair dryer; iron; safe.

Anaheim Plaza Hotel & Suites ⚔ *Value*   Although it's located across the street from Disneyland Resort's main gate, you'll appreciate the way this hotel's clever design shuts out the noisy world. In fact, the seven two-story garden buildings remind me more of 1960s Waikiki than busy Anaheim. The Olympic-size heated outdoor pool and whirlpool are unfortunately surrounded by Astroturf, and the plain motel-style furnishings are beginning to look a little tired. On the plus side, nothing's changed about the light-filled modern lobby, nor the friendly rates, which often drop as low as $49.

1700 S. Harbor Blvd., Anaheim, CA 92802. © **800/228-1357** or 714/772-5900. Fax 714/772-8386. www. anaheimplazahotel.com. 300 units. $79–$150 double; from $185 suite. Rates include continental breakfast. AE, DC, DISC, MC, V. Free parking and Disneyland shuttle. **Amenities:** Restaurant; lounge; outdoor pool; whirlpool; room service (8am–11pm); coin-op laundry; laundry/dry-cleaning service. *In room:* A/C, TV, coffeemaker.

Portofino Inn & Suites ★ *Kids*   Emerging from the rubble of the former Jolly Roger Hotel renovation, this complex of low- and high-rise all-suite buildings sports a yellow exterior and family-friendly interior—just in time for the expanded Disneyland Resort. The location couldn't be better—across the street from California Adventure's back side. You can either walk or take the ART (Anaheim Resort Transit) to the front gate. Designed to work as well for business travelers from the convention center as for Disney-bound families, the Portofino offers contemporary furnishings as well as vacation-friendly rates and suites for any family configuration. Families will want one of the "Kid's Suites," which feature bunk beds and sofa sleeper, plus TV, fridge, and microwave—and that's just in the kids' room; Mom and Dad have a separate bedroom with grown-up comforts like double vanity, shower massage, and their own TV.

1831 S. Harbor Blvd. (at Katella), Anaheim, CA 92802. © **800/482-8389** or 714/782-7600. Fax 714/782-7619. www.portofinoinnanaheim.com. 188 units. $94–$159 double; $109–$219 suite. Midweek, off-season, and other discounts available. AE, DC, DISC, MC, V. Free parking and Disneyland shuttle. **Amenities:** Restaurant; outdoor pool; fitness center; whirlpool; game room; tour desk; laundry/dry-cleaning service; coin-op laundry. *In room:* A/C, TV, dataport, coffeemaker, hair dryer, iron.

INEXPENSIVE

Best Western Anaheim Stardust Inn   Located on the back side of Disneyland, this modest hotel appeals to the budget-conscious traveler who isn't willing to sacrifice everything. All rooms have a refrigerator and microwave, breakfast is served in a refurbished train dining car, and you can relax by the large outdoor heated pool and spa while using the laundry room. The extra-large family rooms accommodate virtually any brood, and shuttles run regularly to the park.

1057 W. Ball Rd., Anaheim, CA 92802. © **800/222-6953** or 714/774-7600. Fax 714/535-6953. www.best western.com. 103 units. $64–$89 double; $105 family room. Rates include full breakfast. AE, DC, DISC, MC, V. Free parking and Disneyland shuttle. **Amenities:** Restaurant; outdoor pool; whirlpool; self-service laundry. *In room:* A/C, TV, fridge.

Candy Cane Inn ★★ *Value*   Take your standard U-shaped motel court with outdoor corridors, spruce it up with cobblestone drives and walkways, old-time street lamps, and flowering vines engulfing the balconies of attractively painted rooms, and you have the Candy Cane. The face-lift worked, making this gem near Disneyland's main gate a treat for the stylish bargain hunter. The rooms are decorated in floral motifs with comfortable furnishings, including queen beds and a separate dressing and vanity area. Breakfast is served in the courtyard, where you can also splash around in a heated pool, spa, or kids' wading pool.

1747 S. Harbor Blvd., Anaheim, CA 92802. © **800/345-7057** or 714/774-5284. Fax 714/772-1305. www.candycaneinn.net. 173 units. $84–$129 double. Rates include expanded continental breakfast. AAA discount available. AE, DC, DISC, MC, V. Free parking and Disneyland shuttle. **Amenities:** Outdoor pool; whirlpool; coin-op laundry; laundry/dry-cleaning service. *In room:* A/C, TV, coffeemaker, hair dryer.

WHERE TO DINE

There's nothing quite like an energetic family vacation to build an appetite, and sooner or later we'll all have to make the inevitable Disney dining decisions: where,

Value **Supercheap Sleeps**

When you simply must shave a few *more* dollars off the hotel tariff, try these bargain-priced chains within easy reach of Disneyland. The **Anaheim at the Park Travelodge**, 1166 W. Katella Ave. (© **800/578-7878** or 714/774-7817; www.travelodge.com), makes up for being a long walk from the resort (no shuttle) by offering regular rates of only $60 to $100—AAA members and seniors can stay for as low as $52. This basic chain motel does boast a nice swimming pool with separate whirlpool, kids' pool, and small playground. The **Super 8 Motel Near Disneyland**, 415 W. Katella Ave. (© **800/777-7123** or 714/778-6900), is a large, impersonal budget property 1 block from the resort. It's clean, basic, and functional, but little extras like a heated swimming pool help—so do the nice low room rates of $55 to $70 (AAA and senior discounts available).

when, and how much? The expanded Disneyland Resort has something for everyone, a respectable lineup that can easily meet your needs for the duration of the typical visit. Until recently, dining options were pretty sparse—limited to those inside Disneyland and some old standbys at the Disneyland Hotel. But Disney's big expansion upped the ante with national theme/concept restaurants along Downtown Disney, and newly competitive dining at the resort hotels. The best of the bunch are reviewed below.

EXPENSIVE

Granville's Steak House ★★ STEAKHOUSE   Located deep inside the Disneyland Hotel tower, this classic steakhouse specializes in thick-cut steaks and seafood in a men's-club-style ambience replete with dark-wood paneling, beveled glass, richly colored carpeting, and scenic paintings depicting the American Southwest. It's perfectly suited for meat-lovers with big appetites and a penchant for fine wines. Dinner starts with a loaf of sourdough bread on a cutting board, followed by a waitperson who brings a small display of the various cuts of beef available—porterhouse, filet mignon, New York—to your table and a chart to determine your particular taste for doneness. Although the prices are expensive—a meal for two will set you back about $150—the tender cuts are very generous, as are the classic steakhouse sides such as baked potatoes, creamed spinach, and Caesar salad. Granville's is also one of the few places where you can get a brief respite from the Disney theme; as such, it's not recommended for children. Dress is casual, though you may feel a bit out of place in your Mickey T-shirt.

1150 W. Magic Way (in the Disneyland Hotel). © **714/956-6755**; reservations 714/956-6755. www.disneyland. com. Reservations recommended. Main courses $24–$31. AE, DC, DISC, MC, V. Daily 5–10pm.

Napa Rose ★★★ CALIFORNIA   In the upscale Grand Californian Hotel, Napa Rose is the first really serious (read: on "foodie" radar) restaurant at the Disneyland Resort. Its warm and light dining room mirrors the Arts and Crafts style of the hotel, down to Frank Lloyd Wright stained-glass windows and Craftsman-inspired seating throughout the restaurant and adjoining lounge. Executive chef Andrew Sutton was lured away from the Napa Valley's chic Auberge du Soleil, bringing with him a Wine Country sensibility and passion for fresh California ingredients and inventive preparations. You can see him busy in the open exhibition kitchen, showcasing specialty items like Sierra golden trout, artisan cheeses from Humboldt County and the Gold Country, and the

Sonoma rabbit in Sutton's signature braised mushroom-rabbit tart. The tantalizing "Seven Sparkling Sins" starter platter (for two) features jewel-like portions of foie gras, caviar, oysters, lobster, and other exotic delicacies; the same attention to detail is evident in seasonally composed main-course standouts like grilled yellowtail with tangerine-basil fruit salsa atop savory couscous, or free-range veal *osso buco* in rich bacon-forest mushroom ragout. Leave room for dessert, to at least share one of pastry chef Jorge Sotelo's creative treats—our favorites are Sonoma goat-cheese flan with Riesling-soaked tropical fruit, and chocolate crepes with house-made caramelized banana ice cream. Napa Rose boasts an impressive and balanced wine list with 45 by-the-glass choices (and the most sommeliers of any restaurant in the world); and outdoor seating is arranged around a fire pit, gazing out across a landscaped arroyo toward California Adventure's Grizzly Peak. *Tip:* You can skip all the pomp and circumstance of a sit-down meal by dining at the restaurant's lounge, which offers full menu service.

1600 S. Disneyland Dr. (in Disney's Grand Californian Hotel). ✆ 714/300-7170. www.disneyland.com. Reservations strongly recommended. Main courses $12–$16 lunch, $19–$30 dinner. AE, DC, DISC, MC, V. Daily 11:30am–2pm and 5:30–10pm.

Yamabuki ★★ JAPANESE   Often ignored by all but their thriving clientele of Asian tourists and business folk—plus in-the-know expense-account suits from surrounding Orange County—Yamabuki has been tucked away for years in the low-profile former Pacific Hotel (now reinvented as Disney's Paradise Pier Hotel). With an upscale and quietly traditional Japanese aesthetic, Yamabuki—the name of a Japanese rose—has a rich interior of deep red lacquer, delicate porcelain vases, discreet teak shutters, and translucent rice-paper screens that together impart a sense of very un-Disney nobility. The staff is elegantly kimono-clad—even at lunch, when the fare includes casual bento boxes, lunch specials, and sushi/sashimi selections. At dinner, tradition demands a languorous procession of courses, from refreshing seafood starters and steaming noodle bowls to grilled teriyaki meats or table-cooked specialties like sukiyaki or *shabu shabu*. The menu, in Japanese and English, rates each dish as "contemporary," "traditional," or "very traditional," presenting the opportunity to try unusual squid, soybean, and pickled root dishes common in the East. If you're willing to spend the time—and the money—Yamabuki is a cultural trip across the globe.

1717 S. Disneyland Dr. (in Disney's Paradise Pier Hotel). ✆ 714/239-5683; reservations 714/956-6755. www.disneyland.com. Reservations recommended at dinner. Main courses $7.50–$11 lunch, $14–$30 dinner. AE, DC, DISC, MC, V. Mon–Fri 11:30am–2pm; daily 5:30–10pm.

MODERATE

Catal Restaurant/Uva Bar ★★ MEDITERRANEAN/TAPAS   Branching out from acclaimed Patina restaurant in Los Angeles, high-priest-of-cuisine Joachim Splichal brings us this Spanish-inspired Mediterranean concept duo at the heart of Downtown Disney. The main restaurant, Catal, features a series of intimate second-floor rooms that combine rustic Mediterranean charm with fine dining. Complemented by an international wine list, the menu is a collage of flavors that borrow from France, Spain, Italy, Greece, Morocco, and the Middle East—all united in selections that manage to be intriguing but not overwhelming. Though the menu will vary seasonally, expect to find selections that range from seared sea scallops over saffron risotto or chorizo-spiked Spanish paella to herb-marinated rotisserie chicken or Sicilian rigatoni with ricotta cheese.

Downstairs, the Uva Bar (*uva* means "grape" in Spanish) is a casual tapas bar offering 40 different wines by the glass in a pleasing outdoor pavilion setting. The affordable menu features the same Pan-Mediterranean influence, even offering many items from the Catal menu; standouts include cabernet-braised short ribs atop horseradish mashed potatoes, marinated olives and cured Spanish ham, and Andalusian gazpacho with rock shrimp.

1580 Disneyland Dr. (at Downtown Disney). ℭ **714/774-4442.** Reservations recommended Sun–Thurs, not accepted Fri–Sat (Catal); not accepted for Uva Bar. Main courses $14–$24; tapas $5–$8. AE, DC, DISC, MC, V. Mon–Thurs 11am–11pm; Fri–Sun 11am–midnight.

Goofy's Kitchen *(Kids* AMERICAN   Your younger kids will never forgive you if they miss an opportunity to dine with their favorite Disney characters at this colorful, lively restaurant inside the Disneyland Hotel. Known for its entertainment and wacky and off-center Toontown-esque decor, Goofy's Kitchen features tableside visits by costumed Disney characters from the classic era (Snow White, Mickey Mouse) to the new generation (Pocahontas, Buzz Lightyear), who thrill the youngsters with miniperformances, autograph signing, and up-close-and-personal encounters. Meals are buffet style and offer an adequate selection of crowd pleasers and standbys from bacon and eggs at breakfast to fried chicken, Caesar salad, deli sandwiches, and Italian pastas at lunch and dinner: This place isn't really about the food, though, and is *not* for kidless grownups (unless you're trying to make up for a deprived childhood). You'll also want to remember a camera for capturing the family's "candid" encounters.

1150 Magic Way (inside the Disneyland Hotel). ℭ **714/956-6755.** www.disneyland.com. Reservations recommended. Buffet prices (child/adult): $10/17 breakfast, $10/$18 lunch, $10/$27 dinner. AE, DC, DISC, MC, V. Daily 7am–9pm.

House of Blues *(* AMERICAN/SOUTHERN   For years fans have been comparing the House of Blues to Disneyland, so this celeb-backed restaurant/nightclub fits right into the Disney compound. Locations in Las Vegas, L.A., Orlando, and so forth all sport a calculated backwoods-bayou-meets-Country-Bear-Jamboree appearance that fits right into the Disneyfied world. The Anaheim HOB follows the formula, filled with made-to-look-old found objects, amateur paintings, uneven wood floors, seemingly decayed chandeliers, and a country-casual attitude. The restaurant features Delta-inspired stick-to-your-ribs cuisine like Louisiana crawfish cakes, Creole seafood jambalaya, cornmeal-crusted catfish, baby back ribs glazed with Jack Daniels sauce, and spicy Cajun meatloaf—plus some out-of-place Cal-lite stragglers like seared *ahi* and pesto pasta. Sunday's Gospel Brunch is an advance-ticket event of hand-clapping, foot-stomping proportions, and the adjacent Company Store offers logo ware interspersed with selected pieces of folk art. HOB's state-of-the-art Music Hall is a welcome addition to the local music scene (advance tickets are highly recommended for big-name bookings).

1530 S. Disneyland Dr. (at Downtown Disney). ℭ **714/778-2583.** www.hob.com. Reservations not accepted for restaurant (tickets required for performance). Main courses $8–$17. AE, DC, DISC, MC, V. Daily 11am–midnight (open from 10am Sun).

Naples Ristorante e Pizzeria *(* ITALIAN   The eye-catching entrance of this better-than-expected Italian concept eatery features a larger-than-life harlequin with an impish expression, wielding a pizza and beckoning you to step inside. Designed to be sophisticated enough for discerning palates while still appropriate for casual families, Naples features a colorful, high-ceilinged dining

---

(*Tips* **Join the Zone**

Sports fans may prefer to dine at the **ESPN Zone** in Downtown Disney, 1545 Disneyland Dr. (℃ **714/300-ESPN;** www.espnzone.com). More than 175 TV monitors allow you to watch just about every current sporting event in the U.S. while dining on American grill food and pub fare.

---

room filled with padded love seats and comfy chairs. Busy chefs work the white-tiled open kitchen's wood-burning oven, while a floor-to-ceiling cherrywood bar anchors the other side of the room. Naples also boasts some of the most scenic outdoor seating in Downtown Disney—request a patio table when reserving. At dinner you can also opt for the quieter ambience of the upstairs dining room. Piedmontese executive chef Corrado Gionatti is a master of the thin-crust Neapolitan pizza and uses an appropriately light hand saucing the menu's selection of pastas. Salads, antipasti, and calzones round out the menu; everything is very good, and—be forewarned—portions are quite large.

1550 Disneyland Dr. (at Downtown Disney). ℃ **714/776-6200.** Reservations strongly recommended. Main courses $11–$16. AE, DC, DISC, MC, V. Daily 11am–11pm.

Rainforest Cafe *Kids* INTERNATIONAL   Designed to suggest ancient temple ruins in an overgrown Central American jungle, this national chain favorite combines entertainment, retail, and family-friendly dining in one fantasy setting. There are waterfalls inside and out, a canopy of lush vegetation, simulated tropical mists, and even a troupe of colorful parrots beckoning shoppers into the "Retail Village." Once seated, diners choose from an amalgam of wildly flavored dishes inspired by Caribbean, Polynesian, Latin, Asian, and Mediterranean cuisines. Masquerading under exotic-sounding names like "Jungle Safari Soup" (a meaty version of minestrone) and "Mojo Bones" (barbecued pork ribs), the food is really fairly familiar: a translated sampling includes Cobb salad, pita sandwiches, potstickers, shrimp-studded pasta, and charbroiled chicken. Fresh-fruit smoothies and tropical specialty cocktails are offered, as well as a best-shared dessert called "Giant Chocolate Volcano." After your meal, you can browse through logo items, environmentally educational toys and games, stuffed jungle animals and puppets, straw safari hats, and other themed souvenirs in the lobby store. There's a children's menu, and the Rainforest Cafe is one of the few Downtown Disney eateries to have full breakfast service.

1515 S. Disneyland Dr. (at Downtown Disney). ℃ **714/772-0413.** www.rainforestcafe.com. Reservations recommended for peak mealtimes. Main courses $9–$21. AE, DC, DISC, MC, V. Sun–Thurs 7am–11pm; Fri–Sat 7am–midnight.

Ralph Brennan's Jazz Kitchen ✦ CAJUN-CREOLE   If you always thought Disneyland's New Orleans Square was just like the real thing, wait till you see this authentically Southern concept restaurant at Downtown Disney. Ralph Brennan, of the New Orleans food dynasty responsible for NOLA landmarks like Commander's Palace and a trio of Big Easy hot spots, commissioned a handful of New Orleans artists to create the handcrafted furnishings that give the Jazz Kitchen its believable French Quarter ambience. Lacy wrought-iron grillwork, cascading ferns, and trickling stone fountains enhance three separate dining choices: The upstairs Carnival Club is an elegant dining salon with silk-draped chandeliers and terrace dining that overlooks the "street scene" below; casual

Flambeaux is downstairs, where a bead-encrusted grand piano hints at the nightly live jazz that sizzles in this room; and the Creole Cafe is a quick stop for necessities like muffulettas or beignets. Expect traditional Cajun-Creole fare with heavy-handed seasonings and rich, heart-stopping sauces—now *that's* authentically New Orleans.

1590 S. Disneyland Dr. (at Downtown Disney). © **714/776-5200**. www.rbjazzkitchen.com. Reservations strongly recommended. Main courses $16–$25 (cafe items $4–$8). AE, DC, DISC, MC, V. Daily 11am–3pm and 5–11pm.

INEXPENSIVE

La Brea Bakery Express & Cafe BAKERY/MEDITERRANEAN   Fresh from the ovens of L.A.'s now-nationally known artisan bakery, this La Brea Bakery duo occupies a coveted position at the beginning of Downtown Disney, right across from the theme parks' ticket kiosks. Each morning still-groggy early-bird park-goers stumble from the parking-lot tram and head straight to La Brea's cafeteria-style Express for a caffeinated pick-me-up or a meal to start the day—light breakfast items are served in addition to creator Nancy Silverton's irresistible breads and pastries. The outdoor patio is comfortably outfitted with woven bistro chairs (plus heat lamps for brisk mornings), and provides a relaxing setting before braving the Disney throngs. Throughout the day, folks stop in for a lunch of sandwiches, filled brioche, or herb-laden focaccia—the kids' menu offers less-grown-up choices like grilled cheese and PB&J.

Beginning at lunchtime, the next-door Cafe joins the team with sit-down meals, complete with wine-by-the-glass selections. Sporting an airy, warm-wood gallery-like setting, the small bistro also features a few outdoor tables alongside the Downtown Disney footpath. Entrees feature the Mediterranean flavors popularized at Silverton's (with husband Mark Peel) acclaimed Campanile restaurant, and range from the lighter side (seared salmon or ahi) to a hearty lamb/sirloin/sausage stew atop creamy polenta.

1556 Disneyland Dr. (at Downtown Disney). © **714/490-0233**. www.labreabakery.com. Reservations recommended for Cafe. Light fare under $5 (Express); main courses $10–$20 (Cafe). AE, DISC, MC, V. Daily 8am–11pm (Express), 11am–11pm (Cafe).

5 Knott's Berry Farm

30 miles SE of downtown L.A.

Although destined to always be in the shadow of Mickey's megaresort, the reality is that Knott's doesn't even attempt to compete with the Disney empire, but instead targets Southern California thrill-seekers (droves of them) by offering a far better selection of scream-inducing thrill rides.

Like Disneyland, Knott's Berry Farm is not without historical background. In 1920 Walter Knott began farming 20 acres of leased land on Highway 39 (now Beach Blvd.). When things got tough during the Depression, Mrs. Knott set up a roadside stand, selling pies, preserves, and home-cooked chicken dinners. Within a year she was selling 90 meals a day. Lines became so long that Walter decided to create an Old West Ghost Town—America's first theme park—in 1940 as a diversion for waiting customers.

Today Knott's amusement park offers a whopping 165 shows, attractions, and state-of-the-art rides that are far more intense than most rides at the Disneyland Resort. Granted, it's less than half the size of the Disney Resort and doesn't have nearly the magical appeal of Disneyland, but if you're more into fast-paced amusement rides than swirling tea cups, spend your money here.

ESSENTIALS
GETTING THERE
Knott's Berry Farm is at 8039 Beach Blvd. in Buena Park. It's about a 10-minute ride north on I-5 from Disneyland. From I-5 or Calif. 91, exit south onto Beach Boulevard. The park is about half a mile south of Calif. 91.

VISITOR INFORMATION
The **Buena Park Convention and Visitors Office,** 6601 Beach Blvd., Suite 200, Buena Park (© **800/541-3953** or 714/562-3560; www.buenapark.com/cvo), provides specialized information on the area, including Knott's Berry Farm. To learn more about the amusement park before you arrive, call © 714/220-5200 or log on to **www.knotts.com.**

ADMISSION PRICES & OPERATING HOURS
Admission to the park, including unlimited access to all rides, shows, and attractions, is $43 for adults and children 12 and over; $33 for seniors 60 or better, nonambulatory visitors, and expectant mothers; $13 for kids 3 to 11; and children under 3 are admitted free. Admission after 4pm (on any day the park is open past 6pm) is $22 for adults and seniors 60 or better and $13 for kids 3 to 11. Parking is $8. Tickets can also be purchased at many Southern California hotels, where discount coupons are sometimes available.

Like Disneyland, Knott's offers discounted admission—$35 for adults and again just $13 for kids 3 to 11—for Southern California residents with zip codes 90000 through 93599, so if you're bringing local friends or family members along, try to take advantage of the bargain. Also like Disneyland, Knott's Berry Farm's hours vary from week to week so call ahead. The park generally is open during the summer daily from 9am to midnight. The rest of the year, it opens at 10am and closes at 6 or 8pm, except Saturday, when it stays open until 10pm. Knott's is closed December 25. Special hours and prices are in effect during Knott's Scary Farm in October. Stage shows and special activities are scheduled throughout the day. Pick up a schedule at the ticket booth.

TOURING THE PARK
Despite all the high-tech multimillion-dollar rides, Knott's Berry Farm still maintains much of its original Old West motif, and also features the Peanuts gang: Snoopy, Charlie Brown, Woodstock, and pals are the official costumed characters of Knott's. The park is divided into six themed areas, each one of which features at least one of the thrill roller coasters that are Knott's claim to fame. The California MarketPlace is located adjacent to, but outside of, the theme park, featuring 14 unique shops and restaurants including the original favorite, Mrs. Knott's Chicken Dinner Restaurant.

GHOST TOWN
The park's original attraction is a collection of authentic 19th-century buildings relocated from deserted Old West towns in Arizona and California. You can pan for gold, ride an authentic stagecoach, take rickety train cars through the Calico Mine, and get held up aboard the Calico Railroad. If you love wooden roller coasters, don't miss the clackity GhostRider.

Calico Railroad   Board this 1881 narrow-gauge steam-engine train—once part of the Denver and Rio Grande Southern Line—for a round-trip tour of half the theme park, interrupted by "bandit" holdups.

Ghost Town Artisans ✸   An entertaining holdover from the earliest days of the park, these living-history booths present old-time crafts and tall tales presented by costumed blacksmiths, woodcarvers, a spinner, and storytellers who help bring Ghost Town to life for curious kids and history buffs.

GhostRider ✸✸✸   Looming 118 feet high, this coaster is the single largest attraction in park history and one of the longest and tallest wooden roller coasters in the world. Riders enter through a replica mine and are strapped into gold-, silver-, or copper-mining cars for an adventure that twists and careens through sudden dips, banked turns, and cheek-flattening G-forces. The ride isn't nearly as smooth and quiet as the steel roller coasters, and that's part of the thrill. Worldwide coaster enthusiasts worship this classic ride.

Silver Bullet ✸✸   Brand-new in 2005, this inverted coaster dangles riders from the steel track that weaves its way through the center of the park. Flying over Reflection Lake from the edge of the stagecoach stop to the top of the Log Ride mountain at a height of 146 feet, this high-speed thriller sends riders head over heels six times with cobra rolls, spirals, corkscrews, and other twists.

Timber Mountain Log Ride ✸   Riders emerge from a dark, twisting "sawmill" waterway and plummet down a 42-foot flume for the grand splash. Compared to the other water rides in the park, this one leaves you only slightly sprinkled.

Wild West Stunt Show   This wild and woolly stunt spectacular is a salute to the Old West presented throughout the day in the open-air Wagon Camp Theater.

FIESTA VILLAGE

Here you'll find a south-of-the-border theme—festive markets and an ambience that suggests old Spanish California. A cluster of carnival-style rides (in addition to the roller coasters listed below) includes a 100-year-old merry-go-round, plus Knott's version of Disneyland's Tea Cups, where you can sit-and-spin your own sombrero. You can stroll the paths of Fiesta Village, which are lined with old-time carnival games and state-of-the-art electric arcades.

Jaguar! ✸✸   Loosely themed around a jungle setting, this roller coaster includes two heart-in-the-mouth drops and a view of Fiesta Village from high above. It's a good family roller coaster for first-timers or the easily frightened.

La Revolucion ✸   A real stomach-churner, this new ride both spins you in circles while swinging back and forth more than 65 feet in the air. It's like being in the rinse cycle of a washing machine that's swinging from a rope.

Montezooma's Revenge ✸   Blasting from 0 to 60 mph in 5 seconds, this not-for-the-fainthearted thriller then propels riders through a giant 360-degree loop both forward and backward.

THE BOARDWALK

The park's most recently added area is a salute to Southern California's beach culture, where colorful architecture and palm trees are the backdrop for a trio of thrill rides. Other amusements include arcade and boardwalk games, the **Dinosaur Discover Center,** and the **Charles M. Schulz Theatre,** where seasonal productions include a Snoopy ice show or holiday pageant (check the marquee or park entertainment schedule for show times).

Boomerang ✸   This corkscrew scream machine sends you twisting through three head-over-heels loops in less than a minute—but it doesn't end there, since you're sent through the track again . . . backwards.

Kingdom of the Dinosaurs Go back in time with this attraction featuring extremely realistic *Jurassic Park*–like creatures.

Lazer Invaders In this adaptation of the classic "Lazer Runner," participants equipped with phasers and fiber-optic vests battle for supremacy in a richly evocative atmosphere. Each combatant must make use of protective walls and laser power to vanquish opponents.

Perilous Plunge 🎡🎡 Just 34 feet shorter than Niagara Falls, this wet adventure sends riders to a height of 127 feet and then drops them down a 115-foot water chute at a 75-degree angle—15 degrees from a sheer vertical. Prepare for a thorough soaking (a boon on hot days, but best experienced before nightfall).

Sky Cabin 🎡 Just when you were thinking all the rides were for hard-core adrenaline-seekers (most are, actually), this quiet ride offers the same spectacular views at a calmer pace. The slowly rotating "cabin" ascends Knott's vertical tower, providing panoramic views of the park and surrounding area.

Supreme Scream 🎡🎡 They could've called this one the "Evil Elevator"— seated and fully exposed riders are hoisted straight up a 30-story tower with their feet dangling in the air, then held at the top just long enough to rattle the nerves before plunging downward faster than gravity at more than 60 mph. The whole descent only takes a bowel-shaking 3 seconds. It's one of the tallest (and most unnerving) thrill rides in the world.

Xcelerator 🎡🎡🎡 It's scary just looking at this stomach-churner. One of the resort's newest attractions, this super-high-tech 1950s-themed roller coaster launches you from 0 to 82 mph in 2.3 seconds, then whips you straight up 20 stories (with a half twist thrown in for added addling) and almost straight back down again. It's like riding on the outer edge of a gigantic paperclip.

CAMP SNOOPY

This will probably be the youngsters' favorite area. The first-ever theme park area dedicated solely for kids, it's meant to re-create a wilderness camp in the High Sierras. Six rustic acres are the playgrounds of Charles Schulz's beagle and his pals Charlie Brown and Lucy, who greet guests and pose for pictures. There are over a dozen rides in the Camp; several kid-size rides are made especially for the younger set, while the entire family can enjoy others. Scaled-down stock cars, locomotives, steamboats, 18-wheeler semis, hot-air balloons, and even the Peanuts gang's school bus give kids a playland of their own. There's also a child-size version of Supreme Scream, called Woodstock's Airmail, and Joe Cool's GR8 SK8, a mini–thrill ride for the whole family. Interactive attractions include the new **Camp Snoopy Theatre** starring the Peanuts gang (little kids are transfixed by this show).

WILD WATER WILDERNESS

This $10-million, 3½-acre area is styled like a turn-of-the-20th-century California wilderness park with a raging white-water river, cascading waterfalls, soaring geysers, and old-style ranger stations.

Bigfoot Rapids 🎡🎡 The centerpiece of Wild Water Wilderness is this outdoor white-water river raft ride, the longest of its kind in the world. Climb aboard a six-seat circular raft, and prepare to be bounced, buffeted, tossed, spun, and splashed along fast-moving currents, under cascading waterfalls, and around soaring geysers. Let there be no doubt: You will get *extremely* wet on this one.

Mystery Lodge 🎡🎡 This amazing high-tech, trick-of-the-eye tribute to the magic of Native American storytelling is a theater attraction for the whole

> ### (Tips Getting Soaked at Knott's
>
> Surf's up at **Knott's Soak City U.S.A.**, a 13-acre water park next door to Knott's Berry Farm. Water thrill-seekers of all ages can get soaked on 21 water rides and attractions, to the theme of surf woodies and long boards of the 1950s Southern California coast. The fun includes tube and body slides, speed slides, an artificial wave lagoon, and an area for youngsters with their own pool and beach-shack fun house. The park is at 8039 Buena Park (© **714/220-5200;** www.knotts.com/soakcity/oc/index.shtml), and admission prices are $25 for adults, $13 for kids 3 to 11, and free for children under 3; parking is $8. Ask about promotions and discount coupons (or check the website). The park is open weekends in May and September, then daily between Memorial Day and Labor Day. Soak City U.S.A. opens at 10am and closes between 6 and 8pm, based on the season.

family. The "Old Storyteller" takes the audience on a mystical, multisensory journey into the culture of local tribes by employing centuries-old legends passed down through oral history.

INDIAN TRAILS

Explore the ride-free Indian Trails cultural area, which offers daily demonstrations of native dance and music by authentically costumed Native American and Aztec dancers, singers, and musicians performed in the round on the Indian Trails stage. In addition, the compound showcases a variety of traditional Native American structures from the Pacific Northwest, Great Plains, and Southwest. The area includes four towering totem poles, standing from 15 to 27 feet high; three authentic tepees, representing the Arapaho, Blackfoot, and Nez Perce tribes; and more. The arts and crafts of Native American tribes from the western part of North America are also demonstrated and displayed. While exploring Indian Trails, visitors can enjoy a sampling of Native American foods, including Navajo tacos, Indian fry bread, and fresh-roasted ears of corn.

WHERE TO STAY

Radisson Resort Knott's Berry Farm (Kids) Within walking distance of Knott's Berry Farm, this spit-shined Radisson also offers a free shuttle to Disneyland, 7 miles away. The pristine lobby has the look of a business-oriented hotel, and that it is. But vacationers can also benefit from the elevated level of service. Ask about "Super Saver" rates, plus Knott's or Disneyland package deals. The rooms in the nine-story tower were tastefully redecorated recently. Doting parents can even treat their kids to a Peanuts-themed room with Snoopy tuck-in service and "Camp Kids" bedtime stories via the in-room phone by the bed. There's also a family pool with children's water-play structure and arcade.

7675 Crescent Ave. (at Grand), Buena Park, CA 90620. © **800/333-3333** or 714/995-1111. Fax 714/828-8590. www.radisson.com/buenaparkca. 320 units. $159 standard; $199 suite. Discount packages available. DC, DISC, MC, V. Free parking and Disneyland shuttle. **Amenities:** 2 restaurants; lounge; outdoor pool; 2 outdoor tennis and basketball courts (lit for night play); fitness center; whirlpool; video arcade; concierge; 24-hr. room service; self-service laundry; laundry/dry-cleaning service. *In room:* A/C, TV w/pay movies, fax, dataport, coffeemaker, hair dryer, iron, safe, bathrobes, video games.

WHERE TO DINE

Mrs. Knott's Chicken Dinner Restaurant (Kids) AMERICAN   Knott's Berry Farm got its start as a roadside diner in 1934, and you can still get a filling—albeit unhealthy—all-American meal without even entering the theme park. Cordelia Knott's down-home cooking was so popular that her husband created a few humble attractions to amuse their patrons. Today more than 1.5 million annual patrons line up around the building to experience Cordelia's original recipe (very similar to the Colonel's, I must admit), served by sweet waitresses in a facility built more for comfort than speed. Looking just as you'd expect—country cute, with window shutters, old black-and-white photos of the original diner, and calico prints aplenty—the restaurant's featured attraction is the original fried chicken dinner, complete with soup, salad, warm buttermilk biscuits, mashed potatoes and chicken gravy, and a slice of famous pie (the boysenberry pie is fantastic). Country fried steak, pot roast, roast turkey, and pork ribs are options, as well as sandwiches, salads, and a terrific chicken potpie. Boysenberries abound, from breakfast jam to traditional double-crust pies, and there's even an adjacent takeout shop that's always crowded. If you're not visiting the amusement park, park in the lot that offers 3 free hours.

8039 Beach Blvd. (near La Palma), Buena Park. ℂ **714/220-5080.** Reservations not accepted. Main courses $7–$10; complete dinners $13. DC, DISC, MC, V. Daily 7am–11pm.

6 The Orange Coast

Seal Beach is 36 miles S of Los Angeles; Newport Beach, 49 miles; Dana Point, 65 miles

Whatever you do, don't say "Orange County" here. The mere name evokes images of smoggy industrial parks, cookie-cutter housing developments, and the staunch Republicanism that prevails behind the so-called "orange curtain." We're talking instead about the Orange Coast, one of Southern California's best-kept secrets—a string of seaside jewels that have been compared with the French Riviera or the Costa del Sol. Forty-two miles of beaches offer pristine stretches of sand, tide pools teeming with marine life, ecological preserves, secluded coves, picturesque pleasure-boat harbors, and legendary surf breaks. My advice? Make it a day trip from L.A.—hit the road early for a scenic cruise down the PCH, stop for lunch at Laguna Beach (the prettiest of all the SoCal beach towns), continue south to Dana Point where the *really* expensive resorts reside, then take the freeway back to L.A. (I-5 to the I-405).

ESSENTIALS

GETTING THERE See "Getting There" in chapter 2 for airport and airline information. By car from Los Angeles, take I-5 or I-405 south. The scenic, shore-hugging Pacific Coast Highway (Calif. 1, or just PCH to the locals) links the Orange Coast communities from Seal Beach in the north to Capistrano Beach just south of Dana Point, where it merges with I-5. To reach the beach communities directly, take the following freeway exits: **Seal Beach,** Seal Beach Boulevard from I-405; **Huntington Beach,** Beach Boulevard/Calif. 39 from either I-405 or I-5; **Newport Beach,** Calif. 55 from either I-405 or I-5; **Laguna Beach,** Calif. 133 from I-5; **San Juan Capistrano,** Ortega Highway/Calif. 74 from I-5; and **Dana Point,** Pacific Coast Highway/Calif. 1 from I-5.

VISITOR INFORMATION The **Seal Beach Chamber of Commerce,** 201 Eighth St., Suite 120, next to City Hall (ℂ **562/799-0179;** www.sealbeach chamber.com), is open Monday through Friday from 10am to 4pm.

The **Huntington Beach Conference & Visitors Bureau,** 301 Main St., Suite 208 (ℂ **800/729-6232** or 714/969-3492; www.hbvisit.com), enthusiastically offers tons of information and personal anecdotes. Open Monday through Friday from 9am to 5pm.

Anaheim Area & Orange Coast Attractions

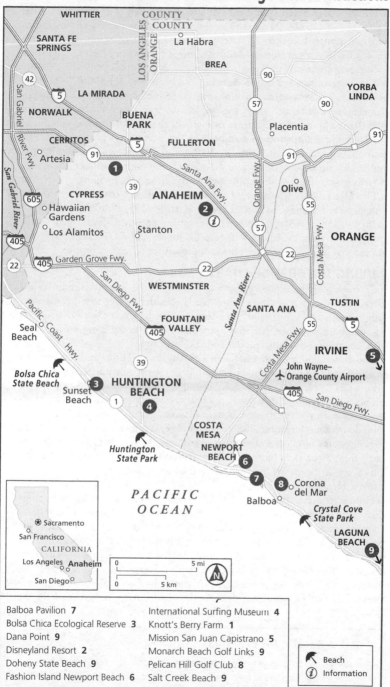

Balboa Pavilion **7**
Bolsa Chica Ecological Reserve **3**
Dana Point **9**
Disneyland Resort **2**
Doheny State Beach **9**
Fashion Island Newport Beach **6**

International Surfing Museum **4**
Knott's Berry Farm **1**
Mission San Juan Capistrano **5**
Monarch Beach Golf Links **9**
Pelican Hill Golf Club **8**
Salt Creek Beach **9**

Beach
Information

The **Newport Beach Conference & Visitors Bureau,** 110 Newport Center Dr., Suite 120 (© **800/94-COAST** or 949/719-6100; www.newportbeach-cvb. com), distributes brochures, sample menus, a calendar of events, and the free *Visitor's Guide.* Call or stop in Monday through Friday from 8am to 5pm (plus weekends in summer).

The **Laguna Beach Visitors Bureau,** 252 Broadway (© **800/877-1115** or 949/497-9229; www.lagunabeachinfo.org), is in the heart of town and distributes lodging, dining, and art gallery guides. It's open Monday through Friday from 9am to 5pm and on Saturday from 10am to 4pm (plus Sun in summer).

The **San Juan Capistrano Chamber of Commerce,** Franciscan Plaza, 31781 Camino Capistrano, Suite 306 (© **949/493-4700;** www.sanjuancapistrano. com), is within walking distance of the Mission and offers a walking-tour guide to historic sites. Open Monday through Friday from 9am to 5pm.

The **Dana Point Chamber of Commerce Visitor Center,** located in the Clocktower Building at the LaPlaza Center (© **800/290-DANA** or 949/496-1555; www.danapoint-chamber.com), is open Monday through Friday from 9am to 5pm, closed noon to 1pm for lunch, and carries some restaurant and lodging information as well as a comprehensive recreation brochure.

DRIVING THE ORANGE COAST

You'll most likely be exploring the coast by car, so the beach communities are covered in order, from north to south. Keep in mind, however, that if you're traveling between Los Angeles and San Diego, the Pacific Coast Highway (Calif. 1) is a breezy scenic detour that adds less than an hour to the commute—so pick out a couple of seaside destinations and take your time.

Seal Beach, on the border between Los Angeles and Orange counties and a neighbor to Long Beach's Naples Harbor, is geographically isolated by both the adjacent U.S. Naval Weapons Station and the self-contained Leisure World retirement community. As a result, the beach town appears untouched by modern development—it's Orange County's version of small-town America. Take a stroll down Main Street for a walk back in time, culminating in the Seal Beach Pier. Although the clusters of sunbathing, squawking seals that gave the town its name aren't around any more, old-timers still fish, lovers still stroll, and families still cavort by the seaside, enjoying great food and retail shops or having a cold drink at Hennessey's tavern.

Huntington Beach—or "Surf City" as it's known—is the largest Orange Coast city; it stretches quite a ways inland and has seen the most urbanization. To some extent this has changed the old boardwalk and pier to a modern outdoor mall where cliques of teens coexist with families and the surfers who continue to flock here, drawn by Huntington's legendary place in surf lore. Hawaiian-born George Freeth is credited with bringing the sport here in 1907, and some say the breaks around the pier and Bolsa Chica are the best in California. The world's top wave riders flock to Huntington each August for the

---

Tips **A Special Arts Festival**

A tradition for 60-plus years in arts-friendly Laguna, the **Festival of Arts & Pageant of the Masters** is held each summer throughout July and August. It's pretty large now, and it includes the formerly "alternative" Sawdust Festival across the street. For more information, log on to www.foapom.com.

rowdy but professional **U.S. Open of Surfing.** If you're around at Christmastime, try to see the gaily decorated marina homes and boats in Huntington Harbor by taking the **Cruise of Lights,** a 45-minute narrated sail through and around the harbor islands. The festivities generally last from mid-December until Christmas; call ℂ **714/840-7542** for schedules and ticket information.

The name **Newport Beach** conjures comparisons to Rhode Island's Newport, where the well-to-do enjoy seaside living with all the creature comforts. That's the way it is here, too, but on a less grandiose scale. From the million-dollar Cape Cod–style cottages on sunny Balboa Island to elegant shopping complexes like Fashion Island and South Coast Plaza (an über-mall with valet parking, car detailing, limo service, and concierge), this is where fashionable socialites, right-wing celebrities, and business mavens can all be found. Alternatively, you could explore **Balboa Peninsula**'s historic Pavilion and old-fashioned pier or board a passenger ferry to Catalina Island.

Laguna Beach, whose geography is marked by bold elevated headlands, coastal bluffs, pocket coves, and a very inviting beach, is known as an artists' enclave, but the truth is that Laguna has became so "in" (read: expensive) that it's driven most of the true bohemians out. Their legacy remains with the annual **Festival of Arts and Pageant of the Masters** (see "A Special Arts Festival," above), as well as a proliferation of galleries mingling with high-priced boutiques along the town's streets. In warm weather, Laguna Beach has an overwhelming Mediterranean-island ambience, which makes *everyone* feel beautifully, idly rich.

San Juan Capistrano, in the verdant headlands inland from Dana Point, is defined by Spanish Missions and its loyal swallows. The Mission architecture is authentic, and history abounds. Think of San Juan Capistrano as a compact, life-size diorama illustrating the evolution of a small Western town—from Spanish-Mission era to rancho period, statehood, and into the 21st century. Surprisingly, Mission San Juan Capistrano (see "Seeing the Sights," below) is once again the center of the community, just as the founding friars intended 200 years ago.

Dana Point, the last town south, has been called a "marina development in search of a soul." Overlooking the harbor stands a monument to 19th-century author Richard Henry Dana, who gave his name to the area and described it in *Two Years Before the Mast.* Activities generally center on yachting and Dana Point's beautiful harbor. Nautical themes are everywhere, particularly the streets named for old-fashioned shipboard lights—a hodgepodge that includes Street of the Amber Lantern, Street of the Violet Lantern, Street of the Golden Lantern, and so on. Bordering the harbor is Doheny State Beach (see "Beaches & Nature Preserves," below), which wrote the book on seaside park and camping facilities.

ENJOYING THE OUTDOORS

BEACHES & NATURE PRESERVES   The **Bolsa Chica Ecological Reserve,** in Huntington Beach (ℂ **714/846-1114**), is a 900-acre restored urban salt marsh that's a haven to more than 200 bird species, as well as a wide variety of plants and animals. Naturalists come to spot herons and egrets as well as California horn snails, jackknife clams, sea sponges, common jellyfish, and shore crabs. An easy 1.5-mile loop trail begins from a parking lot on the Pacific Coast Highway (Calif. 1) a mile south of Warner Boulevard; docents lead a narrated walk the first Saturday of every month. The trail heads inland, over Inner Bolsa Bay and up Bolsa Chica bluffs. It then loops back toward the ocean over a dike that separates the Inner and Outer Bolsa bays and traverses a sand-dune system. This beautiful hike is a terrific afternoon adventure. The Bolsa Chica Conservancy has been working since 1978 on reclaiming the wetlands from oil companies that began drilling here 70 years ago. It's an ongoing process, and you can still see those "see-saw" drills dotting the outer areas of the reserve. *Tip:* Free wetland tours are given the first Saturday of the month from 9 to 10:30am.

Huntington City Beach, adjacent to Huntington Pier, is a haven for volley-ball players and surfers; dense crowds abound, but so do amenities like outdoor showers, beach rentals, and restrooms. Just south of the city beach is 3-mile-long **Huntington State Beach.** Both popular beaches have lifeguards and concession stands seasonally. The state beach also has restrooms, showers, barbecue pits, and a waterfront bike path. The main entrance is on Beach Boulevard, and there are access points all along the Pacific Coast Highway (Calif. 1).

Newport Beach runs for about 5 miles and includes both Newport and Balboa piers. It has outdoor showers, restrooms, volleyball nets, and a vintage boardwalk that just may make you feel as though you've stepped 50 years back in time. **Balboa Bike and Beach Stuff** (℃ 949/723-1516), at the corner of Balboa and Palm near the pier, rents a variety of items, from pier-fishing poles to bikes, beach umbrellas, and body boards. The **Southwind Kayak Center,** 17855 Sky Park Circle, Irvine (℃ **800/768-8494** or 949/261-0200; www. southwindkayaks.com), rents sea kayaks for use in the bay or open ocean at rates starting at $40 per day; instructional classes are available on weekends, with some midweek classes in summer. The center also conducts several easy-going guided outings, including a $55 "Back to Nature" trip that highlights the marine life around Dana Point.

Crystal Cove State Park, which covers 3 miles of coastline between Corona del Mar and Laguna Beach and extends into the hills around El Moro Canyon, is a good alternative to the more popular beaches for seekers of solitude. (There are, however, lifeguards and restrooms.) The beach is a winding, sandy strip, backed with grassy terraces; high tide sometimes sections it into coves. The entire area offshore is an underwater nature preserve. There are four entrances, includ-ing Pelican Point and El Moro Canyon. For information, call ℃ **949/494-3539.**

Salt Creek Beach Park lies below the palatial Ritz-Carlton Laguna Niguel; guests who tire of the pristine swimming pool can venture down the staircase on Ritz-Carlton Drive to wiggle their toes in the sand. The setting is spectacular, with wide white-sand beaches looking out toward Catalina Island (why do you think the Ritz-Carlton was built here?). The park has lifeguards, restrooms, a snack bar, and convenient parking near the hotel.

Doheny State Beach in Dana Point, just south of lovely Dana Point Marina (enter off Del Abispo St.), has long been known as a premier surfing spot and camping site. Doheny has the friendly vibe of beach parties in days gone by: Tree-shaded lawns give way to wide beaches, and picnicking and beach camping are encouraged. There are 121 sites that can be used for either tents or RVs, plus a state-run visitor center featuring several small aquariums of sea and tide-pool life. For more information and camping availability, call ℃ **949/492-0802.**

BICYCLING Biking is the most popular beach activity up and down the coast. A slower-paced alternative to driving, it allows you to enjoy the clean, fresh air and notice smaller details of these laid-back beach towns and harbors. The Newport Beach visitor center (see "Visitor Information," above) offers a free *Bike Ways* map of trails throughout the city and harbor. Bikes and equip-ment can be rented at **Balboa Bike & Beach Stuff,** 601 Balboa Blvd., Newport Beach (℃ **949/723-1516**), and **Laguna Beach Cyclery,** 240 Thalia St. (℃ **949/ 494-1522;** www.lagunacyclery.net).

GOLF   Many golf course architects have used the geography of the Orange Coast to its full advantage, molding challenging and scenic courses from the rolling bluffs. Most courses are private, but two outstanding ones are open to the public. **The Links at Monarch Beach,** 33033 Niguel Rd., Dana Point (© **949/ 240-8247**), is particularly impressive. This hilly, challenging course, designed by Robert Trent Jones, Jr., offers great ocean views. Afternoon winds can sneak up, so accuracy is essential. Weekend greens fees are $185 ($160 weekdays). After 1pm rates drop to $125 weekends and $99 weekdays.

Another challenge is the **Pelican Hill Golf Club,** 22651 Pelican Hill Rd. S., Newport Beach (© **949/760-0707** to reserve a tee time; www.pelicanhill.com), with two Tom Fazio–designed courses. The Ocean North course is heavily bunkered, while the Ocean South course features canyons and ravines; both have large, multitier greens. Weekend greens fees are $250, weekdays $175. And remember—when putting near the ocean, the break is always toward the water.

SEEING THE SIGHTS

Beyond the sights listed below, an excellent attraction is **Balboa Island.** The charm of this pretty little neighborhood isn't diminished by knowing that the island was man-made—and it certainly hasn't affected the price of real estate. Tiny clapboard cottages in the island's center and modern houses with two-story windows and private docks along the perimeter make a colorful and romantic picture. You can drive onto the island on Jamboree Road to the north or take the three-car ferry from Balboa Peninsula ($1.50 per vehicle; $1 per pedestrian). It's generally more fun to park and take the 30-minute ferry ride as a pedestrian, since the island is crowded and lacks parking and the tiny alleys they call streets are more suitable for strolling. **Marine Avenue,** the main commercial street, is lined with small shops and cafes that evoke a New England fishing village. Shaved ices sold by sidewalk vendors will relieve the heat of summer.

Balboa Pavilion 𝕬 (Kids   This historic cupola-topped structure, a California Historical Landmark, was built in 1905 as a bathhouse for swimmers in their ankle-length bathing costumes. Later, during the Big Band era, dancers rocked the Pavilion doing the "Balboa Hop." Now it serves as the terminal for Catalina Island passenger service, harbor and whale-watching cruises, and fishing charters. The surrounding boardwalk is the Balboa Fun Zone, a collection of carnival rides, game arcades, and vendors of hot dogs and cotton candy. For Newport Harbor or Catalina cruise information, call © **949/673-5245;** for sport fishing and whale-watching, call © **949/673-1434.**

400 Main St., Balboa, Newport Beach. © **949/673-5245.** From Calif. 1, turn south onto Newport Blvd. (which becomes Balboa Blvd. on the peninsula); turn left at Main St.

International Surfing Museum   Nostalgic Gidgets and Moondoggies shouldn't miss this monument to the laid-back sport that has become synonymous with California beaches. You'll find gargantuan long boards from the sport's early days, memorabilia of Duke Kahanamoku and the other surfing greats represented on the "Walk of Fame" near Huntington Pier, and a gift shop where a copy of the *Surfin'ary* can help you bone up on your surfer slang even if you can't hang ten.

411 Olive Ave., Huntington Beach. © **714/960-3483.** www.surfingmuseum.org. Admission $2 adults, $1 students, free for kids ages 6 and under. Mid-June to late Sept daily noon–5pm; rest of the year Wed–Sun noon–5pm (hours tend to vary, so call ahead first)

Laguna Art Museum   This beloved local institution is working hard to position itself as the artistic cornerstone of the community. In addition to a small

Biplane, Air Combat & Warbird Adventures: The Thrill of a Lifetime

For anyone with a thirst for adrenaline-pumping excitement, boy have I got a recommendation for you. At a small airport in the coastal town of Carlsbad, about 30 miles north of San Diego, is a company called **Barnstorming Adventures,** run by husband-and-wife team Kate and Tom. Turning a passion for old planes into a thriving business, this cheerful duo offers a knock-out package of nostalgia, romance, fun, and—for the truly adventurous—a mind-blowing chance to fly either a World War II fighter plane or a modern combat aircraft (or both!).

For the mild-mannered, the 1920s-era biplane ride is pure romance: Couples wearing soft leather headgear and goggles (think Snoopy vs. The Red Baron) sit side-by-side at the front of the open cockpit while the pilot—seated in the back—flies a leisurely route along the sunny coast. At your request, the pilot will perform a few dips and lazy eights to add a touch of excitement, but nothing compares to the loops and rolls you'll perform (yes, you, who's never flown a plane in your life) in their big blue AT-6 Texan, a 600-horsepower fighter aircraft equipped with machine-gun barrels that looks like a killer and flies like a pussycat. "Okay, it's your plane," are four words you'll remember forever as the pilot, seated in front, calmly talks you through the aerobatic procedures, which are surprisingly easy to perform (it's one of the most incredible things I've ever done).

Other toys on the tarmac include a pair of modern prop-driven dogfighters. Real fighter pilots from the nearby marine base will give you a preflight lesson on aerial combat maneuvers, then get you airborne and let you fly the plane as you try to blast your partner—flying the "enemy" plane—out of the sky (with simulated bullets, of course). The company's other aircraft is a beautifully restored Beechcraft C-45 World War II transport plane they call the "Beech Belle" (picture the plane in the final scene of Casablanca). The roomy eight-passenger aircraft offers a trip back in time as the twin 450-horsepower Pratt & Whitney engines wind up and the big-band music starts playing in your headphones. For a group of friends, it's a real hoot to fly a 30-minute Coastal Patrol Mission. For more information about Barnstorming Adventures, call ② **800/SKY-LOOP** (800/759-5667) or 760/930-0903. *Tip:* Be sure to visit their website—www.barnstorming. com—for special Internet rates and package deals.

but interesting permanent collection, the museum presents installations of regional works definitely worth a detour. Past examples include a display of surf photography from the coast's 1930s and 1940s golden era, and dozens of plein-air Impressionist paintings (ca. 1900–30) by the founding artists of the original colony. The museum is also open during Laguna Beach Artwalk, the first Thursday each month, when all are admitted free.

307 Cliff Dr., Laguna Beach. ② 949/494-8971. www.lagunaartmuseum.org. Admission $7 adults, $5 students and seniors, free for kids under 12. Daily 11am–5pm.

Mission San Juan Capistrano   The 7th of the 21 California coastal missions, Mission San Juan Capistrano is continually being restored. The mix of old ruins and working buildings is home to small museum collections and various adobe rooms that are as quaint as they are interesting. The intimate Mission chapel with its ornate baroque altar is still used for religious services, and the Mission complex is the center of the community, hosting performing arts, children's programs, and other cultural events year-round.

This mission is best known for its **swallows,** which are said to return to nest each year at their favorite sanctuary. According to legend, the birds wing their way back to the mission annually on March 19, St. Joseph's Day, arriving at dawn; they are said to take flight again on October 23, after bidding the mission farewell. In reality, you'll probably see the well-fed birds here any day of the week, winter or summer.

Ortega Hwy. (Calif. 74), San Juan Capistrano. © **949/234-1300.** www.missionsjc.com. Admission $6 adults, $5 seniors, $4 children. Daily 8:30am–5pm.

WHERE TO STAY

Also consider the **Seal Beach Inn** (© **800/HIDEAWAY** or 562/493-2416; fax 562/799-0483; http://sealbeachinn.com), a romantic 23-room bed-and-breakfast inn 1 block from the beach in a quiet Seal Beach residential neighborhood.

VERY EXPENSIVE

Montage Resort & Spa ☆☆☆   The rich have it good when it comes to vacationing. Spend a few minutes walking around the new 30-acre Montage resort in Laguna Beach and you'll see why. Unfazed by the two luxury resorts—the St. Regis and the Ritz-Carlton Laguna Niguel—just down the road, the investors behind this Arts and Crafts beauty have created yet another reason for big-spenders to unwind along the Orange Coast. You can barely see it from the PCH, and the front entrance is rather understated, but as you walk through the lobby and onto the balcony overlooking the . . . oh my. The change of scenery is so breathtakingly abrupt that it takes composure not to sprint down to the gorgeous mosaic-tiled pool or run barefoot along the sun-kissed beach. It's the same view from the balcony of every room, and you never tire of it.

The Montage Resort is all about style. You don't even check in at the front desk—as soon as you arrive, you're warmly greeted and given a well-rehearsed tour of the resort by attractive khaki-clad employees wearing tailored jackets. The tours ends at the neo-Craftsman-style guest rooms, which are spacious, immaculate, and tastefully decorated with muted color schemes, museum-quality plein-air artwork, huge marble bathrooms with oversize tubs and plush robes, 27-inch flat-screen TVs with DVD players, quality dark-wood furnishings, feather-top beds with goose-down pillows, and very inviting balconies. But don't get too attached: You'll be spending very little time here as you lounge by the infinity-edged pool sipping a lemonade, spend hours exploring the tide pools, stroll through the hotel's impeccably manicured park and pristine beaches, spoil yourself rotten with skin treatments and massages at the oceanfront Spa Montage, then feast on chef James Boyce's superb Mediterranean-style cuisine at the resort's signature restaurant, **Studio.** There's plenty for kids to do as well: They have their own pool and several fun-filled programs to keep them entertained (and, of course, there's the beach). Montage is in a better location than the St. Regis (but no golf course) and has far superior facilities compared to the Ritz-Carlton, so if the higher rate doesn't matter, then, well, there you have it.

30801 S. Coast Hwy., Laguna Beach, CA 92651. © **888/715-6700** or 949/715-6000. Fax 949/715-6100. www. montagelagunabeach.com. 262 units. $475–$735 double; from $1,100 suite. AE, DISC, MC, V. Valet parking $25. **Amenities:** 3 restaurants; lobby lounge with live entertainment; oceanfront fitness facilities and spa; concierge and business services; 24 hr. in-room dining; daily laundry/valet service; newspaper delivery. *In room:* A/C, flat-screen TV and DVD/CD, minibar, hair dryer, iron and ironing board, personal safe, 3 multiline phones with voice mail, high-speed Internet access.

Ritz-Carlton Laguna Niguel ★★★   The Old World meets the Pacific Rim at this regal Dana Point grande dame. Although it's the oldest and most outdated (for now) of the three major resorts in this region—the other two being the St. Regis and Montage—it has one major trump card: the region's most spectacular setting. It's perched right on the edge of a 150-foot-high bluff that fronts an idyllic 2-mile-long beach where some of the world's best surfers play in the waves (truly, you can spend hours on your balcony admiring the ocean view). Lush terraces and colorful flower gardens abound throughout the well-tended property. There's a beautiful marble fireplace in the silk-lined lobby, and the arched Lobby Lounge is perfect for sipping a cocktail while watching the sun set over the Pacific. The service, in typical Ritz-Carlton style, is unassuming and impeccable. The spacious rooms are outfitted with sumptuous furnishings and fabrics, and all come with a terrace, an Italian marble bathroom equipped with double vanity, and the most comfortable feather bed's I've ever slept in; some suites even have fireplaces. The resort's flagship restaurant is the elegant **Dining Room,** but I prefer either the bountiful Friday night seafood buffet at the **Terrace** restaurant or a light lunch or dinner overlooking the ocean at the **Lobby Lounge.** Garden tours, beach shuttles, and excellent kids programs are available as well.

If elegant European ambience and unobstructed ocean views are your criteria, the Ritz property is a better choice than the nearby St. Regis, but if you prefer a more modern and trendsetting hotel, both the St. Regis and Montage are hard to beat. *Note:* A massive remodel of the entire property is scheduled for completion by late 2005. I've seen a peek of the new look and it's surprisingly modish—far more chic and contemporary than your typical Ritz decor.

1 Ritz-Carlton Dr., Dana Point, CA 92629. © **800/241-3333** or 949/240-2000. Fax 949/240-0829. www. ritzcarlton.com. 393 units. From $345 garden/pool-view double; $495 oceanview double; from $525 suite. Children age 17 and under stay free in parent's room. Midweek and special packages available. AE, DC, DISC, MC, V. Parking $25. **Amenities:** 4 restaurants; 2 lounges; 4 outdoor tennis courts; health club; whirlpool; sauna; children's programs; concierge; business center; 24-hr. room service; in-room massage; babysitting; dry-cleaning/laundry service; executive-level rooms; regular shuttle to/from the beach and the golf course. *In room:* A/C, TV w/pay movies, minibar, hair dryer, iron, safe, bathrobes.

St. Regis Monarch Beach Resort & Spa ★★★   Let's cut to the chase: The St. Regis Monarch Beach Resort is one of the finest luxury hotels I have ever had the pleasure of reviewing—and I've reviewed a *lot* of luxury hotels. They nailed it with this one, setting a standard for all other resort hotels to follow. Everything oozes with indulgence here, from the stellar service to the striking artwork, high-tech electronics, absurdly comfortable beds, stellar restaurants, and a 30,000-square-foot spa that will blow your mind. The $240-million, 172-acre resort opened in 2001, with a star-studded gala, and has since been wooing the wealthy with its gorgeous Tuscan-inspired architecture and soothing ocean views.

Perfection is all in the details, and the St. Regis is full of them: a three-lane lap pool with an underwater sound system; a yoga, spinning, and "movement" studio; a full-service Vogue salon; private poolside cabanas; incredible contemporary cuisine at the **Aqua** ★★★ restaurant; couples spa treatment rooms with whirlpool baths and fireplaces; an 18-hole Robert Trent Jones, Jr., golf course; and even a private beach club. Then there's the guest rooms, each loaded with beautiful custom-designed furniture, 32-inch Sony Vega flat-screen TVs with CD-DVD audio systems and a 300-DVD library, huge marble-laden bathroom with glass shower door that must weigh 100 pounds, and the most comfortable bathrobe I've ever worn.

The resort's only caveat is that it's near the beach, but unlike the Ritz-Carlton Laguna Niguel and Montage (see reviews above), it's not on it. Your view is of the terraced pool area and golf course, and complimentary shuttle service is needed to get to the beach. However, hotel guests have exclusive access to the St. Regis Beach Club, where beach attendants set up beach chairs, towels, and umbrellas, and also take food and beverage (including alcohol) orders. You can even hire a "surf butler," who will take your measurements for a wet suit, bring out a long board, and give you surfing lessons. *Tip:* Even if it's a bit beyond your price range, give yourself one heckuva birthday present this year and book a room on the Astor Floor, which comes with your own private butler (trust me, you'll be spoiled for life).

1 Monarch Beach Rd., Dana Point, CA 92629. © **800/722-1543** or 949/234-3200. Fax 949/234-3201. www. stregismonarchbeach.com. 400 units. From $450 resort-view double; from $550 oceanview double; from $875 suites. Golf and spa packages available. AF, DC, DISC, MC, V. Valet parking $25. **Amenities:** 6 restaurants; lounge; wine cellar tasting room; 3 pools; 18-hole golf course; 3 tennis courts (lit for night play); Spa Gaucin and a fitness center; 2 hot tubs; Kid's Club; concierge; 24-hr. business center; 24-hr. room service; in-room massage; babysitting; dry-cleaning/laundry service; executive-level rooms; complimentary local shuttle; retail shops; morning paper; 24-hr. butler service. *In room:* A/C, TV/DVD w/DVD library, minibar, hair dryer, safe, bathrobes, high-speed Internet access, 3 phones, CD player.

Surf and Sand Resort ✮✮ Perhaps the most beloved hotel on the Orange Coast, the Surf and Sand has come a long way since it started in 1948 as a beach-side motor lodge with 13 units. Still occupying the same ocean-side location, it now features 165 top-of-the-line rooms that, despite their simplicity and standard size, feel enormously decadent. They're all bright and beachy; each is done entirely in white and has a private balcony with a dreamy ocean view, a marble bathroom accented handsomely with granite, and plush cotton terry robes. All have whirlpool tubs as well. *Tip:* Try getting one of the deluxe corner rooms, affording an expanded 90-degree view of the California coastline—well worth the additional $40. Also, be sure to check their website for special package deals.

The hotel's Mediterranean-style **Aquaterra Spa** offers a tantalizing array of personalized massage, skin care, and body treatments. You'll find the requisite ocean-inspired treatments, but personal choice is the rule here: The menu features eight different massages, each with your choice of four aromatherapy oils. The spa's four "Couples Rituals" offer themed body treatments followed by a bubble bath for two (the tub has an ocean view), and a massage to finish. **Splashes** restaurant serves three meals daily in an oceanfront setting; the rich Mediterranean cuisine is perfect against a backdrop of sunlight and waves.

1555 S. Coast Hwy. (south of Laguna Canyon Rd.), Laguna Beach, CA 92651. © **888/869-7569** or 949/497-4477. Fax 949/494-2897. www.surfandsandresort.com. 165 units. Jan 3–Mar 28 $290–$485 double, $475–$780 suite; Mar 29–June 27 $295–$375 double, $395–$1,085 suite; June 28–Oct 5 $385–485 double, $475–$1125 suite. AE, DC, DISC, MC, V. **Amenities:** Restaurant; bar; outdoor heated pool; full-service spa; fitness room; whirlpool; summer children's programs; concierge; business center; room service (6:30am–10pm); in-room massage; babysitting; dry-cleaning/laundry service; concierge-level rooms. *In room:* TV w/pay movies, minibar, hair dryer, iron, safe, bathrobes, video games, CD player.

EXPENSIVE

Portofino Beach Hotel ✮ This oceanfront inn, built in a former seaside rail station, is steps away from the Newport Pier, along a stretch of bars and equipment-rental shacks; the beach is across the parking lot. The place maintains a calm, European air even in the face of the midsummer beach frenzy. Although it can get noisy in summer, there are advantages to being at the center of the action. The hotel has its own enclosed parking, and sunsets are spectacular viewed from a plush armchair in the upstairs parlor. Guest rooms, furnished with antique reproductions, are on the second floor—the first is occupied by a guests-only bar and several sitting rooms—and most have luxurious sky-lit bathrooms.

2306 W. Ocean Front, Newport Beach, CA 92663. ℂ 800/571-8749 or 949/673-7030. Fax 949/723-4370. www.portofinobeachhotel.com. 20 units. $169–$339 double. Rates include continental breakfast. Free parking. AE, DC, DISC, MC, V. **Amenities:** Whirlpool; coin-op laundry; dry-cleaning/laundry service. *In room:* A/C, TV.

MODERATE

Blue Lantern Inn 𝒜 A three-story New England–style gray clapboard inn, the Blue Lantern is a pleasant cross between romantic B&B and sophisticated small hotel. Almost all the rooms, which are decorated with reproduction traditional furniture and plush bedding, have a balcony or deck overlooking the harbor. All have a fireplace and whirlpool tub. You can have your breakfast here in private (clad in the fluffy robe provided), or go downstairs to the sunny dining room that also serves complimentary afternoon tea. There's also an exercise room and a cozy lounge with menus for many area restaurants. The friendly staff welcomes you with home-baked cookies at the front desk.

34343 St. of the Blue Lantern, Dana Point, CA 92629. ℂ 800/950-1236 or 949/661-1304. Fax 949/496-1483. www.foursisters.com. 29 units. $175–$500 double. Rates include full breakfast and afternoon wine and hors d'oeuvres. AE, DC, MC, V. **Amenities:** Whirlpool; exercise room; complimentary bicycles; dry-cleaning/laundry service. *In room:* A/C, TV/VCR, minibar, coffeemaker, hair dryer.

Casa Laguna 𝒜 Once you see this terraced complex of Spanish-style cottages amid lush gardens and secluded patios—which offers all the amenities of a B&B *and* affordable prices—you might wonder, What's the catch? Well, the noise of busy PCH wafts easily into Casa Laguna, which might prove disturbing to sensitive ears and light sleepers. Still, the Casa has been a favorite hideaway since Laguna's early days, and now glows under the watchful eye of a terrific owner, who's been upping the comfort ante. Some rooms—especially the suites—are downright luxurious, with fireplace, kitchen, bathrobes, CD player, VCR, and other in-room goodies. Throughout the property, Catalina tile adorns fountains and bougainvillea spills into paths; each room has an individual charm. Breakfast is served in the sunny morning room of the Craftsman-style Mission House, where a cozy living room also invites relaxation and conversation.

2510 S. Coast Hwy., Laguna Beach, CA 92651. ℂ 800/233-0449 or 949/494-2996. Fax 949/494-5009. 21 units. $130–$275 double; $195–$395 suite. Rates include breakfast, afternoon wine, and hors d'oeuvres. Off-season and midweek discounts available. AE, DISC, MC, V. **Amenities:** Heated outdoor pool; whirlpool. *In room:* TV.

Doryman's Inn Bed & Breakfast The rooms at Doryman's Inn are both luxurious and romantic, making this one of the nicest B&Bs to be found along the coast. The rooms are outfitted with French and American antiques, floral textiles, beveled mirrors, and cozy furnishings. Every room has a working fireplace and a sunken marble tub (some have whirlpool jets). King- or queen-size beds, lots of plants, and good ocean views round out the decor. The location, on the Newport Beach Pier Promenade, is also enviable, though some may find it a bit too close to the action. Breakfast includes fresh pastries and fruit, brown eggs, yogurt, cheeses, and international coffees and teas.

2102 W. Ocean Front, Newport Beach, CA 92663. ℂ 949/675-7300. www.dorymansinn.com. 10 units. $190–$380 double; from $265 suite. Rates include continental breakfast. AE, MC, V. Free parking. **Amenities:** Restaurant. *In room:* A/C, TV.

WHERE TO DINE

Options in Seal Beach are limited, but a good choice for seafood is **Walt's Wharf,** 201 Main St. (℗ **562/598-4433**), a bustling, polished restaurant featuring market-fresh selections either plain or with Pacific Rim accents.

EXPENSIVE

5'0" (Five Feet) ✦✦ CALIFORNIA/ASIAN   While 5'0" may no longer break culinary ground, the kitchen still combines the best in California cuisine with Asian technique and ingredients. The restaurant has a minimalist, almost-industrial decor that's brightened by a friendly staff and splendid cuisine. Menu selections run the gamut from tea-smoked filet mignon topped with Roquefort cheese and candied walnuts to a hot Thai-style mixed grill of veal, beef, lamb, and chicken stir-fried with sweet peppers, onions, and mushrooms in curry-mint sauce. The menu changes daily, but you can always find the house specialty, whole braised catfish.

328 Glenneyre, Laguna Beach. ℗ **949/497-4955.** Reservations recommended. Main courses $18–$49. AE, DC, DISC, MC, V. Sun–Thurs 5–10pm; Fri–Sat 5–11pm.

Roy's of Newport Beach ✦ HAWAIIAN REGIONAL/PACIFIC RIM   Any foodie who's been to Hawaii in the past decade knows the name Roy Yamaguchi, father of Hawaiian Regional Cuisine (HRC) and the islands' answer to Wolfgang Puck. Roy's empire expanded to Southern California in 1999, with the opening of this dinner-only restaurant on the fringe of Fashion Island shopping center. Yamaguchi developed a menu that represents his East/West/Polynesian cuisine but can be reliably executed by chefs in far-flung kitchens. Most of each night's specials are fresh Pacific fish, given the patented HRC touch with Japanese, Thai, and even Latin accents. Signature dishes include island-style *ahi poke,* spicy Mongolian-glazed rack of lamb, and blackened yellowfin tuna in soy-mustard-butter sauce. The bar whips up "vacation" cocktails in tropical colors, and there's a to-die-for chocolate soufflé dessert.

453 Newport Center Dr., Fashion Island. ℗ **949/640-ROYS.** Reservations suggested. Main courses $18–$32. AE, DC, DISC, MC, V. Sun–Thurs 5–10pm; Fri–Sat 5–11pm.

MODERATE

Crab Cooker SEAFOOD   Since 1951, folks in search of fresh, well-prepared seafood have headed to this bright-red former bank building. Also a fish market, the Crab Cooker has a casual atmosphere of humble wooden tables, uncomplicated smoked and grilled preparations, and meticulously selected fresh fare. The place is especially proud of its Maryland crab cakes; clams and oysters are also part of the repertoire.

2200 Newport Blvd., Newport Beach. ℗ **949/673-0100.** www.crabcooker.com. Dinner main courses $10–$25; lunch $8–$19. AE, MC, V. Sun–Thurs 11am–9pm; Fri–Sat 11am–10pm.

Harbor Grill SEAFOOD/STEAK   Located in a business/commercial mall right in the center of the Dana Point Marina, the Harbor Grill is enthusiastically recommended by locals for mesquite-broiled ocean-fresh seafood. Hawaiian mahimahi with a mango-chutney baste is on the menu, along with Pacific swordfish, crab cakes, and beef steaks.

34499 St. of the Golden Lantern, Dana Point. ℗ **949/240-1416.** www.harborgrill.com. Reservations recommended. Main courses $10–$23. AE, DC, DISC, MC, V. Daily 11:30am–10pm; Sun brunch 9am–2pm.

Las Brisas *Moments* MEXICAN SEAFOOD   Las Brisas's breathtaking view of the Pacific (particularly at sunset) and potent margaritas are a surefire combination for a *muy romantico* evening. In fact, it's so popular that it can get pretty crowded during the summer months, so be sure to make a reservation. Affordable during lunch but pricey at dinner, the menu consists mostly of seafood recipes from the Mexican Riviera. Even the standard enchiladas and tacos get a zesty update with crab or lobster meat and fresh herbs. Calamari steak is sautéed with bell peppers, capers, and herbs in a garlic-butter sauce, and king salmon is mesquite-broiled and served with a creamy lime sauce. Although a bit on the touristy side, Las Brisas can be a fun part of the Laguna Beach experience.

361 Cliff Dr. (off the PCH north of Laguna Canyon), Laguna Beach. © **949/497-5434.** Reservations recommended. Main courses $10–$24. AE, DC, DISC, MC, V. Mon–Thurs 8am–10pm; Fri–Sat 8am–11pm; Sun 9am–10:30pm. Valet parking $3 lunch, $4 dinner.

Ramos House Cafe ★★ REGIONAL AMERICAN   Hidden away in the historic Rios district next to the train tracks, this converted 1881 cottage brings the flavor of a simpler time to the busy Orange Coast. The small seasonal menu of regional American favorites uses garden-grown herbs, house-baked breads, and hand-turned ice cream. The all-purpose breakfast/lunch menu (dinner only for special events) features warmly satisfying cinnamon-apple beignets, wild-mushroom and sun-dried-tomato omelets, fried green tomatoes sauced with goat cheese, Southern fried chicken salad bathed in pumpkin seed–buttermilk dressing, shrimp and sourdough bread pudding, an always changing but always superb fresh soup, and more comfort food faves with a Southern flair. Seating is outside, on a tree-shaded brick garden patio that invites leisure.

31752 Los Rios St. (off Del Obispo St.), San Juan Capistrano. © **949/443-1342.** Main courses $9–$16. AE, DC, DISC, MC, V. Tues–Sun 8:30am–3pm.

15

The Southern California Desert

by Harry Basch

To the casual observer, Southern California's desert seems desolate—nothing but vast landscapes under a relentless sun. Its splendor is subtle, though; you have to discover its beauty in your own time. For some travelers it will be the surprising lushness of trees, flowering cacti, fragrant shrubs, and other plants—many unique to the region—that have adapted to the harsh climate. The Joshua tree, which some deem majestic and others call ugly, thrives in the upper Mojave Desert. Each spring, the ground throughout the Lancaster area is carpeted with the brilliant golds and oranges of the poppy, California's state flower. Like the autumn leaves in New England, the poppies draw seasonal tourists in droves.

If it looks as though nothing except insects could survive here, look again: You're bound to see a roadrunner or a tiny gecko dart across your path. Close your eyes and listen for the cry of a hawk or an owl. Check the ground for coyote or bobcat tracks. Notice the sparkle of fish in the streams running through palm oases. Check the road signs, which warn of desert tortoise crossings. The tortoise is just one of the many endangered species found only here; fortunately, most of the Southern California desert's flora and fauna is protected by the federal government in a wildlife sanctuary.

Perhaps the beauty you seek is that of personal renewal in the spectacular desert landscape. Whether it's in the shadow of purple-tinged mountains, amid otherworldly rock formations, or beside a sparkling swimming pool, you'll find as much or as little to occupy your time as you desire. Destinations range from gloriously untouched national parks to ultraluxurious resorts—and it's a rare day when the sun doesn't shine out here.

1 En Route to the Palm Springs Resorts

If you're making the drive from Los Angeles via I-10, your first hour or so will be spent just, well, getting out of the L.A. metropolitan sprawl. Soon you'll leave the Inland Empire auto plazas behind, sail past the last of the bedroom-community shopping malls, and edge ever closer to the snowcapped (if you're lucky) San Bernardino and San Jacinto mountain ranges. (Coming from San Diego via I-15, the area discussed below is east of the junction with I-10.)

For frequent travelers on this stretch of highway, there are certain unmistakable signposts. Roadside attractions are part of what makes every moment of the vacation enjoyable. Below are three of our favorites.

Desert Hills Premium Outlets Factory-outlet malls are the rage among bargain hunters, and this one is a cut above the rest—or maybe it's just so massive, the schlock gets lost in the shuffle. Pick up a map to help navigate this behemoth, or you may find yourself browsing Timberland when you'd rather be shopping the Gap. Some of our faves: Kenneth Cole, J. Crew, Eddie Bauer,

---

Fun Fact **Jurassic Park in the Desert**

As the cities give way to pale, dry desert, keep your eyes peeled for the dinosaurs that stand guard over the 24-hour **Wheel Inn Restaurant** (© **909/849-7012**), in Cabazon. That's right, a four-story-tall brontosaurus and his Tyrannosaurus rex pal. You can even climb into the belly of the larger one, where you'll find a remarkably spacious gift shop.

Coach, Barney's New York, A/X Armani Exchange, Donna Karan DKNY, Max Studio, Nike, and Quiksilver. The list goes on; there are 15 shoe stores alone!

But wait, there's more: The newer—but much smaller—**Cabazon Outlets** (© **909/922-3000;** www.cabazonoutlet.com) next door is worth a visit for the Crate & Barrel outlet and others, including Adidas and Puma.

48400 Seminole Dr. (off I-10), Cabazon. © **909/849-6641.** www.premiumoutlets.com. Sun–Thurs 10am–8pm; Fri 10am–9pm; Sat 9am–9pm.

Hadley's Fruit Orchards This friendly emporium has been a fixture here since 1931. It's always packed with folks shopping for dates, dried fruits, nuts, honey, preserves, and other regional products. A snack bar serves the beloved date shake; there are also plenty of gift-packed treats to carry (or ship) home. (For more about the date mystique, see "Sweet Treat of the Desert: The Coachella Valley Date Gardens," on p. 642.)

Just beyond Hadley's is the new high-rise hotel-and-entertainment center that has become part of the Morongo Indian Casino. Now you can stay and play.

48980 Seminole Dr. (off I-10), Cabazon. © **800/854-5655** or 909/849-5255. www.hadleyfruitorchards.com. Mon–Thurs 9am–7pm; Fri–Sun 8am–8pm (call to verify).

Windmill Tours *(Finds* For years, travelers through the San Gorgonio Pass have been struck by an awesome and otherworldly sight: never-ending windmill fields that harness the force of the wind gusting through this passage and convert it to electricity to power air conditioners throughout the Coachella Valley. If you get a charge from them, consider a guided tour offering a look into this alternative energy source. Learn how designers have improved the efficiency of wind turbines (technically they're not windmills), and measure those long rotors against the average human height (about 10 people could lie along one span).

Interstate 10 (Indian Ave. exit), Palm Springs. © **877/449-WIND** or 760/320-1365. www.windmilltours.com. Admission $23 adults, $20 seniors, $10 kids under 14. Tours Wed–Sat at 9am, 11am, and 2pm (varies seasonally).

2 Get Your Kicks on Historic Route 66

There's a way for nostalgia buffs to take a detour down memory lane on their way to desert destinations: Just eschew the fast-paced, faceless I-10 for a very special interstate highway—Route 66.

It's been immortalized in film, song, literature, memory, and the popular imagination. But is anything really left of this great snaking highway, this dependable, comforting spirit John Steinbeck called "the Mother Road"? What of the path to adventure traveled by Tod and Buz in their trademark red Corvette on the namesake 1960s TV series?

The answer is, yes, it's still there. You just have to be willing to look for it.

Until the final triumph of the multilane interstate system in the early 1960s, 2,300-mile-long Route 66 was the only automobile route between the Chicago shores of Lake Michigan and L.A.'s golden Pacific beaches. "America's Main Street" rambled through eight states, and today, in each one, there are organizations dedicated to preserving its remnants. California is fortunate to have a lengthy stretch of the original highway, many miles of which still proudly wear the designation "California State Highway 66." It's not just weed-split abandoned blacktop, either. These are active streets, often the main commercial drag of the community. Many stretches have become clusters of new developments, shopping centers, and fast-food chains. Pretty mundane—until you round a curve and unexpectedly see a vintage wood-frame house, perhaps from a pre–Great Depression ranch. There's poignancy here: That house was probably set way back from the road, amidst a shady grove, before highway workers buried the front yard under asphalt.

ESSENTIALS

THE ROUTE   Our drive begins in Pasadena and ends in downtown San Bernardino, 56 miles west of Palm Springs. In San Bernardino, I-215 intersects Route 66; take it 4 miles south to rejoin I-10 and continue east.

Note: This detour works equally well if your destination is Lake Arrowhead or Big Bear Lake; take I-215 north 3 miles to Calif. 30 and continue into the mountains. For more information, see chapter 14, "Side Trips from Los Angeles." The drive will take anywhere from 2 hours to 3 hours for your trip, depending on how many relics and photo opportunities you stop to enjoy. Some suitably retro meal suggestions are included in case you want to stop for lunch.

VISITOR INFORMATION   For more information, contact the **National Historic Route 66 Federation,** in the Los Angeles area (℃ **909/336-6131;** www.national66.com). There's also a quarterly *Route 66 Magazine;* for information, call ℃ **520/635-4322** or visit www.route66magazine.com.

LET'S HIT THE ROAD!

Although Route 66 officially ended at the picturesque Pacific, there are very few reminders left in the heart of L.A. Besides, I assume you've already seen the city, so Pasadena is the best point to begin your time-warp experience.

One of my favorite places is the **Fair Oaks Pharmacy,** Fair Oaks Avenue and Mission Street, 1½ miles south of Colorado Boulevard (℃ **626/799-1414**), a fixture on this corner since 1915. If you're in the mood for a treat, try an authentic ice-cream soda, a sparkling phosphate, a "Route 66" sundae, or an old-fashioned malt (complete with the frosty mixing can), all served by fresh-faced soda jerks from behind the marble counter. They also serve soup, sandwiches, and snacks. The Fair Oaks is still a pharmacy and offers a variety of gifts, including an abundance of Route 66–themed items. It's open Monday through Friday from 9am to 7pm, Saturday 9am to 5pm, and Sunday from 9am to 8pm.

Perhaps you'd like some driving music. Then, reverse and go north on Fair Oaks to Colorado and turn right. There's no better place than **Canterbury Records,** 805 E. Colorado Blvd., a block west of Lake Avenue (℃ **626/792-7184**). It has L.A.'s finest selection of big bands and pop vocalists on CDs; perhaps you'll choose one of the many renditions of Bobby Troup's, "(Get Your Kicks on) Route 66." The store is open Monday through Saturday from 9am to 9pm and Sunday from 10am to 7pm.

As you continue east on Colorado Boulevard, keep your eyes peeled for **motels** like the Saga Motor Hotel, Vagabond, Astro (fabulous *Jetsons*-style architecture), and Hi-Way Host. In fact, lodgings have proven the hardiest post-66 survivors, and you'll be seeing many frozen-in-time motor courts on the way.

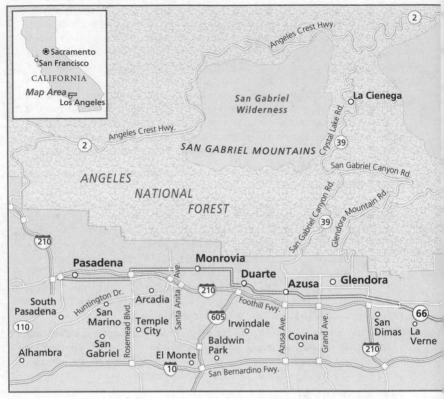

Turn left on Rosemead Boulevard, passing under the freeway (boo, hiss) to Foothill Boulevard. Turning right, you'll soon be among the tree-lined streets of **Arcadia,** home to the Santa Anita Racetrack and the Los Angeles Arboretum, the picturesque former estate of "Lucky" Baldwin, whose Queen Anne cottage has been the setting for many movies and TV shows. Passing into Monrovia, look for the life-size plastic cow on the southeast corner of Mayflower. It marks the drive-thru called **Mike's Dairy**—a splendid example of this auto-age phenomenon. If you're observant, you'll see many drive-thru dairies along my route (mostly Alta-Dena brand). Mike's has all the typical features, including the refrigerated island display case still bearing a vintage DRIFTWOOD DAIRY PRODUCTS price sign.

Next, look for Magnolia Avenue and the **Aztec Hotel** on the northwest corner. Opened in 1925, the Aztec was a local showplace, awing guests with its overscale, dark, Native American–themed lobby, Mayan murals, and exotic Brass Elephant bar. The arcade of shops once held the city's most prominent barbershop, beauty salon, and pharmacy. Little has changed about the interior, and a glance behind the front desk reveals the original cord-and-plug telephone switchboard still in use. If you care to wet your whistle, stop into the bar before continuing on.

Leaving the Aztec, you'll pass splendid Craftsman bungalows and other historic homes. Turn right on Shamrock Avenue and ogle the old gas station with its classic (if ornamental) gas pumps on the northwest corner of Almond

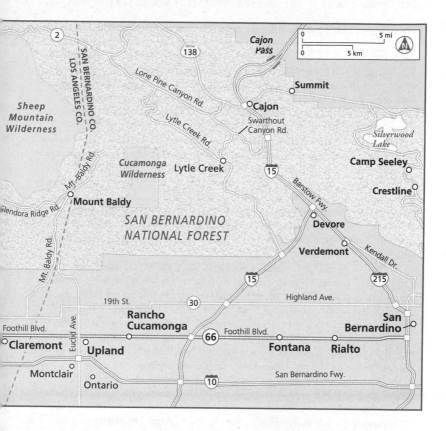

Avenue; continue onward 2 more blocks, then make a left turn on Huntington Drive. Now you're in **Duarte,** where Huntington is lit by graceful and ornate double street lamps on the center median. This stretch also has many fabulous old motor courts; see if you can spot the Ranch Inn, Evergreen, Oak Park, Duarte Inn, and Capri. Check out the **Justice Brothers Racing Museum,** 2734 E. Huntington Dr. in an officelike building at the east edge of town just before the river (open weekdays 8am–5pm).

Crossing over the wide but nearly dry San Gabriel River, glance right from the bridge to see cars streaming along the interstate that supplanted Route 66. In Irwindale—which smells just like the industrial area it is, with plants ranging from a Miller brewery to Health Valley Foods—the street resumes the Foothill Boulevard name. At Irwindale Avenue begins the 30-mile "neon cruise." You'll pass into **Azusa,** with its elegant 1932 **Azusa City Hall and Auditorium,** which features vintage lampposts and a Moorish fountain enhancing a charming courtyard.

Our route swerves right onto Alosta Avenue at the **Foothill Drive-In Theater,** Southern California's last single-screen drive-in. As you cruise by, think of the days when our cars were an extension of our living rooms (with the great snacks Mom wouldn't allow at home), and the outdoor theaters were filled every summer evening by dusk. Alas, the drive-in is in line for demolition, but local history buffs are attempting to save the classic neon signage.

Continuing on Alosta, you'll enter Glendora, named in 1887 by founder George Whitcomb for his wife, Ledora. Look for the **Palm Tropics,** one of the best-maintained old motels along the route. Farther along on the left-hand side is the **Golden Spur,** which began 70 years ago as a ride-up hamburger stand for the equestrian crowd. Unfortunately, the restaurant has been remodeled in boring stucco, leaving only the original sign, with its neon cowboy boot, as a reminder of its colorful past. At the corner of Cataract Avenue, a covered wagon announces the **Pinnacle Peak** restaurant, guarded by a giant steer atop the roof. In a mile or two, you'll pass quickly through San Dimas, a ranchlike community where you must pay attention to the HORSE CROSSING street signs.

Foothill Boulevard enters **La Verne** as you pass underneath the ramps to the I-30 freeway. In a large mall, you'll find a **Route 66 Gift Shop** inside the Cash Plus, between Vons and Target, 2418 Foothill Blvd. (© **909/592-2090**). **La Paloma** Mexican cafe, a fixture on the route for years, is on your left as you leave town. Continue on to Claremont, known these days for the highly respected group of **Claremont Colleges.** You'll pass several of them along this eucalyptus-lined boulevard. In days gone by, drivers would cruise along this route for mile upon mile, through orchards and open fields, the scenery punctuated only by ambling livestock or a rustic wood fence.

At Benson Avenue in Upland, a classic **1950s-style McDonald's** stands on the southeast corner, its golden arches flanking a low, white, walk-up counter with outdoor stools. The fast-food chain has its roots in this region: Richard and Maurice McDonald opened their first burger joint in San Bernardino in 1939. The brothers expanded their business, opening locations throughout Southern California, until entrepreneur Ray Kroc purchased the chain in 1955 and franchised McDonald's nationwide. Farther along, look north at the intersection of Euclid Avenue for the regal **monument to pioneer women.**

Pretty soon you'll be cruising through Rancho Cucamonga, whose fertile soil still yields a reliable harvest. You might see **produce stands** springing up by the side of the road; stop and pick up a fresh snack. If you're blessed with clear weather, gaze north at the gentle slope of the **San Gabriel Mountains** and you'll understand how Foothill Boulevard got its name. The construction codes in this community are among the most stringent in California, designed to respect the region's heritage and restrict runaway development. All new buildings are Spanish-Mediterranean in style and amply landscaped. At the corner of San Bernardino Road, the architectural bones of a wonderful old service station now stand forsaken. Across the street is the **Sycamore Inn,** nestled in a grove of trees and looking very much like an old-style stagecoach stop. This reddish-brown wooden house, dating from 1848, has been a private home and gracious inn; today, it serves the community of Cucamonga as a restaurant and civic hall.

Rancho Cucamonga has preserved two historic wineries. First you'll see the **Thomas Vineyards,** at the northeast corner of Vineyard Avenue, established in 1839. Legend holds that the first owner mysteriously disappeared, leaving hidden treasure still undiscovered on the property. The winery's preserved structures now hold an eatery, coffeehouse, a country crafts store, and a garden-supply boutique housed in the former brandy still tower.

Continuing on to Hellman Avenue, look for the **New Kansan Motel** (on the northeast corner). With that name, it must have seemed welcoming to Dust Bowl refugees. Near the northwest corner of Archibald Avenue, you'll find remnants of a **1920s-era gas station.** Empty now, those service bays have seen many a Ford, Studebaker, and Packard in need of a helping hand. Nearby, on the left, is **Route 66 Memories,** 10150 Foothill Blvd. (© **909/476-3843**), in a three-story classic house with a collection of metallic dinosaurs in the front yard, and a gift shop for

---

> **Tips   A Retro Pit Stop**
>
> If all this driving has made you hungry, consider the **Magic Lamp Inn,** 8189 Foothill Blvd. (© **909/981-8659**), open for lunch and dinner Tuesday through Friday and dinner only on Saturday and Sunday. Built in 1957, the Magic Lamp offers excellent Continental cuisine (nothing nouvelle about Route 66!) in a setting that's part manor house and part *Aladdin* theme park. Dark, stately dining rooms lurk behind a funky banquette cocktail lounge punctuated by a psychedelic fountain/fire pit and a panoramic view. The genie-bottle theme is everywhere, from the restaurant's dinnerware to the plush carpeting, which would be right at home in a Las Vegas casino. Lovers of kitsch and hearty retro fare shouldn't pass this one up.

---

antiques and rustic furniture. Next you'll pass the **Virginia Dare Winery,** at the northwest corner of Haven Avenue, whose structures now house part of a business park/mall, but retain the flourish of the original (1830s) winery logo.

Soon you'll pass the I-15 junction and be driving through Fontana, whose name in Italian means "fountain city." There isn't too much worth stopping for along this stretch, but slow down to have a look at the **motor-court hotels** lining both sides of the road. They're of various vintages, all built to cater to the once-vigorous stream of travelers passing through. Although today they're dingy, the melody of their names conjures up those glory days: Oasis, Rose Motel, Moana, El Rey, Rex, Fiesta, Dragon, Sand & Sage, and Sunset.

As you enter **San Bernardino,** be on the lookout for Meriden Avenue, site of the **Wigwam Motel.** Built in the 1950s (along with an identical twin motor court in Holbrook, Arizona), the whimsy of these stucco tepees lured many a road-weary traveler in for the night. Its catchy slogan, "Sleep in a wigwam, get more for your wampum," has been supplanted today by the more to-the-point "Do it in a teepee." But, as with many of the motor courts we'll pass, you need only picture a few large, shiny Buicks, T-bird convertibles, and "woodie" station wagons pulling in for the night and your imagination will drift back to days gone by.

Soon Foothill Boulevard will become Fifth Street, where the San Bernardino sign must have been a welcome sight for hot and weary westbound travelers emerging from the Mojave Desert. Route 66 wriggled through the steep Cajon Pass into a land fragrant with orange groves, where agricultural prosperity had quickly earned this region a lasting sobriquet: "the Inland Empire."

The year 1928 saw the grand opening of an elegant movie palace, the **California Theatre,** 562 W. Fourth St., only a block from Route 66. From Fifth Street east, turn right at E Street, then make a right on Fourth Street, where you can pull over to view the theater. Lovingly restored and still popular for nostalgic live entertainment and the rich tones of its original Wurlitzer pipe organ, the California was a frequent site of Hollywood "sneak previews." Humorist Will Rogers made his last public appearance here, in 1935. (Following his death, the highway was renamed the "Will Rogers Memorial Hwy.," but it remained popularly known as Route 66.) Notice the intricate relief of the theater's stone facade, and peek into the lobby to see the red velvet draperies, rich carpeting, and gold-banistered double staircase leading up to the balcony.

The theater is the last stop on your time-warp driving tour. Continue west on Fourth Street to the superslab highway only 2½ blocks away—that's I-215, your entry back to the present (see "Essentials" above).

3 The Palm Springs Desert Resorts

120 miles E of L.A.; 135 miles NE of San Diego

Palm Springs had been known for years as a golf-course-studded retirement mecca that's invaded annually by hordes of libidinous college kids on spring break. Well, the city of Palm Springs has been quietly changing its image and attracting a whole new crowd. Former mayor (the late) Sonny Bono's revolutionary "anti-thong" ordinance in 1991 put a lightning-quick halt to the spring-break migration by eliminating public display of the bare derrière, and the upscale fairway-condo crowd has decided to congregate in the outlying resort cities of Rancho Mirage, Palm Desert, Indian Wells, and La Quinta.

These days, there are no billboards allowed in Palm Springs; all the palm trees in the center of town are backlit at night, and you won't see the word "motel" on any establishment. Seniors are everywhere, dressed to the nines in leisure suits and keeping alive the retro-kitsch establishments from the days when Elvis, Liberace, and Sinatra made the desert a swingin' place. But they're not alone: Baby boomers and yuppies nostalgic for the kidney-shaped swimming pools and backyard luaus of the Eisenhower/Kennedy glory years are buying ranch-style vacation homes and restoring them to their 1950s splendor. Hollywood's young glitterati are returning, too. Today, the city fancies itself a European-style resort with a dash of good ol' American small town thrown in—think *Jetsons* architecture and the crushed-velvet vibe of piano bars with the colors and attitude of a laid-back Aegean village. One thing hasn't changed: Swimming, sunbathing, golfing, and playing tennis are still the primary pastimes in this little oasis.

Another important presence in Palm Springs has little to do with socialites and Americana. The Agua Caliente Band of Cahuilla Indians settled in this area 1,000 years before the first golf ball was ever teed up. Recognizing the beauty and spirituality of this wide-open space, they lived a simple life around the mineral springs on the desert floor, migrating into the cool canyons during the summer months. Under a treaty with the railroad companies and the U.S. government, the tribe owns half the land on which Palm Springs is built and works to preserve Native American heritage. It's easy to learn about the American Indians during your visit, and it will definitely add to your appreciation of this part of California.

ESSENTIALS

GETTING THERE   Airlines that service the **Palm Springs International Airport,** 3400 E. Tahquitz Canyon Way (© 760/323-8161), include **Alaska Airlines** (© 800/426-0333; www.alaskaair.com), **American** and **American Eagle** (© 800/433-7300; www.aa.com), **America West Express** (© 800/235-9292; www.americawest.com), **Continental Express** (© 800/525-0280; www.continental.com), **Delta** and **Delta Connection** (© 800/221-1212; www.delta.com), **Horizon Air** (© 800/547-9308; www.horizonair.com), **Northwest** (© 800/225-2525; www.nwa.com), and **United Express** (© 800/241-6522; www.united.com). Flights from Los Angeles take about 40 minutes.

If you're driving from Los Angeles, take I-10 east to the Calif. 111 turnoff to Palm Springs. You'll breeze into town on North Palm Canyon Drive, the main thoroughfare. The trip from downtown L.A. takes about 2 hours if the traffic is light. If you're driving from San Diego, take I-15 north to I-10 east; it takes a little more than 2 hours.

VISITOR INFORMATION   Be sure to pick up *Palm Springs Life* magazine's free monthly, ***Desert Guide.*** It contains tons of visitor information, including a

The Palm Springs Desert Resorts

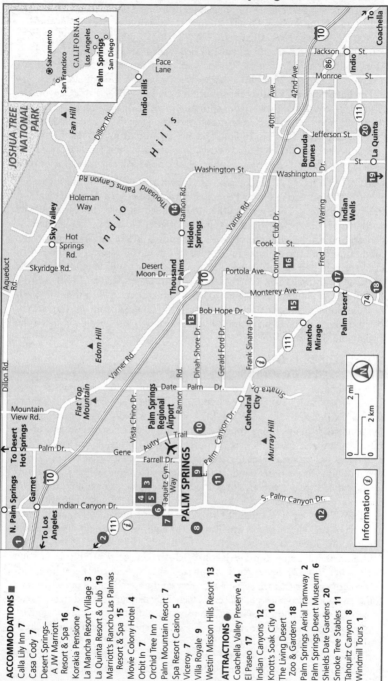

ACCOMMODATIONS ■
Calla Lily Inn **7**
Casa Cody **7**
Desert Springs–
A JW Marriott
Resort & Spa **16**
Korakia Pensione **7**
La Mancha Resort Village **3**
La Quinta Resort & Club **19**
Marriott's Rancho Las Palmas
Resort & Spa **15**
Movie Colony Hotel **4**
Orbit In **7**
Orchid Tree Inn **7**
Palm Mountain Resort **7**
Spa Resort Casino **5**
Viceroy **9**
Villa Royale **9**
Westin Mission Hills Resort **13**

ATTRACTIONS ●
Coachella Valley Preserve **14**
El Paseo **17**
Indian Canyons **12**
Knott's Soak City **10**
The Living Desert
Zoo & Gardens **18**
Palm Springs Aerial Tramway **2**
Palm Springs Desert Museum **6**
Shields Date Gardens **20**
Smoke Tree Stables **11**
Tahquitz Canyon **8**
Windmill Tours **1**

comprehensive calendar of events. Copies are distributed in hotels and newsstands and by the **Palm Springs Desert Resorts Convention & Visitors Authority,** 70-100 Hwy. 111, Rancho Mirage, CA 92270 (© **800/41-RELAX** or 760/ 770-9000). The bureau's office staff can help with maps, brochures, and advice Monday through Friday from 8:30am to 5pm. They also operate a 24-hour information line (© **760/770-1992**) and a website (www.palmspringsusa.com).

The **Palm Springs Visitors Information Center,** 2901 N. Palm Canyon Dr. (© **800/34-SPRINGS;** www.palm-springs.org), offers maps, brochures, advice, souvenirs, and a free hotel reservation service. The office is open Monday through Saturday from 9am to 5pm and Sunday from 8am to 4pm.

Another site worth browsing is **www.thedesertsun.com**, an offshoot of the local newspaper the *Desert Sun* that has information for locals as well as visitors.

ORIENTATION The commercial downtown area of Palm Springs stretches about half a mile along North Palm Canyon Drive between Alejo and Ramon streets. The street is one-way southbound through the heart of town, but its northbound counterpart is Indian Canyon Drive, 1 block east. The mountains lie west and south, while the rest of Palm Springs is laid out in a grid to the southeast. Palm Canyon forks into South Palm Canyon (leading to the Indian Canyons) and East Palm Canyon (the continuation of Calif. 111) traversing the towns of Cathedral City, Rancho Mirage, Palm Desert, Indian Wells, and La Quinta before looping up to rejoin I-10 at Indio. Desert Hot Springs is north of Palm Springs, straight up Gene Autry Trail. Tahquitz Canyon Way creates North Palm Canyon's primary intersection, tracking a straight line between the airport and the heart of town.

WHAT TO SEE & DO
GREAT GOLF COURSES

The Palm Springs Desert Resorts are a mecca for golfers (see "Fairways & Five-Irons, Desert-Style" below). There are 111 public, semiprivate, and private courses in the area. If you're the kind who starts polishing your irons the moment you begin planning your vacation, you're best off staying at one of the valley's many golf resorts, where you can enjoy the proximity of your hotel's facilities as well as smart package deals that can give you a taste of country-club membership. On the other hand, if you'd like to fit a round of golf into an otherwise varied trip and you aren't staying at a hotel with its own links, there are courses at all levels open to the general public, many in Palm Springs, with others down the valley in Cathedral City, Palm Desert, Indian Wells, La Quinta, and Indio. Call ahead to see which will rent clubs or other equipment to the spontaneous player.

Beginners will enjoy **Tommy Jacobs' Bel-Air Greens,** 1001 El Cielo, Palm Springs (© **760/322-6062;** www.tommyjacobsbelairgreens.com), a 9-hole, par-32 executive course that has some water- and sand-trap challenges but also allows for a few confidence-boosting successes. Generally flat fairways and trees characterize the relatively short (3,350-yd.) course. Greens fees range from $15 to $19.

Slightly more intermediate amateurs will want to check out the **Tahquitz Creek Golf Resort,** 1885 Golf Club Dr., Palm Springs (© **760/328-1005**), whose two diverse courses both appeal to mid-handicappers. The "Legend's" wide, water-free holes will appeal to anyone frustrated by the "target" courses popular with many architects, while the Ted Robinson–designed "Resort" course offers all those accuracy-testing bells and whistles more common to lavish private clubs. Greens fees, including cart, range from $69 to $95, depending on the day of the week.

The **Palm Springs Country Club,** 2500 Whitewater Club Dr. (© **760/323-2626**), is the oldest public-access golf course in the city of Palm Springs and is popular with budget-conscious golfers, as greens fees are only $35 to $45, including the required cart. The challenge of bunkers and rough can be amplified by the oft-blowing wind along the 5,885 yards of this unusually laid-out course.

The **Westin Mission Hills Resort Course,** Dinah Shore and Bob Hope drives, Rancho Mirage (© **760/328-3198**), is somewhat more forgiving than most of legendary architect Pete Dye's courses, but don't play the back tees unless you've got a consistent 220-yard drive and won't be fazed by the Dye-trademark giant sand bunkers and elevated greens. Water only comes into play on four holes, and the scenery is an exquisite reward for low-handicappers. Nonguest greens fees are $70 (summer) to $145, including cart. There's also Mission Hills North Course, designed by Gary Player.

One of our favorite desert courses is the **PGA West TPC Stadium Course,** La Quinta Resort & Club, 49499 Eisenhower Dr., La Quinta (© **760/564-4111**), which received *Golf* magazine's 1994 Gold Medal Award for the total golf-resort experience. The par-three 17th has a picturesque island green where Lee Trevino made Skins Game history with a spectacular hole-in-one. The rest of Pete Dye's 7,261-yard design is flat, with huge bunkers, lots of water, and severe mounding throughout. It's one of the most difficult courses in the U.S. Also open for semiprivate play is the **Mountain Course at La Quinta,** another Dye design that regularly appears on U.S. top-100 lists. It's set dramatically against the rocky mountains, which thrust into fairways to create tricky doglegs, and its small Bermuda greens are well guarded by boulders and deep bunkers. Greens fees for nonguests vary seasonally, from $65 to $195. Also at La Quinta Resort is the Pete Dye–designed **Dunes Course,** the (Jack) **Nicklaus Tournament Course,** and the (Greg) **Norman Resort Course.**

A complete **golfer's guide** is available from the Palm Springs Desert Resorts Convention & Visitors Authority (see "Visitor Information" above).

MORE OUTDOOR FUN

BALLOONING This is perhaps the most memorable way to see the desert: floating above the landscape in a colorful hot-air balloon. Choose from specialty themes like sunrise, sunset, or romantic champagne flights. Rides are offered by **Dream Flights** (© **800/933-5628** or 760/321-5154; www.dreamflights.com), and **Fantasy Balloon Flights** (© **800/GO-ABOVE** or 760/568-0997; www.fantasyballoonflights.com). Rates range from $145 to $150 per person for a 60- to 90-minute flight (two per day), including champagne and hors d'oeuvres.

BICYCLING The clean, dry air just cries out to be enjoyed—what could be better than to pedal your way around town or into the desert? **Adventure Bike Tours** (© **760/328-0282**) will outfit you with a bike, helmet, water bottle, and certified guide. Three-hour tours, which meet at local hotels, start at about $50, and bike rentals are $10 per hour or $30 for the day. If you're just looking to rent some wheels and a helmet, **Tri a Bike Rental,** 44841 San Pablo Ave., Palm Desert (© **760/340-2840**), rents road and mountain bikes for the hour ($7–$9), the day ($19–$29), or the week ($65–$95), and offers children's and tandem models. The **Bighorn Bicycle Rental & Tour Company,** 302 N. Palm Canyon (© **760/325-3367**), has hourly ($6–$8) and daily ($20–$29) rental rates in addition to guided bike treks (a 2–4-hr. guided ride/hike is $35–$49 per person including all equipment and snacks). Closed on Wednesday.

Fairways & Five-Irons, Desert-Style

Two hours outside of Los Angeles in the Coachella Valley, strung like ripe dates from I-10, lie the resort cities of Palm Springs, Rancho Mirage, Palm Desert, Indian Wells, and La Quinta. This all-season golfer's paradise boasts more than 100 courses, their lush fairways and velvety greens carved from the arid desert scruff. Both public and resort/semiprivate courses range in difficulty to accommodate low-handicappers and weekend duffers alike, and every imaginable service is available nearby.

If you'd like to sharpen your game, all the principal clubs have resident pros, and there are several schools and clinics, including the **Indian Wells Golf School** at Indian Wells Resort (© 760/346-4653), or the **Golf Center at Palm Desert** (© 760/779-1877). If you're looking to pick up new equipment or golf attire, try the **Roger Dunn Golf Shop** in Cathedral City (© 760/345-3133) and **Lady Golf** in Rancho Mirage (© 760/773-4949).

Many fine resorts offer generous golf packages, among them **Marriott's Desert Springs Spa & Resort** in Palm Desert (© 760/341-2211), **Marriott's Rancho Las Palmas Resort & Spa** in Rancho Mirage (© 760/568-2727), the **Hyatt Grand Champions** in Indian Wells (© 760/341-1000), and **La Quinta Resort & Club** in La Quinta (© 760/346-2904).

Tee times at many courses cannot be booked more than a few days in advance for nonguests, but **Golf à la Carte** (© **877/887-6900** or 760/771-3276; www.palmspringsgolf.com) is able to make arrangements several months earlier and even construct a package for you with accommodations, golf, meals, and other extras. A valuable service for the budget traveler is **Stand-By Golf** (© **866/224-2665** or 760/321-2665; www.stand-bygolf.com), which helps more than 35 area courses—including semiprivate and resort courses—fill their bookings by offering players a last-minute discount of 40% to 60%. For some courses, you can book in advance, but many tee times are for the same or next day; call between 7am and 10pm daily.

For the nonplaying spectator (or anyone longing to see the pros make it look so easy), there are dozens of golf tournaments year-round, including many celebrity and pro-am events in addition to regular PGA, LPGA, and Senior Tour stops. January brings the PGA Tour's **Bob Hope Chrysler Classic** at the Bermuda Dunes Country Club, and the **Frank Sinatra Celebrity Invitational** at Desert Willow Golf Resort in Palm Desert takes place in February (www.sinatragolf.com). In March, catch the LPGA Tour's **Kraft Nabisco Championship** at the Mission Hills Country Club. In November, check out the wacky **Palm Desert Golf Cart Parade** along El Paseo.

A FAMILY WATER PARK   Knott's Soak City, off I-10 south on Gene Autry Trail between Ramon Road and East Palm Canyon Drive (© **760/327-0499;** www.knotts.com/soakcity/ps/index.shtml), is a 16-acre water playground with 12 water slides, body- and board surfing, a wave pool, and more. Dressing rooms, lockers, and private beach cabanas (with food service) are available. Admission is $25 for adults, $13 for kids 3 to 11, and free for kids under 3; rates are discounted after 3pm. The park is open daily mid-March through August, and weekends through October, from 10am to 5pm (later on weekends).

GUIDED JEEP & WAGON EXCURSIONS   Desert Adventures (© 888/ 440-JEEP or 760/324-JEEP; www.red-jeep.com) offers four-wheel-drive eco-tours led by naturalist guides. Your off-road adventure may take you to a replica of an ancient Cahuilla village, the Santa Rosa Mountain roads overlooking the Coachella Valley, or picturesque ravines on the way to the San Andreas Fault. Tours range in duration from 2 to 4 hours and in price from $69 to $99. Advance reservations are required. The company's trademark red Jeeps depart from the Desert Adventures Ranch on South Palm Canyon near the entrance to the Indian Canyons, but most of the longer excursions include hotel pickup and return.

Covered Wagon Tours (© 800/367-2161 or 760/347-2161; www.covered wagontours.com) embraces the pioneer spirit with a 2-hour ride through the Coachella Valley Nature Preserve followed by a good old-fashioned barbecue and live country music. The tours take place 7 days a week from mid-September to mid-June; the cost is $60 for adults, $30 for children ages 7 to 16, and free for kids under 7. Without the "grub," the charge is $36 per adult and $18 per child. Advance reservations are required.

HIKING   The most popular spot for hiking is the nearby **Indian Canyons,** at the end of South Palm Canyon Drive (© 800/790-3398 or 760/325-3400; www.aguacaliente.org). The Agua Caliente tribe made their home here centuries ago, and remnants of their lifestyle can be seen among the streams, waterfalls, and palm groves in Andreas, Murray, and Palm canyons. Striking rock formations and herds of bighorn sheep and wild ponies will probably be more appealing than the "Trading Post" in Palm Canyon, but it does sell detailed trail maps. This is Indian land, and the Tribal Council charges admission of $6 per adult, $4.50 for students, seniors, and military, and $2 for kids ages 6 to 12. The canyons are closed to visitors from late June to early September. The canyons are open 8am to 5pm, and guided hiking tours and ranger lectures are also available.

Don't miss the opportunity to explore **Tahquitz Canyon,** 500 W. Mesquite, west of Palm Canyon Drive, also an Agua Caliente territory. This scenic canyon, which features the waterfall filmed for the classic *Lost Horizon,* was closed to the public for nearly 30 years after it became an all-night party zone for hippies, who vandalized land considered sacred—serious injuries also plagued careless canyon squatters. But now the vegetation is renewed and decades' worth of dumping cleaned up, and in 2001 the tribe began offering 2½-hour ranger-led hikes into their most spiritual and beautiful place. The 2-mile round-trip hike is of moderate difficulty and hikes depart daily at 8am, 10am, noon, and 2pm. The fee is $13 for adults, $6 for children ages 6 to 12; call © 800/790-3398 for recorded information, © 760/416-7044 for reservations (recommended).

Tips **All Kinds of Desert Activities**

Best of the Best Tours (© 760/320-4600 or 760/320-1365; www.bestofthe besttours.com) is a tour operator that handles desert and canyon tours by jeep, outlet-mall excursions, and hiking trips.

Ten miles east of Palm Springs is the 13,000-acre **Coachella Valley Preserve** (© 760/343-1234), which is open daily from sunrise to sunset. There are springs, mesas, both hiking and riding trails, the Thousand Palms Oasis, a visitor center, and picnic areas.

HORSEBACK RIDING   Equestrians from novice to advanced can experience the solitude and quiet of the desert on horseback at **Smoke Tree Stables** (© 760/327-1372). Located south of downtown and ideal for exploring the nearby Indian Canyon trails, Smoke Tree offers guided rides for $25 per hour, $65 for 2 hours. But don't expect your posse leader to be primed with facts on the nature you'll encounter—this is strictly a do-it-yourself experience. Open daily 8am to 4pm. No credit cards.

TENNIS   Virtually all the larger hotels and resorts have tennis courts; but if you're staying at a B&B, you might want to play at **The Tennis Center,** 1300 Baristo Rd. (© 760/323-8272). It has nine courts and offers day and evening clinics for adults, juniors, and seniors, as well as ball machines for solo practice. USPTA pros are on hand.

If you'd like to play for free, the night-lit courts at **Palm Springs High School,** 2248 E. Ramon Rd., are open to the public on weekends, holidays, and in summer. There are also eight free night-lit courts in beautiful **Ruth Hardy Park** at Tamarisk and Caballero streets.

EXPLORING THE AREA

The Living Desert Zoo & Gardens 🅰 *Kids*   This 1,200-acre desert reserve, museum, zoo, and educational center is designed to acquaint visitors with the unique habitats that make up the Southern California deserts. You can walk or take a tram tour through sectors that re-create life in several distinctive desert zones. See and learn about a dizzying variety of plants, insects, and wildlife, including bighorn sheep, mountain lions, rattlesnakes, lizards, owls, golden eagles, and the ubiquitous roadrunner. It's a nonstuffy learning experience for kids, and an interesting way for anyone to learn about the surrounding landscape.

47-900 Portola Ave., Palm Desert. © 760/346-5694. www.livingdesert.org. Admission $11 adults, $9 seniors/military, $6 children 3–12, free for kids under 3. Reduced summer rates. Daily 9am–5pm (last entrance 4pm); summer (mid-June to Aug) 8am–1:30pm.

Palm Springs Aerial Tramway 🅰🅰   To gain a bird's-eye perspective on the Coachella Valley, take this 14-minute ascent up nearly 5,900 feet to the upper slopes of Mount San Jacinto. While the Albert Frey–designed boarding stations retain their 1960s ski-lodge feel, newly installed Swiss funicular cars are sleekly modern and rotate during the trip to allow each passenger a panoramic view. There's a whole other world once you arrive: alpine scenery, a ski-lodge-flavored restaurant and gift shop, and temperatures typically 40° cooler than the desert floor. The most dramatic contrast is during the winter, when the mountaintop is a snowy wonderland, irresistible to hikers and bundled-up kids with saucers. The excursion might not be worth the expense during the rest of the year. Guided mule rides and cross-country ski equipment are available at the top. An upscale restaurant, Elevations, serves cuisine designed by Anthony Gusich that has an Asian flair. Appetizers begin at $8, entrees $29. Wait and take the tram to the top after 4pm for a lower rate. Elevations is open 4 to 8pm daily and reservations are recommended (© 760/327-1590).

Tramway Rd. off Hwy. 111, Palm Springs. © 888/515-TRAM or 760/325-1391. www.pstramway.com. Tickets $21 adults, $19 seniors, $14 children 3–12, free for kids under 3. Mon–Fri 10am–8pm; Sat–Sun 8am–8pm. Tram runs every 30 min., last tram down at 9:45pm.

Here's the Rub: Two Bunch Palms Desert Spa

Since the time of the Native American Cahuilla, who knew how great it felt to soak in the Coachella Valley's natural hot springs, this desert has drawn stressed-out masses seeking relaxation, rejuvenation, and the sigh-inducing pleasure only a health spa can deliver. My number-one, I-can't-recommend-it-enough choice is heavenly **Two Bunch Palms.** Posh yet intimate, this spiritual sanctuary in Desert Hot Springs (about 20 min. north of Palm Springs) has been drawing weary city dwellers since Chicago mobster Al Capone hid out here in the 1930s. Two Bunch Palms later became a playground for the movie community, but today it's a friendly and informal haven offering renowned spa services, bungalows on lush grounds, and lagoons of steaming mineral water. Service is famously—and excellently—discreet; and legions of return guests will attest that the outstanding spa treatments (nine varieties of massage, mud baths, body wraps, facials, salt rubs, and more) and therapeutic waters are what make the luxury of Two Bunch Palms irresistible. Room rates start at $175 (including breakfast) in the high season, with midweek and substantial off-season discounts available. Spa treatments typically cost between $75 and $100 per hour, and money-saving room/meal/spa packages are offered. Don't want to stay over? Then book one of Two Bunch's 6-hour Day Spa packages. The resort is off Palm Drive (Gene Autry Trail) at 67-425 Two Bunch Palms Trail ((C) **800/ 472-4334** or 760/329-8791; www.twobunchpalms.com).

Palm Springs Desert Museum (*&*)   Unlikely though it may sound, this well-endowed museum is worth a look. Exhibits include world-class Western and Native American art collections, the natural history of the desert, and an outstanding anthropology department, primarily representing the local Cahuilla tribe. Traditional Indian life as it was lived for centuries is illustrated by tools, baskets, and other relics. Check local schedules to find out about visiting exhibits (which are usually excellent). Plays, lectures, and other events are presented in the museum's Annenberg Theater.

101 Museum Dr. (just west of the Palm Canyon/Tahquitz intersection), Palm Springs. (C) 760/325-7186. www.psmuseum.org. Admission $7.50 adults, $6.50 seniors 62 and over, $3.50 military and children 6–17, free for children under 6. Tues–Wed and Fri–Sat 10am–5pm; Thurs noon–8pm; Sun noon–5pm. Admission free on Thurs after 4pm.

SHOPPING

Downtown Palm Springs revolves around **North Palm Canyon Drive;** many art galleries, souvenir shops, and restaurants are here, along with a couple of large-scale hotels and shopping centers. This wide one-way boulevard is designed for pedestrians, with many businesses set back from the street—don't be shy about poking around the little courtyards you'll encounter. On Thursday night from 6 to 10pm, the blocks between Amado and Baristo roads are transformed into **VillageFest,** a town street fair. Handicrafts vendors and aromatic food booths compete for your attention with wacky street performers and even wackier locals shopping at the mouthwatering fresh-produce stalls.

Sweet Treat of the Desert: The Coachella Valley Date Gardens

In a splendid display of both wishful thinking and clever engineering, the Coachella Valley has grown into a rich agricultural region, known internationally for grapefruit, figs, and grapes—but mostly for dates. Entrepreneurs, fascinated with Arabian lore and fueled by the Sahara-like conditions of the desert around Indio, planted the area's date palm groves in the 1920s. Launched with just a few parent trees imported from the Middle East, the groves now produce 95% of the world's date crop.

Farmers hand-pollinate the trees, and the resulting fruit is bundled in wind-protective paper while still on the tree, which makes an odd sight indeed. You'll see them along Calif. 111 through Indio, where the road is sometimes referred to as the "Date Highway."

For decades, **Shields Date Gardens,** 80225 Calif. 111 (© **800/414-2555** or 760/347-0996; www.shieldsdates.com), has been enticing visitors into its splendid 1930s Moderne building with banners proclaiming free admission to the continuously running film *The Romance and Sex Life of the Date.* (*Fair warning:* Its racy title is the best part.) Even if you're not interested in the flick, stop by the lunch counter (date shake, anyone?) and store (which sells an endless variety of dates and related goodies) and sample some date ice cream or date crystals, a mysterious sweet product that seems to have many practical uses—until you actually get it home. But the quality and selection of fresh dates is superb; I guarantee you'll find yourself snacking on them before long. Open daily from 8am to 6pm.

There's no more picturesque place in the valley to sample dates than **Oasis Date Gardens,** 59111 Calif. 111 (© **800/827-8017** or 760/399-5665), started in 1912 with nine Moroccan trees and now one of the largest commercial date groves in the United States. It's a drive—about 40 minutes from downtown Palm Springs—but there's a lot to do here. Picnic tables dot an inviting lawn, videos illustrate the history and art of date cultivation, and there's a cool palm arboretum and cactus exhibit, plus a petting zoo for youngsters. Many varieties of dates are laid out for free tasting. Oasis also sells date shakes, ice cream, date pie by the slice, homemade chili and sandwiches, and gourmet food gifts from all over the Southwest. Open daily (except Christmas) from 8am to 5pm.

The northern section of Palm Canyon is becoming known for collectibles and is being touted as the **Antique and Heritage Gallery District.** Check out **Bandini Johnson Gallery,** 750 N. Palm Canyon Dr. (© 760/323-7805), a cramped warren of eclectic treasures; and the **Antiques Center,** 798 N. Palm Canyon Dr. (© 760/323-4443), a discriminating mall-style store whose 35 dealers display wares ranging from vintage linens to handmade African crafts to prized Bakelite jewelry.

GAY & LESBIAN LIFE IN PALM SPRINGS

Don't think the chamber of commerce doesn't recognize that the Palm Springs area is among America's top destinations for gay and lesbian travelers. After just a short while in town, it's easy to see how the gay tourism dollar is courted as aggressively as straight spending. Real-estate agents cater to gay shoppers for vacation properties, while entire condo communities are marketed toward the gay resident. Advertisements for these and scores of other gay-owned businesses can be found in the *Bottom Line* (www.psbottomline.com), the desert's free biweekly magazine of articles, events, and community guides for the gay reader, which is available at hotels, at newsstands, and from select merchants.

Throughout the year, events are held that transcend the gay community to include everyone. In March the **Desert AIDS Walk** benefits the Desert AIDS Project, while one of the world's largest organized gathering of lesbians—the **Dinah Shore Weekend** (www.clubskirts.com)—coincides with the LPGA's **Kraft Nabisco Championship** in mid-March. The predominantly men's **White Party** (www.jeffreysanker.com), the area's largest circuit party event, takes place Easter weekend. **Greater Palm Spring Pride** occurs the first weekend in November, with a parade and 2-day cultural fair (© **760/416-8711;** www.pspride.org).

There are more than two dozen gay hotels, many concentrated on Warm Sands Drive south of Ramon. Known simply as "Warm Sands," this area holds many of the private resorts—mostly discreet and gated inns, many of them clothing-optional. Try the **East Canyon Hotel & Spa,** 288 E. Camino Monte Vista (© **877/324-6835** or 760/320-1928; www.eastcanyonps.com), a men's luxury resort and full-service spa; or **Casitas Laquita,** 450 E. Palm Canyon Dr. (© **760/416-9999;** www.casitaslaquita.com), one of two all-women resorts in town.

The **Palm Springs Visitor and Hotel Information Center** publishes an **Official Gay Visitors Guide.** Obtain it and additional information through their office: 2781 N. Palm Canyon Dr. (© **888/866-2744;** www.palm-springs.org).

WHERE TO STAY

The city of Palm Springs offers a wide range of accommodations, but we particularly like the inns that have opened as new owners renovate the many fabulous 40- to 60-year-old cottage complexes in the wind-shielded "Tennis Club" area west of Palm Canyon Drive. The other desert resort cities offer mostly sprawling complexes, many boasting world-class golf, tennis, or spa facilities and multiple on-site restaurants. Most are destinations in and of themselves, offering activities for the whole family (including a whole lot of relaxing and being pampered). So if you're looking for a good base from which to shop or sightsee, Palm Springs is your best bet.

Regardless of your choice, remember that the rates given below are for high season (winter, generally Nov–May). During the hotter summer months, it's common to find $300 rooms going for $99 or less as part of off-season packages. Even in high season, discounts for midweek stays are common.

PALM SPRINGS
Expensive

La Mancha Resort Village 🏕 The security-gated entry makes La Mancha look like a private community, and it was designed that way. Once you're inside, though, a warmly respectful staff will pamper you, just the way they've coddled the countless celebs who've lent their names to the brochure. Refurbished in 2003, what distinguishes La Mancha from other resorts is its quiet elegance and service, not its modern but unoriginal furnishings. All units are villas, about half of which have private pools filtered with sea salt; the rest have Jacuzzis. All have fireplaces and wet bars. A private fleet of rental cars stands ready should you want to venture the half mile into town, or you can simply relax the days away—how about a massage on your personal patio?

444 Avenida Caballeros, Palm Springs, CA 92262. (℃) **866/673-7501** or 760/323-1773. www.la-mancha.com. 52 units. Villas $259–$499. AE, DC, DISC, MC, V. Free parking. Dogs accepted with $25 fee. **Amenities:** Restaurant; lounge; outdoor heated pool; 5 lit tennis courts; spa; Jacuzzi; room service (11am–5pm); in-room massage. *In room:* A/C, TV/VCR, fridge, coffeemaker, hair dryer, iron, safe.

Orbit In 🐱🐱 This much-hyped renovation of a classic 1950s motel gets our vote as grooviest digs in town, exceeding everyone's expectations with a cocktails-by-the-pool Rat Pack aesthetic and almost scholarly appreciation of the architects and designers responsible for Palm Springs's reign as a mecca of vintage modernism. Serious connoisseurs of interior design will find a museum's worth of furnishings in these rooms, each of which adheres to its theme (Martini Room, Atomic Paradise, and so on) right down to customized lounge-music CDs for your listening pleasure. Contemporary comforts are provided, from cushy double pillow-top mattresses to poolside misters that create an oasis of cool even during midsummer scorchers. Kitchenettes all boast charming restored fixtures, as do the candy-pink-tiled original bathrooms, which have only stall showers but make up for the lack of tubs by being surprisingly spacious—and naturally sunlit. Guests gather at the poolside "boomerang" bar, or in the **Albert Frey Lounge** (homage to the late, great architect whose unique home sits midway up the mountain backdrop); a central "movies, books, and games" closet encourages old-fashioned camaraderie amidst this chic atmosphere. Nearby is the eight-unit Hideaway, a quieter, more secluded hospice with a large saltwater pool; no Jacuzzi but access to the Orbit amenities is available.

562 W. Arenas Rd., Palm Springs, CA 92262. (℃) **877/99-ORBIT** or 760/323-3585. Fax 760/323-3599. www. orbitin.com. 10 units. $209–$269 double. Rates include deluxe continental breakfast and evening hors d'oeuvres. AE, DISC, MC, V. Free parking. **Amenities:** Outdoor heated saltwater pool; Jacuzzi; spa facilities; complimentary Schwinn cruiser bikes; private patios. *In room:* A/C, TV/VCR, dataport, kitchenette, fridge, coffeemaker, hair dryer, iron, safe, CD player.

Viceroy Palm Springs 🐱🐱 Once the choice of Hollywood celebrities, this outstanding historic hotel, formerly the Estrella, is quiet and secluded yet wonderfully close to the action. It's composed of three distinct properties from three different eras, which benefited from a chic transformation in 2002—sort of a Grecian-meets-modern Regency style popular during Palm Springs's golden era. Guest rooms vary widely in terms of size and amenities—some have fireplaces and/or full kitchens, others have wet bars or private balconies—the color scheme is very black-and-white with dramatic lemon yellow accents. The real deals are the studio bungalows, even though they have tiny 1930s bathrooms. Lavish landscaping completes the elegant ambience. The restaurant, Citron, serves lunch and dinner (entrees $24–$34) and has a full bar. There is also pool food service.

415 S. Belardo Rd. (south of Tahquitz Way), Palm Springs, CA 92262. (℃) **800/237-3687** or 760/320-4117. Fax 760/323-3303. www.viceroypalmsprings.com. 74 units. $149–$299 double; $259–$389 suite; $499–$699 villa. AE, DC, MC, V. Free parking. No pets. **Amenities:** 3 outdoor heated pools (including children's pool); 2 Jacuzzis; fitness room; full-service spa. *In room:* A/C, TV, DVD players, fridge, hair dryer.

Moderate

Korakia Pensione 🐱🐱 If you can work within the Korakia's rigid deposit-cancellation policy, you're in for a special stay at this Greek-Moroccan oasis a few blocks from Palm Canyon Drive. This former artist's villa from the 1920s draws a hip international crowd of artists, writers, and musicians. The simply furnished rooms and spacious suites are peaceful and private, surrounded by flagstone courtyards and flowering gardens. Rooms are divided between the main house, a second restored villa across the street, and guest bungalows. Most have kitchens; many have fireplaces. All beds are blessed with thick duvets, and the windows are shaded by flowing white-canvas Mediterranean-style draperies. You also get a sumptuous breakfast served in your room or poolside. *Korakia* is Greek for "crow," and a tile mosaic example graces the pool bottom. *Note:* You must pay a deposit when booking a room, there's a 2-night minimum on weekends, and you have to give at least 2 weeks' cancellation notice (*45 days'* advance notice for holidays) or you'll lose your deposit.

257 S. Patencio Rd., Palm Springs, CA 92262. (C) **760/864-6411.** Fax 760/864-4147. www.korakia.com. 20 units. $129–$199 double; from $289 suite. Rates include breakfast. MC, V. Free parking. **Amenities:** 2 outdoor heated pools; in-room massage. *In room:* A/C, fridge, coffeemaker, safe, hair dryer and iron on request.

Movie Colony Hotel 🞻🞻 Take one classic 1930s hotel designed by prolific and renowned area architect Albert Frey, newly remodeled with black and white 1935 Moderne suites, some two-storied, and you've got a flashback into the reel world.

726 N. Indian Canyon Dr., Palm Springs, CA 92262. (C) **888/953-5700** or 760/320-6340. Fax 760/320-1640. www.moviecolonyhotel.com. 16 units. High season $169–$229 double; $239–$269 suite. Rates include continental breakfast and evening wine. AE, MC, V. Free parking. **Amenities:** Outdoor heated pool; Jacuzzi; massage; patio or balcony; complimentary bicycles. *In room:* A/C, TV w/DVD, minibar, fridge, hair dryer, iron, robes.

Spa Resort Casino This is one of the more unusual choices in town. It's on the Indian-owned parcel of land containing the mineral springs for which Palm Springs was named. The Cahuilla claimed that the springs had magical powers to cure illness. Today's travelers still come here to pamper body and soul by "taking the waters," though now the facility is sleekly modern. There are three pools on the premises: One is a conventional outdoor swimming pool; the other two are filled from the underground natural springs brimming with revitalizing minerals. Inside the hotel's extensive spa are private sunken marble swirl-pools fed by the springs. After your bath, you can avail yourself of the many pampering treatments offered. Despite the addition of the Vegas-style casino (a separate unit across the street), the Cahuilla have truly managed to integrate modern hotel comforts with the ancient healing and Indian spirit this land represents.

100 N. Indian Canyon Dr., Palm Springs, CA 92263. (C) **800/854-1279** or 760/325-1461. Fax 760/325-3344. www.sparesortcasino.com. 229 units. $169–$289 double; from $319 suite. AE, DC, MC, V. Free parking. **Amenities:** Restaurant; 2 bars; 3 outdoor heated pools; fitness center; full-service spa; concierge; car-rental desk; room service. *In room:* A/C, TV, fridge, hair dryer, iron.

Villa Royale 🞻 This charming inn, 5 minutes from the hustle and bustle of downtown, evokes a European cluster of villas, complete with climbing bougainvillea and rooms filled with international antiques and artwork. Uniform luxuries (down comforters and other pampering touches) appear throughout. Rooms vary widely in size and ambience; larger isn't always better, as some of the inn's most appealing rooms are in the smaller, more affordable range. Many rooms have fireplaces, private patios, full kitchens, and a variety of other amenities. A full breakfast is served in an intimate garden setting surrounding the main pool. The hotel's romantic restaurant, **Europa** (p. 648), is a sleeper, offering some of Palm Springs's very best meals.

1620 Indian Trail (off E. Palm Canyon), Palm Springs, CA 92264. (C) **800/245-2314** or 760/327-2314. Fax 760/ 322-3794. www.villaroyale.com. 31 units. $139–$209 double; $269–$329 suite. Rates include full breakfast. Extra person $25. AE, DC, DISC, MC, V. Free parking. **Amenities:** Restaurant; 2 outdoor heated pools; Jacuzzi; in-room massage. *In room:* A/C, TV, dataport, hair dryer, iron.

Inexpensive

Calla Lily Inn   Newly opened after an extensive renovation, this nine-unit inn offers Deluxe rooms with kitchens and Suite poolside rooms, all with tile floors and luxurious beds. Instead of the usual wine at cocktail time, the Calla Lily offers a nighttime cordial or brandy. The tropical decor is enhanced by the lush landscaping with, what else, calla lilies. Two-day minimum on weekends and holidays, no pets, and all rooms are nonsmoking.

350 S. Belardo Rd., Palm Springs, CA 92262. ℂ 888/888-5787 or 760/323-3654. Fax 760/323-4964. www. callalilypalmsprings.com. 9 units. $149 double; $159–$279 suite. AE, DC, DISC, MC, V. **Amenities:** Pool; Jacuzzi; on-site massage. *In room:* A/C, TV w/VCR and DVD, coffeemaker, ironing board, daily newspaper, wireless Internet access, guest robes.

Casa Cody ⍟   Once owned by "Wild" Bill Cody's niece, this 1920s casa with a double courtyard (each with swimming pool) has been restored to fine condition. It now sports a Southwestern decor and peaceful grounds marked by large lawns and mature, blossoming fruit trees. You'll feel more like a houseguest than a hotel client at the Casa Cody. It's located in the residential "Tennis Club" area of town, a couple of easy blocks from Palm Canyon Drive. Many units here have fireplaces and full-size kitchens. Breakfast is served poolside, as are complimentary wine and cheese on Saturday afternoons. Kids are welcome.

175 S. Cahuilla Rd. (between Tahquitz Way and Arenas Rd.), Palm Springs, CA 92262. ℂ 800/231-2639 or 760/320-9346. Fax 760/325-8610. www.casacody.com. 23 units. $89–$149 double; from $159 suite. Rates include expanded continental breakfast. AE, DC, DISC, MC, V. Pets accepted for $10 extra per night. **Amenities:** 2 outdoor heated pools; Jacuzzi; in-room massage. *In room:* A/C, TV, fridge.

Orchid Tree Inn   Billed as a "1930s desert garden retreat," the Orchid Tree is a sprawling complex of buildings from the 1920s to 1950s, just a block from Palm Canyon Drive in the "Tennis Club" district. Dedicated family ownership ensures that the place is impeccably maintained. The inn truly feels like a retreat. The grounds are rich with flowering shrubs, citrus trees, and multitudes of hummingbirds, sparrows, and quail drawn by bird feeders and birdbaths. The rooms are nicer than you'd expect at this price, in keeping with the grace and excellence of the entire neighborhood. Room types range from simple, hotel-style doubles to charming bungalows to pool-front studios with sliding-glass doors.

261 S. Belardo Rd. (at Baristo Rd.), Palm Springs, CA 92262. ℂ 800/733-3435 or 760/325-2791. Fax 760/ 325-3855. www.orchidtree.com. 40 units. $110–$145 double; $170–$255 suite. Extra person $15. Rates include expanded continental breakfast (Nov–May only). AE, DC, DISC, MC, V. **Amenities:** 3 swimming pools; 2 Jacuzzis. *In room:* A/C, TV, hair dryer.

Palm Mountain Resort and Spa *(Kids*   Within easy walking distance of Palm Springs's main drag, this former Holiday Inn welcomes kids under 18 free in their parent's room, making it a good choice for families. The rooms are in the two- or the three-story wing, and many have a patio or balcony, with a view of the mountains or the large Astroturf courtyard. Midweek and summer rates can be as low as $99. For the best rates, book online or ask for "Great Rates."

155 S. Belardo Rd., Palm Springs, CA 92262. ℂ 800/622-9451 or 760/325-1301. Fax 760/323-8937. www. palmmountainresort.com. 119 units. High season $179–$199 double. Children 17 and under stay free in parent's room. AE, DC, DISC, MC, V. Free parking. **Amenities:** Restaurant; lounge; heated pool. *In room:* A/C, TV, fridge, coffeemaker, hair dryer, iron.

RANCHO MIRAGE

Marriott's Rancho Las Palmas Resort & Spa ⍟⍟   The early-California charm of this relaxing Spanish hacienda makes Rancho Las Palmas one of the least pretentious luxury resorts in the desert. Dedicated golfers come to play on the adjoining country club's 27 holes; tennis buffs flock to the 25 hotel courts (three of them red clay); everybody enjoys the world-class health spa plus a separate pool with water slide. Guest rooms are arranged in a complex of low-rise, tile-roofed structures, and the public areas have an easygoing elegance, filled with flower-laden stone fountains, smooth terra-cotta tile floors, and rough-hewn wood trim. Each room has a balcony or patio.

41000 Bob Hope Dr., Rancho Mirage, CA 92270. ⓒ **800/I-LUV-SUN** or 760/568-2727. Fax 760/568-5845. www.rancholaspalmas.com. 450 units. $295–$315 double; from $450 suite. Children 17 and under stay free in parent's room. AE, DISC, MC, V. Self-parking. **Amenities:** 2 restaurants; cocktail lounge; 2 outdoor heated pools; night-lit outdoor tennis courts; health club; full-service spa; 2 Jacuzzis; children's programs; concierge; business center; room service (6am–11pm); babysitting; laundry/dry-cleaning service. *In room:* A/C, TV w/pay movies, dataport, minibar, coffeemaker, hair dryer, iron, safe.

Westin Mission Hills Resort 🏨🏨   Designed to resemble a Moroccan palace surrounded by pools, waterfalls, and lush gardens, this self-contained resort stands on 360 acres. It's an excellent choice for families and for travelers who take their golf game seriously. (Regular desert visitors will note the Westin is situated so Palm Springs and Palm Desert are equally accessible without driving on congested Hwy. 101.) Rooms are arranged around the grounds in a series of two-story buildings, with accommodations that range from basic to palatial. All have terraces and come with an array of creature comforts befitting this price range—including the Westin trademark "Heavenly Bed," an ultracomfy white confection so popular many guests order one for home.

Though the Westin has the business demeanor of a practiced group-and-meeting hotel, it offers a multitude of recreation options for leisure travelers, gamblers attracted to the nearby Agua Caliente Casino, or professionals after the day's business is concluded. In addition to their championship golf course, you'll find a running track, bike trails, lawn games, and the freshly expanded Spa at Mission Hills, a boutiquelike oasis whose treatments range from sports massage to pampering Hawaiian body treatments.

71-333 Dinah Shore Dr. (at Bob Hope Dr.), Rancho Mirage, CA 92270. ⓒ **800/WESTIN-1** or 760/328-5955. Fax 760/321-2955. www.starwood.com. 512 units. $300–$480 double; from $400 suite. Extra person $35. Children under 18 stay free in parent's room. Golf, spa, and family packages available. AE, DC, DISC, MC, V. Free valet and self-parking. **Amenities:** Excellent restaurant serving breakfast all day; 2 lounges; 3 poolside cabana bars; multiple outdoor heated pools and Jacuzzis; night-lit outdoor tennis courts; health club; full-service spa; bike rental; children's activity center; concierge; business center; 24-hr. room service; in-room massage; babysitting; dry-cleaning/laundry service; water slide. *In room:* A/C, TV w/pay movies, dataport, minibar, coffeemaker, hair dryer, iron, safe.

PALM DESERT

Desert Springs—A JW Marriott Resort & Spa 🏨🏨   A tourist attraction in its own right, Marriott's Desert Springs resort is worth a peek even if you're not lucky enough to stay here. Most of the guests are attracted by the golf and tennis facilities, and the luxurious, full-service spa is an added perk. Visitors enter this artificial desert oasis via a sweeping palm-tree-lined road wending its way past a small pond that's home to a gaggle of pink flamingos. Once inside, guests are greeted by a shaded marble lobby "rainforest" replete with interior moat and the squawk of tropical birds; gondolas even ply the lobby's waterways.

While the rooms here are not as fancy as the lobby would lead you to believe, they're exceedingly comfortable, decorated with muted pastels and contemporary furnishings. All have terraces with views of the golf course and the San Jacinto Mountains. Recreational options include a jogging trail, 36 holes of golf, driving range, a unique 18-hole putting range, basketball courts, lawn croquet, and a

---

Tips **A La Quinta Bed & Breakfast Hideaway**

Devotees of bed-and-breakfasts or boutique inns might find the La Quinta Resort's 900-plus rooms a little daunting, but there's a way to enjoy this quiet, affluent end of the valley with a little more intimacy. Check out the hidden-secret **Lake La Quinta Inn,** 78-120 Caleo Bay (© **888/226-4546** or 760/564-7332; www.lakelaquintainn.com), a 13-room Norman-style B&B on the shores of a man-made lake (surrounded by homes) just blocks from the famous resort. Exquisitely outfitted rooms, delightful hosts, on-site massage, and a 24-hour pool and Jacuzzi complete the fantasy. Rates range from $199 to $399; suites are $499 to $599.

---

sunbathing "beach" with volleyball court—you don't have to ever leave the premises if you don't want to.

74855 Country Club Dr., Palm Desert, CA 92260. © 800/331-3112 or 760/341-2211. Fax 760/341-1872. www.desertspringsresort.com. 886 units. $350–$400 double; from $600 suite. Children 17 and under stay free in parent's room. AE, DC, DISC, MC, V. **Amenities:** 5 restaurants; 4 snack bars; 2 lounges; 5 heated outdoor pools; 5 outdoor Jacuzzis; 20 tennis courts (hard, clay, and grass; 7 lit); full-service spa and health club; bike rental; children's programs; game room; concierge; tour desk; car-rental desk; business center; shopping arcade; salon; room service; in-room massage; babysitting; dry-cleaning/laundry service. *In room:* A/C, TV w/pay movies, dataport, minibar, coffeemaker, hair dryer, iron, safe.

LA QUINTA

La Quinta Resort & Club 🏨🏨🏨   A luxury resort amid citrus trees, towering palms, cacti, and desert flowers at the base of the Santa Rosa Mountains, La Quinta is *the* place to be if you're serious about your golf or tennis. The resort is renowned for its five championship golf courses—including one of California's best, Pete Dye's PGA West TPC Stadium Course. All guest rooms are in single-story, Spanish-style buildings throughout the grounds. Each has its own patio and access to one of several dozen small pools, enhancing the feeling of privacy at this retreat. Some units have a fireplace or private Jacuzzi. The tranquil lounge and library in the original hacienda hearkens back to the early days of the resort, when Clark Gable, Greta Garbo, Frank Capra, and other luminaries chose La Quinta as their hideaway. The resort includes **Spa La Quinta,** a Mission-style complex with 35 treatment rooms for every pampering luxury.

49499 Eisenhower Dr., La Quinta, CA 92253. © 800/598-3828 or 760/564-4111. Fax 760/564-7656. www. laquintaresort.com. 800 units. $445–$485 double; from $675 suite. $15 resort fee per night. Extra person $25. Children 17 and under stay free in parent's room. Packages available. AE, MC, V. Free self-parking; valet parking $15. **Amenities:** 5 restaurants (including Azur by Le Bernadin for fine dining and Adobe for Mexican); 3 bars (2 featuring entertainment); 41 outdoor pools w/Jacuzzis; 23 outdoor tennis courts (10 night-lit); full-service spa; bike rental; children's programs; concierge; business center; 24-hr. room service; in-room massage; babysitting; laundry service. *In room:* A/C, TV/VCR w/pay movies, dataport, minibar, coffeemaker, hair dryer, iron, safe.

WHERE TO DINE
PALM SPRINGS
Expensive

Europa Restaurant 🏨🏨 CALIFORNIA/CONTINENTAL   Long advertised as the "most romantic dining in the desert," Europa is a sentimental favorite of many regulars among an equally gay and straight clientele. This European-style hideaway exudes charm and ambience. Whether you sit under the stars on Europa's garden patio or in subdued candlelight indoors, you'll savor dinner prepared by one of Palm Springs's most dedicated kitchens and served by a discreetly attentive staff. Standout dishes include Andalusia Loin of Pork, filet mignon on a bed of crispy onions with garlic butter, and a show-stopping salmon baked in parchment with crème fraîche and dill. For dessert, don't miss the signature chocolate mousse—smooth, grainy, and addictive.

1620 Indian Trail (at the Villa Royale). © 760/327-2314. Reservations recommended. Main courses $22–$34. AE, DC, DISC, MC, V. Tues–Sun 6–9pm; Sun 11:30am–2pm.

Moderate

Edgardo's Café Veracruz ✦ MEXICAN   The pleasant but humble ambience at Edgardo's is a welcome change from touristy Palm Springs. The expert menu features authentic Mayan, Huasteco, and Aztec cuisine. The dark interior boasts an array of colorful masks and artwork from Central and South America, but the postage-stamp-size front patio with a fountain is the best place to sample Edgardo's tangy quesadillas, desert cactus salad, and poblano chiles rellenos—and perhaps even an oyster-tequila shooter from the oyster bar!

494 N. Palm Canyon (at W. Alejo Rd.). © 760/320-3558. Reservations recommended for weekend dinner. Main courses $8–$22 dinner, $7–$11 lunch. AE, DC, DISC, MC, V. Daily 11am–10pm. Free parking.

Las Casuelas Terraza CLASSIC MEXICAN   The original Las Casuelas, a tiny storefront several blocks away, is still open, but the bougainvillea-draped front patio here is a much better place to people-watch. You can order Mexican standards like quesadillas, enchiladas, and mountainous nachos, as well as equally supersized margaritas. Inside, the action heats up with live music and raucous happy-hour crowds (Mon–Fri 4:30–6:30pm). During hot weather the patio and even sidewalk passersby are cooled by the restaurant's well-placed misters, making this a perfect late-afternoon or early-evening choice.

222 S. Palm Canyon Dr. © 760/325-2794. www.lascasuelas.com. Reservations recommended on weekends. Main courses $7–$13. AE, DC, DISC, MC, V. Mon–Fri 11am–10pm; Sat–Sun 10am–10pm.

Inexpensive

Murph's Gaslight PAN FRIED CHICKEN   Join those in the know at this budget-saving lunch-and-dinner rendezvous where the chicken just keeps coming and coming. There are all the trimmings: black-eyed peas, mashed potatoes, corn bread, hot biscuits, country gravy, and fruit cobbler. Call ahead for takeout or join this family-style restaurant on a first-come, first-served basis.

79-860 Ave. 42, near the airport in Bermuda Dunes. © 760/345-6242. $14 for full dinner. MC, V. Tues–Sat 11am–3pm and 5–9pm; Sun 3–9pm.

Mykonos GREEK   Locals have been enjoying Greek specialties at this family-run spot for 10 years. Mykonos is casual, offering simple, candlelit tables (with vinyl tablecloths and the like) in an off-street brick courtyard (entered only from Palm Canyon), but it's a pleasant treat. Traditional lamb shanks over rice, *dolmades* (stuffed grape leaves), moussaka, salads with crumbled feta cheese, and sweet, sticky baklava are among the best items. Be aware that the house wine is Greek.

139 Andreas (just off Palm Canyon). © 760/322-0223. Most items under $15. MC, V. Wed–Mon 11am–2:30pm and 5–9:30pm.

Sherman's Deli and Bakery KOSHER DELI   Join the locals at this indoor and outdoor-patio eatery with 2-inch-thick deli sandwiches, lox and bagels, and a bakery with some of the richest and most delicious cakes and pastries that will put any calorie-conscious dieter into trauma. Iced tea is the drink of the day, but wine and beer are also available. A full lunch can be had on the Lite Lunch Special: chicken or matzo ball soup with a half sandwich of any of the regular deli variety.

401 Tahquitz, Palm Springs, ⓒ **760/325-1199**; and 73-161 Country Club Dr., Palm Desert **760/568-1350.** Breakfast omelets $5.95–$8.95; deli sandwich board $7.95–$12 (includes potato salad); dinner $14–$17. AE, DC, DISC, MC, V. Open daily 7am–9pm.

Simba's BARBECUE   For the best barbecued ribs in the desert, check out Simba's Ribhouse in Palm Springs. You'll also find down-home versions of chicken and dumplings, black-eyed peas, barbecued beans, corn bread, hush puppies, and sweet-potato pie.

190 N. Sunrise Way, in a former bank building. ⓒ **760/778-7630.** $11–$15. MC. V. Tues–Fri 11am–2pm and 5–10pm; Sat–Sun 3–10pm.

PALM DESERT

Louise's Pantry 𝄐 COFFEE SHOP/DINER   A real old-fashioned diner, Louise's has been a fixture in Palm Springs since opening as a drugstore lunch counter in 1945. The original location on Palm Canyon Drive fell victim to sky-rocketing property values, but not before establishing this welcome offshoot decorated with vintage photos of Louise's heyday. Devoted patrons—young and old—still flock in for premium-quality comfort foods such as Cobb salad, Reuben and French dip sandwiches, chicken and dumplings, hearty breakfasts with biscuits and gravy, and tasty fresh-baked pies.

44491 Town Center Way (at Fred Waring Dr. north of Hwy. 111). ⓒ **760/346-9320.** Reservations not accepted. Most menu items under $10. MC, V. Daily 7am–3pm; dinner (except summer) till 8pm.

Palmie 𝄐 CLASSIC FRENCH   Martine and Alain Clerc's cozy bistro is filled with Art Deco posters of French seaside resorts. Chef Alain sends out masterful traditional French dishes such as bubbling cheese soufflé, green lentil salad dot-ted with pancetta, steak au poivre rich with cognac sauce, and lobster raviolis garnished with caviar. In fact, every carefully garnished plate is a work of art. To the charming background strains of French chanteuses, hostess and manager Martine circulates between tables, determined that visitors should enjoy their meals as much as do the loyal regulars she greets by name. Don't leave without sampling dessert: Our favorite is the trio of petite crème brûlées, flavored with ginger, vanilla, and Kahlúa.

44-491 Town Center Way, Suite G, Palm Desert. ⓒ **760/341-3200.** Reservations recommended. Main courses $13–$28. AE, DC, MC, V. Mon–Sat 5:30–9pm.

Tommy Bahama's Tropical Cafe CARIBBEAN   If all this desert makes you long for *de islands, mon,* step upstairs from fashionable Tommy Bahama's bou-tique for a dose of Caribbean relaxation. The decor alone is worth a visit: a fan-tasy port of call, around 1940, with ceiling fans, plenty of rattan and palms, and upholstery in TB's signature tropical prints. Enormous umbrellas shade patio seating with valley views, and spacious indoor booths make for easy relaxing over a series of sweet umbrella drinks. The food is a delicious change of pace, its Caribbean zing not overly spiced; check out coconut shrimp with mango dip, conch fritters, mango shrimp salad, Boca Chica chicken, Jamaican jerk pork, and Key lime pie for dessert. Diners are an entertaining mix of fresh-from-the-courts socialites, always-on-vacation retirees, and well-heeled shoppers.

73595 El Paseo (at Larkspur Ave.). ⓒ **760/836-0288.** Reservations recommended in season. Main courses $8–$16 lunch, $16–$35 dinner. AE, MC, V. Daily 11am–10pm.

THE DESERT RESORTS AFTER DARK

Every month a different club or disco is the hot spot in the Springs, and the best way to tap into the trend is by consulting the *Desert Guide,* the *Bottom Line* (see "Gay & Lesbian Life in Palm Springs," earlier in this chapter), or one of the many other free newsletters available from area hotels and merchants. **Village-Fest** (see "Shopping," earlier in this chapter) turns Palm Canyon Drive into an outdoor party every Thursday night. Below, I've described a couple of the enduring arts and entertainment attractions around the desert resorts.

The **Fabulous Palm Springs Follies,** at the Plaza Theatre, 128 S. Palm Canyon Dr., Palm Springs (© **760/327-0225;** www.psfollies.com), a vaudeville-style show filled with production numbers, is a long-running hit in the historic Plaza Theatre in the heart of town. With a cast of retired showgirls, singers, dancers, and comedians, the revue is hugely popular. The season runs November through May; call for exact schedule. Tickets range from $37 to $75.

The **McCallum Theatre for the Performing Arts,** 73000 Fred Waring Dr., Palm Desert (© **760/340-ARTS**), offers the only cultural high road around. Frequent symphony performances with visiting virtuosos such as conductor Seiji Ozawa or violinist Itzhak Perlman, musicals like *Cats, Chicago,* and *Riverdance,* and pop performers like Olivia Newton John or Michael Finestein are among the theater's recent offerings. Call for upcoming event information.

CASINOS

Native American gaming has been around in the desert for years now, but recently the industry seems to have joined the major leagues, with a professionalism and polish that create a "virtual Vegas."

The best-known and most centrally located casino is the **Spa Resort Casino** in the heart of Palm Springs (p. 645). The gaming rooms that used to be almost an afterthought now share the spotlight with the hot springs. Attendees at the hotel's conference center can often be found playing hooky from business at one or both!

You can't help but be impressed by the brilliant neon fireballs of the **Agua Caliente Casino,** 32-250 Bob Hope Dr., Rancho Mirage (© **760/321-2000;** www.hotwatercasino.com), down the street from the Westin Mission Hills. The complex boasts a full house of dining options plus musical entertainers and boxing matches; it will also eventually include an on-site hotel of its own.

And it was only a matter of time before Donald Trump came to mine gold in the California desert: Check out his venture, the **Trump 29 Casino,** 46-200 Harrison Place, Coachella (© **866/TRUMP-29;** www.trump29.com), about a half-hour from Palm Springs. The land may be tribal-owned, but this sophisticated complex is Vegas all the way, from the big-name shows and a high-roller players club to 24-hour fine dining and even one of those all-you-can-eat prime-rib buffets.

4 Joshua Tree National Park ✮

40 miles NE of Palm Springs; 128 miles E of L.A.

The Joshua trees in this national park are merely a jumping-off point for exploring this seemingly barren desert. Viewed from the roadside, the dry land only hints at hidden vitality, but closer examination reveals a giant mosaic of intense beauty and complexity. From lush oases teeming with life to rusted-out relics of man's attempts to tame the wilderness, from low plains of tufted cacti to mountains of exposed, twisted rock, the park is much more than a tableau of the curious tree for which it is named.

The Joshua tree is said to have been given its name by early Mormon settlers traveling west, for its upraised limbs and bearded appearance reminded them of the prophet Joshua leading them to the promised land. Other observers were not so kind. Explorer John C. Frémont called it "the most repulsive tree in the vegetable kingdom." Nature writer Charles Francis Saunders opined: "The trees themselves were as grotesque as the creations of a bad dream; the shaggy trunks and limbs were twisted and seemed writhing as though in pain, and dagger-pointed leaves were clenched in bristling fists of inhospitality."

That's harsh criticism for this hardy desert dweller, really not a tree but a variety of yucca and member of the lily family. The relationship is apparent when pale-yellow, lilylike flowers festoon the limbs of the Joshuas when they bloom in March, April, or May (depending on rainfall). When Mother Nature cooperates, the park also puts on quite a wildflower display, and you can get an updated report on prime viewing sites by calling the park ranger (see "Essentials" below).

The park, which reaches the southernmost boundary of this special tree's range, straddles two desert environments. There's the mountainous, Joshua tree–studded Mojave Desert forming the northwestern part of the park, while the Colorado Desert—hotter, drier, lower, and characterized by a wide variety of desert flora, including cacti, cottonwood, and native California fan palms—comprises the southern and eastern sections of the park. Between them runs the "transition zone," displaying characteristics of each.

The area's geological timeline is fascinating, stretching back 8 million years to a time when the Mojave landscape was one of rolling hills and grasslands; horses, camels, and mastodons abounded, preyed upon by saber-toothed tigers and wild dogs. Displays at the Oasis Visitor Center show how resulting climatic, volcanic, and tectonic activity have created the park's signature cliffs and boulders and turned Joshua Tree into the arid desert you see today.

Human presence has been traced back nearly 10,000 years with the discovery of Pinto Man, and evidence of more recent habitation can be seen in the form of Native American pictographs carved into rock faces throughout the park. Miners and ranchers began coming in the 1860s, but the boom went bust by the turn of the 20th century. Then a Pasadena doctor, treating World War I veterans suffering from respiratory and heart ailments caused by mustard gas, prescribed the desert's clean, dry air—and the town of Twentynine Palms was (re)born.

In 1994, under provisions of the federal California Desert Protection Act, Joshua Tree was "upgraded" to national park status and expanded to nearly 800,000 acres. The park is popular with everyone from campers to wildflower lovers and even RVers just cruising through. It's a must-see for nature and geology lovers visiting during temperate weather, and more "user-friendly" than the other two hard-core desert parks.

ESSENTIALS
GETTING THERE   From metropolitan Los Angeles, the usual route to the Oasis Visitor Center in Joshua Tree National Park is via I-10 to its intersection with Calif. 62 (some 92 miles east of downtown). Calif. 62 (the Twentynine Palms Hwy.) leads northeast for about 43 miles to the town of Twentynine Palms. Total driving time is around 2½ hours. In town, follow the signs at National Park Drive or Utah Trail to the visitor center and ranger station. Admission to the park is $10 per car (good for 7 days). Camping fees: $5 with no water, $10 with water.

WHEN TO GO   The park is busiest—relatively speaking, since it rarely feels crowded—in the winter months (Nov–Mar). Rock climbers flock to Joshua Tree in winter and spring, along with day-trippers drawn by brilliant wildflower displays (if winter rainfall was sufficient) during March, April, and May. Even the sizzling summer months are popular with international visitors curious about the legendary extremes of temperature, and hardy campers looking for the solitude of balmy evenings.

VISITOR CENTERS & INFORMATION   In addition to the main **Oasis Visitor Center** (© 760/367-5500) at the Twentynine Palms entrance, **Cotton-wood Visitor Center** is at the south entrance, and the privately operated **Park Center** is located in the town of Joshua Tree, close to the West Entrance, unofficially also the portal for rock climbers.

The Oasis Visitor Center is open daily (except Christmas) from 8am to 5pm. Check here for a detailed map of park roads, plus schedules of ranger-guided walks and interpretive programs. Ask about the weekend tours of the Desert Queen Ranch, once a working homestead and now part of the park.

For information before you go, contact the **Park Superintendent's Office,** 74485 National Park Dr., Twentynine Palms, CA 92277 (© 760/367-5500; www.nps.gov/jotr). The Joshua Tree National Park Association is another good resource; reach them at © 760/367-5500; www.joshuatree.org. Another outfit focused on the surrounding communities is **www.desertgold.com**.

EXPLORING THE PARK

An excellent first stop, outside the park's north entrance, is the main **Oasis Visitor Center,** located alongside the Oasis of Mara, also known as the Twentynine Palms Oasis. For many generations, the native Serrano tribe lived at this "place of little springs and much grass." Get maps, books, and the latest in road, trail, and weather conditions before beginning your tour.

From the Oasis Center, drive south to **Jumbo Rocks,** which captures the essence of the park: a vast array of rock formations, a Joshua tree forest, and the yucca-dotted desert, open and wide. Check out Skull Rock (one of the many rocks in the area that appear to resemble humans, dinosaurs, monsters, cathedrals, or castles) via a 1.5-mile nature trail that provides an introduction to the park's flora, wildlife, and geology.

At Cap Rock Junction, the main park road swings north toward the **Wonderland of Rocks,** 12 square miles of massive jumbled granite. This curious maze of stone hides groves of Joshua trees, trackless washes, and several small pools of water. To the south is Keys View Road, which dead-ends at mile-high **Keys View.** From the crest of the Little San Bernardino mountains, enjoy grand desert views that encompass both the highest (Mt. San Gorgonio) and lowest (Salton Sea) points in Southern California.

Don't miss the contrasting Colorado Desert terrain found along Pinto Basin Road—to conserve time, you might plan to exit the park via this route, which ends up at I-10. You'll pass both the **Cholla Cactus Garden** and spindly **Ocotillo Patch** on your way to vast, flat **Pinto Basin,** a barren lowland surrounded by austere mountains and punctuated by trackless sand dunes. The dunes are an easy 2-mile round-trip hike from the backcountry camping board (one of the few man-made markers along this road and one of the only designated parking areas),

---

Tips Load Up on Everything

No restaurants, lodging, gas stations, or stores are found within Joshua Tree National Park. In fact, water is only available at five park locations: Cottonwood Springs, the Black Rock Canyon Campground, the Indian Cove Ranger Station, the West Entrance (the hamlet of Joshua Tree), and the Oasis Visitor Center. Joshua Tree, Twentynine Palms, and Yucca Valley have lots of restaurants, markets, motels, and B&Bs.

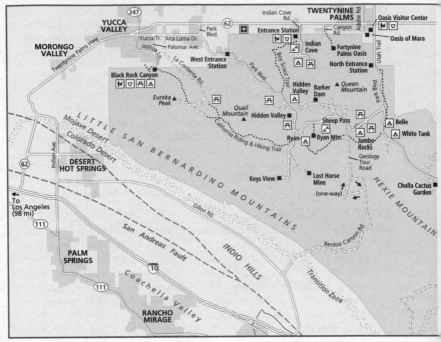

or simply continue to **Cottonwood Springs,** near the southern park entrance. Besides a small ranger station and well-developed campground, Cottonwood has a cool, palm-shaded oasis that is the trail head for a tough hike to Lost Palms Oasis.

HIKING, BIKING & CLIMBING

HIKING & NATURE WALKS   The national park holds a variety of nature trails ranging in difficulty from strenuous challenges to kid-friendly interpretive walks—two of these (**Oasis of Mara** and **Cap Rock**) are paved and wheelchair-accessible. A favorite of the 11 short interpretive trails is **Cholla Cactus Garden,** smack-dab in the middle of the park, where you stroll through dense clusters of the deceptively fluffy-looking "teddy bear cactus."

For the more adventurous, **Barker Dam** is an easy 1-mile loop accessible by a graded dirt road east of Hidden Valley. A small, man-made lake is framed by the majestic Wonderland of Rocks. In addition to scrambling atop the old dam, it's fun to search out Native American petroglyphs carved into the base of cliffs lining your return to the trail head.

The challenging **Lost Horse Mine Trail** near Keys View leads through rolling hills to the ruins of a successful gold-mining operation; once here, a short, steep hike leads uphill behind the ruins for a fine view into the heart of the park.

When you're ready for a strenuous hike, try the **Fortynine Palms Oasis Trail,** accessible from Canyon Road in Twentynine Palms. After a steep, harsh ascent to a cactus-fringed ridge, the rocky canyon trail leads to a spectacular oasis, complete with palm-shaded pools of green water and abundant birds and other wildlife. Allow 2 to 3 hours for the 3-mile round-trip hike.

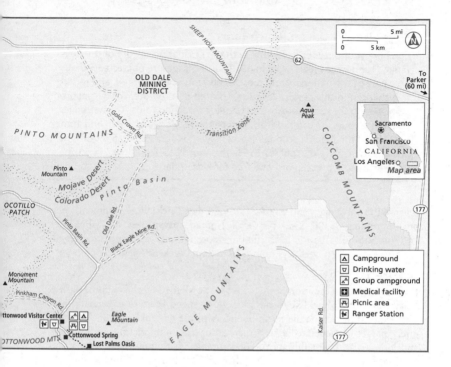

Another lush oasis lies at the end of **Lost Palms Oasis Trail** at Cottonwood Springs. The first section of the 7.5-mile trail is moderately difficult, climbing slowly to the oasis overlook; from here, a treacherous path continues to the canyon bottom, a remote spot that the elusive bighorn sheep find attractive.

MOUNTAIN BIKING   Much of the park is designated wilderness, meaning that bicycles are limited to roads (they'll damage the fragile ecosystem if you venture off the beaten track). None of the paved roads have bike lanes, but rugged mountain bikes are a great tool to explore the park via unpaved roads, where there aren't many cars.

Try the 18-mile **Geology Tour Road,** which begins west of Jumbo Rocks. Dry lake beds contrast with towering boulders along this sandy downhill road, and you'll also encounter abandoned mines.

A shorter but still rewarding ride begins at the **Covington Flats** picnic area. A steep 4-mile road climbs through Joshua trees, junipers, and pinyon pines to Eureka Peak, where you'll be rewarded with a panoramic view.

For other bike-friendly unpaved and four-wheel-drive roads, consult the official park map.

ROCK CLIMBING   From Hidden Valley to the Wonderland of Rocks, the park has emerged as one of the state's premier rock-climbing destinations. The park offers some 4,000 climbing routes, ranging from the easiest of bouldering to some of the sport's most difficult climbs. November through May is the prime season to watch lizardlike humans scale sheer rock faces with impossible grace. Beginners can get into the act with the **Joshua Tree Rock Climbing School** (© **800/890-4745** or 760/366-4745; www.rockclimbingschool.com), which has been operating since 1988 and offers weekend and 4-day group lessons ($110 for

---

> ⓘ **Tips**   **Desert Queen Ranch Tours**
>
> Combine your outdoor adventure with the fascinating history of the Keys family, rugged pioneers who in 1919 settled a desert homestead that's now part of the national park, then for 60 years lived, worked, and raised five children in this remote location. Located in a remote, rocky canyon, admission to the ranch is restricted to guided walking tours. The half-mile, 90-minute tours are offered from October to May daily at 10am and 1pm (call ahead for summer schedule). You may book tours up to 5 months in advance by calling ⓒ **760/367-5555.** The tour is $5 for adults, $2.50 for children 6 to 12 and seniors, and free for kids under 6.

---

1 day, $195 for 2 days, and $390–$490 for 4 days, including equipment), plus private guiding ($300–$330 per day). **Nomad Adventures** in Joshua Tree (ⓒ **760/366-4684**) is the local climbing store for gear sales and shoe rentals ($7.50 a day). Open weekdays from 8am to 8pm, weekends 8am to 6pm.

WHERE TO STAY

If you're staying in the Palm Springs area, it's possible to do the national park as a day trip. But if you'd like to stay close by or spend more time here, Twentynine Palms, just outside the north boundary of the national park on Calif. 62, offers budget-to-moderate lodging; there are also accommodations in Blackrock and Joshua Tree (West Entrance). For a complete listing of Twentynine Palms lodging, contact the **29 Palms Chamber of Commerce,** 6455 Mesquite Rd., Twentynine Palms, CA 92277 (ⓒ **760/367-3445;** www.29chamber.com). Blackrock information is available through the **Yucca Valley Chamber of Commerce,** 56711 Twentynine Palms Hwy., Yucca Valley, CA 92284 (ⓒ **760/ 365-6323;** www.yuccavalley.org). For Joshua Tree (West Entrance), contact the **Joshua Tree Chamber of Commerce,** 61325 Twentynine Palms Hwy. #F, Joshua Tree, CA 92252 (ⓒ **760/366-3723;** www.joshuatreechamber.org).

Near the visitor center in the Oasis of Mara is the rustic **29 Palms Inn** (ⓒ **760/367-3505;** www.29palmsinn.com), a cluster of adobe cottages and old cabins dating from the 1920s; its garden-fresh restaurant is the best in town. There's also the 100-room **Best Western Garden Inn** (ⓒ **760/367-9141;** www. bestwestern.com), a comfortable base from which to maximize your outdoor time. Also recommended in Twentynine Palms is the 53-room **Holiday Inn Express Hotel and Suites,** 71809 Twentynine Palms Hwy. (ⓒ **760/361-4009**).

Nine **campgrounds** scattered throughout the park offer pleasant though often spartan accommodations, with just picnic tables and pit toilets for the most part. Only two—**Black Rock Canyon** and **Cottonwood Springs**—have potable water and flush toilets, for a $10 overnight fee. Indian Cove and West Entrance have water at the ranger station, less than 2 miles from their closest campgrounds. You can make reservations online at **http://reservations.nps.gov** or by calling ⓒ **800/ 365-2267.** Hot showers are available at **Coyote Corner,** 6535 Park Blvd. in Joshua Tree (ⓒ **760/366-9673**); they also rent climbing and camping gear.

5 Anza-Borrego Desert State Park ⓡ

90 miles NE of San Diego; 31 miles E of Julian

The 600,000-acre Anza-Borrego Desert State Park, the nation's largest contiguous state park, lies mostly within San Diego County, and getting to it is almost as much fun as being there. From Julian, the first 20 minutes of the winding hour-long drive feel as if you're going straight downhill; in fact, it's a 7-mile-long drop called Banner Grade. A famous scene from the 1954 movie *The Long, Long Trailer* with Lucille Ball and Desi Arnaz was shot on the Banner Grade, and countless Westerns have been filmed in the Anza-Borrego Desert.

The desert is home to fossils and rocks dating from 540 million years ago; human beings arrived only 10,000 years ago. The terrain ranges in elevation from 15 feet to 6,100 feet above sea level. It incorporates dry lakebeds, sandstone canyons, granite mountains, palm groves fed by year-round springs, and more than 600 kinds of desert plants. After the spring rains, thousands of wildflowers burst into bloom, transforming the desert into a brilliant palette of pink, lavender, red, orange, and yellow. The rare bighorn sheep can sometimes be spotted navigating rocky hillsides, and an occasional migratory bird stops off on the way to the Salton Sea. A sense of timelessness pervades this landscape; travelers tend to slow down and take a long look around.

When planning a trip here, keep in mind that temperatures rise to as high as 115°F (46°C) in summer. Winters days are very comfortable with temperatures in the low to mid 70s (20s Celsius), but note that nighttime temps can drop to freezing—hypothermia is as big a killer out here as the heat.

ESSENTIALS

GETTING AROUND   You don't need a four-wheel-drive vehicle to tour the desert, but you'll probably want to get off the main highways and onto the jeep trails. The Anza-Borrego Desert State Park Visitor Center staff can tell you which jeep trails are in condition for two-wheel-drive vehicles. A Back Country Permit is issued free of charge and is required to camp or use the jeep trails in the park. The Ocotillo Wells area of the park has been set aside for off-road vehicles such as dune buggies and dirt bikes. To use the jeep trails, a vehicle has to be licensed for highway use.

ORIENTATION & VISITOR INFORMATION   In Borrego Springs the Mall is on Palm Canyon Drive, the main drag. Christmas Circle surrounds a grassy park at the entry to town. The **Anza-Borrego Desert State Park Visitor Center** (© 760/767-4205; www.anzaborrego.statepark.org) lies just west of the town of Borrego Springs. It supplies information, maps, and two 15-minute audiovisual presentations, one on the desert's changing faces and the other on wildflowers. The visitor center is open October through May daily from 9am to 5pm, June through September weekends from 9am to 5pm. You might also stop by the **Desert Natural History Association,** 652 Palm Canyon Dr. (tel] **760/767-3098;** www.abdnha.org), whose sleek Borrego Desert Nature Center and Bookstore features an impressive selection of guidebooks, historical resources, educational materials for kids, native plants and regional crafts, and a small museum display that includes a frighteningly real stuffed bobcat. This is also your best source for information on the nearby Salton Sea.

For information on lodging, dining, and activities, contact the **Borrego Springs Chamber of Commerce,** 786 Palm Canyon Dr., Borrego Springs, CA 92004 (© **800/559-5524** or 760/767-5555; www.borregosprings.org).

EXPLORING THE DESERT

Remember that when you're touring in this area, hydration is of paramount importance. Whether you're walking, cycling, or driving, always have a bottle of water at your side. If you will be out after dusk, or anytime during January and February, warm clothing is also essential.

You can explore the desert's terrain on one of its trails or on a self-guided driving tour; the visitor center can supply maps. For starters, the **Borrego Palm Canyon self-guided hike** (1.5 miles each way) starts at the campgrounds near the visitor center. It is beautiful and easy to do, leading to a waterfall and massive fan palms in about 30 minutes. It's grand for photos early in the morning. There is a $4 per vehicle day-use fee.

View spectacular canyons, fossil beds, ancient Native American sites, caves, and more in excursions by desert denizen Paul Ford ("Borrego Paul"), using military-style vehicles. Tours go to the awesome viewpoint at Font's Point, where you can look out on the Badlands—named by the early settlers because it was an impossible area for moving or grazing cattle. Along the way, you'll learn about the history and geology of the area. Tours include drinks, snacks, and pickup at any Borrego Springs lodging; prices start at $69 for the standard 3½-hour adventure. Also inquire about Paul's nighttime tours.

WHERE TO STAY

Borrego Springs is small, but there are enough accommodations to suit all travel styles and budgets. Peak season corresponds with the most temperate weather and wildflower viewing—mid-January through mid-May. Other decent options include **Palm Canyon Resort,** 221 Palm Canyon Dr. (© **800/242-0044** or 760/767-5341; www.pcresort.com), a large complex that includes a moderately priced hotel, RV park, restaurant, and recreational facilities; and, **Borrego Valley Inn,** 405 Palm Canyon Dr. (© **800/333-5810** or 760/767-0311; www. borregovalleyinn.com), a newly built Southwestern complex featuring sand-colored pueblo-style rooms and upscale bed-and-breakfast amenities.

La Casa del Zorro Desert Resort 🏆🏆   This pocket of heaven on earth was built in 1937, and the tamarisk trees that were planted then have grown up around it. So have the many charming tile-roofed casitas, originally neighboring homes bought by the resort's longtime owners, San Diego's Copley newspaper family. Over time the property has grown into a cohesive blend of discreetly private cottages and luxurious two-story hotel buildings—each blessed with personalized service and unwavering standards—that make La Casa del Zorro unequaled in Borrego Springs. Courtesy carts ferry you around the lushly planted grounds, and to the resort's stunning new pool area by the resurfaced tennis courts. It's easy to understand why repeat guests book their favorite casita year after year; some have a fireplace or pool, every bedroom has a separate bathroom, and they all have minifridges and microwaves (though a lack of dishes and utensils is calculated to get you into the Spanish-style main lodge's fine dining room). Outdoor diversions include horseshoes, Ping-Pong, volleyball, jogging trails, basketball, shuffleboard, and a life-size chess set. By the way, *zorro* means fox, and you'll find subtle fox motifs throughout the property.

3845 Yaqui Pass Rd., Borrego Springs, CA 92004. © **800/824-1884** or 760/767-5323. Fax 760/767-5963. www.lacasadelzorro.com. 77 units. $245–$405 double; casitas from $280. Extra person $20. AE, DC, DISC, MC, V. **Amenities:** Restaurant (with dress code Oct–May); lounge; 5 outdoor pools; 9-hole putting green; 6 tennis courts; health club and spa; 4 whirlpools; bike rental; activities desk; courtesy car to golf; business center; salon; room service (7am–11pm); in-room massage; babysitting. *In room:* A/C, TV/VCR w/pay movies, dataport, minibar, coffeemaker, hair dryer, iron.

The Palms at Indian Head 🏆🏆 *(Finds)*   It takes a sense of nostalgia and an active imagination for most visitors to truly appreciate Borrego Springs's only bed-and-breakfast. Its fervent owners, David and Cynthia Leibert, are renovating the once-chic resort. Originally opened in 1947, then rebuilt after a fire in

1958, the Art Deco–style hilltop lodge was a favorite hideaway for San Diego's and Hollywood's elite. It played host to stars like Bing Crosby, Clark Gable, and Marilyn Monroe. The Leiberts rescued it from disrepair in 1993, clearing away some dilapidated guest bungalows and uncovering original wallpaper, light fixtures, and priceless memorabilia. As soon as they'd restored several rooms in luxurious Southwestern style, they began taking in guests.

Now up to 12 rooms, the inn also boasts a restaurant, the **Krazy Coyote** (see "Where to Dine" below), that's a culinary breath of fresh air in town. Also restored is the 42×109-foot pool, soon to be joined by the original subterranean grotto bar behind viewing windows at the deep end. The inn occupies the most envied site in the valley—shaded by palms, adjacent to the state park, with a view across the entire Anza-Borrego region. A hiking trail begins steps from the hotel. The Palms at Indian Head rewards you with charm, comfort, and convenience.

2220 Hoberg Rd., Borrego Springs, CA 92004. ℂ **800/519-2624** or 760/767-7788. Fax 760/767-9717. www. thepalmsatindianhead.com. 12 units. $169–$219 double. Extra person $20. DC, DISC, MC, V. Take S22 into Borrego Springs; at Palm Canyon Dr., S22 becomes Hoberg Rd. Continue north ½ mile. **Amenities:** Restaurant; bar; fantastic outdoor pool; room service (8am–9pm); in-room massage; laundry service. *In room:* A/C, TV, fridge, coffeemaker.

CAMPING

The park has two developed campgrounds. **Borrego Palm Canyon,** with 117 sites, is 2½ miles west of Borrego Springs, near the visitor center. Full hookups are available, and there's an easy hiking trail. **Tamarisk Grove,** at Highway 78 and county road S3, has 27 sites. The overnight rate at both ranges $12 to $20. Both have restrooms with pay showers (bring quarters!) and a campfire program; reservations are a good idea. The park allows open camping along all trail routes. For more information, check with the visitor center (ℂ **760/767-4205;** www. anzaborrego.statepark.org).

WHERE TO DINE

Pickings are slim, but your best bet—if you're not willing to break the bank at La Casa del Zorro's classy but pricey dining room (dinner $28–$41)—is the surprisingly good **Krazy Coyote,** which presents varied ingredients and gourmet preparations previously unheard of in this small town. The **Badlands Market & Cafe,** 561 Palm Canyon Dr., in the Mall (ℂ **760/767-4058**), offers a daily board of gourmet light meals that are great for picnics, plus a prepared-foods deli and store that features imported mustards, marinated sun-dried tomatoes, delicate desserts, and other sophisticated treats; it's open daily, Sunday through Thursday from 7:30am to 4pm, and Friday and Saturday until 7pm. Or you could follow legions of locals into downtown mainstay **Carlee's Place,** 670 Palm Canyon Dr. (ℂ **760/767-3262**), a casual bar and grill with plenty of neon beer signs, a pool table, and fuzzy-sounding jukebox. It's easy to understand why Carlee's is the watering hole of choice for motorcycle brigades that pass through town on recreational rides—and the food is tasty, hearty, and priced just right.

Kendall's Cafe COFFEE SHOP   Here's an economical spot to grab a bite. Buffalo burgers and Mexican dishes are popular. Best bet here is breakfast and anything that can be packed to go if you'd rather dine overlooking the desert.

In the Mall, Borrego Springs. ℂ 760/767-3491. Lunch $4–$8; dinner $6–$11. MC, V. Daily 6am–8pm.

Krazy Coyote Saloon & Grille ⌖ ECLECTIC   The same style and perfectionism that pervades David and Cynthia Leibert's bed-and-breakfast is evident in this casual restaurant, which overlooks the inn's swimming pool and the vast desert beyond. An eclectic menu encompasses quesadillas, club sandwiches, burgers, grilled meats and fish, and individual gourmet pizzas. The Krazy Coyote also offers breakfast (rich and hearty for an active day, or light and healthy for diet-watchers). The evening ambience is welcoming and romantic, as the sparse lights of tiny Borrego Springs twinkle on the desert floor below.

In the Palms at Indian Head, 2220 Hoberg Rd. © 760/767-7788. Lunch $6–$12; dinner $6–$20. AE, MC, V. Open daily; call for seasonal hours.

6 Mojave National Preserve

235 miles E of L.A.; 125 miles SW of Las Vegas

Two decades of park politicking ended in 1994 when President Bill Clinton signed into law the California Desert Protection Act, which created the Mojave National Preserve. Thus far, the Mojave's elevated status has not attracted hordes of sightseers, and devoted visitors are happy to keep it that way. Unlike a fully protected national park, the "national preserve" designation allows hunting and certain commercial land uses, and the continued grazing and mining within the preserve's boundaries are a sore spot for ardent environmentalists.

To most Los Angelenos, the East Mojave is that vast, bleak, interminable stretch of desert to be crossed as quickly as possible while leaving California via I-15 or I-40. Few realize that these highways are the boundaries of what some have long considered the crown jewel of the California desert.

This land is hard to get to know—unlike more developed desert parks, it has no lodgings or concessions, few campgrounds, and only a handful of roads suitable for the average passenger vehicle. It takes a special love of the desert to fully appreciate this stark, spare, spartan, barren terrain. But hidden within this natural fortress are some true gems—the preserve's 1.6 million acres include the world's largest Joshua tree forest; abundant wildlife; spectacular canyons, caverns, and volcanic formations; nationally honored scenic back roads and footpaths to historic mining sites; tabletop mesas; and a dozen mountain ranges.

ESSENTIALS

GETTING THERE I-15, the major route between the Southern California metropolis and the state line for Las Vegas–bound travelers, extends along the northern boundary of Mojave National Preserve. I-40 is the southern access route to the East Mojave. It's a 3½-hour drive from Los Angeles to Kelso Depot, roughly in the center of the preserve. The closest major airport is in Las Vegas.

WHEN TO GO Spring is a splendid time to visit this desert (autumn is another). From March to May the temperatures are mild, the Joshua trees are in bloom, and the lower Kelso Dunes are bedecked with yellow and white desert primrose and pink sand verbena.

VISITOR CENTERS & INFORMATION You can visit the preserve online at **www.nps.gov/moja**. The best source for up-to-date weather conditions and a free topographical map is the **Mojave Desert Information Center,** 72157 Baker Blvd. (under the "World's Tallest Thermometer"), Baker, CA 92309 (© **760/733-4040**), which is open daily from 9am to 5pm and also has a superior selection of books for sale. Additional information and maps are available inside the preserve at the **Hole-in-the-Wall Visitor Center** (© **760/928-2572**), which is open Wednesday to Sunday for most of the year, Friday to Sunday in summer. An additional visitor center was scheduled to open in **Kelso Depot** in early 2005 and become the park's main visitor hub.

EXPLORING THE PARK

One of the preserve's spectacular sights is the **Kelso Dunes,** the most extensive dune field in the West. The 45-square-mile formation of magnificently sculpted sand is famous for "booming": Visitors' footsteps cause miniavalanches and make the dunes go "sha-boom-sha-boom-sha-boom." Geologists speculate that the extreme dryness of the East Mojave Desert, combined with the wind-polished, rounded nature of the individual sand grains, has something to do with their musicality. Sometimes the low rumbling sound resembles a Tibetan gong; other times it sounds like a 1950s doo-wop musical group.

A 10-mile drive from the Kelso Dunes is **Kelso Depot,** built by the Union Pacific in 1924. The Spanish Revival–style structure was designed with a red-tile roof, graceful arches, and a brick platform. The depot continued to be open for freight-train crew use through the mid-1980s, although it ceased to be a railroad stop for passengers after World War II.

On and around **Cima Dome,** a rare geological anomaly, grows the world's largest and densest Joshua tree forest. Botanists say Cima's Joshuas are more symmetrical than their cousins elsewhere in the Mojave. The dramatic colors of the sky at sunset provide a breathtaking backdrop for Cima's Joshua trees, some more than 25 feet tall and several hundred years old.

Tucked into the Providence Mountains, in the southern portion of the preserve, is a treat everyone should try to see. The **Mitchell Caverns** , contained in a state recreation area within the national preserve, is a geological oddity exploited for tourism but still quite fascinating. Regular tours are conducted of these cool rock "rooms"; in addition to showcasing stalactites, stalagmites, and other limestone formations, the caves have proven to be rich in Native American archaeological finds.

Hole-in-the-Wall and **Mid Hills** are the centerpieces of Mojave National Preserve. Both locales offer diverse desert scenery, fine campgrounds, and the feeling of being in the middle of nowhere. The preserve's best drive links the two sites. In 1989 **Wildhorse Canyon Road,** which loops from Mid Hills Campground to Hole-in-the-Wall Campground, was declared the nation's first official "Back Country Byway," an honor federal agencies bestow upon America's most scenic back roads. The 11-mile, horseshoe-shaped road crosses wide-open country dotted with cholla and, in season, purple, yellow, and red wildflowers. Volcanic slopes and flattop mesas tower over the low desert.

Mile-high Mid Hills, so named because of its location halfway between the Providence and New York mountains, recalls the Great Basin Desert topography of Nevada and Utah. Mid Hills Campground offers a grand observation point from which to gaze out at the creamy, coffee-colored Pinto Mountains to the north and the rolling Kelso Dunes shining on the western horizon.

Hole-in-the-Wall is the kind of place Butch Cassidy and the Sundance Kid would have chosen as a hideout. This twisted maze of rhyolite rocks is a form of crystallized red-lava rock. A series of iron rings aids descent into Hole-in-the-Wall; they're not particularly difficult for those who are reasonably agile.

Kelso Dunes, Mitchell Caverns, Cima Dome, and Hole-in-the-Wall are highlights of the preserve that can be viewed in a weekend. But you'll need a week to see all the major sights, and maybe a lifetime to really get to know the East Mojave. And right now, without much in the way of services, the traveler to this desert must be well prepared and self-reliant. For many, this is what makes a trip to the East Mojave an adventure.

HIKING & BIKING

HIKING The free-form ambling climb to the top of the **Kelso Dunes** is 3 miles round-trip. A cool, inviting pinyon pine/juniper woodland is explored by the **Caruthers Canyon Trail** (3 miles round-trip). The longest pathway is **Mid Hills to Hole-in-the-Wall Trail,** a grand tour of basin and range tabletop mesas, large pinyon trees, and colorful cacti; it's 8 miles one-way. If you're not up for a long day hike, the 1-mile trip from **Hole-in-the-Wall Campground** to **Banshee Canyon** and the 5-mile jaunt to **Wildhorse Canyon** offer some easier alternatives. Be sure to pick up trail maps at one of the visitor centers.

MOUNTAIN BIKING Opportunities are as extensive as the preserve's hundreds of miles of lonesome dirt roads. The 140-mile historic **Mojave Road,** a rough four-wheel-drive route, visits many of the most scenic areas in the East Mojave; sections of this road make excellent bike tours. Prepare well: The Mojave Road and other dirt roads are rugged routes through desert wilderness.

CAMPING

The **Mid Hills Campground** is located in a pinyon-pine/juniper woodland and offers outstanding views. This mile-high camp is the coolest in the East Mojave. Nearby **Hole-in-the-Wall Campground** is perched above two canyons. Both campgrounds have pit toilets and potable water but no utility hookups. There is a graded dirt road between the two, but it's suitable for two-wheel-drive passenger cars.

There are also some sites at **Providence Mountain State Recreation Area** (Mitchell Caverns; see "Exploring the Park," above).

One of the highlights of the East Mojave Desert is camping in the open desert all by your lonesome, but certain rules apply. Call the **Mojave Desert Information Center** (© 760/733-4040) for suggestions.

NEARBY TOWNS WITH TOURIST SERVICES

BARSTOW This sizable town has a great many restaurants and motels and is about a 1-hour drive from the center of the preserve. On the east end of Main Street is Barstow Station, looking like a collection of railway cars, but inside is a rambling shop with an amazing collection of tacky souvenirs: Everything from life-size howling wolves made of plaster of Paris to Marilyn Monroe cookie jars. On the other end of Main Street at the Greyhound bus station is a Route 66 museum (© **760/255-1890**). It's only open Friday through Sunday from 11am to 4pm, and admission is free. Of the dozen motels in town, the most reliable are the **Best Western Desert Villa,** 1984 E. Main St., Barstow, CA 92311 (© **760/256-1781**), and the **Ramada Inn,** 1511 E. Main St., Barstow, CA 92311 (© **760/256-5673**).

BAKER Accommodations and food are available in this small desert town, which is a good place to fill up your gas tank and purchase supplies before entering Mojave National Preserve. Inexpensive lodging can be secured at the **Bun Boy Motel,** P.O. Box 130, Baker, CA 92309 (© **760/733-4363**). The Bun Boy Coffee Shop is open 24 hours. For a tasty surprise, hop across the street to the **Mad Greek** (© **760/733-4354**). Order a gyro (pronounced gee-*ro*), Greek salad, souvlaki, or baklava, and marvel at your good fortune for finding such tasty food and pleasant surroundings in the middle of nowhere.

NEWBERRY SPRINGS The only reason for venturing 18 miles southeast of Barstow on Route 66 is to visit the **Bagdad Café** [sic] (© **760/257-3101**). It's

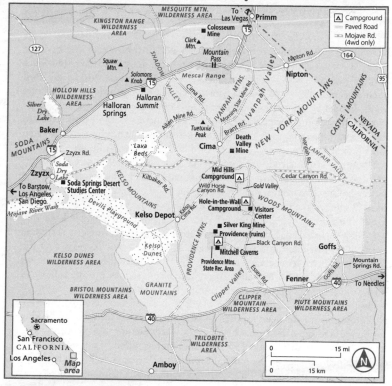

noted for the location of a movie of the same name, which went unnoticed in the States but became a cult favorite of Europeans. They come in busloads to see the site and munch on a Jack Palance burger (with bacon) and mix with some of the colorful locals like General Bob who claims to have designed the Pentagon and can spin some other tall tales.

NIPTON This tiny (pop. 30), charming town boasts a "trading post" that stocks snacks, maps, ice, and native jewelry; and the **Hotel Nipton** (© **760/ 856-2335;** www.nipton.com), a B&B with a sitting room, two bathrooms down the hall, and five guest rooms, each for $70 a night. There are also four eco-tents on platforms that are $60 per night and sleep four. Owners Jerry and Roxanne Freeman, a former hard-rock miner who purchased the entire town in 1984, moved from Malibu to the abandoned ghost town and brought it back to life. Nipton is on Nipton Road, a few miles from I-15 near the Nevada state line.

PRIMM (FORMERLY STATELINE) This privately owned town on the California-Nevada border features three hotel/casinos—Whiskey Pete's, Buffalo Bill's, and Primadonna—each as large and garish as an amusement park and all managed by the same company. Rooms here are pretty nice, cheap, and (if you have a twisted sense of humor) an ironic counterpoint to the wilderness. With a dozen restaurants, including those low-cost Vegas-style buffets, Primm might also be your best dining bet. For reservations, call © **800/FUN-STOP.**

7 Death Valley National Park ⟨★

290 miles NE of L.A.; 120 miles NW of Las Vegas

Park? Death Valley National Park? The Forty-Niners, whose suffering gave the valley its name, would have howled at the notion. To them, other four-letter words would have been more appropriate: gold, mine, heat, lost, dead. And when you trace the whole history, you can imagine a host of other four-letter words shouted by teamsters who drove the 20-mule-team borax wagons.

Americans looking for gold in California's mountains in 1849 were forced to cross the burning sands to avoid severe snowstorms in the nearby Sierra Nevada. Some perished along the way, and the land became known as Death Valley.

Mountains stand naked, unadorned. The bitter waters of saline lakes evaporate into bizarre, razor-sharp crystal formations. Jagged canyons jab deep into the earth. Ovenlike heat, frigid cold, and the driest air imaginable combine to make this one of the most inhospitable locations in the world.

But, human nature being what it is, it's not surprising that people have long been drawn to challenge the power of Mother Nature, even in this, her home court. Man's first foray into tourism began in 1925, a scant 76 years after the Forty-Niners' harrowing experiences (which would discourage most sane folks from ever returning!). It probably would have begun sooner, but the valley had been consumed with lucrative borax mining since the late 1880s.

Death Valley is raw, bare earth, the way it must have looked before life began. Here, forces of the earth are exposed to view with dramatic clarity; just looking out on the landscape, it's impossible to know what year—or what century—it is. It's no coincidence that many of Death Valley's topographical features are associated with hellish images—the Funeral Mountains, Furnace Creek, Dante's View, Coffin Peak, and the Devil's Golf Course. But it can be a place of serenity.

President Herbert Hoover signed a proclamation designating Death Valley a national monument on February 11, 1933. With the stroke of a pen, he not only authorized the protection of a vast and wondrous land but also helped transform one of the earth's least hospitable spots into a tourist destination.

The naming of Death Valley National Monument came at a time when Americans began to discover the romance of the desert. Land that had been considered devoid of life was now celebrated for its spare beauty; places that had been feared for their harshness were now admired for their uniqueness. In 1994, when President Clinton signed the California Desert Protection Act, Death Valley National Park became the largest national park outside Alaska, with over 3.3 million acres. Though remote, it's one of the most heavily visited, and you're likely to hear less English spoken than German, French, and Japanese.

ESSENTIALS

GETTING THERE   There are several routes into the park, all of which involve crossing one of the steep mountain ranges that isolate Death Valley from, well, everything. Perhaps the most scenic entry to the park is via Calif. 190, east of Calif. 178 from Ridgecrest. Another scenic drive to the park is by way of Calif. 127 and Calif. 190 from Baker. For a first-time visitor, take the road 1 mile north of Tocopa, marked to Badwater and Death Valley. It's longer and rougher, but you dip down from the hills into the valley and have the full approach into the region. Otherwise, for the shorter route, continue to 190, which will bring you into Death Valley Center. *Note:* Top off your gas tank in Tocopa—it's pricey but not as bad as in the valley. You'll be required to pay a $10-per-car entrance fee, valid for 7 days. The closest major airport is in Las Vegas.

WHEN TO GO   Death Valley is popular year-round, with the greatest number of visitors during the temperate winter and spring (Nov–Mar). But the park is never deserted, not even in the truly scorching months of July, August, and September, as international visitors and extreme-heat seekers come in ever-increasing numbers to experience record-breaking temperatures. Even during the "cool" months (when evenings can actually become quite chilly), it's essential to wear sunscreen by day to protect against unfiltered rays, and to drink plenty of water to avoid becoming dehydrated in the ultra-arid climate.

VISITOR CENTER & INFORMATION   For information before you go, contact the Superintendent, Death Valley National Park, Death Valley, CA 92328 (© **760/786-3200;** www.nps.gov/deva). The **Furnace Creek Visitor Center & Museum,** 15 miles inside the eastern park boundary on Calif. 190 (© **760/786-3200**), offers interpretive exhibits and an hourly slide program. Ask at the information desk for ranger-led nature walks and evening naturalist programs. The center is open daily from 8am to 6pm in winter (to 5pm in summer).

EXPLORING THE PARK

A good first stop after checking in at the main park visitor center in Furnace Creek is the **Harmony Borax Works**—a rock-salt landscape as tortured as you'll ever find. Death Valley prospectors called borax "white gold," and though it wasn't exactly a glamorous substance, it was a profitable one. From 1883 to 1888, more than 20 million pounds of borax (used to make laundry detergent) were transported from the Harmony Borax Works, and borax mining continued in Death Valley until 1928. A short trail with interpretive signs leads past the ruins of the old borax refinery and some outlying buildings. Transport of the borax was the stuff of legends, too. The famous 20-mule teams hauled the huge loaded wagons 165 miles to the rail station at Mojave. To learn more about this colorful era, visit the Borax Museum at Furnace Creek Ranch and the park visitor center, also located in Furnace Creek.

Badwater—at 282 feet below sea level, the lowest point in the Western Hemisphere—is possibly the hottest place in the world, with regularly recorded summer temperatures of 120°F (49°C). Badwater is mostly a curiosity, and not that much hotter or more brutal than the rest of Death Valley; most folks like to make a brief detour to see the otherworldly landscape and say they were there.

Salt Creek is the home of the **Salt Creek pupfish,** found nowhere else on earth. The little fish, which has made some amazing adaptations to survive in this arid land, can be glimpsed from a boardwalk nature trail. In spring a million pupfish might be wriggling in the creek, but by summer's end only a few thousand remain.

Before sunrise, photographers set up their tripods at **Zabriskie Point** and aim their cameras down at the magnificent panoramic view of Golden Canyon's pale mudstone hills and the great valley beyond. For another spectacular vista, check out **Dante's View,** a 5,475-foot viewpoint looking out over the shimmering Death Valley floor, backed by the high Panamint Mountains.

South of Furnace Creek is the 9-mile loop of **Artists Drive,** an easy must-see for visitors (except those in RVs, which can't negotiate the sharp, rock-bordered curves in the road). From the highway, you can't see the splendid palette of colors splashed on the rocks behind the foothills; once inside, though, stop and climb a hill that offers an overhead view, then continue through to aptly named **Artists Palette,** where an interpretive sign explains the source of nature's rainbow.

Scotty's Castle & the Gas House Museum (© **760/786-2392**), the Mediterranean hacienda in the northern part of the park, is Death Valley's premier tourist attraction. Visitors are wowed by the elaborate Spanish tiles, well-crafted furnishings, and construction that included solar water heating. Even more compelling is the colorful history of this villa in Grapevine Canyon, brought to life by park rangers dressed in 1930s period clothing. Don't be surprised if the castle cook or a friend of Scotty's gives you a special insight into castle life.

Construction of the "castle"—more officially, Death Valley Ranch—began in 1924. It was to be a winter retreat for eccentric Chicago millionaire Albert Johnson. The insurance tycoon's unlikely friendship with prospector, cowboy, and spinner-of-tall-tales Walter Scott put the $2.3-million structure on the map and captured the public's imagination. Scotty greeted visitors and told them fanciful stories from the early hard-rock mining days of Death Valley.

The 1-hour walking tour of Scotty's Castle is excellent, both for its inside look at the mansion and for what it reveals about the eccentricities of Johnson and Scotty. Tours fill up quickly; arrive early for the first available spots (there's an $8 adult, $6 senior, and $4 child fee). A snack bar and gift shop make the wait more comfortable. To learn more about the castle grounds, pick up the pamphlet *A Walking Tour of Scotty's Castle*, which leads you from stable to pool, from bunkhouse to powerhouse. Open daily from 9am to 5pm.

BIKING & HIKING

BIKING   Because most of the park is federally designated wilderness, cycling is allowed only on roads used by cars. Bikes are not allowed on hiking trails.

Good routes for bikers include Racetrack (28 miles, mainly level), Greenwater Valley (30 miles, mostly level), Cottonwood Canyon (20 miles), and West Side Road (40 miles, fairly level with some washboard sections). Artists Drive is 8 miles long and paved, with some steep uphills. A favorite is Titus Canyon, a 28-mile one-way route that starts 2¾ miles east of the park boundary on Nevada Highway 374.

HIKING   The trails in Death Valley range from the half-mile **Salt Creek Nature Trail,** an easy boardwalk path suitable for everyone in the family, to the grueling **Telescope Peak Trail** (14 miles round-trip), an all-day challenge. Telescope Peak is a strenuous, 3,000-foot climb to the 11,049-foot summit, where you'll be rewarded by the view described by one pioneer: "You can see so far, it's just like looking through a telescope." Snow-covered during the winter, the peak is best climbed between May and November.

But there are lots of levels in between. Try the trail into **Mosaic Canyon,** near Stovepipe Wells, where water has polished the marble rock into white, gray, and black mosaics. It's a relatively easy 2.5-mile scramble through long, narrow walls that seem quite "gallery-like"—and provide welcome shade at every turn.

Romping among the **Sand Dunes** on the way to Stovepipe Wells is also fun, particularly for kids. It's a free-form adventure, and the dunes aren't particularly high—but the sun can be merciless. The sand in the dunes is actually tiny pieces of rock, most of them quartz fragments. As with all desert activities, having an adequate water supply is crucial.

Near the park's eastern border, two trails lead from the **Keane Wonder Mill,** site of a successful gold mine. The first is a steep and strenuous 2-mile challenge leading to the mine itself, passing along the way the solid, efficient wooden tramway that carried ore out of the mountain.

If that's beyond your fitness level, try the **Keane Wonder Spring Trail,** leading in another direction. This 2-mile walk is much easier, and the spring that supplied water for the Keane Wonder operation will announce itself with a sulfur smell and piping birdcalls.

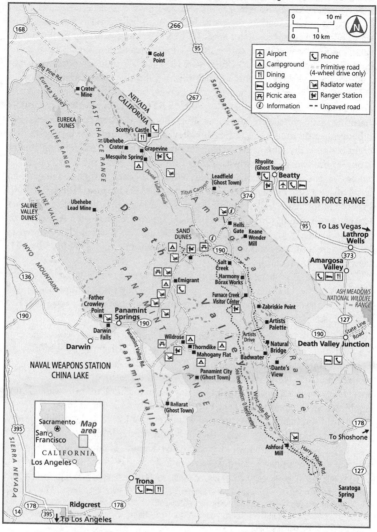

Death Valley National Park

If you're visiting **Ubehebe Crater,** there's a steep but plain trail leading from the parking area up to the crater's lip and around some of the contours. Fierce winds can hamper your progress, but you'll get the exhilarating feeling that you're truly on another planet.

Park rangers can provide topographical maps and detailed directions to these and a dozen other hiking trails within the national park.

WHERE TO STAY

The park's nine campgrounds are at elevations ranging from below sea level to 8,000 feet. In Furnace Creek, **Sunset** offers 1,000 spaces with water and flush toilets. **Furnace Creek Campground** has 200 similarly appointed spaces. **Stovepipe Wells** has 200 spaces with water and flush toilets. Reservations can be made online at **http://reservations.nps.gov** or by calling © **800/365-2267.**

The **Furnace Creek Ranch** (© 760/786-2345; www.furnacecreekresort.com), a private in-holding within the park, has 224 no-frills cottage units with air-conditioning and showers. Rates are $105 to $159. The swimming pool is a popular hangout. Nearby are a coffee shop, saloon, steakhouse, and general store. **Stove Pipe Wells Village** (© 760/786-2387) has 74 modest rooms with air-conditioning and showers, plus a casual dining room that closes between meals.

The only lodging within the park not operated by the official concessionaire is the **Panamint Springs Resort** (© 702/482-7680; www.deathvalley.com), a charming rustic motel, cafe, and snack shop about an hour east of Furnace Creek.

Because accommodations in Death Valley are both limited and expensive, you might consider the money-saving (but inconvenient) option of spending a night at one of the two gateway towns: **Lone Pine,** on the west side of the park, or **Baker,** on the south. **Beatty, Nevada,** which has inexpensive lodging, is an hour's drive from the park's center. The restored **Amargosa Hotel** (© 760/ 852-4441) in Death Valley Junction offers 14 rooms in a historic, out-of-the-way place, 40 minutes from Furnace Creek. If you are there on a winter weekend, check the Amargosa Opera House where dancer Marta Becket painted in 250 spectators on the walls for her dances and pantomimes (© 760/852-4441; www.amargosafilm.com).

Tip: Meals and groceries are exceptionally costly due to the remoteness of the park. If possible, consider bringing a cooler with some snacks, sandwiches, and beverages to last the duration of your visit. Ice is easily obtainable, and you'll also be able to keep water chilled.

Furnace Creek Inn ★★   Like an oasis in the middle of Death Valley, the inn's red-tiled roofs and sparkling blue mineral-spring-fed swimming pool hint at the elegance within. The hotel has equipped its 66 deluxe rooms and suites with every modern amenity while successfully preserving the charm of this 1930s resort. Stroll the palm-shaded gardens before sitting down to a meal in the elegant Dining Room, where the food is excellent but the formality a bit out of place. Don tennis whites for a match in the midwinter sunshine, enjoy 18 holes of golf nearby, take an excursion on horseback—there's even a shuttle from the Furnace Creek airstrip for well-heeled clientele. Reserve early: The inn is booked solid in winter with guests who appreciate a little pampering after a day in the park.

Hwy. 190 (P.O. Box 1), Death Valley, CA 92328. © **800/236-7916** or 760/786-2345. Fax 760/786-2307. www.furnacecreekresort.com. 66 units. $240–$335 double; from $350 suite. Extra person $20. AE, DISC, MC, V. **Amenities:** Restaurant; lounge; naturally heated outdoor pool; nearby golf course (greens fees $35–$55, cart $25); 4 night-lit tennis courts; room service (7am–10pm); in-room massage. *In room:* A/C, TV w/pay movies, fridge, hair dryer, iron.

16

San Diego & Environs

by David Swanson

Best known for its benign climate and fabulous beaches, San Diego is one big outdoor playground. With 70 miles of sandy coastline—plus pretty, sheltered Mission Bay—you can choose from swimming, snorkeling, windsurfing, kayaking, bicycling, in-line skating, and tons of other fun in or near the water. The city is also home to top-notch attractions, including three world-famous animal parks and Balboa Park, a cultural and recreational jewel that's one of the finest urban parks in the country.

Once dismissed as a slow-growth, conservative navy town, San Diego—now the seventh-largest city in the U.S.—has been expanding steadily during the past 2 decades, and now boasts an almost Los Angeles–like diversity of neighborhoods and residents. It also has one of the fastest-rising housing markets in the country,

and a biotech/tourism/telecom economy that—at this writing—fires on all burners. San Diego's military link continues today (yes, it's true: A young John Kerry lived and surfed here before heading off on his second tour of duty in Vietnam). A heightened sensitivity to historical preservation means formerly seedy downtown neighborhoods and architecturally rich suburbs are being carefully restored; they draw a stylish young crowd that's updating the face of San Diego's dining, shopping, and entertainment.

California's first city, San Diego, reflects its Spanish-Mexican heritage in every corner—in fact, bustling Tijuana is just across the border, less than 30 minutes away. So pack a laid-back attitude along with your sandals and swimsuit, and welcome to California's grown-up beach town.

1 Orientation

ARRIVING

BY PLANE

San Diego International Airport, 3707 N. Harbor Dr. (© **619/231-2100;** www.san.org), locally known as Lindbergh Field, is just 2 miles from downtown. All the major domestic carriers fly here, plus **AeroMexico** from Los Cabos and Mexico City. There are three passenger buildings, with short local flights using the Commuter Terminal, a half-mile away.

TRANSPORTATION FROM THE AIRPORT All the major car-rental agencies have offices at the airport, including **Avis** (© **800/230-4898**), **Budget** (© **800/527-0700**), **Dollar** (© **800/800-3665**), and **Hertz** (© **800/654-3131**). If you're driving to downtown from the airport, take Harbor Drive south to Broadway, the main east-west thoroughfare, and turn left. To reach Hillcrest or Balboa Park, exit the airport toward I-5, and follow the signs for Laurel Street. To reach Mission Bay and the beaches, take I-5 north to I-8 west. To reach La Jolla, take I-5 north to the La Jolla Parkway exit, which turns into Torrey Pines Road.

Metropolitan Transit System (MTS) (© **619/233-3004;** www.sdcommute
com) bus route no. 992 provides service between the airport and downtown San
Diego. Route no. 992 bus stops are located at each of the three terminals. The
one-way fare is $2.25. Request a transfer if you're connecting to another bus or
to the San Diego Trolley route downtown. Downtown, route no. 992 stops on
Broadway. The ride takes about 15 minutes; buses come at 10- to 15-minute
intervals. At Broadway and First Avenue is the **Transit Store** (© **619/234-
1060**), where the staff can answer your transit questions and provide free route
maps to help you get where you're going.

Shuttle services run regularly from the airport to points around the city; you'll
see designated pickup areas outside each terminal. The fare is about $5 per per-
son to downtown; Mission Valley and Mission Beach are $8 to $10; La Jolla and
Coronado are $10 to $13—rates to a residence in these areas are usually about
double for the first person. **Taxis** line up outside both terminals and the trip to a
downtown location, usually a 10-minute ride, is about $10 (plus tip); budget $20
to $22 for Coronado or Mission Beach, and about $30 to $35 for La Jolla.

BY CAR

From Los Angeles, you'll enter San Diego via coastal route **I-5.** From points
northeast of the city, you'll come down on **I-15** and **Calif. 163** south to drive
into downtown (where 163 turns into 10th Ave.), or hook up with **I-8** west for
the beaches. From the east, you'll come in on I-8, connecting with Calif. 163
south. The freeways are well marked, pointing the way to downtown streets.

BY TRAIN

San Diego is connected to the rest of the country by **Amtrak** (© **800/USA-
RAIL;** www.amtrak.com), but only via Los Angeles. Trains pull into San Diego's
pretty Mission-style **Santa Fe Train Depot,** 1850 Kettner Blvd. (at Broadway),
within walking distance of some downtown hotels and 1½ blocks from the
Embarcadero. Expect to pay $25 one-way from Los Angeles.

BY BUS

Greyhound (© **800/229-9424;** www.greyhound.com) buses from Los Angeles,
Phoenix, Las Vegas, and other points in the southwest U.S. arrive at the station in
downtown San Diego at 120 W. Broadway. The one-way fare from Los Angeles is
$15. Local buses stop in front, and the San Diego Trolley is nearby.

VISITOR INFORMATION

There are staffed information booths at airport terminals, the train station, and
the cruise ship terminal. Downtown, the Convention & Visitor Bureau's **International Visitor Information Center** (© **619/236-1212;** www.sandiego.org)
is located at 1040½ W. Broadway at Harbor Boulevard (across the street from the
cruise ship terminal). The *Official Visitors Pocket Guide* includes information on
accommodations, dining, activities, attractions, tours, and transportation. Be
sure to ask for the *San Diego Travel Values* pamphlet, which is full of discount
coupons for hotels, restaurants, and attractions. The center is open Monday
through Saturday from 9am to 5pm year-round; it is closed on major holidays.
There is also a walk-up-only facility (that means no phone) at the **La Jolla
Visitor Center,** 7966 Herschel Ave., near the corner of Prospect Street. This
office is open daily: in summer from 10am to 7pm, with a shortened schedule
mid-September through mid-June.

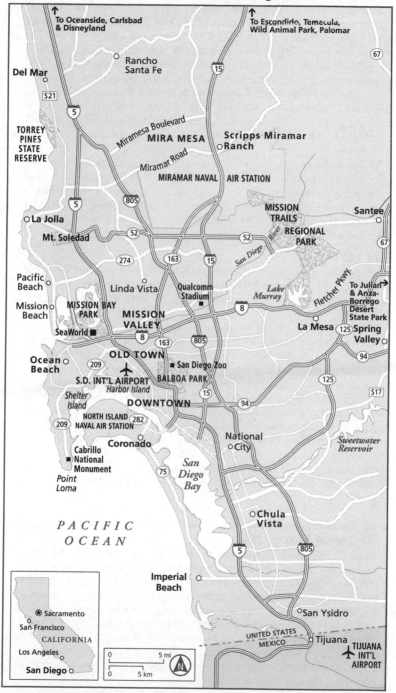

San Diego Area at a Glance

To Oceanside, Carlsbad & Disneyland

To Escondido, Temecula, Wild Animal Park, Palomar

67

15

Del Mar

Rancho Santa Fe

S21

5

TORREY PINES STATE RESERVE

Miramesa Boulevard

MIRA MESA

Scripps Miramar Ranch

Miramar Road

MIRAMAR NAVAL AIR STATION

805

MISSION TRAILS

Santee

La Jolla

5

REGIONAL PARK

67

Mt. Soledad

52

52

San Diego River

Pacific Beach

274

163

15

Lake Murray

Fletcher Pkwy.

To Julian & Anza-Borrego Desert State Park

Linda Vista

Qualcomm Stadium

Mission Beach

MISSION BAY PARK

MISSION VALLEY

8

La Mesa

125

Spring Valley

SeaWorld

8

163

805

94

Ocean Beach

209

OLD TOWN

San Diego Zoo

BALBOA PARK

125

S17

Shelter Island

S.D. INT'L AIRPORT

Harbor Island

DOWNTOWN

15

94

209

NORTH ISLAND NAVAL AIR STATION

282

Coronado

National City

Sweetwater Reservoir

Cabrillo National Monument

Point Loma

75

San Diego Bay

PACIFIC OCEAN

Chula Vista

Imperial Beach

5

805

Sacramento

San Francisco

CALIFORNIA

Los Angeles

San Diego

0   5 mi

0   5 km

N

San Ysidro

UNITED STATES

MEXICO

Tijuana

TIJUANA INT'L AIRPORT

Specialized visitor information outlets include the **Coronado Visitors Center,** 1100 Orange Ave., Coronado (© **619/437-8788**); and **Promote La Jolla,** 1150 Silverado St. (© **858/454-5718;** www.lajollabythesea.com). The **Mission Bay Visitor Information Center,** 2688 E. Mission Bay Dr., San Diego (© **619/276-8200;** www.infosandiego.com), is conveniently located on Mission Bay next to I-5 (exit Clairemont Dr./Mission Bay Dr. and head toward the water). The **San Diego North Convention & Visitors Bureau,** 360 N. Escondido Blvd., Escondido (© **800/848-3336** or 760/745-4741; www.sandiego north.com), can provide information on excursion areas in San Diego County, including Del Mar, Carlsbad, Escondido, Julian, and Anza-Borrego Desert State Park.

To find out what's on at the theater and who's playing in the clubs during your visit, pick up a copy of the *San Diego Weekly Reader* (www.sdreader.com), a free newspaper available all over the city every Thursday; in tourist areas it is distributed in a condensed version under the title the *Weekly.* There's also a Thursday entertainment supplement called "Night & Day" in the city's main daily newspaper, the *San Diego Union-Tribune* (www.signonsandiego.com).

CITY LAYOUT

San Diego has a clearly defined downtown, which is surrounded by several dozen separate neighborhoods—each with its own personality, but all incorporated into the city. The street system is straightforward, so getting around is fairly easy.

Within downtown, Broadway is the main street. Located in the heart of the central business district, it's intersected by Fourth and Fifth avenues (running south and north, respectively). Harbor Drive, hugging the waterfront (Embarcadero), connects downtown with the airport to the northwest and the Convention Center to the south.

The Coronado Bay Bridge leading to Coronado is accessible from I-5 just south of downtown, and I-5 north leads to Old Town, Mission Bay, La Jolla, and North County coastal areas. Balboa Park (home of the San Diego Zoo), Hillcrest, and uptown areas lie north of downtown San Diego. The park and zoo are easily reached by way of Park Boulevard (which would otherwise be 12th Ave.), which leads to the parking lots. Fifth Avenue leads to the Hillcrest and uptown neighborhoods. Highway 163, which heads north from 11th Avenue, leads into Mission Valley.

The Forest Fires of 2003

Although they left the city center and attractions unscathed, San Diego's backcountry suffered devastating forest fires in October 2003. The historic, weeklong disaster came about through the confluence of several years of below-average rainfall, cutbacks in dry brush clearing, and underfunded firefighters (though two of the three concurrent blazes were arson-related). By the end, the fires burned 13% of 4,255-square-mile San Diego County, killed 17 people, destroyed more than 2,200 homes, and cost more than $43 million to battle. The homes are being rebuilt. However, the once-mature forests of Cuyamaca Rancho State Park—south of Julian—will take decades to recover (p. 739).

NEIGHBORHOODS IN BRIEF

Downtown The business, shopping, dining, and entertainment heart of the city encompasses Horton Plaza, the Embarcadero (waterfront), and the Convention Center, sprawling over eight "neighborhoods." This is the most convenient area to stay for those with downtown appointments or attending meetings at the Convention Center. The **Gaslamp Quarter** is the center of a redevelopment kicked off in the mid-1980s with the opening of the Horton Plaza shopping complex; now, the once-seedy area is jam-packed with boutiques, restaurants, and nightspots. Immediately southeast of the Gaslamp is **PETCO Park,** new home of the San Diego Padres. Just northwest, **Little Italy** is an old neighborhood along India Street, between Cedar and Fir, and a great place to find Italian food as well as cutting-edge architecture. Overall, downtown is the easiest place to be based if you don't have your own set of wheels.

Hillcrest & Uptown Hillcrest was the city's first self-contained suburb in the 1920s. Despite the cachet of being close to **Balboa Park** (home of the San Diego Zoo and numerous museums), the area fell into neglect in the 1960s. However, in the late 1970s, legions of preservation-minded residents—particularly its lively gay community—began to restore Hillcrest's charms, making it the local equivalent of a West Hollywood or SoHo. Centrally located and brimming with popular restaurants and avant-garde boutiques, Hillcrest also offers less expensive and more personalized accommodations than any other area in the city. Other uptown neighborhoods of interest are **Mission Hills** to the west of Hillcrest, **University Heights, Normal Heights, North Park,** and **Kensington,** to the east.

Old Town & Mission Valley These two busy areas wrap around the neighborhood of Mission Hills. On one end is the Old Town State Historic Park (where California "began"), Presidio Park, Heritage Park, and numerous museums that recall the turn of the 20th century and the city's beginnings. There's shopping and dining here, too—aimed largely at visitors. Not far from Old Town lies the suburban sprawl of Mission Valley, home to gigantic shopping centers. Hotel Circle is an elongated loop road paralleling the I-8, where a string of moderately priced and budget hotels offer an alternative to the ritzier neighborhoods. In recent years, several major hotel and convention complexes have opened in Mission Valley, and 1990s condo developments have made the valley a residential area.

Mission Bay & the Beaches Here's where they took the picture on the postcard you'll send home. Mission Bay is a watery playground perfect for water-skiing, sailing, and windsurfing. The adjacent communities of **Ocean Beach, Mission Beach,** and **Pacific Beach** are known for their wide stretches of sand, nightlife, and casual dining. Many single San Diegans live here, and once you've visited you'll understand why. The boardwalk, which runs from South Mission Beach to Pacific Beach, is a popular place for skating, biking, people-watching, and sunsets. This is the place to stay if you are traveling with beach-loving children or want to walk barefoot on the sand.

La Jolla With an atmosphere that's somewhere between Rodeo Drive and a Mediterranean village, this seaside community is home to an inordinate number of wealthy folks who could live anywhere. Surrounded by the beach, and the **University of California, San Diego,** La Jolla offers top restaurants, shopping, and medical facilities. Tourists who bed down here can take advantage of the community's attributes without having to buy its high-priced real estate, though all share in La Jolla's problematic parking and traffic snarls. There are really two La Jollas: the so-called "village" is the original seaside community, while residential and business areas that have sprouted along La Jolla Village Drive east of I-8 are of less interest. There's limited public transportation; La Jolla is not an ideal base if you don't have a car.

Coronado   You might be tempted to think of Coronado as an island, as many San Diegans still refer to it. It does have an isolated, resort ambience and is most easily accessed by ferry or sweeping bridge, but the city of Coronado is actually on a bulbous peninsula connected to the mainland by a narrow sand spit, the **Silver Strand.** The northern portion of the peninsula—equally misnamed as North Island—is home to a U.S. Naval Air Station, in use since World War I. The southern sector has a history as an elite playground for snowbirds and represents a charming suburban community. It's also home to more retired admirals than any other community in the country, and quaint shops line the main street, Orange Avenue, and you'll find the Hotel del Coronado astride a lovely beach (one of the area's finest).

2 Getting Around

BY CAR

San Diego has its fair share of traffic, concentrated in the downtown area, and heaviest during the morning and evening commuting hours. Aside from that, it's a very car-friendly town and easy to navigate.

Downtown, many streets run one-way, and finding a parking space can be tricky—but some reasonably priced parking lots are centrally located.

RENTALS   All the large, national car-rental firms have rental outlets at the airport (see "Arriving," above), in the major hotels, and at other locations around the city. Some car-rental companies will allow their cars into Mexico as far as Ensenada, provided that you stop before crossing the border to buy Mexican auto insurance. Insurance is also advised if you drive your own car over the border.

PARKING   Parking meters are common in most San Diego areas, including downtown, Hillcrest, the beaches, and La Jolla. Posted signs indicate operating hours—generally between 9am and 6pm, even on Saturdays; meters devour quarters at a rate of 1 per 12 minutes. Small (paid) lots fringe the busy Gaslamp Quarter, while free parking is the rule in Balboa Park and Old Town.

BY PUBLIC TRANSPORTATION

Both city buses and the San Diego Trolley are operated by the **San Diego Metropolitan Transit System (MTS)** (✆ **619/233-3004;** www.sdcommute.com). The website offers timetables, maps, and fares online, and provides information on how the transit system accommodates travelers with disabilities. Or visit the system's **Transit Store,** 102 Broadway at First Avenue (✆ **619/234-1060**), a complete public-transportation information center, supplying travelers with passes, tokens, timetables, maps, and brochures. Get a copy of the useful pamphlet *Way to Go to See the Sights,* which details routes to the city's most popular tourist attractions. The store is open Monday through Friday from 9am to 5pm.

If you know your route and just need schedule information—or automated answers to FAQs—call **Info Express** (© **619/685-4900**) from any touch-tone phone, 24 hours a day. A $5 **Day-Tripper pass** allows for 1 day of unlimited rides (there's also a 2-day pass for $9, or a 3-day for $12), and is available from the Transit Store and at all Trolley ticket vending machines. *Note:* A fare increase as of July 1, 2004, affected monthly passes with a $2 increase.

BY BUS   San Diego has an adequate bus system encompassing more than 100 routes that will get you to where you're going—eventually. Bus stops are marked by rectangular blue signs every other block or so on local routes, farther apart on express routes. More than 20 bus routes pass through the downtown area. Most fares are $2.25. Buses accept dollar bills, but the driver can't give change. You can request a free transfer as long as you continue on a bus with an equal or lower fare (if it's higher, you pay the difference). Transfers must be used within 90 minutes. You can return to where you started, if you want. Some routes stop at 6pm, while other lines continue to 9pm, midnight, and 2am—ask your bus driver for more specific information. On Saturday a few routes run all night.

BY TROLLEY   The San Diego Trolley is great for visitors, particularly if you're staying downtown and plan to visit Tijuana, Old Town, or Mission Valley. There are two main routes that intersect downtown. The Blue Line travels from the Mexican border north through downtown, Old Town, and then east through Mission Valley. The trip to the border takes 40 minutes from downtown. The Orange Line runs from downtown east through Lemon Grove and El Cajon to the city of Santee. An extension—the Green Line—from Old Town to San Diego State University and on to El Cajon will open in 2005.

Trolleys operate on a self-service fare-collection system; riders buy tickets from machines in stations before boarding. The machines list fares for each destination ($1.25–$3) and dispense change. Tickets are valid for 2 hours from the time of purchase, in any direction. Fare inspectors board trains at random to check tickets. A round-trip ticket is double the price, but is valid all day between the origination and destination points.

Trolleys run every 15 minutes during the day and every 30 minutes at night; during peak weekday rush hours the Blue Line runs every 10 minutes. The trolleys generally operate daily from 5am to about midnight; the Blue Line runs 24 hours Saturday night/Sunday morning.

BY TRAIN   San Diego's express rail commuter service, the **Coaster**, travels between the downtown Santa Fe Depot station and the Oceanside Transit Center, with stops at Old Town, Sorrento Valley, Solana Beach, Encinitas, and Carlsbad. Fares range from $3.50 to $4.75 each way and can be paid by credit card at vending machines at each station. Eligible seniors and riders with disabilities pay half price. The scenic trip between downtown San Diego and Oceanside takes just under an hour. Trains run Monday through Friday about once an hour, with four trains each direction on Saturday (no service Sun); call © **800/ COASTER** for the current schedule.

Amtrak (© **800/USA-RAIL;** www.amtrak.com) trains run between San Diego and downtown Los Angeles about 11 times daily each way. Trains depart from the Santa Fe Depot and stop at Solana Beach, Oceanside, San Juan Capistrano, and Anaheim (Disneyland). A ticket to Los Angeles is $25 each way, or $37 in business class. One-way to Solana Beach is $7, to Oceanside $10.

BY FERRY & WATER TAXI   There's regularly scheduled ferry service between San Diego and Coronado (© **619/234-4111** for information). Ferries leave from the Broadway Pier (1050 N. Harbor Dr., at the intersection of Broadway) on the hour from 9am to 9pm Sunday through Thursday, and until 10pm Friday and Saturday. They return from the Old Ferry Landing in Coronado to the Broadway Pier every hour on the half-hour from 9:30am to 9:30pm Sunday through Thursday and until 10:30pm Friday and Saturday. The ride takes 15 minutes. The fare is $2 each way (50¢ extra if you bring your bike).

Water taxis (© 619/235-TAXI) will pick you up from any dock around San Diego Bay, and operate daily between noon and 10pm, with extended hours in summer. If you're staying in a downtown hotel, this is a great way to reach the beach fronting the Hotel del Coronado. Boats are sometimes available on the spur of the moment, but reservations are advised. Fares are $5 per person to most locations.

BY TAXI

Half a dozen taxi companies serve the area. Rates are based on mileage and can add up quickly in sprawling San Diego—a trip from downtown to La Jolla, for example, will cost $30 to $35. Other than in the Gaslamp Quarter after dark, taxis don't cruise the streets as they do in other cities, so you have to call ahead for quick pickup. If you are at a hotel or restaurant, the front-desk attendant or maitre d' will call one for you. Among the local companies are **Orange Cab** (© 619/291-3333), **San Diego Cab** (© 619/226-TAXI), **Yellow Cab** (© 619/234-6161), **Coronado Cab Company** (© 935/435-6211), and **La Jolla Cab** (© 858/453-4222).

BY BICYCLE

San Diego is on the verge of becoming the nation's preeminent bicycling destination, with millions of dollars earmarked for bicycle paths throughout the city and county. But already, San Diego is cyclist friendly, and named as "one of the top 10 cities in the U.S. to bicycle" by *Bicycling* magazine.

Most major thoroughfares offer bike lanes. Bikes are allowed on the San Diego–Coronado ferry, the San Diego Trolley, and most city buses, at no charge. *Cycling San Diego*, by Nelson Copp and Jerry Schad (Sunbelt Publications), is a good resource for bicyclists and is available at most local bike shops. Or to obtain a detailed map by mail of San Diego County's bike lanes and routes, call **Ride Link Bicycle Information** (© 800/COMMUTE or 619/231-BIKE). You might also want to talk to the **City of San Diego Bicycle Coordinator** (© 619/533-3110) or the **San Diego County Bicycle Coalition** (© 858/487-6063). Always remember to wear a helmet; it's the law.

For information on rentals, see "Outdoor Pursuits," later in this chapter.

FAST FACTS: San Diego

Area Codes San Diego's main area code is **619,** used primarily by downtown, uptown, Mission Valley, Point Loma, Coronado, La Mesa, and El Cajon. The area code **858** is used for northern and coastal areas, including Ocean Beach, Mission Beach, Pacific Beach, La Jolla, Del Mar, and Rancho Santa Fe. Use **760** to reach the remainder of San Diego County, including Encinitas, Carlsbad, Oceanside, Escondido, Julian, and Anza-Borrego.

Babysitters **Marion's Childcare** (© 619/582-5029) has bonded babysitters available to come to your hotel room. **Panda Services** (© 858/292-5503) is also available.

Dentists/Doctors For dental referrals, contact the **San Diego County Dental Society** at 📞 **800/201-0244,** or call 800/DENTIST. Miami-based **Hotel Docs** (📞 **800/468-3537**) is a 24-hour network of physicians, dentists, and chiropractors. They accept credit cards, and their services are covered by most insurance. In a life-threatening situation, dial 📞 **911.**

Emergencies Call 📞 **911** for fire, police, and ambulance.

Hospitals In Hillcrest, near downtown San Diego, **UCSD Medical Center-Hillcrest,** 200 W. Arbor Dr. (📞 **619/543-6400**), has the most convenient emergency room. In La Jolla, **Thornton Hospital,** 9300 Campus Point Dr. (📞 **858/657-7600**), has a good emergency room, and you'll find another in Coronado, at **Coronado Hospital,** 250 Prospect Place, opposite the Marriott Resort (📞 **619/435-6251**). Twenty-four-hour pharmacies include **Sav-On Drugs,** 8831 Villa La Jolla Dr., La Jolla (📞 **858/457-4390**) and 313 E. Washington St., Hillcrest (📞 **619/291-7170**).

Police The downtown police station is at 1401 Broadway (📞 **619/531-2000** or 619/531-2065 for the hearing impaired).

Post Office San Diego's main post office is located at 2535 Midway Dr., just west of Old Town; it is open Monday through Friday from 8am to 5pm, and Saturday from 8am to 4pm. For branch locations, call 📞 **800/ASK-USPS** or log on to www.usps.gov.

Safety Of the 10 largest cities in the United States, San Diego historically has had the lowest incidence of violent crime per capita. Still, it never hurts to take precautions. Virtually all areas of the city are safe during the day. Caution is advised in Balboa Park, in areas not frequented by regular foot traffic. Homeless transients are common—especially downtown, in Hillcrest, and in beach areas. They are rarely a problem, but can be unpredictable when inebriated. Downtown areas to the east of PETCO Park are sparsely populated after dusk, and poorly lighted. Parts of the city that are usually safe on foot at night include the Gaslamp Quarter, Hillcrest, Old Town, Mission Valley, La Jolla, and Coronado.

Taxes Sales tax in restaurants and shops is 7.75%. Hotel tax is 10.5%.

Useful Telephone Numbers For the latest San Diego arts and entertainment information, call 📞 **619/238-0700;** for half-price day-of-performance tickets, call 📞 **619/497-5000;** for a beach and surf report, call 📞 **619/221-8824.** For the correct time, call 📞 **853-1212** (works in all area codes). For local **weather,** call 📞 **619/289-1212.**

3 Where to Stay

The rates listed below are all "rack," or official, rates—you can almost always do better. Rates tend to be highest in summer at beach hotels, and midweek downtown when there's a big convention in town. Remember to factor in the city's 10.5% hotel tax. For good prices in all accommodations categories, contact **San Diego Hotel Reservations** (📞 **800/SAVE-CASH** or 619/627-9300; www.sandiegohotelres.com). Bed-and-breakfasts are available, and several are listed below. For additional choices, contact the **San Diego Bed & Breakfast Guild** (📞 **619/523-1300;** www.bandbguildsandiego.org).

San Diego Accommodations & Dining

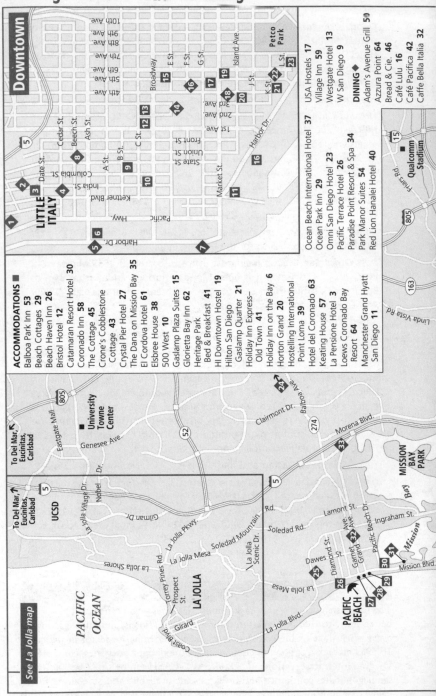

Downtown

ACCOMMODATIONS ■

Balboa Park Inn **53**
Beach Cottages **29**
Beach Haven Inn **26**
Bristol Hotel **12**
Catamaran Resort Hotel **30**
Coronado Inn **58**
The Cottage **45**
Crone's Cobblestone
Cottage **43**
Crystal Pier Hotel **27**
The Dana on Mission Bay **35**
El Cordova Hotel **61**
Elsbree House **38**
500 West **10**
Gaslamp Plaza Suites **15**
Glorietta Bay Inn **62**
Heritage Park
Bed & Breakfast **41**
HI Downtown Hostel **19**
Hilton San Diego
Gaslamp Quarter **21**
Holiday Inn Express–
Old Town **41**
Holiday Inn on the Bay **6**
Horton Grand **20**
Hostelling International
Point Loma **39**
Hotel del Coronado **63**
Keating House **57**
La Pensione Hotel **3**
Loews Coronado Bay
Resort **64**
Manchester Grand Hyatt
San Diego **11**

Ocean Beach International Hotel **37**
Ocean Park Inn **29**
Omni San Diego Hotel **23**
Pacific Terrace Hotel **26**
Paradise Point Resort & Spa **34**
Park Manor Suites **54**
Red Lion Hanalei Hotel **40**
USA Hostels **17**
Village Inn **59**
Westgate Hotel **13**
W San Diego **9**

DINING ◆

Adam's Avenue Grill **50**
Azzura Point **64**
Bread & Cie. **46**
Café Lulu **16**
Cafe Pacifica **42**
Caffe Bella Italia **32**

678

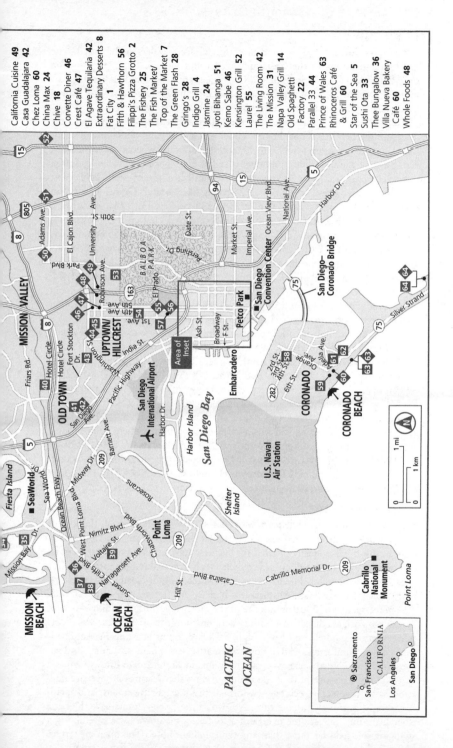

California Cuisine **49**
Casa Guadalajara **42**
Chez Loma **60**
China Max **24**
Chive **18**
Corvette Diner **46**
Crest Café **47**
El Agave Tequilaria **42**
Extraordinary Desserts **8**
Fat City **1**
Fifth & Hawthorn **56**
Filippi's Pizza Grotto **2**
The Fishery **25**
The Fish Market/
  Top of the Market **7**
The Green Flash **28**
Gringo's **28**
Indigo Grill **4**
Jasmine **24**
Jyoti Bihanga **51**
Kemo Sabe **46**
Kensington Grill **52**
Laurel **55**
The Living Room **42**
The Mission **31**
Napa Valley Grill **14**
Old Spaghetti
  Factory **22**
Parallel 33 **44**
Prince of Wales **63**
Rhinoceros Café
  & Grill **60**
Star of the Sea **5**
Sushi Ota **33**
Thee Bungalow **36**
Villa Nueva Bakery
  Café **60**
Whole Foods **48**

DOWNTOWN

San Diego's downtown is a good place for leisure travelers to be based. The nightlife and dining in the Gaslamp Quarter and Horton Plaza shopping are close at hand; Balboa Park, Hillcrest, Old Town, and Coronado are less than 10 minutes away by car; and beaches aren't much farther. It's also the city's public-transportation hub, and thus very convenient for car-free visitors.

Conventions are big business, and the high-rise hotels cater primarily to the meet-and-greet crowd. While they don't offer much personality for leisure travelers, it's not hard to get rooms for 30% to 50% off the rack rates when a convention isn't taking up all the availability. Although their *rack* rates start in the mid–$300s, three chain operations are a good place to test your wheelin'-and-dealin' skills. Start with the city's biggest hotel, the 1,625-room **Manchester Grand Hyatt San Diego** ★★, 1 Market Place (© **800/233-1234** or 619/232-1234; www.hyatt. com), a two-towered behemoth with a 40th-floor cocktail lounge that boasts fabulous views. Then there's the 223-room **Westgate Hotel** ★★★, 1055 Second Ave. (© **800/221-3802** or 619/238-1818; www.westgatehotel.com), where the lobby looks transplanted out of the Palace of Versailles and rooms (remodeled in 2003) are plush, spacious, and bright. New this year is the **Omni San Diego Hotel** ★★ (© **800/THE-OMNI** or 619/231-6664; www.omnihotels.com), a 511-room high-rise located next to the Padres' PETCO Park and opposite the Convention Center—common areas are decorated with baseball memorabilia.

At the other end of the price spectrum, a more moderate choice is the colorful and modern **Bristol Hotel,** 1055 First Ave. (© **800/662-4477** or 619/232-6141; www.bristolhotelsandiego.com), adjacent to the Gaslamp Quarter. In the budget category, the 260-room **500 West,** 500 W. Broadway (© **619/234-5252**), opened just as we went to press, offering small but comfortable rooms for $69 to $89 a night in a seven-story building dating to 1924. It offers contemporary style, history, and a good location. 500 West's only caveat: Bathrooms are down the hall. Cheaper still are downtown's two hostels, where double rooms are about $55 and dorm rooms are under $25: **USA Hostels** (© **800/438-8622** or 619/232-3100; www.usahostels.com), is located in the heart of the Gaslamp at 726 Fifth Ave., while **HI Downtown Hostel** (© **800/909-4776,** ext. 43, or 619/525-1531; http://sandiegohostels.org) is nearby at 521 Market St.

VERY EXPENSIVE

Hilton San Diego Gaslamp Quarter ★★★   With a location at the foot of the Gaslamp Quarter and immediately across the street from the Convention Center, this hotel is ideally situated for business travelers. Yet unlike some of its competition, the Hilton doesn't overwhelm with size, making it a great place for guests who want to be close to the action (which includes loads of restaurants, nightlife, and the ballpark within a few blocks) but not get lost in the shuffle. The hotel opened in 2001 on the site of the old Bridgeworks building—part of San Diego's original wharf of a century ago; much of the brick facade was incorporated into the hotel's polished design. Standard rooms boast up-market furniture, down comforters, and pillow-top mattresses. There are suites and an executive floor, but the snazzy picks are rooms in the intimate Enclave wing, a converted office space next to the main building that features 30 oversize guestrooms with towering ceilings, custom furnishings, Frette linens, and lavish bathrooms sporting whirlpool tubs. No two of the Enclave units have the same floor plan, but they are the handsomest hotel rooms downtown, resembling a swinging loft redo far more than any typical chain hotel. The open-air terrace between the two buildings has a pool and sunning area and a fitness room.

401 K St. (at Fourth Ave.), San Diego, CA 92101. © 800/HILTONS or 619/231-4040. Fax 619/231-6439. 282 units. $295 double; from $395 suite. Children under 12 stay free in parent's room. AE, DC, DISC, MC, V. Valet parking $21. Trolley: Gaslamp Quarter. **Amenities:** 2 restaurants; 2 bars; outdoor pool; health club and full-service spa; Jacuzzi; concierge; business center; salon; 24-hr. room service; laundry service; dry cleaning. *In room:* A/C, TV w/pay movies, dataport, minibar, coffeemaker, hair dryer, iron.

W San Diego San Diego's newest opened in 2003 and quickly took the city by storm with its swanky nightlife—which on Friday and Saturday evenings means there's a line to get into the packed lobby. Fortunately, your room is bright and cheery—like a mod beach cabana beamed into downtown, replete with a sexy shower. *Nouveau nautique* is the theme, with elegant aqua and sand tones accenting the whites, a window seat (great idea) for gazing down on this languid corner of downtown, and a beach-ball-shaped pillow, which should be the only exclamation point needed to remind you that this hotel is supposed to be fun. At the restaurant, **Rice,** and its adjoining bar, cocktail waitresses clad in leather hot pants and fishnets—black, of course—serve blue-tinged cotton candy treats that float through the room like tiny psychedelic clouds. Then there's the **Beach,** up on the third floor, where the developers got really creative: The open-air bar has a sand floor (heated at night), a fire pit, and cabanas—drinks are served in plastic, allowing you to safely roam the terrace barefoot. Shoe check, please. The cacophony mostly dies down by Sunday, when the contingent of mostly Los Angelenos departs, and for a few days the W is the very model of a proper business hotel. Albeit one with a (tiny) pool, a 24-hour open-air gym, and a bank of 18 video screens glowing with an idealized landscape of bubbles floating heavenward. Look closely and you'll notice that each bubble has a floating W logo within it. Self-absorbed? To the max. Fun? Check me in.

421 W. B St. (at State St.), San Diego, CA 92101. © 888/625-5144 or 619/231-8220. Fax 619/231-5779. www.whotels.com/sandiego. 261 units. $359–$469 double; $700 suite. AE, DC, DISC, MC, V. Valet parking $23. Bus: All Broadway routes. Trolley: American Plaza or Civic Center. **Amenities:** Restaurant; 3 lounges; 24-hr. concierge; 24-hr. room service; laundry/dry-cleaning service. *In room:* A/C, TV w/VCR and DVD, dataport, minibar, coffeemaker, hair dryer, iron, CD player.

EXPENSIVE

Holiday Inn on the Bay (Kids) Renovated in 2001, this better-than-average Holiday Inn is reliable and nearly always offers great deals. The three-building high-rise complex is located on the Embarcadero across from the harbor and the Maritime Museum—this scenic spot is only 1½ miles from the airport (you can watch planes landing and taking off) and 2 blocks from the train station and trolley. Rooms, while basic, always seem to sport clean new furnishings and plenty of thoughtful comforts. Although rooms are identical inside, choose carefully; the bay views are marvelous, while city views can be depressing (you're looking at utilitarian older office buildings). In either case, request the highest floor possible.

1355 N. Harbor Dr. (at Ash St.), San Diego, CA 92101-3385. © 800/HOLIDAY or 619/232-3861. Fax 619/232-4924. www.holiday-inn.com/san-onthebay. 600 units. $219 double; from $299 suite. Children under 18 stay free in parent's room. AE, DC, MC, V. Self-parking $15. Bus: All Pacific Hwy. routes. Trolley: American Plaza. Pets accepted with $25 fee and $100 deposit. **Amenities:** 4 restaurants; lounge; outdoor heated pool; exercise room; concierge; business center; room service (6–11am and 5–11pm); babysitting; laundry service; self-service laundry. *In room:* A/C, TV w/pay movies, dataport, coffeemaker, hair dryer, iron.

MODERATE

Horton Grand (Finds) A cross between an elegant hotel and a charming inn, the Horton Grand combines two hotels that date from 1886—the Horton Grand (once an infamous red-light establishment) and the Brooklyn Hotel (which for a time was the Kayle Saddlery Shop where Wyatt Earp resided). Both were saved from demolition, moved to this spot, and connected by an alry atrium lobby filled with white wicker. The facade, with its graceful bay windows, is original. Each room is utterly unique, containing vintage furnishings and gas fireplaces; bathrooms are lush with reproduction floor tiles, fine brass fixtures, and genteel appointments. Rooms overlook either the city or the fig-tree-filled courtyard; they're divided between the clubby and darker "saddlery" side and the pastel-toned and Victorian "brothel" side. The suites (really just large studio-style rooms) are located in a newer wing; choosing one means sacrificing historic character for a sitting area/sofa bed and minibar with microwave. If you're lonely, request room no. 309, where resident ghost Roger likes to hang out.

311 Island Ave. (at Fourth Ave.), San Diego, CA 92101. © 800/542-1886 or 619/544-1886. Fax 619/239-3823. www.hortongrand.com. 132 units. $169–$199 double; from $269 suite. Extra person $20. Children under 18 stay free in parent's room. AE, DC, MC, V. Valet parking $20. Bus: 1, 4, 5, 16, or 25. Trolley: Convention Center. **Amenities:** Restaurant (breakfast, Fri–Sat dinner, and Sun brunch only); bar; business center to open 2005. *In room:* A/C, TV, dataport, hair dryer.

INEXPENSIVE

Gaslamp Plaza Suites 🏔🏔 ⟨Value⟩
You can't get closer to the center of the vibrant Gaslamp Quarter than this impeccably restored late-Victorian edifice. At 11 stories, it was San Diego's first skyscraper, built in 1913. Crafted of Australian gumwood, marble, brass, and exquisite etched glass, the building originally housed San Diego Trust & Savings. Various other businesses (jewelers, lawyers, doctors, and photographers) set up shop here until 1988, when the elegant structure was placed on the National Register of Historic Places and reopened as a boutique hotel. You'll be surprised at the timeless elegance, from the dramatic lobby and wide corridors to guest rooms furnished with European flair. Each bears the name of a writer (Emerson, Swift, Zola, Shelley, Fitzgerald, and so on). Most rooms are spacious and offer luxuries rare in this price range, like pillow-top mattresses and premium toiletries; microwave ovens and dinnerware; and impressive luxury bathrooms. Beware of the cheapest rooms on the back side—they are uncomfortably small (although they do have regular-size bathrooms) and have no view. The higher floors boast splendid city and bay views. Despite the welcome addition of noise-muffling windows, don't be surprised to hear a hum from the street below, especially when the Quarter gets rockin' on the weekends.

520 E St. (corner of Fifth Ave.), San Diego, CA 92101. © 800/874-8770 or 619/232-9500. Fax 619/238-9945. www.gaslampplaza.com. 64 units. $100–$155 double; from $199 suite. Rates include continental breakfast. AE, DC, DISC, MC, V. Valet parking $18. Bus: 1, 3, or 25. Trolley: Fifth Ave. **Amenities:** Room service (lunch and dinner hours). *In room:* A/C, TV w/VCR, dataport, fridge, coffeemaker, hair dryer, iron, safe, microwave.

La Pensione Hotel 🏔 ⟨Value⟩
This place has a lot going for it: modern style, good value, a convenient location in Little Italy within walking distance of the central business district, a friendly staff, and free parking (a premium for small hotels in San Diego). The four-story Pensione is built around a courtyard and feels like a small European hotel. The decor throughout is modern and streamlined, with plenty of sleek black and metallic surfaces, crisp white walls, and modern wood furnishings. Guest rooms are small but make the most of their space and leave you with room to move around. Each room offers a ceiling fan and minifridge; some have a small balcony. *Note:* Rooms don't have air-conditioning, which could be a concern on a hot day; you can open your window, but the street cafes stay busy till midnight on weekends.

606 W. Date St. (at India St.), San Diego, CA 92101. © 800/232-4683 or 619/236-8000. Fax 619/236-8088. www.lapensionehotel.com. 80 units. $75 double. AE, DC, DISC, MC, V. Limited free underground parking. Bus: 5 or 16. Trolley: Little Italy. **Amenities:** Self-service laundry. *In room:* TV, dataport, fridge.

HILLCREST/UPTOWN

Although they're certainly no longer a secret, the gentrified historic neighborhoods north of downtown are still something of a bargain. They're convenient to Balboa Park and offer easy access to the rest of town. Filled with casual and upscale restaurants, eclectic shops, and upbeat nightlife, the area is also easy to navigate. All of the following accommodations cater to the mainstream market but attract a gay/lesbian clientele as well.

In addition to Keating House (below), there are a couple of bed-and-breakfasts that invite consideration. **Crone's Cobblestone Cottage** ⍟, 1302 Washington Place (⟨𝐶⟩ **619/295-4765;** www.cobblestonebandb.com), is a beautifully restored Craftsman bungalow in the beloved older neighborhood of Mission Hills. Tucked into a quiet cul-de-sac is **The Cottage,** 3829 Albatross St. (⟨𝐶⟩ **619/299-1564;** www.sandiegobandb.com/cottage.htm), a 1913 home.

INEXPENSIVE

Balboa Park Inn ⍟   Insiders looking for unusual accommodations head for this small pink inn at the northern edge of Balboa Park. It's a cluster of four Spanish colonial–style former apartment buildings in a mostly residential neighborhood a half mile east of Hillcrest proper. The hotel is popular with gay travelers drawn to Hillcrest's restaurants and clubs, but note that all of these are at least 4 blocks away. All the rooms and suites are tastefully decorated; the specialty suites, however, are over-the-top. There's the "Tara Suite," as in *Gone With the Wind;* the "Nouveau Ritz," which employs every Art Deco cliché, including mirrors and Hollywood lighting; and the "Greystoke" suite, a jumble of jungle, safari, and tropical themes with a completely mirrored bathroom and Jacuzzi tub. Seven rooms have Jacuzzi tubs, and most have kitchens—all have a private entrance, though the front desk operates 24 hours. From here, you're close enough to walk to the San Diego Zoo and other Balboa Park attractions.

3402 Park Blvd. (at Upas St.), San Diego, CA 92103. ⟨𝐶⟩ **800/938-8181** or 619/298-0823. Fax 619/294-8070. www.balboaparkinn.com. 26 units. $99 double; $119–$199 suite. Extra person $10. Children under 12 stay free in parent's room. Rates include continental breakfast. AE, DC, DISC, MC, V. Parking available on street. Bus: 7. From I-5, take Washington St. east, follow signs to University Ave. E. Turn right at Park Blvd. *In room:* TV, fridge, coffeemaker.

Keating House ⍟⍟ *(Finds*   This grand 1880s Bankers Hill mansion, located between downtown and Hillcrest and 4 blocks from Balboa Park, has been meticulously restored by two energetic innkeepers with a solid background in architectural preservation. Doug Scott and Ben Baltic not only know old houses but are also neighborhood devotees filled with historical knowledge. Authentic period design is celebrated throughout, even in the overflowing gardens that bloom on four sides of this local landmark. The house contains a comfortable hodgepodge of antique furnishings and appointments; three additional rooms are in the restored carriage house, opening onto an exotic garden patio. The downstairs entry, parlor, and dining room all have cozy fireplaces; bathrooms—all private—are gorgeously restored with updated period fixtures. Breakfast is served in a sunny, friendly setting; special dietary needs are cheerfully considered. The classy, not frilly, inn draws guests ranging from Europeans to businessmen avoiding the cookie-cutter ambience of a chain hotel.

2331 Second Ave. (between Juniper and Kalmia sts.), San Diego, CA 92101. ⟨𝐶⟩ **800/995-8644** or 619/239-8585. Fax 619/239-5774. www.keatinghouse.com. 9 units. $95–$155 double. Rates include full breakfast. AE, DISC, MC, V. Bus: 1, 3, 11, or 25. From the airport, take Harbor Dr. toward downtown; turn left on Laurel St., then right on Second Ave. *In room:* Hair dryer, no phone.

Park Manor Suites ⭐ *Value* This eight-story building was built as a full-service luxury hotel in 1926 on a prime corner overlooking Balboa Park. Over time the hotel became a popular stopping-off point for celebrities headed for Mexican vacations in the 1920s and 1930s. Although dated, guest rooms are huge and very comfortable, featuring full kitchens, dining rooms, living rooms, and bedrooms with separate dressing areas. A few have glassed-in terraces; request one when you book. The overall feeling is that of a prewar East Coast apartment building, complete with steam heat and lavish moldings. Park Manor Suites does have its weaknesses, particularly bathrooms that have mostly original fixtures and could use some renovation. But prices are quite reasonable, there's a darkly old-world restaurant on the ground floor, laundry service is also available, and a simple continental breakfast buffet is served in the penthouse banquet room. In fact, the penthouse bar becomes a bustling gay social scene on Friday evenings, drawing a horde—the single elevator gets a real workout that night.

525 Spruce St. (between Fifth and Sixth aves.), San Diego, CA 92103. © 800/874-2649 or 619/291-0999. Fax 619/291-8844. www.parkmanorsuites.com. 74 units. $99–$139 studio; from $139 1-bedroom suite. Extra person $15. Children under 12 stay free in parent's room. Rates include expansive continental breakfast. AE, DC, DISC, MC, V. Free parking. Bus: 1, 3, or 25. Take Washington St. exit off I-5, right on Fourth Ave., left on Spruce. **Amenities:** Restaurant/bar; access to nearby health club ($5); laundry/dry-cleaning service; self-service laundry. *In room:* TV, dataport, kitchen, coffeemaker, hair dryer, iron.

OLD TOWN & MISSION VALLEY

Old Town is a popular area for families because of its proximity to Old Town State Historic Park and other attractions that are within walking distance—SeaWorld and the San Diego Zoo are within a 10-minute drive. Around the corner is Mission Valley, where you'll find the city's largest collection of hotels offering rooms under $100 a night. Mission Valley lacks much homegrown personality—this is the spot for chain restaurants and huge shopping malls, not gardens or water views. But it caters to convention groups and leisure travelers drawn by the lower prices and competitive facilities.

Room rates at properties on Hotel Circle are significantly cheaper than those in many other parts of the city. You'll find a cluster of inexpensive chain hotels and motels, including **Best Western Seven Seas** (© **800/421-6662** or 619/291-1300), **Mission Valley Travelodge** (© **800/255-3050** or 619/297-2271), **Motel 6 Hotel Circle** (© **800/4-MOTEL-6** or 619/296-1612), **Ramada Plaza** (© **800/532-4241** or 619/291-6500), and **Vagabond Inn–Hotel Circle** (© **800/522-1555** or 619/297-1691). Although these hotels are a couple miles from the beach, like beach hotels, summer and weekend rates tend to be higher.

MODERATE

Heritage Park Bed & Breakfast Inn ⭐⭐ This exquisite 1889 Queen Anne mansion is set in a Victorian park—an artfully arranged cobblestone cul-de-sac lined with historic buildings saved from the wrecking ball and assembled here, in Old Town, as a tourist attraction. Most of the inn's rooms are in the main house, with a handful of equally appealing choices in an adjacent 1887 Italianate companion. Owner Nancy Helsper is an amiable and energetic innkeeper with an eye for every necessary detail; she's always eager to share tales of these homes' fascinating history and how they crossed paths with Nancy and her husband, Charles. A stay here is about surrendering to the pampering of afternoon tea and candlelight breakfast, and romantic extras (champagne and chocolates, dear?) available for special celebrations. Like the gracious parlors and porches, each room is outfitted with meticulous period antiques and luxurious fabrics; the small staff provides turndown service and virtually anything else you might require. Although the fireplaces are all ornamental, some rooms have whirlpool baths.

2470 Heritage Park Row, San Diego, CA 92110. ℂ 800/995-2470 or 619/299-6832. Fax 619/299-9465. www.heritageparkinn.com. 12 units. $130–$265 double. Extra person $20. Rates include full breakfast and afternoon tea. AE, DC, DISC, MC, V. Free parking. Bus: 5. Take I-5 to Old Town Ave., turn left onto San Diego Ave., then turn right onto Harney St. Trolley: Old Town. *In room:* A/C, hair dryer, iron.

Holiday Inn Express–Old Town 👤 Just a couple of easy walking blocks from the heart of Old Town, this Holiday Inn has a Spanish colonial exterior that suits the neighborhood's theme. Inside you'll find better-than-they-have-to-be contemporary furnishings and surprising small touches that make this hotel an affordable option favored by business travelers and families alike. There's nothing spectacular about the adjacent streets, so the hotel is smartly oriented toward the inside; request a room whose patio or balcony opens onto the pleasant courtyard. Rooms are thoughtfully and practically appointed, with extras like microwave ovens and writing tables. The lobby, surrounded by French doors, features a large fireplace, several sitting areas, and a TV. The hotel entrance, on Jefferson Street, is hard to find but definitely worth the search.

3900 Old Town Ave., San Diego, CA 92110. ℂ 800/451-9846 or 619/299-7400. Fax 619/299-1619. www.ichotelsgroup.com/h/d/hiex/hd/santa. 125 units. $129–$169 double; from $179 suite. Extra person $10. Children under 18 stay free in parent's room. Rates include continental breakfast. AE, DC, DISC, MC, V. Free parking. Bus: 5. Take I-5 to Old Town Ave. exit. **Amenities:** Outdoor pool; whirlpool; laundry/dry-cleaning service. *In room:* A/C, TV, fridge, coffeemaker, microwave.

Red Lion Hanalei Hotel 👤 My favorite hotel along Mission Valley's Hotel Circle has a Polynesian theme and comfort-conscious sophistication that sets it apart from the rest of the pack. Most rooms are split between two eight-story towers, set back from the freeway and cleverly positioned so that the balconies open onto the tropically landscaped pool courtyard or the attractive links of a golf club. A few more rooms are found in the Presidio Building, which is too close to the freeway for my comfort. The heated outdoor pool is large enough for any luau, as is the oversize whirlpool beside it. The hotel boasts an unmistakable 1960s vibe and Hawaiian ambience—the restaurant and bar have over-the-top kitschy decor, with waterfalls, outrigger canoes, and more. But guest rooms are outfitted with contemporary furnishings and conveniences; some have microwaves and refrigerators. Services include a free shuttle to Old Town and the Fashion Valley Shopping Center, plus meeting facilities. Golf packages are also available.

2270 Hotel Circle N., San Diego, CA 92108. ℂ 800/RED-LION or 619/297-1101. Fax 619/297-6049. www.redlion.com. 416 units. $159–$169 double; from $275 suite. Extra person $10. AE, DISC, MC, V. Parking $8. Bus: 6. From I-8, take Hotel Circle exit, follow signs for Hotel Circle N. Pets accepted with $50 deposit. **Amenities:** 2 restaurants; lounge; outdoor pool; nearby golf course; fitness center; whirlpool; game room; activities desk; 24-hr. business center; room service (6am–10pm); laundry/dry-cleaning service; self-service laundry. *In room:* A/C, TV w/pay movies, dataport, coffeemaker, hair dryer, iron.

MISSION BAY & THE BEACHES

If the beach and aquatic activities take a front seat in your San Diego agenda, this part of town may be just the ticket. Even though the beach communities are far removed in atmosphere, downtown and Balboa Park are only a 15-minute drive away. Some hotels are right on Mission Bay, San Diego's water playground; they're usually good choices for families. Ocean Beach, Mission Beach, and Pacific Beach provide a taste of the transient-beach-bum lifestyle—they can be a bit raucous at times, especially on summer weekends, and dining options are largely limited to chain eateries. If you're looking for a more refined landing, head to La Jolla or Coronado (the sections that follow).

(Kids) Family-Friendly Accommodations

Holiday Inn on the Bay (p. 681)   Of the downtown choices, this is the most kid-centric option, is well priced for tight family budgets, and even offers babysitting services for strained parents.

Catamaran Resort Hotel (see below)   Numerous sports facilities and safe bayfront swimming make this resort ideal for families.

Crystal Pier Hotel (p. 687)   Stay on a vintage pier that juts out from Pacific Beach—at night you'll be lulled and gently rocked to sleep by the waves.

Paradise Point Resort & Spa (p. 688)   This self-contained upscale property in the middle of Mission Bay has plenty of space for kids safely to explore, and is just up the street from SeaWorld.

The Sea Lodge (p. 692)   Right smack on the sand at La Jolla Shores, kids can choose between the pool and the ocean. They can even eat in their swimsuits on the patio.

Hotel del Coronado (p. 694)   The kids may not care who Marilyn Monroe was, but they'll love the bustling classic-hotel ambience and beach.

Hostelling International has a 53-bed location in **Point Loma** (© 800/ **909-4776,** ext. 157, or 619/223-4778), 3790 Udall St., about 2 miles inland from Ocean Beach; rates run $19 per person, and private rooms that sleep two are $38. The **Ocean Beach International Hostel,** 4961 Newport Ave. (© **800/339-7263** or 619/223-7873; www.californiahostel.com), has more than 60 beds and is located just 2 blocks from the beach; bunk rates are $20 per person, and they offer free pickup from the airport, train, or bus station. There's an extensive collection of DVDs for guests, and free barbecues are held Tuesday and Thursday.

Rates listed below are for the peak summer season (July–Aug); rates the rest of the year average 20% to 40% lower. Accommodations here tend to book up solid on summer weekends and even weekdays, but discounts can be had, especially for those who dare walk-up bookings on the afternoon of arrival.

EXPENSIVE

Catamaran Resort Hotel (★★) (*Kids*)   Right on Mission Bay, the Catamaran has its own bay and ocean beaches, complete with watersports facilities. Built in the 1950s, the hotel has been fully renovated to modern standards without losing its trademark Polynesian theme; the atrium lobby holds a 15-foot waterfall and full-size dugout canoe, koi-filled lagoons meander through the property, and the pool is surrounded by a real bamboo fence, rather than a fake metal one. The kitschy touches aren't plastic: These were lovingly incorporated before Tiki was tacky. Numerous varieties of bamboo and palm sprout in the lush gardens and tropical birds chirp away; after dark, torches blaze. Guest rooms—in a 13-story building or one of the six 2-story buildings—have subdued South Pacific decor, and each has a balcony or patio. High floors of tower rooms have commanding views, while studios and suites have the added convenience of kitchenettes. The Catamaran is within a few blocks of Pacific Beach's restaurant-and-nightlife scene. It's also steps away from the bay's jogging-and-biking path;

runners with tots in tow can rent jogging strollers at the hotel. The resort's Mississippi-style stern-wheeler, the *Bahia Belle*, cruises the bay Friday and Saturday evenings (nightly in summer) and is free to hotel guests.

3999 Mission Blvd. (4 blocks south of Grand Ave.), San Diego, CA 92109. ℂ 800/422-8386 or 858/488-1081. Fax 858/488-1387. www.catamaranresort.com. 313 units. $275–$385 double; from $389 suite. Children under 12 stay free in parent's room. AE, DC, DISC, MC, V. Valet parking $11; self-parking $9. Bus: 27 or 34. Take Grand/Garnet exit off I-5 and go west on Grand Ave., then south on Mission Blvd. **Amenities:** Restaurant; 2 bars; outdoor pool; fitness room; Jacuzzi; watersports equipment rental; bike rental; children's programs; concierge; limited room service (5am–11pm); in-room massage; laundry service; dry cleaning. *In room:* A/C, TV w/pay movies, dataport, fridge in most units, coffeemaker, hair dryer, iron.

Crystal Pier Hotel *(Kids (Finds* When historic charm is higher on your wish list than hotel-style service, head to this utterly unique cluster of cottages sitting literally over the surf on the vintage Crystal Pier at Pacific Beach. Like renting your own self-contained hideaway, you'll get a separate living room and bedroom, fully equipped kitchen, and private patio with breathtaking ocean views—all within the whitewashed walls of sweet, blue-shuttered cottages that date from 1936 but have been meticulously renovated. Each of the Cape Cod–style cottages has a deck—the more expensive units farthest out have more privacy. There are six units not actually on the pier but still offering sunset-facing sea views; these are cheaper. The sound of waves is soothing, yet the boardwalk action is only a few steps (and worlds) away, and the pier is a great place for watching sunsets and surfers. Guests drive right out and park beside their cottages, a real boon on crowded weekends. But this operation is strictly BYOBT (beach towels!), and the office is only open from 8am to 8pm. Reserve for summer and holiday weekends several months in advance.

4500 Ocean Blvd. (at Garnet Ave.), San Diego, CA 92109. ℂ 800/748-5894 or 858/483-6983. Fax 858/483-6811. www.crystalpier.com. 29 units. $195–$320 double; from $270 for larger units sleeping 4–6. 3-night minimum in summer. DISC, MC, V. Free parking. Bus: 27, 30, or 34. Take I-5 to Grand/Garnet exit; follow Garnet to the pier. **Amenities:** Beach equipment rental. *In room:* TV, kitchen.

Ocean Park Inn *(* This modern oceanfront motor hotel offers simple, attractive, spacious rooms with contemporary furnishings. Although the inn has a smidgeon of sophistication uncommon in this casual, surfer-populated area, you won't find much solitude with the boisterous scene outside. But you can't beat the sand access (directly on the beach) and the view (ditto). Rates vary according to view, but most rooms have at least a partial ocean view; all have a private balcony or patio. Units in front are most desirable, but it can get noisy directly above the boardwalk; try for the second or third floor, or pick one of the three junior suites, which have huge bathrooms and pool views.

710 Grand Ave., San Diego, CA 92109. ℂ 800/231-7735 or 858/483-5858. Fax 858/274-0823. www.ocean parkinn.com. 73 units. $199–$249 double; $239–$269 suite. Rates include continental breakfast. AE, DC, DISC, MC, V. Free indoor parking. Bus: 34 or 34A/B. Take Grand/Garnet exit off I-5; follow Grand Ave. to ocean. **Amenities:** Outdoor pool; Jacuzzi; laundry service; dry cleaning. *In room:* A/C, TV, dataport, fridge, coffeemaker, hair dryer.

Pacific Terrace Hotel *(* The best modern hotel on the boardwalk swaggers with a heavy-handed South Seas–meets–Spanish colonial ambience. Rattan fans circulate in the lobby and hint at the sunny Indonesian-inspired decor in guest rooms, which are named after Caribbean islands. Hands-on owners kicked up the luxury factor (and prices) with a renovation, resulting in a more upscale atmosphere than most of the casual beach pads nearby are able to muster. Located at the north end of the Pacific Beach boardwalk, the more rowdy surfer contingent tends to stay a few blocks south. Large, comfortable guest rooms

each have balconies or terraces and fancy wall safes; bathrooms—designed with warm-toned marble and natural woods—have a separate sink/vanity area. About half the rooms have kitchenettes, and top-floor rooms in this three-story hotel enjoy particularly nice views—you'll find yourself mesmerized by the rhythmic waves and determined surfers below. Management keeps cookies, coffee, and iced tea at the ready throughout the day. The lushly landscaped pool and hot tub overlook a relatively quiet stretch of beach. Five nearby restaurants allow meals to be billed to the hotel, but there's no restaurant on the premises.

610 Diamond St., San Diego, CA 92109. © **800/344-3370** or 858/581-3500. Fax 858/274-3341. www. pacificterrace.com. 75 units. $260–$415 double; from $485 suite. Rates include continental breakfast. AE, DC, DISC, MC, V. Parking $8; limited free parking in off-street lot. Bus: 30 or 34. Take I-5 to Grand/Garnet exit and follow Grand or Garnet west to Mission Blvd., turn right (north), then left (west) onto Diamond. **Amenities:** Pool; access to nearby health club ($5); whirlpool; bike rental nearby; activities desk; room service (11am–10:30pm); in-room massage; laundry/dry-cleaning service; coin-op laundry. *In room:* A/C, TV w/pay movies, dataport, minibar, coffeemaker, hair dryer, iron.

Paradise Point Resort & Spa 🌴🌴 *Kids*   Smack dab in the middle of Mission Bay, this hotel complex is almost as much a theme park as its closest neighbor, SeaWorld (a 3-min. drive). Single-story accommodations are spread across 44 tropically landscaped acres of duck-filled lagoons, lush gardens, and swim-friendly beaches; all have private lanais (patios) and plenty of thoughtful conveniences. The resort was recently updated to keep its low-tech 1960s charm but lose tacky holdovers—rooms now have a refreshingly colorful beach-cottage decor. And despite daunting high-season rack rates, there's usually a deal to be had here. There's an upscale waterfront restaurant, Baleen (fine dining in a contemporary, fun space), and a stunning Indonesian-inspired spa that offers cool serenity and aroma-tinged Asian treatments—this spa is a vacation in itself!

1404 Vacation Rd. (off Ingraham St.), San Diego, CA 92109. © **800/344-2626** or 858/274-4630. Fax 858/ 581-5924. www.paradisepoint.com. 457 units. $269–$459 double; from $479 suite. Extra person $20. Children 17 and under stay free in parent's room. AE, DC, DISC, MC, V. Parking $10. Bus: 9. Follow I-8 west to Mission Bay Dr. exit; take Ingraham St. north to Vacation Rd. **Amenities:** 3 restaurants; lounge; pool bar; 6 outdoor pools; 18-hole putting course; tennis courts; croquet; sand volleyball; basketball; fitness center; full-service spa; whirlpool; bike rental; room service (6am–midnight); laundry/dry-cleaning service. *In room:* A/C, TV w/pay movies, dataport, fridge, coffeemaker, hair dryer, iron.

MODERATE

The Dana on Mission Bay 🌴   The Dana completed a $20-million renovation and expansion in 2004 that added 74 contemporary rooms in a three-story arc wrapping around an infinity pool. While these rooms are a fair upgrade from the sleepy old Dana, the original rooms, in two-story buildings, were spruced up at the same time. Some overlook bobbing sailboats in the recreational marina, others face onto a kidney-shaped pool whose surrounding tiki-torch-lit gardens offer shuffleboard and Ping-Pong. You'll pay a little extra for bay and marina views; if the view doesn't matter, save your money—every one of the old rooms is the same size, with plain but well-maintained furnishings. The new rooms are bigger and feature water views and reclaimed-redwood beam ceilings. Beaches and SeaWorld are a 15-minute walk away (there's a complimentary shuttle). Meals and room service (including poolside food and cocktail ministrations) are available through the new restaurants, **Firefly Bar & Grill** and **Blue Pearl.**

1710 W. Mission Bay Dr., San Diego, CA 92109. © **800/345-9995** or 619/222-6440. Fax 619/222-5916. www. thedana.net. 270 units. $165–$235 double (sleeps up to 4); from $270 suite. AE, DC, DISC, MC, V. Free parking. Bus: 27 or 34. Follow I-8 west to Mission Bay Dr. exit; take W. Mission Bay Dr. **Amenities:** 2 restaurants; outdoor heated pool and Jacuzzi; fitness room; bike rental; watersports equipment rental; limited room service

(7am–8:30pm); coin-op laundry and laundry service; dry cleaning. *In room:* A/C, TV, dataport, fridge, coffeemaker, hair dryer, iron.

Elsbree House ⓐ Katie and Phil Elsbree have turned this modern Cape Cod–style building into an immaculate, exceedingly comfortable B&B, half a block from the water's edge in Ocean Beach. One condo unit with a private entrance rents only by the week; the Elsbrees occupy another. Each of the six guest rooms has a patio or balcony. Guests share the cozy living room (with a fireplace and TV), breakfast room, and kitchen. Although other buildings on this tightly packed street block the ocean view, sounds of the surf and fresh sea breezes waft in open windows, and a charming garden—complete with trickling fountain—runs the length of the house. This Ocean Beach neighborhood is eclectic, occupied by ocean-loving couples, dedicated surf bums, and the occasional contingent of punk skater kids who congregate near the pier. Its strengths are proximity to the beach, a limited but pleasing selection of eateries that attract mostly locals, and San Diego's best antiquing (along Newport Ave.).

5054 Narragansett Ave., San Diego, CA 92107. ⓒ **800/607-4133** or 619/226-4133. www.bbinob.com. 7 units. $135–$149 double; $1,800 per week 3-bedroom condo (lower rates if only 1 or 2 rooms used). Room rates include continental breakfast. MC, V. Bus: 23 or 35. From airport, take Harbor Dr. west to Nimitz Blvd. to Lowell St., which becomes Narragansett Ave. *In room:* Hair dryer, iron, no phone.

INEXPENSIVE

The Beach Cottages This family-owned operation has been around since 1948 and offers a variety of guest quarters, most of them geared to the long-term visitor. It's the 17 cute little detached cottages just steps from the sand that give it real appeal, though some of them lack a view (of anything!); each has a patio with tables and chairs. Adjoining apartments are perfectly adequate, especially for budget-minded families who want to log major hours on the beach—all cottages and apartments sleep four or more and have full kitchens. There are also standard motel rooms that are worn but cheap (most of these sleep two). The property is within walking distance of shops and restaurants and enjoy shared barbecue grills, shuffleboard courts, and table tennis. The cottages themselves aren't pristine but have a rustic charm that makes them popular with young honeymooners and those nostalgic for the golden age of laid-back California beach culture. Reserve the beachfront cottages well in advance.

4255 Ocean Blvd. (1 block south of Grand Ave.), San Diego, CA 92109-3995. ⓒ **858/483-7440**. Fax 858/ 273-9365. www.beachcottages.com. 61 units, 17 cottages. $120–$180 double; from $210 cottages for 4 to 6. Monthly rates available mid-Sept to Mar. AE, DC, DISC, MC, V. Free parking. Bus: 27, 30, or 34. Take I-5 to Grand/Garnet exit, go west on Grand Ave. and left on Mission Blvd. **Amenities:** Self-service laundry. *In room:* TV, fridge, coffeemaker, microwave.

Beach Haven Inn A great spot for beach lovers who can't quite afford to be on the beach, this motel lies 1 block from the sand. Rooms face an inner courtyard, where guests enjoy a secluded ambience for relaxing by the pool. On the street side it looks kind of marginal, but once on the property, you'll find all quarters well maintained and sporting clean, up-to-date furnishings—nearly all units have eat-in kitchens. The friendly staff provides free coffee in the lobby and rents VCRs and movies.

4740 Mission Blvd. (at Missouri St.), San Diego, CA 92109. ⓒ **800/831-6323** or 858/272-3812. Fax 858/272-3532. www.beachhaveninn.com. 23 units. $120–$170 double. 2-night minimum on weekends. Extra person $5. Children under 12 stay free in parent's room. Rates include continental breakfast. AE, DC, DISC, MC, V. Free parking. Bus: 30 or 34. Take I-5 to Grand/Garnet exit, follow Grand Ave. to Mission Blvd. and turn right. **Amenities:** Outdoor pool; whirlpool. *In room:* A/C, TV, kitchenette (most units).

LA JOLLA

The name "La Jolla" is loosely translated from Spanish as "the jewel," a fitting comparison for this section of the city with a beautiful coastline, as well as a compact downtown village that makes for delightful strolling. You'll have a hard time finding bargain accommodations in this upscale, conservative community. But remember, most hotels—even those in our "Very Expensive" category—have occupancy-driven rates, meaning you can score surprising discounts during the off season (winter), when the beds go begging.

All of the hotels listed below are moderate in size. For a more intimate experience, check in to the luxe **Hotel Parisi** 𝆑𝆑𝆑, 1111 Prospect St. (© 877/ 4-PARISI or 858/454-1511; www.hotelparisi.com), a sleek 28-room boutique inn nestled amid fashionable clothing boutiques, and catering to the city-savvy traveler seeking Italy-meets-Zen ambience and relaxation. Two other moderately priced properties provide relatively good value: **Best Western Inn by the Sea** 𝆑, 7830 Fay Ave. (© **800/526-4545** or 858/459-4461; www.bestwestern.com/ innbythesea), located in the heart of La Jolla's village and just a short walk from the cliffs and beach; and the nearby **Empress Hotel of La Jolla** 𝆑, 7766 Fay Ave. (© **888/369-9900** or 858/454-3001; www.thegrandecolonial.com), where you'll find spacious quarters with classy traditional furnishings in a 1960s high-rise.

VERY EXPENSIVE

La Valencia Hotel 𝆑𝆑𝆑   Within its bougainvillea-draped walls and wrought-iron garden gates, this gracious bastion of gentility does a fine job of resurrecting golden-age elegance, when celebrities like Greta Garbo and Charlie Chaplin vacationed here alongside the world's moneyed elite. The bluff-top hotel, which looks much like a Mediterranean villa, has been the centerpiece of La Jolla since opening in 1926, and a $10-million renovation in 2000 refined some of the details and added 15 villas and an enlarged pool, without breaking with its historical glamour. Brides still pose in front of the lobby's picture window, well-coiffed ladies lunch in the dappled shade of the garden patio, and neighborhood cronies quaff libations in the clubby **Whaling Bar** (La Jolla's version of the power lunch). One chooses La Valencia for its history and scenic location, but you won't be disappointed by the old-world standards of service and style.

All rooms are comfortably and traditionally furnished, each boasting lavish appointments and all-marble bathrooms with signature toiletries. Because rates vary wildly according to view (from sweeping to *nada*), my advice is to get a cheaper room and enjoy the scene from one of the many lounges, serene garden terraces, or the amazing pool, which fronts the Pacific and nearby Scripp's Park. Room decor, layouts, and size (starting at a relatively snug 246 sq. ft.) are all over the map, too—a few extra minutes spent with the reservationist will ensure a custom match for you. If you've got the bucks, spring for one of the newer villas, which feature fireplaces and butler service. The hotel's 12-table Sky Room is one of the city's most celebrated dining rooms

1132 Prospect St. (at Herschel Ave.), La Jolla, CA 92037. © **800/451-0772** or 858/454-0771. Fax 858/456-3921. www.lavalencia.com. 117 units. $275–$550 double; from $775 suite or villa. 2-night minimum summer weekends. AE, DC, DISC, MC, V. Valet parking $15. Bus: 30 or 34. Take Torrey Pines Rd. to Prospect Place and turn right. Prospect Place becomes Prospect St. **Amenities:** 3 restaurants; bar; outdoor pool; exercise room w/spa treatments; whirlpool; sauna; concierge; secretarial services; 24-hr. room service; babysitting; laundry/dry-cleaning service. *In room:* A/C, TV w/VCR, dataport, minibar, coffeemaker, hair dryer, iron, safe.

The Lodge at Torrey Pines 𝆑𝆑𝆑   Located 10 minutes north of La Jolla proper, this triumphant *trompe l'oeil* creation at the edge of the Torrey Pines Golf Course is the fantasy of a local hotelier, who took his appreciation for

La Jolla

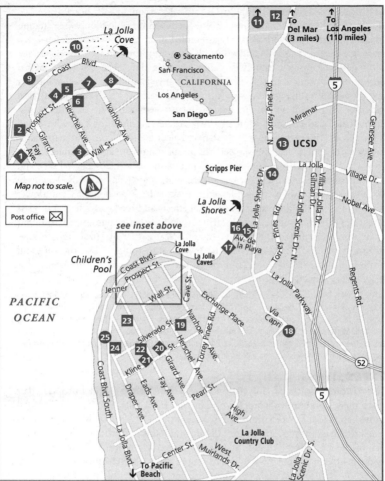

Craftsman-style homes and amplified it into a 175-room upscale hotel. Patterned largely after the 1908 Greene and Greene–designed Gamble House (see chapter 13), the Lodge brims with perfectly assembled nuances of the era: clinker-brick masonry, art glass windows and doors, Stickley furniture, and exquisite pottery. Most guest rooms fall into two main categories. The least expensive are an unstinting 520 square feet, lavished with Tiffany-style lamps, period wallpaper and framed Hiroshige prints, with lots of wood accents. Views face a courtyard carefully landscaped to mimic the rare coastal environment that exists just beyond the hotel grounds. More expensive rooms overlook the golf course and the sea in the distance—most of these have balconies, fireplaces, and giant bathrooms with separate tub and shower. Sumptuous suites are also available.

The 9,500-square-foot **spa** specializes in treatments utilizing coastal sage and other local plants. An excellent **restaurant** named after painter A.R. Valentien features superb seasonal vegetables with most entrees—Valentien's wildflower watercolors line the walls and his personal effects and medals are found in glass bookcases. I find the embrace of local artists and the native natural environment to be absolutely inspired. My only (small) caveat is that in polishing and augmenting Arts and Crafts style for the masses, something is lost: the soul and warmth of a true family home. But the Lodge is unsurpassed as San Diego's ultimate luxury destination, with every whim catered to by a mindful staff.

11480 N. Torrey Pines Rd., La Jolla, CA 92037. © **800/656-0087** or 858/453-4420. Fax 858/453-7464. www. lodgetorreypines.com. 175 units. $450–$625 double; from $900 suite. Children under 18 stay free in parent's room. AE, DC, DISC, MC, V. $14 self-parking, $17 valet parking. Bus: 301. From I-8 take La Jolla Village Dr. W., bear right (north) onto N. Torrey Pines Rd. **Amenities:** 2 restaurants; outdoor pool; whirlpool; fitness center; spa; preferential tee times; concierge and valet; 24-hr. room service. *In room:* A/C, TV, coffeemaker, minibar, hair dryer, in-room safe, fireplace and balcony in most units.

EXPENSIVE

The Grande Colonial ★★ *Finds* Possessed of an old-world European flair that's more London or Georgetown than seaside La Jolla, the Grande Colonial earned accolades for the complete restoration in 2001 of its polished mahogany paneling, brass fittings, and genteel library and lounge. During the original heyday of the La Jolla Playhouse, it was the temporary home for everyone from Groucho Marx to Jane Wyatt. Today a large spray of fresh flowers is the focal point in the lounge, where guests gather in front of the fireplace for drinks—often before enjoying dinner at the hotel's Nine-Ten restaurant. Guest rooms are quiet and elegantly appointed, with beautiful draperies and traditional furnishings. Relics from the early days include oversize closets, meticulously tiled bathrooms, and heavy fireproof doors suspended in the corridors. The hotel is 1 block from the ocean, but many of the rooms have sea views. Numerous historic photos on the walls illustrate the hotel's story, which started as a full-service apartment hotel in 1913. Among La Jolla's minihorde of deluxe properties, the Grande Colonial is sometimes overlooked. In fact, the centrally located hotel is a sleeper that provides comparatively good value.

910 Prospect St. (between Fay and Girard), La Jolla, CA 92037. © **800/826-1278** or 858/454-2181. Fax 858/ 454-5679. www.thegrandecolonial.com. 75 units. $249–$379 double; from $319 suite. AE, DC, DISC, MC, V. Valet parking $14. Bus: 30 or 34. Take Torrey Pines Rd. to Prospect Place and turn right. Prospect Place becomes Prospect St. **Amenities:** Restaurant; outdoor pool; access to nearby health club; limited room service (6:30am–10:30pm); laundry service; dry cleaning. *In room:* A/C, TV w/pay movies, dataport, hair dryer, iron, safe.

The Sea Lodge ★ *Kids* This three-story, 1960s hotel in a mainly residential enclave is under the same management as the exclusive La Jolla Beach & Tennis Club next door. It has an identical on-the-sand location, minus the country club ambience—there are no reciprocal privileges. About half the rooms have some view of the ocean, and the rest look out on the pool or a tiled courtyard. The rooms are pretty basic, with perfunctory, outdated furnishings, priced by view and size. Bathrooms feature separate dressing areas with large closets, balconies or patios are standard, and some rooms have fully equipped kitchenettes. From the Sea Lodge's beach you can gaze toward the top of the cliffs, where La Jolla's village hums with activity (and relentless traffic). Like the "B&T," the Sea Lodge is popular with families but also attracts business travelers looking to balance meetings with time on the beach or the tennis court.

8110 Camino del Oro (at Avenida de la Playa), La Jolla, CA 92037. © 800/640-7722 or 858/459-8271. Fax 858/456-9346. www.ljbtc.com. 128 units. $249–$559 double; $739 suite. Extra person $20. Children under 12 stay free in parent's room. AE, DC, DISC, MC, V. Free covered parking. Bus: 34. Take La Jolla Shores Dr., turn left onto Avenida de la Playa, turn right on Camino del Oro. **Amenities:** Restaurant; swimming pool (plus wading pool for kids); 2 tennis courts; fitness room; whirlpool; babysitting; laundry/dry-cleaning service. *In room:* A/C, TV, dataport, fridge, coffeemaker, hair dryer, iron.

MODERATE

The Bed & Breakfast Inn at La Jolla ★★ *Finds* A 1913 Cubist house designed by San Diego's first important architect, Irving Gill—and occupied in the 1920s by John Philip Sousa and his family—is the setting for this cultured and elegant B&B. Reconfigured as lodging, the house has lost none of its charm, and its appropriately unfrilly period furnishings add to the sense of history. The inn also features lovely enclosed gardens and a cozy library and sitting room. Sherry and fresh-cut flowers await in every room, some of which feature a fireplace or ocean view. Each room has a private bathroom, most of which are compact in size. The furnishings are tasteful and cottage style, with plenty of historic photos of La Jolla. Gourmet breakfast is served wherever you desire—dining room, patio, sun deck, or in your room. Picnic baskets (extra charge) are available with a day's notice. The gardens surrounding the inn were originally planned by Kate Sessions, who created much of the landscaping for Balboa Park.

7753 Draper Ave. (near Prospect), La Jolla, CA 92037. © 800/582-2466 or 858/456-2066. Fax 858/456-1510. www.InnLaJolla.com. 15 units. $179–$359 double; $399 suite. 2-night minimum on weekends. Rates include full breakfast and afternoon wine and cheese. AE, DISC, MC, V. Bus: 30 or 34. Take Torrey Pines Rd. to Prospect Place and turn right. Prospect Place becomes Prospect St.; proceed to Draper Ave. and turn left. *In room:* A/C, hair dryer, iron.

INEXPENSIVE

Wealthy, image-conscious La Jolla is not the best place for deep bargains, but if you're determined to stay here on a budget, try the 30-room **La Jolla Village Lodge,** 1141 Silverado St. (© **858/551-2001;** www.lajollavillagelodge.com), a motel with small, basic rooms; prices reach $120 in July and August, but otherwise rates are under $100 for most of the year.

CORONADO

The "island" of Coronado is a great escape. It offers quiet, architecturally rich streets, a small-town, navy-oriented atmosphere, and laid-back vacationing on one of the state's most beautiful and welcoming beaches. Coronado's resorts are especially popular with Southern California and Arizona families for weekend escapes. Although downtown San Diego is just a 10-minute drive or 20-minute ferry-ride away, you may feel pleasantly isolated in Coronado—it isn't your best choice if you plan to spend most of your time in central parts of the city.

The 438-room **Loews Coronado Bay Resort** ★★, 4000 Coronado Bay Rd. (© **800/81-LOEWS** or 619/424-4000; www.loewshotels.com), is San Diego's most removed hotel, located 6 miles down the Silver Strand, but it works for those who prefer a self-contained resort in a get-away-from-it-all location (it also serves convention groups and has a superlative restaurant, Azzura Point). Far cheaper but with a central location is the vintage **Village Inn,** 1017 Park Place (© **619/435-9318;** www.coronadovillageinn.com). You can walk to all of Coronado's sights, and the rates are a bargain (under $100 a night). The inn's only Achilles' heel is tiny, tiny bathrooms.

VERY EXPENSIVE

Hotel del Coronado 🏆🏆🏆 *(Kids)* Opened in 1888 and designated a National Historic Landmark in 1977, the "Hotel Del," as it's affectionately known, is the last of California's grand old seaside hotels. This monument to Victorian grandeur boasts tall cupolas, red turrets, and gingerbread trim, all spread out over 31 acres. Rooms—almost no two alike—run the gamut from compact to extravagant, and all are packed with antique charm; most have custom-made furnishings. The least expensive are snug and have views of a roof or parking lot. The best are junior suites with large windows and balconies fronting one of the state's finest white-sand beaches, but note that even here, bathrooms are modest in size. There are nine cottages lining the sand that are more private (Marilyn Monroe stayed in the first one during the filming of *Some Like It Hot*). *Note:* Almost half the hotel's rooms are in the seven-story contemporary tower and offer more living space, but none of the historical ambience—personally, I can't imagine staying here in anything but the Victorian structure, but you pay a premium for the privilege (especially for an ocean view), and 2-night minimums often apply.

Even if you don't stay here, don't miss a stroll through the grand, wood-paneled lobby or along the pristine wide beach. Accolades have been awarded to the Prince of Wales, remodeled from a dark, clubby room to an airy, elegant salon with oceanfront dining; cocktails and afternoon tea are served in the wood-paneled lobby and adjoining **Palm Court,** and Sunday Brunch in the **Crown Room** is a San Diego tradition.

1500 Orange Ave., Coronado, CA 92118. © **800/468-3533** or 619/435-6611. Fax 619/522-8238. www. hoteldel.com. 688 rooms. $290–$520 double; from $775 cottage or suite. Children under 18 stay free in parent's room. Additional person $25. Minimum-stay requirements apply most weekends. AE, DC, DISC, MC, V. Valet parking $21, self-parking $16. Bus: 901 or 902. From Coronado Bridge, turn left onto Orange Ave. **Amenities:** 9 restaurants/bars; 2 outdoor pools; 3 tennis courts; health club and spa; 2 whirlpools; bike rental; children's activities; concierge; shopping arcade; 24-hr. room service; babysitting; laundry/dry-cleaning service. *In room:* A/C, TV w/pay movies, dataport, minibar, hair dryer, iron, safe.

MODERATE

Coronado Inn 🏆 Well located and terrifically priced, this renovated 1940s courtyard motel has such a friendly ambience, it's like staying with old friends. Iced tea, lemonade, and fresh fruit are even provided poolside on summer days. It's still a motel, though—albeit with brand-new paint and fresh tropical floral decor—so rooms are pretty basic. The six rooms with bathtubs also have small kitchens; others have microwaves, and hair dryers and irons on request (just ask up front). Rooms close to the street are noisiest—ask for one toward the back. The Coronado shuttle stops a block away; it serves shopping areas and Hotel Del.

266 Orange Ave. (corner of Third St.), Coronado, CA 92118. © **800/598-6624** or 619/435-4121. www. coronadoinn.com. 30 units (most with shower only). $125–$195 double (sleeps up to 4). Rates include continental breakfast. AE, DISC, MC, V. Free parking. Bus: 901 or 902. From Coronado Bridge, stay on Third St. Pets accepted with $10 nightly fee. **Amenities:** Outdoor pool; coin-op laundry. *In room:* A/C, TV, fridge.

El Cordova Hotel 𝒜   This Spanish hacienda across the street from the Hotel del Coronado began life as a private mansion in 1902. By the 1930s it had become a hotel, the original building augmented by a series of attachments housing retail shops along the ground-floor arcade. Shaped like a baseball diamond and surrounding a courtyard with meandering tiled pathways, flowering shrubs, a swimming pool, and patio seating for Miguel's Cocina Mexican restaurant, El Cordova hums pleasantly with activity. Each room is a little different from the next—some sport a Mexican colonial ambience, while others evoke a comfy beach cottage. All feature ceiling fans and brightly tiled bathrooms but lack the frills that would command exorbitant rates. El Cordova has a particularly inviting aura, and its prime location makes it a popular option; reserving several weeks in advance is advised for summer months. Facilities include a barbecue area with picnic table.

1351 Orange Ave. (at Adella Ave.), Coronado, CA 92118. ℂ 800/229-2032 or 619/435-4131. Fax 619/435-0632. www.elcordovahotel.com. 40 units. $129–$209 double; from $269 suite. Children under 12 stay free in parent's room. AE, DC, DISC, MC, V. Parking in neighboring structure $6/day. Bus: 901 or 902. From Coronado Bridge, turn left onto Orange Ave. **Amenities:** Restaurant; outdoor pool; shopping arcade; coin-op laundry. *In room:* A/C, TV.

Glorietta Bay Inn 𝒜𝒜   Right across the street and somewhat in the (figurative) shadow of the Hotel Del, this pretty hotel consists of the charmingly historic John D. Spreckels mansion (1908) and several younger, motel-style buildings. Only 11 rooms are in the mansion, which boasts original fixtures, a grand staircase, and old-fashioned wicker furniture; the guest rooms are also decked out in antiques, and have a romantic and nostalgic ambience. Rooms and suites in the 1950s annexes are much less expensive but are somewhat better than motel-plain; some have kitchenettes and marina views. The least expensive units are small and have parking-lot views. Wherever your room is, you'll enjoy the inn's trademark personalized service including extra-helpful staffers who remember your name and happily offer dining and sightseeing recommendations or arrange tee times; special attention to return guests and families with toddlers; and a friendly continental breakfast. In addition to offering rental bikes and boat rentals on Glorietta Bay across the street, the hotel is within easy walking distance of the beach, golf, tennis, watersports, shopping, and dining. Rooms in the mansion get booked early but are worth the extra effort and expense.

1630 Glorietta Blvd. (near Orange Ave.), Coronado, CA 92118. ℂ 800/283-9383 or 619/435-3101. Fax 619/435-6182. www.gloriettabayinn.com. 100 units. Double $150–$215 annex; from $275 for suite in the mansion. Extra person $10. Children under 18 stay free in parent's room. Rates include continental breakfast and afternoon refreshment. AE, DC, DISC, MC, V. Self-parking $7. Bus: 901 or 902. From Coronado Bridge, turn left on Orange Ave. After 2 miles, turn left onto Glorietta Blvd.; the inn is across the street from the Hotel del Coronado. **Amenities:** Outdoor pool; whirlpool; in-room massage; babysitting; laundry/dry-cleaning service; coin-op laundry. *In room:* A/C, TV w/pay movies, dataport, fridge, coffeemaker, hair dryer.

4 Where to Dine

San Diego's dining scene, once a culinary backwater, has come into its own during the past decade. The spark has been an explosion in the transplant population and cultural diversification, along with a bustling economy, which helps motivate folks to step out and exercise their palates. These new-found foodies have been taught to respect the seasonality of vegetables, allowing chefs to revel in the bounteous agriculture of San Diego County by focusing on vegetables when flavors are at their peak at specialized north county growers like Chino Farms. But don't just take my word for it. In 2003 *Gourmet* magazine announced: "Perhaps for the first time ever, San Diego has a buzzing restaurant scene as engaging as the area's other tourist attractions." Finally, we can be known for something on the table beyond tacos and *frijoles*.

But number one on most every visitor's list of priorities is still Mexican food—a logical choice given the city's history and location. You'll find lots of highly Americanized, often satisfying interpretations of Mexican fare (i.e., combo plates heaped with melted cheddar cheese) along with hidden gems, like El Agave (p. 701), that serve true south-of-the-border cuisine. And don't miss the humble fish taco, the city's favorite fast food, which originated at locally based chain Rubio's.

What follows is an abbreviated sampling of highlights from San Diego's table—the emphasis is on the best of the best in all price categories, locations, and cuisines. For a greater selection of reviews, see *Frommer's San Diego 2005*. To locate these restaurants, see the "San Diego Accommodations & Dining" map on p. 678, and the "La Jolla" map on p. 691.

DOWNTOWN

Downtown was turned on its ear when Horton Plaza was redeveloped in 1985 and swank spots began moving in to the Gaslamp Quarter's restored Victorian buildings. Today there are dozens of eateries (and nightclubs) within the quarter and dozens more nearby.

On evenings when the Padres are playing, or when a big convention has filled the hotels, you'll be competing for parking. Fortunately, pedicabs—three-wheeled bikes that carry two passengers each—are easy to hire. But if you take a taxi or the trolley downtown on game nights, you'll find most restaurants easy to get into once the first pitch is thrown.

The city's top dessert emporium is aptly monikered **Extraordinary Desserts** ☆☆, 1430 Union St. (© **619/294-7001**), where proprietor Karen Krasne produces exquisite cakes and pastries garnished with edible gold, flowers, and exotic fruits. Relocated to Little Italy in 2004, it's open till 11pm (midnight Fri–Sat) to indulge late-night emergency cravings.

VERY EXPENSIVE

Star of the Sea ☆☆☆ SEAFOOD   An Embarcadero fine-dining bastion since 1966, a millennium makeover banished its stuffy, outmoded aura to the past, and the restaurant reopened with a new look, new chef, and new name (to better differentiate it from the unexceptional waterfront fish houses next door, also in the Anthony's restaurant family). Today there's a comfortable, intimate ambience and modern decor matched to the still-glorious harbor view—the tables face the 1863 sailing ship *Star of India*. Stay tuned to the fine dining, though: Executive chef Paul McCabe imbues the menu with sophisticated touches that show he's in touch with today's gourmands. The menu is seasonally composed; representative dishes include striped sea bass with picholine olives and squid, floating in a bisque of Meyer lemons; or perfectly seared diver scallops nuzzling a lobster-and-chanterelle risotto; and northern halibut with fiddlehead ferns, artichokes, and fava beans. There are always a few offerings for carnivores, like a "duo of beef" (short ribs, grilled filet, and roasted bone marrow), or the seared elk loin, but otherwise the always-fresh seafood is accompanied by equally stimulating vegetable creations. There's a reasonably priced wine list and a welcoming bar with its own abbreviated menu.

1360 N. Harbor Dr. (at Ash St.), Embarcadero. © 619/232-7408. www.starofthesea.com. Reservations recommended. Main courses $26–$38. AE, DC, DISC, MC, V. Daily 5:30–9pm (till 10pm Fri–Sat). Valet parking $8. Bus: All Harbor Dr. routes. Trolley: America Plaza.

EXPENSIVE

Chive &&& CALIFORNIA   This big-city-style Gaslamp venue introduced San Diego to sleek and chic dining rooms of the East Coast, and to daring kitchen inventions. The culinary adventure starts with a fashionable cocktail, of course: The local martini is embellished with Gorgonzola-stuffed olives, and Chive's twist on the *mojito,* that rum-and-lime concoction, adds a gingery splash to the Cuban trademark. The menu changes every 6 to 8 weeks, but popular dishes found more often than not include lamb tagine served with *harissa,* the obligatory hot sauce, gnocchi, a roasted baby-beet salad, the caramelized-onion-and-potato pastilla, a nightly "noodle" (pasta) of the chef's whim, and salads that balance crispy greens with pungent, creamy cheeses and sweet fruit accents. But don't be surprised to encounter curiosities like foie gras with banana bread and caramelized bananas—diners who take a chance on such eccentricities are usually richly rewarded. The always-evolving wine list offers many intriguing selections by "cork" or "stem" from all corners of the globe, like quality bottles from South Africa, Temecula, or Mexico. Chive balances its angular, wide space with cozy lighting, warm fabrics, and a pervasive sense of relaxed fun. One lament: In pursuit of elegant modernity, the cement floors and other hard surfaces amplify the noise level.

558 Fourth Ave. (at Market St.), Gaslamp Quarter. © **619/232-4483.** www.chiverestaurant.com. Reservations recommended. Main courses $19–$31. AE, DC, DISC, MC, V. Daily 5–11pm. Live jazz Sat. Bus: 1, 3, 4, 5, 16, or 25. Trolley: Convention Center.

Indigo Grill && CALIFORNIA   Bracing "aboriginal" cuisine of the Pacific coast—from Mexico to Alaska—is showcased at chef Deborah Scott's Little Italy adventure. Root veggies, game, and fruit are integral to the menu, and unusual spices are used liberally. Occasionally the reach is too far, but no matter: This place is a treat for the palates of foodies yearning for something original. Start with Oaxaca Fire, a tequila-based cocktail with a salt-and-pepper rim (lotsa kick), and move on to a salad of spinach, spaghetti squash, and strawberries. The alder-wood plank salmon, served with a tangle of squid-ink pasta spotted with smoky Oaxacan cheese is a wonderful entree, or go for the venison lacquered in wild blueberries—all are extravagantly garnished. Although the menu is primarily meat- and fish-oriented, there are always a couple excellent vegetarian entrees, a throng of meatless appetizers (many of the starters are big enough that two will make a meal), and the ceviche bar is worth investigating.

The room is filled with native iconography, rippling water, and glass dividers that mimic sheets of ice, sharp angles, and masks. Varied textures of wood, stone, metal, and leather invoke elements of the geographical territory encompassed by the menu. Scott made her name in the mid-1990s at **Kemo Sabe** (where Pacific Rim meets Southwestern) and now juggles helming duties there and at this new venture. If you enjoy one, it's worth checking out the other; Kemo Sabe is located at 3958 Fifth Ave., near University Avenue, Hillcrest (© **619/220-6802**).

1536 India St. (at Cedar St.), Little Italy. © 619/234-6802. Reservations recommended. Main courses $9–$13 lunch, $18–$29 dinner. AE, DC, DISC, MC, V. Mon–Fri 11:30am–2pm; Sun–Wed 5–9pm; Thurs 5–10pm; Fri–Sat 5–11pm. Bus: 5 or 16. Trolley: Little Italy.

MODERATE

Fat City AMERICAN   If you need a steak but don't want to get caught up with the Gaslamp's roster of pricey chophouses and also don't want to settle for one of those chain eateries, Fat City is your place. Overlook the vaguely scary name (the owner's name is Tom Fat) and the overly vivid hot-pink paint job (the building is vintage Art Deco), and settle into one of the cushy booths beneath a canopy of Tiffany lamps. Skip the skimpy list of appetizers, since the entrees come with a side of potato or rice, and specials on the blackboard throw in a salad for a couple of bucks more. The steaks are USDA Choice, aged 21 days and grilled to order over mesquite charcoal. Better yet, aim for the USDA Prime top sirloin: A hunky 12-ounce cut is just $15, and miles ahead in flavor of what you get at a Black Angus–type joint. For those who haven't signed on to the Atkins regimen, you'll also find teriyaki salmon, chicken in a peppercorn sauce, and a couple of pasta dishes. I haven't tried those—I come here for the steaks and haven't found a reason to look farther down the menu.

2137 Pacific Hwy. (at Hawthorn), Little Italy. ✆ 619/232-9303. Main courses $11–$21. AE, MC, V. Daily 5–10pm. Free parking. Bus: 34.

The Fish Market ✦ *(Value* SEAFOOD/SUSHI   Ask any San Diegan where to go for the biggest selection of the freshest fish and they'll send you to the bustling Fish Market on the end of the G Street Pier on the Embarcadero. Chalkboards announce the day's catches—be it Mississippi catfish, Maine lobster, Canadian salmon, or Mexican yellowtail. They're sold by the pound or available in a number of classic, simple preparations in the casual, always-packed restaurant. Upstairs, the fancy offshoot **Top of the Market** offers sea fare with souped-up presentations (and jacked-up prices). Either way, the fish comes from the same trough, so I recommend having a cocktail in Top's plush, clubby atmosphere to enjoy the panoramic bay views, and then head downstairs for solidly affordable fare or treats from the sushi and oyster bars.

750 N. Harbor Dr., Embarcadero ✆ 619/232-FISH. www.thefishmarket.com. Reservations not accepted. Main courses $10–$25 lunch, $13–$32 dinner (Top of the Market main courses $13–$35 lunch, $15–$45 dinner). AE, DC, DISC, MC, V. Daily 11am–9:30pm (open till 10pm Fri–Sat). Valet parking $5. Bus: 7/7B. Trolley: Seaport Village.

Napa Valley Grille ✦ CALIFORNIA/MEDITERRANEAN   Proving that a shopping mall doesn't have to be a wasteland when it comes to dining, Napa Valley Grille is a popular, moderately upscale lunch spot for downtown workers, when entree-size salads, sandwiches, and pasta dishes are rolled out. Come back at dinner and the atmosphere is often subdued, and here you'll find a satisfying selection of grilled items: *ahi* tuna with puttanesca, a New York steak with a tomato fondue, plus sea bass crusted in Yukon gold potatoes or the braised lamb shank with French lentils. Despite the mall bustle outside, the dining room is pleasant and appealing.

Horton Plaza Shipping Center (top floor), downtown. ✆ 619/238-5440. Main courses $8–$15 lunch, $12–$27 dinner. AE, DC, DISC, MC, V. Mon–Thurs 11:30am–9pm; Fri–Sat 11:30am–10pm; Sun 11:30am–9:30pm. Bus: All Broadway routes. Trolley: Civic Center.

INEXPENSIVE

Also noteworthy in the Gaslamp is the hip, bohemian **Café Lulu,** 419 F St. (✆ 619/238-0114), a coffee bar with light meals; the spot is open till 1am, 3am on Friday and Saturday. In addition to Filippi's (below), the **Old Spaghetti Factory,** 275 Fifth Ave. (✆ 619/233-4323), is an institution among families for inexpensive pastas.

Filippi's Pizza Grotto *(Kids* *(Value* ITALIAN   For longtime locals, when we think "Little Italy," Filippi's comes to mind—it was a childhood fixture for many of us. To get to the dining area, which is decorated with chianti bottles and red-checked tablecloths, you walk through a "cash and carry" Italian grocery store and deli strewn with cheeses, pastas, wines, bottles of olive oil, and salamis. You might even end up eating behind shelves of canned olives, but don't feel bad—this has been a tradition since 1950. The intoxicating smell of pizza wafts into the street; Filippi's has more than 15 varieties (including vegetarian), plus old-world spaghetti, lasagna, and other pasta. Children's portions are available, and kids will feel right at home under the sweeping mural of the Bay of Naples. The line to get in on Friday and Saturday can look intimidating, but it moves quickly. The original of a dozen branches throughout the county, the other locations include one in **Pacific Beach** at 962 Garnet Ave. (© **858/483-6222**).

1747 India St. (between Date and Fir sts.), Little Italy. © 619/232-5095. No reservations accepted on weekends. Main courses $5–$13. AE, DC, DISC, MC, V. Sun–Mon 9am–10pm; Tues–Thurs 9am–10:30pm; Fri–Sat 9am–11:30pm. Free parking. Bus: 5. Trolley: Little Italy.

HILLCREST/UPTOWN

Hillcrest and the other gentrified uptown neighborhoods to its west and east brim with great food for any palate (and any wallet). Some are old standbys filled nightly with loyal regulars; others are cutting-edge experiments that might be gone next year. Whether ethnic food, French food, health-conscious bistro fare, retro comfort food, specialty cafes and bakeries, or California cuisine (as in the restaurant of the same name)—they're most often mastered with the innovative panache you'd expect in the most nonconformist part of town.

This is also the place to stock up on Balboa Park picnic supplies. **Bread & Cie. Bakery and Cafe** ☆☆, 350 University Ave. (© **619/683-9322**), is San Diego's top bakery, in the traditions of European artisan bread-making—sandwiches here are delicious. The popular **Whole Foods** supermarket, 711 University Ave. (© **619/294-2800**), has a mouthwatering deli and robust salad bar—you can take out or eat at the tables up front. Families should consider a nostalgic crowd-pleaser, the 1950s flashback **Corvette Diner,** 3946 Fifth Ave. (© **619/542-1001**), where chummy waiters lavish kids with entertainment.

VERY EXPENSIVE

Laurel ☆☆☆ FRENCH/MEDITERRANEAN   Laurel is one of my favorite spots for a special meal. The Bankers Hill location is close to downtown and Hillcrest, the decor is sophisticated yet understated, and the crowd is reliably elegant. Throw in a wine list with the city's best selection of French Rhône and extravagant Napa cabernets, and a well-composed menu of southern French country dishes with the occasional Moroccan accent, and it's no wonder this restaurant continues to be at the top of its game. Live piano music adds to the panache of this graceful room. Start by choosing from an extensive selection of tantalizing appetizers, including saffron-tinged red-pepper-and-shellfish soup, veal sweetbreads with salsify and truffle, and warm caramelized-onion-and-Roquefort tart. Main courses include mouthwatering crisp duck confit with Toulouse sausage, or the seafood specials like sautéed monkfish cheek with braised baby fennel and lemony couscous. If you're overwhelmed by the choices, succumb to the five-course tasting menu ($75 with four wine pairings). One of the most reliable upscale choices outside downtown and La Jolla, Laurel has New York–style ambience coupled with San Diego's slightly more temperate prices.

505 Laurel St. (at Fifth Ave.), Hillcrest. © 619/239-2222. www.laurelrestaurant.com. Reservations recommended. Main courses $22–$32. AE, DC, DISC, MC, V. Daily 5–10pm. Valet parking $6. Bus: 1, 3, or 25.

EXPENSIVE

California Cuisine ☆☆ CALIFORNIA   The kitchen at this long-popular restaurant got an overhaul in 2003. The menu was slimmed down to bring back the qualities that put this restaurant on the map when it originally opened in

1982. Since these trademarks—no freezers, no can openers—are now well established at many serious restaurants across town, it's not as easy to stand out from the crowd, but the menu here is once again fresh and contemporary. The spare, understated dining room and delightfully romantic patio set the stage as a smoothly professional and respectful staff proffers fine dining at fair prices to a casual crowd. The menu changes regularly but contains mouthwatering appetizers like sesame-seared ahi with spicy mango culée, or Prince Edward Island mussels in a Thai coconut broth. Main courses are composed with equal care and might include maple-glazed pork loin with yam spaetzle and grilled radicchio, or herb-crusted rack of lamb, topped with whole-grain-mustard sherry sauce. And don't miss scintillating desserts by pastry chef Laurel Hufnagle, who tries inventive twists on old standards, like the jasmine-and-green-tea crème brûlée. Allow time to find parking, which can be sparse.

1027 University Ave. (east of 10th St.), Hillcrest. ℂ 619/543-0790. www.californiacuisine.cc. Reservations recommended for dinner. Main courses $7–$15 lunch, $17–$30 dinner. AE, DISC, MC, V. Tues–Fri 11am–3pm; Tues–Sun 5–10pm. Bus: 908.

Parallel 33 🏵🏵 *Finds* INTERNATIONAL Inspired by a theory that all locales along the 33rd parallel (San Diego's latitude) of the globe might share the culinary traditions of the Tigris-Euphrates Valley (birthplace of civilization), chef Amiko Gubbins presents a cuisine that combines flavors from Morocco, Lebanon, India, China, and Japan. Even if the globe-girdling concept doesn't quite make sense, sit back and savor the creativity displayed in a menu that leaps enthusiastically from fragrant Moroccan chicken *b'stilla* to oven-roasted *za'atar* chicken with basmati rice, English peas, and *harissa*. The *ahi poke* (raw tuna) appetizer fuses a Hawaiian mainstay with Asian pear and mango and Japanese wasabi—it's a winner! The restaurant is nice but not fancy, just an upscale neighborhood joint that's easily overlooked by visitors. The Indian/African/Asian decor throws soft shadows throughout, inviting conversation and leisurely dining. The intimate dining room was instantly popular after opening, and in 2004 expanded to encompass a small house next door. Still, the number of devout fans shows no signs of waning—you'll want to reserve a table in advance.

741 W. Washington St. (at Falcon), Mission Hills. ℂ 619/260-0033. Reservations recommended. Main courses $18–$27. AE, DISC, MC, V. Mon–Thurs 5:30–10pm; Fri–Sat 5:30–11pm. Bus: 3, 16, or 908.

MODERATE

Fifth & Hawthorn 🏵 *Value* AMERICAN You won't find a sign in front of this neighborhood hideaway—just look for the street-sign marking the intersection of Fifth and Hawthorn, a few blocks north of downtown, and aim for the red neon OPEN sign. Inhabited by a slew of regulars, the comfortable room is somewhat dark, vaguely romantic—just enough, anyway, to take your mind off the planes coming in for a landing overhead. The menu has pretty much stayed the same for 16 years: You won't find anything daring, but you will find lots of well-executed basics, like a filet mignon in green peppercorn sauce and linguine with clams, white wine, and garlic. There are a few dishes Fifth & Hawthorn excels at: The mustard-crusted catfish is simple and delicious, and the calamari, sautéed "abalone-style," are rendered tender and sweet. The restaurant also offers a terrific four-course meal: appetizer, soup or salad, one of six entrees, and dessert for $50 per couple, *including* a bottle of wine to share.

515 Hawthorn St. (at Fifth Ave.), Hillcrest. ℂ 619/544-0940. Main courses $15–$25. AE, MC, V. Mon–Thurs 5–9pm; Fri–Sat 5–10:15pm; Sun 4:30–8:30pm. Street parking usually available. Bus: 1, 3, or 25.

INEXPENSIVE

Crest Cafe AMERICAN/BREAKFAST   This long-popular Hillcrest diner is a great refuge from sleek designer food and swank settings. The cheery pink interior announces 1940s style, and the room bubbles with upbeat waiters and comfort food doled out on Fiestaware. Church pew–like booths are comfortable enough, but the small stucco room doesn't do much to mask the clang of plates. No matter: Burger lovers will fall in love with the "butter burger"—a dollop of herb butter is buried in the patty before cooking (it's even better than it sounds). And the east Texas fried chicken breast crusted with hunks of jalapeño peppers is none too subtle either, but it's tasty. A variety of sandwiches and salads, the popular steamed-vegetable basket, and broiled chicken dishes are healthier options. During the early evening, the joint brims with neighborhood bohemians in search of a cholesterol fix, while later the club contingent swoops in; the breakfast of omelets or crème brûlée French toast is a happy eye-opener.

425 Robinson Ave. (between Fourth and Fifth aves.), Hillcrest. ☎ 619/295-2510. www.crestcafe.net. Reservations not accepted. Main courses $5–$14. AE, MC, V. Daily 7am–midnight. Bus: 1, 3, 25, or 908.

OLD TOWN & MISSION VALLEY

Visitors usually have at least one meal in Old Town, and although this area showcases San Diego at its most touristy, I can't argue with the appeal of dining in California's charming original settlement. Mexican food reigns supreme at most Old Town restaurants—combo plates and bathtub-size margaritas are the focus, liberally spiced with mariachi music and colorful decor.

Old Town is also the gateway to decidedly less-historic Mission Valley. Here you'll find plenty of chain eateries, both good and bad, and not discussed in depth below. In the very busy Fashion Valley Shopping Center complex lies Cheesecake Factory, California Pizza Kitchen, and P.F. Chang's—expect long waits for a table at each. In or near the Mission Valley Shopping Center is an Outback Steakhouse, Hooter's, and Mimi's Cafe.

EXPENSIVE

Cafe Pacifica 🐟🐟 CALIFORNIA/SEAFOOD   You can't tell a book by its cover: Inside this cozy Old Town casita, the decor is cleanly contemporary (but still romantic) and the food anything but Mexican. Established in 1980, Cafe Pacifica serves upscale, imaginative seafood at decent prices and produces kitchen alumni who go on to enjoy local fame. Among the temptations are crab-stuffed portobello mushrooms topped with grilled asparagus, anise-scented bouillabaisse, and daily fresh-fish selections served grilled with your choice of five sauces. Signature items include Hawaiian ahi with shiitake mushrooms and ginger butter, griddled mustard catfish, and the "Pomerita," a pomegranate margarita. To avoid the crush, arrive before 6:30pm—you'll also get to take advantage of the early-bird special: entree with soup or salad for $23.

2414 San Diego Ave., Old Town ☎ 619/291-6666. www.cafepacifica.com. Reservations recommended. Main courses $16–$29. AE, DC, DISC, MC, V. Mon–Sat 5–10pm; Sun 5–9:30pm. Valet parking $5. Bus: 5/5A. Trolley: Old Town.

El Agave Tequileria 🐟🐟 MEXICAN   Don't be misled by this restaurant's less-than-impressive location above a liquor store. This warm, bustling eatery continues to draw local gourmands for the regional Mexican cuisine and rustic elegance that leave the touristy fajitas-and-cerveza joints of Old Town far behind. El Agave is named for the agave plant from which tequilas are derived, and they boast more than 850 boutique and artisan tequilas from throughout the Latin world—bottles of every size, shape, and jewel-like hue fill shelves and cases throughout the dining room. But even teetotalers will enjoy the restaurant's authentically flavored mole sauces (from Chiapas, rich with peanuts; tangy tomatillo from Oaxaca; and the more familiar dark mole flavored with chocolate and sesame), along with giant shrimp and sea bass prepared in a dozen variations, or El Agave's signature beef filet with goat cheese and dark tequila sauce. On the other hand, I could almost make a meal out of the warm watercress salad dressed with onions and bacon, folded into tortillas. Lunches are simpler affairs without the exotic sauces, and inexpensive.

2304 San Diego Ave., Old Town. © **619/220-0692**. www.elagave.com. Reservations recommended. Main courses $7–$10 lunch, $16–$32 dinner. AE, MC, V. Daily 11am–10pm. Street parking. Bus: 5. Trolley: Old Town.

MODERATE

Casa Guadalajara (Finds) (Kids) MEXICAN   The best of the minichain of restaurants operated by Bazaar del Mundo, Casa Guadalajara is actually located a block away from the shops, which provides another advantage: it's often less crowded than its counterparts (though waits of 30 min. or more are not unusual here Fri–Sat). Mariachi tunes played by strolling musicians accent the room nightly, and you can also dine alfresco in a picturesque courtyard occupied by a 200-year-old pepper tree. Huge margaritas start most meals, while dining ranges from gourmet Mexican to simpler south-of-the-border fare. My favorite is the *tacos de cochinita*—two soft corn tacos bulging with achiote-seasoned pork and marinated red onions—but the extensive menu features all the fajita and combo plates most people expect. This place (like the Bazaar, where there are four more venues serving Mexican food) is touristy, but it's where I bring out-of-towners for reliable old-California ambience and food.

4105 Taylor St. (at Juan St. in Old Town). © **619/295-5111**. www.casaguadalajara.com. Reservations recommended. Main courses $8–$16. AE, DC, DISC, MC, V. Sun–Thurs 11am–10pm; Fri–Sat 11am–11pm. Free parking. Bus: 5/5A. Trolley: Old Town.

INEXPENSIVE

The Living Room COFFEE & TEA/LIGHT FARE   You're liable to hear the buzz of conversations from students on break from nearby universities, who use this spot as a sort of off-campus study hall. Grab a sidewalk table and enjoy splendid people-watching any time of day; indoors you'll find faux antiques—appropriately weathered to give a lived-in feel. I think the pastries and coffee fall a bit short, but this local minichain is known for temptingly good light meals that make it a good choice for early risers and insomniacs alike. Breakfast includes omelets and waffles, while the rest of the day finds a chalkboard menu: try the turkey lasagna, chicken Dijon, tuna melt, or one of several hearty entree salads. Plus you'll find exotic iced or hot coffees, like the Emerald Isle (espresso, white chocolate, and mint). Additional locations are found in **La Jolla** at 1010 Prospect St. (© 858/459-1187), **Hillcrest** at 1417 University Ave. (© 619/295-7911), the **Sports Arena** area at 1018 Rosecrans (© 619/222-6852), and near **San Diego State University,** at 5900 El Cajon Blvd. (© 619/286-8434).

2541 San Diego Ave. © **619/523-4445**. www.livingroomcafe.com. Main courses $6–$8; $3–$8 breakfast. AE, MC, V. Sun–Thurs 7am–10pm; Fri–Sat 7am–midnight. Bus: 5. Trolley: Old Town.

MISSION BAY & THE BEACHES

Generally speaking, dining at the beach exists primarily to provide an excuse for sitting and gazing at the water. Because this activity is most commonly accompanied by steady drinking, it stands to reason that the food isn't often remarkable. One not-too-expensive place, slightly off the beaten track, for solid Continental fare and a wine list that heralds excellent value is **Thee Bungalow** ☆☆, 4996 W. Point Loma Blvd., Ocean Beach (ⓒ **619/224-2884**). Or, if all you need is a beach and a view, **The Green Flash,** 701 Thomas Ave., Pacific Beach (ⓒ **858/ 270-7715**), offers a glassed-in patio that is probably the city's best place for people-watching (or -ogling, if that's your game).

MODERATE

Caffè Bella Italia ☆☆ ITALIAN   If the odd-looking stucco exterior in a less-than-promising section of PB looks like a dry cleaner adorned with umbrellas, well, it once was a spot for all your 1-hour Martinizing needs. But in just a few short years, this charmer has found a niche in the community. Although located well away from the surf, it's lovely inside, and the food can knock your socks off. It's the best spot in the area for shellfish-laden pasta, wood-fired pizzas, and management that welcomes guests like family. Romantic lighting, sheer draperies, and warmly earthy walls create a vaguely North African ambience, assisted by the lilting Milan accents of the staff. Every item on the menu bears the unmistakable flavor of freshness and homemade care—even the simplest curled-edge ravioli stuffed with ricotta, spinach, and pine nuts is elevated to culinary perfection, while salmon is dealt with unusually firmly, endowed with olives, capers, and thick hunks of tomato in wine and garlic. You may leave wishing you could be adopted by this gracious family. A second location is in Kearny Mesa, 4411 Mercury St. (ⓒ **858/278-5367**).

1525 Garnet Ave. (between Ingraham and Haines), Pacific Beach. ⓒ **858/273-1224.** www.caffebella italia.com. Reservations suggested for dinner. Main courses $8–$13 lunch, $10–$28 dinner. AE, MC, V. Tues–Fri 11am–2:30pm; Tues–Sun 5–10:30pm. Free (small) parking lot. Bus: 9 or 27.

The Fishery ☆ *Finds* SEAFOOD   You're pretty well guaranteed to get fresh-off-the-boat seafood at this off-the-beaten-track establishment: It's really a wholesale warehouse and retail fish market with a casual restaurant attached. The decor is clean and calm without being overly utilitarian, and the prices are fair. Regular menu favorites include spicy mahimahi, chargrilled and topped with jalapeño butter; king salmon Oscar, layered with garlic mashed potatoes and grilled asparagus, Dungeness crab, and hollandaise; or—the favorite—Chilean sea bass, charbroiled with a soy-ginger marinade. You can keep it simple at lunch or dinner with bacon-wrapped scallops over a delectable salad, or the very reliable fish and chips, and there's always a couple of vegetarian stir-fry entrees. The menu is printed fresh daily, and a loyal crowd ventures away from the Mission/Garnet/Grand strips to enjoy this neighborhood haunt.

5040 Cass St. (at Opal, ¾ miles north of Garnet), Pacific Beach. ⓒ **858/272-9985.** Reservations not accepted, but "preferred seating" available. Main courses $6–$21 lunch, $8–$27 dinner. AE, DC, DISC, MC, V. Daily 11am–10pm. Street parking usually available. Bus: 9.

Gringo's ☆ MEXICAN   Aiming for a more accurate reflection of south-of-the-border cooking, the awkwardly monikered Gringo's is located at PB's busiest intersection, providing visitors and locals alike with an option beyond the neighborhood's ubiquitous fast-food emporiums. The discretely upscale space is agreeable, with warm woods, cool flagstone, and trendy lighting providing a modern feel, and a large patio is primed with heaters and fire pits most evenings—the venue bears little resemblance to typical Mexican restaurants (no off-key mariachis here!). Although the menu does offer a tip of the hat to dishes the average gringo will recognize (quesadillas, fajitas, burritos), flip it over and you'll find regional specialties from all over Mexico: the food of Oaxaca, the Yucatan, and Mexico's Pacific coast. So, a chicken breast is stuffed with goat cheese and corn, then lathered in a sauce of *huitlacoche* (a delicious fungus that grows on corn); a poblano chile is stuffed with picadillo and draped in walnut-cream sauce and a drizzle of pomegranate. The margarita options are worth inspection, as are the selection of Mexican wines—drink specials run Sunday through Thursday. Sunday brunch is available from 10am to 3pm.

4474 Mission Blvd. (at Garnet Ave.), Pacific Beach. ✆ 858/490-2877. www.gringoscantina.com. Reservations suggested for weekends. Main courses $8–$14 lunch, $11–$27 dinner. AE, DC, DISC, MC, V. Daily 10am–11pm. Bus: 27 or 34.

Sushi Ota ✿✿ SUSHI   Masterful chef-owner Yukito Ota creates San Diego's finest sushi. This sophisticated, traditional restaurant (no Asian fusion here) is a minimalist bento box with stark white walls and black furniture, softened by indirect lighting. The sushi menu is short, because discerning regulars look first to the daily specials posted behind the counter. The city's most experienced chefs, armed with nimble fingers and seriously sharp knives, turn the day's fresh catch into artful little bundles accented with mounds of wasabi and ginger. The rest of the varied menu features seafood, teriyaki-glazed meats, tempura, and a variety of small appetizers perfect to accompany a sushi order. This restaurant is difficult to find, mainly because it's hard to believe that such outstanding dining would hide behind a laundromat and convenience store in the rear of a mini-mall. It's also in a nondescript part of Pacific Beach, a stone's throw from the I-5, but none of that should discourage you from seeking it out.

4529 Mission Bay Dr. (at Bunker Hill), Pacific Beach. ✆ 858/270-5670. Reservations strongly recommended on weekends. Main courses $6–$9 lunch, $9–$20 dinner; sushi $4–$12. AE, MC, V. Tues–Fri 11:30am–2pm; daily 5:30–10:30pm. Free parking (additional lot behind the mall). Bus: 27.

INEXPENSIVE

The Mission ✿ ✿*Value* BREAKFAST/LIGHT FARE   Located alongside the funky surf shops, bikini boutiques, and alternative galleries of bohemian Mission Beach, The Mission is the neighborhood's central meeting place. But it's good enough to attract more than just locals, and now has additional siblings near the ballpark and east of Hillcrest. The menu features all-day breakfasts, from traditional pancakes to nouvelle egg dishes to burritos and quesadillas—standouts include tamales and eggs with tomatillo sauce, chicken-apple sausage with eggs and a mound of rosemary potatoes, and cinnamon French toast with blackberry purée. At lunch, the menu expands for sandwiches, salads, and a few Chino-Latino items like ginger-sesame chicken tacos. Seating is casual, comfy, and conducive to lingering (tons of students, writers, and surfers hang out here), if only with a soup-bowl-size latte. The other locations are at 2801 University Ave., in North Park (✆ 619/220-8992), and 1250 J St., downtown (not yet opened when we went to press). Expect waits of half an hour or more on weekends.

3795 Mission Blvd. (at San Jose), Mission Beach. ✆ 858/488-9060. All items $5–$9. AE, MC, V. Daily 7am–3pm. Bus: 27 or 34.

LA JOLLA

As befits an upscale community with time (and money) on its hands, La Jolla seems to have more than its fair share of good restaurants. Happily, they're not all expensive and are more ethnically diverse than you might expect in a community that still supports a haberdashery called The Ascot Shop.

Other choices include the stylish **Roppongi** ✿, 875 Prospect St., at Fay Avenue (✆ 858/551-5252), where the cuisines of Japan, Thailand, China, Vietnam, and India collide in a creative explosion of flavorful dishes that are perfect for sharing. At **Trattoria Acqua** ✿✿, 1298 Prospect St. (✆ 858/454-0709), northern Italian is nurtured with a relaxed ambience and top-drawer wine list (reserve for a table with a sea view).

VERY EXPENSIVE

George's at the Cove 🎭🎭🎭 CALIFORNIA   You'll find host and namesake George Hauer at his restaurant's door most nights; he greets loyal regulars by name, and his confidence assures newcomers that they'll leave impressed with this beloved La Jolla institution. Regularly voted San Diego's most popular restaurant, George's wins consistent praise for impeccable service, gorgeous views of the cove, and outstanding cuisine. The menu presents many inventive seafood options, filtered through the myriad influences of chef Trey Foshee, selected as one of America's top 10 chefs by *Food & Wine*. Foshee starts each day with a trek up to Chino Farms to select the evening's produce, which work their way into exquisite starters like the Jerusalem-artichoke-and-leek soup. Mains combine divergent flavors with practiced artistry, ranging from the Neiman Ranch pork tasting to roasted lamb loin and braised lamb shoulder with a spicy medjool-date couscous and baby spinach. George's signature smoked chicken, broccoli, and black-bean soup is still a mainstay at lunch; they'll even give out the recipe for this local legend. As an alternative to dinner's pricey main courses, try the tasting menu, which offers a seasonally composed five-course sampling for $55 per person. George's **Ocean Terrace Café** 🎭🎭 is upstairs, and offers casual, moderately priced dining on a splendid rooftop terrace.

1250 Prospect St., La Jolla. ⓒ 858/454-4244. www.georgesatthecove.com. Reservations strongly recommended for dinner. Main courses $12–$15 lunch, $26–$38 dinner. AE, DC, DISC, MC, V. Daily 11:30am–2:30pm; Sun–Thurs 5:30–10pm; Fri–Sat 5–10:30pm. Valet parking $7. Bus: 34.

The Marine Room 🎭🎭🎭 *Moments* FRENCH/CALIFORNIA   For more than 6 decades, San Diego's most celebrated dining room has been this shorefront institution, perched within kissing distance of the waves that snuggle up to La Jolla Shores. But it wasn't until the 1994 arrival of executive chef Bernard Guillas of Brittany that the food finally lived up to its glass-fronted room with a view, and today the Marine Room is the city's top "special occasion" destination. Guillas and *chef de cuisine* Ron Oliver never hesitate to pursue unusual flavors from other corners of the globe. So, a favored entree includes barramundi, a delicate white fish from Australia, encrusted with a hazelnut fennel pollen, garnished with flowering chive and a lacy crisp of fried lotus root. Then there's the ingot of foie gras sitting atop paper-thin slices of duck breast—the buttery concoction is smartly cut with a garnish of young tomatillo. The vigilant service is charmingly deferential, yet never condescending. The Marine Room is filled to the gills on weekends; weekdays it's much easier to score a table, and the four-course tasting menu available Monday through Wednesday for $58 ($72 paired with wines) is an excellent value. Ideally, schedule your reservation a half-hour or so before sunset—this will give you a chance to enjoy the scampering sandpipers and fishing pelicans while the sand takes on a honeyed aura at dusk.

2000 Spindrift Dr., La Jolla. ⓒ 858/459-7222. www.marineroom.com. Reservations recommended, especially weekends. Main courses $14–$19 lunch, $26–$37 dinner. AE, DC, DISC, MC, V. Tues–Sat 11:30am–2pm; Sun brunch ($35) 11am–2pm; Sun–Thurs 5:30–9pm; Fri–Sat 5:30–10pm. Complimentary valet parking. Bus: 34.

EXPENSIVE

Fresh 🎭🎭 CALIFORNIA/SEAFOOD   La Jolla never quite got the point of the *nuevo latino* Tamarindo restaurant, so the owners went back to the drawing board and created this fine seafood-plus restaurant, which was a hit right from its 2003 debut. Chef Matthew Zappoli created the moderately adventurous menu, which starts with a mouthwatering lobster Napoleon made with delicate potato chips, or the poached seafood salad tossed with a Meyer-lemon vinaigrette. Entrees include a surprisingly delicate coriander-crusted mahimahi, and there's a good quantity of "land" offerings, like duck two ways, prepared with an apple-quince compote and calvados reduction, and braised veal shank *osso buco*, served with seasonal vegetables. A raw bar is available, and the desserts (also overseen by Zappoli) are well worth investigating. The dining room got a soothingly modern redesign, with billowing waves of fabric across the elevated ceilings and broad windows that successfully integrate the outside dining area. Fresh is one of La Jolla's favorite new haunts.

1044 Wall St. (at Hershel), La Jolla. ℂ 858/551-7575. www.freshseafoodrestaurant.com. Reservations strongly recommended. Main courses $9–$17 lunch, $18–$30 dinner. AE, DISC, MC, V. Daily 11:30am–9:30pm (Fri–Sat till 10:30pm). 2-hr. validated parking. Bus: 34.

MODERATE

Piatti 🅰 ITALIAN/MEDITERRANEAN   La Jolla's version of the neighborhood hangout is this pasta-centric trattoria a couple blocks inland from La Jolla Shores. Come here on Friday or Saturday evening—well, any night, really—and you're likely to be surrounded by a crew of regulars that pops in once or twice a week and knows all the staff by name. You won't feel left out, however, and the food is well priced. Lemon-herb-roasted chicken, peppercorn-crusted *bistecca* (rib-eye), plus the Thursday night special of *osso buco* with risotto lead the short list of entrees, but it's the pastas that parade out to most tables. Try *orecchiette* bathed in Gorgonzola, grilled chicken and sun-dried tomatoes, or pappardelle "fantasia"—shrimp-crowned ribbons of saffron pasta, primed with garlic, tomato, and white wine. The outdoor patio, beneath the sprawl of an enormous ficus tree, is ideal for dining any night.

2182 Avenida de la Playa. ℂ 858/454-1589. Reservations recommended. Main courses $13–$25; Sat–Sun brunch $8–$11. AE, DC, MC, V. Sun–Thurs 11am–10pm; Fri–Sat 11am–11pm. Street parking usually available. Bus: 34.

Spice & Rice Thai Kitchen 🅰 THAI   This attractive restaurant is a couple of blocks from the village's traffic crush—far enough to ensure easier parking. The lunch crowd consists of shoppers and curious tourists, while dinner is quieter; all the local businesses have shut down. The food is excellent, with polished presentations and expert renditions of the classics like pad Thai, satay, curry, and glazed duck. The starters often sound as good as the entrees—consider making a grazing meal of house specialties like "gold bags" (minced pork, vegetables, glass noodles, and herbs wrapped in crispy rice paper) or prawns with yellow-curry lobster sauce; crispy calamari is flavored with tamarind sauce and chile sauce. The romantically lit covered front patio has a secluded-garden feel, and inside tables also have indirect lighting.

7734 Girard Ave. ℂ 858/456-0466. Reservations recommended. Main courses $8–$13. AE, MC, V. Mon–Sat 11am–3pm; Sun–Thurs 5–10pm; Fri–Sat 5–11pm. Bus: 34.

INEXPENSIVE

The Cottage BREAKFAST/CALIFORNIA   La Jolla's best—and friendliest—breakfast is served at this turn-of-the-20th-century bungalow on a sunny village corner. Newly modernized, the cottage is light and airy, but most diners opt for tables outside, where a white picket fence encloses the trellis-shaded brick patio. Omelets and egg dishes feature Mediterranean, Asian, or classic American touches; my favorite has creamy mashed potatoes, bacon, and melted cheese folded inside. The Cottage bakes its own muffins, breakfast breads, and—you can quote me on this—the best brownies in San Diego. While breakfast dishes are served all day, toward lunch the kitchen begins turning out freshly made soups, light meals, and sandwiches. Summer dinners (never heavy, always tasty) are a delight, particularly when you're seated before dark on a balmy seaside night.

7702 Fay Ave. (at Kline St.). © 858/454-8409. www.cottagelajolla.com. Reservations accepted for dinner only. Main courses $9–$15 dinner, $7–$11 lunch, $6–$9 breakfast. AE, DISC, MC, V. Daily 7:30am–3pm; dinner (June–Sept only) Tues–Sat 5–9:30pm. Bus: 34.

CORONADO

Rather like the conservative, old-school navy aura that pervades the entire "island," Coronado's dining options are reliable and often quite good, but the restaurants aren't breaking new culinary ground. Notable exceptions are the resort dining rooms, which seem to be waging a little rivalry over who can attract the most prestigious, multiple-award-winning executive chef. If you're in the mood for a special-occasion meal, one of two to consider is **Azzura Point** at Loews Coronado Bay Resort (© 619/424-4000), where a view-endowed, stylish dining room wins raves from deep-pocketed San Diegans looking for inventive California-Mediterranean creations. The other, the Hotel del Coronado's fancy **Prince of Wales** (© 619/522-8496), is equally scenic, gazing at the beach across the hotel's regal Windsor Lawn; the eclectic California menu always showcases seasonally fresh ingredients.

EXPENSIVE

Chez Loma FRENCH   This intimate Victorian cottage filled with antiques and subdued candlelight makes for romantic dining. The house dates from 1889, the French-Continental restaurant from 1975. Tables are scattered throughout the house and on the enclosed garden terrace; an upstairs wine salon, reminiscent of a Victorian parlor, is a cozy spot for coffee or conversation. Among the entrees are salmon with smoked-tomato vinaigrette, and roast duckling with lingonberry, port, and burnt-orange sauce; main courses are served with soup or salad, rice or potatoes, and fresh vegetables. Follow dinner with a silky crème caramel or Kahlúa crème brûlée. California wines and American microbrews are available, in addition to a full bar, and early birds enjoy specially priced meals: $25 for a three-course meal before 6pm. The restaurant's only downfall—predictability—is also its main strength.

1132 Loma (off Orange Ave.), Coronado. © 619/435-0661. www.chezloma.com. Reservations recommended. Main courses $20–$29. AE, DC, MC, V. Daily 5–10pm. Bus: 901, 902, or 904.

MODERATE

Rhinoceros Cafe & Grill AMERICAN   With its quirky name and something-for-everyone menu, this light, bright bistro is a welcome addition to the Coronado dining scene. It's more casual than it looks from the street and offers large portions, though the kitchen can be a little heavy-handed with sauces and spices. At lunch, every other patron seems to be enjoying the popular penne a la vodka in creamy tomato sauce; favorite dinner specials are Italian cioppino, Southwestern-style meatloaf, and simple herb-roasted chicken. Plenty of crispy fresh salads balance out the menu. There's a fair wine list, or you might decide to try Rhino Chaser's American Ale.

1166 Orange Ave., Coronado. © 619/435-2121. Main courses $10–$22. AE, DISC, MC, V. Daily 11am–2:45pm; Sun–Thurs 5–9pm; Fri–Sat 5–10pm. Street parking usually available. Bus: 901, 902, or 904.

INEXPENSIVE

Villa Nueva Bakery Café 🍴 *Value* BREAKFAST/LIGHT FARE Formerly known as Primavera Pastry Caffe, this wonderful little cafe is the best of its kind on the island. In addition to fresh-roasted coffee and espresso drinks, it serves omelets, bagels and lox, and other breakfast treats (until 2pm), deli sandwiches on their delicious house bread, and a daily fresh soup. It's the kind of spot where half the customers are greeted by name. Locals rave about the "Yacht Club" sandwich, a croissant filled with yellowfin tuna, and the breakfast croissant, topped with scrambled eggs, ham, and cheddar cheese. Those fat, gooey cinnamon buns are every bit as good as they look.

956 Orange Ave., Coronado. ℂ 619/435-4191. Main courses $5–$8. MC, V. Mon–Thurs 6:30am–4pm; Fri–Sun 6:30am–5pm. Bus: 901, 902, or 904.

SPECIAL FINDS IN THE BURBS

Don't limit your dining experience in San Diego to the main tourist zones outlined above. Five minutes north of Mission Valley is the mostly business neighborhood of Kearny Mesa, home to San Diego's best Asian venues. One to try is **Jasmine** 🍴🍴, 4609 Convoy St. (ℂ **858/268-0888**), which at lunch showcases wonderful Hong Kong–style dumplings that are wheeled around the room on carts; dinners are more elaborate, with seafood and Peking duck two ways a good choice. Nearby is **China Max** 🍴, 4698 Convoy St. (ℂ **858/650-3333**), which occupies a nondescript building in an Asian minimall near the junction of the 805 and 163 freeways; the room is spare, but the kitchen exhibits finesse with southern Chinese delicacies and always has excellent (sometimes pricey) fish specials.

Just east of Hillcrest (south and parallel to Mission Valley) is Adams Avenue, one of the city's streets of character, with antiques shops and bistros en route to Kensington. Here you'll find the **Kensington Grill** 🍴🍴, 4055 Adams Ave., next to the Ken Cinema (ℂ **619/281-4014**), owned by the same crew in charge of the Gaslamp's hip Chive and featuring contemporary American cuisine in a chic setting that draws lots of neighborhood types. In nearby Normal Heights, **Jyoti Bihanga,** 3351 Adams Ave. (ℂ **619/282-4116**), caters to followers of Sri Chinmoy and delivers a vegetarian menu of Indian-influenced salads, wraps, and curries; the "neatloaf" is a winner. All items are priced under $10. And close to Park Boulevard (and Hillcrest) is the **Adams Avenue Grill** 🍴, 2201 Adams Ave. (ℂ **619/298-8440**), a friendly neighborhood joint that serves comfort food with international accents.

5 The Three Major Animal Parks

San Diego Zoo 🍴🍴🍴 *Kids* More than 4,000 creatures reside at this celebrated and influential zoo, operated by the Zoological Society of San Diego. Started in 1916, in the early days the zoo's founder, Dr. Harry Wegeforth, traveled around the world and bartered native Southwestern animals such as rattlesnakes and sea lions for more exotic species. The zoo is also an accredited botanical garden, lavished with more than 700,000 plants; "Dr. Harry" brought home plants from every location where animals were acquired, ensuring what would become the zoo's naturalistic and mature environment.

The zoo is one of only three in the U.S. with giant pandas, but there are many other rare species: Buerger's tree kangaroos of New Guinea, long-billed kiwis from New Zealand, wild Przewalski's horses from Mongolia, lowland gorillas from Africa, and giant tortoises from the Galapagos. The Zoological Society is involved with animal preservation efforts around the world and has engineered many "firsts" in breeding. The zoo was also a forerunner in creating barless, moated enclosures that allow animals to roam in sophisticated environments resembling their natural ones.

Among the noteworthy exhibits is **Absolutely Apes,** a habitat that opened in 2003 to showcase orangutans and siamangs of Indonesia; it marked the first time these primates of a single ecosystem share an enclosure at the zoo. Next door is **Gorilla Tropics,** where two troops of Western lowland gorillas roam an 8,000-square-foot habitat. Despite the hype, I find the **Panda Discovery Center** *not* worth the hassle when a long line is in place (lines are shortest first thing in the morning or toward the end of the day). More noteworthy is **Ituri Forest,** which simulates a central African rainforest with forest buffalos, otters, okapis, and hippos, which are superbly viewed underwater from a glassed-in enclosure; and the **Polar Bear Plunge,** where you'll find a 2¼-acre summer tundra habitat inhabited by Siberian reindeer, yellow-throated martens, and diving ducks, along with the playful titular heroes. The **Children's Zoo** features a nursery with baby animals and a petting area where kids can cuddle up to sheep, goats, and the like. There's also a **sea lion show** at the 3,000-seat amphitheater (this is easy to skip if you're headed to SeaWorld).

If a lot of walking—some of it on steep hills—isn't your passion, a 40-minute **Guided Bus Tour** provides a narrated overview and covers about 70% of the facility. It costs $10 for adults, $5.50 for children 3 to 11, and is included in the so-called "Best Value" admission package. Since you get only brief glimpses of the enclosures and animals won't always be visible, you'll want to revisit some areas, and included in the bus ticket is access to the un-narrated **Express Bus,** which allows you to get on and off at one of five different stops along the same route. You can also get an aerial perspective from the **Skyfari,** which costs $2.50 per person each way, though you won't see many creatures. Ideally, take the complete bus tour first thing in the morning, when the animals are more active (waits for the bus tour can top an hour by midday). After the bus tour, take the Skyfari to the far side of the park and wend your way back on foot or by Express Bus to revisit animals you missed.

In addition to several fast-food options, the restaurant **Albert's** is a beautiful oasis at the lip of a canyon and a lovely place in which to break up the day.

2920 Zoo Dr., Balboa Park. ⓒ 619/234-3153 (recorded info), or 619/231-1515. www.sandiegozoo.org. Admission $20 adults, $12 children 3–11, free for military in uniform. The "Best Value" package (admission, guided bus tour, round-trip Skyfari aerial tram) $32 adults, $29 seniors, $20 children. AE, DISC, MC, V. Sept to mid-June daily 9am–4pm (grounds close at 5 or 6pm); mid-June to Aug daily 9am–9pm (grounds close at 10pm). Bus: 7, 7A/B. Interstate 5 south to Pershing Dr., follow signs.

⟮Value Now That's What I Call a Deal!

Always aware of what side their tourism bread is buttered on, San Diego's three main animal attractions have joined forces with combo ticket deals that reward big savings to visitors with recreational stamina. Here's how it works: If you plan to visit both the zoo and Wild Animal Park, a two-park ticket (the "Best Value" zoo package, plus Wild Animal Park admission) is $53 for adults, $35 for children 3 to 11 (a $59/$39 value). You get one visit to each attraction, to be used within 5 days of purchase. Or throw in SeaWorld within the same 5 days—this combo works out to $89 for adults, $63 children ages 3 to 9 (a $103/$74 value).

If the museums of Balboa Park rate high with the zoo on your agenda, check out "Balboa Park Money-Savers," below.

San Diego Attractions

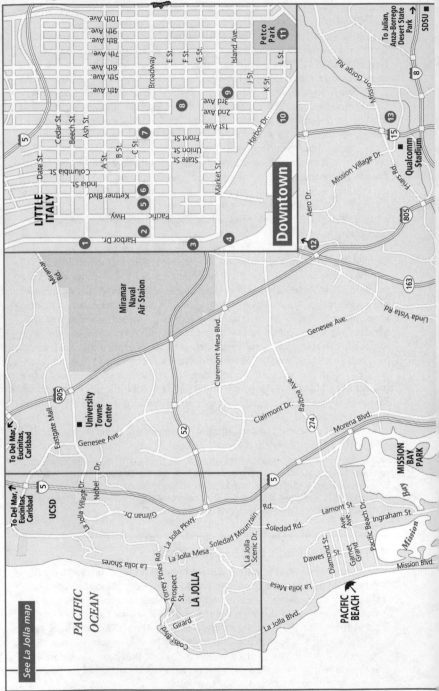

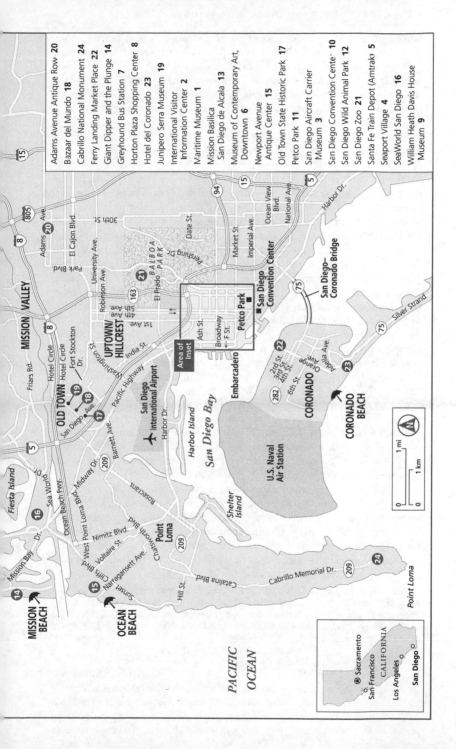

Adams Avenue Antique Row **20**
Bazaar del Mundo **18**
Cabrillo National Monument **24**
Ferry Landing Market Place **22**
Giant Dipper and the Plunge **14**
Greyhound Bus Station **7**
Horton Plaza Shopping Center **8**
Hotel del Coronado **23**
Junipero Serra Museum **19**
International Visitor
Information Center **2**
Maritime Museum **1**
Mission Basilica
San Diego de Alcala **13**
Museum of Contemporary Art,
Downtown **6**
Newport Avenue
Antique Center **15**
Old Town State Historic Park **17**
Petco Park **11**
San Diego Aircraft Carrier
Museum **3**
San Diego Convention Center **10**
San Diego Wild Animal Park **12**
San Diego Zoo **21**
Santa Fe Train Depot (Amtrak) **5**
Seaport Village **4**
SeaWorld San Diego **16**
William Heath Davis House
Museum **9**

SeaWorld San Diego ★★ *(Kids)*   One of California's best-marketed attractions, SeaWorld is a chief draw for many San Diego visitors. The park opened in 1964, and with each passing year the educational pretext increasingly takes a back seat to slick shows and rides, but the aquatic theme park—owned by the Anheuser-Busch corporation—is perhaps the country's premiere showplace for marine life, made politically correct with a nominally informative atmosphere. At its heart, SeaWorld is a shore-side family entertainment center where the performers are dolphins, otters, sea lions, walruses, and seals. The 20-minute shows run several times each during the day, with visitors cycling through the various open-air amphitheaters.

Several successive 4-ton black-and-white killer whales have functioned as the park's mascot, and the **Shamu Adventure** is SeaWorld's most popular show. Performed in a 5,500-seat stadium, the stage is a 7-million-gallon pool lined with plexiglass walls that offer magnified views of the huge performers. But think twice before you sit in the seats down front—a highlight of the act is multiple drenchings in the first 12 or so rows of spectators. The slapstick **Fools With Tools** (sea lions and otters), the fast-paced **Dolphin Show,** and the **Pet's Playhouse** are other performing animal routines, all in huge venues seating more than 2,000. There's a "4-D" movie, *R.L. Stine's Haunted Lighthouse,* starring a roster of multisensory effects. There is also a small collection of rides, led by **Journey to Atlantis,** a 2004 arrival that combines a roller coaster and log flume with Atlantis mythology and a simulated earthquake. **Shipwreck Rapids** is a splashy adventure on raftlike inner tubes through caverns, and **Wild Arctic** is a motion simulator helicopter trip to the frozen North.

Guests disembarking Wild Arctic (or those using the ride bypass) find themselves in the midst of one of SeaWorld's real specialties: carefully simulated marine environments. In this case it's an **arctic research station,** surrounded by beluga whales and polar bears. Other animal environments worth seeing are **Manatee Rescue, Shark Encounter,** and the **Penguin Encounter.** The 2-acre hands-on area called **Shamu's Happy Harbor** encourages kids to handle things—and features everything from a pretend pirate ship, with plenty of netted towers, to tube crawls, slides, and chances to get wet.

The **Dolphin Interaction Program** is an opportunity for people to meet bottlenose dolphins. Although the program stops short of allowing you to swim with the dolphins, it does offer the opportunity to wade waist-deep and to stroke the mammals and try giving training commands. This program includes some classroom time before you wriggle into a wet suit and climb into the water for 20 minutes with the dolphins. It costs $140 per person (not including park admission); participants must be age 6 or older.

500 Sea World Dr., Mission Bay. (✆) 800/380-3203 or 619/226-3901. www.seaworld.com. Admission $47 adults, $38 children 3–9, free for children under 3. AE, DISC, MC, V. Open daily. Hours vary seasonally, but always open 10am–5pm; most weekends and during summer the park opens at 9am and stays open as late as 10pm during peak periods. Parking $7. Bus: 9 or 27. From I-5, take Sea World Dr. exit; from I-8, take W. Mission Bay Dr. exit to Sea World Dr.

San Diego Wild Animal Park ★★★ *(Kids)*   Located 34 miles north of San Diego, outside of Escondido, this terrific "zoo of the future" will transport you to the African plains and other faraway landscapes. Originally started as a breeding facility for the San Diego Zoo, the 1,800-acre Wild Animal Park now holds 3,500 animals representing 429 different species. What makes the park unique is that many of the animals roam freely in vast enclosures, allowing giraffes to interact with antelopes, much as they would in Africa. You'll find the largest crash of rhinos at any zoological facility in the world, an exhibit for the critically endangered California condor, and a mature landscape of exotic vegetation from many corners of the globe. Although the San Diego Zoo may be "world-famous," it is the Wild Animal Park that many visitors celebrate as their favorite—to me, both are essential components of the San Diego experience.

The central focus is the 5-mile **Wgasa Bush Line Railway**, a 60-minute monorail ride that's included in the price of admission. Trains leave every 10 minutes or so from the station, and lines build up by late morning—make this your first or last attraction of the day (the animals are more active anyway). The monorail passes through areas designated as East Africa, South Africa, Asian Plains, and the Asian Waterhole, through swaying grasses and along rocky outcrops. Although many of the animals can be hundreds of feet away, the monorail is not meant to give you the up-close experience of a traditional zoo but to experience the open plains and wildlife diversity.

Other exhibits bring you closer to the animals, like the three self-guided **walking tours,** which visit various habitats. **Nairobi Village** is the commercial hub of the park, but even here are interesting animal exhibits, including the **nursery area,** where irresistible young 'uns can be seen frolicking, being bottle-fed, and sleeping; a **petting station;** the **lowland gorillas;** and the **South American Aviary.** There are amphitheaters for a bird show and another featuring elephants, scheduled two or three times daily. Within Nairobi Village are souvenir stores and several spots for mediocre dining. Visitors should be prepared for sunny, often downright hot weather (it's not unusual for temperatures to be 5°–10° warmer here than in San Diego).

If you want to get up-close-and-personal with the animals, take one of the park's **Photo Caravans,** which shuttle groups of eight in flatbed trucks out into the open areas that are not accessible to the general public. Crossing the fence to meet the rhinos, ostriches, zebras, and deer on their home turf, even getting nose-to-nose with giraffes along the way, makes for an excellent adventure. There are two different itineraries available, each 1¾ hours long, and you'll want to make reservations ahead of your visit (© **619/718-3050**). The price is $90 per person for one caravan (park admission not included), or $130 for both; children must be at least 8 years old, and ages 8 through 17 must be accompanied by an adult.

15500 San Pasqual Valley Rd., Escondido. © **760/747-8702.** www.wildanimalpark.org. Admission $27 adults, $24 seniors 60 and over, $20 children 3–11, free for children under 3 and military in uniform. AE, DISC, MC, V. Daily 9am–4pm (grounds close at 5pm); extended hours during summer and Festival of Lights (2 weekends in Dec). Parking $6. Take I-15 to Via Rancho Pkwy.; follow signs for about 3 miles.

6 Beaches

San Diego County is blessed with 70 miles of sandy coastline and more than 30 individual beaches, probably the state's best collection. The beaches cater equally to surfers, snorkelers, swimmers, sailors, divers, walkers, volleyballers, sunbathers—you get the drift. Even in winter and spring, when water temps drop to the high 50s (teens Celsius), they are great places to walk and jog, and surfers happily don wet suits to pursue their passion. In summer the beaches teem with locals and visitors alike—the bikinis come out, the pecs are bared, and a spring-break atmosphere threatens to break loose. Fortunately, common sense and good taste usually prevail and a good time is had by all.

One party pooper can be **June Gloom,** a local phenomenon caused as inland deserts heat up at the end of spring and suck the marine layer—a thick bank of fog—inland for a few miles. Be prepared for clammy mornings and evenings at our beaches from mid-May through mid-July.

Here's a list of San Diego's best, each with its own personality and devotees. They are listed geographically from south to north.

CORONADO 🐾 Lovely, wide, and sparkling, this beach is conducive to strolling and lingering, especially in the late afternoon. At the north end, you can watch fighter jets in formation flying from the Naval Air Station, while in the center is the pretty section fronting Ocean Boulevard and the Hotel del Coronado. Waves are gentle here, so the beach draws many Coronado families—and their dogs, which are allowed off-leash at the most northwesterly end. South of the Hotel Del, the beach becomes the beautiful, often deserted, **Silver Strand.**

OCEAN BEACH The northern end of Ocean Beach Park is officially known as **Dog Beach,** and is one of only a few in the county where your pooch can roam freely on the sand. Surfers congregate around the O.B. Pier, mostly in the water but often at the snack shack on the end. Rip currents can be strong—check with the lifeguard stations. Facilities at the beach include restrooms, showers, picnic tables, volleyball courts, and plenty of metered parking lots. To reach the beach, take West Point Loma Boulevard all the way to the end.

MISSION BEACH Anchored by the 80-year-old **Giant Dipper** roller coaster, the sands and wide cement "boardwalk" sizzle with activity and great people-watching for most of the year; at the southern end there's always a volleyball game going on. Parking can be tough, with your best bet being the public lots around the Giant Dipper or at the south end of West Mission Bay Drive. This street is the centerline of a 2-block-wide isthmus that leads a mile north to . . .

PACIFIC BEACH There's always action here, particularly along **Ocean Front Walk,** a paved promenade featuring a human parade akin to that at L.A.'s Venice Beach boardwalk. It runs along Ocean Boulevard (just west of Mission Blvd.) to the pier. Surfing is popular year-round, in marked sections, and the beach is well staffed with lifeguards. You're on your own to find street parking. A half-mile north of the pier is **Tourmaline Surfing Park,** where the sport's old guard gathers to surf waters where swimmers are prohibited.

MISSION BAY PARK This *inland,* 4,600-acre aquatic playground contains 27 miles of bay front, picnic areas, children's playgrounds, and paths for biking, in-line skating, and jogging. The bay lends itself to windsurfing, sailing, water-skiing, and fishing. There are dozens of access points; at the southwest corner is **Bonita Cove,** a protected inlet with calm waters, grassy picnic areas, and playground equipment. The water is cleaner for swimming here than in the northeastern reaches. Get there from Mission Boulevard in south Mission Beach.

LA JOLLA COVE 🐾🐾 These protected, calm waters—celebrated as the clearest along the coast—attract snorkelers and scuba divers, along with a fair share of families. The stunning setting offers only a small sandy beach, as well as the **Children's Cove,** inhabited most of the year by a colony of harbor seals. Smaller fish huddle in the tide pools between the two beaches. The cove is terrific for swimming, cramped for sunbathing, and accessible from Coast Boulevard; parking nearby is free, if sparse.

LA JOLLA SHORES The wide, flat mile of sand at La Jolla Shores is popular with joggers, swimmers, and beginning body- and board surfers, as well as families. In summer you need to shuffle your feet entering the water so as not to step on occasional (harmless) jellyfish. Weekend crowds can be enormous, though, quickly occupying both the sand and the metered parking spaces in the lot. There are restrooms, showers, and picnic areas here, as well the grassy, palm-lined Kellogg Park across the street.

BLACK'S BEACH 🐾   The area's unofficial (and illegal) nude beach, 2-mile-long Black's lies north of La Jolla Shores, at the base of steep, 300-foot-high cliffs. It is out of the way and not easy to reach, but draws scores with its secluded beauty and good swimming conditions—the spectacle of hang gliders launching from the cliffs above adds to the show. To get here, take North Torrey Pines Road, park at the Glider Port, and clamber down the makeshift path, staying alert to avoid one of several false trails. To bypass the cliff descent, you can walk to Black's from beaches north (Torrey Pines) or south (La Jolla Shores). *Note:* Lifeguards are usually present from spring break through October; there are no restroom facilities. Citations for nude sunbathing, however, are rarely issued.

TORREY PINES 🐾   At the north end of Black's Beach, at the foot of the Torrey Pines State Park, is this fabulous, underused strand, accessed by a pay parking lot at the entrance to the park. Combining a visit to the park with a day at the beach is my concept of the quintessential insider's San Diego experience. It's rarely crowded, though you need to be aware of high tide (when most of the sand gets a bath)—in almost any weather, it's a great beach for walking.

7 Exploring the Area

BALBOA PARK

New York has Central Park, San Francisco has Golden Gate Park. San Diego's crown jewel is 1,174-acre Balboa Park, the nation's largest urban cultural park. The Park was established in 1868 in the heart of the city. Tree plantings began in the late 19th century, while the initial buildings were created to host the 1915–16 Panama-California Exposition; another expo in 1935–36 brought additional developments. Today Balboa Park's most distinctive features include mature landscaping, the architectural beauty of the Spanish-Moorish buildings lining El Prado, and an outstanding and diverse collection of museums. You'll also find **The Old Globe** theater complex (p. 729) and the **San Diego Zoo** (p. 708).

Entry to Balboa Park is free, as is parking, but most of the museums have admission charges and varying open hours (most are open daily). A free tram will transport you around the park. Get details from the **Balboa Park Visitor Center,** located in the House of Hospitality (© **619/239-0512;** www.balboapark.org).

⟨*Tips* Balboa Park Money-Savers

Most Balboa Park attractions are open free of charge one Tuesday each month; there's a rotating schedule so two or three participate each Tuesday (the visitor center has a schedule). If you plan to visit more than three of the park's museums, buy the **Passport to Balboa Park,** a coupon booklet that allows entrance to 13 major museums and is valid for 1 week for $30. If you plan to spend a day at the zoo and return for the museums, buy the **Best of Balboa Park Combo,** which provides one ticket to the zoo, and 3 days' admission to the 13 museums, for $55. The passports can be purchased at any museum or the visitor center.

The visitor center is also the starting point for several free tours of the park that focus on the architecture, horticulture, and so on. Top museums include:

Mingei International Museum 𝒜𝒜   This captivating museum (pronounced *Min*-gay, meaning "art of the people" in Japanese), offers changing exhibitions generally describable as folk art. The rotating exhibits—usually four at a time—feature artists from countries across the globe; displays include textiles, costumes, jewelry, toys, pottery, paintings, and sculpture. The permanent collection includes whimsical contemporary sculptures by the late French artist Niki de Saint Phalle, who made San Diego her home in 1993. It is one of only two major museums in the United States devoted to folk crafts on a worldwide scale (the other is in Santa Fe, New Mexico) and is well worth a look.

1439 El Prado, in the House of Charm. 𝒞 619/239-0003. www.mingei.org. Admission $6 adults, $3 children 6–17 and students with ID, free for children under 6. Free 3rd Tues of each month. AE, MC, V. Tues–Sun 10am–4pm. Bus: 7 or 7A/B.

Museum of Photographic Arts 𝒜𝒜   If names like Ansel Adams and Edward Weston stimulate your fingers to do the shutterbug, then don't miss a taste of the 7,000-plus collection of images housed by this museum—one of few in the United States devoted exclusively to the photographic arts (which, at MOPA, encompasses cinema, video, and digital photography). Provocative traveling exhibits change every few months, while photos by Alfred Stieglitz, Margaret Bourke-White, Imogen Cunningham, Paul Strand, and Manuel Alvarez Bravo are all in the permanent collection, and the plush cinema illuminates classic films Friday, Saturday, and some weeknights.

1649 El Prado. 𝒞 619/238-7559. www.mopa.org. Admission $6 adults; $4 seniors, students and military; free for children under 12 with adult; cinema admission $7 adults, $6 seniors, students, and children. Free 2nd Tues of each month. Daily 10am–5pm (Thurs until 9pm). Bus: 7 or 7A/B.

Reuben H. Fleet Science Center 𝒜 *(Kids*   A park highlight for kids, this tantalizing collection of interactive exhibits and rides is designed to provoke the imagination and teach scientific principles. The Virtual Zone includes Deep Sea, a motion simulator ride that lurches you into a virtual ocean floor. The Fleet also houses a 76-foot-high IMAX Dome Theater, and the Fleet has a spiffy simulator for planetarium shows (held the first Wed of each month).

1875 El Prado. 𝒞 619/238-1233. www.rhfleet.org. Fleet Experience admission includes 1 IMAX film and exhibit galleries: $12 adults, $10 seniors 65 and over, $9 children 3–12 (exhibit gallery can be purchased individually). Free 1st Tues of each month (exhibit galleries only). AE, DISC, MC, V. Open daily 9:30am; closing times vary but always until at least 5pm. Bus: 7 or 7A/B.

San Diego Museum of Art 𝒜   This museum is known in the art world for its collection of Spanish baroque painting and possibly the largest horde of Indian paintings outside India. The American collection includes works by Georgia O'Keeffe and Thomas Eakins. Only a small percentage of the 12,000-piece permanent collection is on display at any given time, in favor of varied, often prestigious touring shows. In 2005 *Maxfield Parrish—Master of Make Believe* should be a big hit, featuring 70 fanciful works by the early-20th-century artist (the show runs July 16–Sept 11).

1450 El Prado. 𝒞 619/232-7931. www.sdmart.org. Admission $9 adults 25 and older; $7 seniors, military, and youths 18–24; $4 children 6–17; free for children under 6. Admission to traveling exhibits varies. Free 3rd Tues of each month. Tues–Sun 10am–6pm (Thurs until 9pm). Bus: 7 or 7A/B.

Timken Museum of Art 𝒜 *(Finds*   This jewel-like repository houses the Putnam Foundation's collection of 19th-century American paintings and works by European old masters, as well as a worthy display of Russian icons. Yes, it's a

Balboa Park

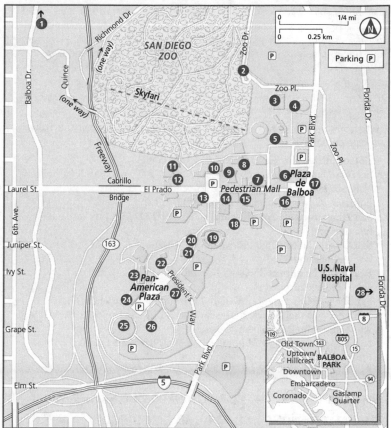

small horde, but it's free, and the marquee attractions include Peter Paul Reubens's *Portrait of a Young Man in Armor;* San Diego's only Rembrandt, *St. Bartholomew;* and a masterpiece by Eastman Johnson, *The Cranberry Harvest.* You'll find a spot apiece for works by Bierstadt, Pissarro, Corot, and Cézanne. The petite Timken also makes for an easy introduction to fine art for younger travelers (pick up a copy of the *Children's Gallery Guide* for $2).

1500 El Prado. ⓒ 619/239-5548. www.timkenmuseum.org. Free admission. Tues–Sat 10am–4:30pm; Sun 1:30–4:30pm. Closed Sept. Bus: 7 or 7A/B.

Other noteworthy attractions—with their locations shown on the Balboa Park map on p. 717—include:

- **Botanical Building and Lily Pond** 𝆏 (no phone)
- **Japanese Friendship Garden** (ⓒ 619/232-2721; www.niwa.org)
- **Marston House Museum** 𝆏 (3525 Seventh Ave., at Upas St., in the northwest corner of the park; ⓒ **619/298-3142**)
- **San Diego Automotive Museum** 𝆏 (ⓒ **619/231-2886**; www.sdauto museum.org)
- **San Diego Hall of Champions Sports Museum** (ⓒ **619/234-2544;** www.sdhoc.com)
- **San Diego Historical Society Museum** (ⓒ **619/232-6203;** www.sandiegohistory.org)
- **San Diego Miniature Railroad and Carousel** 𝐾𝑖𝑑𝑠 (no phone)
- **San Diego Model Railroad Museum** 𝆏 𝐾𝑖𝑑𝑠 (ⓒ **619/696-0199;** www.sdmodelrailroadm.com)
- **San Diego Museum of Man** (ⓒ **619/239-2001;** www.museum ofman.org)
- **San Diego Natural History Museum** 𝐾𝑖𝑑𝑠 (ⓒ **619/232-3821;** www.sdnhm.org)
- **Spreckels Organ Pavilion** (ⓒ **619/226-0819;** www.serve.com/sosorgan)

MORE ATTRACTIONS IN & AROUND SAN DIEGO
DOWNTOWN & BEYOND

Downtown, you can wander through the turn-of-the-20th-century **Gaslamp Quarter** 𝆏𝆏, which consists of 16½ blocks of restored historic buildings. You'll find many of San Diego's best restaurants and our most vigorous nightlife scene here. More information about the Gaslamp Quarter, and walking tours on Saturdays at 11am, are available at the **William Heath Davis House,** a museum within downtown's oldest structure, and home to the quarter's historical foundation; it's at 410 Island Ave., at Fourth Avenue (ⓒ **619/233-4692;** www. gaslampquarter.org). At **Horton Plaza** 𝆏, you can shop, stroll, snack or dine, and people-watch—all within a unique and playful village framework (p. 727).

In 2004 the city completed the $474-million **PETCO Park.** Mired in litigation and revelations of influence peddling that drove a city councilperson from office, the 42,000-seat ballpark incorporated seven historic structures into the stadium, including the Western Metal Supply building, a four-story brick edifice dating to 1909 that now sprouts left-field bleachers from one side. The San Diego Padres play April through September. PETCO parking is limited, and costly—for a space within a couple blocks of the facility, expect to pay at least $17. Better yet, take the San Diego Trolley. For schedules, information, and tickets, call ⓒ **877/374-2784** or 619/795-5000, or visit www.padres.com.

Cabrillo National Monument 𝆏𝆏 Breathtaking views mingle with the early history of San Diego, which began when Juan Rodríguez Cabrillo arrived in 1542. This tip of Point Loma is also a vantage point for migrating Pacific gray whales en route from Alaska to Baja California December through March. A tour of the restored lighthouse (1855) illuminates what life was like here more than a century ago. National Park Service rangers lead walks at the monument, and there are tide pools at the base of the peninsula that beg for exploration. Free 30-minute films on Cabrillo, tide pools, and the whales are shown on the hour daily from 10am to 4pm. The drive from downtown takes about a half-hour.

1800 Cabrillo Memorial Dr., Point Loma. (C) 619/557-5450. www.nps.gov/cabr. Admission $5 per vehicle, $3 for walk-ins. Daily 9am–5:15pm. Take I-8 west to Rosecrans St., right on Canon St., left on Catalina, and follow signs. Bus: 26.

Maritime Museum 𝐴𝐴 (Kids)   This quartet of classic ships is led by the full-rigged merchant vessel *Star of India* (1863), whose impressive masts are an integral part of the San Diego cityscape. The ship is a National Historic Landmark and the world's oldest ship that still goes to sea; in her day, the *Star* sailed around the globe 21 times, and carried salmon fishermen to Alaska and British emigrants to New Zealand. The gleaming white San Francisco–Oakland steam-powered ferry *Berkeley* (1898) worked round-the-clock to carry people to safety following the 1906 San Francisco earthquake; you'll find a museum with fine ship models on display. There's also the elegant *Medea* (1904), one of the world's few remaining large steam yachts, and *Pilot* (1914), which was San Diego Bay's official pilot boat for 82 years. You can board and tour each vessel.

1306 N. Harbor Dr. (C) 619/234-9153. www.sdmaritime.com. Admission $8 adults; $6 seniors over 62, youths 13–17, and active military with ID; $5 children 6–12; free for children under 6. Daily 9am–8pm (open till 9pm in summer). Bus: 2, 4, 20, 23, or 29. Trolley: America Plaza.

San Diego Aircraft Carrier Museum   The USS *Midway*'s 47-year military history began 1 week after the Japanese surrender of World War II in 1945. By the time *Midway* was decommissioned in 1991, the aircraft carrier had patrolled the Taiwan Straits in 1955, operated in the Tonkin Gulf, and served as the flagship from which Desert Storm was conducted—in all, more than 200,000 men served aboard the warship. The carrier is now moored at the Embarcadero and in 2004 became San Diego's first naval museum. A self-guided audio tour takes visitors to several levels of the ship, telling the story of life onboard the ship. The highlight is climbing up the superstructure to the bridge and gazing down on the 1,001-foot-long flight deck, with various aircraft poised for duty. What really brings the experience to life is how the ship has not been restored cosmetically—incomplete paint jobs litter the walls with the occasional graffiti; the austere bunkers look like the inhabitants just stepped out.

900 N. Harbor Dr. (at Navy Pier). (C) 619/544-9600. www.midway.org. Admission $13 adults, $10 seniors and veterans, $7 youths 6–17, free for children under 5 and military in uniform. Daily 10am–5pm. $7 parking. Bus: 7/7B. Trolley: American Plaza.

OLD TOWN & BEYOND: CALIFORNIA'S BEGINNINGS

The birthplace of San Diego—indeed, of California—Old Town takes you back to the Mexican California, which existed here until the mid-1800s. Today the spot suffers a tourist invasion daily, many of them headed to **Bazaar del Mundo** 𝐴𝐴, a one-time 1930s-era motel that is now a terrific collection of shops and restaurants for those seeking well-chosen south-of-the-border wares and birdbath-size margaritas (see "Where to Dine," earlier in this chapter and "Shopping," later in this chapter).

Mission Valley, which starts at Presidio Park and heads straight east, is anything but old—until Highway 8 was built in the 1950s, it was little more than cow pastures with a couple of dirt roads. Shopping malls, motels, a golf course, condos, car dealerships, and a massive sports stadium fill its girth today.

Old Town and Mission Valley are easily accessed via San Diego Trolley.

Junípero Serra Museum   Perched on the hill above Old Town, this iconic Spanish Mission-style **building** *RR* built in 1929 overlooks the slopes where, in 1769, the first mission, first presidio (fort), and first non-native settlement on the west coast of the United States and Canada were founded. The museum's exhibits introduce visitors to the Native American, Spanish, and Mexican people who first called this place home. On display are their belongings, from cannons to cookware; a Spanish furniture collection; and one of the first paintings brought to California, which survived being damaged in an Indian attack. From the 70-foot tower, visitors can compare the spectacular view with historic photos to see how this land has changed over time. Designed by William Templeton Johnson, the structure can be seen from miles around.

2727 Presidio Dr., Presidio Park. ✆ 619/297-3258. Admission $5 adults; $4 seniors, students, and military; $2 children 6–17; free for children under 6. Fri–Sun 10am–4:30pm. Bus: 5, 5A, or 6. Trolley: Old Town. Take I-8 to the Taylor St. exit. Turn right on Taylor, then left on Presidio Dr.

Mission Basilica San Diego de Alcala   This was the first link in a chain of 21 missions founded by Spanish missionary Junípero Serra (the mission was moved from Old Town to this site in 1774 for agricultural reasons, and to separate Native American converts from the fortress that included the original building). The mission was burned by Indians a year after it was built—Father Serra rebuilt the structure using 5- to 7-foot-thick adobe (mud) walls and clay tile roofs, rendering it harder to burn. In the process he inspired a bevy of 20th-century California architects. A few bricks belonging to the original mission are in Presidio Park in Old Town. Mass is said daily in this active Catholic parish.

10818 San Diego Mission Rd., Mission Valley. ✆ 619/281-8449. Admission $3 adults, $2 seniors and students, $1 children under 13. Free Sun and for daily Masses. Daily 9am–4:45pm; Mass daily 7am and 5:30pm. Bus: 13. Trolley: Mission San Diego. Take I-8 to Mission Gorge Rd. to Twain Ave., which turns into San Diego Mission Rd.

Old Town State Historic Park *R*   Dedicated to re-creating the early life of the city as it was from around 1821 to 1872, this is where San Diego's Mexican heritage shines brightest—the stars and stripes weren't raised over Old Town until 1846. Seven of the park's 20 structures are original, including homes made of adobe (clay). Among the sites are La Casa de Estudillo, which depicts the living conditions of a wealthy family in 1872; and Seeley Stables, named after A. L. Seeley, who ran the stagecoach and mail service in these parts from 1867 to 1871. Pick up a map at Park Headquarters, and peruse the model of Old Town as it looked in 1872. On Wednesday and Saturday, costumed park volunteers reenact life in the 1800s with cooking and crafts demonstrations, a working blacksmith, and parlor singing. Free 1-hour walking tours leave daily at 11am and Saturday and Sunday at 2pm from the Robinson-Rose House.

4002 Wallace St., Old Town. ✆ 619/220-5422. Free admission (donations welcome). Daily 10am–5pm. Bus: 5, 5A, or 6. Trolley: Old Town.

MISSION BAY & THE BEACHES

Mission Bay is a man-made, 4,600-acre aquatic playground created in 1945 by dredging tidal mud flats and opening them to sea water. Today this is a great area for walking, jogging, in-line skating, biking, and boating. The boardwalk connecting **Mission Beach** and **Pacific Beach** is almost always bustling and colorful. A wooden roller coaster, the **Giant Dipper**, still screams away—daily in summer, weekends the rest of the year—providing a thrill for $4. Dedicated swimmers head for **The Plunge,** the classic, 175-foot-long indoor pool at the foot of the Giant Dipper. For all of these activities, see the appropriate headings in "Outdoor Pursuits," later in this chapter. For **SeaWorld San Diego,** see p. 712.

LA JOLLA

One of San Diego's most scenic spots—star of postcards for more than 100 years—is **La Jolla Cove** and the **Ellen Browning Scripps Park** on the bluff above it. The walk through the park, along Coast Boulevard, offers some of California's most resplendent coastal scenery, and just south is the **Children's Pool,** a beach where dozens of harbor seals can be spotted lazing in the sun (sorry, no swimming here). For a fine scenic drive, follow La Jolla Boulevard to Nautilus Street and turn east to get to 800-foot-high **Mount Soledad** ✿, which offers a 360-degree view of the area.

Birch Aquarium at Scripps ✿✿   This beautiful facility is both aquarium and museum, operated as the interpretive arm of the world-famous Scripps Institution of Oceanography. To make the most of it, pick up a visitor guide from the information booth just inside the entrance, and take time to read about each of the exhibits. The aquarium affords close-up views of the Pacific Northwest, the California coast, Mexico's Sea of Cortez, and the tropical seas, all presented in 33 marine-life tanks. The giant kelp forest is particularly impressive, replete with tiger sharks and eels, and don't miss the tanks of fanciful white anemones and ethereal moon jellies (which look like living parachutes). The sea-horse propagation program here has met with excellent results—nine different species of sea horse are on display. The rooftop demonstration tide pool not only shows visitors marine coastal life but also offers an amazing view of Scripps Pier and La Jolla. Free tide-pool talks are offered on weekends, which are also when the aquarium is most crowded, and off-site adventures are conducted year-round.

2300 Expedition Way. ✆ 858/534-FISH. www.aquarium.ucsd.edu. Admission $10 adults, $8.50 seniors, $7 college students with ID, $6.50 children 3–17, free for kids under 3. Parking $3. AE, MC, V. Daily 9am–5pm. Bus: 34. Take I-5 to La Jolla Village Dr. exit, go west 1 mile, and turn left at Expedition Way.

Museum of Contemporary Art San Diego ✿✿   Focusing on works produced since 1950, this museum is known internationally for its permanent collection and thought-provoking exhibitions. The 3,000-plus holdings include every major art movement of the past half-century, with a strong representation by California artists. You'll see particularly noteworthy examples of minimalism, light and space work, conceptualism, installation, and site-specific sculptures. The museum is perched on a bluff overlooking the ocean, and the views from the galleries are gorgeous. The original building was the residence of the legendary Ellen Browning Scripps, designed by Irving Gill in 1916. More than a dozen exhibitions are presented each year, and guided docent tours are available daily at 2pm, with a second tour Thursdays at 5:30pm. There is a small satellite location in downtown San Diego at 1001 Kettner Blvd., across from the Santa Fe depot (✆ 619/234-1001). There are usually two exhibits here and admission is free.

700 Prospect St. ✆ 858/454-3541. www.mcasandiego.org. Admission $6 adults; $2 students, seniors, and military; free for children under 12. Free 1st Sun and 3rd Tues of each month. Fri–Tues 11am–5pm; Thurs 11am–7pm (closed Wed). Bus: 30, 34, or 34A. Take the La Jolla Pkwy. exit off I-5 north or the La Jolla Village Dr. west exit off I-5 south. Take Torrey Pines Rd. to Prospect Place and turn right. Prospect Place becomes Prospect St.

Torrey Pines State Reserve ✿✿ (Moments   The rare torrey pine tree grows only two places in the world: Santa Rosa Island 175 miles northwest of San

Diego and here, at the north end of La Jolla. Even if the twisted shape of these awkwardly beautiful trees doesn't lure you to this spot, the equally scarce undeveloped coastal scenery should. The 1,750-acre reserve encompasses the 300-foot-high, water-carved limestone bluffs, which provide a precarious footing for the trees. A half-dozen trails under 1½ miles in length travel from the road to the cliff edge or down to the beach, and there's a small visitor center, built in the traditional adobe style of the Hopi Indians, featuring a lovely 12-minute video about the park. For a taste of what Southern California's coast looked like a couple hundred years ago, this delicate spot is one of San Diego's unique treasures. *Note:* There are no facilities for food or drinks inside the park.

Hwy. 101, La Jolla. © 858/755-2063. www.torreypine.org. Admission $4 per car, $3 for seniors. Daily 8am–sunset. Bus: 101. From I-5, take Carmel Valley Rd. exit west; left at Hwy. 101.

CORONADO

It's hard to miss San Diego Bay's most noteworthy landmark: the **San Diego–Coronado Bay Bridge** ﷼. Completed in 1969, this graceful five-lane bridge spans 2¼ miles and links the city and the "island" of Coronado. At 246 feet in height, the bridge was designed to be tall enough for the navy's aircraft carriers to pass through but it still looks more elegant than utilitarian, with a sweeping curve that maximizes the view, which encompasses Mexico and the shipyards of National City to the left, the San Diego skyline to the right, and Coronado, the naval station, and Point Loma in front of you (designated drivers have to promise to keep their eyes on the road!). Bus no. 901 from downtown will also take you across the bridge. Also worth checking out, even if you're not checking in, is the **Hotel del Coronado** ﷼﷼, a turreted Victorian seaside resort that remains an enduring, endearing national treasure (see p. 694 for a review).

SIGHTSEEING TOURS

Hornblower Cruises   A fleet of seven different yachts ranging from a 40-passenger to a three-deck, 880-passenger behemoth invite guests on a 2-hour narrated harbor tour—you'll see the *Star of India,* cruise under the San Diego–Coronado Bridge, visit the Hotel Del and the Submarine Base, and swing by an aircraft carrier or two; a 1-hour itinerary is also available. Guests can visit the captain's wheelhouse for a photo op, and harbor seals and sea lions on buoys are a regular sighting. Whale-watching trips (mid-Dec through late Mar) are a blast, and there's also a 2-hour Sunday (and Sat in summer) champagne brunch cruise at 11am, and nightly dinner cruises.

1066 N. Harbor Dr. © 800/ON-THE-BAY or 619/686-8715. www.hornblower.com. Harbor tours $15–$20 adults; $2 off for seniors and military; ½ price children 4–12. The brunch cruise is $45; whale-watching trips are $25 (both $2 off for seniors and military, ½ price for children). Bus: 2. Trolley: Embarcadero.

Old Town Trolley Tours   Not to be confused with the public transit trolley, these narrated excursions are an easy way to get an overview of the city, especially if you're short on time or lacking your own set of wheels. The trackless trolleys do a 30-mile circular route, and you can hop off at any one of eight stops, explore at leisure, and reboard when you please (trolleys run every half-hour). Stops include Old Town, the Gaslamp Quarter, Coronado, the San Diego Zoo, and Balboa Park. You can begin wherever you want, but you must purchase tickets before boarding (not all stops have a ticket kiosk).

Old Town Trolley also operates **Sea and Land Adventures,** a 2-hour tour that conquers the city in amphibious vehicles that hold 50 passengers. After cruising the streets of the Gaslamp Quarter, Old Town, and Coronado, you'll take a dip into the bay to experience the maritime and military history of San Diego. The trip costs $25 for adults and $15 for kids 4 to 12. Or opt for the humor-fueled **Ghosts & Gravestones** tour, a 90-minute twilight excursion to haunted and historical houses that concludes with a walk through one of the city's oldest cemeteries. The tour costs $28 and is restricted to ages 8 and up.

4040 Twiggs St., Old Town. © 619/298-TOUR. www.historictours.com. Tickets $25 adults, $15 for kids 4–12, free for children 3 and under. The route by itself takes about 2 hr. Old Town Trolleys operate 9am–5pm in winter, 9am–6pm in summer.

San Diego Harbor Excursion   This company also offers daily 1- and 2-hour narrated tours of the bay, using its fleet of seven boats ranging from a 1940s passenger launch to a modern, paddle-wheel-style vessel. The 1-hour itinerary covers 12 miles including the *Star of India,* U.S. Navy surface fleet, San Diego–Coronado Bridge, and shipyards; the 25-mile 2-hour route also visits the Submarine Base and North Island Naval Air Station. In winter, whale-watching excursions feature naturalists from the Birch Aquarium, and the 2-hour Sunday brunch cruise aboard a sleek yacht is popular; dinner cruises sail nightly.

1050 N. Harbor Dr. (foot of Broadway). © 800/44-CRUISE or 619/234-4111. www.sdhe.com. Harbor tours $15–$20 ($2 off for seniors and military; half price for children 4–12). Brunch cruise $40 adults, $30 children; whale-watching trips $25 adults, $21 seniors, $15 children. Bus: 2. Trolley: Embarcadero.

8 Outdoor Pursuits

BALLOONING & SCENIC FLIGHTS   A peaceful dawn or dusk balloon ride reveals sweeping vistas of the Southern California coast, the wine country surrounding Temecula (70 min. north of downtown), or rambling estates and golf courses around Rancho Santa Fe (25 min. north of downtown). For a champagne-fueled glimpse of the county at sunrise or sunset, followed by an hors d'oeuvres party, contact **Skysurfer Balloon Company** (© 800/660-6809 or 858/481-6800; www.sandiegohotairballoons.com) or **California Dreamin'** (© 800/373-3359 or 760/438-3344; www.californiadreamin.com). Rates range from $118 to $148 (the higher rates apply on weekends).

BIKING   The paths around **Mission Bay** are great for leisurely rides, although the oceanfront **boardwalk** between Pacific Beach and Mission Beach can get very crowded, especially on weekends (but that's half the fun). The road out to **Point Loma** (Catalina Dr.) offers moderate hills and wonderful scenery. Traveling old **State Route 101** (aka the Pacific Coast Hwy.) from La Jolla north to Oceanside offers terrific coastal views, along with plenty of places to refuel with coffee, a snack, or a swim.

For rentals, call **Bike Tours San Diego,** 509 Fifth Ave. (© 619/238-2444), which offers free delivery as far north as Del Mar. Rates for a city/hybrid bike start at $18 for a day, and include helmets, locks, maps, and roadside assistance. Other rental outlets include **Mission Beach Club,** 704 Ventura Place, off Mission Boulevard at Ocean Front Walk (© 858/488-8889), for one-speed beach cruisers, and **Cheap Rentals** on Mission Boulevard (© 858/488-9070) for mountain bikes and more. In La Jolla, try **California Bicycle,** 7462 La Jolla Blvd. (© 858/454-0316), for front-suspended mountain bikes. In Coronado, check out **Bikes and Beyond,** 1201 First St., at the Ferry Landing Marketplace (© 619/435-7180), for beach cruisers and mountain bikes. Expect to pay $6 and up per hour for bicycles, $30 for 24 hours.

BIRD-WATCHING   San Diego's birding scene is huge: More than 480 species have been observed in the county, more than in any other in the United States. The area is a haven along the Pacific Flyway—the migratory route along the Pacific Coast—and the diverse range of ecosystems also helps to lure a wide range of winged creatures. From the tidal marshes to the desert, it's possible for birders to enjoy four distinct bird habitats in a single day.

Among the best places for bird-watching is the **Chula Vista Nature Center** at **Sweetwater Marsh National Wildlife Refuge** (© **619/409-5900;** www.chulavistanaturecenter.org), where you may spot rare residents like the light-footed clapper rail and the western snowy plover, as well as predatory species like the American peregrine falcon and northern harrier. Also noteworthy is the **Torrey Pines State Reserve** (p. 721), a protected habitat for swifts, thrashers, woodpeckers and wrentits. Inland, the **Anza-Borrego Desert State Park** (see chapter 15) makes an excellent day trip from San Diego—268 species of birds have been recorded there.

Obtain the free brochure *Birding Hot Spots of San Diego* through the Port Administration Building, 3165 Pacific Hwy., or at the San Diego Zoo, Wild Animal Park, San Diego Natural History Museum, or Birch Aquarium. It is also found on the **Port of San Diego** website at www.portofsandiego.org/sandiego_environment/bird_brochure.asp. The **San Diego Audubon Society** is another source of birding information: © **619/682-7200;** www.sandiego audubon.org.

FISHING   Summer and fall are ideal for boat fishing, when the waters around **Point Loma** are brimming with bass, bonito, and barracuda; the **Islas los Coronados,** which belong to Mexico but are only about 18 miles from San Diego, are popular for abalone, yellowtail, yellowfin, and big-eyed tuna. Some outfitters will take you deeper into Baja California waters on multi-day trips. Fishing charters depart from Harbor and Shelter islands, Point Loma, Imperial Beach, and Quivira Basin in Mission Bay. Participants over age 16 need a California fishing license, but anglers of any age can fish free of charge without a license off any **municipal pier** in the state, including those of Shelter Island, Ocean Beach, and Imperial Beach.

San Diego's sport-fishing fleet consists of more than 75 large commercial vessels and several dozen private charter yachts, and a variety of half-, full-, and multi-day trips are available. Rates for trips on a large boat average $35 for half a day or $70 for three-quarters of a day. Or spring $90 for a 20-hour overnight trip to the Islas los Coronados—call around and compare prices. Rates are lower for kids, and discounts are often available for twilight sailings; charters or "limited load" rates are also available. The following outfitters offer short or extended outings with daily departures: **H & M Landing,** 2803 Emerson (© **619/222-1144;** www.hmlanding.com); **Lee Palm Sportfishers,** 2801 Emerson (© **619/224-3857;** www.redrooster3.com); **Point Loma Sportfishing,** 1403 Scott St. (© **619/223-1627;** www.pointlomasportfishing.com); and **Seaforth Sportfishing,** 1717 Quivira Rd. (© **619/224-3383;** www.seaforthlanding.com).

GOLF   With 90-plus courses, more than 50 of them open to the public, San Diego County offers golf enthusiasts endless opportunities to play. For a full listing of area courses, visit **www.golfsd.com**, or request the *Golf Guide* from the San Diego Convention and Visitors Bureau (© **619/236-1212;** www.sandiego.org). **San Diego Golf Reservations** (© **800/905-0230** or 858/964-5980; www.sandiegogolfreservations.com) can arrange tee times for you at San Diego's premiere golf courses. They will consult with you on the courses, charging a $10 per person/per tee time coordination fee.

The city's most famous links are found at the **Torrey Pines Golf Course** 𝕽𝕽, a pair of 18-hole championship courses on the cliffs between La Jolla and Del

Mar. Home of the Buick Invitational Tournament, and the setting for the 2008 U.S. Open, the biggest challenge at Torrey Pines is getting a tee time, which are taken starting at 7pm, 7 days in advance, by automated telephone. Greens fees on the south course are $105 Monday through Friday, $125 Saturday and Sunday; the north course is $65 and $75, respectively. Cart rentals are $30, and twilight rates are available. Golf packages double the cost but give you much better odds of actually getting onto the course. Tee times: (C) **858/570-1234** ((C) 858/ 452-3226 for the pro shop and packages; www.torreypinesgolfcourse.com).

In addition to Torrey Pines, other acclaimed, newer links include: **Four Seasons Resort Aviara Golf Club** in Carlsbad ((C) 760/603-6900; www. fourseasons.com); **The Meadows Del Mar** ((C) 858/792-6200; www.meadows delmar.com), **Maderas Golf Club** in Poway ((C) 858/726-4653; www.maderas golf.com), **Barona Creek** in Lakeside ((C) 619/387-7018; www.barona.com), and **The Auld Course** in Chula Vista ((C) 619/482-4666; www.theauld course.com). More convenient for most visitors is the **Riverwalk Golf Club** ((C) 619/296-4653), links that wander along the Mission Valley floor. Nonresident greens fees, including cart, are $79 Monday through Thursday, $89 Friday, and $99 Saturday and Sunday; twilight and bargain evening rates are available.

HIKING & WALKING   The best **beaches** for walking are Coronado, Pacific Beach, La Jolla Shores, and Torrey Pines, but pretty much any shore is a good choice. You can also walk around most of Mission Bay on a series of connected footpaths. If a four-legged friend is your walking companion, head for Dog Beach in Ocean Beach or Fiesta Island in Mission Bay—two of the few areas where dogs can legally go unleashed. The **Coast Walk** in La Jolla offers supreme surf-line views (see "La Jolla," earlier in this chapter). Other places for hikes listed earlier in this chapter include **Torrey Pines State Reserve** (p. 721) and **Cabrillo National Monument** (p. 718).

The **Sierra Club** sponsors many hikes in the San Diego area, and nonmembers are welcome to participate. Most are free. For a recorded message about outings, call (C) **619/299-1744**, or contact the office ((C) **619/299-1743**). Volunteers from the **Natural History Museum** ((C) **619/232-3821**; www.sdnhm.org) also lead nature walks throughout San Diego County.

Walkabout International, 4639 30th St., Suite C, San Diego ((C) **619/ 231-7463**; www.walkabout-int.org), sponsors more than 100 free walking tours every month that are led by local volunteers and are listed on the website. Walking tours hit all parts of the county, including the Gaslamp Quarter, La Jolla, and the beaches, and there's a hike in the mountains most Wednesdays and Saturdays.

SAILING & MOTOR YACHTS   Sailors have a choice of the calm waters of 4,600-acre **Mission Bay,** with its 26 miles of shoreline; the exciting **San Diego Bay,** which is one of the most beautiful natural harbors in the world; or out onto the open **Pacific Ocean,** sailing south to the Islas los Coronados (that is, the trio of uninhabited islets on the Mexico side of the border).

The **Maritime Museum of San Diego** ((C) **619/234-9153**; www.sdmaritime. org) offers sailing trips aboard the *Californian,* the official tall ship of the state, a replica of an 1847 cutter that sailed the coast during the Gold Rush. Half-day sails depart most days at 1pm from the Maritime Museum and are priced at $30 for adults, $21 for seniors over 65, juniors ages 13 to 17, and active military, and $17 for kids 12 and under (not recommended for children under 10). Full-day sails, overnight trips to the Catalina Islands, and weeklong excursions up the coast are also offered; call or check the website for details.

Based at Shelter Island Marina, **Classic Sailing Adventures** (© **800/659-0141** or 619/224-0800; www.classicsailingadventures.com) offers two 4-hour sailing trips daily aboard *Soul Diversion*, a 38-foot Ericson. The afternoon cruise leaves at 1pm and a champagne sunset sail departs at 5pm. The yacht carries a maximum of six passengers (minimum two), and the $65-per-person price includes beverages and snacks. From mid-December through March the company offers similarly priced whale-watching excursions.

If you have sailing or boating experience, there are options for nonchartered rentals. **Seaforth Boat Rental,** 1641 Quivira Rd., Mission Bay (© **888/834-2628** or 619/223-1681; www.seaforthboatrental.com), has a variety of boats for bay or ocean. It rents 15- to 240-horsepower powerboats ranging from $55 to $115 an hour, 14- to 25-foot sailboats for $20 to $40 an hour, and ski boats and jet skis starting at $70 an hour. Half- and full-day rates are available. Canoes, kayaks, and pedal boats also available, as well as fishing boats and equipment. Seaforth has a location downtown at the Marriott San Diego Hotel, 333 W. Harbor Dr. (© **619/239-2628**), and in Coronado at 1715 Strand Way (© **619/437-1514**). **Mission Bay Sportcenter,** 1010 Santa Clara Place (© **858/488-1004;** www.missionbaysportcenter.com), rents sailboats, catamarans, sailboards, kayaks, and motorboats. Prices range from $18 to $95 an hour, with discounts for 4-hour and full-day rentals. Private instruction is available for $30 per hour.

SCUBA DIVING & SNORKELING   San Diego's underwater scene ranges from the magnificent giant kelp forests of Point Loma to a nautical graveyard off Mission Beach called Wreck Alley, where a 366-foot Canadian destroyer and other ships sit on the sea floor. There is an aquatic Ecological Reserve off the La Jolla Cove—fishing and boating activity is banned in the 533-acre reserve, but diving and snorkeling is welcome, and it's a reliable place to spot the rare garibaldi, California's state fish, as well as rare giant black sea bass. Shore diving here, or at nearby La Jolla Shores, is common, and there are dive shops to help you get set up. But boat dives are the rule, particularly to the Islas los Coronados, a trio of uninhabited islets off Tijuana, where seals, sea lions, eels, and more cavort against a landscape of boulders. Water visibility in San Diego is best in the fall, while in the spring, plankton blooms can reduce visibility to 20 feet.

The **San Diego Oceans Foundation** (© **619/523-1903;** www.sdoceans.org) is a local organization devoted to the stewardship of local marine waters. The website contains good info about the local diving scene. **San Diego Divers Supply,** 4004 Sports Arena Blvd. (© **619/224-3439**) and 5701 La Jolla Blvd. (© **858/459-2691**), will set you up with scuba and snorkeling equipment. **Blue Escape Dive and Charter** (© **619/223-3483**) and **Scuba San Diego** (© **800/586-3483** or 619/260-1880; www.scubasandiego.com) are other good outfits.

SKATING   Gliding around San Diego, especially the Mission Bay area, on in-line skates is the quintessential Southern California experience. In Pacific Beach, rent a pair of regular or in-line skates from **Resort Watersports** (© **858/488-2582**), based at the Catamaran Resort, 3981 Mission Blvd.; or **Pacific Beach Sun and Sea,** 4539 Ocean Blvd. (© **858/483-6613**). In Coronado, go to **Bikes and Beyond,** 1201 First St. and at the Ferry Landing (© **619/435-7180**). Be sure to ask for protective gear.

SURFING   San Diego is popular as a year-round surf destination. Some of the best spots include La Jolla Shores, Windansea, Pacific Beach, Mission Beach, Ocean Beach, and Imperial Beach. In North County you might consider Carlsbad State Beach and Oceanside. If you didn't bring your own board, they are available for rent at stands at many popular beaches. Local surf shops also rent equipment; they include **La Jolla Surf Systems,** 2132 Avenida de la Playa, La Jolla Shores (© **858/456-2777**), and **Emerald City–The Boarding Source,** 1118 Orange Ave., Coronado (© **619/435-6677**).

For surfing lessons, check with **San Diego Surfing Academy** (© **800/447-SURF** or 760/230-1474; www.surfsdsa.com/index.htm), which offers lessons at Tourmaline in Pacific Beach and San Elijo State Beach in Cardiff by the Sea; and **Surf Diva** (© **858/454-8273;** www.surfdiva.com), the world's first surfing school for women and girls (with one instructor dude), based in La Jolla.

9 Shopping

Okay, so we've embraced the suburban shopping mall with vigor. Many San Diegans do the bulk of their shopping at two massive complexes in Mission Valley where every possible need is represented. Downtown has even adopted the mall concept at Horton Plaza, and historic Old Town reveals textiles and colors from south-of-the-border lands with great flair.

Sales tax in San Diego is 7.75%, and savvy out-of-state shoppers have larger items shipped directly home at the point of purchase, thereby avoiding the tax.

DOWNTOWN

The Disneyland of shopping malls, **Horton Plaza** ⍟, 324 Horton Plaza (© **619/238-1596;** www.westfield.com/us/centres/california/hortonplaza), is in the heart of the revitalized city center. The multilevel facility has more than 130 specialty shops, including art galleries, clothing and shoe stores, and several fun shops for kids. There's a 14-screen cinema, three major department stores, several restaurants, and a roster of short-order eateries. It transcends its genre with a conglomeration of rambling paths, bridges, towers, piazzas, sculptures, fountains, and live greenery. Designed by the local Jerde Partnership, Horton Plaza opened in 1985 to rave reviews and provided an initial catalyst for the Gaslamp's redevelopment. The parking garage (3 hr. free with validation) is confusing, and temporarily losing your car is part of the Horton Plaza experience.

The ersatz, 14-acre **Seaport Village,** 849 W. Harbor Dr. (© **619/235-4014;** www.seaportvillage.com), snuggled alongside San Diego Bay, was built to resemble a small Cape Cod community, but the 75 shops are very much the Southern California cutesy variety. Still the waterfront atmosphere is pleasant, and 2 hours' free parking is provided with purchase.

Seekers of serious art might want to head to Little Italy's **Studio Arts Complex,** north of downtown. Among the galleries housed at 2400 Kettner Blvd. is **David Zapf Gallery,** no. 104 (© **619/232-5004**), which features painting, sculpture, drawings, or furniture; they also distribute the *Arts Down Town* guide. The **Pratt Gallery,** no. 106 (© **619/236-0211**) has a changing display space, often featuring innovative paintings, photography, or other individualistic work.

HILLCREST/UPTOWN

Compact Hillcrest is an ideal shopping destination for browsing unique and often wacky shops, but also for buying things at the area's vintage-clothing stores, memorabilia shops, recognizable chains, and bakeries and cafes. Start at the neighborhood's axis, the intersection of University and Fifth avenues. Street parking is available.

A half-mile east of Hillcrest is the start of the **Adams Avenue Antique Row.** It lies along Park Boulevard (beginning at Robinson Ave.) and on Adams Avenue (extending from Park east to around 40th St.). Antiques and collectibles stores, vintage-clothing boutiques, and dusty used-book stores line this L-shaped district, providing many hours of happy browsing and treasure hunting. There are plenty of coffeehouses, pubs, and small restaurants to break up the excursion. For more information and an area brochure with a map, contact the **Adams Avenue Business Association** (© 619/282-7329; www.GoThere.com/AdamsAve).

OLD TOWN & MISSION VALLEY

Old Town Historic Park is a restoration of some of San Diego's historic sites and adobe structures, a number of which now house shops that cater to tourists. Many have a "general-store" theme and carry gourmet treats and inexpensive Mexican crafts alongside the obligatory T-shirts, baseball caps, and other San Diego–emblazoned souvenirs. Sixteen interconnected shops are found in **Bazaar del Mundo** 🌸🌸, 2754 Calhoun St. (© 619/296-3161; www.bazaardelmundo. com), featuring one-of-a-kind folk art, home furnishings, clothing, and textiles from Mexico and Central and South America, which are arranged around a fountain courtyard.

Mission Valley is home to two giant malls (**Fashion Valley** and **Mission Valley**), with more than enough stores to satisfy any shopper, and free parking—both can be reached via San Diego Trolley from downtown. Book lovers will find local outposts of **Barnes & Noble,** 7610 Hazard Center Dr. (© **619/220-0175**), and **Borders,** 1072 Camino del Rio N. (© **619/295-2201**).

MISSION BAY & THE BEACHES

The beach communities all offer laid-back shopping in typical California fashion: plenty of surf shops, recreational gear, and casual garb stores. If you're in need of a new bikini, the best selection is at **Pilar's,** 3745 Mission Blvd., Pacific Beach (© 858/488-3056), where dozens of racks are meticulously organized. Across the street is **Liquid Foundation Surf Shop,** 3731 Mission Blvd. (© 858/488-3260), which specializes in board shorts for guys.

San Diego's greatest concentration of antiques stores is found in the **Ocean Beach Antique District,** along the 4800 block of Newport Avenue. Several of the stores are mall-style, featuring multiple dealers under one roof. The hundreds of individual sellers cover the gamut—everything from Asian antiquities to vintage watches to mid-20th-century collectibles. A good place to start is the **Newport Ave. Antique Center,** 4864 Newport Ave. (© 619/222-8686), with 18,000 square feet of retail, and even a small espresso bar. Most of the O.B. antiques stores are open daily from 10am to 6pm, with reduced hours Sunday.

LA JOLLA

It's clear from the look of La Jolla's village that shopping is a major pastime in this upscale community of moneyed professionals and retirees. Women's-clothing boutiques tend toward conservative and costly, like those lining Girard and Prospect streets (Ann Taylor, Armani Exchange, Polo/Ralph Lauren, Talbots, and Sigi's Boutique), but you'll also find mainstream (that is, less pricey) venues like Banana Republic and Dansk.

Even if you're not in the market for furnishings and accessories, the many home-decor boutiques make for great window-shopping, as do La Jolla's ubiquitous jewelers: Swiss watches, tennis bracelets, gems, and pearl necklaces sparkle at you from windows along every street. No visit to La Jolla is complete without seeing **John Cole's Book Shop,** 780 Prospect St. (© 858/454-4766), an eclectic, family-run local favorite set in a charming old cottage.

CORONADO

This rather insular, conservative navy community doesn't have a great many shopping opportunities; what there is lines Orange Avenue at the western end of the island. In addition to some scattered housewares and home-decor boutiques, as well as several small women's boutiques, there are gift shops at Coronado's major resorts. The **Ferry Landing Marketplace,** 1201 First St., at B Avenue (© **619/435-8895**), is an unexciting faux-seaport with shops, restaurants, and a sweeping view of the bay and the downtown skyline.

10 San Diego After Dark

Historically, San Diego's cultural scene has lounged in the shadows of Los Angeles and San Francisco, content to take a back seat to the beach, the zoo, our meteorologically inspired state of affairs. But the dot-com influence brought new blood and money into the city, and arts organizations felt the impact. The biggest winner was the San Diego Symphony, which in 2002 received the largest single donation to a symphony anywhere, ever. But don't think "after dark" in this city is limited to high-falutin' affairs for the Lexus crowd—it also means night *lively:* rock and pop concerts, swank martini bars and nightclubs, and, of course, our newly stadium-enriched baseball team, the Padres.

THE PERFORMING ARTS

For a rundown of major events, the San Diego Convention and Visitors Bureau has an **Art + Sol** campaign which provides a calendar of events and profiles of 11 member institutions; check it out at www.sandiegoartandsol.com. The San Diego Performing Arts League produces *What's Playing?,* a performing-arts guide, every 2 months. You can pick one up at the ARTS TIX booth or write to 701 B St., Suite 225, San Diego, CA 92101-8101 (© **619/238-0700;** www.sandiegoperforms.com).

Half-price tickets to theater, music, and dance events are available at the **ARTS TIX** booth, in Horton Plaza Park at Broadway and Third Avenue. For a daily listing of offerings, call © **619/497-5000** or visit www.sandiegoperforms.com.

THEATER

A complex of three performance venues inside Balboa Park, **The Old Globe** is best known for the 581-seat Old Globe Theatre—fashioned after Shakespeare's—but also includes the 225-seat Cassius Carter Centre Stage and the 612-seat open-air Lowell Davies Festival Theatre. Between them, they mount 15 plays annually, from world premieres of such subsequent Broadway arrivals as Tina Howe's *Pride's Crossing* or *The Full Monty,* to excellent summer Shakespeare. Leading performers regularly grace the stage, and tours are offered Saturday and Sunday at 10:30am ($5 per person). Tickets range from $19 to $52. For more information, call © **619/239-2255** or log on to www.theoldglobe.org.

Equally respected is the **La Jolla Playhouse**, which boasts a Hollywood pedigree (it was founded in 1947 by Gregory Peck, Dorothy McGuire, and Mel Ferrer) and a 1993 Tony Award for outstanding American regional theater. The Playhouse stages seven productions each year (May–Dec) at three fine theaters on the UCSD campus. Past hits include Matthew Broderick in *How to Succeed in Business Without Really Trying* and the 2000 revival of *Thoroughly Modern Millie; The Who's Tommy* and *Big River* also premiered at the Playhouse before going on to Broadway acclaim. Tickets are $28 to $57, but for each show, one Saturday matinee is a "pay what you can" performance, and every night unsold tickets are $15 each in a "public rush" sale 10 minutes before curtain. More information: ℂ 858/550-1010; www.lajollaplayhouse.com.

Also noteworthy is the **San Diego Repertory Theatre,** which mounts plays and musicals at the Lyceum Theatres in Horton Plaza (ℂ 619/544-1000; www.sandiegorep.com). In Coronado **Lamb's Players Theatre** (ℂ 619/437-0600; www.lambsplayers.org) is a professional rep company whose season runs February through December. And, founded in 1948, the **San Diego Junior Theatre,** at Balboa Park's Casa del Prado Theatre (ℂ 619/239-8355; fax 619/239-5048; www.juniortheatre.com), is the country's oldest continuously producing children's theater. Students make up the cast and crew of six shows each year.

CLASSICAL MUSIC, OPERA & DANCE

Like a phoenix from the ashes, the **San Diego Symphony** ✮ is on the verge of major triumph following a spate of financial problems. Stability arrived in 2002 with the announcement of a $120-million bequest by Joan and Irwin Jacobs (of Qualcomm Inc.). The donation allows the organization—now "placed firmly on the nation's musical landscape" (the *New York Times*)—to lure top talent, starting with the arrival of a new resident conductor, Jahja Ling. The symphony's home is the restored Fox Theatre, a 1929-era, French-rococo-style downtown landmark, now known as Symphony Hall. The season runs October through May, while a Summer Pops series, with programs devoted to an eclectic mix of big band, Broadway, Tchaikovsky, and sundry "pops," is held weekends late June through August at the Embarcadero. Tickets range $12 to $85. Additional information: ℂ 619/235-0804; www.sandiegosymphony.com.

The respected **La Jolla Music Society** ✮ has been bringing marquee names to San Diego since 1968, including Pinchas Zukerman, Emanuel Ax, Joshua Bell, and the American Ballet Theatre. Most of the 40-plus annual shows are held October through May in La Jolla's Sherwood Auditorium, at the Museum of Contemporary Art. The annual highlight is SummerFest, a 3-week series of concerts, forums, open rehearsals, talks, and artist encounters—it's held in early August and is broadcast nationally live on NPR. Tickets range from $20 to $105; for more information: ℂ 858/459-3728; www.lajollamusicsociety.org.

The **San Diego Opera** ✮✮ has grown into one of the community's most successful arts organizations. The annual season runs from late January through mid-May, with five offerings at downtown's 3,000-seat Civic Theatre, ranging from well-trod warhorses like *Madame Butterfly* to new productions such as 2004's *Pearl Fishers,* all performed by local singers and name talent from around the world. Tickets run $20 to $150. More information: ℂ 619/570-1100 (box office) or 619/232-7636; www.sdopera.com.

The **San Diego Dance Alliance** is the umbrella organization for the local dance community (ℂ 619/230-8623; www.sandiegodance.org). The alliance puts on the **Nations of San Diego International Dance Festival,** held each January and spotlighting the city's ethnic dance groups and emerging artists. The website provides links to 22 local dance outfits.

THE CLUB & MUSIC SCENE

The most comprehensive listings are found in the free *San Diego Weekly Reader* (www.sdreader.com), published Thursdays and distributed all over town (in tourist areas, it's a condensed version called the *Weekly*).

LIVE ROCK, POP, FOLK, JAZZ & BLUES

You'll find live music nightly at **Croce's Nightclubs,** 802 Fifth Ave. at F Street (ℂ 619/233-4355; www.croces.com), a mainstream gathering place in the

Gaslamp. Two separate clubs operate a couple doors apart—one provides a venue for traditional jazz, the other is rhythm and blues on Friday and Saturday. The cover charge is waived if you eat at the (expensive) restaurant. Near Little Italy is **The Casbah,** 2501 Kettner Blvd. at Laurel (© **619/232-HELL;** www. casbahmusic.com), which has a total-dive ambience but also boasts a well-earned rep for showcasing alternative and rock bands that either are, were, or will be famous. In summer, San Diegans flock to **Humphrey's** ✿, 2241 Shelter Island Dr. (© **619/523-1010;** www.humphreysconcerts.com), a 1,300-seat outdoor venue on the water. The lineup covers the spectrum of entertainment—rock and jazz to comedy, blues, folk, and international music.

DANCE CLUBS & DISCOS

The Gaslamp Quarter is the hub of nightlife, but much of it is concentrated into just 2 nights a week, Friday and Saturday, when late-night dance clubs spring into action. Leading the crowd is **On Broadway,** 615 Broadway at Sixth Avenue (© **619/231-0011**), a swanky hangout in a converted 1925 bank building with five rooms covering the musical gamut: house, techno, hip-hop, and R&B— using a 90,000-watt sound system—plus a sushi bar with live jazz and a billiards room in the former bank vault. Dress to impress, as this is the city's most high-end dance club. Miami South Beach Art Deco flair meets high-tech dance club at **Deco's,** 731 Fifth Ave. (© **619/696-3326**), which means candy-colored neon, "VIP beds," and, of course, an open-air lounge. **The Bitter End,** 770 Fifth Ave. (© **619/338-9300;** www.thebitterend.com), has three levels for its Brit-themed martini bar, late-night dance club, and relaxing cocktail lounge. For Latin-themed fun, visit **Olé Madrid,** 751 Fifth Ave. (© **619/557-0146**), a loud, energetic club with tapas and sangria from the adjoining Spanish restaurant; or **Sevilla,** 555 Fourth Ave. (© **619/233-5979**), where you can learn to salsa (lessons Tues–Thurs and Sun at 8pm, followed by live bands), or nibble on tapas.

BARS & COCKTAIL LOUNGES

The Beach, the rooftop bar of the W Hotel at 421 B St. downtown (© **619/ 231-8220**), features a heated sand floor, cabanas, and fire pit—very popular among trendoids, but don't forget your flip-flops, shovel, and pail. The **Onyx Room,** 852 Fifth Ave., Gaslamp Quarter (© **619/235-6699**), is an underground (literally) club where the atmosphere is lounge, the drinks are up, and the music is cool. San Diego's ultimate bar with a view, **Top of the Hyatt,** 1 Market Place, at Harbor Drive (© **619/232-1234**), is the 40th floor of the West Coast's tallest waterfront building—you'll get a wide view of the city, harbor, and Coronado. For a real retro trip, swing over to North Park's **Red Fox Room,** 2223 El Cajon Blvd., 1 mile east of Park Boulevard (© **619/297-1313**), where the Always Entertaining Shirley Allen tickles the ivories Wednesday through Saturday at this hipster haunt.

GAY & LESBIAN CLUBS & BARS

Club Montage, 2028 Hancock St. (© **619/294-9590;** www.clubmontage. com/main/index.html), is the city's state-of-the-art dance club, with all the bells and whistles, while the **Brass Rail,** 3796 Fifth Ave., Hillcrest (© **619/298-2233**), is San Diego's oldest gay bar, with energetic dancing, bright lights, and come-as-you-are attitude. Located opposite each other, **Numbers,** 3811 Park Blvd. (near University Ave.), Hillcrest (© **619/294-9005**) and **The Flame,** 3780 Park Blvd. (© **619/ 295-4163**), are popular dance emporiums with theme nights. On the busiest night, Saturday, Numbers is for the boys and The Flame is for the girls, but a mixed crowd is always welcome. **Kickers,** 308 University Ave., at Third Avenue, Hillcrest (© **619/491-0400**), is a country-western dance hall that attracts both sexes for two-stepping, line-dancing Thursday through Saturday, and the adjacent Hamburger Mary's restaurant. **Bourbon Street,** 4612 Park Blvd., University Heights (© **619/291-0173**), is a jazzy and elegant piano bar with a New Orleans–esque patio. Finally, **Rich's,** 1051 University Ave., between 10th and 11th avenues (© **619/295-2195,** or 619/497-4588 for upcoming events; www.richs-sandiego. com), is a high-energy, high-image dance club, with house music and a video bar.

11 North County Beach Towns

The necklace of picturesque beach towns that dot the coast of San Diego County from Del Mar to Oceanside make great day-trip destinations for sun worshipers and surfers. Be forewarned: You'll be tempted to spend the night.

ESSENTIALS

It's a snap: **Del Mar** is only 18 miles north of downtown San Diego, **Carlsbad** about 33 miles. If you're driving, follow I-5 north; Del Mar, Solana Beach, Encinitas, Carlsbad, and Oceanside all have freeway exits. The farthest point, Oceanside, will take about 45 minutes. The other choice by car is to wander up the coast road, known along the way as Camino del Mar, the "PCH" (Pacific Coast Hwy.), Old Highway 101, and County Highway S21.

From downtown San Diego, the **Coaster** commuter train provides service to Solana Beach, Encinitas, Carlsbad, and Oceanside, and **Amtrak** stops in Solana Beach—just a few minutes north of Del Mar—and Oceanside. The Coaster makes the trip almost hourly weekdays, four times on Saturday; Amtrak passes through 11 times daily each way. Call © **619/685-4900** for local transit information, or for Amtrak call © **800/USA-RAIL** (www.amtrak.com).

DEL MAR 🕸🕸

Just 18 miles up the coast lies Del Mar, a small community with just over 4,500 inhabitants in a 2-square-mile municipality. The town has adamantly maintained its independence, eschewing incorporation into the city of San Diego. It's one of the most upscale communities in the greater San Diego area, yet Del Mar somehow manages to maintain a casual, small-town ambience that radiates personality and charm. Come summer, the town swells as visitors flock in for the thoroughbred horseracing season and the county's San Diego Fair.

The history and popularity of Del Mar are inextricably linked to the **Del Mar Racetrack & Fairgrounds,** 2260 Jimmy Durante Blvd. (© **858/753-5555;** www.delmarfair.com). In 1933, actor Bing Crosby developed the Del Mar Turf Club, enlisting the help of Pat O'Brien and other celebrity friends. Soon, Hollywood stars like Lucille Ball, Desi Arnaz, Betty Grable, and Bob Hope were seen around Del Mar, and the town experienced a resurgence. A new $80-million grandstand opened in 1993, built in the Spanish mission style of the original structure. Racing season is late July through mid-September.

Two excellent beaches flank Del Mar: **Torrey Pines State Beach** to the south and **Del Mar State Beach.** Both are wide, well-patrolled strands popular for sunbathing, swimming, and surfing (in marked areas). The sand stretches north to the mouth of the San Dieguito Lagoon, where people bring their dogs for a romp in the sea. Beyond the surf and the turf, the hub of activities for most residents and visitors is **Del Mar Plaza,** a multistory modern structure at the corner of Camino Del Mar and 15th Street. Though it lacks the quaint, lived-in atmosphere that most of the community shares, there are good restaurants and shops, and super views to the sea, especially at sunset.

For more information about Del Mar, contact or visit the **Del Mar Regional Chamber of Commerce Visitor Information Center,** 1104 Camino del Mar #1, Del Mar, CA 92014 (© **858/755-4844;** www.delmarchamber.org), which also distributes a detailed folding map of the area. Open hours vary according to volunteer staffing but usually approximate weekday business hours. There's also a city-run website (www.delmar.ca.us).

WHERE TO STAY

Del Mar Motel on the Beach *Finds*　The only property in Del Mar right on the beach, this simply furnished little white-stucco motel has been here since 1946. All rooms are of good size and are well kept (except for a number of worn-out lampshades)—upstairs units have one king-size bed; downstairs rooms have two double beds. Most of them have little in the way of a view, but two ocean-front rooms sit right over the sand (and are dressed up with faux plants and larger bathrooms). This is a good choice for beach lovers, because you can walk along the shore for miles, and families can be comfortable knowing a lifeguard station is right next door, as are popular seaside restaurants Poseidon and Jake's.

1702 Coast Blvd. (at 17th St.), Del Mar, CA 92014. © **800/223-8449** for reservations, or 858/755-1534. www.delmarmotelonthebeach.com. 44 units (upper units with shower only). $169–$219 double. AE, DC, DISC, MC, V. Take I-5 to Via de la Valle exit. Go west, then south on Hwy. 101 (Pacific Coast Hwy.); veer west onto Coast Blvd. *In room:* A/C, TV, fridge, coffeemaker.

L'Auberge Del Mar Resort and Spa *ﾊﾊﾊ*　On the site of the historic Hotel del Mar (1909–69), the luxurious yet intimate L'Auberge manages to attract casual weekenders as easily as the rich-and-famous horse set, who flock here during summer racing season. In 2002 the resort enhanced the lower-level full-service spa, polished up the poolside ambience, and revamped the dining room. The result is an atmosphere of relaxation and welcome. Guest rooms exude the elegance of a European country house, complete with marble bathrooms, architectural accents, well-placed casual seating, and the finest bed linens and appointments. Twenty-five rooms boast fireplaces; all have a private balcony or terrace (several with an unadvertised view to the ocean). The hotel is across the street from Del Mar's main shopping and dining scene, and a short jog from the sand. **J. Taylor's,** the hotel's California/Mediterranean dining room, easily stands as one of Del Mar's finest restaurants.

1540 Camino del Mar (at 15th St.), Del Mar, CA 92014. © **800/245-9757** or 858/259-1515. Fax 858/755-4940. www.laubergedelmar.com. 120 units. $300–$365 double; from $600 suite. AE, DC, MC, V. Valet parking $19. Take I-5 to Del Mar Heights Rd. west, then turn right onto Camino del Mar Rd. **Amenities:** Restaurant; lounge; 2 swimming pools; tennis courts; indoor/outdoor fitness center; full-service spa; whirlpool; concierge; courtesy van; room service (6:30am–10pm); laundry/dry-cleaning service. *In room:* A/C, TV w/pay movies, dataport, minibar, coffeemaker, hair dryer, iron.

Les Artistes *Finds*　What do you get when you take a 1940s motel, put it in the hands of Sulana Sae-Onge, a Thai architect with a penchant for prominent painters, and wait while she transforms each room, one at a time? The answer is an intriguingly funky, disarmingly informal hotel, just a few blocks from down-town Del Mar. Although none of the rooms has an ocean view, and an ugly empty lot sits awkwardly between the hotel and busy Camino del Mar, there are still so many charming touches—like a lily-and-koi pond, Asian chimes, and climbing bougainvillea—that you feel only privacy. At last count, eight rooms had been redone as tributes to favored artists, two more were given a Japanese makeover, leaving two tastefully decorated but decidedly standard units. Artists spotlighted include Diego Rivera—this gives you the feeling of stepping into a warm Mexican painting—while the Monet room has an almost distractingly abstract swirl of color. Other subjects include Georgia O'Keeffe, Erté, Remington, and Gauguin, while the Japanese Furo room is so authentic that a soaking tub is carved into the bathroom floor—the details are eye-filling. Downstairs rooms in the two-story structure have tiny private garden decks.

944 Camino del Mar, Del Mar, CA 92014. ℂ 858/755-4646. www.lesartistesinn.com. 12 units. $115–$195 double. Rates include continental breakfast. DISC, MC, V. Free parking. From I-5 go west on Del Mar Heights Rd., then left onto Camino Del Mar Rd. Pets accepted with $50 cash deposit plus $20 cleaning fee. In room: TV.

WHERE TO DINE

Head to the upper level of the centrally located Del Mar Plaza, at Camino del Mar and 15th Street. Here you'll find **Il Fornaio Cucina Italiana** ⭐ (ℂ 858/755-8876) for pleasing Italian cuisine and an *enoteca* (wine bar) that is great for ocean views; **Pacifica Del Mar** ⭐⭐ (ℂ 858/792-0476), which serves outstanding seafood; and **Epazote** ⭐ (ℂ 858/259-9966), where Southwestern meets Asian, with a terrific house margarita on offer.

Arterra ⭐⭐⭐ CALIFORNIA   The name of this restaurant derives from "art of the earth," and under the stewardship of Bay Area chef Bradley Ogden, Arterra proves the moniker is no mere marketing gimmick. Housed in a drab, modern Marriott hotel, the broad dining room is impressive, cast in gold and purple tones, with accents of glass and copper, and plush leather banquettes. On-site kitchen master Carl Shroeder crafts his menu based on what's on the shelves at Chino's or Be Wise, the Encinitas farms specializing in heirloom vegetables. Needless to say, the menu is regularly adapted to meet the schedule of mother earth. You'll never eat rigid hot-house tomatoes—that's because Arterra doesn't serve them in winter, when tomatoes don't grow naturally in San Diego. But come in summer and you'll feast on a plate of ravishing heirloom tomatoes lightly garnished with pickled corn and warm goat cheese. The entrees are no slouch: wild striped bass with asparagus and garlic risotto, or chardonnay-braised pork with baby potatoes and glazed baby vegetables are recent offerings. The breakfast, by the way, is superlative, and worth the trip by itself.

11966 El Camino Real (next to I-5 in the Marriott Del Mar), Carmel Valley. ℂ 858/369-6032. www.arterra restaurant.com. Main courses $21–$29 dinner, $12–$18 lunch, $7–$13 breakfast. AE, DC, DISC, MC, V. Nightly 5:30–9:30pm; breakfast Mon–Fri 6:30–10:30am, Sat–Sun 7–11:30am; lunch Mon–Fri 11:30am–2:30pm. Free parking with validation, or $3 for valet parking.

Jake's Del Mar ⭐ SEAFOOD/CALIFORNIA   The spirit of Aloha permeates this Hawaiian-owned seafood-and-view outpost. Occupying a building originally constructed in 1910, Jake's has a perfect seat next to the sand so that diners get straight-on views of the beach scene—sunbathers, surfers, and the occasional school of dolphins pass by (lunch here is "Endless Summer" no matter the weather). The predictable menu can't live up to the panorama, but it's prepared competently and service is swift (too swift, actually—don't let them rush you). At lunch you'll find pan-roasted Atlantic salmon in ponzu sauce, or shrimp fettuccini Provençal; sandwiches and salads round out the offerings. Dinner brings in the big boys: Maine lobster tails, giant scampi, rack of lamb, and so on. To enjoy the scene without the wallet wallop, come for happy hour when a shorter bar/bistro menu is half-price and the mai tais are just $3.

1660 Coast Blvd. (at 15th St.), Del Mar. ℂ 858/755-2002. Main courses $8–$14 lunch, $16–$36 dinner. AE, DC, DISC, MC, V. Tues–Sat 11:30am–2:30pm; Sun brunch 11am–2pm; nightly 5–9pm. Happy hour Mon–Fri 4–6pm, Sat 2:30–4:30pm. Valet parking $2–$3. Bus: 101.

SOLANA BEACH, ENCINITAS & CARLSBAD ⚓

North of Del Mar and a 45-minute drive from downtown San Diego, the pretty communities of Solana Beach, Encinitas, and Carlsbad provide many reasons to linger on the California coast: good swimming and surfing beaches, small-town atmosphere, an abundance of antiques and gift shops, and a seasonal display of the region's most beautiful flowers.

Carlsbad was named for Karlsbad, Czechoslovakia, because of the similar mineral (some say curative) waters they both produced, but the town's once-famous artesian well has long been plugged up. Carlsbad is also a noted commercial-flower-growing region, along with its neighbor Encinitas. A colorful display can be seen at **Carlsbad Ranch** (© 760/431-0352) each spring, when 45 acres of solid ranunculus fields bloom into a breathtaking rainbow visible even from the freeway. In December the nurseries are alive with holiday poinsettias.

The **Solana Beach Visitor Center** is near the train station at 103 N. Cedros (© 858/350-6006; www.solanabeachchamber.com). The **Encinitas Visitors Center** is located in a nondescript shopping mall immediately west of the I-5, at 138 Encinitas Blvd. (© 800/953-6041 or 760/753-6041; www.encinitas chamber.com). The **Carlsbad Visitor Information Center,** 400 Carlsbad Village Dr. (in the old Santa Fe Depot; © 800/227-5722 or 760/434-6093; www. carlsbadca.org), has information on flower fields and nursery touring.

FUN THINGS TO SEE & DO

Going from south to north, the hub of activity for **Solana Beach** is South Cedros Avenue, 1 block east of and parallel to the Pacific Coast Highway. In a 2-block stretch are many of San Diego County's best furniture and home-design shops, antiques stores, art dealers, and boutiques selling imported goods, and the **Belly Up Tavern,** an appealing concert venue that sometimes hosts high-profile acts.

In **Encinitas** everyone flocks to **Moonlight Beach,** where you'll find plenty of facilities, including free parking, volleyball nets, restrooms, showers, picnic tables, and fire grates. The beach entrance is at the end of B Street (at Encinitas Blvd.). A mile south is the appropriately serene **Swami's Beach,** named for the adjacent spiritual retreat (see below). This lovely little beach is surfer central in the winter. It adjoins little-known **Boneyard Beach,** directly to the north. Here, low-tide coves provide shelter for romantics and nudists; this isolated stretch can be reached only from Swami's Beach. There's a free parking lot at Swami's, plus restrooms and a picnic area.

The **Self Realization Fellowship** was founded in 1920 by guru Paramahansa Yogananda, and the exotic-looking domes are what remain of the retreat originally built in 1937 (the rest was built too close to the cliff-edge and tumbled into the sea). Today the site serves as a spiritual sanctuary for holistic healers and their followers, with meditation gardens and a gift shop that sells Fellowship publications and arts and crafts from India. The serene, immaculate gardens line a cliff, with beautiful flower displays in spring, and koi ponds—they're a terrific place to cool off on a hot day. The gardens are entered at 215 K St., at the south end of Encinitas, and are open Tuesday through Sunday; admission is free. The bookstore is located at 1105 Second St., between J and K streets (© 760/753-2888; www.yogananda-srf.org).

Carlsbad is a great place for antiquing. Whether you're a serious shopper or seriously window-shopping, park the car and stroll the 3 blocks of **State Street** between Oak and Beech streets. There are about two dozen shops in this part of town, where diagonal street parking and welcoming merchants lend a village atmosphere. Wares range from estate jewelry to country quilts, from inlaid side-boards to Depression glass.

Carlsbad State Beach runs alongside downtown. It's a great place to stroll along a wide concrete walkway, surrounded by like-minded outdoors types walk-ing, jogging, and in-line skating, even at night (thanks to good lighting). Enter on Ocean Boulevard at Tamarack Avenue; there's a $4 fee per vehicle. South of town is **South Carlsbad State Beach,** almost 3 miles of cobblestone-strewn sand. A state-run campground at the north end is immensely popular year-round, and the southern portion is favored by area surfers. There's a $4 fee at the beach's entrance, along Carlsbad Boulevard at Poinsettia Lane.

LEGOLAND California *Kids*   The ultimate monument to the world's most famous plastic building blocks, LEGOLAND is the third such theme park—following branches in Denmark and Britain that proved enormously successful. In addition to 5,000 Lego models, the Carlsbad park is beautifully landscaped with 1,360 bonsai trees and other plants from around the world, and features more than 50 rides, shows, and attractions. Attractions include hands-on interactive dis-plays; a life-size menagerie of animals; scale models of international landmarks (the Eiffel Tower, Sydney Opera House, and so on)—all constructed of real LEGO bricks. To give the park a little more weight for older kids, there are three relatively gentle roller coasters, but the park is geared toward children ages 2 to 12—as I found with my 3-year-old nephew, there was more than enough to keep him wide-eyed and smiling for a day. *A touring tip:* When the park opens, many visitors hop in line for the first rides encountered (neither of which are special)—it's better to head to the back side of the park where lines are shorter for the first hour or so.

1 Legoland Dr. *C* **877/534-6526** or 760/918-LEGO. www.legoland.com. $42 adults, $35 seniors and kids 3–12, free for children under 3. AE, DISC, MC, V. Summer (late June to Aug) daily 10am–8pm; off season Thurs–Mon 10am–5 or 6pm. Closed Tues–Wed Sept–May, but open daily during Christmas and Easter vaca-tion periods. Parking $7. From I-5 take the Cannon Rd. exit east, following signs for Legoland Dr.

Quail Botanical Gardens *rit*   You don't have to possess a green thumb to be satisfied with an afternoon at this wonderful botanical facility. Boasting the country's largest bamboo collection, plus 30 acres of California natives, exotic tropicals, palms, cacti, Mediterranean, Australian, and other unusual collections, this serene compound is crisscrossed with scenic walkways, trails, and benches. Guided tours are given Saturdays at 10am, and there's a gift shop and nursery. The gardens are free to everyone on the first Tuesday of the month.

230 Quail Gardens Rd., Encinitas. *C* **760/436-3036.** www.qbgardens.com. Admission $8 adults, $5 seniors and military, $3 children 5–12, free for children under 5. AE, MC, V. Daily 9am–5pm. From San Diego take I-5 north to Encinitas Blvd.; go ½ mile east, left on Quail Gardens Dr.

WHERE TO STAY

Beach Terrace Inn   At Carlsbad's only beachside hostelry (others are across the road or a little farther away), the rooms and the swimming pool/whirlpool all have ocean views. This downtown Best Western property is tucked between rows of high-rent beach cottages and proffers its scenic location as its best quality. The rooms are extralarge, and although they suffer from generic "furnished bachelor pad"–style interiors, some have balconies, fireplaces, and kitchenettes. Suites are affordable and have separate living rooms and bedrooms, making this a good choice for families. VCRs and videos are available at the front desk. You can walk everywhere from here—except LEGOLAND, which is a 5-minute drive away.

2775 Ocean St., Carlsbad, CA 92008. *C* **800/433-5415** or 760/729-5951. Fax 760/729-1078. www. beachterraceinn.com. 49 units. $165 double; from $215 suite. Children 12 and under stay free in parent's room. Extra person $20. Rates include continental breakfast. AE, DC, DISC, MC, V. Free parking. **Amenities:** Outdoor pool; whirlpool; dry-cleaning service; self-service laundry. *In room:* A/C, TV w/pay movies, dataport, fridge, coffeemaker, hair dryer, iron, safe.

Four Seasons Resort Aviara 😊😊😊   In 1997 the Four Seasons chain opened their first oceanview golf-and-tennis resort in the continental United States, and Aviara quickly won over skeptical local residents, who head here for summer jazz concerts and an exceptional Friday night seafood buffet. The resort offers every over-the-top comfort with the never-off-putting ease that sets Four Seasons apart; when not wielding club or racquet, guests can lie by the dramatically perched pool, relax in a series of carefully landscaped gardens, or luxuriate in the newly expanded spa, where treatments incorporate regional flowers and herbs. Rooms are decorated with soothing neutrals and nature prints that evoke the many birds in the surrounding Batiquitos Lagoon. In fact, the name Aviara is a nod to the egrets, herons, and cranes that are among the 130 bird species nesting in the protected coastal wetlands. The hotel's Arnold Palmer–designed golf course was designed to keep the wetlands intact, and incorporates native marshlike plants throughout its 18 holes to help blend with the surroundings. The once-barren hills around the Four Seasons have since been built up with multimillion-dollar homes, but you can quickly escape to the wildness of the lagoon on a nature trail with several different access points.

7100 Four Seasons Point, Carlsbad, CA 92009. ✆ **800/332-3442** or 760/603-6800. Fax 760/603-6801. www. fourseasons.com/aviara. 329 units. $395–$510 double; from $620 suite. Kids 17 and under stay free in parent's room. AE, DISC, MC, V. Valet parking $18. From I-5, take Poinsettia Lane east to Aviara Pkwy. S. **Amenities:** 4 restaurants; 2 lounges; 2 outdoor pools; golf course (see above); 6 tennis courts; health club; 15,000-sq.-ft. spa; whirlpool; bike rental; concierge; business center; 24-hr. room service; in-room massage; babysitting; laundry/dry-cleaning service. *In room:* A/C, TV w/pay movies, dataport, minibar, coffeemaker, hair dryer, iron, safe.

Pelican Cove Inn 😊   Located 2 blocks from the beach, this Cape Cod–style bed-and-breakfast hideaway combines romance with luxury. Hosts Kris and Nancy Nayudu see to your every need, from furnishing guest rooms with soft feather beds and down comforters to providing beach chairs and towels or preparing a picnic basket (with 24 hr. notice). Each room features a fireplace and private entrance; some have private spa tubs. The Pacific room is most spacious, while the airy La Jolla room has bay windows and a cupola ceiling. Breakfast can be enjoyed in the garden if weather permits. Courtesy transportation from the Carlsbad or Oceanside train stations is available.

320 Walnut Ave., Carlsbad, CA 92008. ✆ **888/PEL-COVE** or 760/434-5995. www.pelican-cove.com. 10 units. $90–$210 double. Rates include full breakfast. Extra person $15. AE, MC, V. Free parking. From downtown Carlsbad, follow Carlsbad Blvd. south to Walnut Ave.; turn left and drive 2½ blocks. *In room:* TV, no phone.

WHERE TO DINE

Always crowded is **Fidel's,** known for reliably tasty Mexican food and kickin' margaritas. The restaurant has a location in Solana Beach at 607 Valley Ave. (✆ **858/755-5292**), and there's a **Fidel's Norte** branch in Carlsbad at 3003 Carlsbad Blvd. (✆ **760/729-0903**).

In Encinitas look for **Vigilucci's,** 505 S. Hwy. 101 (✆ **760/942-7332**), where the wafting fragrance of garlic always draws a crowd in for authentic southern Italy trattoria fare served in a lively atmosphere accented with old-world touches like stained glass and a grand mahogany bar. **Meritage** 😊, 897 S. Coast Hwy. 101 (✆ **760/634-3350**), is an appealing charmer that embraces light California styles—on Monday and Wednesday nights, wine lovers are treated to half-off on almost all bottles. At **Siamese Basil,** 527 S. Coast Hwy. 101 (✆ **760/753-3940**), an innocuous facade and bland interior belie a well-deserved reputation for zesty Thai food and a friendly attitude—choose your spice quotient, from toddler-safe 1 to fire-alarm 10.

The architectural centerpiece of Carlsbad is **Neiman's,** 2978 Carlsbad Blvd. (© 760/729-4131; www.neimans.com), a restored Victorian mansion complete with turrets, cupolas, and waving flags. Inside, there's a casual cafe and bar; the Sunday brunch is a vast buffet of breakfast and lunch items, and the daily happy hour (11am–6pm) offers draft beers and well drinks for $2. There's live music, a DJ, or karaoke most evenings. Located in the Carlsbad Company Stores outlet mall is **Bellefleur,** 5610 Paseo del Norte (© 760/603-1919; www.bellefleur. com), which celebrates the "wine country experience" with wood-fired grills, a tasting bar, and glassed-in aging room. Lunchtime sandwiches and salads surpass shopping-mall standards.

12 Julian: Gold, Apple Pies & a Slice of Small-Town California

60 miles NE of San Diego; 31 miles W of Anza-Borrego Desert State Park

A trip to Julian (pop. 3,000) is a trip back in time. The old gold-mining town, now best known for its apples, has a handful of cute B&Bs, but its popularity is based on the fact that it provides a chance for city-weary folks to get away from it all, an asset best appreciated if you visit weekdays, when things are a little quieter here.

People first ventured into these fertile hills—elevation 4,225 feet—in search of gold in the late 1860s. They discovered it in 1870 near where the Julian Hotel stands today, and 18 mines sprang up like mushrooms. During all the excitement, four cousins—all former Confederate soldiers from Georgia, two with the last name Julian—founded the town of Julian. The mines produced up to an estimated $13 million worth of gold in their day.

In October 2003, Julian was virtually engulfed by the devastating Cedar Fires. Firefighters made a stand to protect the town against what seemed insurmountable odds. For a few days it was touch-and-go, and hundreds of homes in the surrounding hillsides were lost. But the central historic part of Julian was saved, along with all of the town's famed apple orchards. Today you can stand on Main Street again without knowing a catastrophe visited just a few hundred yards away. But keep in mind that most of Julian's residents *do* live on the outskirts, and more than a third lost their homes and livelihoods.

ESSENTIALS

GETTING THERE   The 90-minute drive can be made via Calif. 78 or I-8 to Calif. 79. Calif. 78 traverses open country and farmland, while Calif. 79 winds through scenic Cuyamaca Rancho State Park.

VISITOR INFORMATION   For a brochure on what to see and do, contact the **Julian Chamber of Commerce,** corner of Main and Washington streets, P.O. Box 413, Julian, CA 92036 (© 760/765-1857; www.julianca.com), where staffers offer enthusiastic suggestions. The office is open daily 10am to 4pm.

EXPLORING THE TOWN

This 1880s gold-mining town has managed to retain a rustic, woodsy sense of its historic origins. Radiating the dusty aura of the Old West, Julian offers an abundance of early California history, quaint Victorian streets filled with apple-pie shops and antiques stores, crisp fresh air, and friendly people. *Be forewarned:* Julian's charming downtown can be exceedingly crowded during the fall harvest season, so consider making your trip during another time in order to enjoy this unspoiled relic with a little privacy (rest assured, apple pies are baked year-round).

At an elevation of 4,225 feet, the autumn air is crisp and bracing, and Julian sees a dusting (and often more) of snow during the winter months.

The best way to experience tiny Julian is on foot. After stopping in at the **chamber of commerce** in the old town hall—check out the vintage photos of Julian's yesteryear—cross the street to the **Julian Drug Store & Miner's Diner,** 2134 Main St. (© 760/765-3753), an old-style soda fountain serving sparkling sarsaparilla, conjuring images of boys in buckskin and girls in bonnets. The **Eagle and High Peak Mines** (ca. 1870) at the end of C Street (© 760/765-0036), although seemingly a tourist trap, offers an interesting and educational look at the town's one-time economic mainstay. The town's **Pioneer Cemetery** is a must-see for graveyard buffs; contemporary graves belie the haphazard, overgrown look of this hilly burial ground, and eroded older tombstones tell the intriguing story of Julian's rough pioneer history.

There are lots of **roadside fruit stands** and **orchards** in the Julian hills; during autumn they're open all day, every day, but in the off season, many are open only on weekends. Most stands sell apples, pears, peaches, cider, jams, jellies, and other homemade foodstuffs. Many are along Highway 78 between Julian and Wynola; there are also stands along Farmers Road, a scenic country lane leading north from downtown Julian. But apple pie represents the town's mainstay, and the **Julian Pie Company,** 2225 Main St. (© 760/765-2449), is the most charming pie shop of them all. It serves original, Dutch, apple–mountain berry, and no-sugar-added pies, as well as other baked goodies. Another great bakery is the aptly named **Mom's Pies,** 2119 Main St. (© 760/765-2472), whose special attraction is a sidewalk plate-glass window through which you can observe the mom-on-duty rolling crust, filling pies, and crimping edges. Nearby is the **Julian Cider Mill,** 2103 Main St. (© 760/765-1430), where you can see cider presses at work October through March; it offers free tastes of the fresh nectar and sells jugs to take home.

OUTDOOR PURSUITS

Within 10 miles of Julian are numerous hiking trails that traverse rolling meadows, high chaparral, and thick pine forests; however, many trails were closed by the 2003 fires. The most spectacular hike—not affected by the fires—is at **Volcan Mountain Preserve,** north of town along Farmers Road; the trail to the top is a moderately challenging hike of around 3.5 miles round-trip, with a 1,400-foot elevation gain. From the top, hikers have a panoramic view of the desert, mountains, and sea.

The 26,000-acre **Cuyamaca Rancho State Park,** along Highway 79 between Julian and the I-8, was badly burned during the October 2003 forest fires. Rangers started to reopen park trails in summer 2004. For a map and further information about park status, stop in at **park headquarters** on Highway 79 (© 760/765-0755; www.cuyamaca.us).

Eight miles south of Julian, **Lake Cuyamaca** is a tiny community that centers around lake activities, primarily boating and fishing for trout (stocked year-round), plus bass, catfish, bluegill, and sturgeon. There's a general store and restaurant. The fishing fee is $5 per day, $2.50 per day for kids 8 to 15, free for children under 8. A California state fishing license is required and sold here: $11 for the day or $31 per year. Rowboats are $14 per day, and motorboat rentals run $35 for the day ($30 after 1pm). Canoes and paddleboats can be rented by the hour for $10. For boat rental, fishing information, and RV or tent sites, call © 877/581-9904 or 760/765-0515 or see www.lakecuyamaca.org.

For a different way to tour, try **Llama Trek** (© 800/LAMAPAK or 760/765-1890; www.wikiupbnb.com). You'll lead the llama, which carries packs, for hikes to see rural neighborhoods, a historic gold mine, mountain and lake views, and apple orchards. Rates for the 4-hour trips run $95 per person ($75 for children under 12) and include lunch.

WHERE TO STAY

Julian is B&B country, and they fill up months in advance for the fall apple harvest season. Many (but not all) are affiliated with the **Julian Bed & Breakfast Guild** (© 760/765-1555; www.julianbnbguild.com), a terrific resource for personal assistance in locating accommodations. The 15 members also include private cabins and other options.

Julian Gold Rush Hotel ⚜ Built in 1897 by freed slave Albert Robinson, this frontier-style hotel is a living monument to the area's gold boom days—it's the oldest continually operating hotel in Southern California. Located right downtown, the hotel isn't as secluded or plush as some of the many B&Bs, but if you seek historically accurate lodgings in Queen Anne style to complete your weekend time warp, this is the place. The 14 rooms and 2 cottages have been authentically restored (with nicely designed private bathrooms added where necessary) and boast antique furnishings; some rooms are also authentically tiny, so claustrophobics should inquire when reserving! Upstairs rooms are engulfed by a mélange of colorful wallpapers. An inviting private lobby is stocked with books, games, literature on local activities, and a wood-burning stove.

2032 Main St. (at B St.), Julian, CA 92036. © **800/734-5854** or 760/765-0201. Fax 760/765-0327. www.julianhotel.com. 16 units. $100–$145 double; $140–$195 cottages. Rates include full breakfast and afternoon tea. AE, MC, V. *In room:* No phone.

Orchard Hill Country Inn ⚜⚜ *Value* Hosts Darrell and Pat Straube offer the most upscale lodging in Julian, a surprisingly posh, two-story Craftsman lodge and 12 cottages on a hill overlooking the town. Ten guest rooms, a guests-only dining room (open 5 nights a week), and a great room with a massive stone fireplace are in the lodge. The 12 cottages are spread over 3 acres and offer romantic hideaways. All units feature contemporary, nonfrilly country furnishings and snacks. While rooms in the main lodge feel somewhat hotel-ish, the cottage suites are secluded and luxurious, with private porches, fireplaces, wet bars, whirlpool tubs in most, and robes. Several hiking trails lead from the lodge into adjacent woods. Check for midweek specials on the website.

2502 Washington St., at Second St. (P.O. Box 2410), Julian, CA 92036. © **800/71-ORCHARD** or 760/765-1700. Fax 760/765-0290. www.orchardhill.com. 22 units. $164–$240 double; from $228 for cottages. Extra person $25. 2-night minimum stay if including Sat. Rates include breakfast and hors d'oeuvres. AE, MC, V. From Calif. 79, turn left on Main St., then right on Washington St. *In room:* A/C, TV/VCR.

WHERE TO DINE

There is a variety of adequate restaurants in Julian, all of them serving apple pie for dessert. Set in a cozy cottage festooned with lacy draperies, flickering candles, and a warm hearth, the **Julian Grille**, 2224 Main St. (© **760/765-0173**), is the town's nicest eatery, with lunches of soups, sandwiches, large salads, charbroiled burgers, and hearty omelets. Dinner features grilled and broiled meats, seafood, and prime rib. Occupying a historic farmhouse just off Main Street, **Romano's Dodge House**, 2718 B St. (© **760/765-1003**), is a home-style Italian spot, with red-checked tablecloths and straw-clad chianti bottles. The signature dish, pork Juliana, is loin chops in a whisky-apple-cider sauce.

Index

Travel Tip: He who finds the best hotel deal has more to spend on facials involving knobbly vegetables.

Hello, the Roaming Gnome here. I've been nabbed from the garden and taken round the world. The people who took me are so terribly clever. They find the best offerings on Travelocity. For very little cha-ching. And that means I get to be pampered and exfoliated till I'm pink as a bunny's doodah.

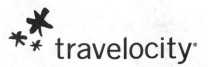

travelocity®

1-888-TRAVELOCITY / travelocity.com / America Online Keyword: Travel

2004 Travelocity.com LP. All rights reserved. TRAVELOCITY, the Stars Design and The Roaming Gnome are trademarks of Travelocity.com LP. CST# 2056372-50.

Travel Tip: Make sure there's customer service for any change of plans — involving friendly natives, for example.

One can plan and plan, but if you don't book with the right people you can't seize le moment and canoodle with the poodle named Pansy. I, for one, am all for fraternizing with the locals. Better yet, if I need to extend my stay and my gnome nappers are willing, it can all be arranged through the 800 number at, oh look, how convenient, the lovely company coat of arms.

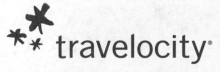

1-888-TRAVELOCITY / travelocity.com / America Online Keyword: Travel